C000144146

ISBN 978-0-428-19368-3
PIBN 10249430

SIXTH BIENNIAL REPORT

OF THE

BOARD OF DIRECTORS

OF THE

Kansas State Historical Society,

6 - 9

FOR THE PERIOD

COMMENCING JANUARY 19, 1887, AND ENDING NOVEMBER 20, 1888.

TOPEKA.
KANSAS PUBLISHING HOUSE: CLIFFORD C. BAKER, STATE PRINTER.
1889.

OFFICERS FOR THE YEARS 1887-88.

DANIEL W. WILDER, Hiawatha, ... PRESIDENT, 1887.
EDWARD RUSSELL, Lawrence, ... PRESIDENT, 1888.
HENRY H. WILLIAMS, Osawatomie, ... VICE PRESIDENT, 1887.
WM. A. PHILLIPS, Salina, ... VICE PRESIDENT, 1888.
THOMAS A. McNEAL, Medicine Lodge, ... VICE PRESIDENT, 1887-8.
FRANKLIN G. ADAMS, Topeka, ... SECRETARY.
JOHN FRANCIS, Topeka, ... TREASURER.

EXECUTIVE COMMITTEE.
JOHN A. MARTIN, T. DWIGHT THACHER, P. I. BONEBRAKE, N. A. ADAMS, F. P. BAKER.

LEGISLATIVE COMMITTEE.
BENJ. F. SIMPSON, E. R. PURCELL, EDWARD RUSSELL.

1707509

DIRECTORS.

Members of the Board of Directors for the year ending January 15, 1889:

ADAMS, F. G.,	Topeka.	LOWE, P. G.,	Leavenworth.
ADMIRE, J. V.,	Osage City.	MARTIN, GEO. W.,	Kansas City.
BLAIR, C. W.,	Leavenworth.	MILLER, SOL.,	Troy.
BLUE, R. W.,	Pleasanton.	MOHLER, MARTIN,	Osborne.
BONEBRAKE, P. I.,	Topeka.	MURDOCK, M. M.,	Wichita.
BUCHAN, W. J.,	Kansas City.	PECK, GEO. R.,	Topeka.
CARR, E. T.	Leavenworth.	RICHARDSON, J. R.,	Hiawatha.
CARROLL, ED.,	Leavenworth.	SHEAN, W. M.,	Gardner.
DALLAS, E. J.,	Topeka.	SIMPSON, BENJ. F.,	Topeka.
ELLIOTT, L. R.,	Manhattan.	SLAVENS, W. H.,	Yates Center.
EDWARDS, W. C.,	Larned.	SMITH, JAMES,	Topeka.
ESBERY, J. S.,	Lawrence.	SMITH, W. W.,	Topeka.
FINCH, L. E.,	Burlingame.	STEELE, J. W.,	Topeka.
GILLETT, ALMERIN,	Emporia.	STOTLER, JACOB,	Wellington.
GOSS, N. S.,	Topeka.	THACHER, T. D.,	Topeka.
HOLLIDAY, C. K.,	Topeka.	WOOD, S. N.,	Woodsdale.
JONES, C. J.,	Garden City.		

Members of the Board of Directors for the term ending January 21, 1890:

ABBOTT, J. B.,	DeSoto.	LELAND, CYRUS,	Troy.
ADAMS, N. A.,	Manhattan.	MCAFEE, J. B.,	Topeka.
AMOS, J. WAYNE,	Gypsum City.	McNEAL, T. A.,	Medicine Lodge.
BURTON, J. R.,	Abilene.	MURDOCK, T. B.,	El Dorado.
CLOGSTON, J. B.,	Eureka.	OSBORN, THOMAS A.,	Topeka.
COLEMAN, A. L.,	Centralia.	PRATT, JOHN G.,	Maywood.
CREW, E. B.,	Delphos.	PRENTIS, NOBLE L.,	Newton.
DOTY, GEO. W.,	Burlingame.	PURCELL, E. R.,	Manhattan.
DOWNING, J. H.,	Hays City.	RICE, JOHN H.,	Fort Scott.
FAULKNER, C. E.,	Salina.	SCOTT, JOHN W.,	Iola.
HAUN, T. S.,	Jetmore.	SMITH, A. W.,	McPherson.
HUDSON, J. K.,	Topeka.	TAYLOR, T. T.,	Hutchinson.
JOHNSON, A. S.,	Topeka.	TILTON, W. S.,	Wa-Keeney.
KELLY, H. B.,	McPherson.	VEALE, G. W.,	Topeka.
KELLOGG, L. B.,	Emporia.	WILLIAMSON, CHAS.,	Washington.
KIMBALL, C. H.,	Parsons.	WILLIAMS, H. H.,	Osawatomie.
KNAPP, GEO. W.,	Clyde.		

Members of the Board of Directors for the term ending January 20, 1891:

ANTHONY, D. R.,	Leavenworth.	LANE, V. J.,	Kansas City.
BAILEY, L. D.,	Garden City.	LEGATE, JAS. F.,	Leavenworth.
BAKER, F. P.,	Topeka.	LESTER, H. N.,	Syracuse.
BALL, VOLNEY,	Lincoln.	McBRIDE, WM. H.,	Osborne.
ENGLISH, A. N.,	Wichita.	McINTIRE, T.,	Arkansas City.
ESKRIDGE, C. V.,	Emporia.	MARTIN, JOHN A.,	Atchison.
FRANCIS, JOHN,	Topeka.	MOORE, H. MILES,	Leavenworth.
GLICK, GEO. W.,	Atchison.	PHILLIPS, W. A.,	Salina.
GOODNOW, ISAAC T.,	Manhattan.	REYNOLDS, M. W.,	Genda Springs.
GREENE, A. R.,	Cedarvale.	RIDDLE, A. P.,	Minneapolis.
GREER, ED. P.,	Winfield.	ROBINSON, CHAS.,	Lawrence.
HAMILTON, J. W.,	Wellington.	RUSSELL, EDWARD,	Lawrence.
HILLER, C. A.,	Salina.	SPEER, JOHN,	Sherlock.
HOLT, JOEL,	Beloit.	WARE, E. F.,	Fort Scott.
HUMPHREY, L. U.,	Independence.	WILDER, D. W.,	Hiawatha.
JONES, JOHN P.,	Coldwater.	WRIGHT, R. M.,	Dodge City.
KINGMAN, S. A.,	Topeka.		

SIXTH BIENNIAL REPORT,

OF THE

BOARD OF DIRECTORS,

OF THE

nsas State Historical Society,

FOR THE PERIOD

MENCING JANUARY 19, 1887, AND ENDING NOVEMBER 20, 1888.

TOPEKA.
KANSAS PUBLISHING HOUSE: CLIFFORD C. BAKER, STATE PRINTER.
1889.

CONTENTS.

REPORT.

The Board of Directors met in the rooms of the Society, Tuesday, November 20, 1888, at 3:30 P. M., the following members being present: Hon. John Francis, Hon. V. J. Lane, Hon. F. P. Baker, Judge S. A. Kingman, Hon. D. W. Wilder, Hon. James Smith, Maj. Benjamin F. Simpson, Hon. James F. Legate, Hon. W. C. Edwards, Hon. E. J. Dallas, Hon. Martin Mohler, Hon. T. D. Thacher, and the Secretary, F. G. Adams.

Letters were read from Hon. Edward Russell, President of the Society, and from Prof. I. T. Goodnow and Hon. L. R. Elliott, expressing regrets at their inability to be present at the meeting.

The President and Vice-Presidents being absent, Judge Kingman was called to the chair, on motion of Hon. F. P. Baker.

The Secretary then read the report, which was approved on motion of Mr. Legate, and ordered for publication.

On motion of Mr. Legate, it was voted that a committee be appointed, composed of three citizens of Topeka, to act in connection with the President and Secretary of the Society, to confer with the Executive Council and the Legislature, and to take charge of the matter of procuring suitable rooms in the State House, when completed, for the library and collections of the Society. The President appointed F. P. Baker, T. D. Thacher and John Francis members of the committee.

The Secretary called the attention of the Board to a letter from Senator Plumb, transmitting a letter of Col. R. J. Hinton, in which the latter proposes to dispose of some historical manuscripts and papers which he has collected. On motion, the Secretary was directed to confer with Colonel Hinton upon the subject.

On motion of Mr. Edwards, the following resolution was adopted, and ordered to be submitted to the annual meeting for its consideration:

Whereas, The Kansas State Historical Society has always considered that its library and collections were being gathered and made up wholly as the property of the State; and, whereas, the Legislature, by act of March 10, 1879, declared the Society to be a trustee of the State, and its library and collections of every kind to be the inalienable property of the State: therefore,

Resolved, That this Society hereby formally declares it to be the intention of the Society, that its library and collections hitherto gathered, and all that shall hereafter be gathered, are, and are to become the exclusive property of the State of Kansas, for the use of the people of the State; and the Society fully accepts the terms and conditions expressed and contained in said act of March 10, 1879.

On motion, the meeting adjourned.

REPORT OF THE BOARD OF DIRECTORS, NOV. 20, 1888.

By vote of the Board of Directors at the meeting of January 17th, 1888, the time for concluding the yearly work of the Society and making up the annual report was changed from the third Tuesday of January to the third Tuesday in November. This change was made for the object of giving time for the printing of the Society's biennial reports previous to their presentation to the annual meeting, and before the meeting of the Legislature. The report here presented, then, exhibits the work of the Society during the period commencing with January 18th, 1887, and ending with November 19th, 1888, or about one year and ten months, instead of for the full period of two years, as has been the case with former biennial reports.

SUMMARY.

During the period covered by this report there have been added to the library of the Society, of bound volumes, 1,619; unbound volumes and pamphlets, 9,250; volumes of newspapers and periodicals, 1,995; single newspapers, 1,734; maps, atlases and charts, 116; manuscripts, 662; pictures and works of art, 275; scrip, currency, coins and medals, 32; war relics, 12; miscellaneous contributions, 229.

The library additions of books, pamphlets, and newspaper files, not including duplicates, number 12,864 volumes. Of these, 12,001 have been procured by gift, and 863 by purchase.

The whole number of volumes in the library at the present time is as follows, namely: 9,971 bound volumes; 30,353 unbound volumes; 7,981 bound newspaper files and volumes of periodicals; in all, 48,305 volumes.

YEARLY GROWTH OF THE LIBRARY.

The following is a statement of the yearly growth of the library in thirteen years, 1876 to 1888, inclusive:

Date.	Volumes books.	Volumes newspapers and periodicals.	Pamphlets.	Total yearly accessions.	Yearly total of the library.
1876	280	54	74	408	408
1877	115	150	501	766	1,174
1878	1,237	710	1,184	3,131	4,305
1879	290	275	491	1,056	5,361
1880	448	448	1,146	2,042	7,403
1881	414	375	1,127	1,916	9,319
1882	1,669	513	2,721	4,903	14,222
1883	307	403	1,088	1,798	16,020
1884	732	807	2,763	4,302	20,322
1885	1,088	678	2,033	3,799	24,121
1886	1,772	1,573	7,975	11,320	35,441
1887	753	1,007	1,543	3,303	38,744
1888	866	988	7,707	9,561	48,305
Totals	9,971	7,981	30,353	48,305	

The tables which the report contains show perhaps as well as tables and exhibits can, the character and extent of the work done by the Society during the period which the report covers.

Included in the pamphlet accessions are 5,393 newspaper cuttings, which have been mounted and placed in the library classification. These are the accumulations of many years. They relate chiefly to Kansas history, local and general, to biography, proceedings of local pioneer gatherings, and of various State societies and associations. Mounted in scrap-books and placed in the library, they are thus made convenient for reference.

MENTION OF SOME DONATIONS.

Among the most liberal of the donors of books and pamphlets may be mentioned Rev. S. L. Adair, of Osawatomie; Hon. F. P. Baker, Hon. T. D. Thacher, Mr. A. S. Huling and Hon. D. M. Valentine, of Topeka; Prof. I. T. Goodnow and Mrs. B. F. Mudge, of Manhattan; Hon. Geo. W. Martin, Kansas City; Hon. Eli Thayer, of Worcester, Massachusetts; Dr. Samuel A. Green, Secretary of the Massachusetts Historical Society, Boston; and the Essex Institute, Salem, Massachusetts. Prof. Goodnow has given from his thirty-three years' savings in Kansas a mass of historical material of inestimable value, consisting of books, pamphlets, magazines, manuscripts, maps, newspaper files and other papers. Hon. D. M. Valentine has given the Society ninety-four pamphlets, chiefly consisting of Kansas political and other publications thoughtfully saved by him during his thirty years' residence in Kansas. One of the most valuable gifts of books to the Society has been that made by Hon. George W. Martin, now of Kansas City, Kansas, consisting of 100 copies of "Wilder's Annals," 1875 edition. This book has been much sought for by libraries and institutions with which our Society makes exchanges, and the gift enables us to effect exchanges securing the augmentation of our library by many valuable volumes otherwise beyond our reach.

Of the 602 manuscript papers contributed, there are many which are of historical interest. Among such may be mentioned the record books of early Topeka social organizations, given by Mrs. Ashbaugh; the muster-rolls, given by Judge L. D. Bailey, containing a record of the first military organization in what is now Lyon county; Dr. George W. Brown's contributions to anti-slavery and early Kansas history; the contributions made to John Brown history by John Brown, jr., Theodore Botkin, Hon. Horace L. Jones, Hon. O. E. Morse, Col. William A. Phillips, and Capt. J. A. Pike; the autobiographical sketches by lady editors of Kansas newspapers; the mass of petitions of the women of Kansas for municipal suffrage, presented to the Legislature of 1887; and the voluminous original records of Kansas history contained in the contributions made by Mrs. Lawrence, the widow of Amos A. Lawrence, a most liberal benefactor of Kansas in the earliest days of trial. These manuscripts contain a large portion of the records of

the work of the New England Emigrant Aid Company, of which Mr. Lawrence was the treasurer.

Of maps and atlases donated to the library, the atlas to accompany the Ohio Geological Survey, given by Mr. Robert Clarke, of Cincinnati, accompanied as the gift was by that of the volumes of the Survey, is worthy of special mention; as is also the gift by Mr. F. E. Jerome, of Russell, of the atlas to accompany the Michigan Geological Survey. Mr. John P. Edwards, of Quincy, Illinois, has added to the gifts before made by him of Kansas maps and atlases, by contributing large wall maps of three Kansas and one Missouri county. Professor Goodnow's very large gift to the Society was acccompanied by eighteen valuable maps. The gift made by J. H. Meacham of his voluminous illustrated atlas of Brown and Nemaha counties is an important contribution to the materials of Kansas history. The Iowa atlas given by Mr. A. W. Stubbs is a valuable record of the history of a neighboring State. Messrs. Wasser and Flint, of Girard, have added again to their contributions of Kansas maps. Mr. Henry Kuhn's gift of Boudinot's map of the Indian Territory is an important contribution. Rand, McNally & Co. have added largely to the gifts which they had before made of maps of the States and Territories. The archæological map made and given to the Society by Mr. William Griffing is an interesting record of original investigation of the antiquities of Kansas.

Noteworthy among the pictures added to the gallery is a crayon portrait of Senator Ingalls, a gift of the artist, Mr. A. Montgomery; a crayon portrait of Col. Alexander S. Johnson, given by himself by special request; and a portrait of Chester Thomas, sr., given by members of his family. Mr. Robert Tracy, of St. Joseph, Mo., has given photo portraits of Maj. William P. Richardson and Dr. John H. Stringfellow, both prominent figures in the earliest period of Kansas Territorial history; the family and friends of Prof. B. F. Mudge have given a portrait of that most prominent early worker in Kansas science; Thomas W. Heatley has given an original photo portrait of Richard Realf, and a fine crayon copy of this portrait has been given the Society by Mrs. Peacock, who executed it; H. T. Martin, the photographer, has contributed cabinet photos of members of the Legislature and the executive officers of 1887–8, 136 in number. Numerous other portraits and pictures have also been contributed to the Society's very large collection of this class of historical material. Ex-Gov. Frederick P. Stanton, now a resident of Farmwell, Virginia, has given the Society a fine marble bust of himself, executed many years ago by Horatio Stone. This gift will ever be regarded by the Society and by the people of Kansas as an interesting memorial of one whose official career was marked by invaluable services in times of great need.

Conspicuous among the contributions is the gold medal which was presented by Victor Hugo and his associates in France, in 1874, to the widow of Capt. John Brown, in testimony of the recognition by the donors of the

supreme sacrifice made by the Kansas martyr in behalf of human rights. The medal has been deposited with the Historical Society by Capt. John Brown, jr., and his brothers and sisters, regarding as they do our Society as the appropriate custodian of the memorials of their illustrious father.

Of war memorials may be mentioned the gift by Maj. James B. Abbott of his sword, a relic of the early troubles in Kansas, as well as of the war of the Rebellion, also the gift by the same of an English musket, a relic of Confederate arms employed on our border in Price's raid, and a Pro-Slavery flag, a relic of the Kansas Territorial troubles; the gift by Mrs. Hannah Ritchie of the sword and gun of Gen. John Ritchie, memorials of the services rendered by a distinguished and honored pioneer citizen of Kansas in the war for the preservation of the Union. Hon. A. Washburn gives an interesting relic of the war of the Revolution, and Dr. S. B. Prentiss the same of the Pro-Slavery troubles of 1856. Interesting relics of the war of the Rebellion have been given by Mrs. Lititia Watkins, Mr. W. A. Warreu, J. W. Richardson, W. E. Richey, and Mrs. Sophia Ashbaugh.

Of files of newspapers, Rev. S. L. Adair has given thirty-six volumes, Hon. F. P. Baker sixteen, and Prof. I. T. Goodnow sixty-two. These with the others contributed swell the number of files given the Society in addition to those contributed in regular issues, to one hundred and twenty-eight in number. These added to the volumes of newspapers and periodicals which have accumulated through regular newspaper issues received, chiefly from gifts, make up 1,995 volumes of this most valuable class of historical materials received during the period covered by the report.

CHARACTER OF THE LIBRARY.

The lists and tables which this report contains show that there is being made up by this Society for the use of the people of Kansas a library of history and reference, remarkable in its growth, and still more remarkable in the character and value of the materials which it contains. They show that notwithstanding much embarrassment the growth of the library and collections has steadily continued from year to year during the thirteen years of the Society's existence, and that in that time there have been placed on the library shelves more than forty-eight thousand volumes of books, newspaper files and pamphlets; and in addition to these, this and former reports show a collection of manuscripts, pictures, statuary, relics and objects of historical illustration of every kind and description almost countless in number.

The character of these materials is such as was contemplated in the organization of the Society and such as the law directs the Society to bring into its library and collections. They are chiefly the printed and written records of the people of Kansas; records which go to show the sacrifices and achievements of our first settlers in establishing freedom on our soil; records of the daily, weekly, monthly and yearly transactions of the people

in social, moral, educational and material progress; in the building-up of
our towns, with their depots of trade, their manufactories, and varied industrial establishments; records which show the unexampled progress in the
construction of lines of railroad transportation; in the opening and planting of farms, orchards and vineyards; records of the march, year by year,
of our frontier people toward the border, still experimenting with the powers
of nature, and still subduing obstacles which for all the ages before had
been deemed insurmountable. The history of the struggles and triumphs
of the people of Kansas, from the earliest day to the present, have been
and are being more fully recorded by pen and printing-press than ever before was that of any people; and our Historical Society is very fully gathering in and placing accessibly on its shelves the record as thus being made
up. The published statistics of the libraries of the country show that the
library of the Kansas Historical Society is the largest historical library
west of the Mississippi river, and the largest but one west of the Alleghany
Mountains. When it is considered that this library is not composed of
evanescent books of the literature of the day, written and printed for the
amusement of the hour, and then no longer sought for reference or for any
other use, but that it chiefly contains the original records of the facts in
the history of our own pioneer people, of the first generation of the founders
and builders of the State, it may be well said that when we speak of its
remarkable growth in the number of its volumes, we present a feature of
but slight consideration compared with that of the character of the volumes
which it contains as original materials of history.

And not only is the history of our own people being gathered into this
library, but as the law directs, the library is being made one of very widely
extended reference, in general history, in science, and in all subjects of
social, educational, and literary research.

RELATION OF THE SOCIETY TO THE STATE.

The kind of work being done by the Society, and the relation which it sus-
tains to the State, are peculiar; hence the duties imposed, and the privileges
conferred upon it by law, are not so well understood as they should be. There
is but one other institution in the country so nearly like this in object and
scope, and in its connection with the State, as to admit of comparison. The
Wisconsin Historical Society is much like ours, and afforded the model
upon which our work in its incipiency was planned and in the main has
since been carried forward. Both are voluntary associations. Their members and officers are private citizens elected by the societies. Their mode of
work has been devised, and is being carried forward upon plans, rules and
regulations made by themselves. But what they do is for the people of the
State. Their library and all their collections are the property of the State,
placed in rooms provided by the State, and are inalienable and irremovable.
The expenses of the work of the Society are chiefly defrayed by the State.

This relation of the State Historical Society to the State is essential to the existence of a historical society in a new State where there are no opulent citizens to found and maintain such a society. So far as there has been any experience in such work, it is the relation best calculated to secure the making up of a public historical collection in any State; a work which it is everywhere conceded every State should have by some means done for it, and the neglect of which is greatly deplored where it has been left undone. Such a society is greatly stimulated to exertion to fulfill the public requirements. Where by law the society is made the trustee and servant of the State its work is not perfunctory like that of the State official, whose term of service is determined upon political considerations. The existence of the Society and its continued support are dependent upon its fulfillment of the public demand and expectation year by year and continually. This has been and must ever be the experience of such a relation to the State of a voluntary association of this character.

LEGAL REQUIREMENTS.

The act of the Legislature of 1879, by which the Society was made the trustee of the State and its collections the property of the State, makes it the duty of the Society to make up a library of "books, maps and other materials illustrative of the history of Kansas in particular and the West generally; . . . to purchase books to supply deficiencies in the various departments of its collections, and to procure by gift and exchange such scientific and historical reports of the Legislatures of other States, of railroads, reports of geological and other scientific surveys, and such other books, maps, charts and materials as will facilitate the investigation of historical, scientific, social, educational and literary subjects, and to cause the same to be properly bound; to catalog the collections of the said Society for the more convenient reference of all persons who may have occasion to consult the same; to biennially prepare for publication a report of its collections and such other matter relating to its transactions as may be useful to the public; and to keep its collections arranged in convenient and suitable rooms, to be provided and furnished by the Secretary of State, as the Board of Directors shall determine."

Considering the novelty of such a relation of a State to an association of its private citizens, it is not surprising that the duties thus imposed by the State and the compensation given for performing them should not for a time be properly adjusted. The Society has not been in the habit of complaining of lack of appreciation and compensation; for the public appreciation has always and everywhere been made most manifest, and the Society has always been confident that the lack of adequate means for carrying on its work would prove to be but temporary. The membership of the Society now extends to every county in the State. The most valuable part of the current accessions to its library, namely the newspaper issues, and locally

printed matter, are being freely contributed by members of the Society,
from every county in the State. The faithful performance of the most important part of its work, that of caring for these local contributions, employs
more than half the time of the clerical force of the Society. It is not to be
supposed that a society whose work is being done wholly for the people of
the State, whose working membership embraces every part of the State, and
the results of whose work have come to be appreciated by all classes of intelligent people in the State, will remain for a much longer period in a state
of embarrassment for want of means to carry forward the work assigned to it.

BROAD FIELD OF WORK.

The duty imposed by the Legislature upon the Society to place in its
library with the publications of our own State, those of other States and
those of learned, social and scientific institutions generally, so as to make
up a library which shall give every citizen of the State facilities for the investigation of "historical, social, educational and literary subjects," are so
comprehensive that its library undertaking may be said to be unlimited in
its object and scope.

The broad field from which the materials of this library are being gathered
has proven to be a very fruitful one. While our best garnerings are from
within our own State, the limits of the work of the Society are boundless.
So interwoven has been the history of Kansas with that of the principal
events of the whole country, and so much has the work of the Society
enlisted a general interest, its library has come to be the recipient, largely
by gift, of not only the materials of the history of the whole country, but
of everything of a literary and scientific character relating to all parts of
the country. The library is becoming, at a cost involving little more than
that of freight and postage, care and keeping, a library of reference very
broad in its scope. Its growth would be far more rapid, and its accessi-
bility and consequent usefulness to the public would be far greater, were
adequate means given the Society to employ a sufficient clerical force, and
if the State had been able to fulfill its undertaking to furnish "suitable and
convenient rooms for the collections."

The State of Kansas in legalizing the work of the State Historical Society and giving such a breadth and scope to the objects aimed to be accomplished by it, intended no half-way work. The action of the Legislature
was prompted by the conviction which has always rested in the minds of
our people, that Kansas has made and is making a history unique in its
character and unparalleled in the magnitude of the principles which had
been and are being vindicated and exemplified on our soil. The materials
of our own history, and of our world-wide related history, are such as no
State ever before had spread out for the gathering.

And the willing helpers in the work are as widespread as are the materials. The interest in the work of the Kansas Historical Society is as broad

as the country itself. Said the Secretary of the Massachusetts Historical Society: " Massachusetts helped to redeem and make Kansas,—it will help its Historical Society." Said Henry Ward Beecher in accepting a membership in our Society: "I need not say how deep an interest I have taken in her noble progress and renowned prosperity. She well deserves the title 'New England of the West.'" Said William Lloyd Garrison: "The formation of such a society is cause for special congratulation, and an event of historical importance far beyond the limits of the State;—for there is nothing more thrilling in American history than the struggle to secure freedom and free institutions to Kansas—a struggle which, if it had terminated otherwise than it did, would have been fraught with appalling consequences not only to the State itself, but to the whole country. How different would have been the fate of Kansas, if slavery had been successfully established upon her soil! Under the plastic hand of freedom, how astonishing has been her growth in intelligence, industry, enterprise, population, and material prosperity; and at the present time what strides she is making in developing her ample resources, and how irresistible is the magnetism by which she is drawing to herself from all quarters a mighty immigration that can scarcely fail to place her, ere long, in the front rank of States. This is her fitting recompense for having gone through a baptism of blood and an ordeal of fire with such firmness and devotion to the sacred cause of freedom. May her 'peace be as a river,' and her 'prosperity as the waves of the sea.'"

It is in the preservation of the materials of the history of the growth and development of Kansas during the past thirteen years that the work of the Society is most complete and comprehensive. Before our Society had begun its work, the printed materials of the history of the earlier days had in large part been dissipated and destroyed. The materials of the present day, as they are daily and weekly being issued from more than a thousand busy printing-presses, are all being saved in the library of our Society. In its growth and development Kansas has gone forward until it has reached, with all the appliances of the best civilization the world has ever known, the remotest boundaries of our State; and now are to be found newspaper presses in every county. These papers make a record, week by week, of all the events occurring in the growth of these new counties, and complete files of all are being preserved in the library of the State Historical Society, the gift of their generous and thoughtful publishers.

PROVINCE OF A HISTORICAL SOCIETY.

That the Kansas State Historical Society is well fulfilling the mission assigned it by the Legislature, and according to the highest standards established for an institution charged by a State with the duty of forming a library of historical and other materials for the use of the people, may be quoted here a single testimonial as to what ought to be done for the accom-

plishment of such object. It is the testimony of Dr. Henry A. Homes, who for forty years, and till his death a few months since, was the eminent librarian of the general library of the State of New York. It is found in an article prepared by him contained in the United States Government publication entitled, "Public Libraries in the United States of America; their History, Condition, and Management," published by the Department of the Interior, in 1876. In a paragraph in which he makes a statement of the special province of a general State library, as distinct and separate from that of a library of law reports, statutes, journals of the Legislature, and State documents, he says:

"A State library will, of course, make it one of its special aims to collect works of American history in general just so far as the means at its disposal will admit. But of all the purposes for which it exists, none respond so directly to the wants of the largest number of the citizens of a State as to aim to collect all the materials accessible to illustrate the history of the State, its counties, its towns, and its citizens. The authorities of the library will therefore be attentive to secure all local histories and biographies, manuscript collections of the papers of its eminent citizens, the official proceedings of all counties and towns, reports of all societies, charitable, commercial, manufacturing, military and secret, and as many of the newspapers printed in the State as can be obtained, with its almanacs, and business and town directories. To these will naturally be added works in science and the arts which relate more particularly to the productions of the State. An honorable historic consciousness will be promoted by securing works of merit of all kinds written by citizens of the State."

NEWSPAPERS AS MATERIALS OF HISTORY.

The following is quoted from the same high authority:

"Much might be said regarding the value of the different classes of books just mentioned, a value which grows with successive years. We will, however, single out from among them for particular notice the class of newspapers. For many towns and counties they are the only printed record of the earliest facts of local history. Their value in libraries is already recognized in our Western States. The Indiana State Library receives twenty-eight newspapers as an annual gift; Minnesota was receiving forty in 1862; and Ohio received twenty-eight. The New Jersey Library invites donations of the same kind. There can be little doubt that the publishers of a large proportion of the newspapers of any State would preserve and give to the State the file of each year, on the single condition that it should be promptly bound and be made accessible to the public. It would be equitable and useful to provide by statute that each publisher sending a newspaper should receive a copy of the laws of the session."

This eminent librarian singles out from among the most important of all the subjects of collection the local newspaper. And yet what a meager showing he makes as to what the State libraries of the country were twelve years ago doing in this department of work: Indiana, twenty-eight newspapers; Minnesota, forty; Ohio, twenty-eight. And they are doing no better to-day. State libraries never have effectively done the most appropriate work for a library of local history and general reference for the

people. They have a paramount object besides, and to that their chief work is naturally and necessarily confined.

It was left to the voluntary associations of private citizens forming the Wisconsin Historical Society and the Kansas Historical Society, to properly inaugurate and carry forward this kind of work. The board of directors of the Wisconsin Historical Society at their annual meeting in January last, reported as contained in their library, 5,240 volumes of newspaper files; and to this class of library materials they particularly refer as being "the fountain-head of modern history."

SPIRIT OF THE KANSAS PRESS.

The New York State Librarian suggested that publishers should be compensated for their newspapers. That might do for New York, Indiana, and Ohio. But Kansas newspaper publishers see the matter in a different light; it was they who organized the Society, and no sooner was it organized than they began freely to give their regular issues. Not only that, but the veteran editor who had published his paper from away back in the early history of Kansas Territory got together his scattered duplicates until he had made up for the Society a complete file, not a number missing. At least one file thus given we have, covering a period now of more than thirty years. So the publisher of the newspaper starting in a frontier county, hearing of the work our Society is doing, of which he is pretty sure to hear even before his first issue is out, with alacrity puts the State Historical Society on his mail book. Thus the work of the newspaper man's enterprise, zeal and ambition goes to posterity. And who shall say that he will not do better work; more for the good of the people a history of whose doings he records, than if he felt that the issues from his press were but for a day, speedily to pass from the face of the earth as has been the common experience where no historical society has existed to save the issues of the press and place them between fire-proof walls built by the State for the preservation of its sacred archives. The newspaper men and women of Kansas are putting it in the power of the Historical Society which they founded to do better work in making up a library of the best materials of local history than is being done by any other society or institution in the world.

That the publishers of Kansas newspapers appreciate the work being done by the Historical Society which they established, a single quotation may be given from among hundreds. Says the editor of a leading daily:

"This Society, as its name implies, is the custodian and conservator of the history of Kansas. A copy of almost every newspaper published in this State, from its organization, and prior to that period, through its earliest Territorial days, may be found on file in its rooms. From that established in 1854 down to the journals of to-day, a copy of each is there carefully preserved, thus making a continuous and unbroken history of the State to-day. A copy of every book written, by Kansans, may be found on its shelves; so of thousands of foreign newspapers and pamphlets; and all the addresses and speeches embodying matters relating to Kan-

sas affairs are there compiled and stowed away. A copy of each annual Agricultural
Report, which, by the way, are the fullest, completest, and most accurate reports of the
kind prepared by any State in the Union, is there preserved. Copies of the proceedings of every Legislature and every State convention, a record of the minutes
of every important public gathering ever held in Kansas, are kept there. The walls
and cases of this office are adorned with portraits of Governors of Kansas, of many
other historial characters, and of the various Territorial and State Legislatures.
Glass cases arranged about the rooms contain Kansas relics of all sorts, conveniently
placed. In short, everything of an historical character is being gathered up and
consigned to its proper place in the archives of this Society.

"The value of our State Historical Society, aside from its general purposes, as
the custodian of Kansas history, as an aid in litigation, can hardly be overestimated.
A prominent attorney of this city a few years ago, in an important patent case,
found himself compelled to establish a certain date and fact vital to his client. He
searched high and low, far and near, without avail. At last it occurred to him that
he might at least get a clue from the State Historical Society. He went to Topeka
and was handed by the Secretary of the Society the public directory containing the
very date and fact he needed.

"The men who organized this Society builded better than they knew. Their
efforts to maintain it through all these years have already been amply rewarded in
the practical as well as sentimental benefit it has conferred upon the citizens of
Kansas, and the appropriations made by the Legislature for its support have been
among the best investments the State has ever made. Its utility will be more appreciated from year to year, and long after its projectors and present patrons have
passed from the stage of action, its work and accumulations will abide among the
most cherished possessions of the Kansans who are to be."

THE WORK EXCEEDS THE MEANS.

The law makes it the duty of the Society to catalog this library. This
calls for consideration the subject of the long-continued embarrassment of
the Society for want of adequate appropriations by the Legislature to carry
on its work, a subject which has been repeatedly presented before in these
reports. The present very poorly paid clerical force is insufficient to properly perform the current work of the Society, which has hitherto been
necessarily confined to that of gathering in the accumulations, making a record of them, having them bound, classifying and arranging them on the
shelves, acknowledging gifts, and conducting the very extensive correspondence involved in reaching out for material, widely scattered as are the
people who have for manifest causes had connection with the events of
Kansas history from the earliest days. It has thus far been impossible to
comply with the requirement to catalog the library. The meager appropriations have compelled the payment to the clerks employed of less than
one-half the amount paid to employés in other departments of the State.
Double the amount should be paid to present employés, and an additional
force should be employed. The scanty provision made by the State to enable the Society to perform its work has no precedent in the legislation of
any State. While Kansas gives $4,250 to its Historical Society, Wisconsin
has for many years given annually more than $9,000.

LACK OF ROOM.

The present embarrassment of the Society for lack of room for its collections, and the urgent demand at this time that provision shall be made in the State Capitol when completed for the future needs of this library, must again be mentioned.

The law, as has been quoted, has made it the duty of the Secretary of State to furnish convenient and suitable rooms for the library and collections, such as the Board of Directors of the Society shall determine. Of course it has been thus far out of the power of the Secretary of State or any other authority to comply with this requirement in the uncompleted state of the Capitol building. But in view of the progress being made toward the completion of the Capitol, at the annual meeting two years ago, the Board presented the subject in its report to the Society, and, during the session of the Legislature following, a conference was held between the legislative committee of the Society and the joint committee of the Legislature on the State Library, to whom the Governor's recommendation, that proper legislation should be had for the maintenance of the work of the Society, had been referred. The committee of the Legislature responded to the wishes of our committee, and the following concurrent resolution was introduced by the committee in the House of Representatives, and was adopted:

HOUSE CONCURRENT RESOLUTION No. 22, 1887.—*"Be it resolved by the House of Representatives, the Senate concurring therein,* That the State House Commissioners be, and they are hereby instructed, that in the preparation of the plan of the main building of the State House, and in the assignment of rooms, ample provision be made for the valuable collections of historical material of the State Historical Society, and for its future growth."

When the resolution came before the Senate it failed to pass. A committee has been appointed by the Board of Directors to confer with the Executive Council and the Legislature in relation to rooms for the library and collections of the Society in the Capitol when completed.

SOCIETY'S SEAL.

During last year, at the suggestion of President Wilder, an engraved seal for the Society's use, with a design deemed appropriate, was procured to be made in Washington, through the kind offices of Senator Plumb. The design combines the seal of the State of Kansas, with the coats of arms of France and Spain at the periods of the sovereignty of those powers over Louisiana Territory, of which the territory within the bounds of Kansas formed a part.

ADDRESSES BEFORE THE SOCIETY.

At the annual meeting, January 17, 1888, addresses were delivered by the following persons:

Hon. D. W. Wilder delivered the annual address, briefly sketching the

history of the Society. Other addresses were delivered upon subjects pertaining to Kansas history, as follows:

Prof. I. T. Goodnow, Manhattan, Personal Reminiscences, being an account of the founding of Manhattan by a New England Emigrant Aid party in 1855, of which party Prof. Goodnow was the leader.

Hon. S. A. Kingman, Topeka, on the Growth and Development of Kansas.

Prof. W. H. Carruth, Lawrence, on the subject of the Origin of Kansas Geographical Names.

C. A. Hiller, Esq., Salina, on the Padouacas, and other Aboriginal Tribes of Kansas.

C. F. Scott, Iola, on the subject of the Pioneer Press of Kansas.

Hon. H. N. Lester, Syracuse, on the Colonization of the Upper Arkansas Valley in Kansas.

Hon. J. Ware Butterfield, Florence, on the subject of the Kansas Historical Society, the character of its work, and the importance of maintaining it.

Columbus Borin, of Oberlin, on Kansas, her History, her History-makers, and her Historical Society.

Hon. James F. Legate, Leavenworth, on the Pioneers of Kansas, referring particularly to the services of Joel K. Goodin, Samuel C. Pomeroy, John Brown, and some others.

Noble L. Prentis, Newton, on the subject of the Swedish, Bohemian, Irish, and other colonies of foreigners in Kansas.

Historical papers were prepared and presented to the meeting by persons who were not present, as follows:

John P. Jones, of Coldwater, on the subject of the alleged Exploration of Lieut. Du Tisne, in 1719, of the country of the Osages, Pawnees and Padouacas.

J. S. Painter, of Garden City, on Southwestern Kansas, its settlement, development, and transformation.

Prof. C. A. Swensson, of Lindsborg, on the History of the Swedish American settlements in Kansas.

Printed or manuscript copies of most of these addresses and papers are in the files of the Society, and should form a part of a volume of collections which should be published at an early day.

TERM OF OFFICE OF PRESIDENT.

At the annual meeting in January, 1888, Hon. D. W. Wilder, having held the office of President for one year, resigned the position, and Hon. Edward Russell of Lawrence was elected in his stead for the unexpired term of one year. This was done in pursuance of the suggestion made by Gen. Wilder and approved by a vote of the Board of Directors, that it would be better for the interests of the Society that the term of the office of President should be but for one year, instead of two years as provided in the constitution.

An amendment of the constitution for this object has been proposed and placed in the minutes of the Society for consideration at the annual meeting in 1889. It is in the following words:

"The elective officers of the Society shall consist of a President and two Vice-Presidents, who shall hold their offices for the term of one year, and until their successors shall be chosen; a Secretary and a Treasurer, who shall hold their offices for the term of two years, and until their successors shall be chosen; said officers to be chosen by the Board of Directors from their members, their election to be made at the first meeting of the Board subsequent to the annual meeting of the Society, and their terms of office shall begin at the date of their election and qualification in office."

At this meeting, also, Hon. William A. Phillips, of Salina, was elected one of the Vice-Presidents, in the place of Hon. Henry H. Williams, who has removed from the State.

FINANCES, 1887.

The finances of the Society for the year ending January 17, 1888, including the Treasurer's account of receipts and expenditures and the expenditures from the appropriations made by the Legislature, as shown at the annual meeting, 1888, were as follows:

RECEIPTS.

1887.

Jan. 18, Appropriations to June 30, 1887	$1,135 39
" 18, Balance in hands of Treasurer of Society, fees	3 20
" 18, Balance of miscellaneous appropriation	322 62
July 1, Appropriation to June 30, 1888	4,250 00
Receipts from membership fees	54 00
Total	$5,765 21

EXPENDITURES.

Salaries and clerk hire from general appropriations	$2,447 55	
Clerk hire from miscellaneous appropriations	322 62	
Clerk hire from membership receipts	14 40	
Purchase of books	653 78	
Postage, freight and contingent	485 73	3,924 08
Balance		$1,841 13

FINANCES, 1888.

The finances for the period commencing January 18, and ending November 20th, 1888, are as follows:

RECEIPTS.

1888.

Jan. 17, Balance of appropriation to June 30, 1888	$1,798 33
" 17, Balance in hands of Treasurer of Society, fees	42 80
July 1, Appropriation to June 30, 1889	4,250 00
Receipts from membership fees	54 00
Total	$6,145 13

Forward, total receipts...$6,145 13

EXPENDITURES.

Salaries and clerk hire.......................................	$2,500 00	
Purchase of books..	745 11	
Postage, freight and contingent............................	206 47	
Expenditures from membership fees........................	64 80	3,516 38
Balance..		$2,628 75

PRINCIPAL LIBRARY ACCESSIONS.

The following classified lists show the principal accessions of books and pamphlets to the library during the period covered by the report:

BIBLIOGRAPHY AND JOURNALISM.—Indexes to 16 vols. New York Daily Tribune; Clarke's Globe Dictionary of the English Language; Publishers' Trade-List Annual, 1888; Bulletins of the Library Company of Philadelphia; Hammett's Bibliography of Newport, Rhode Island; Proceedings of the Mississippi Press Association, 1885–6; Norton's History of the Texas Press; Perrin's Pioneer Press of Kentucky; English Catalogue of Books for 1887; Annual American Catalogue, 1887; Poole's Index to Periodical Literature; Continuous Index to Periodicals; Prof. M. M. Campbell's Publications on the Improvement of the English Alphabet, 5 pamphlets; Knudsen's Spelling Reform Publications, 3; Gibson's Bibliography of Short-hand; Sampson's History of Advertising; Bates's Advertiser's Handy Guide; Bates's Advertiser's Guide Book, 1888; Alden's American Newspaper Catalogue, 1886; Rowell's American Newspaper Directories, 7 vols.; Ayer's Newspaper Annual, 1886, 1887.

RELIGION, TEMPERANCE, MORMONISM.—Walsh's Echoes of Bible History; Reports of American Sunday School Union; The Policy of the M. E. Church, 1842; Kerr's People's History of Presbyterianism; Pingree and Rice's Debate on the Doctrine of Universal Salvation; Bradlee's Sermons for All Sects; Mayo's Graces and Powers of the Christian Life; History of the American Missionary Association; Adams's Bohemian Work in Chicago; The West Church, Boston, Commemorative Services, 1887; Cooke's History of the Clapboard Trees Parish, Dedham, Mass.; Kidder's Mormons, 1852; Gunnison's Mormons or Latter Day Saints; Hyde's Mormonism, Its Leaders and Designs; Annual Report Kansas Y. M. C. A., 1888; Historical Sketch of the First Presbyterian Church of Lawrence, Kansas, 1888; Kansas Baptist Annual, 1886; Clubb's Maine Liquor Law and Life of Neal Dow; Proceedings of the United Grand Commandery Knights Templar, 1886; Armstrong's Temperance Reformation.

UNITED STATES PUBLIC DOCUMENTS.—Congressional Documents, 172 vols.; Presidents' Messages and Documents, 1873–1882, 13 vols.; Reports of the Secretary of U. S. Treasury; Annual Report U. S. Commissioner of Pensions, 1888; Report of the U. S. Commissioner of Patents, 1884; Statistics of the United States Domestic Commerce of 1863; Nimmo's Internal

Commerce of the United States; Nimmo's Commerce and Navigation; Reports, Commerce and Navigation of the United States, 6 vols.; Commercial Relations of the United States, 1862; Index to U. S. Consular Reports; Statistics and Preliminary Reports of the U. S. Census, 1860; Reports of the Director of U. S. Mint, 7 vols.; Proceedings of National Prison Reform Congress; Proceedings of the U. S. Conference of Charities and Corrections; Report of the U. S. Commissioner of Labor, 1887; Proceedings of the National Convention of Bureaus of Statistics and Labor, 4 vols.; Bulletins of U. S. Fish Commissioner, 1881–4; Bulletins of U. S. Commissioner of Fisheries, vols. 2, 3 and 4; Annual Report of the U. S. Commissioner of Fish and Fisheries; Goode's Fisheries and Fish Industries of the United States; Bulletins and Proceedings of the U.S. National Museum, 11 vols.; Report of U. S. Chief Signal Officer, 1887; Report of the U. S. Chief Signal Office; Reports of the Chief Signal Officer of the United States, 4 vols.; Annual Reports of the U. S. Light House Board, 1886 and 1887, 2 vols.; U. S. Life-Saving Service Report; Annual Reports and Maps of the U. S. Coast Survey, 5 vols.; U. S. Official Postal Guide; Annual Report of the U. S. Superintendent of Public Documents.

STATE DOCUMENTS.— Reports of Illinois Railroad and Warehouse Commissioners; Reports of Iowa, Massachusetts, Minnesota, and New York Railroad Commissioners; Reports of Iowa State Veterinary Surgeon; Reports Iowa State Library, 9 vols.; Census of the State of New York, 1875; Year Book of Charleston, South Carolina, 1887; Report of the Massachusetts Board of Lunacy and Charity, 1887; Reports of Ohio Meteorological Bureau; Bulletins Nebraska and Missouri Weather Service; Annual Reports of the Governors of Idaho, Montana, New Mexico, Washington, and Wyoming Territories; Publications of Montana Territory, 16 vols.; Reports of the Indiana, Louisiana, Michigan and Wisconsin State Boards of Health; Reports of the New Jersey and New York Bureaus of Statistics of Labor; Michigan Registration of Vital Statistics, 1872; Ohio State Statistical Report; Reports of Indiana Department of Statistics.

POLITICS, POLITICAL ECONOMY.— Journal of Debates in the Massachusetts Convention, 1820–21; Discussions on the Massachusetts Constitution of 1853; Pamphlets on the Constitution of the United States; Stanwood's History of Presidential Elections; Bartlett's Presidential Candidates, 1860.; Henry's Messages of President Buchanan; Benton's Thirty Years' View; Works of William H. Seward, 5 vols.; Mill's Essay on Liberty; McPherson's Hand-Book of Politics, 1868, 1872, 1880, 1888; Proceedings in the Cases of the Impeachment of Kansas State Officers, 1862; Trumbull's American Lesson of the Free Trade Struggle in England; Lieb's Protective Tariff; Peffer's Tariff Manual; Oglesby's Usury; Prohibition Party Campaign Documents, 1886, 1888; The Knight's Book, the Principles and Aims of the Knights of Labor; Gunton's Wealth and Progress; Kellogg's Labor and Capital; Smith's Hard Times, Suggestions to Workers and Hints

—2

to the Rich; Jacobson's Hints Toward Settling the Labor Troubles; Foreman's Big Wages and How to Earn Them; Gilmore's Republican Campaign Songs, 1888; Colton's Labor Songs; Ingalls' Social Wealth; Norcross' History of Democracy; Lumry's National Suicide and Its Prevention; Parsons' Rights of a Citizen of the United States; Quarantine Laws of the United States; Endicott's Immigration Laws of the United States, State and National; Cullin's China in America; Dillon's Oddities of Colonial Legislation; Chapman's Right and Wrong in Massachusetts; Hale's How They Lived in Hampton; Woman Suffrage in Kansas; Reynolds's History of the Grand Lodge of Illinois; Proceedings of the Grand Lodge of Kansas, 1870–1875; Proceedings of the M. W. Grand Lodge of Kansas, 1886–8; Proceedings of the Grand Commandery of Kansas, 1868–1885; Proceedings of the Grand Chapter of Kansas, 1866–1874.

SLAVERY.—Elliot's Bible and Slavery; Clarkson's Essay on Slavery; Alcot's African Colonization; Channing's West India Emancipation; The Boston Slave Riot and Trial of Anthony Burns; The Abolitionist, 1833; Stearns's Notes on Uncle Tom's Cabin; Jones's Negro Myths from the Georgia Coast; Cable's The Negro Question.

FINANCE.—Financial History of the United States from 1774 to 1885, 3 vols.; Knox's History of the Issues of United States Paper Money; Baker's, The Subject of Money; Report of the Silver Commission of the United States, 1876; Dye's Coin Encyclopedia.

MILITARY AND NAVAL.—Scott's General Regulations for the U. S. Army, 1821; U. S. Army Regulations, 1881; Hamersly's Army and Navy Register, 1776–1887; Hamersly's Army Register, U. S., for one hundred years, 1779–1879; Official Army Registers of the United States, 1887, 1888; Scribner's Navy in the Civil War, 3 vols.; Reports Chief of Engineers, U. S. Army; Report of the Chief of Ordnance, U. S. A., 1886; Report of the Secretary of U. S. Navy, 2 vols., 1885 and 1886; Congressional Report on Ordnance and War Ships; War Series, Information from Abroad; Naval Resources, Information from Abroad; Chadwick's Training of Seamen in England and France; Soley's Foreign Systems of Naval Education; Iowa Adjutant General's Report, 8 vols.; Report of the Adjutant General of Pennsylvania, 1866.

EDUCATION.—Kiddle & Schem's Cyclopædia of Education; Painter's History of Education; Low & Pulling's History of English Education; Rosenkranz's Philosophy of Education; Preyer's The Mind of the Child; Froebel's Education of Man; Lancaster Improvements in Education, 1807; Baldwin's Elementary Psychology and Education; White's European Schools of History and Politics; Laurie's Rise and Early Constitution of Universities; Adams's Study of History in American Colleges and Universities; Record of the Commemoration of the 250th Anniversary of Harvard University; Bowditch's History of Yale University; Hough's Historical and Statistical Sketch of the University of the State of New York; Alex-

SCIENCE.—Silliman's American Journal of Science and Arts, 36 numbers; The American Journal of Science, 1818; Woodward's Modern Philosophical Conceptions of Life; Good's Book of Nature; Annual Report Smithsonian Institution, 1849, 1884, 1885; Miscellaneous Publications of same, 9 vols.; Smithsonian Miscellaneous Collections, vols. 28 to 33; Smithsonian Contributions to Knowledge, 6 vols.; Reports of the American Philosophical Society; Proceedings of the American Philosophical Society, 1887; Proceedings of the American Philosophical Society, vol. 25, 1888; Proceedings of the Philadelphia Academy of Natural Sciences, 1888; Bulletins of the Washington Philosophical Society; Transactions of the Kansas Academy of Science; Journal of the Cincinnati Society of Natural History; Proceedings of the Cincinnati Society of Natural History, 1887; Essex Institute Bulletins, 18 vols., 1869–1886; Annales de Société des Sciences Naturelles, La Rochelle, France, 1886; Bulletin de Société des Sciences, Lettres et Arts, De Pau, France, 1885 to 1887, 2 vols.; Memoires de l'Académié de Sciences et Belles Lettres, de Dijon, France, vol. 9, 1887; American Ephemeris and Nautical Almanac, 1888; Proctor's Half-Hours With the Stars; Atkinson's Elements of Electric Lighting; Blodget's Climatology of the United States; Dawson's Geological History of Plants; Kellerman's Analytical Flora of Kansas, 1888; Hall's Catalogue of the Unionidæ of the Mississippi Valley; Keep's West Coast Shells; Allen's History of the American Bison; Patton's Natural Resources of the United States; Mineral Resources of the United States, 1867; Raymond's Mineral Resources West of the Rocky Mountains, 1877; Report of the Director of the U. S. Mint on Precious Metals, 1884; Annual Reports of the California State Mineralogist, 1885, '86, and '87; Reports of the Colorado State School of Mines, 1885–1887; De la Beche's Geological Manual; Hull's Geological History; Reports of U. S. Geological Survey; Emmons's Geology and Mining Industry of Leadville, Colo.; Emmons's Atlas of the Geology of Leadville; Worthen's Illinois Geological Report,

1875; Lyon, Cox and Lesquereux's Kentucky Geological Report, 1851; Owen's Kentucky Geological Report, 1858–9; Jackson's Maine Geological Report, 1837, 5 vols.; Jackson's Maine Geological Report, 1839; Broadhead, Meek & Shumard's Geological Report of Missouri, 1855–1871; Pumpelly's Missouri Geological Report, 1872; Shumard & Swallow's New Fossils from Missouri and Kansas; Swallow's Geology of the Southwest Branch of the Missouri Pacific Railroad; Leidy's Ancient Fauna of Nebraska, 1853; Geological History of Lake Lahontan, Nevada; Ohio Geological Reports, 6 vols., and maps; Rogers's Pennsylvania Geological Report, vols. 1 and 2, 1858; White's Pennsylvania Geological Report, 1878; Lesquereux's Atlas to the Coal Flora of Pennsylvania, 1879; Lesquereux's Text to accompany the same, 1880; Buckley's Reports of the Geological and Agricultural Survey of Texas, 1874, 1876; Dutton's Tertiary History of the Grand Cañon District, with atlas; Hager's Vermont Geological Reports, 1861; Whitfield's Paleontology of the Black Hills; Jenney's Mineral Wealth, etc., of the Black Hills, 1876; Billing's Canada Geological Report, 1861–5; Browne's Boston and New England Medical Register, 4 vols.; Stimson's History of Express Companies and Railroads; Wood's Practical Treatise on Railroads, 1832; Poor's Directory of Railroads, 1886.

ARCHÆOLOGY AND ETHNOLOGY.—Reports of the Peabody Museum of American Archæology and Ethnology; Baldwin's Ancient America; Read's Archæology of Ohio; Griffing's Archæological Chart of Manhattan and Vicinity; Büchner's Man in the Past, Present and Future; Thurston's Mound Builders; Report of the U. S. Bureau of Ethnology, 1881–1882; Cushing's Zuni Bread Stuff.

AGRICULTURE, HORTICULTURE AND FORESTRY.— Reports of Statistician of the U. S. Department of Agriculture, 14 vols.; Botanical Division U. S. Department of Agriculture, Bulletin Nos. 2, 3, 5 and 6; U. S. Department of Agriculture, 2d Report Bureau of Animal Industry, 1885; Annual Report U. S. Commissioner of Agriculture, 1887; Division of Entomology, U. S. Department of Agriculture, Bulletin No. 19; Division of Entomology, U. S. Department of Agriculture, Periodical Bulletins, vol. 1, Nos. 1, 2 and 3; Chemical Division, U. S. Department of Agriculture, Bulletins Nos. 2, 3, 6, 12, 13, 14, 15, 16, 17, and 18; Ohio State Forestry Review, 1886; Consular Reports on the Forestry of Europe; U. S. Agricultural Department's Report of Forestry Conditions of the Rocky Mountains; Proceedings of the Annual Conventions of American Florists, 1886–7; Alkali Lands, Irrigation and Drainage in California; Report of the Alabama Commissioner of Agriculture, 1888; Transactions of the Massachusetts Horticultural Society, 1887; Report of the Michigan State Pomological Society, 1878; Transactions of the Michigan State Agricultural Society, 14 years; Bulletins 34–38, Michigan Agricultural Farm Department; Reports of the Michigan State Board of Agriculture for 11 years; Proceedings of the Mississippi Horticultural Society, 1883; Twelve Bulletins of the Missouri State Agri-

cultural College; Ohio Agricultural Reports, 12 vols.; Report of the Commissioner of Agriculture of South Carolina, 1886; Tennessee Agricultural and Geological Map, 1888; Memoires Publier Par La Société Nationale d'Agriculture de France, 1888; Beal's Grasses of North America; Brisbin's Beef Bonanza, or How to Get Rich on the Plains; Brisbin's Trees and Tree Planting; Food and Food Adulterants, Wiley, Richardson and Crampton; U. S. Bulletin of Sugar-Producing Plants; Bulletins of the Connecticut Cornell University, Illinois, Kansas, Kentucky, Maine, Massachusetts, Michigan, Minnesota, Missouri, North Carolina, New Hampshire, Ohio, Pennsylvania, Vermont, and Wisconsin Agricultural Experiment Stations.

LITERATURE AND MISCELLANY.— Gov. John A. Martin's Addresses Delivered in Kansas; Peffer's Geroldine; or, What May Happen; Mrs. Hudson's Esther. The Gentile; Picard's Old Boniface; Peacock's Poems of the Plains, and Songs of the Solitudes; John P. Campbell's Poetical Works, Queen Sylvia and Other Poems, The Summerless Sea and Other Poems, and Merle of Medevon and other Prose Writings, 4 vols. in all; Jos. E. Badger's Stories and Tales of the West; Poems of Celeste May; Bartlett's Familiar Quotations; Hitchcock's Poetical Dictionary; Frey's Sobriquets and Nicknames; R. W. Emerson's Miscellanies; Hale's Books That Have Helped Me; Higginson's Hints on Writing and Speechmaking; Fiske's Mirror Annual and Directory of Theaters for 1888; William Wirt's Letters of the British Spy; Keim's Society in Washington; The Columbian Orator; Thompson's Seasons; Coates Kinney's Lyrics; W. M. Paxton's Poems; Poems of Phillis Wheatley; Humphrey's Miscellaneous Works.

HISTORY, GEOGRAPHY, DESCRIPTIVE, TRAVELS.— Memoires Société Historique, Litteraire, Artistique et Scientifique du Cher., vol. 3, 1887; Bulletin de la Société Nationale des Antiquaries de France, 1885 and 1886, 2 vols.; Archivos do Museu Nacional do Rio de Janeiro, vol. 7, 1887; Proceedings Canadian Institute, 1888; Proceedings New Hampshire Historical Society, 1884–8; Proceedings of the Massachusetts Historical Society, 1884–6; Massachusetts Historical Society Collections, vol. 2, sixth series: "Sewall's Letter-book"; Essex Institute Historical Collections, 23 vols., 1859–1886; Proceedings Bunker Hill Monument Association, 1888; Proceedings of the Rhode Island Historical Society, 1887–8; New York Historical Society Collections, 9 vols.; Publications of the Buffalo, New York, Historical Society, vols. 1 and 2; Proceedings of the New Jersey Historical Society; Southern Historical Society, vol. 15, 1887; Collections of the Virginia Historical Society, vol. 7, 1888; Georgia Historical Collections, 2 vols., 1840–2; Publications of the Western Reserve and Northern Ohio Historical Society, 7 vols.; Catalogue of the Minnesota Historical Society; Transactions of the Nebraska State Historical Society; Contibutions to the Historical Society of Montana, 1876; Papers of the Califoria Historical Society; Rawlinson's Ancient History; Stoke's Mediæval History; Patton's Modern History; Prescott's Encyclopedia of History,

Biography and Travel; Murray's. Encyclopedia of Geography; Morlitz's Travels in England in 1782; Atkinson's Oriental and Western Siberia; Margry, Memoires et Documents, Origines Francaises des Pays d'Outre-Mer, 1679–1754, 6 vols.; Historical Writings of Francis Parkman, 7 vols.; Kingsford's History of Canada, 1679–1725; Bryce's Short History of the Canadian People; Bryce's Old Settlers of the Red River, Canada; Bryce's Holiday Rambles Between Winnipeg and Victoria; Bryce's Manitoba, Its Infancy, Growth and Present Condition; Sullivan and Blake's Mexico, Picturesque, Political and Progressive, 1888; Hamilton's Mexican Handbook; Solis's History of the Conquest of Mexico by the Spaniards; Prescott's Conquest of Mexico, 3 vols.; Chevalier's Mexico, Ancient and Modern; Ruxton's Adventures in Mexico and the Rocky Mountains, 1846–7; Barrister's Trip to Mexico, 1849–50; Cubas' Republic of Mexico in 1876; Wilson's Mexico and Its Religion; Curtis's Capitals of Spanish America; Squier's Nicaragua, Its People, Scenery and the Proposed Oceanic Canal, 1852, 2 vols.; Stout's Nicaragua; Account of Miranda's Expedition; Pumpelly's Across America and Asia and Around the World; Jenkins's Exploring Expeditions of Wilkes d'Urville, Ross and Lynch; Nourse's American Explorations in the Ice Zone; International Polar Expedition to Point Barrow, Alaska, during the years 1881–1883, by Lieut. P. H. Ray; Schley's Greely Relief Expedition, 1884; Joel Barlow's Vision of Columbus; Bancroft's History of the United States, vols. 4–6; Winsor's Narrative and Critical History of the United States, 2 vols.; Henry's Normal History of the United States; Chevalier's Society in United States; Carnegie's Triumphant Democracy, or Fifty Years' March of the Republic; Pearse's History of Iron Manufacture in the American Colonies; Mellen's Book of the United States, 1836; Colerick's Adventures of Pioneer Children; Abbott's Blue Jackets of '76, Naval Battles of the Revolution; Conover's Journals of Sullivan's Expedition; Mrs. Grant's Memoirs of an American Lady; Baxter's British Invasion from the North, Campaigns of Carleton and Burgoyne, with Digby's Journal; Brown's Views of the Campaigns of the Northwestern Army, 1815; Cutts's Conquest of California and New Mexico; Tour to Northern Mexico with Doniphan's Expedition, 1846 and 1847, Wislizenus; Melish's Travels in the United States in 1806–11; Mitchell's Traveler's Guide Through the United States, 1833; Hodgson's Journey Through North America; Pope's Tour of the United States; Loskiel's Journey from Bethlehem, Penn, to Goshen, Ohio, in 1803; Dixon's Tour Through the United States and Canada; Barneby's Life and Labors in the Far West; Steele's Overland Guide, 1888; Gleed's Overland Guide; Clemens' Life on the Mississippi; Forman's Narrative of a Journey Down the Ohio and Mississippi, 1789–90; Whymper's Travel and Adventure in the Territory of Alaska; Emory's Mexican Boundary Survey, 2 vols., 1857–8; Reports of the Mexican Border Commission, 1875; McClure's Three Thousand Miles Through the

Rocky Mountains; Cox's Adventures on the Columbia River; Sitgreaves' Expedition Down the Zuni and Colorado Rivers, 1854; Stansbury's Exploration of Utah;. W. Hepworth Dixon's White Conquest; Palmer's Rocky Mountain Travels; Perkins' Check List for American Local History; Barber's History and Antiquities of New England, 1841; Stearns's History of Rindge, N. H.; Goodwin's Pilgrim Republic, Colony of New Plymouth; Stearns's History of Ashburnham, Mass.; Bates' Records of the Town of Braintree, Mass.; Celebration of the 250th Anniversary of Dedham, Mass.; Lewis's History of Linn, Mass.; Green's History of Springfield, Mass.; Mason's History of the Town and City of Springfield, Mass., 1636–1886; Winchester, Massachusetts, Historical Record; Providence Plantations for 250 Years, 1636 to 1886; Atwater's History of New Haven; Brooks's Story of New York; Clute's Annals of Staten Island, N. Y.; Broadhead's Towns along the Mohawk River from 1630–1634; Hough's History of Jefferson County, New York; Hotchkins's History of the Settlement of Western New York; Hawes's Buffalo Fifty Years Ago; Evert's History of Monroe County, New York; Parker's Rochester, New York, a Historical Story; Cornell's History of Pennsylvania; Howe's Historical Collections of New Jersey; Shaw's History of Essex and Hudson Counties, N. J.; Clay's Annals of the Swedes on the Delaware; Minutes of the Council of the State of Delaware, 1776–1792; McSherry's History of Maryland, 1634–1848; Polk's Hand-Book of North Carolina, 1879; Carroll's South Carolina, 1836; Year Book of Charleston, South Carolina, 1886; White's Historical Collections of Georgia; Meek's Romantic Passages in Southwestern History; Duane's Account of Louisiana, 1803; Stiff's Texas Emigrant; Smith's Reminiscences of the Texas Republic; McCalla's Adventures in Texas, 1840; Parker's Expedition of Captain Marcy Through Texas in 1854; Parker's Notes of Marcy's Expedition Through Texas in 1854; Phelan's History of Tennessee; Andrews' Admission of Kentucky, Tennessee and Ohio Into the Union; Historical Writings of Orasmus H. Marshall, in Relation to the West; Hale's Trans-Alleghany Pioneers; Gilmore's Advance Guard of Western Civilization; Hall's Legends of the West; The Old Northwest, Hinsdale; Drake's Making of the Great West; Mitchener's Ohio Annals, Historic Events in the Tuscarawas and Muskingum Valleys; Graham's History of Coshocton County, Ohio; Venable's Foot-Prints of the Pioneers in the Ohio Valley; Rickoff's Ohio, a Centennial Poem; History of Wayne County, Ohio; Norton's History of Knox County, Ohio; Alderman's Centennial Souvenir of Marietta, Ohio; Perrin's History of Stark County, Ohio; Black's Story of Ohio; Walker's History of Athens County, Ohio; Graham's History of Richland County, Ohio; Beers's History of Clark County, Ohio; Goodrich & Tuttle's Illustrated History of Indiana; Sheahan & Upton's Great Conflagration in Chicago; Reynolds' Pioneer History of Illinois; Blois' Gazetteer of Michi-

gan, 1839; History of Dane County, Wisconsin; Seymour's Sketches of Minnesota, with a map, 1850; Belton's Annals of St. Louis, Under the French and Spanish Domination; History of Vernon County, Missouri; History of Clay and Platte Counties, Missouri; McNamara's Three Years on the Kansas Border; W. W. Sargent's Holton, the County Seat of Jackson County, Kansas, 1888; Savage's Visit to Nebraska, 1842; Scidmore's Alaska; Priest's American Antiquities and Discoveries in the West; Buffalo Bill, His Wild West Show; McClung's Sketches of Western Adventure; Mrs. Custer's Tenting on the Plains, or General Custer in Kansas and Texas; Exploration for a Railroad Route from the Mississippi River to the Pacific Ocean, 1860; Dixon's New America; Bancroft's Pacific States Histories, 27 vols.; Marryat's Mountains and Mole Hills, California; Widney's California of the South; Nicolay's Oregon Territory, 1846; Houghton, Mifflin & Co.'s American Commonwealths, 9 vols.; Koster's Travels in Brazil, 1817; Kidder's Sketches of Residence and Travels in Brazil, 1845; Herndon's Exploration of the Valley of the Amazon, with atlas, 1854; King's Twenty-four Years in the Argentine Republic; Antonio de Ulloa's Noticias Americanos (Central and North), Madrid, 1792.

GAZETTEERS, DIRECTORIES, ALMANACS.—Ure's Dictionary of Arts, Manufactures of Mines, 2 vols.; Morse's American Gazetteer, 1797; Centennial Gazetteer of the United States, 1876; Zell's Business Directory, 1886; Ames's Almanac for 1765; Whig Almanac, N. Y., 1847–54, and Tribune Almanac, 1856–87, 14 years; American Almanac, 15 years, completing set from 1830; Brown's Western Gazetteer, 1817; Boston Municipal Register, 1861; Dickman's Kansas Medical Directory, 1881; Elk County Directory, 1888; Radges's Topeka City Directory, 1888–9.

MAPS, ATLASES, CHARTS.— Mitchell's New General Atlas; Labberton's Historical Atlas and General History; Historical Map of the United States; Monthly Pilot Charts of the North Atlantic Ocean; Map of the Great Central Route between the Atlantic and Mississippi, 1854; Maps of the Yellowstone Country; Andreas' Illustrated Historical Atlas of the State of Iowa; Rand, McNally & Co.'s Maps, (see list of map donations); Map of the Platte Country, Missouri, 1854; Meacham's Illustrated Atlas of Brown and Nemaha Counties, Kansas; Eleven Maps of Kansas and parts of Kansas. (See list of donors of maps, atlases, and charts.)

BIOGRAPHY.— Morley's English Writers; Groser's Men Worth Imitating; Simmons's Men of Mark; Victor's Life and Events; Angell's Autobiographical Sketches; Appleton's Cyclopædia of American Biography, 5 vols.; American Men of Letters, 10 vols.; Houghton, Mifflin & Co.'s American Statesmen, 18 vols.; Miller's Bench and Bar of Georgia; Lynch's Bench and Bar of Mississippi; Everett's Address on Charles Francis Adams; Life of P. T. Barnum; Biography of Rev. Henry Ward Beecher; Knox's Life

and Work of Henry Ward Beecher; Rosevelt's Life of Thomas Hart Benton; Hayden's Biographical Sketch of Oliver Brown; Curtis's Life of James Buchanan, 2 vols.; Hensel and Parker's Lives of Cleveland and Thurman; Life, Journals and Correspondence of Rev. Manasseh Cutler, 2 vols.; DeLesseps' Recollections of Forty Years; Life and Times of Frederick Douglass; Mansfield's Memoirs of Daniel Drake, and of the Early Settlement of Cincinnati; Biographical Sketch of Lyman C. Draper and M. M. Jackson; Hayden's Gen. Roger Enos, of Arnold's Expedition to Canada, 1775; Life of John B. Finch; McMaster's Benjamin Franklin as a Man of Letters; Memoirs of John C. Fremont; Hale's Franklin in France, parts 1 and 2; Austin's Life of Elbridge Gerry; Greeley's Recollections of a Busy Life; Reminiscences of General W. S. Hancock; Taylor's Memoirs of Joseph Henry; Jackson's Life of William Henry Harrison; Grigg and Elliot's Life of General William H. Harrison; Wallace and Townsend's Lives of Harrison and Morton; Danvers's Thomas Jefferson; Life of Amos A. Lawrence; Arnold's Life of Abraham Lincoln; Rice's Reminiscences of Abraham Lincoln; Wells's Lincoln and Seward; Dawson's Life and Services of Gen. John A. Logan; Rudd and Carleton's Life and Writings of Gen. Nathaniel Lyon; Woodward's Life of Gen. Nathaniel Lyon; Adams's Lives of Madison and Monroe; Magruder's Biography of John Marshall; Weems's Life of William Penn; Jenkins's President Polk and His Administration; Reminiscences of Ben: Perley Poore; Memoirs, Correspondence and Reminiscences of William Renick; Diary of Thomas Robbins; Life of Emery A. Storrs; Harsha's Life of Charles Sumner; Byrce's Biographical Sketch of John Tanner; Life and Writings of Grant Thorburn; Autobiography of Lorenzo Waugh, 4th edition; Hall's Life of George Washington; Lossing's Home of Washington; Autobiography of Thurlow Weed; Memoirs of Thurlow Weed; Hayden's Weitzel Memorial.

GENEALOGY.— Burke's General Armory of England, Scotland, Ireland and Wales, 1883; Savage's Genealogical Dictionary, 4 vols.; New England Historic Genealogical Society Proceedings; Hughes' American Ancestry; Munsell's American Ancestry; Rupp's thirty thousand names of German, Swiss, Dutch, French and other Immigrants in Pennsylvania; Austin's Genealogical Dictionary of Rhode Island; Dedham, Massachusetts, Record of Marriages, Births and Deaths, 1635–1845; Genealogy of the Family of Ralph Earle; Genealogy of the Family of George Marsh, of Hingham, Mass., by E. J. Marsh; The Genealogy of John Marsh, of Salem, Mass.; Genealogy of the Perrin Family; Hayden's Pollock's Descendents.

INDIANS.— Cleveland's Lost Tribes; Lake Mohonk Conference of the friends of the Indians, 1887; Helen Jackson's Century of Dishonor; Barrow's The Indians' Side of the Indian Question; Harrison's Studies on Indian Reservations; Life of John Eliot, The Apostle to the Indians; Jacobs's No-

nantum and Natiek, Mass.; Ojibway New Testament, 1844; Powell's Introduction to the Study of Indian Languages; Hayden's Silver and Copper
Indian Medals; Compiled Laws of the Cherokee Nation, from 1839–1875;
Blackbird's History of the Ottawa and Chippewa Indians; Lang and Taylor's Visit to Indians West of the Mississippi, 1843; Newsom's Scenes Among
the Indians, and Custer's Last Fight; Johnston's Capture by the Indians in
1790; Col. James Smith's Captivity with the Indians, 1755–9; Jewett's Captivity among the Savages of Nootka Sound, 1815; Pattie's Narrative, Timothy
Flint; Seaver's Life of Mary Jemison; Foster's Sequoyah; Mrs. Eastman's
Dahcotah, or Life and Legends of the Sioux; Brisbin's Belden, The White
Chief.

REBELLION.—Greeley's American Conflict; Nicolay's Outbreak of the
Rebellion; Moore's Rebellion Record, 12 vols.; Raymond's History of the
Administration of President Lincoln; Compte De Paris, History of the
Civil War in America, 4 vols.; Campaigns of the Civil War, 13 vols.;
Official Army Register of the volunteer force of the United States Army,
1861–5, parts 3 and 6; Reports on the Conduct of the War, 1865, 3 vols.;
Official Records, War of the Rebellion, 7 vols.; Medical and Surgical His-
tory of the War of the Rebellion, vol. 1, part 3; Reports of the Woman's
Relief Corps; Bigelow's France and the Confederate Navy, 1862–8; Wil-
liams's Negro Troops in the War of the Rebellion; Wilson's, The Black
Phalanx; A History of the Negro Soldiers of the U. S.; Higginson's Army
Life in a Black Regiment; Pinkerton's Spy of the Rebellion; Pitman's
Trials for Treason; Glisan's Journal of Army Life; Steele's Frontier Army
Sketches; Swinton's Campaigns of the Army of the Potomac; Van Horne's
History of the Army of the Cumberland; Gen. Logan's Volunteer Soldier
of America; Gen. McClellan's Own Story, The War for the Union; Auto-
biography of Private Dalzell; Lee's Army Ballads and Other Poems;
Brown's Bugle Echoes, Poetry of the Civil War, Northern, and Southern;
True's Maine in the War of the Union; Schouler's Massachusetts in the
Civil War; Laciar's Patriotism of Carbon County, Penn., During the War
of the Rebellion; Sprenger's Camp and Field Life of the 122d Regiment
Pennsylvania Volunteers; Jacob's Rebel Invasion of Maryland and Penn-
sylvania; Capt. D. J. Wright's History of the 8th Regiment Kentucky
Volunteer Infantry; Ohio Official Roster of Soldiers; Roster of the Ohio
Soldiers in the War of the Rebellion, 3 vols.; Merrill's Soldier of Indiana
in the War of the Union; Admire's Memoranda of Company E, 65th Regiment Indiana Infantry; List of ex-Soldiers, Sailors and Marines living in
Iowa; Kelso's Reign of Terror in Missouri; Dunnet's Roster of Michigan
Soldiers in Kansas; Moser's Roster of Iowa Soldiers in Kansas; Ellen Williams's History of the 2d Colorado Regiment; Stephens's Constitutional View
of the War Between the States.

DONORS OF BOOKS AND PAMPHLETS.

The following is a list of gifts made to the Society of books and pamphlets by individuals and institutions, including exchanges and gifts of State publications for exchanges with other societies and institutions:

Donors.	Books.	Pamp
Abbott, J. B., DeSoto	2	1
Abbott, Willis J., Kansas City, Mo	1	....
Academie de La Rochelle, Société de Sciences Naturelles, La Rochelle, France	2	....
Academie des Belles-lettres, Sciences et Arts, La Rochelle, France	1	....
Academie des Sciences et Belles-lettres, Dijon, France	1	....
Adair, Rev. S. L., Osawatomie	9	42
Adams, F. G., Topeka	1	4
Adams, Frank Scott, Waterville	....	1
Adams, John W., Topeka	....	2
Adams, Rev. Edwin E., Chicago, Ill	....	1
Admire, J. V., Ossage City	1	9
Admire, W. W., Topeka	8	....
Alabama Commissioner of Agriculture, Montgomery	1	....
Alden, Edwin, Cincinnati, O.	1	....
Alexander, W. L., Des Moines, Ia	1	....
Allen, A. T., Topeka	2	31
Allen, Hon. E. B., Topeka	63	....
Allison, W. M., editor Visitor, Wichita	....	1
Alrich, L. L., Cawker City	....	1
American Bell Telephone Co., Boston, Mass	....	1
American Congregational Association, Boston, Mass	....	1
American Historical Association, Washington, D. C.	....	5
American Home Missionary Society, New York	3	5
American Humane Association, Chicago, Ill	....	12
American Institute of Electrical Engineers, New York city	4	....
American Museum of Natural History, New York city	....	4
American Philosophical Society, Philadelphia, Pa	2	1
American Protective Tariff League, New York city	....	11
American Sunday-School Union, Philadelphia, Pa	....	4
American Tract Society, New York city	....	1
Ames, John G., Washington, D. C.	....	5
Anderson, Hon. John A., Washington, D. C.	....	1
Andrews, Dr. Israel Ward, Marietta, O.	....	1
Angell, George T., Boston, Mass	2	51
Anthony, D. R., Leavenworth	....	2
Anthony, Gov. George T., Leavenworth	....	1
Appleton, F. H., Boston, Mass	4	2
Arkansas Deaf-Mute Institute, Little Rock	....	1
Armstrong and Moyer, editors Gazette, Wyandotte	....	4
Astor Library, New York	....	1
Atchison, Topeka & Santa Fé Railroad Co., Boston, Mass	....	2
Atwood, G. A., editor Republican, Manhattan	....	1
Austin Industrial School, Knoxville, Tenn	....	7
Ayer, N. W. & Son, Philadelphia, Pa	3	....
Badger, Joseph E., Frankfort	....	21
Baker, C. C., Topeka	....	7
Baker, F. P., Topeka	68	83
Baldwin, W. H., Boston, Mass	1	....
Ball, Mrs. Bell, Topeka	....	1
Ball, R. W., Harper	....	1
Bancroft Bros., San Francisco, Cal	1	....
Barnes, J. S., Sec., Phillipsburg	....	3
Barnes, Mrs. Charles, Manhattan	....	1
Barnes, W. H., Sec., Independence	....	10
Barton, C. M., Worcester, Mass	....	10
Bass, A. & Co., McPherson	....	3
Bates, J. H., New York city	1	1
Battell, Robbins and Miss Anna, Norfolk, Conn	1	....
Beadle & Adams, New York city	....	62
Beegley, J. F., Sec., Girard	....	8
Belfield, Henry H., Chicago, Ill	....	4
Belrose, Louis, Washington, D. C.	....	2
Bennett and Benham, editors Prohibitionist, Columbus	....	2
Betton, Hon. Frank H., Topeka	2	18
Bigelow, John, New York city	....	4
Biggers, Mrs. Kate H., Longton	....	1
Black, George, Olathe	....	1
Blake, C. C., Richland	....	1
Bonham and Palmer, editors Dispatch, Clay Center	....	2
Boston Public Library, Boston, Mass	2	2
Boston Public Schools, Boston, Mass	....	....

DONORS OF BOOKS AND PAMPHLETS—CONTINUED.

Donors.	Books.	Pamp
Boudinot, W. P., Tahlequah, I. T.	6	....
Boutwell, D. W., Topeka	....	1
Bowes, G. W., Topeka	....	3
Brackett, George C., Lawrence	1	....
Bradford, Hon. S. B., Topeka	2	2
Bradford, Mrs. M. F., Atchison	....	1
Bradlee, Rev. C. D., Boston, Mass.	4	85
Branner, A. J., Clifton	1	....
Brigham, Sarah M., Junction City	....	1
British and American Archæological Society, Rome, Italy	....	2
Brooklyn Library, Brooklyn, N. Y.	....	4
Brown, Capt. John, jr., Put-in-Bay Island, Ohio	....	1
Brown, Dr. Francis H., Boston, Mass.	4	3
Brown, George W., Rockford, Ill.	....	4
Brown, John H., Kansas City, Kas.	4	1
Brown, Joseph M., Atlanta, Ga.	....	1
Brown, Orville C., Adams, N. Y.	....	3
Brown, Rev. Duncan, Highland	....	7
Browne, J. C., editor Bugle, Burdett	....	9
Buffalo Historical Society, Buffalo, N. Y.	2	1
Bureau of Press Cuttings, New York city, N. Y.	....	1
Burnett, H. C., Santa Fé, N. M.	....	2
Burton & Black, editors Times, Ness City	....	5
Bushell, W., Camden, N. J.	....	2
Caldwell, E. F., Lawrence	....	1
California Historical Society, Berkeley, Cal.	1	1
California State Mining Bureau, San Francisco.	3	....
California University, Berkeley	4	7
Campbell, J. B., Haddam	....	1
Campbell, John Preston, Abilene	4	....
Campbell, J. P., and D. A. Valentine, editors of the Times, Clay Center	....	3
Campbell, M. M., North Topeka	....	10
Canadian Institute, Toronto	1	4
Caruthers, E. P., editor Index, Medicine Lodge	....	1
Case, Nelson, Oswego	....	1
Caspar, C. N., Milwaukee, Wis.	....	1
Cassell & Co., New York City	1	4
Cavanaugh, Thomas H., Olympia, W. T.	....	4
Century Company, New York City	1	3
Chaffee, Rev. H. W. Ottawa	....	3
Chamberlain, A. F., Toronto, Canada	....	2
Chambers, W. L., Stockton	....	5
Chapman, E. L., editor Register, Great Bend	....	3
Chapman, J. B., editor Tribune, Fort Scott	....	2
Chicago Board of Public Works, Chicago, Ill.	1	....
Chicago Historical Society, Chicago, Ill.	5	3
Children's Aid Society, New York city	....	11
Children's Hospital, Boston, Mass.	....	1
Childs, George W., Philadelphia, Pa	....	1
Church Home for Orphan and Destitute Children, Boston, Mass.	....	2
Church Temperance Society, New York City.	....	5
Cincinnati Society of Natural History, Cincinnati, Ohio	....	6
Clapp, Rev. A. H., D. D., New York City	1	1
Clark, A. P., editor Republic, Washington, D. C.	....	1
Clark, Arthur, Leavenworth	....	1
Clark, Geo. A., editor Republican, Junction City	....	2
Clark, S. H. H., St. Louis	....	1
Clarke, Robert, Cincinnati, Ohio	....	11
Clarke, S. H., Clyde, N. Y.	....	14
Clarkson, Harrison, Topeka	....	4
Clement, G. W., Wichita	1	4
Clough, J. F., secretary, Sabetha	....	1
Cochrane, John C., Chicago, Ill	....	1
Collet, C. D., London, England	....	18
Collins, J. S. & Co., Topeka	....	2
Colorado State Agricultural College, Fort Collins	....	1
Colorado State School of Mines, Denver	3	....
Cone, William W., Topeka	2	10
Congregational Sunday-school Publication Society, Boston, Mass.	1	....
Connecticut Agricultural Experiment Station, New Haven	1	2
Cooke, Gen. P. St. George, Detroit, Mich.	....	1
Corbin, Caroline F., Chicago, Ill.	....	2
Cornell University, Ithaca, N. Y.	1	3
Cornell University Agricultural Experiment Station, Ithaca, N. Y.	1	2
Courtenay, William A., Charleston, S. C.	2	....
Cragin, F. W., Topeka	....	5
Crane, Geo. W., Topeka	....	4
Crawford, Gov. Samuel J., Topeka	1	7
Criswell, Ralph L., Gove City	....	1

DONORS OF BOOKS AND PAMPHLETS—Continued.

Donors.	Books.	Pamp
Crosby, D. R., Minneapolis		1
Cruce, W. P., El Dorado		1
Cullin, Stewart, Philadelphia, Pa		1
Cummins, C. S., Caneua		1
Currier, Charles, Leavenworth		1
Cuthbertson, M. D., Voltaire		1
Cutter, C. A., Boston, Mass		1
Darling, C. W., Utica, N. Y	1	11
Davenport Academy of Science, Davenport, Iowa		1
Davie, W. O., Cincinnati, Ohio	8	10
Davis, Charles S., editor Tribune, Junction City		3
Dedham Historical Society, Dedham, Mass	1	1
DeGeer, Mrs. M. E., Topeka		2
Delaware Historical Society, Wilmington	1	
DeMotte, McK., editor Independent, Enterprise		1
Dennis, H. J., Topeka	3	
DesMoines Academy of Science, DesMoines, Iowa		2
Dewey, A. T., San Francisco, Cal		1
Dewey, Melvil, New York City		4
Doane College, Crete, Neb		1
Doniphan, Col. John, St. Joseph, Mo	1	2
Dowling, Thomas, Washington, D. C		1
Drummond, Frank, Topeka	1	
Dunnett, D. W., Howard		1
Earle, Pliny, Northampton, Mass	1	
Easley, Ralph, editor News, Hutchinson		1
Eastman, Dr. B. D., Topeka	6	
Eaton, Ben. A., editor Beacon, Wichita		2
Egle, Dr. W. H., Harrisburg, Pa	2	
Eldridge, J. L., Topeka		6
Elliott, L. R., Manhattan		57
Essex Institute, Salem, Mass	41	10
Fairchild, George T., Manhattan		17
Farmers Loan Company, Winfield		2
Field, Millard L., Osawatomie		1
Filson, T. A., and P. M., editors Times, Concordia		1
Findlay, George W., Topeka		3
Fish, H. S., editor Chieftain, LaCrosse		1
Fisk, Clinton B., New York city		41
Fiske, Daniel, Minneapolis, Minn		7
Foley, J. M., Chicago, Ill		5
Foote, A. E., Philadelphia, Pa		1
Forde, E. M., Emporia		1
Foster, Joseph, London, Eng	1	
Frenow, B. E., Washington, D. C		6
Frost, Harry W., editor Lance, Topeka		2
Fuller, Mrs. Mary, Washington, D. C		1
Funk, John J., Sec., Peabody		1
Funston, Hon. E. H., Washington, D. C		3
Gallagher, F. W., Sec., St. Marys		1
Galloway, John M., Topeka		13
Gast, Hallie A., Fremont, Ohio	1	
Gazette Company, St. Joseph, Mo		4
Georgia Historical Society, Savannah, Ga		1
Gerard, Charles B., Anderson, Ind	1	
Gile, W. S., Venango		3
Gillman, H. A., Supt. State Hospital for the Insane, Mount Pleasant, Iowa		1
Gilmore, John S., Fredonia		1
Girls' Higher School, Chicago, Ill		1
Globe-Democrat Co., St. Louis, Mo		3
Goepel, Frank, Sec., Cawker City		6
Goodnow, Rev. I. T., Manhattan	2	512
Graham, I. D., Manhattan	1	20
Grand Chapter, Kansas	1	
Grand Commandery, Kansas	2	
Green, Dr. Samuel A., Boston, Mass	21	336
Green, Samuel S., Worcester, Mass		1
Greer, Ed. P., editor Courier, Winfield		1
Griffin, Albert, New York city		39
Griswold, W. M., Washington, D. C		1
Guild, E. B., Topeka		2
Hadley, T. J., Olathe		1
Haffa, S. A., editor Nugget, Dorrance		1
Hamilton, Hon. James W., Topeka	3	
Hampton, E. S., Detroit, Mich		3
Hard, N. J., Topeka	8	
Harding, W. J., Hillsboro		1
Harper, Rev. Joel, Wichita		3
Harrington, Grant W., Lawrence		2

DONORS OF BOOKS AND PAMPHLETS—CONTINUED.

Donors.	Books.	Pamp
Hart, Rev. O. E. Minneapolis		1
Harvard University, Cambridge, Mass	7	2
Haskell, W. H., Atchison	1	
Hayden, Rev. Horace Edwin, Wilkesbarre, Pa		15
Heatley, T. W. Wyandotte		3
Heely, P. J., San Francisco		9
Hein, O. L., Leavenworth		1
Hendy, Rev. J. F., Emporia		6
Herald Company, St. Joseph, Mo		7
Higgins, L. L., Topeka		2
Higginson, Thomas W., Cambridge, Mass	1	
Hile, J. W., Valley Falls		1
Hill, Dr. G. H., Independence, Ia		1
Hill, William L., St. Louis, Mo		1
Hinckley, Howard V., Topeka		1
Hinton, R. J., New York city		1
Hirons, C. C., Topeka	2	
Historical and Philosophical Society of Ohio, Cincinnati		1
Historical Society of Southern California, Los Angeles		1
Hodgdon, D. P., editor Prohibitionist, Lyons		2
Hoffman, Rev. R. A., Downs		2
Holliday, C. K., Topeka	1	
Holman, Rev. C., North Topeka		1
Holt, L. H. & Co., Topeka		2
Horton, Hon. A. H., Topeka		2
Howe, E. W., editor Globe, Atchison		4
Howland, Joseph A., Worcester, Mass		1
Hudson, J. K., Topeka		3
Hudson, Mrs. M. W., Topeka	1	
Hulbert, E. W., Sec., Fort Scott		1
Huling, Alden S., Topeka	34	
Humphrey, Mrs. Mary A., Junction City	1	
Hutchins, B. S., editor Leader, Kingman		6
Iliff, J. M., Mound City		1
Illinois Agricultural Experiment Station		2
Illinois Industrial University, Champaign, Ill	13	
Indian Rights Association, Philadelphia, Pa	1	8
Indiana Department of Statistics, Indianapolis	1	
Indiana Historical Society, Indianapolis		1
Indiana State Board of Health, Indianapolis	2	
Indianapolis Public Library, Indianapolis, Ind		1
Industrial Education Association, New York City		26
Industrial League, Philadelphia, Pa		7
Ingalls, Hon. John J., Washington, D. C	6	2
Iowa, Adjutant General of	6	2
Iowa State Agricultural College, Ames, Iowa	9	10
Iowa State Board of Health, DesMoines		1
Iowa State Historical Society, Iowa City		1
Iowa State Library, DesMoines, Iowa	8	3
Iowa State Veterinary Department		2
Jackson, H. M., Atchison	1	
Jenkins, W. L., Boston, Mass		1
Jerome, F. E., Russell		33
Johns Hopkins University, Baltimore, Md	2	23
Johns, Mrs. Laura M., Salin		11
Johnston, John C., Secretary, Newton		4
Journal Company, Kansas City, Mo		6
Kansas Academy of Science, Topeka	60	
Kansas Board of Railroad Commissioners, Topeka	100	3
Kansas State Teachers' Association		17
Kaufman, A C., Charleston, S. C		1
Kellam, T. J., Topeka		1
Kellerman, W. A., Manhattan	1	2
Kelly, H. B, editor Freeman, McPherson		4
Kenea & Lane, editors Journal, LaCygne		8
Kentucky Agricultural Experiment Station		13
Kessler, D., Willis		1
Kilmer, Fred. B, New Brunswick, N. J		5
Knapp, F. A., Topeka		31
Knapp, George W., Kendall		3
Knight Brothers, New York City		1
Knox, Rev. J. D., Topeka		5
Knox, Rev. M. V. B., Littleton, N. H		2
Knox, W. C. & Co., Topeka		5
Knudsen, C, W., Norwalk, Conn	3	
Kost, Dr. J., Tallahasse, Fla		2
Ladd, Rev. H. O., Santa Fé, N. M		2
Lamb, C. J., editor Independent, Kirwin		1
Lane, Ed. C., LaCygne		4

DONORS OF BOOKS AND PAMPHLETS—CONTINUED.

Donors.	Books.	Pamp
Langford & Stoke, editors Graphic, Great Bend		1
Lathy, W. E., Newton		1
Latimer, J. W., secretary, Pleasanton		3
Lawhead, Hon. J. H., Topeka	63	....
Lawrence, C. H., secretary, Hiawatha		1
Lawrence. Mrs. Sarah E., Brookline, Mass		4
Layton, William E., Newark, N. J		1
Leahy, D. D., Kiowa	1	
Leavenworth, Mrs. J. C., Haverford College, Pa		1
Lee, Ed. G., editor Democrat, Frisco		1
Lee, John I., editor Clipper, Ashland		2
Leicester, Massachusetts, Public Library		1
Leslie, Gov. Preston H., Helena. Montana		1
Library Bureau, Boston, Massachusetts		2
Library Company of Philadelphia, Philadelphia, Pa		3
Linn, John Blair, Bellefonte, Pa		1
Lippincott, Dr. J. A., Lawrence		41
Livingston County, New York, Historical Society, Danville, N. Y		1
Lockley, Fred., editor Traveler, Arkansas City		1
Logan, Rev. N. Rogers, Oskaloosa		1
Long Island Historical Society, Brooklyn, N. Y		1
Loue, Adolph, Cincinnati, Ohio	1	1
Louisiana State Board of Health, New Orleans	6	1
Lovett, J. T., Little Silver, N. J		1
Loy, William E., San Francisco, Cal		3
Lykins, W. H. R., Kansas City, Mo		1
Lyons, J. A., DesMoines, Iowa	12	1
MacLennan, Frank P., editor Journal, Topeka		1
McAllaster, O. W., Lawrence		2
McBride, Rev. R. F., Washington, Kas		2
McCarthy, Hon. Timothy, Topeka	57	....
McChesney, John W., Red Wing, Minn		1
McConnell, W. K., Sec., Greenleaf		2
McCrary, George W., Kansas City, Mo		7
McDowell, S. O., Topeka		6
McGill, G. M., editor Jacksonian, Cimarron		3
McGregor, R. P., Baxter Springs		7
McHarg, Rev. ——, Blue Rapids		1
McIlravy, E. L, Lawrence		7
McIntire, T., editor Democrat, Arkansas City		1
McVicar, Dr. P., Topeka		1
Maimonides Library, New York city		1
Maine Agricultural Experiment Station, Orono, Me		6
Manchester, Rev. Alfred, Providence, R. I		3
Marsh, E. J., Leominster, Mass	1	....
Marshall, Mary, Beloit		1
Marston, C. W., Cedar Junction		1
Martin, George W., editor of the Union, Junction City	100	9
Martin, Gov. John A., Topeka	1	15
May, Mrs. Celeste, Nelson, Neb	1	
Massachusetts Board of Lunacy and Charity, Boston	2	....
Massachusetts Bureau of Statistics of Labor	1	....
Massachusetts Charitable Eye and Ear Infirmary, Boston		2
Massachusetts Historical Society, Boston	4	2
Massachusetts Horticultural Society, Boston	3	2
Massachusetts School for Feeble-Minded, Boston		2
Massachusetts Society for Promoting Agriculture, Boston	4	2
Massachusetts State Agricultural Experiment Station, Amherst		19
Mead, J. R., Wichita	4	12
Meade and Dunham, editors Republican, McPherson		1
Merrill, Miss Catherine, Indianapolis, Ind	2	....
Michigan Agricultural College, Agricultural College P. O	10	10
Michigan Agricultural Experiment Station, Agricultural College P. O		1
Michigan Agricultural Farm Department, Constantine		5
Michigan State Agricultural Society, Lansing	14	....
Michigan State Board of Health, Lansing	1	....
Mickey Bros. & Co., Stockton		2
Midland College, Atchison		1
Milford, M. E., Vinita, I. T		1
Miller, J. H., Holton		2
Miller, Sol., Troy		10
Milliken, Robert. Emporia		1
Mills, T. B., Las Vegas, N. M		5
Miner, E. N and L. A., New York city		1
Minnesota Agricultural College. St. Paul		1
Minnesota Agricultural Experiment Station, St. Anthony Park		4
Minnesota Historical Society, St. Paul		4
Mississippi Press Association, Vicksburg	2	
Mississippi State Agricultural College, Jackson	1	2

DONORS OF BOOKS AND PAMPHLETS—CONTINUED.

Donors.	Books.	Pamp
Missouri Agricultural Experiment Station, Columbia		3
Missouri School of Mines and Metallurgy, Rolla		1
Missouri State Agricultural College, Columbia		12
Missouri Weather Service, Director of, St. Louis		7
Mitchell, Joshua, Sec., Seneca		1
Mohler, Martin, Topeka		101
Montana Historical Society, Helena	1	
Montana Territorial Library, Helena	7	10
Moon, E. G., Topeka		2
Moonlight, Gov. Thomas, Cheyenne. Wyoming		4
Moore, Robert R., Topeka		2
Moriarty, F. A., Sec., Council Grove		3
Moser, O. A., Emporia		2
Motter, John L., St. Joseph, Mo		1
Mudge, Mrs. B. F., Manhattan	11	143
Mulvane, Kansas Building and Loan Association, Mulvane		2
Munn & Co., New York city	1	
Murdock, T. B., editor Republican, El Dorado		3
Murdock, M. M., editor Eagle, Wichita		1
National Museum of Brazil, Rio Janeiro		1
National Young Woman's Christian Association, Chicago, Ill		2
Nebraska State Historical Society, Lincoln	1	
Nebraska Weather Service, Director of, Crete, Neb		7
New England Historic Genealogical Society, Boston, Mass		3'
New England Methodist Historical Society, Boston, Mass		6
New England Society, New York city		2
New Hampshire Agricultural Experiment Station, Hanover		3
New Hampshire Historical Society, Concord		1
New Jersey Bureau of Statistics of Labor, Trenton	2	
New Jersey Historical Society, Newark	1	1
New York Bureau of Statistics of Labor, Albany	2	1
New York Institution for Deaf Mutes, New York city		1
New York Life Insurance Co., New York city		1
New York State Library, Albany	16	1
Newberry, Horace J., Topeka		1
Newberry Library, Chicago		1
Newlon, Dr. W. S., Oswego		1
Nichols, C. D., Sec., Columbus		3
North, F. W., Wichita	1	
North Carolina Agricultural Experiment Station, Raleigh	3	7
North Carolina Board of Agriculture, Raleigh		2
Norton, A. B., Dallas, Tex	1	1
Norton, C. A., Beloit	1	67
Ohio, Adjutant General of, Columbus	3	
Ohio Agricultural Experiment Station, Columbus		7
Ohio Meteorological Bureau, Columbus	1	7
Ohio, Secretary of State. Columbus	3	1
Ohio State School of Agriculture, Columbus		2
Olney, Mrs. Emeline A., Madison, Wis		1
Omaha Public Library, Omaha, Neb		1
Oregon State Agricultural College, Corvallis		2
Osgoodby, W. W., Rochester, N. Y		2
Owen, Col. Richard, New Harmony, Ind		7
Ozias, J. W., Ottawa		1
Parmalee, G. F., Topeka		3
Paxton, W. M., Platte City, Mo	1	
Peabody Museum of American Archæology and Ethnology, Cambridge, Mass	1	17
Peacock, T. B., Topeka	1	1
Peck, Miss Ada H., Topeka		6
Pecker, J. E., Concord, N. H		1
Peffer, W. A., Topeka	1	2
Pennsylvania Agricultural Experiment Station, State College, Pa		1
Pennsylvania Board of Agriculture, Harrisburg		3
Pennsylvania Museum and School of Industrial Art, Philadelphia		1
Pennsylvania State Penitentiary, Philadelphia	2	2
Pennsylvania University, Philadelphia	2	
Perine, A. B., Topeka		5
Perine, Mary E., Topeka		1
Perine, Miss Emma G., Topeka		1
Peters, Hon. S. R., Washington, D. C		4
Pettilon, W. T., editor Democrat, Dodge City		2
Philadelphia Academy of Natural Sciences, Philadelphia, Pa		5
Phillips, Henry, jr., Philadelphia, Pa		7
Phillips, William A., Salina	1	4
Philosophical Society of Washington, D. C		13
Pilling, J. C., Washington, D. C		1
Plumb, P. B., Washington, D. C		2
Pomeroy, S. C., Washington, D. C	2	4
Porter, W. G., Colby		1

DONORS OF BOOKS AND PAMPHLETS—CONTINUED.

Donors.	*Books.*	*Pamp*
Powell, F. M., Glenwood, Ia		3
Powell, Mrs. Ella, Washington	1	4
Pratt, W. D., Jetmore		1
Prentis, Noble L., editor Republican, Newton		3
Price, Viola V., Emporia		1
Pritchett, C. W., Glasco, Mo	1	
Prohibition National Committee, New York city		22
Providence Athenæum, Providence, R. I		1
Railway Age Co., Chicago, Ill		1
Rastall, Mrs. Fanny H., Burlingame		1
Rathbone, Charles, Sec., Peabody		3
Redden, A. L., El Dorado		1
Redden, Dr. J. W., Topeka		2
Redington, J. C. O., Topeka		1
Reid, John M., Morrill		1
Republican Editors of Washington		2
Reynolds, R. E., Kingman		24
Rhode Island Historical Society, Providence	1	2
Rhodes, Rev. M., Atchison		1
Rice, Allen Thorndike, New York city	1	
Rice, Franklin B., Worcester, Mass	2	36
Rice, Hon. James, Denver, Col	1	12
Rice, John H. and sons, editors Monitor, Fort Scott		6
Ricksecker, J. H., and W. H. Page, Sterling		2
Riser, H. C., Topeka		1
Roberts, F. H., editor Independent, Oskaloosa		1
Roe, A. S., Worcester, Mass		1
Rohrer, G. W. C., editor Gazette, Abilene		9
Rolling, H., Topeka		2
Romero, M., Washington, D. C	1	
Root, F. A., North Topeka		14
Ross, Gov. E. G., Santa Fé, N. M		6
Roudebush, J. W., Topeka		1
Rudisill, Rev. L. A., Topeka		1
Russell, Ed., Lawrence		2
Rust University, Holly Springs, Miss		6
Ryan, Hon. Thomas, Washington, D. C		2
Sampson, F. A., Sedalia, Mo		1
San Francisco Public Library, Cal		1
Sanborn, F. B., Concord, Mass		1
Sargent, W. W., Holton		4
Savage, James W., Omaha, Neb	1	1
Sawyer, Mrs. A. H., Topeka		1
Seabrook, S. L., Topeka	1	
Searl, A. D., Leadville, Col	1	
Semple, Gov. Eugene, Olympia, W. T		4
Schulein, S., Ft. Scott		5
Shelden, Alvah, editor Times, El Dorado		6
Sheltering Arms, New York city		2
Shelton, Prof. E. M., Manhattan		3
Shepard, R. B., Anthony	2	4
Shiner & Codding, editors Recorder, Westmoreland		1
Shinn, A. C., Ottawa		1
Sikes, J. R., Loudonville, Ohio		1
Simmons, Dr. N., Lawrence		1
Sims, Hon. William, Topeka	77	225
Slonecker, J. G., Topeka		1
Smith, B. F., Lawrence		1
Smith, George W., Topeka	5	346
Smith, G. Y., & Co., Kansas City, Mo		1
Smithsonian Institution, Washington, D. C	8	3
Snyder, Edwin, Sec., Oskaloosa		1
Snyder, J. H., San Diego, Cal		1
Spengler, John, Kansas City, Mo		1
Société des Sciences, Lettres et Arts, De Pau, France	2	1
Société Historique, Littéraire, Artistique, et Scientifique, du Cher, Bourges	1	
Société Nationale d'Agriculture de France, Paris	2	
Société Nationale des Antiquaries de France, Paris	4	
Sone, F. D., Philadelphia, Pa		1
South Carolina Department of Agriculture, Columbia		2
South End Industrial School, Roxbury, Mass		3
Southwick, Henry L., Boston, Mass		1
Spangler, William W., Indianapolis, Ind		1
Spelman's Seminary and Normal School, Atlanta, Ga		1
Stacy, A. G., Topeka		1
Stamp, Miss M. J., Topeka	1	
Stearns, J. N., New York city		21
Stearns, Mrs. Mary E., Medford, Mass		2
Stebbins, L. A., Lawrence		1

—3

DONORS OF BOOKS AND PAMPHLETS—Continued.

Donors.	Books.	Pamp
Stevens, Thomas, Hiawatha	1	
Stevens, Gov. E. A., Boise City, Idaho		4
Stewart, William J., Boston, Mass		3
Swarr, D. M., Lancaster, Pa	1	1
Swarthout, R. B., editor Journal, Caldwell		1
Swezey, G. D., Crete, Neb		5
Taylor, A. R., Emporia		6
Taylor, Hawkins, Washington, D. C		4
Tennessee State Board of Health, Nashville		5
Thacher, T. D., Topeka	33	560
Thayer, Albert F., Maple Hill		4
Thayer, Eli, Worcester, Mass		48
Thomann, G., New York city	2	
Thomas, Chester, jr., Sec., Topeka		4
Thomas, Don Lloyd, New York city	1	
Thompson, Dr. A. H., Topeka		2
Thompson, Tom E., Howard		17
Thurston, G. P., Nashville, Tenn		1
Tilley, R. H., Newport, R. I		1
Times Company, Kansas City, Mo		6
Trimble, John, Lansing, Mich	1	
Underwood, R. F., Chicago, Ill		1
U. S. Army Adjutant General, Washington, D. C	13	6
U. S. Army Surgeon General, Washington, D. C	1	
U. S. Attorney General, Washington, D. C	1	2
U. S. Bureau of Navigation, Washington, D. C	2	
U. S. Bureau of Statistics, Treasury Department, Washington, D. C	7	1
U. S. Chief of Engineers, U. S. A., Washington, D. C	7	
U. S. Chief of Ordnance, U. S. A., Washington, D. C	2	
U. S. Commissioner of Agriculture, Washington, D. C	8	92
U. S. Commissioner of Education, Washington, D. C	4	3
U. S. Commissioner of Labor, Washington, D. C		1
U. S. Commissioner of Patents, Washington, D. C	1	
U. S. Commissioner of Pensions, Washington, D. C	1	
U. S. Fish Commissioner, Washington, D. C	5	3
U. S. Geological Survey, Director of, Washington, D. C	7	7
U. S. Hydrographic Office, Washington, D. C		1
U. S. Inter-State Commerce Commission, Washington, D. C	1	
U. S. Life-Saving Service, Washington, D. C	1	
U. S. Lighthouse Board, Washington, D. C	2	
U. S. Mint, Director of, Washington, D. C	7	
U. S. Nautical Almanac, Supt. of, Washington, D. C	1	1
U. S. Naval Academy, Annapolis, Md		2
U. S. Naval Observatory, Washington, D. C		1
U. S. Secretary of State, Washington, D. C	13	13
U. S. Secretary of the Interior, Washington, D. C	225	4
U. S. Secretary of the Navy, Washington, D. C	10	3
U. S. Secretary of the Treasury, Washington, D. C	3	2
U. S. Secretary of War, Washington, D. C	1	1
U. S. Signal Office, Washington, D. C		1
U. S. Signal Service, Washington, D. C	10	
U. S. Signal Station, Observer of, Leavenworth		22
Unknown	2	10
Utley, H. M., Detroit, Mich		10
Vail, Bishop T. H., Topeka		1
Valentine, Hon. D. M., Topeka		94
Van Hoesen, I. N., Sec., Lawrence		1
Vermont Agricultural Experiment Station, Burlington		14
Virginia Department of Agriculture, Richmond		7
Virginia Granger, editor of, Portsmouth, Va		1
Virginia Historical Society, Richmond	3	
Votaw, Daniel, Independence		1
Wait, Mrs. Anna C., editor Beacon, Lincoln		1
Wakefield, W. H. T., editor Anti-Monopolist, Enterprise		2
Walker, I. H., Adams, Ind		1
Wallace, H. B., Sec., Salina		4
Waller, W. F., editor Republican, Council Grove		4
Ward, Henry A., Rochester, N. Y		1
Ward, Mrs. Jennie M., Ottawa		6
Ward, Rev. M. L., Ottawa		3
Washington, B. T., Tuskegee, Ala		3
Wasser & Flint, editors Press, Girard		1
Waugh, Rev. Lorenzo, Petaluma, Cal	2	16
Webb, W. D., Atchison		1
Weber, G. A., St. Louis		8
Weeks, Stephen B., Chapel Hill, N. C		2
Welsh, Herbert, Philadelphia, Pa		1
Welsh, L. A., Leavenworth		2
Western Reserve and Northern Ohio Historical Society, Cleveland, O	1	8

DONORS OF BOOKS AND PAMPHLETS—Concluded.

Donors.	Books.	Pamp
Western Unitarian Association, Chicago, Ill.	....	1
Wharton, Francis, Washington, D. C.	3	....
Whitman, Albery A., Topeka.	....	2
Whittemore, L. D., Topeka.	....	1
Whittlesey, Frederick A., Rochester, N. Y.	....	2
Wilcox, P. P., Denver, Col.	....	1
Wilder, D. W., Topeka.	12	474
Wilder, E., Topeka.	....	1
Wilder, Mrs. C. F., Manhattan.	....	6
Wiley, H. W., Washington, D. C.	....	1
Wilson, W. J., Sec., Winfield.	....	10
Winchester Historical Genealogical Society, Winchester, Mass.	1	5
Wisconsin Agricultural Experiment Station, Madison.	2	3
Wisconsin Board of Health, Madison.	2	....
Wisconsin State Grange, Neenah.	....	1
Wisconsin State Historical Society, Madison.	3	4
Wollstein, M., Kansas City, Mo.	....	1
Woman's Medical College, Philadelphia, Pa.	....	1
Woman's National Republican Committee, New York city.	....	17
Wood, S. N., Woodsdale.	....	2
Woodford, J. E., Sec., Burlington.	....	2
Woodward, C. L., New York city.	1	....
Wooster, L. C., Eureka.	....	1
Worcester Free Public Library, Worcester, Mass.	....	3
Worcester Society of Antiquity, Worcester, Mass.	....	2
Worrall, Harvey, Topeka.	....	1
Wright, T. J., Atchison.	1	....
Wright, W. S., Stockton.	....	1
Wyoming Historical and Geological Society, Wilkesbarre.	....	1
Yale University, New Haven, Conn.	1	2
Yoe, W. T., and C., editors Tribune, Independence.	....	2
Yonge, H. A., editor Democrat, Beloit.	....	1
Young, H. W., Independence.	....	2
Young Men's Christian Association, Topeka.	....	14
Yuran, Jason, Blue Rapids.	....	1
Zirkle, H. W., Burrton	....	1

DONORS OF MANUSCRIPTS.

Abbott, James B., DeSoto: Pen-and-ink sketch of an early citizen of Kansas, written by Gen. James G. Blunt; Manuscript muster-roll of the Sewannoe (Shawnee) Company, Co. G., mustered for the protection of Kansas Territory.

Adams, H. J., Topeka: Poll-book of the election in school district number 22, Shawnee county, Kansas, August 28, 1886.

Alexander, Mrs. Loise L., Lawrence: Biographical sketch of Louis S. Leary, of Oberlin, Ohio, who was killed at Harper's Ferry, Va., October 17, 1859, in John Brown expedition.

Alrich, Mrs. E. B., Cawker City: Autobiographical sketch, with editorial experiences of donor, dated December 22, 1887.

Ashbaugh, Mrs. Sophia, Topeka: By-laws and minutes of N. E. Sewing Society of Topeka, from November 7, 1861, to March 24, 1864, (four-quire blank book); Constitution, by-laws and minutes of the Topeka Woman Suffrage Association, from November, 1867, to November, 1875, (three-quire blank book); Constitution and proceedings of the Topeka Busy-Bee Society, from February 19, 1877, to May 25, 1881, (three-quire blank book); the same from May 12, 1881, to July 12, 1883, (three-quire blank book.)

Bailey, L. D., Garden City: Five muster-rolls and one exemption-roll of Kansas Militia, 1858, for the precincts of Columbia, Russell, Eagle Creek, Florence and Shellrock Falls, in Madison (now Lyon) county, Kansas, in the 7th Brigade, commanded by Gen. John W. Whistler, the enrollment having been made by donor as enrolling officer under his oath of office, February 26, 1858, which is indorsed on the roll for Russell precinct.

Baker, C. C., Topeka: Petitions presented to the Kansas Legislature, 1887, on the subject of Woman Suffrage; petition of 85 boys and girls of Galena, Kansas, for passage of laws for their protection from the manufacture and sale of alcoholic beverages.

Botkin, Theo., Attica: Statement of donor relative to a conference between John Brown, Augustus Wattles and James Montgomery, concerning John Brown's Harper's Ferry expedition.

Bowman, Mrs. Mary M., Abilene: Autobiographical sketch with editorial experiences of donor, dated December 1, 1887.

Bray, Miss Olive P., Topeka: Autobiographical sketch with editorial experiences of donor, dated November 30, 1887.

Britton, R., Oakland, Iowa: Copy of donor's poem entitled "Kansas."

Brown, Dr. George W., Rockford, Ill.: Letter of donor containing historical reminiscences of Kansas; Account of the founding of Emporia, Kansas, dated October 8, 1887; Letter of James Christian, dated Arkansas City, Kansas, September 29, 1887, containing an account of the recovery of writer's eyesight; Letter of donor relative to pamphlet entitled "The Man With The Branded Hand," dated April 25th, 1887, and addressed to Rev. Photius Fisk; Letter of George N. Hill, relating to foregoing, dated Boston, Mass., May 22, 1887.

Brown, John, jr., Put-in-Bay Island, Lake Erie, Ohio; Copy of letter of Marshall Johnson to donor, dated Jefferson, Ashtabula county, Ohio, January 24, 1860, and letter of donor in reply, dated Dorset, Ashtabula county, January 25, 1860; having reference to the effort of the marshal to arrest Captain Brown for complicity in the Harper's Ferry invasion; Original manuscript entitled "Phrenological Description of John Brown, as given by O. S. Fowler," dated New York, February 27, 1847.

Burton, Mrs. Mary L., Jamestown: Autobiographical sketch and editorial experiences of donor, dated December 6, 1887.

Casselle, Charles, Horton: Letter of donor, dated Oct. 1, 1888, giving his recollections of steamboating on the Kansas river, in 1855.

Clark, Arthur, Leavenworth: Letter of Col. Philip St. George Cooke, dated May 19, 1855, in reply to inquiries made by Dr. Samuel F. Few and George Russell of Leavenworth, relative to the custody of certain persons accused of crimes or political offenses.

Clarke, S. H., Clyde, N. Y.: Letter written by Hon. S. C. Pomeroy to George S. Park, dated April 24, 1855, relative to the destruction of the

Parkville Luminary, Parkville, Мо., by Pro-slavery men; letters written by S. C. Pomeroy to donor, Oct. 19, 1855, and July 30, and Dec. 7, 1859 relative to Kansas affairs; certificate of membership in New York State Kansas Emigration Company, share No. 848, $5, dated March, 1857.

Cuthbertson, М. D., Voltaire: Letter written by Gen. John A. Logan, dated June 15, 1885, to donor, acknowledging letter of congratulation on the reëlection of Gen. Logan to the United States Senate.

Darling, C. W., Utica, N. Y.: Proceedings of the Oneida Historical Society, November 28, 1887; "Ancestry of Darling."

Emerson, Joseph W., Zeandale: Reminiscences of donor's early Kansas experiences.

Fisk, Rev. Photius, Boston, Мass.: Autograph of Captain John Brown, given donor in 1859, as the giver was about to leave Мassachusetts for Harper's Ferry, Virginia.

Flenniken, B. F., Clay Center: Hand-made newspaper published February 4th, 1878, by Elias Cunningham, of Мiddletown, Conn., vol. 3, No. 136, entitled "The Young American."

Goodnow, Prof. I. T., Мanhattan: Personal reminiscences of emigration to Kansas in 1855, paper read at the meeting of the Kansas State Historical Society, January 17, 1888; letter written to donor by George Walter, dated New York, November 22, 1854, relative to the Kansas American Settlement Company, proposing the settlement at Council City, now Burlingame, Osage county, Kansas; letter of Hon. Eli Thayer to donor, dated Worcester, Мass., February 25, 1888, relative to the settlement of the Мanhattan, Kansas, colonies in 1855, under the auspices of the New England Emigrant Aid Company.

Harding, Benjamin, Wathena: Мinutes of the Union League of America, No. 68 of Wathena, from August 14, 1863, to June 23, 1864.

Hogbin, Mrs. Flora P., Sabetha: Autobiographical sketch with editorial experiences of donor, dated April 13, 1888.

Holcombe, R. I., Мonticello, Mo.: Letter of donor dated Kirksville, Мo., July 19, 1887, on Мissouri bibliography.

Hughes, Thomas, Мound City: Autograph letter of Gen. William H. Harrison addressed to his wife, Mrs. Anna Harrison, Cincinnati, Ohio, dated Headquarters, Franklinton, June 12, 1813.

Hunter, Mrs. М. J., Salina: Autobiographical sketch with editorial experiences of donor, dated November 30, 1887.

Jeffers, D. B., McPherson, Kansas: Portion of letter envelope addressed to donor from Edinburgh, Scotland, lost in the mail by the sinking of the steamer Oregon off Fire Island, N. Y., Мarch 14, 1886; recovered July 1–4, 1886, and forwarded to donor by the postmaster of New York City, with explanatory note attached.

Jones, Horace L., Salina: Letter written by T. W. Scudder, Topeka, to John H. Kagi, dated May 22, 1857; discharge of John H. Kagi from

service in Co. B, 2d Reg. Kas. Vols., invasion of 1856, signed by Capt. W. F. Creitz and Col. C. Whipple (Aaron Dwight Stevens), dated October 1, 1856; letter of L. Clephane to John H. Kagi, written for G. Bailey, jr., editor of the National Era, Washington, D. C., dated January 26, 1857, relating to Kansas correspondence.

Kansas House of Representatives, 1887, by resolution: One hundred and sixty-five petitions for municipal suffrage for women, presented to the Kansas Legislature of 1887, by Mrs. Fanny H. Rastall, President of the Kansas Woman's Temperance Union, and Mrs. Laura M. Johns, President of the Kansas Equal Suffrage Association.

Knapp, George W., Clyde: Paper written by D. L. Chandler, giving an account of the naming of Cloud county, Kansas, dated March 13, 1885.

Lane, V. J., Wyandotte: Copy of a manuscript letter of credit, confidence and good-will, written by Gov. Sam Houston, of Texas, in behalf of James St. Louis, a Delaware Indian chief, dated April 15, 1843.

Lawrence, Mrs. Sarah E., Longwood, Brookline, Mass.: Ten manuscript books of the New England Emigrant Aid Company, 1854–1862, consisting of accounts of original shares of stock, with names of shareholders, namely, one cash book, one journal, three ledgers, two books of quitclaims, and one book containing 256 type-writer copies of letters written by Amos A. Lawrence, while treasurer of the Emigrant Aid Company from 1854 to 1861 inclusive, all relating to Kansas; 12 papers relating to the affairs of the Kansas land trust fund, of dates from 1856 to 1870.

Maloy, John, Council Grove: Letter of donor, August 4, 1888, relative to the naming of Dorn county, now Cherokee county, Kansas.

Marple, Ezekiel, North Topeka: "Pass" given by a pro-slavery committee at Chillicothe, Mo., September 10, 1856, addressed to Lieut. Col. Jeff. Thompson, St. Joseph, giving donor passport with wagons through Missouri to Kansas, signed, H. D. Renney, Ed. S. Darlington, N. J. Bliss.

Martin, Gov. John A., Atchison: Letter written by Mrs. Mary Martin, Claflin, Barton county, July 22, 1888, to Gov. Martin, transmitting photo portrait, group of triplets, children of John W. and Mary Martin, 15 months old, Loy C., Roy B. and Floy G. Martin.

Moore, Milton R., Topeka: Day-book of the Kansas Magazine Company, Topeka, entries from January 1, 1872, to October 15, 1873, 143 pages; ledger of same, 215 pages; subscription book of same with alphabetic lists of subscribers to the magazine; scrap book containing editorial notices of the Kansas Magazine. (See miscellaneous list.)

Morse, O. E., Mound City: Letter of donor, dated July 27, 1887, relating to the attempted rescue of Capt. John Brown from the Charlestown, Va., prison, by Col. James Montgomery and others.

Northrop, H. M., Wyandotte: Certificate of donation of $1,000, made by Mrs. Margaret Northrop, April 15, 1867, to secure to the citizens of Kan-

sas a pew in the Metropolitan Memorial M. E. Church at Washington, D. C., with autographs of Gen. U. S. Grant, Chief Justice S. P. Chase, and others; letter of donor transmitting the foregoing, dated Wyandotte, July 6, 1887.

Phillips, William A., Salina: Autograph letter of John H. Kagi, addressed to donor, dated Tabor, Iowa, Feb. 7, 1859, relating to the last party of fugitive slaves escorted by John Brown from Missouri through Kansas; letter of donor, dated Jan. 12, 1888, transmitting foregoing.

Pike, J. A., Florence: Letter of donor, June 23, 1887, relative to the attempted rescue of Captain John Brown from Charlestown, Va., prison, by Col. James Montgomery and others.

Pritchard, Miss L. D., Millbrook: Autobiographical sketch, with editorial experiences of donor, dated Dec. 11, 1887.

Prouty, S. S., Topeka: Volume containing 117 letters written by contributors, in 1885–6, to Hon. J. V. Admire, concerning the one-thousand-dollar Prouty Fund.

Reed, Miss Adele, Westphalia: Autobiographical sketch with editorial experiences of donor, dated Dec. 6, 1887.

Remington, J. B., Osawatomie: Copies of original manuscripts now in the possession of Maj. Remington, being official and semi-official papers of the Confederate Government in the War of the Rebellion, and which came into the possession of Maj. Remington at the residence of Jefferson Davis at the capture of Richmond in April, 1865, 7 papers. Given to the Society at the solicitation of Capt. John Brown, jr.

Salter, Mrs. S. M., Argonia: Autograph card and portrait of donor, Mayor of Argonia, 1887.

Sherman, A. C., Rossville: Letter of Dr. W. R. Sherman, written to his daughter, Alice M. Sherman, and dated Mt. Pleasant, Iowa, Nov. 6, 1856; speaks of the proposed extension of slavery and of the outrages in Kansas.

Simpson, Mrs. W. H., Topeka: Order, dated Hartford, Conn., Dec. 2, 1776, directed to Chauncey Whittlesey, great-grandfather of donor, by Gov. Jonathan Trumbull.

Smith, Charles W., Lawrence: The six original poll-books of the city election at Lawrence, April 5, 1887— the first city election at which women voted in Kansas.

Smith, George W., Topeka: Manuscript receipt book of Docket Clerk, Kansas House of Representatives, 1887, containing autographs of members; book containing petitions of settlers of Finney, Hodgeman and Ford counties, Kansas, praying the Legislature of 1887 to establish a new county to be called Banner county; subscription book containing autographs of members of Kansas House of Representatives, 1887, contributors to the purchase of a gold watch for Chaplain J. A. Bright; petition of residents of Butler county, Kansas, praying the Legislature of 1887

to prohibit county commissioners from building a bridge across Whitewater river in Augusta township; petition of residents of Osage county
to Senate of 1887 for an appropriation for an Industrial School for girls;
pledge of members of House of Representatives of 1883 to the support
of certain railroad legislation.

Thayer, Eli, Worcester, Mass.: Letter of donor, dated October 13, 1887, relating to a meeeting held at Cambridge, Mass., November 17, 1856, for
the purpose of discussing the "Kansas Question."

Wait, Mrs. Anna C., Lincoln: Autobiographical sketch with editorial experiences of donor, dated December 6, 1887.

Washburn, A., Topeka: Manuscript account of Revolutionary powder-horn
given by him to the Historical Society.

Wilcox, P. P., Denver, Colo.: Manuscript letters, March and April, 1887;
Original letter of Rev. Pardee Butler to Hon. P. P. Wilcox of Denver,
dated Framingham, Kansas, January 25, 1887, relating to early Kansas
affairs.

Wilder, D. W., Topeka: Copy of Col. John A. Martin's official report of ac-
tions of the Third Brigade, First Division 20th Army Corps, dated Chattanooga, Tenn., September 28, 1863.

Yates, E. N., Leavenworth: Original confederate muster-roll, captured by
donor, while marching with Sherman's army through Georgia, in 1864.

DONORS OF MAPS, CHARTS, AND ATLASES.

Andrews and Payne, Salina: Copy of Phil. Q. Bond's plat of Salina, Kansas, January 16, 1887.

Baker, F. P., Topeka: Pilot charts of the North Atlantic ocean, May, June
and July, 1887.

Bartholomew & Co., Topeka: Map of the city of Topeka, 1887.

Bartlett, J. R., Washington, D. C.: Monthly pilot charts of the Northern
Atlantic ocean for the years 1887, 1888, 24 maps.

Bass, A. & Co., McPherson: Map of College Place addition to the city of
McPherson.

Bennett, J. H., Holton: Pocket map of Shawnee and Wyandotte lands in
Kansas Territory, compiled from U. S. surveys by Robert L. Lawrence,
March, 1857.

Black, John C., Washington, D. C.: Holman & Cowdons's statistical map
of the United States, 1888.

Bradlee, Rev. Dr. C. D., Boston, Mass.: Copy of Edward E. Clark's map
of the city of Boston, 1885.

Clark, Arthur, Leavenworth: Map of Kansas and the Pike's Peak region,
1859.

Clark, Robert, Cincinnati, Ohio: Atlas to accompany reports of geological
survey of Ohio, 1873.

Criswell, Ralph L., Gove City: Map of Gove City, Kansas, 1888.

Edwards, John P., Quincy, Ill.: Wall maps of Douglas county, Kansas, 1887, of Johnson county, Kansas, 1886, Wyandotte county, Kansas, 1886, and Jackson county, Missouri, 1887.

Goodnow, Prof. I. T., Manhattan: Map of Greenwood County, Kansas, showing lands of M. K. & T. Rly., 1871; Map of Wilsonton, 1888; Map of Pottawatomie Reserve Lands; Map of part of Kansas Pacific Railway lands; Map of M. K. & T. Railway lands in Woodson county; Map of part of the land of the A. T. & S. F. Railroad Company in Kansas; Map of Ashland, Riley county, 1857; Map of St. George, Pottawatomie county, K. T.; Adams & Elliott's Map of Kansas; Map of M. K. & T. Railway lands in Neosho Valley; Phillips' Map of the United States, Liverpool; Map of Denver & Rio Grande Railway and connections, Chicago, 1877; Four New York Tribune war maps, 1861 and 1862; Map of the War in Europe, 1870; Map of the Great Central Route between the Atlantic and the Mississippi, 1854; Map of the lands of the Ontario Colony, San Bernardino county, California.

Griffing, William J., Manhattan: Archæological chart of Manhattan and vicinity, 1888, made by donor, showing results of explorations and investigations made by him and other members of the Agricultural College Scientific Club.

Hale, George D., Topeka: Map of Denver, Colorado, 1888.

Hall & O'Donald, Topeka: Chart containing roster of Kansas State, county, and Federal officers, May, 1888.

Heath, D. C. & Co., Boston, Mass.: Four outline maps of the United States.

Hord, B. M., Nashville, Tenn.: Tennessee Agricultural and Geological Map, 1888.

Jerome, F. E., Wilson: Atlas containing plates to accompany the second volume of the Geological Survey of Wisconsin, 1876.

Kansas Railroad Commissioners, James Humphrey, Almerin Gillett and A. R. Greene, Topeka: Railroad maps of Kansas, 1886 and 1887, 20 copies.

Kenea, J. P. and Ed. C. Lane, LaCygne: Map showing the Congressional districts of Kansas, published in LaCygne Journal, March 10, 1883.

Krarup, M. C., Ellis: Map showing the lands of W. T. Hansen, in Graham, Trego, Rooks and Ellis counties, Kansas.

Kuhn, Henry, Rhoades, Kansas: Copy of E. C. Boudinot's map of the Indian Territory, 1879.

Kurtz, Charles H., Newton: Map of Newton, Kas., 1887.

Lawrence, Mrs. Sarah E., Longwood, Brookline, Mass.: Colton's map of Nebraska and Kansas, 1854.

Marston, C. W., Cedar Junction: Map entitled "An Accurate Map of North America, Showing the British and Spanish Dominions According to the Treaty of Paris, of February 10, 1763." London.

Meacham, J. H., Sabetha: Meacham's Illustrated Atlas of Brown and Nemaha counties, Kas., 1887.

Mohler, Martin, Topeka: Map of Gove City, Kansas, 1888.

Mudge, Mrs. B. F., Manhattan: Six maps of the Yellowstone country.

Perine, Clara E., Topeka: Map of Wabaunsee county, Kansas, 1887.

Radges, Samuel, Topeka: Two maps of Kansas, showing new counties as established by the Legislature of 1887.

Rand, McNally & Co., Chicago, Ill.: Large sectional map of southern California; indexed map of Nebraska; pocket maps of Louisiana, Utah and the Indian Territory, 1887; commercial map of the United States and Canada, 1887; official railroad map of United States and Canada, 1887; pocket maps of Minnesota, Washington Territory, Arizona Territory, and Dakota Territory; pocket map and shippers' guide of Kansas, 1888; pocket map of Colorado, 1887.

Ricksecker, J. H., and W. H. Page, Sterling: Map of the city of Sterling, October, 1886; map of Rice county, Kansas, September, 1886.

Ross, Robbins & Co., Topeka: Map of Topeka and additions, 1887.

Secretary of the Interior, Washington, D. C.: Atlas to accompany Herndon & Gibbon's Report of Exploration of the Valley of the Amazon, 1854; 60 maps of the Coast Survey, 1855.

Sherrill, J. E., Danville, Ind.: Map of Mertilla, Kansas, containing price list of lots, 1887.

Sims, William, Topeka: Map of Kansas with new counties, 1887.

Stubbs, A. W., Santa Fé, Kansas: Illustrated historical atlas of the State Iowa, 1875.

Talbott, Albert G., Wyandotte: Map of Kansas City Kansas and vicinity, 1887.

Thacher, T. D., Topeka: Military map of Kansas, Rand, McNally & Co., Chicago, 1886.

Wasser & Flint, Girard: Map of Girard, Kansas, 1886; Map of Crawford county, Kansas, 1886; Map showing line of Chicago, Jefferson City, Girard & Pacific Railroad through Missouri and Kansas, in Girard Press, May, 4, 1887.

Watson, George W., Topeka: Map of Florence, Kansas, 1887; Map of the city of Topeka, 1887.

DONORS OF PICTURES.

Abbott, J. B., De Soto: Miniature monogram of the members of the Kansas House of Representatives, Republican and Democratic separate, 1868.

Abbott, Mrs. James B., De Soto: Photo portrait of donor.

Adams, F. G., Topeka: Nine of Winslow & Homer's Campaign Sketches of the War of the Rebellion, by L. Prang & Co.; portrait of Gen. Benjamin Harrison, Republican candidate for President, 1888.

Adams, Mrs. Daniel M., North Topeka: Large photo portrait of Chester Thomas, sr., gilt frame.

Admire, W. W., Topeka: Photo picture of the grave of Mrs. Nancy Hanks Lincoln, mother of Abraham Lincoln, at Boonville, Indiana.

Alrich, Mrs. E. B., Cawker City: Cabinet photo portrait of donor, 1887.

Amos, J. Wayne, Salina: Cabinet photo portrait of donor.

Anthony, Daniel R., Leavenworth: Lithograph picture of donor's stock farms at Baileyville, Nemaha county, and Huron, Atchison county, Kansas, also of the Leavenworth Times building, and of donor's private residence in Leavenworth city; steel engraved portrait of donor.

Armstrong, John, Topeka: Cabinet photo portrait of donor, 1888.

Bailey, Zachariah, Topeka: Lithograph monogram, portraits of Miss Frances E. Willard, Gov. John P. St. John, Hon. Alfred Colquitt, and Gen. Neal Dow.

Baker, C. C., Topeka: Photo group, caricature, of Gen. Ben Butler and Sand Lot Kearney; photo view of Commonwealth office and State capitol; stereoscopic view of the Gunnison Review office, Gunnison, Colo.

Bixby, Charles S., Osawatomie: Stereoscopic view of Osawatomie gas well, No. 1, 1887.

Bradlee, Rev. Dr. C. D., Boston, Mass.: Photo portrait of donor.

Brown, Dr. George W., Rockford, Ill.: Cabinet photo portrait of Rev. Photius Fisk, with inscription by donor; and cabinet photo portrait of donor.

Burton, Mrs. Mary L., Jamestown: Cabinet photo portrait of donor.

Butler, Rev. Pardee, Farmington: Cabinet photo portrait of donor.

Century Company, New York City, N. Y.: Portraits of Lincoln banner, belonging to the Historical Society; Photos of certificate and autograph of Gov. John W. Geary, with the seal of the Territory of Kansas attached to the pardon of Milton Kinzler, dated March 2, 1857.

Clarke, S. H., Clyde, N. Y.: Cabinet portrait of donor, 1888; Photo portraits of Secretary Edwin M. Stanton, President Andrew Johnson, Frederick Douglass, William H. Seward, Anna Dickinson; of Washington and Lincoln, grouped; and of P. T. Barnum and Gen. Tom Thumb and Commodore Nutt and their wives, grouped.

Coon, G. L., Jewell City: Photo of Ashtabula, Ohio, railroad disaster, December 29, 1876.

Copeland, Mrs. Delila, Oberlin, Ohio: Photo portrait of John A. Copeland, associate of John Brown, executed at Charlestown, Virginia, December 16, 1859.

Drake, A. W., Century Co., N. Y.: Proofs of Kansas pictures in Century Magazine, illustrating the Abraham Lincoln serial, 1887, 12 engravings.

Emerson, Joseph W., Zeandale: Photo portrait of donor.

Everest, H. W., Wichita: Garfield University Memorial Picture, Wichita, Kansas.

Farnsworth, H. W., Topeka: Cabinet photo portrait of donor, taken Feb. 1, 1887.

Fisk, Rev. Photius, Boston, Mass.: Ambrotype picture of Dr. John Doy and the members of the party who rescued him from jail at St. Joseph, Missouri, July 23, 1859.

Foley, J. M., Chicago, Ill.: Monogram containing portraits of the seven anarchists condemned for throwing dynamite bombs, May 4, 1886.

Goodnow, Prof. I. T., Manhattan: Two cabinet photo portraits of donor, taken, one in 1852, the other in 1886.

Harding, Benjamin, Wathena: Cabinet photo of donor.

Harris, E. P., Topeka: Cabinet photo of donor, 1886.

Heatley, Thomas W., Wyandotte: Photo portrait of Richard Realf, the original from which the engraved portrait of the poet was taken for Lippincott's Magazine, March, 1879.

Hogbin, Mrs. Flora P., Sabetha: Cabinet photo of donor.

Hubbard, H. R., R. P. McGregor, A. N. Chadsey, E. H. Brown, L. D. Kirkman, members of the House of Representatives, 1887: Monogram containing photo portraits of sixty-nine ex-soldiers, members and officers of the Kansas House of Representatives, 1887.

Hubbard, J. M., Middletown, Conn.: Cabinet photo portrait of donor, 1887.

Ingalls, John J., Atchison: Photograph of fly-leaves of John Brown's bible, containing inscription to John F. Blessing, Charlestown, Virginia, and autograph of Captain Brown.

Jerome, F. E., Wilson: Cabinet photo portraits of donor and his daughter.

Johnson, Col. Alexander S., Topeka: Life-size crayon portrait of donor.

Kagy, Joseph R., Findlay, Ohio: Photo portrait of John Henry Kagi, of Kansas and Harper's Ferry.

Lawrence, Mrs. Sarah E., Longwood, Brookline, Mass.: The Albion Gallery, N. Y., 1843, a volume of seven engravings, with text; "Picturesque Sketches in Spain," London, 1837, a volume containing 26 sketches, principally of Spanish architecture, by David Roberts.

Lescher, T. H., Topeka: Portrait of donor, printed by Blue process, 1887.

McGregor, R. P., Baxter Springs: Photograph of soldiers' monument erected by the U. S. Government to the memory of the officers and soldiers killed in the battle of Baxter Springs, Kansas, October 6, 1863, and other engagements in this vicinity, who are buried near the monument, and whose names are inscribed thereon.

Martin, Gov. John A., Atchison: Photo portraits, group of triplets, children of John W. and Mary Martin, Claflin, Barton county, Kansas, 15 months old, July, 1888 — Loy C., Roy B., and Floy G. Martin.

Martin, H. T., Topeka: Cabinet photo portrait of Louis S. Leary, associate of John Brown, copied from daguerrotype in possession of his daughter, Louise Leary Alexander, of Douglas county, Kansas; cabinet photo portraits of Kansas State officers and members of the Legislature of 1887, 1888, 136 in number.

Moffett, C. W., Montour, Iowa: Photo portrait of John H. Kagi, of early Kansas and Harper's Ferry.

Montgomery, A., Topeka: Photograph of donor's drawing from Munkacsy's

picture of Christ Before Pilate; large crayon portrait of Senator John J. Ingalls, executed by donor.

Mudge, Mrs. B. F., Manhattan; A. H. Thompson, N. S. Goss and F. G. Adams, Topeka; J. R. Meade, Wichita; R. J. Brown, Leavenworth, and J. D. Parker, Manhattan: Oil-painted portrait of Prof. B. F. Mudge, by Woodman.

Newberry, Horace J., Topeka: Monogram of Senate reporters, Legislature of 1887.

Peacock, Mrs. Ida E.: Large crayon portrait of Richard Realf, from the engraving accompanying Rossiter Johnson's sketch in Lippincott's Magazine.

Peacock, Miss Nina, Topeka: Large crayon portrait of Thomas Brower Peacock, executed by donor.

Perine, Miss Clara E., Topeka: Cuts representing the school houses of Wabaunsee county, Kansas, in Matt. Thompson's map of the county.

Perine, Miss Emma G., Topeka: Cabinet photo portrait of donor.

Reed, Miss Adele, Westphalia: Cabinet photo portrait of donor.

Rupe, Mrs. M. L., Clyde: Photo of log cabin in Elk township, Cloud county, built in 1865 and occupied by Hon. John B. Rupe and Frank Rupe.

Salter, Mrs. S. M., Argonia: Portrait of donor, 1887.

Stanton, Fred. P., Farmwell, Va.: Marble bust of donor, executed by Horatio Stone, of Washington, D. C.

Stout, J. W. & Co., Topeka: Pencil sketch, design of monument to the memory of Gen. U. S. Grant, designed and drawn for the Kansas Grant Monument Association by W. H. Fernald and George M. Stone, Topeka, 1887.

Stringfellow, B. F., Topeka: Large photo portrait of donor; the same, cabinet size.

Stringham, T. L., Topeka: Bird's-eye view of the western part of Topeka and suburbs.

Swayze, O. K., Topeka: Programme of grand concert, Marshall's Military Band, Topeka, Feb. 4, 1888, containing photo portrait of J. B. Marshall, director.

Thompson, Tom E., Howard: Photograph of Elk county court house, Howard, 1887.

Towner, W. E., Topeka: Cabinet-photo portrait of donor.

Tracy, Robt., St. Joseph, Mo.: Cabinet photo portrait of Maj. Gen. William P. Richardson, of the Kansas Territorial Militia, 1855–6; cabinet photo portrait of Dr. John H. Stringfellow, Speaker of the first Kansas House of Representatives.

Triplett, C. S., Leoti: Photo group of first officers of Wichita county, Kansas, elected February 8, 1887; photograph of first agricultural display in Wichita county, made by Dunham and Barker at Bank of Leoti City, 1887.

Van Antwerp, Bragg & Co., Cincinnati, O.: Engraved portraits of authors of publications of the donors; namely, of Dr. Joseph Ray, J. C. Ridpath, A. Schuyler, E. E. White, W. H. McGuffey, H. W. Harvey, Alfred Holbrook, and W. J. Milne, eight portraits.

Vance, W. O., New Albany, Ind.: Photographic view of school house in the mountains of Maryland, used by Captain John Brown as an arsenal, also of swivel gun and pike employed by Captain Brown in the Harper's Ferry invasion, October 16, 1859.

Waugh, Rev. Lorenzo, Petaluma, Cal.: Picture of Old John Street (N. Y.) M. E. Church, the first in America.

Wheeler & Teitzel, Junction City: Monogram containing portraits of the 115 members of the Kansas M. E. Conference, at Junction City, March, 1887; photographic view of the remains of the first Territorial capitol, at Pawnee, near Fort Riley, as remaining 1887.

Wilcox, P. P., Denver, Colo.: Bird's-eye view of Denver, 1887.

DONORS OF SCRIP, COINS, AND MEDALS.

Baker, C. C., Topeka: Three-dollar note of the Bullion Bank of Washington, D. C., dated July, 1862.

Banner, A. J., Clifton: Piece of North Carolina Colonial scrip, two shillings six pence, 1771.

Bolmar, C. P., North Topeka: A Democratic bronze medal of the Presidential campaign of 1840, with medallion of President Van Buren on one side and on the other side an eagle with shield and motto, "Independent Treasury, July 4, 1840."

Brown, John, jr., Put-in-Bay Island, Ottawa county, Ohio, deposited by himself and the other surviving children of John Brown, of Osawatomie and Harper's Ferry: The Golden Medal which was presented in 1874 to Mrs. Mary A. Brown, widow of John Brown, by Victor Hugo and others, members of a subscription committee in Paris, France; also the original letter accompanying the gift signed by the members of the committee; also a copy of the letter written by John Brown, jr., on behalf of his mother and family, addressed to the committee in acknowledgment of the gift.

Cunningham, E. W., Emporia: Bond No. 25 of School District No. 1, Lyon county, Kansas, dated July 1st, 1863, for $100, supposed to be the first legal issue of Kansas school-district bonds.

Darling, Charles W., Utica, N. Y.: A $500 note of the Bank of Monroe, Mich., 1835; autograph of John Quincy Adams.

Harbord, J. G., Manhattan: Tippecanoe medal of 1840, showing on one side profile bust of Gen. William H. Harrison, surrounded by the words, "Maj. Gen. William H. Harrison, born February 9, 1773;" on the other side an eagle with Tippecanoe banner.

Losch, William, Topeka: Coins—Swedish, 1 ore, 1870, copper; French, 2 of the Third Empire, cinq. centimes, 1855, and dix centimes, 1856,

copper; Canadian, one half-penny token, Bank of Upper Canada, 1857, copper; German, 1 Kreuzer, 1875, 6 Kreuzer, 1835, 2 copper coins; 1 pfennig, 1849, 1 do, 1851, 1 do, 1871, 20 do, 1874, first three copper, last silver; 1 Kreuzer, 1871, Baden; 1 Sechsling, 1855, Hamburg, copper; 1 Dreiling, 1855, Hamburg; Russian, 1 K. K. Aesterreichische Scheide-munze, 1861; Hungarian, 1 Magyr Kiralyi Valto Penz, 1868; 3 U. S. copper cents, 1 1876, 2 1881.

Patton, David, Atchison: Piece of Continental money, 14 shillings, issue of 1775.

Pratt, E., Cottonwood Falls: Piece of Maryland colonial scrip, denomination $200, dated Annapolis, April 10, 1774; also piece of U. S. Continental scrip, denomination $50, issued under act of Congress, January 14, 1779.

Shepard, William J., Blue Mound: Copper Whig Harrison medal, of the campaign of 1840 — on one side scales labeled "Whigs and Democrats," the latter "Weighed in the Balance and Found Wanting." The other side, worn smooth, the word "Buren" only remaining.

Stone, R. C., Piedmont: Claim debt bond of Kansas Territory, No. 852, $1,000, payable to William Stone, under act for the adjustment and payment of claims, approved February 7, 1859, signed by H. J. Strickler, Auditor, and dated December 1, 1859.

Walch, C. J., Burden: Coins —1 U. S. copper cent, 1843; 1 alloy do, 1857; 1 Canadian five-cent piece, 1883; 1 Chinese one-fourth De, 1860.

WAR RELICS.

Abbott, J. B., De Soto: English musket found by Col. A. S. Johnson on the battle-field of Westport, Mo., and presented by him to Maj. Abbott, battle fought Oct. 23, 1864; sword, procured by donor in 1855, from the manufacturer at Cabotville, Conn., and used by him through the Kansas Territorial troubles and Price's raid; Border-Ruffian flag which was placed in the Hartford, Conn., Atheneum, by James D. Farren, afterward returned to Mrs. Abbott.

Ashbaugh, Mrs. Sophia, Topeka: Candlestick of stone or clay, made by Dr. A. Ashbaugh while in charge of a small-pox hospital at Paola, Kansas, during the War of the Rebellion.

Kansas Republican State Convention, July, 1888, Topeka, by resolution: Gavel made from block of wood from battle-field of Chickamauga, Tenn., with bullet imbedded; the handle made of wood from the battle-field of Stone river, Tenn.; (presented to the Convention by Hon. W. E. Richey, of Harveyville, Kansas.)

McCarthy, Timothy, Topeka: Antique Colt's navy revolver, found on farm of donor near Fort Larned, 1887.

Prentiss, Dr. S. B., Lawrence: The leaden bullet extracted by donor from the body of John Jones, who was shot and killed by Pro-Slavery men at Blanton's bridge, Douglas county, Monday, May 19, 1856.

Richardson, J. W., Marquette: Biscuit presented by the wife of a Confederate soldier to J. B. Dock, a Union soldier marching through North Carolina.

Ritchie, Mrs. Hannah, Topeka: The sword and gun of Gen. John Ritchie, used by him during the period of his service in the army in the War of the Rebellion.

Washburn, A., Topeka: Powderhorn made in October, 1775, by Nathan Washburn, a Connecticut Revolutionary soldier, while in camp at Roxbury, Mass., during the investment of Boston. The horn was given by Mr. Washburn to his grandson, the donor.

Wasson, W. A., Lane, Kansas: Fragment of the vest, with button attached, of Capt. Nick L. Beuter, Company C, 12th Kansas Infantry, who was shot and killed near Hot Springs, Arkansas, April 2, 1864.

Watkins, Mrs. Lititia V., Barnard: Revolving pistol No. 2769, the property of Col. James Montgomery during the Pro-Slavery troubles in Kansas Territory, and during the War of the Rebellion.

DONORS OF MISCELLANEOUS CONTRIBUTIONS AND RELICS.

Abbott, Jas. B., De Soto: Blanks relating to payment of Quantrill raid claims, appropriation of 1887.

Adams, F. G., Topeka: Complimentary ticket and badge given to members of the Legislative excursion to Wichita, Feb. 18–19, 1887; programme, ticket, and badge, Northwest Kansas Editorial Association, May 23–25, 1888.

Adams, H. J., Topeka: Shawnee county, Kansas, election tickets, fall of 1885.

Barnes, J. S., Sec., Phillipsburg: Invitation cards to Phillips County Fair, 1887 and 1888.

Barnes, W. H., Sec., Independence: Cards, circulars, &c., Montgomery County Fair, 1876, 1880–1887.

Bayley, Samuel, Hartford: Two flint-scrapers, one spear-head, and five fragments of Indian pottery, found sec. 5, T. 20, R. 14 E., California township, Coffey county, Kansas.

Beezley, J. F., Sec., Girard: Posters, &c., Crawford County Fairs, 1878–1887, except 1882–3.

Bethany College, Lindsborg: Invitation card, commencement exercises, June, 1887.

Botkin, Theo., Attica: Fragment of mastodon's tooth, found at Attica, five and a half feet below the surface, April, 1887.

Bowes, George W., Topeka: Book of blank notes of Topeka Bank and Savings Institution.

Bradlee, Rev. C. D., Boston, Mass.: Card of Title Insurance Company.

Carson, Hampton L., Sec., Philadelphia: Invitation card to Constitutional Centennial Celebration, Philadelphia, September 15–17, 1887.

Carter, Joe H., Lexington: Sandstone pebble, form of linch-pin for ox-bow key, found in bed of Bluff creek, Clark county, Kansas, 1887.

Clarke, W. B., Kansas City, Mo.: Copy of memorandum book and calendar of the Merchants' National Bank, Kansas City.

Crosby, D. R., Minneapolis: Premium lists, posters, etc., of the Ottawa County Fair, 1888.

Cuthbertson, A. D., Voltaire: Badge worn at first annual reunion of the old soldiers of Sherman county, Kansas, at Voltaire, September 12–14, 1887; and badge worn at the first reunion of the soldiers of Sherman county, Kansas, Eustis, September 1–3, 1887.

Daniel, S. A., Eskridge: Election ticket used in the first city election, Eskridge, Kansas, 1887—candidates all women.

Elliott, L. R., Manhattan: Handbill, dated April 25, 1887, and extra of the Leonardville (Riley county) Monitor, April 26, 1887, mementoes of the Rock Island Railroad bond vote in Riley county.

Fast, Henry H., Hillsboro: Plate for the printing of cloth, made and used by the grandfather of donor, in Russia, as early as 1775.

Fee, S., Wamego: Stamped envelope of 1876, United States postage 3 cents, engraving showing post-rider in 1776, and mail car in 1876.

Fisher, J. R., Topeka: Section of oak tree with branch so bent and grown into the trunk as to form a loop, or looped-handle.

Frankey, J. F., Dodge City, Kansas: Card of invitation to the laying of the corner-stone of the Presbyterian College at Dodge City, April 5, 1888.

Goodnow, Prof. I. T., Manhattan: Broadside proclamation of the Executive Committee of Kansas, under the Topeka Constitution, dated November 24, 1855, giving notice of the election to be held December 15, 1855, on the adoption of the Constitution, signed by J. H. Lane, Chairman, and J. K. Goodin, Secretary.

Hale, George D., Topeka: Ancient vase of pottery, procured by H. E. Nickerson from a mound in section 33, township 11, range 7, east, on the banks of the Little river, Poinsett county, Arkansas, 1887.

Hubert, Mrs. A. G., Topeka: Piece of granite from Texas State capitol, Austin.

Hulbert, E. W., Secretary, Fort Scott: Posters of Bourbon county fair, 1887.

Kenea, J. P., and Ed. C. Lane, La Cygne: Calendars of the La Cygne Journal for 1887—8 cards.

Latimer, J. W., Pleasanton: Posters of Pleasanton (Linn county) fair, 1887.

McClelland, W. B., Bird City: Poster Bird City Driving Park Association, 1887.

McConnell, W. K., Greenleaf: Card of invitation to Washington County Fair, 1888.

McLain, F. E., Sec., Hays City: Posters of the fair of the Western Kansas Agricultural Association, Hays City, 1886.

Magill, J. S., Sec., Marysville: Posters of meetings of Marshall county pioneers at Marysville, Sept. 12, 1888.

Meade, J. R., Wichita: Piece of pottery found by donor in 1885, in the western part of New Mexico, thirty miles north of Grant station, on the A. & P. Rly., and given by him to the Society Feb. 19, 1887.

Mills, T. B., Las Vegas, N. M.: Poster relative to lot sale in Las Vegas, August 4, 1887.

Mitchell, David, McPherson: Circulars, &c., of stock sale, May 4, 1887.

Mitchell, Joshua, Seneca: Posters of the Nemaha County Fair, 1888.

Moon, E. G., Sec., Topeka: Card of invitation to State Fair, Topeka, 1888; posters, cards, &c., of the same.

Moore, Milton R., Topeka: Scrap-book containing editorial notices of the Kansas Magazine, Topeka, 1872–1873.

Munz, A., Ogden: Two flint spear-heads found six miles north of Fort Riley, in bed of Three-Mile creek, Riley county, Kansas.

Murdock, M. M., Wichita: Pocket tally-sheets of Kansas Republican Convention, Wichita, July 25, 1888, and card containing the electoral vote of 1884.

Nichols, C. D., Sec., Columbus: Programs and posters of the Cherokee county fair, 1887.

Patrick, A. G., Valley Falls: Copies of donor's political broadsides, Nov. 1887.

Pope Manufacturing Co., Boston, Mass: Donor's bicycle calendar for 1888.

Reinch, A., Lawrence: Skeleton of an Osage Indian, exhumed near Walnut river, Cowley county, Kansas.

Richards, J. H., Wichita, Kansas: Pass over St. L. Ft. S. & Wichita Railroad, 1887, design of sunflower engraved thereon.

Sims, A. C., Winona: Specimen of nickel ore from mine near Winona, Logan county, Kansas.

Snow, William M., Manhattan: Scrap-book made by Dr. Amory Hunting of Manhattan, containing newspaper clippings relating to Kansas Territorial affairs.

Stewart, Mrs. M., Wichita: Silk badge worn by the Wichita delegation to San Francisco, Cal., at the 20th National Encampment G. A. R., August, 1886, with grasshopper and sunflower painted thereon by donor.

Thacher, T. D., Topeka: Card of invitation of the Irish National League, to attend the meeting at the Grand Opera House, Topeka, April 12th, 1887, addressed by Hon. John J. Ingalls and Hon. Thomas Ryan.

Thomas, Chester, jr., Topeka: Posters, cards, circulars, etc., Kansas State Fair, 1887.

Van Hoesen, I. N., Sec., Lawrence: Card of invitation, posters, cards, etc., of the Western National Fair, Bismarck Grove, 1888.

Vance, D. J., Sec., Mankato: Card of invitation to Jewell County Fair, 1888.

Walch, C. I., Burden: One flint arrow-head.

Wilson, W. J., Secretary, Winfield: Copies of circulars, postal cards, etc., of Cowley county fair, Winfield, 1887; 37 posters, cards, blanks, badges, etc., of Cowley county fair, 1888.

Worrall, Isaac W., Pratt, Kansas: Carving of peach pit, made to represent an Indian head.

DONORS OF SINGLE NEWSPAPERS.

Abbott, James B., De Soto: Supplement to Hartford (Conn.) Post, of January 5, 1887, containing brief biographical mention of the members of the Connecticut Legislature of 1887; Hartford Post of January 29, 1887, containing biographical sketch of Mark Howard, President National Fire Insurance Company; Weekly Underwriter, Hartford, supplement, January 15, 1887, containing biographical sketches of Hartford underwriters.

Adair, Rev. S. L., Osawatomie: Thirty-two copies miscellaneous newspapers.

Adams, Frank S., Waterville: Waterville Telegraph, February 4, 1887, containing biographical sketches of Waterville business men.

Adams, J. W., Topeka: Copy of the Union and Advertiser, Rochester, N. Y., March 23, 1888, containing a review of the history and progress of Rochester.

Andrews & Payne, Salina: Salina (Kansas) Republican, illustrated edition, May, 1888.

Anthony, Daniel R., Leavenworth: Supplement to the Leavenworth Times, 1888, containing press comments on donor's candidacy for Governor.

Atchison, Topeka & Santa Fé Railroad, General Offices, Topeka: Copy of the Madagascar Times, Antananarivo, November 12, 1887.

Ball, Dr. J. Parker, Coldwater: Comanche County Sun, Coldwater, Nos. 1 and 2, September 10 and 29, 1888.

Barnes, M. E. and M. J. Packard, Atlanta, Ga.: Copies of Spellman Messenger, November and December, 1887.

Bradlee, Rev. Dr. C. D., Boston, Mass.: Unitarian Record, Chelmsford, Mass., February, 1887, and of the Southern Letter, February, 1887, Tuskegee, Ala.; Boston Evening Traveller, June 11, 1888, containing donor's poem, "In Memoriam," to Rev. James Freeman Clarke; copy of the Christian Register, Boston, December 1, 1887; copy of Our Best Words, Shelbyville, Ill., 1888.

Burleigh, Rev. C. H., Cheney: The Conference Daily, Winfield, March 10–15, 1887, five newspapers.

Bushell, W., Camden, N. J.: Copy of the North American, Phila., Sept. 16, 1887, containing fac-simile of the first printed copy of the constitution of the United States.

Caldwell, E. F., Lawrence: Copy of the Southern Kansan, January, 1887.

Call Publishing Co., Wichita: Copy of Wichita Daily Call, Feb. 19, 1887,

giving list of persons attending Legislative excursion to Wichita, Feb. 18–19, 1887, with proceedings of entertainment, while in that city.

Cameron, Hugh, Lawrence: Copy of the Journal of United Labor, Phila., March 19, 1887.

Chandler, Dr. Daniel L., Ogden: Twenty-eight copies of Herald of Freedom, Lawrence, K. T., 1857; 2 copies of the Topeka Tribune, Jan. 12 and June 6, 1857; copy Kansas Freeman, Topeka, Nov. 14, 1855; copy of Lecompton Union, Feb. 21, 1857; copy of New York Republican, Nov. 22, 1856.

Christian Cynosure, Chicago, Publishers of: Issues of March 31, 1887, containing articles relating to John Brown, written by Hon. S. C. Pomeroy, Rev. C. C. Foote and others.

Clark, Arthur, Leavenworth: Copy of the Truth-Teller, a half-sheet newspaper, Topeka, February 24, 1862.

Clarke, Sylvester H., Clyde, N. Y.: Copy of "Social Visitor, Magazine," containing biographical sketch of W. C. Quantrill and account of Lawrence raid, August 21, 1863.

Cooper, F. N. and Co., Lyons: Lyons Daily Democrat, Sept. 29, 1887, descriptive of Lyons and Rice county, Kansas.

Corey, Wells, Editor Quid-Nunc, Wellington: Copy of New Year's edition, Jan. 1, 1888.

Criswell, Ralph L., Gove City: Copy of the Gove City Advocate, April 2, 1888.

Darling, C. W., Utica, N. Y.: Fac-simile number of the Utica Morning Herald, 1887.

Davis, Charles S., Junction City: Conference Daily Tribune, Junction City, March 17–22, 1887, 5 newspapers.

Dignon, T. D., Topeka: Copy Ulster County Gazette, Princeton, N. Y., January 4, 1880, (reprint), containing account of the death of Gen. George Washington.

Dixon, J. J. A. T., Bunker Hill: Copies of the Bunker Hill News of November 26, December 10, 17, 24 and 31, 1886.

Easley, C. G., South Hutchinson: Saturday Review, South Hutchinson, Kansas, October 1, 1887, descriptive edition.

Elliott & Rosser, Coffeyville: Six copies of Southern Kansas Journal and Land Buyer's Guide, Coffeyville, March, 1887.

Elliott, L. R., Manhattan: Copies of the Manhattan Methodist, October and December, 1886; Assembly Herald, Ottawa, June 22 and July 3, 1886; Kansas Banner, Parsons, Y. M. C. A., September 21, 1886; copy of the Y. M. C. A. Argus, vol. 2, No. 1, first quarter, 1888; and The Crank, Gueda Springs, September 11, 1886.

Foote, A. E., Philadelphia, Pa.: Philadelphia Inquirer, containing lecture of donor on the minerals of the United States.

Garrison, Francis J., Boston, Mass.: Copies of The Liberator, Boston,

March 21 and December 5, 1845, and March 13, 1846, to supply deficiencies in files.

Goodnow, Prof. I. T., Manhattan: Two numbers of the Salt Lake Tribune, Utah, March 13 and 14, 1888; copy of Jonathan's Whittlings of War, New York, April 22, 1854; copy of the New York Amulet, March 1, 1831; copy of the Brownsville (Nebraska) Advertiser of September 12, 1867; copy of the Portland, Maine Advertiser, May 18, 1827; copy of "Boston, 1630–1880," dated September 17, 1880; forty numbers of the Oxford Observer, Paris, Maine, 1826–1832; ninety-two numbers of the Oxford (Maine) Democrat, 1856–1860; one hundred and twenty-three numbers of Zion's Herald, Boston, Mass., 1877–1887; eight numbers of the American Agriculturist, 1864–1872; five copies of the Norway (Maine) Advertiser, 1845–1850; thirty-two numbers of the New York Weekly Witness, 1872–1876; eighteen numbers of the Land Owner, Chicago, Ill., 1874–1876; one hundred and two numbers of the Globe-Democrat, St. Louis, Mo., 1862–1880; ten numbers of the New York Independent, 1870–1875; fifty-two numbers, daily and weekly, of the Chicago Inter-Ocean, 1885–1887; twenty-three numbers of the Hearth and Home, Washington, D. C., 1884–1887; forty-two numbers of the New York Weekly Tribune, 1870–1885; eight numbers of the Herald of Health, New York, 1865–1867; forty-four numbers of the Advance, Chicago, Ill., 1870–1875; one hundred and sixteen numbers of the Topeka Weekly Capital, 1883–1887; eight numbers of the Kansas Farmer, vol. 1, 1863–1864, and thirty-two numbers of the same, 1865–1872; fifty-four numbers of the Kansas Methodist, Topeka, 1881–1888; nine numbers of the Literary Review, Agricultural College, Manhattan, February to December, 1872; copy of the Emporia News, July 8, 1865; thirteen numbers of the Manhattan (Kansas) Express, 1869; fifty-eight numbers of the Manhattan Republic, 1884–1887; twenty numbers of the Manhattan Independent, 1862–1867; eighteen numbers of the Manhattan Beacon, 1872; one hundred and twenty-four numbers of the Manhattan Nationalist, 1874–1882; five numbers of the Kansas M. E. Conference Daily, Topeka, March, 1888; one hundred and fifty-one miscellaneous Kansas newspapers, 1873–1887; two hundred and forty-one numbers miscellaneous newspapers of other States; Kansas City Times, November 25, 1879, containing biography of Prof. B. F. Mudge; 1,457 in all.

Greer, Ed. P., Winfield: Copy of Winfield Courier, June 8, 1887, containing illustrations of Winfield statistics, &c.

Hoffman, Rev. R. A., Downs: Ellsworth Daily Democrat, March 24–28, 1887, containing proceedings of Northwest Kansas M. E. Conference, 1887, 4 newspapers.

Hughes, Mrs. Thomas, Albuquerque, N. M.: Santa Fé Daily New Mexican, February 4, 5, 7, 8, 10, 1887, containing matter relating to the New Mexico Legislature then in session.

Jerome, Frank E., Russell and Wilson: Copies of Wakefield (England) Express, March 19, 1887, and Manchester Courier of May 3 and 5, and June 6 and 11, 1887, containing an account of the Queen's jubilee; Copy of the Ulster County Gazette, Kingston, N. Y., January 4, 1800, (reprint;) Copies of the Gleaner and Luzern Advertiser, Wilkesbarre, Pa., October 11 and 18, and November 1, 15, 22, and 29, 1811.

Lee, Ed. G., Frisco: Morton County (Kansas) Democrat, Frisco, February 5, 1887, containing paragraph relating to valuable historical papers in possession of Judge Frybarger, Syracuse, Kansas.

Litts, L. H., & Co., Abilene: Illustrated Abilene Reflector, April 12, 1887; two copies.

Lykins, W. H. R., Kansas City, Mo.: Copy of Agassiz Companion, Wyandotte, October, 1887, containing article written by donor on Indian names.

McCrary, George W., Kansas City, Mo.: Copy of Our Best Words, Shelbyville, Ill., April 15, 1887.

Maffet, George W., Anthony: Copies of Anthony (Kansas) Republican, vol. 9, Nos. 38 and 39, boom edition, 1888; 2.

Marston, C. W., Cedar Junction: Copies Cherokee (I. T.) Advocate, Tahlequah, August 14, 1885, and Indian Chieftain, Vinita, I. T., January 27 and February 3, 1887.

Martin, G. W., Junction City: Junction City Union, February 12, 1887, containing a paper written by Lemuel Knapp, dated December 23, 1856, giving his experiences at Pawnee City in 1854-55.

Menager, E. S. and S. A., Menager, Kansas: Copy of "Cincinnati, 1788 and 1888," a centennial newspaper.

Mueller, Ernest, Topeka: Copy of the Berliner Tageblatt, March 16, 1888, official paper of the German empire, containing an account of the life, death and funeral of Emperor William, proclamations, etc.

Miller, J. H., Holton: Copy of the Normal Advocate, Holton, May 1, 1887.

Mills, T. B., & Son, Las Vegas, N. M., Investors' Review, vol. 1, No. 1, October, 1887.

Nixon, Thomas, Wellington: Newcastle Weekly Chronicle, England, August 29, 1885, containing an account of Washington Hall, at Washington, Eng., formerly the property of George Washington's ancestors.

Olney, Henry C., Gunnison, Colo.: Copy of Rocky Mountain News, Denver, holiday edition, December 29, 1887.

Owens & Mendenhall, Dodge City: Newspapers containing a business review of the products and progress of Dodge City, Kansas, 1888.

Ozias, J. W., Ottawa or Wichita: Northwestern Christian Advocate, April 30, 1862, and Buchanan County Bulletin, Independence, Iowa, Oct. 29, 1869.

Pratt, Captain R. H., Carlisle, Penn.: Copies of "Eadle Keatah Toh," vol. I., No. 2., and of the Morning Star, vol. V., No. 2, publications of Indian Industrial School, Carlisle.

Schulein, S., Fort Scott: Cuttings from newspapers relative to commercial agencies.

Swarr, D. M., Lancaster, Pa.: Fac-simile copy of the Philadelphia Public Ledger, vol. I., No. 1, March 25, 1836; copies of the Philadelpia Press, of March 13 and 14, 1888, containing account of the eastern blizzard of the 12th and 13th; copies of Der Volks-Freund, Lancaster, Pa., of Dec. 29, 1835 and Jan. 26 and March 1, 1836; copy of the Manheim (Pa.) Monitor, April 5, 1888.

Thayer, Eli, Worcester, Mass.: Four copies of Boston Herald, April 24, 1887, containing articles by donor, relating to saving Kansas to freedom. Two newspaper clippings relating to the work of the New England Emigrant Aid Society, articles by donor.

Thompson, Tom E., Howard: Copy of Elk County Courant, Elk City, June 17, 1874; copies of Elk County Herald, Howard, Kas., vols. 1 to 9, Aug. 20 to Oct. 14, 1881; the same of the Howard City Beacon, Nos. 3 to 22, July 24 to Nov. 27, 1875, and six duplicates.

Valentine, D. A., Clay Center: Times, Clay Center, March 31, 1887, containing views of that city in 1877 and 1886.

Walker, John, Hunnewell: Copy of the Sentinel, Richmond, Va., March 14, 1865, containing message of President Jeff. Davis to the Confederate Congress, and other matters of historical interest.

Waugh, Rev. Lorenzo: Biggs (Cal.) Argus, Feb. 24, 1887, containing personal mention of donor, and his moral work among the children; copy of the Christian Advocate, N. Y., May 21, 1888, containing proceedings of the Twenty-fifth General Conference, and a letter of donor; copy of Chico (Cal.) Chronicle, Feb. 17, 1887, giving paragraph relating to Rev. Lorenzo Waugh, also to J. B. Robinson and W. B. Mott, early Californians; Sacramento (Cal.) Daily Bee, immigration edition, 1887.

Wilcox, P. P., Denver, Colo.: Copies of Denver Republican of Jan. 30, 1887, containing an account of stage-robbing in June, 1881, near Lake City, Colorado.

Wilder, D. W., Hiawatha: Daily Brown County World, Oct., 1887, Fair edition.

Willson, H. C., Waterville: Waterville Telegraph, Jan. 7, 14, 21, 28, and Feb. 11, 1887, containing biographical sketches of Waterville business men.

DONORS OF NEWSPAPER FILES.

The following is a list of newspaper files and volumes of periodicals donated, other than those received in current issues:

Adair, Rev. S. L., Osawatomie: Files of the New York Evangelist, from January 9, 1845, to February 11, 1847; of the Advance, Chicago, for 1873 to 1875, 1877, 1879, 1884, and partial files for 1876, 1878, 1882 and 1883; of the Sunday School Times, Philadelphia, for 1879, 1880, 1884, 1885, 1886, and partial files for 1878 and 1883; and of the National Sunday School Teacher, Chicago, for 1869–1881, and partial files for 1868 and 1882—thirty-six files in all.

Angell, George T., Boston, Mass.: Files of "Our Dumb Animals," Boston, from July, 1882, to January, 1885.

Baker, Dr. W. S., Topeka: Files of the New York Semi-Weekly Tribune for 1886 and 1887.

Baker, F. P., Topeka: Four files of the Weekly Commonwealth, 1883, 1886 and 1887; two files of the Daily Commonwealth, 1884; four files of the Daily Commonwealth, 1887; files of the Daily Commonwealth, Topeka, January 2, to December 30, 1883, and from July 10 to December 30, 1883; the same of the Weekly Commonwealth, January 1, 1881, to December 28, 1882, and from July 19 to December 27, 1883; sixteen files in all.

Bawden, W. J., Fort Scott: Files of the Fort Scott Monitor, weekly, for 1868 and 1869.

Beers, Dr. G. L., Topeka: Files of the Christian Union, New York, from June 17, 1886, to June 30, 1887; New York Independent, from June 17, 1886, to December 30, 1887; The Christian Advocate, N. Y., from June 24 to December 30, 1886.

Bell, G. H., Battle Creek, Mich.: File of the Fireside Teacher, Battle Creek, from May, 1886, to April, 1887.

Burleigh, C. H., Cheney: Two files of Southwestern Kansas Conference Daily, Winfield, March 10 to 15, 1887.

Campbell, M. M., North Topeka: File of the Phonographic Magazine, Cincinnati, Ohio, 1887.

Evans, Mrs. A. R., Topeka: File of The Delineator, N. Y., 1886.

Goodnow, Prof. I. T., Manhattan: Two files of the Oxford Observer, Paris, Maine, from July 8, 1824, to June, 1826; 6 files of the Oxford Democrat, 1871–1876; 6 files of Zion's Herald, Boston, Mass., 1868, 1869, 1870, 1879, 1880, 1883; 5 files of the Great Southwest, St. Louis, Mo., vols. 1, 2, 3, 6, and 7, 1874–1880; 2 files of the American Agriculturist, 1860–1861; 2 files of the Norway (Maine) Advertiser, January 2, 1872 to December 31, 1875; 4 files of the Land Owner, Chicago, Ill., 1870–1873; 8 files of the Kansas Farmer, 1865–1872; file of the New York Independent, 1874; 6 files of the New York Weekly Tribune, 1879–1884; 2 files of the Advance, Chicago, Ill., 1872 and 1873; 3 files of the Manhattan Kansas Express, 1860, 1861, 1862; file of the Manhattan Independent, 1864; 2 files of the Manhattan Beacon, 1873 and 1874; 11 files of the Manhattan Nationalist, 1871, 1873, 1875, 1878, 1879, 1883, 1884–1887; sixty-two files in all.

Holbrook, E. A., Chicago, Ill.: File of the Western Trail, Rock Island route, 1886 and 1887.

Johns Hopkins University, Baltimore, Md.: File of the University circular from December, 1879, to August, 1882.

McLaren, J. D., Kansas City, Mo.: File of the Normal Institute Record, Minneapolis, Kansas, July 15 to August 9, 1878; Kansas Educational Journal, Emporia and Topeka, file from June, 1871, to April, 1873.

Moore, Robert R., Topeka: File of Dye's Government Counterfeit Detector, 1887, 1888.

Rank, D. H., Publishing Company, Indianapolis, Ind.: Millstone and Corn Miller, files for 1884 and 1885.

Robinson, Mrs. E. S., Topeka: Files of the Evangelical Magazine and Gospel Advocate, Utica, N. Y., vols. 4, 5 and 9, 1833, 1834 and 1838, duplicate of 1833; files of Utica, N. Y., Evangelical Magazine, vols. 2 and 3, April 5, 1828, to December 26, 1829; five files in all.

Smalley, Ellis, Council Grove: Files of the Diamond, 1840–1842, a monthly periodical published in New York in the interest of radical reform.

St. John, E., Rock Island Railway, Chicago, Ill.: Files of the Western Trail, from May, 1886, to April, 1888.

Swayze, Oscar K., Topeka: File of the Topeka Daily Blade from January 7, 1875, to February 17, 1876.

Thompson, Tom. E., Howard: File of the Winfield Courier from February 1, 1873, to May 29, 1874.

Tincher, G. W., Topeka: File of the Temperance Rural, Cherokee, Kansas 1878 and 1879.

BOUND NEWSPAPERS AND PERIODICALS.

The following is a statement of bound newspaper files and bound volumes of periodicals in the library of the Society, November 20, 1888, including the volumes which become complete December 31, 1888, numbering 7,990 volumes; of which 5,751 are of Kansas, and 2,239 are of other States and countries, and of which 2,004 have been added during the two years covered by this report. (Volumes not otherwise described are of weekly newspapers.)

BOUND NEWSPAPER FILES AND PERIODICALS, KANSAS.

Newspapers.	Years.	No. vols.
ALLEN COUNTY.		
Iola Register	1873–1888	16
Allen County Independent, Iola	1879,1880	1
Allen County Courant, Iola	1884–1888	5
Allen County Democrat, Iola	1886–1888	1
Democrat-Courant, Iola	1888	1
Humboldt Union	1876–1888	13
Inter-State, Humboldt	1878–1888	9
Independent Press, Humboldt	1882	1
The Humboldt Herald	1887–1888	1
Moran Herald	1885–1888	3
ANDERSON COUNTY.		
Garnett Weekly Journal	1876–1888	13
Garnett Plaindealer	1876–1884	9
Anderson County Republican, Garnett	1883,1884	1
Republican-Plaindealer, Garnett	1884–1888	5
Anderson County Democrat, Garnett	1885–1887	2
Garnett Eagle	1886–1888	2
The Greeley Tribune	1880,1881	1
The Greeley News	1881–1888	7
The Colony Free Press	1882–1884	7
Westphalia Times	1885–1888	3
Kincaid Kronicle	1886,1887	2
The Kincaid Dispatch	1888	1
ATCHISON COUNTY.		
Squatter Sovereign, Atchison	1856,1857	1
Freedom's Champion, (1861 lacking,) Atchison	1857–1863	4
Atchison Daily Free Press	1865–1868	7
Atchison Weekly Free Press, (four files each of 1866 and 1867,)	1866–1868	3
Champion and Press (weekly), Atchison	1868–1873	4

BOUND NEWSPAPER FILES AND PERIODICALS, KANSAS—CONTINUED.

Newspapers.	Years.	No. vols.
ATCHISON COUNTY—concluded.		
Atchison Daily Champion	1876–1888	23
Atchison Weekly Champion, (lacking from 1878–1885,)	1873–1888	8
Kansas Zeitung, Atchison, (duplicates of vol. 1,)	1857,1858	1
Atchison Union, (broken files,)	1859–1861	3
Atchison Patriot, daily, (from July, 1876, to July, 1879, lacking,)	1876–1888	13
Atchison Patriot (weekly)	1874–1888	15
Atchison Courier	1876–1879	4
Atchison Globe (daily)	1878–1888	19
Atchisonian, Atchison	1877	1
Atchison Banner	1878,1879	1
The New West, Atchison	1878–1880	2
The Sunday Morning Call, Atchison	1882,1883	2
Atchison Telegraph	1882	1
Kansas Staats-Anzeiger, Atchison	1881–1885	4
Atchison Journal (daily)	1881,1882	2
Western Mercury, Atchison	1884–1886	2
Atchison Sunday Morning Sermon	1884	1
The Western Recorder, Atchison	1884	1
The Trades-Union, Atchison	1885,1886	1
The Atchison Times	1888	1
The Prairie Press, Lancaster	1888	1
Messachorean (monthly), Atchison	1888	1
Muscotah Record, (missing from August, 1886, to January, 1887,)	1885–1887	2
The Effingham Times	1887,1888	1
BARBER COUNTY.		
Barber County Mail, Medicine Lodge	1878,1879	1
Medicine Lodge Cresset	1879–1888	10
The Barber County Index, Medicine Lodge	1881–1888	7
Medicine Lodge Chief	1886–1888	1
Hazelton Express	1884–1888	5
The Kiowa Herald, New Kiowa	1884–1888	4
The Kiowa Journal	1886–1888	2
Sharon News	1884–1886	2
The Union, Sun City	1884–1888	4
The Ætna Clarion	1885–1887	2
Kansas Prairie Dog, Lake City	1885–1887	3
The Lake City Bee	1888	1
BARTON COUNTY.		
Great Bend Register	1876–1888	13
Inland Tribune, Great Bend	1876–1888	13
Arkansas Valley Democrat, Great Bend	1877–1882	6
Kansas Volksfreund, Great Bend	1878,1879	1
Barton County Democrat, Great Bend	1886–1888	2
Daily Graphic, Great Bend	1887,1888	2
The Ellinwood Express	1878–1888	10
Pawnee Rock Leader	1886–1888	3
The Echo, Hoisington	1888	1
Claflin Gazette	1888	1
BOURBON COUNTY.		
Fort Scott Daily Monitor	1880–1888	18
Fort Scott Weekly Monitor, (1870–1876 lacking,)	1867–1888	15
Fort Scott Pioneer	1876–1878	2
Camp's Emigrant's Guide, Fort Scott	1877	1
New Century, Fort Scott	1877,1878	1
The Fort Scott Herald	1878–1882	5
Republican-Herald, Fort Scott	1879–1882	4
Herald and Record, Fort Scott	1882–1884	2
Evening Herald, daily, Fort Scott	1882–1885	6
Medical Index, monthly, Fort Scott	1881–1884	4
The Banner, Fort Scott	1882–1884	2
Fort Scott Daily Tribune	1884–1888	8
Fort Scott Weekly Tribune	1884–1888	4
Kansas Staats-Zeitung, Fort Scott	1886,1887	2
The Fort Scott Union	1887,1888	1
Bronson Pilot	1884–1888	4
The Fulton Independent	1884–1888	4
The Telephone, Uniontown	1885–1888	3
The Garland Gleaner	1886,1887	2
BROWN COUNTY.		
Hiawatha Dispatch	1876–1882	6
The Hiawatha World	1882–1888	7
Kansas Herald, Hiawatha	1876–1883	8
The Kansas Sun, Hiawatha	1879,1880	2

BOUND NEWSPAPER FILES AND PERIODICALS, KANSAS—CONTINUED.

Newspapers.	Years.	No. vols.
BROWN COUNTY—*concluded.*		
Weekly Messenger, Hiawatha	1882–1884	2
The Kansas Democrat, Hiawatha	1884–1888	5
Free Press, Hiawatha	1887,1888	1
Everest Reflector	1885,1886	2
Horton Headlight	1886–1888	2
Horton Daily Headlight	1887,1888	2
BUTLER COUNTY.		
Augusta Republican, (1875–1880 lacking,)	1873–1883	4
Southern Kansas Gazette, Augusta	1876–1886	11
Augusta Advance	1883,1884	1
Augusta Electric Light	1884–1886	2
Augusta Weekly Journal	1888	1
Walnut Valley Times, El Dorado	1874–1888	15
Daily Walnut Valley Times, El Dorado	1887–1888	3
El Dorado Press	1877–1883	7
El Dorado Daily Republican	1885–1888	6
El Dorado Republican	1883–1888	5
Butler County Democrat, El Dorado	1881–1888	8
The El Dorado Eagle	1882	1
The New Enterprise, Douglass	1879,1880	2
Douglass Index	1880–1883	3
The Douglass Tribune	1884–1888	5
Leon Indicator, (missing from February to September, 1887,)	1880–1888	7
The Leon Quill	1886,1887	1
The Benton Reporter	1884,1885	1
The Towanda Herald	1885–1888	4
The Brainerd Sun	1885,1886	1
Latham Journal	1885,1886	1
Latham Signal	1887,1888	2
The Beaumont Business	1886–1888	2
Potwin Messenger	1888	1
The Brainerd Ensign	1887,1888	2
CHASE COUNTY.		
Chase County Courant, Cottonwood Falls	1874–1888	14
Chase County Leader, Cottonwood Falls	1875–1888	14
Strong City Independent	1881–1887	6
Chase County Republican, Strong City	1887,1888	1
CHAUTAUQUA COUNTY.		
Chautauqua Journal, Sedan	1875–1884	9
The Chautauqua County Times, Sedan	1878–1881	3
Sedan Times	1882–1884	3
Sedan Times-Journal	1885–1888	4
The Border Slogan, Sedan	1883,1884	1
The Graphic, Sedan	1884–1888	4
Chautauqua News, Peru	1877–1881	5
The Peru Times	1886,1887	1
The Weekly Call, Peru	1888	1
The Chautauqua Springs Spy	1882,1883	1
Chautauqua Springs Mail	1887	1
The Cedar Vale Star	1884–1888	5
CHEROKEE COUNTY.		
Republican-Courier, Columbus	1876–1878	3
The Columbus Courier	1879–1888	9
Columbus Democrat	1876	1
Border Star, Columbus	1877–1886	9
The Columbus Vidette	1877,1878	1
The Times, Columbus	1882–1886	5
Kansas Bee-Keeper, Columbus	1882–1885	2
Lea's Columbus Advocate	1882–1888	6
The Daily Advocate, Columbus	1886,1887	2
The Daily News and The Weekly News, Columbus	1882,1883	1
The Expository, Girard and Columbus	1883,1884	1
The Sprig of Myrtle (monthly), Columbus	1883–1885	2
The Kansas Prohibitionist, Columbus	1886	1
Baxter Springs Republican	1876,1877	1
The Times, Baxter Springs	1878–1881	3
Baxter Springs News	1882–1888	7
Baxter Springs Delta	1887	1
Galena Miner	1877–1880	4
Galena Miner (second)	1888	1
Short Creek Weekly Banner, Galena	1878	1
The Galena Messenger	1879	1
Short Creek Republican, Galena	1883–1888	6

Newspapers.	Years.	No. vols.
CHEROKEE COUNTY—*concluded.*		
Empire City Echo	1877–1879	3
The Ionian Casket (monthly), Quakervale	1878,1879	1
Western Friend (monthly), Quakervale	1880–1888	7
The Laborer's Tribune, Weir	1884–1888	6
CHEYENNE COUNTY.		
Cheyenne County Rustler, Wano	1885–1888	3
Plaindealer, Wano	1886–1888	2
Bird City News	1886–1888	2
Cheyenne County Democrat, Bird City	1886–1888	2
The Gleaner, Jaqua	1887,1888	1
CLARK COUNTY.		
Clark County Clipper, Ashland	1884–1888	4
Republican Herald, Ashland	1886,1887	2
Ashland Journal	1887,1888	2
Clark County Chief, Englewood	1885–1887	3
The Englewood Chief	1888	1
Englewood Enterprise	1888	1
Appleton Kansas Era	1885–1887	2
The Lexington Leader	1886–1888	2
The Minneola Era	1887,1888	1
Clark County Republican, Minneola	1888	1
Cash City Cashier	1887,1888	1
CLAY COUNTY.		
Clay County Dispatch, Clay Center	1876–1888	13
The Localist, Clay Center	1879–1881	3
The Democrat, Clay Center	1879,1880	2
The Cresset, Clay Center	1882,1883	1
The Times, Clay Center	1882–1888	7
The Times (daily), Clay Center	1886–1888	5
The Kansas Baptist, Clay Center	1881–1884	3
The Monitor, Clay Center	1883,1884	1
Clay Center Eagle	1885,1886	1
Republican Valley Democrat, Clay Center	1886–1888	3
Morganville News and Sunflower	1885–1887	3
The Clay County Sentinel, Morganville	1887,1888	2
The Idana Journal	1886,1887	1
Wakefield Advertiser	1887,1888	2
The Herald, Industry	1887,1888	1
CLOUD COUNTY.		
Republican Valley Empire, Clyde and Concordia	1870–1872	3
Concordia Empire	1876–1882	7
The Republican-Empire, Concordia	1883–1886	4
Concordia Empire	1887,1888	2
The Concordia Republican	1882,1883	2
The Concordia Expositor	1877–1881	5
The Cloud County Blade, Concordia	1879–1881	3
Kansas Blade, Concordia	1882–1888	7
Concordia Daily Blade	1884–1888	6
Cloud County Critic, Concordia	1882–1888	7
The Concordia Times	1884–1888	5
Concordia Democrat, and Daylight	1886–1888	3
Clyde Democrat	1880–1882	2
The Clyde Herald	1878–1888	10
Cline's Press, Clyde	1884	1
The Clyde Mail	1884–1887	3
The Clyde Argus	1888	1
Glasco Tribune	1881,1882	1
The Glasco Sun	1883–1888	6
Cloud County Kansan, Jamestown	1881–1888	7
The Miltonvale News	1882–1888	8
Miltonvale Star	1886	1
Miltonvale Chieftain	1888	1
Ames Advocate	1885,1886	1
The Ames Bureau	1887	1
The Weekly Courier, Ames	1888	1
COFFEY COUNTY.		
Neosho Valley Register, Burlington	1859,1860	1
Kansas Patriot, Burlington, (duplicate of 1867,)	1864–1868	5
Burlington Patriot	1876–1886	10
Burlington Republican	1882–1886	4
The Republican-Patriot, Burlington	1886	1
Burlington Daily Republican-Patriot	1887	1
The Burlington Independent	1876–1888	13

BOUND NEWSPAPER FILES, AND PERIODICALS, KANSAS — CONTINUED.

Newspapers.	Years.	No. vols.
COFFEY COUNTY — *concluded.*		
Burlington Daily Star	1878	1
The Burlington Nonpareil	1887–1888	2
Leroy Reporter	1879–1888	9
The Leroy Eagle	1888	1
The Lebo Light	1884, 1888	5
The Waverly News	1885, 1888	4
The Gridley Gazette	1887, 1888	2
COMANCHE COUNTY.		
Comanche Chieftain, Nescatunga	1884–1886	2
The Western Kansan, Nescatunga	1885, 1887	3
Nescatunga Enterprise	1886–1888	3
Coldwater Review	1884–1888	4
The Western Star, Coldwater	1885–1888	4
Republican, Coldwater	1885, 1886	1
Coldwater Echo	1887, 1888	2
Comanche County Citizen, Avilla	1885, 1886	2
The Avilla Democrat	1886, 1887	1
Protection Echo	1885–1887	3
The Protection Press	1886, 1887	1
Kansas Weekly Ledger, Protection	1887	1
The Leader, Protection	1888	1
Evansville Herald	1885–1887	2
Comanche City News	1886–1888	1
COWLEY COUNTY.		
Winfield Courier	1873–1888	15
Winfield Daily Courier	1885–1888	7
Winfield Plow and Anvil	1876	1
Cowley County Telegram, Winfield	1876–1888	13
Winfield Daily Telegram, (1883–1886 lacking,)	1879–1888	10
Winfield Semi-Weekly	1879, 1880	1
Cowley County Monitor, Winfield	1880	1
Cowley County Courant, Winfield	1881, 1882	1
Winfield Daily Courant	1881, 1882	1
The Daily Visitor, Winfield	1886–1888	6
The Winfield Tribune	1884–1888	4
The American Nonconformist, Winfield	1887, 1888	2
Southwestern Kansas Conference Daily, Winfield	1887	1
Arkansas City Traveler and Republican-Traveler	1876–1888	13
Arkansas Valley Democrat, Arkansas City	1879–1888	9
The Arkansas City Republican	1884–1886	3
Republican-Traveler (daily), Arkansas City	1886–1886	4
Canal City Daily Dispatch, Arkansas City	1887, 1888	3
Canal City Dispatch (weekly), Arkansas City	1887, 1888	2
The Fair Play, Arkansas City	1888	1
The New Enterprise, Burden	1880, 1881	2
Burden Enterprise	1882–1888	7
Burden Eagle	1885–1888	4
Cambridge Commercial	1881	1
The News, Cambridge	1882–1886	3
The Eye, Dexter	1884–1888	4
The Udall Sentinel	1885, 1886	1
The Udall Record	1886, 1887	2
The Cambridge News	1888	1
CRAWFORD COUNTY.		
Girard Press	1874–1888	15
Crawford County News, Girard	1876–1880	4
Girard Herald	1880–1888	9
The Kansas Workman, monthly, Girard	1882–1884	2
Cherokee Index	1876, 1877	2
The Young Cherokee, Cherokee	1876, 1877	1
Cherokee Banner	1877, 1878	1
The Temperance Rural, Cherokee, (one duplicate,)	1878, 1879	1
Sentinel on the Border, Cherokee	1879–1882	4
The Cherokee Sentinel	1883–1888	5
The Saturday Cyclone, Cherokee	1885–1887	3
The Smelter, Pittsburg	1881–1888	8
The Headlight, Pittsburg	1886–1888	3
The Daily Headlight, Pittsburg	1887	1
The McCune Standard	1881, 1882	1
The McCune Times	1882–1888	6
The Brick, McCune and Pittsburg	1886, 1887	2
Walnut Journal	1882–1888	7
The Educational Advocate, Walnut	1884	1
The Arcadia Reporter	1882–1887	5

BOUND NEWSPAPER FILES AND PERIODICALS, KANSAS—Continued.

Newspapers.	Years.	No. vols.
CRAWFORD COUNTY — concluded.		
The Christian Worker, Arcadia	1888	1
The Hepler Leader	1883	1
The Hepler Banner	1887, 1888	2
The Farlington Plaindealer	1885, 1886	1
Farlington Gem	1886, 1887	1
Mulberry Grove Gazette	1886	1
DAVIS COUNTY.		
Junction City Union, (triplicates of '75, '76, '77, '78, and duplicates of '79–'86,)	1865–1888	25
The Junction City Daily Union	1887	1
Junction City Tribune	1873–1888	16
The Youths' Casket (monthly), Junction City	1878	1
Davis County Republican, Junction City	1882–1888	6
The Junction City Methodist	1886, 1887	1
DECATUR COUNTY.		
The Oberlin Herald	1879–1888	8
The Eye, Oberlin	1883–1888	5
The Oberlin World and Democrat	1885, 1886	1
Oberlin Opinion	1886–1888	3
The Norcatur Register	1886–1888	1
The Allison Breeze and Times	1887, 1888	2
DICKINSON COUNTY.		
Dickinson County Chronicle, Abilene	1876–1888	13
Kansas Gazette, Enterprise and Abilene	1876–1888	13
Abilene Daily Gazette	1886–1888	6
The Weekly Democrat, Abilene	1880–1882	2
The Abilene Reflector	1883–1888	5
The Abilene Daily Reflector	1887, 1888	3
The Solomon Sentinel, Solomon City	1879–1888	9
Enterprise Register	1883, 1884	2
The Anti-Monopolist, Enterprise	1884–1888	4
The Chapman Star	1884–1886	2
The Chapman Courier	1887, 1888	2
The Herington Tribune	1885–1888	4
The Hope Herald	1885–1888	4
The Hope Dispatch	1886–1888	3
Carlton Advocate	1886–1888	2
The Banner Register, Banner City	1887, 1888	2
The Manchester Sun	1887, 1888	1
DONIPHAN COUNTY.		
White Cloud Chief, (7 duplicates,)	1857–1872	16
Weekly Kansas Chief, Troy, (1 duplicate,)	1876–1888	16
Troy Reporter	1866, 1867	1
Doniphan County Republican, Troy, (1873 lacking,)	1871–1875	5
Troy Weekly Bulletin	1877–1879	2
The Troy Times	1886–1888	2
Elwood Advertiser, (1 duplicate,)	1857, 1858	1
Kansas Free Press, Elwood, (1 duplicate,)	1858, 1859	1
Elwood Free Press, (1 duplicate,)	1859–1861	2
Wathena Reporter, (1868–1873 lacking,)	1867–1877	5
Highland Sentinel	1878, 1879	1
The Central State, Highland	1880–1882	2
White Cloud Review	1880–1887	7
Enterprise, Severance, (and Centralia, Nemaha county,)	1883	1
DOUGLAS COUNTY.		
Herald of Freedom, Lawrence, (7 duplicates,)	1854–1859	6
Kansas Free-State, Lawrence	1855, 1856	1
Lawrence Republican, (volumes 1 and 3, incomplete,)	1857–1860	2
The Western Home Journal, Lawrence	1869–1884	14
The Weekly Kansas Journal, Lawrence	1886–1888	3
Republican-Journal (daily), Lawrence	1877–1880	•8
Lawrence Daily Journal	1880–1888	13
The Congregational Record, monthly, (Lawrence, January, 1859, to December, 1864; Topeka, June, 1865, to May, 1867,)	1859–1867	8
The Tribune, Lawrence, (lacking 1873 and 1875,)	1868–1883	13
The Semi-Weekly Tribune, and the Weekly Herald-Tribune, Lawrence	1884, 1885	2
The Lawrence Tribune	1885–1888	3
The Tribune, daily, (1875, 1878, 1879, and part of 1877 lacking; duplicates,) Lawrence	1873–1884	17
Herald-Tribune, daily, Lawrence	1884, 1885	3
Evening Tribune, Lawrence	1886–1888	6
Spirit of Kansas, Lawrence	1875–1882	7
Kansas Collegiate, Lawrence	1875–1879	5
The University Courier, Lawrence	1878, 1879	1

BOUND NEWSPAPER FILES AND PERIODICALS, KANSAS—Continued.

Newspapers.	Years.	No. vols.
DOUGLAS COUNTY—*concluded.*		
University Courier, Lawrence	1882–1886	6
The Kansas Review (monthly), Lawrence	1879–1888	9
Lawrence Standard	1877–1879	3
Kansas Monthly, Lawrence	1878–1881	4
The Daily Reporter, Lawrence	1879	7
Kansas Temperance Palladium, Lawrence	1879,1880	1
Die Germania, Lawrence	1880–1888	1
The Kansas Liberal (monthly), Lawrence, July to September, 1882, (see Valley Falls,)		
The Lawrence Gazette	1882–1888	6
Lawrence Daily Gazette	1884,1885	1
Western Recorder, Lawrence	1883,1884	1
Kansas Churchman (monthly), Lawrence	1883–1885	2
Kansas Daily Herald, Lawrence	1883,1884	2
The Head Center and Daily Morning Sun, Lawrence	1883	1
The Daily Morning News, Lawrence	1883,1884	1
Once a Week, Lawrence	1883–1885	2
Sigma Nu Delta (bi-monthly), Lawrence	1886–1888	2
Evening Telegram, Lawrence	1885	1
Lawrence Daily Democrat	1885	1
The Kansas Zephyr, Lawrence	1884–1887	3
North Lawrence Leader	1884,1885	1
Freeman's Champion, Prairie City	1857,1858	1
Baldwin Criterion	1883–1885	1
The Baldwin Visitor	1884	1
The Baldwin Ledger	1885–1888	4
The Baldwin Index, Baker University	1886	1
Lecompton Monitor	1885,1886	1
The Eudora News	1887,1888	1
EDWARDS COUNTY.		
Edwards County Leader, Kinsley	1877–1880	4
Valley Republican, (bound with Kinsley Graphic, 1878,)	1877,1878	1
Kinsley Republican	1878–1881	4
The Kinsley Graphic, (except 1882,)	1878–1887	8
Kinsley Republican-Graphic	1882	1
Edwards County Banner, Kinsley	1887	1
Weekly Banner-Graphic, Kinsley	1887,1888	1
Kansas Staats-Zeitung, Kinsley	1878,1879	1
The Kinsley Mercury	1883–1888	5
Kinsley Daily Mercury	1887,1888	2
The Wendell Champion	1885–1888	1
Belpre Beacon	1888	1
ELK COUNTY.		
The Courant, Howard	1875–1877	3
The Courant-Ledger, Howard	1878–1880	3
Industrial Journal, Howard	1878–1880	2
The Howard Courant	1880–1888	8
Kansas Rural, Howard	1881	1
The Howard Journal	1880–1883	3
The Howard Democrat	1884–1888	4
Kansas Traveler, Howard	1886,1887	1
Howard Daily Traveler	1887	1
The Broad Axe, Howard	1883	1
Elk County Ledger, Elk Falls	1876,1877	2
The Weekly Examiner, Elk Falls	1878	1
Elk Falls Signal	1880–1882	2
The Pioneer, Longton	1880,1881	2
The Times, Longton	1881–1888	8
Longton Leader	1887	1
Moline News	1880	1
Moline Mercury, (1883 and 1884 lacking,)	1882–1888	5
The Moline Free Press	1883–1885	6
Grenola Argus	1880–1882	2
The Grenola Chief	1883–1888	5
Grip, Howard	1883,1884	1
The Cave Springs Globe	1882	1
The Herald, Cana Valley	1882,1883	1
The Grenola Hornet	1884,1885	1
ELLIS COUNTY.		
Ellis County Star (lacking from December 7, 1876, to April 11, 1879,) Hays City	1876–1881	4
Hays Sentinel, Hays City	1877–1881	5
The Star-Sentinel, and Hays City Sentinel	1880–1888	8
German-American Advocate, Hays City	1882–1886	4
Ellis Weekly Headlight, Hays City	1882–1888	7
Hays City Times, Hays City	1886	1

BOUND NEWSPAPER FILES AND PERIODICALS, KANSAS—Continued.

Newspapers.	Years.	No. vols.
ELLIS COUNTY—concluded.		
Ellis County Democrat and Ellis County Free Press, Hays City	1886–1888	3
Ellis Review, Hays City	1886–1888	3
Democratic Times, Hays City	1888	1
The Republican, Hays City	1888	1
Walker Journal	1887,1888	1
ELLSWORTH COUNTY.		
Ellsworth Reporter	1875–1888	14
The Rural West, Ellsworth	1882	1
The Ellsworth News	1883,1884	2
The Ellsworth Democrat	1885–1888	3
Wilson Index	1878,1879	1
The Wilson Echo	1880–1888	9
The Wilson Wonder	1886,1887	2
Cain City News	1882–1886	3
The Kanopolis Journal	1886–1888	2
The Holyrood Enterprise	1887,1888	2
The Wilson Hawkeye	1887,1888	1
FINNEY COUNTY.		
The Irrigator, Garden City	1882–1886	4
Garden City Herald, (1884-7 lacking,)	1883–1888	2
Garden City Herald (daily)	1886–1888	6
Garden City Sentinel	1884–1888	4
Garden City Sentinel (daily)	1886–1888	6
The Cultivator and Herdsman, monthly and weekly, Garden City	1884–1886	1
The Western Times, Garden City	1885	1
Finney County Democrat, Garden City	1887,1888	2
Pierceville Courier	1886,1887	1
Terry Enterprise	1886,1887	1
The Terry Eye	1887,1888	2
Locomotive, Loco	1886,1887	1
The Hatfield News	1887,1888	1
FOOTE COUNTY.		
(See Gray county.)		
The New West and the Optic, Cimarron	1879–1881	2
The Signet, Cimarron	1880	1
FORD COUNTY.		
Dodge City Times	1876–1888	13
Ford County Globe, Dodge City	1878–1884	7
The Globe Live-Stock Journal, Dodge City	1884–1887	3
Dodge City Democrat	1884–1888	5
Kansas Cowboy, Dodge City	1884,1885	1
The Sun, Dodge City	1886,1887	1
Ford County Republican, Dodge City	1887,1888	2
Speareville Enterprise	1878	1
Speareville News	1878–1880	1
Speareville Blade	1885–1888	4
Ford County Record, Speareville	1885,1886	1
Ford County Democrat, Speareville and Fonda	1886,1887	2
The Ryansville Boomer, and The Boomer, Ford City	1885–1887	2
Wilburn Argus	1886,1887	2
Bucklin Standard	1887,1888	1
The Bucklin Herald	1887,1888	1
The Weekly Telegram, Bloom	1888	1
FRANKLIN COUNTY.		
Western Home Journal, Ottawa	1865–1868	3
Ottawa Journal	1870–1874	5
The Triumph, Ottawa	1876	1
Ottawa Journal and Triumph	1877–1888	12
Ottawa Campus, occasional, (vols. 1 and 2,)	1864–1888	3
Ottawa Republican, (1875 lacking,)	1874–1888	14
Ottawa Daily Republican	1879–1888	19
Kansas Home News, Ottawa	1879,1880	1
Ottawa Gazette	1879	1
Ottawa Leader	1880	1
Kansas Free Trader (monthly), Ottawa	1883	1
Queen City Herald, Ottawa	1883–1887	2
Jefferies Western Monthly, Ottawa	1884,1885	1
Daily Local News, Ottawa	1886–1888	5
Williamsburg Review	1879	1
Weekly Gazette, Williamsburg	1880–1883	2
The Eagle, Williamsburg	1885–1888	4
Lane Advance	1881,1882	1

BOUND NEWSPAPER FILES AND PERIODICALS, KANSAS—Continued.

Newspapers.	Years.	No. vols.
FRANKLIN COUNTY—*concluded.*		
The Commercial Bulletin, Lane.	1886–1888	3
The Wellsville News.	1882	1
The Wellsville Transcript.	1882,1883	1
The Wellsville News (second).	1884–1886	3
The Wellsville Exchange.	1887,1888	1
The Pomona Enterprise.	1885–1888	2
Richmond Recorder.	1885–1888	3
Princeton Progress.	1885–1888	3
Fireside, Factory and Farm, Ottawa.	1886–1888	1
The Kansas Lever, Ottawa.	1887,1888	2
The Bee (daily and weekly), Ottawa.	1887,1888	1
GARFIELD COUNTY.		
Ravanna Chieftain.	1885–1888	3
Ravanna Sod-House.	1886,1887	1
Ravanna Record.	1887,1888	1
The Ravanna Enquirer.	1887,1888	1
The Kal Vesta Herald.	1886–1888	2
The Essex Sunbeam.	1887	1
The Garfield County Call, Eminence.	1887,1888	1
Garfield County Journal, Loyal.	1887,1888	1
GOVE COUNTY.		
Buffalo Park Express.	1880	1
Buffalo Park Pioneer.	1885,1887	3
The Golden Belt Republican, Grinnell.	1885,1888	3
Cap Sheaf, Grainfield.	1885,1888	3
Gazette, Gove City.	1885–1888	3
Gove County Graphic, Gove City.	1887,1888	1
The Settler's Guide, Quinter.	1886–1888	2
The Smoky Globe, Jerome.	1887,1888	1
GRAHAM COUNTY.		
The Western Star, Hill City.	1879,1880	1
Hill City Lively Times.	1881	1
The Hill City Reveille.	1884–1888	4
Hill City Democrat.	1887,1888	1
Graham County Lever, Gettysburg.	1879,1880	1
The Millbrook Times.	1879–1883	10
Graham County Republican, Millbrook.	1881	1
Millbrook Herald.	1882,1883	1
Millbrook Herald (second).	1885–1888	2
The Graham County Democrat, Millbrook.	1885–1888	3
Roscoe Tribune.	1880,1881	1
Western Cyclone, Nicodemus.	1886–1888	2
Nicodemus Enterprise.	1887	1
The Fremont Star.	1886–1888	2
The Fremont Press.	1888	1
GRANT COUNTY.		
Grant County Register, Ulysses.	1885–1888	3
Ulysses Tribune.	1887,1888	2
The Post, Surprise.	1886,1887	1
Shockeyville Eagle.	1886,1887	1
Golden Gazette.	1887,1888	2
Zionville Sentinel.	1887,1888	1
The Commercial, Cincinnati and Appomattox.	1887,1888	2
The Standard-Democrat, Cincinnati and Appomattox.	1887,1888	1
The Lawson Leader.	1887,1888	1
Conductor Punch.	1887,1888	1
GRAY COUNTY.		
The New West, Cimarron and Echo.	1885–1888	4
Cimarron Herald and Kansas Sod House.	1885,1886	1
The Jacksonian, Cimarron.	1885–1888	3
Gray County Echo, Ingalls and Cimarron.	1886–1888	2
Ingalls Union.	1887,1888	1
Gray County Republican, Ingalls.	1888	1
The Montezuma Chief.	1886–1888	2
Ensign Razzoop.	1887,1888	1
GREELEY COUNTY.		
Greeley County Gazette, Greeley Center and Horace.	1886–1888	2
Greeley County News, Greeley Center and Horace.	1886–1888	1
Horace Messenger.	1888	1

—5

BOUND NEWSPAPER FILES AND PERIODICALS, KANSAS — Continued.

Newspapers.	Years.	No. vols.
GREELEY COUNTY—concluded.		
Hector Echo	1886	1
Greeley County Tribune, Tribune, and Reid	1886,1887	1
Greeley County Enterprise, Tribune	1887,1888	1
Greeley County Republican, Reid	1887,1888	1
Colokan Graphic	1887,1888	1
GREENWOOD COUNTY.		
Eureka Censorial	1876–1879	3
Eureka Herald	1876–1888	13
The Graphic, Eureka	1879–1882	3
The Eureka Republican	1879,1880	2
Greenwood County Republican, Eureka	1880–1888	8
The Eureka Sun	1879,1880	1
Greenwood County Democrat, Eureka	1882–1884	2
Democratic Messenger, Eureka	1884–1888	5
Madison Times	1877,1878	1
The Madison News	1879–1885	9
The Zenith, and the Madison Times	1886–1888	3
Fall River Times	1881–1888	7
Fall River Echo	1883–1886	3
Fall River Courant	1886–1888	2
Severy Pioneer	1882	1
Southern Kansas Journal, Severy	1884–1887	3
Severy Liberal	1885,1886	2
Severy Record	1887,1888	2
The Kansas Clipper, Severy	1887,1888	1
The Sunflower, Reece	1885,1886	2
Greenwood Review, Virgil	1887,1888	1
HAMILTON COUNTY.		
The Syracuse Journal	1885–1888	3
Syracuse Sentinel, (removed from Johnson City, Stanton county,)	1886–1888	3
Syracuse Democrat	1887	1
Democratic Principle, Syracuse	1887,1888	1
West Kansas News, Syracuse	1887	1
Border Ruffian, Coolidge	1885–1887	1
Coolidge Citizen	1886–1888	2
Coolidge Times	1887,1888	1
Surprise Post	1886	1
The Signal, Kendall	1886,1887	1
The Kendall Boomer	1886–1888	3
Kendall Republican	1886,1887	1
Kendall Gazette	1887	1
Johnson City Sentinel, (since in Stanton county,)	1886–1888	3
Enfield Tribune	1886,1887	1
HARPER COUNTY.		
The Anthony Republican	1879–1888	9
Anthony Daily Republican	1886–1888	5
Harper County Enterprise, Anthony	1885–1888	4
The Harper County Democrat, Anthony	1886–1888	2
Anthony Free Press, daily	1887,1888	1
Anthony Journal	1878–1884	5
Anthony Daily Journal	1885	1
Harper County Times, Harper	1878–1885	7
The Sentinel, Harper	1882–1888	5
The Daily Sentinel, Harper	1886–1888	3
Harper Graphic	1883–1888	4
Harper Daily Graphic	1886	1
Bluff City Tribune	1886–1888	2
The Danville Courant	1883,1884	1
The Danville Express	1885,1886	1
The Attica Advocate	1885–1888	4
Attica Bulletin	1886–1888	2
Attica Daily Advocate	1887	1
Freeport Leader	1885–1888	1
Midlothian Sun, Freeport	1885,1886	1
The Freeport Tribune, (changed from Sun,)	1886	1
The Crisfield Courier	1885–1888	3
HARVEY COUNTY.		
Zur Heimath, (semi-monthly), Halstead	1875–1881	7
The Halstead Independent	1881–1888	8
The Halstead Clipper	1884–1886	2
Halstead Herald	1887,1888	2
Harvey County News, Newton	1876–1879	4
The Newton Republican, (changed from Harvey County News,)	1879–1888	9

BOUND NEWSPAPER FILES AND PERIODICALS, KANSAS—CONTINUED.

Newspapers.	Years.	No. vols.
HARVEY COUNTY—concluded.		
Newton Daily Republican	1886–1888	6
Newton Kansan	1876–1888	13
Newton Daily Kansan	1887,1888	2
The Golden Gate, Newton	1879–1882	3
Das Neue Vaterland, Newton	1879	1
The Newton Democrat	1883–1887	3
Newton Anzeiger	1887,1888	1
The Kansas Commoner, Newton	1887,1888	1
The Kansas Chronicle, Newton	1888	1
The Burrton Telephone	1878–1881	3
The Burrton Monitor	1881–1888	7
The Burrton Graphic	1886–1888	2
The Jayhawker and Palladium, Sedgwick	1842–1884	2
The Pantagraph, Sedgwick	1884–1888	5
Walton Independent	1886–1888	2
HASKELL COUNTY.		
Ivanhoe Times	1886–1888	3
Santa Fé Trail	1886,1887	2
Santa Fé Champion	1887,1888	1
Haskell County Review, Santa Fé	1887,1888	1
Haskell County Republican, Santa Fé	1888	1
The Santa Fé Leader	1888	1
HODGEMAN COUNTY.		
Agitator, Hodgeman Center	1879,1880	1
Republican, Fordham	1879	1
The Buckner Independent, Jetmore	1879–1881	2
The Jetmore Reveille	1882–1888	7
Hodgeman County Scimitar, Jetmore	1886–1888	3
Jetmore Siftings	1886–1888	1
Jetmore Journal	1887,1888	1
The Orwell Times	1885,1886	1
JACKSON COUNTY.		
Holton Express	1872–1875	4
Holton Recorder	1875–1888	14
The Holton Argus	1877	1
The Holton Signal	1878–1888	11
Jackson County Federal, Holton	1886,1887	1
The Bee (daily and weekly), Netawaka and Holton	1879,1880	1
The Whiting Weekly News	1883–1888	6
The Hoyt Times	1887	1
JEFFERSON COUNTY.		
The Kansas Educational Journal, Grasshopper Falls. (See Leavenworth county.)		
The Kansas New Era, Grasshopper Falls	1866,1867	1
Valley Falls New Era	1873–1888	16
The Valley Falls Liberal and the Kansas Liberal (monthly), Valley Falls and Lawrence	1880–1883	3
Lucifer, (the Light-Bearer,) Valley Falls	1883–1888	5
Valley Falls Register	1881–1888	8
The Oskaloosa Independent	1870–1888	19
Sickle and Sheaf, Oskaloosa	1878–1879	7
Oskaloosa Weekly Sickle	1879–1886	7
The Winchester Argus	1879–1888	9
The Winchester Herald	1888	1
The Kaw Valley Chief, Perry	1879–1882	3
The Perry Monitor and Kaw Valley Chief (second), Perry	1883,1884	1
The Nortonville News	1885–1888	4
Meriden Report	1885–1888	3
The Osawkie Times	1885,1886	1
The McLouth Times	1887,1888	1
JEWELL COUNTY.		
Jewell County Diamond, Jewell City	1876,1877	2
Jewell County Republican, Jewell City	1879–1888	9
Jewell County Monitor, Jewell Center	1876,1877	2
Jewell County Monitor and Diamond, Jewell Center	1878,1879	2
Jewell County Monitor, Jewell Center and Mankato	1880–1888	9
Jewell County Review, Jewell Center and Mankato	1879–1882	3
Mankato Review	1883–1888	6
Mankato Daily Review	1887	1
The Kansas Jewellite, Mankato	1882,1883	1
The Jacksonian, Mankato	1888	1
White Oak Independent	1879	1
Jewell County Journal, Omio	1879,1880	1
Western Advocate, Omio	1882	1

BOUND NEWSPAPER FILES AND PERIODICALS, KANSAS—CONTINUED.

Newspapers.	Years.	No. vols.
JEWELL COUNTY—concluded.		
The Omio Mail	1884	1
Burr Oak Rereille	1880–1884	5
Burr Oak Herald	1883–1888	6
Burr Oak Rustler	1886,1887	1
Independent Republican, Burr Oak	1886,1887	1
Salem Chronicle	1882	1
Salem Argus	1883–1888	5
The People's Friend, Salem	1885–1887	3
Randall Register	1885–1888	3
Randall Tribune	1887,1888	1
JOHNSON COUNTY.		
Olathe Mirror	1866–1868	2
Mirror and News-Letter, Olathe	1876–1882	6
The Olathe Mirror, (1884–6, see below,)	1882–1888	3
Olathe Mirror-Gazette	1883–1886	4
Western Progress, Olathe	1876–1880	4
Kansas Star, Olathe	1876–1888	13
Olathe Leader	1879–1882	3
Olathe Gazette	1879–1883	3
Educational Advocate, Olathe	1880	1
Johnson County Democrat, Olathe	1882–1888	7
Kansas Patron, Olathe	1882–1888	7
The Olathe Republican	1884,1885	2
Kansas Register, Spring Hill	1878	1
Weekly Review, Spring Hill	1881,1882	1
Spring Hill New Era	1883–1885	1
KEARNEY COUNTY.		
Lakin Herald	1882–1884	3
The Kearney County Advocate, Lakin	1885–1888	3
Pioneer Democrat, Lakin	1885–1888	3
Hartland Times	1886,1887	2
Hartland Herald	1886–1888	3
Kearney County Coyote, Chantilly, and Omaha	1887,1888	2
KINGMAN COUNTY.		
The Kingman Mercury	1878–1880	2
The Kingman Blade	1880	1
The Kingman County Citizen, Kingman	1879–1884	4
The Kingman County Republican, Kingman	1882–1884	2
Citizen-Republican, Kingman	1884	1
Southern Kansas Democrat, Kingman	1883–1888	5
The Kingman Courier	1884–1888	5
Kingman Daily Courier	1887,1888	3
Kingman Leader	1884–1888	4
Kingman News	1886–1888	2
Kingman Daily News, (November, 1887, to February, 1888, lacking,)	1886–1888	2
Voice of the People, Kingman	1888	1
News, Norwich	1886–1888	3
Ninnescah and Cunningham Herald	1886–1888	2
The Spivey Dispatch	1887,1888	2
New Murdock Herald	1887	1
The Penalosa News	1887,1888	1
The Nashville News	1888	1
KIOWA COUNTY.		
Wellsford Register	1885	1
Wellsford Republican	1886,1887	1
Kiowa County Democrat, Wellsford	1887,1888	2
The Democrat and Watchman, Dowell post office	1885,1886	1
Comanche Chief and The Kiowa Chief, Reeder	1886	1
Greensburg Signal	1886–1888	3
Greensburg Rustler	1886–1888	3
Greensburg Republican	1887,1888	1
Mullinville Mallet	1886–1888	2
The Weekly Telegram, Mullinville	1886,1887	1
The Haviland Tribune	1887,1888	1
LABETTE COUNTY.		
Parsons Sun	1876–1888	13
Parsons Sun, daily	1884–1888	10
Parsons Eclipse	1876–1888	13
Parsons Daily Eclipse	1881–1888	15
Daily Outlook, Parsons	1877,1878	1
Daily Infant Wonder, Parsons	1878–1880	3
Daily Republican, Parsons	1880,1881	2

BOUND NEWSPAPER FILES AND PERIODICALS, KANSAS—Continued.

Newspapers.	Years.	No. vols.
LABETTE COUNTY—*concluded.*		
Parsons Palladium..	1883–1888	6
The Daily Evening Star, Parsons, (April 6 to October 19, 1881,).............	1881	1
Southern Kansas Advance, Chetopa..	1876–1878	2
Chetopa Advance..	1878–1888	11
Chetopa Herald..	1876–1878	2
Chetopa Statesman	1885–1888	3
The Chetopa Democrat	1888	1
Oswego Independent..	1876–1888	13
Labette County Democrat, Oswego...	1880–1888	9
The Oswego Republican..	1881–1886	5
The Oswego Daily Republican..	1881–1883	3
The Oswego Bee..	1887,1888	2
The Oswego Daily Bee..	1887,1888	3
Mound Valley Herald	1885–1888	3
Mound Valley News...	1886,1887	1
The Altamont Sentinel..	1886–1888	3
The Edna Star..	1887,1888	1
LANE COUNTY.		
Lane County Gazette, California...	1880–1882	2
Lane County Herald, Dighton..	1885–1888	3
The Dighton Journal..	1886–1888	3
Dighton Republican..	1887,1888	1
LEAVENWORTH COUNTY.		
Kansas Herald, Leavenworth...	1854–1859	5
Kansas Territorial Register, Leavenworth.......................................	1855	1
Leavenworth Conservative, daily, (January to June, 1867, lacking,).........	1861–1868	16
Times and Conservative, Leavenworth (daily)	1869,1870	3
Leavenworth Times, daily, (July to October, 1878, lacking,).................	1870–1888	37
Leavenworth Times (weekly)...	1876–1880	5
Leavenworth Daily Commercial..	1873–1876	4
Kansas Freie Presse, Leavenworth (weekly)....................................	1876–1886	10
Kansas Freie Presse, Leavenworth (daily)......................................	1876–1886	18
Leavenworth Appeal........	1876–1878	3
Leavenworth Appeal and Herald..	1879	1
Leavenworth Appeal and Tribune...	1879,1880	1
Public Press, Leavenworth (weekly)...	1877–1883	6
Public Press, Leavenworth, daily, (from July, 1877, to June, 1879, lacking).	1877–1882	8
Home Record, Leavenworth (monthly)...	1876–1888	13
Democratic Standard, Leavenworth (weekly)...................................	1880–1882	3
Kansas Farmer, Leavenworth (monthly)...	1867–1872	8
Leavenworth Evening Standard.......	1881–1888	16
The Kansas Educational Journal, monthly: Leavenworth, January, 1864, to August, 1865; Grasshopper Falls, September, 1865, to January, 1866; Topeka, June, 1866, to August, 1867; Emporia, September, 1867, to April, 1871; Emporia and Topeka, May, 1871, to April, 1873...........	1864–1873	9
Orphan's Friend, Leavenworth (monthly).......................................	1878–1888	10
The Western Homestead, Leavenworth (monthly)..............................	1878–1882	3
The Workingman's Friend, Leavenworth...	1881–1883	2
Leavenworth Weekly Chronicle...	1883,1884	1
The Visitor, Leavenworth	1883–1884	2
The Catholic, Leavenworth..	1885–1888	4
The Kansas Prohibitionist, Leavenworth...	1883,1884	1
Kansas Commoner, Leavenworth..	1884,1885	1
Truth, monthly, Leavenworth..	1886,1887	1
The Daily Sun, Leavenworth..	1887,1888	2
Leavenworth Post (daily)..	1888	2
The Tonganoxie Mirror...	1882–1888	6
The Tonganoxie News, changed from Linwood Leader........................	1885–1887	2
The Linwood Leader....	1883,1884	1
LINCOLN COUNTY.		
Lincoln County News, Lincoln Center..	1873	1
Saline Valley Register, Lincoln Center...	1876–1879	4
Lincoln Register, Lincoln Center...	1879,1840	1
Saline Valley Register, Lincoln Center...	1841–1883	2
Lincoln Banner, Lincoln Center..	1884–1886	2
Lincoln Republican, Lincoln Center...	1886–1888	3
The Argus and Beacon, Lincoln Center..	1880	1
The Beacon of Lincoln County, Lincoln Center.................................	1881–1884	3
The Lincoln Beacon, Lincoln Center..	1884–1888	5
Lincoln County Democrat, Lincoln	1886–1888	2
The Sylvan Grove Sentinel...	1887,1888	1

BOUND NEWSPAPER FILES AND PERIODICALS, KANSAS—CONTINUED.

Newspapers.	Years.	No. vols.
LINN COUNTY.		
Border Sentinel, Mound City	1866–1874	8
Linn County Clarion, Mound City	1876–1888	13
Mound City Progress	1884–1888	5
La Cygne Weekly Journal	1876–1888	13
La Cygne Leader	1887, 1888	1
The Pleasanton Observer	1876–1888	13
The Pleasanton Herald	1882–1888	7
The Prescott Eagle	1888–1888	5
The Blue Mound Sun	1883–1888	5
LOGAN COUNTY.		
The Oakley Opinion	1885–1888	3
The Oakley Republican	1887, 1888	1
Oakley Saturday Press	1888	1
Logan County Times, Oakley and Russell Springs	1887, 1888	1
The Courier, Ennis and Monument	1886–1888	1
The Scout, Gopher and Winona, (bound with Winona Messenger,)	1886–1888	3
The Winona Clipper	1887, 1888	1
McAllaster Weekly Record	1887, 1888	1
Augustine Herald	1887, 1888	1
The Leader, Russell Springs	1887, 1888	1
The Record, Russell Springs	1887	1
The Logan County Republican, Russell Springs	1888	1
LYON COUNTY.		
Emporia News	1866–1888	23
Emporia Daily News	1878–1888	20
Kansas Educational Journal, Emporia, (see Leavenworth county,)		
Emporia Ledger	1876–1880	5
The Hatchet (monthly), Emporia	1877, 1878	1
The Educationalist (monthly,) Emporia	1879–1880	2
Emporia Sun	1878, 1879	2
The Kansas Greenbacker, and the National Era, Emporia	1878, 1879	2
The Emporia Journal	1880, 1881	2
The Kansas Sentinel, Emporia	1880–1882	3
Daily Bulletin, Emporia	1881	1
Emporia Daily Republican	1881–1888	15
The Emporia Republican	1886–1888	2
Emporia Democrat	1882–1888	7
Emporia Daily Globe	1886, 1887	2
The Fanatic, Emporia	1887, 1888	1
The Hartford Enterprise	1879, 1880	1
The Hartford Weekly Call	1879–1888	9
Americus Weekly Herald	1881, 1882	1
The Americus Ledger	1885–1888	4
The Neosho Vivifier, Neosho Rapids	1885, 1886	1
The Neosho Valley Press, Neosho Rapids	1886, 1887	1
The Admire City Free Press	1887, 1888	1
The Allen Tidings	1887, 1888	1
M'PHERSON COUNTY.		
The McPherson Independent	1876–1879	4
The McPherson Freeman	1878–1888	11
McPherson Daily Freeman	1887, 1888	2
The McPherson Republican	1879–1888	9
McPherson Daily Republican	1887, 1888	4
The Comet, McPherson	1881, 1882	1
Industrial Liberator, McPherson	1882	1
The McPherson Independent, McPherson	1882–1884	4
The McPherson Press	1884, 1885	1
The McPherson County Champion, McPherson	1883, 1887	2
The Democrat, McPherson	1886–1888	2
Kansas State Register, McPherson	1887	1
The McPherson Anzeiger	1887, 1888	2
Lindsborg Localist	1879–1888	3
Smoky Valley News, Lindsborg	1881–1888	7
Kansas Posten, Lindsborg	1882, 1883	1
The Canton Monitor	1880	1
Canton Carrier	1883, 1888	3
The Windom Record	1884–1886	2
The Windom Enterprise	1886–1888	2
The Moundridge Leader	1887, 1888	2
Marquette Monitor	1887, 1888	2

BOUND NEWSPAPER FILES AND PERIODICALS, KANSAS—CONTINUED.

Newspapers.	Years.	No. vols.
MARION COUNTY.		
Marion County Record, Marion Center	1875–1888	13
The School Galaxy, Marion Center	1877	1
Central Kansas Telegraph, Marion Center	1880	1
Marion Banner, Marion Center	1880,1881	2
Marion Graphic, Marion Center	1882,1883	1
Marion County Democrat and Independent, Marion Center	1883,1884	1
The Marion Register, Marion	1885,1888	2
The Marion Tribune	1886,1887	1
The Cottonwood Valley Times, Marion	1887,1888	2
Marion Daily Times	1888	2
The Marion County Anzeiger, Marion and Hillsboro	1887,1888	1
The Peabody Gazette	1876–1888	13
The Peabody Daily Gazette	1887	1
Peabody Reporter	1880	1
The Peabody Post	1882	1
Marion Graphic, Peabody	1883–1888	5
Florence Herald, (1886 lacking,)	1876–1888	12
Florence Tribune	1884–1886	2
Florence Weekly News	1886,1887	1
The Florence Weekly Bulletin	1887,1888	2
Hillsboro Phonograph	1881	1
The Intelligencer, Hillsboro	1881,1882	1
Freundschafts-Kreis, Hillsboro	1885,1886	2
Hillsboro Herald	1886,1887	2
Canada Arcade	1887	1
MARSHALL COUNTY.		
The Marysville Enterprise (volumes 1 and 3)	1866–1868	2
The Lantern, Marysville	1876	1
The Marshall County News, Marysville	1876–1888	13
Kansas Staats-Zeitung, Marysville	1879–1881	2
Marysville Signal	1881–1883	2
Marysville Post, (German,)	1881–1888	7
Marshall County Democrat, Marysville	1883–1888	6
The Bugle Call, Marysville	1885,1886	1
The True Republican, Marysville	1886–1888	2
The Waterville Telegraph, (1874 and 1875 lacking,)	1870–1888	17
Blue Rapids Times	1876–1888	13
The Blue Rapids Lyre	18–6,1887	1
Irving, Blue Valley Gazette	1876–1878	3
The Irving Citizen	1880	1
The Irving Leader	1886–1888	2
Frankfort Record	1876–1879	4
The National Headlight, Frankfort	1879–1881	2
The Frankfort Bee	1881–1888	8
The Frankfort Sentinel	1886–1888	2
The Beattie Boomerang	1883,1884	1
The North Star, Beattie	1884,1885	1
The Star, Beattie	1885–1888	4
The Visitor, Axtell	1883,1884	1
Axtell Anchor	1883–1888	5
Lincolnville Star	1887,1888	1
MEADE COUNTY.		
Fowler City Graphic	1885–1888	3
The Fowler City Advocate	1886	1
Meade County Globe, Meade Center	1885–1888	3
Meade Center Press	1885,1886	1
The Press-Democrat, Meade Center	1886–1888	
Meade Center Telegram	1886	1
The Meade Republican, Meade Center	1887,1888	1
The Hornet, Spring Lake, and Artois, Artesian City	1885–1888	3
The Guardian, West Plains	1886,1887	1
The West Plains News and Democrat	1887,1888	1
Meade County Times, Mertilla	1886–1888	2
MIAMI COUNTY.		
The Western Spirit, Paola	1874–1888	15
The Miami Republican, Paola	1876–1888	13
Republican-Citizen, Paola	1878–1880	2
Miami Talisman, Paola	1881,1882	1
Paola Times	1882–1888	7
The Border Chief, Louisburg	1879–1881	2
Watchman, Louisburg	1881	1
The Louisburg Herald	1887,1888	1
Osawatomie Times	1880,1881	1
The Osawatomie Sentinel	1885,1886	2

BOUND NEWSPAPER FILES AND PERIODICALS, KANSAS—CONTINUED.

Newspapers.	Years.	No. vols.
MIAMI COUNTY—concluded.		
Osawatomie Gaslight	1887,1888	1
Graphic, Osawatomie	1888	1
Fontana News	1885–1888	3
MITCHELL COUNTY.		
Beloit Gazette, (duplicates from April, 1872, to April, 1873; 1873, 1874 and 1875 lacking;)	1872–1888	13
Beloit Weekly Record	1877–1879	3
The Beloit Courier	1879–1888	10
Beloit Weekly Democrat	1878–1880	2
Western Democrat, Beloit, (1882 and 1883 lacking,)	1880–1888	5
The Western Nationalist, Beloit	1882,1883	2
The Echo, Cawker City	1876–1878	2
The Cawker City Free Press	1878–1883	5
Cawker City Journal	1880–1888	8
The Public Record, Cawker City	1883–1888	6
Glen Elder Key	1880	1
Glen Elder Herald	1885–1888	3
Simpson Siftings	1884–1886	2
Scottsville Independent	1886–1888	3
MONTGOMERY COUNTY.		
Independence Courier	1874,1875	2
Independence Kansan	1876–1884	9
The Star, Independence	1882–1884	3
The Star and Kansan, Independence	1885–1888	4
The South Kansas Tribune, Independence	1876–1888	13
The Workingman's Courier, Independence	1877–1879	3
The Living Age, Independence	1881	1
The Evening Reporter, Independence, (lacking from 1883 to February 17, 1886,)	1882–1888	7
The Independence News (daily and weekly)	1886	1
Montgomery Argus, Independence	1886	1
Coffeyville Journal	1876–1888	13
The Gate City Enterprise, Coffeyville	1884,1885	1
Gate City Gazette, Coffeyville	1886, 1887	1
The Sun, Coffeyville	1886–1888	2
Cherryvale Leader	1877	1
Cherryvale Globe	1879–1882	3
Cherryvale News	1881,1882	1
Cherry Valley Torch, Cherryvale	1882–1885	3
Cherryvale Globe-News	1882–1884	3
The Globe and Torch, Cherryvale	1885–1888	3
Daily Globe and Torch, Cherryvale	1885–1887	4
The Weekly Clarion, Cherryvale	1885	1
Cherryvale Bulletin	1884–1888	5
The Cherryvale Republican	1886–1888	2
The Cherryvale Champion	1887,1888	1
The Elk City Globe	1882–1887	5
The Elk City Star	1884–1886	1
The Elk City Democrat	1885,1886	1
The Elk City Eagle	1886–1888	2
The Caney Chronicle	1885–1888	3
The Havana Vidette	1885,1886	1
Havana Weekly Herald	1887,1888	1
Liberty Light	1886	1
The Liberty Review	1886–1888	2
MORRIS COUNTY.		
Morris County Republican, Council Grove	1876,1877	1
Council Grove Democrat	1876,1877	2
Republican and Democrat, Council Grove	1877–1879	2
Council Grove Republican	1879–1888	10
Morris County Times, Council Grove	1880,1881	2
The Kansas Cosmos, Council Grove, (January to July, 1885, lacking; October 15, 1886, Cosmos consolidated with Council Grove Republican,)	1881–1886	6
The Council Grove Guard	1884–1888	4
The Anti-Monopolist, Council Grove	1884	1
Morris County Enterprise, Parkerville	1878–1884	7
The Parkerville Times	1887,1888	1
The Morris County News, White City	1886–1888	2
The Dwight Wasp	1887,1888	2
MORTON COUNTY.		
Frisco Pioneer	1886,1887	1
Morton County Democrat, Frisco	1886–1888	1
The Richfield Leader	1886,1887	1
The Leader-Democrat, Richfield	1888	1

BOUND NEWSPAPER FILES AND PERIODICALS—CONTINUED.

Newspapers.	Years.	No. vols.
MORTON COUNTY—*concluded.*		
The Richfield Republican	1887, 1888	1
The Great Southwest, Richfield	1887, 1888	1
The Taloga Star	1887, 1888	1
NEMAHA COUNTY.		
Seneca Weekly Courier	1875–1884	10
Seneca Courier-Democrat	1885, 1888	4
The Seneca Tribune	1879–1888	10
Our Mission, Seneca	1885, 1886	1
Nemaha County Republican, Sabetha	1876–1888	13
The Sabetha Advance	1876, 1877	2
Sabetha Weekly Herald	1884–1888	5
The Oneida Journal	1879–1882	3
The Oneida Chieftain, Democrat, and Dispatch	1883, 1884	1
The Oneida Monitor	1885, 1886	1
The Wetmore Spectator, (lacking from August, 1884, to August, 1885,)	1882–1888	5
The Centralia Enterprize	1883, 1884	1
The Centralia Journal	1885–1888	4
The Goff's News	1887, 1888	1
NEOSHO COUNTY.		
Neosho County Journal, Osage Mission	1876–1888	13
The Temperance Banner, Osage Mission	1878–1880	2
Neosho Valley Enterprise, Osage Mission	1840–1882	2
The Neosho County Democrat, Osage Mission	1883–1888	5
Neosho County Record, Erie	1876–1886	11
The Neosho County Republican, Erie	1884–1886	3
The People's Vindicator, Erie	1888	1
Republican-Record, Erie	1886–1888	2
Chanute Times	1876–1888	13
The Chanute Democrat	1879–1882	3
The Chanute Chronicle	1882, 1883	2
Chanute Blade	1883–1888	5
The Chanute Vidette	1887, 1888	1
Head Light, Thayer	1876–1888	13
The Thayer Herald	1885, 1886	1
Star of Hope, Urbana	1878	1
NESS COUNTY.		
The Pioneer, Clarinda & Sidney	1879–1882	3
The Advance, Sidney	1882–1883	1
Ness City Times	1880–1888	8
The Truth, Ness City	1883–1884	1
The News, Ness City	1884–1888	4
The Ness City Graphic	1886	1
Walnut Valley Sentinel, Ness City	1886–1888	2
The Globe, Schoharie	1883, 1884	1
The Harold Boomer and Record	1887, 1888	2
Nonchalanta Herald	1887, 1888	1
The Bazine Register	1887, 1888	1
NORTON COUNTY.		
Norton County Advance, Norton	1878–1882	5
Norton County People, Norton	1880–1883	2
The Norton Courier	1883–1888	6
Norton Champion	1884–1888	4
The Norton Democrat, and Weekly New Era	1886–1888	2
The Lenora Leader	1882–1888	6
The Kansas Northwest, Lenora	1884, 1885	1
The Kansas Monitor, Lenora	1885, 1886	1
The Common People, Lenora	1886, 1887	1
The Lenora Record	1887, 1888	1
The Norton County Badger, and } The Edmond Times, Edmond. }	1886–1888	3
The Almena Star	1885–1888	3
Almena Plaindealer	1888	1
The Oronoque Magic	1886	1
OSAGE COUNTY.		
Osage County Chronicle, Burlingame, (1872 lacking)	1868–1888	19
Osage County Democrat, Burlingame	1881–1887	4
Burlingame Herald	1881–1884	2
Burlingame Independent, (changed from Carbondale Calendar, January 28 to April 1, 1886; Carbondale Independent, April 8 to May 13, 1886, then moved to Burlingame,)	1886–1888	2
Burlingame News, amateur	1886–1888	1
Osage City Free Press	1876–1888	13
The Kansas Times, Osage City, (moved from Lyndon,)	1879–1881	3
The Osage City Republican	1882, 1883	1

BOUND NEWSPAPER FILES AND PERIODICALS, KANSAS—CONTINUED.

Newspapers.	Years.	No. vols.
OSAGE COUNTY — concluded. *		
Osage County Democrat, Osage City	1886,1887	1
The Kansas People, Osage City	1887,1888	2
Kansas People (daily), Osage City	1887,1888	3
Lyndon Times	1876–1879	3
The Lyndon Journal	1882–1888	6
The Lyndon Leader	1882,1883	2
Kansas Plebeian, Lyndon and Scranton	1882	1
Osage County Times, Scranton	1883	1
The Carbondale Journal	1879	1
Carbondale Independent	1882–1884	2
Astonisher & Paralyzer, Carbondale	1885–1887	2
The Carbondalian, Carbondale	1887,1888	2
The Carbondale Record	1888	1
Kansas Workman, Scranton and Quenemo	1883–1888	5
Osage County Republican, Quenemo	1886–1888	2
Melvern Record	1884–1888	4
OSBORNE COUNTY.		
Osborne County Farmer, Osborne	1876–1888	13
The Truth Teller, Osborne	1880	1
Daily News, Osborne	1881	1
Osborne County News, Osborne	1883–1888	6
Western Odd Fellow (monthly). Osborne	1886–1888	1
Osborne County Journal, Osborne	1886–1888	2
Bull's City Post	1880	1
Osborne County Key, Bull's City	1881,1882	1
The Western Empire, Bull's City	1883–1885	2
The Western Empire, Alton	1885–1888	4
Downs Times	1880–1888	9
Downs Chief	1886–1888	2
Portis Patriot	1881–1888	7
OTTAWA COUNTY.		
The Solomon Valley Mirror, Minneapolis	1874–1886	12
The Sentinel, Minneapolis	1876–1883	8
Minneapolis Messenger, (successor to Sentinel,)	1883–1885	4
The Daily Messenger, Minneapolis	1887	1
Minneapolis Independent	1876–1881	6
Ottawa County Index, Minneapolis	1880–1888	4
The Progressive Current, Minneapolis	1883,1884	1
Solomon Valley Democrat, Minneapolis	1884–1888	4
The Daily Institute, Minneapolis, Nos. 1 to 20	1885	1
Kansas Workman, monthly, Minneapolis	1885–1888	4
Minneapolis School Journal	1885,1886	1
The Sprig of Myrtle, monthly, Minneapolis	1886–1888	2
Ottawa County Commercial, Minneapolis	1886–1888	2
The Delphos Herald	1879,1880	2
Delphos Carrier	1881–1888	7
Bennington Star	1883–1888	4
The Bennington Journal	1885	1
The Tescott Herald	1887,1888	1
PAWNEE COUNTY.		
Larned Press	1876–1878	3
The Pawnee County Herald, Larned	1877,1878	2
The Larned Enterprise-Chronoscope	1878–1888	11
Larned Daily Chronoscope	1887,1888	3
The Larned Optic	1878–1884	6
The Larned Weekly Eagle-Optic	1885–1888	4
Garfield Letter	1885,1886	1
The Garfield News	1887,1888	1
The Burdett Bugle	1880–1888	2
Pawnee County Republican	1886,1887	1
PHILLIPS COUNTY.		
The Kirwin Chief	1876–1888	13
Kirwin Progress and Kirwin Democrat	1877,1878	2
The Independent, Kirwin	1880–1888	8
Kirwin Republican	1883,1884	1
Phillips County Herald, Phillipsburg	1878–1888	11
The Phillipsburg Times	1884,1885	1
The Phillipsburg Dispatch	1886–1888	2
Phillipsburg Democrat	1887,1888	1
Logan Enterprise	1879–1883	5
Phillips County Freeman, Logan	1883–1888	5
The Logan Republican	1886–1888	3
The Long Island Argus	1885	1
Long Island Leader	1886–1888	2
Phillips County Democrat, Long Island	1886	1

BOUND NEWSPAPER FILES AND PERIODICALS, KANSAS—CONTINUED.

Newspapers.	Years.	No. vols.
PHILLIPS COUNTY—*concluded.*		
Phillips County Inter-Ocean, Long Island.	1887,1888	2
Marvin Monitor.	1886,1887	1
Woodruff Gazette and Republican	1886,1887	1
POTTAWATOMIE COUNTY.		
Pottawatomie Gazette, Louisville, (vols. 1, 2, 3, 4, and duplicate vol. 1,)	1867–1870	5
Kansas Reporter, Louisville	1870–1887	17
Pottawatomie County Herald, Louisville	1879	1
The Louisville Republican (and The Semi-Weekly Republican)	1882–1886	5
The Louisville Indicator	1887,1888	2
Weekly Kansas Valley, Wamego	1869–1871	2
The Wamego Blade	1876	1
The Wamego Tribune	1877–1882	6
Kansas Agriculturist, Wamego	1879–1888	10
Wamego Democrat	1885,1886	1
The Daily Wamegan, Wamego	1887,1888	3
St. Marys Times	1876,1877	2
St. Marys Democrat	1878	1
Pottawatomie Chief, St. Marys	1878,1879	2
St. Marys Express	1880–1888	7
St. Marys Star	1884–1888	5
St. Marys Gazette	1888	1
Inkslingers' Advertiser, Westmoreland	1878	1
The Weekly Period, Westmoreland	1882–1885	3
The Westmoreland Recorder	1885–1888	4
The Onaga Journal	1878–1885	8
The Onaga Democrat	1885–1887	2
Independent and Morning News, Havensville	1880–1882	2
The Olsburg News-Letter	1887,1888	2
PRATT COUNTY.		
The Stafford Citizen	1877,1878	1
Pratt County Press, Iuka	1878–1887	9
Pratt County Times, Iuka	1881–1883	7
The Iuka Traveler	1886–1888	1
The Saratoga Sun	1885–1887	3
Pratt County Democrat, Saratoga	1885,1886	1
The Cullison Banner	1886–1888	2
Pratt County Register, Pratt	1886–1888	2
The Pratt County Republican, Pratt	1888	1
The Preston Herald	1887,1888	1
Springvale Advocate	1888	1
RAWLINS COUNTY.		
Atwood Pioneer	1879–1882	3
Republican Citizen, Atwood	1880–1888	8
Rawlins County Democrat, Atwood and Blakeman	1885–1888	3
The Atwood Journal	1888	1
The Ludell Settler	1884–1887	3
The Celia Enterprise	1885–1888	3
The Blakeman Register	1887–1888	1
The Herndon Courant	1888	1
RENO COUNTY.		
Hutchinson News	1876–1888	13
Hutchinson Daily News	1886–1888	5
Hutchinson Herald	1876–1885	9
The Interior, Hutchinson	1877–1885	8
The Interior-Herald, Hutchinson	1885–1888	4
Hutchinson Daily Interior-Herald	1887	1
The Sunday Democrat, The Dollar Democrat, The Democrat, and The Hutchinson Democrat	1883–1888	6
The Hutchinson Call (daily)	1888	1
The Argosy, Nickerson	1878–1888	10
The Nickerson Register	1884–1888	4
The Arlington Enterprise	1885–1888	3
The Nickerson Daily Register	1887	1
The South Hutchinson Leader	1886,1887	1
The Saturday Review, South Hutchinson	1887,1888	1
Sylvia Telephone	1886–1888	2
The Haven Independent	1886–1888	2
The Turon Rustler	1886–1888	2
Partridge Cricket and Press	1886,1887	1
Lerado Ledger	1886–1888	1

BOUND NEWSPAPER FILES AND PERIODICALS, KANSAS—CONTINUED.

Newspapers.	Years.	No. vols.
REPUBLIC COUNTY.		
The Belleville Republic	1876	1
The Belleville Telescope	1876–1888	13
The Weekly Record, Belleville	1883–1885	2
The Belleville Democrat	1886–1888	2
Scandia Republic	1877	1
The Republic County Journal, Scandia	1878–1880	4
Republican-Journal, Scandia	1881	1
Scandia Journal	1882–1888	7
Republic County Independent, Scandia	1883–1884	1
Republic County Chief, Scandia	1885,1886	1
The Scandia Independent	1887,1888	1
White Rock Independent	1879	1
Republic City News	1883–1888	5
Conservative Cuban, Cuba	1884–1886	2
Republic County Pilot, Cuba	1885–1888	4
The Wayne Register	1885–1887	3
The Warwick Leader	1886,1887	1
RICE COUNTY.		
Rice County Gazette, Sterling	1876–1880	5
Sterling Gazette	1881–1888	8
Weekly Bulletin, and The Sterling Bulletin	1877–1888	11
The Lyons Republican	1879–1888	9
The Daily Republican, Lyons	1882	1
The Lyons Daily Republican	1887,1888	3
Central Kansas Democrat, (1882 and 1883 lacking,) Lyons	1879–1887	7
Central Kansas Democrat, daily, Lyons	1886,1887	2
The Lyons Prohibitionist	1885–1888	3
The Soldiers' and Lyons Tribune	1887,1888	1
The Rural West, Little River	1881,1882	2
The Little River Monitor	1886–1888	2
The Chase Dispatch	1884,1885	1
The Weekly Record, Chase	1886–1888	2
The Daily Bulletin, Sterling	1887,1888	2
Sterling Republican, weekly	1886,1887	1
Sterling Republican, daily	1887	1
The Arkansas Valley Times, Sterling	1888	1
The Saturday Republican	1888	1
Geneseo Herald	1887,1888	2
The Raymond Independent	1887,1888	1
The Cain City Razzooper	1887,1888	1
Partridge Press	1887	1
Independent, Frederick	1888	1
The Alden Herald	1888	1
RILEY COUNTY.		
Manhattan Express	1860–1862	3
The Kansas Radical, Manhattan, (duplicate of 1867 and 1868,)	1866–1868	3
The Manhattan Independent, (1865 lacking,)	1864–1868	3
The Manhattan Standard, (triplicate of 1869 and duplicate of 1870,)	1868–1870	3
Manhattan Homestead	1869–1878	7
The Nationalist, Manhattan, (eleven duplicates,)	1870–1888	18
The Literary Review, Manhattan	1872	1
Manhattan Beacon, (two duplicates,)	1872–1875	3
The Industrialist, Manhattan, (twelve duplicates,)	1875–1888	14
Manhattan Enterprise	1876–1882	6
The Kansas Telephone, Manhattan	1881–1888	8
The Manhattan Republic	1882–1888	7
Manhattan Daily Republic	1887,1888	3
The Independent, Manhattan	1883	1
The Mercury, Manhattan	1884–1888	4
The Golden Cresset (monthly), Manhattan	1884,1885	1
The Journal of Mycology (monthly), Manhattan	1885–1888	3
The Riley Times	1887,1888	1
The Independent, Riley Center	1879–1882	2
Randolph Echo	1882–1887	5
Leonardville Monitor	1884–1888	5
ROOKS COUNTY.		
The Stockton News and the Western News, (except 1881, see Plainville News,)	1876–1888	11
Rooks County Record, Stockton	1879–1888	9
Stockton Democrat	1883–1884	3
Stockton Eagle	1887,1888	1
The Plainville News, (moved from Stockton for one year,)	1881	4
The Plainville Press	1883,1886	1
Plainville Echo	1884–1886	2
Plainville Times	1886–1888	3

BOUND NEWSPAPER FILES AND PERIODICALS, KANSAS—CONTINUED.

Newspapers.	Years.	No. vols.
ROOKS COUNTY—*concluded.*		
Webster Eagle	1885–1887	2
Webster Enterprise	1888	1
Woodston Saw and Register	1886–1888	2
Cresson Dispatch	1887,1888	1
RUSH COUNTY.		
Rush County Progress, Rush Center, and LaCrosse Eagle	1877,1878	2
LaCrosse Chieftain	1882–1888	7
LaCrosse Democrat	1887,1888	1
The Blade, Walnut City	1878–1882	5
The Herald, Walnut City	1883–1886	4
Walnut City Gazette, Rush Center	1886–1888	3
The Democrat, Walnut City	1886–1888	2
Walnut City News (daily)	1887,1888	2
The McCracken Enterprise	1887,1888	2
RUSSELL COUNTY.		
Russell County Record, Russell	1876–1888	13
Russell County Advance, Russell	1878	1
Russell Independent	1879–1881	2
The Russell Hawkeye	1882,1883	1
Russell Live-Stock Journal, and Russell Journal	1885–1888	4
Russell Review, and Democratic Review, Russell	1886–1888	1
Bunker Hill Advertiser	1880,1881	2
Bunker Hill Banner	1882,1883	1
Bunker Hill Banner (second)	1884,1885	1
The Bunker Hill News	1887,1888	1
Bunker Hill Gazette	1883	1
The Dorrance Nugget	1886–1888	2
Luray Headlight	1887,1888	1
ST. JOHN COUNTY.		
The Oakley Opinion	1885,1886	1
SALINE COUNTY.		
The Salina Herald	1876–1888	13
Salina Daily Herald	1887,1888	3
Saline County Journal, Salina	1876–1888	13
Saline County Daily Journal, Salina	1887,1888	2
Farmers' Advocate, Salina	1876–1879	4
The Weekly Democrat, Salina	1878,1879	1
Svenska Herolden, Salina	1878–1881	3
The Salina Independent	1882–1885	3
The Salina Republican	1886–1888	3
The Rising Sun, Salina	1885–1888	3
Brookville Independent	1880	1
Brookville Transcript	1881–1888	7
Brookville Times	1887,1888	1
Chico Advertiser	1886,1887	1
The Gypsum Banner	1886,1887	1
Gypsum Valley Echo	1886–1888	2
Assaria Argus	1887,1888	2
SCOTT COUNTY.		
Western Times, Scott City	1885,1886	1
Scott County News, Scott City	1886–1888	3
Scott County Herald, Scott City	1886–1888	3
The Scott Sentinel, Scott City	1886–1888	2
Grigsby City Scorcher	1887	1
The Pence Phonograph	1887,1888	1
SEDGWICK COUNTY.		
Wichita Vidette, (August 25, 1870, to March 11, 1871,)	1870,1871	1
Wichita City Eagle, (1873–1876 lacking,)	1872–1888	14
Wichita Daily Eagle	1884–1888	9
Wichita Weekly Beacon	1874–1888	15
The Wichita Daily Beacon	1884–1888	9
Wichita Herald	1877–1879	3
Stern des Westens, Wichita	1879	1
National Monitor, Wichita	1879,1880	1
Daily Republican, Wichita	1880,1881	2
Wichita Republican	1880,1881	1
Wichita Daily Times	1881–1884	7
Sedgwick Jayhawker and Palladium, Wichita	1882,1883	2
The New Republic, Wichita	1883–1888	6
Wichita Daily Evening Resident	1886	2
The Arrow, Wichita	1880–1888	3

BOUND NEWSPAPER FILES AND PERIODICALS, KANSAS—Continued.

Newspapers.	Years.	No. vols.
SEDGWICK COUNTY—*concluded.*		
Kansas Staats-Anzeiger, Wichita	1886-1888	3
Wichita Herald	1885-1888	3
The Wichita Citizen, Labor Union, Union Labor Press, and Independent	1886-1888	2
The Wichita District Advocate	1886-1888	1
Sunday Growler, Wichita	1886-1888	2
Wichita Daily Journal	1887, 1888	4
Wichita Daily Call	1887	1
Wichita Globe	1887	1
Western Evangelist, Wichita	1887, 1888	1
The Leader, (prohibition,) Wichita, (see Topeka,)	1888	1
Cheney Journal	1884-1886	5
The Cheney Weekly Blade	1888	1
Valley Center News	1885-1888	3
The Mount Hope Mentor	1885-1888	3
Clearwater Leader	1886-1888	3
The Colwich Courier	1887, 1888	2
Garden Plain Herald	1887, 1888	1
SEQUOYAH COUNTY.		
(See Finney County.)		
The Garden City Paper	1879	1
The Irrigator, Garden City	1882	1
SEWARD COUNTY.		
The Prairie Owl, Fargo Springs	1885-1888	2
Seward County Democrat, Fargo Springs	1886-1888	3
The Fargo Springs News	1886-1888	2
Springfield Transcript	1886-1888	2
Springfield Soap-Box	1887, 1888	1
Seward County Courant, Springfield	1887, 1888	1
Seward Independent	1887, 1888	1
The Arkalon News	1888	1
The Liberal Leader	1888	1
SHAWNEE COUNTY.		
Daily Kansas Freeman, Topeka, (October 24 to November 7,)	1885	1
The Kansas Tribune, Topeka	1855-1858	2
Topeka Tribune, (two sets,)	1858-1861	4
The Topeka Tribune	1866, 1867	1
Topeka Daily Tribune, (January 12 to March 1,)	1864	1
The Congregational Record, Topeka, (see Douglas county).		
Weekly Kansas State Record, Topeka, (1863-1867 lacking, and 7 duplicates,)	1859-1875	16
Daily Kansas State Record, Topeka, (January to June, 1870, lacking)	1868-1871	8
Daily Kansas State Record, Topeka, (duplicates of above)	1868-1871	10
Fair Daily Record, Topeka, (duplicate volume,)	1871	1
The Kansas Farmer, monthly, (Topeka, May, 1863, March and April, 1864; Lawrence, January, 1865, to July, 1867; Leavenworth, September, 1867, to December, 1873; Topeka, weekly, 1873 to 1884,) eight duplicates	1863-1888	25
Kansas Educational Journal, Topeka, (see Leavenworth county).		
Topeka Leader, (1866 and 1867, duplicates,)	1865-1869	6
Commonwealth, daily, Topeka, (50 duplicates,)	1869-1888	83
The Weekly Commonwealth, Topeka, (13 duplicates,)	1874-1888	13
Tanner and Cobbler, Topeka	1872	1
Kansas Magazine (monthly), Topeka	1872, 1873	4
Topeka Daily Blade, (1874 not published, 1 duplicate,)	1873-1879	10
Topeka Weekly Blade	1876-1879	4
Kansas State Journal (daily), Topeka	1879-1888	19
Kansas Weekly State Journal, Topeka	1879-1886	7
Kansas Democrat, Topeka	1874-1882	8
American Young Folks (monthly), Topeka	1876-1882	7
Times (daily), Topeka	1876	1
The Kansas Churchman, monthly, Topeka, (1883-1885, Lawrence,)	1876-1886	7
Commercial Advertiser, Topeka	1877	1
Educational Calendar (monthly), Topeka	1877, 1878	1
Colored Citizen, Topeka	1878, 1879	2
Der Courier, Topeka	1878-1880	2
The Daily Capital, Topeka	1879-1888	20
Weekly Capital and Farmers' Journal, Topeka	1883-1888	5
Kansas Staats-Anzeiger, Topeka	1879-1881	2
The Kansas Methodist and Kansas Methodist-Chautauqua, Topeka, (monthly 1879, 1880, and weekly 1881-1886,)	1879-1888	10
The Topeka Tribune	1880, 1881	2
North Topeka Daily Argus, and Times	1880, 1881	3
The Topeka Post (daily)	1880	1
The Whim-Wham, Topeka	1880, 1881	2
The Educationist, Topeka	1880-1884	4
Western School Journal (monthly), Topeka	1885-1888	4
The Kansas Telegraph, Topeka	1881-1888	8

BOUND NEWSPAPER FILES AND PERIODICALS, KANSAS—Concluded.

Newspapers.	Years.	No. vols.
SHAWNEE COUNTY—*concluded.*		
Good Tidings, Topeka	1881–1886	5
Daily Democrat and Daily State Press, Topeka	1881, 1882	1
The Colored Patriot, Topeka	1882	1
The Evening Herald, Topeka	1882	1
The Faithful Witness (semi-monthly), Topeka	1882–1888	4
The National Workman, Topeka	1882	1
Saturday Evening Lance, Topeka	1883–1888	5
The Kansas Newspaper Union, Topeka	1883–1888	5
The Topeka Tribune	1883–1885	2
Anti-Monopolist, Topeka	1883, 1884	1
The Daily Critic, Topeka	1884	1
New Paths in the Far West (German monthly), Topeka	1884, 1885	1
Light (Masonic monthly), Topeka	1884–1888	4
The Kansas Knight and Soldier (semi-monthly), Topeka	1884–1888	4
The Spirit of Kansas, Topeka	1884–1888	3
Western Baptist	1884–1888	4
City and Farm Record and Real Estate Journal (monthly), Topeka	1884–1888	4
The Kansas Law Journal, Topeka	1885–1887	4
The Citizen (daily), Topeka	1885, 1886	1
The Washburn Argo (monthly), Topeka	1883–1888	3
The Washburn Reporter, Topeka	1887, 1888	2
The Kansas Democrat (daily), Topeka	1886–1888	6
Our Messenger (monthly), Topeka	1886–1888	3
Welcome, Music and Home Journal (monthly), Topeka	1885–1888	3
Kansas Home (monthly), Topeka	1886–1888	1
The Lantern, Topeka	1887, 1888	1
North Topeka Daily Courier	1887, 1888	1
Topeka Times, North Topeka, (March, 1873, to February, 1874, lacking,)	1871–1874	3
North Topeka Times	1876–1885	10
The Evening Republic, North Topeka	1882	1
North Topeka Mail	1882–1888	6
The North Topeka News	1888	1
News (daily), North Topeka	1888	1
Kansas Valley Times, Rossville	1879–1782	4
The Rossville News	1883, 1884	1
Carpenter's Kansas Lyre, Rossville	1884–1888	3
Silver Lake News	1882	1
The Future, monthly, Richland	1885–1887	2
SHERIDAN COUNTY.		
Sheridan County Tribune, Kenneth	1881, 1882	1
Weekly Sentinel, Kenneth and Hoxie	1884–1888	4
Democrat, Kenneth and Hoxie	1885–1888	3
Sheridan Times	1887, 1888	1
SHERMAN COUNTY.		
The New Tecumseh, Gandy, Leonard and Itasca	1885, 1886	1
Sherman County Republican, Itasca, Sherman Center and Goodland	1886–1888	2
Voltaire Adviser	1885, 1886	1
Sherman County News, Voltaire	1886–1888	2
Sherman County Dark Horse, Eustis	1886–1888	2
Sherman County Democrat, Eustis	1887, 1888	1
Sherman Center News, Sherman Center and Goodland	1886, 1887	1
SMITH COUNTY.		
Smith County Pioneer, Smith Centre	1876–1888	13
The Daily Pioneer, Smith Centre	1887, 1888	2
The Kansas Free Press, Smith Centre	1879–1881	2
Smith County Record, Smith Centre	1882, 1883	2
Smith County Weekly Bulletin, Smith Centre	1884–1888	5
The Bazoo, Smith Centre	1885–1888	4
Gaylord Herald	1879–1888	9
The Toiler and Independent, Harlan	1879, 1880	1
The Harlan Weekly Chief	1884, 1885	2
The Harlan Advocate	1885–1887	1
The Harlan Enterprise	1887, 1888	1
The Cedarville Telephone	1883	1
The Cedarville Review	1884, 1885	1
Cedarville Globe	1886–1888	2
The Dispatch, Reamsville	1884–1886	1
The Cora Union	1886, 1887	1
The Lebanon Criterion	1887, 1888	1
The People's Friend, Reamsville	1887, 1888	1
STAFFORD COUNTY.		
Stafford County Herald, Stafford	1879–1886	6
Stafford County Republican, Stafford	1886–1888	3
The St. John Advance	1880–1888	8

BOUND NEWSPAPER FILES AND PERIODICALS, KANSAS—CONTINUED.

Newspapers.	Years.	No. vols.
STAFFORD COUNTY — *concluded.*		
The Sun, St. John	1885–1888	3
County Capital, St. John	1887, 1888	2
The Stafford County Bee, Milwaukee	1882, 1883	1
The Macksville Times	1886–1888	3
The Cassody Herald	1886, 1887	1
The Cassody Mirage	1887, 1888	1
Stafford County Democrat, Stafford	1885–1888	3
The Weekly Telegram, Stafford	1886–1888	2
STANTON COUNTY.		
Veteran Sentinel, and Johnson City and Syracuse Sentinel	1886	1
The Johnson City World	1886–1888	2
Stanton County Eclipse, Johnson City	1887, 1888	1
Johnson City Journal	1888	1
The Mitchellville Courier	1887, 1888	1
The Border Rover, Borders	1887, 1888	1
Stanton Telegram, Goguac	1888	1
STEVENS COUNTY.		
Hugo Herald, Hugoton	1886–1888	3
Hugoton Hermes	1887, 1888	1
Woodsdale Democrat	1887, 1888	1
Dermot Enterprise	1887, 1888	1
The Voorhees Vindicator	1887, 1888	1
Zella Gazelle and Moscow Review	1887, 1888	1
SUMNER COUNTY.		
Sumner County Press, Wellington	1873–1888	16
Wellington Daily Press	1886, 1887	3
Sumner County Democrat, Wellington	1877–1879	3
Wellington Semi-Weekly Vidette	1879	1
The Wellingtonian, Wellington	1881–1885	5
The Wellington Democrat	1882–1884	2
Sumner County Standard, Wellington	1884–1888	4
Daily Standard, Wellington	1887, 1888	3
The Daily Postal Card, Wellington	1886, 1887	2
The Republican, Wellington	1886	1
The Wellington Monitor	1886–1888	3
Kansas Weather Observer, Wellington	1886	1
Wellington Morning Quid Nunc (daily)	1887, 1888	3
Wellington Quid Nunc	1887, 1888	1
Wellington Daily Telegram	1887	1
Oxford Independent	1876–1879	4
Oxford Reflex and Weekly	1880–1881	1
The Oxford Register	1884–1888	4
Caldwell Post	1879–1883	5
Caldwell Journal	1883–1888	6
Caldwell Daily Journal	1887	1
Oklahoma War Chief, Wichita, January 12 to March 9, 1883; Geuda Springs, March 23 to July 19, 1883; Oklahoma Territory, April 26 and May 3, 1884; Arkansas City, May 10, 1884; Geuda Springs, August 30, 1884; South Haven, October 23 to December 4, 1884; Arkansas City, February 3 to June 11, 1885; Caldwell, June 18, 1885, to August 12, 1886	1883–1886	3
Caldwell Commercial	1880–1883	3
Caldwell Standard	1884	1
The Free Press, Caldwell	1885, 1886	1
Times, Caldwell	1886, 1887	1
The Caldwell News, daily and weekly	1887, 1888	1
The Industrial Age, Caldwell	1887, 1888	1
Belle Plaine News	1879–1888	9
The Kansas Odd Fellow, Belle Plaine	1882, 1883	1
The Resident, Belle Plaine	1885, 1886	1
Mulvane Herald	1880–1882	2
Mulvane Record	1885–1888	4
Geuda Springs Herald	1882–1888	6
Argonia Clipper	1884, 1888	5
Conway Springs Star	1884–1888	3
The Weekly News, South Haven	1885, 1886	1
The South Haven New Era	1886–1888	3
THOMAS COUNTY.		
Thomas County Cat, Colby	1885–1888	4
The Democrat, Colby	1886–1888	2
The Hastings & Brewster Gazette	1888	1

BOUND NEWSPAPER FILES AND PERIODICALS, KANSAS—CONTINUED.

Newspapers.	*Years.*	*No. vols.*
TREGO COUNTY.		
The Wa-Keeney Weekly World	1879-1888	10
Kansas Leader, Wa-Keeney	1879,1880	1
Trego County Tribune, Wa-Keeney	1885-1888	3
Globe, Cyrus	1882,1883	1
Trego County Gazette, Wa-Keeney	1887,1888	1
WABAUNSEE COUNTY.		
The Wabaunsee County Herald, Alma	1869-1871	2
The Alma Weekly Union	1871,1872	1
Wabaunsee County News, Alma	1876-1888	13
The Blade, Alma	1877,1878	1
Wabaunsee County Herald, Alma	1879-1881	2
The Alma Enterprise	1884-1888	4
The Land-Mark, Eskridge, (not published from December, 1874, to June 30, 1888,)	1873-1883	2
The Home Weekly, Eskridge	1881-1883	7
The Eskridge Star	1883-1888	5
Wabaunsee County Democrat, Eskridge	1886	1
The Alta Vista Register	1887,1888	1
WALLACE COUNTY.		
Wallace County Register, Wallace	1886-1888	3
Wallace County News	1886,1887	1
Wallace Weekly Herald	1888	1
The Western Times, Sharon Springs	1886-1888	2
Sharon Springs Leader	1887,1888	2
WASHINGTON COUNTY.		
Western Observer, and Washington Republican, (broken files,)	1869,1870	1
Washington Republican and Watchman	1870,1871	2
Washington Republican	1876-1888	13
Washington County Register, Washington	1881-1888	7
Washington County Daily Register, Washington	1884,1885	2
Weekly Post, Washington	1883-1888	5
Washington Daily Post	1887	1
Washington Daily Times	1887,1888	1
Western Independent, Hanover	1876,1877	2
Washington County Sun and Hanover Democrat	1878	1
The Hanover Democrat	1878-1888	11
Grit, Hanover	1884,1885	1
The Clifton Localist	1878	1
Clifton Journal and Review	1878-1880	3
Clifton Review	1881-1888	8
The Local News, and The Semi-Weekly News, Clifton	1885-1888	3
The Greenleaf Journal	1881-1883	3
The Greenleaf Independent	1882,1883	1
The Independent-Journal, Greenleaf	1883-1887	4
Greenleaf Journal	1887,1888	1
Greenleaf Herald	1883-1888	5
The Haddam Weekly Clipper	1883-1888	5
The New Era, Haddam	1886,1887	1
Palmer Weekly Globe	1884	1
Palmer Pioneer	1888	1
The Barnes Enterprise	1885-1888	3
WICHITA COUNTY.		
Wichita Standard, Bonasa and Leoti City	1885-1888	3
Leoti Lance	1886,1887	1
Wichita County Democrat, Leoti City	1886,1887	1
The Leoti Transcript, Leoti City	1887,1888	1
Wichita County Herald, Coronado	1886,1887	1
The Coronado Star	1886-1888	1
Wichita County Farmer, Coronado, Farmer City and Leoti	1888	1
WILSON COUNTY.		
Wilson County Citizen, Fredonia	1870-1888	19
Fredonia Tribune	1878,1879	2
Fredonia Democrat	1882-1888	1
The Times, Fredonia	1883-1885	1
Fredonia Chronicle	1885-1888	3
Neodesha Free Press	1876-1882	7
Neodesha Gazette	1881,1882	1
Neodesha Register	1883-1888	5
Neodesha Independent	1887,1888	1
Altoona Advocate	1886,1887	1
The Benedict Echo	1886-1888	2
Buffalo Clipper	1887	1
Buffalo Express	1888	1
The Coyville Press	1887,1888	1

BOUND NEWSPAPER FILES AND PERIODICALS, KANSAS—Concluded.

Newspapers.	Years.	No. vols.
WOODSON COUNTY.		
Woodson County Post, Neosho Falls...	1873–1883	10
Neosho Falls Post	1883–1888	6
Woodson County Republican and Independent, Neosho Falls...................	1886,1887	1
Weekly News, Yates Center, and the Yates Center News.......................	1877–1888	12
Yates Center Argus...	1882,1883	2
Woodson Democrat, Yates Center..	1884–1888	4
The Sun and Independent-Sun, Yates Center....................................	1886–1888	2
The Toronto Topic...	1883–1888	5
Register, Toronto..	1886,1887	1
WYANDOTTE COUNTY.		
Quindaro Chindowan...	1857,1858	1
Wyandotte Gazette, (1869 and 1873 lacking,)....................................	1866–1883	19
The Kansas City Daily Gazette..	1887,1888	4
Wyandotte Herald, (1873 lacking,)..	1872–1888	16
The Kawsmouth Pilot, Wyandotte...	1881	1
Equitable Aid Advocate (monthly), Wyandotte.................................	1881–1883	3
Wyandotte Republican (daily and weekly)......................................	1881,1882	2
The Wyandotte Chief...	1883,1885	2
Kansas Pionier, Wyandotte..	1883–1888	5
The Pioneer, Kansas City, Kansas..	1878–1880	3
The Kansas Pilot, Kansas City, Kansas..	1879,1881	2
The Stock Farm and Home Weekly, Kansas City, Kansas......................	1880	1
The Spy, Kansas City, Kansas...	1881,1882	1
The Globe and the Sun and Globe, Kansas City, Kansas.......................	1884,1886	2
Light, Kansas City, Kansas...	1884–1886	1
The Kansas Weekly Cyclone, Kansas City, Kansas............................	1887,1888	1
The Wasp, Rosedale...	1884,1885	1
Rosedale Record..	1888	1
Argentine Republic...	1887,1888	1
The Argentine Advocate..	1888	1
Cromwell's Kansas Mirror, Armourdale...	1887,1888	1

BOUND NEWSPAPERS, ETC., OF OTHER STATES AND COUNTRIES.

Newspapers.	Years.	No. vols.
ALABAMA.		
The Nationalist, Mobile..	1865–1868	3
ARIZONA.		
Arizona Weekly Journal-Miner, Prescott	1887,1888	1
CALIFORNIA.		
Overland Monthly, San Francisco, f. s..	1868–1875	15
Overland Monthly, San Francisco, s. s..	1883–1888	12
San Francisco Weekly Post...	1879–1888	11
The Alaska Appeal, San Francisco..	1879,1880	1
The Pacific Rural Press, San Francisco	1882–1888	7
California Patron and Agriculturist, San Francisco...........................	1886–1883	3
American Sentinel, Oakland...	1886–1888	3
Signs of the Times, Oakland	1886–1888	3
Pacific Health Journal (monthly), Oakland....................................	1886–1888	2
COLORADO.		
Silver World, Lake City	1877–1888	11
Weekly Rocky Mountain News, Denver...	1878–1888	11
The Rocky Mountain Presbyterian, Denver and Cincinnati...................	1879–1880	1
The Gunnison Review (weekly)...	1880,1881	2
The Gunnison Daily and Tri-Weekly Review-Press...........................	1882–1888	11
Mountain Mail, Salida..	1880–1888	8
Denver Daily Tribune..	1884	2
Grand Junction News..	1884	1
White Pine Cone	1884–1888	4
The Denver Republican (daily)...	1887,1888	2
The Queen Bee (monthly), Denver...	1887,1888	1

BOUND NEWSPAPERS, ETC., OF OTHER STATES AND COUNTRIES—CONTINUED.

Newspapers.	Years.	No. vols.
CONNECTICUT.		
The Connecticut Courant, Hartford	1796–1799	3
Middlesex Gazette, Middletown, 1804, 1805 and 1817	1804–1817	3
Silliman's Journal of Science and Arts, New Haven, vols. 1, and 37 to 48	1818–1869	13
Quarterly Journal of Inebriety, Hartford	1876–1888	12
Travelers' Record (monthly), Hartford	1886–1888	3
DAKOTA.		
Dakota Teacher, Huron, August, 1885, to June, 1886	1885,1886	1
Bismarck Weekly Tribune	1887,1888	1
DISTRICT OF COLUMBIA.		
Kendall's Expositor, Washington	1841	1
The National Era, Washington	1847–1859	13
The Council Fire, Washington	1879–1882	3
The Alpha, Washington	1881–1888	8
The Washington World	1882–1884	2
National Tribune	1883,1884	2
United States Government publications, monthly catalogue, Washington	1885–1888	4
The Official Gazette of the United States, Patent Office, Washington	1885–1888	12
Public Opinion, Washington and New York	1887,1888	1
FLORIDA.		
The Florida Dispatch, Jacksonville	1885–1888	3
GEORGIA.		
Southern Industrial Record (monthly), Atlanta	1885–1888	3
Atlanta Constitution	1887,1888	1
ILLINOIS.		
Religio-Philosophical Journal, Chicago	1868–1877	10
The Inter-Ocean, Chicago	1874–1881	8
Semi-Weekly Inter-Ocean, Chicago	1879–1888	10
Faith's Record (monthly), Chicago	1874–1881	6
Commercial Advertiser, Chicago	1877–1879	2
Industrial World and Commercial Advertiser, Chicago	1880–1882	3
Industrial World and Iron Worker, Chicago	1882–1888	6
American Antiquarian (quarterly), Chicago	1878–1888	12
Weekly Drovers' Journal, Chicago	1879–1888	9
The Standard, Chicago	1880–1888	8
Farmers' Review, Chicago	1880,1881	2
Chicago Journal of Commerce	1881	1
National Sunday School Teacher (monthly), Chicago	1869–1881	13
Land Owner, Chicago	1870–1873	4
Chicago Advance, (files for 1872, 1873, 1874, 1875, 1877, 1879, 1884, and one duplicate,)	1872–1884	7
The Dial, Chicago	1881–1888	8
Brown and Holland's Short-Hand News (monthly), Chicago	1882–1885	4
The Watchman (semi-monthly), Chicago	1882–1888	6
The Weekly Magazine, Chicago	1882–1885	3
The New Era, Chicago	1883,1884	1
The Odd Fellows' Herald, Bloomington	1883–1888	5
The Weekly News, Chicago	1884–1886	2
The Western Plowman, Moline	1885–1888	4
The Grange News, River Forest	1885,1886	1
Svenska Amerikanaren, Chicago	1885–1888	4
The Unitarian (monthly), Chicago	1886,1887	1
The Union Signal, Chicago	1886–1888	3
The Penman's Gazette (monthly), Chicago and New York	1886	1
Pravda (monthly), Chicago	1886–1888	2
The Western Trail (monthly), Chicago	1886–1888	1
Gaskell's Magazine (monthly), Chicago	1887,1888	1
The Open Court, Chicago	1887,1888	2
The Conrade (bi-monthly), Chicago	1887,1888	2
The National Educator (monthly), Chicago	1887,1888	2
The Chicago Express	1888	1
INDIAN TERRITORY.		
The Cherokee Advocate, Tahlequah	1881–1888	7
The Cheyenne Transporter, Darlington	1883–1886	4
Indian Chieftain, Vinita	1884–1888	5
INDIANA.		
Indiana State Journal, Indianapolis	1878–1888	11
Our Herald, La Fayette	1882,1883	2
The Millstone and The Corn Miller (monthly), Indianapolis	1884–1888	5
Mennonitische Rundschau, Elkhart	1886–1888	3
Indiana Student (monthly), Bloomington	1886–1888	2

BOUND NEWSPAPERS, ETC., OF OTHER STATES AND COUNTRIES—CONTINUED.

Newspapers.	Years.	No. vols.
IOWA.		
Davenport Gazette..................	1878	1
The Weekly Hawk-Eye, Burlington...........................	1881–1885	4
The Burlington Hawk-Eye (daily)...........................	1882–1885	5
The Iowa Historical Society (quarterly), Iowa City.................	1885–1888	4
KENTUCKY.		
Weekly Courier-Journal, Louisville....	1878–1880	2
Southern Bivouac (monthly), Louisville.....................	1886, 1887	1
LOUISIANA.		
South-Western Christian Advocate, New Orleans..................	1879–1888	9
The Times-Democrat (daily), New Orleans.................	1883–1885	5
MAINE.		
Oxford Observer, Paris.................	1824–1826	2
Oxford Democrat, Paris..................	1871–1876	6
Maine Advertiser, Norway	1872–1875	2
MARYLAND.		
Johns Hopkins University Circular, Baltimore, (1882–1884 lacking,)..................	1879–1883	4
Jottings (monthly), Baltimore..................	1887, 1888	2
The American Journal of Psychology, Baltimore, (quarterly)	1888	1
MASSACHUSETTS.		
The Boston Chronicle, Dec. 21, 1767, to Dec. 19, 1768..................	1767, 1768	1
Federal Orrery, Boston, Oct. 20, 1794, to April 18, 1796, and scattering duplicates from Oct. 20, 1794, to Oct. 12, 1795..................	1794–1796	2
Massachusetts Mercury, Boston, May 11, 1798, to Aug. 9, 1799..................	1798–1799	2
The Independent Chronicle and the Universal Advertizer, Boston, from Jan. 1, 1798, to Dec. 17, 1801..................	1798–1801	4
The Independent Chronicle, Boston, Dec. 21, 1801, to Dec. 30, 1804..................	1801–1804	8
Boston Patriot, from April 7, 1809, to Sept. 12, 1810; from March 2 to Dec. 25, 1811; from March 14, 1812, to Sept. 8, 1813; and scattering duplicates from March 3, 1809, to March 10, 1815..................	1809–1813	7
Independent Chronicle and Boston Patriot (semi-weekly), Jan. 11, 1832, to Aug. 10, 1837..	1832–1837	4
Columbian Centinel and Massachusetts Federalist, Boston, from June 29, 1799, to Aug. 31, 1805; from Jan. 3, 1807, to Oct. 3, 1810; from Jan. 2, 1811, to July 1, 1812; and scattering duplicates from Feb. 28, 1801, to Dec. 29, 1802..................	1799–1812	13
Boston Gazette, from Jan. 9 to Oct. 29, 1804; from Aug. 19, 1815, to Aug. 19, 1816; from Dec. 27, 1817, to Dec. 25, 1819; from April 23, 1827, to Nov. 28, 1828..................	1804–1828	6
Boston Commercial Gazette (daily), from Dec. 29, 1817, to Dec. 25, 1819..................	1817–1819	2
Massachusetts Spy or Worcester Gazette..................	1805, 1806	2
The National Ægis, Worcester, Dec. 2, 1801, to Dec. 25, 1811; from Jan. 23, 1813, to May 4, 1814; from Jan. 5, 1815, to Dec. 25, 1816; from Dec. 15, 1824, to June 8, 1825; and years 1823, 1830, 1838–1840..................	1801–1825	19
Boston Spectator, from Jan. 4, 1814, to Feb. 5, 1815..................	1814, 1815	1
North American Review, Boston, (Nos. 3–6, 10, 11, 13, 14, 15, 19, 20, 21 and 130 lacking,) 1879, 1880, 1888..................	1815–1888	108
Essex Register, Salem, from Jan. 1 to Dec. 17, 1817..................	1817	1
The Missionary Herald, Boston, vols. 17–80..................	1821–1884	63
The Massachusetts Spy (weekly), Worcester..................	1822	1
New England Galaxy, Boston, from Oct. 31, 1823, to Dec. 26, 1828; and scattering duplicates from Oct. 15, 1824, to April 6, 1827..................	1823–1828	7
Christian Examiner, Boston, vols. 1–19, 1824–1836, and 12 vols. between 1840 and 1867....	1824–1868	31
Boston Recorder, from Jan. 2, 1832, to Dec. 25, 1835..................	1832–1835	4
The Liberator, Boston, (lacking 1834–1837 and 1839,)..................	1833–1865	28
Evening Journal, Boston, from Jan. 3, 1837, to Dec. 30, 1843; from Jan. 4 to Dec. 30, 1844; and from Feb. 4 to Dec. 30, 1845..................	1837–1845	9
The Commonwealth, Boston, Jan. 1 to July 3, 1851; and from Jan. 1 to Sept. 21, 1854..................	1851–1854	3
The Commonwealth, Boston, from Sept. 1, 1866, to Aug. 28, 1869..................	1866–1869	3
Youth's Companion, Boston, from Oct. 21, 1852, to April 17, 1856, and 1886–1888	1852–1888	7
Daily Transcript, Worcester, from Feb., 1853, to Dec., 1855..................	1853–1855	6
Evening Telegraph (daily), Boston, from Sept. 27, 1854, to March 31, 1855..................	1854, 1855	1
Quarterly Journal of American Unitarian Association, Boston..................	1854–1859	5
Monthly Journal of the American Unitarian Association, Boston..................	1860–1869	9
Anglo-Saxon, Boston, from Jan. 5 to Dec. 16, 1856..................	1856	1
The Atlantic Monthly, Boston, vols. 1–50..................	1857–1882	50
The Atlas and Daily Bee, Boston, from June 15 to Dec. 31, 1858..................	1858	1
Worcester Daily Spy, from Jan. to Dec., 1859; from Jan., 1868, to Dec.,.1884; and from July, 1885, to July, 1886..................	1859–1886	38
Worcester Evening Gazette, from Jan. to Dec., 1866; from Jan., 1867, to July 18, 1881; and from Jan., 1882, to Dec., 1885..................	1868–1885	38
Zion's Herald, Boston, (1868, 1869, 1870, 1879, 1880, 1883,)..................	1868–1883	6
Banner of Light, Boston..................	1869–1872	4
Worcester Daily Press, from June, 1873, to Dec., 1876..................	1873–1876	7
Boston Journal of Chemistry..................	1873–1877	4
Ægis and Gazette, Worcester, (part of 1877 lacking,)..................	1875–1880	5

BOUND NEWSPAPERS, ETC., OF OTHER STATES AND COUNTRIES—CONTINUED.

Newspapers.	Years.	No. vols.
MASSACHUSETTS—*concluded.*		
The New England Historical and Genealogical Register (quarterly), Boston	1876–1888	11
The Woman's Journal	1879–1888	10
Harvard University Bulletin (quarterly)	1880–1888	4
Civil Service Record, Boston	1881,1882	2
United States Official Postal Guide (monthly), Boston	1881–1886	6
Our Dumb Animals (monthly), Boston	1882–1885	2
Science, Cambridge, (see New York,)	1883–1885	6
The Citizen (monthly), Boston	1886–1888	2
The Evening Traveller (daily), Boston, from January to June, 1886	1886	1
The Popular Science News, Boston	1885–1888	4
The Unitarian Review and Religious Magazine, Boston	1885–1888	4
Political Science Quarterly, Boston	1886–1888	3
Abolitionist, Boston	1833	1
The Writer (monthly), Boston	1887,1888	2
The Estes & Lauriat Book Bulletin (monthly), Boston	1887,1888	1
American Teacher (monthly), Boston	1887,1888	1
Evening Gazette, Boston	1888	1
The New Jerusalem Magazine (monthly), Boston	1888	1
Spelling (quarterly), Boston	1887,1888	1
Library Notes (monthly), Boston	1888	1
Martha's Vineyard Herald, Cottage City	1887,1888	1
MICHIGAN.		
The Fireside Teacher (monthly), Battle Creek	1886–1882	2
The Unitarian, Ann Arbor	1887,1888	1
MINNESOTA.		
Pioneer-Press, St. Paul and Minneapolis	1878,1879	1
MISSOURI.		
The Western Journal, (and Civilian, monthly), St. Louis	1848–1854	11
Organ and Reveille, St. Louis	1851	1
St. Joseph Free Democrat	1860	1
American Journal of Education (monthly), St. Louis	1873–1888	14
Kansas City Times, daily, (1875 lacking,)	1873–1888	26
The Great Southwest (monthly), St. Louis, vols. 1, 2, 3, 6 and 7	1874–1880	5
St. Joseph Herald, daily, (1878 and to July, 1879, lacking,)	1876–1888	22
St. Joseph Herald	1877–1888	12
St. Joseph Gazette	1877–1888	11
The Kansas City Review of Science and Industry, monthly	1877–1884	8
Weekly Journal of Commerce, Kansas City	1877–1879	3
Kansas City Daily Journal	1879–1888	20
Mirror of Progress, Kansas City	1879–1881	3
Kansas City Price Current	1880,1881	1
Santa Fé Trail (monthly), Kansas City, volume 1, number 1 to 8	1880,1881	1
Camp's Emigrant Guide to Kansas, Kansas City	1880–1884	4
Fonetic Teacher (monthly), St. Louis, volume 2	1881	1
American Home Magazine, Kansas City	1881,1882	3
The Communist and Altruist (bi-monthly), St. Louis	1881–1888	3
Kansas City Live-Stock Indicator	1882–1888	7
The Mid-Continent, Kansas City	1882–1888	7
Srenska Herolden, Kansas City	1882–1884	3
Western Newspaper Union, Kansas City	1883–1888	6
The Centropolis, Kansas City	1883–1888	4
American Journalist (monthly), St. Louis	1883–1885	1
The Kansas City Medical Index	1884–1888	7
Kansas City Live-Stock Record and Price Current	1884–1888	4
The Kansas City Record	1885–1888	3
Missouri and Kansas Farmer, Kansas City	1886–1888	3
The Kansas City Star, daily	1886–1888	5
The Faithful Witness (monthly), Kansas City	1886,1887	1
The Herald, Kansas City	1886–1888	2
The Kansas Magazine (monthly), Kansas City	1886–1888	2
The St. Louis Evangelist	1887,1888	1
St. Louis Globe-Democrat, daily	1887,1888	2
The Central Christian Advocate, St. Louis	1888	1
The Evening News, Kansas City	1888	1
Kansas City Daily Traveler	1888	1
NEBRASKA.		
The Western Newspaper Union, Omaha	1886–1888	2
The Woman's Tribune (monthly and weekly), Beatrice	1887,1888	2
Western Resources (monthly), Lincoln	1887,1888	2
Nebraska State Journal (daily), Lincoln	1887,1888	2
Nebraska State Journal, Lincoln	1887,1888	1

BOUND NEWSPAPERS, ETC., OF OTHER STATES AND COUNTRIES — Continued.

Newspapers.	Years.	No. vols.
NEW JERSEY.		
The Journal of American Orthoëpy (monthly), Ringos........................	1884–1888	5
Orchard & Garden (monthly), Little Silver	1887,1888	2
NEW MEXICO.		
Santa Fé New Mexican...	1881–1883	4
Albuquerque Weekly Journal..	1881–1886	6
Mining World, Las Vegas..	1880–1882	2
New Mexican Mining News, Santa Fé...	1881–1883	2
Las Vegas Weekly Optic..	1883,1884	1
The Santa Fé Weekly Leader...	1885,1886	2
The Daily Citizen, Albuquerque..	1887,1888	3
Daily New Mexican, Santa Fé...	1887,1888	2
NEW YORK.		
New York American, New York City..	1827,1828	2
Evangelical Magazine, Utica, (vols. 2 and 3,)...................................	1828,1829	2
Evangelical Magazine and Gospel Advocate, Utica, (vols. 4, 5, and 9, 1833, 1834 and 1838,)	1833–1838	3
The Anti-Slavery Record, New York...	1836	1
The Emancipator, New York, (from February 3, 1837, to February 14, 1839,)...	1837–1839	2
The New-Yorker, New York..	1837–1840	3
The Jeffersonian, Albany..	1838,1839	1
The Diamond, New York..	1840–1842	3
The Northern Light, Albany...	1841–1843	2
Workingman's Advocate, New York...	1841,1845	1
New York Evangelist..	1845–1847	2
Scientific American, New York, (lacking from 1861 to 1884,)................	1819–1888	18
New York Daily Tribune, (lacking from 1870 to 1874, and from 1876 to 1879,)..	1849–1888	69
New York Semi-Weekly Tribune, (lacking 1876, 1883, 1884,)................	1871–1887	14
New York Weekly Tribune, (lacking 1871–1878,)...............................	1869–1884	8
Propagandist, New York..	1850,1851	1
The Home Missionary, New York...	1850–1888	38
Harper's Monthly Magazine, New York...	1851–1854	8
Harper's Weekly, New York...	1857–1888	32
New York Illustrated News...	1853	1
The Industry of All Nations, New York...	1853	1
Putnam's Monthly, New York..	1853–1857	14
Daily Times, New York, (incomplete,)..	1854–1856	4
The Phonographic Intelligencer, New York......................................	1857	1
The Printer, New York..	1858–1863	4
New York Independent, New York, (1874 duplicate,).........................	1859–1887	39
U. S. Service Magazine (monthly), New York...................................	1864–1866	5
The Galaxy (monthly), New York	1866,1877	24
American Agriculturist (monthly), New York, (lacking 1862–1866,).........	1860–1889	4
The Revolution, New York	1868–1870	5
The Spectator, New York and Chicago..	1870–1880	11
Scribner's Monthly and the Century Magazine, New York...................	1870–1888	36
Popular Science Monthly, New York...	1872–1885	27
Fruit Recorder and Cottage Gardner, Palmyra..................................	1874–1876	3
The Christian Union, New York...	1874–1887	14
The Iron Age, New York	1876	1
The Library Journal (monthly), New York..	1876–1888	13
The Magazine of American History (monthly), New York.....................	1877–1888	20
Brown's Phonographic Monthly, New York.......................................	1878–1883	6
The National Citizen and Ballot Box, (from May, 1878, to October, 1881,) New York, (see Ballot Box, Ohio,)...	1878–1881	4
The Cultivator and Country Gentleman, Albany.................................	1879,1880	2
The Daily Register, New York...	1879–1888	20
America, New York..	1879–1881	3
The Sheltering Arms (monthly), New York.......................................	1879–1888	9
The Union, Brooklyn..	1879–1882	3
The Bee Keepers' Exchange (monthly), Canajoharie...........................	1879–1882	4
The Publishers' Weekly, New York..	1879–1888	17
The American Missionary, New York..	1880–1888	9
The Nation, New York..	1882–1888	7
John Swinton's Paper, New York...	1883–1887	4
Appleton's Literary Bulletin (bi-monthly), New York.........................	1883–1888	5
Phonetic Educator, New York and Cincinnati...................................	1884,1885	1
The Literary News, New York.......................R.............................	1884,1885	3
The Student's Journal (phonographic monthly), New York...................	1884–1888	5
The Phonographic World (monthly), New York..................................	1885–1888	4
New York Weekly Witness...	1885–1888	3
The Irish World, New York..	1885–1888	3
The Christian Advocate (from April, 1885, to Dec. 30, 1886), New York	1885,1886	3
The Coöperative Index to Periodicals (quarterly), New York................	1885–1888	4
The Protestant Episcopal Mission Leaf (monthly), New York................	1886	1
The National Temperance Advocate, New York.................................	1886–1888	3
Science, New York..	1886–1888	6

BOUND NEWSPAPERS, ETC., OF OTHER STATES AND COUNTRIES—CONTINUED.

Newspapers.	Years.	No. vols.
NEW YORK—concluded.		
The American Book-Maker (monthly), New York	1885,1886	2
The New Princeton Review (semi-monthly), New York city	1886–1888	6
The Husbandman, Elmira	1886–1888	3
Sabbath Reading, New York	1886–1888	2
The Delineator (monthly), New York	1886	1
Electrical Review, New York	1886–1888	2
Scribner's Magazine (monthly), New York	1887,1888	4
Agricultural Science (monthly), New York	1887,1888	2
The Swiss Cross (monthly), New York	1887,1888	2
The Voice, New York	1887,1888	2
The Decorator and Furnisher (monthly), New York	1887,1888	3
The Public Service Review (monthly), New York	1887,1888	1
Home Knowledge (monthly), New York	1887,1888	2
Judge, New York	1888	1
New York Pioneer	1887,1888	1
The Curio, New York	1887,1888	1
Demorest's Monthly, New York	1888	1
Tariff League Bulletin, New York	1888	1
Library Bulletin of Cornell University (monthly)	1887,1888	2
Political Science Quarterly, New York	1886–1888	3
OHIO.		
The Ohio Cultivator, Columbus	1845,1846	2
Weekly Phonetic Advocate, Cincinnati	1850–1853	4
Phonetic Advocate Supplement, Cincinnati	1850–1852	2
The Masonic Review	1853–1862	17
Type of the Times, Cincinnati	1854,1855	2
American Phonetic Journal, Cincinnati	1858	1
The Crisis, (from January 31, 1861, to January 23, 1863,) Columbus	1861–1863	2
The Ballot Box, from June 1876, to May 1878, Toledo, (see National Citizen, New York)	1876–1878	2
Nachrichten aus der Heidenwelt, Zanesville	1877–1880	4
Cincinnati Weekly Times	1878–1888	11
The Phonetic Educator, Cincinnati	1878–1883	5
The Christian Press, Cincinnati	1880–1888	8
The American Journal of Forestry, Cincinnati	1882–1883	1
The Christian Standard, Cincinnati	1883–1888	6
Magazine of Western History (monthly), Cleveland	1884–1888	3
Farm and Fireside (semi-monthly), Springfield	1884–1888	3
The American Grange Bulletin, Cincinnati	1886	1
Ohio Archæological and Historical Quarterly, Columbus	1887–1888	1
Phonographic Magazine (monthly), Cincinnati	1887	1
PENNSYLVANIA.		
The American Naturalist, Philadelphia	1867–1880	14
The Press (daily), Philadelphia	1878–1880	6
Progress, Philadelphia	1878–1885	7
Public Ledger (daily), Philadelphia	1879–1888	20
Faith and Works (monthly), Philadelphia	1879–1888	10
Eadle Keatah Toh—The Morning Star and the Red Man, Carlisle	1881–1888	8
Sunday School Times, (files for 1879, 1880, 1884, 1885, 1886), Philadelphia	1879–1886	5
Naturalist's Leisure Hour (monthly), Philadelphia	1880–1888	7
Historical Register, (vols. 1 and 2), Harrisburg	1883,1884	2
The Farmer's Friend, Mechanicsburg	1886–1888	3
Dye's Government Counterfeit Detector, Philadelphia	1886–1888	2
The Building Association and Home Journal (monthly), Philadelphia	1887,1888	2
The Book Mart (monthly), Philadelphia	1887,1888	1
Paper and Press (monthly), Philadelphia	1888	1
American Manufacturer and Iron World, Pittsburg	1888	1
TEXAS.		
Live-Stock Journal, Fort Worth	1882–1888	7
Texas Wool Grower, Fort Worth	1882,1883	2
El Paso Times (daily)	1883	1
Texas Review (monthly), Austin	1886	1
The Canadian Free Press	1887,1888	1
The Canadian Crescent	1888	1
VERMONT.		
The Woman's Magazine (monthly), Brattleboro	1885–1888	4
The National Bulletin (monthly), Brattleboro	1886,1887	1
VIRGINIA.		
The Richmond Standard	1880,1881	1
Southern Workman and Hampton School Record, Hampton	1886	3
WASHINGTON TERRITORY.		
Whatcom Reveille	1884–1886	2

Newspapers.	Years.	No. vols.
WISCONSIN.		
Wisconsin State Journal, Madison..	1878–1888	11
Western Farmer and Wisconsin Grange Bulletin, Madison...	1886	1
ENGLAND.		
London Illustrated News..	1842–1879	62
Diplomatic Review, (vols. 1–25,) London	1855–1877	25
The Fonetic Journal, Bath.............	1879	1
The Labour Standard, London...	1882–1884	3
Forestry, a magazine for the country (monthly), Edinburgh and London......................	1884,1885	3
FRANCE.		
Bulletin de la Société Protectrice des Animaux (monthly), Paris....................................	1878–1882	5
Bulletin de la Société de Geographie, Paris..	1878–1888	11
Société de Geographie compte rendu des Séances de la Commission Centrale (semi- monthly), Paris...	1882–1888	7
Chronique de la Société des Gens de Lettres (monthly), Paris......................................	1879–1888	10
Bulletin Mensuel de la Société des Gens de Lettres, Paris..	1878–1880	1
Bulletin des Séances de la Société Nationale d'Agriculture (monthly), Paris...................	1879–1886	9

KANSAS NEWSPAPERS AND PERIODICALS NOW RECEIVED.

The following is a list of the newspapers and periodicals published in Kansas, corrected up to January 1, 1889. The regular issues of these, with very few exceptions, are now being received by the Kansas State Historical Society. They are the free gift of the publishers to the State. They are bound in annual or semi-annual volumes, and are preserved in the library of the Society in the State Capitol for the free use of the people. They number 827 in all. Of these 45 are dailies, 1 is semi-weekly, 733 weeklies, 40 monthlies, 1 is semi-monthly, 2 are bi-monthlies, 4 are quarterlies, and 1 is occasional. They come from all of the 106 counties of Kansas, and record the history of the people of all the communities and neighborhoods.

ALLEN COUNTY.

The Humboldt Union, Republican; W. T. McElroy, publisher and proprietor, Humboldt.

The Humboldt Herald, Democratic; S. A. D. Cox, editor and publisher, Humboldt.

The Iola Register, Republican; W. W. Scott, publisher, Iola.

Allen County Courant, Democratic; J. C. Hamm & Bro., publishers and proprietors, Iola.

The Moran Herald, Republican; G. D. Ingersoll, editor and proprietor, Moran.

ANDERSON COUNTY.

Garnett Weekly Journal, Democratic; J. T. Highley, publisher, Garnett.

The Republican-Plaindealer, Republican; Anderson County Republican Company and Howard M. Brooke, publishers, Garnett.

The Garnett Eagle, Republican; W. A. Trigg, editor, publisher and proprietor, Garnett.

The Greeley News, neutral; W. O. Champe, editor, Greeley.

The Colony Free Press, Republican; J. J. Burke, editor, Colony.

Westphalia Times, independent; Adele D. Reed, editor and proprietor, Misses Adele D. and Bertie Reed, publishers, Westphalia.

The Kincaid Dispatch, Republican; J. E. Scruggs and J. G. Cash, publishers, Kincaid.

ATCHISON COUNTY.

The Atchison Champion, (daily and weekly,) Republican; John A. Martin, proprietor, Alf. H. Martin, business manager, Atchison.

Atchison Patriot, (daily and weekly,) Democratic; C. S. Wilson, editor, R. B. Drury, business manager, Patriot Publishing Company, publishers, Atchison.

Atchison Globe, (daily and weekly,) independent; Edgar W. Howe & Co., editors and proprietors, Atchison.

The Atchison Times, Union Labor; J. A. Sunderland, publisher, Atchison.

The Messachorean, Midland College, (monthly,) educational; W. B. Glanding, managing editor, Atchison.

Muscotah Record, Republican; L. H. and Chas. Miller, editors and proprietors, Muscotah.

The Effingham Times, independent; Wilson Cohoon and Coleman Martin, editors and proprietors, Effingham.

The Prairie Press, Democratic; W. C. Adkins, publisher, Lancaster.

BARBER COUNTY.

Medicine Lodge Cresset, Republican; L. M. Axline, editor, publisher and proprietor, Medicine Lodge.

The Barber County Index, Democratic; E. P. Caruthers, editor and proprietor, Medicine Lodge.

The Hazelton Express, Republican; W. A. E. Adams, editor and publisher, Hazelton.

The Kiowa Herald, Democratic; J. E. Hall, editor and publisher, Kiowa.

The Kiowa Journal, Republican; W. C. Charles and D. A. Woodworth, editors and publishers, Kiowa.

The Union, Democratic; J. D. Youart, editor and proprietor, Sun City.

The Lake City Bee, independent; A. B. Hoffman, editor and proprietor, Lake City.

BARTON COUNTY.

The Great Bend Register, Republican; R. A. Charles, editor, E. L. Chapman, proprietor, Great Bend.

Great Bend Tribune, Republican; C. P. Townsley, editor and proprietor, Great Bend.

Barton County Democrat, Democratic; Will E. Stoke, editor and proprietor, Great Bend.

The Ellinwood Advocate, Democratic; J. D. Quillen, editor, Ellinwood.

Pawnee Rock Leader, Republican; M. E. Heynes, editor, publisher and proprietor, Pawnee Rock.

BOURBON COUNTY.

Fort Scott Monitor, (daily and weekly), Republican; John H. Rice, editor, W. M. Rice, associate editor, R. P. Rice, business manager, H. V. Rice, traveling solicitor, Fort Scott.

Fort Scott Tribune, (daily and weekly,) Democratic; J. B. Chapman, editor, Fort Scott.

Fort Scott Weekly Globe, Union Labor; H. L. Burdett and A. L. Preston, publishes, Fort Scott.

The Bronson Pilot, neutral; W. M. Holeman, proprietor, Bronson.

The Fulton Independent, independent; A. W. Felter, editor and proprietor, Fulton.

The Telephone, Republican; G. J. McQuad, editor and proprietor.

BROWN COUNTY.

Brown County World, Republican; D. W. Wilder, editor and proprietor, Ewing Herbert, associate editor and manager, Hiawatha.

The Kansas Democrat, Democratic; George T. Williams, editor and publisher, Hiawatha.

Horton Headlight, Republican; Harley W. Brundige and Samuel E. Bear, editors and publishers, Horton.

The Horton Gazette, Republican; Charles O. Bartruff, editor, publisher and proprietor, Horton.

Horton Commercial, Democratic; Clyde McManigal, editor, J. S. Sherdeman and Clyde McManigal, publishers, Horton.

The Horton Railway Register, Republican; C. N. Whitaker, managing editor, Harry Whitaker, city editor, Horton.

The Everest Enterprise, independent; T. A. H. Lowe, editor and business manager, T. A. H. Lowe and J. B. Green, publishers, Everest.

Fairview Enterprise, independent; S. O. Groesbeck, editor, Fairview.

BUTLER COUNTY.

The Augusta Journal, Republican; W. J. Speer, editor, publisher and proprietor, Augusta.

Walnut Valley Times, (daily and weekly,) Republican; Alvah Shelden, editor, publisher and proprietor, El Dorado.

El Dorado Republican, Republican; T. B. Murdock, editor and proprietor, El Dorado.

Butler County Jeffersonian, Democratic; J. B. Crouch, editor and proprietor, El Dorado.

Douglass Tribune, Republican; J. M. Satterthwaite, editor, publisher and proprietor, Douglass.

The Leon Indicator, Republican; C. R. Noe, editor and publisher, Leon.

The Herald, independent; E. Davis, jr., editor, publisher and proprietor, Towanda.

Latham Signal, Republican; Tom C. Copeland, editor, publisher and proprietor, Latham.

The Brainerd Ensign, Republican; R. P. Morrison, editor, publisher and proprietor, Brainerd.

Potwin Messenger, neutral; J. M. Worley, publisher, Potwin.

CHASE COUNTY.

Chase County Courant, Democratic; W. E. Timmons, editor, publisher and proprietor, Cottonwood Falls.

Chase County Leader, Republican; William A. Morgan, editor and publisher, Cottonwood Falls.

Chase County Republican, Republican; W. Y. Morgan, editor and proprietor, Strong City.

CHAUTAUQUA COUNTY.

The Sedan Times-Journal, Republican; Adrian Reynolds, editor, publisher and proprietor, Sedan.

The Sedan Graphic, Democratic; A. D. Dunn, publisher, Sedan.

The Weekly Call, Republican; F. M. Gwyn, editor and publisher, Peru.

Chautauqua Springs Express, neutral; W. J. Wright, editor and publisher, Chautauqua Springs.

The Cedar Vale Star, independent; F. G. Kenesson, editor, publisher and proprietor, Cedar Vale.

CHEROKEE COUNTY.

The Columbus Star-Courier, Democratic; N. T. Allison and W. P. Eddy, editors and proprietors, Columbus.

The Columbus Advocate, Republican; A. T. Lea & Son, editors, publishers and proprietors, Columbus.

Baxter Springs News, neutral, M. H. Gardner, editor and publisher, Baxter Springs.

Short Creek Republican, Republican; L. C. Weldy, editor and proprietor, Galena.

Galena Miner, Union Labor; J. F. McDowell, publisher, Galena.

The Western Friend, (monthly,) religious; Cyrus W. Harvey, editor, Varck.

Weir City Tribune, independent; Wm. Hawley, editor, The Tribune Printing Co. publishers and proprietors, Weir.

Weir City Eagle, Republican; John McKillop, editor and manager, Weir City.

CHEYENNE COUNTY.

Cheyenne County Rustler, Republican; C. E. Denison, editor, publisher and proprietor, St. Francis.

The Plaindealer, Democratic; C. F. Woodward, editor, Plaindealer Publishing Co., publishers, St. Francis.

Bird City News, Republican; Geo. W. Murray, editor and publisher, Bird City.

Cheyenne County Democrat, Democratic; Will C. Hydon, editor and manager, Bird City.

CLARK COUNTY.

Clark County Clipper, Democratic; John I. Lee editor, Lee Bros. publishers and proprietors, Ashland.

Ashland Weekly Journal, Republican; Charles C. Moore and Myron G. Stephenson editors and proprietors, Ashland.

The Englewood Enterprise, neutral; J. R. Axsom, editor and proprietor, Englewood.

The Englewood Chief, Republican; J. M. Grasham, editor, J. M. Grasham and G. S. Watt, publishers, Englewood.

CLAY COUNTY.

The Dispatch, Republican; E. J. Bonham and J. B. Palmer, editors, J. B. Palmer, manager, Dispatch Publishing Company, publishers, Clay Center.

The Times, Republican; J. P. Campbell and D. A. Valentine, editors, owners and publishers, Clay Center.

Republican Valley Democrat, Democratic; R. O. Lewis, editor, Democrat Publishing Co., publishers, Clay Center.

The Clay County Sentinel, Republican; C. W. Hoyt, editor and publisher, Morganville.

The Herald, Republican; E. P. Ellis, editor and proprietor, Chas. H. Jones, local editor and business manager, Oak Hill.

The Echo, Republican; J. C. Cline, editor, Frank A. Cline, publisher, Oak Hill.

Wakefield Advertiser, Democratic; J. J. L. Jones, editor, Wakefield.

CLOUD COUNTY.

Concordia Empire, Republican; T. A. Sawhill, editor and proprietor, Concordia.

Kansas Weekly Blade, Republican; J. M. Hagaman, publisher, Concordia.

The Concordia Times, Republican; T. A. Filson, editor and publisher; S. Z. Filson, associate editor, Concordia.

Weekly Daylight, Democratic; E. Marshall & Co., editors and proprietors, Concordia.

The Clyde Herald, Republican; J. B. and M. L. Rupe, editors and proprietors, Clyde.

The Clyde Argus, Republican; Chas. A. Morley and Owen V. Smith, editors and publishers, Clyde.

The Glasco Sun, independent; Miss Katie Hubbard, editor and proprietor, Glasco.

The Miltonvale News, Republican; J. C. Cline, editor and proprietor, Miltonvale.

The Kansan, Republican; James and Mary L. Burton, editors, publishers and proprietors, Jamestown.

The Quill, Republican; W. W. Pinkerton, proprietor; Mark G. Woodruff, associate editor, Jamestown.

COFFEY COUNTY.

Burlington Republican and Patriot, Republican; C. O. Smith, editor, publisher and proprietor, Burlington.

The Burlington Independent, Democratic; John E. Watrous, publisher, Burlington.

The Burlington Nonpareil, Republican; Brown Printing Company, publishers, Burlington.

LeRoy Reporter, independent; Frank Fockele, publisher and proprietor, LeRoy.

The Lebo Light, neutral; F. M. Burnham, editor and proprietor, Lebo.

Waverly News, independent; L. E. Smith, publisher and proprietor, Waverly.

The Gazette, Union Labor; Dan K. Swearingen, publisher, Burlington.

COMANCHE COUNTY.

The Western Star, Democratic; W. M. Cash, editor and proprietor, Coldwater.

The Coldwater Review, Democratic; Review Publishing Company, publishers, Coldwater.

Coldwater Echo, Republican; E. G. Phelps, editor, J. E. Hutchison, publisher, Coldwater.

Coldwater Enterprise, Republican; N. S. Mounts, editor, Geo. W. Newman, publisher, Mounts & Newman, proprietors, Coldwater.

The Leader, Democratic; Joe H. Carter, editor, Protection.

COWLEY COUNTY.

The Winfield Courier, (daily and weekly,) Republican; Ed. P. Greer, editor, Frank H. Greer, city editor, Winfield.

Winfield Telegram, Democratic; J. R. Clark, editor and proprietor, Winfield.

Saturday Evening Tribune, Republican; E. B. Buck, editor, Tribune Company, publishers, Winfield.

The Winfield Visitor, (daily and weekly,) independent; A. L. Schultz and M. L. Harter, editors, publishers and proprietors, Winfield.

The American Nonconformist, Union Labor; H. Vincent, editor, J. H. Randall, associate editor, H. and L. Vincent, publishers and proprietors, Winfield.

Republican Traveler, (daily and weekly,) Republican; T. W. Eckert, editor, T. W. Eckert and R. A. Howard, publishers, Arkansas City.

Arkansas Valley Democrat, Democratic; T. McIntire, editor, C. M. McIntire, local editor, L. M. M'Intire, publisher, Arkansas City.

Canal City Dispatch, (daily and weekly,) Democratic; Geo. W. Wagner and B. A. Wagner, editors and publishers, Arkansas City.

The Fair Play, Union Labor; W. B. Wagner, editor and proprietor, Arkansas City.

The Burden Enterprise, Republican; W. L. Hutton, editor, W. K. McComas, publisher and proprietor, Burden.

Burden Eagle, Republican; J. G. and J. H. Crawford, editors and proprietors, Burden.

The Udall Record, Republican; W. H. Hornaday, editor and publisher, Udall.

The Cambridge News, Republican; A. V. Wilkinson, editor, Samuel B. Sherman, Henry F. Hicks, and A. V. Wilkinson, proprietors, Cambridge.

Atlanta Cricket, Republican; Milo A. Copeland, publisher, Atlanta.

Dexter Free Press, independent; P. W. Craig, editor and publisher, Dexter.

CRAWFORD COUNTY.

The Girard Press, Republican; E. A. Wasser and Dudley C. Flint, editors, publishers and proprietors, Girard.

The Girard Herald, Union Labor; W. A. Bailey, editor and proprietor, Girard.

The Cherokee Sentinel on the Border, Republican; F. W. Doughty and Willis Swank, publishers, Cherokee.

Pittsburg Smelter, Republican; John P. Morris, editor, Pittsburg.

The Pittsburg Headlight, (daily and weekly,) Republican; Wm. Moore & Son (C. W. Moore), editors and publishers, Pittsburg.

Pittsburg Democrat, Democratic; G. S. McCartney, publisher, Pittsburg.

The McCune Times, Republican; Alfred Jett, editor and publisher, McCune.

Walnut Journal, Republican; H. Quick and —— Martin, editors, publishers and proprietors, Walnut.

The Arcadian, Republican; Willis Swank, editor, publisher and proprietor, Lawrence Galliher, local editor and business manager, Arcadia.

Arcadia Democrat, Democratic; J. M. Swan, editor, J. M. Swan and J. C. Pasley, proprietors, Arcadia.

The Hepler Banner, Republican; Henry F. Canutt, editor, H. F. Canutt and Son, publishers, Hepler.

DAVIS COUNTY.

The Junction City Union, Republican; W. C. Moore, editor, John Montgomery and E. M. Gilbert, publishers, Junction City.

The Junction City Tribune, Union Labor; John Davis, editor, Chas. S. Davis, associate editor and business manager, John Davis & Sons, proprietors, Junction City.

The Junction City Republican, Republican; Geo. A. Clark, editor, publisher and proprietor, Junction City.

Insurance Messenger, (monthly;) G. F. Little, editor and proprietor, M. L. Little, associate editor, Junction City.

DECATUR COUNTY.

Oberlin Herald, Democratic; Fred. L. Henshaw, editor and proprietor, Oberlin.

Oberlin Opinion, Republican; F. W. Casterline, editor, publisher and proprietor, Oberlin.

The Eye, Republican; C. Borin, editor; Eye Publishing Company, publishers, Oberlin.

The Oberlin Farmer, (monthly,) agricultural; G. Webb Bertram, editor and proprietor, Oberlin.

The Norcatur Register, neutral; H. H. Hoskins, editor and publisher, Norcatur.

The Jennings Times, Democratic; John Shields and —— Lewis, editors, Jennings.

Jennings Echo, Republican; J. W. Page and R. M. Day, editors, publishers and proprietors, Jennings.

DICKINSON COUNTY.

Abilene Weekly Chronicle, Republican; R. B. Claiborne, editor, publisher and proprietor, Chronicle Publishing Company, publishers, Abilene.

The Abilene Gazette, Democratic; the Gazette Printing Company, publishers, Abilene.

Abilene Reflector, (daily and weekly,) Republican; Chas. M. Harger, city editor,

Dickinson County News, Democratic; B. F. Strother, editor, Strother Bros., publishers, Abilene.

Solomon Sentinel, Republican; E. B. Burnett, editor and publisher, Solomon City.

The Enterprise Independent; Enterprise Publishing Company, publishers, Enterprise.

The Kansas Miller and Manufacturer, (monthly,) manufacturing interests; C. B. Hoffman, editor, W. T. Hopkins, business manager, Enterprise.

The Hope Herald, Republican; Geo. Burroughs, editor, publisher and proprietor, Hope.

Hope Dispatch, Republican; A. M. Crary, editor, M. C. Hemenway, proprietor, Hope.

The Herington Tribune, neutral; V. C. Welch and Frank I. Sage, publishers, Herington.

The Herington Headlight, Republican; Tom Gallagher, publisher, Herington.

The Chapman Courier, independent; J. H. Engle, editor, publisher and proprietor, Chapman.

The Manchester Sun, neutral; A. S. Green, editor, Manchester.

DONIPHAN COUNTY.

The Weekly Kansas Chief, Republican; Sol. Miller, editor, publisher and proprietor, Troy.

The Troy Times, Republican; F. L. Finch, editor and publisher, W. H. Finch, proprietor, Troy.

White Cloud Review, neutral; Sanders Bros., publishers, White Cloud.

DOUGLAS COUNTY.

The Evening Tribune, (daily,) Republican; O. E. Learnard, publisher and proprietor, H. M. Greene, editor, Lawrence.

Lawrence Journal, (daily and weekly,) Republican; O. E. Learnard, publisher and proprietor, H. M. Greene, editor, Lawrence.

Die Germania, (German,) Edward Grün, publisher, Lawrence.

The Lawrence Gazette, Democratic; Osbun Shannon, editor, Gazette Publishing Co., publishers, Frank L. Webster, manager, Lawrence.

The University Review, (monthly,) educational; V. L. Kellogg, editor-in-chief, W. T. Caywood and A. L. Wilmoth, business managers, Kansas University Publishing Co., publishers, Lawrence.

The Weekly University Courier, educational; Richard Horton, editor-in-chief, Courier Co., publishers, Chas. H. Johnson, president, E. C. Esterly, secretary, P. T. Foley, printer, Lawrence.

University Times, educational; Edgar Martindale, editor-in-chief, C. E. Street and J. Frank Craig, business managers, Lawrence.

Delta of Sigma Nu, (bi-monthly,) college society magazine; Grant W. Harrington, managing editor, Lawrence.

The Progressive Educator, (monthly,) educational; Prof. J. A. Stotler, editor and proprietor, Lawrence.

The College Review, Business College, (quarterly;) E. McIlravy, editor, Lawrence Business College, publishers, P. T. Foley, printer, Lawrence.

Baldwin Ledger, Republican; W. H. Finch, editor, Baldwin.

The Baker University Index, (monthly,) educational; C. K. Woodson, editor-in-chief, J. A. Hyden, jr., business manager, College literary societies, publishers, Lawrence.

College Echo, (monthly,) educational; F. P. Jacoby, editor, Lane University, publishers, Lecompton.

The Eudora News, neutral; M. R. Cain, editor and proprietor, Eudora.

EDWARDS COUNTY.

The Weekly Kinsley Mercury, Republican; W. S. Hebron, editor, publisher and proprietor, Kinsley.

Weekly Banner-Graphic, Democratic; J. M. Springer, editor, Kinsley.

ELK COUNTY.

The Howard Courant, Republican; Asa, Tom. E. and John A. Thompson, editors, publishers and proprietors, Howard.

The Howard Democrat, Democratic; James Robert Hall, editor and publisher, Howard.

The Broad Axe, Union Labor; Harry E. Bird, editor and publisher, Howard.

The Longton Times, independent; Geo. M. Flory, editor and publisher, Longton.

Moline Mercury, Republican; Geo. C. Armstrong, editor and proprietor, Moline.

The Grenola Chief, Union Labor; Brice E. Davis, editor and proprietor, Grenola.

Kansas Weekly Ledger, Republican; William Root, editor and publisher, Elk Falls.

ELLIS COUNTY.

Hays City Sentinel, Republican; W. P. Montgomery, manager and publisher; Hays City.

Free Press, (semi-weekly,) Republican; Harry Freese, editor, publisher and proprietor, Hays City.

Democratic Times, Democratic; G. W. Sweet, editor and publisher, Hays City.

The Republican, Republican; George P. Griffith, editor, Hays City.

The Ellis Headlight, Republican; Edgar M. Baldwin, editor and publisher, Ellis.

The Ellis Review, neutral; Frank J. Brettle, editor and publisher, Ellis.

ELLSWORTH COUNTY.

Ellsworth Reporter, Republican; Geo. Huycke, editor, publisher and proprietor, Ellsworth.

Ellsworth Democrat, Democratic; G. A. Collett and F. S. Foster, editors and publishers, Ellsworth.

The Weekly Herald, Republican; H. D. Morgan, editor, Ellsworth.

The Wilson Echo, Republican; S. A. Coover, editor, Coover & Hutchison, proprietors, C. S. Hutchison, foreman, Wilson.

Wilson Eagle, Democratic; R. J. Coffey, editor, Wilson.

The Kanopolis Journal, Republican; R. V. Morgan, editor and publisher, Kanopolis.

The Holyrood Enterprise, Republican; M. G. Woodmansee, editor and proprietor, Holyrood.

FINNEY COUNTY.

Finney County Democrat, Democratic; L. H. Barlow and M. B. Hundley, editors and publishers, Garden City.

Garden City Sentinel, (daily and weekly,) Republican; J. W. Gregory, publisher and proprietor, Garden City.

Garden City Weekly Herald, Republican; J. S. Painter, editor, W. W. Wallace, business manager, Herald Printing Company, publishers, Garden City.

The Terry Eye, Democratic; E. L. Stephenson, editor, publisher and proprietor, Terry.

The Hatfield News, neutral; M. B. Crawford & Co., proprietors, Hatfield.

The Queen City Herald, Democratic; J. B. Kessler, editor, publisher and proprietor, Ottawa.

The Kansas Lever, Prohibition; E. W. Frick and Frank Muth, Ottawa Printing Company, publishers and proprietors, Ottawa.

The Ottawa Campus, (monthly,) collegiate; William J. Cowell, editor-in-chief, J. W. Griffith, business manager, Ottawa University Oratorical Association, publishers, Ottawa.

The Eagle, Republican; T. W. Fields, editor, publisher and proprietor, Williamsburg.

Wellsville Exchange, neutral, Mrs. L. A. Fields, editor, publisher and proprietor, Wellsville.

The Pomona Enterprise, neutral; T. L. Newcomb, editor, Enterprise Publishing Company, publishers, Pomona.

GARFIELD COUNTY.

Ravanna Chieftain, Republican; W. F. Ellsworth, editor, Ravanna.

Ravanna Record, Democratic; Thos. A. Davies, publisher, Ravanna.

Garfield County Call, Independent Democratic; E. L. Cline, editor and proprietor, Eminence.

The Garfield County Journal, independent; S. J. Myers, editor, C. F. Hoadley, publisher and proprietor, Loyal.

GOVE COUNTY.

Grainfield Cap Sheaf, Independent Democratic; C. M. and E. L. M'Clintock, editors, and publishers, Grainfield.

Gove County Gazette, Democratic; E. J. Killean, editor, Gazette Printing Company, publishers, Gove City.

Gove County Republican, Republican; J. E. Hart, editor, W. J. Lloyd, publisher, Gove City.

The Settlers' Guide, Republican; S. W. Baker, editor, J. H. Baker, manager, Quinter.

GRAHAM COUNTY.

The Millbrook Times, Republican; Benj. B. F. Graves and Merritt L. Graves, publishers and proprietors, Millbrook.

Graham County Democrat, Democratic; Louis M. Pritchard and Milt. L. Singrey, editors and publishers, Millbrook.

The Hill City Reveille, Republican; H. D. Clayton, editor, publisher and proprietor, Hill City.

Hill City Democrat, Democratic; J. F. Stewart and H. Kampmeier, editors, publishers and proprietors, Hill City.

Hill City Star, Republican; J. H. Wright and H. S. Hogue, publishers, Hill City.

Hill City Sun, Union Labor; T. H. McGill, editor, publisher and proprietor, Hill City.

The Fremont Press, Democratic; E. E. Bright and R. S. Stout, editors and proprietors, Fremont.

The Bogue Signal, Republican; F. F. McBride, editor and proprietor, Bogue.

GRANT COUNTY.

Grant County Register, Democratic; Herbert L. Gill, editor and proprietor, Ulysses.

The Tribune-Commercial, Republican; John M. Ruckman and Geo. W. Perry, editors, publishers and proprietors, Ulysses.

Golden Gazette, Democratic; J. A. Harman, editor, publisher and proprietor, J. O. Johnson, associate editor, Golden.

Shockeyville Plainsman, Republican; T. R. Hornaday, editor and proprietor, Shockey.

GRAY COUNTY.

The Jacksonian, Democratic; E. S. Garten, editor and manager, Jacksonian Printing Company, publishers and proprietors, Cimarron.

New West Echo, Republican; N. B. Klaine, editor, S. S. Logan, business manager, New West Printing Company, publishers, Cimarron.

The Montezuma Chief, Democratic; J. H. Hebard, editor and manager, Chief Publishing Company, publishers, T. B. Pyles, proprietor, Montezuma.

Ingalls Union, independent; R. H. Turner, editor, Union Publishing Company, publishers, Ingalls.

GREELEY COUNTY.

The Horace Champion, Republican; Clarke H. White and Henson B. Lemmon, proprietors, Horace.

The Horace Messenger, Democratic; A. J. Hunter and A. C. Fulkerson, editors and proprietors, Horace.

The Greeley County Enterprise, Democratic; Carter Hutchinson, editor and manager, Tribune.

Greeley County Republican, Republican; J. M. Hawkins, publisher, Tribune.

GREENWOOD COUNTY.

The Eureka Herald, Republican; Z. Harlan, editor, publisher and proprietor, Eureka.

The Greenwood County Republican, (daily and weekly,) Republican; W. E. Doud, editor and proprietor, Eureka.

Democratic Messenger, Democratic; T. W. Morgan, editor, Eureka.

The Madison News, Republican; W. O. and V. E. Lunsford, editors and proprietors, Madison.

—7

The Severy Record, Republican; Geo. H. Doud, editor, Geo. H. Doud and H. W. Bailey, proprietors, Severy.

The Kansas Clipper, Democratic; C. E. Wainscott, editor and proprietor, Severy.

Fall River Times, Union Labor; J. A. Somerby, editor, Fall River.

Saturday Morning Sun, neutral; J. H. Morse, editor and proprietor, Fall River.

HAMILTON COUNTY.

The Syracuse Journal, Republican; H. N. Lester, editor, G. W. Reed, business manager, Journal Publishing Company, publishers, Syracuse.

Syracuse Sentinel, Republican; Will C. Higgins and Ed. V. Higgins, managing editors and proprietors, Sentinel Company, publishers, Syracuse.

The Democratic Principle, Democratic; F. M. Dunlavy, editor and proprietor, T. S. Hurd, associate editor, Syracuse.

The Kendall Boomer, Democratic; Henry Block, editor, publisher and proprietor, Kendall.

The Coolidge Citizen, Republican; O. H. Knight and J. H. Borders, editors and proprietors, Coolidge.

The Coolidge Times, Democratic; L. I. Purcell, editor, publisher and proprietor, Coolidge.

HARPER COUNTY.

The Anthony Republican, (daily and weekly,) Republican; George W. Maffet, editor, publisher and proprietor; Lafe. Merritt, city editor, Anthony.

Harper County Enterprise, Democratic; T. H. W. McDowell, editor, publisher and proprietor; W. L. Hutchinson, general business manager, Anthony.

Anthony Journal, Republican; J. R. Hammond, editor; Anthony Journal Co., publishers, Anthony.

The Harper Sentinel, Democratic; J. L. Isenberg, editor and publisher, Harper.

The Prophet, Union Labor, —— ——, editor and manager, Harper.

Harper Normal School and Business College Journal, (monthly,) educational; R. W. Ball, editor and publisher, Harper.

The Harper Republican, (daily and weekly,) Republican; M. A. Hull, editor and publisher, Harper.

The Attica Advocate, Republican; L. A. Hoffman, editor; Hoffman & Son, (A. B.,) publishers and proprietors, Attica.

Freeport Leader, Republican; Mervin O. Cissel, publisher, Freeport.

Bluff City Herald, Republican; James Glover, editor and proprietor, Bluff City.

The Crisfield Courier, independent; B. Wilson, editor; Henry Anderson and L. B. Wilson, proprietors, Crisfield.

HARVEY COUNTY.

The Newton Republican, (daily and weekly,) Republican; Noble L. Prentis, editor; Newton Publishing Company, publishers, Newton.

Newton Kansan, Republican; Charles H. Kurtz, editor and proprietor, Newton.

Newton Anzeiger, German; C. D. Heinrich, editor and publisher, Newton.

The Kansas Commoner, Union Labor; J. R. Rogers, editor, B. E. Kies, business manager, Newton.

The Newton Weekly Journal, Democratic; John A. Reynolds, publisher, Newton.

The Halstead Independent, Republican; Joe F. White, editor and proprietor, Halstead.

The Burrton Graphic, Republican; M. L. Sherpy, editor and proprietor, Burrton.

The Sedgwick Pantagraph, Republican: Cash M. Taylor, editor and publisher, Sedgwick.

HASKELL COUNTY.

The Ivanhoe Times, Democratic; T. B. Pyles, editor, Times Publishing Company, publishers, Ivanhoe.

The Santa Fé Leader, Democratic; C. R. Cravens, editor, Leader Publishing Company, publishers, Santa Fé.

The Santa Fé Monitor, Republican; J. W. Richardson, editor and publisher, Santa Fé.

HODGEMAN COUNTY.

Jetmore Reveille, Republican; Roando C. Orndorff, managing editor, H. Orndorff, proprietor, Jetmore.

The Jetmore Weekly Scimitar, Democratic; William J. Fuller, editor and manager, Jetmore.

Jetmore Siftings, Republican; L. C. Miller, editor and proprietor, Jetmore.

Jetmore Journal, Republican; E. E. Hood, editor, S. A. Sheldon, proprietor, Jetmore.

JACKSON COUNTY.

The Holton Weekly Recorder, Republican; M. M. Beck, editor and proprietor, Holton.

The Holton Weekly Signal, Democratic; W. W. Sargent, editor and proprietor, Holton.

The Normal Advocate, (monthly,) educational; E. J. Hoenshel, editor and proprietor; J. J. Rippetoe, associate editor, Holton.

The Whiting Weekly News, Republican; J. S. Clark, editor, publisher and proprietor, Whiting.

Soldier City Tribune, neutral; A. P. Shaw, publisher, Soldier.

JEFFERSON COUNTY.

The Oskaloosa Independent, Republican; F. H. Roberts, editor and publisher, Oskaloosa.

Valley Falls New Era, Republican; A. W. Robinson, editor and proprietor, Valley Falls.

The Valley Falls Register, Democratic; T. W. Gardner, editor and publisher, Valley Falls.

Lucifer, (The Light Bearer,) Liberal; Moses Harmon, editor and publisher, Valley Falls.

Fair Play, Liberal; E. C. Walker, editor; E. C. Walker and Lillian Harmon, publishers, Valley Falls.

The Winchester Herald, Republican; Oscar C. Kirkpatrick, publisher, Winchester.

The Nortonville News, Republican; Robert A. Wright, editor and proprietor, Nortonville.

Meriden Report, Democratic; John Gish and John Groshong, editors and publishers, Meriden.

The McLouth Times, Republican; A. B. Mills, editor and publisher, McLouth.

JEWELL COUNTY.

Jewell County Monitor, Republican; R. F. Vaughan, editor and proprietor, Mankato.

Jewell County Review, Republican; S. M. Weed, editor and proprietor, Mankato.

Kansas Labor Clarion, Union Labor; J. Dunton, editor and proprietor, Mankato.

The Jacksonian, Democratic; George W. Reed, editor, S. S. Mason, publisher, Mankato.

Jewell County Republican, Republican; Benjamin Musser and W. C. Palmer, publishers, Jewell City.

Burr Oak Herald, Republican; H. F. Faidley, editor and proprietor, Burr Oak.

JOHNSON COUNTY.

The Olathe Mirror, Republican; H. A. Perkins, editor, publisher and proprietor, Olathe.

The Kansas Patron, Grange; Geo. Black, editor, H. C. Livermore, manager, Johnson County Coöperative Association, publishers, Olathe.

The Kansas Star; published by the pupils of the Deaf and Dumb Institution, Olathe.

The Olathe Baptist Builder, (monthly,) religious; R. P. Stephenson, editor and publisher, Olathe.

Spring Hill New Era, Prohibition; J. W. Sowers, editor, Spring Hill.

The Johnson County Democrat, Democratic; David Hunt, publisher, Olathe.

KEARNEY COUNTY.

The Kearney County Advocate, Republican; C. O. Chapman, editor and proprietor, Lakin.

Lakin Pioneer Democrat, Democratic; John T. Griffith, editor and publisher, Lakin.

Hartland Herald, Democratic; Jos. Dillon, editor and proprietor, Hartland.

Kearney County Coyote, Democratic; Lon. Whorton, editor and proprietor, Hartland.

The Standard, Democratic; Jo. W. Merifield, editor, Hartland.

KINGMAN COUNTY.

Kingman County Democrat, Democratic; W. A. Eaton, editor and publisher, Kingman.

The Kingman Courier, (daily and weekly), Republican; J. Malcom Johnston, editor, J. A. Maxey, business manager, C. M. Bay, publisher, Kingman.

Kingman Leader, Republican; Morton Albaugh, editor, Kingman.

Voice of The People, Union Labor; C. L. Swartz, editor, N. V. Van Patten, manager, Kingman.

Norwich News, Republican; J. O. Graham, editor and publisher, Norwich.

The Cunningham Herald, independent Republican; J. Geo. Smith, editor and publisher, Cunningham.

The Spivey Dispatch, independent; Al. D. Krebs and W. J. Krebs, editors and proprietors, Spivey.

The Spivey Index, neutral; Geo. W. Kelley, editor, B. V. Kelley, publisher, Spivey.

KIOWA COUNTY.

The Kiowa County Signal, Republican; Will. E. Bolton, editor, publisher and proprietor, Greensburg.

Greensburg Rustler, Democratic; S. B. Sproule, editor, publisher and proprietor, Greensburg.

Kiowa County Times, independent; H. B. Graves, editor, Coke Eberly, publisher, Greensburg.

Wellsford Reformer, Democratic; S. W. Herring, editor, W. S. Neal, proprietor, Wellsford.

Haviland Tribune, Union Labor; Will. S. Neal, proprietor, Haviland.

The Parsons Sun, (daily and weekly,) Republican; H. H. Lusk, editor, publisher and proprietor, Parsons.

The Parsons Eclipse, (daily and weekly,) independent; J. B. Lamb & Sons, (C. L. and —— Lamb,) editors and proprietors, Parsons.

Parsons Palladium, Democratic; Will W. Frye, editor, Frank W. and Will W. Frye, publishers and proprietors, Parsons.

The Weekly Clarion, Republican; A. H. Tyler, editor, and business manager, L. K. Sheward, publisher and proprietor, Parsons.

The Chetopa Advance, Republican; J. M. Cavaness, editor, Chetopa.

Chetopa Statesman, Union Labor; Nelson Abbott, editor, Chetopa.

The Chetopa Democrat, Democratic; J. J. Rambo, publisher, Chetopa.

The Oswego Independent, Republican; Nelson Case, editor, Mrs. Mary McGill, publisher, W. F. McGill, local editor, Oswego.

Labette County Democrat, Democratic; J. M. Landis, editor and publisher, Oswego.

The Oswego Bee, (daily and weekly,) Union Labor; Wright, Macon & Company, publishers, J. H. Macon, business manager, Oswego.

The Mound Valley Herald, Republican; W. F. Thrall, editor and publisher, Mound Valley.

Altamont Sentinel, independent; Mrs. Lizzie Newlon, publisher, C. S. Newlon, proprietor, Altamont.

The Wilsonton Journal, neutral; Mrs. Augustus Wilson, editor and proprietor, E. G. Cushing, associate editor and manager, Wilsonton.

Lane County Herald, Democratic; J. C. Riley, jr., editor; Riley & Egger, publishers and proprietors, Dighton.

The Dighton Journal, Republican; Ben L. Green, editor and proprietor; H. E. Woolheater, local editor, Dighton.

Lane County Republican, Republican; M. H. Curts, editor, publisher and proprietor, Dighton.

The Leavenworth Times, (daily and weekly,) Republican; Z. A. Smith, editor, A. C. Lamborn, manager, Leavenworth Times Publishing Company, publishers, Leavenworth.

The Standard, (daily and weekly,) Democratic; T. A. Hurd, president, Edward Carroll, secretary, Frank T. Lynch, treasurer and manager, Leavenworth.

The Sun, (daily,) independent; Sun Publishing Company, publishers, Leavenworth.

Leavenworth Post, (German,) independent; Max Gronefeld, editor, Franz F. Metschan, publisher, Leavenworth.

The Kansas Catholic, religious; John O'Flanagan, editor, Kansas Catholic Publishing Company, publishers, Leavenworth.

The Home Record, (monthly,) charitable; Mrs. C. H. Cushing, editor, Home for the Friendless, publishers, Leavenworth.

The Orphan's Friend, (monthly,) charitable; Mrs. Thomas Carney, editor and business manager, Mrs. DeForest Fairchild, associate editor, Leavenworth.

The Lance, independent; James Paddock, editor and publisher, Leavenworth.

Central Business College Journal, (monthly,) educational; Leach & Parker, principals, Leavenworth.

The Tonganoxie Mirror, Republican; William Heynen, editor, publisher and proprietor, Tonganoxie.

The Blue Mound Sun, Republican; John N. Barnes and W. S. Platt, editors and publishers, Blue Mound.

The Prescott Republican, Republican; Charles Henry Bigwood and James Stewart Beckwith, editors and publishers, Prescott.

LOGAN COUNTY.

Monument Obelisk, Republican; J. W. Taylor, editor and publisher, Monument.

Oakley Opinion, Democratic; Edward Kleist, editor and publisher, Oakley.

Oakley News Letter, Republican; John A. Goodier, editor and publisher, Oakley.

Winona Weekly Messenger, Democratic; A. S. Booton, editor and publisher, Winona.

The Winona Clipper, Republican; J. P. Israel, editor, Winona.

Logan County Republican, Republican; C. V. Kinney, editor; J. K. Hupp, proprietor, Russell Springs.

Logan County Leader, Democratic; S. W. Grove, editor; S. W. Grove and Geo. Egger, publishers, Russell Springs.

Augustine Herald, Republican; N. Fenstemaker, editor, publisher and proprietor, Augustine.

LYON COUNTY.

The Emporia News, (daily and weekly,) independent; J. F. O'Connor, editor; H. D. Hammond, business manager; News Company, publishers, Emporia.

Emporia Republican, (daily and weekly,) Republican; C. V. Eskridge, editor, publisher and proprietor, Emporia.

The Emporia Democrat, Democratic; J. M. McCown, editor and proprietor, Emporia.

The Kansas Workman, Union Labor; Cyrus Corning, editor; Kansas Workman Publishing Company, publishers, Emporia.

The Fanatic, Prohibition; Joseph Langellier, editor and publisher, Emporia.

Emporia Sunday Gazette, Republican; W. F. Craig, editor and proprietor, Emporia.

The Hartford Call, Republican; W. J. Means, editor and publisher, Hartford.

The Americus Ledger, Republican; C. A. and William Moore, editors, publishers, and proprietors, Americus.

Allen Tidings, Republican; Major A. Paul, editor and proprietor, Allen.

M'PHERSON COUNTY.

The McPherson Freeman, Republican; H. B. Kelly, editor, publisher and proprietor, McPherson.

The McPherson Republican and Weekly Press, (daily and weekly,) Republican; S. G. Mead, editor, publisher and proprietor, McPherson.

The Democrat, Democratic; Warren Knaus, editor, publisher and proprietor, McPherson.

McPherson Anzeiger, (German;) J. F. Harms, editor, Western German Publishing Company, publishers, McPherson.

Our Opinion, Union Labor; Geo. C. Findley, editor and business manager, Our Opinion Publishing Company, publishers, McPherson.

The School, Fireside and Farm, (monthly,) educational; S. Z. Sharp, editor-in-chief, George E. Studebaker, business manager, McPherson College, publishers, McPherson.

The Lindsborg News, Republican; A. Ringwald, publisher, Lindsborg.

The Canton Republican, Republican; W. R. Davis, editor and publisher, Canton.

The Moundridge Leader, independent; James M. Coutts, editor, Moundridge Publishing Company, proprietors, Moundridge.

The Marquette Monitor, Republican; S. W. Hill, editor and proprietor, Marquette.

The Galva Times, neutral; James A. Harris, publisher, Galva.

Framat, (Swedish,) educational; Jonas Westling, manager, Bethany Book Concern, publishers, Lindsborg.

MARION COUNTY.

Marion Record, Republican; E. W. Hoch, editor, B. C. Hastings, manager, Marion.

The Cottonwood Valley Times, Democratic; W. W. Wheeland, editor, "The Times" Publishing Company, J. H. Buchanan, president, M. O. Billings, business manager, publishers, Marion.

Marion County Anzeiger, German; J. F. Harms, editor, Western German Publishing Company, publishers, Hillsboro.

The Lower Light, (monthly,) religious; O. L. Clarke, secretary, Y. M. C. A., publishers, Marion.

The Peabody Gazette, Republican; W. H. Morgan and Son (Geo. E.), editors, publishers and proprietors, Peabody.

The Peabody Graphic, Republican; R. L. Cochran, editor, D. McKercher, publisher, Peabody.

The Florence Herald, Republican; W. H. Booth, editor and proprietor, Florence.

Florence Weekly Bulletin, Democratic; J. B. Crouch, editor, Florence.

Hillsboro Herald, (German,) Republican; John Dole, proprietor, Hillsboro.

The Lost Springs Courier, Republican; J. C. Padgett, publisher, Lost Springs.

MARSHALL COUNTY.

arshall County News, Republican; Geo. T. Smith, editor and proprietor, Marsvill<small>M</small>

Marshall County Democrat, Democratic; O. J. Morse and W. T. Ecks, editors and managers, Marysville.

Marysville Post, (German,) Democratic; William Becker, editor, publisher and proprietor, Marysville.

The True Republican, Union Labor; P. D. Hartman, editor, Marysville. ·

The Waterville Telegraph, Republican; Henry C. Willson, editor, publisher and proprietor, Waterville.

Blue Rapids Times, Republican; E. M. Brice and Edward Skinner, editors, publishers and proprietors, Blue Rapids.

The Frankfort Bee, Republican; W. J. Granger, editor, publisher and proprietor, Frankfort.

The Frankfort Sentinel, Union Labor; S. H. Peters, editor, publisher and proprietor, Frankfort.

The Axtell Anchor, Republican; J. M. Ross and Thomas Nye, publishers, Axtell.

The Star, Republican; Dan M. Mabie, editor and publisher, Beattie.

The Irving Leader, Republican; J. R. Leonard, editor and proprietor, Irving.

MEADE COUNTY.

The Meade County Globe, Republican; Frank Fuhr, editor, publisher and proprietor, Meade Center.

Meade County Press-Democrat, Democratic; H. Wilts. Brown, editor and publisher, Meade Center.

The Meade Republican, Republican; T. J. Palmer, editor and proprietor, Meade Center.

Fowler City Graphic, Republican; I. A. Strauss, editor, O. S. Hurd, publisher and proprietor, Fowler City.

The West Plains Mascott, Republican; H. B. Stone, editor and publisher, West Plains.

The Hornet, Republican; Chas. K. Sourbeer, editor, Sourbeer Bros., publishers, Artesian City.

MIAMI COUNTY.

· The Western Spirit, Democratic; B. J. Sheridan, editor, publisher and proprietor Paola.

The Miami Republican, Republican; W. D. Greason, editor, publisher and proprietor, Paola.

The Paola Times, Republican; Aaron D. States, editor; Harry W. Land, publisher; States & Land, proprietors, Paola.

The Louisburg Herald, Republican; R. H. Cadwallader, editor, publisher and proprietor, Louisburg.

Osawatomie Graphic, independent; Frank Pyle and Merritt E. Springer, editors and proprietors, Osawatomie.

Osawatomie Advertiser, neutral; published by Osawatomie Printing Co., A. F. Meek, president; W. H. Campbell, secretary; G. N. Marley, publisher, Osawatomie.

The Fontana News, neutral; M. Bramblet, editor and publisher, Fontana.

MITCHELL COUNTY.

The Beloit Gazette, Republican; S. H. Dodge, editor, publisher and proprietor, Beloit.

Beloit Weekly Courier, Republican; W. H. Caldwell, editor and proprietor, Beloit.

The Western Democrat, Democratic; H. A. Yonge, publisher and proprietor, Beloit.

Cawker City Journal, Republican; by Ferd. Prince, Cawker City.

Public Record, Republican; L. L. Alrich, editor and publisher, Cawker City.

The Weekly Times, Republican; J. W. McBride, editor and proprietor, Cawker City.

Glen Elder Herald, Republican; N. F. Hewett, editor, Glen Elder.

Scottsville Independent, Republican; Frank M. Coffey, editor and publisher, Scottsville.

MONTGOMERY COUNTY.

The Star and Kansan, Democratic; H. W. Young, editor, publisher and proprietor, Independence.

South Kansas Tribune, Republican; W. T. and C. Yoe, editors, publishers and proprietors, Independence.

The Evening Reporter, (daily,) neutral; T. N. Sickels, editor, publisher and proprietor, Independence.

The Refugees' Lone Star, (occasional,) charitable; D. Votaw, editor, Freedman's Relief Association, publishers, Independence.

The Coffeyville Journal, Republican; D. Stewart Elliott, editor, W. G. Waverling, business manager and publisher, Coffeyville.

The Sun, Republican; W. A. Peffer, jr., editor and publisher, Coffeyville.

The Eagle, Democratic; H. M. Stewart, editor, Stewart & Hetherington, publishers, Coffeyville.

Daily Globe and Torch, and The Republican, (weekly,) Republican; C. P. Buffington, editor, Republican Publishing Company, (C. C. Kincaid, C. P. Buffington, W. A. Cormack and O. F. Carson,) publishers, Cherryvale.

Cherryvale Champion, Republican; S. P. Moore, editor, F. G. Moore, publisher and proprietor, Cherryvale.

The Elk City Eagle, Republican; W. F. Kingston, editor, publisher and proprietor, Elk City.

The Caney Chronicle, Republican; J. T. McKee, editor, J. T. McKee & Sons, proprietors, Caney.

The Liberty Review, Union Labor; A. S. Duley, editor and publisher, Liberty.

The Havana, Herald, independent; V. O. Prather, editor and proprietor, E. G. Smith and V. O. Prather, publishers, Havana.

MORRIS COUNTY.

The Council Grove Republican, Republican; Frank Moriarty and W. F. Waller, editors and proprietors, Council Grove.

Council Grove Guard, Democratic; E. J. Dill, editor and publisher, Council Grove.

The Anti-Monopolist, Union Labor; W. H. T. Wakefield, editor, publisher and proprietor, Council Grove.

The Dunlap Reporter, independent; Daniel W. Murphy, editor, Dunlap.

The White City News, independent; Banna F. Cress, editor, publisher and proprietor, White City.

The Dwight Wasp, Republican; Joseph O. Clayton, editor and manager; Dwight Printing Company, publishers, Dwight.

MORTON COUNTY.

The Leader-Democrat, Democratic; Q. A. Robertson, editor, Richfield.

The Richfield Republican, Republican; R. G. Price, publisher, Richfield.

The Taloga Star, Prohibition; H. W. Worthington, editor and publisher; Samuel Worthington, associate editor, Taloga.

Westola Wave, neutral; W. C. Calhoun, editor and proprietor, Westola.

Cundiff Journal, Democratic; Colver & Wester, editors and proprietors, Cundiff.

Morton County Monitor, Republican; Glenn S. Van Gundy, editor; Frank Van Gundy, publisher, Morton.

The Herald; —— Gilbert, editor and proprietor, Morton.

Seneca Courier-Democrat, Democratic; A. P. and C. H. Herold, editors, publishers and proprietors, Seneca.

The Seneca Tribune, Republican; W. H. and G. F. Jordan, editors and publishers, Seneca.

Nemaha County Republican, Republican; J. F. Clough, editor and proprietor, · W. H. Whelan, associate editor, Sabetha.

The Sabetha Herald, Republican; Flora P. Hogbin, editor, A. C. Hogbin, publisher, Sabetha.

Nemaha County Spectator, Republican; John Stowell, editor, Wetmore.

Centralia Journal, Republican; Bert Patch, editor, B. H. Patch, publisher and proprietor, Centralia.

The Goff's News, neutral; Thomas A. Kerr, editor, publisher and proprietor, Goff's.

Neosho County Journal, Democratic; John R. Brunt, publisher and proprietor, Osage Mission.

Chanute Weekly Times, Republican; Cyrus T. Nixon, editor and publisher, Chanute.

The Chanute Blade, Democratic; C. E. Allison and J. P. Bell, editors and publishers, Chanute.

Chanute Vidette, Republican; G. M. Dewey, publisher and proprietor, Chanute.

Republican Record, Republican; Ben. J. Smith, editor and proprietor, Erie.

The People's Vindicator, Union Labor; Wm. George and W. E. Hardy, editors and publishers, Erie.

Head Light, Republican; C. T. Ewing, publisher, Thayer.

Galesburg Enterprise, Republican; J. R. Schoonover, publisher, Galesburg.

Ness City Times, Republican; Steele L. Moorhead, editor and proprietor, Ness City.

Ness County News, Republican; James K. Barnd, editor and proprietor, Ness City.

Walnut Valley Sentinel, Democratic; D. E. McDowell and R. G. Weisell, editor, publisher and proprietor, Ness City.

Harold Record, Republican; Robert Findlay, sr., editor and proprietor, Harold.

Nonchalanta Herald, neutral; H. C. Notson, editor and publisher, Nonchalanta.

The Norton Courier, Republican; F. M. Duvall, manager, Norton.

The Champion, Republican; J. W. Conway, editor and proprietor, Norton.

Weekly New Era and Norton Democrat, Democratic; W. H. Hiles, editor, Norton.

Lenora Record, Democratic; Charles T. Bogert, editor, publisher and proprietor, Lenora.

The Edmond Times, Republican; Mark J. Kelley, editor, Times Printing Company, publishers, Edmond.

The Almena Star, Republican; Marion J. Munday, publisher, Almena.

The Almena Plaindealer, Republican; A. J. McKinney, editor and publisher, Almena.

The Osage County Chronicle, Republican; J. N. McDonald, editor, publisher and proprietor, Burlingame.

The Burlingame Democrat, Democratic; W. D. Jacobs and J. L. Cooper, editors and proprietors, E. J. Dill, W. D. Jacobs and J. L. Cooper, publishers, Burlingame.

The Burlingame News, (amateur monthly;) Dick Taylor, editor, publisher and proprietor, Burlingame.

The Beech Brook Breeze, (amateur monthly;) Nettie B. Woodzelle, editress, W. H. Mundy, publisher, Burlingame.

The Burlingame Echo, (amateur monthly;) W. H. Mundy, editor, proprietor and publisher, Miss Lulu Harris, associate editor, Burlingame.

The Oage City Free Press, Republican; J. V. Admire, editor, D. J. Roberts, superintendent, Free Press Company, publishers, Osage City.

Kansas People, independent; Miles W. Blain and Elijah Mills, editors and publishers, Osage City.

The Lyndon Journal, Republican; W. A. Madaris, editor, publisher and proprietor, Lyndon.

Osage County Graphic, Republican; R. A. Miller, editor, Graphic Publishing Company, publishers, Lyndon.

The Carbondalian, Republican; Reuben F. Playford, editor, publisher and proprietor, Carbondale.

The Osage County Republican, Republican; W. F. Cochran and M. B. Evans, editors and publishers, Quenemo.

The Melvern Record, Republican; W. S. Rilea, editor and publisher, Melvern.

Osage County Times, Union Labor; James Cox, editor and proprietor, Scranton.

OSBORNE COUNTY.

Osborne County Farmer, Republican; C. W. Crampton and C. W. Landis, editors, publishers and proprietors, C. W. Crampton, business manager, Osborne.

Osborne County News, Democratic; W. D. Gerard & Co., editors and publishers, Osborne.

Osborne County Journal, Republican; F. H. Barnhart and John G. Eckman, proprietors, Osborne.

Downs Times, Republican; E. D. and Q. R. Craft, publishers, Downs.

The Downs Chief, Democratic; W. H. Whitmore, editor and proprietor, Downs.

Western Empire, Republican; Israel Moore and D. E. Goddard, publishers, Alton.

Portis Patriot, Republican; M. H. Hoyt, publisher and proprietor, Portis.

The Downs Globe, Republican; Benj. T. Baker, editor, Benj. T. Baker and James Bower, proprietors, Downs.

OTTAWA COUNTY.

The Minneapolis Messenger, Republican; A. P. Riddle and C. M. Dunn, editors and publishers, A. P. Riddle, proprietor, Minneapolis.

Solomon Valley Democrat, Democratic; Park S. Warren, managing editor, Minneapolis.

Minneapolis Commercial, Republican; H. R. Campbell, editor, H. R. and E. K. Campbell, publishers, Minneapolis.

Kansas Workman, (monthly,) A. O. U. W.; A. P. Riddle, editor and proprietor, Minneapolis.

The Sprig of Myrtle, (monthly,) Knights of Pythias; A. P. Riddle, editor and proprietor, Minneapolis.

The School Room Journal, (monthly,) educational; A. P. Warrington, editor, Minneapolis.

Delphos Republican, Republican; J. M. Waterman, editor and proprietor, Delphos.

Bennington Star, Union Labor; D. B. Loudon, editor and proprietor, D. K. Kirkland, local editor, Bennington.

The Tescott Herald, Republican; Guy A. Adams, editor and proprietor, Tescott.

Larned Weekly Chronoscope, Republican; The Larned Printing Company, publisher, Fred S. Hatch, managing editor, Larned.

The Larned Eagle-Optic, Democratic; Optic Steam Printing Company, publishers, Thomas E. Leftwich, managing editor, A. B. Leftwich, business manager, Larned.

The Labor News, Union Labor; W. M. Goodner, editor and business manager, Larned.

Larned Democrat, Democratic; B. B. Crawford, editor and proprietor, Larned.

The Burdett Bugle, Democratic; J. C. Browne, publisher, Burdett.

The Kirwin Chief, Republican; R. J. Palmer, and C. E. Anderson, publishers, R. J. Palmer, manager, Kirwin.

Phillipsburg Herald, Republican; E. F. Korns and R. A. Dague, publishers and proprietors, Phillipsburg.

Phillipsburg Democrat, Democratic; W. D. Covington, proprietor, Phillipsburg.

The Phillipsburg Dispatch, Republican; J. M. McNay, editor, J. M. McNay & Co., publishers, Phillipsburg.

Phillips County Freeman, anti-monopoly; H. N. Boyd, editor, publisher and proprietor, Logan.

The Logan Republican, Republican; Lew and Chas. Cunningham, publishers, Logan.

Long Island Leader, Republican; J. N. Curl, editor, publisher and proprietor, Long Island.

Phillips County Inter Ocean, Republican; E. M. Weed, editor, and proprietor, Long Island.

The Louisville Indicator, Republican; E. D. Anderson, editor and publisher, Louisville.

Kansas Agriculturist, Republican; Ernest A. Weller, editor, publisher and proprietor, Wamego.

Daily Wamegan, Republican; Ernest A. Weller, editor and proprietor, Wamego.

The Kansas Reporter, Republican; W. P. Campbell, editor and publisher, Wamego.

St. Marys Star, Democratic; James Graham, editor; C. W. and L. J. Graham, associate editors and publishers, St. Marys.

St. Marys Gazette, Republican; J. S. Carpenter, editor; J. S. Carpenter and A. C. Sherman, publishers, St. Marys.

The Westmoreland Recorder, Republican; J. W. Shiner, editor and publisher, Westmoreland.

The Onaga Democrat, Democratic; A. W. Chabin, editor and publisher, Onaga.

The Olsburg Newsletter, Republican; Lewis Havermale, editor, publisher and proprietor, Olsburg.

The Pratt County Republican, Republican; F. A. Lanstrum and C. T. Warren, editors and proprietors, Pratt.

Pratt County Times, Republican; James Kelly, editor; James Kelly and J. W. Naron, publishers, Pratt Center.

Pratt County Register, Democratic; Dilday & Van Senden, editors, publishers and proprietors, Pratt Center.

Cullison Tomahawk, Democratic; J. S. M'Anarney, editor; Cullison Publishing Company, publishers; C. Y. Martin, manager, Cullison.

Preston Enterprise, independent; Charles T. Allen, editor and publisher, Preston.

RAWLINS COUNTY.

The Republican Citizen, Republican; James D. Greason, editor and publisher, Atwood.

The Atwood Journal, Democratic; R. S. Hendricks, editor and proprietor, Atwood.

The Rawlins County Democrat, Democratic; L. A. Hannigan, editor, Blakeman.

The Blakeman Register, Republican; F. F. Coolidge, editor and proprietor, Blakeman.

The Ludell Gazette, Republican; R. H. Chase, editor, Ludell.

The McDonald Times, Republican; Fred H. Eno, editor, J. R. Sedgwick, publisher, McDonald.

The Herndon Courant, Republican; E. H. Rathbone, publisher, Herndon.

RENO COUNTY.

Hutchinson News, (daily and weekly,) Republican; Ralph M. Easley, president and managing editor, Hutchinson News Company, publishers, Hutchinson.

. Weekly Interior Herald, Republican; Fletcher Meridith, editor and proprietor, Hutchinson.

The Weekly Democrat, Democratic; M. J. Keys, editor and publisher, Hutchinson.

The Saturday Review, Democratic; Y. A. Hartman, editor, South Hutchinson.

The Nickerson Argosy, Republican; W. F. Hendry and J. E. Humphrey, editors and publishers, Nickerson.

The Nickerson Register, Republican; Harry W. Brown and Harry Brightman, editors and publishers, Nickerson.

The Arlington Enterprise, Republican, John L. Sponsler, editor, publisher and proprietor, Arlington.

Sylvia Telephone, Republican; F. D. Roberts & Co., proprietors, Sylvia.

The Haven Dispatch, Republican; George S. Astle and G. W. Duke, editors and proprietors, Haven.

The Turon Rustler, Republican; M. A. Smedley and R. S. Smedley, editors and publishers, Turon.

The Journal, Republican; R. H. Chittenden, editor, H. T. Chittenden, jr., publisher, South Hutchinson.

The Weekly Press, Republican; F. G. Guyer, editor and proprietor, Olcott.

The Torch Light, Prohibition; L. D. Abbott, editor and proprietor, Plevna.

REPUBLIC COUNTY.

The Belleville Telescope, Republican; E. E. Brainerd, editor, publisher and proprietor, Belleville.

The Belleville Democrat, Democratic; C. M. McLaury, editor, J. and C. M. McLaury, publishers and proprietors, Belleville.

Scandia Journal, Republican; I. C. Ware, editor, Ware & Co., publishers, Scandia.

The Scandia Independent, independent; H. J. Newton, publisher and proprietor, Scandia.

Republic City News, Republican; Gomer T. Davies, editor, publisher and proprietor, Republic City.

The Cuba Union, Republican; T. A. Cordry, editor, publisher and proprietor, Cuba.

The Cuba Daylight, Republican; Joseph Shimek, editor, publisher and proprietor, Cuba.

RICE COUNTY.

Sterling Gazette, Republican; E. B. Cowgill, editor and publisher, A. L. McMillan, associate editor, Sterling.

The Sterling Bulletin, Republican; J. E. Junken and S. H. Steele, publishers, W. J. Benn, city editor, Sterling.

Sterling Weekly Champion, Republican; Thos. L. Powers, editor, publisher and proprietor, Sterling.

The Lyons Republican, Republican; Clark Conkling, publisher, Lyons.

The Lyons Prohibitionist, Prohibition; D. P. Hodgdon, editor and proprietor, Lyons.

The Lyons Tribune, Democratic; Soldiers' Tribune Publishing Company, publishers, Lyons.

The Chase Record, independent; D. W. Stone, editor and proprietor, Chase.

The Little River Monitor, Republican; W. G. Greenbank, editor and business manager, E. B. Pulliam, publisher, Little River.

Geneseo Herald, Republican; W. R. White and M. W. Smith, editors, Geneseo.

Cain City Razzooper, Democratic; Will J. McHugh, editor and publisher, B. Grant Jefferis, associate editor, Cain City.

Frederick Independent, Republican; Ira H. Clark, editor and proprietor, Frederick.

RILEY COUNTY.

The Nationalist, Republican; Rev. R. D. Parker, Geo. F. Thompson, and L. B. Parker, editors, publishers and proprietors, Manhattan.

The Industrialist, educational and agricultural; edited by the Faculty of the State Agricultural College, Geo. T. Fairchild, president, Manhattan.

The Manhattan Republic, (daily and weekly,) Republican; G. A. Atwood, editor and publisher, Manhattan.

The Mercury, Democratic; J. J. Davis, editor and proprietor, Manhattan.

The Kansas Telephone, (monthly,) religious; Rev. R. D. Parker, editor and publisher, Manhattan.

Journal of Mycology, (monthly,) scientific; Prof. W. A. Kellerman, editor and publisher, Manhattan.

The Argus, (quarterly,) religious; Manhattan Y. M. C. A., publishers, Manhattan.

The Saturday Signal, Union Labor; Jas. W. and Emmett McDonald, publishers, Manhattan.

Randolph Enterprise, Republican; J. H. Colt. editor and proprietor, Randolph.

Leonardville Monitor, Republican; P. S. Loofbourrow, editor, Leonardville.

The Riley Times, Union Labor; Dudley Atkins, editor and publisher, Riley.

ROOKS COUNTY.

The Western News, Republican; E. and O. Owen, editors and proprietors, Stockton.

Rooks County Record, Republican; W. L. Chambers, editor, publisher and proprietor, Stockton.

Rooks County Democrat, Democratic; H. T. Miller, editor and publisher, Stockton.

Stockton Eagle, Republican; R. D. Graham and Mart. H. Hoyt, editors, Stockton.

Stockton Academician, educational, (monthly;) edited by the Faculty, I. F. Mather, principal, Stockton.

The Plainville Times, Republican; W. E. Powers, editor and proprietor, Plainville.

Labor Tablet, Union Labor; James and William Butler, editors and publishers, Plainville.

Woodston Register, independent; D. E. Cole, editor, M. L. McIntyre & Co., publishers, Woodston.

Cresson Dispatch, neutral; Frank M. Boyd, proprietor, Cresson.

RUSH COUNTY.

Rush Centre Gazette, Republican; R. A. Russell, editor and publisher, R. A. and H. A. Russell, proprietors, Rush Centre.

Rush County News, Republican; Tom J. Stumbaugh, editor and manager, News Publishing Company, publishers, Rush Centre.

La Crosse Chieftain, Republican; John E. Frazer, editor, John E. Frazer and F. H. Davis, proprietors, La Crosse.

The La Crosse Democrat, Democratic; J. M. Tracy, editor and publisher, La Crosse.

McCracken Enterprise, Republican; W. B. Newton, editor and publisher, McCracken.

RUSSELL COUNTY.

The Russell Record, Republican; James Jones, editor and publisher, W. S. Keller, foreman, Russell.

Russell Journal, Democratic; E. J. Collins, editor, Collins and Merrill, proprietors, Russell.

Bunker Hill Gazette, Republican; J. C. Gault and A. J. Ulsh, editors, J. C. Gault, publisher, Bunker Hill.

The Dorrance Nugget, Republican; Samuel H. Haffa, editor and proprietor, Dorrance.

Luray Headlight, independent; J. M. McAfee, editor and publisher, Luray.

The Lucas Advance, Republican; C. E. Hughey, editor, publisher and proprietor, Lucas.

Waldo Enterprise, independent; F. M. Case, editor and publisher, Waldo.

SALINE COUNTY.

Saline County Journal, Republican; M. D. Sampson, editor, publisher and proprietor, Salina.

Salina Herald, Democratic; J. M. Davis, publisher, Salina.

The Salina Republican, (daily and weekly,) Republican; J. Leeford Brady, editor, publisher and proprietor, Salina.

The Rising Sun, Prohibition; D. M. Gillespie, editor and publisher, Salina.

Normal Register, (quarterly,) educational; L. O. Thoroman, managing editor, Salina.

The Western Odd Fellow, (semi-monthly,) secret society; D. J. Richey, publisher, Salina.

Vade Mecum, (monthly,) in the interests of agents and advertisers; F. F. Oakley, publishers, Salina.

Brookville Transcript, Republican; Frank Honeywell, editor and publisher, Brookville.

The Gypsum Valley Echo, Republican; J. Wayne Amos, editor and publisher, Gypsum City.

The Assaria Argus, Republican; Dursley Sargent, publisher and proprietor, Assaria.

Scott County News, Republican; Harvey Fleming and N. D. Adams, editors and publishers, Scott City.

The Sentinel-Herald, Democratic; D. F. Hall, editor, J. M. Beadles, managing editor, Scott City.

The Pence Phonograph, Democratic; R. W. Black, editor and proprietor, Pence.

Wichita Eagle, (daily and weekly,) Republican; Marshall M. Murdock, editor, M. M. and R. P. Murdock, publishers and proprietors, Wichita.

The News-Beacon, (daily,) and The Wichita Beacon, (weekly,) Democratic; John S. Richardson, editor, Frederick N. Peck, publisher, Wichita.

Wichita New Republic, Republican; J. S. Jennings, editor and proprietor, Wichita.

The Arrow, neutral; Lon Hoding, publisher, Wichita.

Wichita Herold, (German,) Democratic; John Hoenscheidt, editor, Wichita.

Kansas Staats-Anzeiger, (German,) Democratic; John Hoenscheidt, editor, Wichita.

The Wichita Independent, neutral; H. W. Sawyer, editor and manager, Wichita.

The Mirror, society; R. E. Ryan and E. L. Mackenzie, editors and publishers, Wichita.

The Wichita Journal, (daily and weekly,) Democratic; John Hoenscheidt, managing editor, Leo. L. Redding and Samuel A. Harburg, associate editors, Journal Publishing Company, publishers, Wichita.

Monthly Echoes, Y. M. C. A.; A. Baird, general secretary, Wichita.

University Review, (quarterly,) educational; Rev. Warren B. Hendryx, president and business manager, Wichita.

The Wichita Weekly Express, Union Labor; Robert E. Neff, editor, G. T. Demaree, managing editor, Enterprise Publishing Company, publishers, Wichita.

Wichita Commercial Bulletin, neutral; J. Hulaniski, editor, C. L. Hammack, business manager, Hulaniski & Hammack, publishers, Wichita.

The Wichita Commercial, neutral; Ralph Field, editor and publisher, Whit C. Mitchell, associate editor, Wichita.

Wichita Diocesan News, religious; Rev. John Begley, editor, Wichita.

The Valley Center News, Republican; Dwight Beach, editor, Dewing & Beach, proprietors, Valley Center.

The Weekly Mount Hope Mentor, Republican; E. V. Welch, publisher and proprietor, Mount Hope.

The Colwich Courier, independent; Willis B. Powell, editor, publisher and proprietor, Colwich.

The Clearwater Sun, Republican; F. B. Brown, editor and publisher, Clearwater.

The Cheney Blade, Republican; Warren Foster, editor and proprietor, Cheney.

The Liberal Leader, Democratic; Lambert Willstaedt, editor and publisher, Liberal.

Southwest Chronicle, Republican; Griff B. Newcom, editor and manager, Chronicle Printing Co., publishers, Liberal.

The Arkalon News, Republican; A. K. Stoufer, editor and proprietor, Arkalon.

Springfield Transcript, Democratic; L. P. Kemper, editor and proprietor, Springfield.

The Capital-Commonwealth, (daily and weekly,) Republican; J. K. Hudson, editor, publisher and proprietor, Topeka.

State Journal, (daily and weekly,) Republican; Frank P. MacLennan, editor and publisher, Topeka.

The Kansas Democrat, (daily,) Democratic; The Kansas Democrat Publishing Co., C. K. Holliday, jr., president, W. P. Tomlinson, vice-president, Harry Garvey, secretary, treasurer, manager and publisher, J. L. Thornton, business manager, Topeka.

Kansas Farmer, agricultural; Kansas Farmer Company, publishers, Samuel J. Crawford, president, J. B. McAfee, vice-president, H. A. Heath, business manager, W. A. Peffer, managing editor, Topeka.

Kansas Telegraph, (German,) Democratic; H. Von Langen, editor and publisher, Topeka.

The Kansas Churchman, (monthly,) religious; Rt. Rev. Bishop Vail, editor, Topeka.

The Western Baptist, religious; L. H. Holt and C. S. Sheffield, editors, publishers and proprietors, Topeka.

Saturday Evening Lance, literary; Harry W. Frost, editor and publisher, Topeka.

The Kansas Newspaper Union; F. P. Baker, editor, N. R. Baker, manager, Topeka.

Western School Journal, (monthly,) educational; John MacDonald, editor, publisher and proprietor, Topeka.

The Weekly Knight and Soldier, G. A. R.; M. O. Frost, editor and publisher, Topeka.

The American Citizen, (colored,) Republican; J. Hume Childers, editor, A. Morton, manager, J. L. Sims, assistant manager, Morton & Co., publishers, Topeka.

The Christian Citizen, general newspaper; Richard Wake, editor, Riley & Wake Printing Company, publishers, A. T. Riley, business manager, Topeka.

The Sunday Ledger, literary; J. P. Limeburner, editor, George W. Reed, business manager, The Ledger Company, publishers, Topeka.

The Light, (monthly,) Masonic; Charles Spalding, editor and publisher, Topeka.

Our Messenger, (monthly,) W. C. T. U.; Olive P. Bray, editor, Topeka.

The Welcome, (monthly,) musical; E. B. Guild, editor and publisher, Topeka.

The Washburn Argo, (monthly,) literary; A. W. Brewster, editor-in-chief, Samuel W. Naylor, business manager, Topeka.

The Washburn Reporter, collegiate; Robert Stone, editor-in-chief, C. P. Donnell, D. H. Platt, H. M. Olson and J. L. Poston, associate-editors, L. S. Dolman, business manager, Topeka.

The Night Hawk; Washburn College, occasional, Topeka.

Kansas United Presbyterian, (monthly,) religious; Rev. M. F. McKirahan, publisher, R. M. McGaw, local editor, W. J. Neely and J. E. Kirkpatrick, business managers, Topeka.

The Leader, Prohibition; Lee H. Dowling, editor, Topeka.

Topeka Argus, Republican-Prohibition, equal suffrage, human rights and Western immigration; Mrs. M. E. DeGeer, editor-in-chief, Miss Laura Keeve, publisher, Topeka.

The Kansas Financier, (semi-monthly;) S. L. Seabrook, editor and proprietor, Topeka.

The Printer Girl, (monthly,) literary; Mary Abarr, editor and manager, Printer Girl Publishing Co., publishers. Topeka.

What Now, (monthly;) published by Railroad Department of the Y. M. C. A., R. L. Roberts, editor, Topeka.

—8

The Association Reflector, (monthly,) Y. M. C. A.; T. P. Day, editor, G. W. Garland, business manager, Topeka.

The Season Signal, (monthly,) advertising; J. M. Shepherd, publisher, Topeka.

The Budget, (monthly,) advertising; J. F. Daniels, publisher, Topeka.

The Kansas News, (monthly,) advertising; C. E. Prather, editor, Kansas News Co., publishers, Topeka.

National Passenger, (monthly,) railroad; James L. King, editor, Geo. M. Ewing, business manager, Topeka.

The Topeka Mail, Republican; Frank A., Albert C. and George A. Root, editors and publishers, North Topeka.

The North Topeka News, (daily and weekly,) neutral; G. F. Kimball, editor, Kansas News Co., publishers, North Topeka.

The Spirit of Kansas, Prohibition and anti-monopoly; G. F. Kimball, editor and publisher, North Topeka.

The Rossville Times, neutral; G. A. Weller, editor and publisher, Rossville.

SHERIDAN COUNTY.

The Hoxie Sentinel, Republican; W. L. Humes, editor and proprietor, Hoxie.

The Hoxie Democrat, Democratic; S. P. Davidson, editor and proprietor, Hoxie.

The Selden Times, Republican; J. F. Thompson, publisher, Selden.

SHERMAN COUNTY.

Sherman County Democrat, Democratic; Frank Parks, editor, publisher and proprietor, Goodland.

Sherman County Dark Horse, Republican; J. H. Tait, editor, publisher and proprietor, Goodland.

The Goodland News, Democratic: E. F. Tennant, editor and publisher, Goodland.

Sherman County Republican, Republican; J. H. Stewart, publisher, J. J. Crofut, soliciting editor, Goodland.

State Line Register, neutral; Chas. A. Fitch, editor, J. Frank Longanecker, proprietor, Kanorado.

SMITH COUNTY.

Kansas Pioneer, (daily and weekly;) J. N. Beacom, managing editor and publisher. J. J. Hafer, local editor, Smith Centre.

The Smith County Bulletin, Republican; John Q. Royce, editor and proprietor, Smith Centre.

The Bazoo, Democratic; Jack W. Stewart, editor and proprietor, Smith Centre.

Gaylord Herald, Republican; Lew C. Headley, editor and proprietor, Gaylord.

Cedarville Globe, Republican; A. Barron, editor and proprietor, Cedarville.

The Lebanon Criterion, Republican; J. A. Wright, editor and publisher, Lebanon.

Union Labor Trumpet and The People's Friend, Union Labor; M. L. and Katie Lockwood, publishers, Kensington.

The Kensington Mirror, Republican; O. L. Reed, editor, Kensington.

The Athol News, Union Labor; M. L. and Katie Lockwood, publishers, Athol.

STAFFORD COUNTY.

Stafford County Herald, Republican and Democratic; R. M. Blair and L. M. Steele, editors, Herald Publishing Company, proprietors, M. Benefiel, publisher.

Stafford County Republican, Republican-Prohibition; Dr. Geo. W. Akers, editor, Art. B. Akers, business manager, Akers & Son, proprietors, Stafford.

The St. John Weekly News, Republican; W. K. P. Dow, editor and business manager, The News Publishing Company, publishers, St. John.

County Capital, Democratic; John B. Hilmes, editor and publisher, St. John.

The Macksville Times, Republican; A. H. Dever, editor, Welch & Woodford, managers, John S. Welch, business manager, Macksville.

The Cassoday Mirage, Democratic; Hosea Hammitt, editor and publisher, Cassoday.

STANTON COUNTY.

Johnson City Journal, Republican; John A. Webster and N. R. Spencer, editors, Johnson City.

The Border Rover, Democratic; Lou Cravens, editor and publisher, T. B. Pyles, proprietor, Borders.

Stanton Telegram, Republican; E. W. Cross, editor and proprietor, Goguae.

STEVENS COUNTY.

The Hugo Weekly Herald, Democratic; Geo. W. McClintick, editor and proprietor, Hugoton.

Woodsdale Democrat, Democratic; S. N. Wood & M. L. Wood, editors, Woodsdale Publishing Company, publishers, D. W. Walker, manager, Woodsdale.

The Hermes, Republican; Chas. M. Davis, editor and publisher, Hugoton.

Moscow Review, Democratic; Lee A. Walton, editor, James Moody, publisher, T. B. Pyles, proprietor, Moscow.

The Voorhees Vindicator, Democratic; O. R. Wright, editor, T. B. Pyles, proprietor, Voorhees.

SUMNER COUNTY.

The Sumner County Press, Republican; Jacob Stotler, editor and manager, Will R. Stotler, assistant editor, Press Printing Company, publishers, Wellington.

Sumner County Standard, (daily and weekly,) Democratic; Luke Herring, editor and publisher, Wellington.

The Wellington Monitor, Republican; J. G. Campbell and Chas. Hood, editors and publishers, Wellington.

The Christian Reminder, (monthly,) religious; Rev. J. G. M. Hursh, editor and publisher, Wellington.

Stars and Stripes for Young America, (bi-monthly,) amateur; Fred F. Heath, Milwaukee, Wis., and John T. Nixon, editors, Wellington.

The Mocking Bird, Republican; A. A. Richards. publisher, Oxford.

The Caldwell Journal, Democratic; David Leahy, editor, R. B. Swarthout, publisher, Caldwell.

The Caldwell News, Republican; Robert T. Simons, editor and publisher, Caldwell.

The Industrial Age, Union Labor; S. C. Whitwam, editor, Wellington.

Belle Plaine News, independent; Emera E. Wilson, editor, Wilson, Turley & Co., proprietors, Belle Plaine.

Mulvane Record, independent; G. L. Reed, editor, publisher and proprietor, Mulvane.

Geuda Springs Herald, Republican; M. W. Reynolds, editor and proprietor, Geuda Springs.

The Argonia Clipper, independent; S. W. Duncan, editor and proprietor, Argonia.

Conway Springs Star, Republican; Geo. W. Cain and P. W. Bast, publishers, Conway Springs.

The South Haven New Era, neutral; Boone Denton, editor and proprietor, South Haven.

THOMAS COUNTY.

Thomas County Cat, Republican; Joseph A. Gill, editor, Thomas County Publishing Company, proprietors, Colby.

The Democrat, Democratic; Howard Carpenter, editor and proprietor, Colby.

The Colby Tribune, Republican; I. A. Kelley, editor and proprietor, Colby.

The Brewster Gazette, Republican; G. F. Roberts, editor, Brewster.

TREGO COUNTY.

Western Kansas World, Republican; W. S. Tilton, editor, publisher and proprietor, Wa-Keeney.

Wa-Keeney Tribune, Democratic; C. L. Cain, publisher and proprietor, Wa-Keeney.

Trego County Republican, Republican; Geo. J. Shepard, editor and publisher, Wa-Keeney.

WABAUNSEE COUNTY.

The Wabaunsee County News, Republican; I. D. Gardiner, editor, publisher and proprietor, Alma.

The Alma Enterprise, Republican; V. C. Welch and Frank I. Sage, editors, publishers and proprietors, Alma.

The Eskridge Star, Republican; E. H. Perry, editor, publisher and proprietor, Eskridge.

The Alta Vista Register, Republican; S. A. Stauffer, editor, Register Co., publishers, Alta Vista.

The Paxico Courier, Republican; L. E. Hoffman, editor, Paxico.

WALLACE COUNTY.

Wallace County Register, Republican, S. L. Wilson, editor; S. L. Wilson & Co., publishers, Wallace.

Wallace Weekly Herald, Democratic; A. S. Booton, editor, A. S. Booton and J. L. Bornt, publishers, Wallace.

The Western Times, Republican; Mrs. Kate B. Russell, editor, publisher and proprietor, Sharon Springs.

Sharon Springs Leader, Republican; C. N. Banks, editor, publisher and proprietor, Tune Bentley, local editor and manager, Sharon Springs.

The Weskansan, independent; Mark Scott, editor, Weskan Publishing Company, publishers, Weskan.

WASHINGTON COUNTY.

Washington Republican, Republican; H. C. Robinson and L. J. Sprengle, editors, publishers and proprietors, Washington.

The Washington Register, Republican; J. B. Besack & Son (W. H.), editors, Washington.

The Washington Post, Democratic; Samuel Clarke, editor, Washington.

The Hanover Democrat, Democratic; J. M. Hood, editor, J. M. Hood and —— Munger, publishers, Hanover.

The Clifton Review, Republican; J. A. Branson, editor and proprietor, Clifton.

The Local News, Republican; L. A. Palmer, editor, publisher and proprietor, Clifton.

Greenleaf Journal, Republican; J. W. Bliss, editor, Frank D. Bliss, publisher and proprietor, Greenleaf.

The Greenleaf Herald, independent; Frederick Amelung, editor and proprietor, Greenleaf.

Haddam Weekly Clipper, Republican; J. B. Campbell, editor, publisher and proprietor, Haddam.

The Haddam Investigator, neutral; Ray E. Chase, editor, T. C. Baldwin, manager, Haddam.

The Barnes Enterprise, Republican; M. H. Williams and M. O. Reitzel editors, Enterprise Publishing Company, publishers, Barnes.

Palmer Pioneer, Republican; F. T. Cook, editor, Palmer.

Hollenberg Record, Republican; Charles E. Williamson, editor, Hollenberg.

WICHITA COUNTY.

Wichita Standard, Republican; C. S. Triplett, editor, publisher and proprietor, Leoti.

The Leoti Transcript, Democratic; W. R. Gibbs, editor and proprietor, Leoti.

The Western Farmer, neutral; D. T. Armstrong, editor and proprietor, Leoti.

WILSON COUNTY.

Wilson County Citizen, Republican; John S. Gilmore, editor, publisher and proprietor, Fredonia.

Fredonia Democrat, Democratic; H. L. Crittenden, editor, publisher and proprietor, Fredonia.

Neodesha Register, Republican; J. K. Morgan, editor, publisher and proprietor, Neodesha.

Neodesha Independent, independent; Harry A. Armstrong, editor and publisher, Neodesha.

Buffalo Express, Union Labor; W. H. Jones, editor and publisher, Buffalo.

Altoona Journal, independent; M. A. Rhea, editor and publisher, Altoona.

WOODSON COUNTY.

The Post, Republican; J. N. Stout, editor, publisher and proprietor, Neosho Falls.

The News, Republican; I. M. Jewitt and R. H. Trueblood, publishers and proprietors, Yates Center.

Woodson Democrat, Democratic; R. R. Wells, editor and proprietor, Yates Center.

The Toronto Republican, Republican; N. B. Buck and C. A. Buck, publishers and proprietors, Toronto.

WYANDOTTE COUNTY.

The Wyandotte Herald, Democratic; V. J. Lane & Co., editors, publishers and proprietors, Kansas City.

The Kansas City Gazette, (daily and weekly,) Republican; the Gazette Company, publishers, Geo. W. Martin, president and editor, J. J. Maxwell, city editor and treasurer, J. W. Wert, secretary, Kansas City.

Kansas Pioneer, Republican; Louis Weil, editor and publisher, Kansas City.

The Agassiz Companion, (monthly,) scientific; Will H. Plank, editor and publisher, Kansas City.

Rosedale Record, Democratic; F. M. B. Norman, editor and proprietor, Rosedale Publishing Company, publishers, Rosedale.

The Armourdale Advocate, (daily and weekly,) Republican; John E. Rastall, editor and proprietor, F. O. Rodell, local editor, Armourdale post office, Kansas City.

Cromwell's Kansas Mirror, Republican; Mark Cromwell, editor and proprietor, Armourdale post office, Kansas City.

Argentine Republic, neutral; Joseph T. Landrey, editor and proprietor, Argentine.

NEWSPAPERS AND PERIODICALS OF OTHER STATES AND COUNTRIES NOW RECEIVED.

ARIZONA.

Arizona Weekly Journal-Miner, Republican; Arizona Publishing Company, publishers, J. C. Martin, editor and manager, Prescott.

CALIFORNIA.

The Weekly Post; Post Company, publishers, San Francisco.

Pacific Rural Press; Dewey & Co., publishers, A. T. Dewey and W. B. Ewer, editors, San Francisco.

The Overland Monthly; Overland Monthly Company, publishers, San Francisco.

California Patron and Agriculturist; A. T. Dewey, manager, San Francisco.

The Signs of The Times; International Missionary Society, publishers, E. J. Waggoner and Alonzo T. Jones, editors, Oakland.

Pacific Health Journal and Temperance Advocate, (monthly;) Pacific Press Company, publishers, J. N. Loughborough, J. E. Caldwell, M. D., and C. P. Bollman, editors, Oakland.

The American Sentinel, (monthly;) Pacific Press Publishing Company, publishers, E. J. Waggoner and Alonzo T. Jones, editors, Oakland.

COLORADO.

Weekly Rocky Mountain News; News Company, publishers, John Arkins, president and manager, Denver.

The Denver Republican, (daily;) Republican Publishing Company, publishers, Denver.

Queen Bee, woman suffrage; Mrs. C. M. Churchill, publisher and proprietor, Denver.

Colorado School Journal, (monthly;) Aaron Gove, editor, J. D. Dillenback, publisher, Denver.

Hinsdale Phonograph; Walter E. Mendenhall, editor, W. E. Mendenhall and D. C. Loudon, proprietors, Lake City.

Gunnison Review-Press, (tri-weekly,) Republican; H. C. Olney, manager, Review-Press Publishing Company, publishers, Gunnison.

White Pine Cone, Republican; Geo. S. Irwin, editor, Gunnison.

The Salida Mail, (semi-weekly;) C. F. Brown, editor, J. F. Erdlen, publisher, Erdlen & Brown, proprietors, Salida.

Law and Gospel, (monthly;) W. H. Bauser, publisher, Springfield.

CONNECTICUT.

Quarterly Journal of Inebriety; T. D. Crothers, M. D., editor, published by the American Association for the Cure of Inebriates, Hartford.

Travelers' Record, (monthly;) Travelers' Insurance Company, publishers, Hartford.

DISTRICT OF COLUMBIA.

The Official Gazette of the United States Patent Office, (weekly,) Washington.

United States Official Postal Guide; The Brodix Publishing Co., Washington.

Public Opinion; Public Opinion Co., publishers, Washington, A. H. Lewis, resident manager, 140 Nassau street, New York.

The National Tribune; Geo. E. Lemon, editor, Washington.

United States Government Publications, (monthly catalogue;) J. H. Hickcox, publisher, Washington.

DAKOTA.

Bismarck Weekly Tribune, Republican; M. H. Jewell, publisher, Bismarck.

FLORIDA.

The Florida Weekly Dispatch; Chas. W. Da Costa, publisher, A. K. Hammond, manager, Jacksonville.

Southern Industrial Railroad Record; conducted by A. L. Harris, Record Publishing Co., publishers, Atlanta.

The Atlanta Constitution. Atlanta.

Spelman Messenger, (monthly;) L. A. Upton and M. J. Packard, editors, E. O. Werden, publisher, Atlanta.

Semi-Weekly Inter-Ocean; Inter-Ocean Publishing Company, Chicago.

Industrial World and Iron Worker; F. W. Palmer, editor, Melvin M. Cohen, assistant manager, Chicago.

The Standard, (religious;) Justin A. Smith, D. D., editor, Edward Goodman, E. R. and J. S. Dickerson, proprietors, Chicago.

The Weekly Drovers' Journal; H. L. Goodall & Co., publishers, Chicago.

The Svenska Amerikanaren; Swedish American Printing Co., publishers, Bonggren and Waerner, editors, A. E. G. Wingard, business and advertising manager, Chicago.

The American Antiquarian, and Oriental Journal, (bi-monthly;) Rev. Stephen D. Peet, editor and publisher, Mendon and Chicago.

The Union Signal, organ of W. N. T. U.; Mary Allen West, editor, Julia Ames, associate editor, Woman's Temperance Publication Association, publishers, Geo. C. Hall, business manager, Chicago.

The Open Court; Dr. Paul Carus, editor, Open Court Publishing Company, publishers, Chicago.

The Comrade, (monthly;) H. E. Gerry, managing editor, Chicago.

The Dial, (monthly;) A. C. McClurg & Co., publishers, Chicago.

Watchman, (semi-monthly,) Y. M. C. A.; S. A. Taggart, editor, W. W. Vanarsdale, publisher, Chicago.

The Chicago Express, Union Labor; D. P. Hubbard, editor and manager, Express Printing Co., publishers, Chicago.

The Humane Journal, (monthly;) Albert W. Landon, publisher, Chicago.

Pravda, mission work; A. E. Adams, publisher, Chicago.

The Newspaper Union, (monthly;) J. F. Cramer, president, C. E. Strong, manager, Chicago.

The Kindergarten, (monthly;) Cora L. Stockham and Emily A. Kellogg, editors, Alice B. Stockham & Co., publishers, Chicago.

The Western Trail; published in the interest of the Rock Island Railroad, Chicago.

Liberty Library; J. M. Foley, publisher, Chicago.

The Odd Fellows' Herald; G. M. Adams, editor and manager, M. T. Scott, publisher, Bloomington.

Western Plowman; J. W. Warr, editor, L. B. Kuhn, business manager, Warr & Kuhn, proprietors, Moline.

The National Educator; J. Bonham, editor and publisher, Rev. Francis Springer, associate editor, Springfield.

The Cherokee Advocate; W. P. Boudinot, editor, J. L. Springston, translator, Tahlequah.

Indian Chieftain; John L. Adair, editor, M. E. Milford, manager, Chieftain Publishing Co., publishers, Vinita.

The Indiana State Journal; Journal Newspaper Co., publishers, Indianapolis.

The Millstone and the Corn Miller, (monthly;) the D. H. Ranck Publishing Co.,

(D. H. Ranck, president, A. K. Hallowell, vice-president, Louis H. Gibson, secretary,) publishers, Indianapolis.

Indiana Student, (semi-monthly;) Robertson & Dresslar, editors, Bloomington.

Mennonitische Rundschau, Mennonite Publishing Co., publishers, Elkhart.

IOWA.

The Iowa Historical Record, (quarterly;) published by the State Historical Society, M. W. Davis, secretary, Iowa City.

LOUISIANA.

Southwestern Christian Advocate; A. E. P. Albert, editor, published by the Methodist Book Concern, New Orleans.

MARYLAND.

Johns Hopkins University Circulars, (monthly;) printed by John Murphy & Co., Baltimore.

The American Journal of Psychology, (quarterly;) G. Stanley Hall, editor, E. C. Sanford, publisher, Baltimore.

Jottings, (monthly,) insurance; Jottings Co., proprietors, Baltimore.

MASSACHUSETTS.

New England Historical and Genealogical Register, (quarterly;) John Ward Dean, editor, N. E. Historic Genealogical Society, publishers, Boston.

The Woman's Journal; Lucy Stone, H. B. Blackwell and Alice Stone Blackwell, editors, Boston.

The Unitarian Review and Religious Magazine, (monthly;) Jos. Henry Allen, editor, Boston.

The Youth's Companion; Perry Mason & Co., publishers, Boston.

Popular Science News, (monthly;) Austin P. Nichols, editor, W. J. Rolfe, associate editor, Seth C. Bassett, manager, Boston.

Harvard University Bulletin; Justin Winsor, editor, Cambridge.

Library Notes, (quarterly;) Melvil Dewey, editor, Library Bureau, publishers, Boston.

Estes and Lauriat's Monthly Book Bulletin, Boston.

Saturday Evening Gazette; Henry G. Parker, editor and publisher, Boston.

Journal of American Folk-Lore, (quarterly;) Franz Boas, T. Frederick Crane, J. Owen Dorsey, editors, W. W. Newell, general editor, Boston.

The Writer, (monthly;) W. H. Hills, editor and publisher, Boston.

The New-Jerusalem Magazine, (monthly,) religious; Massachusetts New-Church Union, publishers, Boston.

American Teacher, (monthly,) educational; A. E. Winship and W. E. Sheldon, editors, New England Publishing Company, publishers, Boston.

Spelling, (quarterly,) organ of the Spelling Reform Association; Melvil Dewey, editor, Boston.

Martha's Vineyard Herald, Chas. Strahan, publisher, Cottage Hill.

MICHIGAN.

The Fireside Teacher, (monthly,) home culture; G. H. Bell, publisher, Battle Creek.

Advent Review and Sabbath Herald; Uriah Smith, editor, L. A. Smith, associate editor, Seventh-Day Adventist Publishing Association, Battle Creek.

The Unitarian, (monthly;) J. T. Sunderland, publisher, Ann Arbor.

MISSOURI.

Kansas City Times, (daily;) Morrison Munford, president and manager, Charles E. Hasbrook, secretary, Times Publishing Co., publishers, Kansas City.

Kansas City Daily Journal; Journal Co., publishers, Kansas City.

The Kansas City Star, (daily,) Kansas City.

The Evening News, (daily;) Willis J. Abbott, editor, N. E. Eisenlord, business manager, Kansas City.

Kansas City Daily Traveler; Traveler Printing Co., H. B. Cooper, manager, Kansas City.

Kansas City Live-Stock Indicator; The Indicator Publishing Company, publishers, Kansas City.

The Kansas City Live-Stock Record and Farmer; J. H. Ramsey Printing Co., proprietors, Kansas City.

Lanphear's Kansas City Medical Index, (monthly;) S. Emory Lanphear, editor and publisher, Kansas City.

The Kansas City Record; A. N. Kellogg Newspaper Co., publishers, J. F. Guiwits, manager, Kansas City.

Western Newspaper Union, Kansas City.

The Mid-Continent, religious; Rev. A. A. E. Taylor, editor, Rev. William J. Lee, associate editor, Presbyterian Newspaper Co., publishers, Kansas City.

The New West, (monthly;) Warren Watson, editor, The New West Publishing Co., publishers, Kansas City.

The Herald; Herald Publishing Co., publishers, Kansas City.

Missouri and Kansas Farmer, (monthly;) Cliffe M. Brooke, editor and publisher, Kansas City.

Western Advocate, or Camp's Emigrant Guide, (monthly;) C. Rollin Camp, editor and publisher, Kansas City.

The Sun, (bi-monthly;) C. T. Fowler, publisher, Kansas City.

St. Joseph Herald, (daily and weekly;) William M. Shepherd, manager, Herald Publishing Co., publishers, St. Joseph.

St. Joseph Weekly Gazette; Gazette Publishing Co., publishers, E. E. McCammon, secretary, St. Joseph.

St. Louis Globe-Democrat, (daily;) Globe Printing Company, publishers, D. M. Houser, president, S. Ray, secretary, St. Louis.

American Journal of Education, (monthly;) J. B. Merwin, managing editor, St. Louis.

The Central Christian Advocate; Benj. St. James Fry, editor, Cranston & Stowe, publishers, St. Louis.

The Christian Evangelist; J. H. Garrison and B. W. Johnson, editors, J. J. Haley, office editor, Christian Publishing Company, publishers, St. Louis.

The Altruist, (monthly;) devoted to common property and community homes; A. Longley, editor, St. Louis.

St. Louis Herald, (monthly;) Charles A. Mantz, publisher, St. Louis.

The Church Builder and Western Evangelist; H. C. Scotford, editor and publisher, Kansas City, Mo., and Wichita, Kas.

NEBRASKA.

Western Resources; H. S. Reed, managing editor, Resources Publishing Company, publishers, Lincoln.

The Woman's Tribune; Clara Bewick Colby, editor and publisher, Beatrice.

Western Newspaper Union; Newspaper Union Publishing Company, publishers, Omaha.

Nebraska Congregational News; H. A. French, publisher, Lincoln.

Nebraska State Journal, (daily and weekly;) Lincoln.

The Journal of American Orthoëpy, (monthly;) C. W. Larisun, editor, Ringos.

Orchard and Garden; published by J. T. Lovett, Little Silver.

The Daily Citizen; Thos. Hughes, editor and proprietor, Albuquerque.

Las Vegas Daily Optic; R. A. Kistler, editor and proprietor, East Las Vegas.

Santa Fé Daily New Mexican; New Mexican Printing Company, publishers, Santa Fe.

New York Tribune, (daily,) New York.

The Daily Register; the New York law journal, New York.

The Century Illustrated Monthly Magazine; Century Company, publishers, Wm. W. Ellsworth, secretary, New York.

Harper's Weekly; Harper & Bros., New York.

Magazine of American History, (monthly;) Mrs. Martha J. Lamb, editor, New York.

Scientific American; O. D. Munn and A. E. Beach, editors and proprietors, New York.

Science; Science Company, N. D. C. Hodges, publishers, New York.

The Swiss Cross; Harlan H. Ballard, editor, N. D. C. Hodges, publisher, New York.

Electrical Review; Geo. Worthington, editor, Chas. W. Price, associate editor, New York.

The Library Journal, (monthly;) official organ of the American Library Association; C. A. Cutter and R. R. Bowker, editors, New York.

The Coöperative Index to Periodicals, (quarterly;) W. I. Fletcher, editor, New York.

The American Missionary, (monthly;) published by the American Missionary Association, Rev. W. M. Taylor, D. D., LL. D., president, New York.

The Home Missionary, (monthly;) published by the American Home Missionary Society, Alexander H. Clapp, D. D., Treasurer, New York.

The Nation, New York.

Political Science Quarterly; edited by the Faculty of Political Science of Columbia College, Ginn & Co., publishers, New York.

Appleton Literary Bulletin; D. Appleton & Co., publishers, New York.

The Irish World; Patrick Ford, editor and proprietor, New York.

New York Weekly Witness; John Dougall & Co., publishers, New York.

The Voice; Funk & Wagnalls, publishers, New York.

The Decorator and Furnisher, (monthly;) T. A. Kennett, editor, W. P. Wheeler, business manager, The Art Trades Publishing Company, publishers, New York.

Student's Journal; Andrew J. Graham, editor and proprietor, New York.

Sabbath Reading; John Dougall & Co., publishers, New York.

The Phonographic World, (monthly;) E. N. Miner, publisher, New York.

The Library Magazine, John B. Alden, publisher, New York.

The National Temperance Advocate; J. N. Stearns, secretary and publishing agent, New York.

The Publishers' Weekly, (a book trade journal;) R. R. Bowker, manager, New York.

The Husbandman, Elmira.

Public Opinion; Public Opinion Co., publishers, New York and Washington.

The New York Pioneer; John Dougall & Co., publishers, New York.

The New Princeton Review, (bi-monthly;) A. C. Armstrong & Son publishers, New York.

The Tariff League Bulletin; published by the American Protective Tariff League, New York.

Demorest's Monthly Magazine; W. Jennings Demorest, publisher, New York.

The North American Review, (monthly;) Allen Thorndike Rice, editor, New York.

Sheltering Arms, (monthly,) New York.

Scribner's Magazine, (monthly;) Chas. Scribner's Sons, publishers, New York.

The Globe; The North American Exchange Company, publishers, New York.

Judge; I. M. Gregory, editor, W. J. Arkell, publisher, New York.

The Standard; Henry George, editor and proprietor, New York.

The Book Buyer, (monthly;) Chas. Scribner's Sons, New York.

The Bibliographer, (monthly;) Moulton, Weuborne and Co., publishers, Buffalo.

Garden and Forest; conducted by Prof. C. S. Sargent, The Garden and Forest Publishing Company, publishers, New York.

Book Chat; Brentano's, publishers, New York.

The Literary News, (monthly,) New York.

The Library Bulletin of Cornell University, Ithaca.

The Book Mart, (monthly;) Halkett Lord, literary editor, New York.

The Youth's Temperance Banner; J. N. Stearns, corresponding secretary and publishing agent, New York.

OHIO.

Magazine of Western History, (monthly;) J. H. Kennedy, editor, Cleveland.

Ohio Archæological and Historical Quarterly; Prof. George W. Knight, Prof. W. H. Venable, Prof. B. A. Hinsdale and Prof. G. F. Wright, editorial committee, A. H. Smythe, publisher, Columbus.

Weekly Times, Cincinnati.

The Christian Press; published by the Western Tract Society, Cincinnati.

Christian Standard; Isaac Errett, editor-in-chief, Cincinnati.

American Grange Bulletin; F. P. Wolcott, editor, Cincinnati.

Farm and Fireside, (semi-monthly;) Mast, Crowell & Kirkpatrick, editors and proprietors, Springfield and Philadelphia, Pa.

PENNSYLVANIA.

Public Ledger, (daily;) G. W. Childs, editor and publisher, Philadelphia.

Faith and Works; published by the Woman's Christian Association; Miss H. V. Wriggins, business manager, Miss A. C. Webb, editor, Philadelphia.

The Naturalist's Leisure Hour, (monthly;) A. E. Foote, editor and publisher, Philadelphia.

Farmers' Friend and Grange Advocate; R. H. Thomas, editor, Mechanicsburg.

Building Association and Home Journal, (monthly;) Michael J. Brown, editor and proprietor, Philadelphia.

Paper and Press, (monthly;) W. M. Patton, publisher and proprietor, Philadelphia.

American Manufacturer and Iron World; Jos. D. Weeks, editor, Pittsburgh.

Poultry Keeper, (monthly;) P. H. Jacobs, editor, Poultry Company, publishers, Parkesburg and Philadelphia.

Book News; John Wanamaker, publisher, Philadelphia.

The Book Mart, (monthly;) Halkett Lord, literary editor, Book Mart Publishing Co., publishers, Pittsburgh.

The Red Man, (monthly;) printed by Indian boys at the Indian School, M. Burgess, business manager, Carlisle.

Agricultural Science, (monthly;) Chas. S. Plumb, editor, Knoxville.

Canadian Free Press; L. V. Harm, editor and proprietor, Canadian.

The Canadian Crescent; Freeman E. Miller, Canadian.

Texas Live-Stock Journal; Stock Journal Publishing Company, publishers, Fort Worth.

The Southern Mercury; State Alliance Publishing Company, P. S. Browder, business manager, Dallas.

The Woman's Magazine, (monthly;) Esther T. Housh, editor, Frank E. Housh & Co., publishers, Brattleboro.

Southern Workman and Hampton School Record; S. C. Armstrong, H. W. Ludlow and M. F. Armstrong, editors, F. N. Gilman, business manager, printed by negro and Indian students, Hampton.

Wisconsin State Journal; David Atwood, proprietor, Madison.

The Herald, phonetic; The Herald Publishing Co., publishers, Toronto.

Société de Géograpie, Compte rendu des Séances de la Commission Centrale, (semi-monthly;) Paris.

Bulletin de la Société de Géographie, (quarterly,) Paris.

Chronique de la Société des Gens de Lettres, (monthly,) Paris.

Bulletin des Séances de la Société Nationale d'Agriculture de France, (monthly,) Paris.

Bulletin de la Ministére de l'Agriculture, (monthly,) Paris.

SEVENTH BIENNIAL REPORT

OF THE

BOARD OF DIRECTORS

OF THE

KANSAS STATE HISTORICAL SOCIETY,

FOR THE PERIOD

COMMENCING NOVEMBER 21, 1888, AND ENDING NOVEMBER 18, 1890.

――――――――

TOPEKA.
KANSAS PUBLISHING HOUSE: CLIFFORD C. BAKER, STATE PRINTER.
1891.

OFFICERS FOR THE YEARS 1889-91.

WILLIAM A. PHILLIPS, Salina...President, 1889.
CYRUS K. HOLLIDAY, Topeka..President, 1890.
JAMES S. EMERY, Lawrence...President, 1891.
CYRUS K. HOLLIDAY, Topeka..Vice President, 1889.
JAMES S. EMERY, Lawrence...Vice President, 1889-90.
LYMAN U. HUMPHREY, Independence.....................................Vice President, 1890.
THOMAS A. OSBORN, Topeka...Vice President, 1891.
SAMUEL N. WOOD, Woodsdale...Vice President, 1891.
FRANKLIN G. ADAMS, Topeka...Secretary, 1889-91.
JOHN FRANCIS, Topeka ....Treasurer, 1889-90.
T. DWIGHT THACHER, Topeka ....Treasurer, 1891.

EXECUTIVE COMMITTEE:
C. K. HOLLIDAY, L. U. HUMPHREY, J. N. IVES, F. P. BAKER, D. W. WILDER.

LEGISLATIVE COMMITTEE:
T. D. THACHER, S. N. WOOD, B. F. SIMPSON, A. R. GREENE, GEO. D. HALE.

DIRECTORS.

Members of the Board of Directors for the year ending January 19, 1892:

ADAMS, F. G .... Topeka.	JONES, C. J................ Garden City.
BOOTH, HENRY............... Larned.	LOWE, P. G............... Leavenworth.
CARR, E. T................ Leavenworth.	MARTIN, GEO. W.......... Kansas City.
CARROLL, ED............... Leavenworth.	McTAGGART, D............. Liberty.
CHRISTIAN, JAMES.. .... Arkansas City.	MEAD, J. R.............. Wichita.
DALLAS, E. J.................. Topeka.	MOODY, JOEL .... Mound City.
EDWARDS, W. C............... Larned.	PECK, GEORGE R............. Topeka.
ELLIOTT, L. R.............. Manhattan.	REYNOLDS, ADRIAN .... Sedan.
EMERY, J. S................. Lawrence.	SCHILLING, JOHN.......... Hiawatha.
GOSS, N. S.................. Topeka.	SIMPSON, B. F.............. Topeka.
HANNA, B. J. F............... Wa-Keeney.	STOTLER, JACOB........... Wellington.
HAYS, R. R.................. Osborne.	STREET, W. D............. Decatur.
HEIZER, D. N................ Great Bend.	SWENSSON, C. A........... McPherson.
HILLS, F. M................. Cedar Vale.	THACHER, T. D.............. Topeka.
HOLLIDAY, C. K .... Topeka.	WALROND, Z. T.............. Osborne.
HOPKINS, SCOTT .... Horton.	WELLHOUSE, F............. Fairmount.
HUMPHREY, JAMES............... Junction City.	

Members of the Board of Directors for the year ending January 17, 1893:

ABBOTT, J. B.................. DeSoto.	KELLY, H. B.......... McPherson.
ADAMS, N. A................. Manhattan.	KIMBALL, C. H............ Parsons.
ANTHONY, GEO. T............ Ottawa.	LIPPINCOTT, J. A.......... Topeka.
BLACKMAR, F. W............... Lawrence.	McCARTHY, TIMOTHY.......... Larned.
CANFIELD, JAMES H........... Lawrence.	McNEAL, T. A............ Medicine Lodge.
CORDLEY, RICHARD........... Lawrence.	McVICAR, PETER........... Topeka.
DOWNING, J. H............... Hays City.	MILLER, SOL............... Troy.
ELLIOTT, R. G............... Lawrence.	MURDOCK, M. M............ Wichita.
ELLISTON, HENRY........... Atchison.	MURDOCK, T. B............ El Dorado.
FAIRCHILD, GEO. T........... Manhattan.	PRENTIS, NOBLE L........... Newton.
HALE, GEO. D................ Topeka.	RICE, WM. M............... Fort Scott.
HIGGINS, WM................ Topeka.	SCOTT, CHAS. F........... Iola.
HOCH, E. W................. Marion.	SMITH, A. W............ McPherson.
HOWE, EDGAR W............... Atchison.	TAYLOR, A. R............ Emporia.
HUDSON, J. K................ Topeka.	QUAYLE, W. A........... Baldwin City.
JOHNSON, A. S............... Topeka.	VALENTINE, D. A........... Clay Center.
KELLOGG, L. B................ Emporia.	

Members of the Board of Directors for the year ending January 16, 1894:

ANDERSON, J. W. D............. Elk City.	McBRIDE, WM. H............ Osborne.
ANTHONY, D. R............... Leavenworth.	McINTIRE, T............ Arkansas City.
BAILEY, L. D............... Garden City.	OSBORN, THOS. A........... Topeka.
BAKER, F. P................ Topeka.	PHILLIPS, WM. A........... Salina.
BERRY, ED. A............... Waterville.	RIDDLE, A. P........... Minneapolis.
BROWN, A. Z............... Guilford.	ROBINSON, CHAS........... Lawrence.
COBUN, M. W................ Hoisington.	RUSSELL, EDWARD........... Lawrence.
DOTY, W.................. Oketo.	SPEER, JOHN............ Sherlock.
ELDER, P. P................ Ottawa.	STEWART, SAM'L J........... Humboldt.
ESKRIDGE, C. V............ Emporia.	WARE, E. F............ Fort Scott.
GLICK, GEO. W............... Atchison.	WEBB, W. C............ Topeka.
GOODNOW, I. T............. Manhattan.	WEIGHTMAN, M............ Topeka.
GREENE, A. R............... Lecompton.	WHEELER, S. C........... Concordia.
HUMPHREY, L. U............. Independence.	WHITTINGTON, A. N........... Lincoln.
IVES, J. N................ Sterling.	WILDER, D. W............ Hiawatha.
KINGMAN, S. A............... Topeka.	WOOD, S. N............ Woodsdale.
LEGATE, JAS. F............... Leavenworth.	

CONTENTS.

REPORT.

THE Board of Directors presents the following report of the work of the Society during the two years ending November 18, 1890.

Bound volumes added to the library, 2,260; unbound volumes and pamphlets, 5,208; volumes of newspapers and periodicals, 2,153; single newspapers and newspaper cuttings containing special historical matter, 5,950; maps, atlases and charts, 99; manuscripts, 951; pictures and other works of art, 514; scrip, currency and coin, 43; war relics, 19; miscellaneous contributions, 525.

From this statement it will be seen that the library additions proper, of books, pamphlets and periodicals during the two years number 9,621 volumes. Of these, 9,237 have been procured by gift and exchanges, and 384 by purchase.

The total of the library at the present time is as follows, namely: 12,231 bound volumes, 35,561 unbound volumes and pamphlets, and 10,134 bound newspaper files and volumes of periodicals; in all, 57,926 volumes.

YEARLY GROWTH OF THE LIBRARY.

The following is a statement of the yearly growth of the library in fifteen years, 1876 to 1890, inclusive:

Date.	Volumes books.	Volumes newspapers and periodicals.	Pamphlets.	Total yearly accessions.	Yearly total of the library.
1876	280	54	74	408	408
1877	115	150	501	766	1,174
1878	1,237	710	1,184	3,131	4,305
1879	290	275	491	1,056	5,361
1880	448	448	1,146	2,042	7,403
1881	414	375	1,127	1,916	9,319
1882	1,669	513	2,721	4,903	14,222
1883	307	403	1,088	1,798	16,020
1884	732	807	2,763	4,302	20,322
1885	1,088	678	2,033	3,799	24,121
1886	1,772	1,573	7,975	11,320	35,441
1887	753	1,007	1,543	3,303	38,744
1888	866	988	7,707	9,561	48,305
1889	1,269	1,053	2,248	4,570	52,875
1890	901	1,100	2,960	4,967	57,926
Totals	12,231	10,134	35,561	57,926	....

CHARACTER OF THE LIBRARY.

The library accessions have somewhat exceeded in number the average of former periods. They have been of the same general character. The purchases of books have been chiefly confined to works more or less directly

pertaining to Kansas. Gifts and exchanges have been more miscellaneous. As formerly, they have been largely the publications of the educational, scientific, social, charitable and economic departments of other States and of the United States Government; and of the publications of the voluntary societies and institutions of this and of foreign countries. These go to enrich our library in those departments which so much at the present time engage the attention of students and writers seeking full and exact information as to the social and economic problems of the day. Our library is constantly consulted by such inquirers, not merely of the locality of Topeka, but from all parts of the State.

While our accessions have been largely such as pertain to the history and progress of the State and country in the more remote past, they have been complete in the collection of the materials of the history of Kansas for the period of the two years covered by this report. It is the work of saving the materials of the history and of the intellectual and moral life of the present, that a historical society in the final summing-up has been found to have been most useful. The books and pamphlets issued from the press of Kansas have been more numerous during the past two years than in any other like period. These have all been gathered into our library. They embrace a wide range of subjects, historical, social, political, scientific, and literary.

The addition to the number of volumes of our newspapers and periodicals continues to be a marked feature in the growth of our library. Experience brings constant proof of the great value of this department. We have now 10,050 volumes of this class. Of these, nearly 8,000 volumes are of Kansas newspapers. These represent every county and considerable town in the State. They contain the social, political and economic history of every county and locality. In very large part they are the only files of such papers that have been preserved, and therefore are the only records in existence of a large portion of the local information which they contain. These files are consulted by people of all classes. They are consulted by teachers, students, and local historians and writers for information as to the early settlements, the organization of societies, churches, schools, corporations, and municipal government; by political and other writers for the proceedings of political conventions and all public gatherings, and for the records of public men; and they are consulted by attorneys and public officers for official and legal notices.

Historical writers in these days seek for original information as to the early beginnings and the every-day progress of the social life of the people. And they have come to learn that it is in the columns of the daily and weekly newspaper that this information has been most fully recorded, and that nowhere else are exact data to be found. Teachers and students in our educational institutions are more and more learning that the study of the history and development of their own State and locality are worthy of their attention, and our files are frequently being consulted by attendants upon schools and colleges in all parts of the State. No little of the correspondence of the Secretary is employed in giving information sought by students, teachers, and

other inquirers for such local information. It is a matter of congratulation and pride that in its number of volumes of newspapers, our library far exceeds, in its own local domain, that of any other library in any other State or country.

The regular issues of all newspapers and periodicals now being published in Kansas are being freely given to the Society by the publishers; of all classes, parties and creeds. The bound files are being constantly consulted by people of all classes; for facts of local and general history, of science, public economy, and social life. The truth of the testimony of the best librarians of the country as to the usefulness of newspaper files, is every day being verified in the use which the people are making of the files in our library. In organizing this branch of the work of the Society, we were guided in the outset by such advice as that given by Hon. A. R. Spofford, who has long been the librarian of the Congressional Library at Washington, the largest library in America. That veteran librarian says:

"While the files of the journals of any period furnish, unquestionably, the best instruments for the history of that epoch, it is lamentable to reflect that so little care has ever been taken to preserve a fair representation of those of any age. The destiny of nearly all newspapers is swift destruction, and even those which are preserved, commonly survive in a provokingly fragmentary state. The obvious causes of the rapid disappearance of periodical literature are its volume, necessarily increasing every year, the difficulty of lodging the files of any long period in our narrow apartments, and the continual demand for paper for the uses of trade. To these must be added the great cost of binding files of journals, increasing in the direct ratio of the size of the volumes. As so formidable an expense can be incurred by very few private subscribers to periodicals, so much the more important is it that the public libraries should not neglect a duty which they owe to their generation as well as to those that are to follow. These poor journals of to-day, which everybody is ready to stigmatize as trash not worth the room to store or the money to bind, are the very materials which the man of the future will search for with eagerness, and for some of which he will be ready to pay their weight in gold. These representatives of the commercial, industrial, inventive, social, literary, political, moral and religious life of the times, should be preserved and handed down to posterity with sedulous care. No historian, or other writer on any subject, who would write conscientiously or with full information, can afford to neglect this fruitful mine of the journals, where his richest materials are to be found."

During the past few months a great change has taken place in the political character of Kansas newspapers. Nearly one hundred have been established to promote the political views of an organization new to Kansas politics; or have changed from allegiance to other organizations to support the views of this. Whether it shall prove that this change shall mark the beginning of a permanent era in political progress, or whether it shall prove to have been but a manifestation of temporary discontent as the result of temporary depression, it is certain that our Historical Society has preserved the fullest record of the history of a widespread and profound political agitation among the people ever preserved in any State or country. Fifteen years ago the Kansas State Historical Society was organized, as was said in the first paper drawn in contemplation of its organization, "for the purpose of saving the

present and past records of our twenty-one years of eventful history." These words looked backward to the gathering of the materials of the proud history which Kansas had before that time made. But Kansas had not then stopped making history. The work has since gone steadily forward. The State Historical Society succeeded beyond all expectations in gathering up the materials of the former history. At the same time it has carefully and industriously saved the materials of the history of current events, and of all social, material and political movements since it was organized. It is now found that the record of the history since the Society was formed is of little less value than that of what had occurred before. As individuals, or as members of social organizations, or political parties, we may not always be satisfied with the record; the record may, indeed, be that of sore disappointment. But in the final summing-up, when the people of the future generations for whom the work of the Historical Society is done, shall pass upon the usefulness to them of our collections, they will bless us that we have preserved all the materials of the history of all that has transpired.

Among the larger gifts of books and pamphlets, besides those coming from our own citizens have been as usual many from the East; given by persons whose life-work seems to be largely that of aiding to build up libraries, as a means of promoting education among the people, and whose attention has been drawn to Kansas by influences which have ever made this the favorite State for the expenditure of benevolences, and for the promotion of enterprises in the interest of human progress. Of the larger contributors the following names may be mentioned: Dr. Samuel A. Green, Rev. Dr. Caleb D. Bradlee, and Mr. J. P. Mendum, all of Boston; Prof. A. S. Gatschet, of Washington, D. C.; and, of our own State, Hon. D. W. Wilder, Rev. J. W. D. Anderson, Rev. M. O. Harrington, Rev. D. D. Proper, and Messrs. A. S. Huling, L. R. Elliott, Frank A. Root, F. O. Popenoe, and C. E. Pond.

The manuscript accessions as usual have been large, and the papers acquired are of much historical interest. Those contributed by Col. D. H. Horne, Rev. Dr. Bradlee, Col. William A. Phillips, Benjamin Singleton, Sidney Hayden, W. H. R. Lykins, and William Barnes, are especially worthy of mention. Those of Mr. Lykins relate to early movements among Kansas settlers in securing titles to their lands and in the sale and distribution of town-lot interests. Those given by Mr. Barnes are papers which show the work of an Eastern emigrant aid organization in promoting the colonization of Kansas, influenced largely by an interest in the Free-State side of the great political struggle which convulsed the country during the early years of the Territorial period.

The accessions of pictures and portraits have been large. Noteworthy among these are the portraits of members of the Legislature, and State officers, and of other public men and prominent citizens of the State; some of which, as those of Hon. E. P. McCabe, Hon. F. P. Baker, Hon. E. N. Morrill, Gov. John A. Martin, and of Chief Justice A. H. Horton, are of large size, and executed in a high style of the photographic art or of that of the painter's

skill. A gift to the Society of a plaster copy of Brackett's bust of John Brown, given by Mrs. Mary E. Stearns, of Medford, Massachusetts, is worthy of special mention, especially as this is but one of eight given by the donor and her friends in Massachusetts to different societies and institutions in Kansas. A lifelike statuette of Henry Ward Beecher, given by Maj. J. B. Pond, of New York, is an attractive object in our rooms.

Among the larger accessions of volumes of newspaper files will be noticed those contributed to the library by Prof. I. T. Goodnow, Hon. John Speer, Hon. F. P. Baker, Hon. James R. Mead, Dr. Caleb D. Bradlee, and Hon. John Maloy.

Interesting war and other relics have been given the Society by Hon. John Davis, W. W. Phillips, Esq., Hon. L. D. Bailey, W. H. H. Fox, Rev. Dr. Bradlee, Hon. Sol. Miller, Hon. A. D. Walker, Mr. T. A. Stanley, and Manhattan Lodge of I. O. O. F., the last mentioned being that of the sword of Gov. Green, of the war of the Rebellion.

CATALOG.

The last Legislature increased the appropriation for the Society in the item of clerk hire with the view to the cataloging of our library. Much time has been given during the past year and a half to this work. It is a measure of great importance, as it is intended through such catalog to exhibit to the public a detailed showing of what the library contains, and to make its entire contents accessible for reference. This work has so far progressed as to promise the early publication of a first volume. It was confidently expected that such a volume would have been issued before the present time. It is a work requiring the greatest care in order to insure accuracy and completeness; and all experience in library cataloging has shown that the measure of time within which such work can be accomplished cannot be correctly estimated.

The first volume, now in preparation, will consist of and be confined to a catalog of matter exclusively pertaining to Kansas. It will show the works of Kansas history, literature, science, and all books and pamphlets which have been written and published in Kansas or about Kansas, with indexes in many instances showing their particular contents. It will show the various Kansas church and society publications. It will give an index to Kansas documentary history, showing the publications of the Legislature, of the State executive departments, and the State charitable, educational, and other institutions. It will point out those numerous Congressional and executive papers of the United States Government, issued during the period of our Territorial history, and published in the United States documentary volumes, with full indexes to the most important of this class. Subsequent volumes of the catalog will show the manuscript and museum collections of the Society and the various works of history, science, political and social economy, which go to make up the general library.

FOURTH VOLUME.

During the present year the Secretary has compiled and had published the fourth volume of the Collections of the Society. This volume makes an exhibit of the work of the Society during the four years preceding the period covered by this report, and includes the historical papers presented at the several annual and other meetings held in that time. It also contains the official correspondence pertaining to the office of Governor of Kansas Territory during the latter part of Gov. Shannon's administration in 1856, and of Governor Geary's administration from September 9, 1856, to March 10, 1857, including the official executive minutes kept by Gov. Geary. These documents relate to a considerable portion of the most stirring period of Kansas Territorial history. They have been gathered from Congressional documents published about that period. These documents have hitherto lain hidden from the general public, and much of what they contain will be found to be new to students of Kansas history. The book has an alphabetical index of sixty pages, pointing to every subject and almost every name contained in it; also a chronological index to the contents of the public documents. These official papers, added to those pertaining to the administrations of Gov. Reeder and Gov. Shannon contained in our third volume of Collections, make a full record of this class of historical material through the first three and a half years of Kansas Territorial history.

ROOMS.

As the Capitol building is soon to be completed, it is to be hoped that not many months will elapse before the Society will have given it suitable accommodations for its library and collections and ample provision for its future growth. This subject will no doubt have the careful attention of the appropriate committee of the Society.

UNION OF LIBRARIES.

The State Senate at the last session of the Legislature appointed a committee to devise and to recommend to the Senate at the coming session of the Legislature measures of legislation, amendatory of existing laws, for the more effective and economical administration of the State government in its various departments. The committee invited our State Historical Society to make suggestions of changes which might be desirable in the law governing the Society. The subject was considered by members of your executive committee, and a draft of a bill to take the place of the present law was prepared and given the Senate committee. The proposed bill contained substantially the provisions of the existing law; making the Society the trustee of the State, responsible to the State for all its work, and making its entire collections the property of the State, to be kept in the State Capitol for the use of all the people for all time. The bill placed the financial administration and general management of the Society more under the care and control of the executive officers of the State, by

providing that the Governor and other constitutional State officers shall, by virtue of office, be members of the Board of Directors, and that they shall compose a majority of the committee to audit accounts, to make rules governing the care of the library, and to supervise the purchase of books, and the expenditure of all moneys appropriated by the Legislature for the use of the Society.

It seems that the Senate committee, instead of approving the legislation proposed by our committee, propose a consolidation of the State Historical Society with the State Library, virtually abolishing the State Historical Society. But it is hardly to be presumed that the Legislature would seriously entertain a proposition of this kind.

Such legislation as would bring the two institutions into relations which would harmonize and economize the library work of the State would no doubt be desirable; for economy to the State, for the convenience of users of the two libraries, and as promotive of efficient work in the collection of such library materials as should be brought together in the State Capitol for public use. Such a measure, or one virtually contemplating the same object, was, early in the existence of the State Historical Society, considered by our board of directors in conference with the Trustees of the State Library. The Board of Directors proposed to the trustees that a line of distinction should be drawn between the two libraries; that the State Library should be confined to what is always the primary and essential work of State libraries, that of making up a library of books of law and of such works of reference as may be needed for the use of the Supreme Court and attorneys practicing therein, and by State officers and the Legislature; and that the State Historical Society should have given to it the miscellaneous department of the State Library; the work of which has been, so far as it has gone, essentially of the same character as that of the State Historical Society. This would be a clear line of demarkation; and it is one which experience in other States has proven to be practicable and efficient. In the State of New York, under the care of the Regents of the State University, the State Library has grown up with such a division, there being separate libraries and separate librarians for the law and for the miscellaneous, or the general library, as it is there called. In Wisconsin, where of all States the State Library work has been done most efficiently, this line of distinction has been for thirty-five years in force. There the State Library has the law side and the State Historical Society has the miscellaneous and historical side. The one has grown up with ample maintenance for official and judicial use, and the other is equally well supported in gathering a library of the materials of the history of the State and of the social, political and scientific history of the country. No other State in the Union possesses so valuable a general, historical and miscellaneous library as does Wisconsin.

But the Trustees of the State Library, upon consideration found that existing laws did not authorize them to accept the proposal of the State Historical Society. Such authority has not yet been given by the Legislature;

and for fifteen years the two libraries have been growing up in more or less conflict, and with more or less detriment to public economy and to public usefulness. This legislation, it would seem, should now be had; legislation clearly defining the work of the two institutions, giving to the State Library its essential and appropriate work of providing for the needs of the Supreme Court, and to the State Historical Society that of making up a reference library of history, science, political and social economy, and of such materials as will be useful to students of the history of their State and of the country.

There are but few examples showing the experience of other States in an effort to make up a full general or historical library; in but few of the States are such libraries being built up and maintained by the State. In almost all of the States there is one so called State Library. This is under the control of the Governor, or of the judicial department of the State, and the collection of books is almost exclusively confined to law books and books of reference for the use of the Supreme Court. Beyond this object little attention is given to the building up of a library. But in States where historical societies have been maintained by the State, their chief object being the making up of a library of the materials of the State, and all its localities, such institutions have become the pride and glory of the people. And where the State has failed to have this work done the neglect has eventually come to be deplored by all.

All experience has proven that historical societies, connected with the State and made responsible to the State, as is our society, do the work of building up a general library and a library of historical materials for the use of the people far more effectively than do State libraries however managed. The general side, the miscellaneous side, the historical side of a State library, by whatever name it may be called, if under the management of a sole executive officer of the State or of the judicial department of the State, is more remotely in contact with the people, is less directly in sympathetic communication with the people; its managing board is not so immediately responsible to the people; and above all, its entire work is not done for the use of the whole people. What is done on the popular side is only of secondary consideration compared with the primary object of the existence of the library.

On the other hand, with the suggested line of separation, the historical or miscellaneous side of the work given to a State historical society composed of an interested membership of the more intelligent citizens of the State, residing in all parts of the State, the work is carried on efficiently and with a view to the benefit of the whole people. Such a society engages the popular interest. Its library comes to be held in esteem by all the people, as a place where all may resort for the examination of original sources of information, as to the earliest and latest events. The citizen takes pride in contributing to such a library, and its accessions come to be made up in large part, from year to year, by voluntary gifts. Besides the gratification of serving the State through contributions to an honored institution of the State, and in so

doing contributing to that which will promote the education of the people, it often happens that donors find here a means by which their library treasures, which might otherwise become scattered and lost to good uses, may be kept together and made of perpetual benefit. The increase of such libraries is found to be in greater ratio year by year. They seem to contain within themselves a principle of acceleration, and to illustrate the truth of the maxim that "To him that hath shall be given." Such has been the experience in the growth of our Historical Society. For fifteen years it has been maintained by the State, and has sustained a growth and popularity unprecedented.

The Board of Directors calls attention to this subject at the present time, because it is one of vital interest to the Society. The just demand of the people for an economical administration of public affairs applies to the library work of the State, and should be enforced. The library materials of the State must soon be given new places in the completed Capitol building. There is every reason why the Legislature should permanently establish a plan for the State Library work. It is the duty of the Society to see to it that the work in which it has been so long engaged at the demand of the people and with their manifest approval, should not be sacrificed or its efficiency impaired.

MEETINGS, 1889–90.

THIRTEENTH ANNUAL MEETING.

The thirteenth annual meeting of the Society was held in the hall of the House of Representatives, Tuesday evening, January 15, 1889; Hon. Edward Russell, President of the Society, in the chair.

An address was delivered by Hon. James Humphrey, of Junction City, on the subject "Kansas, West of Topeka, Prior to 1865;" a paper prepared by John C. McCoy, of Kansas City, Mo., on the subject of the "Survey of the Indian Lands of Kansas," was read by Hon. T. D. Thacher; and a paper on the subject of the "Rescue of Dr. John Doy," was read by Maj. James B. Abbott, of DeSoto.

On motion, the amendment to the constitution of the Society submitted at the annual meeting, 1888, was adopted, in the following words:

"The elective officers of the Society shall consist of a President and two Vice-Presidents, who shall hold their offices for the term of one year, and until their successors shall be chosen; and a Secretary and a Treasurer, who shall hold their offices for the term of two years, and until their successors shall be chosen; said officers to be chosen by the Board of Directors from their members, their election to be made at the first meeting of the Board subsequent to the annual meeting of the Society, and their terms of office shall begin at the date of their election and qualification in office."

On motion of Hon. D. W. Wilder, Hon. Joel Moody, of Linn county, was invited to deliver an address before the Society at some time during the winter.

The committee on nominations reported the following names for members of the Board of Directors for the term ending January 19, 1892:

F. G. Adams, Topeka; Henry Booth, Larned; E. T. Carr, Leavenworth; Ed. Carroll, Leavenworth; James Christian, Arkansas City; E. J. Dallas, Topeka; W. C. Edwards, Larned; L. R. Elliott, Manhattan; J. S. Emery, Lawrence; N. S. Goss, Topeka; B. J. F. Hanna, Wakeeney; R. R. Hays, Osborne; D. N. Heizer, Great Bend; F. M. Hills, Cedar Vale; C. K. Holliday, Topeka; Scott Hopkins, Horton; James Humphrey, Junction City; C. J. Jones, Garden City; P. G. Lowe, Leavenworth; Geo. W. Martin, Kansas City; D. McTaggart, Liberty; J. R. Mead, Wichita; Joel Moody, Mound City; George R. Peck, Topeka; Adrian Reynolds, Sedan; John Schilling, Hiawatha; B. F. Simpson, Topeka; Jacob Stotler, Wellington; W. D. Street, Decatur; C. A. Swensson, McPherson; T. D. Thacher, Topeka; Z. T. Walrond, Osborne; F. Wellhouse, Fairmount.

The persons so nominated were elected.

The following committees were appointed for the ensuing year:

Executive Committee—Governor L. U. Humphrey, Hon. T. Dwight Thacher, Hon. Albert R. Greene, Hon. N. A. Adams, Hon. F. P. Baker.

Legislative Committee—Hon. James S. Emery, Hon. F. P. Baker, Hon. T. Dwight Thacher, Col. C. K. Holliday, Hon. A. R. Greene.

The meeting then adjourned.

SPECIAL MEETING FEBRUARY 4, 1889.

On call of the President and Secretary, a meeting of the Historical Society was held in its rooms Monday evening, February 4th, 1889, to hear a paper read by Senator Joel Moody, on the subject, "Alvar Nuñez Cabeça de Vaca." The meeting was called to order by Vice-President Hon. James S. Emery, of Lawrence.

At the conclusion of Senator Moody's address, a vote of thanks was extended to him, and a copy of his address solicited for publication in the Transactions of the Society.

SPECIAL MEETING FEBRUARY 11' 1889.

On Monday evening, February 11, 1889, the Historical Society met in the Senate Chamber, for the purpose of listening to an address delivered by Senator H. B. Kelly, in accordance with an invitation which had been extended by vote of the Society. The subject was, "No Man's Land." At the conclusion of the reading, the thanks of the Society were extended to the Senator, together with a request for a copy of his address for publication in its Transactions.

FOURTEENTH ANNUAL MEETING.

At the annual meeting, January 21, 1890, in the absence of President Wm. A. Phillips, Vice-President C. K. Holliday presided.

Hon. T. D. Thacher read the annual address prepared by President Phillips, entitled "Lights and Shadows of Kansas History."

Hon. Percival G. Lowe read a paper entitled "Kansas as seen in the Indian Territory."

Hon. A. R. Greene read an eulogium, prepared by Hon. B. F. Simpson, on the late Gov. John A. Martin.

Col. A. S. Johnson, Col. Thomas Ewing, Hon. Edward Russell, Hon. John Brady and Rev. John G. Pratt were, by vote, invited to prepare papers to present to the next annual meeting.

The following officers were elected for the ensuing year:

President, Col. Cyrus K. Holliday, Topeka; Vice-Presidents, Hon. James S. Emery, Lawrence, and Governor Lyman U. Humphrey, Independence.

The following were elected members of the Board of Directors for the term ending January 17, 1893:

J. B. Abbott, De Soto; N. A. Adams, Manhattan; Geo. T. Anthony, Ottawa; F. W. Blackmar, Lawrence; James H. Canfield, Lawrence; Richard Cordley, Lawrence; J. H. Downing, Hays City; R. G. Elliott, Lawrence; Henry Elliston, Atchison; Geo. T. Fairchild, Manhattan; Geo. D. Hale, Topeka; Wm. Higgins, Topeka; E. W. Hoch, Marion; Edgar W. Howe, Atchison; J. K. Hudson, Topeka; A. S. Johnson, Topeka; H. B. Kelly, McPherson; L. B. Kellogg, Emporia; C. H. Kimball, Parsons; J. A. Lippincott, Topeka; Timothy McCarthy, Larned; T. A. McNeal, Medicine Lodge; Peter McVicar, Topeka; Sol. Miller, Troy; M. M. Murdock, Wichita; T. B. Murdock, El Dorado; Noble L. Prentis, Newton; Wm. M. Rice, Fort Scott; Chas. F. Scott, Iola; A. W. Smith, McPherson; A. R. Taylor, Emporia; W. A. Quayle, Baldwin City; D. A. Valentine, Clay Center.

FINANCES, 1889.

The finances of the Society for the year ending November 19, 1889, including the Treasurer's account of receipts and expenditures and the expenditures from the appropriations made by the Legislature, as shown at the annual meeting, 1889, were as follows:

1888.   RECEIPTS.

Nov. 21, Balance of appropriations to June 30, 1889	$2,596 75	
Nov. 21, Balance in hands of the Treasurer of the Society	32 00	
1889.		
July 1, Appropriation to June 30, 1890	5,500 00	
Receipts from membership fees	51 00	
Total	$8,179 75	

EXPENDITURES.

Salaries and clerk hire	$3,413 30	
Purchase of books	641 80	
Postage, freight and contingent	417 74	
		4,472 84
Balance		$3,706 91

FINANCES, 1890.

The finances for the year ending November 18, 1890, are as follows:

1889.   RECEIPTS.
Nov. 20, Balance of appropriations to June 30, 1890...................... $3,623 91
Nov. 20, Balance in hands of the Treasurer of the Society...............   83 00
1890.
July 1. Appropriations to June 30, 1891.............................   6,000 00
         Receipts from membership fees...............................   26 00

         Total.. $9,732 91

                          EXPENDITURES.
Salaries and clerk hire............................. .... $4,355 28
Purchase of books...   249 55
Postage, freight and contingent...........................   928 16   5,532 99

         Balance... $4,199 92

DONORS OF BOOKS AND PAMPHLETS.

The following is a list of gifts made to the Society, of books and pamphlets by individuals and institutions, including exchanges and gifts of State publications, for exchanges with other societies and institutions:

Donors.	Books	Pamp
Abbott, J. B., DeSoto........................	3	......
Academie de La Rochelle, Société des Sciences Naturelles, La Rochelle, France......	1	......
Academie de Jaçon, France....................	1	......
Academie des Sciences et Belles-lettres, Dijon, France..................	1	......
Academy of Natural Sciences, Philadelphia, Pa...................	1	1
Adams, D. M., jr., Topeka...................	3	......
Adams, F. G., Topeka.......................	......	18
Adams, Harriet, Topeka.....................	......	8
Adams, H. J., Topeka.......................	......	20
Adams, N. A., Manhattan....................	......	1
Adams, W. M., Neosho Rapids................	......	1
Adkins, W. C., Lancaster...................	......	1
Admire, W. W., Topeka.....................	2	......
Alabama Agricultural Experiment Station, Auburn.......	......	18
Alabama Agricultural Experiment Station, Montgomery...........	......	14
Alabama Commissioner of Agriculture, Montgomery.............	1	1
Alderman, L. A., Lakeside, Ohio..............	......	1
Alderman, Mrs. L. A., Marietta, Ohio........	1	1
Allen, A. T., Topeka........................	......	294
Allen, E. B., Topeka........................	......	20
Allen, H. L., Secretary, Russell Springs.......	......	1
Allen, Martin, Hays City....................	1	......
Alrich, L. L., Cawker City..................	......	4
Ambrose, Wm. H., Lane.....................	......	1
American Bell Telephone Company, Boston, Mass.....	......	1
American Congregational Association, Boston, Mass......	......	2
American Florists, Society of, Boston, Mass......	......	1
American Florists, Society of, Buffalo, N. Y......	......	1
American Historical Association, Washington, D. C......	......	1
American Home Missionary Society, New York......	......	5
American Institute of Electrical Engineers, New York City......	1	......
American Missionary Association Bible House, New York City......	......	2
American Museum of Natural History, Central Park, New York......	1	6
American Philosophical Society, Philadelphia, Pa......	3	5
Ames, John G., Washington, D. C.............	2	......
Anderson, Rev. J. W. D., Elk City...........	5	66
Anthony, Miss Susan B., Rochester, N. Y.....	1	......
Arkansas Agricultural Experiment Station, Fayetteville, Ark......	1	11
Armstrong, Rev. James A., Waverly..........	......	4
Atchison Public Schools, Superintendent of, Atchison......	......	1
Atchison, Topeka & Santa Fé Railroad, Boston, Mass......	1	1
Atkins, Dudley, Randolph....................	......	1
Attwood, G. A., Manhattan..................	......	1
Axline, H. A., Columbus, O..................	2	......
Ayer, Dr. J. C. & Co., Lowell, Mass........	1	......
Badger, Joseph E., Jr., Frankfort...........	......	29
Baker, Benjamin, Reed City, Mich...........	......	1

DONORS OF BOOKS AND PAMPHLETS—Continued.

Donors.	Books	Pamp
Baker, C. C., Topeka	48	193
Baldwin, Evelyn B., Oswego		1
Ball, Mrs. Belle, Kansas City, Mo.		1
Ball, R. W., Harper		4
Ballard, E. T., Ballard Falls		4
Bangor, Maine, Public Library		3
Banter, J. E., Hiawatha		1
Barber, Ed. T., Iola		2
Barnes, William, Albany, N. Y.		2
Barnhart & Eckman, Osborne		1
Barratt, Rev. J., North Topeka		5
Barrow, Mrs. J. W., New York City, N. Y.	1	
Barteldes, F. & Co., Lawrence		1
Bass, A. & Co., McPherson		1
Bates, J. H., New York City, N. Y.	2	3
Bates, Phineas, Boston, Mass.		1
Beadle & Adams, New York City		162
Beer, William, Topeka		1
Bennett & Son, Topeka		3
Bethel College, Newton		1
Betton, Frank, Topeka	120	2
Biggers, Mrs. Kate H., Longton	1	
Bixby, C. S., Osawatomie		1
Black, George, Olathe	1	2
Black, S. W., Chanute		1
Blackmar, Frank W., Lawrence		1
Blakesley, Rev. L., Topeka		3
Blanchard, Wm. H., Koloko		1
Bland, Richard P., Washington, D. C.		1
Bleavaness, A. A., Baldwin		1
Bodwell, Rev. Lewis, Clifton Springs, N. Y.	1	
Bogert, C. F., Lenora		1
Bollard, W. W., Topeka		3
Booth, Henry, Larned		2
Boston Children's Mission to the Children of the Destitute, Massachusetts		1
Boston Public Library, Boston, Mass.	2	
Boston Public Schools, Superintendent of		2
Boutwell, D. W., Topeka		2
Bowers, George W., Halifax, Nova Scotia		2
Bowes, Geo. W., Topeka		3
Bowker, R. R., New York City		1
Brackett, G. C., Lawrence	60	
Bradlee, Rev. C. D., Boston, Mass.		96
Branch, V. H., Sec., Cawker City		1
Breckinridge, C. R., Washington, D. C.		6
Brewer, Prof. F. P., Grinnell, Ia.		4
Brewster, A. W., Topeka		1
Bright, Rev. J. A., Abilene		1
Broad, L. P., Topeka		2
Broadhead, L. W., Delaware Water Gap, Pa.		1
Brooklyn Library, Brooklyn, N. Y.		4
Brooks, Frank, Topeka		6
Brown, Bestor G., Topeka		14
Brown, C. H., Topeka		3
Brown, Duncan, Highland		5
Brown, Frank J., Topeka		3
Brown, Dr. G. W., Rockford, Ill.	1	2
Brown, John, jr., Put-in-Bay, O.		13
Brown, John H., Kansas City, Kas.	2	
Brown, O. C., Adams, N. Y.		1
Brown, R. J., Leavenworth		7
Brown, T. B., Topeka		4
Brummitt, Dan. B., Baldwin		1
Bryan, George D., Charleston, S. C.	1	
Bryan, J. W., Lake Charles, La.		1
Buffalo Historical Society, Buffalo, N. Y.		2
Burdett, Samuel F., Leavenworth	8	
Burnell, Rev. A. T., Eureka		5
Burnett, E. B., Solomon City		2
Burnett, W. S., Helena, Ark.		1
Burton, James and Mary L., Jamestown	2	1
Butterworth, Ben., Cincinnati, Ohio	13	
Caldwell, John C., Topeka	1	
California Academy of Sciences, San Francisco	2	19
California Agricultural Experiment Station, Berkeley	2	
California Bureau of Labor Statistics, San Francisco		2
California Board of Trade, San Francisco		

DONORS OF BOOKS AND PAMPHLETS — CONTINUED.

Donors.	Books	Pamp
California State Mining Bureau, Sacramento, Cal	2	......
California Superintendent of Public Instruction, Sacramento	1	......
Cameron, A. C., Chicago, Ill	1	......
Cameron, Joseph G., Washington, D. C.	......	4
Campbell, A. B., Topeka	679	121
Campbell, E. F., Secretary, Mound City	......	1
Campbell, G. Mound Valley	......	1
Campbell, John Preston, Abilene	3	......
Campbell, J. P., and D. A. Valentine, Clay Center	......	1
Campbell, Matthew M., North Topeka	......	3
Campbell, W. P., Wamego	1	......
Campdoras, Mrs. E. M., North Topeka	4	......
Canadian Institute, Toronto, Canada	......	4
Canebrake Agricultural Experiment Station, Uniontown, Ala	......	21
Canfield, James H., Lawrence	1	8
Capital Grange Library, Topeka	21	......
Case, F. M., Waldo	......	1
Case, Nelson, Oswego	......	1
Cavaness, A. A. B., Baldwin City	......	7
Chambers, W. L., Stockton	......	2
Chandler, William E., Washington, D. C.	1	15
Chapman Bros., Chicago, Ill	1	......
Chesney, E. E., Topeka	......	5
Chesney, Mrs. Rinda E., Topeka	......	11
Chicago Board of Public Works, Chicago, Ill.	1	......
Chicago, Historical Society, Chicago, Ill	1	8
Chicago Manual Training School, Chicago, Ill	......	4
Chicago Public Library, Chicago, Ill	......	12
Chicago, Rock Island & Pacific Railroad	......	1
Children's Aid Society, New York City	......	1
Children's Hospital, Boston, Mass	......	2
Childs, George W., Philadelphia, Pa	......	2
Chittenden, Rev. E. P., Salina	1	......
Christian Publishing House, Dayton, O.	......	1
Church, Gov. L. K., Bismarck, N. D.	......	4
Church Home for Orphan and Destitute Children, Boston, Mass	......	2
Cincinnati Public Library, Cincinnati, O.	......	1
Cincinnati Society of Natural History, Cincinnati, O.	......	2
Clark, G. M., Topeka	......	1
Clark & Runnels, Marysville	......	1
Clarke, George K., Boston, Mass	1	......
Clarke, Robert, Cincinnati, O.	1	......
Clarke, Hon. Sidney, Lawrence	......	1
Clarke, Sylvester H., Clyde, N. Y.	1	3
Clayborn, R. B. & Son, Abilene	......	1
Clifton, Frederick, Rockford, Ill	1	......
Clinton, C. W., Salina	......	1
Coan, C. H., Leoti	1	1
Cobden Club, London, Eng.	4	13
Coburn, F. D., Kansas City, Kansas	......	16
Codding, J. S., Louisville	......	1
Coffin, H. A., Jr., Sec., Hill City	......	4
Coffin, J. H., Jewell City	......	6
Coffman, S., Jewell City	......	1
College for the Training of Teachers, New York	......	2
College of the Sisters of Bethany, Topeka	......	6
Collet, C. D., London, England	......	20
Colorado Agricultural Experiment Station, Fort Collins	2	9
Colorado Agricultural College, Fort Collins, Col	......	......
Colorado Bureau of Labor Statistics, Denver	1	......
Colorado Commissioner of Immigration, Denver, Col.	......	3
Colquitt, A. H., Washington, D. C.	......	3
Columbia College, New York City	......	1
Comer, W. H., Holton	......	3
Concord, City of, N. H	1	......
Cone, Frank W., Boston, Mass	1	......
Cone, R. L., Taunton, Mass	......	1
Cone, W. W., Topeka	......	31
Connecticut Agricultural Experiment Station, New Haven	1	15
Connecticut Adjutant General, Hartford	2	......
Connecticut Bureau of Labor Statistics, Hartford	3	......
Connecticut Historical Society, Hartford	1	......
Cooke, Josiah Parsons, Boston, Mass	......	1
Corgan, John N., McPherson	......	1
Cornell Agricultural Experiment Station, Ithaca, N. Y	......	18
Cornell University, Ithaca, N. Y.	2	5
Cornell University Christian Association, Ithaca, N. Y.	......	1

DONORS OF BOOKS AND PAMPHLETS—CONTINUED.

Donors.	Books	Pamp
Cotton, John M., Omaha, Neb.,	.....	1
Cougher, John G., Wyandotte.	1	......
Craft, E. D. & Son, Downs	.....	1
Cragin, F. W., Topeka	.....	2
Crampton & Landis, Osborne.	1	......
Crane, George W., Topeka	3	2
Crawford, Geo. A., Grand Junction, Col	.....	2
Crawford, Samuel J., Topeka.	.....	1
Credit Foncier Company, New York	.....	13
Crisp, Charles F., Washington, D. C.	.....	1
Croasdale, Wm. T., New York City	.....	3
Culverwell, James, Dentonia.	.....	2
Cunningham, R. W., Secretary, Kansas City, Mo.	.....	1
Curtis, William E., Washington, D. C.	1	5
Cutcheon, Byron M., Washington, D. C.	.....	1
Dall, C. C., Atchison	1	......
Dakota Agricultural and Experimental Station, Brookings, S. D.	.....	12
Dana, F. L., Topeka.	1	18
Daniel, John W., Washington, D. C.	.....	11
Darling, General C. W., Utica, N. Y.	.....	5
Davis, Buel T., Atchison	.....	4
Davis, John, Junction City.	8	14
Davis, Olin S., Topeka.	.....	5
Day, Albert, Boston, Mass.	.....	17
Day, G. W., Topeka.	.....	1
De Long, James, Wichita.	.....	1
Dedham Historical Society, Dedham, Mass.	1	5
Dennis, H. J., Topeka.	6	4
Detroit Public Library, Michigan.	.....	1
Detwiler, J. R., Topeka.	.....	2
Dewey, Melville, Albany, N. Y.	3	3
Doane College, Crete, Neb	.....	13
Dockery, Alexander M., Washington, D. C.	.....	2
Dodge, S. H., Beloit.	.....	1
Dodge School of Theology of the Methodist Episcopal Church, Dodge City.	.....	1
Dornblaser, Rev. T. F., Topeka.	.....	1
Dowell, M. R., Edinburgh, Scotland.	.....	1
Dowling, Thomas, Washington, D. C.	.....	1
Downing, R. F. & Co., New York City	.....	1
Day, W. S., Ithaca, Mich.	.....	1
Drowne, Henry Thayer, New York City	.....	1
Durham, T. W., Topeka.	.....	1
Durrie, Daniel S., Madison, Wis.	.....	1
Dury, Charles, Cincinnati, Ohio.	.....	1
Eames, Wilberforce, New York City.	.....	1
Eckert, T. W., Arkansas City	.....	1
Eldorado Springs, Superintendent of, Cedar county, Mo.	.....	2
Elliott, Chas. S., Topeka	.....	4
Elliott, L. R., Manhattan	12	48
Emery, A. L., Topeka.	1	......
Eshelman, M. M., McPherson.	1	......
Eskridge, C. V., Emporia.	.....	3
Essex, J. A., Clifton.	.....	2
Essex Institute, Salem, Mass.	.....	15
Everest, Harvey W., Chancellor, Garfield University, Wichita.	.....	2
Ewing, Gen. Thomas, New York City.	.....	1
Fairchild, Geo. T., Manhattan	1	56
Farnsworth, H. W., Topeka.	.....	6
Faubion, Rev. J. W., Effingham.	.....	2
Faulkner, Chas. J., Washington, D. C.	.....	2
Fee, S., Wamego.	.....	120
Fegtly, J. J., Wichita.	1	......
Ferril, Will C., Denver, Colorado.	1	......
Figge, S. N., Barnard.	.....	1
Filley, C. E., Burlingame.	.....	1
Finch, C. S., Lawrence.	1	......
Finch, C. O., Baldwin.	1	......
Findlay, G. W., Topeka.	70	......
Firmin, Emile, Florence.	.....	1
Fisher, Geo. S., Topeka.	.....	4
Fisher, J. A., Florence	.....	1
Florida State Agricultural Experiment Station, Lake City.	.....	9
Flower, Roswell P., New York City.	.....	5
Fortine, J. A., Downs.	.....	1
Forsyth, Capt. S. K., Washington, D. C.	.....	2
Foster, C. A., Quincy, Mass.	.....	1

DONORS OF BOOKS AND PAMPHLETS—Continued.

Donors.	Books	Pamp
Foster, C. M., Topeka..	......	1
Fox, G. W., Boston, Mass..	......	8
Franklin, Gen. Wm. B., Hartford, Conn...........................	1	......
Frazier, W. T. Salina..	......	2
Free Public Library, Worcester, Mass.............................	1	1
Fritch, E. H., Wichita...	......	1
Funston, Edward H., Washington, D. C............................	......	2
Gage, Norris L., Topeka..	......	2
Gast, Harriet A., Fremont, O.....................................	......	1
Gates, F. M., Topeka...	......	2
Gatschet, Albert S., Washington, D. C............................	......	27
Gear, John H., Washington. D. C.................................	......	2
Genet, T. E., Mound Ridge.......................................	......	1
Geological and Natural History Survey, Ottawa, Canada..........	2	2
Geological Survey of the State of New Jersey, New Brunswick.....	1	......
George, Rev. A. P., Cimarron....................................	......	2
Georgia Historical Society. Savannah.............................	......	1
Georgia Agricultural Experiment Station, Griffin.................	......	4
Georgia Agricultural Experiment Station, Athens.................	......	5
Gerard, W. D. & Co., Osborne....................................	......	1
German-American Stenographic Society, New York.................	......	2
Gillespie, D. M., Salina..	1	1
Gleed & Gleed. Topeka...	......	1
Goerz, David, Halstead...	......	1
Goodnow, Prof. I. T., Manhattan.................................	......	354
Goodwine, John, Sec., Dodge City................................	......	1
Gotwald, Rev. George D., Kansas City, Mo........................	......	7
Gove, J. L., Sec., Mound City....................................	......	1
Graham, Prof. I. D., Manhattan..................................	......	2
Granger, Mrs. A. P., Canandaigua, N. Y..........................	......	10
Graves, A. R., Sec., Troy..	......	1
Gray, P. L., Bendena...	1	2
Graybill, J. M., Leavenworth.....................................	......	2
Green, S. S., Worcester, Mass....................................	......	3
Green, Samuel A., Boston, Mass..................................	92	329
Green, Dr. C. C., Winfield.......................................	1	......
Greene. Albert R., Topeka..	......	1
Griffin, Albert, New York City, N. Y.............................	......	48
Grosvenor, Charles H., Washington, D. C.........................	......	1
Grove, Archibald, New York......................................	......	1
Guthrie, John, Topeka...	......	1
Guthrie, Miss Lou, Helena, Montana.............................	......	7
Hackbusch, H. C. F., Leavenworth...............................	8	......
Hagaman, J. M., Concordia.......................................	......	1
Halderman, I. D., Topeka..	......	1
Hale, George D., Topeka...	1	5
Hampton Normal and Agricultural Institute, Hampton, Va........	......	4
Harrington, Grant W., Lawrence..................................	1	12
Harrington, H. B., Topeka..	......	6
Harrington, Rev. M. O., Topeka..................................	12	82
Harris, Rev. Theo., Topeka.......................................	......	1
Harris Institute Library, Woonsocket, R. I.......................	......	2
Hart, Jas. W., Kansas City, Mo..................................	......	1
Harvard University, Cambridge, Mass.............................	......	4
Haskell, W. H. & Son, Atchison..................................	5	......
Haverford College, Haverford, Pa................................	1	......
Havermale, Lewis, Olsburg.......................................	......	1
Hay, John, Junction City..	......	7
Hayden, Rev. Horace Edwin, Wilkes-Barre, Pa....................	......	6
Hayden, Sidney, Holton..	1	......
Hays, Robert R., Osborne..	......	1
Heatley, W. H., Topeka..	......	1
Heizler, Edward C., LaSalle, Ill.................................	......	1
Heizer, D. N., Great Bend..	......	1
Henrie, C. A., Topeka..	......	3
Henry, Mrs. J. O., Olathe..	......	4
Hesper Academy, Hesper..	......	2
Higgins, I. L., Topeka...	......	3
Higgins, William, Topeka...	310	45
Highland University, Highland....................................	......	5
Hildeburn, Charles R., Philadelphia, Pa..........................	......	1
Hilton, Mrs. C. A., Tama, Ia.....................................	1	......
Hinricks, Dr. Gustavus, Iowa City, Ia............................	......	5
Hirons, C. C., Topeka..	3	......

DONORS OF BOOKS AND PAMPHLETS—Continued.

Donors.	Books	Pamp
Foster, C. M., Topeka............	......	1
Fox, G. W., Boston, Mass........	......	8
Franklin, Gen. Wm. B., Hartford, Conn........................	1	......
Frazier, W. T. Salina.......	......	2
Free Public Library, Worcester, Mass.....................	1	1
Fritch, E. H., Wichita........	......	1
Funston, Edward H., Washington, D. C...............	......	2
Gage, Norris L., Topeka..........	......	2
Gast, Harriet A., Fremont, O........	......	1
Gates, F. M., Topeka........	......	2
Gatschet, Albert S., Washington, D. C........	......	27
Gear, John H., Washington, D. C............	......	2
Genet, T. E., Round Ridge.............	......	1
Geological and Natural History Survey, Ottawa, Canada.......	2	2
Geological Survey of the State of New Jersey, New Brunswick...............	1	......
George, Rev. A. P., Cimarron........	......	2
Georgia Historical Society, Savannah........	......	1
Georgia Agricultural Experiment Station, Griffin........	......	4
Georgia Agricultural Experiment Station, Athens........	......	5
Gerard, W. D. & Co., Osborne........	......	1
German-American Stenographic Society, New York........	......	2
Gillespie, D. M., Salina.......................	1	1
Gleed & Gleed. Topeka........	......	1
Goerz, David, Halstead........	......	1
Goodnow, Prof. I. T., Manhattan........	......	354
Goodwine, John, Sec., Dodge City........	......	1
Gotwald, Rev. George D., Kansas City, Mo........	......	7
Gove, J. L., Sec., Mound City........	......	1
Graham, Prof. I. D., Manhattan........	......	2
Granger, Mrs. A. P., Canandaigua, N. Y........	......	10
Graves, A. R., Sec., Troy........	......	1
Gray, P. L., Bendena.....	1	2
Graybill, J. M., Leavenworth........	......	2
Green, S. S., Worcester, Mass........	......	3
Green, Samuel A., Boston, Mass........	92	329
Green, Dr. C. C., Winfield........	1	......
Greene, Albert R., Topeka........	......	1
Griffin, Albert, New York City, N. Y........	......	48
Grosvenor, Charles H., Washington, D. C........	......	1
Grove, Archibald, New York........	......	1
Guthrie, John, Topeka........	......	1
Guthrie, Miss Lou, Helena, Montana........	......	7
Hackbusch, H. C. F., Leavenworth........	8	......
Hagaman, J. M., Concordia........	......	1
Halderman, I. D., Topeka	......	1
Hale, George D., Topeka	1	5
Hampton Normal and Agricultural Institute, Hampton, Va........	......	4
Harrington, Grant W., Lawrence........	1	12
Harrington, H. B., Topeka........	......	6
Harrington, Rev. J. O., Topeka........	12	82
Harris, Rev. Theo., Topeka........	......	1
Harris Institute Library, Woonsocket, R. I........	......	2
Hart, Jas. W., Kansas City, Mo........	......	1
Harvard University, Cambridge, Mass........	......	4
Haskell, W. H. & Son, Atchison........	5	......
Haverford College, Haverford, Pa........	1	......
Havermale, Lewis, Olsburg........	......	1
Hay, John, Junction City........	......	7
Hayden, Rev. Horace Edwin, Wilkes-Barre, Pa........	......	6
Hayden, Sidney, Holton........	......	1
Hays, Robert R., Osborne........	......	1
Heatley, W. H., Topeka........	......	1
Heigler, Edward C., LaSalle, Ill........	......	1
Heizer, D. N., Great Bend........	......	1
Henrie, C. A., Topeka	......	3
Henry, Mrs. J. O., Olathe........	......	4
Hesper Academy, Hesper........	......	3
Higgins, L. L., Topeka........	......	3
Higgins, William, Topeka........	310	45
Highland University, Highland........	......	5
Hildeburn, Charles R., Philadelphia, Pa........	......	1
Hilton, Mrs. C. A., Tama, Ia........	1	......
Hinricks, Dr. Gustavus, Iowa City, Ia........	......	5
Hirons, C. C., Topeka........	3	......

DONORS OF BOOKS AND PAMPHLETS—Continued.

Donors.	Books	Pamp
Historical and Philosophical Society of Ohio. Cincinnati	169	252
Historical Society of Southern California. Los Angeles		1
Hoenshel, E. J., Holton		1
Hoffman, R. A., Smith Center		1
Hoisington, P. M., Secretary, Newton		1
Holcombe, A. A., Topeka		1
Holt, Rev. L. H., Topeka		22
Hunnewell, James F., Charlestown, Mass	1	
Hope, William. Ottawa		26
Hornbeck, E. A., National City, Cal		4
Howe, Mrs. Julia W., Boston, Mass		4
Hubbard, Col. A. S., San Francisco, Cal		2
Hubbard, Jeremiah, Erie	1	1
Hubbard, Josiah M., Middletown, Conn		2
Hubbard, Kate, Glasco		1
Huling, Alden S., Topeka		306
Humphrey, Gov. Lyman U., Topeka		55
Hunt, Rev. J. P., Ellsworth		3
Hunter, George H., Wellington		2
Husted Investment Company, Kansas City, Kan		3
Iliff, J. M., Mound City		2
Illinois Agricultural Experiment Station. Champaign		9
Illinois Bureau of Labor Statistics, Springfield	1	
Illinois Press Association, Morris		1
Illinois Woman's Press Association. Chicago		1
Indian Rights Association. Philadelphia, Pa		31
Indiana Agricultural Experiment Station. Lafayette		31
Indiana Department of Geology and Natural History, Indianapolis	2	
Indiana Department of Statistics, Indianapolis	1	
Indiana State Board of Health, Indianapolis	2	
Indiana State Grange, Adams		1
Indiana State Library, Indianapolis		1
Industrial Education Association. New York City		10
Ingalls, John J., Washington, D. C	32	49
Investment Banking Company, Topeka		1
Iowa Agricultural Experiment Station. Ames		7
Iowa State Historical Society, Iowa City		1
Iowa State Library, Des Moines	1	
Iowa Statistics of Labor, Des Moines	1	
Italian Bureau of Agriculture. Florence, Italy	1	
Ivison, Blakeman & Co., New York City	1	
Jackson, Lydia J., Topeka	1	
Jacobs, Rev. S. P., Sabetha		10
Janes, C. H., Hiawatha		1
Jenkins, William R., New York City		2
Jennings, T. B., Topeka		18
Johns, Mrs. Laura M., Salina		3
Johns Hopkins University, Baltimore, Md	1	17
Johnson, Dr. G. H. T., Atchison		3
Johnson, Robert U., New York City		3
Jones, Charles H., St. Louis, Mo		3
Jones, John P., Washington, D. C		4
Jones, Seward A., Scottsville		1
Jordan, Josiah. Topeka	1	
Julian, Geo. W., Centerville, Ind		10
Kansas Academy of Science. Topeka	60	
Kansas Board of Railroad Commissioners, Topeka	120	83
Kansas City Board of Education		3
Kansas Phonograph Company, Topeka		1
Kansas State Library, Topeka	1	
Kansas State Penitentiary. Lansing		2
Kansas State Republican Resubmission Club		1
Kansas State Teachers' Association. Topeka		20
Kansas Wesleyan University. Lawrence		1
Karr, Earnest P., Winchester		1
Kellerman, W. A., Manhattan	1	1
Kelley, Harrison. Burlington		10
Kellogg, L. B., Topeka	40	
Kelly, H. B., McPherson		5
Kellion, Dwight H., Quincy, Mich	1	6
Kemp, E. L., Wichita		1
Kennedy, J. J., Secretary, Winfield		1
Kentucky Agricultural Experiment Station, Lexington		42
Kilmer, Fred. B., New Brunswick, N. J		4
Kimble, Sam'l, Manhattan		1
Kirk, L. K., Garnett	1	
Klock, J. E., Emporia		2

—2

DONORS OF BOOKS AND PAMPHLETS—CONTINUED.

Donors.	Books	Pamp
Knox, Rev. John D., Topeka		22
Koester, Chas. F., Marysville		1
Lacey, John F., Washington, D. C.		4
Lane, J. R. & Co., Agra		1
Lanham, S. M., Topeka		8
Lansing, G. L., San Francisco, Cal		1
Lasher, Esmeralda, Topeka		5
Latimer, J. W., Secretary, Pleasanton	1	2
Lawhead, J. H., Topeka	1	
Lawrence Business College, Lawrence		1
Leavenworth, F. P., Haverford College, Pennsylvania		2
Lee, Charles S., Denver, Col		1
Legate, Miss Nellie, Topeka	4	
Leicester, Massachusetts, Public Library		1
Lettner, G. W., Working. Eng		1
Lewis, D. W., Topeka	1	
Library Bureau, Boston. Mass		2
Library Company of Philadelphia. Pa		5
Lick Observatory, Mt. Hamilton. Cal	2	
Limerick, Mrs. Alice G., Winfield	1	
Linehaw, John C., Manchester, N. H	1	
Lippincott, Dr. J. A., Lawrence		3
Lippincott, J. B., Company, Philadelphia, Pa		1
Livingston County, New York, Historical Society, Danville		1
Lodge, H., Erie		1
Lodge, Henry C., Washington, D. C.		6
Longley, Alcander, St. Louis, Mo	1	
Longley, Elias, Pasadena, Cal		1
Longshore, E. W., Topeka	2	4
Los Angeles Public Library, Los Angeles, Cal		1
Lothrop, D., Boston, Mass		1
Louisiana Agricultural Experiment Station, Baton Rouge		5
Louisiana Commissioner of Immigration, New Orleans		6
Louisiana State Board of Agriculture, Baton Rouge	2	
Lykins, William H. R., Kansas City, Mo	2	
Lyman, Miss Eunice A., Topeka		3
McAlaster, O. W., Lawrence		2
McBride, J. W., Cawker City		1
McCarthy, Timothy, Topeka	60	3
McClintock, John N., Concord, N. H		1
McConaugh, A. D., Atchison		5
McCook, Anson G., Washington, D. C.		1
MacDonald, John, Topeka		23
MacDonald, William, Lawrence		1
McFarland, N. C., Topeka		1
McNay, J. M., Phillipsburg		2
McPherson, Edward, editor, New York City		1
McPherson College, McPherson		2
McRoberts, J. W., Secretary, Mankato		2
McVicar, Dr. Peter, Topeka		11
Maher & Grosh, Toledo, O		1
Maine Agricultural Experiment Station		3
Maine Bureau of Industrial Labor Statistics, Augusta	2	
Maloy, John, Council Grove	2	1
Manchester, Alfred, Providence, R. I.	1	18
Manchester, D. W., Cleveland, O.		1
Manderson, Charles F., Washington, D. C.		2
Marshall, Frank A., Leavenworth		2
Marshall, John, Howard		2
Marston, C. W., Cedar Junction	1	18
Martin, Geo. W., Kansas City, Kas		3
Martin, J. C., Prescott, Arizona		1
Martin, John A., Atchison		3
Mary F. Seymour Publishing Company, New York City		1
Maryland Agricultural Experiment Station. College Park, Prince George's county		12
Massachusetts Agricultural College. Amherst	3	13
Massachusetts Bureau Statistics of Labor, Boston	4	
Massachusetts Historical Society, Boston	3	18
Massachusetts Horticultural Society, Boston	1	
Massachusetts Infant Asylum, Boston		13
Massachusetts Institute of Technology, Boston	1	14
Massachusetts Public Library, Salem		2
Massachusetts School for the Feeble-Minded, Boston		2
Massachusetts Society for the Prevention of Cruelty to Children, Boston		1
Massachusetts State Board of Lunacy and Charity, Boston	2	
Massachusetts State Library, Boston	24	
Mathews, Henry S., San José, Cal	1	
Mead, J. R., Wichita		1

DONORS OF BOOKS AND PAMPHLETS — CONTINUED.

Donors.	Books	Pamp
Mendum, J. P., editor Investigator, Boston, Mass.	19	.....
Mercantile Library Association, New York City	1	33
Merchantile Library Association of San Francisco, Cal	.....	1
Merrill, Nathan C., Ness City.	.....	16
Michigan Agricultural College, Agricultural College P. O.	29	23
Michigan Bureau of Labor Statistics, Lansing.	6	.....
Michigan Public Library, Detroit.	.....	1
Michigan State Board of Health, Lansing.	1	1
Michigan State Library, Lansing.	57	12
Middaugh & Powers, Plainville.	.....	1
Miller, C. W., Hays City	.....	2
Miller, J. H., Howard.	1	.....
Miller, W. H., Kansas City, Mo.	.....	20
Mills, A. B., McLouth.	.....	1
Mills, F. B., Las Vegas, N. M.	.....	1
Milwaukee Public Library, Wis.	2	4
Miner, Rev. S. J., Sabetha.	.....	5
Minneapolis Public Library, Minneapolis, Minn.	.....	3
Minnesota Academy of Natural Sciences, Minneapolis.	.....	1
Minnesota Agricultural Experiment Station, St. Anthony Park.	1	5
Minnesota Historical Society, St. Paul.	1	1
Minnie, Dr. J. E., Topeka.	1	.....
Minor, Mrs. Virginia L., St. Louis, Mo.	.....	1
Mississippi Agricultural Experiment Station, Agricultural College.	.....	15
Missouri Agricultural Experiment Station, Columbia	.....	13
Missouri Bureau of Statistics of Labor, Jefferson City.	2	.....
Missouri Press Association, Columbia, Mo.	.....	1
Missouri Weather Service, Director of, St. Louis.	.....	22
Mitchell, C. R., Geuda Springs.	.....	1
Mitchell, J. K., Osborne.	.....	1
Mitchell, Mrs. Jennie S., York, Neb.	.....	3
Mitchell, John H., Washington, D. C.	.....	7
Mohler, M., Topeka.	66	707
Monroe, Harriet Earhart, Phila., Pa.	1	.....
Montgomery, James Mortimer, New York City.	1	.....
Moon, E. G., Secretary, Topeka.	.....	4
Moon, John E., Hiawatha.	.....	10
Moore, John T., Lawrence.	.....	4
Moore, Robert R., Topeka.	.....	125
Moriarty & Thorpe, Bogue.	.....	1
Morrill, Edmund N., Hiawatha.	.....	4
Morrill, Justin S., Washington, D. C.	.....	10
Muir, W. G., Secretary, Harper.	.....	1
Munsell's, Joel, Sons, Albany, N. Y.	.....	2
National Grange, Topeka.	1	.....
National Society Sons American Revolution	2	.....
National Temperance Society, N. Y.	.....	7
Nebraska Agricultural Experiment Station, Lincoln.	.....	3
Nebraska Bureau of Labor Statistics, Lincoln.	1	.....
Nebraska Historical Society, Lincoln.	3	15
Nebraska Weather Service, Director of, Crete.	.....	25
Nelander, Edward, Lindsborg.	.....	1
Neosho Rapids Seminary, Neosho Rapids.	.....	1
Nevins, J. S., Secretary, Independence.	.....	1
Nevins Memorial Library, Methuen, Mass.	2	.....
Newberry, Horace J., Chicago, Ill.	.....	3
Newberry Library, Chicago, Ill.	.....	2
New England Historic Genealogic Society, Boston, Mass.	.....	2
New England Hospital for Women and Children, Boston, Mass.	.....	2
New England Society, New York City.	1	3
New Hampshire Adjutant General, Manchester.	1	.....
New Hampshire Agricultural Experiment Station, Hanover.	.....	12
New Hampshire Bank Commissioners of, Manchester.	1	.....
New Hampshire Board of Railroad Commissioners, Manchester.	1	1
New Hampshire Historical Society, Concord, N. H.	1	.....
New Hampshire Insurance Commissioner, Concord.	.....	1
New Hampshire State Board of Agriculture, Concord.	1	.....
New Hampshire State Board of Health, Concord.	2	.....
New Hampshire State Grange of the Patrons of Husbandry.	.....	1
New Jersey Agricultural Experiment Station, New Brunswick.	3	.....
New Jersey Bureau of Statistics of Labor, Trenton, N. J.	2	2
New Jersey Free Public Library, Paterson.	.....	2
New Jersey Geological Survey, New Brunswick.	1	.....
New Jersey Historical Society, Newark, N. J.	39	40
New Jersey State Treasurer, Trenton, N. J.	1	.....
New London Historical Society, Connecticut.	.....	1
Newton, W. S., Oswego.	.....	1
New York Agricultural Experiment Station, Geneva.	5	1
New York Bureau of Statistics of Labor, Albany.	5	.....

DONORS OF BOOKS AND PAMPHLETS—Continued.

Donors.	Books	Pamp
New York Children's Aid Society, New York City		1
New York College for the Training of Teachers, New York City		48
New York Institution for Deaf Mutes, New York City		2
New York State Library, Albany	3	1
Nicholson, George T., Topeka		1
Nipher, Francis E., St. Louis, Mo.		3
North Carolina Agricultural Experiment Station, Raleigh		13
North Carolina, University of, Chapel Hill	1	
Northrup, H. M., Kansas City, Kas.		1
Norton, C. A., Topeka	1	
Norton, Charles Elliott, Cambridge, Mass.		12
Nubert, Gus. J., Kansas City, Kas.		16
Nye, M. J., Hiawatha		1
Oates, Wm. C., Washington, D. C.		13
Ohio Adjutant General, Columbus.	2	5
Ohio Agricultural Experiment Station, Columbus.	3	35
Ohio Bureau of Statistics of Labor, Columbus	3	
Ohio Meteorological Bureau, Columbus	3	140
Ohio State Archæological and Historical Society, Columbus.	12	11
Ohio State Forestry Bureau, Columbus.	1	
Oldroyd, O. H., Springfield, Ill.		1
Olney, Mrs. Emeline, Madison, Wis.		1
Oneida Historical Society, Utica, N. Y.	1	22
Ontario Department of Agriculture, Bureau of Statistics, Guelph, Canada		2
Ontario Agricultural College and Experiment Farm, Guelph, Canada		7
Opdyke, Charles Wilson, New York City.	1	
Oregon Immigration Board, Portland		4
Ormsbee, Talcott, Topeka.		1
Outhwaite, J. H., Washington, D. C.		4
Owen, Prof. Richard, New Harmony, Ind.		3
Owen Brothers, Stockton.		1
Ozias, J. W., Wichita		1
Palmer & Anderson, Kirwin.		1
Parker, Rev. John D., Fort Riley.		1
Parks, C. W., Troy, N. Y.		4
Parks, Frank, Goodland.		1
Parsons, H. N., Topeka.		4
Payne, Albert Bigelow, Fort Scott.		1
Peabody Institute, Baltimore, Md.		7
Peabody Public Library, Peabody.		1
Pease, Granville S., Anoka, Minn.		1
Peck, Ada H., Topeka.		1
Peck, Geo. C., Junction City	2	
Peck, Geo. R., Topeka.		4
Pecker, Col. J. E., Concord, N. H.	4	15
Pennsylvania, Adjutant General of, Harrisburg.	1	
Pennsylvania Agricultural Experiment Station, State College, Center County	2	6
Pennsylvania Historical Society, Philadelphia	1	
Pennsylvania Penitentiary, Philadelphia.	1	
Pennsylvania State Penitentiary, Philadelphia.		2
Perine, Miss Emma G., Topeka.		3
Perine, Mrs. Mary E., Topeka		1
Perkins, Bishop W., Washington, D. C.		5
Pernin, H. M.? Detroit, Mich.	1	3
Perry, Fred. H., Apopka, Fla.		1
Phelps, Rev. A. D., Wichita		7
Philadelphia Academy of Natural Sciences, Philadelphia, Pa.		2
Philadelphia Library Company, Philadelphia, Pa.		1
Phillips, Wm. A., Salina		2
Philosophical Society of Ohio, Cincinnati		1
Pierce, Gilbert A., Washington, D. C.		2
Pike & Ellsworth, Pasco County, Fla.		1
Pilling, James C., Washington D. C.		1
Plumb, P. B., Washington, D. C.	2	
Poinsett, Wm. B., Lansing.	2	
Polk, R. L. & Co., Chicago, Ill.	1	
Pomeroy, S. C., Washington, D. C.		6
Pond, Chester E., Topeka.		16
Poor, H. V. & H. W., New York.		2
Popenoe, F. O., Topeka.	2	157
Popenoe, Mrs. F. O., Topeka.		3
Porter, A. N., Sterling.		1
Powell, Mrs. Ella, Washington, Kas.		
Pratt, John G., Maywood.	2	
Price, Rev. Samuel, Wellington.		5
Proctor Bros., Gloucester, Mass.		5
Proper, Rev. D. D., Atchison.		83
Providence Athenæum, Providence, R. I.		1
Purdue University, LaFayette, Ind.		2

DONORS OF BOOKS AND PAMPHLETS — CONTINUED.

Donors.	Books	Pamp
Queen, J. W. & Co., Philadelphia, Pa................	.....	1
Radges, Samuel, Topeka....	1	.....
Raffensperger, Mrs. A. F., Marion, O'.........	2	.....
Rash, Howard C., Salina.............	.....	3
Rastall, Mrs. Fannie, Topeka...........	.....	2
Redden, Dr. J. W., Topeka..........	120	5
Reed, G. L., editor, Sulvane............	.....	1
Reagan, John H., Washington, D. C..........	.....	4
Republican Resubmission Club, Topeka.........	.....	1
Reynolds, Rev. J. B., Pratt.......	.....	2
Reynolds, John M., Atchison........	1	.....
Reynolds Library, Rochester, N. Y............	.....	1
Rhea, M. A., Altoona	.....	1
Rhode Island Agricultural Experiment Station, Kingston........	.....	13
Rhode Island Bureau of Industrial Statistics, Providence.........	1	1
Rhode Island Historical Society, Providence...........	1	6
Rice, Franklin P., Worcester, Mass...	.....	2
Richardson, Rev. A. M., Lawrence.........	.....	2
Richter, Rudolph, Kansas City, Mo.......	.....	1
Riddle, A. P., and C. M. Dunn, Minneapolis.........	.....	1
Riley, Z. F., Topeka........	1	.....
Robb, S. C., Ogallah.........	.....	1
Roberts, J. N., Topeka..........	60	.....
Roberts and Hill, Osage City............	.....	1
Robinson, A. A., Topeka............	.....	1
Robinson, A. W., Valley Falls.........	.....	1
Robinson, John C., Washington, D. C........	1	.....
Robinson & Co., Richmond, Ind.......	.....	1
Robinson & Springle, Washington.........	.....	1
Root, Frank A., North Topeka..........	1	74
Root, W. L., Topeka...........	.....	1
Ropes, George, Topeka...........	.....	1
Ross, D. M., Guthrie, Ok............	1	1
Ross, Gov. Edmund G., Deming, N. M........	.....	2
Rondebush, J. W., Topeka........	.....	1
Rutgers College, New Brunswick, N. J.......	7	22
Ryan, Thomas, Topeka...........	216	.....
St. Louis Public Library, St. Louis, Mo........	.....	2
St. Marys College, St. Marys............	.....	2
Samuels, Prof. H., Topeka............	.....	1
Sanborn, F. B., Concord, Mass..........	.....	1
San Francisco Free Public Library, Cal........	.....	1
San Francisco Mercantile Library, Cal.........	.....	1
Sarah Fuller Home, Boston, Mass...........	.....	1
Sargent, W. W., Holton............	.....	1
Sawhill, T. A., Concordia	.....	1
Sawin, Rev. A. G., Clifton...........	.....	8
Schuyler, Rev. Aaron, Salina	.....	2
See, A. N., editor, Salina............	.....	1
Sefrit, M. L. & Son, Washington, Ind............	.....	2
Severance, Mrs. Sarah M., Gilroy, Cal.......	.....	4
Sharder, J. W., Sec., Oskaloosa...........	.....	3
Shaw, A. P., Soldier	.....	1
Shaw, Wm., Boston, Mass..........	.....	5
Sheldon, Rev. C. M., Topeka............	.....	4
Sheldon, E. M., Ottawa............	.....	1
Sheltering Arms, New York City..........	.....	1
Shelton, E. M., Manhattan............	1	146
Shepard, R. B., Anthony............	.....	5
Sherrill, John B., Concordia	.....	1
Shinn, C., Ottawa............	1	.....
Simpson, B. F., Topeka............	.....	1
Simpson, J. Lea, Tonganoxie..........	.....	1
Sims, William, Topeka............	3	1
Smith, B. F., Lawrence...........	.....	2
Smith, Chester A., Yates Center............	1	1
Smith, Ed. R., Mound City..........	.....	1
Smith, George W., Topeka............	46	1,075
Smith, Wm. F., Kiowa............	.....	3
Smithsonian Institution, Washington, D. C..........	12	10
Smyth, B. B., Topeka............	20	2
Snow, Francis H., Lawrence...........	.....	31
Snyder, J. H., San Diego, Cal.........	.....	1
Société Archeologique du Department de Constantine, Alger, Africa........	2	.....
Société de Geographie, Paris, France........	.....	7
Société de Geographie Commerciale de Nantes, France.........	.....	3
Société de Geographie Commerciale de Paris, France.........	.....	3
Société de Geographie Commerciale du Havre, France.........	.....	3
Société de Geographie de Lyon, France.........	.....	3

DONORS OF BOOKS AND PAMPHLETS—CONTINUED.

Donors.	Books	Pamp
Sociéte Geographie de Toulouse, France		3
Société Havraise d'Etudes, Le Havre, France		2
Société Historique, Litteraire, Artistique, et Scientifique, du Cher, Bourges, France	2	
Société de Horticulture et de Botanique de Marseilles, France		2
Société Nationale D' Agriculture, Paris, France		1
Société Nationale des Antiquaries de France, Paris	2	
Société Neuchateloise, de Geographie, Neuchatel, France		6
Société Royale de Botanique de Belgique, Brussels, France		1
Society of American Florists, Boston, Mass		1
South Carolina Agricultural Experiment Station, Columbia	2	
South Carolina Commissioner of Education, Columbia	1	3
South Dakota Agricultural Experiment Station, Brookings		2
Southeran, Henry & Co., Piccadilly, London		1
Southern California Historical Society, Los Angeles		1
Spaulding, Charles, Topeka		22
Spellman Seminary, Atlanta, Ga		1
Spooner, John C., Washington, D. C		5
Sproat, Mrs. Kate, Topeka		1
Stacey, A. G., Topeka	1	
Stanley, E., Lawrence		1
Stanley, T. A., Osawatomie	1	13
State Agricultural College, Manhattan		7
Sterling, Wilson, Lawrence		1
Stevenson, Governor E. A., Boise City, Idaho		2
Stewart, C. H., Secretary, Seneca		1
Stewart, M., Wichita	1	
Stewart, W. H., Washington, D. C		18
Stonestreet, Frederick M., Topeka	15	1
Storch, George, Atchison		1
Storrs School Agricultural Experiment Station, Mansfield, Conn		6
Stotler, Jacob, Wellington	1	
Stotler, Joseph, Lawrence		2
Stowell, John and J. F., Briston, Wetmore		1
Strang, Judge J. C., Larned	5	
Strong, C. A., Waterville		1
Stryker, William, Great Bend		1
Stumm, Ewing, Hutchinson		2
Sutherland, George, Ottawa		7
Swensson, Rev. C. A., Lindsborg	1	3
Tauber, George, Topeka	1	
Taylor, A. R., Emporia	1	68
Taylor, Edw. F., Kansas City, Kas		1
Taylor, Rev. R. B., Stillwater, Ok	3	
Teller, H. M., Washington, D. C		2
Tennessee Bureau of Agriculture, Nashville		1
Tennessee State Board of Health, Nashville		4
Tenney, Mrs. Harriet A., Lansing, Mich		1
Texas Agricultural Experiment Station, College Station, Brazos county		11
Thayer Eli, Worcester, Mass	1	4
Thomann, G., New York City		1
Thomas, Robert H., Mechanicsburg, Pa		1
Thomas, Rev. E. S., Salina		1
Thompson, J. F., Sabetha		3
Thompson, Tom E., Howard		2
Thoroman, L. O., Salina		2
Thwing, Rev. Edward P., Brooklyn, N. Y	2	20
Tilley, R. H., Newport. R. I		3
Tousey, M. S., Clay Center		1
Tribune Association, New York City		2
Tribune Publishing Company, Los Angeles, Cal		1
Troup, Ira S., Lincoln		1
Troutman, James A., Topeka		15
Tucker, Rev. E. B., Ada		4
Turner, B. H., Newton		3
Tweeddale, Col. W., Topeka		1
Tyler, A. H., Parsons		1
U and I Club, Lawrence		1
Union, Geography du nord de la France, Douar, France		7
U. S. Agricultural Experiment Station, Washington, D. C		1
U. S. Army Adjutant General, Washington, D. C	3	
U. S. Brewers' Association, New York City		4
U. S. Bureau of Labor, Washington, D. C	15	3
U. S. Bureau of Navigation, Washington, D. C	1	
U. S. Bureau of Statistics, Treasury Department, Washington, D. C	2	3
U. S. Cavalry Association, Ft. Leavenworth	5	9
U. S. Chief of Engineers, U. S. A., Washington, D. C	9	
U. S. Chief of Ordnance, U. S. A., Washington, D. C	2	
U. S. Commissioner of Education, Washington, D. C	9	13
U. S. Commissioner of Patents, Washington, D. C		1

DONORS OF BOOKS AND PAMPHLETS—CONTINUED.

Donors.	Books	Pamp
U. S. Commissioner of Pensions, Washington, D. C.	......	2
U. S. Department of Agriculture, Washington, D. C.	10	71
U. S. Fish Commissioner, Washington, D. C.	11	......
U. S. Geological Survey, Director of, Washington, D. C.	11	18
U. S. Interstate Commerce Commission, Washington, D. C.	2	......
U. S. Life-Saving Service, Washington, D. C.	2	......
U. S. Lighthouse Board, Washington, D. C.	2	......
U. S. Mint, Director of, Washington, D. C.	5	......
U. S. Nautical Almanac office, Bureau of Equipment, Navy Department, Washington, D. C.	1	3
U. S. Naval Academy, Annapolis.	......	1
U. S. Naval Observatory, Washington, D. C.	3	......
U. S. Secretary of Agriculture, Washington, D. C.	2	6
U. S. Secretary of Interior, Washington, D. C.	439	2
U. S. Secretary of State, Washington, D. C.	46	20
U. S. Secretary of the Treasury, Washington, D. C.	25	60
U. S. Secretary of War, Washington, D. C.	4	......
U. S. Signal Office, Washington, D. C.	32	256
U. S. Signal Station, Observer of, Leavenworth.	......	6
University of California, Berkeley.	8	36
University of Kansas, Lawrence.	......	87
University of Nebraska, Lincoln.	......	1
Unknown.	......	6
Vail, Rev. A. L., Emporia.	......	2
Vail, Bishop T. H., Topeka.	......	5
Vanderbilt Benevolent Association, Charleston, S. C.	......	1
Van Dyke, H. N., Princeton, N. J.	......	1
Van Rensselaer, Rev. Munsell, New York.	1	......
Vermont Agricultural Experiment Station, Burlington.	......	9
Vincent, H., Winfield.	......	2
Vincent, H. & L., Winfield.	......	6
Virginia Agricultural Experiment Station, Blacksburg.	......	6
Von Langen, H., Topeka.	......	2
Votel, Rev. Henry J., St. Mary's.	......	1
Waldin, Horace G., Washington, D, C.	1	......
Walker, S. T., Olathe.	......	2
Wallace, J. W., Garden City.	......	1
Wanamaker, John, Philadelphia, Pa.	......	1
Ward, Mrs. Jennie M., Ottawa.	......	3
Ward, Dr. M. B., Topeka.	......	3
Ward, W. J., Kansas City, Mo.	1	......
Warkentin, B., Newton.	......	2
Warner, George T., Austin, Texas.	......	1
Warren, L. J., Clay Center.	......	2
Waterman, A. A., Boston, Mass.	......	1
Waterman, J. N., Delphos.	......	1
Watson, Miss Carrie M., Lawrence.	1	......
Waugh, Lorenzo, San Francisco, Cal.	......	19
Welburn, J. B., Effingham.	......	1
Weller, Ernest A., Wamego.	......	2
West Virginia Agricultural Experiment Station, Morgantown.	......	7
Western Reserve and Northern Ohio Historical Society, Cleveland.	......	1
Weston, J. A., Secretary, Frankfort.	......	1
Whaley, W. E., Manhattan.	......	1
White, H. F., Topeka.	......	13
Whitmore, W. H., Downs.	......	1
Wichita Public Schools, Superintendent of.	1	......
Wickersham, J. A., Terre Haute, Ind.	1	......
Wight, R. A., Rochester, N. Y.	1	......
Wilder, D. W., Topeka.	146	92
Wiles, C. K., Winfield.	......	3
Willard, Miss Frances E., Chicago, Ill.	......	5
Wilkinson, J. N., Emporia.	......	1
Williams, A. L., Topeka.	......	1
Williams, George T., Chicago, Ill.	......	1
Williams, H., New York.	2	......
Williams, Col. James A., Trinidad, Col.	......	1
Williams, John Fletcher, St. Paul, Minn.	......	1
Wilson, Mrs. Augustus, Wilsonton.	......	1
Winans, George W., Topeka.	60	......
Winthrop, Robert C., Boston, Mass.	......	1
Wisconsin Agricultural Experiment Station, Madison.	2	8
Wisconsin Bureau of Labor and Industrial Statistics, Madison	1	1
Wisconsin State Board of Health, Appleton, Wis.	......	1
Wisconsin State Grange, Neenah.	......	1
Wisconsin State Historical Society, Madison.	38	11
Wolcott, E. O., Washington, D. C.	......	2
Wolf, Right Rev. Innocent, Atchison.	......	1
Wolford, A. G., Topeka.	1	......

DONORS OF BOOKS AND PAMPHLETS — CONCLUDED.

Donors.	Books	Pamp
Woman's Temperance Publication Society, Chicago, Ill.	......	6
Wood, M. F., Cherry Vale.	......	1
Woodford, J. E., Secretary, Burlington.	......	1
Woodman, Selden J., Los Angeles, Cal.	......	1
Woodruff, Wilford, Salt Lake City, Utah.	1	......
Woods, M. H., Secretary, Garnett.	......	8
Woodward, Brinton W., Lawrence.	1	......
Worcester Society of Antiquity, Worcester, Mass.	1	2
Worrall, Harvey, Topeka.	......	19
Wray, E. W., Guthrie, I. T.	1	......
Wright, J. M., Dodge City.	......	6
Wright, Rezin A., New York City.	9	2
Wynn, Prof. W. H., Atchison.	......	8
Wyoming Historical and Geological Society, Wilkes-Barre, Pa	......	2
Yates, Lorenzo G., Santa Barbara, Cal.	......	7
Ye Little Olde Book Store, Springfield, Mass.	3	......
Yingling, Dr. W. A., Nonchalanta.	......	1
Young, I. D., Beloit.	......	2
Zercher, D. C., Olathe.	......	1
Zinn, L. W., Hutchinson.	......	1

DONORS OF MANUSCRIPTS.

Abarr, Miss Mary, Topeka: Invitation to the Leslie Club social, December 21, 1888, Music Hall, Topeka.

Abbott, George, Osawkee: Share number 241, of stock in the town of Osawkee, Kansas Territory, dated July 25, 1857, signed by George C. Wright, president.

Abbott, Major J. B., De Soto: Letter of donor addressed to Hon. Joel K. Goodin, dated Topeka, March 14, 1888; also letter of Mr. Goodin in reply, dated Ottawa, Kansas, January 25, 1889. The correspondence relates to the arrest at Topeka of twenty or twenty-five Free-State men, members of the Topeka Legislature, January 5, 1857, by Deputy United States Marshall Pardee, on indictment of grand jury at Tecumseh, for object of getting Governor Geary into trouble with the administration and thereby securing his removal.

Adams, Henry J., Topeka: Biographical sketch of Captain Samuel A. Williams, member first Territorial Legislature, by J. T. Williams.

Alrich, L. L., Cawker City: Register of attendance at the meeting of Cawker City Old Settlers' Association, January 1, 1889.

Anderson, Rev. J. W. D., Elk City: Fac-simile of the ordination certificate given by John Wesley to Bishop Coke, the first Methodist Bishop in America; list of books about Kansas, or of which citizens of Kansas are the authors; mostly in the possession of Mr. Anderson; also in the library of the State Historical Society.

Barnes, William, Albany, N. Y.: The records and papers of the New York State Kansas Committee of 1856 and 1857, of which Mr. Barnes was the secretary, together with the tin case in which the records and papers were preserved by him, namely: Manuscript record book, (also contains the record of Wm. Barnes as the treasurer of the Hungarian Liberty Association of the city of Albany, 1852); 27 letters from Dr. Thomas H. Webb and other

officers of the New England Emigrant Aid Company; 39 letters from National Kansas Aid Committee, Chicago; 22 letters from Daniel R. Anthony, Rochester, N. Y.; 10 letters from J. P. Filer; 35 letters from Rev. A. H. Shurtliff; 4 letters from O. C. Brown; 25 letters from J. L. Wilde; 18 letters from B. B. Newton; 7 letters from Eli Thayer; 9 letters from Russell Hubbard; 1 letter from Capt. John Brown; 1 letter from Thaddeus Hyatt; 1 letter from Horace Greeley; 412 miscellaneous letters; 15 resolutions; 11 receipts, etc.; 1 subscription paper to New York State Kansas Fund; 19 certificates of credentials of delegates to the Free-State Kansas Convention held at Buffalo, July 9th and 10th, 1856, with list of delegates; 4 blank subscription books of the National Kansas Committee appointed at Buffalo, July 9th, 1856; 1 pamphlet report of the proceed-- ings of the convention of delegates from Kansas aid societies in different States, held at Cleveland, O., June 20th and 21st, and adjourned and held at Buffalo, N. Y., July 9th and 10th, 1856, A. H. Reeder, president, Wm. Barnes and W. F. M. Arny, secretaries, 21 pages; 1 pamphlet prospectus and description of the city of Burlingame, Kansas, 1857; 657 manuscripts in all. (See lists of Donors of Books and Pamphlets, of Pictures, of Scrip, Currency, etc., of War Relics, and of Miscellaneous Contributions.)

Benson, Harry Darius, St. Francis: Autobiographical sketch of donor, delegate to the Legislature, 1889–90.

Bonham, Jeriah, Springfield, Ill.: Manuscript press article entitled "Farmers' Organizations in Kansas and Other States; some history connected with them; their failure as political factors." Dated Springfield, Ill., October 23, 1890; 8 pages.

Botkin, G. W., publisher of the Hutchinson *Republican*, Hutchinson: Autographical sketch of donor, dated June 27, 1889.

Bradlee, Rev. C. D., Boston, Mass.: Autographs of Rev. Dr. Frederic H. Hedge, Cambridge, Mass.; Rev. J. H. Allen, editor Unitarian *Review;* Rev. Dr. A. P. Peabody, LL.D., Harvard University; autograph letter addressed to donor from First Congregational Church, Quincy, Mass., March 1, 1889; brief autobigraphical sketch of donor; autograph letter of R. C. Waterson, dated October 18, 1886. Seven acknowledgment certificates from societies and institutions: Three Geneva, Switzerland; one Paris; two Florence, Italy; one New York.

Brown, Geo. W., Rockford, Ill.: Letter of donor dated Rockford, September 29, 1890, relating to incidents of Governor Geary's administration.

Caine, William W., Witoka, Minn.: Account of Wakarusa war and other Kansas reminiscences, letter of donor addressed to Secretary of the Historical Society, dated Witoka, February 28, 1889; reminiscences of donor in Kansas, 1855–6.

Coburn, F. D., Kansas City, Kansas: Letter of John J. Ingalls, addressed to donor, relative to seal of Kansas, dated Washington, D. C., October 10,

1888; also letter of donor relative to the foregoing, dated Kansas City, Kas., January 14, 1889.

Corey, C. A., Topeka: Biographical sketch of Albert Samuel Corey, printer, dated August 28, 1889.

Corgan, John N., McPherson: Letter of Capt. John C. Brand to donor dated [Jeff.] Davis Plantation, (near Vicksburg), July —, 1864; letter of Col. B. L. E. Bonneville, dated Benton Barracks, Mo., May 31, 1864; letter of Lieut. H. Hemriges, dated Camp, Vicksburg, Miss., April 20, 1864; description of Bedloe's Island, N. Y., written by donor, as in 1848; letter of Fred Shattner, County Clerk of Sedgwick county, Kas., dated Aug. 24, 1871, relative to the boundaries of Black Kettle township; also 10 other letters and papers of a later date; 15 in all.

Davis, E., sr., Towanda: Parchment indenture of donor as an apprentice in England, dated 1837.

Dodge, S. H., Beloit: Fac-simile of the indenture of Hon. Simon Cameron, of Pennsylvania, as an apprentice to Andrew Kennedy, printer, May 14, 1861.

Elder, D. M., El Dorado: Autobiographical sketch of donor, member of the Legislature, 1889–90, Sixty-third District, dated Feb. 14, 1889.

Emery, Rufus Marion, Seneca: Autobiographical sketch of donor, State Senate, 1889–91, Twenty-first Senatorial District, dated January 30, 1889.

Emery, J. S., Lawrence: Address of donor delivered before an Oklahoma mass meeting, Arkansas City, Feb. 20, 1889.

Eshelman, Rev. M. M., McPherson: Autobiographical sketch of donor.

Fairchild, G. T., Manhattan: Autobiography of donor, President of the State Agricultural College, March, 1889.

Ford, W. D., Pittsburg, member of the Legislature, Twenty-fourth District, 1889–90: Autobiographical memorandum of donor.

Forney, Josephus W., Belle Plaine, State Senator, 1889–91, Twenty-eighth Senatorial District: Autobiographical sketch of donor.

Gleed, C. S., Topeka: Letter of Sylvester Baxter, to donor, dated Malden, Mass., July 11, 1889, relative to tobacco-pouch relic. (See Miscellaneous Contributions, C. S. Gleed.)

Goodnow, Prof. I. T., Manhattan: Sermon of Rev. Joseph Denison, delivered at Tecumseh, M. E. Church, April 21, 1889, and reported by his son, Henry L. Denison.

Greene, A. R., Topeka: Autobiography of donor, State Railroad Commissioner, dated Jan. 16, 1889.

Griffith, Geo. P., Hayes City: Original Lease given by Samuel Winfield to Thomas Abbott, Dec. 24, 1767, of a windmill at Ohoroton, in Nottingham county, England, for fifty years from date, written on parchment 21x 27 inches in size.

Hale, James H. Rose, member of the Legislature, Thirty-sixth District, 1889–90: Autobiographical sketch of donor.

Hawes, Alex. G., San Francisco, Cal.: Manuscript account by donor, of the battle of Osawatomie, Aug. 30, 1856.

Hayden, Sidney, Holton: Original of bill of particulars filed in court in Prince George county, Md., June 10, 1727, in the case of Ed. Moberly vs. Wyatt's executors; original writ of fieri facias, directed to the Sheriff of Prince George's county, Md., in the name of King George II, in the case of Epes vs. Raney, dated May 30, 1739; manuscript deed from James Morris, of Reading, Berks county, to Benjamin Davies, same place, for 8,668 acres of land in Mifflin county, Pa., dated July 30, 1821.

Hebbard, J. C., Topeka: Manuscript relative to the naming of the towns of Seneca and Sabetha.

Hitt, James J., Topeka: Autograph of John Quincy Adams, attached to land patent of David Jackson, of Howard county, Mo., April 1st, 1825; autograph of James Monroe, attached to land patent of David Jackson, of Boone county, Mo., Aug. 20, 1824.

Holman, Rev. C., North Topeka: Manuscript record book containing the record of the Kansas M. E. Conference for the years 1873–1881. [Conditional deposit.]

Horne, D. H., Oceanside, Cal.: Letter of Marie L. Horne, dated Topeka, April 16, 1855, addressed to her mother and sisters, Susan and Bell; recruiting order addressed to donor, dated Headquarters Kansas Brigade, Camp Mitchell, Oct. 3, 1861, and signed by J. H. Lane, commanding Kansas Brigade, and by T. J. Anderson, acting Assistant Adjutant General; note addressed to "President, Directors, and other parties in interest of the Union Pacific Railroad Company, E. D.," introducing donor, delegated to present the claims of Topeka as a point in the line of said road, signed by C. K. Holliday, late President, H. W. Farnsworth, Jacob Safford, F. L. Crane, and S. N. Wood, Directors, dated Topeka, Feb. 10, 1864.

Jerome, F. E., Topeka: Letter of donor, relating to the history of the John Brown song, dated Topeka, Dec. 23, 1888.

Jones, John P., Coldwater: List of papers, translations from Spanish and French, relating to Coronado's Expedition, in possession of donor.

Julian, N. P., Liverpool: Biographical sketch of donor, 1889.

King, James L., Topeka: Two letters of Gov. John A. Martin, dated Dec. 29, and 31, 1887, addressed to donor, giving biographical sketch of his wife, Mrs. Ida Challiss Martin, for use in an article afterward published in the Chicago *Tribune*.

Lewis, D. W., Topeka: Manuscript saved from the Cincinnati fire of 1884.

Lockard, F. M., Norton: Biographical sketch of donor, State Senator, 1889–91, Thirty-fourth Senatorial District.

Lykins, William H. R., Kansas City, Mo.: Parchment float issued by President Andrew Johnson to Joel Walker, June 14, 1865, for one section of land; the following manuscript papers relating to original shares and lots in Lawrence, and dated 1854 to 1860; 22 drawings of shares by donor;

letter of Gov. A. H. Reeder to donor; manuscript book of proceedings of trustees of Robitaille float, 1858; brief in the case of the Reeder float; 12 miscellaneous papers; 37 applications for registry preëmption claims.

McDowell, John S., commissioner of State Reformatory, Smith Center: Autobiographical sketch of donor, dated January 28, 1889.

Martin, William Wallace, Fort Scott, member of the Senate, Seventh Senatorial District, 1889–91: Autobiographical sketch of donor.

Maule, Chas. Ingersoll, Strong City, member of the Legislature, Sixty-fourth District, 1889–90: Autobiographical sketch of donor.

Miller, Fremont, Admire, member of the Legislature, Fifty-fifth District 1889–90: Autobiographical sketch of donor.

Mitchell, Clinton Robert, Regent State University, Geuda Springs: Autobiographical sketch of donor.

Mitchell, Mrs. Jennie S., York, Neb.: Letter written by Geo. A. Crawford, dated Leavenworth City, May 29th, 1862, addressed to Col. Sam Stambaugh, of Pennsylvania, introducing Gen. R. B. Mitchell.

Montgomery, Mrs. Clarinda, Castle Rock, W. T.: Letter of donor, dated Castle Rock, Oct. 13, 1889, giving account of personal appearance of Col. James Montgomery, her husband.

Moore, Thomas P., Regent and Loan Commissioner, State Agricultural College, Holton: Autobiographical sketch of donor.

Morgan, L. J., Springdale, member of the Legislature, 1889, 1890, Eighth District: Autobiographical sketch of donor.

Morse, O. E., Mound City: Letter of donor relating to the history of the John Brown song, dated January 7, 1889.

Murphy, Eugene F., Goodland: Autobiographical sketch of donor, Delegate to the Legislature, Sherman county, 1889, 1890.

Newlon, W. S., Oswego: Oswego Town Company stock certificate, number 25, dated April 11, 1868, in favor of donor; also certificate of Oswego Town Company entitling donor to deed of warranty to town lots in Oswego.

Nicholls, Archibald, Chardon: Autobiographical sketch of donor, member of the Legislature, 1889, 1890; One Hundred and Twenty-fourth District; dated February 15, 1889.

Painter, J. S., editor *Garden City Herald*, Garden City: Autobiographical sketch of donor.

Paramore, Ed. H., Huntsville, Ala.: Promissory note of A. H. Thurston, for payment of $40.88, hire of a negro woman from January 1, 1846, to January 1, 1847, dated March 5, 1846, with payments indorsed on back.

Phillips, Colonel William A., Salina: Certificate of ownership of Romeo, a negro slave, by the President and people of the United States, dated July 22, 1845, signed by Major-General Thomas S. Jesup, of the Seminole war; also donor's letter of transmittal, dated August 28, 1889. Also, letter of John H. Kagi, written to donor from Chambersburg, Pa., a few days before the attack on Harper's Ferry, with explanatory memorandum. Also,

topographical report of the Cherokee Neutral Land Commission made in 1867 and 1868. The lands were 800,000 acres lying in Bourbon, Crawford and Cherokee counties. The report contains description, topography, names of original settlers, price, minerals, etc., slope of the lands, creeks, water, timber, etc.; eighteen mauuscript books.

Rankin, John C., Quenemo; member of the Senate, Sixteenth District, 1889–91: Autobiographical sketch of donor.

Reader, Samuel J., North Topeka: Poem by donor entitled, "The Battle of Big Blue, Price's Raid," giving, in rhyme, a brief history of the battle.

Reeder, Gen. Frank, Easton, Pa.: Letter of donor, dated October 11th, 1889, giving personal description of Gov. Andrew J. Reeder.

Rice, William Montgomery, Fort Scott, member of the Legislature, Twenty-second District, 1889–90: Autobiographical sketch of donor.

Roach, Thomas Kirkpatrick, Holton, member of the Legislature, Forty-third District, 1889–90: Autobiographical sketch of donor.

Roy, G. D., Prescott: Old settlers' register of Sheridan township, Linn county, names procured at meeting held at Holmes's Grove, August 18th, 1888, and August 8th, 1889.

Russell, Edward, Lawrence: Oath of allegiance of D. R. Anthony, number 417, dated Post of Gainsville, Ala., June 8, 1865, sworn to and subscribed before Chas. A. Hubbard, captain 93d Ind. Vols. and Provost Marshal.

Rutledge, G. O., Parkville, Mo.: Two letters of Robert S. Kelley, addressed to —— Miller, dated Atchison, K. T., August 19th and 22d, 1855, relating to political affairs in Kansas; also poem addressed to Hon. David R. Atchison.

Sapp, F. H., Moody, Texas: Reminiscences of Kansas in 1856, account of battles of Franklin, and other events, Feb. 5, 1890; biographical sketch of author and donor, Feb. 17, 1890.

Senate and House of Representatives, Topeka, by concurrent resolution: Penitentiary Investigation, testimony taken by the joint committee of the Legislature, vols. 1 and 2, 1889.

Singleton, Benjamin, Kansas City, Mo.: Certificate of incorporation of the Edgefield Real Estate Association, a colored exodus organization, Davidson county, Tenn., in office of Secretary of State, Nashville, Sept. 12, 1874, Chas. N. Gibbs, Secretary. The incorporators are "W. A. Sizemore, Benjamin Petway, Houston Molloy, Washington Anthony, sr., A. McClure, Washington Anthony, jr., Thomas Weston, Richard Battle, and donor, all of Davidson county, Tenn." Certificate of incorporation of Singleton Colony of Morris and Lyon counties, Kansas, June 25, 1879; five manuscripts, dated Dunlap, Kansas, Aug. 9, 1879, containing list of names of heads of families in Singleton Colony, with number of individuals in each family, and number of acres selected for each family; commendation of donor, dated Topeka, Kansas, Oct. 22, 1879, and signed by Gov. John P. St. John, Albert H. Horton, N. C. McFarland, F. G. Adams, and W. A. Sizemore;

appeal made by Singleton Colony, soliciting help towards first payment on their lands, fall of 1879, signed by 37 members of the colony, and authorizing donor to receive money for such object; deed to donor of four lots in town of Dunlap, dated Oct. 3, 1882, also six letters relative to same; four letters addressed to donor from his children in Tennessee; letter of A. D. De Frantz, addressed to Pap Singleton, dated Jan. 25, 1887.

Stewardson, James M., Colby, member of the Legislature, One Hundred and Twenty-third District, 1889–90: Autobiographical sketch of donor.

Smith, Geo. W., Topeka: Petitions for bridge at Kansas City from citizens; Price Raid petition; petition from Atchison Industrial School for girls; letter of Geo. Ropes, addressed to Hon. J. N. High, chairman sub-committee for investigation of claim of donor against State of Kansas, Topeka, Feb. 20, 1889.

Smith, H. B., Osawatomie, Account-book of Henry Crane, of Durham, Conn., dates running from Feb. 3, 1743, to Nov. 10, 1810, bound in vellum; formerly the property of Chas. H. Crane, who settled in Osawatomie in 1855.

Smith, Horace J., Ottawa, member of the Legislature, Sixteenth District, 1889–90: Autobiographical sketch of donor.

Spencer, Orsemus Hale, McPherson, member of the Legislature, Eightieth District, 1889–90: Autobiographical sketch of donor.

Thayer, Eli, Worcester, Mass.: Letter of donor, dated Sept. 24, 1889, with inclosure of printed slip containing letters from Dr. LeBarron Russell, relative to the influence of the N. E. Emigrant Aid Company in making Kansas a free State.

Thompson, Geo. F., Manhattan: Autograph letter of Prudence Crandall Philleo, with poem entitled "Address to Farmers," written to donor, dated Elk Falls, June 16, 1886.

Triplett, C. S., Leoti, Delegate to the Legislature from Wichita county: Autobiographical sketch of donor, dated Feb. 14, 1889.

Younkman, David M., Goff's, member of the Legislature, Forty-fifth District, 1889–90: Autobiographical sketch of donor.

Wallace, William W., manager *Garden City Herald*, Garden City: Autobiographical sketch of donor.

Weed, Geo. W., Topeka: Commission of donor as resident Commissioner for the State of Kansas at the Garfield Monument Fair, held in the Capitol, Washington, from November 25 to December 3, 1882; certificate of donor's membership in Payne's Oklahoma Colony, Wichita, February 6, 1884; autograph of D. L. Payne.

White, Charles Longton, member of the Legislature, Fifty-seventh District, 1889–90: Autobiographical sketch of donor, dated January 7, 1889.

Wright, Rezin A., New York city, N. Y.: Manuscripts, military letters and papers relating to the late war, given by Brigadier General M. R. Patrick, to donor; also ten other autographs.

Wilder, D. W., Topeka: A brief outline of the life of John A. Martin; by donor before the Eighth Kansas Volunteers, Topeka, October 8, 1890. Letter of William Kaucher, addressed to donor, dated Hamlin, December 17, 1888, relative to French burr millstone, supposed to be one of the first brought to Kansas.

Wilkinson, J. N., Emporia: Register of Kansas teachers at the National Teachers' Association, San Francisco, Cal., August, 1889.

Williamson, J. D., Troy, member of the Legislature, First District, 1889-90: Autobiographical sketch of donor.

Wood, L. M., Denver, Colo.: Copy of a commission to Capt. William H. Leeman, by John Brown, dated near Harper's Ferry, Md., Oct. 15, 1859, presented to donor by Colonel J. T. Gibson, Charlestown, Jefferson county, W. Va.

Wright, John K., Junction City, member of the Senate, 1889-90, Twentieth Senatorial District: Autobiographical sketch of donor.

Wright, Jonathan Joel, Emporia, member of the Legislature, Fifty-fourth District, 1889-90: Autobiographical sketch of donor, inclosed in his letter of April 23, 1890.

DONORS OF MAPS, CHARTS, AND ATLASES.

Bradlee, Dr. C. D., Boston, Mass.: Map of the city of Boston, 1890.

Campbell, A. B., Topeka: Military map of Kansas, 1886, four copies.

Clark, Sylvester H., Clyde, N. Y.: A copy of the engraved chart, entitled "The Triumph of Freedom Over Slavery," containing an engraved copy of the Thirteenth Amendment to the Constitution of the United States, abolishing slavery, with autographs as follows: Abraham Lincoln, President; H. Hamlin, Vice President; Schuyler Colfax, Speaker of the House of Representatives; J. W. Forney, Secretary of the Senate; Edward McPherson, Clerk of the House of Representatives; and of the members of the Senate and House of Representatives who voted for the Amendment, which passed the Senate April 8, 1864, and the House of Representatives January 30, 1865, and was approved by President Abraham Lincoln February 1, 1865; also key to the above chart.

Clarkson, Harrison, Topeka: Sanborn Fire Map of Topeka, 1885.

Cook, Geo. H., State Geologist, New Brunswick, N. J.: Geological map of New Jersey, from original surveys, 1889, by donor; atlas of New Jersey, geological survey; the State map of New Jersey, and the relief map of the State of New Jersey, 1888, by donor.

Coyell, E. E., Topeka: Topeka Guide and Business Directory — chart.

Day, W. H., Tyrone: Map of the city of Tyrone, Seward county, Kansas, incorporated May 7, 1888.

Geological Natural History Survey of Canada, Ottawa: Plan of Asbestos Areas, Part K, annual report, 1887; part M, annual report, 1887, sheet number 17, N. E. New Brunswick.

Goerz, David, Halstead: Map showing the A. T. & S. F. R. R. and extensions in Kansas.

Goodnow, Prof. I. T., Manhattan: Township map of eastern Kansas, by Whitman & Searl; atlas to Warren's System of Geography; system of map drawing, by F. L. Ripley; map of Kansas, 1888,. Manhattan *Republic* supplement, containing also pictures of buildings, public and private, in Manhattan; map of State Agricultural College lands in Washington, Marshall, Clay, Riley and Dickinson counties (no date); map of northern and eastern portions of Kansas, also schedule of State Agricultural College lands, 1889; map of State of California, compiled, for Immigration Association of San Francisco, California (no date); three maps of the seat of war in Europe, in 1854 and 1855; map of the Baltic Sea, presented to subscribers of Boston *Chronicle*, war of 1854–55.

Green, Samuel A., Boston, Mass.: Fac-simile of Hubbard's map of New England, with text by donor.

Halderman, Gen. John A., Washington, D. C.: Map showing location of the Diplomatic and Consular Offices of the U. S. of America, March 1, 1888.

Hall & O'Donald Lithographing Co., Topeka: Two charts giving list of county, State and Federal officers of Kansas, April, 1889.

Historical and Philosophical Society, of Ohio, Cincinnati: Three United States maps.

Jennings, T. B, Topeka: Twenty-six rain charts to accompany Kansas Weather-Crop Bulletins.

Kansas Railroad Commissioners, Topeka: James Humphrey, Geo. T. Anthony, Albert R. Greene, Topeka; railroad map of Kansas, 1889, 12 copies; Campbell's commercial map, 1884, issued by Missouri Railroad Commissioners; railroad map of Kansas, 1890, 60 copies.

Kilmer, Fred B., New Brunswick, N. J.: Map of Oregon and Upper California, to accompany Fremont's Survey, by Charles Preuss, 1848.

Lykins, William H. R., Kansas City, Mo.: Map of Lawrence, Kansas, 1855, by A. D. Searl.

Mohler, Martin, Topeka: Map of Kansas, published by the State Board of Agriculture, 1889.

Ohio Archæological and Historical Society, Columbus: Map of Ohio, 1888.

Popenoe, F. O., Topeka: Atlas of the Santa Fé route.

Powell, J. W., Washington, D. C.: Mineral productions of the United States, 1882 to 1887, tabulated statement by donor, dated October 15, 1888.

Rutgers College, New Brunswick, N. J.: Atlas of geology of New Jersey, 1868, by Geo. H. Cook.

Ryan, Thomas, Topeka: Map of the Missouri river, surveys, 1878 to 1881, by D. W. Wellman.

Selwyn, Dr. Alfred R. C., Ottawa, Canada: Maps, etc., to accompany Annual Report of the Geological and Natural History Survey of Canada, vol. 3, 1887–88.

Smith, Geo. W., Topeka: Fourteen Senatorial apportionment maps, State of
Kansas, 1888; map of Rice county, 1886; two maps of Lyons, Rice county.

Smith, H. B., Osawatomie: MacLean & Lawrence's sectional map of Kansas
Territory, compiled by C. P. Wiggin, April, 1857.

Stonebraker, S. A., Black Jack: Map of Prairie City, surveyed February,
1857, by A. D. Searl.

Tenney, Mrs. Harriet A., State Librarian, Lansing, Mich.: Atlas of maps
accompanying geological survey of Michigan, Upper Peninsula, vols. 1,
2, 4.

Times, Kansas City, Mo.: Map of Oklahoma, April, 1889.

Union Pacific R. R. Company: Map of the overland route.

U. S. Department of State, Washington, D. C.: Atlas of joint maps of the
northern boundary of the U. S. from the Lake of the Woods to the summit
of the Rocky Mountains; eight maps showing the location of the Diplomatic and Consular offices of the U. S. of America, March 1st, 1888.

U. S. Geological Survey, Washington, D. C.: Atlas to accompany a Monograph on the Geology of the Quicksilver Deposits of the Pacific Slope, by
Geo. F. Becker.

Unknown: Map of the City of Washington, D. C., showing route of inaugural
parade, March 4, 1889.

Wilder, D. W., Topeka: Map of portions of Kansas, Nebraska and Missouri,
1859, by J. H. Colton; sketch of the country near the southern boundary
of Kansas, by J. E. Johnston.

World, Wichita: Map of Indian Territory and Oklahoma Territory, supplement to Wichita *World*, of March 30, 1889.

DONORS OF PICTURES.

Adams, Helen W., Waterville: Three views of watermelon field in Washington county, 1888.

Adams, W. M., Neosho Rapids: Photo of Neosho Rapids Seminary.

Admire, W. W., Topeka: Portrait of Governor Wilson Shannon, in frame;
engraving of the ruins of the first Kansas Capitol Building, at Pawnee;
engraving of ex-Governor A. H. Reeder, taken from a painting in the
State Historical Rooms; also one from a photo of his disguise when fleeing
from the Kansas Territory.

Aldrich, Emma B., Cawker City: Photo portrait of the Woman's Hesperian
Library Club, Cawker City.

Arment, A. B., Winfield: Photo of sample ear of Cowley county corn, 1890.

Bailey, Judge L. D., Garden City: Cabinet photo portrait of donor.

Baker, C. C., Topeka: Engraved portrait of donor.

Baker, Floyd P., Topeka: Nearly life-size photo portrait of donor, neatly
framed, 1890.

Barnes, William, Albany, N. Y.: Portrait of John Brown, upon which is
the following inscription: "This is an original photograph of John Brown,

—3

taken for me in Albany, N. Y., about the year 1857; it is a good picture of him at that time. (Signed) William Barnes, Albany, N. Y., December 8, 1888."

Beets, Mary F., editor *Young Kansan*, Gardner: Cabinet-size photo portrait of donor.

Bradlee, Rev. C. D., Boston, Mass.: Engraved portrait of Rev. Dr. and Prof. E. P. Thwing, of Brooklyn, N. Y.; engraved portrait of Rev. Caleb Bradley, born at Dracut, Mass., March 12, 1771, died June 2, 1861, in his ninetieth year; engraved portrait of Major-General William Moultrie; cabinet size photos of Edward P. Jackson, Edwin T. Horne, Rev. Joseph Weeks.

Bright, Rev. J. A., Abilene: Photograph of donor, Chaplain of Kansas House, session 1887, and of Senate, 1889–90.

Brooks, Frank, Topeka: Cabinet photo of donor.

Campbell, W. P., Wamego: Picture group, (blue process,) representing amateur dramatic company cast for the drama "Corene."

Carpenter, J. S., St. Marys: Photo group of Pottawatomie county editors, 1889.

Cedar Vale Corps, No. 160, W. R. C., Cedar Vale: Photographic portraits of the members, 1890.

Chapman, James G., North Topeka: Photograph of Belvoir, dwelling of John D. Knox, north of Potwin Place, 1888.

Christian, James, Arkansas City: Cabinet photo of Gen. James H. Lane; also cabinet photo of donor.

Cone, W. W., Topeka: Photo of grape-vine, in fruit, Topeka, Aug. 15, 1889.

Corey, C. A., Topeka: Photographic portrait of Albert S. Corey.

Crane, Geo. W. & Co., Topeka: Album of Topeka, 1888, fifty-five views of the city; engraving of Kansas State Historical room, by donor.

DuPuy, Maria Wilder, Rochester, N. Y.: Steel portrait of Thaddeus Stevens, 1867, John Sartain, engraver.

Eshelman, Rev. M. M., McPherson: Cabinet photo portrait of donor.

Farnham, Capt. G. W., Chicago, Ill.: Photos of Gen. Geo. W. Deitzler; of Gen. Robt. B. Mitchell; of Gen. James G. Blunt, and of Col. Geo. H. Hoyt.

Farrow, W. F., Topeka: Three photo views of Kansas State Historical rooms, 1889.

Ford, W. D., member of the Legislature, Pittsburg: Photo portrait of donor, 1889.

Goss, Col. N. S., Topeka: Cabinet photo of donor.

Gotwald, Rev. Geo. D., Kansas City, Mo.: Photo view of car-load of flour for the Johnstown sufferers, from the citizens of Salina.

Gove, Alonzo, Osawatomie: Tintype taken at Butler, Mo., in 1863, of the following persons: C. P. Casey, Dwight Chapell, Edger Cone, Geo. R. Fer-

ris; all residents of Osawatomie, and all members of Co. I, Col. Jennison's regiment, war of the Rebellion.

Halderman, John A., Washington, D. C.: Engraved view of the city of Hobart, Tasmania, Australia.

Harrington, N. O., Topeka: View of buildings Williston Seminary, East Hampton, Mass.

Hays, Robert R., Senator, Osborne: Photo portrait of donor, 1889.

Hill, W. R., Hill City: Photo of donor and wife, Mrs. Lydia Hill; two photo cards exhibiting the process of cutting, cleaning,.and curing of broom corn on farm of donor, in Graham county, Sept. 10, 1889; 10 views in Hill City, Graham county, including that of the pioneer house, which existed from 1880–89; photograph of Harvest Home Festival at First Baptist Church, Hill City, Sept. 10, 1889; photo of Pomeroy's special train at Hill City, Oct. 22, 1888, and Pomeroy House, at same place, in all 17 views.

Hopkins, T. R., Topeka: Two photographic views of Baptist Indian Mission buildings, west of Topeka.

Horton, Albert H., Topeka: Photo portrait of donor, framed.

Jamison, Capt. Jacob, Cherokee: Photo of Marquer, and grounds of donor, July 1, 1890.

Johnson, Col. A. S., Topeka: Cabinet-size photo portrait of donor, 1888.

Kamensky, Theodore, New York City, N. Y.: Photo of donor's sketch models for the tympanum of the north and south pediments of the Kansas Capitol building; photo of donor's model of a statue of Ceres, for the dome of the Capitol.

Kavanagh, N. Jos., publisher *News*, Blaine: Cabinet photo of donor.

Knox, Rev. John D., Topeka: Photo view of the ruins of the great fire in Boston, Nov. 9 and 10, 1872.

Lewis, D. W., Topeka: Photo of Sir Marcus Goodwillie, the largest and heaviest man in the world.

Lockard, F. M., State Senator, Norton: Photo portrait of donor.

McCoy, J. C., jr., Kansas City, Mo.: Cabinet photo of the late J. C. McCoy, sr.

McCray, D. O., Topeka: Cabinet photo of donor.

McDowell, John S., Commissioner State Industrial Reformatory, Smith Center: Cabinet photo portrait of donor.

McLeod, photographer, Atchison: Photo, view showing the devastation caused by the flood at Atchison, 1890.

Manchester, Alfred, Providence, R. I.: Cabinet photo portrait of donor.

Martin, H. T., Topeka: Cabinet photo portraits of President Geo. T. Fairchild, and of T. P. Moore of Holton, A. P. Forsyth of Liberty, and Joshua Wheeler of Nortonville, Regents of State Agricultural College; of J. H. Franklin, Russell, Regent State Normal School, and J. S. McDowell, Smith Center, Director of State Penitentiary; of 23 Senators and 148 members, officers and employés of the House of Representatives, 1889, and 8 of the Pages of the House and Senate.

Matherson, Miss Ida, New Cumberland, W. Va.: Steel-engraved portrait of Dr. H. D. McCarty.

Morrill, E. N., Hiawatha: Life-size photo portrait of donor, 1889.

Murphy, E. F., Goodland; member of the Legislature, 1889: Photo portrait of the donor.

Otis, Alfred G., Atchison, Regent of the State University: Cabinet size of photo of donor.

Parker, Rev. John D., Ft. Riley, Chaplain U. S. A.: Cabinet photo portrait of donor, 1888.

Pautot, V., photographer, St. Marys: Photo. of the editors and publishers in Pottawatomie county, 1889.

Peck, Geo. R., C. J. Brown, and others, members of the Topeka bar: Life-size oil-painting of Chief Justice A. H. Horton, neatly framed; by Selden J. Woodman.

Pond, Maj. James B., New York city, N. Y.: Statuette in clay of Henry Ward Beecher, by John Rodgers.

Popenoe, F. O., Topeka: Photo portrait of the new Ingleside building, Topeka, erected in 1889.

Prather, C. E., Topeka: Cabinet photo portrait of donor.

Prentice, C. T. K., Lawrence: Photo of Martin F. Conway, taken during the time he was serving as U. S. Consul to Marseilles under appointment of President Lincoln.

W. F. Johnson, H. W. Rolfe, B. F. Foster, Geo. W. Cable, and Geo. W. Smith, committee for colored people of Shawnee county: Life-size portrait of Hon. E. P. McCabe, State Auditor of Kansas, 1883–1886, by Miss Nina Peacock.

Reader, Samuel J., Topeka: Two prohibition pictures, one representing "Thirsty Spook" soliloquizing; the other representing Satan and the Dragon petitioning for high license; photographic copy of his painting of the "Battle of Big Blue"; photo of "The Horse and the Neglected Bridge," (with fable in rhyme.)

Riddle, J. R., Topeka: Negatives of Kansas and Colorado views and portraits, and groups of soldiers stationed at forts in Colorado, New Mexico, Arizona, etc., mostly unnamed.

Robb, S. C., Ogallah: Cabinet photo of Forestry Committee of Kansas; three views of Forestry Station at Ogallah, Kansas.

Roberts, H. S., Manhattan: Engravings of the Riley county prize exhibit. Manhattan, July 31, 1889, as taken from Frank Leslie's illustrated newspaper of October 9, 1889.

Root, F. A., Topeka: Scrap containing wood cut of Chicago in 1831.

Ropes, Geo., Topeka: Sketch for south pediment of Kansas capitol building, November, 1889, by donor; photo portrait of donor, cabinet size.

Salter, Mrs. Susanna M., Argonia (mayor of Argonia, 1887): Cabinet photo of donor.

Sixth Kansas Cavalry Veterans Association: Group of the survivors of the

Sixth Regiment Kansas Cavalry who attended the reunion at Fort Scott, Aug. 20–22, 1888.

Sproat, Mrs. Kate, Topeka: Cabinet photo portrait of Capt. Lewis Stafford, after whom Stafford county is named.

Stanley, T. A., Osawatomie: Engraving of the capture of Jefferson Davis, by the Union Army, 1865.

Stearns, Mrs. Mary E., Medford, Mass.: Plaster bust of Capt. John Brown of Harper's Ferry; also engraving of model of life-size statue of Capt. John Brown.

Thomas, D. W., Topeka: Photo portrait of Kit Carson, card size.

Unknown, Ft. Dodge, Kas.: Officers' quarters and barracks, 1888.

Vandergrift, F. L., Atchison: Nearly life-size photo portrait of Edgar W. Howe, editor of the Atchison *Globe*.

Ward, Mrs. Jennie M., Ottawa: Lithographic copy of commission of Gen. George Washington, to be General and Commander-in-Chief of the Army of the United Colonies, dated Philadelphia, June 19, 1775, and conferred by order of the Congress, John Hancock, President, Albert Chas. Thompson, Secretary.

Wilder, D. W., Topeka: Cabinet photo portrait of donor; nearly life-size photo portrait of ex-Gov. John A. Martin; photo portrait of Rev. William Henry Channing, enlarged from daguerreotype, presented to donor by Mrs. Maria G. Porter, of Rochester, N. Y.; photo copies of receipt given by James Redpath to Capt. P. B. Plumb for seventy-six Colt's revolvers, dated Topeka, Sept. 27, 1856; of letter of James Redpath to P. B. Plumb, dated Malden, Kansas, April 7, 1859; of the commission of P. B. Plumb as superintendent of enrollment of the people of Kansas for the protection of the ballot-box, dated July 20, 1857, signed by James H. Lane; of permit addressed to Capt. D. B. Sackett, authorizing bearer to visit the treason prisoners, Gov. Robinson and others, at Lecompton, dated July 9, 1856, signed, Samuel J. Jones; also photo of addresses of envelope; photo copy of poem relating to the *Herald of Freedom*, after the manner of "Who Killed Cock Robin?" by Richard Realf; of notice of appointment as Aid-de-Camp to the Major General of the Kansas Militia, under the act of Dec. 16, 1857, signed by James H. Lane; of franked envelope addressed by Eli Thayer to P. B. Plumb, Emporia, Kansas; portraits of F. D. Huntington, Prof. Asa Gray, Phillips Brooks, Joseph Lovering, James Walker, Winfield Scott, and Henry Carey; also engraved portraits of Tycho Brahe, Henricus Cornelius Agrippa, Albertus Magnus, Nicholas Copernicus; also of Lord Brougham, William Penn, Jacob Behmen, Geo. Withers, Robert Fludd, Joseph Justus Scalizer, William Lilly, Roger Bacon.

Winch, S. G., Wichita: Album of Wichita, Kansas, 1888.

Wood, L. M., Denver, Col.: Original pencil-drawing of original design for portion of Senate Chamber, Kansas Capitol, Topeka, 1885, designed by donor.

DONORS OF SCRIP, COINS, AND MEDALS.

Abbott, Maj. James B., De Soto: U. S. Nickel coin three cents, 1865.

Adams, Miss Zu, Topeka: Canadian silver coin of five cents, 1874; U. S. silver dime, 1836.

Barnes, Wm., Albany, N. Y.: 36 blank certificates of contributions to the fund for the relief of the Free-State citizens of Kansas, and the establishment of freedom in the Territory.

Bradlee, Dr. C. D., Boston, Mass.: Whig medal of Harrison and VanBuren, campaign of 1837; Brazilian coin of 1869, "Petrus 2nd," "10 Rs." (10 reals); Australian silver coin of the reign of Francis 1st, 1832.

Glendening, Miss Stella, Oakland: Five-hundred-dollar Confederate note, dated Richmond, Va., Feb. 17, 1864.

Higinbotham, William, Clay Center: Five-dollar bill Farmers' and Merchants' bank, Memphis, Tenn., March, 1852.

Kelley, Mark J., Edmond: Silver coin of Denmark and Norway, 1620, reign of Christianus, 4th.

Stanley, T. A., Osawatomie: Four certificates of shares in the Minneola Town Company, in favor of Turner Sampson, numbered 291, 292, 293, and 294, signed by J. K. Goodin, president, and O. A. Bassett, secretary, and dated April 7, 1858; warrant on the Treasurer of the Territory of Kansas for $220.75, dated June 6, 1859, in favor of Turner Sampson, signed by H. J. Strickler, Auditor, and issued under an act entitled "An act providing for the adjustment and payment of claims, approved Feb. 7, 1859"; promissory note of Turner Sampson of $40, payable to William R. Richardson, for the hire of a negro slave named Betty, dated Jan. 1st, 1849.

Smith, Chester A., Yates Center: Certificate of stock, Meade Center Town Company, Meade county, No. 1490, to Paul Hahn, for $25, signed by Rev. Cyrus G. Allen, president, H. H. Rayon, secretary, dated July 20, 1885.

Weed, Geo. W., Topeka: Fac-simile $8, Continental currency, 1776.

DONORS OF WAR RELICS.

Adams, John W., Topeka: Piece of brick found in Charleston harbor after the bombardment of Ft. Sumter, by Colonel John Pratt, of Mass., who presented it to donor, then living in Rochester, N. Y.

Barnes, Wm., Albany, N. Y.: One box of percussion caps for Sharps rifles furnished to emigrants to Kansas in 1855.

Bailey, Judge, L. D., Garden City: Pike-head taken from one of the first battle-fields of the war by David G. Peabody, supposed to have belonged to a member of a Georgia regiment, armed with pikes in default of better weapons. The staff of the pike had been shot away, and a man was killed by the same ball that severed the staff.

Davis, John, Junction City: Bullets, leather, and iron, picked up from the battle-fields of Seven Pines, east of Richmond, Va., by donor, November,

1888; marble from battle-field monument, New Orleans, January 8, 1815, (Chalmette,) Gen. Andrew Jackson in command.

Driggs, Master Willie, Topeka: One-and-one-half-pound cannon ball picked up by donor in Kearney's Gap, a short distance northwest of Las Vegas, N. M.

Edwards, J. W., Newton: Gun barrel and lock of Sharps rifle No. 68,520, picked up by donor on the battle-field of the Wilderness, Parker's store, Va., June, 1884, twenty years after the battle; bullet imbedded in oak board, labeled by donor, "This bullet was shot into an oak tree at the battle of the Wilderness in 1864, from which the board was sawed in June, 1884." Canteen with bullet-hole through lower part, picked up by donor on the battle-field of the Wilderness, June, 1884.

Gove, Alonzo, Osawatomie: Canister shot found in Mine street, Osawatomie, a relic of the sacking of that place, August 30, 1856.

Manhattan Lodge No. 17, I. O. O. F., Manhattan: Sword of Governor Nehemiah Green, with a costly and elegantly engraved silver plate inscribed in the following words: "Sword carried during the War of the Rebellion, 1861 to 1865, by Governor Nehemiah Green, fourth Governor of Kansas, and by him presented to Manhattan Lodge No. 17, I. O. O. F., Manhattan, Kansas, April 13, 1882." Presented by the Lodge to the State Historical Society February 13, 1890.

Millard, H. L., Sterling: Gavel of oak from a tree on the battle-field of Stone river, Tennessee, December 26, 1862, to January 3, 1863, with leaden bullet imbedded, presented by W. E. Richey, of Wabaunsee county, to the Kansas House of Representatives, and accepted by that body February 20, 1889.

Montgomery, Mrs. James, Castle Rock, Wyoming: Knapsack belonging to Captain James Montgomery, and carried by him during the Kansas border troubles.

Phillips, W. W., Topeka; Policeman's mace made from a piece of the original flooring of Libby Prison, Richmond, Va., procured by donor May 17, 1889, while in the company of John W. Woodward, who had charge of the removal of Libby to Chicago.

Wagner, F. X., Cimarron: A six-pounder cannon sight, found on the battle-field of Lexington, Mo.

DONORS OF MISCELLANEOUS CONTRIBUTIONS AND RELICS.

Adams, F. G., Topeka: Five cards relative to the fifth annual convention of the National Editorial Association, 1889; twelve miscellaneous railroad folders; memoriam badge and crape bow worn at the funeral services of ex-Gov. John A. Martin, by the State officers, October 2, 1889; National Editorial Association badges worn by the donor and Miss Harriet Adams at Minister Palmer's log cabin, Detroit, Mich., August 27, 1889; also badges worn by same at the fifth annual convention, Detroit, Mich., August 27–31,

1889; passes over the following roads of Kansas for the year 1888: Union Pacific; Atchison, Topeka & Santa Fé; Kansas City, Fort Scott & Gulf; Chicago, Kansas & Nebraska; and Missouri Pacific.

Bailey, Judge L. D., Garden City: Flax spinning-wheel, given to the mother of donor, by his grandmother, at the time of the former's marriage.

Barnes, William, Albany, N. Y.: Thirty-seven circulars of the New York State Kansas Committee of 1856, 1857; Forty-six blank emigrant certificates and notices of committee meetings.

Bates, Alanson H., Topeka: Bullseye watch, once the property of Capt. Nathaniel Hunt, who was born in Seekonk, Bristol county, Mass., December 3, 1758, died February 5, 1832, the great-grandfather of donor.

Bradlee, Rev. C. D., Boston, Mass.: Chinese card with words in Chinese, "Los Angeles, Canton."

Branch, V. H., Secretary, Cawker City: Posters and complimentary invitation Cawker City District Fair, 1889.

Brown, John, Arkalon: Petrified bone supposed to be from the leg of mastodon, found by donor.

Campbell, E. F., Secretary, Mound City: Poster, &c., of Linn County Fair Association, 1890.

Campbell, W. P., Wamego: "Corene," cast of the four-act drama by donor.

Canfield, James H. Lawrence: Membership badge presented to members of the National Educational Association, by the city of Oakland, Cal., on the occasion of meeting of the Association at San Francisco, July 1, 1889.

Clark, S. H., Clyde, N. Y.: Broadside entitled the "Bonnie Blue Flag," and reply to same, war songs, 1862.

Cone, W. W., Topeka: Badge worn by Ed. Gillis, of Rochester, N. Y., at the meeting of the Supreme Legion of the A. O. U. W., of the world, held at Topeka, October, 1885.

Coney, P. H., and Martin J. Cuff, Topeka: Banner of the Irish-American Republican League of Kansas, made in June, 1884, and swung across Kansas avenue, Topeka, in national campaigns of 1884 and 1888.

Corgan, John N., McPherson: Obituary card of Chas. Williams, who was buried at Llanwenarth church, Abergavany, Wales, March 26, 1882.

Crane, Geo. W., Topeka: Invitation and program to reception and inaugural ball, January 14, 1888; remnant of the staff of the embroidered silk flag presented by Gov. Thomas A. Osborn to the members of the Republican party of Shawnee county, Kas., in recognition of their zeal in having secured a larger Republican majority than any other Kansas county at the Presidential and State elections, November 6, 1888.

Davis, John, Junction City: Fragment of bone from sand of Republican river; pyrites of iron from Trego county; also Dakota sandstone from same county, containing impression of a fossil leaf; gypsum, white crystals, from Saline county, red and white mixed from a twenty-foot well in Davis county; chalk used as building stone from Graham county; bone and tooth

from Republican river, Davis county; lead ore from Cherokee county; natural lime, to be used with or without burning, from Graham county; conglomerate of fossil shells and clay, Davis county; fragment of wood taken in 1880 from the belfry of Independence Hall, Philadelphia, from above where the bell hung; marble from capstone of Washington monument, D. C., picked up by Mrs. Maj. Powell, when the workmen were cutting the stone; iron hatchet plowed up by Geo. A. Taylor in bottom land of Smoky Hill, Davis county; remains of Mound-Builders, taken from a mound on a farm formerly owned by donor, three miles northwest of Junction City; thirty-nine fragments of pottery; nine arrow-heads; one spear-head; one large scraper; twenty-seven fragments of flint implements; forty-six fragments of human bones; fifty human teeth; fragment of cottonwood bark, taken from a tree in Davis county, Feb. 21, 1888, by J. A. Smith (the circumference of tree at base being twenty-four feet, diameter of stump, 6–8 feet; making about 25 cords of 16-inch wood); scales found in earth near a Southern negro's cabin, and supposed to have been brought with him from the South as a charm. They are probably scales of an alligator.

Davis, William, Gognac: Aboriginal Anlace steel dagger or arrow-head found by donor on his farm in Stanton county; paleontological specimen found by donor 40 feet below the surface while digging a well on his farm.

Filley, C. E., Secretary, Burlingame: Poster of the Osage County Fair Association, 1889.

Fox, William Henry Harrison, Auburn: Cane of Henry Fox, given to him by a friend who had made it; the stick of English hawthorn, and the knob from a fragment of marble broken from a mantel in Jefferson Davis's country residence near Vicksburg, Miss., during the late war.

Frazier, W. T., Salina: Piece of stone from sea wall at St. Augustine, Fla.; cap to holy water fount in old cathedral at St. Augustine, Fla.; piece of stone from the wall of the old Catholic cathedral, at St. Augustine, Fla.; shells picked up on sea when at Trujillo, Honduras, Central America; acorns picked in the cemetery at Andersonville; a stone from wall of the oldest house in America, located at St. Augustine, Fla.; rock-salt mineral from Louisiana; cassava, or Indian bread, from Honduras, Central America, made from the root of a plant, baked in the sun; piece of rock from the prison wall in old Fort Marion, St. Augustine, Fla., the place where prisoners of war were confined; stone from walls of burial vault in dungeon of Fort Marion; piece of stone from the old city gate of Fort Marion; stone from tower of old Fort Marion; piece of brick from Jackson's monument, battle-field of New Orleans.

Gleed, C. S., Topeka: Tobacco pouch made of the complete skin of a yellow house cat, captured from an emigrant train by the Cheyenne Indians, in western Kansas, in the raid of September, 1878.

Goodwin, John, Secretary, Dodge City: Poster, Ford County Agricultural Association, 1889.

Graves, A. R., Secretary, Troy: Card of invitation and posters, Doniphan County Fair Association, 1889.

Gove, J. L., Secretary, Mound City: Posters, cards and complimentary invitation, Linn County Fair Association, 1889.

Hale, Geo. D., Topeka: Tissue ballot, Charleston, S. C., election of 1876.

Hall & O'Donald, Topeka: Roster of State, judicial, and county officers, two copies.

Hayden, Sidney, Holton: Fac-simile of charter granted by Charles II to William Penn, for the province of Pennsylvania.

Heatley, W. H., Topeka: Specimen of iron ore found near Richmond, Va.; also Indian whetstone, found near Warwick, Chesterfield county, Va.

Hosington, P. M., Secretary, Newton: Five posters of the Harvey County Fair Association, 1889; also complimentary invitations to same.

Husted Investment Co., Kansas City, Kas.: Business cards and calendars issued by, 1889 and 1890.

Jennings, T. B., Topeka: Twenty-six Kansas weather-crop bulletins, with rain chart.

Jerome, Frank E.: G. A. R. badge given to donor as author of the John Brown song by comrades at campfire at Beloit, returning from reunion at Cawker City, June 1, 1888. The badge is attached to a grasshopper pin, and has a brazen sunflower suspended from it.

Jordan, William, Alma: Piece of box in which Sharps rifles were shipped to Kansas by Gen. Geo. W. Deitzler, in 1855.

Kenca & Lane, LaCygne: Republican ticket voted in every township in Linn county, November 6, 1888.

Kenneday, W. J., Secretary, Winfield: Poster of the Cowley County Fair and Driving Park Association, 1890.

Lasher, Esmeralda, Topeka: Piece of gold ore picked up from Canadian gold mines by Jacob H. Moore, 1867.

Latimer, J. W., Secretary, Pleasanton: Poster, etc., of the Pleasanton Fair Association, 1889.

Lewis, D. W., Topeka: Piece of fresco taken from one of the ruined pillars in front of Hamilton county court house, Cincinnati, Ohio, immediately after the fire of 1884, memorial of the great riot; piece of cinder from the great Chicago fire, 1871.

Lindas, H. E., Pawnee Rock: Pyramid of marble from Sun City, Barber county, Kansas.

Losch, William, Topeka: Card photo representation of statues erected at Geneva, Switzerland, 1869, in commemoration of the fiftieth anniversary of the Union of the Canton of Geneva with the Swiss Confederation; also, badge pin used on the occasion of the celebration of the erection of the statues, September 20 to 23, 1869. The Union was effected in 1864, but the statues were not completed until 1869, when the celebration was had.

McTaggart, D., Liberty: Broadside, supplement to the *Cherryvale Republican*, Friday, March 17, 1890.

Manchester, Rev. Alfred, Providence, R. I.: Program of the Centennial Anniversary Club of Providence (R. I.) Association of Mechanics and Manufacturers, February 27, 1889.

May, Enoch, East Farmington: Rude flint arrow-head picked up on the old Caleb May farm, October 4, 1890, by donor, who still lives on the old homestead.

Miller, Sol., Troy: Piece of wood cut from the limb of a beech tree in Washington county, East Tenn., June 8, 1890, by John B. Zimmerman, of Troy, Kas.; the tree bearing the inscription now plainly visible, "Daniel Boone cild barr, this tree, October, 1767;" oaken mallet made from a rib of the U. S. war ship Constitution, "Old Ironsides," by Denton McCoy, an old-time ship carpenter employed in the Washington Navy Yard; presented to donor by Arthur Jaques, who requested him to present it to the Kansas State Historical Society, for preservation.

Moon, E. G., Secretary, Topeka: Posters of the Kansas State Fair Association, 1889.

Nevins, J. M., Secretary, Independence: Poster and program of the Montgomery County Agricultural Society, 1889.

Payne, Geo. B., North Topeka: Hornet's nest from Green river, Butler county, Ky., 1884.

Pickering, L. M., Secretary, Columbus: Posters, Cherokee County Breeders' Association, 1889; also card of invitation to same.

St. John, E., General Manager, Chicago, Ill.: Calendar issued by the Great Rock Island Route.

Scott, G. W., Secretary, Edgerton: Premium lists, handbills, streamers, posters, and premium tags of Johnson County Fair Association, 1889, 1890.

Sharrai, Napoleon, Topeka: Whale's tooth, "said to be," deposited by donor September, 1890; has been in possession of his family fourteen years. The portrait engraved on it is supposed to be that of Commodore Perry.

Sheldon, Rev. Chas. M., Topeka: Dedicatory hymn, Central Congregational church, July 21, 1889, card.

Sheldon, E. M., secretary, Ottawa: Posters of the Franklin County Agricultural Society, 1890.

Singleton, Benjamin, Kansas City, Mo.: Scrap-book of donor, the originator of the negro exodus to Kansas, containing much information relative to the emigration, 1878.

Sixth Kansas Cavalry Veteran Association: Program of the reunion of the regiment at Junction City, September 11–13, 1889.

Stacey, A. G., Topeka: A piece of stone chipped from the ancient castle of Heidelberg, Germany, built in the twelfth century, and destroyed by fire in 1764.

Stanley, T. A., Osawatomie: Broadside, entitled "A Pilgrimage Song," by Martha A. Burdick.

Stark, J. J., La Cygne: Fragment of coffin in which one of the victims of the Hamilton raid, May 19, 1858, was buried.

Stewart, C. H., secretary, Seneca: Posters, cards, Nemaha County Fair Association, 1889.

Smith, Wm. F., Kiowa: Circular letter of Baracklow Post, No. 384, G. A. R., Kiowa, August 1st, 1890, relating to a reunion of old soldiers, to be held at Kiowa, October 6–8, 1890.

Walker, A. D., Holton: County seal of Calhoun county, Kansas Territory, upon which is an engraving representing a negro in the act of chopping down a pine tree, and cattle and a log cabin in the distance, encircled by the words, "County Court, Calhoun County, Kansas Territory."

Walz, F. J., Leavenworth: Meteorological summary, station for Leavenworth, ten in all.

Weed, Geo. W., Topeka: Five cards of admission to U. S. House of Representatives during the counting of the vote for President and Vice-President, Electoral Commission "8–7," February, 1877, Feb. 21, 22, 23, 24, and 26; badge of donor when on Governor's staff, Kansas State Militia National Drill, Washington, D. C., May 23 to 30, 1887; admission ticket closing ceremonies of National International Exhibition, Philadelphia, Pa., 1876; Kansas badge, Garfield Monument Fair, Washington, D. C., 1882; also, admission and membership tickets to the same.

Weston, J. A., Secretary, Frankfort: Poster of Frankfort Fair Association, 1890.

Whittemore, L. D., Topeka: Program sixth annual meeting Academy of Language, Literature and Art, Topeka, Nov. 29, 30, 1889.

Wight, Rezin, New York City, N. Y.: Blank Confederate tax-roll, under the act of February 17, 1864.

Wood, L. M., Denver, Colo.: Beer mug taken from the beer garden of John Walruff, in Lawrence, Kansas, 1881, by donor.

Yuran, Jason, Blue Rapids: Delegate and press badges of the Interstate Deep-Harbor Convention, held at Topeka Oct. 1, 1889.

DONORS OF SINGLE NEWSPAPERS.

Anderson, J. W. D., Elk City: Copy of Japanese old newspaper.

Baker, C. C., Topeka: Copy of the San Francisco Chronicle, vol. 51, June 22, 1890; copy of the Credit Foncier, of Sinaloa, Topolobampo, Sinaloa, Mexico, vol. 4, No. 45, July 15, 1890.

Ball, Volney, Beverley: Fac-simile copy of the Boston Gazette, and County Journal, March 12, 1770.

Becker, O. M., Norton: The Normal-Insti-Tooter, August, 1888, and August, 1889.

Beers, Dr. Geo. L., Topeka: Copy of the New York Independent, September 5, 1889.

Bradlee, Rev. C. D., Boston, Mass.: Copy of the Dorchester Beacon, October 12, 1889; copy of the Southern Letter, Tuskogee, Ala., October, 1889; copy of the Southern Letter, Tuskogee, Ala., vol. 7, No. 2, February, 1890; copy of the Union, Boston, November, 1889; copy of the Sounding-Board.

Quincy, Mass., vol. 1, No. 2, February 27, 1889; copy of the Mountain Echo, Delaware Water Gap, Pa., July 27, 1889, July 19, 1890; copy of the Boston Budget, Mass., July 20, 1890; also copy of the Mountain Echo, Delaware Water Gap, Pa.

Brown, Orville C., Adams, N. Y.: Copy of Jefferson County Journal, Adams, N. Y., November 4, 1890, containing obituary notice of Horace Brown, with poem written by donor.

Burnell, Rev. A. T., Eureka: Copy of the Academy Student, Eureka, vol. 2, No. 4, November 8, 1889.

Campbell, W. P., Wamego: Copy of the Kansas Reporter, November 9, 1888, containing account of " Harrison's election."

Chapman, J. B., Fort Scott: Copy of the Fort Scott Daily Tribune, January, 1889, New Year's edition.

Clark, Sylvester H., Clyde, N. Y.: Copy of the Grin and Bear It, September 27, 1884.

Clinton, C. W., Salina: Copy of the Sentinel, containing prospectus of college work, St. John's School, Salina.

Coburn, F. D., Kansas City: Copy of the Kansas City Daily Gazette, January 11, 1889, containing "The Story of the Great State of Kansas;" copy of the Daily Graphic, New York, November 27, 1883, containing illustrations and description of Kansas City, Kansas, and Kansas City, Missouri.

Crawford, Gov. Geo. A., Grand Junction, Colo.: Copy of the Daily News, Denver, March 23, 1890, containing historic sketch of Grand Junction, Colorado.

Darling, Gen. C. W., Utica, N. Y.: Copy of the Home Journal, N. Y., August 20, 1890, containing "The Lost Ten Tribes," by donor; copy of the Saturday Globe, Utica, December 15, 1888, containing portrait and biographical sketch of donor; copy of the Seattle Times, Washington Territory, January 28, 1889, containing matter relative to name of Washington Territory.

Dedham Historical Society, Dedham, Mass.: Copy of the Dedham Transcript, September 1, 1888, giving ancestry of Chief Justice Fuller, by D. G. Hill; the Dedham Transcript, September 28, 1886, containing proceedings of the 250th anniversary of the incorporation of the town of Dedham; Dedham Standard, September 21, 1886, special anniversary number.

Drake, J. F., Emporia: Journal of the Kansas State Sunday School Association, January 1, 1883, April, 1884, October, 1884 and 1885, July, 1887 containing minutes of the Association.

Elliott, H. S., Tallahassee, Fla.: The Monthly Bulletin, Tallahassee, Fla., vol. 1, Nos. 1–7, 1889, 1890.

Elliott, L. R., Manhattan: Copy of the Manhattan Homestead, March, 1889.

Frazier, W. T., Salina: Copy of the Daily Picayune, New Orleans, February 17, 1885; three copies of the Mascot, New Orleans, January 31, Feb-

ruary 6, 14, 1885; carnival edition of the Times-Democrat, Mardi Gras eve, New Orleans, February 16, 17, 1885; The Naturalist in Florida, St. Augustine, vol. 1, No. 3, 1885, tourist edition.

Friend, J. C., publisher, Rawlins, Wyoming: Copy of Carbon County Journal, May 11, 1889, containing illustrated description of the county and State.

Goodnow, Prof. I. T., Manhattan: Herald of Freedom, Lawrence, 122 scattering numbers, 1855–1859; Garden City Sentinel, 1887, 28 numbers containing historical sketches by Judge L. D. Bailey; Conference edition Lawrence Daily Tribune, March 6–12, 1889, 6 numbers; Frank Leslie's Illustrated Newspaper, N. Y., 62 scattering numbers in 1859, '61, '62, '64, '65; Gleason's Pictorial, N. Y., 13 scattering numbers, 1852–54; Illustrated Weekly, 1876, 10 numbers, Harper's Weekly, N. Y., 39 scattering numbers, 1864, 1865; The Christian Citizen, 24 numbers in 1888 and 1889; Ballou's Pictorial, Boston, January 10, 1857, containing illustrated description of Lynn, Mass.; 26 miscellaneous newspapers.

Graham, Prof. I. D., Manhattan: Copy of the Industrialist, Manhattan, May 25, 1889, containing historical sketch of State Agricultural College, 9 copies; two copies of the Industrialist, June 8, 1889, containing history, endowments, objects, course of study, etc., of Kansas Agricultural College, by Prof. J. D. Walters; Kansas Printers' Specimen Extra, The Industrialist, June 8, 1889, by J. S. C. Thompson.

Green, Dr. Samuel A., Boston, Mass.: The Centennial, Philadelphia, 1873, and February, 1874, April and May, 1874; copy of the New York Herald, April 19, 1875, containing "Journalism in 1875;" fac-similes of the accounts of the battle of Lexington, etc.

Hale, George D., Topeka: The Mail and Express, New York, April 29, 30, 1889; The Sun, New York, May 2, 1889; New York Times, April 30 and May 1, 1889, and part of New York World, April 30, 1889, containing account of Centennial of Washington's Inauguration, April 30, 1889.

Harrington, Rev. M. O., Topeka: Two copies of the Christian Express, July 2, 1883, and September 1, 1885.

Howe, E. W., Atchison: Copy of the Grasshopper, vol. 1, No. 1, published at Grasshopper Falls, (Valley Falls,) June 12, 1858, S. Ward Smith, publisher; J. A. Cody, editor and proprietor; H. Rees Whiting, associate editor.

Lescher, T. H., Topeka: Copy of the Easton Weekly Argus, Easton, Pa., May 9, 1890, also copy of the Daily Argus, May 5, 1890, containing Easton Centennial celebration—1790 to 1890.

Lubers, H. L., Las Animas, Colo.: Copy of the Bent County Democrat, Las Animas, Colo., December 29, 1888, illustrated holiday number, containing description of Bent county.

Lykins, William H. R., Kansas City, Mo.: Copy of Herald of Freedom, October 30, 1858, containing article by donor, relating to railroads in Kan-

sas; copy of Weekly Rocky Mountain News, Denver, Colo., October 5, 1864.

Manchester, Alfred, Providence, R. I.: Copy of the Providence Daily Journal, September 29, 1890, with supplement containing proceedings of the Slater Cotton Centennial Convention held at Pawtucket, R. I., September, 1890.

McCammon, E. E., Secretary, St. Joseph, Mo.: Copy of the St. Joseph Daily Gazette, January 1, 1889, annual trade edition.

Newlon, W. S., Oswego: Copy of the Oswego Graphic, vol. 1, No. 4, February, 1882.

Parker, Rev. R. D., Manhattan: Copy of the Kansas Telephone, Manhattan, January, 1889, containing biographical sketch of Mrs. Mary Parker.

Perine, Mrs. Mary E., Oakland: Three copies of the Japan Daily Mail, Yokohama, October 21, 23, 24, 1889; copy of the Temperance Union, October 4, 1888, in English, market reports only in Chinese.

Pillsbury & Ellsworth, Tulare, Cal.: Copy of the Weekly Tulare Register, December 28, 1888.

Pond, Chester E., Topeka: Copy of the Western School Journal, Topeka, vol. 4, No. 12, November, 1888.

Pool, T. W., New Orleans, La.: Bulletin of the Louisiana Commissioner of Immigration.

Popenoe, Fred O., Topeka: Student's Journal, N. Y., March, 1874, and July, 1876.

Pratt, Rev. John G., Maywood: Copy of the Weekly Southern Democrat, June 30, 1855, Parkville, Mo., containing item referring to donor.

Reading Circle Association, Chicago, Ill.: Copy of the Union Reading Circle and Office Visitor, December 15, 1888.

Reilley, A., editor, San Francisco, Cal.: Pacific Coast Commercial Record, September and December, 1887, February, June, August and November, 1888, containing matter relating to the commercial, financial, manufacturing, and natural resources of California.

Rice, John H. & Son, Fort Scott: Two copies of the Fort Scott Monitor, New Year's edition, January 1, 1889.

Roe, A. S., Worcester, Mass.: Three copies of the Old Guard, Worcester, Mass., February 5, 6, 7, 1889, published in connection with the G. A. R. Fair, under auspices of George H. Ward Post.

Rolfe, H. W., editor, Topeka: Copy of the American Citizen, February 1, 1889, containing portrait and biographical sketch of Hon. Albert Fairfax, member of the Legislature from Chautauqua county, 1889.

Root, F. A., North Topeka: Copy of the Hoof and Horn, Prescott, Arizona, August 11, 1887; copy of the Primitive Catholic, Brooklyn, N. Y., September 29, 1888; Topeka Argus, May 18, 1888; two newspapers.

Rudisill, L. A., Topeka: Copy of the Kansas Siftings, Topeka, vol. 3, No. 4, May 22, 1890, containing program, etc., of the Kansas Chautauqua Assem-

bly; copy of the Kansas Church Tidings, Topeka, vol. 2, No. 4, May 19, 1890, containing program, etc., of the Kansas Chautauqua Assembly, June 24 to July 24, 1890.

Scott, G. W., Edgerton: Two copies of the Fair Journal, Edgerton, containing premium list, rules and regulations, sixth annual fair of the Johnson County Fair Association, September 11–13, 1889.

Sheldon, Alvah, El Dorado: Copy of the Daily Citizen, Vicksburg, Miss., July 2, 1863.

Speer, John, Sherlock: The Lawrence Republican, Lawrence, October 25, 1860, April 4, 1861, July 10, 1862, three newspapers; Kansas Free-State, Lawrence, January 3 and 31, February 14 and 24, April 14, May 7, June 4 and 18, and July 2 and 16, 1855; and October 31, 1857; Herald of Freedom, Lawrence, February 3, 1855; January 12, 1856; Kansas Tribune, January 24, February 21, and March 14, 1855; October 3, 1863, and July 14, 1855. [Conditional deposit. See donors of newspaper files.]

Stebbins, H. P., Yellwood, Fla.: Six newspapers, published at Apopka, Tampa, Jacksonville, Orlando, March, April, June, August, 1890.

Stonebraker, S. A., Black Jack: Copy of the Freeman's Champion, Prairie City, Kas., vol. 1, August 27, 1857.

Striker, William, Great Bend: Copy of the Normal Quarterly, vol. 1, No. 2, January 1889.

"True Blue," Pittsburg: Copy of the St. Louis Globe-Democrat, November 5, 1888, inciting St. Louis voters to support David G. Francis for Governor.

Unknown: Copy of the Coast Commercial Herald, San Francisco, Cal., March, 1888; copy of the Philadelphia Press, November 2, 1889, containing sketch of John Brown's early days. Senator Delamater's (of Crawford county, Pa.) connection with old Osawatomie's family; copy of the Massachusetts Spy, Worcester, August 20, 1823.

Vermont, Ed. V., New York City, N. Y.: Copy of Illustrated Journal of Useful Inventions, vol. 1, No. 3, July, 1889.

Weed, G. W., Topeka: Fac-simile copy of the Philadelphia Public Ledger, vol. 1, No. 1, March 25, 1836.

White, H. F., Topeka: Copy of the American, New York, May 15, 1819.

Wilder, D. W., Topeka: Copy of Canterbury Press, and Kent County News, July 26, 1890, England; also copy of the Times, London, England, July 28, 1890; copy of the Centennial, N. Y., No. 3, July, 1857; the Rochester Campus, vol. 5, No. 3, December, 1877; the Wichita Daily Eagle, Wichita, January 12, 1890, containing "The Journey of Alvar Nuñez Cabeça de Vaca," address of Senator Moody on that subject, criticised by J. P. Jones.

Winterbourne, Rev. Geo., editor, Horton: Copy of Horton Headlight, (conference extra edition,) March 8, 1890, containing conference proceedings of the First M. E. Church.

Zinn, L. W., Hutchinson: Copy of the Educator, Hutchinson, February 15, 1889, vol. 1, No. 1.

DONORS OF NEWSPAPER FILES.

The following is a list of newspaper files and volumes of periodicals donated, other than those received in current issues:

Baker, Dr. William S., Topeka: File of the New York Semi-Weekly Tribune, Jan. 3 to Dec. 28, 1888.

Baker, F. P., Topeka: Bound files of the New York American, Jan. 1, 1830, to July 31, 1835, vol. 9-16.

Beers, G. L., Topeka: The Christian Union, July 7, 1887, to May 30, 1889; The Independent, New York, July 7, 1887, to May 30, 1889; file of the Independent, New York, June 6 to Sept. 12, 1889; The Christian Union, June 6 to Sept. 12, 1889.

Bradlee, Rev. C. D., Boston, Mass.: Files of the Evening Gazette from Jan. 8, 1888, to Nov. 18, 1890.

Buckingham, Henry, Lawrence: Files of the Republican Valley Empire, Clyde and Concordia, from May 31, 1870, to Nov. 23, 1872.

George, Rev. A. P., Cimarron: File of Our Methodist, Dodge City, 1888 to 1889.

Goodnow, Isaac T., Manhattan: Files of the Whim-Wham, Topeka, Oct. 9, 1880, vol. 1, No. 1, to Oct. 9, 1881, except No. 14, vol. 2, Nov. 2, 1881, (and daily, Sept. 17-19, and Oct. 18, 1881); the National Tribune, Washington, D. C., 1886, 1887, and 1888; file of the American Phrenological Journal, N. Y., 1864; Emery's Journal of Agriculture, July 1, 1858, to Dec. 16, 1858; Gazette and Courier, May 28, 1888, to March 30, 1889; files of the Oxford Observer, Norway, Maine, 1829.

Kansas Board of Railroad Commissioners, Topeka: Northwestern Railroader, incomplete file, Jan. 4, 1888, to June 14, 1889.

Mead, J. R., Wichita: Files of the Wichita Weekly Eagle, April 12, 1872, No. 1, vol. 1, to March 28, 1878, except from April 10, 1873, to April 9, 1874.

Mendum, J. P., Boston, Mass.: Files of the Boston Investigator, April 27, 1859, to April 29, 1863, vols. 29-32; April 29, 1874, to April 21, 1875, vol. 44; April 25, 1877, to April 11, 1883, vols. 47-52; April 15, 1885, to April 3, 1889, vols. 55-58.

Maloy, John, Council Grove: File of the Council Grove Democrat, to December, 1886; partial files of the Kansas Press, Cottonwood Falls and Council Grove, 1859, 1860, 1861, 1863, and 1864.

Moore, R. R., Topeka: File of Dye's Government Counterfeit Detector, Philadelphia, Pa., March to December, 1889, January, 1890.

Popenoe, F. O., Topeka: Files of the Student's Journal, New York, 1878-1881, four volumes.

—4

Roustadt, J. D., Ellinwood: Files of the Rural Register, vols. 1 and 2, July 1, 1859, to June 1, 1861.

Speer, John, Sherlock: Bound files of the New Orleans Weekly Picayune, 1841, 1842, 1843, 1844, 1845, 1846, 1847; the Daily Enquirer, Jefferson City, Ao., December 19, 1850, to Aarch 2, 1851; the Kansas Daily Tribune, Lawrence, from November 29, 1863, to February 3, 1871. [Conditional deposit. See donors of single newspapers.]

Winterbourne, Rev. Geo., Wamego: File of Conference Daily, Kansas Conference A. E. Church, Topeka, Aarch 14 to Aarch 21, 1888; file of the Lawrence Evening Tribune, conference edition, Kansas Conference, Lawrence, Aarch 6 to 13, 1889.

Zinn, L. W., Hutchinson: File of the Western Business College and Normal School Journal, Hutchinson, 1888 and 1889.

BOUND NEWSPAPERS AND PERIODICALS.

The following is a statement of bound newspaper files and bound volumes of periodicals in the library of the Society, November 18, 1890, including the volumes which become complete December 31, 1890, numbering 10,143 volumes; of which 7,472 are of Kansas, and 2,671 are of other States and countries, and of which 2,153 have been added during the two years covered by this report. (Volumes not otherwise described are of weekly newspapers.)

BOUND NEWSPAPER FILES AND PERIODICALS, KANSAS.

Newspapers.	Years.	No. vols.
ALLEN COUNTY.		
Iola Register	1873–1890	18
Allen County Independent. Iola	1879,1880	1
Allen County Courant, Iola	1884–1888	5
Allen County Democrat. Iola	1886–1888	1
Democrat-Courant, Iola	1888	1
The Farmers' Friend, Iola	1890	1
Humboldt Union	1876–1890	15
Inter-State, Humboldt	1878–1888	9
Independent Press, Humboldt	1882	1
The Humboldt Herald	1887–1890	3
The Rural Kansan, Humboldt	1873,1874	1
Moran Herald	1885–1890	5
ANDERSON COUNTY.		
Garnett Weekly Journal	1876–1890	15
Garnett Plaindealer	1876–1884	9
Anderson County Republican, Garnett	1883,1884	1
Republican-Plaindealer, Garnett	1884–1890	7
Anderson County Democrat, Garnett	1885–1887	2
Garnett Eagle	1886–1890	4
The Greeley Tribune	1880,1881	1
The Greeley News	1881–1890	9
The Colony Free Press	1882–1890	9
Westphalia Times	1885–1890	5
Kincaid Kronicle, (April, 1888, to September, 1889, lacking,)	1886–1890	4
The Kincaid Dispatch	1888–1890	3
ATCHISON COUNTY.		
Squatter Sovereign, Atchison	1856,1857	1
Freedom's Champion, (1861 lacking,) Atchison	1857–1863	4
Atchison Daily Free Press	1865–1868	7
Atchison Weekly Free Press, (four files each of 1866 and 1867,)	1866–1868	3
Champion and Press (weekly), Atchison	1868–1873	4
Atchison Daily Champion	1876–1890	27

BOUND NEWSPAPER FILES AND PERIODICALS, KANSAS — Continued.

Newspapers.	Years.	No. vols.
ATCHISON COUNTY — *concluded.*		
Atchison Weekly Champion, (lacking from 1878-1885,)	1873-1890	10
Kansas Zeitung, Atchison, (duplicates of vol. 1,)	1857,1858	1
Atchison Union, (broken files.)	1859-1861	3
Atchison Patriot (daily), (from July, 1876, to July, 1879, lacking,)	1876-1890	22
Atchison Patriot (weekly)	1874-1890	17
Atchison Courier	1876-1879	4
Atchison Globe (daily)	1878-1890	23
Atchisonian, Atchison	1877	1
Atchison Banner	1878,1879	1
The New West, Atchison	1878-1880	2
The Sunday Morning Call, Atchison	1882,1883	2
Atchison Telegraph	1882	1
Kansas Staats-Anzeiger, Atchison	1881-1885	4
Atchison Journal (daily)	1881,1882	2
Western Mercury, Atchison	1884-1886	2
Atchison Sunday Morning Sermon	1884	1
The Western Recorder, Atchison	1884	1
The Trades-Union, Atchison	1885,1886	1
The Atchison Times	1888-1890	3
Messachorean (monthly), Atchison	1888	2
The Prairie Press, Lancaster	1888-1890	2
Muscotah Record, (missing from August, 1886, to January, 1887,)	1885-1888	3
The Effingham Times	1887-1890	2
Huron Graphic	1890	1
BARBER COUNTY.		
Barber County Mail, Medicine Lodge	1878,1879	1
Medicine Lodge Cresset	1879-1890	12
Barber County Index, Medicine Lodge	1881-1890	9
Medicine Lodge Chief	1886-1888	1
Hazelton Express	1884-1890	7
The Kiowa Herald, New Kiowa	1884-1890	6
The Kiowa Journal	1886-1890	4
Sharon News	1884-1886	2
The Union, Sun City	1884-1888	4
The Ætna Clarion	1885-1887	2
Kansas Prairie Dog, Lake City	1885-1888	3
The Lake City Bee	1888,1889	1
BARTON COUNTY.		
Great Bend Register	1876-1890	15
Inland Tribune, Great Bend	1876-1890	15
Arkansas Valley Democrat, Great Bend	1877-1882	6
Kansas Volksfreund, Great Bend	1878,1879	1
Barton County Democrat, Great Bend	1886-1890	4
Daily Graphic, Great Bend	1887,1888	2
The Ellinwood Express	1878-1888	10
The Ellinwood Advocate	1888-1890	2
Pawnee Rock Leader	1886-1890	5
The Echo, Hoisington	1887-1889	1
Hoisington Dispatch	1889,1890	1
Claflin Gazette	1888	1
BOURBON COUNTY.		
Fort Scott Daily Monitor	1880-1890	22
Fort Scott Weekly Monitor (1870-1876 lacking)	1867-1890	17
Fort Scott Pioneer	1876-1878	2
Camp's Emigrants' Guide, Fort Scott	1877	1
New Century, Fort Scott	1877,1878	1
Fort Scott Herald	1878-1882	5
Republican-Record, Fort Scott	1882-1882	4
Herald and Record, Fort Scott	1882-1884	2
Evening Herald, daily, Fort Scott	1882-1885	6
Medical Index, monthly, Fort Scott	1881-1884	4
The Banner, Fort Scott	1882-1884	2
Fort Scott Daily Tribune	1884-1890	12
Fort Scott Weekly Tribune	1884-1890	6
Kansas Staats-Zeitung, Fort Scott	1886,1887	2
The Fort Scott Union	1887,1888	1
The Sunday Call, Fort Scott	1889	1
The Spectator, Fort Scott	1890	1
Bronson Pilot	1884-1890	6
The Fulton Independent	1884-1890	6
The Telephone, Uniontown	1885-1888	3
The Garland Gleaner	1886,1887	2
The Telephone, Mapleton	1889	1
Mapleton Dispatch	1889,1890	2

Newspapers.	Years.	No. vols.
BROWN COUNTY.		
Hiawatha Dispatch...	1876–1882	6
The Hiawatha World..	1882–1890	9
Kansas Herald, Hiawatha...	1876–1883	8
The Kansas Sun, Hiawatha..	1879,1880	2
Weekly Messenger, Hiawatha..	1882–1884	2
The Kansas Democrat, Hiawatha..	1884–1890	6
Free Press, Hiawatha...	1887,1888	1
The Hiawatha Journal..	1883,1890	2
Everest Reflector..	1883,1886	2
The Everest Enterprise..	1888–1890	2
Horton Headlight.........,...	1886–1890	4
Horton Daily Headlight........*...	1887–1889	3
The Horton Railway Register..	1888,1889	1
Horton Telegram...	1889,1890	1
Horton Commercial...	1889,1890	2
Hamlin News Gleaner..	1889,1890	1
Fairview Enterprise..	1888–1890	3
Morrill News...	1890	1
BUTLER COUNTY.		
Augusta Republican, (1875–1880 lacking,).....................................	1873–1883	4
Southern Kansas Gazette, Augusta..	1876–1886	11
Augusta Advance...	1883,1884	1
Augusta Electric Light...	1884–1886	2
Augusta Weekly Journal...	1888–1890	3
The Augusta News..	1889,1890	1
Walnut Valley Times. El Dorado...	1874–1890	17
Daily Walnut Valley Times, El Dorado..	1887–1890	7
El Dorado Press.........................*..	1877–1883	7
El Dorado Daily Republican..	1885–1888	6
El Dorado Republican..	1883–1890	7
Butler County Democrat, El Dorado, (lacking from Oct. '88 to Nov. '89,)....	1881–1890	9
The El Dorado Eagle...	1882	1
Butler County Jeffersonian, El Dorado..	1888,1889	2
Kansas Workman, Emporia and El Dorado......................................	1888–1890	3
The New Enterprise, Douglass...	1879,1880	2
Douglass Index...	1880–1883	3
The Douglass Tribune..	1884–1890	7
Leon Indicator, (missing from February to September, 1887.).................	1880–1890	9
The Leon Quill...	1886,1887	1
The Benton Reporter...	1884,1885	1
The Towanda Herald...	1885–1890	6
The Brainerd Sun..	1885,1886	1
The Brainerd Ensign...	1887,1889	2
Latham Journal..	1885,1886	1
Latham Signal...	1887–1890	3
The Latham Times...	1890	1
The Beaumont Business..	1886–1888	2
Potwin Messenger...	1888,1889	2
Whitewater Tribune..	1889,1890	2
CHASE COUNTY.		
Chase County Courant, Cottonwood Falls.......................................	1874–1890	16
Chase County Leader, Cottonwood Falls..	1875–1890	16
Strong City Independent...	1881–1887	6
Chase County Republican, Strong City..	1887–1890	3
CHAUTAUQUA COUNTY.		
Chautauqua Journal, Sedan..	1875–1884	9
The Chautauqua County Times, Sedan..	1878–1881	3
Sedan Times..	1882–1884	3
Sedan Times-Journal..	1885–1890	6
The Border Slogan, Sedan...	1883,1884	1
The Graphic, Sedan..	1884–1890	6
Chautauqua News, Peru...	1877–1881	5
The Peru Times...	1886,1887	1
The Weekly Call, Peru..	1888,1889	2
The Peru Eagle...	1890	1
The Chautauqua Springs Spy..	1882,1883	1
Chautauqua Springs Mail..	1887	1
The Chautauqua Springs Express..	1888,1889	1
The Cedar Vale Star...	1884–1890	7
Cedar Vale Commercial..	1889,1890	1

BOUND NEWSPAPER FILES AND PERIODICALS KANSAS — CONTINUED.

Newspapers.	Years.	No. vols.
CHEROKEE COUNTY.		
Republican-Courier, Columbus	1876–1878	3
The Columbus Courier	1879–1888	9
The Columbus Star-Courier	1889,1890	2
Columbus Democrat	1876	1
Border Star, Columbus	1877–1886	9
The Columbus Vidette	1877,1878	1
The Times, Columbus	1882–1886	5
Kansas Bee-Keeper, Columbus	1881–1885	3
Lea's Columbus Advocate	1882–1888	6
The Columbus Advocate	1889,1890	2
The Daily Advocate, Columbus	1886,1887	2
The Daily News and the Weekly News, Columbus	1882,1883	1
The Expository, Girard and Columbus	1883,1884	1
The Sprig of Myrtle (monthly), Columbus	1883–1885	2
The Kansas Prohibitionist, Columbus	1886	1
Baxter Springs Republican	1876,1877	1
The Times, Baxter Springs	1878–1881	3
Baxter Springs News	1882–1890	9
Baxter Springs Delta	1887	1
Galena Miner	1877–1880	4
Galena Miner (second)	1888,1889	1
Short Creek Weekly Banner, Galena	1878	1
The Galena Messenger	1879	1
Short Creek Republican, Galena	1883–1890	8
Empire City Echo	1877–1879	3
The Ionian Casket (monthly), Quakervale	1878,1879	1
Western Friend (monthly), Quakervale	1880–1890	8
The Laborer's Tribune, Weir	1884–1888	5
Weir City Tribune	1889,1890	2
The Weir Journal	1889,1890	2
CHEYENNE COUNTY.		
Cheyenne County Rustler, Wano	1885–1890	5
Plaindealer, Wano	1886–1888	2
Bird City News	1886–1890	4
Cheyenne County Democrat, Bird City	1886–1890	3
The Gleaner, Jaqua	1887,1888	1
Weekly Review, St. Francis	1889,1890	1
Cheyenne County Herald. St. Francis	1889,1890	1
CLARK COUNTY.		
Clark County Clipper, Ashland	1884–1890	6
Republican Herald, Ashland	1886,1887	2
Ashland Journal	1887–1890	4
Clark County Chief, Englewood	1885–1887	3
The Englewood Chief	1888,1889	1
Englewood Enterprise	1887–1889	1
Appleton Kansas Era	1885–1887	2
The Lexington Leader	1886–1888	2
The Minneola Era	1887,1888	1
Clark County Republican, Minneola	1888	1
Cash City Cashier	1887,1888	1
CLAY COUNTY.		
Clay County Dispatch. Clay Center	1876–1890	15
The Localist, Clay Center	1879–1881	3
The Democrat, Clay Center	1879,1880	2
The Cresset, Clay Center	1882,1883	1
The Times, Clay Center	1882–1890	9
The Times (daily), Clay Center	1886–1888	5
The Kansas Baptist, Clay Center	1881–1884	3
The Monitor, Clay Center	1883,1884	1
Clay Center Eagle	1885,1886	1
Republican Valley Democrat, Clay Center	1886–1889	5
The Clay Center Democrat	1890	1
Morganville News and Sunflower	1885–1887	3
The Clay County Sentinel, Morganville	1887–1890	4
The Idana Journal	1886,1887	1
Wakefield Advertiser	1887,1890	4
The Herald, Industry	1887,1888	1
Oak Hill Herald	1888–1889	1
Oak Hill Echo	1889	1

BOUND NEWSPAPER FILES AND PERIODICALS, KANSAS—CONTINUED.

Newspapers.	Years.	No. vols.
CLOUD COUNTY.		
Republican Valley Empire, Clyde and Concordia	1870–1872	3
Concordia Empire	1876–1882	7
The Republican-Empire. Concordia	1883–1886	4
Concordia Empire	1887–1890	4
The Concordia Republican	1882,1883	2
The Concordia Expositor	1877–1881	5
The Cloud County Blade. Concordia	1879–1881	3
Kansas Blade, Concordia	1882–1890	9
Concordia Daily Blade	1884–1888	6
Cloud County Critic, Concordia	1882–1888	7
The Concordia Times	1884–1890	7
Concordia Democrat, and Daylight	1886–1888	3
The Concordia Weekly Daylight	1889,1890	2
Clyde Democrat	1880–1882	2
The Clyde Herald	1878–1890	12
Cline's Press, Clyde	1884	1
The Clyde Mail	1884–1887	3
The Clyde Argus	1888–1890	3
Glasco Tribune	1881,1882	1
The Glasco Sun	1883–1890	8
Cloud County Kansan. Jamestown	1881–1890	9
The Quill, Jamestown	1888–1890	2
The Miltonvale News	1882–1890	10
Miltonvale Star	1886	1
Miltonvale Chieftain	1888	1
Ames Advocate	1885,1886	1
The Ames Bureau	1887	1
The Weekly Courier, Ames	1888	1
COFFEY COUNTY.		
Neosho Valley Register, Burlington	1859,1860	1
Kansas Patriot, Burlington, (duplicate of 1867,)	1864–1868	5
Burlington Patriot	1876–1886	10
Burlington Republican	1882–1886	4
The Republican-Patriot, Burlington	1886–1890	5
Burlington Daily Republican-Patriot	1887	1
The Burlington Independent	1876–1890	15
Burlington Daily Star	1878	1
The Burlington Nonpareil	1887–1890	4
Leroy Reporter	1879–1890	11
The Leroy Eagle	1888	1
The Lebo Light	1884–1888	5
The Lebo Courier	1889,1890	2
The Waverly News	'83,'85–'89	4
The Gazette, Waverly	1889–1890	2
The Gridley Gazette	1887,1888	2
The Standard, Gridley	1889,1890	1
COMANCHE COUNTY.		
Comanche Chieftain, Nescatunga	1884–1886	2
The Western Kansan, Nescatunga	1885–1887	3
Nescatunga Enterprise	1886–1888	3
Coldwater Review	1884–1890	6
Coldwater Enterprise	1889,1890	2
The Western Star, Coldwater	1885–1890	6
Republican, Coldwater	1885,1886	1
Coldwater Echo	1887–1890	4
Comanche County Citizen, Avilla	1885,1886	2
The Avilla Democrat	1886,1887	1
Protection Echo	1885–1887	3
The Protection Press	1886,1887	1
Kansas Weekly Ledger, Protection	1887	1
The Leader, Protection	1888	1
Evansville Herald	1885–1887	2
Comanche City News	1886–1888	1
COWLEY COUNTY.		
Winfield Courier	1873–1890	17
Winfield Daily Courier	1885–1890	11
Winfield Plow and Anvil	1876	1
Cowley County Telegram, Winfield	1876–1890	15
Winfield Daily Telegram, (1883–1886 lacking,)	1879–1888	10
Winfield Semi-Weekly	1879,1880	1
Cowley County Monitor, Winfield	1880	1
Cowley County Courant, Winfield	1881,1882	1
Winfield Daily Courant	1881,1882	1
The Daily Visitor, Winfield	1886–1889	8

BOUND NEWSPAPER FILES AND PERIODICALS, KANSAS — CONTINUED.

Newspapers.	Years.	No. vols.
COWLEY COUNTY — *concluded.*		
The Winfield Tribune	1881–1890	6
The Winfield Visitor	1887–1889	2
The American Nonconformist, Winfield	1887–1890	4
Southwestern Kansas Conference Daily, Winfield	1887	1
Industrial Free Press, Winfield	1890	1
Arkansas City Traveler and Republican-Traveler	1876–1890	15
Arkansas Valley Democrat, Arkansas City	1879–1890	11
The Arkansas City Republican	1884–1886	3
The Arkansas City Republican (daily)	1886,1887	2
Republican-Traveler (daily), Arkansas City	1887	1
Arkansas City Traveler (daily)	1888–1890	6
Canal City Daily Dispatch, Arkansas City	1887–1889	4
Evening Dispatch, Arkansas City	1889,1890	3
Canal City Dispatch (weekly), Arkansas City	1887–1890	4
The Fair Play, Arkansas City	1888–1890	3
The New Enterprise, Burden	1880,1881	2
Burden Enterprise	1882–1890	9
Burden Eagle	1885–1889	5
Cambridge Commercial	1881	1
The News, Cambridge	1882–1886	3
The Cambridge News	1888–1890	3
The Eye, Dexter	1884–1888	4
Dexter Free Press	1888–1890	2
The Udall Sentinel	1885,1886	1
The Udall Record	1886–1890	4
CRAWFORD COUNTY.		
Girard Press	1874–1890	17
Crawford County News, Girard	1876–1880	4
Girard Herald	1880–1890	11
The Kansas Workman, monthly, Girard	1882–1884	2
Cherokee Index	1876,1877	2
The Young Cherokee, Cherokee	1876,1877	1
Cherokee Banner	1877,1878	1
The Temperance Rural, Cherokee, (one duplicate,)	1878,1879	1
Sentinel on the Border, Cherokee	1879–1882	4
The Cherokee Sentinel	1883–1890	7
The Saturday Cyclone, Cherokee	1885–1887	3
The Smelter, Pittsburg	1881–1890	10
The Headlight, Pittsburg	1886–1890	5
The Daily Headlight, Pittsburg	1887	1
Pittsburg Democrat	1888,1889	1
The Pittsburg Kansan	1889,1890	2
The McCune Standard	1881,1882	1
The McCune Times	1882–1890	8
The Brick, McCune and Pittsburg	1886,1887	2
Crawford County Democrat, McCune	1889,1890	1
Walnut Journal	1882–1890	9
The Educational Advocate, Walnut	1884	1
The Arcadia Reporter	1882–1887	5
The Christian Worker, Arcadia	1888	1
Arcadia Democrat	1888–1890	2
The Hepler Leader	1889,1890	2
The Hepler Banner	1887–1889	3
The Farlington Plaindealer	1885,1886	1
Farlington Gem	1886,1887	1
Mulberry Grove Gazette	1886	1
DAVIS COUNTY. (See Geary.)		
Junction City Union, (triplicates of '75, '76, '77, '78, and duplicates of '79–'86	1863–1888	25
The Junction City Daily Union	1887	1
Junction City Tribune	1873–1888	16
The Youths' Casket, monthly, Junction City	1878	1
Davis County Republican, Junction City	1882–1888	6
The Junction City Methodist	1886,1887	1
DECATUR COUNTY.		
The Oberlin Herald	1879–1890	10
The Eye, Oberlin	1883–1890	7
The Oberlin World and Democrat	1885,1886	1
Oberlin Opinion	1886–1890	5
The Norcatur Register	1886–1890	3
The Allison Breeze and Times	1887,1888	2
Jennings Echo	1888–1890	2
Jennings Times	1888,1889	1
The Alliance Times, Jennings	1890	1
The Star, Dresden	1890	1

BOUND NEWSPAPER FILES AND PERIODICALS, KANSAS—CONTINUED.

Newspapers.	Years.	No. vols.
DICKINSON COUNTY.		
Dickinson County Chronicle, Abilene	1876–1890	13
Kansas Gazette, Enterprise and Abilene	1876–1889	14
Abilene Daily Gazette	1886–1888	6
The Weekly Democrat, Abilene	1880–1882	2
The Abilene Reflector	1883–1890	7
The Abilene Daily Reflector	1887–1890	4
The Dickinson County News, Abilene	1888–1890	2
The Solomon Sentinel, Solomon City	1879–1890	11
Enterprise Register	1883,1884	2
Kansas Miller and Manufacturer, Enterprise	1888–1890	3
Enterprise Independent	1888–1890	3
The Anti-Monopolist, Enterprise	1884–1888	4
The Chapman Star	1884–1886	2
The Chapman Courier	1887–1890	4
The Herington Tribune	1885–1890	6
Herington Headlight	1888,1889	1
Herington Vindicator	1890	1
The Hope Herald	1885–1890	6
The Hope Dispatch	1886–1890	5
Carlton Advocate	1886–1888	2
The Banner Register, Banner City	1887,1888	2
The Manchester Sun	1887–1890	3
DONIPHAN COUNTY.		
White Cloud Chief, (7 duplicates,)	1857–1872	16
Weekly Kansas Chief, Troy, (1 duplicate,)	1879–1890	18
White Cloud Review	1888,1889	7
White Cloud Review, (second,)	1880–1887	1
Troy Reporter	1866,1867	1
Doniphan County Republican, Troy, (1873 lacking,)	1871–1875	5
Troy Weekly Bulletin	1877–1879	2
The Troy Times	1846–1890	4
Elwood Advertiser, (1 duplicate.)	1857,1838	1
Kansas Free Press, Elwood, (1 duplicate.)	1858,1859	1
Elwood Free Press, (1 duplicate,)	1859–1861	2
Wathena Reporter, (1868–1873 lacking,)	1857–1877	5
Wathena Gazette	1889,1890	2
Highland Sentinel	1878,1879	1
The Central State, Highland	1880–1882	2
Enterprise, Severance, (and Centralia, Nemaha county,)	1883	1
Severance News	1889,1890	2
DOUGLAS COUNTY.		
Herald of Freedom, Lawrence, (7 duplicates,)	1854–1859	6
Kansas Free-State, Lawrence	1855,1856	1
Lawrence Republican, (volumes 1 and 3, incomplete.)	1857–1860	2
The Western Home Journal, Lawrence	1860–1884	14
The Weekly Kansas Journal, Lawrence	1886–1888	3
The Lawrence Weekly Journal-Tribune	1889,1890	2
Republican-Journal (daily), Lawrence	1877–1880	8
Lawrence Daily Journal	1880–1888	18
The Congregational Record, monthly, (Lawrence, January, 1859, to December, 1864; Topeka, June, 1865, to May, 1867,)	1859–1867	8
The Tribune, Lawrence, (lacking 1873 and 1875,)	1868–1883	13
The Semi-Weekly Tribune, and the Weekly Herald-Tribune, Lawrence	1884,1885	2
The Lawrence Tribune	1885–1888	3
The Tribune, daily, (1875, 1878, 1879, and part of 1877 lacking; duplicates,) Lawrence	1873–1884	17
Herald-Tribune, daily, Lawrence	1884,1885	3
Evening Tribune, Lawrence	1886–1888	6
Spirit of Kansas, Lawrence	1875–1882	7
Kansas Collegiate, Lawrence	1875–1879	5
The University Courier, Lawrence	1878,1879	1
University Courier, Lawrence	1882–1886	6
The Kansas Review (monthly), Lawrence	1879–1886	10
Lawrence Standard	1877–1879	3
Kansas Monthly, Lawrence	1878–1881	4
The Daily Reporter, Lawrence	1879	7
Kansas Temperance Palladium, Lawrence	1879,1880	1
Die Germania, Lawrence	1880–1890	3
The Kansas Liberal (monthly), Lawrence, July to September, 1882, (see Valley Falls,)		
The Lawrence Gazette	1882–1890	8
Lawrence Daily Gazette	1884,1885	1
Western Recorder, Lawrence	1883,1884	1
Kansas Churchman (monthly), Lawrence	1883–1885	2
Kansas Daily Herald, Lawrence	1883,1884	2
The Head Center and Daily Morning Sun, Lawrence	1883	1

BOUND NEWSPAPER FILES AND PERIODICALS, KANSAS — CONTINUED.

Newspapers.	Years.	No. vols.
DOUGLAS COUNTY — *continued.*		
The Daily Morning News. Lawrence	1883, 1884	1
Once a Week, Lawrence	1883–1885	2
The Kansas Zephyr. Lawrence	1884–1887	3
Sigma Nu Delta (bi-monthly), Lawrence	1886–1889	2
Evening Telegram. Lawrence	1888	1
Lawrence Daily Democrat	1888	1
University Times, Lawrence	1888, 1889	1
The Weekly Record, Lawrence	1889, 1890	1
University Kansan, Lawrence	1889, 1890	1
The Daily Record, Lawrence	1889, 1890	3
North Lawrence Leader	1884, 1885	1
Freeman's Champion, Prairie City	1857, 1858	1
Baldwin Criterion	1883–1885	1
The Baldwin Visitor	1884	1
The Baldwin Ledger	1885–1890	6
The Baldwin Index, Baker University, (1887 lacking,)	1881–1889	4
The Baker Beacon. Baldwin	1889, 1890	1
Lecompton Monitor	1885, 1886	1
The Lecompton Ledger	1890	1
College Echoes, Lecompton	1888–1890	2
The Eudora News	1887–1890	3
EDWARDS COUNTY.		
Edwards County Leader, Kinsley	1877–1880	4
Valley Republican, (bound with Kinsley Graphic, 1878,)	1877, 1878	1
Kinsley Republican	1878–1881	4
The Kinsley Graphic. (except 1882,)	1878–1887	8
Kinsley Republican-Graphic	1882	1
Edwards County Banner, Kinsley	1887	1
Weekly Banner-Graphic, Kinsley	1887–1889	2
Weely Graphic, Kinsley	1890	1
Kansas Staats-Zeitung, Kinsley	1878, 1879	1
The Kinsley Mercury	1883–1890	7
Kinsley Daily Mercury	1887, 1888	2
The Wendell Champion	1885–1888	1
Belpre Beacon	1888	1
ELK COUNTY.		
The Courant, Howard	1875–1877	3
The Courant-Ledger, Howard	1878–1880	3
The Howard Courant	1880–1890	10
Industrial Journal, Howard	1878–1880	2
Kansas Rural, Howard	1881	1
The Howard Journal	1880–1883	3
The Howard Democrat	1884–1890	6
Kansas Traveler. Howard	1886, 1887	1
Howard Daily Traveler	1887	1
The Broad Axe, Howard	1888	1
Grip, Howard	1883, 1884	1
Elk County Ledger, Elk Falls	1876, 1877	2
The Weekly Examiner. Elk Falls	1878	1
Elk Falls Signal	1880–1882	2
The Pioneer, Longton	1880, 1881	2
The Times, Longton	1881–1890	10
Longton Leader	1887	1
Longton Signal	1890	1
Moline News	1880	1
Moline Mercury, (1883 and 1884 lacking,)	1882–1889	6
The Moline Free Press	1883–1885	2
The Moline Republican	1889, 1890	1
Grenola Argus	1880–1882	2
The Grenola Chief	1883–1890	7
The Grenola Hornet	1884, 1885	1
The Cave Springs Globe	1882	1
The Herald, Cana Valley	1882, 1883	1
ELLIS COUNTY.		
Ellis County Star, (lacking from December 7, 1876, to April 11, 1879,) Hays City	1876–1881	4
Hays Sentinel, Hays City	1877–1881	5
The Star-Sentinel, and Hays City Sentinel	1880–1890	11
German-American Advocate, Hays City	1882–1886	4
Ellis County Democrat and Advocate. Hays City	1884, 1885	1
Ellis Weekly Headlight, Hays City	1882–1890	9
Hays City Times, Hays City	1886	1
Ellis County Democrat and Ellis County Free Press, Hays City	1886–1890	5
Ellis County Free Press, Hays City	1888–1890	2

BOUND NEWSPAPER FILES AND PERIODICALS, KANSAS — CONTINUED.

Newspapers.	Years.	No. vols.
ELLIS COUNTY — concluded.		
Ellis Review, Hays City	1886–1890	5
Democratic Times, Hays City	1888–1890	3
The Republican, Hays City	1888–1890	3
Walker Journal	1887,1888	1
ELLSWORTH COUNTY.		
Ellsworth Reporter	1875–1890	16
The Rural West, Ellsworth	1882	1
The Ellsworth News	1883,1884	2
The Ellsworth Democrat	1885–1890	5
The Weekly Herald, Ellsworth	1888–1890	1
The Ellsworth Republican	1890	1
Wilson Index	1878,1879	1
The Wilson Echo	1880–1890	11
The Wilson Wonder	1886,1887	2
The Wilson Hawkeye	1887,1888	1
Cain City News	1882–1886	3
The Kanopolis Journal	1886–1890	4
Kanopolis Kansan	1890	1
The Holyrood Enterprise	1887–1890	3
FINNEY COUNTY.		
The Irrigator, Garden City	1882–1886	4
Garden City Herald, (1884–7 lacking.)	1883–1890	4
Garden City Herald (daily)	1886–1890	8
Garden City Sentinel	1884–1890	6
Garden City Sentinel (daily)	1889–1888	6
The Cultivator and Herdsman, monthly and weekly, Garden City	1881–1886	1
The Western Times, Garden City	1885	1
Finney County Democrat, Garden City	1887–1890	4
The Garden City Imprint	1889–1890	2
Pierceville Courier	1886,1887	1
Terry Enterprise	1886,1887	1
The Terry Eye	1887–1889	3
Locomotive, Loco	1886,1887	1
The Hatfield News	1897–1889	1
FOOTE COUNTY. (See Gray county.)		
The New West and the Optic, Cimarron	1879–1881	2
The Signet, Cimarron	1880	1
FORD COUNTY.		
Dodge City Times	1876–1890	15
Ford County Globe, Dodge City	1878–1884	7
The Globe Live-Stock Journal, Dodge City	1884–1887	3
Dodge City Democrat, (May to Dec., 1889, lacking,)	1884–1890	6
Kansas Cowboy, Dodge City	1884,1885	1
The Sun, Dodge City	1886,1887	1
Ford County Republican, Dodge City	1887–1889	3
The Globe-Republican, Dodge City	1890	1
Spearville Enterprise	1878	1
Spearville News	1878–1880	1
Spearville Blade	1885–1890	6
Ford County Record, Spearville	1885,1886	1
Ford County Democrat, Spearville and Fonda	1886–1888	2
The Ryansville Boomer, and The Boomer, Ford City	1885–1887	2
Ford Gazette	1886–1890	5
Wilburn Argus	1896,1897	2
Bucklin Standard	1887,1888	1
The Bucklin Herald	1887,1888	1
The Bucklin Journal	1888–1890	2
The Weekly Telegram, Bloom	1888,1889	2
Western Kansas Ensign, Bellefont	1889,1890	2
FRANKLIN COUNTY.		
Western Home Journal, Ottawa	1865–1868	3
Ottawa Journal	1870–1874	5
The Triumph, Ottawa	1876	1
Ottawa Journal and Triumph	1877–1890	14
Ottawa Campus (occasional), (vols. 1 and 2.)	1864–1890	5
Ottawa Republican, (1875 lacking,)	1874–1890	16
Ottawa Daily Republican	1879–1890	23
Kansas Home News, Ottawa	1879,1880	1
Ottawa Gazette	1879	1
Ottawa Leader	1880	1
Kansas Free Trader (monthly), Ottawa	1883	1

BOUND NEWSPAPER FILES AND PERIODICALS, KANSAS—Continued.

Newspapers.	Years.	No. vols.
FRANKLIN COUNTY—*concluded.*		
Queen City Herald. Ottawa.	1883–1887	2
Jefferies Western Monthly, Ottawa.	1884,1885	1
Daily Local News, Ottawa.	1886–1888	5
Fireside, Factory and Farm, Ottawa.	1886–1888	1
The Kansas Lever. Ottawa.	1887–1890	4
The Bee (daily and weekly), Ottawa	1887,1888	1
Ottawa Tribune.	1889,1890	1
The Ottawa Herald	1889,1890	2
Williamsburg Review.	1879	1
Weekly Gazette, Williamsburg.	1880–1883	2
The Eagle, Williamsburg.	1885–1889	5
The Enterprise, Williamsburg.	1889,1890	2
Lane Advance .	1881,1882	1
The Lane Star .	1889,1890	1
The Lane Leader.	1890	1
The Commercial Bulletin, Lane.	1886–1888	3
The Wellsville News.	1882	1
The Wellsville Transcript.	1882,1883	1
The Wellsville News (second).	1884–1886	3
The Wellsville Exchange.	1887–1889	2
The Pomona Enterprise.	1885–1890	4
Republican, Pomona.	1889,1890	1
Richmond Recorder	1885–1888	3
Princeton Progress.	1885–1888	3
GARFIELD COUNTY.		
Ravanna Chieftain.	1885–1890	5
Ravanna Sod-House.	1886,1887	1
Ravanna Record.	1887,1889	2
The Ravanna Enquirer.	1887,1888	1
The Kal Vesta Herald .	1886–1888	2
The Essex Sunbeam.	1887	1
The Garfield County Call. Eminence	1887–1890	3
Garfield County Journal, Loyal.	1887–1889	2
GEARY COUNTY. (See Davis.)		
Junction City Union.	1889,1890	2
Junction City Tribune.	1889,1890	2
Davis County Republican, Junction City.	1889,1890	2
The Junction City Sentinel.	1889	1
The Democratic Sentinel.	1890	1
GOVE COUNTY.		
Buffalo Park Express.	1880	1
Buffalo Park Pioneer.	1885–1887	3
The Golden Belt, Grinnell.	1885–1890	5
Cap-Sheaf, Grainfield.	1885–1890	5
Gazette, Gove City.	1886–1890	5
Gove County Graphic, Gove City.	1887,1888	1
Gove County Republican, Gove City.	1888–1890	1
The Settler's Guide, Quinter.	1886–1888	2
Quinter Republican.	1889,1890	2
The Smoky Globe, Jerome.	1887,1888	1
GRAHAM COUNTY.		
The Western Star, Hill City.	1879,1880	1
Hill City Lively Times.	1881	1
The Hill City Reveille.	1884–1890	6
Hill City Democrat.	1887–1890	3
Hill City Sun.	1888,1889	1
Hill City Star.	1888,1889	1
Graham County Lever. Gettysburg.	1879,1880	1
The Millbrook Times.	1879–1889	10
Graham County Times, Millbrook.	1889,1890	2
Graham County Republican, Millbrook.	1881	1
Millbrook Herald.	1882,1883	1
Millbrook Herald (second).	1885–1888	2
The Graham County Democrat, Millbrook.	1885–1888	3
Roscoe Tribune.	1880,1881	1
Western Cyclone, Nicodemus.	1886–1888	2
Nicodemus Enterprise.	1887	1
The Fremont Star.	1886–1888	2
The Fremont Press.	1888,1889	1
Fremont Eagle.	1889,1890	1
The Bogue Signal.	1888–1890	2
The Times, Penokee.	1889,1890	1

BOUND NEWSPAPER FILES AND PERIODICALS, KANSAS — CONTINUED.

Newspapers.	Years.	No. vols.
GRANT COUNTY.		
Grant County Register, Ulysses..........................	1885–1890	4
Ulysses Tribune........................	1887–1890	3
Ulysses Tribune and Grant County Register....................	1890	1
Ulysses Plainsman..........................	1880,1890	1
The Post, Surprise........................	1886,1887	1
Shockeyville Eagle........................	1886,1887	1
Shockeyville Plainsman........................	1889	1
Golden Gazette........................	1887–1889	3
Zionville Sentinel........................	1887,1888	1
The Commercial, Cincinnati and Appomattox................	1887,1888	2
The Standard-Democrat, Cincinnati and Appomattox............	1887,1888	1
The Lawson Leader........................	1887,1888	1
Conductor Punch........................	1887,1888	1
GRAY COUNTY.		
The New West, Cimarron and Echo........................	1885–1888	4
The West, Echo........................	1889,1890	2
Cimarron Herald and Kansas Sod House....................	1885–1886	1
The Jacksonian, Cimarron........................	1885–1890	5
Gray County Echo, Ingalls and Cimarron....................	1886–1888	2
Ingalls Union........................	1887–1890	3
Gray County Republican, Ingalls........................	1888	1
The Weekly Messenger, Ingalls........................	1889,1890	1
The Montezuma Chief........................	1886–1889	2
Gray County Republican, Montezuma........................	1889	1
Ensign Razzoop........................	1887,1888	1
GREELEY COUNTY.		
Greeley County Gazette, Greeley Center and Horace...........	1886–1888	2
Greeley County News, Greeley Center and Horace.............	1886–1888	1
Horace Messenger........................	1888	1
Horace Champion........................	1888,1889	2
Hector Echo........................	1888	1
Greeley County Tribune, Tribune and Reid....................	1886,1887	1
Greeley County Enterprise, Tribune........................	1887,1888	1
Greeley County Republican, Tribune........................	1889,1890	2
Greeley County Journal, Tribune........................	1890	1
Greeley County Republican, Reid........................	1887,1888	1
Colokan Graphic........................	1887,1888	1
GREENWOOD COUNTY.		
Eureka Censorial........................	1876–1879	3
Eureka Herald........................	1876–1890	15
The Graphic Eureka........................	1879–1882	3
The Eureka Republican........................	1879,1880	2
Greenwood County Republican, Eureka.....................	1880–1890	10
The Eureka Sun........................	1879,1880	1
Greenwood County Democrat, Eureka...	1882–1884	2
Democratic Messenger, Eureka........................	1884–1890	7
Kansas Alliance Union, Eureka........................	1890	1
The Academy Student, Eureka........................	1889,1890	1
Madison Times........................	1877,1878	1
The Madison News........................	1879–1890	11
The Zenith, and the Madison Times........................	1886–1888	3
Fall River Times........................	1881–1890	9
Fall River Echo........................	1883–1886	3
Fall River Courant........................	1886–1888	2
Saturday Morning Sun, Fall River........................	1888,1889	1
Severy Pioneer........................	1882	1
Southern Kansas Journal, Severy........................	1884–1887	3
Severy Liberal........................	1885,1886	2
Severy Record........................	1887–1890	4
The Kansas Clipper, Severy........................	1887–1889	1
Severyite, Severy........................	1889,1890	2
The Sunflower, Reece........................	1885,1886	2
Greenwood Review, Virgil........................	1887–1890	2
The Hamilton Broadaxe........................	1889,1890	1
HAMILTON COUNTY.		
The Syracuse Journal........................	1885–1890	5
Syracuse Sentinel, (removed from Johnson City, Stanton county,)...	1886,1889	3
Syracuse Democrat........................	1887	1
Democratic Principle, Syracuse........................	1887–1890	3
West Kansas News, Syracuse........................	1887	1
Border Ruffian, Coolidge........................	1885–1887	1

BOUND NEWSPAPER FILES AND PERIODICALS, KANSAS—CONTINUED.

Newspapers.	Years.	No. vols.
HAMILTON COUNTY—*concluded.*		
Coolidge Citizen	1886–1890	4
Coolidge Times	1887–1890	2
Surprise Post	1886	1
The Signal, Kendall	1886, 1887	1
The Kendall Boomer	1886–1889	3
Kendall Republican	1886, 1887	1
Kendall Gazette	1887	1
The Kendall Free Press	1889, 1890	1
Johnson City Sentinel, (since in Stanton county,)	1886–1888	3
Enfield Tribune	1886, 1887	1
HARPER COUNTY.		
The Anthony Republican	1879–1890	11
Anthony Daily Republican	1886–1889	6
Harper County Enterprise, Anthony	1885–1890	6
The Harper County Democrat, Anthony	1886–1888	2
Anthony Free Press, daily	1887, 1888	1
Anthony Journal	1878–1884	5
Anthony Journal, (second,)	1888–1890	3
Anthony Daily Journal	1888	1
Harper County Times, Harper	1878–1885	7
The Sentinel, Harper	1882–1890	7
The Daily Sentinel, Harper	1886–1888	5
Harper Graphic	1883–1888	4
Harper Daily Graphic	1886	1
The College Journal, Harper	1888, 1889	1
The Prophet, Harper	1888	1
Bluff City Tribune	1886–1888	2
Bluff City Herald	1888–1890	3
The Danville Courant	1883, 1884	1
The Danville Express	1885, 1886	1
The Attica Advocate	1885–1890	6
Attica Bulletin	1886–1888	2
Attica Daily Advocate	1887	1
Freeport Leader	1885–1890	3
Midlothian Sun, Freeport	1885, 1886	1
The Freeport Tribune (changed from Sun,)	1886	1
The Crisfield Courier	1885–1890	4
HARVEY COUNTY.		
Zur Heimath (semi-monthly), Halstead	1875–1881	7
The Halstead Independent	1881–1890	10
The Halstead Clipper	1884–1886	2
Halstead Herald	1887, 1888	2
The Halstead Tribune	1890	1
Harvey County News, Newton	1876–1879	4
The Newton Republican, (changed from Harvey County News,)	1879–1890	11
Newton Daily Republican	1886–1890	10
Newton Kansan	1876–1890	15
Newton Daily Kansan	1887, 1888	2
The Golden Gate, Newton	1879–1882	3
Das Neue Vaterland, Newton	1879	1
The Newton Democrat	1883–1887	3
Newton Anzeiger	1887–1890	3
The Kansas Commoner, Newton	1887–1890	3
The Kansas Chronicle, Newton	1888	1
Newton Weekly Journal	1888–1890	2
The Burrton Telephone	1878–1881	3
The Burrton Monitor	1881–1888	7
The Burrton Graphic	1886–1890	5
The Free Lance, Burrton	1890	1
The Jayhawker and Palladium, Sedgwick	1882–1884	2
The Pantagraph, Sedgwick	1884–1890	7
Walton Independent	1886–1888	2
The Walton Reporter	1890	1
HASKELL COUNTY.		
Ivanhoe Times	1886–1890	5
Santa Fé Trail	1886, 1887	2
Santa Fé Champion	1887, 1888	1
Haskell County Review, Santa Fé	1887, 1888	1
Haskell County Republican, Santa Fé	1888	1
The Santa Fé Leader	1888	1
Santa Fé Monitor	1888–1890	3

BOUND NEWSPAPER FILES AND PERIODICALS, KANSAS—CONTINUED.

Newspapers.	Years.	No. vols.
HODGEMAN COUNTY.		
Agitator, Hodgman Center	1879,1880	1
Republican, Fordham	1879	1
The Buckner Independent, Jetmore	1879–1881	2
The Jetmore Reveille	1882–1890	9
Hodgeman County Scimitar, Jetmore	1886–1889	4
Jetmore Siftings	1886–1890	3
Jetmore Journal	1887–1889	2
The Jetmore Sunflower	1889,1890	1
The Orwell Times	1885,1886	1
The Cowland Chieftain	1885	1
JACKSON COUNTY.		
Holton Express	1872–1875	4
Holton Recorder	1875–1890	16
The Holton Argus	1877	1
The Holton Signal	1878–1890	13
Jackson County Federal, Holton	1886,1887	1
The Bee (daily and weekly), Netawaka and Holton	1879,1880	1
Independent Tribune, Holton	1890	1
The Whiting Weekly News	1883–1890	8
The Hoyt Times	1887	1
Soldier City Tribune	1888,1890	2
The Denison Star	1889,1890	1
JEFFERSON COUNTY.		
The Kansas Educational Journal, Grasshopper Falls. (See Leavenworth County.)		
The Kansas New Era, Grasshopper Falls	1866,1867	1
Valley Falls New Era	1873–1890	18
The Valley Falls Liberal and the Kansas Liberal (monthly), Valley Falls and Lawrence.	1880–1883	3
Lucifer, (the Light-Bearer,) Valley Falls	1883–1890	7
Valley Falls Register	1881–1890	10
Fair Play, Valley Falls	1888–1890	2
Valley Falls Republican	1889,1890	1
The Oskaloosa Independent	1870–1890	21
Sickle and Sheaf, Oskaloosa	1873–1879	7
Oskaloosa Weekly Sickle	1879–1886	7
The Winchester Argus	1879–1888	9
The Winchester Herald	1888–1890	3
The Kaw Valley Chief, Perry	1879–1882	3
The Perry Monitor and Kaw Valley Chief (second), Perry	1883,1884	1
The Nortonville News	1885–1890	6
Meriden Report	1885–1888	3
Meriden Weekly Tribune	1890	1
The Osawkie Times	1885,1886	1
The McLouth Times	1887–1890	3
JEWELL COUNTY.		
Jewell County Diamond, Jewell City	1876,1877	2
Jewell County Republican, Jewell City	1879–1890	11
Jewell County Monitor, Jewell Center	1876,1877	2
Jewell County Monitor and Diamond, Jewell Center	1878,1879	2
Jewell County Monitor, Jewell Center and Mankato	1880–1888	9
Jewell County Monitor, Mankato	1889,1890	2
Jewell County Review, Jewell Center and Mankato	1880–1882	3
The Jewell County Review, Mankato	1880,1890	2
Mankato Review	1883–1888	6
Mankato Daily Review	1887	1
The Kansas Jewellite, Mankato	1882–1883	1
The Jacksonian, Mankato	1888,1890	3
The Labor Clarion, Mankato	1889	1
White Oak Independent	1879	1
Western Advocate, Omio	1889,1890	1
Jewell County Journal, Omio	1882	1
The Omio Mail	1884	1
Burr Oak Reveille	1880–1884	5
Burr Oak Herald	1883–1890	8
Burr Oak Rustler	1886,1887	1
Independent Republican, Burr Oak	1886,1887	1
Salem Chronicle	1882	1
Salem Argus	1883–1890	6
The People's Friend, Salem	1885–1887	3
Randall Register	1885–1888	3
Randall Tribune	1887,1888	1
The Beacon, Randall	1889,1890	1

BOUND NEWSPAPER FILES AND PERIODICALS, KANSAS — CONTINUED.

Newspapers.	Years.	No. vols.
JOHNSON COUNTY.		
Olathe Mirror......	1866–1868	2
Mirror and News-Letter, Olathe........	1876–1882	6
The Olathe Mirror. (1884–6. see below,).......	1882–1890	5
Olathe Mirror-Gazette	1883–1886	4
Western Progress, Olathe........	1876–1880	4
Kansas Star, Olathe......	1876–1890	15
Olathe Leader	1879–1882	3
Olathe Gazette.......	1879–1883	3
Educational Advocate, Olathe......	1880	1
Johnson County Democrat, Olathe.....	1882–1890	9
Kansas Patron, Olathe.....	1882–1890	9
The Olathe Republican	1884,1885	2
Kansas Register, Spring Hill.....	1878	1
Weekly Review, Spring Hill	1881,1882	1
Spring Hill New Era, (1886 to Aug. 1888, lacking,).....	1883–1890	3
The Young Kansan, Gardner.....	1889,1890	2
KEARNY COUNTY.		
Lakin Herald.....	1882–1884	3
The Kearny County Advocate, Lakin.....	1885–1890	5
Pioneer Democrat, Lakin.....	1885–1890	4
Hartland Times.....	1886,1887	2
Hartland Herald.....	1886–1890	5
Kearny County Coyote, Chantilly and Omaha.....	1887,1890	3
KINGMAN COUNTY.		
The Kingman Mercury......	1878–1880	2
The Kingman Blade	1880	1
The Kingman County Citizen, Kingman	1879–1884	4
The Kingman County Republican. Kingman	1882–1884	2
Citizen-Republican, Kingman.....	1884	1
Southern Kansas Democrat, Kingman.....	1883–1888	5
The Kingman County Democrat.....	1889,1890	2
The Kingman Courier	1884–1889	6
Kingman Daily Courier......	1887,1888	3
Kingman Leader......	1884–1889	4
Kingman Leader-Courier.....	1890,1890'	1
Kingman News......	1886–1888	2
Kingman Daily News, (November, 1887, to February, 1888, lacking,).....	1886–1888	2
Voice of the People, Kingman.....	1888,1889	2
The Kingman Weekly Journal.....	1890	1
News, Norwich.....	1886–1890	5
Ninnescah and Cunningham Herald.....	1886–1888	2
Cunningham Herald.....	1889,1890	2
The Spivey Disputch.....	1887,1888	2
Spivey Index.....	1889,1890	2
New Murdock Herald	1887	1
The Penalosa News.....	1887,1888	1
The Nashville News.....	1888	1
KIOWA COUNTY.		
Wellsford Register......	1885	1
Wellsford Register (second).....	1890	1
Wellsford Republican.....	1886,1887	1
Kiowa County Democrat, Wellsford.....	1887,1888	2
The Democrat and Watchman, Dowell post-office.....	1885,1886	1
Comanche Chief and The Kiowa Chief, Reeder.....	1886	1
Greensburg Signal.....	1886–1888	3
The Kiowa County Signal, Greensburg.....	1889,1890	2
The Kiowa County Times, Greensburg.....	1888–1890	2
Greensburg Rustler.....	1886–1888	3
Greensburg Republican.....	1887,1888	1
Mullinville Mallet.....	1886–1888	2
The Weekly Telegram, Mullinville.....	1886,1887	1
The Haviland Tribune.....	1887–1889	2
LABETTE COUNTY.		
Parsons Sun.....	1876–1890	15
Parsons Sun, daily.....	1884–1890	14
Parsons Eclipse.....	1876–1890	15
Parsons Daily Eclipse.....	1881–1890	13
Daily Outlook, Parsons.....	1877,1878	1
Daily Infant Wonder, Parsons.....	1878–1880	3
Daily Republican, Parsons.....	1880,1881	2
Parsons Palladium.....	1883–1890	8
The Daily Evening Star, Parsons, (April 6 to October 19, 1881,).....	1881	1

BOUND NEWSPAPER FILES AND PERIODICALS, KANSAS—Continued.

Newspapers.	Years.	No. vols.
LABETTE COUNTY—*concluded.*		
The Weekly Clarion, Parsons	1888-1890	3
Southern Kansas Advance, Chetopa	1876-1878	2
Chetopa Advance	1878-1890	13
Chetopa Herald	1876-1878	2
Chetopa Statesman	1883-1889	4
The Chetopa Democrat	1888-1890	3
Oswego Independent	1876-1890	15
Labette County, Democrat, Oswego	1880-1890	11
The Oswego Republican	1881-1886	5
The Oswego Daily Republican	1881-1883	3
The Oswego Bee	1887,1888	2
The Oswego Daily Bee	1887,1888	3
Labette County Statesman, Oswego	1889,1890	1
The Oswego Courant	1889,1890	2
Mound Valley Herald	1885-1890	6
Mound Valley News	1886,1887	1
The Altamont Sentinel	1886-1890	5
Mills's Weekly World, Altamont	1889,1890	2
The Edna Star	1887,1888	1
The Wilsonton Journal	1888-1890	3
LANE COUNTY.		
Lane County Gazette, California	1880-1882	2
Lane County Herald, Dighton	1885-1890	5
Dighton Journal	1886-1890	5
Dighton Republican	1887-1889	2
LEAVENWORTH COUNTY.		
Kansas Herald, Leavenworth	1854,1859	5
Kansas Territorial Register, Leavenworth	1855	1
Leavenworth Conservative, daily, (January to June, 1867, lacking,)	1861-1868	16
Times and Conservative, Leavenworth (daily)	1869,1870	3
Leavenworth Times, daily, (July to October, 1878, lacking,)	1870-1890	41
Leavenworth Times (weekly)	1876-1880	5
Leavenworth Daily Commercial	1873-1876	4
Kansas Freie Presse, Leavenworth (weekly)	1876-1886	10
Kansas Freie Presse, Leavenworth (daily)	1876-1886	18
Leavenworth Appeal	1876-1878	3
Leavenworth Appeal and Herald	1879	1
Leavenworth Appeal and Tribune	1879,1880	1
Public Press, Leavenworth (weekly)	1877-1883	6
Public Press, Leavenworth, daily, (from July, 1877, to June, 1879, lacking,)	1877-1882	8
Home Record, Leavenworth (monthly)	1876-1890	15
Democratic Standard, Leavenworth (weekly)	1880-1882	3
Kansas Farmer, Leavenworth (monthly)	1867-1872	8
Leavenworth Evening Standard	1881-1890	20
The Kansas Educational Journal, monthly; Leavenworth, January, 1864, to August, 1865; Grasshopper Falls, September, 1865, to January, 1866: Topeka, June, 1866, to August, 1867; Emporia, September, 1867, to April, 1871; Emporia and Topeka, May, 1871, to April, 1873	1864-1873	9
Orphans'Friend, Leavenworth (monthly)	1878-1890	12
The Western Home-stead, Leavenworth (monthly)	1878-1882	3
The Workingman's Friend, Leavenworth	1881-1883	2
Leavenworth Weekly Chronicle	1883,1884	1
The Visitor, Leavenworth	1892-1884	2
The Catholic, Leavenworth	1885-1889	5
The Kansas Prohibitionist, Leavenworth	1883,1884	1
Kansas Commoner, Leavenworth	1884,1885	1
Truth, monthly, Leavenworth	1886,1887	1
The Daily Sun, Leavenworth	1887-1890	6
Leavenworth Post (daily)	1888-1890	6
Journal of the U. S. Cavalry Association, Leavenworth (quarterly)	1888-1890	3
The Leavenworth Advocate	1888-1890	2
The Tonganoxie Mirror	1882-1890	8
The Tonganoxie News, changed from Linwood Leader	1885-1887	2
The Tonganoxie Sentinel	1889,1890	2
The Linwood Leader	1883,1884	1
LINCOLN COUNTY.		
Lincoln County News, Lincoln Center	1873	1
Saline Valley Register, Lincoln Center	1876-1879	4
Lincoln Register, Lincoln Center	1879-1880	1
Saline Valley Register, Lincoln Center	1881-1883	2
Lincoln Banner, Lincoln Center	1884-1886	2
Lincoln Republican, Lincoln Center	1886-1890	5
The Argus and Beacon, Lincoln Center	1890	1

BOUND NEWSPAPER FILES AND PERIODICALS, KANSAS—Continued.

Newspapers.	Years.	No. vols.
LINCOLN COUNTY—*concluded.*		
The Beacon of Lincoln County, Lincoln Center	1881–1884	3
The Lincoln Beacon, Lincoln Center	1884–1890	7
Lincoln County Democrat, Lincoln	1886–1890	4
The Sylvan Grove Sentinel	1887–1890	3
Barnard Times	1888–1890	2
LINN COUNTY.		
La Cygne Weekly Journal	1876–1890	15
La Cygne Leader	1887,18-8	1
Border Sentinel, Mound City	1866–1874	8
Linn County Clarion, Mound City	1876–1890	15
Mound City Progress	1884–1890	7
The Torch of Liberty, Mound City	1888–1890	3
The Pleasanton Observer	1876–1890	15
The Pleasanton Herald	1882–1890	9
The Prescott Eagle	1883–1888	5
The Prescott Republican	1888,1889	1
Prescott Enterprise	1889	1
The Blue Mound Sun	1883–1890	7
The Parker Pilot	1889,1890	2
Goodrich Graphic	1890	1
LOGAN COUNTY.		
The Oakley Opinion	1885–1889	4
The Oakley Republican	1887,1888	1
Oakley Saturday Press	1888	1
Logan County Times, Oakley and Russell Springs	1887,1888	1
Oakley News Letter	1889	1
Oakley Graphic	1889,1890	1
The Courier, Ennis and Monument	1886–1888	2
The Monument Obelisk	1888,1889	2
The Monument Observer	1890	1
The Scout, Gopher and Winona, (bound with Winona Messenger,)	1886–1888	3
The Winona Clipper	1887–1890	3
Winona Messenger	1887–1889	2
McAllaster Weekly Record	1887,1888	1
Augustine Herald	1887–1890	3
The Leader, Russell Springs	1887–1889	2
The Record, Russell Springs	1887	1
The Logan County Republican, Russell Springs	1888–1890	3
Page City Messenger	1889,1890	1
LYON COUNTY.		
Emporia News	1866–1889	24
Emporia Daily News	1878–1889	22
Kansas Educational Journal, Emporia, (see Leavenworth county.)		
Emporia Ledger	1876–1880	5
The Hatchet (monthly), Emporia	1877,1878	1
The Educationalist (monthly), Emporia	1879,1880	2
Emporia Sun	1878,1879	2
The Kansas Greenbacker, and the National Era, Emporia	1878,1879	2
The Emporia Journal	1880,1881	2
The Kansas Sentinel, Emporia	1880–1882	3
Daily Bulletin, Emporia	1881	1
Emporia Daily Republican	1881–1890	19
The Emporia Republican	1886–1890	4
Emporia Democrat	1882–1890	8
The Primitive Friend, Emporia	1883–1885	2
Emporia Daily Globe (1888 lacking)	1886–1889	3
The Fanatic, Emporia	1887,1888	1
The Weekly News-Democrat, Emporia	1889,1890	1
Emporia News-Democrat (daily)	1889,1890	1
The Semi-Weekly Miniature, Emporia	1887	1
The Normal Quarterly, Emporia	1889,1890	1
Kansas Workman, Emporia, (see Butler county.)		
College Life, Emporia	1890	1
The Hartford Enterprise	1879,1880	1
The Hartford Weekly Call	1879–1890	11
Hartford News	1890	1
Americus Weekly Herald	1881,1882	1
The Americus Ledger	1885–1889	4
The Neosho Vivifier, Neosho Rapids	1885,1886	1
The Neosho Valley Press, Neosho Rapids	1886,1887	1
The Neosho Rapids Pilot	1889,1890	2
The Admire City Free Press	1887,1888	1
The Allen Tidings	1887–1890	3

—5

BOUND NEWSPAPER FILES AND PERIODICALS, KANSAS — CONTINUED.

Newspapers.	Years.	No. vols.
M'PHERSON COUNTY.		
The McPherson Independent.	1876–1879	4
The McPherson Freeman.	1878–1890	13
McPherson Daily Freeman.	1887,1888	2
The McPherson Republican.	1879–1890	11
McPherson Daily Republican.	1887–1890	8
The Comet, McPherson.	1881,1882	1
Industrial Liberator, McPherson.	1882	1
The McPherson Independent.	1882–1884	4
The McPherson Press.	1884,1885	1
The McPherson County Champion, McPherson.	1885–1887	2
The Democrat, McPherson.	1886–1890	4
Kansas State Register. McPherson.	1887	1
The McPherson Anzeiger.	1887–1890	4
Our Opinion, McPherson.	1888–1890	2
The Educator and Companion.	1888–1890	3
The Industrial Union, McPherson.	1890	1
Lindsborg Localist.	1879–1883	3
Smoky Valley News, Lindsborg.	1881–1888	7
Kansas Posten, Lindsborg.	1882,1883	1
Framat, Lindsborg.	1889	1
The Lindsborg News.	1889,1890	2
The Canton Monitor.	1880	1
Canton Carrier.	1885–1888	3
The Republican, Canton.	1889,1890	2
The Windom Record.	1884–1886	2
The Windom Enterprise.	1886–1888	2
The Moundridge Leader.	1887–1890	4
Marquette Monitor.	1887,1888	2
Marquette Tribune.	1889,1890	2
Galva Times.	1888–1890	2
MARION COUNTY.		
Marion County Record, Marion Center.	1875–1890	15
The School Galaxy, Marion Center.	1877	1
Central Kansas Telegraph. Marion Center.	1880	1
Marion Banner, Marion Center.	1880,1881	2
Marion Graphic. Marion Center.	1882,1883	1
Marion County Democrat and Independent, Marion Center.	1883,1884	1
The Marion Register, Marion.	1885–1888	4
The Marion Tribune.	1886,1887	1
The Cottonwood Valley Times, Marion.	1887–1889	3
Marion Daily Times.	1888	2
The School Gleaner, Marion.	1889,1890	1
The Rural Kansan, Marion.	1889,1890	2
The Scimeter, Marion.	1890	1
The Marion County Anzeiger, Marion and Hillsboro.	1887–1890	3
The Peabody Gazette.	1876–1890	15
The Peabody Daily Gazette.	1887	1
Peabody Reporter.	1880	1
The Peabody Post.	1882	1
Marion Graphic, Peabody.	1883–1890	7
Florence Herald, (1886 lacking).	1876–1890	14
Florence Tribune.	1884–1886	2
Florence Weekly News.	1886,1887	1
The Florence Weekly Bulletin.	1887–1890	4
Hillsboro Phonograph.	1881	1
The Intelligencer, Hillsboro.	1881,1882	1
Freundschafts-Kreis, Hillsboro.	1883,1886	2
Hillsboro Herald.	1886–1888	3
Canada Arcade.	1887	1
Lincolnville Star.	1887,1888	1
The Weekly Courier, Lost Springs.	1888,1889	1
Burns Monitor.	1889,1890	1
MARSHALL COUNTY.		
The Marysville Enterprise, (volumes 1 and 3,).	1866,1868	2
The Lantern, Marysville.	1876	1
The Marshall County News, Marysville.	1876–1890	15
Kansas-Staats-Zeitung, Marysville.	1879–1881	2
Marysville Signal.	1881–1883	2
Marysville Post, (German.).	1881–1890	9
Marshall County Democrat, Marysville.	1883–1890	8
The Bugle Call, Marysville.	1885,1886	1
The True Republican, Marysville.	1886–1890	4
The Daily Free Press, Marysville.	1889,1890	3
The Waterville Telegraph, (1874 and 1875 lacking,).	1870–1890	19

BOUND NEWSPAPER FILES AND PERIODICALS, KANSAS — Continued.

Newspapers.	Years.	No. vols.
MARSHALL COUNTY— *concluded.*		
Blue Rapids Times...	1876–1890	15
The Blue Rapids Lyre..	1886, 1887	1
Blue Valley Gazette, Irving......................................	1876–1878	3
The Irving Citizen..	1890	1
The Irving Leader..	1886–1890	4
Frankfort Record..	1876–1879	4
The National Headlight, Frankfort.................................	1879–1881	2
The Frankfort Bee..	1881–1890	10
The Frankfort Sentinel..	1886–1890	4
The Beattie Boomerang..	1883, 1884	1
The North Star, Beattie...	1884, 1885	1
The Star, Beattie...	1885–1890	6
The Visitor, Axtell...	1883, 1884	1
Axtell Anchor...	1883–1890	7
The Summerfield Sun...	1889, 1890	2
The Oketo Sun...	1889, 1890	1
MEADE COUNTY.		
The Pearlette Call..	1879, 1880	1
Fowler City Graphic..	1885–1890	4
The Fowler City Advocate.......................................	1886	1
Meade County Globe, Meade Center...............................	1885–1890	5
Meade Center Press...	1885, 1886	1
The Press-Democrat, Meade Center................................	1885–1890	4
Meade Center Telegram..	1886	1
The Meade Republican, Meade Center.............................	1887–1890	3
Meade County Democrat, Meade..................................	1890	1
The Hornet, Spring Lake, and Artois, Artesian City................	1885–1889	4
The Guardian, West Plains.......................................	1886, 1887	1
The West Plains News and Democrat...............................	1887, 1888	1
The West Plains Mascott..	1888, 1889	1
Meade County Times, Mertilla....................................	1886–1888	2
MIAMI COUNTY.		
The Western Spirit, Paola..	1874–1890	17
The Miami Republican, Paola.....................................	1876–1890	15
Republican-Citizen, Paola..	1878–1880	2
Miami Talisman, Paola..	1881, 1882	1
Paola Times...	1882–1890	9
The Miami School Journal, Paola..................................	1889, 1890	1
The Border Chief, Louisburg.....................................	1879–1881	2
Watchman, Louisburg...	1881	1
The Louisburg Herald...	1887–1890	3
Osawatomie Times..	1880, 1881	1
Osawatomie Gaslight..	1887, 1888	1
Graphic, Osawatomie..	1888–1890	3
Osawatomie Advertiser..	1888–1890	1
Farmers' Signal, Osawatomie.....................................	1890	1
Fontana News...	1885–1889	4
MITCHELL COUNTY.		
Beloit Gazette, (dups. from April, 1872, to April, 1873; 1873, 1874 and 1875 lacking,).....	1872–1890	15
Beloit Weekly Record...	1877–1879	3
The Beloit Courier...	1879–1890	12
Beloit Weekly Democrat...	1878–1880	2
Western Democrat, Beloit, (1882 and 1883 lacking,)................	1880–1890	7
The Western Nationalist, Beloit..................................	1882, 1883	2
Beloit Dental Herald..	1888, 1889	1
The Echo, Cawker City..	1876–1878	2
The Cawker City Free Press......................................	1878–1883	5
Cawker City Journal..	1880–1890	9
The Public Record, Cawker City..................................	1883–1890	8
Cawker City Times...	1888–1890	3
Glen Elder Key..	1890	1
Glen Elder Herald..	1885–1890	4
The Kansas Herald, Glen Elder...................................	1890	1
Simpson Siftings...	1884–1886	2
Scottsville Independent..	1886–1889	4
Tri-County News, Scottsville.....................................	1889, 1890	2
MONTGOMERY COUNTY.		
Independence Courier...	1874, 1875	2
Independence Kansan...	1876–1884	9
The Star, Independence...	1882–1884	3
The Star and Kansan, Independence...............................	1883–1890	6
The South Kansas Tribune, Independence..........................	1876–1890	15

BOUND NEWSPAPER FILES AND PERIODICALS, KANSAS — CONTINUED.

Newspapers.	Years.	No. vols.
MONTGOMERY COUNTY—*concluded.*		
The Workingman's Courier, Independence	1877–1879	3
The Living Age, Independence	1881	1
The Evening Reporter, and The Morning Reporter, Independence, (lacking from 1883 to February 17, 1886.)	1882–1890	11
The Independence News (daily and weekly)	1886	1
Montgomery Argus, Independence	1886	1
Coffeyville Journal	1876–1890	15
The Gate City Enterprise, Coffeyville	1884, 1885	1
Gate City Gazette, Coffeyville	1886, 1887	1
The Sun, Coffeyville	1886–1888	2
The Eagle, Coffeyville	1888–1890	1
The Index, Coffeyville	1889, 1890	1
The News, Coffeyville	1890	1
Cherryvale Leader	1877	1
Cherryvale Globe	1879–1882	3
Cherryvale News	1881, 1882	1
Cherry Valley Torch, Cherryvale	1882–1885	3
Cherryvale Globe-News	1882–1884	3
The Globe and Torch, Cherryvale	1885–1888	3
Daily Globe and Torch, Cherryvale	1885–1887	4
The Weekly Clarion, Cherryvale	1885	1
Cherryvale Bulletin	1884–1888	5
The Cherryvale Republican	1886–1890	4
The Cherryvale Champion	1887–1890	3
The Elk City Globe	1882–1887	5
The Elk City Star	1884–1886	1
The Elk City Democrat	1885, 1886	1
The Elk City Eagle	1886–1890	4
Elk City Times	1886	1
The Elk City Enterprise	1889, 1890	1
The Caney Chronicle	1885–1890	5
The Caney Times	1889, 1890	2
The Havana Vidette	1885, 1886	1
Havana Weekly Herald	1887, 1888	1
The Havana Recorder	1889	1
The Havana News	1890	1
Liberty Light	1886	1
The Liberty Review	1886–1890	4
MORRIS COUNTY.		
Morris County Republican, Council Grove	1876, 1877	1
Council Grove Democrat	1876, 1877	2
Republican and Democrat, Council Grove	1877–1879	2
Council Grove Republican	1879–1890	12
Morris County Times, Council Grove	1880, 1881	2
The Kansas Cosmos, Council Grove, (January to July, 1885, lacking; October 15, 1886, Cosmos consolidated with Council Grove Republican,)	1881–1886	6
The Council Grove Guard	1884–1890	6
The Anti-Monopolist, Council Grove	1888	1
Morris County Enterprise, Parkerville	1878–1884	7
The Parkerville Times	1887, 1888	1
The Morris County News, White City	1886–1888	2
The White City News	1888, 1889	1
White City Register	1889, 1890	2
The Dwight Wasp	1887–1890	4
The Dunlap Courier	1889, 1890	1
Wilsey Bulletin	1890	1
MORTON COUNTY.		
Frisco Pioneer	1886, 1887	1
Morton County Democrat, Frisco	1886–1888	1
The Richfield Leader	1886, 1887	1
The Leader-Democrat, Richfield	1888, 1889	1
The Richfield Republican	1887–1890	2
The Monitor-Republican, Richfield	1890	1
The Great Southwest, Richfield	1887, 1888	1
The Taloga Star	1887–1890	3
Cundiff Journal	1888, 1889	1
The Morton County Monitor, Morton	1888–1890	1
The Westola Wave	1888, 1889	1
NEMAHA COUNTY.		
Seneca Weekly Courier	1875–1884	10
Seneca Courier-Democrat	1885–1890	6
The Seneca Tribune	1879–1890	12
Our Mission, Seneca	1885, 1886	1

BOUND NEWSPAPER FILES AND PERIODICALS, KANSAS—Continued.

Newspapers.	Years.	No. vols.
NEMAHA COUNTY—concluded.		
Nemaha County Republican, Sabetha	1876–1890	15
The Sabetha Advance	1876,1877	2
Sabetha Weekly Herald	1884–1890	7
The Oneida Journal	1879–1882	3
The Oneida Chieftain, Democrat and Dispatch	1883,1884	1
The Oneida Monitor	1885,1886	1
The Wetmore Spectator, (lacking from August, 1884, to August, 1885)	1882–1890	7
The Centralia Enterprise	1883,1884	1
The Centralia Journal	1885–1890	6
The Goff's News	1887–1890	3
The Bern Press	1889,1890	2
NEOSHO COUNTY.		
Neosho County Journal, Osage Mission	1876–1890	15
The Temperance Banner, Osage Mission	1878–1880	2
Neosho Valley Enterprise, Osage Mission	1880–1882	2
Neosho County Democrat, Osage Mission	1883–1888	5
Neosho County Record, Erie	1876–1886	11
Neosho County Republican, Erie	1884–1886	3
The People's Vindicator, Erie	1888,1880	1
Republican-Record, Erie	1886–1890	4
The Erie Sentinel	1889,1890	1
Chanute Times	1876–1890	15
The Chanute Democrat	1879,1882	3
The Chanute Chronicle	1882,1883	2
Chanute Blade	1883–1890	7
The Chanute Vidette	1887–1890	3
Railroad Employés' Companion, Chanute	1889,1890	1
Head Light, Thayer	1876–1890	15
The Thayer Herald	1885,1886	1
Star of Hope, Urbana	1878	1
NESS COUNTY.		
The Pioneer, Clarinda and Sidney	1879–1882	3
The Advance, Sidney	1882,1883	1
Ness City Times	1880–1890	10
The Truth, Ness City	1883,1884	1
The News, Ness City	1884–1890	6
The Ness City Graphic	1886	1
Walnut Valley Sentinel, Ness City	1886–1890	4
The Globe, Schoharie	1883,1884	1
The Harold Record	1887–1889	3
Harold Boomer	1887	1
Nonchalanta Herald	1887,1888	1
The Bazine Register	1887,1888	1
Bazine Leader	1889	1
NORTON COUNTY.		
Norton County Advance, Norton	1878–1882	
Norton County People, Norton	1880–1883	2
The Norton Courier	1883–1890	8
Norton Champion	1884–1890	6
The Norton Democrat	1886–1888	2
The Farmers' Advance, Norton	1890	1
Weekly New Era, Norton	1888–1890	2
The Lenora Leader	1882–1888	6
The Kansas Northwest, Lenora	1884,1885	1
The Kansas Monitor, Lenora	1885,1886	1
The Common People, Lenora	1886,1887	1
The Lenora Record	1887–1890	3
The Norton County Badger, and } The Edmond Times, Edmond, }	1886–1890	5
The Almena Star	1885–1888	3
Almena Plaindealer	1888–1890	3
The Almena Advance	1889,1890	1
The Oronoque Eagle	1886	1
The Calvert Gazette	1889,1890	1
OSAGE COUNTY.		
Osage County Chronicle, Burlingame, (1872 lacking,)	1868–1890	21
Osage County Democrat, Burlingame	1881–1887	
Burlingame Herald	1881–1884	3
Burlingame Independent, (changed from Carbondale Calendar, January 28 to April 1, 1886: Carbondale Independent, April 8 to May 13, 1886: then moved to Burlingame,)	1886–1888	2
Burlingame News, (amateur,)	1886–1889	1
The Burlingame Democrat	1888–1890	1

BOUND NEWSPAPER FILES AND PERIODICALS, KANSAS—CONTINUED.

Newspapers.	Years.	No. vols.
OSAGE COUNTY—concluded.		
The Burlingame Echo	1888–1890	2
Osage City Free Press	1876–1890	13
The Kansas Times, Osage City, (moved from Lyndon,)	1879–1881	3
The Osage City Republican	1882,1883	1
Osage County Democrat, Osage City	1886,1887	1
The Kansas People, Osage City	1887–1890	4
Kansas People (daily), Osage City	1887,1888	3
Lyndon Times	1876–1879	3
The Lyndon Journal	1882–1890	8
The Lyndon Leader	1882,1883	2
Kansas Plebeian, Lyndon and Scranton	1882	1
Osage County Graphic, Lyndon	1888–1890	2
Osage County Times, Scranton and Burlingame	1888–1890	3
The Scranton Gazette	1890	1
The Carbondale Journal	1879	1
Carbondale Independent	1882–1884	2
Astonisher & Paralyzer, Carbondale	1885–1887	2
The Carbondalian, Carbondale	1887–1890	4
The Carbondale Record	1888	1
Kansas Workman, Scranton and Quenemo	1883–1888	5
Osage County Republican, Quenemo	1886–1890	4
The Quenemo Leader	1889,1890	2
Melvern Record	1884–1890	6
Overbrook Herald	1889,1890	2
OSBORNE COUNTY.		
Osborne County Farmer, Osborne	1876–1890	15
The Truth Teller, Osborne	1880	1
Daily News, Osborne	1881	1
Osborne County News, Osborne	1883–1890	8
Western Odd Fellow (monthly), Osborne	1886–1888	1
Osborne County Journal, Osborne	1886–1889	3
Bull's City Post	1880	1
Osborne County Key, Bull's City	1881–1882	1
The Western Empire, Bull's City	1883–1885	2
The Western Empire, Alton	1885–1890	6
Downs Times	1880–1890	11
Downs Chief	1886–1890	4
Downs Globe	1888–1890	2
Portis Patriot	1881–1890	9
The Whisperer, Portis	1890	1
OTTAWA COUNTY.		
The Solomon Valley Mirror, Minneapolis	1874–1886	12
The Sentinel, Minneapolis	1876–1883	8
Minneapolis Messenger, (successor to Sentinel,)	1883–1890	6
The Daily Messenger, Minneapolis	1887	1
Minneapolis Independent	1876–1881	6
Ottawa County Index, Minneapolis	1880–1883	4
The Progressive Current, Minneapolis	1883,1884	1
Solomon Valley Democrat, Minneapolis	1884–1890	6
The Daily Institute, Minneapolis, Nos. 1 to 20	1885	1
Kansas Workman (monthly), Minneapolis	1885–1890	6
Minneapolis School Journal	1883,1886	1
The Sprig of Myrtle (monthly), Minneapolis	1886–1890	4
Ottawa County Commercial, Minneapolis	1886–1890	4
The Delphos Herald	1879,1880	2
Delphos Carrier	1881–1888	7
The Delphos Republican	1889–1890	2
Bennington Star	1883–1888	4
The Bennington Journal	1885	1
Herald and Star, Bennington	1889,1890	1
The Tescott Herald	1887–1890	3
PAWNEE COUNTY.		
Larned Press	1876–1878	3
The Pawnee County Herald, Larned	1877,1878	2
The Larned Enterprise-Chronoscope	1878–1888	11
Larned Chronoscope	1880,1890	2
Larned Daily Chronoscope	1887,1888	3
The Larned Optic	1878–1884	6
The Larned Weekly Eagle-Optic	1885–1890	6
The Labor News, Larned	1888,1889	1
Pawnee County Republican, Larned	1886,1887	1
Garfield Letter	1885,1886	1
The Garfield News	1887,1888	1
The Burdett Bugle	1886–1888	2

BOUND NEWSPAPER FILES AND PERIODICALS, KANSAS — CONTINUED.

Newspapers.	Years.	No. vols.
PHILLIPS COUNTY.		
The Kirwin Chief................................	1876–1890	15
Kirwin Progress and Kirwin Democrat................	1877,1878	2
The Independent, Kirwin............................	1880–1888	8
The Independent, Kirwin, (second,)...................	1889,1890	1
Kirwin Republican.................................	1883,1884	1
Kirwin Graphic....................................	1889	1
Phillips County Herald, Phillipsburg.................	1878–1890	13
The Phillipsburg Times.............................	1884,1885	1
The Phillipsburg Dispatch...........................	1886–1890	4
Phillipsburg Democrat..............................	1887–1890	3
Logan Enterprise..................................	1879–1883	5
Phillips County Freeman, Logan......................	1883–1890	7
The Logan Republican..............................	1886–1890	5
The Long Island Argus..............................	1885	1
Long Island Leader................................	1886–1890	3
Phillips County Democrat, Long Island................	1886	1
Phillips County Inter-Ocean, Long Island..............	1887–1890	4
Marvin Monitor...................................	1886,1887	1
Woodruff Gazette and Republican.....................	1886,1887	1
POTTAWATOMIE COUNTY.		
Pottawatomie Gazette, Louisville, (vols. 1, 2, 3, 4, and duplicate vol. 1,)................	1867–1870	4
Kansas Reporter, Louisville..........................	1870–1887	17
Pottawatomie County Herald, Louisville...............	1879	1
The Louisville Republican (and The Semi-Weekly Republican)................	1882–1886	5
The Louisville Indicator............................	1887–1889	3
Pottawatomie County Times, Louisville................	1889,1890	1
Weekly Kansas Valley, Wamego.......................	1869–1871	2
The Wamego Blade.................................	1876	1
The Wamego Tribune...............................	1877–1882	6
Kansas Agriculturist, Wamego.......................	1879–1890	12
Wamego Democrat.................................	1885,1886	1
The Daily Wamegan, Wamego........................	1887–1889	5
The Kansas Teacher, Wamego........................	1889,1890	1
St. Marys Times...................................	1876,1877	2
St. Marys Democrat................................	1878	1
Pottawatomie Chief, St. Marys.......................	1878,1879	2
St. Marys Express.................................	1880–1888	7
St. Marys Star....................................	1884–1890	7
St. Marys Gazette.................................	1888–1890	3
The Dial, St. Marys................................	1890	1
Inkslingers' Advertiser, Westmoreland.................	1878	1
The Weekly Period, Westmoreland....................	1882–1885	3
The Westmoreland Recorder.........................	1885–1890	6
The Westmoreland Indicator.........................	1889,1890	1
The Onaga Journal.................................	1878–1885	5
The Onaga Democrat...............................	1885–1889	3
The Onaga Herald.................................	1890	1
Independent and Morning News, Havensville............	1880–1882	2
The Havensville Register............................	1889,1890	1
The Olsburg News-Letter............................	1887–1890	4
The Belvue Dodger................................	1889	1
Butler City News..................................	1889,1890	1
PRATT COUNTY.		
The Stafford Citizen...............................	1877,1878	1
Pratt County Press, Iuka............................	1878–1887	9
Pratt County Times, Iuka...........................	1881–1890	9
The Iuka Traveler.................................	1886–1888	1
The Saratoga Sun..................................	1885–1887	3
Pratt County Democrat, Saratoga.....................	1885,1886	1
The Cullison Banner...............................	1886–1888	2
Cullison Tomahawk................................	1888–1890	1
Pratt County Register, Pratt.........................	1886–1890	4
The Pratt County Republican, Pratt...................	1889–1890	3
Pratt County Union, Pratt...........................	1890	1
The Preston Herald................................	1887,1888	1
The Preston Plain Dealer............................	1889,1890	1
Springvale Advocate...............................	1888	1
RAWLINS COUNTY.		
Atwood Pioneer...................................	1879–1882	3
Republican Citizen, Atwood.........................	1880–1890	10
Rawlins County Democrat, Atwood and Blakeman.......	1885–1890	5
The Atwood Journal................................	1888	1
The Ludell Settler.................................	1884–1887	3

BOUND NEWSPAPER FILES AND PERIODICALS, KANSAS—Continued.

Newspapers.	Years.	No. vols
RAWLINS COUNTY—concluded.		
Ludell Gazette..................................	1887–1890	2
The Celia Enterprise............................	1885–1888	3
The Blakeman Register...........................	1887–1890	3
The Herndon Courant.............................	1888–1890	3
McDonald Times..................................	1888–1890	2
RENO COUNTY.		
Hutchinson News.................................	1876–1890	15
Hutchinson Daily News...........................	1886–1890	7
Hutchinson Herald...............................	1876–1885	9
The Interior, Hutchinson........................	1877–1885	8
The Interior-Herald, Hutchinson.................	1885–1890	6
Hutchinson Daily Interior-Herald................	1887	1
The Sunday Democrat, The Dollar Democrat, The Democrat, and The Hutchinson Democrat........	1889–1890	8
The Hutchinson Call, daily......................	1888	1
Hutchinson Republican...........................	1880,1890	2
The Hutchinson Times............................	1880,1890	1
The Clipper, Hutchinson.........................	1889,1890	2
Kansas Herald, Hutchinson (German)..............	1888–1890	2
The South Hutchinson Leader.....................	1886,1887	1
The Saturday Review, South Hutchinson...........	1887–1890	2
The Journal, South Hutchinson...................	1888,1889	1
The Argosy, Nickerson...........................	1878–1890	12
The Nickerson Register and The Nickerson Industry	1884–1890	6
The Nickerson Daily Register....................	1887	1
The Arlington Enterprise........................	1885–1890	5
Sylvia Telephone................................	1886–1889	2
The Sylvia Herald...............................	1889,1890	2
The Sylvia Banner...............................	1889,1890	1
The Haven Independent...........................	1886–1890	3
The Turon Rustler...............................	1886,1889	2
Turon Headlight.................................	1889,1890	2
Partridge Cricket and Press.....................	1886,1887	1
Lerado Ledger...................................	1886–1888	1
The Weekly Press, Olcutt........................	1889	1
The Torch Light, Plevna.........................	1888,1889	1
REPUBLIC COUNTY.		
The Belleville Republic.........................	1876	1
The Belleville Telescope........................	1876–1890	15
The Weekly Record, Belleville...................	1883–1885	2
The Belleville Democrat.........................	1886–1890	4
Republic County Press, Belleville...............	1889,1890	1
Scandia Republic................................	1877	1
The Republic County Journal, Scandia............	1878–1880	4
Republican-Journal, Scandia.....................	1881	1
Scandia Journal.................................	1882–1890	9
Republic County Independent, Scandia............	1883–1884	1
Republic County Chief, Scandia..................	1885,1886	1
The Scandia Independent.........................	1887–1889	2
White Rock Independent..........................	1879	1
Republic City News..............................	1883–1890	7
Conservative Cuban, Cuba........................	1884–1886	2
Republic County Pilot, Cuba.....................	1885–1888	4
The Cuba Union and The Union Pilot, Cuba........	1888–1890	2
The Cuba Daylight...............................	1890	1
The Wayne Register..............................	1885–1887	3
The Warwick Leader..............................	1886,1887	1
Cortland Register...............................	1889,1890	2
RICE COUNTY.		
Rice County Gazette, Sterling...................	1876–1880	5
Sterling Gazette................................	1881–1890	10
Weekly Bulletin, and The Sterling Bulletin......	1877–1890	13
Sterling Weekly Champion........................	1888–1890	2
The Daily Bulletin, Sterling....................	1887–1889	2
Sterling Republican, weekly.....................	1886,1887	1
Sterling Republican, daily......................	1887	1
The Arkansas Valley Times, Sterling.............	1888	1
The Saturday Republican, Sterling...............	1888	1
The Lyons Republican............................	1879–1890	11
The Daily Republican, Lyons.....................	1882	1
The Lyons Daily Republican......................	1887,1888	3
Central Kansas Democrat, (1882, 1883, 1888, 1889 lacking,) Lyons.	1879–1890	8
Central Kansas Democrat, daily, Lyons...........	1886,1887	2

BOUND NEWSPAPER FILES AND PERIODICALS, KANSAS — Continued.

Newspapers.	Years.	No. vols.
RICE COUNTY — *concluded.*		
The Lyons Prohibitionist..	1885–1890	4
The Soldiers' Tribune, Lyons...	1887,1888	1
The Lyons Tribune...	1888–1890	2
Rice County Eagle, Lyons..	1890	1
The Lyons Democrat..	1889,1890	1
The Rural West, Little River...	1881,1882	2
The Little River ɔonitor...	1886–1890	4
The Chase Dispatch..	1884,1885	1
The Weekly Record, Chase..	1886–1890	4
Geneseo Herald..	1887–1890	4
The Raymond Independent..	1887,1888	1
The Cain City Razzooper..	1887,1888	1
Partridge Press..	1887	1
Independent, Frederick...	1888,1889	1
The Alden Herald..	1888	1
RILEY COUNTY.		
ɔanhattan Express...	1860–1862	3
The Kansas Radical, ɔanhattan, (duplicate of 1867 and 1868,)......................	1865–1868	3
The ɔanhattan Independent. (1865 lacking.)..	1864–1868	3
The ɔanhattan Standard, (triplicate of 1869 and duplicate of 1870,)...............	1868–1870	3
ɔanhattan Homestead..	1869–1890	7
The Nationalist, ɔanhattan, (eleven duplicates,)..................................	1870–1890	20
The Literary Review, ɔanhattan..	1872	1
ɔanhattan Beacon. (two duplicates,)...	1872–1875	3
The Industrialist, ɔanhattan, (twelve duplicates,)................................	1875–1890	16
ɔanhattan Enterprise...	1876–1882	6
The Kansas Telephone, ɔanhattan...	1881–1890	10
The ɔanhattan Republic...	1882–1890	9
ɔanhattan Daily Republic...	1887–1890	7
The Independent, ɔanhattan...	1888	1
The ɔercury, ɔanhattan...	1884–1890	6
The Golden Cresset (monthly), ɔanhattan..	1884,1885	1
The Journal of ɔycology (monthly), ɔanhattan......................................	1885–1888	3
The Saturday Signal, ɔanhattan..	1888,1889	1
The Signal, ɔanhattan...	1890	1
The ɔidget, ɔanhattan...	1890	1
Randolph Echo...	1882–1887	5
The Randolph Enterprise..	1888–1890	2
The Riley Times...	1887–1889	2
The Independent, Riley Center...	1879–1882	2
The Riley Regent..	1889,1890	1
Leonardville ɔonitor..	1884–1890	7
Bala City Advance..	1890	1
ROOKS COUNTY.		
The Stockton News and the Western News, (except 1881, see Plainville News,)........	1876–1890	13
Rooks County Record, Stockton...	1879–1890	11
Stockton Democrat...	1885–1889	4
Stockton Eagle..	1887,1888	1
Stockton Academician, (quarterly,)..	1888–1890	1
The Plainville News, (moved from Stockton for one year,)...........................	1881	4
The Plainville Press...	1885,1886	1
Plainville Echo...	1884–1886	2
Plainville Times..	1886–1890	5
Webster Eagle...	1885–1887	2
Webster Enterprise..	1888	1
Woodston Saw and Register...	1886–1889	3
Cresson Dispatch..	1887,1888	1
RUSH COUNTY.		
Rush County Progress, Rush Center, and LaCrosse Eagle.............................	1877,1878	2
LaCrosse Chieftain..	1882–1890	9
LaCrosse Clarion..	1889,1890	1
LaCrosse Democrat...	1887–1890	3
The Blade, Walnut City..	1878–1882	5
The Herald, Walnut City...	1883–1886	4
Walnut City Gazette, Rush Center...	1886–1888	3
The Democrat, Walnut City...	1886–1888	2
Walnut City News (daily)..	1887,1888	2
Rush Center Gazette...	1888–1890	3
Rush County News, Rush Center...	1888–1890	3
The McCracken Enterprise..	1887–1890	4

BOUND NEWSPAPER FILES AND PERIODICALS, KANSAS—CONTINUED.

Newspapers.	Years.	No. vols.
RUSSELL COUNTY.		
Russell County Record, Russell	1876–1890	15
Russell County Advance, Russell	1878	1
Russell Independent	1879–1881	2
The Russell Hawkeye	1882,1883	1
Russell Live-Stock Journal, and Russell Journal	1885–1890	6
Russell Review, and Democratic Review, Russell	1886–1888	1
Russell County School Signal, Russell	1889–1890	2
Bunker Hill Advertiser	1880,1881	2
Bunker Hill Banner	1882,1883	1
Bunker Hill Banner (second)	1884,1885	1
The Bunker Hill News	1887,1888	1
Bunker Hill Gazette	1888,1889	1
The Dorrance Nugget	1886,1889	2
Luray Headlight	1887–1890	3
The Lucas Advance	1888–1890	3
Waldo Enterprise	1888–1890	2
ST. JOHN COUNTY. (See Logan.)		
The Oakley Opinion	1885,1886	1
SALINE COUNTY.		
The Salina Herald	1876–1890	15
Salina Daily Herald	1887,1888	3
Saline County Journal, Salina	1876–1890	15
Saline County Daily Journal, Salina	1887,1888	2
Farmers' Advocate, Salina	1876–1879	4
The Weekly Democrat, Salina	1878,1879	1
Svenska Heroiden, Salina	1878–1881	3
The Salina Independent	1882–1885	3
The Salina Republican	1886–1890	5
Salina Daily Republican	1888–1890	4
The Rising Sun, Salina	1885–1889	4
The Salina Sun	1889–1890	1
Wesleyan Advocate, Salina	1888,1889	2
The Normal Register, Salina	1885–1890	1
Vade Mecum (monthly), Salina	1890	1
Woman's Mission Star, Salina	1889,1890	1
Western Odd Fellow, Salina, (monthly,)	1888–1890	2
The Evening News, Salina	1889–1890	3
Salina Gazette	1889	1
The Weekly Tidings, Salina	1887–1890	3
Brookville Independent	1890	1
Brookville Transcript	1881–1890	9
Brookville Times	1887,1888	1
Chico Advertiser	1886,1887	1
The Gypsum Banner	1886,1887	1
Gypsum Valley Echo	1886–1890	4
Assaria Argus	1887–1889	2
SCOTT COUNTY.		
Western Times, Scott City	1885,1886	1
Scott County News, Scott City	1886–1890	5
Scott County Herald, Scott City	1886–1888	3
The Scott Sentinel, Scott City	1886–1888	2
The Sentinel-Herald, Scott City	1889,1890	2
Grigsby City Scorcher	1887	1
The Pence Phonograph	1887–1889	2
SEDGWICK COUNTY.		
Wichita Vidette, (August 25, 1870, to March 11, 1871,)	1870,1871	1
Wichita City Eagle, (1873–1876 lacking,)	1872–1890	16
Wichita Daily Eagle	1884–1890	13
Wichita Weekly Beacon	1874–1890	17
The Wichita Daily Beacon, (the Evening News-Beacon, 1880–90, 3 volumes,)	1884–1890	13
Wichita Herald	1877–1879	3
Stern des Westens, Wichita	1879	1
National Monitor, Wichita	1879,1880	1
Daily Republican, Wichita	1880,1881	2
Wichita Republican	1880,1881	1
Wichita Daily Times	1881–1884	7
Sedgwick Jayhawker and Palladium, Wichita	1882,1883	2
The New Republic, Wichita	1883–1890	8
Wichita Daily Evening Resident	1886	2
The Arrow, Wichita	1886–1890	5
Kansas Staats-Anzeiger, Wichita	1886–1890	5
Wichita Herald	1885–1890	5

BOUND NEWSPAPER FILES AND PERIODICALS, KANSAS—CONTINUED.

Newspapers.	Years.	No. vols.
SEDGWICK COUNTY—*concluded.*		
The Wichita Citizen, Labor Union, Labor Union Press, and Independent	1886–1888	2
The Wichita District Advocate	1886–1888	1
Sunday Growler, Wichita	1886–1888	2
Wichita Daily Journal	1887–1890	7
Wichita Daily Call	1887	1
Wichita Globe	1887	1
Western Evangelist, Wichita	1887, 1888	1
The Leader, (prohibition,) Wichita, (see Topeka,)	1888	1
The Wichita Commercial	1887–1889	1
The Mirror, Wichita	1888–1890	2
The Journal, Wichita	1888–1890	3
The Democrat, Wichita	1890	1
Western Methodist, Wichita	1889–1890	1
Cheney Journal	1884–1886	5
The Cheney Weekly Blade	1888–1890	3
Valley Center News	1885–1890	5
The Mount Hope Mentor	1885–1890	5
Clearwater Leader	1886–1888	3
The Clearwater Sun	1888–1890	2
The Colwich Courier	1887–1890	4
Garden Plain Herald	1887–1888	1
The Weekly Report, Goddard	1889–1890	1
SEQUOYAH COUNTY. (See Finney county.)		
The Garden City Paper	1879	1
The Irrigator, Garden City	1882	1
SEWARD COUNTY.		
The Prairie Owl, Fargo Springs	1885–1888	2
Seward County Democrat, Fargo Springs	1886–1888	3
The Fargo Springs News	1886–1888	2
Springfield Transcript	1886–1889	3
Springfield Soap-Box	1887, 1888	1
Springfield Republican	1889, 1890	2
Seward County Courant, Springfield	1887, 1888	1
Seward Independent	1887, 1888	1
The Arkalon News	1888–1890	3
The Liberal Leader	1888–1890	3
Southwest Chronicle, Liberal	1888–1890	1
SHAWNEE COUNTY.		
Daily Kansas Freeman, Topeka, (October 24 to November 7,)	1855	1
The Kansas Tribune, Topeka	1855–1858	2
Topeka Tribune, (two sets,)	1858–1861	4
The Topeka Tribune	1866, 1867	1
Topeka Daily Tribune, (January 12 to March 1,)	1864	1
The Congregational Record, Topeka, (see Douglas county).		
Weekly Kansas State Record, Topeka, (1863–1867 lacking, and 7 duplicates,)	1859–1875	16
Daily Kansas State Record, Topeka, (January to June, 1870, lacking, and 10 duplicates,),	1868–1871	8
Fair Daily Record, Topeka, (duplicate volume,)	1871	1
The Kansas Farmer, monthly, (Topeka, May, 1863, March and April, 1864: Lawrence, January, 1865, to July, 1867: Leavenworth, September, 1867, to December, 1873: Topeka, weekly, 1873 to 1884,) eight duplicates	1863–1890	27
Kansas Educational Journal, Topeka, (see Leavenworth county).		
Topeka Leader, (1866 and 1867, duplicates,)	1865–1869	6
Commonwealth, daily, (50 duplicates,)	1869–1888	83
The Weekly Commonwealth, Topeka, (13 duplicates,)	1874–1888	13
Tanner and Cobbler, Topeka	1872	1
Kansas Magazine (monthly), Topeka	1872, 1873	4
Topeka Daily Blade, (1874 not published, 1 duplicate,)	1873–1879	10
Topeka Weekly Blade	1876–1879	4
Kansas State Journal (daily), Topeka	1879–1890	23
Kansas Weekly State Journal, Topeka	1879–1886	7
Kansas Democrat, Topeka	1874–1882	8
American Young Folks (monthly), Topeka	1876–1882	7
Times (daily), Topeka	1876	1
The Kansas Churchman, monthly, Topeka, (1883–1885, Lawrence,)	1876–1886	7
Commercial Advertiser, Topeka	1877	1
Educational Calendar (monthly), Topeka	1877, 1878	1
Colored Citizen, Topeka	1878, 1879	2
Der Courier, Topeka	1878–1880	2
The Daily Capital, Topeka	1879–1890	24
Weekly Capital and Farmers' Journal, Topeka	1883–1888	5
Kansas Staats-Anzeiger, Topeka	1879–1881	2

BOUND NEWSPAPER FILES AND PERIODICALS, KANSAS—Continued.

Newspapers.	Years.	No. vols.
SHAWNEE COUNTY—*concluded.*		
The Kansas Methodist and Kansas Methodist-Chautauqua, Topeka, (monthly 1879, 1880, and weekly 1881-1886,)......................•...........................	1879-1888	10
	1880,1881	2
The Topeka Tribune.......................	1880,1881	3
The Topeka Post (daily)....................	1880	1
The Whim-Wham, Topeka...................	1880,1881	2
The Educationist, Topeka...................	1880-1884	4
Western School Journal (monthly), Topeka......	1885-1890	6
The Kansas Telegraph, Topeka...............	1881-1890	10
Good Tidings, Topeka......................	1881-1886	5
Daily Democrat and Daily State Press, Topeka.....	1881,1882	1
The Colored Patriot, Topeka................	1882	1
The Evening Herald, Topeka................	1882-	1
The Faithful Witness (semi-monthly), Topeka....	1882-1886	4
The National Workman, Topeka..............	1882	1
Saturday Evening Lance, Topeka.............	1883-1890	7
The Kansas Newspaper Union, Topeka.........	1883-1890	7
The Topeka Tribune.......................	1883-1885	2
Anti-Monopolist, Topeka...................	1883,1884	1
The Daily Critic, Topeka...................	1884	1
New Paths in the Far West (German monthly), Topeka	1884,1885	1
Light (Masonic monthly), Topeka............	1884-1889	5
The Kansas Knight and Soldier (semi-monthly), Topeka	1884-1889	4
The Spirit of Kansas, Topeka...............	1884-1890	5
Western Baptist.........................	1884-1889	5
City and Farm Record and Real Estate Journal (monthly), Topeka	1884-1889	5
The Kansas Law Journal, Topeka.............	1885-1887	4
The Citizen (daily), Topeka................	1885,1886	1
The Washburn Argo (monthly), Topeka........	1885-1890	5
The Washburn Reporter, Topeka.............	1887-1890	4
The Kansas Democrat (daily), Topeka.........	1886-1890	10
Our Messenger (monthly), Topeka...........	1886-1890	5
Welcome, Music and Home Journal (monthly), Topeka	1885-1888	3
Kansas Home (monthly), Topeka.............	1886-1888	1
The Lantern, Topeka......................	1887,1888	1
The Printer Girl, Topeka...................	1888,1889	1
The Christian Citizen, Topeka..............	1888,1889	1
The Association Reflector, Topeka...........	1888-1890	1
The Kansas Financier, Topeka..............	1888-1890	2
The Jeffersonian, Topeka....................	1889,1890	1
Villa Range, Topeka......................	1890	1
Sunday Ledger, Topeka....................	1888-1890	3
The Topeka Republican....................	1889,1890	1
The Western Veteran, Topeka...............	1889,1890	2
The Advocate, Meriden and Topeka...........	1889,1890	1
The Alliance Tribune, Topeka...............	1889,1890	1
Kansas Medical Journal, Topeka.............	1889,1890	2
The Western Poultry Breeder, Topeka........	1889,1890	1
Topeka Times, North Topeka, (March, 1873, to February, 1874, lacking,)	1871-1874	3
North Topeka Times......................	1876-1885	10
North Topeka Daily Argus, and Times.........	1880,1881	3
The Evening Republic, North Topeka..........	1882	1
North Topeka Mail........................	1882-1890	8
North Topeka Daily Courier................	1887,1888	1
The North Topeka News...................	1888-1890	3
News (daily), North Topeka...............	1888	1
Potwin Tribune, Potwin Place..............	1889-1890	1
Kansas Valley Times, Rossville.............	1879-1882	4
The Rossville News.......................	1883,1884	1
Carpenter's Kansas Lyre, Rossville..........	1884-1888	4
The Rossville Times......................	1888-1890	2
Silver Lake News........................	1882	1
The Future (monthly), Richland.............	1885-1887	2
SHERIDAN COUNTY.		
Sheridan County Tribune, Kenneth..........	1881,1882	1
Weekly Sentinel, Kenneth and Hoxie.........	1884-1890	6
Democrat, Kenneth and Hoxie...............	1885-1890	5
Sheridan Times..........................	1887,1888	1
Selden Times...........................	1883,1890	2
SHERMAN COUNTY.		
The New Tecumseh, Gandy, Leonard, and Itasca...	1885,1886	1
Sherman County Republican, Itasca, Sherman Center, and Goodland	1886-1890	4
Sherman Center News, Sherman Center and Goodland	1886,1887	1
The Goodland News.......................	1887-1890	3
Voltaire Adviser.........................	1885,1886	1
Sherman County News, Voltaire.............	1886-1888	2

BOUND NEWSPAPER FILES AND PERIODICALS, KANSAS — CONTINUED.

Newspapers.	Years.	No. vols.
SHERMAN COUNTY — *concluded.*		
Sherman County Dark Horse, Eustis...	1886–1890	4
Sherman County Democrat, Eustis...	1887–1889	2
State Line Register, Lamborn...	1888–1890	2
SMITH COUNTY.		
Smith County Pioneer, Smith Centre..	1876–1890	15
The Daily Pioneer, Smith Centre...	1887,1888	2
The Kansas Free Press, Smith Centre...	1879–1881	2
Smith County Record, Smith Centre..	1882,1883	2
Smith County Weekly Bulletin, Smith Centre.................................	1884–1890	7
The Bazoo, Smith Centre	1885–1889	4
Stewart's Bazoo, Smith Centre...	1889,1890	2
Gaylord Herald..	1879–1890	11
The Toiler and Independent, Harlan...	1879,1880	1
The Harlan Weekly Chief...	1884,1885	2
The Harlan Advocate	1885–1887	1
The Harlan Enterprise..	1887,1888	1
The Cedarville Telephone...	1883	1
The Cedarville Review..	1884,1885	1
Cedarville Globe..	1886–1890	1
The Dispatch, Reamsville...	1884–1886	1
The People's Friend, Reamsville..	1887,1888	1
The Cora Union...	1886–1887	3
The Lebanon Criterion..	1887,1890	1
Lebanon Journal..	1889,1890	1
The Union Labor Trumpet, Kensington.......................................	1888–1890	2
The Kensington Mirror..	1888–1890	2
Union Labor Trumpet, The Athol News, The People's Friend...................	1888,1889	1
STAFFORD COUNTY.		
Stafford County Herald, Stafford, (1887 and 1888 lacking,)...................	1879–1890	7
Stafford County Republican, Stafford...	1886–1890	5
Stafford County Democrat, Stafford...	1885–1888	3
The Weekly Telegram, Stafford...	1886–1888	2
The Alliance Herald, Stafford..	1890	1
Plain Truth, Stafford...	1889	1
The St. John Advance...	1880–1890	10
The Sun, St. John...	1885–1888	3
County Capital, St. John..	1887–1890	4
Stafford County Rustler, St. John..	1889,1890	1
St. John Weekly News...	1888–1890	2
The Stafford County Bee, Milwaukee..	1892,1883	1
The Jacksville Times..	1886–1888	3
Jacksville Telephone..	1889,1890	1
The Cassody Herald	1886,1887	1
The Cassody Mirage	1887–1889	1
Seward Independent...	1889,1890	1
STANTON COUNTY.		
Veteran Sentinel, and Johnson City and Syracuse Sentinel....................	1888	1
The Johnson City World	1886–1888	2
Stanton County Eclipse, Johnson City...	1887,1888	1
Johnson City Journal..	1888–1890	3
Stanton Telegram, Gognac and Johnson City..................................	1888–1889	2
Stanton County Republican, Johnson City	1889,1890	1
The Mitchellville Courier..	1887,1888	1
The Border Rover, Borders..	1887–1889	1
STEVENS COUNTY.		
Hugo Herald, Hugoton...	1886–1889	4
Hugoton Hermes..	1887–1890	2
Woodsdale Democrat..	1887–1889	1
Woodsdale Sentinel..	1889,1890	2
Stevens County Tribune, Woodsdale..	1890	1
Dermot Enterprise..	1887,1888	1
The Voorhees Vindicator..	1887–1890	3
Zella Gazette and Moscow Review..	1887,1888	1
SUMNER COUNTY.		
Sumner County Press, Wellington...	1878–1890	18
Wellington Daily Press..	1886,1887	3
Sumner County Democrat, Wellington..	1877–1879	3
The Wellington Semi-Weekly Vidette..	1879	1
The Wellingtonian, Wellington..	1881–1885	5
The Wellington Democrat,...	1882–1884	2
Sumner County Standard, Wellington...	1884–1890	6

BOUND NEWSPAPER FILES AND PERIODICALS, KANSAS—Continued.

Newspapers.	Years.	No. vol.
SUMNER COUNTY—*concluded.*		
Daily Standard, Wellington..	1887–1889	5
The Daily Postal Card, Wellington......	1886, 1887	2
The Republican, Wellington.....	1886	1
The Wellington Monitor.................................	1886–1890	5
Kansas Weather Observer, Wellington................................	1886	1
Wellington Morning Quid Nunc, (daily,)...........................	1887, 1888	3
Wellington Quid Nunc...............................	1887, 1888	1
Wellington Daily Telegram.................................	1887	1
The Christian Reminder, Wellington.........................	1889–1890	1
The Daily Mail, Wellington................................	1889, 1890	1
Wellington Gazette, daily...........................	1889, 1890	2
Oxford Independent..................................	1876–1879	4
Oxford Reflex and Weekly..............................	1880, 1881	1
The Mocking Bird, Oxford.........................	1888–1890	3
The Oxford Register............................	1884–1888	4
Caldwell Post........................	1879–1883	5
Caldwell Journal......................	1883–1890	8
Caldwell Daily Journal...................	1887	1
Oklahoma War Chief, Wichita, January 12 to March 9, 1883; Genda Springs, March 23 to July 19, 1883; Oklahoma Territory, April 26 and May 3, 1884; Arkansas City, May 10, 1884; Geuda Springs, August 30, 1884; South Haven, October 23 to December 4, 1884; Arkansas City, February 3 to June 11, 1885; Caldwell, June 18, 1885, to August 12, 1886...	1883–1886	3
Caldwell Commercial.....................	1890–1883	3
Caldwell Standard.......................	1884	1
The Free Press, Caldwell..............	1885, 1886	1
Times, Caldwell............	1886, 1887	1
The Caldwell News, daily and weekly.......................	1887–1890	3
The Industrial Age, Caldwell........................	1887–1889	1
Geuda Springs Herald.........................	1882–1890	8
Belle Plaine News..................................	1879–1890	11
The Kansas Odd Fellow, Belle Plaine.............	1882, 1883	1
Tha Resident, Belle Plaine.....................	1885, 1886	2
Mulvane Herald.....................	1880–1882	2
Mulvane Record...................	1885–1890	6
Argonia Clipper..................	1884–1890	7
Conway Springs Star...............	1885–1890	5
The Weekly News, South Haven..................	1885, 1886	1
The South Haven New Era..................	1886–1890	5
The South Haven Rustler..................	1889, 1890	1
The Patrick Henry, South Haven............	1890	1
THOMAS COUNTY.		
Thomas County Cat, Colby....................	1885–1890	6
The Democrat, Colby.........................	1886–1888	2
The Free Press, Colby.....	1889, 1890	1
The Colby Tribune.......................	1888–1890	3
The Hastings and Brewster Gazette.................	1888	1
The Brewster Gazette.......................	1889, 1890	2
TREGO COUNTY.		
The Wa-Keeney Weekly World............................	1879–1890	12
Kansas Leader, Wa-Keeney.......................	1879, 1880	1
Trego County Tribune, Wa-Keeney.....................	1885–1889	5
Trego County Gazette, Wa-Keeney..................	1887, 1888	1
Trego County Republican, Wa-Keeney..............	1889	1
Globe, Cyrus........................	1882, 1883	1
WABAUNSEE COUNTY.		
The Wabaunsee County Herald, Alma...................	1869–1871	2
The Alma Weekly Union.........................	1871, 1872	1
Wabaunsee County News, Alma.....................	1876–1890	15
The Blade, Alma.....................	1877, 1878	1
Wabaunsee County Herald, Alma	1879–1881	2
The Alma Enterprise..................	1889–1890	6
The Alma Signal.................	1889, 1890	1
The Land-Mark, Eskridge, (not published from December, 1874, to June 30, 1883,).....	1873–1883	2
The Home Weekly, Eskridge.....................	1881–1888	7
The Eskridge Star.................	1883–1890	7
Wabaunsee County Democrat, Eskridge.................	1886	1
The Alta Vista Register..... ...	1887–1889	1
The Alta Vista Bugle.................	1889, 1890	1
The Alta Vista Record	1890	1
The Paxico Courier.........................	1888, 1889	1

BOUND NEWSPAPER FILES AND PERIODICALS, KANSAS — CONTINUED.

Newspapers.	Years.	No. vols.
WALLACE COUNTY.		
Wallace County Register, Wallace	1886–1890	4
Wallace County News	1886, 1887	1
Wallace Weekly Herald	1888, 1889	1
Wallace County Gazette, Wallace	1890	1
The Western Times, Sharon Springs	1886–1890	4
Sharon Springs Leader	1887–1890	4
The Weskansan, Weskan	1888–1890	2
WASHINGTON COUNTY.		
Western Observer, and Washington Republican, (broken files,)	1869, 1870	1
Washington Republican and Watchman	1870, 1871	2
Washington Republican	1876–1890	15
Washington County Register. Washington	1881–1890	9
The Washington County Daily Register, Washington	1884, 1885	2
Weekly Post, Washington	1883–1890	7
Washington Daily Post	1887	1
Washington Daily Times	1887, 1888	1
Western Independent, Hanover	1876, 1877	2
Washington County Sun, and Hanover Democrat	1878	1
The Hanover Democrat	1878–1890	13
Brit, Hanover	1884, 1885	1
The Clifton Localist	1878	1
Clifton Journal and Review	1878–1880	3
Clifton Review	1881–1890	10
The Local News, and The Semi-Weekly News, Clifton	1885–1890	5
The Greenleaf Journal	1881–1883	3
The Greenleaf Independent	1882, 1883	1
The Independent-Journal, Greenleaf	1883–1887	4
Greenleaf Journal	1887–1890	3
Greenleaf Herald	1883–1889	6
The Haddam Weekly Clipper	1883–1890	7
The New Era, Haddam	1886, 1887	1
Haddam Politician	1880	1
Palmer Weekly Globe	1884	1
Palmer Pioneer	1889–1890	3
The Barnes Enterprise	1885–1890	5
The Record, Hollenberg	1889	1
The Linn Gazette	1889, 1890	1
WICHITA COUNTY.		
Wichita Standard, Bonasa and Leoti City	1885–1890	5
Leoti Lance	1886, 1887	1
Wichita County Democrat, Leoti City	1886, 1887	1
The Leoti Transcript, Leoti City	1887–1890	2
The Western Farmer, Leoti	1889, 1890	2
Wichita County Herald, Coronado	1886, 1887	1
The Coronado Star	1886–1888	1
Wichita County Farmer, Coronado, Farmer City, and Leoti	1888	1
The Selkirk Graphic	1889, 1890	1
WILSON COUNTY.		
Wilson County Citizen, Fredonia	1870–1890	21
Fredonia Tribune	1878, 1879	1
Fredonia Democrat	1882–1890	9
The Times, Fredonia	1883–1885	1
Fredonia Chronicle	1885–1888	3
Neodesha Free Press	1876–1882	7
Neodesha Gazette	1881, 1882	1
Neodesha Register	1883–1890	7
Neodesha Independent	1887, 1888	1
Altoona Advocate	1886, 1887	1
Altoona Journal	1887–1890	4
The Benedict Echo	1886–1890	3
Buffalo Clipper	1887	1
Buffalo Express	1888	1
The Buffalo Advocate	1889, 1890	2
The Coyville Press	1887, 1888	1
WOODSON COUNTY.		
Woodson County Post, Neosho Falls	1873–1883	10
Neosho Falls Post	1883–1890	8
Woodson County Republican and Independent, Neosho Falls	1886, 1887	1
Weekly News, Yates Center, and The Yates Center News	1877–1890	14
Yates Center Argus	1882, 1883	2
Woodson Democrat, Yates Center	1884–1890	6
The Sun and Independent-Sun, Yates Center	1886–1888	2

BOUND NEWSPAPER FILES AND PERIODICALS, KANSAS — CONCLUDED.

Newspapers.	Years.	No. vols.
WOODSON COUNTY—concluded.		
Yates Center Tribune.	1889	1
The Toronto Topic.	1883–1888	5
Register, Toronto.	1886, 1887	1
The Toronto Republican.	1888–1890	2
WYANDOTTE COUNTY.		
Quindaro Chindowan.	1857, 1858	1
Wyandotte Gazette, (1869 and 1873 lacking,).	1866–1888	19
Wyandotte Herald. (1873 lacking.)	1872–1890	18
The Pioneer, Kansas City.	1878–1880	3
The Kansas Pilot, Kansas City.	1879, 1881	2
The Kawsmouth Pilot. Wyandotte.	1881	1
Equitable Aid Advocate (monthly), Wyandotte	1881–1883	3
Wyandotte Republican (daily and weekly).	1881, 1882	2
The Wyandotte Chief.	1883, 1885	2
Kansas Pioneer, Wyandotte.	1883–1889	5
The Kansas City Gazette.	1880, 1890	2
The Kansas City Daily Gazette.	1887–1890	8
The Stock Farm and Home Weekly, Kansas City.	1880	1
The Spy, Kansas City.	1881, 1882	1
The Globe and The Sun and Globe, Kansas City.	1884, 1886	2
Light, Kansas City.	1884–1886	1
The Kansas Weekly Cyclone, Kansas City	1887, 1888	1
The Chronicle, Kansas City.	1890	1
Kansas Herald (German), Kansas City	1890	1
The Kansas Catholic. Leavenworth and Kansas City.	1890	1
The Weekly Press, Kansas City.	1890	1
The Wasp, Rosedale.	1884, 1885	1
Rosedale Record.	1888	1
Rosedale Era.	1889, 1890	1
Argentine Republic.	1887–1890	3
The Argentine Advocate	1888	1
Cromwell's Kansas Mirror, Armourdale.	1887–1890	3

BOUND NEWSPAPERS, ETC., OF OTHER STATES AND COUNTRIES.

Newspapers.	Years.	No. vols.
ALABAMA.		
The Nationalist, Mobile.	1865–1868	3
ALASKA.		
The Alaska Free Press, Juneau.	1889, 1890	2
The Alaskan, Sitka.	1889, 1890	1
ARIZONA.		
Arizona Weekly Journal-Miner, Prescott.	1887–1890	3
CALIFORNIA.		
Overland Monthly, San Francisco, f. s.	1868–1875	15
Overland Monthly, San Francisco, s. s.	1883–1890	16
San Francisco Weekly Post.	1879–1888	11
The Alaska Appeal, San Francisco.	1879, 1880	1
The Pacific Rural Press, San Francisco.	1882–1890	8
California Patron and Agriculturist, San Francisco.	1886–1888	3
The California Prohibitionist, San Francisco.	1889, 1890	1
American Sentinel, Oakland	1886–1889	4
Signs of the Times, Oakland.	1886–1890	5
Pacific Health Journal (monthly), Oakland.	1886–1890	4
COLORADO.		
Silver World, Lake City.	1877–1888	11
Hinsdale Phonograph, Lake City.	1888, 1889	1
Weekly Rocky Mountain News, Denver.	1878–1890	13
Denver Daily Tribune.	1884	2
The Denver Republican (daily).	1887–1890	6
The Queen Bee (monthly), Denver.	1887–1890	2
The Commonwealth (monthly), Denver.	1889, 1890	2
The Great Divide (monthly), Denver	1889, 1890	1

BOUND NEWSPAPERS, ETC., OF OTHER STATES AND COUNTRIES—Continued.

Newspapers.	Years.	No. vols.
COLORADO—concluded.		
Colorado School Journal, Denver	1887–1889	1
The Denver Press	1889,1890	2
The Rocky Mountain Presbyterian, Denver and Cincinnati	1879,1880	1
The Gunnison Review. (weekly.)	1880,1881	2
The Gunnison Daily and Tri-Weekly Review-Press	1882–1890	13
Mountain Mail (semi-weekly), Salida	1880–1890	10
Grand Junction News	1884	1
Grand Valley Star, Grand Junction	1890	1
White Pine Cone	1884–1890	6
The Otero County Eagle, La Junata	1889,1890	1
Law and Gospel (monthly), Springfield	1886–1890	2
The Fruita Star	1889,1890	1
CONNECTICUT.		
The Connecticut Courant, Hartford	1796–1799	3
Quarterly Journal of Inebriety, Hartford	1876–1890	14
Travelers Record (monthly), Hartford	1886–1890	5
Middlesex Gazette, Middletown, 1804, 1805 and 1817	1804–1817	3
Silliman's Journal of Science and Arts, New Haven, vols. 1, and 37 to 48 (bi-monthly)	1818–1869	13
DAKOTA.		
Dakota Teacher, Huron	1885,1886	1
Bismarck Weekly Tribune	1887–1890	3
Pierre Daily Capital	1890	2
DISTRICT OF COLUMBIA.		
Kendall's Expositor, Washington	1841	1
The National Era, Washington	1847–1859	13
The Council Fire. Washington	1879–1882	3
The Alpha, Washington	1881–1888	8
The Washington World	1882–1884	2
National Tribune, Washington. (1885 and 1887 lacking,)	1883–1889	3
United States Government publications, monthly catalogue, Washington	1885–1890	6
The Official Gazette of the United States, Patent Office, Washington	1885–1890	14
Public Opinion, Washington and New York	1887–1890	3
FLORIDA.		
The Florida Dispatch, Jacksonville	1835–1890	5
The Advertiser, Apopka	1890	1
The Monthly Bulletin, Tallahassee	1889,1890	1
GEORGIA.		
Southern Industrial Record (monthly), Atlanta	1835–1890	5
Atlanta Constitution	1887,1888	1
Spelman Messenger (monthly), Atlanta	1889–1890	2
ILLINOIS.		
Religio-Philosophical Journal, Chicago	1868–1877	10
The Inter-Ocean. Chicago	1874–1881	8
Semi-Weekly Inter-Ocean. Chicago	1879–1890	12
Faith's Record (monthly), Chicago	1874–1881	6
Commercial Advertiser, Chicago	1877–1879	2
Industrial World and Commercial Advertiser, Chicago	1880–1882	3
Industrial World and Iron Worker, Chicago	1882–1890	8
American Antiquarian (quarterly), Chicago	1878–1890	14
Weekly Drovers' Journal, Chicago	1879–1890	11
The Standard, Chicago	1880–1890	10
Farmers' Review. Chicago	1880,1881	2
Chicago Journal of Commerce	1881	1
National Sunday School Teacher (monthly), Chicago	1869–1881	13
Land Owner, Chicago	1870–1873	4
Chicago Advance, (files for 1872, 1873, 1874, 1875, 1877, 1879, 1884, and one duplicate,)	1881–1890	10
The Dial (monthly), Chicago	1881–1890	10
Brown and Holland's Short-Hand News (monthly), Chicago	1882–1884	4
The Watchman (semi-monthly), Chicago	1882–1889	7
The Weekly Magazine, Chicago	1882–1885	3
The New Era, Chicago	1883–1885	2
The Weekly News, Chicago	1884–1886	2
Svenska Amerikanaren, Chicago	1885–1890	6
The Unitarian (monthly), Chicago	1886,1887	1
The Union Signal, Chicago	1886–1890	5
The Penman's Gazette (monthly), Chicago and New York	1886	1
Privada (monthly), Chicago	1886–1890	4
The Western Trail (monthly), Chicago	1886–1890	2

BOUND NEWSPAPERS, ETC., OF OTHER STATES AND COUNTRIES — CONTINUED.

Newspapers.	Years.	No. vols.
ILLINOIS — *concluded.*		
Gaskell's Magazine (monthly), Chicago...	1887,1888	1
The Open Court. Chicago..	1887,1890	4
The Comrade (bi-monthly). Chicago..	1887,1888	2
Soldier and Citizen (monthly). Chicago..	1889,1890	1
The National Educator (monthly) Chicago...	1887,1888	2
The Chicago Express..	1888-1890	3
Newspaper Union (monthly), Chicago..	1888-1890	2
The Lever, Chicago...	1890	1
Unity, Chicago...	1889,1890	1
National Journalist (monthly), Chicago..	1889,1890	2
The Inland Printer (monthly), Chicago..	1889,1890	2
Young Men's Era, Chicago..	1890	1
National Reveille, Chicago..	1890	1
Humane Journal (monthly), Chicago...	1889,1890	1
The Kindergarten, Chicago..	1888-1890	2
National W. C. T. U. Bulletin, Evanston..	1889,1890	1
The Odd Fellows' Herald (semi-monthly), Bloomington..............................	1883-1890	7
The Western Plowman (monthly), Moline..	1885-1890	6
The Grange News, River Forest...	1885,1886	1
The Gospel Messenger, Mt. Morris...	1889,1890	1
INDIAN TERRITORY AND OKLAHOMA.		
The Cherokee Advocate, Tahlequah...	1881-1890	9
The Cheyenne Transporter, Darlington..	1883-1886	4
Indian Chieftain, Vinita..	1884-1890	7
The Oklahoma Capital. Guthrie...	1889,1890	2
The Oklahoma Daily Capital, Guthrie...	1889	1
Oklahoma Optic, Guthrie...	1889	1
Evening Democrat, Guthrie...	1890	2
The Frisco Herald..	1889,1890	1
Hennessey Clipper...	1890	1
The Courier, Hennessey..	1890	1
The Evening Gazette, Oklahoma..	1889,1890	3
Oklahoma Daily Journal..	1890	2
Oklahoma City Daily Times...	1890	2
The Mulhall Monitor..	1890	1
INDIANA.		
Indiana State Journal, Indianapolis...	1878-1890	13
The Millstone and The Corn Miller (monthly), Indianapolis.........................	1884-1890	7
Our Herald, La Fayette...	1882,1883	2
Mennonitische Rundschau, Elkhart...	1886-1890	5
Indiana Student (monthly), Bloomington..	1886-1888	2
IOWA.		
Davenport Gazette...	1878	1
The Weekly Hawk-Eye, Burlington..	1881-1885	4
The Burlington Hawk-Eye (daily)...	1882-1885	5
The Iowa Historical Record (quarterly), Iowa City.................................	1885-1890	6
The Christna (semi-monthly), Tabor..	1889,1890	1
KENTUCKY.		
Weekly Courier-Journal, Louisville...	1878-1880	2
Southern Bivouac (monthly), Louisville..	1886,1887	1
LOUISIANA.		
South-Western Christian Advocate, New Orleans....................................	1879-1890	11
The Times-Democrat (daily,) New Orleans..	1883-1885	3
MAINE.		
Oxford Observer, Paris...	1824-1826	2
Oxford Democrat, Paris..	1871-1876	6
Maine Advertiser, Norway..	1872-1875	2
The Kennebec Journal, Augusta..	1889,1890	1
MARYLAND.		
Johns Hopkins University Circular, Baltimore, (1882 and 1884 lacking,).............	1879-1888	4
Jottings (monthly), Baltimore..	1887,1888	2
The American Journal of Psychology, Baltimore, (quarterly,).......................	1888	1
MASSACHUSETTS.		
The Boston Chronicle, Dec. 21, 1767, to Dec. 19, 1768.............................	1767,1768	1
Federal Orrery, Boston, Oct. 20, 1794, to April 18, 1796, and scattering duplicates from Oct. 20, 1794, to Oct. 12, 1795	1794-1796	2
Massachusetts Mercury, Boston, May 11, 1798, to Aug. 9, 1799.....................	1798-1799	2
The Independent Chronicle and the Universal Advertizer, Boston, from Jan. 1, 1798, to Dec. 17, 1801......	1798-1801	4

BOUND NEWSPAPERS, ETC., OF OTHER STATES AND COUNTRIES—Continued.

Newspapers.	Years.	No. vols.
MASSACHUSETTS—concluded.		
he Independent Chronicle, Boston, Dec. 21. 1801, to Dec. 30, 1804........	1801–1804	3
oston Patriot, from April 7, 1809. to Sept. 12, 1810: from March 2 to Dec. 25, 1811: from March 14, 1812, to Sept. 8, 1813: and scattering duplicates from March 3, 1809, to March 10, 1813........	1809–1813	7
ndependent Chronicle and Boston Patriot (semi-weekly), Jan. 11, 1832, to Aug. 10, 1837..	1832–1837	4
olumbian Centinel and Massachusetts Federalist, Boston, from June 29, 1799. to Aug. 31, 1805: from Jan. 3. 1807, to Oct. 3. 1810: from Jan. 9, 1811, to July 1, 1812; and scattering duplicates from Feb. 28, 1801, to Dec. 29, 1802........	1799–1812	13
oston Gazette. from Jan. 9 to Oct. 29, 1804: from Aug. 19, 1815, to Aug. 19, 1816; from Dec. 27, 1817, to Dec. 25, 1819: from April 23, 1827. to Nov. 28, 1828........	1804–1828	6
oston Commercial Gazette (daily), from Dec. 29, 1817, to Dec. 25, 1819........	1817–1819	2
oston Spectator, from Jan. 4, 1814. to Feb. 5, 1815........	1814–1815	1
orth American Review, Boston (Nos. 3–6, 10, 11, 13, 14, 15, 19, 20, 21 and 130 lacking), 1879, 1880, 1888........	1815–1888	108
he Missionary Herald. Boston. vols. 17–80........	1821–1884	63
ew England Galaxy. Boston, from Oct. 31, 1823, to Dec. 26, 1828; and scattering duplicates from Oct. 15. 1824, to April 6, 1827........	1823–1828	7
hristian Examiner, Boston. vols. 1–19. 1824–1836, and 12 vols. between 1840 and 1867....	1824–1868	31
oston Recorder, from Jan. 2, 1832. to Dec. 25. 1835........	1832–1835	4
he Liberator, Boston. (lacking 1834–1837 and 1839.)........	1833–1865	28
vening Journal, Boston, from Jan. 3. 1837, to Dec. 30, 1843; from Jan. 4 to Dec. 30, 1844; and from Feb. 4 to Dec. 30, 1845........	1837–1845	9
he Commonwealth (daily), Boston, Jan. 1 to July 3. 1851; and from Jan. 1 to Sept. 21, 1854........	1851–1854	3
he Commonwealth, Boston, from Sept. 1, 1866, to Aug. 28, 1869........	1866–1869	3
outh's Companion, Boston, from Oct. 21, 1852 to April 17, 1856, and 1886–1890........	1852–1890	9
vening Telegram (daily), Boston, from Sept. 27, 1854, to March 31, 1855........	1854–1855	1
uarterly Journal of American Unitarian Association, Boston........	1854–1859	5
onthly Journal of the American Unitarian Association, Boston........	1860–1869	9
nglo-Saxon, Boston, from Jan. 5 to Dec. 16. 1856........	1856	1
he Atlantic Monthly, Boston. vols. 1–50........	1857–1882	50
he Atlas and Daily Bee. Boston. from June 15 to Dec. 31, 1858........	1858	1
lon's Herald. Boston, (1868, 1869. 1870, 1878, 1880, 1883,)........	1868–1883	6
anner of Light, Boston........	1869–1872	4
oston Journal of Chemistry........	1873–1877	4
he New England Historical and Genealogical Register (quarterly), Boston........	1876–1800	13
he Woman's Journal. Boston........	1879–1890	12
ivil Service Record. Boston........	1881,1882	2
nited States Official Postal Guide (monthly), Boston........	1881–1886	6
ur Dumb Animals (monthly), Boston........	1882–1885	2
he Citizen (monthly), Boston........	1883–1885	6
he Evening Traveller (daily), Boston, from January to June, 1886........	1886	1
he Popular Science News. Boston........	1885–1890	5
he Unitarian Review, Boston........	1885–1890	6
olitical Science Quarterly, Boston........	1886–1888	3
bolitionist, Boston........	1833	1
ne Writer (monthly), Boston........	1887–1890	4
ne Estes & Lauriat Book Bulletin (monthly), Boston........	1887–1888	1
merican Teacher (monthly), Boston........	1887–1890	3
vening Gazette, Boston........	1888–1890	3
ne New Jerusalem Magazine (monthly), Boston........	1888–1890	3
elling (quarterly), Boston........	1887–1888	1
brary Notes (monthly), Boston........	1888	1
oston Investigator. (1864, 1873, 1876 lacking,)........	1859–1890	12
ne Golden Rule, Boston........	1890	1
artha's Vineyard Herald, Cottage City........	1887, 1888	1
orcester Daily Press, from June. 1873. to Dec. 1876........	1873–1876	7
assachusetts Spy or Worcester Gazette........	1805, 1806	2
ne Massachusetts Spy (weekly), Worcester........	1822	1
orcester Daily Spy, from Jan. to Dec. 1859: from Jan. 1868, to Dec. 1884; and from July 1885, to July 1886........	1859–1886	38
ne National Ægis, Worcester, Dec. 2, 1801, to Dec. 25, 1811; from Jan. 20, 1813, to May 4, 1814; from Jan. 5, 1815, to Dec. 25, 1816; from Dec. 15, 1824, to June 8, 1825; and years 1823, 1830, 1838–1840........	1801–1825	19
ily Transcript, Worcester, from Feb. 1853 to Dec. 1855........	1853–1855	6
orcester Evening Gazette, from Jan. to Dec. 1866; from Jan. 1867 to July 18, 1881; and from Jan. 1882 to Dec. 1885........	1868–1885	38
tis and Gazette. Worcester, (part of 1877 lacking,)........	1875–1880	5
rvard University Bulletin (occasional), Cambridge........	1880–1890	6
rvard University Bulletin (quarterly), Cambridge........	1880–1888	4
ience, Cambridge (see New York,)........	1883–1885	6
dham Historical Record (quarterly)........	1890	1
sex Register, Salem. from Jan. 1 to Dec. 17, 1817........	1817	1
lletin of the Essex Institute, Salem, (1873 and 1874 lacking,)........	1869–1890	20
storical Collections of the Essex Institute, Salem........	1859–1889	26

BOUND NEWSPAPERS. ETC., OF OTHER STATES AND COUNTRIES—Continued.

Newspapers.	Years.	No. vols.
MICHIGAN.		
The Fireside Teacher (monthly), Battle Creek....................................	1886–1889	3
The Advent Review, Battle Creek..	1886–1890	4
The Unitarian (monthly), Ann Arbor..	1887–1890	3
The Plaindealer, Detroit..	1889,1890	2
MINNESOTA.		
Pioneer-Press, St. Paul and Minneapolis..	1878,1879	1
MISSOURI.		
The Western Journal (and Civilian, monthly), St. Louis.........................	1848–1854	11
Organ and Reveille, St. Louis...	1851	1
American Journal of Education (monthly), St. Louis.............................	1873–1888	14
The Great Southwest (monthly), St. Louis, vols. 1, 2, 3, 6, and 7	1874–1880	5
Fonetic Teacher (monthly), St. Louis, vol. 2...................................	1881	1
The Communist and Altruist (bi-monthly), St. Louis............................	1881–1890	4
American Journalist (monthly), St. Louis......................................	1883–1885	1
The St. Louis Evangelist...	1887,1888	1
The St. Louis Globe-Democrat (daily)..	1887–1890	6
The Central Christian Advocate, St. Louis......................................	1888–1890	3
The Christian Evangelist, St. Louis..	1889,1890	2
St. Joseph Free Democrat	1860	1
St. Joseph Herald, daily, (1878 and to July, 1879, lacking,)...................	1876–1890	22
St. Joseph Herald..	1877–1890	14
St. Joseph Gazette:..	1877–1890	13
Kansas City Times, daily, (1875 lacking,).....................................	1873–1890	30
The Kansas City Review of Science and Industry (monthly).....................	1877–1884	8
Weekly Journal of Commerce, Kansas City.....................................	1877–1879	3
Kansas City Daily Journal	1879–1890	24
Mirror of Progress, Kansas City..	1879–1881	3
Kansas City Price Current	1880–1881	1
Santa Fé Trail (monthly), Kansas City, vol. 1, Nos. 1 to 8....................	1880–1881	1
Camp's Emigrant Guide to Kansas, Kansas City...............................	1880–1884	4
American Home Magazine, Kansas City..	1881,1882	3
Kansas City Live-Stock Indicator..	1882–1890	9
The Mid-Continent, Kansas and St. Louis......................................	1882–1890	9
Svenska Herolden, Kansas City...	1882–1884	3
Western Newspaper Union, Kansas City..	1883–1890	8
The Centropolis, Kansas City...	1883–1888	4
The Kansas City Medical Index (monthly)......................................	1884–1890	9
Kansas City Live-Stock Record and Price Current..............................	1884–1888	4
The Kansas City Record...	1885–1890	4
Missouri and Kansas Farmer (monthly), Kansas City..........................	1886–1888	3
Kansas City Star...	1890	1
The Kansas City Star (daily)...	1846–1890	9
The Faithful Witness (monthly), Kansas City..................................	1886,1887	1
The Herald, Kansas City...	1886–1889	3
The Kansas Magazine (monthly), Kansas City.................................	1886–1888	2
The Evening News, Kansas City...	1888–1890	5
Kansas City Daily Traveler...	1888–1889	3
Hoisington Bank Reporter (semi-monthly), Kansas City.......................	1889,1890	1
Christian Era, Kansas City...	1890	1
Kansas City Globe..	1889,1890	4
Border's Odd Fellow (monthly), Kansas City...................................	1890	1
NEBRASKA.		
The Western Newspaper Union, Omaha..	1886–1890	3
The Woman's Tribune (monthly and weekly), Beatrice.........................	1887–1890	4
Western Resources (monthly), Lincoln..	1887–1890	4
Nebraska State Journal (daily), Lincoln..	1887–1890	4
Nebraska State Journal, Lincoln..	1887–1890	3
Nebraska Congregational News (monthly), Lincoln..............................	1887–1890	2
NEW JERSEY.		
The Journal of American Orthoëpy (monthly), Ringos..........................	1884–1890	7
Orchard & Garden (monthly), Little Silver.....................................	1887–1890	4
NEW MEXICO.		
Santa Fé New Mexican..	1881–1883	4
Daily New Mexican, Santa Fé...	1887–1890	6
New Mexican Mining News, Santa Fé..	1881–1883	2
The Santa Fé Weekly Leader..	1885,1886	2
Albuquerque Weekly Journal..	1881–1886	6
The Daily Citizen, Albuquerque...	1887–1890	7
Mining World, Las Vegas..	1880–1882	2
Las Vegas Weekly Optic...	1883,1884	1
Las Vegas Daily Optic	1888–1890	4
San Marcial Reporter...	1889,1890	2

BOUND NEWSPAPERS, ETC., OF OTHER STATES AND COUNTRIES — CONTINUED.

Newspapers.	Years.	No. vols.
NEW YORK.		
New York American, New York City	1827,1828	2
The Anti-Slavery Record, New York	1836	1
The Emancipator, New York, (from February 8, 1837, to February 14, 1839,)	1837,1839	2
The New-Yorker, New York	1837-1840	3
The Diamond, New York	1840-1842	3
Workingman's Advocate, New York	1844,1845	1
New York Evangelist	1845-1847	2
Scientific American, New York, (lacking from 1861 to 1884,)	1849-1890	20
New York Daily Tribune, (lacking from 1870 to 1874, and from 1876 to 1879,)	1849-1890	70
New York Semi-Weekly Tribune, (lacking 1876, 1883, 1884,)	1871-1887	14
New York Weekly Tribune, (lacking 1871-1878,)	1869-1884	8
Propagandist, New York	1850,1851	1
The Home Missionary (monthly), New York	1850-1890	40
Harper's Monthly Magazine, New York	1851-1854	8
Harper's Weekly, New York	1857-1888	32
New York Illustrated News	1853	1
The Industry of All Nations, New York	1853	1
Putnam's Monthly, New York	1853-1857	14
Daily Times, New York, (incomplete,)	1854-1856	4
The Phonographic Intelligencer, New York	1857	1
The Printer, New York	1858-1863	4
New York Independent, New York, (1874 duplicate,)	1859-1887	30
U. S. Service Magazine (monthly), New York	1864-1866	5
The Galaxy (monthly), New York	1866-1877	24
American Agriculturist (monthly), New York, (lacking 1862-1866,)	1860-1869	4
The Revolution, New York	1868-1870	5
The Spectator, New York and Chicago	1870-1880	11
Scribner's Monthly and the Century Magazine, New York	1870-1888	36
Popular Science Monthly, New York	1872-1885	27
The Christian Union, New York	1874-1887	14
The Iron Age, New York	1876	1
The Library Journal (monthly), New York	1876-1890	15
The Magazine of American History (monthly), New York	1877-1888	20
Brown's Phonographic Monthly, New York	1878-1883	6
The National Citizen and Ballot-Box, (from May, 1878, to October, 1881,) New York, (see Ballot-Box, Ohio,)	1878-1881	4
The Daily Register, New York	1879-1888	20
America, New York	1879-1881	3
The Sheltering Arms (monthly), New York	1879-1890	11
The Publishers' Weekly, New York	1879-1890	19
The American Missionary (monthly), New York	1880-1890	11
The Nation, New York	1882-1888	7
John Swinton's Paper, New York	1883-1887	4
Appleton's Literary Bulletin (bi-monthly), New York	1881-1889	6
Phonetic Educator, New York and Cincinnati	1884,1885	1
The Literary News, New York	1884-1890	8
The Student's Journal (phonographic monthly), New York	1884-1890	7
The Phonographic World (monthly), New York	1885-1890	6
New York Weekly Witness	1885-1890	5
The Irish World, New York	1885-1890	5
The Christian Advocate, (from April, 1885, to December 30, 1886,) New York	1885,1886	3
The Coöperative Index to Periodicals (quarterly), New York	1885-1888	4
The Protestant Episcopal Mission Leaf (monthly), New York	1886	1
The National Temperance Advocate (monthly), New York	1886-1890	5
Science, New York	1886-1888	6
The American Book-Maker (monthly), New York	1885,1886	2
The New Princeton Review (semi-monthly), New York city	1886-1888	6
Sabbath Reading, New York	1886-1890	4
The Delineator (monthly), New York	1886	1
Electrical Review, New York	1886-1890	5
Scribner's Magazine (monthly), New York	1887,1888	4
Agricultural Science (monthly), New York	1887,1882	2
The Swiss Cross (monthly), New York	1887-1889	3
The Voice, New York	1887-1890	4
The Decorator and Furnisher (monthly), New York	1887-1890	5
The Public Service Review (monthly), New York	1887,1888	1
Home Knowledge (monthly), New York	1887,1888	2
Judge, New York	1888	1
New York Pioneer	1887-1890	3
The Curio, New York	1887,1888	1
Demorest's Monthly, New York	1888	1
Tariff League Bulletin, New York	1888	1
Political Science Quarterly, New York	1886-1890	5
Insurance, New York	1884,1885	2
The Standard, New York	1888,1889	1
Literary Digest, New York	1890	1

BOUND NEWSPAPERS, ETC., OF OTHER STATES AND COUNTRIES — Continued.

Newspapers.	Years.	No. vols.
NEW YORK — *concluded.*		
American Economist, New York	1890	1
The Silver Cross (monthly), New York	1889,1890	1
The Critic, New York	1887–1889	1
The Saturday Globe, New York	1888–1890	3
Twentieth Century, New York	1889,1890	1
The Nation, New York	1889,1890	1
College for the Training of Teachers, leaflet, New York	1887–1890	3
The American Sentinel, New York	1890	1
The Business Woman's Journal (bi-monthly), New York	1889,1890	2
Evangelical Magazine, Utica, (vols. 2 and 3,)	1828,1829	2
Evangelical Magazine and Gospel Advocate, Utica, (vols. 4, 5, and 9,1833, 1834, and 1838,)	1833–1838	3
The Jeffersonian, Albany	1838,1839	2
The Northern Light, Albany	1841–1843	1
The Cultivator and Country Gentleman, Albany	1879,1880	2
The Union, Brooklyn	1879–1882	3
Fruit Recorder and Cottage Gardener, Palmyra	1874–1876	3
The Bee Keepers' Exchange (monthly), Canajoharie	1879–1882	4
The Husbandman, Elmira	1886–1890	5
Library Bulletin of Cornell University (monthly), Itnaca	1887–1888	2
OHIO.		
The Ohio Cultivator, Columbus	1845,1846	2
The Crisis, (from January 31, 1861, to January 23, 1863,) Columbus	1861–1863	2
Ohio Archæological and Historical Quarterly, Columbus	1887,1889	1
Weekly Phonetic Advocate, Cincinnati	1850–1853	4
Phonetic Advocate Supplement, Cincinnati	1850–1852	2
The Masonic Review, Cincinnati	1853–1862	17
Type of the Times, Cincinnati	1854,1855	2
American Phonetic Journal, Cincinnati	1858	1
Cincinnati Weekly Times	1878–1890	13
The Phonetic Educator, Cincinnati	1878–1883	5
The Christian Press (monthly), Cincinnati	1880–1890	10
The American Journal of Forestry, Cincinnati	1882,1883	1
The Christian Standard, Cincinnati	1883–1890	8
The American Grange Bulletin, Cincinnati	1886–1890	5
Phonographic Magazine (monthly), Cincinnati	1887	1
The Ballot-Box, (from June, 1876, to May, 1878,) Toledo, (see National Citizen, New York)	1876–1878	2
Nachrichten aus der Heidenwelt, Zanesville	1877–1880	4
Magazine of Western History (monthly), Cleveland	1884–1890	5
Farm and Fireside (semi-monthly), Springfield	1884–1890	5
Herald of Gospel Liberty, Dayton	1889,1890	2
OKLAHOMA TERRITORY.		
(See Indian Territory.)		
PENNSYLVANIA.		
The American Naturalist, Philadelphia	1867–1880	14
The Press (daily), Philadelphia	1878–1880	6
Progress, Philadelphia	1878–1885	7
Public Ledger (daily), Philadelphia	1879–1890	24
Faith and Works (monthly), Philadelphia	1879–1890	11
Sunday School Times, (files for 1879, 1880, 1884, 1885, 1886,) Philadelphia	1879–1886	5
Naturalist's Leisure Hour (monthly), Philadelphia	1880–1890	9
Dye's Government Counterfeit Detector, Philadelphia	1886–1889	3
The Building Association and Home Journal (monthly), Philadelphia	1887–1889	3
The Book Mart (monthly), Philadelphia	1887–1890	3
Paper and Press (monthly), Philadelphia	1888–1890	3
Book News (monthly), Philadelphia	1889,1890	1
Food, Home & Garden, Philadelphia	1889,1890	1
Eadle Keatah Toh — The Morning Star and the Red Man (monthly), Carlisle	1881–1890	9
Historical Register (vols. 1 and 2), Harrisburg	1883,1884	2
The Farmer's Friend, Mechanicsburg	1886–1890	5
American Manufacturer and Iron World, Pittsburgh	1887–1890	3
Poultry Keeper (monthly), Parkersburg and Philadelphia	1888,1889	1
TEXAS.		
Live-Stock Journal, Fort Worth	1882–1890	9
Texas Wool Grower, Fort Worth	1882,1883	2
El Paso Times (daily)	1883	1
Texas Review (monthly), Austin	1886	1
The Canadian Free Press	1887–1889	2
The Canadian Crescent	1888,1889	1
Southern Mercury, Dallas	1888–1890	2

BOUND NEWSPAPERS, ETC., OF OTHER STATES AND COUNTRIES — Concluded.

Newspapers.	Years.	No. vols.
VERMONT.		
The Woman's Magazine (monthly), Battleboro.	1885–1890	5
The National Bulletin (monthly), Brattleboro.	1886,1887	1
VIRGINIA.		
The Richmond Standard.	1880,1881	1
Southern Workman and Hampton School Record, Hampton.	1886–1890	6
WASHINGTON.		
Whatcom Reveille.	1884–1886	2
WISCONSIN.		
Wisconsin State Journal, Madison.	1878–1889	11
Western Farmer and Wisconsin Grange Bulletin. Madison.	1886	1
WYOMING.		
Laramie Boomerang (daily).	1889	1
ENGLAND.		
London Illustrated News.	1842–1879	62
Diplomatic Review, (vols. 1-25,) London.	1855–1877	25
The Labour Standard, London.	1882–1884	3
Forestry, a magazine for the country, (monthly,) Edinburgh and London.	1884,1885	3
The Fonetic Journal, Bath.	1879	1
FRANCE.		
Bulletin de la Société Protectrice des Animaux (monthly), Paris.	1878–1882	5
Bulletin de la Société de Geographie, Paris.	1878–1883	11
Société de Geographie compte rendu des Séances de la Commission Centrale (semi-monthly), Paris.	1882–1890	9
Chronique de la Société des Gens des Lettres (monthly), Paris.	1879–1890	12
Bulletin Mensuel de la Société des Gens des Lettres, Paris.	1878–1880	1
Bulletin des Séances de la Société Nationale d'Agriculture (monthly), Paris.	1879–1886	9

KANSAS NEWSPAPERS AND PERIODICALS NOW RECEIVED.

The following is a list of the newspapers and periodicals published in Kansas, corrected up to January 1, 1891. The regular issues of these, with very few exceptions, are now being received by the Kansas State Historical Society. They are the free gift of the publishers to the State. They are bound in annual or semi-annual volumes, and are preserved in the library of the Society in the State Capitol for the free use of the people. They number 793 in all. Of these 33 are dailies, 1 is semi-weekly, 718 weeklies, 36 monthlies, 2 are semi-monthlies, 1 is bi-monthly, and 2 are quarterlies. They come from all of the 106 counties of Kansas, and record the history of the people of all the communities and neighborhoods.

ALLEN COUNTY.

Humboldt Union, Republican; W. T. McElroy, publisher and proprietor, Humboldt.

Humboldt Herald, Democrat; S. A. D. Cox, editor and publisher, Humboldt.

Iola Register, Republican; Charles F. Scott, editor and publisher, Iola.

Farmers' Friend, People's Party; A. H. Harris, publisher, Iola.

Allen County Herald, Democratic; S. A. D. Cox, editor and manager, C. T. Cox, assistant editor, Iola.

Moran Herald, Republican; George D. Ingersoll and Leo Fesler, editors, publishers and proprietors, Moran.

Elsmore Eagle, neutral; N. B. Webber, editor, Elsmore.

ANDERSON COUNTY.

Garnett Weekly Journal, Democratic; I. T. Highly, editor and proprietor, Garnett.

Republican-Plaindealer, Republican; Howard M. Brooke, publisher, Garnett.

Garnett Eagle, Republican; W. A. Trigg, editor, publisher, and proprietor, Garnett.

Kansas-Agitator, People's Party; W. O. Champe, editor and publisher, Garnett and Greeley.

Greeley News, People's Party; W. O. Champe, editor and publisher, Greeley.

Colony Free Press, Republican; S. L. Tathwell, editor and publisher, Colony.

Westphalia Times, independent: Ancil F. Hatten, editor and proprietor, J. Hatten & Son, publishers, Westphalia.

Kincaid Chronicle, People's Party; W. C. Routzong, editor, W. C. Routzong & Son, proprietors.

Kincaid Dispatch, Republican; J. E. Scruggs, jr., editor, Scruggs Bros. publishers, Kincaid.

ATCHISON COUNTY.

Atchison Champion (daily and weekly), Republican; L. C. Challiss, editor and manager, owned by John A. Martin estate, Atchison.

Atchison Patriot (daily and weekly), Democratic; R. T. Hazzard, editor, Patriot Publishing Co., publishers, Atchison.

Atchison Globe (daily and weekly), independent; Edgar W. Howe, editor and publisher, Atchison.

Atchison Times, People's Party; J. A. Sunderland, editor and publisher, Atchison.

Atchison Baptist, (monthly), religious; Rev. D. D. Proper, editor, Atchison.

Midland College Monthly, educational; edited by the faculty and students, Atchison.

Business College Review (monthly), educational; edited by the faculty and students, Atchison.

Muscotah Record, neutral; Fred. W. Badger, editor and publisher, Muscotah.

Effingham Times, neutral; W. W. Cahoon, editor, publisher and proprietor, Effingham.

Huron Graphic, Democratic; W. C. Adkins, editor and publisher, Huron.

BARBER COUNTY.

Medicine Lodge Cresset, Republican; L. M. Axline, editor, publisher, and proprietor, Medicine Lodge.

Barber County Index, People's Party; W. G. Musgrove, editor, Medicine Lodge.

Barber County Herald, Democratic; John L. Brady, editor, E. F. Widner, proprietor, Medicine Lodge.

Hazelton Express, People's Party; W. F. Hatfield, editor, publisher, and proprietor, Hazelton.

Kiowa Journal, Republican; Wm. McKean, editor and publisher, Kiowa.

BARTON COUNTY.

Great Bend Register, Republican; Morgan Caraway, editor, publisher and proprietor, Great Bend.

Great Bend Tribune, Republican; C. P. Townsley, editor and proprietor, Great Bend.

The Daily News, neutral; C. P. Townsley, editor, publisher and proprietor, Great Bend.

Barton County Democrat, Democratic; Will E. Stoke, editor, publisher and proprietor, Great Bend.

Barton County Beacon, People's Party; D. T. Armstrong, editor and publisher, Great Bend.

Ellinwood Advocate, Democratic; W. P. Feder, jr., editor and proprietor, Ellinwood.

Pawnee Rock Leader, Republican; H. R. Lewis, editor and publisher, Pawnee Rock.

Hoisington Dispatch, Republican; Ira H. Clark, editor, publisher and proprietor, Hoisington.

Barton County Banner, Independent; O. E. O'Bleness, editor and proprietor, Claflin.

BOURBON COUNTY.

Fort Scott Monitor (daily and weekly), Republican; W. M. Rice, R. P. Rice and H. V. Rice, editors, publishers and proprietors, Fort Scott.

Fort Scott Tribune, (daily and weekly), Democratic; J. B. Chapman, editor, Martin and Chapman, proprietors, Fort Scott.

The Spectator, Democratic; Ralph Richards, editor, Spectator Publishing Company, publishers, Fort Scott.

Industrial Union, People's Party; H. B. Frye, editor, Fort Scott.

The Normal Journal, educational; D. E. Sanders, editor, W. H. Kerr, business manager, Fort Scott.

Bronson Pilot, neutral; W. M. Holeman, editor and proprietor, Bronson.

Fulton Independent, independent; A. W. Felter, editor and proprietor, Fulton.

Fulton Rustler, independent; S. B. De Lano, editor, Fulton.

The Lantern, People's Party; Lockhart & Waterman, editors and proprietors, Mapleton.

Mapleton Despatch, Republican; H. S. Brimhall, editor and publisher, Mapleton.

BROWN COUNTY.

Brown County World, Republican; D. W. Wilder, proprietor, Ewing Herbert, manager, Hiawatha.

The Kansas Democrat, Democratic; B. F. Hildebrand, editor and proprietor, Hiawatha.

The Hiawatha Journal, People's Party; Journal Publishing Company, publishers, Hiawatha.

Delta Sigma Nu (bi-monthly); Grant W. Harrington, editor and publisher, Hiawatha.

Horton Weekly Headlight, Republican; H. W. Whitaker and L. C. Clark, publishers, Horton.

Horton Commercial, Democratic; Clyde McManigal, editor, publisher and proprietor, Horton.

The Everest Enterprise, Democratic; N. F. Hess, editor and proprietor, Everest.

Fairview Enterprise, Democratic; S. O. Groesbeck, editor, Fairview.

The Morrill News, Republican; J. P. Grinstead, editor and publisher, Morrill.

BUTLER COUNTY.

The Augusta Journal, Republican; W. H. Cady, editor, Augusta.

The Industrial Advocate, People's Party; Walter L. Holcomb, editor, Olin Meacham, business manager, Augusta.

Walnut Valley Times (daily and weekly), Republican; Alvah Shelden, editor and publisher, El Dorado.

El Dorado Republican, Republican; T. B. Murdock, editor and publisher, El Dorado.

Butler County Democrat, Democratic; J. C. Riley, jr., editor and proprietor, El Dorado.

The Daily Eli, People's Party; A. J. Miller, editor, El Dorado.

Kansas Workman, People's Party; Cyrus Corning, A. J. Miller, A. W. Florea, editors, Kansas Workman Publishing Co., publishers, El Dorado.

Douglass Tribune, Republican; J. M. Satterthwaite, editor and publisher, Douglass.

The Leon Indicator, Republican; C. R. Noe, editor and publisher, G. W. Tracy, proprietor, Leon.

The Herald, People's Party; E. Davis, jr., editor and proprietor, Towanda.

The Latham Times, Independent; Jay Shafer, editor, publisher, and proprietor, Latham.

The Whitewater Tribune, Republican; H. W. Bailey, editor, Whitewater.

CHASE COUNTY.

The Chase County Courant, Democratic; W. E. Timmons, editor and publisher, Cottonwood Falls.

Chase County Leader, Republican; William A. Morgan, editor, publisher and proprietor, Cottonwood Falls.

The Reveille, People's Party; E. W. Ellis, editor, Cottonwood Falls.

Chase County Republican, W. Y. Morgan, editor and proprietor, Strong City.

CHAUTAUQUA COUNTY.

The Sedan Times-Journal, Republican; Adrian Reynolds, editor and publisher, Sedan.

Sedan Republican, Republican; T. B. Ferguson, editor and proprietor, Sedan.

The Cedar Vale Star, independent; F. G. Kenesson, editor and proprietor, Cedar Vale.

The Cedar Vale Commercial, Republican; W. M. Jones, editor, Cedar Vale.

The Peru Eagle, People's Party; W. T. Gwyn, editor and proprietor, Peru.

CHEROKEE COUNTY.

The Columbus Star-Courier, Democratic; N. T. Allison and W. P. Eddy, editors and proprietors, Columbus.

The Columbus Advocate, Republican; L. M. Dillman, editor; A. T. Lea & Son, publishers, Columbus.

Baxter Springs News, Neutral; M. H. Gardner, editor and publisher, Baxter Springs.

Short Creek Republican, Republican; L. C. Weldy, editor and proprietor, Galena.

The Galena Times, Democratic; C. T. Dana, editor, Galena Publishing Company, publishers, Galena.

Weir City Tribune, Independent; H. Hayden, publisher, Weir.

The Weir Journal, Republican; T. G. Robison, editor and proprietor, Weir.

CHEYENNE COUNTY.

Bird City News, Republican; George W. Murray, editor and publisher, Bird City.

Cheyenne County Rustler-Review, Republican; C. E. Dennison and R. M. Jaque, publishers, St. Francis.

CLARK COUNTY.

Clark County Clipper, Democratic; W. L. Cowden, editor, Ashland.

The Ashland Weekly Journal, Republican; M. G. Stevenson, editor, Journal Company, publishers, Ashland.

CLAY COUNTY.

The Dispatch, Republican; Bion S. Hutchins, editor, publisher and proprietor, Clay Center.

The Times, Republican; J. P. Campbell and D. A. Valentine, editors, publishers and proprietors, Clay Center.

The Clay County Critic, People's Party; Enoch Weekly, editor, W. J. A. Montgomery, publisher, Clay Center.

The Clay County Sentinel, Republican; W. A. Stacy, editor, Morganville.

The News, Republican; L. A. Palmer, editor, publisher and proprietor, Clifton.

Wakefield Advertiser, neutral, J. J. L. Jones, editor and publisher, Wakefield.

CLOUD COUNTY.

Concordia Empire, Republican; T. A. Sawhill, editor, Concordia.

The Concordia Blade, Resubmission; J. M. Hagaman, editor, Blade Publishing Co., publishers, Concordia.

The Concordia Times, Republican; T. A. Filson, editor, S. Z. Filson, associate editor, Concordia.

Concordia Daylight, Republican; E. Marshall, editor and proprietor, Concordia.

The Alliant, People's Party; Ferd. Prince, editor and publisher, Concordia.

The Clyde Herald, Republican; J. B. & M. L. Rupe, editors, publishers and proprietors, Clyde.

The Clyde Argus, Republican; Charles A. Morley and Owen V. Smith, editors and proprietors, Clyde.

Jamestown New Era, Republican; John W. McCoy, editor, Jamestown.

The Glasco Sun, Republican; Kate Hubbard, editor, Glasco.

Miltonvale Review, Republican; M. O. Burdick, editor and proprietor, Miltonvale.

COFFEY COUNTY.

Burlington Republican, Republican; C. O. Smith, editor, publisher and proprietor, Burlington.

Burlington Independent, Democratic; John E. Watrous, editor, publisher and proprietor, Burlington.

The Burlington Nonpareil, independent; A. D. Brown, editor, publisher and proprietor, Burlington.

The Farm Record, Alliance; I. W. Pack, editor and proprietor, Burlington.

LeRoy Reporter, independent; Frank Fockele, editor, publisher and proprietor, LeRoy.

The Lebo Courier, independent; G. W. Neiberger, editor and proprietor, Lebo.

Waverly Gazette, independent; Dan K. Swarengin, publisher, Waverly.

COMANCHE COUNTY.

The Western Star, Democratic; W. M. Cash, editor, proprietor and publisher, Coldwater.

The Coldwater Review, Democratic; John A. Templeman and Henry E. Oldfather, publishers, Coldwater.

Coldwater Echo, Republican; E. G. Phelps, editor, Coldwater.

Coldwater Enterprise, Republican; J. E. Hutchison, editor, Coldwater.

The People's Advocate, People's Party; N. S. Mounts, editor, Coldwater.

The Coldwater Voice, Farmers' Alliance; M. S. and H. A. Boyce, editors and proprietors, Coldwater.

The Winfield Courier (daily and weekly), Republican; Ed. P. Greer, editor, Winfield.

The Winfield Telegram, People's Party; M. L. Garrigus, editor, H. and L. Vincent, publishers, Winfield.

The Winfield Tribune (daily and weekly), Republican; S. E. Burger, editor, M. L. Harter and Company, publishers, Winfield.

The American Nonconformist, People's Party; Henry Vincent, editor, Henry and Leo Vincent, publishers and proprietors, Winfield.

Winfield Newspaper Union; Ed. P. Greer, editor, Winfield.

The Industrial Free Press, People's Party; P. W. Craig, editor, Winfield.

The Western Reveille; A. H. Limerick, editor, Winfield.

The Monthly Herald, Baptist; Rev. Geo. P. Wright, editor, Winfield.

Economic Quarterly, political economy; C. Vincent, editor, H. and L. Vincent, publishers, Winfield.

Republican Traveler (daily and weekly), Republican; T. W. Eckert and R. C. Howard, editors, Arkansas City.

Arkansas Valley Democrat, Democratic; Timothy McIntire, editor and publisher, Arkansas City.

Canal City Dispatch (daily and weekly), People's Party; G. W. and B. A. Wagner, editors and proprietors, Arkansas City.

Fair Play, People's Party; H. B. Funk, editor, Arkansas City.

The Burden Enterprise, Republican; W. L. Hutton, editor, W. K. McComas, publisher and proprietor, Burden.

The Udall Record, neutral; B. F. Baker, editor and proprietor, Udall.

The Girard Press, Republican; E. A. Wasser and D. C. Flint, editors, publishers and proprietors, Girard.

The Western Herald, People's Party; Percy Daniels, editor, Girard.

The Cherokee Sentinel on the Border, Republican; Swank & Price, editors and publishers, Cherokee.

Pittsburg Smelter, Republican; John R. Morris & Co., editors, publishers and proprietors, Pittsburg.

The Pittsburg Headlight (daily and weekly), Republican; Wm. Moore and C. W. Moore, editors, publishers and proprietors, Pittsburg.

Pittsburg Herold (German), Democratic; John G. Burkhart, editor, Burkhart & Muser, publishers, Pittsburg.

The Weekly World, independent; W. C. L. Beard, president, World Publishing Company, publishers, Pittsburg.

Pittsburg Kansan, Democratic; J. C. Buchanan, editor, Pittsburg.

McCune Times, Republican; Merritt E. Springer and J. C. Bogard, editors, publishers and proprietors, McCune.

Crawford County Democrat, Democratic; J. M. Mahr and W. D. Bevans, editors and proprietors, McCune.

Walnut Journal, neutral; Lewis Martin, editor, publisher and proprietor, Walnut.

Arcadia News, Republican; L. R. Jewell, editor and proprietor, Arcadia.

Oberlin Herald, Democratic; Dr. W. B. Mead, editor; Herald Publishing Co., publishers, Oberlin.

Oberlin Opinion, Republican; F. W. Casterline, publisher, Oberlin.

The Eye, Republican; C. Borin, editor and proprietor, Oberlin.

Alliance Times. People's Party; John Shields, editor and proprietor, Oberlin.

The Norcatur Register, Republican; H. H. Hoskins, publisher, Norcatur.

Dresden Star, Republican; E. E. Van Epps, publisher and proprietor; L. W. Brewer, local editor, Dresden.

Jennings Echo, Republican; Geo. W. Shook, editor and publisher, Jennings.

DICKINSON COUNTY.

Abilene Weekly Chronicle, Republican; R. B. Claiborne, editor, R. B. Claiborne & Son, publishers, Abilene.

Abilene Reflector (daily and weekly), Republican; Chas. Morean Harger, editor, Reflector Publishing Co., publishers, Abilene.

The Dickinson County News, Democratic; L. B. Strother and F. K. Strother, publishers, Abilene.

The Alliance Monitor, People's Party; D. G. Smith, editor and publisher, Abilene.

Solomon Sentinel, Republican; E. B. Burnett, editor and publisher, Solomon City.

Enterprise Journal, Republican; J. C. Gault, editor, Enterprise Publishing Co., publishers, Enterprise.

Kansas Miller and Manufacturer (monthly); C. B. Hoffman, editor, Enterprise.

The Hope Herald, Republican; Geo. Burroughs, editor and publisher, Hope.

Hope Dispatch, Republican; M. C. Hemenway, editor and publisher, Hope.

The Herington Times, Republican; A. M. Crary, editor and proprietor, Herington.

The Chapman Courier, Republican; Chas. G. Bear, Chapman.

The Manchester Sun, Republican; A. S. Green, editor and publisher, Manchester.

DONIPHAN COUNTY.

The Weekly Kansas Chief, Republican; Sol. Miller, editor, publisher and proprietor, Troy.

The Troy Times, Democratic; Frank L. Finch, editor and publisher, Troy.

The Weekly News, neutral; W. T. Pandolph, editor, publisher and proprietor, Severance.

Highland University Nuncio, Educational; G. E. Partch, editor, Highland.

DOUGLAS COUNTY.

Lawrence Journal (daily and weekly), Republican; O. E. Learnard, proprietor; C. S. Finch, editor, Lawrence.

Daily and Weekly Record, independent Republican; Record Publishing Co., proprietors, H. M. Greene, editor, Lawrence.

Die Germania (German); Edward Grün, editor and publisher, Lawrence.

Lawrence Gazette, Democratic; Frank L. Webster, editor and proprietor, Lawrence.

The Jeffersonian, Alliance; W. H. T. Wakefield, editor and proprietor, Lawrence.

University Review (monthly), college; Review Publishing Co., Harold Barnes, editor, Lawrence.

University Courier, college; Courier Publishing Co., R. R. Whitman, editor, Lawrence.

The Select Friend (monthly). organ of the order of Select Friends; J. S. Boughton, editor, J. S. Boughton Publishing Co., publishers, Lawrence.

Baldwin Ledger, Republican; J. N. Moorehead & Son, editors and proprietors, Baldwin.

Baker Beacon, college; Beacon Publishing Co., Baldwin.

Baker University Index; S. McRoberts, editor, Baldwin.
College Echoes, college; Echoes Publishing Co., J. O. Rankin, Lecompton.
Eudora News, Republican; George C. Brune, editor and proprietor, Eudora.

EDWARDS COUNTY.

The Kinsley Mercury, Republican; Fred D. Smith, editor, and publisher, Kinsley.
The Kinsley Graphic, Democratic; Henry R. Griggs and Ed. W. Creviston, editors and proprietors, Kinsley.
The Kinsley Chronicle, religious; C. A. Greenlees, editor, Kinsley.

ELK COUNTY.

The Howard Courant, Republican; Asa, Tom E. and John A. Thompson, editors, publishers and proprietors, Howard.
The Howard Democrat, Democratic; James Robert Hall, editor and publisher, Howard.
The Longton Times, independent; Geo. M. Flory, editor and publisher, Longton.
Longton Signal, Republican; Tom C. Copeland, editor and publisher, Longton.
The Moline Republican, Republican; Geo. C. Armstrong, editor, publisher and proprietor, Moline.
Weekly Crisis, Sol. L. Long, editor, Grenola.

ELLIS COUNTY.

The Review-Headlight, Republican; F. M. Robinson, Ellis.
Hays City Sentinel, Republican; W. P. Montgomery, manager, Hays City.
Free Press, Republican; Harry Freese, editor and proprietor, Hays City.
Democratic Times, Democratic; G. W. Sweet, editor and publisher, Hays City.
The Republican, Republican; Geo. P. Griffith, editor, Hays City.
Our Church Mirror, (monthly,) religious; Rev. J. W. Funk, editor, Claud O. Funk, publisher, Howard.

ELLSWORTH COUNTY.

Ellsworth Reporter, Republican; George Huycke, editor and proprietor, Ellsworth.
Ellsworth Democrat, Democratic; G. A. Collett and F. S. Foster, editors and proprietors, Ellsworth.
Ellsworth Republican, Republican; M. D. Morgan and R. V. Morgan, Ellsworth.
The Wilson Echo, Republican; S. A. Coover, editor, Wilson.
The Kanopolis Kansan, People's Party; T. K. Griffith, editor and publisher, Kanapolis.

FINNEY COUNTY.

Finney County Democrat, Democratic; M. B. Hundley, editor and publisher, Garden City.
Garden City Sentinel, Republican; J. W. Gregory, editor and publisher, Garden City.
Garden City Weekly Herald, Republican, J. F. Kirkpatrick, editor; R. E. Gray, publisher, Garden City.
The Garden City Imprint, Republican; D. A. Mims, editor, S. G. Norris and W. W. Pegg, publishers, Garden City.

FORD COUNTY.

The Dodge City Times, Democratic; F. H. Mendenhall, editor, Times Publishing Company, publishers, Dodge City.
The Dodge City Democrat, Democratic; W. F. Petillon, editor, Petillon Brothers, publishers, Dodge City.

The Globe-Republican, Republican; D. M. Frost, editor, Globe-Republican Publishing Company, publishers, Dodge City.

Western Kansas Ensign, Republican; J. A. Cline, editor and publisher, Bellefont.

FRANKLIN COUNTY.

Ottawa Journal and Triumph, People's Party; E. H. Snow, editor, publisher and proprietor, Ottawa.

Ottawa Republican (daily and weekly), Republican; Wm. Hope, editor, Ottawa.

Ottawa Herald, Democratic; John B. Kessler, editor and publisher, Ottawa.

The Ottawa Lever, Prohibition; W. M. Preshaw, editor, publisher and proprietor, Ottawa.

Ottawa Tribune, Republican; T. W. Fields and A. Gould, editors and proprietors, Ottawa.

Ottawa Campus, educational (monthy), W. H. Isely, editor-in-chief.

The Pomona Enterprise, independent; T. L. Newcomb, editor, Enterprise Publishing Co., publishers, Pomona.

The Enterprise, neutral; T. J. Swaney and A. D. Zimmerman, editors and publishers, Williamsburg.

The Wellsville Globe, neutral; F. S. Rice and E. L. Rice, editors and proprietors, Wellsville.

Lane Leader, Republican; Dursley Sargent, editor and publisher, Lane.

GARFIELD COUNTY.

Ravanna Chieftain, Republican; M. L. Hart, editor and publisher, Ravanna.

Garfield County Call, Republican; W. B. Smith, editor and publisher, Eminence.

GEARY COUNTY.

The Junction City Union, Republican; John Montgomery, E. M. Gilbert, and W. C. Moore, publishers, Junction City.

The Junction City Tribune, People's Party; Chas. S. Davis, editor, publisher and proprietor, Junction City.

The Junction City Republican, Republican; Geo. A. Clark, editor, publisher and proprietor, Junction City.

Democratic Sentinel, Democratic; A. W. Chabin, editor and publisher, Junction City.

Mid-Continental Review (monthly), literary and political; John Hay, editor, Junction City.

Insurance Messenger (monthly), insurance; G. F. Little, editor and proprietor, Junction City.

Kansas Wheelmen's Library (monthly), road improvement; Kansas Division, L. A. W., publishers.

GOVE COUNTY.

Grainfield Cap Sneaf, Republican; I. T. Purcell, editor and publisher, Grainfield.

Gove County Gazette, Republican; O. B. Jones and J. F. Jones, editors and publishers, Gove City.

Quinter Republican, independent; A. K. Teimmer, editor and proprietor, Quinter.

GRAHAM COUNTY.

Graham County Times, Republican; J. H. Wright, editor and publisher, Hill City.

Hill City Democrat, Democratic; J. F. Stewart, editor and publisher, Hill City.

Hill City Republican, Republican; W. H. Hill, editor; W. R. Hill, publisher and proprietor, Hill City.

Hill City Reveille, Republican; H. D. Clayton, editor and proprietor, Hill City.

The People's Advocate, People's Party; L. C. Chase, editor and publisher, Hill City.

Bogue Signal, Republican; Frank P. Graves, editor and publisher, Bogue.

GRANT COUNTY.

Ulysses Tribune and Grant County Register, Republican; Geo. W. Perry, editor and publisher, Ulysses.

GRAY COUNTY.

The Jacksonian, Democratic; Ellis S. Garten, editor, publisher and proprietor, Cimarron.

New West Echo, Republican; N. B. Klaine, editor and publisher, Cimarron.

Ingalls Union, Republican; R. H. Turner, editor, Union Publishing Company, publishers, Ingalls.

GREELEY COUNTY.

The Greeley County Republican, Republican; L. M. Riley, editor and publisher, Brown & Donahue, proprietors, Tribune.

Greeley County Journal, People's Party; C. E. Wightman, editor, Journal Company, publishers, Tribune.

GREENWOOD COUNTY.

The Eureka Herald, Republican; Z. Harlan, editor, publisher, and proprietor, Eureka.

Greenwood County Republican, Republican; W. E. Doud, editor, publisher and proprietor, Eureka.

Democratic Messenger, Democratic; T. W. Morgan, editor and publisher, Eureka.

Kansas Alliance-Union, People's Party; O. C. Woodrow, editor, Alliance-Union Publishing Company, publishers, Eureka.

Madison News, Republican; W. O. Lunsford, editor and proprietor, Madison.

The Severy Record, Republican; Geo. H. Doud, editor and proprietor, Severy.

Severyite, Republican; C. G. Pierce, editor and proprietor, Severy.

The Fall River Times, People's Party; J. A. Somerby, editor and publisher, Fall River.

Virgil Review, People's Party; G. S. McCartney, editor and publisher, Virgil.

HAMILTON COUNTY.

The Syracuse Journal, Republican; H. N. Lester, editor, Journal Publishing Company, publishers, Syracuse.

The Democratic Principle, Democratic; F. M. Dunlavy, editor, Syracuse.

Hamilton County Bulletin, Republican; John W. Bishop, editor and proprietor, Coolidge.

HARPER COUNTY.

The Anthony Republican, Republican; Geo. W. Maffet, editor and publisher, Anthony.

Harper County Enterprise, Democratic; T. H. McDowell, editor and publisher, Anthony.

Anthony Journal, Republican; J. R. Hammond, editor, S. C. Hammond, publisher, Anthony.

The Harper Sentinel, Independent; Jonas Cook, editor and publisher, Harper.

The Alliance Bulletin, People's Party; W. Whitworth, editor and proprietor, Geo. H. Coulson, assistant editor, Harper.

The College Journal (monthly), educational; R. W. Ball, editor and publisher, Harper.

Harper Semi-Weekly Graphic, Republican; Minerva D. Walker, editor, Harper.

The Attica Advocate, People's Party; L. A. Hoffman, editor, Hoffman & Son, publishers, Attica.

HARVEY COUNTY.

The Newton Republican (daily and weekly), Republican; T. J. Norton, editor, Republican Publishing Company, publishers, Newton.

Newton Kansan, Republican; Chas. H. Kurtz, editor, publisher and proprietor, Newton.

Newton Anzeiger, German; C. D. Heinrich, editor and publisher, Newton.

The Weekly Journal, Democratic; J. A. Reynolds and M. J. Reynolds, editors and publishers, Newton.

The Halstead Independent, Republican; Joe F. White, editor and publisher, Halstead.

The Halstead Tribune, Republican; J. C. Gaiser, editor and publisher, Halstead.

The Burrton Weekly Graffic, Republican; Osborn & Kent, editors and publishers, Burrton.

The Free Lance, People's Party; Leslie P. Purcell, editor and publisher, Burrton.

The Sedgwick Pantagraph, Republican; Cash. M. Taylor, editor and publisher, Sedgwick.

The Walton Reporter, Republican; H. A. Brush, editor, Walton.

HASKELL COUNTY.

Ivanhoe Times, Republican; F. Gray and R. E. Blair, editors, publishers and proprietors, Ivanhoe.

Santa Fé Monitor, Republican; John J. Miller, editor and publisher, Santa Fé.

HODGEMAN COUNTY.

Jetmore Reveille, Republican; P. N. Bernard, editor and proprietor, Jetmore.

Jetmore Siftings, Republican; L. C. Miller, editor and proprietor, Jetmore.

The Jetmore Sunflower, Republican; O. E. Hardy, publisher and proprietor, Jetmore.

JACKSON COUNTY.

The Holton Weekly Recorder, Republican; M. M. Beck, editor and proprietor, Holton.

The Holton Weekly Signal, Democratic; W. W. Sargent, editor and proprietor, Holton.

Independent Tribune, independent; Armer P. Shaw and Chas. V. Hamm, editors and publishers, Holton.

The Whiting Weekly News, independent; Mrs. Anna Van Moon, editor and proprietor, Whiting.

JEFFERSON COUNTY.

The Oskaloosa Independent, Republican; F. H. Roberts, editor, Oskaloosa.

The Valley Falls New Era, Republican; A. W. Robinson, editor and publisher, Valley Falls.

The Valley Falls Register, Democratic; T. W. Gardiner, editor and publisher, Valley Falls.

The Farmers' Vindicator, People's Party; N. H. Harman, editor and publisher, Valley Falls.

The Winchester Herald, Republican; Ernest P. Karr, editor, publisher, and proprietor, Winchester.

The Nortonville News, Republican; R. M. Cook, editor and proprietor, Nortonville.

Meriden Weekly Tribune, Republican; J. W. Cook and A. C. Kious, editors, publishers, and proprietors, Meriden.

The McLouth Times, Republican; A. B. Mills, editor and publisher, McLouth.

Perry News, Republican; H. W. Spangler, editor, Perry.

—7

Jewell County Monitor, Republican; R. F. Vaughn, editor and proprietor, Mankato.

Jewell County Review, Republican; S. M. Weed, editor and proprietor, Mankato.

Jewell County Republican, Republican; Benjamin Musser and W. C. Palmer, publishers, Jewell City.

Burr Oak Herald, Republican; Walter B. Tibbals, editor and proprietor, Burr Oak.

The Western Advocate, Alliance; William E. Bush and Mattie E. Convis, editors and proprietors, Burr Oak.

The Olathe Mirror, Republican; H. A. Perkins, editor, publisher and proprietor, Olatha.

The Kansas Patron, Grange; George Black, editor, Johnson County Coöperative Association, publisher, Olathe.

The Kansas Star; published by the students of the Deaf and Dumb Institution, Olathe.

The Johnson County Democrat, Democratic; Wm. Williams & Son, editors, publishers and proprietors, Olathe.

Spring Hill New Era, Prohibition; J. W. Sowers, editor, publisher and proprietor, Spring Hill.

The Kansan, neutral; E. L. McKee, editor and publisher, Gardner.

Kearny County Advocate, Republican; W. B. Logan, editor, L. P. Kimball, publisher, Lakin.

The Lakin Index, Republican; F. R. French, editor and proprietor, Lakin.

Hartland Herald, Democratic; Joseph Dillon, editor and proprietor, Hartland.

Kingman County Democrat, Democratic; W. A. Eaton, editor and publisher, Kingman.

The Leader-Courier, Republican; Morton Albaugh, editor, publisher, and proprietor, Kingman.

The Kingman Journal, People's Party; J. A. Maxey, editor and publisher, Kingman.

Norwich News, Republican; J. O. Graham, editor and publisher, Norwich.

The Cunningham Herald, Republican; J. Geo. Smith, editor and publisher, Cunningham.

The Spivey Index, Republican; Geo. W. Kelley, editor and publisher, Spivey.

The Kiowa County Signal, Republican; Will E. Bolton, editor, proprietor and publisher, Greensburg.

Kiowa County Times, People's Party; C. F. Mingenback, editor, Greensburg.

The Republican, Republican; M. M. Lee, editor, M. M. Lee and H. B. Graves, publishers, Greensburg.

The Parsons Sun (daily and weekly), Republican; H. H. Lusk, editor, publisher, and proprietor, Parsons.

The Parsons Eclipse (daily and weekly), independent; J. B. Lamb's Sons, editors and proprietors, Parsons.

Parsons Palladium, Democratic; Frank W. Frye, editor and publisher, Parsons.

Weekly Clarion, Republican; L. A. Sheward, editor, publisher, and proprietor, Parsons.

Journal, Republican; H. C. Lombeer, editor, Parsons.

Oswego Courant, Republican; S. C. Steinberger, editor, publisher, and proprietor, Oswego.

Labette County Statesman, People's Party; Abbott & Abbott, editors, publishers, and proprietors, Oswego.

The Oswego Independent, Republican; M. A. McGill & Sons, editors and publishers, Oswego.

Labette County Democrat, Democratic; J. M. Landis, editor and publisher, Oswego.

The Chetopa Advance, Republican; J. M. Cavaness, editor and publisher, Chetopa.

The Chetopa Democrat, Democratic; J. J. Rambo, editor, publisher, and proprietor, Chetopa.

The Mound Valley Herald, Republican; W. F. Thrall, editor and publisher, Mound Valley.

Mills' Weekly World, People's Party; Harry Mills, editor and publisher, Altamont.

The Wilsonton Journal, neutral; Mrs. Augustus Wilson, editor and proprietor, Wilsonton.

The Edna Independent, independent; A. C. Veach, editor and publisher, Edna.

LANE COUNTY.

Lane County Herald, Republican; F. P. Stearns, editor and proprietor, Dighton.

Dighton Journal, Republican; Ben. L. Green, editor and proprietor, Dighton.

Lane County Farmer, People's Party; Ed. Lucas, editor and publisher, Dighton.

LEAVENWORTH COUNTY.

The Leavenworth Times (daily and weekly), Republican; D. R. Anthony, editor and publisher, Leavenworth.

The Evening Standard, Democratic; T. A. Hurd, president, Frank T. Lynch, treasurer and manager, Leavenworth.

The Evening Sun, independent; Evening Sun Publishing Company, publishers, Leavenworth.

The Leavenworth Post (daily), Democratic; Max Gronefeld, editor, German Publishing Company, publishers, Leavenworth.

The Leavenworth Advocate, Republican; W. B. Towsend and B. K. Bruce, editors and publishers, Leavenworth.

The Orphan's Friend (monthly), charitable; Mrs. Thos. Carney, editor, Mrs. De-Forest Fairchild, associate editor, Leavenworth.

Home Record (monthly), charitable; Mrs. C. H. Cushing, editor, Leavenworth.

Taps (monthly), neutral; Andrew J. Smith, editor, Rev. W. J. Gillespie, associate editor, W. B. Shockley, publisher, National Military Home.

The Tonganoxie Mirror, Republican; Wm. Heynen, editor and proprietor, Tonganoxie.

The Weekly Sentinel, neutral; W. A. Brice, editor and proprietor, Tonganoxie.

LINCOLN COUNTY.

The Lincoln Republican, Republican; Tell W. Walton, editor, publisher and proprietor, Lincoln.

The Lincoln Beacon, People's Party; W. S. and Anna C. Wait, editors and publishers, Lincoln.

Lincoln County Farmer, People's Party; A. W. Woody, editor, Lincoln.

Barnard Times, Independent; John Lewis, editor, I. A. Ballard, publisher, Barnard.

La Cygne Weekly Journal, Republican; J. P. Kenea and Ed. C. Lane, editors, publishers and proprietors, La Cygne.

The Visitor (monthly), M. E. Church; Rev. D. F. Holtz, editor and publisher, La Cygne.

The Pleasanton Observer, Republican; J. P. Kenea, Ed. C. Lane and J. Frank Smith, editors, publishers and proprietors, Pleasanton.

The Pleasanton Herald, People's Party; J. E. Latimer, editor and publisher, Pleasanton.

Mound City Progress, Republican; N. Campbell and Frank Waymire, editors and proprietors, Mound City.

The Torch of Liberty, People's Party; G. H. Townsley & Son, publishers and proprietors, Geo. H. Townsley, editor, Mound City.

Linn County Clarion, Republican; C. J. and F. C. Trigg, editors and publishers, Mound City.

The Blue Mound Sun, Republican; J. N. Barnes, editor, J. N. and S. E. Barnes, publishers, Blue Mound.

Goodrich Graphic, Neutral; C. M. Brown, editor and publisher, Goodrich.

Parker Weekly Pilot, Republican; Carl Brann, editor and publisher, Parker.

The Western Observer, Republican; W. H. Cotton, editor, W. J. Neil, proprietor, Monument.

The Oakley Graphic, Republican; C. V. Kinney, editor, Graphic Publishing Company, publishers, Oakley.

Winona Clipper, Republican; Park R. Mitten, editor, publisher and proprietor. Winona.

Augustine Herald, neutral; E. P. & E. L. Stephenson, editors and proprietors, Augustine.

Logan County Republican, Republican; J. K. Hupp and C. E. Bickel, editors and proprietors, Russell Springs.

The Emporia Republican (daily and weekly), Republican; C. V. Eskridge, editor, publisher and proprietor, Emporia.

The Emporia Standard, People's Party; J. R. Graham & Co., editors, publishers. and proprietors, Emporia.

The Emporia Gazette (daily), independent; J. R. Graham & Co., editors, publishers and proprietors Emporia.

College Life (monthly), literary; H. M. Kingrey, editor, Emporia.

Baptist Visitor; Rev. L. H. Holt, editor and publisher, Emporia.

Columbia; W. D. Evans, Emporia.

Normal Quarterly, literary; W. C. Stevenson, editor, Emporia.

The Hartford Call, Republican; W. J. Means, editor and publisher, Hartford.

Hartford News, independent; C. C. Rogan, editor and publisher, Hartford.

The Americus Greeting, neutral, C. V. Alrich and Eva Alrich, editors and publishers, Americus.

The Tidings, Republican; Major A. Paul, editor and proprietor, Allen.

Neosho Rapids Pilot, W. M. Adams, editor and proprietor, Neosho Rapids.

The McPherson Freeman, Republican; H. B. Kelly, editor and publisher, McPherson.

The McPherson Republican, Republican; S. G. Mead, editor, publisher and proprietor, McPherson.

The Democrat, Democratic; Warren Knaus, editor, publisher and proprietor McPherson.

The Industrial Union, People's Party; George C. Findley, editor, Union Publishing Co., publishers, McPherson.

Kansas Vim, Republican; George P. Hall, editor, George P. Hall and F. Potter, publishers, McPherson.

Alliance Index, Alliance; S. Ruckman, editor and manager, McPherson.

The Educator and Companion (monthly), educational; J. M. Snyder, editor and publisher, McPherson. (Organ of McPherson College.)

The Lindsborg News, Republican; A. Ringwald, editor and publisher, Lindsborg.

The Canton Republican, Republican; D. W. Stone, editor and publisher, Canton.

The Moundridge Leader, neutral; G. H. Wichman, editor, Moundridge.

The Marquette Tribune, Republican; Banna F. Cress, editor and publisher, Marquette.

The Galva Times, People's Party; J. H. Baker, editor and publisher, Galva.

MARION COUNTY.

Marion Record, Republican; E. W. Hoch, editor and publisher, Marion.

Marion Weekly Globe, Republican; C. N. Whitaker, editor, Whitaker & Jones, publishers, Marion.

Marion Times, Republican; C. E. Foote, editor, H. Kuhn, proprietor. Marion.

Hillsboro Anzeiger, Republican (German); J. F. Harms, editor and proprietor, Hillsboro.

The Peabody Gazette, Republican; W. H. Morgan, editor and publisher, Peabody.

The Peabody Graphic, Republican; Will G. Christ, editor, Graphic Publishing Co., publishers, Peabody.

The Florence Herald, Republican; W. H. Booth, editor and publisher, Florence.

Florence Bulletin, Democratic; J. B. Crouch, editor and publisher, Florence.

Burns Mirror, Republican; Will H. Peter, editor and publisher, Burns.

MARSHALL COUNTY.

The Marshall County News, Republican; Geo. T. Smith, publisher and proprietor, Marysville.

Marshall County Democrat, Democratic; Wm. Becker, editor and publisher, Marysville.

Marysville Post; Wm. Becker, editor and publisher, Marysville.

Evening Democrat; Wm. Becker, editor and publisher, Marysville.

The People's Advocate, Union Labor; Clark & Runneals, editors and publishers, Marysville.

Waterville Telegraph, Republican; Henry C. Willson, editor and publisher, Waterville.

Blue Rapids Times, Republican; E. M. Brice, editor and publisher, Blue Rapids.

Blue Rapids Motor, Republican; R. A. & H. A. Russell, editors, publishers and proprietors, Blue Rapids.

Holiness War News, religious; Bradford and Sarah Washburn, editors and proprietors, (printed for editors by E. M. Brice,) Blue Rapids.

The Frankfort Bee, Republican; W. J. Granger, editor and proprietor, Frankfort.

The Frankfort Sentinel, Alliance; S. H. Peters, publisher, Frankfort.

The Axtell Anchor, Republican; Ross & Nye, publishers, Axtell.

The Star, Republican; Dan. M. Mabie, editor and publisher, Beattie.

The Irving Leader, Republican; Hugh Thompson, editor and publisher, Irving.

The Oketo Sun; C. E. Williamson, editor, Oketo.

The Summerfield Sun, Moore & Kendall, editors and publishers, Summerfield.

MEADE COUNTY.

The Meade County Globe, Republican; Frank Fahr, editor and publisher, Meade.

Meade County Democrat, Democratic; Sam Lawrence, editor, L. J. Smith, manager, Democrat Publishing County, publishers, Meade.

The Meade Republican, Republican; T. J. Palmer, editor and·proprietor, Meade.

MIAMI COUNTY.

Western Spirit, Democratic; B. J. Sheridan, editor, publisher and proprietor, Paola.

The Miami Republican, Republican; W. D. Greason, editor, publisher and proprietor, Paola.

The Paola Times, Republican; John W. Bell, editor and publisher, Paola.

The Louisburg Herald, Republican; R. H. Cadwallader, editor and publisher, Louisburg.

Osawatomie Graphic, Republican; Frank Pyle, editor and publisher, Osawatomie.

Farmers' Signal, People's Party; John W. Hall, editor, Hall & Carter, publishers, Osawatomie.

Fontana News, independent; J. B. Bomar, editor and publisher, Fontana.

MITCHELL COUNTY.

The Beloit Gazette, Republican; S. H. Dodge, editor and publisher, Beloit.

Beloit Weekly Courier, Republican; W. H. Caldwell, editor and publisher, Beloit.

The Western Call, People's Party; J. W. and J. S. Parks, editors, Beloit.

The Public Record, Republican; L. L. Alrich, editor and publisher, Cawker City.

The Cawker City Times, Republican; J. W. McBride, editor, publisher and proprietor, Cawker City.

Northwest Expositor (monthly), religious; Rev. M. R. Myer, editor, L. L. Alrich, publisher, Cawker City.

The Grellett Student, educational; Erwin Stanley and students, editors, L. L. Alrich, publisher, Cawker City.

The Kansas Herald, Republican; F. J. Hulaniski, editor and publisher, Glen Elder.

Tri-County News. Republican; Seward Jones, editor, C. H. Sawyer, publisher and proprietor, Scottsville.

MONTGOMERY COUNTY.

Star and Kansan, Democratic; H. W. Young, publisher and proprietor, Independence.

South Kansas Tribune, Republican; W. T. and C. Yoe, editors, publishers and proprietors, Independence.

The Evening Reporter, neutral; T. N. Sickels, editor and proprietor, Independence.

The Journal, Republican; D. Stewart Elliott, editor, Coffeyville

The News, Democratic; E. W. Lyon, editor and proprietor, Coffeyville.

Cherryvale Champion, Republican; F. G. Moore, publisher, S. P. Moore, editor. Cherryvale.

Cherryvale Republican, Republican; Republican News Co., publishers, Cherryvale.

Southern Kansas Farmer, Republican; —— Richardson, editor, Farmer Publishing Co., publisher, Cherryvale.

The Elk City Enterprise, Alliance; J. R. Chariton, publisher, Elk City.

The Caney Chronicle, Republican; J. T. McKee & Sons, Caney.

The Caney Times, Alliance; C. J. Reynolds, editor, Times Publishing Co., publishers, Caney.

The Liberty Review, Union Labor; A. S. Duley, editor, Miss Florence Duley, assistant editor, Liberty.

The Havana Globe, neutral; O. L. Cullison and C. P. Buffington, editors, Havana.

MORRIS COUNTY.

The Council Grove Republican, Republican; W. F. Waller, editor, Republican Printing Company, publishers, Council Grove.

Council Grove Guard, Democratic; Dill, Bell & Sharp, editors, publishers and proprietors, Council Grove.

The Dunlap Courier, independent; S. M. Padgett, publisher, Dunlap.

White City Register, Republican; W. G. Means & Co., publishers, White City.

The Dwight Wasp, Republican; J. D. & H. F. Parsons, editors and publishers, Dwight.

Wilsey Bulletin, People's Party; G. W. Coffin, jr., editor, Wilsey.

MORTON COUNTY.

The Monitor Republican, Republican; Glenn S. and Frank Van Gundy, editors and publishers, Richfield.

The Taloga Star, Prohibition; H. W. Worthington, editor and publisher, Taloga.

NEMAHA COUNTY.

Seneca Courier-Democrat, Democratic; A. P. and C. H. Herold, editors, publishers, and proprietors, Seneca.

The Seneca Tribune, Republican; W. H. & G. F. Jordon, editors, Seneca.

The Seneca News, People's Party; James M. Jones, editor and proprietor, Mrs. James M. Jones, associate editor, Seneca.

Nemaha County Republican, Republican; J. F. Clough, editor, publisher and proprietor, Sabetha.

The Sabetha Herald, Republican; Flora P. Hogbin, editor, A. C. Hogbin, publisher, Sabetha.

Nemaha Spectator, Republican; J. T. Briston, editor, publisher and proprietor, Wetmore.

Centralia Journal; A. J. Birchfield, editor, Journal Publishing Co., publishers, Centralia.

The Bern Press, neutral; F. P. Harbour, editor, publisher and proprietor, Bern.

NEOSHO COUNTY.

The Osage Mission Journal, Democratic; John R. Brunt, editor, publisher and proprietor, Osage Mission.

Chanute Weekly Times, Republican; C. T. Nixon and M. H. Ruff, editors, Times Publishing Company, publishers, Chanute.

The Chanute Blade, Democratic; John A. Cross, editor, Blade Publishing Company, publishers, Chanute.

Chanute Vidette, Republican; G. M. Dewey and J. H. Williams. editors and publishers, Chanute.

Republican-Record, Republican; Benjamin J. Smith and C. E. Harbough, editors and publishers, Erie.

The Erie Sentinel, People's Party; John W. Locke, editor and publisher, Erie.

Head Light, Republican; C. T. Ewing, editor and publisher, Thayer.

NESS COUNTY.

Ness City Times, Republican; S. L. Moorhead, editor and proprietor, Ness City.

Ness County News, Republican; J. K. Barnd, editor and proprietor, Ness City.

Walnut Valley Sentinel, Democratic; J. W. Brown, editor, Ness City.

The Norton Courier, Republican; F. M. Duvall, editor, Norton.

The Champion, Republican; J. W. Conway, editor, publisher and proprietor, Norton.

Weekly New Era, People's Party; W. H. Hiles, editor, Norton.

The Almena Plaindealer, Republican; John Dyatt and S. C. Youngman, publishlishers and proprietors, Almena.

The Osage County Chronicle, Republican; J. N. McDonald, editor, publisher and proprietor, Burlingame.

The National Echo, neutral; Kate Wathren, editor, W. H. Mundy, publisher and proprietor, Burlingame.

Osage City Free Press, Republican; D. J. Roberts, editor, J. V. Admire, associate editor, D. J. Roberts and R. J. Hill, proprietors, Osage City.

Kansas People, Republican; Elijah Mills, editor, Osage City.

The Osage County Times, People's Party; George Hoover, editor, Burlingame.

The Lyndon Journal, Republican; W. A. Madaris, editor and publisher, Lyndon.

Osage County Graphic, Republican; R. A. Miller, editor, Graphic Publishing Company, publishers, Lyndon.

The People's Herald, People's Party; A. C. Easter, editor, Geo. Rogers, publisher, Lyndon.

The Carbondalian, Republican; Reuben F. Playford, editor and proprietor, Carbondale.

The Osage County Republican, Republican; Miller and Ellis, editors, Quenemo.

The Scranton Gazette, neutral; Ralph M. Parker and Q. K. Stakebake, editors and proprietors, Scranton.

The Overbrook Herald, Republican; S. A. Stauffer and M. R. Stauffer, publishers, Overbrook.

Melvern Review, neutral; I. and J. E. Farley, editors, A. R. Ball, publisher, Melvern.

Osborne County Farmer, Republican; W. S. Tilton and C. W. Landis, editors, publishers and proprietors, Osborne.

Osborne County News, People's Party; W. D. Gerard & Co., editors and publishers, Osborne.

Downs Times, Republican; E. D. Craft & Son, editors, publishers and proprietors, Downs.

The Downs Chief, Democratic; W. H. Whitmore, editor, Chief Publishing Company, publishers, Downs.

Western Empire, Republican; H. M. Fletcher & Co., editors and publishers, Alton.

The Minneapolis Messenger, Republican; A. P. Riddle, editor, publisher and proprietor, Minneapolis.

Solomon Valley Democrat, Democratic; Park S. Warren, managing editor, Minapolis.

The Minneapolis Commercial, Republican; W. M. Campbell, editor and proprietor, W. M. & E. K. Campbell, publishers, Minneapolis.

Kansas Union, People's Party; J. C. & F. O. Cline, editors and proprietors, Minneapolis.

Kansas Workman (monthly), A. O. U. W.; A. P. Riddle, editor and proprietor, Minneapolis.

The Sprig of Myrtle (monthly), Knights of Pythias; A. P. Riddle, editor and proprietor, Minneapolis.

The Delphos Republican, Republican; J. M. Waterman, editor, J. M. Waterman & Son, publishers, Delphos.

Herald and Star, Democratic; D. B. Loudon, editor and publisher, Bennington.

The Tescott Herald, Republican; Guy A. Adams, editor and proprietor, Tescott.

PAWNEE COUNTY.

Larned Chronoscope (weekly), Republican; Frank J. Davis and Wm. G. Stevens, editors, The Larned Printing Co., publishers, Larned.

The Larned Eagle-Optic, Democratic; T. E. Leftwich, managing editor, A. B. Leftwich, business manager, Optic Steam Printing Co., publishers, Larned.

PHILLIPS COUNTY.

The Kirwin Chief, Republican; John R. Lane, editor and publisher, Kirwin.

The Independent, independent; H. W. and S. C. Landes, editors, publishers and proprietors, Kirwin.

Phillipsburg Herald, Republican; R. A. Dague and E. E. Brainerd, publishers and proprietors, Phillipsburg.

Phillipsburg Democrat, Democratic; F. S. Brong, publisher and proprietor, Phillipsburg.

The Phillipsburg Dispatch, Republican; J. M. McNay & Co., publishers, Phillipsburg.

The Logan Republican, Republican; A. W. Crippin, publisher, Logan Printing Co., proprietors, Logan.

Long Island Leader, People's Party; J. N. Curl, editor, publisher and proprietor, Long Island.

Phillips County Inter-Ocean, Republican; H. S. Montgomery, publisher, Long Island.

POTTAWATOMIE COUNTY.

Pottawatomie County Times, Independent ; Sylvester Fowler, editor, R. M. Chilcott and Sylvester Fowler, publishers and proprietors, Louisville.

The Kansas Agriculturist, Republican; Ernest A. Weller, editor, publisher and proprietor, Wamego.

St. Marys Star, People's Party; P. J. Jackson and C. W. Graham, editors, publishers and proprietors, St. Marys.

St. Marys Gazette, Republican; J. S. Carpenter, editor, publisher and proprietor, St. Marys.

The Dial (monthly), literary; W. John Garvey, editor-in-chief, Francis E. Carroll, exchange editor, Patrick O'Sullivan, business manager, published by the students of St. Marys College, St. Marys.

The Westmoreland Recorder, Republican; W. F. Hill, editor, publisher and proprietor, Westmoreland.

The Westmoreland Indicator, Republican; Anderson Bros., Westmoreland.

Alliance News, People's Party; J. C. Stanley, editor, publisher and proprietor, Westmoreland.

The Onaga Herald, Republican; F. S. Haughawout, editor, publisher and proprietor, Onaga.

Olsburg News Letter, Republican; Lewis Havermale, editor, publisher and proprietor, Olsburg.

Havensville Register, Republican; C. A. Hill and W. A. Hill, editors and publishers, Havensville.

The Times-Republican, Republican; —— Sponsler, J. L. Sponsler and —— Carr, editors and proprietors, Hutchinson.

The Alliance Gazette, People's Party; Warren Foster, editor and publisher, Hutchinson.

The Clipper, society and dramatic; W. A. Loe, publisher, Hutchinson.

The Nickerson Argosy, Republican; W. F. Hendry and J. E. Humphrey, editors and publishers, Nickerson.

The Nickerson Register, Republican; Harry H. Brightman, editor and publisher. Nickerson.

Arlington Enterprise, Republican; Eaton & Morton, editors and publishers, Arlington.

The Sylvia Banner, People's Party; Jeff. Bower, editor, M. P. Womack, manager. Sylvia.

The Haven Independent, People's Party; Warren Foster, proprietor, C. A. Hamlin, editor, Haven.

Turon Headlight, independent; E. F. Koontz, editor, M. Benefiel, business manager, Turon.

REPUBLIC COUNTY.

The Belleville Telescope, Republican; J. C. Humphrey, publisher and proprietor, Belleville.

The Belleville Democrat-Press, Democratic; W. J. A. Montgomery, editor and publisher, Belleville.

Republic County Freeman, People's Party; H. N. Boyd, publisher and proprietor, Belleville.

Scandia Journal, Republican; I. C. Ware, editor and publisher, Scandia.

Republic City News, Republican; Gomer T. Davies, editor, publisher and proprietor, Republic City.

The Cuba Daylight, Republican; J. J. Shimek, editor, Daylight Publishing Co., publishers, Cuba.

Cuba Dispatch; H. G. McDonald, editor and publisher, Cuba.

Cortland Register, Republican-Alliance; Joe A. Litsinger, editor and publisher, Cortland.

RICE COUNTY.

Sterling Gazette, Republican; W. H. Hornaday, editor, publisher and proprietor, Sterling.

The Bulletin, Republican; J. E. Junkin, editor, Junkin & Steele, publishers, Sterling.

Sterling Weekly Champion, independent; Thos. L. Powers, editor and publisher, Sterling.

The Lyons Republican, Republican; Clark Conkling, editor, Frank E. Hoyt, manager, Lyons.

The Lyons Tribune, Republican; Elbert W. Hoyt, editor, A. W. Hoyt, publisher, Lyons.

Central Kansas Democrat, Democratic; Fred. N. Cooper, editor, Minnie Wood Cooper, publisher, Lyons.

Rice County Eagle, People's Party; D. P. Hodgdon, editor and proprietor, Lyons.

The Chase Record, independent; Geo. W. Loman, editor and proprietor, Chase.

The Little River Monitor, Republican; W. G. Greenbank, editor and publisher, Little River.

Geneseo Herald, Republican; W. R. White, publisher, Geneseo.

Rice County News, neutral; H. T. Murray, editor and publisher, Frederick.

RILEY COUNTY.

The Nationalist, Republican; R. D. Parker and Geo. F. Thompson, editors, publishers and proprietors, Manhattan.

The Industrialist, educational and agricultural; edited by the President and Faculty, Geo. T. Fairchild, president, Manhattan.

The Manhattan Republic (daily and weekly), independent; A. A. Stewart, editor and publisher, Manhattan.

The Mercury, Democratic; J. J. Davis, editor and publisher, Manhattan.

The Signal, People's Party; McDonald, Atkins & Co. (Jas. W. McDonald and Dudley Atkins), proprietors, D. Atkins, publisher, Valdy Atkins, local editor, Manhattan.

The Kansas Telephone (monthly), religious; Rev. R. D. Parker, editor and publisher, Manhattan.

The Manhattan Homestead (monthly), real estate; L. R. Elliott, editor, F. B. Elliott, assistant, Manhattan.

Manhattan District Methodist (monthly), religious; Rev. James Lawrence, editor and publisher, Manhattan.

The Enterprise, Republican; J. H. Colt, editor and publisher, Randolph.

Leonardville Monitor, Republican; P. S. Loofbourrow, editor and publisher, Leonardville.

The Bala City Advance, Republican; Samuel Johnson, publisher, Bala City Advance Publishing Co., proprietors, Bala City.

The Riley Regent, Republican; Chas. A. Southwick, editor, Chas. A. Southwick and Geo. W. Southwick, publishers, Riley.

ROOKS COUNTY.

The Western News, Republican; E. Owen, editor, E. Owen and O. T. Owen, publishers and proprietors, Stockton.

Rooks County Record, Republican; W. L. Chambers, editor, publisher and proprietor, Stockton.

The Salina Sun, Republican; W. H. Johnson, editor, publisher and proprietor, Salina.

The Weekly Tidings, religious; Rev. A. N. See, editor, publisher and proprietor, Salina.

The Salina Union, People's Party; A. C. Pattee and Frank Honeywell, publishers, Salina.

The Evening News, independent; J. H. Padgett, editor, Salina.

Woman's Mission Star, religious; C. M. Williams, editor and manager, Salina.

The Western Odd Fellow (monthly); A. L. Voorhis, editor, publisher and proprietor, Salina.

Vade'Mecum, advertising agent; F..F. Oakley, editor and publisher, Salina.

The Kansas Churchman (monthly), religious; Rev. E. P. Chittenden, editor, Salina.

The Normal Register (quarterly), educational; L. O. Thoroman, editor and manager, Salina.

The Gypsum Advocate, Republican; J. Wayne Amos, editor and publisher, Gypsum City.

The Earth, independent; M. S. Amos, editor, Brookville.

SCOTT COUNTY.

Scott County News, Republican; N. D. Adams, editor and proprietor, Scott City.

The Sentinel-Herald, People's Party; D. F. Hall, editor and publisher, Frank A. Capps, managing editor, Scott City.

SEDGWICK COUNTY.

The Wichita Eagle (daily and weekly), Republican; M. M. Murdock, editor, R. P. Murdock, business manager, Wichita.

The Wichita Beacon (daily and weekly), Democratic; John S. Richardson, editor and publisher, Wichita.

Wichita Republic, Independent; J. S. Jennings, editor, publisher and proprietor, Wichita.

The Arrow, Republican; Lon. Hoding, publisher, Wichita.

Wichita Herold (German), Democratic; John Hoenscheidt, manager, Wichita.

Kansas Staats Anzeiger (German), Democratic; John Hoenscheidt, manager, Wichita.

The Mirror (society), E. L. McKenzie, editor and publisher, Wichita.

The Kansas Commoner, People's Party; E. Kies, editor, Industrial Publishing Co., publishers, Wichita.

The Kansas Sunflower, Republican, J. B. Gibbs, jr.. editor, J. W. Gibbs, publisher, Wichita.

Western Methodist, religious; Rev. J. D. Botkins, editor, W. M. Starr, publisher, Wichita.

The Opinion; Opinion Printing Co., publishers, Wichita.

The Leader (monthly); G. W. Collings, editor.

The Wichita Record; A. N. Kellogg Newspaper Co., Wichita.

The Wichita Poultry Home; G. W. C. Jones, editor, Wichita.

The Kansas Cultivator and Stockman; Kansas Cultivator and Stockman, publishers, Wichita.

The Kansas Star, Democratic; W. E. Huttman, publisher, Henry W. Huttman, managing editor, Wichita.

The Valley Center News, Republican; Whitmore & Beach, publishers, Valley Center.

Colwich Courier, Independent; J. A. Mahuran, editor and proprietor, Colwich.

The Weekly Mount Hope Mentor, Republican; C. V. Welch, editor and proprietor.

SEWARD COUNTY.

The Liberal Leader, Democratic; Lambert Willstaedt, editor and publisher, Liberal.

The Liberal Lyre, Republican; H. V. Nichols, editor and publisher, Liberal.

The Arkalon News, Republican; A. K. Staufer, editor and proprietor, Arkalon.

The Springfield Republican, Republican; H. F. Thompson, editor and publisher, Springfield.

SHAWNEE COUNTY.

The Topeka Capital (daily and weekly), Republican; J. K. Hudson, editor and president, James L. King, vice-president, Dell Keiser, secretary and business manager, Herold T. Chase, treasurer, Topeka.

State Journal (daily), Republican; Frank P. MacLennan, editor and publisher, Topeka.

The Kansas Democrat (daily), Democratic; C. K. Holliday, jr., president; W. P. Tomlinson, vice-president, Harry Garvey, publisher, Kansas Democrat Publishing Company, proprietors, Topeka.

Kansas Farmer (agricultural), Kansas Farmer Publishing Company, publishers, Samuel J. Crawford, president, J. B. McAfee, vice-president, D. C. Nellis, secretary, H. A. Heath, manager, W. A. Peffer, editor, Topeka.

Kansas Telegraph (German), Democratic; H. Von Langen, editor, Kansas Telegraph Publishing Company, publishers, Topeka.

The Lance, literary; Harry Frost, editor and publisher, Topeka.

The Kansas Newspaper Union; F. P. Baker, editor, Topeka.

Western School Journal, educational; John MacDonald, editor and publisher, Topeka.

The Sunday Ledger, literary; Geo. W. Reed, editor, Topeka.

Our Messenger (monthly), W. C. T. U.; Olive P. Bray, editor, Topeka.

The Washburn Argo (monthly), literary; Albert Tucker, editor-in-chief, Harry E. Mills and Eugene L. Smith, business managers, Topeka.

Kansas United Presbyterian (monthly), religious; M. F. McKirahan, publisher, W. J. Neeley, business manager, Topeka.

Kansas Medical Journal (monthly); J. E. Minney, editor-in-chief, Topeka.

The Kansas Financier (semi-monthly); S. L. Seabrook, editor and proprietor, Topeka.

Western Veteran, G. A. R.; O. H. Coulter and Lewis Hanback, editors, Topeka.

The Grand Army Journal, G. A. R.; T. R. Hornaday, editor and publisher, Topeka.

The Advocate, People's Party; S. McLallin, editor, Mrs. Anna L. Diggs and J. C. Hebbard, associate editors, Topeka.

The Alliance Tribune, People's Party; G. K. Estes, editor, Alliance Tribune Publishing Company, publishers.

The Association Reflector, Y. M. C. A.; W. H. Holmes, editor, Young Men's Christian Association, publishers, Topeka.

The Budget, (monthly), advertising; J. F. Daniels, editor and manager, Topeka.

The Illustrated Weekly, E. L. Shelton, editor and publisher, Topeka.

The Topeka Republican, Republican; J. C. Thomas, editor, M. R. Chesney, business manager, Topeka.

Lucifer—The Light Bearer; M. Harman, editor and publisher, Topeka.

Kansas Church Tidings, (monthly), religious; L. A. Rudisell, editor, Topeka.

Washburn Reporter, literary; J. F. Lawson, editor-in-chief, J. L. Posten, business manager, Topeka.

Kansas Trade Journal (monthly), advertising; J. F. Daniels, publisher, Topeka.

The Western Poultry Breeder; Thos. Owen, editor, Owen & Co., publishers, Topeka.

Ham and Eggs or the Hog and the Hen; Thos. Owen, editor, Owen & Co., publishers, Topeka.

Kansas Methodist Times (semi-monthly), religious; Rev. James Lawrence, editor and publisher, Topeka.

The Detective World; Fred L. McPherson, manager, World Publishing Company, publishers, Topeka.

The Topeka News, Republican; G. F. Kimball, editor, Kimball Printing Company, publishers, North Topeka.

Spirit of Kansas, Republican; G. F. Kimball, editor, Kimball Printing Company, publishers, North Topeka.

The Topeka Mail, Republican; Frank A. Root, editor, North Topeka.

The Rossville Times, neutral; Geo. A. Weller, editor and publisher, Rossville.

The Oakland News, Republican; L. A. Rudisell, editor, L. A. Rudisell, B. T. Williams and T. J. Nichols, publishers, Oakland.

Potwin Tribune; Edward Epps, editor and publisher, Potwin.

SHERIDAN COUNTY.

The Hoxie Sentinel, Republican; W. L. Humes, editor and proprietor, Hoxie.

The Hoxie Democrat, People's Party; S. P. Davidson, editor, publisher, and proprietor, Hoxie.

The Selden Times, Republican; E. E. Van Epps, publisher, Selden.

SHERMAN COUNTY.

Sherman County Dark Horse, Republican; J. H. Tait, editor and proprietor, Goodland.

The Goodland News, People's Party; E. F. Tennant, editor and publisher, Goodland.

The Goodland Republican, Republican; J. H. Stewart, editor, Helena Stewart, assistant editor, Goodland.

The Academy Microscope and Messenger, literary; G. M. Caldwell, editor and publisher, Goodland.

State Line Register, People's Party; Charles A. Fitch, editor, J. Frank Longanecker, publisher, Lamborn.

SMITH COUNTY.

The Pioneer Bulletin, Republican; J. N. Beacom and W. H. Nelson, publishers, Smith Center.

Stewart's Bazoo, Democratic; Jack Stewart, editor and proprietor, Smith Center.

Smith County Journal, People's Party; M. L. Lockwood and K. Lockwood, editors and publishers, Smith Center.

Gaylord Herald, Republican; Lew C. Headley, editor, publisher and proprietor, Gaylord.

The Lebanon Criterion, Republican; W. H. Wahl, editor and publisher, Lebanon.

Lebanon Journal, People's Party; J. A. Wright, editor and publisher, Lebanon.

The Kensington Mirror, Republican; O. L. Reed, editor, Kensington.

STAFFORD COUNTY.

Stafford Semi-Weekly Republican, Republican; Dr. Geo. W. Akers, editor, Geo. W. and Art B. Akers, proprietors, Stafford.

The Alliance Herald, People's Party; May Garvin, editor and publisher, Stafford.

The St. John Weekly News, Republican; W. A. Potter, editor and proprietor, St. John.

County Capital, People's Party; John B. Hilmes, editor, St. John.

The Advance, Republican; W. K. P. Dow, publisher, St. John.

STANTON COUNTY.

The Johnson City Journal, Republican; J. A. Webster, editor, publisher and proprietor, Johnson City.

The Stanton County Republican, Republican; P. J. Haas, editor and proprietor, Johnson City.

STEVENS COUNTY.

Woodsdale Sentinel, People's Party; S. N. Wood and Ada McClure, editors, A. C. McClure, publisher, Woodsdale.

Stevens County Tribune, People's Party; A. A. Dunmire, editor, A. A. Dunmire and J. C. Gerrond, proprietors, Woodsdale.

The Voorhees Vindicator, People's Party; O. R. Wright, editor, Voorhees.

Hugoton Hermes, Republican; C. M. Davis, editor and proprietor, Hugoton.

SUMNER COUNTY.

The Sumner County Press, Republican; Jacob Stotler, editor and manager, Will R. Stotler, assistant, Wellington.

Sumner County Standard, Democratic; Luke Herring, editor, Wellington.

The Wellington Monitor, Republican; J. G. Campbell and Chas. Hood, editors and publishers, Wellington.

The Christian Reminder, religious; J. G. M. Hursh, editor, Wellington.

People's Voice, People's Party; Lyman Naugle, editor and publisher, Wellington.

The Daily Mail, J. H. Shade, editor, Fred. Bohanna, publisher, Wellington.

The Methodist News (monthly), religious; Rev. L. M. Hortley and Rev. S. Price, editors, Wellington.

The Mocking Bird, Republican; Wm. M. Massey, publisher and proprietor, E. L. Cline, manager, Oxford.

The Caldwell Journal, People's Party; R. B. Swartout, publisher, Caldwell.

The Caldwell News, Republican; Robert T. Simons, publisher, Caldwell.

Belle Plaine News, independent; D. M. Turley, editor, Belle Plaine.

The Mulvane Record, independent; G. L. Reed, editor, publisher and proprietor, Mulvane.

Geuda Springs Herald, Republican; W. C. Barnes, editor and proprietor, Geuda Springs.

The Argonia Clipper, independent; S. W. Duncan, publisher, Argonia.

Conway Springs Star, Republican; D. W. Cain and P. W. Bast, publishers, Conway Springs.

The South Haven New Era, independent; C. A. Branscombe, editor, publisher and proprietor, South Haven.

The Patrick Henry, Anti-Monopolist; Samuel Nutt, editor, published by the U. O. A. M., South Haven.

THOMAS COUNTY.

The Thomas County Cat, Republican; G. F. Roberts, editor and proprietor, Colby.

The Colby Tribune, Republican; P. A. Troutfetter, editor and proprietor, Colby.

The Free Press, Democratic; J. L. Loar, editor, W. T. Logan, publisher, Colby.

TREGO COUNTY.

Western Kansas World, Republican; S. R. Cowick and C. E. Cosby, Wakeeney.

WABAUNSEE COUNTY.

The Alma News, People's Party; I. D. Gardiner, editor, publisher and proprietor, Alma.

Alma Enterprise, Republican; V. C. Welch and Frank I. Sage, editors, publishers and proprietors, Alma.

The Alma Signal, Democratic; Matt. Thomson, editor, publisher and proprietor, Alma.

The Eskridge Star, Republican; W. H. Melrose, editor, publisher and proprietor, Eskridge.

The Alta Vista Record, Republican; J. C. Padgett, editor, publisher and proprietor, Alta Vista.

WALLACE COUNTY.

The Western Times, Republican; Mrs. Kate Russell-Doering, editor and proprietor, Sharon Springs.

The Sharon Springs Leader, Republican; Tune Bentley, editor and proprietor, Sharon Springs.

The Alliance Echo, People's Party; J. K. Laycock and O. J. Benjamin, editors and proprietors, Sharon Springs.

The Weskansan, Republican; Ed. Carter, editor and proprietor, Weskan.

Wallace County Gazette, Republican; N. Fenstemaker, editor and proprietor, Wallace.

WASHINGTON COUNTY.

Washington Republican, People's Party; by L. J. Sprengle, Washington.

The Washington Register, Republican; J. B. Besack, editor, J. B. and J. E. Besack, publishers, Washington.

The Washington Post, Democratic; J. T. Hole and S. W. Veatch, editors, Washington.

The Hanover Democrat, Democratic; J. M. Hood, editor, J. M. Hood, and —— Munger, publishers, Hanover.

The Clifton Review, Republican; J. A. Branson, editor and proprietor, Clifton.

Greanleaf Journal, Republican; J. W. Bliss, editor, Frank D. Bliss, publisher, Greenleaf.

Haddam City Clipper, Republican; A. Tansel, editor, S. T. Yoder, local editor, Haddam.

The Barnes Enterprise, Republican; M. O. Reitzel, editor and publisher, Barnes.

Linn Local Record, independent; Lewis Cobb, editor and publisher, Linn.

WICHITA COUNTY.

Leoti Standard, Republican; C. S. Triplett, editor and publisher, Leoti.

Western Kansan; J. B. Milford, editor and publisher, Leoti.

The Selkirk Graphic; E. P. & L. L. Stephenson, editors and publishers, Selkirk.

WILSON COUNTY.

Wilson County Citizen, Republican; John S. Gilmore, editor, publisher and proprietor, Fredonia.

Fredonia Democrat, Democratic; T. Sherk, editor, Fredonia.

Neodesha Register, Republican; J. Kansas Morgan, editor and publisher, J. K. and J. B. Morgan, proprietors, Neodesha.

Altoona Journal, independent; M. A. Rhea, editor, publisher and proprietor, Altoona.

The Buffalo Advocate, Republican; Grant Keesling, editor and publisher, Buffalo.

WOODSON COUNTY.

The Post, Republican; J. M. Stout, editor and proprietor, Neoeho Falls.

The News, Republican; C. C. Clevenger, editor, Trueblood & Stephenson, proprietors, Yates Center.

The Woodson Democrat, Democratic; R. R. Wells, editor, publisher and proprietor, Yates Center.

The Farmers' Advocate, People's Party; N. A. and C. A. Macoubrie, publishers and proprietors, Yates Center.

The Toronto Republican, Republican; N. B. Buck and C. A. Buck, editors, publishers, and proprietors, Toronto.

WYANDOTTE COUNTY.

The Wyandotte Herald, Democratic; by V. J. Lane & Co., Kansas City.

The Kansas City Gazette (daily and weekly), Republican; George W. Martin, editor, Gazette Publishing Company, publishers, Kansas City.

Cromwell's Kansas Mirror, Republican; Mark Cromwell, editor and proprietor, Kansas City (Armourdale).

The Kansas Catholic, religious; John O'Flanagan, editor, Kansas Catholic Publishing Company, publishers, Kansas City.

Kansas City Sun, Republican; E. F. Heisler, editor, Sun Printing Company, Kansas City.

—8

The Overland Monthly, Overland Monthly Co., publishers, San Francisco.

The California Prohibitionist, Prohibition Publishing Co., publishers, A. G. Shehan, editor-in-chief, San Francisco.

The Signs of the Times, E. J. Waggenor and M. C. Wilcox, editors, Oakland.

Pacific Health Journal and Temperance Advocate (monthly), Pacific Press Co., publishers, J. N. Loughborough and W. P. Burke, editors, Oakland.

COLORADO.

Weekly Rocky Mountain News; Rocky Mountain News Co., publishers, Thos. A. Patterson and John Arkins, proprietors, Denver.

The Denver Republican (daily); Republican Publishing Company, publishers, Denver.

The Denver Press, Republican; V. P. Wilson, editor, V. P. Wilson & Son, publishers, Denver and Highland.

The Commonwealth (monthly); the Commonwealth Publishing Co., publishers, Denver.

The Great Divide; Stanley Wood, editor, Great Divide Publishing Co., publishers, Denver.

The West Side Citizen, Republican; Lewis L. Gray, editor; Villa Park.

Gunnison Review-Press, Republican; Henry C. Olney, editor and manager, Gunnison.

The Otero County Republican, Republican; George Henry, editor and publisher, La Junta.

The Salida Mail (semi-weekly); M. D. Snedicor, editor, J. F. Erdlen & Co., proprietor, Salida.

The White Pine Cone, Republican; George S. Irwin, editor, White Pine.

Grand Valley Star; Grand Junction Publishing Company, publishers, Grand Junction.

CONNECTICUT.

Quarterly Journal of Inebriety; T. D. Crothers, M.D., editor, published by The American Association for the Cure of Inebriates, Hartford.

Travelers Record (monthly); Travelers Insurance Company, publishers, Hartford.

DISTRICT OF COLUMBIA.

The Official Gazette of the United States Patent Office (weekly); Washington.

United States Official Postal Guide; The Brodix Publishing Co., Washington.

Public Opinion; Public Opinion Co., publishers, Washington.

The Washington Book Chronicle and Bulletin of Government Publications (monthly); Washington.

The National Tribune; George E. Lemon, editor, Washington.

United States Government Publications (monthly catalogue); J. H. Hickox, publisher, Washington.

FLORIDA.

The Florida Dispatch; Stephen Powers, editor, De Costa & Powers, publishers, Jacksonville.

The Advertiser; Fred. H. Perry, proprietor, Apopka.

Monthly Bulletin; Published by Bureau of Immigration, Department of Agriculture, Tallahassee.

GEORGIA.

Southern Industrial Railroad Record (monthly); conducted by A. L. Harris, Record Publishing Co., publishers, Atlanta.

Spelman Messenger (monthly); L. H. Upton and M. J. Packard, editors, E. O. Werden, publisher, Atlanta.

ILLINOIS.

Semi-Weekly Inter-Ocean; Inter-Ocean Publishing Company, Chicago.

Industrial World and Iron Worker; David H. Mason, editor, Melvin M. Cohen, assistant manager, Chicago.

The Standard, religious; Justin A. Smith, D. D., editor, Edward Goodman, E. R. and J. S. Dickerson, proprietors, Chicago.

The Weekly Drovers' Journal; H. L. Goodall & Co., publishers, Chicago.

The Svenska Amerikanaren; Swedish American Printing Co., publishers, Bonggren and Waerner, editors, A. E. G. Wingard, business and advertising manager, Chicago.

The American Antiquarian and Oriental Journal (bi-monthly); Rev. Stephen D. Peet, editor and publisher, Mendon and Chicago.

The Union Signal, organ of W. N. T. U.; Mary Allen West and Julia Ames, editors, Woman's Temperance Publication Association, publishers, Geo. C. Hall, business manager, Chicago.

The Open Court; Dr. Paul Carus, editor, Open Court Publishing Company, publishers, Chicago.

The Chicago Express; Alfred Clark and Mrs. Marion Todd, editors and managers Express Printing Co., publishers, Chicago.

The Humane Journal (monthly); Albert W. Landon, publisher, Chicago.

Pravda (monthly), mission work; A. E. Adams, publisher, Chicago.

The Newspaper Union (monthly); J. F. Cramer, president, C. E. Strong, manager, Chicago.

The Kindergarten (monthly); Cora L. Stockham, editor, Alice B. Stockham & Co., publishers, Chicago.

The Western Trail (monthly); published in the interest of the Rock Island Railroad, Chicago.

The Dial (monthly); A. C. McClurg & Co., publishers, Chicago.

Young Men's Era; H. F. Williams, editor, Chicago.

National Journalist (monthly); National Journalist Publishing Co., publishers, Chicago.

National Reveille, Sons of Veterans (semi-monthly); G. B. Abbott, editor, James I. Lyons, publisher and proprietor, Chicago.

The Lever; The Center-Lever Publishing Co., Chicago.

National Stenographer (monthly); Isaac S. Dement, editor and publisher, Chicago.

The Inland Printer; A. C. Cameron, editor, Chicago.

The Morist (quarterly); Open Court Publishing Co., publishers, Chicago.

The National W. C. T. U. Bulletin; Alice E. Briggs, editor, Evanston.

The Gospel Messenger; H. B. Brumbaugh, editor, Mt. Morris.

The Odd Fellows' Herald (semi-monthly); G. M. Adams, editor and manager, M. T. Scott, publisher, Bloomington.

Western Plowman (monthly); W. F. Eastman, editor, Moline.

INDIAN TERRITORY.

The Cherokee Advocate; R. F. Wyly, editor, Tahlequah.

The Indian Chieftain; M. E. Milfôrd, manager, Chieftain Publishing Co., publishers, Vinita.

The Territorial Topic; Miller & Covington, publishers and proprietors, Purcell, Chickasaw Nation.

Minco Minstrel; Lewis N. Hornbeck, editor, publisher and proprietor, Minco, Chickasaw Nation.

INDIANA.

Indiana State Journal; Indianapolis Journal Newspaper Co., publishers, Indianapolis.

The Millstone & Corn Miller (monthly), published by the D. H. Ranck Publishing Co., Indianapolis.

Mennonetische Rundschan; Mennonite Publishing Co., publishers, Elkhart.

IOWA.

The Christna (semi-monthly); James Vincent, sen., editor and proprietor, Tabor.

The Iowa Historical Record (quarterly); published by the State Historical Society, Iowa City.

LOUISIANA.

Southwestern Christian Advocate; published by Methodist Book Concern, New Orleans.

MAINE.

The Kennebec Journal; Chas. B. Burleigh and Chas. F. Flynt, publishers, Augusta.

MARYLAND.

Johns Hopkins University Circulars, printed by John Murphy & Co., Baltimore.

MASSACHUSETTS.

New England Historical and Genealogical Register, (quarterly;) John Ward Dean, editor, N. E. Historic Genealogical Society, publishers, Boston.

The Woman's Journal; Lucy Stone, H. B. Blackwell and Alice Stone Blackwell, editors, Boston.

The Unitarian Review, (monthly;) Jos. Henry Allen, editor, Boston.

The Youth's Companion; Perry Mason & Co., publishers, Boston.

Harvard Univesity Bulletin; Justin Winsor, editor, Cambridge.

Saturday Evening Gazette; Henry G. Parker, editor and publisher, Boston.

Journal of American Folk-Lore, (quarterly;) Franz Boas, T. Frederick Crane, J. Owen Dorsey, editors, W. W. Newell, general editor, Boston.

The Writer (monthly); W. H. Hills, editor and publisher, Boston.

The New-Jerusalem Magazine, (monthly,) religious; Massachusetts New-Church Union, publishers, Boston.

The Boston Investigator; L. K. Washburn, editor. Joseph P. Mendum, Boston.

Technology Quarterly; James P. Munroe, editor, Boston.

The Golden Rule; Francis E. Clark, editor, Golden Rule Publishing Co., publishers, Boston.

MICHIGAN.

Advent Review and Sabbath Herald; Uriah Smith, editor, L. A. Smith, associate editor, Seventh-Day Adventist Publishing Association, Battle Creek.

The Unitarian (monthly); J. T. Sunderland, editor and publisher, Ann Arbor.

The Plaindealer; The Plaindealer Publishing Co., publishers, Detroit.

MINNESOTA.

The Illustrated Monthly Northwest Magazine ; E. V. Smalley, editor and publisher, St. Paul.

MISSOURI.

Kansas City Times (daily); Morrison Munford, president and manager, Charles E. Hasbrook, secretary, Times Publishing Co., publishers, Kansas City.

Kansas City Daily Journal; Journal Co., publishers, Kansas City.

The Kansas City Star (daily and weekly); Kansas City.

Kansas City Live-Stock Indicator, Record and Farmer; The Indicator Publishing Co., publishers, Kansas City.

Lanphear's Kansas City Medical Index (monthly); Emory Lanphear, editor and publisher, Kansas City.

The Kansas City Record; A. N. Kellogg Newspaper Co., publishers, J. F. Guiwits, manager, Kansas City.

Western Newspaper Union, Kansas City.

The Mid-Continent, religious; Rev. A. A. E. Taylor, editor, Rev. D. M. Hazlett, assistant editor, Presbyterian Newspaper Company, publishers, St. Louis and Kansas City.

Missouri and Kansas Farmer (monthly); Cliff M. Brooke, editor and publisher, Kansas City.

The Kansas City Globe (daily); Globe Newspaper Company, publishers, Louis Hammerslough, president, Kansas City.

Real Estate Journal; Walter & Brodie, publishers, Kansas City.

Hoisington Bank Reporter (semi-monthly); A. J. Hoisington, president, Joe H. Borders, secretary and manager, Kansas City.

Borders' Odd Fellow (monthly); Joe H. Borders, editor, Hoisington Publishing Company, publishers, Kansas City.

The Christian Era; Rev. H. C. Scotford, editor, Christian Era Publishing company, publishers, Kansas City.

St. Joseph Herald (daily and weekly); William M. Shepherd, manager, Herald Publishing Company, publishers, St. Joseph.

St. Joseph Weekly Gazette; Gazette Publishing Company, publishers, C. F. Cochran, editor, St. Joseph.

St. Louis Globe-Democrat (daily); Globe Printing Company, publishers, D. M. Houser, president, S. Ray, secretary, St. Louis.

American Journal of Education (monthly); J. B. Merwin, managing editor, St. Louis.

The Central Christian Advocate; Benj. St. James Fry, editor, Cranston & Stowe, publishers, St. Louis.

The Christian Evangelist; J. H. Garrison and B. W. Johnson, editors, G. A. Hoffman, assistant editor, Christian Publishing Company, publishers, St. Louis.

The Altruist, (monthly), devoted to common property and community homes; A. Longley, editor, St. Louis.

The Amoret Chief; T. Trickett, publisher, Amoret.

NEBRASKA.

The Woman's Tribune; Clara Bewick Colby, editor and publisher, Beatrice.

Western Resources (published once every ten days); H. S. Reed, editor and manager, Lincoln.

Nebraska State Journal (daily and weekly); Lincoln.

University Studies; L. A. Shearman, editor, published by the University of Nebraska, Lincoln.

Nebraska Congregational News (monthly); H. A. French, editor, Lincoln.

Western Newspaper Union; Henry C. Akin, manager, Omaha.

NEW MEXICO.

Santa Fé New Mexican (daily); New Mexican Printing Co., publishers, Santa Fé.

San Marcial Reporter; J. A. Whitmore, editor and publisher, San Marcial.

The Daily Citizen; Thos. Hughes, Albuquerque.

Las Vegas Daily Optic; R. A. Kistler, editor, Los Vegas.

NEW JERSEY.

Orchard and Garden (monthly); J. T. Lovett & Co., publishers, H. G. Corney, editor, Little Silver.

NEW YORK.

New York Tribune (daily); New York.

Magazine of American History (monthly); Mrs. Martha J. Lamb, editor, New York.

Scientific American; O. D. Munn and A. E. Beach, editors and proprietors, New York.

Electrical Review; Geo. Worthington and Chas. W. Price, editors, New York.

The Library Journal (monthly); official organ of the American Library Association, C. A. Cutter and R. R. Bowker, editors, New York.

The Coöperative Index to Periodicals (quarterly); W. I. Fletcher, editor, New York.

The American Missionary (monthly); published by the American Missionary Association, Rev. W. M. Taylor, D. D., LL. D., president, New York.

The Home Missionary (monthly); published by the American Home Missionary Society, Alexander H. Clapp, D. D., treasurer, New York.

Political Science Quarterly; edited by the Faculty of Political Science of Columbia College, Ginn & Co., publishers, New York.

The Irish World; Patrick Ford, editor and proprietor, New York.

New York Weekly Witness; John Dougall & Co., publishers, New York.

The Voice; Funk & Wagnalls, publishers, New York.

The Decorator and Furnisher (monthly); W. R. Bradshaw, editor, W. P. Wheeler, business manager, The Art Trades Publishing Company, publishers, New York.

The Student's Journal (monthly); Andrew J. Graham, editor and proprietor, New York.

Sabbath Reading; John Dougall & Co., publishers, New York.

The Phonographic World (monthly); E. N. Miner, publisher, New York.

The National Temperance Advocate (monthly); J. N. Stearns, secretary and publishing agent, New York.

The Publishers' Weekly (a book trade journal); R. R. Bowker, manager, New York.

Public Opinion; Public Opinion Co., publishers, New York and Washington.

The Literary News, (monthly), New York.

The Literary Digest, Funk & Wagnalls, publishers. New York.

The Saturday Globe, a weekly Democratic review, New York.

The American Sentinel, Alonzo T. Jones, editor. Pacific Press Publishing Co., publishers, New York.

Building and Loan News (monthly); devoted to the interests of Building Associations, Louis H. Cornish, business manager, New York.

American Economist, American Protective Tariff League, New York.

The Silver Cross (monthly); Organ of the King's Daughters, New York.

The Business Woman's Journal (bi-monthly); Mary F. Seymour, managing editor New York.

The Library Bulletin of Cornell University, Ithaca.

The Husbandman, Elmira.

NORTH DAKOTA.

Bismarck Tribune (daily and weekly); M. H. Jewell, editor and publisher, Bismarck.

SOUTH DAKOTA.

Pierre Daily Capital, Republican; Goddard, Ireland & Patterson, editors and proprietors, Pierre.

OHIO.

Magazine of Western History (monthly); J. H. Kennedy, editor, Cleveland.

Weekly Times, Cincinnati.

The Christian Press (monthly); published by the Western Tract Society, Cincinnati.

Christian Standard; Isaac Errett, editor-in-chief, Cincinnati.

American Grange Bulletin; F. P. Wolcott, editor, Cincinnati.

Herald of Gospel Liberty; J. P. Watson, editor, Dayton.

OKLAHOMA.

The Evening Gazette; Evening Gazette Company, publishers, Oklahoma.

Oklahoma City Daily Times; Hamlin W. Sawyer, editor and publisher, Oklahoma.

Oklahoma Daily Journal; J. J. Burke, editor, E. E. Brown, city editor, Oklahoma.

Weekly Oklahoma State Capital; Frank H. Greer, editor, State Capital Publishing Company, publishers, Guthrie.

The Norman Transcript; Ed. P. Ingle, editor, Norman.

The Courier; N. H. Thorpe, editor and proprietor, Kingfisher.

The New World; Ellis, Ross & Ellis, editors, publishers and proprietors, Kingfisher.

The Mulhall Monitor; Ed. F. Watts, editor and proprietor, Mulhall.

Edmond Sun; A. H. Classen, editor and publisher, Edmond.

Hennessey Clipper; J. B. Campbell, editor and publisher, Hennessey.

El Reno Herald, Republican; L. F. Grove, editor and publisher, El Reno.

The Frisco Herald; Herald Publishing Company, publishers, Frisco.

OREGON.

Fire and Hammer (monthly); W. T. Ellis, editor, Portland.

PENNSYLVANIA.

Public Ledger (daily); G. W. Childs, editor and publisher, Philadelphia.

Faith and Works (monthly); published by the Woman's Christian Association, Philadelphia.

The Naturalist's Leisure Hour (monthly); A. E. Foote, editor and publisher, Philadelphia.

Farm and Fireside; Mast, Crowell & Kirkpatrick, editors and publishers, Philadelphia and Springfield, Ohio.

The Sugar Beet (monthly); Lewis S. Ware, editor, Henry Carey Baird & Co., publishers, Philadelphia.

The Sunday School Times; John D. Wattles, publisher, Philadelphia.

Annals of the American Academy (quarterly); Edmund J. James, editor, Philadelphia.

Food, Home and Garden (monthly); Vegetarian Society of America, Philadelphia.

Paper and Press (monthly); W. M. Patton, publisher and proprietor, Philadelphia.

Poultry Keeper (monthly); P. H. Jacobs, editor, Poultry Co., publishers, Parkersburg and Philadelphia.

Book News (monthly); John Wanamaker, publisher, Philadelphia.

Stowell's Petroleum Reporter (monthly); Pittsburg.

American Manufacturer and Iron World; Joseph D. Weeks, editor, Pittsburg.

The Book Mart (monthly); Halkett Lord, literary editor, Book Mart Publishing Co., publishers, Pittsburg.

Farmers' Friend and Grange Advocate; R. H. Thomas, edtior, Mechanicsburg.

The Red Man (monthly); printed by Indian boys at the Indian School, M. Burgess, business manager, Carlisle.

TENNESSEE.

State Board of Health Bulletin; J. Berrien Lindsley, Secretary, Nashville.

TEXAS.

Texas Live Stock Journal; Stock Journal Publishing Co., publishers, Fort Worth.

Southern Mercury; State Alliance Publishing Co., publishers, Dallas.

VIRGINIA.

Southern Workman and Hampton School Record; S. C. Armstrong, Helen W. Ludlow, and Alice M. Bacon, editors, Hampton.

WYOMING.

The Wyoming Commonwealth, C. G. Coutant, editor and publisher, Cheyenne.

The Daily Boomerang; Laramie.

FRANCE.

Société de Géograpie, Compte rendu des Séances de la Commission Centrale (semi-monthly), Paris.

Bulletin de la Société de Géographie (quarterly), Paris.

Chronique de la Société des Gens de Lettres (monthly), Paris.

Bulletin du Ministère de l'Agriculture (monthly), Paris.

Bulletin de la Société de Géographie Commerciale, Paris.

Bulletin des Séances de la Société Nationele d'Agriculture de France (monthly), Paris.

Bulletin de la Société de Géographie de Lyon (monthly), Lyon.

Union Géographique du Nord de la France (bi-monthly), Douai.

Bulletin de la Société Languedocienne de Géographie, Montpellier.

Bulletin de la Société de Géographie de l'est (bi-monthly), Nancy.

Bulletin de la Société de Géographie Commerciale, Du Havre.

Bulletin de la Société de Géographie de Toulouse (bi-monthly), Toulouse.

Bulletin de la Société de Géographie de Rochefort (quarterly), Paris et Rochefort.

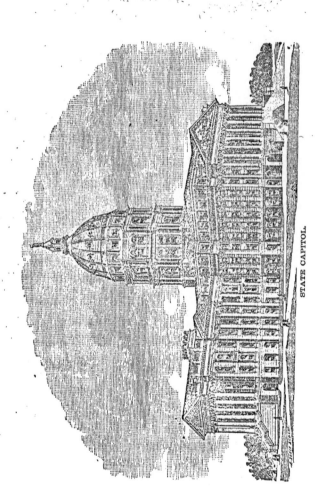

STATE CAPITOL.

EIGHTH BIENNIAL REPORT

OF THE

BOARD OF DIRECTORS

OF THE

KANSAS STATE HISTORICAL SOCIETY,

FOR THE PERIOD

COMMENCING NOVEMBER 18, 1890, AND ENDING NOVEMBER 15, 1892.

TOPEKA.
PRESS OF THE HAMILTON PRINTING COMPANY;
EDWIN H. SNOW, State Printer.

1892.

OFFICERS FOR THE YEARS 1891-'92.

JAMES S. EMERY, Lawrence.. { PRESIDENT, 1891.
....{ PRESIDENT, 1892.
THOMAS A. OSBORN, Topeka... VICE-PRESIDENT, 1891.
SAMUEL N. WOOD, Woodsdale... VICE-PRESIDENT, 1891.
BENJAMIN F. SIMPSON, Topeka....................................... VICE-PRESIDENT, 1892.
ALBERT R. GREENE, Lecompton...................................... VICE-PRESIDENT, 1892.
FRANKLIN G. ADAMS, Topeka.. SECRETARY, 1891-'92.
T. DWIGHT THACHER, Topeka... TREASURER, 1891-'92.

EXECUTIVE COMMITTEE.
C. K. HOLLIDAY, L. U. HUMPHREY, J. N. IVES, F. P. BAKER, D. W. WILDER, A. R. GREENE.

LEGISLATIVE COMMITTEE.
T. D. THACHER, S. N. WOOD, B. F. SIMPSON, A. R. GREENE, GEO. D. HALE.

COLUMBIAN EXPOSITION COMMITTEE.
J. S. EMERY, J. B. ABBOTT, CHAS. S. GLEED, F. G. ADAMS, E. J. DALLAS.

NOMINATING COMMITTEE.
F. P. BAKER, P. G. LOWE, S. C. WHEELER, A. N. WHITTINGTON, B. F. SIMPSON.

DIRECTORS.

Members of the Board of Directors for the year ending January 17, 1893:

ABBOTT, J. B..............De Soto.	KELLY, H. B...............McPherson.
ADAMS, N. A...............Manhattan.	KIMBALL, C. H.............Parsons.
ANTHONY, GEO. T...........Ottawa.	LIPPINCOTT, J. A..........Topeka.
BLACKMAR, F. W............Lawrence.	McCARTHY, TIMOTHY........Larned.
SNOW, FRANK H.............Lawrence.	McNEAL, T. A.............Medicine Lodge.
CORDLEY, RICHARD..........Lawrence.	McVICAR, PETER...........Topeka.
DOWNING, J. H.............Hays City.	MILLER, SOL..............Troy.
ELLIOTT, R. G.............Lawrence.	MURDOCK, M. M............Wichita.
ELLISTON, HENRY...........Atchison.	MURDOCK, T. B............El Dorado.
FAIRCHILD, GEO. T.........Manhattan.	PRENTIS, NOBLE L.........Newton.
HALE, GEO. D..............Topeka.	RICE, WM. M..............Fort Scott.
HIGGINS, WM...............Topeka.	SCOTT, CHAS. F...........Iola.
HOCH, E. W................Marion.	SMITH, A. W..............McPherson.
HOWE, EDGAR W.............Atchison.	TAYLOR, A. R.............Emporia.
HUDSON, J. K..............Topeka.	QUAYLE, W. A.............Baldwin.
JOHNSON, A. S.............Topeka.	VALENTINE, D. A..........Clay Centre.
KELLOGG, L. B.............Emporia.	

Members of the Board of Directors for the year ending January 16, 1894:

ANDERSON, J. W. D.........Elk City.	McBRIDE, WM. H...........Osborne.
ANTHONY, D. R.............Leavenworth.	McINTIRE, T..............Arkansas City.
ECKERT, T. W..............Arkansas City.	OSBORN, THOS. A..........Topeka.
BAKER, F. P...............Topeka.	PHILLIPS, WM. A..........Salina.
BERRY, ED. A..............Waterville.	RIDDLE, A. P.............Minneapolis.
BROWN, A. Z...............Guilford.	ROBINSON, CHAS...........Lawrence.
COBURN, M. W..............Hoisington.	RUSSELL, EDWARD..........Lawrence.
DOTY, W...................Oketo.	SPEER, JOHN..............Sherlock.
ELDER, P. P...............Ottawa.	STEWART, SAM'L J.........Humboldt.
ESKRIDGE, C. V............Emporia.	WARE, E. F...............Fort Scott.
GLICK, GEO. W.............Atchison.	COLLINS, J. S............Topeka.
GOODNOW, I. T.............Manhattan.	WEIGHTMAN, M.............Topeka.
GREENE, A. R..............Lecompton.	WHEELER, S. C............Concordia.
HUMPHREY, L. U............Independence.	WHITTINGTON, A. N........Lincoln.
IVES, J. N................Sterling.	WILDER, D. W.............Hiawatha.
KINGMAN, S. A.............Topeka.	WOOD, MRS. MARGARET L....Woodsdale.
LEGATE, JAS. F............Leavenworth.	

Members of the Board of Directors for the year ending January 15, 1895:

ADAMS, F. G...............Topeka.	MARTIN, GEO. W...........Kansas City.
CALDWELL, ALEX............Leavenworth.	MARTIN, JOHN.............Topeka.
CARROLL, ED...............Leavenworth.	MEAD, J. R...............Wichita.
DALLAS, E. J..............Topeka.	MOODY, JOEL..............Mound City.
ELLIOTT, L. R.............Manhattan.	MORRILL, E. N............Hiawatha.
EMERY, J. S...............Lawrence.	PECK, GEO. R.............Topeka.
GLEED, CHAS. S............Topeka.	PRICE, JOHN M............Atchison.
GUTHRIE, JOHN.............Topeka.	REYNOLDS, ADRIAN.........Sedan.
HAYS, R. B................Osborne.	SIMPSON, B. F............Topeka.
HOLLIDAY, C. K............Topeka.	SIMS, WILLIAM............Topeka.
HOPKINS, SCOTT............Horton.	SMITH, W. H..............Marysville.
HORTON, ALBERT H..........Topeka.	STOTLER, JACOB...........Wellington.
HUMPHREY, JAMES...........Junction City.	SWENSSON, C. A...........McPherson.
JOHNSON, J. B.............Topeka.	THACHER, T. D............Topeka.
LANE, V. J................Wyandotte.	WELLHOUSE, FRED..........Leavenworth.
LOWE, P. G................Leavenworth.	WRIGHT, JOHN K...........Junction City.
MALOY, JOHN...............Council Grove.	

TABLE OF CONTENTS.

REPORT.

Herewith the Board of Directors of the Kansas State Historical Society presents the report of the work of the Society during the two years ending November 15, 1892.

There have been added to the library of the Society during the two years, 2,183 volumes of books; unbound volumes and pamphlets, 7,710; volumes of newspapers and periodicals, 2,499; single newspapers containing matter of special historical interest, 734; maps, atlases, and charts, 3,253; manuscripts, 556; pictures and other works of art, 183; scrip, currency, and coin, 81; war relics, 23; miscellaneous contributions, 443.

From this statement it will be seen that the library additions proper, of books, pamphlets, newspapers, and periodicals, during the two years, number 12,392 volumes. Of these, 11,796 have been procured by gift and exchanges, and 596 by purchase.

The total of the library at the present time is as follows, namely: 14,414 bound volumes; 43,271 unbound volumes and pamphlets; and 12,633 bound newspaper files and volumes of periodicals; in all, 70,318 volumes.

YEARLY GROWTH OF THE LIBRARY.

The following is a statement of the yearly growth of the library in 17 years, from 1876 to 1892, inclusive:

DATE.	Volumes books.	Volumes newspapers and periodicals.	Pamphlets.	Total yearly accessions.	Yearly total of the library.
1876	280	54	74	408	408
1877	115	150	501	766	1,174
1878	1,237	710	1,184	3,131	4,305
1879	290	275	491	1,056	5,361
1880	448	448	1,146	2,042	7,403
1881	414	375	1,127	1,916	9,319
1882	1,660	513	2,721	4,903	14,222
1883	307	403	1,088	1,798	16,020
1884	732	807	2,763	4,302	20,322
1885	1,088	678	2,033	3,799	24,121
1886	1,772	1,573	7,975	11,320	35,441
1887	753	1,007	1,543	3,303	38,744
1888	866	988	7,707	9,561	48,305
1889	1,269	1,053	2,248	4,570	52,875
1890	991	1,100	2,960	4,967	57,926
1891	719	1,280	4,591	6,590	64,516
1892	1,464	1,219	3,119	5,802	70,318
Totals	14,414	12,633	43,271	70,110	....

The Kansas State Historical Society had its origin in action taken by the editors and publishers of Kansas. At a meeting of the State Editors' and Publishers' Association in 1875, a resolution was adopted, under which a committee was appointed, in the language of the resolution, "for the purpose of saving the present and past records of our 21 years of eventful history." The events of 17 years have since been added to those of the period named. The Society began as a voluntary association, without recognition by the State. But it brought its collections into the State House from the first. Soon the value of its work became recognized by the State; means were appropriated by the Legislature for its support, and rooms in the Capitol building were designated for its use. In 1879 a law was passed making the Society the trustee of the State, and defining its duties and its relations to the State. The law declares the collections of the Society to be the property of the State, and the Society has accepted the conditions imposed by this provision. The law broadened the scope of the work of the Society beyond that of a mere collection of Kansas historical materials, to that of making up a general library of reference. especially in the departments of history, science, sociology, and the useful arts. To augment its collections, the law gives the Society 60 bound copies each of the publications of the State and its various institutions, for use in exchanges with other societies and institutions; and for the yearly use of the Society, a small sum is appropriated for the purchase of books to supply deficiencies in the various departments.

Under these fostering provisions, a library of reference in the departments contemplated has grown up not exceeded in the number of its volumes and in their value as such materials by more than one library west of the Alleghany mountains. There are other historical society libraries which have long been receiving far greater appropriations for the purchase of library accessions, but not one has grown more rapidly. This fact of the rapid growth of our library by gifts is no doubt in no small measure attributable to the prominence which Kansas has had from the beginning of its history in affairs of world-wide interest. The events of the territorial period of our history were the prelude to the civil war. From that time to the present, Kansas has been eventful in social progress and in political agitation. The fact that such a State is making up a historical, scientific and political library has attracted the attention of the libraries and institutions, not only of this entire country, but of the world. Our society makes exchanges with libraries and institutions in all of the States, and in many foreign countries. Thus this library is being made up with little cost to the State.

From lists and statements appended to this report, it will be seen that the growth of the library and collections, has been equal to that of former periods, and, in important respects, greater. Our lists of acknowledgments show that the accessions by gift and exchange during the past two years have come from more than 2,000 different sources. More than half of the persons, societies and institutions giving these publications reside outside of Kansas.

The gifts relate to the history and progress of the country, from the earliest to the latest period. They are very largely of those classes of library materials which record in particular detail the events of the period covered by the report, events in all the affairs of human activity; they record the thoughts, the sentiments, the social movements, and the efforts at human progress in all respects.

BOOKS.

The growth of the library in books of historical reference of permanent value has been very gratifying. By exchanges effected through the Interior Department at Washington, 331 volumes of the publications of the United States Government of a political and scientific character have the past two years been added. The gift of 513 volumes of books, made by the Thomas Crane Library, of Quincy, Mass., is one of great interest. The books are largely United States Government records, beginning with those of the First Congress, which met in New York in 1789. These contain the definite and detailed history of the very beginnings of our permanent national existence. These books came from the home of two Presidents of the United States. Some of them contain the autograph of one of these, John Quincy Adams, of whose library they once formed a part. They are the direct gift of Hon. Chas. Francis Adams, a worthy descendent of the line, who is the present trustee of the library which held these books as duplicates. To our former Kansas citizen of the territorial period, Hon. Chas. A. Foster, of Osawatomie, the Society is indebted for the thoughtful act of calling the attention of Mr. Adams to the appropriateness of this gift. The gift is an illustration of the fact that, in its effort to preserve the materials of its history, Kansas has the interest and sympathy of intelligent and liberal people throughout the country.

Hon. Thomas Ryan, United States Minister to Mexico, always a liberal contributor to the library of the Society, has given, during the two years, 197 volumes of books from his private collection. Prof. I. T. Goodnow, a devoted literary collector through all the years of Kansas life, has given from his own store 13 books and 837 pamphlets. Dr. Samuel A. Green, of the Massachusetts Historical Society, has continued to enrich our library, by the gift, during the two years, of 35 books and 187 pamphlets. The long list of contributors of this class is remarkable, as showing the sources of the growth of our library.

PAMPHLETS.

The pamphlet accessions, 7,502 in number, are in large part the reports of societies and institutions. These show the work of numberless thoughtful and earnest people, engaged in individual or in associated endeavor to promote some movement or some measure intended to benefit mankind. Of the historical value of this class of library materials, Lord Beaconsfield once said: "Pamphlets, those leaves of an hour, and volumes of a season, and even of a week, slight and evanescent as they appear, and scorned at by opposite par-

ties, while each cherishes its own, are in truth the records of the public mind
—the secret history of a people."

NEWSPAPERS AND PERIODICALS.

It is with gratification that we refer to the continued evidences of the usefulness of the newspaper department of our Society. While at all times our
newspaper files are found the best source of information as to what has transpired in all affairs in all parts of the State, their usefulness is made more
especially apparent during the progress of great political canvasses. It is
then that the political platforms of the past are reëxamined, and the records
which have been made by candidates in former years are scrutinized. In
these times of quick and close communication, by telegraph, telephone, and
railroads, the people of the State are at such times brought into the closest
communication. The whole people confer together as in one assembly. Every
possible thing bearing upon questions at issue and upon the characters of
men up for office is discussed by all. What a county platform may contain,
adopted years ago in the farthest corner of the State, comes to be considered
of prime importance, as affecting the present status of a party or a candidate.
Our library, the only place where the facts in full may be established, is at
once consulted. Our 9,054 volumes of Kansas newspaper files contain the
political records of men and parties in Kansas for all the years that have
gone before.

This is but one feature of the value of newspaper files as materials of the
history of the past. They contain a record of all in human thought and in
human activity in the past. In the language of the late Gov. John A. Martin,
who was among the founders and builders up of this Society, these newspaper
files contain "every essential fact connected with the growth and development of the communities in which they are published: marriages and deaths;
the establishment of business and manufacturing enterprises, and their changes;
transfers of property; the erection of all important buildings; the results of
elections; the opening of streets; the building of railroads; fires and floods;
the municipal policies suggested, discussed, and adopted; and the daily life,
thoughts, hopes, triumphs and disappointments of an aspiring and energetic
community." Such is the character of the historical information in the Kansas newspaper files in the library of our State Historical Society respecting
every county and every community in the State. There is no part of the
State whose history in all these particulars is not here to be found.

What Kansas is doing in saving materials of the history of the State
through its newspaper files is being done to a considerable extent by other
Western historical societies, but by none to so great an extent as by our Society. Our example is awakening Eastern historical societies to the importance of this work. Says the report of the Connecticut Historical Society for
1891: "It is admitted by all that newspapers are the one great source of
printed material for the making of history. Also that the historical societies

of the East are far behind those at the West in collecting this material. We should certainly keep files of the Connecticut papers."

The manuscript accessions have been unusually large. Among the most valuable of this class ever received into the library of the society is the journal kept by the missionary, Rev. Jotham Meeker, the gift of Mrs. William T. Keith, of Oakland, Cal., the surviving daughter of Mr. Meeker. This journal consists of three books, containing in all 732 closely-written foolscap pages. The entries begin with September 10, 1832, and end with January 4, 1855, the last entry having been made eight days before the death of Mr. Meeker. They give an account of his journey in 1832 from Cincinnati, by the way of the Ohio river, the Ohio canal, and the lakes, to Sault Ste. Marie; of his residence there for a few months, and then of his removal to the Indian Territory—now Kansas—and of his continued residence here until his death. While at Sault Ste. Marie, he invented his remarkable phonetic alphabet, which he adjusted to all Indian languages, and which came to be employed by many missionaries in their early work among the Indians. Coming to the Indian Territory, Mr. Meeker brought with him from Cincinnati a printing press, which he set up at the Shawnee Baptist Mission, a few miles out from Kansas City, and began printing in March, 1834. He printed editions of many instruction books, hymn books, tracts, and portions of the Bible, in the Shawnee, Delaware, Ottawa, and other languages. The alphabet used being strictly phonetic, the task of learning to read was practically only that of learning the characters of the alphabet. Children and adults alike were quickly enabled to read the Bible and other books in their own tongues. Missionary effort became greatly stimulated through the use of this remarkable invention. This journal of Mr. Meeker contains the whole history of his printing. The library of the society contains several of the small books printed by Mr. Meeker in this alphabet. But the Indian languages were not languages of civilization, and no abiding results followed the use of the Meeker phonetic alphabet, except as its use opened to the untutored mind of the Indian the nature and power of the white man's books, and influenced him to have his children taught the white man's language and literature.

The manuscript journal exhibits the daily life of the missionary and his family in the wilderness, and the life and customs, and, in too many instances, the degraded condition, of the rude aborigines, greatly demoralized and corrupted as they were through intercourse with the frontier white people, from contact with whom they had been removed from further east, only again to be subjected to like influences in their new homes in the new Territory.

This journal had remained in the possession of different members of Mr. Meeker's family for more than 37 years since his death. The generous thoughtfulness of the daughter in finally placing it in the library of our Society must always be held in grateful appreciation.

Valuable gifts of manuscripts have been made to the Society by former residents of Kansas who have long been absent. Hon. William Hutchinson, a prominent citizen of Kansas during the territorial period, but who has resided for 30 years past in Washington city, has given upwards of 70 manuscript papers, consisting chiefly of letters of prominent persons who were active in early Kansas affairs. Among the writers appear the names of Dr. W. W. Updegraff, Jas. Redpath, Justin S. Morrill, C. K. Holliday, Henry Harvey, Hugh S. Walsh, W. W. Ross, R. J. Hinton, E. P. Watson, Thos. Ewing, jr., S. C. Pomeroy, Lucy Larcom, Henry J. Adams, Geo. W. Collamore, Marcus J. Parrott, Henry J. Raymond, Gov. A. H. Reeder, Gov. Chas. Robinson, Geo. W. Brown, Dr. Jos. P. Root, Eli Thayer, Augustus Wattles, William Hutchinson, W. Y. Roberts, A. Curtis, Thos. W. Higginson, C. C. Parker, E. B. Whitman, Mrs. Jennie E. Eddy, Mrs. J. M. Howard, H. Miles Moore, G. W. Hutchinson, O. C. Brown, and W. H. Russell.

Mr. Hutchinson was a member of the Wyandotte constitutional convention, and during the territorial period was a correspondent of the New York *Times*, the Boston *Journal*, and other Eastern papers. He was among the victims of the Lawrence raid of May 21, 1856. Besides the manuscripts mentioned, Mr. Hutchinson has given from his collections a large number of pamphlets and newspapers of great interest as containing materials of Kansas history.

Col. Richard J. Hinton, who was also a citizen of Kansas during the territorial times, as an active newspaper correspondent, and who has been prominent in literary and scientific work at Washington and elsewhere since, has given the Society many valuable manuscripts, chiefly of Kansas territorial and war history, and others of literary interest. Among the writers of these appear the names of President Andrew Jackson, Martin F. Conway, W. D. Howells, Jos. Medill, Fred. P. Stanton, John Swinton, Gen. John McNeil, Gen. S. R. Curtis, Walt Whitman, Richard Realf, Edward E. Ropes, Frank J. Merriam, and S. Hatch. Colonel Hinton was a correspondent of the New York *Tribune*, the Chicago *Tribune*, and other papers. He is the author of the valuable Kansas book entitled, "The Army of the Border," published in 1864, and which contains a very full history of the raid of Gen. Sterling Price, which threatened the destruction of Kansas, and which was repelled by our people. With the manuscripts are also given newspapers, newspaper clippings and other papers containing matter relating to the Kansas territorial history and the history of the civil war.

Orville C. Brown, of Adams, N. Y., has given many manuscripts and papers of much historical interest. Mr. Brown was, more than any other person, the founder of Osawatomie, having, in 1854, settled there with the company that selected the town-site. He possessed comparatively large means, which he expended in improvements. He was one of the largest sufferers from the repeated raids which were made by Pro-Slavery parties upon the town in 1856. The manuscripts given relate in considerable part to Mr. Brown's son, Spen-

cer Kellogg Brown, who, a boy 12 years of age, was taken a prisoner into Mis-, souri at the sacking of Osawatomie, August 30, 1856. Young Brown became an active and daring soldier in the War of the Rebellion, largely in scouting service. He was finally captured by Confederate troops, was confined for a long time in the Mississippi Penitentiary, then taken to Castle Thunder, Richmond, and was there tried, convicted and executed as a spy, under circumstances which left on his father's mind the full belief of his innocence of the offense for which his life was sacrificed in the cause of the Union. The manuscripts and other materials in our library relating to the history, perils and sacrifices of this intrepid boy would make a volume of thrilling interest.

From J. DeWitt Walsh, of North Topeka, have been received 108 manuscript papers of the late Territorial Secretary, Hon. Hugh S. Walsh, relating to the Territorial Legislature of 1858 (the first Free-State Legislature), including vouchers and accounts of members and officers of the Legislature; of W. W. Ross, legislative printer; and of numerous persons furnishing supplies; certified to by Gov. J. W. Denver, C. W. Babcock, President of the Council, G. W. Deitzler, Speaker of the House of Representatives, and Geo. F. Warren, Sergeant-at-Arms. Included in this gift is also a large number of bills and papers relating to the legislative proceedings.

Mr. Samuel Bernstein, of Cincinnati, has given the Society a copy of his eulogy delivered at the funeral of the late Col. John C. Vaughan, in the chapel of the Cincinnati Crematory, on the 26th of September last; also a copy of a letter written by Col. Joseph Medill, of Chicago, containing reminiscences of Colonel Vaughan. These, with other papers which the Society has collected, afford quite full materials for a sketch of the life of a man long prominent in the history of Kansas, and who, before Kansas had a history, had made a national reputation as connected with historical events of great interest.

PICTURES.

The pictures added to the collections are chiefly portraits of citizens of the State of more or less prominence in affairs of the State's history. Ex-Gov. Samuel J. Crawford has added to our portraits of former chief executives of the State a life-size, oil-painted portrait of himself, by Woodman. The John Brown portraiture, before so largely represented in our collections, has received the accession, by gift of the artist, of Woodman's original oil-painted portrait, so widely known through the engraved copy published in the Century Magazine in 1882. Among other portrait accessions, the following are worthy of note: A large, life-like photograph of the late Senator Plumb, the gift of Mrs. Plumb; photograph of Hon. A. Carter Wilder; of Gen. John A. Halderman; Col. R. J. Hinton; Lieut. Gov. Joseph P. Root; Col. John C. Vaughan, Sec. Hugh S. Walsh; Rev. Pardee Butler; Rev. S. L. Adair; Horace Greeley, and Oliver Johnson. Other portraits of interest will be found in the list, elsewhere in this report.

In our lists of war relics and miscellaneous contributions are mentioned

interesting gifts made by Prof. I. T. Goodnow, Maj. J. Arrell Johnson, Prof. Edwin A. Popenoe, Hon. Chas. J. Jones, Miss Hattie W. Lovell, Hon. Sol. Miller, Geo. J. Remsburg, Hon. Chas. A. Foster, Col. Richard J. Hinton, Granville W. Hume, Hon. E. N. Morrill, Hon. Jacob Nixon, Prof. O. St. John, and many other contributors. In our lists of donors of single newspapers, mention is made of large numbers of miscellaneous newspapers contributed by Prof. I. T. Goodnow, Col. Richard J. Hinton, Hon. William Hutchinson, and others.

CATALOGING.

The subject of cataloging of the library of the Society is one to which reference is again to be made, with regret that no catalog volume has yet been published. The work of preparing such a volume has gone forward with as much activity as has been practicable with the force of library workers employed. The labor of cataloging a library of historical materials, such as ours, cannot be estimated in comparison with that of the work of cataloging libraries of books alone, such as make up other libraries. Our library of Kansas history is composed of an innumerable multitude of books, pamphlets, magazines, newspapers, newspaper scraps, State documents, reports of State institutions, reports of railroads, and charitable, scientific and many other societies. All these our Society is cataloging in full, with contents where the book contains a variety of subjects, and with bibliographical and biographical notes. This kind of cataloging will not only show what the library contains, but will point to the political, literary, social and scientific history of the State. Items are now prepared sufficient for a catalog volume. This will soon be published.

WORLD'S FAIR.

On application to the Kansas Board of Managers for the World's Columbian Exposition, a room has been assigned for the use of the Society in the Kansas building at Chicago for a historical exhibition. The Board of Directors has appointed a committee to take into consideration the subject of the kind of display which should be made by the Society. The prominence which Kansas has, during nearly 40 years past, occupied in the history of the country makes it appropriate that our State should have a full representation from its historical collections at the greatest of all historical expositions.

REPUBLICATION.

The editions of the earlier volumes of the collections of the Society have long been exhausted and should be republished. The editions are limited to 2,500 copies. These scarcely serve to supply the demand of persons whose names appear in the publications as donors to the library and collections. There is a large demand besides which can only be partially supplied. Not only should the out-of-print editions be republished, but the editions of future publications should be larger. The Society should have for use in connection

with the Kansas World's Columbian Exposition at least a small supply of
the several editions of its publications, in effecting exchanges with other institutions, and in supplying other imperative demands.

ROOM FOR THE SOCIETY.

The subject of the need of additional room for the library and collections
of the Society again demands mention in this report. For the proper shelving of our library and the proper placing of our portraits and museum collections, there is need of four times as much room as that now occupied. Our
Board has made careful estimates of our needs. The library materials which
the Society possesses have from the first been carefully entered upon our accession records, and full statements of their number and character have been
made from year to year in the reports of the Society. Our collections now
fill every nook and corner of the main room of the Society, from floor to
ceiling; they occupy cases in the corridors, and they occupy three rooms in
the cellar of the State House. This library and these collections are in all
respects the kind of materials which the Society is by law required to gather
into the State Capitol for the use of the people. They do not consist of trash
or valueless matter in any respect. They consist of the very materials which
go to make up the history of the State and the country. One single room in
the State House cellar, only reached through darkness, grime, and dust, contains upwards of 5,000 volumes of papers, which contain the actual history
of every county in the State during the past 17 years, and in large part the
history of Kansas for all the years from the earliest settlement of Kansas
Territory. In other cellar rooms and corridors are more than 100 large boxes
of books, which contain the actual political history of the country since the
foundation of the Government. The amount of proper library space which
these books demand, in order that they may be properly placed, is determined
by the well-established rules of library architecture and shelf room. It is
readily shown to be four times the room space now given the Society in the
Capitol building. Our large collections of museum relics, of intense interest
to the youth and masses of our people, are so crowded and huddled into the
few cases which our scant room gives them that they cannot be seen with the
least satisfaction.

The Board has made all possible effort to have adequate room provided for
our present and future needs in the Capitol building when it shall be completed. No designated or contemplated rooms for the Society are to be seen
in the present plans of the building. In order that there may be provision
made, our Board has asked from the State Executive Council directions to
to the Board of Public Works and State Architect to reëxamine the plans of
the building, together with such assignments as are contemplated for the various departments of the State, with a view to determine in what part of the
building rooms may yet be provided for the Society. It is hoped that this
examination will be made, and that information will be elicited which will
lead to provision for adequate accommodations for the Society.

The fifteenth annual meeting of the Society was held in the hall of the House of Representatives, Tuesday evening, January 20, 1891; Hon. C. K. Holliday, President, in the chair.

President Holliday delivered his annual address, on the subject, "The Fremont Campaign, 1856."

At the close of the President's address, Hon. Edward Russell read a paper on the subject of "The Administration of Gov. Thomas Carney."

Hon. James F. Legate then made a few remarks on the same subject.

The following were elected members of the Board of Directors for the term of three years, ending January 16, 1894: J. W. D. Anderson, D. R. Anthony, L. D. Bailey, F. P. Baker, Ed. A. Berry, A. Z. Brown, N. W. Cobun, W. Doty, P. P. Elder, C. V. Eskridge, Geo. W. Glick, I. T. Goodnow, A. R. Greene, L. U. Humphrey, J. N. Ives, S. A. Kingman, James F. Legate, William H. McBride, T. McIntire, Thomas A. Osborn, William A. Phillips, A. P. Riddle, Chas. Robinson, Edward Russell, John Speer, Samuel J. Stewart, E. F. Ware, W. C. Webb, N. Weightman, S. C. Wheeler, A. N. Whittington, D. W. Wilder, S. N. Wood.

MEETING OF THE BOARD OF DIRECTORS.

At a meeting of the Board of Directors held on the adjournment of the annual meeting, January 20, 1891, the following officers and members of the Society were elected:

President, James S. Emery; Vice-Presidents, Thomas A. Osborn and Samuel N. Wood; Treasurer, T. Dwight Thacher; Secretary, Franklin G. Adams. Honorary members: John Brown, jr., Put-in-Bay Island, Ohio, and Geo. W. Julian, Irvington, Indiana. Active member, W. E. Richey, Harveyville.

Legislative Committee: T. D Thacher, S. N. Wood, B. F. Simpson, A. R. Greene, Geo. D. Hale.

Executive Committee: C. K. Holliday, L. U. Humphrey, J. N. Ives, F. P. Baker, D. W. Wilder.

SPECIAL MEETINGS.

An informal meeting of the Board of Directors was held October 12, 1891, at which were present Hon. J. S. Emery, Col. C. K. Holliday, Hon. F. P. Baker, Hon. J. G. Haskell, and F. G. Adams. On motion of Colonel Holliday, it was voted that the Board of Directors be advised to request the Executive Council to procure, through the Board of Public Works, information as to what rooms may be provided in the completed Capitol building for the use of the State Historical Society.

At a meeting of the Board of Directors held in the rooms of the Society January 19, 1892, a resolution was adopted recognizing the Kansas Legisla-

tive Association of 1868, of which Hon. John N. Price is president, and Hon. John T. Norton is secretary, as an auxiliary of the State Historical Society.

SIXTEENTH ANNUAL MEETING.

The sixteenth annual meeting was held in the hall of the House of Representatives, Tuesday evening, January 19, 1892; the President, Hon. James S. Emery, in the chair.

The President read his annual address, entitled, "History and Historical Composition."

Rev. Dr. Peter McVicar read a paper on the subject, "Some Reminiscences concerning School Lands on the Osage Reservation in Kansas."

The following persons were elected members of the Board of Directors for the term of three years, ending January 15, 1895: F. G. Adams, Topeka; Alex. Caldwell, Leavenworth; Ed. Carroll, Leavenworth; E. J. Dallas, Topeka; L. R. Elliott, Manhattan; Jas. S. Emery, Lawrence; Chas. S. Gleed, Topeka; John Guthrie, Topeka; R. R. Hays, Osborne; C. K. Holliday, Topeka; Scott Hopkins, Horton; Albert H. Horton, Topeka; James Humphrey, Junction City; J. B. Johnson, Topeka; V. J. Lane, Wyandotte; P. G. Lowe, Leavenworth; John Maloy, Council Grove; Geo. W. Martin, Kansas City; John Martin, Topeka; J. R. Mead, Wichita; Joel Moody, Mound City; E. N. Morrill, Hiawatha; Geo. R. Peck, Topeka; John N. Price, Atchison; Adrian Reynolds, Sedan; B. F. Simpson, Topeka; William Sims, Topeka; W. H. Smith, Marysville; Jacob Stotler, Wellington; C. A. Swensson, McPherson; T. D. Thacher, Topeka; Fred. Wellhouse, Leavenworth; John K. Wright, Junction City.

To fill vacancies caused by the death of Col. Samuel N. Wood, for the term ending January 16, 1894, Mrs. Margaret L. Wood; and in the place of Hon. W. C. Webb, declined, J. S. Collins, of Topeka, for the term ending January 16, 1894; and in the place of Hon. L. D. Bailey, deceased, T. W. Eckert, of Arkansas City, for the term ending January 16, 1894; and in the place of Prof. James H. Canfield, removed from the State, Chancellor Frank H. Snow, of Lawrence, for the term ending January 17, 1893.

MEETING OF THE BOARD OF DIRECTORS.

On adjournment of the annual meeting, January 19, 1892, the Board of Directors convened, and elected the following officers and members of the Society:

President, Thomas A. Osborn; Vice-Presidents, Benjamin F. Simpson and Albert R. Greene. Corresponding members: Dr. Stephen D. Peet, Avon, Ill.; Hon. Wm. Harden, Savannah, Ga.; Prof. Henry Badger, Howard University, Washington, D. C.; Hon. E. A. Steedman, London, Eng.; Richard D. Mobley, Grand Junction, Colo.; Hon. Thomas S. Parvin, Cedar Rapids, Iowa.

SPECIAL MEETING.

At a meeting in the rooms of the Society August 31, 1892, the following committees were appointed:

To present to the Executive Council an application that the Board of Public Works be directed by the Council to examine the plans of the Capitol building and contemplated assignments for the officers of the various departments of the State, with a view of determining what portion of the building can best be prepared for the use of the State Historical Society, the following committee: James F. Legate, Wm. Sims, Dr. S. McLallin, and F. G. Adams.

To present to the Kansas Board of Managers of the World's Columbian Exposition an application for room in the Kansas building, for the use of the Society for a historical exhibit, the following committee: T. D. Thacher, F. P. Baker, and F. G. Adams.

MEETING OF THE BOARD OF DIRECTORS.

The Board of Directors met in the rooms of the Society at 3 P. M., Tuesday, the 15th of November, 1892, to consider the eighth biennial report of the Society. The following members were present:

Maj. B. F. Simpson and Col. C. K. Holliday, Topeka; Hon. S. C. Wheeler, Concordia; Judge J. S. Emery, Lawrence; Maj. J. K. Hudson and Chas. S. Gleed, Topeka; L. R. Elliott, Manhattan; Maj. J. B. Abbott, De Soto; Judge S. A. Kingman, Judge John Guthrie, and Hon. Wm. Sims, Topeka; Hon. Fred. Wellhouse, Leavenworth; Hon. John M. Price, Atchison; Hon. F. P. Baker, Topeka; Hon. Martin Mohler, Osborne; Hon. P. G. Lowe, Leavenworth; Geo. D. Hale, Esq., E. J. Dallas, and F. G. Adams, Secretary, Topeka.

Vice-President Benjamin F. Simpson presided.

The Secretary read the report of the Board of Directors, which, on motion of Mr. Baker, was approved for publication.

The President appointed the following committee to audit the accounts of the Secretary and Treasurer: C. K. Holliday, E. J. Dallas, and P. G. Lowe.

The chair reported the following resolutions, which were adopted:

Resolved, That grateful thanks are hereby extended by the Kansas State Historical Society to the Hon. Charles Francis Adams, of Quincy, Mass., for his generous thoughtfulness, as trustee of the Thomas Crane Public Library, of Quincy, in giving to our Society more than 500 volumes of books, chiefly of documents relating to the political history of the country.

Resolved, That special thanks are also given our former citizen, Hon. Charles A. Foster, of Osawatomie, for his thoughtful action in relation to this gift.

Resolved, That the Secretary be directed to give copies of these resolutions to the persons named therein.

The following resolution, proposed by Major Simpson, was offered by Mr. Gleed, and unanimously adopted:

Resolved, That section 5 of the constitution of the Society be so amended as to read as follows:

5. The annual meeting of the Society shall be held at Topeka on the 29th day of

January, or on the following Monday; and those members, not less than 10, who meet at any annual or special meeting of the Society, upon the call of the Board of Directors, shall be a quorum for the transaction of business.

On motion of Mr. Gleed, the following resolution was adopted:

Resolved, That Capt. Henry King, of the St. Louis *Globe-Democrat;* Hon. J. R. Mead, of Wichita; and Hon. Jacob Stotler, of Wellington, be requested to deliver addresses at our next annual meeting, January 17, 1893.

On motion of Mr. Baker, the chair appointed the following committee on nominations: F. P. Baker, P. G. Lowe, S. C. Wheeler, A. N. Whittington, B. F. Simpson.

Judge Kingman stated that, in behalf of Judge Guthrie, Judge Emery, and himself, who had been designated by the chair for that duty, he would offer the following resolution:

Resolved, That the Directors and officers of the State Historical Society have heard with the most profound sorrow of the death of Mrs. Julia D. Osborn, the lovely and accomplished wife of our President, and we extend to him and family our sympathy and condolence in this, their great bereavement.

On motion of Mr. Baker, the resolution was adopted.

Colonel Holliday, from the Executive Committee, made the annual financial report, which was adopted.

Mr. Baker, from the committee appointed to confer with the Kansas Board of World's Fair Managers, reported that the application of the Society for room for the Kansas historical exhibit had been granted.

On motion of Judge Guthrie, a committee was appointed to take into consideration the subject of the kind of display which should be made by the Society, and to report upon the same at the annual meeting in January next, as follows: J. S. Emery, J. B. Abbott, Chas. S. Gleed, F. G. Adams, and E. J. Dallas.

On motion of Mr. Lowe, Gen. Frank Wheaton, U. S. A., in charge of the department of Texas, at San Antonio, was elected an honorary member of the Society.

Secretary Adams offered the following resolution, which, on motion of Judge Guthrie, was adopted:

Resolved, That Monday, the 30th day of January next, be observed by the Society as "Kansas Day," and that D. W. Wilder, Eugene F. Ware, Charles F. Scott, J. C. Hebbard, Mrs. J. K. Hudson, A. R. Greene, and Noble L. Prentis, with such other persons as they may choose to add to their number, form a committee to make arrangements for a proper observance of the day, and that the exercises be of a character calculated to invite a reunion of Kansas authors and writers, especially of the authors of books and pamphlets which have been contributed to the library of this Society, and that the exercises also have particular reference to John G. Whittier, as in a large sense the poet of Kansas.

—2

The finances of the Society for the year ending November 17, 1891, are as follows:

RECEIPTS.

Nov. 18, 1890. Balance of appropriations to June 30, 1891	$4,177 50	
Nov. 18, 1890. Balance in hands of the Treasurer of the Society........	19 00	
July 1, 1891. Appropriation to June 30, 1892.........................	5,500 00	
Receipts from membership fees.......................................	32 00	
Total...	$9,728 50	

EXPENDITURES.

Salaries and clerk hire.............................	$4,783 00	
Purchase of books..	556 59	
Postage, freight, and contingent...........................	554 35	5,893 94
Balance..............................		$3,834 56

The finances for the year ending November 15, 1892, are as follows:

RECEIPTS.

Nov. 17, 1891. Balance of appropriations to June 30, 1892.............	$3,783 56	
Nov. 17, 1891. Balance in hands of the Treasurer of the Society........	51 00	
July 1, 1892. Appropriation to June 30, 1893........................	5,500 00	
Receipts from membership fees.......................................	52 00	
Total...	$9,386 56	

EXPENDITURES.

Salaries and clerk hire....................................	$4,555 58	
Purchase of books.......................................	664 27	
Postage, freight, and contingent...........................	592 40	5,812 25
Balance		$3,574 31

DONORS OF BOOKS AND PAMPHLETS.

The following is a list of books and pamplets given the Society by individuals and institutions, including those received in exchange, and State publications given the Society by the State for use in making exchanges:

DONORS.	Bks.	Pam.
Abbott, James Burnett, De Soto........	8	1
Académie de Macon, Sociétie des Arts, Sciences, Belles-lettres et d' Agricul., Macon, France	2	......
Académie des Sciences, Arts et Belles-lettres de Dijon, France...........................	1	......
Academy of Natural Sciences, Philadelphia..........................	1	......
Adams, Chas. Francis, jr., Boston, Mass	519	.....
Adams, F. G., Topeka........................	3	9
Adams, Harriet E., Topeka................	......	23
Adams, H. J., Topeka........	......	1
Adams, Maggie L., Topeka............	...	1
Adams Nervine Asylum, Boston, Mass.........	......	5
Adams, Paul, Topeka.......	......	1
Adams, Samuel, Topeka.........	......	1
Adler, Dr. Cyrus, U. S. National Museum, Washington, D. C....	......	1
Admire, W. W., Chicago, Ill....	......	1
Advertiser, Daily, Boston, Mass....	......	3
Aërmotor Company, Chicago, Ill.	......	3
Ahlborn, Ida A., Baldwin.........	......	1
Alabama Agricultural Experiment Station, Auburn....	......	39
Alabama Department of Agriculture, Montgomery......	......	2
Alabama Polytechnic Institution, Auburn	......	1
Albee, F. A., Goodland........	......	2
Alford, D. S., Lawrence...........	......	2
Allen, Rev. C. G., Meade...........	......	12
Allen, Martin, Ogallah...........	......	12
Alliance News, Westmoreland.	......	1
Altman, Rev. D. S., Ottawa	......	5
American Academy of Political and Social Sciences, Philadelphia, Pa............	......	1
American Antiquarian Society, Worcester, Mass............	1	3
American Bell Telephone Company, Boston, Mass....	......	1
American Catholic Historical Society, Philadelphia, Pa...........	2	1
American College and Education Society, Boston, Mass.	......	5
American Congregational Association, Boston, Mass.........	......	2
American Dialect Society, Cambridge, Mass....	......	2
American Historical Society, Washington, D. C........	1	......
American Home Missionary Society, New York city........	1	......
American Library Association, Washington, D. C......	......	1
American Metrological Association, New York city...........	......	1
American Missionary Association, Bible House, New York city	......	2
American Museum of Natural History, Central Park, New York	2	2
American Philosophical Society, Philadelphia, Pa.........	......	8
American Society for the Prevention of Cruelty to Animals, New York city..........	......	1
American Society of Microscopists, Pittsburg, Pa............	......	1
Anderson, H. C. L., Sydney, New South Wales, Australia	1	4
Anderson, Rev. J. W. D., Hot Springs, S. D....	5	......
Anderson, Thomas J., Topeka.........	......	2
Anthony, Miss Susan B., Rochester, N. Y.....	......	2
Arizona Agricultural Experiment Station, Tucson	......	3
Arkansas Agriculture Experiment Station, Fayetteville....	......	7
Armstrong, D. T., Great Bend........	......	1
Associated Charities of Boston, Mass.........	......	28
Associated Charities, San Francisco, Cal........	......	1
A. T. & S. F. R. R., Passenger Department, Topeka........	......	4
Atkins, Dudley, Manhattan	......	2
Attwater, Henry R., Sedan.......	......	3
Badger, Joseph E., jr., Frankfort....	......	18
Bailey, E. H. S., Lawrence, Kas.....	......	11
Bailey, Mrs. Elizabeth, Lawrence, Kas.....	......	1
Baker, C. C., Topeka........	10	......
Ball, Mrs. Belle, Kansas City, Mo.......	3	4
Ballou, L. M., Woonsocket, R. I.....	1	......
Balston, G. B., Palmer.........	1	
Bancroft, Hubert H., San Francisco, Cal.....	......	2
Bangor Public Library, Bangor, Me	......	3
Banta, J. Edward, Hiawatha.....	......	3
Barnes, Harold, Lawrence.........	......	2

DONORS OF BOOKS AND PAMPHLETS — CONTINUED.

DONORS.	Bks.	Pam.
Barnwell, James G., Librarian, Philadelphia, Pa...........	......	1
Bates, J. H., New York city..........	......	1
Baxter, L. W., Emporia..........	......	18
Beacon, Publishers of, Great Bend..........	......	1
Beebe, John W., Kingman..........	1	......
Beers, William H., New York city, N. Y..........	......	1
Beer, William, Topeka..........	1	2
Belden, S. C., Horton..........	..	2
Belden, S. C., S. P., and Eliza Felch, Horton..........	1	......
Bellamy, Edward, Boston, Mass..........	......	2
Ben Franklin Publishing Company, Philadelphia, Pa..........	......	1
Berry, John M., Worcester, Mass..........	......	1
Betton, Frank H., Topeka..........	121	3
Bible House, Alleghany, Pa..........	......	6
Biological Society of Washington, D. C..........	......	14
Black, Geo., Olathe..........	1	5
Blackmar, Prof. F. W., Lawrence..........	......	2
Blakesley, Rev. L., Topeka..........	......	3
Blanchard, Rev. W. H., Koloko..........	......	3
Blow, Susan E., Avon, N. Y..........	......	3
Bodwell, Rev. Lewis, Clifton Springs, N. Y..........	......	11
Bolton, Rev. C. S., Topeka..........	......	6
Bonham, Jeriah, Sparland, Ill..........	......	2
Boomer, J. M., Fairview..........	......	1
Borin, Bruce, and Hiskey, Tom. B., Oberlin..........	1	......
Boss, Henry R., Chicago, Ill..........	2	26
Boston Chamber of Commerce, Boston, Mass..........	1	......
Boston Public Library, Boston, Mass..........	......	11
Boston Public Schools, Superintendent of..........	9	2
Boswell Observatory, Doane College, Crete, Neb..........	......	4
Bourne, Geo. S., Hutchinson..........	......	1
Bowes, Geo. W., Topeka..........	......	1
Brackett, G. C., Lawrence..........	40	......
Bradlee, Rev. Caleb D., Boston, Mass..........	......	33
Bray, Olive P., Topeka..........	...	2
Breck, Sam'l, Washington, D. C..........	1	......
Bright, Rev. J. A., Topeka..........	......	1
Brinton, Dr. Dan'l G., Media, Pa..........	......	1
British and American Archæological Society, Rome, Italy..........	......	1
Broad, Rev. L. P., Topeka..........	A	......
Brockway, Francis E., Oswego, N. Y..........	1	......
Broderick, Case, Washington, D. C..........	......	2
Brookline Library, Mass..........	......	1
Brooklyn Library, Brooklyn, N. Y..........	......	10
Brooks, Frank, Topeka..........	......	1
Brooks, William Henry, Boston, Mass..........	1	1
Brotherhood of Christian Unity, New York city..........	....	3
Brown, Bestor G., Topeka..........	......	6
Brown, John H., Kansas City..........	3	5
Brown, Rev. John S., Lawrence..........	......	37
Brown, Joseph M., Atlanta, Ga..........	......	1
Brown, Orville C., Adams, N. Y..........	......	1
Bryan, Geo. D., Charleston, S. C..........	2	......
Bryan, Wm. J., Washington, D. C..........	......	1
Buck, L. A., Peabody..........	......	13
Buffalo Historical Society, Buffalo, N. Y..........	......	7
Bulkley, Mrs. A. L., Brooklyn, N. Y..........	1	......
Brumbaugh, J. M., Concordia..........	......	13
Brummitt, Dan. B., Baldwin..........	......	13
Burgner, Jacob, Oberlin, O..........	1	......
Burleigh, Chas., Saco, Me..........	1	......
Burnell, H. L., Topeka..........	1	......
Burnz, Mrs. Eliza B., New York city..........	7	21
Bushnell, Wm., Camden, N. J..........	......	1
Butler, J. C., Washington, D. C..........	......	3
Butterfield, J. Ware, Topeka..........	......	3
Butterworth, Ben., Washington, D. C..........	......	8
California Agricultural Experiment Station, Berkeley..........	......	8
California Bureau of Labor Statistics, San Francisco..........	......	8
California University, Berkeley..........	1	1
California Weather Bureau, Sacramento..........	2	12
Callette, A. M., Emporia..........	......	1
Call, Prof. R. Ellsworth, Des Moines, Iowa..........	......	19
Campbell, J. M., North Topeka..........	......	4
Canadian Institute, Toronto, Canada..........	2	5
Canebrake Agricultural Experiment Station, Uniontown, Ala..........	......	6
Canfield, J. H., Lawrence..........	1	.....(
Carr, E. T., Leavenworth..........	1	......
Caso, Rev. F. A., Girard..........	......	1
Case, Geo. H., Lansing..........	......	13

DONORS OF BOOKS AND PAMPHLETS — CONTINUED.

DONORS.	Bks.	Pam.
Case, L. W., Chicago, Ill.......	2	......
Caswell, Mrs. H. S..........	......	1
Central College, Enterprise.....	......	1
Chace, Mrs. T. W., New York city...............	......	9
Chandler, Geo., Washington, D. C...............	1	4
Chapman Bros., Chicago, Ill........	3	......
Chapman, Dr. J., Exeter, N. H............	2	......
Charity Organization Society, New York.....	1	49
Chase, Rev. Lyman C., Hill City........	1	......
Chesbro. S. K. J., Chicago, Ill............	1	1
Chicago Board of Trade, Chicago, Ill....	20	......
Chicago Daily News, Chicago, Ill.......	1	......
Chicago Historical Society, Ill............	......	7
Chicago Public Library, Ill..........	......	17
Chicago University, Chicago, Ill............	......	1
Childs, Geo. W., Philadelphia, Pa...........	......	1
Chism, B. B., Little Rock, Ark.......	7	......
Church Home, Boston, Mass.......	......	1
Church Home for Orphan and Destitute Children, Topsfield, Mass.....	......	1
Chrader, J. W., Oskaloosa........	......	1
Christian, James, Arkansas City	......	1
Christian, S. P., Girard....	......	1
Cilley, J. P., Rockland, Me	......	1
Cincinnati Chamber of Commerce and Merchants' Exchange, Cincinnati, Ohio.....	11	......
Cincinnati Public Library, Cincinnati, Ohio........	......	3
Clarke, Alonzo Howard, curator National Museum, Smithsonian Institute, Washington, D. C.........	......	2
Clarke, Sylvester H., Clyde, New York....	6	19
Clarkson, John V. B., New York city......	......	7
Clayton, B. F., Macedonia, Iowa.....	......	1
Clemenson Agricultural College Experiment Station, Fort Hill, S. C.....	......	3
Cleveland Public Library, Cleveland, Ohio........	1	......
Cline, J. B , Topeka	......	1
Clubb, Henry S., Philadelphia, Pa	1	......
Clute, O., Agricultural College, Mich........	3	1
Cobb, Wm. H., Boston, Mass......	11	......
Cobun, J. W., Great Bend	......	1
Coffman, S., Jewell......	......	1
Colby, Mrs. Clara B., Beatrice, Neb........	......	1
Colby University, Waterville, Me......	......	46
Cole, Frank T., Columbus, Ohio.....	1	......
Cole, Geo. E., Girard......	......	1
College for the Training of Teachers, New York city......	......	2
Collet, A. M., Emporia......	......	10
Collet, C. D., London, Eng.......	......	87
Colorado Agricultural Experiment Station, Fort Collins....	1	10
Colorado Bureau of Labor Statistics, Denver......	......	1
Colorado Commissioner of Forestry, Denver......	1	1
Colorado Scientific Society, Denver......	......	6
Colorado State Inspector of Coal Mines, Denver......	1	1
Cone, W. W., Topeka........	......	1
Conference of Charities, New Orleans, La.....	......	2
Connecticut Agricultural Experiment Station, New Haven.....	......	69
Connecticut Bureau of Labor Statistics, Hartford......	1	......
Connecticut Historical Society, Hartford......	1	2
Connecticut Society of Sons of the American Revolution, Hartford.....	......	1
Cooper, Mrs. S. B., San Francisco, Cal......	......	2
Cornell University, Agricultural Experiment Station, Ithaca, N. Y.....	2	24
Cornell University, Ithaca, N. Y......	3	3
Cougher, John G., Topeka......	......	1
Cragin, Francis W., Topeka......	......	1
Crane, Geo. W., Topeka.......	......	10
Credit Foncier Company, New York city......	3	18
Crosdale, William T., New York city........	......	5
Cutter, C. A., Boston Athenæum, Mass.....	......	1
Cutter, Nahum S., Greenfield, Mass......	1	57
Dana, J. C., Denver, Colo......	1	6
Daniels, Percy, Girard......	......	6
Darling, Chas. W., Utica, N. Y.....	......	12
Dauchy & Co., New York city......	......	1
Davis, Chas., Junction City......	......	4
Davis, C. Wood, Goddard......	......	1
Davis, John, Washington, D. C......	1	5
Dean, John Ward, Boston......	......	3
Dedham Historical Society, Dedham, Mass......	......	1
Deering, Dr. Benj. T., Paris, France......	......	1
Defouri, Rev. James H., Santa Fé, N. M......	......	1
Delaware Agricultural Experiment Station, Newark......	......	18
Delaware Historical Society, Wilmington......	......	2
Dennis, H. J., Topeka	4	9

DONORS OF BOOKS AND PAMPHLETS — Continued.

DONORS.	Bks.	Pam.
Denver Public Library, Denver, Colo	......	1
Detroit Board of Education, Mich	......	1
Detroit Heating and Lighting Company, Mich	......	1
Detroit Public Library, Mich.	......	2
Dimond, Edwin R., San Francisco, Cal	1	......
Diplomatic Review, London, England	......	46
Ditto, Frank S., Topeka	......	11
Dixon, Wm. Bradford, Kansas City. Mo	1	......
Dodge School of Theology. Dodge City	......	1
Doniphan, John, St. Joseph, Mo	......	7
Doolittle, Miss L. A., Topeka	......	1
Double Chloride of Gold Club, Western Branch, Soldiers' National Home, Leavenworth	......	1
Downs, S. H., Topeka	......	1
Downs, Rev. T. C., Bucyrus	......	1
Doyle, Mrs. C. W., Wichita	1	......
Drexel Institute, Philadelphia, Pa	......	1
Dupuy, Mrs. Maria Wilder, Rochester, N. Y	......	1
Dury, Chas., Cincinnati, Ohio	......	1
Duvall, Linda M., Delaware, Ohio	......	1
Eastman, Dr. B. D., Topeka	12	2
Edmonds, John, Philadelphia, Pa	......	1
Edwards, E. A., Topeka	......	1
Edwards, James E., Dubuque, Iowa	......	1
Elliott, Chas. S., Topeka	1	5
Elliott, L. R., Manhattan	......	1
Emery, Mark P., Portland, Me	1	......
Essex Institute, Salem, Mass	9	6
Evans, D. J., U. S. Navy Department, Washington, D. C	......	1
Fairchild, Geo. T., Manhattan	17	94
Fairchild, Thos. A., Holton	......	1
Farnsworth, Claudius B., Pawtucket, R. I	1	......
Felter, A. W., Fulton	......	1
Felts, W. B., Russell Springs	......	4
Ferguson, D. M., Paola	......	1
Filson, T. A., Concordia	......	1
Findley, John T., Pittsburg, Pa	1	......
Fink, Rev. L. M., Leavenworth	2	......
Florida Agricultural Experiment Station, Lake City	......	8
Foley, John S., Chicago, Ill	......	1
Foote, A. E., Philadelphia, Pa	......	1
Forde, E. S., Emporia	......	5
Foster, Chas. A., Quincy, Mass	......	9
Foster, J. J., W. London, England	......	2
Foster, Rev. R. B., Stillwater, Ok. Ter	......	1
Free Kindergarten Association, Providence, R. I	......	2
Free Public Library, Jersey City, N. J	......	1
French, John Marshall, Milford, Mass	......	2
Friends' Book Committee, Philadelphia, Pa	36	17
Frost, H. W., Topeka	1	......
Frow, John A., Ottawa	......	1
Funk & Wagnalls, New York city	......	5
Garrison, Wendell Phillips, New York	......	1
Geological and Natural History Survey of Canada, Ottawa	1	......
Geological Survey of Missouri, Jefferson City	1	......
George, Rev. A. P., Cimarron	......	4
Georgia Agricultural Experiment Station, Experiment	......	17
Georgia Historical Society, Savannah	......	1
Georgia State Department of Agriculture, Atlanta	6	6
Giles, F. W., Topeka	6	7
Gillespie, Dr. D. M., Clay Centre	1	......
Given, Rev. A., Boston, Mass	1	......
Goldthwaite, W. T., New Orleans, La	2	......
Goodnow, Isaac T., Manhattan	13	817
Goodrich, E. J., Oberlin, Ohio	......	2
Goodspeed, Thomas W., Chicago, Ill	......	1
Goodwin, James J., Hartford, Conn	1	......
Gordon, H. L., Minneapolis, Minn	1	......
Goss, N. S., Topeka	1	......
Goulding, J. H., Rutland, Vt	......	9
Graham, W. O., Kansas City, Mo	......	3
Gray, P. L., Bendena	1	1
Graybill, J. M., Leavenworth	......	1
Green, Chas. R., Lyndon	......	3
Green, Dr. Sam'l A., Boston, Mass	35	187
Green, Samuel S., Worcester, Mass	......	11
Greene, Albert R., Topeka	1	6
Greer, Frank H., Guthrie, Ok	......	1
Grubb, Mrs. S. F., Lawrence	......	94
Gruwell, J. P., Alliance, Ohio	......	1
Guild, Howard R., Providence, R. I	......	1

DONORS OF BOOKS AND PAMPHLETS—CONTINUED.

DONORS.	Bks.	Pam.
Gunn's Unclaimed Money and Estate Agency, London, N. W., England		1
Guthrie, John, Topeka		246
Halderman, John, Leavenworth		1
Hale, George D., Topeka	2	
Hall, E. W., Waterville, Me		1
Hall & O'Donald, Topeka	1	
Hall, Theo. Parsons, Detroit, Mich	1	
Hanback, Mrs. Lewis, Topeka		4
Handy, N. F., Topeka		1
Harper & Brothers, New York city	2	
Harrington, Rev. J. O., Topeka	11	10
Hartford Theological Seminary, Hartford, Conn		1
Hartzell, J. C., Cincinnati, Ohio	1	1
Harvard University, Cambridge, Mass	4	3
Harvard University Library, Cambridge, Mass		28
Haskell Printing Company, Atchison	1	
Hatch Agricultural Experiment Station, Amherst, Mass		23
Havelland, Laura S., Cottonwood, Cal	1	
Hay, John, Junction City		1
Hayden, Rev. Horace Edwin, Wilkes Barre, Penn	1	3
Hazen, Rev. Henry A., Auburndale, Mass	1	
Heath, D. C. & Co., Boston, Mass	1	34
Hebbard, J. C., Topeka		2
Hemenway Expedition, Boston, Mass	1	
Hendy, Rev. John F., Emporia		1
Henrie, C. A., Topeka		1
Hermann, Binger, Washington, D. C		1
Hickok, E. P., Winfield		6
Higgins, William, Topeka	198	
Hill, O. C., Hiawatha	1	
Hiller, Charles A., Salina		1
Hinton, Col. Richard J., Washington, D. C		13
Hirons, C. C., Topeka	1	1
Historical and Philosophical Society of Ohio, Cincinnati		2
Hobbs, Rev. A. L., Collier		1
Hoffman, C. B., Enterprise		9
Hogue, Isaac, Topeka		1
Hoisington, A. J. and E. M., Kansas City, Mo	3	17
Holman, Rev. C., North Topeka		3
Holt, Henry & Co., New York		1
Hopkins, Prof. George E., Topeka		9
Hornbeck, E. A. National City, Cal		1
Hovey, Charles M., Topeka	1	46
Howard, George E., Lincoln, Neb		1
Howard, Prof. W. F., Lakin		2
Howe, E. W., Atchison	1	
Howe, Gilman Bigelow, Northborough, Mass	1	
Huffman, G. M., Lecompton		1
Huguenot Society of America, New York		1
Huling, A. S., Topeka		1
Humphreys, Dr. F., New York		1
Humphrey, Gov. Lyman U., Topeka	5	33
Hunt & Eaton, New York city		2
Hurst, Keenan. Howard		13
Hutchins, Bion S., Clay Centre		2
Hutchinson, William, Washington, D. C		25
Huxley, H. E., Neenah, Wis		1
Hyde Park Historical Society, Hyde Park, Mass	2	16
Iliff, Rev. J. M., Sound City		1
Illinois Agricultural Experiment Station, Champaign		7
Illinois Historical State Library, Springfield		3
Illinois Press Association, Jerseyville		1
Illinois State Board of Health, Springfield	3	
I. O. O. F. Sovereign Grand Lodge, Columbus, Ohio	1	
Indian Rights Association, Philadelphia, Penn		27
Indiana Agricultural Experiment Station, La Fayette		13
Indiana Bureau of Statistics, Indianapolis	2	
Indiana Historical Society, Indianapolis		2
Indiana State Board of Health, Indianapolis	2	
Indiana State Grange, Adams		3
Indiana Weather Service, Indianapolis		1
Ingalls, John J., Atchison	38	1
Inman, Henry, Topeka		4
International American Conference, Washington, D. C	1	
Interstate Commerce Commission, Washington, D. C	2	
Iowa Agricultural Experiment Station, Ames		1
Iowa Historical Society, Iowa City	95	
Iowa State University, Iowa City		1
Irwin, Rev. A. B., Highland		1
Ives, J. N., Topeka	60	

DONORS OF BOOKS AND PAMPHLETS — CONTINUED.

DONORS.	Bks.	Pam.
Jackman, A. C., Minneapolis...		1
Jackson, Miss Mary E., Topeka...	2	......
Jennings, T. B., Topeka...	1	49
Jersey City (N. J.) Free Public Library.................................	1	3
Johns Hopkins University, Baltimore, Md..............................	2	7
Johns, Mrs. Laura M., Salina...	......	2
Johnson, Chas. F., Topeka...	......	1
Johnson, Thos. L., Washington, D. C....................................	......	1
Jones, Rev. J. W., Labette..	......	4
Jones of Binghampton, Binghampton, N. Y.............................	......	6
Jordan, Josiah, Topeka...	......	1
Julian, Geo. W., Centerville, Ind..	......	2
Julian, Isaac H., San Marcos, Texas.....................................	......	1
Junkerman, Mrs. Clara E., Wichita......................................	......	1
Kansas Equal Suffrage Association, Topeka.	......	1
Kansas Institute for the Deaf and Dumb, Olathe......................	......	3
Kansas Library Association, Topeka.....................................	......	24
Kansas Mutual Life Association, Hiawatha..............................	......	4
Kansas State Board of Railroad Commissioners, Topeka.............	120	1
Kansas State Normal School, Emporia..................................	......	2
Kansas Telegraph, Topeka..	......	1
Kellam Book & Stationery Co., Topeka..................................	......	3
Kellogg, Geo. F., Sterling...	......	9
Kellogg, Vernon L., Lawrence...	......	6
Kelly, Harrison, Washington, D. C.......................................	......	3
Kelly, Clarence E., Haverhill, Mass.....................................	1	......
Kelton, Dwight H., Quincy, Mich..	......	1
Kennedy, Wm., Pottsville, Pa...	......	1
Kentucky Agricultural Experiment Station, Lexington................	......	20
Kenyon Military Academy and Harcourt Place Seminary, Gambier, Ohio.	......	1
Kern County Land Company, Bakersfield, Cal..........................	1	5
Kiddoo, H. G., Russell Springs...	......	1
King, J. L., Topeka..	......	2
King, S. S., Kansas City, Kas...	......	2
Knox, Rev. J. D., Topeka..	1	63
Larimer, J. B., Topeka...	......	5
Larison, C. W., Ringos, N. J..	1	......
Lasswell, Jess R., Adrian..	1	......
Lathrop, Rev. Jas. H., Topeka..	......	7
Lawrence, H. & Co., Denver, Colo.......................................	1	......
Lawrence, Dr. Robt. M., Lexington, Mass..............................	1	......
Ledyard, H. B., Detroit, Mich..	......	1
Leech, Edward O., Washington, D. C....................................	1	......
Leicester Town Library, Leicester, Mass................................	......	2
Leland Stanford Junior University, Palo Alto, Cal	......	1
Leonard Scott Publishing Company, New York.........................	......	1
Lewis, A. G., Topeka...	......	1
Lewis, Virgil A., Charleston-Kanawha, W. Va..........................	3	11
Library Company of Philadelphia, Pa...................................	......	2
Lick Observatory, Sacramento, Cal......................................	1	......
Lindsay, Dr. W. S., Topeka..	......	1
Longshore, E. W., Topeka...	......	1
Los Angeles Public Library, California..................................	......	6
Loudon, W. D...	......	1
Louisiana Agricultural Experiment Station, Baton Rouge............	......	43
Lydecker, John E., Kingman..	1	......
McAllaster, O. W., Lawrence...	......	1
McBride, William H., Topeka...	73	......
McCabe, Dr. F. S., Topeka..	......	1
McCarthy, Timothy, Topeka..	1	......
McClurg & Co., Chicago, Ill..	1	......
McDonough, Jos., Albany, N. Y..	......	1
McKeen, John G., Russell..	......	6
McNair, W. P., Wichita..	......	2
McVicar, Dr. Peter, Topeka...	......	1
Magers, J. S., La Cygne...	......	2
Maine Agricultural Experiment Station, Orono........................	2	37
Maine Bureau of Labor Statistics, Augusta............................	1	......
Maine Historical Society, Portland......................................	1	......
Manchester, Alfred, Providence, R. I....................................	......	2
Markham, O. G., Baldwin...	......	4
Marsland, Geo., secretary, New York...................................	2	1
Marston, C. W., Argentine..	......	1
Martin, Mrs. Sophia Smith, Hartford. Conn...........................	1	......
Maryland Agricultural Experiment Station, College Park, Prince George's county.	......	26
Massachusetts Agricultural College, Boston...........................	......	....
Massachusetts Agricultural Experiment Station, Amherst............	6	9
Massachusetts Board of Education, Boston..............................	8	....
Massachusetts Bureau of Statistics of Labor, Boston..................	12	11
Massachusetts Historical Society, Boston...............................	4	1

DONORS OF BOOKS AND PAMPHLETS — Continued.

DONORS.	Bks.	Pam.
Massachusetts Homœopathic Hospital and Ladies' Aid Association, Boston.............	.....	1
Massachusetts Horticultural Society, Boston..	3	6
Massachusetts Institute of Technology, Boston..	2	23
Massachusetts Secretary of State, Boston....	.....	2
Massachusetts School for the Feeble-Minded, Boston..	.....	2
Massachusetts Society for Promoting Agriculture, Boston....................................	.....	2
Massachusetts State Board of Agriculture, Boston..	12	29
Massachusetts State Board of Health. Boston...............	.....	4
Massachusetts State Board of Lunacy and Charity, Boston..................	2	......
May, Samuel P., Newton, Mass.	1	......
Mellott, Clell, Leavenworth.......	.....	2
Mercantile Library Association, San Francisco, Cal....	.....	1
Mercantile Library, Chamber of Commerce, Denver, Colo..................	1	......
Merrill, Frank P., Boston, Mass.	.....	2
Merry, Miss Maggie M., Topeka.......	.....	1
Meserve, Chas. F., Haskell Institute, Lawrence............	.....	1
Methodist Book Concern, New York city..................	.....	2
Mexico Secretary of Agriculture, City of Mexico	1	6
Michigan Agricultural College, Agricultural College P. O....	.....	7
Michigan Agricultural Experiment Station. Agricultural College....	.....	28
Michigan Bureau of Labor and Industrial Statistics, Lansing..................	3	.....
Michigan Secretary of State, Lansing........	4	10
Michigan State Board of Agriculture. Agricultural College.......	1	.....
Michigan State Board of Health, Lansing...............	8	36
Michigan State Library, Lansing............................	6	1
Michigan Weather Service, Lansing..................	.....	1
Miles, John D., Lawrence..................	.....	1
Milwaukee, Wisconsin, Superintendent of Schools..................	12	4
Mims, D. A., Garden City............	.....	1
Miner, Rev. S. J., Sabetha..........	.....	7
Minnesota Academy of Natural Sciences, Minneapolis........	.....	1
Minnesota Agricultural Experiment Station, St. Anthony Park..................	.....	10
Minnesota Bureau of Labor Statistics, Minneapolis..................	2	.....
Minnesota Historical Society, St. Paul..................	1	2
Minney, Dr. J. E., Topeka....	.....	1
Mississippi Agricultural Experiment Station, Agricultural College....	.....	13
Missouri Agricultural Experiment Station, Columbia..................	.....	9
Missouri Bureau of Labor Statistics, Jefferson City..................	1	2
Missouri Geological Survey, Jefferson City..................	.....	5
Missouri River Improvement Association, Kansas City, Mo..................	.....	1
Missouri State Mine Inspector, Jefferson City..................	1	......
Missouri Weather Service, St. Louis	.....	8
Mitchell, John M., Washington, D. C....	.....	2
Mobley, R. D., Grand Junction, Colo..................	.....	1
Mohler, Martin, Topeka	61	785
Montgomery, Jas. Mortimer, New York city..................	1	......
Moore. J. Howard, Cawker City..................	.....	2
Moore, John T., Lawrence..................	.....	1
Moore, Robert R., Topeka..................	21	12
Moore, W. H., Brockport, N. Y..................	.....	1
Morgan, George H., St. Louis, Mo..................	2	5
Morgan, John T., Washington, D. C....	.....	2
Morgan, Nina Lillian, Lawrence........	1	......
Morgridge, Dr. G. O., Los Cerrillos, N. M..................	6	......
Morrill, Justin S., Washington, D. C..................	.....	1
Morris, Jonathan Flynt, Hartford, Conn..................	1	......
Mosher, John B., Alfred Center, N. Y..................	.....	1
Mottram, Mrs. Myra, Ottawa..................	.....	2
Mulvane, J. R., Topeka..................	.....	2
Munn & Co., New York city	.....	4
Mutual League, Boston. Mass.	.....	2
Muybridge, Edward, Philadelphia, Pa..................	.....	1
Nasmith, Rev. J. S., Beloit..................	.....	4
National Grange, Patrons of Husbandry, Washington, D. C..................	2	9
National Prohibition Committee, New York city..................	.....	1
National Republican League, New York city..................	.....	48
National Temperance Society, New York city..................	.....	2
Nebraska Agricultural Experiment Station, Lincoln..................	1	20
Nebraska Bureau of Labor Statistics, Lincoln..................	1	.....
Nebraska Historical Society, Lincoln..................	4	25
Nebraska State Board of Agriculture, Lincoln..................	2	......
Nebraska Weather Service, Doane College, Crete..................	.....	20
Nebraska Wesleyan University, Lincoln..................	.....	2
Neinhiser, Henry, Denver, Colo..................	.....	2
Neubert, Gus. J., Kansas City..................	.....	2
Nevada Agricultural Experiment Station, Reno..................	.....	14
Newbury Library, Chicago, Ill..................	.....	4
New England Historical and Genealogical Society, Boston, Mass..................	.....	4
New England Methodist Historical Society, Boston, Mass..................	.....	1
New England Hospital for Women and Children, Boston, Mass..................	.....	1

DONORS.	Bks.	Pam.
New Hampshire Adjutant General, Concord	1	......
New Hampshire Agricultural Experiment Station, Hanover	......	15
New Hampshire Department of Public Instruction, Concord	1	......
New Hampshire Insurance Commissioner, Concord	1	......
New Hampshire State Board of Agriculture, Concord	1	......
New Hampshire State Board of Health, Manchester	......	1
New Hampshire State Library, Concord	4	......
New Hampshire State Treasurer, Concord	......	1
New Jersey Adjutant General, Trenton	1	......
New Jersey Agricultural Experiment Station, Camden	1	18
New Jersey Statistics of Labor and Industries, Trenton	14	......
New Jersey Free Public Library, Jersey City	......	1
New Jersey State Historical Society, Newark	19	39
New Jersey Pharmaceutical Association, Bayonne	3	......
New Jersey State Reform School, Jamesburg	......	1
New Mexico Agricultural Experiment Station, Las Cruces	......	8
New Mexico Territorial Fair Association, Albuquerque	......	1
New West Education Commission, Chicago, Ill.	......	10
New York Agricultural Experiment Station, Geneva	2	17
New York Bond and Investment Company, New York city	......	1
New York Bureau of Statistics of Labor, Albany	2	1
New York College for the Training of Teachers, New York city	......	9
New York Kindergarten Association, New York city	......	1
New York Life Insurance Company, New York city	......	1
New York State Board of Health, Albany	5	......
New York State Library, Albany	5	12
New York State Reformatory, Elmira	......	6
New York State University, Albany	......	1
Nicaragua Construction Company, New York city	1	9
Nicholson, Geo. T., Topeka	1	1
Norrborn, Rev. A., Topeka	......	1
North Branch Academy, North Branch	......	20
North Carolina Agricultural Experiment Station, Raleigh	......	20
North Carolina Bureau of Statistics, Raleigh	3	......
Northrup, H. M., Kansas City	......	1
Numismatic and Antiquarian Society of Philadelphia, Pa.	......	2
Oates, William C., Washington, D. C.	......	4
Oberlin College, Ohio	1	......
O'Brien, Dr. M., Topeka	61	2
Ohio Agricultural Experiment Station, Columbus	......	39
Ohio Archæological and Historical Society, Columbus	......	3
Ohio Bureau of Labor Statistics, Columbus	1	......
Ohio Department of Inspection, Columbus	1	4
Ohio Historical and Philosophical Society, Cincinnati	......	......
Ohio Inspector of Mines, Columbus	1	......
Ohio Meteorological Bureau, Columbus	......	12
Ohio State Board of Agriculture, Columbus	......	4
Ohio State Board of Health, Columbus	4	......
Ohio State Bureau of Labor, Columbus	2	......
Ohio State Forestry Bureau, Cincinnati	1	......
Ohio Weather and Crop Service, Columbus	......	3
Old Colony Historical Society, Taunton, Mass.	......	3
Oldroyd, O. H., Springfield, Ill.	......	1
Olney, Emeline, Madison, Wis.	......	2
Olney, Henry C., Gunnison, Colo.	......	2
Omaha Public Library, Nebraska	......	1
Oneida Historical Society, Utica, N. Y.	3	16
Onondaga Salt Springs, Syracuse, N. Y.	......	3
Ontario Agricultural College, Guelph, Canada	2	7
Ontario Agricultural Experiment Station, Guelph, Canada	......	21
Ontario Department of Agriculture, Toronto	1	5
Orange Judd Company, New York city	......	2
Oregon Agricultural College, Corvallis	......	3
Oregon Agricultural Experiment Station, Portland	......	31
Osborn, Gov. Thomas A., Topeka	2	......
Osmond, Rev. S. M., Elkton, Md	1	......
Otis, John G., Topeka	......	10
Page, Mrs. Carrie E., Brandon, Vt.	4	12
Palmer, Josiah, Executors of, Brooklyn, N. Y.	2	1
Park, Stanton, Atchison	......	1
Parker, Mrs. Joel, and family, Freehold, N. J.	1	......
Parson, E., Topeka	......	1
Parvin, T. S., Cedar Rapids, Iowa	......	1
Patterson, Geo. A., Oskaloosa	......	2
Paxton, W. M., Platte City, Mo.	......	2
Peabody Academy of Science, Salem, Mass.	......	3
Peabody Institute, Baltimore, Md.	......	2
Peabody Museum of American Archæology and Ethnology, Cambridge, Mass.	......	4
Pecker, J. E., Concord, N. H	......	8

DONORS OF BOOKS AND PAMPHLETS—Continued.

DONORS.	Bks.	Pam.
Peffer Wm. A., Washington. D. C....	2	......
Pennsylvania Adjutant General, Harrisburg....	4	1
Pennsylvania Agricultural Experiment Station, State College, Center county, Pa....	......	13
Pennsylvania Department of Internal Affairs, Harrisburg....	1	......
Philadelphia Public Schools, Superintendent of, Pennsylvania....	......	1
Pennsylvania State College, State College, Pennsylvania....	8	1
Pennsylvania State Penitentiary, Inspectors for Eastern District, Philadelphia....	......	4
Perkins, B. W., Washington, D. C....	7	16
Perry, Leslie J., Washington, D. C....	6	2
Prohibition National Committee, New York....	......	1
Providence Atheneum, Rhode Island....	......	1
Philadelphia Public Library Company, Philadelphia, Pa....	......	1
Philadelphia Society for Organizing Charity, Philadelphia, Pa....	......	26
Phillips, John K., Portland, Ore....	......	1
Plaindealer, Preston....	......	1
Plumb, P. B., Washington, D. C....	28	31
Plumb, Mrs. Preston B., Emporia....	1	......
Polen, H. O. & Co., Kansas City, Mo....	......	1
Pond, J. B., New York city....	......	2
Prescott, B. F., Concord, N. H....	1	......
Pratt Institute, Brooklyn, N. Y....	......	3
Prather, Charles Edgar, Topeka....	1	......
Pope, A. A., Boston, Mass....	......	1
Popenoe, Edwin A., Manhattan....	......	2
Popenoe, F. O., Topeka....	......	28
Portillo, A. & Co., City of Mexico....	2	2
Pounds, L. H., Topeka....	......	7
Powers, Ada Wilmans, Douglasville, Ga....	......	2
Pueblo Board of Trade Association, Colorado....	......	1
Putnam, Prof. F. W., Harvard University, Cambridge, Mass....	......	21
Queensland Department of Agriculture, Brisbane, Australia....	3	15
Quayle, Pres. W. A., Baldwin....	......	3
Ramabai Association, Boston, Mass....	......	3
Rash, Howard C., Cincinnati, O....	......	2
Rathbone, F. B., Oberlin....	......	2
Redden, Dr. J. W., Topeka....	60	......
Reiche, Rev. Gustave, Topeka....	......	1
Reid, W. R., Fort Scott....	......	1
Religious Society of Friends, Philadelphia, Pa....	......	1
Remsburg, Geo. J., Oak Mills....	......	4
Reynolds Library, Rochester, N. Y....	......	2
Rhode Island Agricultural Experiment Station, Kingston....	......	15
Rhode Island Bureau of Industrial Statistics, Providence....	1	1
Rhode Island Historical Society, Providence....	......	2
Rhodes, John S., Topeka....	2	......
Rice, Franklin P., Worcester, Mass....	......	1
Richardson, Rev. A. M., Lawrence....	1	4
Riddle, A. P., Minneapolis...	......	5
Riggs, C. W., Station "C," Cincinnati, O....	......	1
Riley, G. T., Marion....	......	2
Riley, Z. F., Topeka....	6	......
Ritchie, Ryerson, Kansas City, Mo....	2	......
Roberts, Rev. W. H., Cincinnati, O....	1	......
Robinson, Gov. Chas., Lawrence....	1	......
Robinson, Fred. B., Huntsville, Texas....	......	1
Robinson & Co., Richmond, Ind....	......	1
Root, F. A., North Topeka....	1	197
Root, Geo. A., Topeka....	......	236
Ropes, E. E., Astor, Fla....	......	1
Ross, Theodore A., Columbus, O....	13	......
Rossman, J. B. Hamline, Minn....	......	1
Rochester Historical Society, Rochester, N. Y....	1	......
Rowell, Geo. P. & Co., New York city....	1	......
Royal Academy of Belles-lettres, History, and Antiquity, Stockholm, Sweden....	15	......
Royer, Salem B., Mount Morris, Ill....	......	2
Rust, Albert D., Waco, Texas....	1	......
Ryan, Thomas, City of Mexico....	197	4
St. Louis Engineers' Club, St. Louis, Mo....	......	3
St. Louis Mercantile Library Association, Missouri....	......	2
St. Louis Public Library, Missouri....	......	2
Salem Public Library, Salem, Mass....	......	2
Sanborn, F. B., Concord, Mass....	1	......
San Francisco Free Public Library, California....	......	1
San Francisco Mercantile Library Association, San Francisco, Cal....	1	......
San Francisco Produce Exchange....	......	5
Schenck, Dr. W. L., Topeka....	......	1
Scherer, Rev. J. T., Garnett....	......	2
Schmitt, M. J., Emporia....	......	1
Scott, Chas. F., Iola....	1	......

DONORS OF BOOKS AND PAMPHLETS—Continued.

DONORS.	Bks.	Pam.
Scudder, Rev. John L., Jersey City, N. J.		4
Seaver, Edwin P., Boston, Mass.		3
See, Rev. A. N., Salina.		1
Seeds, Mrs. Alice M., Abilene		1
Seventh Day Adventists' Central Publication Association, Battle Creek, Mich.	1	8
Shafer, J. D., Stroudsburg, Pa.	2	12
Shaw, Mrs. Quincy, Boston, Mass.		3
Sheffield, C. S., Topeka.		66
Shelden, Alvah, El Dorado.		6
Sheldon, Rev. Charles M., Topeka.	1	1
Shelton, E. M., Brisbane, Queensland, Australia.		1
Shepard, R. B., Anthony.		1
Sheppard, Wm. D., Springfield, Mo.		3
Sims, William, Topeka.	60	11
Sims, Mrs. William, Topeka		1
Simpson, Jerry, Washington, D. C.	3	5
Smith, Andrew, Albuquerque, N. M.		1
Smith, Col. Andrew J., Leavenworth.		1
Smith, Cassius C., Denver, Colo.		1
Smith, Geo. W., Topeka.	2	87
Smithsonian Institution, Washington, D. C.	28	13
Smithsonian Institution, Bureau of Ethnology, Washington, D. C.	5	1
Smyth, B. B., Topeka.	50	12
Snow, Chancellor F. H., Lawrence.		123
Snow, Miss Florence L., Neosho Falls.		2
Snyder, John H., San Diego, Cal.		2
Snyder, W. A., Topeka.	1	
Société Archeologique du Department de Constantine, Algeria, Africa.	1	
Société de Géographie Commerciale du Havre, France.		1
Société des Sciences Naturelles de la Charente Inferieure, La Rochelle, France.	1	
Société Havraise d'Etudes Diverses, Lé Havre, France.		4
Société Nationale d'Agriculture, Paris, France.	1	
Société Neuchateloise de Géographie, Neuchatel, France.	1	
Society of American Florists, Boston, Mass.		1
Sons of the American Revolution, Washington, D. C.		1
Sons of the Revolution, New York Society, New York city.		1
Southbridge Public Library, Southbridge, Mass.	2	2
South Carolina Experiment Station, Fort Hill.		7
South Dakota Agricultural Experiment Station, Brookings.		30
Southern California Historical Society, Los Angeles.		1
Southern Pacific Railroad Company, San Francisco, Cal.		6
Southwestern Business College, Wichita.		1
Spelman Seminary, Atlanta, Ga.		2
Spencer, Robt. C., Milwaukee, Wis.		1
Spooner, Geo. A., Leavenworth.	2	
Stall, Rev. Sylvanus, Philadelphia, Pa.	3	1
Stanard, L. E., Media.		2
Standard, The, New York.	3	2
Stanley, E., Lawrence.		1
Stanley, T. A., Osawatomie.		1
Stearns, J. N., New York city.		1
Stewart, John T., Scammon.		25
Stewart, W. M., Washington, D. C.		1
Stitt, Geo. P., Hutchinson.		8
Stitt, Geo. S., New York city.		1
Stone, Mrs. Lucy, Boston, Mass.		77
Stonestreet, Fred., Topeka.		1
Storrs School Agricultural Experiment Station, Mansfield, Conn.	1	2
Strickler, Mrs. Harriet S., Topeka.		1
Strong, C. M., U. S. Signal Service, Columbus, O.		2
Sunset Club, of Chicago, Ill.	1	
Swan, Sonnenschein & Co., London, England.	1	
Swensson, Rev. C. A., Lindsborg.		1
Tanner, O. R., Barry.		2
Taylor, A. R., Emporia.		54
Tennessee Agricultural Experiment Station, Knoxville.	1	23
Tennessee State Board of Health, Nashville.		1
Texas Agricultural Experiment Station, College Station, Brazos county.	1	25
Thomas, Rev. A. R., Hahnemann Medical College, Philadelphia, Pa.	1	
Thomas, Rev. Elisha S., Topeka.		2
Thompson, A. H., Topeka.		3
Thompson, Chas. H., Lansing, Mich.	1	
Thwing, Rev. E. P., Brooklyn, N. Y.		1
Tipton, A. W., Topeka.	1	
Torrey, D., Detroit, Mich.		1
Townsend, H. H., North Branch.		4
Trimble, John, Washington, D. C.	1	
Tuttle, Gov. Hiram A., Concord, N. H.	1	
Twentieth Century Publishing Company, New York.		1
Twining, Thomas J., Fort Wayne, Ind.	1	

DONORS OF BOOKS AND PAMPHLETS—Continued.

DONORS.	Bks.	Pam.
United Presbyterian Board of Publication, Pittsburg, Pa.	1	19
U. S. Army, Adjutant General, Washington, D. C.	1	1
" Board on Geographic Names, Washington, D. C.	1	......
" Bureau of American Republics, Washington, D. C.	1	10
" Bureau of Labor, Washington, D. C.	2	......
" Bureau of Rolls and Library, Washington, D. C.	......	1
" Census Office, Robt. P. Porter, Superintendent, Washington, D. C.	......	228
" Chief of Engineers, U. S. A., Washington, D. C.	10	......
" Chief of Ordinance, U. S. A., Washington, D. C.	2	......
" Civil Service Commission, Washington, D. C.	1	6
" Coast and Geodetic Survey, Washington, D. C.	......	1
" Commissioner of Education, Washington, D. C.	25	10
" Commissioner of General Land Office, Washington, D. C.	1	......
" Commissioner of Indian Affairs, Washington, D. C.	7	......
" Commissioner of Labor Statistics, Washington, D. C.	1	......
" Commissioner of Patents, Washington, D. C.	2	......
" Commissioner of Pensions, Washington, D. C.	......	1
" Department of Agriculture, Washington, D. C.	8	58
" Department of Agriculture, Botanical Division. Washington, D. C.	......	5
" Department of Agriculture, Bureau of Animal Industry, Washington, D. C.	1	......
" Department of Agriculture, Division of Chemistry, Washington, D. C.	2	14
" Department of Agriculture, Division of Entomology, Washington, D. C.	......	18
" Department of Agriculture, Division of Forestry, Washington, D. C.	......	2
" Department of Agriculture, Division of Ornithology, Washington, D. C.	......	8
" Department of Agriculture, Division of Pathology, Washington, D. C.	......	5
" Department of Agriculture, Division of Pomology, Washington, D. C.	......	1
" Department of Agriculture, Division of Statistics, Washington, D. C.	1	32
" Department of Agriculture, Division of Vegetable Pathology, Washington, D. C.	......	3
" Department of Agriculture, Office of Experiment Stations, Washington, D. C.	......	40
" Department of Agriculture, Weather Bureau, Washington, D. C.	......	4
" Fish Commissioner, Washington, D. C.	3	......
" Geological Survey, Washington, D. C.	13	17
" Life-Saving Service, Washington, D. C.	1	......
" Light-House Board, Washington, D. C.	3	......
" Military Academy, West Point, N. Y.	......	6
" Naval Academy, Annapolis, Md.	......	1
" Naval Observatory, Washington, D. C.	2	2
" Navy Department, Bureau of Equipment, Nautical Almanac Office, Washington, D. C.	4	......
" Navy Department, Hydrographic Office, Washington, D. C.	4	14
" Postmaster General, Washington, D. C.	......	5
" Secretary of State, Washington, D. C.	10	32
" Secretary of the Interior, Washington, D. C.	315	16
" Secretary of the Treasury, Washington, D. C.	13	......
" Signal Office, Washington, D. C.	1	6
" Treasury Department, Bureau of Statistics, Washington, D. C.	10	8
" Weather Bureau, Washington, D. C.	2	15
Unity Publishing Committee, Chicago, Ill.	......	50
University of California, Berkeley.	3	72
University of Denver, and Colorado Seminary, Denver.	......	1
University of Minnesota, Minneapolis.	......	1
University of Nevada, Reno.	......	1
University of Vermont, Burlington.	......	1
University of Worcester, Mass.	......	1
Utah Agricultural Experiment Station, Logan.	1	11
Unknown.	1	11
Vermont Agricultural Experiment Station, Burlington.	......	14
Veteran Association, 55th Regiment Illinois Volunteer Infantry, Davenport, Iowa.	1	......
Vincent, C., Winfield.	4	......
Vincent Bros., Winfield.	1	......
Vincent, H. & L., Winfield.	1	......
Vincent, W. D., Clay Centre.	......	1
Virginia Agricultural Experiment Station, Blacksburg, Va.	......	17
Votel, Rev. Henry J., St. Mary's.	......	3
Vuilleumier, Jean, Battle Creek, Mich.	......	5
Wallace, Mrs. Catherine P., Melbourne, Australia.	......	28
Wallace, H. B., Salina.	1	......
Waller, D. J., Harrisburg, Pa.	......	1
Walsh, J. DeWitt, Grantville.	1	240
Wanamaker, John, Washington, D. C.	......	......
Ward, Mrs. Jennie Decker, Ottawa.	......	9
Ward, Dr. M. B., Topeka.	......	1
Ware, Emma F., Milton, Mass.	......	1
Warren, Francis E., Cheyenne, Wyo.	......	1
Waugh, Rev. Lorenzo, San Francisco, Cal.	......	6
Webb, Leland J., Topeka.	1	......
Webb, Col. and Mrs Leland J., Topeka.	......	2
Wedderburn, Alexander J., Washington, D. C.	......	3
Welch, Herbert, Philadelphia, Pa.	......	1
Welch, L. A., Leavenworth.	......	4
Wentworth, Moses, Chicago, Ill.	3	......

DONORS OF BOOKS AND PAᴙPHLETS—Concluded.

DONORS.	Bks.	Pam.
Westchester Historical Society, White Plains, N. Y.	......	2
Western Advocate, ᴙankato	......	1
Western Reserve Historical Society, Cleveland, Ohio.	2	1
West Virginia Agricultural Experiment Station, ᴙorgantown.	......	27
Wheeler, Joshua, Nortonville.	......	1
Whiston, E. A., Boston, Mass.	......	54
White, H. F., Topeka.	......	4
White, M. L., Garnett.	......	1
White, W. H., Topeka.	......	1
Whiting, Fanny, Chicago, Ill.	1	......
Whittaker, A. S., North Denver, Colo.	..·..	1
Whittaker, Thomas, New York.	7	......
Whittemore, Henry, New York city.	......	5
Wilder, Mrs. C. F., ᴙanhattan.	......	1
Wilder, D. W., Kansas City, Mo.	......	⁓223
Williams, H., New York city.	......	4
Williams, J. Fletcher, St. Paul, Minn.	3	......
Wilson, Mrs. Augustus, Wilsonton.	......	1
Wilson, Wm. L., Washington, D. C.	......	1
Winans, Geo. W., Topeka.	48	42
Winchell, W. H., ᴙinneapolis, Minn.	......	1
Wisconsin Agricultural Experiment Station, Madison.	2	15
Wisconsin Dairymen's Association, ᴙadison.	2	......
Wisconsin Farmers' Institute, ᴙadison.	1	......
Wisconsin State Board of Health, ᴙadison.	......	1
Wisconsin State Historical Society, ᴙadison.	28	44
Wisconsin University, ᴙadison.	......	1
Wittlesey, E., Washington, D. C.	6	......
Woman's Republican Association, Washington, D. C.	......	1
Wood, M. F., Independence.	......	1
Wood, Mrs. S. N., Woodsdale.	......	1
Woodford, J. E., Burlington.	......	2
Woodward, Chas. L., New York city.	......	1
Worcester Free Public Library, Worcester, Mass.	......	1
Worcester Society of Antiquity, ᴙassachnsetts.	......	9
World's Fair Columbian Exposition, Chicago, Ill.	......	339
World's Congress Auxiliary of the World's Columbian Exposition, Chicago, Ill.	......	6
World's Fair Transportation and Trust Company, Topeka.	......	1
Worrall, Harvey, Topeka.	..·..	3
Wyoming Historical and Geneaological Society, Wilkes Barre, Pa.	......	1
Yale University, New Haven, Conn.	2	130
Yarger, Rev. H. L., Lawrence.	......	4
Yonkers Historical and Library Association, New York.	......	1
Yurann, Jason, Blue Rapids.	......	5

DONORS OF MANUSCRIPTS.

.ms, D. M., Rome: A description written by donor of a hail storm in Sumner :ounty, Kansas, in June, 1886, and of a cyclone in the same county, August 6, 1888.

:ander, J. M., Welda: Autobiographical sketch of donor, Representative from Twentieth District, Legislature of 1891.

:erson, J. W. D., Hot Springs, S. D.: Manuscript bibliography of Kansas, to October 11, 1890, containing 220 titles.

ey, Mrs. Elizabeth A., Lawrence: Manuscripts written by Judge L. D. Bailey, as 'ollows — Kansas Day address, January 29, 1890; letter from Kansas, October 12, 1886, Garden City; the story of Lawrence, 1887; words of welcome, a poem, July j, 1858; first impressions of Kansas, May, 1857; names selected for a projected Kansas State Historical Society, 1865.

ard, David E., Ballard's Falls: Original manuscript proceedings of a meeting of >fficers and soldiers of Kansas regiments at the office of Capt. M. S. Adams, in :amp in Arkansas, August 1, 1864, to take action in reference to a representation >f the Kansas soldiers in the field at the Republican convention, Topeka, September J, 1864, for the nomination of State officers.

nstein, Samuel, Cincinnati, Ohio: A paper containing a biographical sketch of ind eulogy on the late Col. John C. Vaughan, written by donor, and read by him in he chapel at the Cincinnati crematory on the occasion of the funeral of Colonel · 7aughan, Monday, September 26, 1892; 6 letters written by donor, dated Cincinnati,)hio, October and November, 1892, in relation to biography and portraiture of Jol. John C. Vaughan; also copy of a letter by donor to Hon. Joseph Medill, lated October 28, 1892, on the same subject, together with copies of two letters rom Mr. Medill to donor in reply, dated Chicago, October 31 and November 4, 1892.

twell, D. W., Topeka: Letter of Gen. G. Norman Lieber, acting Judge-Advocate 3eneral, to donor, dated Washington, D. C., January 20, 1888, relative to files in he Advocate General's office, pertaining to 5th Kansas Cavalry.

llee, Rev. C. D., Boston, Mass.: Certificate of appointment of Joseph Williams is justice of the peace, county of Suffolk, Province of Massachusetts Bay, in New England, January 12, 1761.

winski, R. V., St. Joseph, Mo.: Letter to donor from War Department, May 8, 1891, with autograph signature of G. Norman Lieber, acting Judge-Advocate General.

wn, Geo. W., Rockford, Ill.: Letter under date of November 2, 1892, relating to lonor's "Reminiscences of Governor Walker," and also to incidents concerning Governor Geary's administration.

wn, Orville C., Adams, N. Y.: Thirty letters written by his son, Spencer Kellogg 3rown, chiefly during the years 1861, 1862, and 1863, while in service as a soldier n the Union army, written from Independence, Jefferson Barracks, St. Louis, and 3pringfield, Mo., from Newport, Ky., from U. S. gunboat Essex, from Jackson, Miss., and from Castle Thunder, Richmond, Va.; diary, of 14 pages, written in ackson, Miss., Penitentiary while a prisoner of war, in 1863; sketch of his army nd prison experiences, written while a prisoner at Richmond, Va.; brief sketches,

headed "Penitentiary Literature;" also manuscript papers of donor, including a receipt of James Redpath for Osawatomie town shares, dated May 21, 1858; petition of Josiah Goodwin to Claim Commissioners Hoogland, Adams, and Kingman; the same of Ephraim Husted; certificate of S. C. Pomeroy relating to the town of Osawatomie, vouching for O. C. Brown; certificate of ownership by O. C. Brown of 100 Osawatomie town shares, signed by the trustees, S. C. Pomeroy, O. C. Brown, William Ward, Samuel Geer, and William Chestnut, and by M. F. Conway, witness; certified copy of indictment in the U. S. court, second judicial district, for Lykins county, against O. C. Brown, John Brown, sr., John Brown, jr., O. V. Dayton, Alexander Gardner, Richard Mendenhall, Chas. A. Foster, Chas. Crane, William Partridge, and William Chestnut, 6; letter of Matthew M. Campbell, agent of the American Bible Society, Monrovia, Kas., June 26, 1860; note of sympathy signed G. B. and H.; letter of O. C. Brown to the Osawatomie monument committee, dated August 21, 1877; 10 miscellaneous letters, and an autograph of Com. W. D. Porter; American seamen's protective paper, in favor of O. C. Brown, dated Sag Harbor, May 26, 1834, signed John P. Osborne, collector; 2 Osawatomie town-share certificates; letters from Mrs. M. A. Brown, December 16, 1855; Orville C. Brown, March 18, 1856; Mrs. M. A. Brown, November 4, November 5, and November 11, 1860, and May 9, 1861; Spencer Kellogg Brown, May 11, 1861, and September 25, 1862; Senator S. C. Pomeroy, January 20, 1862; Com. W. D. Porter, May 25, 1863; Fred. C. Starr [Treasury Department], May 29, 1863; Admiral D. D. Porter, June 5, 1863; Gen. G. M. Locke, June 19, 1863; Adjt. G. T. Sprague, July 21, 1863: Col. W. Hoffman, August 12, 1863; Capt. Geo. D. Wise, October 10, 1863; Spencer Kellogg Brown, September 23, 1863; Senator Roscoe Conkling, September 25, 1863; Ben. J. Lossing, March 22, 1864, and November 4, 1864; Mrs. E. Alberti, August 20, 1865; Mr. Crane's appeal for aid, September 4, 1865; Mrs. Charlotte Crane, New York, September 8, 1865, and October 10, 1865; Jas. H. Sherman, November 18, 1869; list of authors; biographical sketch of Spencer Kellogg Brown; letter written by donor, signed "Chester," and dated Lawrence, Kas., September 2, 1856, giving an account of Kansas affairs at that time, movements of Free-State and Pro-Slavery forces, battle of Osawatomie, etc.; Spencer Kellogg Brown's rules of conversation; letter of Spencer Kellogg Brown, from Osawatomie, dated June 6, 1860, to [A. G.] Boone, asking employment; manuscript relating to Spencer Kellogg Brown's "Experience in Secessia," dated St. Louis, May 6, 1862; letter from Spencer Kellogg Brown to his sister, dated July 20, 1863; fragment of letter of O. C. Brown to Senator S. C. Pomeroy relating to slavery, dated December 12, 1861; letter of O. C. Brown to his wife, dated January 10, 1862, also fragments of two letters to his wife, no dates; 33 manifold copies of letters written by O. C. Brown, mostly from Osawatomie, during the years from 1856 to 1862; letter of Fannie Brown to her parents, dated March 9, 1863; letter of J. T. Carpenter, chaplain of Castle Thunder, dated September 26, 1863, giving an account of Spencer Kellogg Brown's conviction at Richmond, Va., as a spy; telegram from Rev. Wm. G. Scandlin, dated September 24, 1863, announcing Spencer Kellogg Brown's trial at Richmond; letter of same, dated Washington, September 25, 1863, relating to the imprisonment of Spencer Kellogg Brown, and letters, dated Grafton, October 19, 1865, and October 16, 1869, concerning Spencer Kellogg Brown's biography; in all, 46 manuscripts; manuscript of 87 pages, containing an account of the pioneer life of donor in Kansas, from 1854 to 1861; also a manuscript of 15 pages, written by Spencer Kellogg Brown, giving an account of the battle of Osawatomie, copied from his diary.

Brown, W. E., Newton: Autobiographical sketch of donor, Representative Eighty-first District, Legislature of 1891.

Case, Mrs. Lucia O., Topeka: Petition presented to Gov. L. U. Humphrey by the women of Topeka and Salina in behalf of the appointment of Maj. J. K. Hudson to the vacancy in the U. S. Senate caused by the death — December 20, 1891 — of Preston B. Plumb.

Clarke, Sylvester H., Clyde, N. Y.: Letter of donor, August 30, 1891, giving an account of public sentiment in Kansas City, Mo., at the time of the threatened robbery of the American hotel, May, 1855.

Covert, John C., Cleveland, Ohio: Manuscript letter, dated Cleveland, Ohio, October 11, 1892, containing reminiscences of John C. Vaughan.

Dickerson, Luther, Atchison: Commission issued by Gov. Chas. Robinson to donor as captain of Company B, Kansas State Militia, 1861; also order dated May 10, 1861, issued by John A. Martin, inspector for Atchison, addressed to Captain Dickerson.

Dupuy, Mrs. M. W., Rochester, N. Y.: Letter from Oliver Johnson, the distinguished editor and anti-slavery writer, to Hon. D. W. Wilder.

Giles, F. W., Topeka: Letter of Henry George, written to donor, Topeka, April 23, 1888.

Goodnow, I. T., Manhattan: Affidavit of H. A. Wilcox and David Ambrose, relative to jumping the claim of Wm. E. Goodnow by I. Haskell, in May, 1855, dated Juniata, Kas., June 29, 1855; memorandum of testimony relative to the jumping of claim of Wm. E. Goodnow in May, 1855; original House bill, an act locating State University at Manhattan, vetoed by Gov. C. Robinson.

Green, C. R., Lyndon: Manuscript memoranda, notes relating to Capt. John Brown, Hon. L. D. Bailey, and Quenemo (Sac and Fox Indian); manuscript roster of ex-soldiers, sailors, militiamen, and their widows and orphans, residing in Burlingame township, Osage county, 1889; same as above in Scranton township, 1889; manuscript poem, entitled "General Sherman and the War," in two parts; 6 manuscript orders issued by Gen. James G. Blunt at Fort Leavenworth, May, 1862, found in Kentucky by donor, where they had been left by Kansas troops with surplus baggage; manuscript passes, orders, and various military papers of donor, relating to Sherman's Atlanta campaign, 1864, 41 in all; memorandum book carried by donor through part of the War of the Rebellion, containing accounts, list of letters written, clothing drawn, and army incidents, etc.

Greene, Albert R., Topeka: Biographical sketch of Gen. Thos. J. B. B. Cramer, Treasurer of Kansas Territory, written by donor; manuscript sketch by donor, entitled "A Few Remarks about the Town of Lecompton."

Guthrie, John, Topeka: Commission of donor as United States presidential elector, dated Topeka, November 30, 1872, signed "W. H. Smallwood, Secretary of State."

Halderman, John A., Leavenworth: 109 manuscript letters, documents, and legal papers, principally of dates during the Kansas territorial period and that of the civil war, and bearing the following signatures: O. Diefendorf, Wm. S. Yohe, J. H. Day, trustees of Leavenworth Association, John W. Forman, W. H. Russell, Hugh Ewing, C. H. McLaughlin, Wm. B. Hutchinson, Hon. Wm. Bigler, Judge Rush Elmore, Gen. John H. Morgan (of the Confederate army), Sheriff Sam'l J. Jones, H. D. McMeekin, E. L. Berthoud, J. L. Byers, Gen. Frank J. Marshall, Henry Addoms, W. S. Brewster, Surgeon General Wm. A. Hammond, Gen. Nathaniel Lyon, John N. Dyer, Col. C. W. Adams, Gen. Henry Stanberry, Judge Martin F. Conway, S. S. Marshall, Gen. H. J. Strickler, A. McDonald, Hugh S. Walsh, Gen. W. E. Walker, Hon. J. P. Usher, Alex. Repine, Gen. Powell Clayton,

E. Hensley, Geo. R. Hines, Gov. Geo. A. Crawford, W. A. Shannon, Orrin T. Welch, Gen. S. C. Pomeroy, Bishop Vail, D. H. Armstrong, H. Miles Moore, Geo. W. Gist. Robt. Wilson, Sam'l Paul, C. B. Donalson, G. P. Lowrey, W. R. Montgomery, Gov. Andrew H. Reeder, Judge Sam'l D. Lecompte, A. Dawson, Thos. A. Minard, John Donalson, W. H. Hutter, Abram Barry, Thos. Sherwood, Johnston Lykins; H. M. Hook, C. C. Andrews, Thos. T. Slocum, Sam'l J. Jones, A. G. Otis, Wm. L. Blair, Vice-President Thos. A. Hendricks, Aristides Rodrique, Maj. S. Macklin, Gen. J. W. Whitfield, Chas. Mundee, John P. Slough, Cyrus F. Currier, N. S. Goss, Gov Henry A. Wise, Geo. W. Brown, Orlin Thurston, W. C. P. Breckinridge, Gen. Geo. W. Deitzler, Gov. Thos. Moonlight, J. N. Halloway, Ruggles & Plumb, Gov. T. T. Crittenden, John M. Haberlein, P. I. B. Ping, John J. Ingalls, Hon. Dudley C. Haskell, Gen. Rufus Ingalls, Frank M. Tracey, T. J. Hudson; autograph letter of donor relating to the battle of Wilson's Creek, dated Washington, D. C., July 24, 1882.

Hardick, Cornelius Fonda, Louisville: Autobiographichal sketch of donor, Representative Fiftieth District, Legislature, 1891.

Harrington, Grant W., Hiawatha: Copy of certificate No. 144, Claytonville Town Company, Brown county, Kansas, dated March 9, 1857.

Harris, Rev. Theo. W., Topeka: Resolution of the Topeka Ministerial Union in favor of prohibiting the sale of liquor in the national Capitol.

Henry, Rev. S., Rutland: Autobiographical sketch of donor, Representative Thirty-first District, Legislature of 1891.

Hinton, Col. R. J., Washington, D. C.: Manuscript paper containing the message of President Andrew Jackson, dated January 3, 1830, to the Senate in relation to the treaty at Dancing Rabbit creek with the Choctaw Indians, bearing the autograph signature of President Jackson; 3 letters of Martin F. Conway, dated June 15, 1859, February 9 and 21, 1861; letter of W. D. Howells, dated Columbus, Ohio, August 24, 1860; letter of Joseph Medill, January 21, 1862; letter of Fred. P. Stanton, June 22, 1862; letter of John Swinton, 1863 or 1864; copy of letter of Gen. John McNeil, dated "Headquarters, Fort Smith, December 20, 1863;" letter of Gen. S. R. Curtis, April 4, 1865; 2 letters of Walt Whitman, October 22, and November 8, 1866; original lecture written by Richard Realf, on "Shakespeare," and delivered by him at the U. S. Government Library, at Governor's Island, N. Y., February 4, 1869; letter of Edward E. Ropes, dated Lake View, Fla., March 14, 1871; paper in the handwriting of Frank J. Merriam, of Boston, one of John Brown's Harper's Ferry party, containing a list of five secret-writing inks, for use in army and other secret correspondence; provost marshal permit, dated January 15, 1852, permitting donor to pass beyond the limits of the city of St. Joseph, Mo., to go to Hannibal, signed "S. Hatch, Lieutenant 16th Ill. Regt. and Provost Marshal," with a description of donor and oath of loyalty attached. sworn to before the provost marshal; letter of C. B. Carpenter, dated Tolono, Ill., May 10, 1863, relative to a missing contraband woman; manuscript letter of U. S. Senator John Sherman, dated February 26, 1864, relating to the legality of the election of Thos. Carney to the U. S. Senate from Kansas by the Legislature of 1864; also one from Senator James Harlan, of Iowa, of the same date, and on the same subject.

Hutchinson, Wm., Washington, D. C.: 120 manuscripts pertaining to early Kansas history—letters of Dr. W. W. Updegraff, Osawatomie, August 5, 1856; James Redpath, Chicago, October 28, 1856; Justin S. Morrill, Washington, December 24, 1856; Col. C. K. Holliday, Topeka, November 11, 1857; Henry Harvey, Brownsville, January 23 and March 2, 1858; Hugh S. Walsh, Lecompton, February 25,

1858; W. W. Ross, Topeka, April 21, 1858; R. J. Hinton, Boston, December 28, 1858; E. P. Watson, Marion, Mass., July 26, 1860; Thomas Ewing, jr., Leavenworth, April 14, 1860; S. C. Pomeroy, Atchison, July 10, ——; Lucy Larcom, Bethel, Maine, August 27, 1879; 7 letters from Henry J. Adams, Washington, D. C., from April to November, 1860; 4 letters from Geo. W. Collamore, written in 1856, '57,' '58, '59; 2 letters of Marcus J. Parrott, 1856 and 1860; 10 letters of Henry J. Raymond, of the New York *Times*, 1856 to 1860; 5 letters of Gov. A. H. Reeder, 1856-'61; 2 letters of Gov. Charles Robinson, 1856 and 1858; letter of Geo. W. Brown, 1856; 4 letters of Dr. Joseph P. Root, 1856-'57; 2 letters of Eli Thayer, Worcester, Mass., 1859; 2 letters of Augustus Wattles, Moneka and Fort Scott, April and November, 1858; letter of Wm. Hutchinson to W. Y. Roberts, June 26, 1857; letters relating to relief distribution, 1856 and 1857, written by A. Curtis, Thos. W. Higginson, C. C. Parker, E. B. Whitman (2), Mrs. Jennie E. Eddy, Richmond, Ind., Mrs. J. M. Howard, Detroit, Mich., H. Miles Moore, G. W. Hutchinson, and O. C. Brown. Miscellaneous papers: Report of Wm. Hutchinson to the national Kansas committee relative to condition of hostility in Kansas, in August, 1856; call for convention to nominate State officers under the Leavenworth constitution, April 28, 1858; address of Wm. Hutchinson before the House of Representatives, Topeka, June, 1857, on his election as Speaker *pro tem.;* speech of Wm. Hutchinson at the territorial convention at Lawrence, December 3, 1857, on the question of voting under the Lecompton constitution; vigilance club obligation, Kansas, 1855; declaration of principles at State Republican convention; report of committee on the charter election, in Lawrence, March, 1858; a bill to incorporate the Scientific and Historical Society of Kansas; appeal from the merchants of Lawrence to the merchants of St. Louis against the interruption by Missourians of the transit of goods through Missouri to Kansas; letter of W. H. Russell, Lexington, Mo., to J. Riddlesbarger & Co., Kansas City, relative to a box on board the steamer Genoa, containing a piano, supposed by Missourians to contain guns for Kansas, March 21, 1856; reward of $100 offered by E. B. Whitman for apprehension of the robbers of the Lawrence relief store; list of persons composing the second regular party sent by the New England Emigrant Aid Company for Kansas Territory, March 20, 1855, in charge of J. T. Farwell, manufacturer of tools, Fitchburg, Mass.; historical sketch of Lawrence, Kansas, written by donor in 1860.

Iliff, Rev. J. M., Mound City: Manuscript records of the South Kansas Conference, M. E. Church, 1873-'84, in three volumes. [Special deposit.]

Ingram, Joseph Thomas, Republic City: Autobiographical sketch of donor, Representative Seventy-third District, Legislature of 1891.

Johnson, Maj. John Arrell, North Topeka: Manuscript military history of donor.

Keith, Mrs. W. T. [Eliza Meeker], Oakland, Cal.: Three manuscript books containing the daily journal kept by her father, the Rev. Jotham Meeker, missionary to the Indians in Michigan and Kansas, beginning with September 10, 1832, and ending with January 4, 1855; notes taken from a letter of Mrs. Jotham Meeker to her daughter Emma, a short time after Mr. Meeker's death, January, 1855.

Larcom, Miss Lucy, Boston, Mass.: Autograph copy of her poem entitled "A Call to Kansas," written in February, 1855, as a prize poem for the New England Emigrant Aid Company, and for which the sum of $50 was paid by Dr. Thomas H. Webb, the secretary of the company.

Kingman, Judge Samuel A., Topeka: Biographical sketch of Hon. W. B. Barnett, Kansas State Senator, 1861.

Lawrence, W, W. H. Painesville, Ohio: Manuscript relating an incident in the early

days in Kansas, pertaining to the election, August 2, 1858, on the Lecompton constitution, as submitted by the English bill.

Lines, Family of the late Chas. B., Wabaunsee: Manuscript book containing the minutes of the meetings of the Connecticut Kansas colony, better known as the "Beecher Bible and Rifle Colony," organized in New Haven, Conn., March 7, 1856, and settled at Wabaunsee in April the same year.

McKinnie, Geo. Henry: Autobiographical sketch of donor, Representative from the One-hundredth District, Legislature of 1891.

McKonkey, Geo., Minneapolis: Autobiographical sketch of donor, Representative Seventy-seventh District, Legislature of 1891.

Medill, Joseph, Chicago, Ill.: Manuscript letter, dated Chicago, October 31, 1892, containing reminiscences of Col. John C. Vaughan.

Morrison, Philip A., Altamont: Autobiographical sketch of donor, Representative Twenty-ninth District, in the Legislature of 1891.

Morse, O. E., Mound City: Letter relating to the execution by hanging, October 30, 1863, of Wm. Griffith, one of the participants in the Marais des Cygnes massacre.

Noble, Peter Stryker, Webster City, Iowa: Autobiographical sketch of donor, dated Washington, D. C., August 10, 1892.

Phillips, J. H., Paola: Biographical sketch of James Armstrong Phillips.

Prentis, Noble L., Newton: Manuscript of his address before the State Editorial Association at Winfield, May 10, 1883, on the subject, "Facts and Failures of Journalism."

Scott, W. W., Canal Dover, Ohio: Photo. of lines written in the album of Miss Fanny Dawson, Bloomfield, Ky., by the guerrilla, William Clark Quantrill, 69 days previous to receiving his death wound within five miles of that place.

Stephens, John Phares, Hoyt: Autobiographical sketch of donor, Representative of Sixteenth District, Legislature of 1891.

Tappan, Saml. F., Washington, D. C.: Eight manuscripts written by donor, and given by him to the Society in November, 1890, as follows: Personal recollections of debate in U. S. Senate, February 27, 1859, on the bill for the admission of Kansas under the Lecompton constitution, relating to speeches of John P. Hale, Stephen A. Douglass, Albert G. Brown; Gwin, of California; Green, of Missouri; Jefferson Davis, and others; 2 papers relating to the history of the congressional debate on the Lecompton constitution; paper containing an account of a tour of Kansas by writer with Hon. Martin F. Conway, in June and July, 1855; visit to Neosho Valley, Fort Riley, Manhattan, etc.; mention of Big Springs convention; account of Branson's rescue; incident of the Wakarusa war; sketches of Sheriff S. J. Jones and C. W. F. Leonhardt; paper containing a statement of the attitude of Col. Thos. H. Benton and D. R. Atchison on the Kansas question: chronology of Kansas debate in Congress, 1852, –'53, –'54; a poem entitled "Telemachus, and John Brown;" a paper on the illegality of slavery in the United States.

Vail, Chas., Colby: Autobiographical sketch of donor, Representative One Hundred and Twenty-third District, 1891.

Walsh, J. DeWitt, Grantville: One hundred and eight manuscript papers of the late Secretary Hugh S. Walsh, relating to the Territorial Legislature of 1858, including vouchers and accounts of members and officers of the Legislature, legislative printer, and bills for supplies, certified to by Gov. J. W. Denver, C. W. Babcock, President of the Council; G. W. Deitzler, Speaker of the House of Representatives; and George F. Warren, Sergeant-at-Arms.

Whittaker, David, Topeka: Autobiographical sketch of donor, dated Topeka, July

30, 1892, together with gift of letter of John A. Martin to donor, dated Topeka, June 3, 1861.

Whittier, John G., Amesbury, Mass.: Autograph copy of his poem entitled, "Song of the Kansas Emigrants," written in 1854.

World's Fair Columbian Exposition, Chicago, Ill.: Weekly letters relating to the World's Columbian Exposition.

Worrall, Harvey, Topeka: Letter written in Roman alphabet, phonetic, with dia-critical marks to denote pronunciation.

DONORS OF MAPS, ATLASES, AND CHARTS.

Adams, F. G., Topeka: Map showing stage lines to all principal mining camps in San Luis Valley, Colo.

Bradlee, Rev. C. D., Boston, Mass.: Map of the city of Boston for 1891.

Credit Foncier Company, New York: Jones's combination map and chart; map of the Fuerte Valley from Topolobampo Bay, Mexico; 1 map of Frete Valley, Topolobampo Bay.

Ditto, Frank S., Topeka: Outline map of Kansas, with all county boundary lines.

Geological and Natural History Survey of Canada, Ottawa: Maps to accompany Fourth Annual Report, new series, 1888–'89.

Geological Survey of Missouri, Jefferson City: The Higginsville sheet, La Fayette county, April, 1892.

Goodnow, Isaac T., Manhattan: Map of Kansas State Agricultural College lands Washington, Marshall, Clay, Riley and Dickinson counties; map of Kentucky geological survey; Jones's Combination Chart and map of the United States, 1891; 14 miscellaneous Kansas and other maps; Worcester's Historical Atlas, Boston, 1830, folio, 41 pages.

Green, C. R., Lyndon: War map of country within 30 miles of Richmond, Va., May 3, 1864.

Ingalls, John J., Atchison: Atlas to accompany the official records of the War of the Rebellion, parts 1 to 8.

Jennings, T. B., Topeka: Precipitation charts of the Kansas Weather Service, April 14, 23, May 5, 12, 19, 26, June 11, 18, 25, July 2, 9, 16, 23, 30, August 6, 13, 20, 27, September 3, 10, 17, 1892; weather charts; official forecast at Kansas City, Mo., from October, 1888, to February, 1892; 2,000 charts.

Johnson, A. S., Topeka: Vest-pocket map of Kansas, with a table of distances from Kansas City.

Kansas State Board of Railroad Commissioners, Topeka: 60 Kansas railroad maps 1891; official railroad map of Kansas, 1892, 60 copies.

Missouri Commissioner of Labor, Jefferson City: Map of Missouri, showing commodities, marked by counties.

Otis, J. G., Washington, D. C.: Post-route map of Kansas and Nebraska to October, 1891.

Queensland, Australia, Department of Agriculture, Brisbane: Map of Queensland water supply department, 1890, 1891.

Root, Geo. A., Topeka: Map of the city of Topeka, Shawnee county, 1887.

Rossman, J. B., Hamline, Minn.: Map of St. Paul and Minneapolis, Minn.

Ryan, Daniel J., Columbus, Ohio: 6 railroad, political and statistical maps of Ohio.

Smith, Geo., Topeka: Map of Kansas issued by the State Board of Railroad Commissioners, 1887 (5 copies).

Southern Pacific R. R. Co., San Francisco, Cal.: The unique map of California.

Unknown: Map of the city of St. Louis.

U. S. Commissioner of Indian Affairs, Washington, D. C.: Map showing Indian reservations within the limits of the United States, compiled under the direction of T. J. Morgan, Commissioner, 1890.

U. S. Department of the Interior, General Land Office, Washington, D. C.: Map of the United States, 1888.

U. S. Geological Survey, Washington, D. C.: 57 geological atlas maps, all of Kansas.

U. S. Navy Department, Hydrographer's Office, Washington, D. C.: Pilot chart of the North Atlantic ocean, November, 1887; February, September, October, 1888; December, 1888, to January, 1891; November, 1891; November, 1892; pilot chart, hurricanes of November 21-28, 1888.

U. S. Secretary of Agriculture: Album of Agricultural Graphics; values per acre of crops of the United States—1 atlas.

U. S. Signal Office, Washington, D. C.: Tri-daily meteorological record, May to December, 1878 — 720 charts; daily international charts, July to December, 1884, October, 1886, to December, 1887 — 274 charts.

U. S. Weather Bureau, Washington, D. C.: 13 weather and other charts.

World's Fair Columbian Exposition, Chicago, Ill.: 2 maps.

DONORS OF PICTURES.

Adams, F. G., Topeka: Photograph group of National Editorial Association at Senator Palmer's log cabin, at the annual convention at Detroit, August 27-30, 1889.

Baker, Wm., Washington, D. C.: Cabinet photograph of donor, Congressman Sixth District, Kansas.

Bell, Mrs. Lydia, Fancy Creek: Card photograph of Catholic Church, Atchison.

Benton, W. R., Oakland: 10 views showing plans of World's Columbian Exposition buildings and grounds, Chicago; monogram of the 23 Republican members of the House of Representatives, 1891, who voted for John J. Ingalls for United States Senator.

Bernstein, Samuel, Cincinnati, Ohio: Cabinet photograph of Col. John C. Vaughan.

Buffalo Historical Society, Buffalo, N. Y.: Two views of the monument erected to the memory of Red Jacket.

Butler, Mrs. Sybil S., Farmington: Large crayon portrait of Rev. Pardee Butler.

Cabrera, Daniel, City of Mexico, Mexico: Lithograph portraits of Melchor Ocampo, Vicente Guerrero, Ignacio Allende, Lic. Sebastian Lerdo de Tejada; also lithograph of Monumento á Cuauhtemoc.

Chapman, E. L., Great Bend: Photograph of donor, State Senator Thirty-sixth District, 1889.

Clarke, Sylvester H., Clyde, N. Y.: Daguerreotype of Horace Greeley, taken at Clyde, N. Y., October, 1860; presented to donor by Mr. Greeley.

Coöperative News, Cincinnati, Ohio: Supplement containing photo-lithographs of the offices of the Ohio Building Association League.

Corwin, H. C., Topeka: Photographs showing progress of the work on the Kansas river dam at Topeka, November 6 and 18, 1891 — 3 pictures.

Crawford, Gov. Saml. J., Topeka: Life-size oil painting of donor.

Dunbar, W., Washington, D. C.: Copper-plate portraits of Senator John J. Ingalls, Hon. Thos. B. Reed, Gov. W. R. Merriam, and Gov. Jas. E. Campbell.

Dupuy, Mrs. M. W., Rochester, N. Y.: Photo. portrait of Oliver Johnson, the last survivor of the N. E. Anti-Slavery Society of 1832; cabinet photograph of Hon. A. Carter Wilder.

Elder, P. P., Princeton: Photo. portrait of donor, Speaker of the House of Representatives, 1891.

Farrow, W. F., Topeka: Photograph set of six views, showing the funeral procession of Senator P. B. Plumb, at Topeka, December 23, 1891.

Goodman, Mrs. Mary C., Philadelphia, Pa.: Photo. portrait of ex-Gov. John W. Geary.

Goodnow, Isaac T., Manhattan: One photograph group.

Halderman, John A., Leavenworth: Large photo. portrait of donor.

Herbert, Ewing, Hiawatha: Photo. group, portraits of Will. A. White, Vernon L. Kellogg, and Ewing Herbert.

Hinton, Col. Richard J., Washington, D. C.: Framed photo. portrait of donor.

Hutchins, Bion S., Wellington: Life-size crayon portrait of Wirt W. Walton.

Jones, C. J., Omaha, Neb.: Large photograph of buffalos harnessed; also herd of donor's buffalos and crosses (catalos).

Keagy, Franklin, Chambersburg, Pa.: Photograph of the house of Mrs. Ritner, in Chambersburg, in which John Brown, John H. Kagi and others tarried while organizing the Harper's Ferry raid.

Kelly, Harrison, Burlington: Cabinet photograph of donor.

Kent, Orson, Burlington: Cabinet photograph of Hiram McAllister; card photograph of Andrew Franklin.

Leonard, J. H., Topeka: Photograph of the W. H. R. Lykins log cabin, Lawrence, 1855; photo. portrait of Capt. John Brown; photograph of John Brown whistle.

Longton, Geo. R., North Topeka: Photograph of State fair grounds, Topeka, 1871; photograph of Tefft House, in Topeka, taken by J. Lee Knight.

Losch, Wm., Topeka: Photograph of Wartburg Castle, in which Martin Luther was detained by the Elector of Saxony after being taken prisoner while coming from the Diet of Worms, and where he translated the Bible; also photograph of the interior of Luther's room in the castle.

Lydecker, John E., Kingman: Bird's-eye view of Fargo Springs, Seward county.

Martin, H. T., Topeka: Two photographs showing the South Carolina red flag brought to Kansas by Capt. F. G. Palmer, of the Atchison South Carolina company of Pro-Slavery men, in 1856, displayed at Lawrence at the "sacking," May 21, 1856, and captured with the company at the battle of Slough Creek, September 11, 1856, by Col. Jas. A. Harvey's forces.

Natural Science Association of America, New York city: Three colored plates, viz., 11, 65, and 95 — birds of America.

Neeley, S. F., Leavenworth: Photo. portrait of donor, Representative, Legislature of 1891, Seventh District.

Neiswander, W. A., Topeka: Photograph of decorations at Westminister Presbyterian Church, Topeka, Thanksgiving Day, 1890, with portrait of Rev. T. W. Harris, pastor.

Newby, J., Milford: Photo. views of the battle ground of Palmyra, or Black Jack — two pictures.

Noble, Peter Stryker, Washington, D. C.: Cabinet-sized photograph of donor, formerly Adjutant General of Kansas.

Orner, Theo. F., Topeka: Colossal oil-painted portrait of Pres. Benj. Harrison.

Plumb, Mrs. Preston B., Emporia: Framed photo. portrait of the late Senator Preston B. Plumb.

Popenoe, Edwin A., Manhattan: Photo. group of the faculty of the State Agricultural College, 1890; stereoscopic view of a buffalo killed for the hide.

Popenoe, F. O., Topeka: Photograph view of ruin of the first Baptist meeting-house built in Rawlins county, Kansas, a sod house; also photograph view of Swedish sod meeting-house in Rawlins county, with congregation, photographed April, 1891; stereoscopic views of the Bender murder place, Cherry Vale; also stereoscopic view of the first settlers on the prairie.

Read, F. W., Lawrence: Photograph copy of painting of Lawrence as in 1858; also stereoscopic view of the same.

Reader, S. J., North Topeka: Photograph views of house built by Gen. W. T. Sherman in Soldier township, Shawnee county, Kansas, 1859, and taken by donor October 22, 1891.

Remsburg, Geo. J., Oak Mills: Cabinet photograph of John E. Remsburg.

Remington, J. B., Osawatomie: Cabinet photograph of Rev. S. L. Adair, of Osawatomie.

Rice, Oscar, Fort Scott: Photograph, front and rear views of John Brown's fort at Harper's Ferry, Va.

Root, Frank A., North Topeka: Bird's-eye view of buildings to be erected by Topeka wheel factory, Seymour Davis, architect.

Root, Dr. J. P., jr., Kansas City, Kas.: Photograph of Gov. J. P. Root, taken about 1879.

Shafer, J. D., Stroudsburg, Pa.: Photograph of donor and student in donor's law office at Leavenworth city, 1885.

Shockley, Maj. W. B., Fort Scott: Photograph of the Confederate General, John Morgan, and his wife, representing General Morgan in uniform, sitting, and his wife standing by his side.

Simpson, Jerry, Washington D. C.: Cabinet photograph of donor.

Smith, Dr. L. Anton, Topeka: Card photograph showing west side of Kansas avenue, Topeka, between Fifth and Sixth streets, about 1870.

Stevenson, E. S., El Dorado: Eight photograph views showing the ruins and remains of Towanda as left by the cyclone of March 31, 1892.

Stewart, Sam'l J., Humboldt: Photo. of donor and his brother, Watson Stewart.

Unknown: Lithographs of Kenyon Military Academy and Harcourt Place Seminary.

Vandercook & Co., Chicago, Ill.: Two sheets of illustrations of half-tone process specimens of engraving.

Walker, Col. Samuel, Lawrence: Life-size crayon portrait of donor.

Walsh, J. DeWitt, Grantville: Cabinet photo. portrait of his father, the late Hon. Hugh S. Walsh.

Woodman, Seldon J., Topeka: His original oil-painted portrait of John Brown, an engraving from which was published in the Century Magazine of July. 1883, upon which high encomiums were passed by John G. Whittier, Mrs. John Brown. and others; photo. picture showing portrait of Hon. S. C. Pomeroy, seated in his carriage in front of his residence, Washington, D. C.; photo. portrait of donor; cabinet photo. portrait of Gen. J. H. Lane.

World's Fair Columbian Exposition, Chicago: Official bird's-eye views, showing grounds and designs of the buildings — 5 pictures; plan of Machinery Hall, Chicago, 1893; 10 views showing the plans of buildings and grounds.

DONORS OF SCRIP, COINS, AND MEDALS.

Attwater, Henry R., Sedan: Funding bonds of Montgomery county (1871), Lincoln county (1874), Reno county (1874), Howard county (1874).

Barnd, J. K., Ness City: The Ness City *News's* sight draft, 50 cents.

Bondi, August, Salina: Certificate of share No. 46, issued to Ed. Lotz by the Coöperative Meat Market, Salina, February, 1884.

Bradlee, Rev. C. D., Boston, Mass.: Seven Spanish coins, of dates from 1767 to 1821.

Emery, Judge J. S., Lawrence: Share No. 67 of stock issued by the Leavenworth, Lawrence & Fort Gibson Rld. Co., February 10, 1865, to donor, for $2,000; shares Nos. 258 and 259, stock in the town of Minneola, Kas., issued by the Minneola Town Company, March 10, 1858.

Harrington, Rev. M. O., Topeka: Five pieces of Confederate currency, Richmond, Va.; 29 pieces of fractional currency issued during the War of the Rebellion by banks and private individuals and corporations in Columbus, Augusta, Macon, and other towns in Georgia, and one in Chattanooga, Tenn.; 10 notes issued by the Manufacturers' Bank and other banks at Macon, Ga., Chattanooga, Tenn., and by the State Bank of Alabama—in all, 44 pieces; 12 copper coins, English farthings, of dates 1860, '63, '64, '66, '67, '68, '73, '75, '78.

Klink, C. F., Horton: Spanish quarter-dollar, 1786; U. S. copper cent, 1857; and U. S. 13-link coin, 1787—3 coins; also a Leavenworth shinplaster, 5 cents.

Lewis, Virgil A., Charleston-Kanawha, W. Va.: Two Virginia treasury notes of $1 each, dated October 21, 1862.

Raymond, S. S., Frederick: Continental currency, 1 piece, $7.

Wyoming Historical and Geological Society, Wilkes Barre, Pa.: Medal commemorating the battle and massacre at Wyoming, Pa., July 7, 1779.

DONORS OF WAR RELICS.

Goodnow, Prof. I. T., Manhattan: Burnside rifle No. 84, manufactured by Bristol Fire-Arms Co., Providence, R. I.; invented by Gen. A. E. Burnside while on duty in the Mexican War, and adopted by him for Rhode Island troops in the War of the Rebellion. Given to donor by Governor Jackson, of Rhode Island, in December, 1860, for introduction in the West. Shown by donor to Governor Wood, of Illinois, and Col. Ephraim Elmer Ellsworth at Springfield, January 17, 1861; also, a box of ammunition for the same.

Green, C. R., Lyndon: Wallet labeled "War Treasury; served through part of the War; kept for the good it has done."

Johnson, Maj. J. Arrell, Topeka: Mementoes presented to him by his comrades of the 6th Kansas Vol. Regt. as testimonials of their respect and confidence in him as a brave soldier in the War for the Union, namely: A pair of silver-mounted, gold-plated cylinder Remington revolvers; a sword of Damascus steel, with silver hilt and gold-plated guards, the scabbard gold plated, with silver trimmings; a cross composed of gold, silver and copper ore, mingled with crystals and Indian relics; a 7th Army Corps pin of solid gold; also, an antique gold watch, an heirloom of Major Johnson's family, presented to Major Johnson by his father, Maj. Fielding Johnson.

Miller, Sol., Troy: Hat and sword taken from the body of a dead bushwhacker on an Arkansas battle field, 1863, by Rev. Ozem B. Gardner, who presented it to donor.

Popenoe, Edwin A., Manhattan: 3 canister shots, 6 bullets, and a fragment of shell, all from the battle field of Pea Ridge, Ark. (fought March 6, 7, and 8, 1862), procured by donor in 1890 — 10 war relics.

DONORS OF MISCELLANEOUS CONTRIBUTIONS AND RELICS.

Adams, F. G., Topeka: Badge of the Northwest Kansas Editorial Association, Clay Centre, Colorado excursion, June, 1891; 4 railroad folders; badges of the seventh annual convention of the National Editorial Association, St. Paul, Minn., July 14-17, 1891; 14 out-of-date railroad passes; cards and programs relating to Northwestern Kansas Editorial Association; circular and program of the Eastern Kansas Editorial Association, August 12, 1892.

Adams, Miss Harriet E., Topeka: Program of graduating exercises, Washburn College, Topeka, twenty-sixth commencement, June, 1891.

A. T. & S. F. R. R. Co., passenger department, Topeka: Two folders descriptive of the country through which the road passes.

Bailey, E. H. S., Lawrence: Notice of the twenty-fourth annual meeting, Kansas Academy of Science, Ottawa, October 14-16, 1891.

Balston, Mrs. G. B., Palmer: Model fire-escape.

Banta, J. Edward, Hiawatha: Program third annual commencement exercises of Hiawatha Academy, 1891.

Beer, Wm., Topeka: Fragment of wood from the stairs in the hotel, Alexandria, Va., where Ephraim E. Ellsworth was shot, May 24, 1861.

Bradlee, Rev. C. D., Boston, Mass.: Invitation to anniversary exercises of the home for aged couples, Roxbury, Mass., June 12, 1891.

Brown, Orville C., Adams, N. Y.: Lock of cotton slivers taken from the ram Arkansas, by Spencer Kellogg Brown, after the boat was disabled by the gunboat Essex, September, 1862; reception invitation card to donor and daughter.

Callen, A. W., Junction City: Skull of a blacktail deer, from Callen's mining camp Placertias, Ariz.

Cannon, Austin, New Richmond, Pa.: Two pieces of clapboard from old John Brown tannery, taken out in 1890, by donor, who is the present owner; cane made from the timber of old John Brown tannery, wood taken out in 1890 by donor.

Coan, Chas., Leoti: Concretion from bituminous shale, found in Wichita county.

Cole, Geo. E., secretary, Girard: Premium list, posters, etc., Crawford county fair, September 1-4, 1891.

Duffy, R. W., secretary, Iola: Program of first annual fair, Iola Park Association, August 6-8, 1891.

Fairchild, Pres. Geo. T., Manhattan: Invitation and program, exercises of commencement week, Kansas State Agricultural College, June 7-10, 1891.

Fergusson, S. W., San Francisco, Cal.: A broadside descriptive of Kern county, California, 1892.

Flanders, Chas. E., secretary, Wellington: Premium list, posters, etc., Sumner county fair, August 25-28, 1891.

Foote, J. W. D., secretary, Winona: Premium list, etc., of the third annual fair, Logan county, September 30 to October 2, 1891.

Foster, Chas. A., Quincy, Mass.: Parchment marriage settlement by the Rev. Robt. Pregion Huston, of estates in Freeston and Butterwick, in the county of Lincoln, England, upon the marriage of his daughter Mary with Joseph Sikes, dated July 3, 1779.

Frow, John A., secretary, Ottawa: Four posters of the Franklin County Agricultural Association, 1892.

Furguson, D. M., secretary, Paola: Four large posters of the Miami County Fair Association, 1892.

Gillett, H. F., secretary, Cottonwood Falls: Premium list, posters, etc., Chase County Fair Association, October 7-9, 1891.

Glore, D. H., secretary, Lane: Two posters of the District Agricultural Fair Association, 1892.

Green, Miss Louise J., Whiting: Program of piano recital for graduation, by donor, June 18, 1891.

Green, Dr. Samuel A., Boston, Mass.: Proclamation of Gov. W. E. Russell, of Massachusetts, commemorative of the four hundredth anniversary of the discovery of America by Columbus.

Grubb, Mrs. S. F., Lawrence: Two cards of the National W. C. T. U., department of foreign work, printed in the German and Spanish languages.

Hale, George D., Topeka: Advertising card of the Interstate Artificial Rain Company, Goodland, October 30, 1891.

Hall & O'Donald, Topeka: Roster of Kansas State, judicial and county officers, mounted.

Heath, Mrs., Seward county: Fragment of petrified sponge (?) from the Cimarron, in Seward county; petrified bone taken from a well in Santa Fé, Kansas, at a depth of 200 feet.

Hewett, R. H., secretary, Cawker City: Premium list, posters, etc., of the sixth annual fair of the Cawker City District Fair Association, September 22-25, 1891.

Higgins, L. L., Topeka: Three calendars.

Hilliard, Franklin, Richland: 14 specimens of stones gathered by donor in the Wakarusa river.

Hinton, Col. Richard J., Washington, D. C.: Broadside circular containing a letter of Gov. W. F. M. Arny, addressed to Gov. John W. Geary, December 8, 1856, in relation to public education in Kansas; handbill dated Independence, Mo., December 12, 1861, offering a reward of $100 for the return to Henry J. Brown of his runaway slave, Nelson (this slave afterwards became a soldier in the First Kansas Colored Volunteers); circular appeal of the Kansas Emancipation League to the public for aid in taking care of the 4,000 contrabands already thrown upon Kansas; card of J. H. Lane, July 18, 1857, addressed to speakers in the political campaign, calling attention to provisions to be made for the protection of the ballot-boxes at the approaching election; 2 orders issued by General Lane relating to the protection of the ballot-boxes at the elections in 1857; broadside circular of the National Kansas Committee, dated Chicago, March 23, 1857, giving information for emigrants to Kansas, signed by Edward Daniels, agent.

Horr, Mrs. R. B., Paola: A saddle, at one time the property of Maj. James B. Abbott, presented to donor by the widow of Gen. C. W. F. Leonhardt.

Hume, Granville W., Strasburg, Mo.: An image of pottery, supposed to be an idol of the mound builders, or Aztecs, found in a mound near Akron, Independence county, Arkansas, 1886. [Conditional deposit.]

Hutchinson, Wm., Washington, D. C.: Three posters relating to the Lawrence charter election, February, 1859, and of the old settlers' celebration, September, 1879.

Irwin, Rev. A. B., Highland: Programs of university commencement exercises, 1891.

John Brown Fort Co., Chicago, Ill.: Invitation and ticket to the opening of John Brown's fort, October 15, 1892.

Jones, Chas. J., McCook, Neb.: Hose and mittens made of the wool of the buffalo, the American bison, presented to the Historical Society by donor, "Buffalo Jones," March 5, 1892, as a memento of the noble animal at one time so numerous on the plains of Kansas, and the existence of which on the face of the earth Mr. Jones, with patience and perseverance, is endeavoring to perpetuate.

Junkerman, Mrs. Clara E., Wichita: Woman's Relief Corps convention badge, worn by donor at the eight annual convention, Atchison, February 24–26, 1892.

Kansas State Institution for the Education of the Deaf and Dumb, at Olathe: Program of commencement exercises, June 10, 1889.

Kenneday, W. J., secretary, Winfield: Premium list and posters ninth annual exhibition, Cowley County Fair and Driving Park Association, September 1–4, 1891.

Kiddoo, H. G., secretary, Russell Springs: Three cards of Logan County Agricultural Fair Association, 1892.

Klink, C. F., Horton: Turtle shell found in the Indian Territory in 1891.

Knox, John D., Topeka: Real-estate and loan envelope of donor, rescued from the Johnstown flood, of June 1, 1889.

Lane University, Lecompton: Invitation to exercises of the twenty-sixth annual commencement, with program, June 18, 1891.

Losch, Mrs. Wm., Topeka: Ancient clock, made by Eli Ferry & Son, Plymouth, Conn. [Conditional deposit.]

Lovell, Miss Hattie W., Topeka: Walking-stick procured by Abraham Lincoln at Mt. Vernon, 1848; presented by Mr. Lincoln to Hon. Wm. Henry, Bellows Falls, Vt., and by Mr. Henry to his sister, Mrs. E. W. Lovell, of Michigan. [Conditional deposit.]

Lovell, Miss Sue, Topeka: A military pass given by Capt. H. H. Cushing, assistant provost marshal at Nashville, Tenn., to donor and party, on all turnpikes leading to Nashville, dated May 19, 1865.

McNair, William P., secretary, Wichita: Premium list, posters, etc., of Southern Kansas District Fair, September 28 to October 3, 1891.

McNemee, Lloyd, secretary, La Crosse: Poster of the sixth annual fair of the Rush County Fair Association, La Crosse, September 24–26, 1891.

Maloy, John, Council Grove: A block of limestone bearing a deeply-impressed imprint of a mule's shoe. (Quarried by H. C. Richardson, seven miles southwest of Council Grove, Kas.)

Markham, O. G., Baldwin: Programs of commencement exercises, Baker University, June, 1891; program, circulars, etc., of the commencement exercises of Baker University, June 3–7, 1892.

Mills, J. B., secretary, Wamego: Two posters of Pottawatomie and Wabaunsee County Fair Association, Wamego, September 20–23, 1892.

Moon, E. G., Topeka: Premium list, posters, etc., Kansas State Fair, Topeka, September 14–19, 1891.

Morrill, Hon. E. N., Hiawatha: The pen with which the Morrill disability pension bill was signed by President Benjamin Harrison, June 27, 1890; a brick taken from the inside of the wall of the John Brown fort at Harper's Ferry, in September, 1890.

Murdock, R. P., Wichita: *Eagle* calendar for 1891.

Neiswanger, W. A., Topeka: Impacted ball of hair from a bovine's stomach.

New Jersey Free Public Library, Jersey City: 10 cards relating to the library.

Nicholson, Geo. T., Topeka: Folders of the A. T. & S. F. R. R.

Nixon, Jacob, Kellogg post office: A Pawnee Indian fife or flute, procured from a

Pawnee Indian at Winfield, Kas., during the removal of that tribe from Nebraska to the Indian Territory, 1873-'76.

Oakes, Miss F., Hutchinson: Fragment of first flag-staff erected on Pike's Peak.

Parsons, C. H., Des Moines, Iowa: An ornamental carving in Kansas white magnesian limestone.

Pounds, L. H., secretary, Topeka: Premium list, posters and cards relating to the Kansas State Fair, Topeka, September 12-17, 1892 — in all, 29.

Queen, Rev. Chas. N., Fort Scott: Service program for the First Congregational Church, Ft. Scott, Nos. 1-16, June 5 to September 25, 1892.

Rambo, J. J., Chetopa: Two pieces of cloth from pants worn by Bob and Grat Dalton, when killed at Coffeyville, Kas., October 5, 1892.

Rathbone, F. B., Oberlin: Folder relating to northwest Kansas and its resources.

Remsburg, Geo. J., Atchison: Relics taken from Indian mounds and Indian village sites, as follows: Five arrows, 5 spear-heads, 5 fragments of arrow and spearheads, 9 flint chips, 9 fragments of pottery, 2 shells, 1 fragment of tooth, and 3 fragments of bone; 15 fragments of bone, pottery, and flint chips, from an Indian mound eight miles northwest of Oak Mills, in Atchison county; 13 relics found on the site of an Indian village on Owl creek, in Walnut township, Atchison county, near Oak Mills; 3 broken arrow-heads, 3 fragments of pottery, 5 flint chips; fragments of pottery found at an old Indian village site, Port William, eight miles southeast of Atchison and two miles northwest of Oak Mills, Atchison county; 9 pottery fragments, arrow-heads and chips of flint, from a field on Walnut creek, five miles southeast of Atchison.

Rice, Rev. C. R., Independence: Squaw hoe found in a garden near Independence, Kas., on lands formerly occupied by the Osage Indians.

Root, Frank A., North Topeka: Fifty-seven cards, loan, investment and other companies.

Root, Geo. A., Topeka: Kansas election tickets, 1892.

Roudebush Bros., Topeka: Roudebush writing system, 4 charts.

St. John, Prof. O., Topeka: Pair of Indian ball bats, from the Choctaw Nation, Indian Territory.

Scott, G. W., Edgerton: Premium list, posters, etc., of the Johnson County Fair Association, September 22, 1891.

Shafer, J. D., Stroudsburg, Pa.: Tilden ballot, fourth ward, Leavenworth city, 1876.

Walker, William, jr., secretary, Goodland: Rules, regulations, premium list and poster, fifth annual exhibition Sherman county fair, Goodland, September 22-25, 1891.

White, M. L., secretary, Garnett: Premium list, posters, etc., nineteenth Anderson county fair, August 26-28, 1891.

Wallace, H. B., secretary, Salina: Posters, cards, etc., tenth annual exhibition Saline County Fair Association, September 8-11, 1891; 2 posters of the Saline County Agricultural Association, 1892.

Washburn College, Topeka: Program annual musical recital, May 22, 1891.

Welch, Uriah, Niagara Falls, N. Y.: Descriptive folder relating to International Hotel, Niagara Falls.

White, M. L., secretary, Garnett: Four posters of the Anderson County Fair Association, Garnett, August 30 to September 2, 1892.

Wilson, W. W., secretary, Neosho Falls: Premium list, posters, etc., Neosho Valley District Fair, September 14-19, 1891.

Wisconsin Historical Society, Madison: Memorial card, death of Danl. Steele Durrie, Librarian.

Adams, F. G., Topeka: Copy of the Pueblo (Colo.) *World*, June 27, 1891, containing historical sketches relating to Manitou; copies of the Chicago *Herald*, August 2 and 5, 1891; copy of the *War Cry*, New York, July 11, 1891; *Harper's New Monthly Magazine*, New York, vol. 83, No. 494, July, 1891.

A. T. & S. F. R. R. Co., Chicago: 35 copies of the *Santa Fé Trail*, spring of 1892, illustrating the city of Hutchinson.

Baker, C. C., Topeka: Copy of daily paper in Arabic, Cairo, Egypt, March 5, 1891.

Bardeen, C. W., Syracuse, N. Y.: *The School Bulletin and New York State Educational Journal*, Syracuse, vol. 18, Nos. 1 and 2, September and October, 1891 — 2 newspapers.

Barnes, Wm., Albany, N. Y.: Albany *Evening Journal*, of November 25, 1890, containing article on Kansas in 1856.

Beer, William, Topeka: 11 copies miscellaneous Kansas educational monthlies; 1 copy of *The Florida School Room*, June, 1890; newspaper clipping containing a poem entitled, 'Ellworth's Avengers," by A. Lora Hendson.

Bernstein, Samuel, Cincinnati, O.: Clipping from the *Commercial Gazette*, Cincinnati, O., September 26, 1892, containing an obituary notice of Col. John C. Vaughan.

Blackmar, Prof. F. W., Lawrence: *Seminary Notes*, vol. 1, No. 1, May, 1891 — 1 magazine.

Bonham, Jeriah, Springfield, Ill.: Copy of *Marshall County Democrat*, Lakin, Ill., April 15, 1892, containing an article entitled "Compulsory Education; Historical Facts connected with it."

Boston Public Library, Massachusetts: Bulletin Nos. 4-86, 1868-'91, except 19-22, 24, 28, 34-37, 44, 46, 52, 54-56, 58, 68-77, 84 — 55 magazines.

Bowes, Geo. W., Topeka: Two broadsides, showing the names of county clerks and treasurers in Kansas, 1892.

Bradlee, Dr. C. D., Boston, Mass.: Copy of the Boston *News*, vol. 1, No. 16, June 18, 1891; copy of the *Military Journal*, Boston, Mass., February 8, 1892; copy of the *Mountain Echo*, Delaware Water Gap, Pa., July 30, 1892; the *Magazine of Poetry*, vol. 3, No. 3, Boston, July, 1891; *Food and Health Exposition*, Boston, October 6, 13, 1891; copies of the *Sounding Boaı ḍ*, Boston, November 22, 1890, vol. 2, Nos. 8, 9, and 10, December, January and February, 1891; copies of Boston newspapers of March, 1891, relating to Delaware Water Gap; the *Orange Belt*, Alessandro.

Brown, Orville C., Adams, N. Y.: Copy of the Osawatomie *Graphic*, July 2, 1892. containing an article entitled "Reminiscence of 1856, Scenes and Incidents of the Border War," from the private diary of Spencer Kellogg Brown; biographical sketch of Dr. Johnston Lykins; also 6 miscellaneous newspaper cuttings.

Bushell, W., Camden, N. J.: The Philadelphia *Record*, souvenir edition, January 1, 1892.

Campbell, Geo., Mound Valley: Newspaper clipping containing a history of the Farmers' Alliance and Industrial Union.

Chittenden, Rev. E. P., Salina: *The Sentinel*, Fort Leavenworth, vol. 1, Nos. 7-12, 1888-'89; Salina, vol. 2, Nos. 1-6, 8, 9, 11, 12, 1889-'90.

Christian Literature Company, New York: *The Magazine of Christian Literature*, vol. 4, No. 3, June, 1891.

Clarke, Sylvester H., Clyde, N. Y.: Copies of the *Evening Press*, Rochester, N. Y., December 13, 1877; the *National Journal* and *New York Palladium*, New York, November 2, 1878; the *Independent and Advertiser*, Clyde, N. Y., May 4, 1881;

copy of the *Great Republic* monthly, vol. 2, No. 1, July, 1859; *Hunt's Merchants' Magazine*, vol. 36, No. 4, April, 1857; vol. 40, No. 5, 1859 — 2 magazines; clippings from the Kansas City *Enterprise*, May 11, 1855, relating to threatened robbing of the American Hotel, Kansas City; from the Boston *Telegraph*, June 1, 1855, relating to the destruction of the Parkville, Mo., *Luminary* office. and addresses of M. J. Patterson and S. C. Pomeroy on the subject; and from the St. Louis *Republican* relating to Wm. C. Quantrill.

Covert, John C., Cleveland, O.: Clippings from the Cleveland *Leader*, of September 27 and October 3, 1892, containing reminiscences of Col. John C. Vaughan.

Cranston, Arthur, Parsons: Copy of *El Telegrama*, Guadalajara, Mex., No. 66, November 13, 1886. (Said to be the smallest paper published in the world.)

Crawshay, Geo., Working, Eng.: *The Imperial and Asiatic Quarterly Review and Oriental and Colonial Record*, July, 1891 — 1 magazine.

Ditto, F. S., Topeka: Copy of the *Daily Citizen*, Vicksburg, Miss., July 2, 1863 (reprint); The *Nighthawk*, Washburn College, Topeka, vol. 1' Nos. 1 and 2, 1888.

Drowne, Henry T., New York: *New Amsterdam Gazette*, New York, (extra edition,) vol. 7, No. 4, June 24 to September 10, 1891.

Duncan, Alexander, Angola: Newspaper clipping containing the early history of Canada township, Labette county.

Elliott, L. R., Manhattan: Copy of the *Daily Christian Advocate*, Omaha, Neb. May 21, 1892.

Goodnow, Isaac T., Manhattan: Manhattan *Enterprise*, December 5' 1879; copy of daily *Tribune*, Salt Lake City, Utah, September 15, 1890, containing an article entitled "Prohibition;" the *Nation*, April 3-24, 1890, 4 numbers; *Our Country Home*, 1884-'87, 12 numbers; the *Defecator*, 1883-'84, 11 numbers; *Scientific American*, 1878-'91, 10 numbers; the *Chronicle*, San Francisco, Cal., 1883-'89, 29 numbers; *Midland Christian Advocate*, Kansas City and Topeka, 1889-'90, 12 numbers; *Times*, Denver, Colo., June, 1890, to January, 1891, 8 numbers; *Daily Republican*, Springfield, Mass., January 13, 1871, to April 25, 1891, 13 numbers; *Kansas and Colorado Farmer*, Omaha, Neb., January to December, 1890, 7 numbers; *Colman's Rural World*, St. Louis, Mo., 1879-'91, 21 numbers; *Zion's Herald*, Boston, Mass., January 7, 1885, to February 18, 1891, 25 numbers; miscellaneous newspapers: California 18, Illinois 49, New York 23, Missouri 29, Georgia 7, Massachusetts 15, Utah 18, Rhode Island 10, Texas 8, Ohio 14, and 116 other miscellaneous newspapers and magazines — in all, 563.

Green, C. R., Lyndon: *Osage County Graphic* supplement, February 11, 1891, containing historical matter.

Greene, A. R., Lecompton: The *Evening Star*, Washington, D. C., September 19 to 24, 1892, containing an account of the National Encampment of the G. A. R. at Washington, 1892 — 6 newspapers.

Grinsted, Chas. R., Kingfisher, Ok.: Copy of Cincinnati *Daily Times*, December 3, 1855.

Halderman, Gen. John A., Washington, D. C.: Copy of the *Straits Times* (Straits of Malacca, Asia), Singapore, December 24, 1890.

Hartzell, J. C., Cincinnati, Ohio: The *Christian Educator*, vol. 1, No. 1, October, 1889, to vol. 2, No. 3, April, 1891 — 1 magazine.

Harvard College Library, Cambridge, Mass.: *Bulletin*, Nos. 8 and 9, 1878; Nos. 11, 12, 13, 1879; No. 14, 1880; No. 44, 1889 — 7 magazines.

Heisler, E. F., Kansas City: Three copies of the New Year's edition, 1891, of the Kansas City *Sun*, containing historical matter relating to the establishment of the Shawnee Baptist Mission in Kansas, and of the introduction of the first printing press in Kansas, 1834.

Hinton, Col. Richard J., Washington, D. C.: The *Western Dispatch*, extra, Independence, Mo., September 3, 1856, warning the people of western Missouri against an impending invasion of Missouri by Jas. H. Lane, with 3,000 lawless Kansas abolitionists; copies of the *Equal Rights Gazette*, a Confederate newspaper, Springfield, Mo., August 28, 1861, and September 21, 1861, containing accounts of battles of Wilson's Creek, August 10, 1861, and of Lexington, September 20, 1861; clipping from a Boston newspaper giving the proceedings of an anti-slavery convention held in Boston May 29, 1860, in which donor and Jas. Redpath participated; part of the *Liberator*, Boston, June 15, 1860, containing proceedings of the before-mentioned convention and a speech by Wendell Phillips at Melodeon Hall, Boston, May 31, 1860, on the imprisonment of Thaddeus Hyatt—imprisoned in Washington jail, under arrest as a witness in the Harper's Ferry investigation; clipping from the Jefferson (Ohio) *Sentinel,* December 5, 1860, containing an account of troubles in southern Kansas, written by donor.

Hoffman, C. B. Enteprise: Five newspapers relating to the Credit Foncier Company.

Horton, A. H., Topeka: Copy of the *Graphic*, Chicago, vol. 5, No. 5, August 1, 1891.

Huling, A. S., Topeka: Newspaper clipping containing obituary of Edmund J. Huling.

Hutchinson, Wm., Washington, D. C.: Copies of the New York *Times*, Boston *Liberator*, Boston *Journal*, *Anti-Slavery Standard*, and other newspapers of dates from 1853 to 1868, containing speeches of Wm. H. Seward, Rufus Choate, Gerrit Smith, John G. Palfrey, Samuel Hoar, Douglass Jerrold, Louis Kossuth, Lucy Stone, Joshua R. Giddings, John P. Hale, Henry Ward Beecher, Theodore Clapp, Edward Everett, Salmon P. Chase, Stephen A. Douglas, Abraham Lincoln, Thaddeus Stevens, Wendell Phillips, John Savory, Geo. B. Cheever, Mary Grew, and Cora L. V. Daniels, besides much information relating to early Kansas affairs, the War of the Rebellion, reconstruction and the political history of the country covered by these dates; also copy of the Atchison *Champion* containing the address of John J. Ingalls, delivered at the dedication of the monument to John Brown and his associates at Osawatomie, August 30, 1877; copy of the Lawrence *Republican-Journal* of September 17, 1870, containing the address of Senator S. C. Pomeroy at the old settlers' meeting; also the Lawrence *Republican* of January 1, 1870, containing a history and description of Lawrence; copies of Lawrence papers containing proceedings of the old settlers' celebration at Bismarck Grove, September 15 and 16, 1879; of the Lawrence *Journal* of October 28, 1884, containing articles relating to the candidacy of Governor Robinson for the State Senate; the Lawrence *Tribune* of September 5, 1887, containing the Fourth of July address of Wm. Hutchinson at Lawrence in 1855; a paper containing the proceedings of a reunion of Lawrence pioneers at the residence of Mr. and Mrs. Paul R. Brooks, in 1890; a part of the Chicago *Inter-Ocean* of December 2, 1889, containing proceedings of the Chicago Bar Association, in which is a sketch of John Hutchinson, an early pioneer of Kansas; scrap from the St. Louis *Democrat* of February 26, 1859, containing the proceedings of the celebration of the opening of the Hannibal & St. Joseph Railroad; supplement to the Washington *Chronicle*, containing a biographical sketch of Thaddeus Stevens, who died August 11, 1868; newspaper scrap containing the address of Ralph Waldo Emerson, January 16, 1872, on the subject "Home"; cutting from the Washington *Chronicle*, September 28, 1872, containing the history of the origin of the so-called Liberal Republican party — 40 newspapers and 5 newspaper scraps.

Jersey City Free Public Library, New Jersey: The *Library Record*, Jersey City, vol. 1, No. 1, February 15, 1892.

Julian, Isaac H., San Marcus, Tex.: Copy of the *Daily Post*, Houston, Tex., March 27, 1892, containing "Biographical Sketch of Israel B. Donalson, a life coevâl with our national history."

Keagy, Franklin, Chambersburg, Pa.: Copy of *Public Opinion*, Chambersburg, February 13, 1891, containing an article by donor on John Brown and his men, relating particularly to John H. Kagi.

Langston, J. S., Topeka: Copy of the *Deseret News*, Salt Lake City, Utah, dated December 28, 1850, found by J. Rutherford in 1891 in a house which he was repairing called the "Bee Line," which had been the residence of Brigham Young. The paper was given to donor by Mr. Rutherford.

Lasher, Esmeralda, Topeka: Detroit *Tribune*, August 4 and 5, 1891, containing proceedings of the National Encampment of the G. A. R., held at Detroit, Mich., August 5–8, 1891; *Washington Post*, Detroit, Mich., August 4, 1891, containing same; copy of Denver, Colo., *Times* of August 1, 1891, containing historical sketch of Idaho Springs, Colo.

Learnard, O. E., Lawrence: Holiday number of the Lawrence *Journal*, December 25, 1890.

Leonard Scott Publication Company, New York city, N. Y.: *Nineteenth Century*, No. 171, May, 1891; the *Fortnightly Review*, No. 289, January, 1891; *Contemporary Review*, March, 1891; *Westminster Review*, vol. 135, February, 1891—4 magazines.

Manchester, Rev. A., Providence. R. I.: Copy of the *North Star*, February, 1892.

Marston, C. W., Cedar Junction: *Kawkab America* (*Star of America*), an Oriental weekly, New York, vol. 1, Nos. 1 and 2, April 15 and 22, 1892, the first Arabic newspaper printed in America.

Martin, Geo. W., Kansas City: Copy of New Year's edition of Kansas City *Gazette*, 1890.

Mead, J. R., Wichita: Copy of the *Daily Eagle*, Wichita, April 3, 1892, containing account of the Towanda sufferers from the cyclone; also historical sketch of Towanda, by donor.

Medill, Joseph, Chicago, Ill.: Clipping from the Chicago *Tribune*, September 29, 1892, containing an article copied from the Cleveland *Leader* of September 27, 1892, relating to Col. John C. Vaughan, with notes by donor.

Mills, T. B., Las Vegas, N. M.: Copy of the Las Vegas *Daily Optic*, N. M., January 1, 1892, containing history-and description of Las Vegas.

Mobley, R. D., Grand Junction, Colo.: Copy of the *Field and Farm*, Denver, Colo., April 2, 1892, containing reminiscences of the Arickaree fight.

Morehouse, Geo. P., Council Grove: Council Grove *Republican* of December 5, 1890, containing an article on ancient books in Kansas.

Nicaragua Construction Company, New York city: Reprint from *Engineering News*, of September 14, 1889; also 2 papers relating to the inter-ocean canal of Nicaragua—3 newspapers.

Olney, Henry C., Gunnison, Colo.: Copies of 13 Colorado and Utah newspapers, of dates from December 21, 1890, to January 1, 1891; copy of the Salt Lake *Tribune*, Salt Lake City, Utah, January 1, 1892, containing historical sketch of Salt Lake City; the Minneapolis, Minn., *Tribune Annual*, January 1, 1892—2 newspapers.

Oneida Historical Sociaty, Utica, N. Y.: Four newspapers containing proceedings of the annual meeting, January, 1891; address of Gen. C. W. Darling at the annual meeting of the American Historical Society, Washington, January 1, 1891; proceedings of the Jefferson County (New York) Historical Association, January, 1891.

Page, Mrs. Carrie E. H., Brandon, Vt.: *Vermont Quarterly Gazetteer*, Nos. 6, 7, 8, 9, 10, and 11—6 magazines.

—4

Parmelee, Geo. F., Topeka: Copy of the Derby (England) *Mercury*, January 10, 1788.

Pasteur-Cumberland Filter Company, Dayton, Ohio: One copy *Le Pasteur*, January, 1891.

Popenoe, F. O., Topeka: *Santa Fé Trail* of spring of 1892, No. 4, containing illustrations of Hutchinson; the upper South, its Republican probabilities and possibilities.

Riley, Z. F., Topeka: *Union County Star*, New Berlin, Pa., June 9, 16, 23, 30, February 24, March 10, 17, 24, 31, April 7, 14, 21, 28, May 5, 1853; January 19, 26, February 2, 9, 1854 — 18 numbers.

Root, Geo. A., North Topeka: Five copies daily *Sunflower*, Topeka, 1888; 3 copies daily *Bulletin*, New York, 1888; copy of the *American Volunteer*, Carlisle, Pa., August 12, 1891; the *Commonwealth*, Denver, Colo., vols. 1 and 2, March and April, 1889; 3 miscellaneous newspapers; 10 miscellaneous Mexican newspapers.

Roudebush Bros., Topeka: Copy of *Good Writing*, vol. 1, No. 1.

Schulein, S., Kansas City, Mo.: Broadside relating to cause of hard times, depression of trades, etc. etc.; addresses delivered, 1878 — 2 broadsides.

Sheppard, Wm. D., Springfield, Mo.: Copy of *The Southwest*, St. Louis, vol. 1, No. 3, March 1, 1888, containing historical sketch of Springfield, Mo., and surroundings.

Standard, New York, The: Copy of the *Standard*, New York., extras Nos. 1–7, 9, 10, 1891 — 9 newspapers.

Times Publishing Company, Kansas City, Mo.: Copy of the *Times* containing biographical sketch of Gov. Geo. A. Crawford (who died at Grand Junction, Colo., January 26, 1891).

Trouslot, R. B., Kansas City, Mo.: *The Hoosier Naturalist*, Valparaiso, Ind., 1885–'87 — 19 numbers.

Votaw, D., Independence, Kas.: *Refugees' Lone Star*, Independence, November, 1889, and October, 1892.

Vuilleumier, Jean, Battle Creek, Mich.: Copy of *Les Signes des Temps*, March 3, 1891 — 1 newspaper.

Waugh, Rev. Lorenzo, San Francisco, Cal.: Copies of California newspapers containing biographical information relative to donor.

Ward, Capt. W. H., Topeka: Copy of the *Statesman Patriot*, Milledgeville, Ga., May 1, 1830; the *Standard of Union and Free-Trade Advocate*, Sparta, Ga., May 4, 1833; the *Enterprise*, Forsyth, Ga., September 12, 1843; the *Federal Union*, Milledgeville, Ga., May 7, 1844; the *Southern Democrat*, Oglethorpe, Ga., May 20, 1853; and of the Savannah *Republican*, Ga., June 29, 1861 — 6 newspapers.

Webb, Leland J., Topeka: Buffalo *Morning Express*, September, 1888, extra number issued as a souvenir of the International Industrial Fair, September 4–14, 1888; copy of the *Globe*, Kansas City, Mo., February 10, 1890; New York *Sunday World*, April 13, 1890, special supplement containing photo.-illustrated interview with John J. Ingalls.

Wilder, D. W., Topeka: Newspaper containing a review by John P. Jones of Joel Moody's address on Cabeza de Vaca; copy of the Grand Junction *Daily Star*, containing a biographical sketch of Gov. Geo. A. Crawford (who died at Grand Junction, Colo., January 26, 1891).

Wilson, Rev. E. F., Sault Ste. Marie, Ont.: Newspaper entitled *Our Forest Children*, Christmas number, 1888.

World's Fair Columbian Exposition, Chicago, Ill.: Broadside entitled *No Lack of Information*.

DONORS OF NEWSPAPER FILES.

The following is a list of newspaper files and volumes of periodicals donated, other than those received in current issues:

Adams, Charles Francis, jr., Boston, Mass.: *The Nation*, New York, 1866–'81, except 1870; file of *Potter's American Magazine*, Philadelphia, 1876; *Knights of Honor Reporter*, scattering numbers, 1878 to 1888; Lossing's American Historical Record, Philadelphia, vols. 1, 2, 3, 1872, '73, '74·

American College and Education Society, Boston, Mass.: Six volumes of the Quarterly Register, 1830–'42.

Baker, F. P., Topeka: Bound files *Kansas Newspaper Union*, Topeka, July, 1890, to July, 1892.

Beers, Dr. Geo. L., Topeka: Files of *The Christian Union*, New York, 1890, also 17 extra numbers, 1889; *The Independent*, New York, vols. 41 and 42, 1889 and 1890.

Bradlee, Rev. Caleb D., Boston, Mass.: *Evening Gazette*, Boston, 1891–'92; *The Unitarian*, Boston, 1891–'92.

Colby, Mrs. Clara B., Beatrice, Neb.: File of *The National Bulletin*, September, 1890, to April, 1892.

Collet, C. D., London, Eng.: *Free·Press*, London, vols. 3–13, 1856–'70, incomplete.

Elliott, L. R., Manhattan: File of *Daily Christian Advocate*, Omaha, Neb., May 2–27, 1892.

Goodnow, Prof. I. T., Manhattan: Files of the *National Tribune*, Washington, D. C., May 9, 1889, to April 23, 1891; *Weekly Press*, Philadelphia, February 20 to December 11, 1889; *Zion's Herald*, Boston, Mass., January 2 to November, 1884, January 15 to December, 1890; *Gazette and Courier*, Greenfield, Mass., 1879 to 1890; the *Mountain Echo*, Keyser, Mineral county, W. Va., March 1, 1889, to November 7, 1890; the *Weekly Progress*, Kansas City, Mo., April 12, 1890, to January 9, 1891; Colman's *Rural World*, St. Louis, Mo., 1881–'90.

Graham, I. D., Manhattan: Bound file of *The Industrialist*, August 23, 1890, to June 27, 1891.

Green, Dr. Saml. A., Boston, Mass.: Files of the *Christian Examiner*, 1854, 1855, Boston, Mass.

Harrington, Rev. M. O., Topeka: *Bibliotheca Sacra*, Andover, Mass., and Oberlin, Ohio, vol. 34, 1877, to vol. 46, 1889; the *Hebrew Student*, Chicago, vol. 2, Nos. 1–10, 1882; the *Old Testament Student*, Chicago, vol. 3, Nos. 1–3, 1883, Nos. 5–10, 1884, vol. 4, Nos. 1–4, 1884, Nos. 5–10, 1885, vol. 5, Nos. 1–4, 1885, Nos. 5–8, 1886.

Knerr, E. B., Atchison: *Midland College Monthly*, Atchison, vol. 1, Nos. 1–10, May, 1890, to April, 1891.

Perry, Alfred T., librarian, Hartford, Conn.: *Hartford Seminary Record*, vol. 1, Nos. 1–6, 1890–'91.

Queen, Rev. Chas. N., Ft. Scott: File of *Amicus Life-Line*, Fredonia, vol. 1, Nos. 1–9, October to June, 1892.

Roe, Alfred S., Worcester, Mass.: Files of· *Light*, published at Worcester, vols. 1, 2 and 3, 1890–'91.

Wallace, Catharine P., Melbourne, Australia: File of the *Alliance Record*, Melbourne, January 10 to December 30, 1891.

BOUND NEWSPAPERS AND PERIODICALS.

'The following is a statement of bound newspaper files and bound volumes of periodicals in the library of the Society, November 15, 1892, including the volumes which become complete December 31, 1892, numbering 12,633 volumes; of which 9,054 are of Kansas, and 3,579 are of other States and countries, and of which 2,456 have been added during the two years covered by this report. Volumes not otherwise described are of weekly newspapers. Added to some of the county lists below are volumes which contain short-lived newspapers, such as suspended publication after a few issues, and which have been bound together in one book, as indicated:

NEWSPAPERS.	Years.	No. vols.
ALLEN COUNTY.		
Iola Register	1873–1892	20
Allen County Independent, Iola	1879,1880	1
Allen County Courant, Iola	1884–1889	5
Allen County Democrat, Iola	1886–1888	1
Democrat-Courant, Iola	1888	1
The Farmers' Friend, Iola	1890–1892	3
Allen County Herald, Iola	1890–1892	3
The Rural Kansan, Humboldt	1873,1874	1
Humboldt Union	1876–1892	17
Inter-State, Humboldt	1878–1888	9
Independent Press, Humboldt	1882	1
The Humboldt Herald	1887–1892	5
Moran Herald	1855–1892	7
Elsmore Eagle	1890–1892	2
Savonburg Progress	1891,1892	1
ANDERSON COUNTY.		
Garnett Weekly Journal	1876–1892	17
Garnett Plaindealer	1876–1884	9
Anderson County Republican, Garnett	1883,1884	1
Republican-Plaindealer, Garnett	1884–1892	9
Anderson County Democrat, Garnett	1885–1887	2
Garnett Eagle	1886–1892	6
Kansas Agitator, Garnett	1890–1892	2
The Greeley Tribune	1880,1881	1
The Greeley News	1881–1892	11
Greeley Graphic	1892	1
The Light, Greeley	1892	1
The Colony Free Press	1882–1892	11
Westphalia Times	1885–1892	7
Kincaid Kronicle, (April, 1888, to September, 1889, lacking,)	1886–1892	6
The Kincaid Dispatch	1888–1992	5
ATCHISON COUNTY.		
Squatter Sovereign, Atchison	1856,1857	1
Freedom's Champion, Atchison, (1861 lacking,)	1857–1863	4
Atchison Daily Free Press	1865–1868	7
Atchison Weekly Free Press, (four files each of 1866 and 1867,)	1866–1868	3
Champion and Press (weekly), Atchison	1868–1873	4
Atchison Daily Champion	1876–1892	31
Atchison Weekly Champion, (lacking from 1878–1885,)	1873–1892	12
Kansas Zeitung, Atchison, (duplicates of vol. 1,)	1857,1858	1
Atchison Union, (broken files,)	1859–1861	3
American Journal of Education. (See Missouri — St. Louis.)		
Atchison Patriot (daily), (from July 1876, to July, 1879, lacking,)	1876–1892	26
Atchison Patriot (weekly)	1874–1892	19
Atchison Courier	1876–1879	4
Atchison Globe (daily)	1878–1892	27
Atchisonian, Atchison	1877	1
Atchison Banner	1878,1879	1
The New West, Atchison	1878–1880	2
The Sunday Morning Call, Atchison	1882,1883	2

BOUND NEWSPAPER FILES AND PERIODICALS, KANSAS—Continued.

NEWSPAPERS.	Years.	No. vols.
ATCHISON COUNTY—*Concluded.*		
Atchison Telegraph	1882	1
Kansas Staats-Anzeiger, Atchison	1881–1885	4
Atchison Journal (daily)	1881,1882	2
Western Mercury, Atchison	1884–1886	2
Atchison Sunday Morning Sermon	1884	1
The Western Recorder, Atchison	1884	1
The Trades-Union, Atchison	1885,1886	1
The Atchison Times	1888–1891	3
Messachorean (monthly), Atchison	1888	2
Midland College Monthly, Atchison	1891,1892	1
The Midland (monthly), Atchison	1892	1
Atchison Baptist (monthly)	1890–1892	2
The College Review (monthly), Atchison	1891,1892	2
The Kansas Churchman (monthly), Atchison	1891,1892	1
The New Kansas Magazine (monthly), Atchison	1892	1
The Prairie Press, Lancaster	1888–1890	1
Muscotah Record, (missing from August, 1886, to January, 1887,)	1885–1892	7
The Effingham Enterprise	1886	1
The Effingham Times	1887–1891	3
The Graphic, Effingham	1891,1892	1
Huron Graphic	1890,1891	1
The Huron Herald	1891,1892	2

Atchison county short lived, vol. 1:
    The Public Ledger, Atchison, Aug. to Oct.,1880; Sunday Morning Facts, Atchison,
    Sept. 2, 1883, to Feb. 3, 1884; Der Humorist, Atchison, Feb. 2, 1884; Atchison Sunday Morning Sermon, June and July, 1884; Atchison Advance, Nov., 1884, to Jan.,
    1885; Daily Atchison Bee, March and April, 1889; Muscotah News, June 6, 1880;
    The Huron Headlight, March 13, 1884; The Huron Messenger, July 2, 1884
		1

BARBER COUNTY.		
Barber County Mail, Medicine Lodge	1878,1879	1
Medicine Lodge Cresset	1879–1892	14
Barber County Index, Medicine Lodge	1881–1892	11
Medicine Lodge Chief	1886–1888	1
Barber County Herald, Medicine Lodge	1890,1891	1
Hazelton Express	1884–1892	9
The Herald, New Kiowa and Medicine Lodge	1884–1891	6
The Kiowa Journal	1886–1892	6
The Alliance Review, Kiowa	1891,1892	2
Sharon News	1884–1886	2
The Union, Sun City	1884–1888	4
The Ætna Clarion	1885–1887	2
Kansas Prairie Dog, Lake City	1885–1888	3
The Lake City Bee	1888,1889	1
BARTON COUNTY.		
Great Bend Register	1876–1892	17
Inland Tribune, Great Bend	1876–1892	17
Arkansas Valley Democrat, Great Bend	1877–1882	6
Kansas Volks Freund, Great Bend	1878,1879	1
Barton County Times, Great Bend	1883	1
Barton County Democrat, Great Bend	1886–1892	6
Daily Graphic, Great Bend	1887,1888	2
Evening News (daily), Great Bend	1890–1892	4
Barton County Beacon, Great Bend	1890–1892	2
The Ellinwood Express	1878–1888	10
The Ellinwood Advocate	1888–1892	4
Pawnee Rock Leader	1886–1892	7
Fun, Pawnee Rock	1891	1
The Alliance Globe, Pawnee Rock	1891,1892	1
The Echo, Hoisington	1887–1889	1
Hoisington Dispatch	1889–1892	4
The Hoisington Blade	1892	1
Claflin Gazette	1888	1
Barton County Banner, Claflin	1890–1892	2

Barton county short lived, vol. 1:
    The Barton County Times, Great Bend, July 26 to September 27, 1883; The Crank,
    Pawnee Rock, March 7 to 28, 1888; Fun, Pawnee Rock, February 2 to March 30,
    1891; The Hoisington Mascot, August 17 to October 18, 1888		

BOURBON COUNTY.		
Fort Scott Daily Monitor	1880–1892	25
Fort Scott Weekly Monitor, (1870–1876 lacking,)	1867–1891	18
Fort Scott Pioneer	1876–1878	2
Camp's Emigrants' Guide, Fort Scott	1877	1
New Century, Fort Scott	1877,1878	1

BOUND NEWSPAPER FILES AND PERIODICALS, KANSAS—CONTINUED.

NEWSPAPERS.	Years.	No. vols.
BOURBON COUNTY—*Concluded.*		
Fort Scott Herald................................	1878–1882	5
Republican-Record, Fort Scott................	1879–1882	4
Herald and Record, Fort Scott................	1882–1884	2
Evening Herald (daily), Fort Scott...........	1882–1885	6
Medical Index (monthly), Fort Scott.........	1881–1884	4
The Banner, Fort Scott........................	1882–1884	2
Fort Scott Daily Tribune......................	1884–1892	16
Fort Scott Weekly Tribune....................	1884–1892	8
Kansas Staats-Zeitung, Fort Scott............	1886,1887	2
The Fort Scott Union..........................	1887,1888	1
The Fort Scott Evening Globe (daily)........	1888,1889	1
The Sunday Call, Fort Scott...................	1889	1
Fort Scott Weekly News.......................	1889,1890	1
Fort Scott Herold, (see Pittsburg, Crawford county,).........	1890	1
The Spectator, Fort Scott.....................	1890–1892	3
Fort Scott Industrial Union...................	1890,1891	1
The Normal Journal (monthly), Fort Scott...	1891,1892	1
The Lantern, Fort Scott	1891,1892	1
The Southern Argus, Fort Scott.	1891,1892	1
Bronson Pilot..................................	1884–1892	8
The Fulton Independent.......................	1884–1892	8
The Fulton Rustler (monthly)	1890–1892	2
The Telephone, Uniontown....................	1885–1888	3
The Garland Gleaner...........................	1886,1887	2
The Telephone, Mapleton......................	1889	1
Mapleton Dispatch.............................	1889–1892	3
The Lantern, Mapleton........................	1890,1891	1
Bourbon county short lived, vol. 1:		
Fort Scott Weekly News, November, 1889, to March, 1890; Broom-Corn Reporter (monthly), Fort Scott, September, 1886, to September, 1887; Fort Scott Herald (German), April to May, 1890..................................		4
BROWN COUNTY.		
Hiawatha Dispatch..	1876–1882	6
The Hiawatha World...........................	1882–1892	11
Kansas Herald, Hiawatha......................	1876–1883	8
The North Kansan, Hiawatha..................	1878	1
The Kansas Sun, Hiawatha....................	1879,1880	2
Weekly Messenger, Hiawatha..................	1882–1884	2
The Kansas Democrat, Hiawatha..............	1884–1892	8
Free Press, Hiawatha..........................	1887,1888	1
The Hiawatha Journal..........................	1889–1892	4
The Delta of Sigma Nu (bi-mo.), Hiawatha...	1891,1892	2
Everest Reflector..............................	1885,1886	2
The Everest Enterprise........................	1888–1892	4
Horton Headlight..............................	1886–1892	6
Horton Daily Headlight........................	1887–1889	3
The Horton Railway Register..................	1888,1889	1
Horton Daily Railway Register.	1889	1
Horton Telegram...............................	1889,1890	1
Horton Commercial............................	1889–1892	4
Hamlin News Gleaner..........................	1889,1890	1
Fairview Enterprise............................	1888–1892	5
Morrill News...................................	1890–1892	3
The Robinson Reporter.........................	1891,1892	1
Brown county short lived, vol. 1:		
The North Kansan, Hiawatha, Sept. 7 to Nov. 30, 1878; The Morrill Journal, July 5, to Oct. 18, 1882; Brown County Herald, Morrill, July 9 to Aug. 20, 1886; Horton Gazette, Jan. 5 to May 11, 1889; Brown County Star, Horton, Jan. 1 to April 23, 1889		4
BUTLER COUNTY.		
Augusta Republican, (1875-1880-lacking,)...	1873–1883	4
Southern Kansan Gazette, Augusta............	1876–1886	11
Augusta Advance.	1883,1884	1
Augusta Electric Light........................	1884–1886	2
Augusta Weekly Journal.......................	1888–1892	5
The Augusta News.............................	1889,1890	1
The Industrial Advocate, Augusta............	1890–1892	2
Walnut Valley Times, El Dorado...............	1874–1892	19
Daily Walnut Valley Times, El Dorado........	1887–1892	11
El Dorado Press................................	1877–1883	7
El Dorado Daily Republican....................	1885–1888	6
El Dorado Republican	1883–1892	9
Butler County Democrat, El Dorado, (lacking from Oct. 1888 to Nov. 1889,).........	1881–1891	9
Butler County Jeffersonian, El Dorado, (see Democrat,).........	1888,1889	1
The El Dorado Eagle...........................	1882	1

BOUND NEWSPAPER FILES AND PERIODICALS, KANSAS—CONTINUED.

NEWSPAPERS.	Years.	No. vols.
BUTLER COUNTY—*Concluded.*		
Kansas Workman, Emporia and El Dorado......................	1888–1891	3
The Daily Eli, El Dorado......................	1890,1891	1
The New Enterprise, Douglass........................	1879,1880	2
Douglass Index......................	1880–1883	3
The Douglass Tribune......................	1884–1892	9
Leon Indicator, (missing from February to September, 1887,)...............	1880–1892	11
The Leon Quill......................	1886,1887	1
The Benton Reporter......................	1884,1885	1
The Towanda Herald......................	1885–1892	8
The Brainerd Sun......................	1885,1886	1
The Brainerd Ensign......................	1887–1889	2
Latham Journal......................	1885,1886	1
Latham Signal......................	1887–1890	3
The Latham Times......................	1890–1892	3
The Beaumont Business......................	1886–1888	2
Potwin Messenger......................	1888,1889	2
White Water Tribune......................	1889–1892	4
CHASE COUNTY.		
Chase County Courant, Cottonwood Falls......................	1874–1892	18
Chase County Leader, Cottonwood Falls......................	1875–1892	18
The Reveille, Cottonwood Falls......................	1890–1892	2
Strong City Independent......................	1881–1887	6
Chase County Republican, Strong City......................	1887–1892	4
Strong City Derrick......................	1892	1
CHAUTAUQUA COUNTY.		
Chautauqua Journal, Sedan......................	1875–1884	9
The Chautauqua County Times, Sedan......................	1878–1881	3
Sedan Times......................	1882–1884	3
Sedan Times-Journal......................	1885–1892	8
The Border Slogan, Sedan......................	1883,1884	1
The Graphic, Sedan......................	1884–1890	6
Sedan Republican......................	1890–1892	2
Chautauqua News, Peru......................	1877–1881	5
The Peru Times......................	1886,1887	1
The Weekly Call, Peru......................	1888,1889	2
The Peru Eagle......................	1890,1891	1
The Freemen's Lance, Peru......................	1891	1
The Chautauqua Springs Spy......................	1882,1883	1
Chautauqua Springs Mail......................	1887	1
The Chautauqua Springs Express......................	1888,1889	1
The Cedar Vale Star......................	1884–1892	9
Cedar Vale Commercial......................	1889–1892	3
CHEROKEE COUNTY.		
Republican-Courier, Columbus......................	1876–1878	3
The Columbus Courier......................	1879–1888	9
The Columbus Star-Courier......................	1889–1892	4
Columbus Democrat......................	1876	1
Border Star, Columbus......................	1877–1886	9
The Columbus Vidette......................	1877,1878	1
The Times, Columbus......................	1882–1886	5
Kansas Bee-Keeper, Columbus......................	1881–1885	3
Lea's Columbus Advocate......................	1882–1888	6
The Columbus Advocate......................	1889–1892	4
The Daily Advocate, Columbus......................	1886,1887	2
The Daily News and the Weekly News, Columbus......................	1882,1883	1
The Expository, Girard and Columbus......................	1883,1884	1
The Sprig of Myrtle (monthly), Columbus......................	1883–1885	2
The Kansas Prohibitionist, Columbus......................	1886	1
Modern Light, Columbus......................	1891,1892	2
Baxter Springs Republican......................	1876,1877	1
The Times, Baxter Springs......................	1878–1881	3
Baxter Springs News......................	1882–1892	11
Baxter Springs Delta......................	1887	1
The Southern Argus, Baxter Springs......................	1891	1
Galena Miner......................	1877–1880	4
Galena Miner (second)......................	1888,1889	1
Short Creek Weekly Banner, Galena......................	1878	1
The Galena Messenger......................	1879	1
Short Creek Republican, Galena......................	1883–1892	10
The Galena Times......................	1890–1892	2
Cherokee County Teacher (monthly), Galena......................	1891,1892	1
Empire City Echo......................	1877–1879	3
The Ionian Casket (monthly), Quakervale......................	1878,1879	1

BOUND NEWSPAPER FILES AND PERIODICALS, KANSAS—Continued.

NEWSPAPERS.	Years.	No. vols.
CHEROKEE COUNTY—*Concluded.*		
Western Friend (monthly), Quakervale...	1880–1890	8
The Laborer's Tribune, Weir	1884–1888	5
Weir City Tribune	1889–1892	4
The Weir Journal	1889–1892	4
The Scammon Register	1891	1
The Globe-Miner, Scammon	1892	1
Cherokee county short lived, vol. 1: The Young Cherokee, June 10 to Aug. 12, 1876; The Daily Courier, Cherokee, Nov. 28 to Dec. 6, 1882; The Gospel Mirror, Columbus, Sept. 18 to Oct. 2, 1880; The Refugees' Star of Hope, Columbus, Jan. to Nov., 1882; Baptist Banner (semi-monthly), Columbus, April, May, 1887; The Christian Polemic (monthly), Galena, Feb. to Apr., 1879; The Baxter Springs Mirror, Nov. 27, 1880, to May 24, 1881; The Daily News, Baxter Springs, Oct. 7 to Oct. 11, 1884		1
CHEYENNE COUNTY.		
Cheyenne County Rustler, Wano, St. Francis	1885–1892	7
Plaindealer, Wano	1886–1888	2
Bird City News	1886–1892	6
Cheyenne County Democrat, Bird City	1886–1890	3
The Gleaner, Jaqua	1887,1888	1
Weekly Review, St. Francis	1889,1890	1
Cheyenne County Herald, St. Francis	1889,1890	1
People's Defender, St. Francis	1892	1
CLARK COUNTY.		
Clark County Clipper, Ashland	1884–1892	8
Republican Herald, Ashland	1886,1887	2
Ashland Journal	1887–1892	6
Clark County Chief, Englewood	1885–1887	3
The Englewood Chief, (suspended June 19, 1889, to August 19, 1891,)	1888–1892	2
Englewood Enterprise	1887–1889	1
Appleton Kansas Era	1885–1887	2
The Lexington Leader	1886–1888	2
The Minneola Era	1887,1888	1
Clark County Republican, Minneola	1888	1
Cash City Cashier	1887,1888	1
CLAY COUNTY.		
Clay County Dispatch, Clay Center	1876–1892	17
The Localist, Clay Center	1879–1881	3
The Democrat, Clay Center	1879,1880	2
The Cresset, Clay Center	1882,1883	1
The Times, Clay Center	1882–1892	11
The Times (daily), Clay Center	1886–1888	5
The Kansas Baptist, Clay Center	1881–1884	3
The Monitor, Clay Center	1883,1884	1
Clay Centre Eagle	1885,1886	1
Republican Valley Democrat, Clay Center	1886–1889	5
The Clay Center Democrat	1890,1891	2
The Holiness War News (monthly), Clay Center	1890,1891	1
The Weekly Sun, Clay Center	1891,1892	1
The Pentecost Trumpet, Clay Center	1891,1892	1
Morganville News and Sunflower	1885–1887	3
The Clay County Sentinel, Morganville	1887–1891	4
Uncle Sam's Live-Stock Journal, Morganville	1891,1892	1
The Advance, Morganville	1891,1892	1
The Idana Journal	1886,1887	1
Wakefield Advertiser	1887–1892	6
The Herald, Industry	1887,1888	1
Oak Hill Herald	1888,1889	1
Oak Hill Echo	1889	1
The Times, Clifton	1892	1
CLOUD COUNTY.		
Republican Valley Empire, Clyde and Concordia	1870–1872	3
Concordia Empire	1876–1882	7
The Republican-Empire, Concordia	1883–1886	4
Concordia Empire	1887–1892	6
The Concordia Republican	1882,1883	2
The Concordia Expositor	1877–1881	5
The Cloud County Blade, Concordia	1879–1881	3
Kansas Blade, Concordia	1882–1892	11
Concordia Daily Blade	1884–1888	6
Cloud County Critic, Concordia	1882–1886	7
The Concordia Times	1884–1891	8
Concordia Democrat, and Daylight	1886–1888	3
The Concordia Weekly Daylight	1889–1892	4

BOUND NEWSPAPER FILES AND PERIODICALS, KANSAS—CONTINUED.

NEWSPAPERS.	Years.	No. vols.
D COUNTY—*Concluded.*		
e Alliant, Concordia..........	1890–1892	2
rde Democrat	1880–1882	2
e Clyde Herald	1878–1892	14
ne's Press, Clyde.........	1884	1
e Clyde Mail.........	1884–1887	3
e Clyde Argus.........	1888–1892	5
e Farmers' Voice, Clyde.........	1891,1892	2
isco Tribune.........	1881,1882	1
e Glasco Sun.........	1883–1892	10
iud County Kansan, Jamestown.........	1881–1890	9
e Quill, Jamestown	1888–1890	2
nestown New Era	1890–1892	2
e Miltonvale News.....	1882–1891	11
Itonvale Star.........	1886	1
Itonvale Chieftain.........	1888	1
ies Advocate.........	1885,1886	1
e Ames Bureau.........	1887	1
e Weekly Courier, Ames.........	1888	1
EY COUNTY.		
osho Valley Register, Burlington.........	1859,1860	1
nsas Patriot, Burlington, (duplicate of 1867,).........	1864–1868	5
rlington Patriot.........	1876–1886	10
rlington Republican.........	1882–1886	4
e Republican-Patriot, Burlington.........	1886–1892	7
rlington Daily Republican-Patriot.........	1887	1
e Burlington Independent.........	1876–1892	17
rlington Daily Star.........	1878	1
e Burlington Nonpareil.........	1887–1892	6
e Farm Record, Burlington.........	1890–1892	1
e Courier, Burlington.........	1891,1892	1
oy Reporter.........	1879–1892	13
e Leroy Eagle.........	1888	1
e Lebo Light.........	1884–1888	5
e Lebo Courier.........	1889–1891	2
e Lebo Enterprise.........	1891,1892	2
e Waverly News.........	'83,'85–'89	4
e Gazette, Waverly.........	1889–1892	4
e Gridley Gazette.........	1887,1888	2
e Standard, Gridley.........	1889,1890	1
NCHE COUNTY.		
nanche Chieftain, Nescatunga.........	1884–1886	2
e Western Kansan, Nescatunga.........	1885–1887	3
catunga Enterprise.........	1886–1888	3
dwater Review.........	1884–1891	6
dwater Enterprise.........	1889–1892	4
e Western Star, Coldwater.........	1885–1892	8
ublican, Coldwater.........	1885,1886	1
Iwater Echo.........	1887–1892	6
e People's Advocate, Coldwater	1890,1891	1
manche County Citizen, Avilla.........	1885,1886	2
e Avilla Democrat.........	1886,1887	1
tection Echo.........	1885–1887	3
e Protection Press.........	1886,1887	1
nsas Weekly Ledger, Protection.........	1887	1
e Leader, Protection.........	1888	1
e Protection Press (second)	1891	1
nsville Herald.........	1885–1887	2
nanche City News.........	1886–1888	1
EY COUNTY.		
nfield Courier.........	1873–1892	19
nfield Daily Courier.........	1885–1890	11
field Plow and Anvil.........	1876	1
ley County Telegram, Winfield.........	1876–1890	15
nfield Daily Telegram, (1883–1886 lacking,).........	1879–1848	10
field Semi-Weekly.........	1879,1880	1
ley County Monitor, Winfield.........	1880	1
ley County Courant, Winfield	1881,1882	1
field Daily Courant.........	1881,1882	1
Daily Visitor, Winfield.........	1886–1889	8
Winfield Tribune.........	1884–1892	8
Winfield Visitor.........	1887–1889	2
American Nonconformist, Winfield.........	1887–1891	5
hwestern Kansas Conference Daily, Winfield.........	1887	1

BOUND NEWSPAPER FILES AND PERIODICALS, KANSAS—Continued.

NEWSPAPERS.	Years.	No. vols.
Cowley County — *Concluded.*		
Industrial Free Press, Winfield	1890–1892	3
Winfield Newspaper Union	1890–1892	2
Western Reveille (monthly), Winfield	1891, 1892	2
The Monthly Herald (Baptist), Winfield	1891, 1892	1
Arkansas City Traveler and Republican-Traveler	1876–1892	17
Arkansas Valley Democrat, Arkansas City	1879–1892	13
The Arkansas City Republican	1884–1886	3
The Arkansas City Republican (daily)	1886, 1887	2
Republican-Traveler (daily), Arkansas City	1887	1
Arkansas City Traveler (daily)	1888–1892	10
Canal City Daily Dispatch, Arkansas City	1887–1889	4
Evening Dispatch, Arkansas City	1889–1892	7
Canal City Dispatch (weekly), Arkansas City	1887–1892	6
The Fair Play, Arkansas City	1888–1892	5
The Bugle Call, Arkansas City, Howard	1888	1
People's Leader, Arkansas City	1891	1
The New Enterprise, Burden	1880, 1881	2
Burden Enterprise-Siftings	1882–1891	9
Burden Eagle	1885–1889	5
The Spirit of the West, Burden	1891, 1892	1
Cambridge Commercial	1881	1
The News, Cambridge	1882–1886	3
The Cambridge News	1888–1890	3
The Eye, Dexter	1884–1888	4
Dexter Free Press	1888–1890	2
The Udall Sentinel	1885, 1886	1
The Udall Record	1886–1892	6
Atlanta Cricket	1888, 1889	1
Crawford County.		
Girard Press	1874–1892	19
Crawford County News, Girard	1876–1880	4
Girard Herald	1880–1890	11
The Western Herald, Girard	1890–1892	2
The Kansas Workman (monthly), Girard	1882–1884	2
Cherokee Index	1876, 1877	2
The Young Cherokee, Cherokee	1876, 1877	1
Cherokee Banner	1877, 1878	1
The Temperance Rural, Cherokee, (one duplicate,)	1878, 1879	1
Sentinel on the Border, Cherokee	1879–1882	4
The Cherokee Sentinel	1883–1892	9
The Saturday Cyclone, Cherokee	1885–1887	3
The Smelter, Pittsburg	1881–1891	11
The Headlight, Pittsburg	1886–1892	7
The Daily Headlight, Pittsburg	1887	1
Pittsburg Democrat	1888, 1889	1
The Pittsburg Kansan	1889, 1892	4
The Pittsburg Star	1891, 1892	1
The Weekly World, Pittsburg	1891, 1892	1
The World (daily), Pittsburg	1890–1892	2
Pittsburg Herald	1890, 1891	1
Sunday Morning Mail, Pittsburg	1892	1
Walnut Comet	1892	1
The McCune Standard	1881, 1882	1
The McCune Times	1882–1891	9
The Brick, McCune and Pittsburg	1886, 1887	2
Crawford County Democrat, McCune	1889–1892	3
Walnut Journal	1882–1892	10
The Educational Advocate, Walnut	1884	1
The Arcadia Reporter	1882–1888	5
The Christian Worker, Arcadia	1888	1
Arcadia Democrat	1888–1890	2
Arcadia News	1890–1892	2
The Hepler Leader	1889, 1890	2
The Hepler Banner	1887–1889	3
The Farlington Plaindealer	1885, 1886	1
Farlington Gem	1886, 1887	1
Mulberry Grove Gazette	1886	...
Davis County. (See Geary.)		
Junction City Union, (triplicates of '75, '76, '77, '78, and duplicates of '79-'86,)	1865–1888	23
The Junction City Daily Union	1887	1
Junction City Tribune	1873–1888	16
The Youths' Casket (monthly), Junction City	1878	1
Davis County Republican, Junction City	1882–1888	6
The Junction City Methodist	1886, 1887	1

BOUND NEWSPAPER FILES AND PERIODICALS, KANSAS—Continued.

NEWSPAPERS.	Years.	No. vols.
ECATUR COUNTY.		
The Oberlin Herald..	1879–1892	12
The Eye, Oberlin..	1883–1892	9
The Oberlin World and Democrat..............................	1885,1886	1
Oberlin Opinion...	1886–1892	7
Alliance Times, Oberlin..	1890–1892	2
The Rathbone Family Historian (monthly), Oberlin.......	1892	1
The Norcatur Register..	1886–1892	5
The Allison Breeze and Times..................................	1887,1888	2
Jennings Echo...	1888–1892	4
Jennings Times..	1888,1889	1
The Alliance Times, Jennings...................................	1890	1
The Star, Dresden..	1890–1892	3
CKINSON COUNTY.		
Dickinson County Chronicle, Abilene.........................	1876–1892	17
Kansas Gazette, Enterprise and Abilene.....................	1876–1889	14
Abilene Daily Gazette..	1886–1888	6
The Weekly Democrat, Abilene.................................	1880–1882	2
The Abilene Reflector..	1883–1892	9
The Abilene Daily Reflector.....................................	1887–1892	8
The Dickinson County News, Abilene.........................	1888–1892	4
The Alliance Monitor, Abilene..................................	1890–1892	2
The Solomon Sentinel, Solomon City.........................	1879–1892	13
Enterprise Register...	1883,1884	2
Kansas Miller and Manufacturer, Enterprise................	1888–1892	5
Enterprise Independent..	1888–1890	3
The Anti-Monopolist, Enterprise..............................	1884–1888	4
The Integral Coöperator, Enterprise..........................	1891,1892	1
The Enterprise Journal...	1890–1892	2
The Chapman Star..	1884–1846	2
The Chapman Courier..	1887–1891	4
The Chapman Howitzer...	1891,1892	2
The Herington Tribune...	1885–1890	6
Herington Headlight..	1888,1889	1
Herington Vindicator...	1890	1
The Herington Times...	1889–1892	3
The Herington Signal...	1891,1892	1
The Hope Herald..	1885–1892	7
The Hope Dispatch..	1886–1892	7
Carlton Advocate..	1886–1888	2
The Banner Register, Banner City.............................	1887,1888	2
The Manchester Sun..	1887–1892	5
NIPHAN COUNTY.		
White Cloud Chief, (7 duplicates,)............................	1857–1872	16
Weekly Kansas Chief, Troy, (1 duplicate,)..................	1872–1892	20
White Cloud Review..	1880–1887	1
White Cloud Review (second)..................................	1888,1889	7
The White Cloud News (bi-weekly)............................	1891,1892	1
Troy Reporter	1866,1867	1
Doniphan County Republican, Troy, (1873 lacking,)......	1871–1875	5
Troy Weekly Bulletin..	1877–1879	2
The Troy Times...	1886–1892	6
Elwood Advertiser, (1 duplicate,).............................	1857,1858	1
Kansas Free Press, Elwood, (1 duplicate,)..................	1858, 1859	1
Elwood Free Press, (1 duplicate,).............................	1859–1861	2
Wathena Reporter, (1868–1873 lacking,)....................	1867–1877	5
Wathena Gazette,...	1889–1890	2
Highland Sentinel...	1878, 1879	1
The Central State, Highland....................................	1880–1882	2
Highland University Nuncio (bi-weekly).....................	1890–1892	2
The Vidette, Highland..	1892	1
Enterprise, Severance, (and Centralia, Nemaha county,)..	1883	1
Severance News..	1889–1892	4
UGLAS COUNTY.		
Herald of Freedom, Lawrence, (7 duplicates,).............	1854–1859	6
Kansas Free-State, Lawrence..................................	1855, 1856	1
Lawrence Republican, (volumes 1 and 3, incomplete,)....	1857–1860	2
The Western Home Journal, Lawrence.......................	1869–1884	14
The Weekly Kansas Journal, Lawrence, (1890, see Journal-Tribune,)..	1886–1892	6
The Lawrence Weekly Journal-Tribune.......................	1890	1
Lawrence Journal-Tribune (daily).............................	1890	2
Republican-Journal (daily), Lawrence.......................	1877–1880	8
Lawrence Daily Journal, (1890, see Journal-Tribune,)....	1880–1892	24
The Congregational Record, monthly, (Lawrence, January, 1859, to December, 1864; Topeka, June, 1865, to May, 1867,)............	1859–1867	8

BOUND NEWSPAPER FILES AND PERIODICALS, KANSAS—CONTINUED.

NEWSPAPERS.	Years.	No. vols.
DOUGLAS COUNTY—Concluded.		
The Tribune, Lawrence, (lacking 1873 and 1875,)	1868–1883	13
The Semi-Weekly Tribune, and the Weekly Herald-Tribune, Lawrence	1884, 1885	2
The Lawrence Tribune	1885–1888	3
The Tribune, daily, (1875, 1878, 1879, and part of 1877 lacking; duplicates,) Lawrence,	1873–1884	17
Herald-Tribune (daily), Lawrence	1884, 1885	3
Evening Tribune, Lawrence	1886–1888	6
Spirit of Kansas, Lawrence	1875–1882	7
Kansas Collegiate, Lawrence	1875–1879	5
The University Courier, Lawrence	1878, 1879	1
University Courier, Lawrence	1882–1892	10
The Kansas Review (monthly), Lawrence	1879–1892	13
Lawrence Standard	1877–1879	3
Kansas Monthly, Lawrence	1878–1881	4
The Daily Reporter, Lawrence	1879	1
Kansas Temperance Palladium, Lawrence	1879, 1880	1
Die Germania, Lawrence	1880–1892	5
The Kansas Liberal (monthly), Lawrence, July to September, 1882, (see Valley Falls.)		
The Lawrence Gazette	1882–1892	10
Lawrence Daily Gazette	1884, 1883	1
Western Recorder, Lawrence	1883, 1884	1
Kansas Churchman (monthly), Lawrence	1883–1885	2
Kansas Daily Herald, Lawrence	1883, 1884	2
The Head Center and Daily Morning Sun, Lawrence	1883	1
College Review and Progressive Educator, Lawrence	1885–1889	4
Evening Telegram, Lawrence	1888	1
University Times, Lawrence	1888, 1889	1
University Kansan, Lawrence	1889, 1890	1
The Daily Record, Lawrence	1889–1892	5
The Weekly Record, Lawrence	1890–1892	2
The Select Friend (monthly), Lawrence	1890–1892	2
The Jeffersonian, Lawrence	1890–1892	2
Smith's Small Fruit Farmer (quarterly), Lawrence	1891, 1892	1
Seminary Notes (monthly), Lawrence	1891, 1892	2
Lawrence Weekly Press	1891	1
The World (daily and weekly), Lawrence	1892	2
The Daily Morning News, Lawrence	1883, 1884	1
Once a Week, Lawrence	1883–1885	2
The Kansas Zephyr, Lawrence	1884–1887	3
Sigma Nu Delta (bi-monthly), Lawrence	1886–1889	2
Evening Telegram, Lawrence	1888	1
Lawrence Daily Democrat	1888	1
University Times, Lawrence	1888, 1889	1
The Weekly Record, Lawrence	1889, 1890	1
University Kansan, Lawrence	1889, 1890	1
The Daily Record, Lawrence	1889, 1890	3
North Lawrence Leader	1884, 1885	1
Freeman's Champion, Prairie City	1857, 1858	1
Baldwin Criterion	1883–1885	1
The Baldwin Visitor	1834	1
The Baldwin Ledger	1885–1892	8
The Baldwin Index, Baker University, (1887 lacking,)	1881–1892	7
The Baker Beacon, Baldwin	1889–1892	3
Lecompton Monitor	1885, 1886	1
The Lecompton Ledger	1890	1
College Echoes, Lecompton	1888–1891	2
The Lecompton Sun	1891, 1892	2
The Eudora News	1887–1892	5
EDWARDS COUNTY.		
Edwards County Leader, Kinsley	1877–1880	4
Valley Republican, (bound with Kinsley Graphic, 1878,)	1877, 1878	1
Kinsley Republican	1878–1881	4
The Kinsley Graphic, (except 1882,)	1878–1887	8
Kinsley Republican-Graphic	1882	1
Edwards County Banner, Kinsley	1887	1
Weekly Banner-Graphic, Kinsley	1887–1889	2
Weekly Graphic, Kinsley	1890–1892	3
Kansas Staats-Zeitung, Kinsley	1878, 1879	1
The Kinsley Mercury	1883–1892	8
Kinsley Daily Mercury	1887, 1888	2
The Wendell Champion	1885–1888	1
Belpre Beacon	1888	1
ELK COUNTY.		
The Courant, Howard	1875–1877	3
The Courant-Ledger, Howard	1878–1880	3

BOUND NEWSPAPER FILES AND PERIODICALS, KANSAS—CONTINUED.

NEWSPAPERS.	Years.	No. vols.
ELK COUNTY — *Concluded.*		
The Howard Courant.........	1880–1892	12
Industrial Journal, Howard	1878–1880	2
Kansas Rural, Howard	1881	1
The Howard Journal........	1880–1883	3
The Howard Democrat.........	1884–1891	6
Elk County Citizen, Howard.........	1891,1892	2
Kansas Traveler, Howard.......	1886,1887	1
Howard Daily Traveler.........	1887	1
The Broad Axe, Howard........	1888	1
Grip, Howard.	1883,1884	1
Our Church Mirror, Howard, (see Harvey county—Halstead.)		
Elk County Ledger, Elk Falls........	1876,1877	2
The Weekly Examiner, Elk Falls........	1878	1
Elk Falls Signal........	1880–1882	2
The Pioneer, Longton	1880,1881	2
The Times, Longton	1881–1892	11
Longton Leader	1887	1
Longton Signal.........	1890–1892	2
Moline News........	1880	1
Moline Mercury, (1883 and 1884 lacking,)	1882–1889	6
The Moline Free Press........	1883–1885	2
The Moline Republican........	1889–1892	3
The Grenola Argus........	1880–1882	2
The Grenola Chief, (see Crisis, 1891,)........	1883–1892	8
The Weekly Crisis, Grenola	1890,1891	1
The Grenola Hornet........	1884,1885	1
The Cave Springs Globe	1882	1
The Herald, Cana Valley........	1882,1883	1
ELLIS COUNTY.		
Ellis County Star, (lacking from December 7, 1876, to April 11, 1879,) Hays City.......	1876–1881	4
Hays Sentinel, Hays City........	1877–1881	5
The Star-Sentinel, and Hays City Sentinel........	1880–1892	13
German-American Advocate, Hays City	1882–1886	4
Ellis County Democrat and Advocate, Hays City........	1884,1885	1
Ellis Weekly Headlight, Hays City........	1882–1890	9
The Ellis Review-Headlight........	1890–1892	2
Hays City Times, Hays City........	1886	1
Ellis County Democrat and Ellis County Free Press, Hays City........	1886–1890	5
Ellis County Free Press, Hays City........	1888–1892	4
Ellis Review, Hays City........	1886–1890	5
Democratic Times, Hays City........	1888–1891	3
The Republican, Hays City........	1888–1892	5
Walker Journal........	1887,1888	1
ELLSWORTH COUNTY.		
Ellsworth Reporter........	1875–1892	18
The Rural West, Ellsworth........	1882	1
The Ellsworth News........	1883,1884	2
The Ellsworth Democrat........	1885–1891	5
The Weekly Herald, Ellsworth	1888–1890	1
The Ellsworth Republican........	1890	1
Ellsworth Messenger........	1891,1892	1
Wilson Index........	1878,1879	1
The Wilson Echo........	1880–1892	13
The Wilson Wonder........	1886,1887	2
The Wilson Hawkeye........	1887,1888	1
Cain City News........	1882–1886	3
The Kanopolis Journal........	1886–1890	4
Kanopolis Kansan........	1890–1892	3
The Holyrood Enterprise........	1887–1890	3
The Sentinel, Holyrood........	1891,1892	1
FINNEY COUNTY.		
The Irrigator, Garden City........	1882–1886	4
Garden City Herald, (1884-'87 lacking)........	1883–1892	6
Garden City Herald (daily)........	1886–1890	8
Garden City Sentinel........	1884–1892	8
Garden City Sentinel (daily)........	1886–1888	6
The Cultivator and Herdsman (monthly and weekly), Garden City........	1884–1886	1
The Western Times, Garden City........	1885	1
Finney County Democrat, Garden City........	1887–1891	4
The Garden City Imprint........	1889–1892	4
The Lookout, Garden City........	1891,1892	1
Pierceville Courier........	1886,1887	1
Terry Enterprise........	1886,1887	1

BOUND NEWSPAPER FILES AND PERIODICALS, KANSAS—Continued.

NEWSPAPERS.	Years.	No. vols.
FINNEY COUNTY—*Concluded.*		
The Terry Eye	1887–1889	3
Locomotive, Loco	1886,1887	1
The Hatfield News	1887–1889	1
FOOTE COUNTY. (See Gray county.)		
The New West and the Optic, Cimarron	1879–1881	2
The Signet, Cimarron	1880	1
FORD COUNTY.		
Dodge City Times	1876–1892	16
Dodge City Times-Ensign (and Bellefont)	1892	1
Ford County Globe, Dodge City	1878–1884	7
The Globe Live-Stock Journal, Dodge City	1884–1887	3
Dodge City Democrat, (May to December, 1889, lacking,)	1884–1892	8
Kansas Cowboy, Dodge City	1884,1885	1
The Sun, Dodge City	1886,1887	1
Ford County Republican, Dodge City	1887–1889	3
Our Methodist (monthly), Dodge City	1888,1889	1
The Globe-Republican, Dodge City	1890–1892	3
Speareville Enterprise	1878	1
Speareville News	1878–1880	1
Speareville Blade	1885–1890	6
Ford County Record, Speareville	1885–1886	1
Ford County Democrat, Speareville and Fonda	1886–1888	2
The Ryansville Boomer, and The Boomer, Ford City	1885–1887	2
Ford Gazette	1886–1890	5
Wilburn Argus	1886,1887	2
Bucklin Standard	1887,1888	1
The Bucklin Herald	1887,1888	1
The Bucklin Journal	1888–1890	2
Bucklin Weekly Bulletin	1892	1
The Weekly Telegram, Bloom	1888,1889	2
Western Kansas Ensign, Bellefont	1889–1891	3
FRANKLIN COUNTY.		
Western Home Journal, Ottawa	1865–1868	3
Ottawa Journal	1870–1874	5
The Triumph, Ottawa	1876	1
Ottawa Journal and Triumph	1877–1892	16
Ottawa Campus (occasional), (vols. 1 and 2)	1864–1892	7
Ottawa Republican, (1875 lacking,)	1874–1892	18
Ottawa Daily Republican	1879–1892	27
Kansas Home News, Ottawa	1879,1880	1
Ottawa Gazette	1879	1
Ottawa Leader	1880	1
Kansas Free Trader (monthly), Ottawa	1883	1
Queen City Herald, Ottawa	1883–1887	2
Jefferies Western Monthly, Ottawa	1884,1885	1
Daily Local News, Ottawa	1886–1888	5
Fireside, Factory and Farm, Ottawa	1886–1888	1
The Kansas Lever, Ottawa	1887–1892	6
The Bee (daily and weekly), Ottawa	1887,1888	1
Ottawa Tribune	1889–1892	3
Ottawa Daily Tribune	1891,1892	2
The Ottawa Herald	1889–1892	4
Ottawa Chautauqua Assembly Herald	1891,1892	1
The Ottawa Baptist (monthly)	1892	1
Williamsburg Review	1879	1
Weekly Gazette, Williamsburg	1880–1883	2
The Eagle, Williamsburg	1885–1889	5
The Enterprise, Williamsburg	1889–1892	4
Lane Advance	1881,1882	1
The Lane Star	1889,1890	1
The Lane Leader	1890–1892	3
The Commercial Bulletin, Lane	1886–1888	3
The Wellsville News	1882	1
The Wellsville Transcript	1882,1883	1
The Wellsville News (second)	1884,1886	3
The Wellsville Exchange	1887–1892	2
The Pomona Enterprise	1885–1892	6
Republican, Pomona	1889,1890	1
Richmond Recorder	1885–1888	3
Princeton Progress	1885–1888	3
Wellsville Globe	1891,1892	2

BOUND NEWSPAPER FILES AND PERIODICALS, KANSAS—Continued.

NEWSPAPERS.	Years.	No. vols.
GARFIELD COUNTY.		
Ravanna Chieftain	1885–1892	7
Ravanna Sod-House	1886,1887	1
Ravanna Record	1887–1889	2
The Ravanna Enquirer	1887,1888	1
The Kal Vesta Herald	1886–1888	2
The Essex Sunbeam	1887	1
The Garfield County Call, Eminence	1887–1892	5
Garfield County Journal, Loyal	1887–1889	2
GEARY COUNTY. (See Davis.)		
Junction City Union	1889–1892	4
Junction City Tribune	1889–1892	4
Davis County Republican, Junction City	1889–1892	4
The Junction City Sentinel, The Democratic Sentinel	1889–1892	4
The Mid-Continental Review (monthly), Junction City	1890–1891	2
The Kansas Wheelmen's Library (monthly), Junction City	1891,1892	2
GOVE COUNTY.		
Buffalo Park Express	1880	1
Buffalo Park Pioneer	1885–1887	3
The Golden Belt, Grinnell	1885–1890	5
Cap-Sheaf, Grainfield	1885–1892	7
Gazette, Gove City	1886–1892	7
Gove County Graphic, Gove City	1887,1888	1
Gove County Republican, Gove City	1888–1890	1
Gove County Echo, Gove City	1891,1892	1
The Settler's Guide, Quinter	1886–1888	2
Quinter Republican	1889–1892	4
The Smoky Globe, Jerome	1887,1888	1
GRAHAM COUNTY.		
The Western Star, Hill City	1879,1880	1
Hill City Lively Times	1881	1
The Hill City Reveille	1884–1892	8
Hill City Democrat	1887–1890	3
Hill City Sun	1888,1889	1
Hill City Star	1888,1889	1
Hill City Republican	1890–1892	2
The People's Advocate, Hill City	1891,1892	1
Graham County Lever, Gettysburg	1879,1880	1
The Millbrook Times	1879–1889	10
Graham County Times, Millbrook	1889,1890	2
Graham County Republican, Millbrook	1881	1
Millbrook Herald	1882,1883	1
Millbrook Herald (second)	1885–1888	2
The Graham County Democrat, Millbrook	1885–1888	3
Roscoe Tribune	1880,1881	1
Western Cyclone, Nicodemus	1886–1888	2
Nicodemus Enterprise	1887	1
The Fremont Star	1886–1888	2
The Fremont Press	1888,1889	1
Fremont Eagle	1889,1890	1
The Bogue Signal	1888–1890	2
The Times, Penokee	1889,1890	1
GRANT COUNTY.		
Grant County Register, Ulysses	1885–1890	4
Ulysses Tribune, Tribune-Commercial, and Grant County Register, (Enfield, 1887,)	1887–1892	6
Ulysses Plainsman	1889,1890	1
Grant County Republican, Ulysses	1892	1
The Post, Surprise	1886,1887	1
Shockeyville Eagle	1886,1887	1
Shockeyville Plainsman	1889	1
Golden Gazette	1887–1889	3
Zionville Sentinel	1887,1888	1
The Commercial, Cincinnati and Appomattox, (see Ulysses Tribune,)	1887,1888	2
The Standard-Democrat, Cincinnati and Appomattox	1887,1888	1
The Lawson Leader	1887,1888	1
Conductor Punch	1887,1888	1
GRAY COUNTY.		
The New West, Cimarron and Echo	1885–1888	4
The West, Echo, and Cimarron New West	1889–1892	4
Cimarron Herald and Kansas Sod House	1885,1886	1
The Jacksonian, Cimarron	1885–1892	7

BOUND NEWSPAPER FILES AND PERIODICALS, KANSAS—CONTINUED.

NEWSPAPERS.	Years.	No. vols.
GRAY COUNTY—*Concluded.*		
Gray County Echo, Ingalls and Cimarron	1886–1888	2
Ingalls Union	1887–1892	5
Gray County Republican, Ingalls	1888	1
The Weekly Messenger, Ingalls	1889,1890	1
The Montezuma Chief	1886–1889	2
Gray County Republican, Montezuma	1889	1
Ensign Razzoop	1887,1888	1
GREELEY COUNTY.		
Greeley County Gazette, Greeley Center and Horace	1886–1888	2
Greeley County News, Greeley Center and Horace	1886–1888	1
Horace Messenger	1888	-1
Horace Champion	1883,1889	2
Hector Echo	1886	1
Greeley County Tribune, Tribune and Reid	1886,1887	1
Greeley County Enterprise, Tribune	1887,1888	1
Greeley County Republican, Tribune	1889–1892	4
Greeley County Journal, Tribune	1890–1892	2
Greeley County Republican, Reid	1887,1888	1
Colokan Graphic	1887,1888	1
GREENWOOD COUNTY.		
Eureka Censorial	1876–1879	3
Eureka Herald	1876–1892	17
The Graphic, Eureka	1879–1882	3
The Eureka Republican	1879,1880	2
Greenwood County Republican, Eureka	1880–1892	12
The Eureka Sun	1879,1880	1
Greenwood County Democrat, Eureka	1882–1884	2
Democratic Messenger, Eureka	1884–1892	9
Kansas Alliance Union, Eureka	1890–1892	3
The Academy Student, Eureka	1889,1890	1
Madison Times	1877,1878	1
The Madison News	1879–1892	12
The Zenith, and the Madison Times	1886–1888	3
Fall River Times	1881–1891	10
Fall River Echo	1883–1886	3
Fall River Courant	1886–1888	2
Saturday Morning Sun, Fall River	1888,1889	1
Severy Pioneer	1882	1
Southern Kansas Journal, Severy	1884–1887	3
Severy Liberal	1885,1886	2
Severy Record	1887–1891	4
The Kansas Clipper, Severy	1887–1889	1
Severyite, Severy	1889–1892	4
The Sunflower, Reece	1885,1886	2
Greenwood Review, Virgil	1887–1892	4
The Hamilton Broadaxe	1889,1890	1
The Severy Telegram	1891,1892	2
The Fall River Chief	1891	1
HAMILTON COUNTY.		
The Syracuse Journal	1885–1892	7
Syracuse Sentinel, (removed from Johnson City, Stanton county,)	1886–1889	3
Syracuse Democrat	1887	1
Democratic Principle, Syracuse	1887–1892	5
West Kansas News, Syracuse	1887	1
Hamilton County Bulletin, Coolidge and Syracuse	1890–1892	2
Border Ruffian, Coolidge	1885–1887	1
Coolidge Citizen	1886–1890	4
Coolidge Times	1887–1890	2
Surprise Post	1886	1
The Signal, Kendall	1886,1887	1
The Kendall Boomer	1886–1889	3
Kendall Republican	1886,1887	1
Kendall Gazette	1887	1
The Kendall Free Press	1889,1890	1
Johnson City Sentinel, (since in Stanton county,)	1886–1888	3
Enfield Tribune, (Enfield and Ulysses; see Grant county,)	1886,1887	1
HARPER COUNTY.		
The Anthony Republican	1879–1892	13
Anthony Daily Republican	1886–1889	6
Harper County Enterprise, Anthony	1883–1891	7
The Harper County Democrat, Anthony	1886–1888	2
Anthony Free Press (daily)	1887,1888	1

BOUND NEWSPAPER FILES AND PERIODICALS, KANSAS — CONTINUED.

NEWSPAPERS.	Years.	No. vols.
HARPER COUNTY — *Concluded.*		
Anthony Journal	1878–1884	5
Anthony Journal (second)	1888–1892	5
Anthony Daily Journal	1888	1
The Weekly Bulletin, Anthony	1891,1892	1
Harper County Times, Harper	1878–1885	7
The Sentinel, Harper	1882–1892	9
The Daily Sentinel, Harper	1886–1888	5
Harper Graphic, (suspended August, 1888, to September, 1890,)	1883–1892	6
Harper Daily Graphic	1886	1
The College Journal, Harper	1888,1889	1
The Prophet, Harper	1888	1
The Alliance Bulletin, Harper	1890,1891	1
The Advocate, Harper	1891,1892	1
Bluff City Tribune	1886–1888	2
Bluff City Herald	1888–1890	3
Bluff City Independent	1891,1892	1
The Danville Courant	1883,1884	1
The Danville Express	1885,1886	1
The Attica Advocate	1885–1891	7
Attica Daily Advocate	1887	1
Attica Bulletin	1886–1888	2
Attica Tribune	1891,1892	1
Freeport Leader	1885–1890	3
Midlothian Sun, Freeport	1885–1886	1
The Freeport Tribune, (changed from Sun,)	1886	1
The Crisfield Courier	1885–1890	4
HARVEY COUNTY.		
Zur Heimath (semi-monthly), Halstead	1875–1881	7
The Halstead Independent	1881–1892	12
The Halstead Clipper	1884–1886	2
Halstead Herald	1887,1888	2
The Halstead Tribune	1890–1892	3
Harvey County News, Newton	1876–1879	4
The Newton Republican, (changed from Harvey County News,)	1879–1892	13
Newton Daily Republican	1886–1892	14
Newton Kansan	1876–1892	17
Newton Daily Kansan, (1889 to 1891 lacking,)	1887–1892	4
The Golden Gate, Newton	1879–1882	3
Das Neue Vaterland, Newton	1879	1
The Newton Democrat	1883–1887	3
Newton Anzeiger	1887–1892	4
The Kansas Commoner, Newton	1887–1890	3
The Kansas Chronicle, Newton	1888	1
Newton Weekly Journal	1888–1892	4
The School Journal (monthly), Newton	1891,1892	1
The Ladies' Magazine (monthly), Newton	1891,1892	1
The Burrton Telephone	1878–1881	3
The Burrton Monitor	1881–1888	7
The Burrton Graphic	1884–1892	7
The Free Lance, Burrton	1890–1892	3
The Jayhawker and Palladium, Sedgwick	1882–1884	2
The Pantagraph, Sedgwick	1884–1892	9
Walton Independent	1886–1888	2
The Walton Reporter	1890–1892	3
HASKELL COUNTY.		
Ivanhoe Times	1886–1892	7
Santa Fé Trail	1886,1887	2
Santa Fé Champion	1887,1888	1
Haskell County Review, Santa Fé	1887,1888	1
Haskell County Republican, Santa Fé	1888	1
The Santa Fé Leader	1888	1
Santa Fé Monitor	1888–1892	5
HODGEMAN COUNTY.		
Agitator, Hodgeman Center	1879,1880	1
Republican, Fordham	1879	1
The Buckner Independent, Jetmore	1879–1881	2
The Jetmore Reveille	1882–1892	10
Hodgeman County Scimitar, Jetmore	1886–1889	4
Jetmore Siftings	1886–1892	5
Jetmore Journal	1887–1889	2
The Jetmore Sunflower	1889–1892	3
The Orwell Times	1885,1886	1
The Cowland Chieftain	1885	1
Western Herald, Jetmore	1892	1

—5

BOUND NEWSPAPER FILES AND PERIODICALS, KANSAS — CONTINUED.

NEWSPAPERS.	Years.	No. vols.
JACKSON COUNTY.		
Holton Express..	1872–1875	4
Holton Recorder.....................................	1875–1892	18
The Holton Argus...................................	1877	1
The Holton Signal........ ...	1878–1892	15
Jackson County Federal, Holton..............	1886, 1887	1
The Bee (daily and weekly), Netawaka and Holton....	1879, 1880	1
Independent Tribune, Holton.....................	1896, 1897	3
The Fraternal Aid (monthly), Holton.........	1891, 1892	1
The Whiting Weekly News.........................	1883–1892	10
The Hoyt Times.....................................	1877	1
Soldier City Tribune	1858–1890	2
The Denison Star....................................	1889, 1890	1
The Soldier City Clipper..........................	1891, 1892	2
The Kansas Bazaar, Circleville..................	1891, 1892	1
JEFFERSON COUNTY.		
The Kansas Educational Journal, Grasshopper Falls. (See Leavenworth county.)		
The Kansas New Era, Grasshopper Falls.....	1866, 1867	1
Valley Falls New Era..............................	1878–1892	20
The Valley Falls Liberal and the Kansas Liberal (monthly), Valley Falls and Lawrence.......	1880–1883	3
Lucifer, (the Light-Bearer,) Valley Falls......	1883–1890	7
Valley Falls Register..............................	1881–1891	11
Fair Play, Valley Falls............................	1888–1890	2
Valley Falls Republican..........................	1889, 1890	1
Farmers' Vindicator, Valley Falls..............	1890–1892	2
The Oskaloosa Independent.......................	1870–1892	23
Sickle and Sheaf, Oskaloosa.....................	1878–1879	7
Oskaloosa Weekly Sickle.........................	1879–1886	7
The Oskaloosa Times...............................	1891, 1892	2
The Winchester Argus.............................	1879–1888	9
The Winchester Herald.............................	1888–1892	5
The Kaw Valley Chief, Perry.....................	1879–1882	3
The Perry Monitor and Kaw Valley Chief (second), Perry......	1883, 1884	1
The Perry News......................................	1891, 1892	2
The Nortonville News..............................	1885–1892	5
Meriden Report......................................	1885–1888	3
Meriden Weekly Tribune...........................	1890–1892	3
The Osawkie Times...................................	1885, 1886	1
The McLouth Times..................................	1887–1892	5
JEWELL COUNTY.		
Jewell County Diamond, Jewell City............	1876, 1877	2
Jewell County Republican, Jewell City........	1879–1892	13
Jewell County Monitor, Jewell Center........	1876, 1877	2
Jewell County Monitor and Diamond, Jewell Center....	1878, 1879	2
Jewell County Monitor, Jewell Center and Mankato....	1880–1892	13
Jewell County Review, Jewell Center and Mankato....	1879–1882	3
The Jewell County Review, Mankato...........	1889–1892	4
Mankato Review......................................	1883–1888	6
Mankato Daily Review..............................	1887	1
The Kansas Jewellite, Mankato..................	1882, 1883	1
The Jacksonian, Mankato..........................	1888–1890	3
The Labor Clarion, Mankato......................	1889	1
White Oak Independent............................	1879	1
Jewell County Journal, Omio.....................	1889, 1890	1
Western Advocate, Omio...........................	1882	1
The Omio Mail.......................................	1884	1
The Western Advocate, Mankato.................	1890–1892	2
The Jewell County News, Jewell City..........	1891, 1892	1
Burr Oak Reveille..................................	1880–1884	5
Burr Oak Herald.....................................	1883–1892	10
Burr Oak Rustler....................................	1886, 1887	1
Independent Republican, Burr Oak..............	1886, 1887	1
Salem Chronicle.....................................	1882	1
Salem Argus..	1883–1890	6
The People's Friend, Salem.......................	1885–1887	3
Randall Register.....................................	1885–1888	3
Randall Tribune......................................	1887, 1888	1
The Beacon, Randall................................	1889, 1890	1
The Exponent, Randall	1890–1892	2
JOHNSON COUNTY.		
Olathe Mirror.......................................	1866–1868	2
Mirror and News-Letter, Olathe.................	1876–1882	6
The Olathe Mirror, (1884–'86, see below,)....	1882–1892	7

BOUND NEWSPAPER FILES AND PERIODICALS, KANSAS—Continued.

NEWSPAPERS.	Years:	No. vols.
Johnson County—*Concluded.*		
Olathe Mirror-Gazette	1883–1886	4
Western Progress, Olathe	1876–1880	4
Kansas Star, Olathe	1876–1892	17
Olathe Leader	1879–1882	3
Olathe Gazette	1879–1883	3
Educational Advocate, Olathe	1880	1
Johnson County Democrat, Olathe	1882–1891	10
Kansas Patron, Olathe	1882–1892	11
The Olathe Republican	1884,1885	2
The Olathe Leader (second)	1891,1892	1
Kansas Register, Spring Hill	1878	1
Weekly Review, Spring Hill	1881,1882	1
Spring Hill New Era, (1886 to August, 1888, lacking,)	1883–1892	5
The Young Kansan, Gardner	1889,1890	2
The Kansan, Gardner	1890,1891	1
Gardner Graphic	1891,1892	1
Kearny County.		
Lakin Herald	1882–1884	3
The Kearny County Advocate, Lakin	1885–1892	7
Pioneer Democrat, Lakin	1885–1890	4
The Lakin Index	1890–1892	2
Hartland Times	1886,1887	2
Hartland Herald	1886–1891	5
Kearny County Coyote, Chantilly and Omaha	1887–1890	3
Kingman County.		
The Kingman Mercury	1878–1880	2
The Kingman Blade	1880	1
The Kingman County Citizen, Kingman	1879–1884	4
The Kingman County Republican, Kingman	1882–1884	2
Citizen-Republican, Kingman	1884	1
Southern Kansas Democrat, Kingman	1883–1888	5
The Kingman County Democrat	1889–1892	4
The Kingman Courier	1884–1889	6
Kingman Daily Courier	1887,1888	3
Kingman Leader	1884–1889	4
Kingman Leader-Courier	1889–1892	3
Kingman News	1886–1888	2
Kingman Daily News, (November, 1887, to February, 1888, lacking,)	1886–1888	2
Voice of the People, Kingman	1884,1889	2
The Kingman Weekly Journal	1890–1892	3
News, Norwich	1886–1892	7
Ninnescah and Cunningham Herald	1886–1888	2
Cunningham Herald	1889–1892	4
The Spivey Dispatch	1887,1888	2
Spivey Index	1889–1891	3
New Murdock Herald	1887	1
The Penalosa News	1887,1888	1
The Nashville News	1888	1
Kiowa County.		
Wellsford Register	1885	1
Wellsford Register (second)	1890	1
Wellsford Republican	1886,1887	1
Kiowa County Democrat, Wellsford	1887,1888	2
The Democrat and Watchman, Dowell post office	1885,1886	1
Comanche Chief and The Kiowa Chief, Reeder	1886	1
Greensburg Signal	1886–1888	3
The Kiowa County Signal, Greensburg	1880–1892	4
The Kiowa County Times, Greensburg	1888–1892	4
Greensburg Rustler	1886–1888	3
Greensburg Republican	1887,1888	1
The Republican, Greensburg	1890,1891	1
Republican Banner, Greensburg	1891,1892	2
Mullinville Mallet	1886–1888	2
The Weekly Telegram, Mullinville	1886,1887	1
The Haviland Tribune	1887–1889	2
Labette County.		
Parsons Sun	1876–1892	17
Parsons Sun, daily	1884–1892	18
Parsons Eclipse	1876–1892	17
Parsons Daily Eclipse	1881–1892	23
Daily Outlook, Parsons	1877,1878	1
Daily Infant Wonder, Parsons	1878–1880	3

BOUND NEWSPAPER FILES AND PERIODICALS, KANSAS — Continued.

NEWSPAPERS.	Years.	No. vols.
LABETTE COUNTY — *Concluded.*		
Daily Republican, Parsons.	1880,1881	2
Parsons Palladium.	1883–1892	10
The Daily Evening Star, Parsons, (April 6 to October 19, 1881,).	1881	1
The Weekly Clarion, Parsons.	1888–1891	3
The Daily Eli, Parsons.	1890,1891	3
Kansas Workman and State Alliance, Parsons.	1891	1
Our Home Visitor (monthly), Parsons.	1891,1892	1
Mills's Weekly World, Parsons.	1891,1892	1
Southern Kansas Advance, Chetopa.	1876–1878	2
Chetopa Advance.	1878–1892	15
Chetopa Herald.	1876–1878	2
Chetopa Statesman.	1885–1889	4
The Chetopa Democrat	1888–1892	5
Oswego Independent.	1876–1892	17
Labette County Democrat, Oswego.	1880–1892	13
The Oswego Republican.	1881–1886	5
The Oswego Daily Republican.	1881–1883	3
The Oswego Bee.	1887,1888	2
The Oswego Daily Bee.	1887,1888	3
Labette County Statesman, Oswego.	1889–1892	3
The Oswego Courant.	1889,1890	2
Mound Valley Herald.	1885–1892	7
Mound Valley News.	1886,1887	1
The Altamont Sentinel.	1886–1890	5
Mills's Weekly World, Altamont.	1889–1891	3
The Edna Star.	1887,1888	1
The Edna Independent.	1891,1892	1
The Wilsonton Journal.	1888–1892	5
LANE COUNTY.		
Lane County Gazette, California.	1880–1882	2
Lane County Herald, Dighton.	1885–1892	7
Dighton Journal.	1886–1892	6
Dighton Republican.	1887–1889	2
Lane County Farmer, Dighton.	1890,1891	1
LEAVENWORTH COUNTY.		
Kansas Herald, Leavenworth.	1854–1859	5
Kansas Territorial Register, Leavenworth.	1855	1
Leavenworth Conservative, daily, (January to June, 1867, lacking,).	1861–1868	16
Times and Conservative, Leavenworth (daily).	1869,1870	3
Leavenworth Times, daily, (July to October, 1878, lacking,).	1870–1892	45
Leavenworth Times (weekly).	1876–1880	5
Leavenworth Daily Commercial.	1873–1876	4
Kansas Freie Presse, Leavenworth (weekly).	1876–1886	10
Kansas Freie Presse, Leavenworth (daily).	1874–1886	18
Leavenworth Appeal.	1876–1878	3
Leavenworth Appeal and Herald.	1879	1
Leavenworth Appeal and Tribune.	1879,1880	1
Public Press, Leavenworth (weekly).	1877–1883	6
Public Press, Leavenworth, daily, (from July, 1877, to June, 1879, lacking,).	1877–1882	8
Home Record, Leavenworth (monthly).	1876–1892	17
Democratic Standard, Leavenworth (weekly).	1880–1882	3
Kansas Farmer, Leavenworth (monthly).	1867–1872	8
Leavenworth Evening Standard.	1881–1892	24
The Kansas Educational Journal, monthly: Leavenworth, January, 1864, to August, 1865; Grasshopper Falls, September, 1865, to January, 1866; Topeka, June, 1866, to August, 1867; Emporia, September, 1867, to April, 1871; Emporia and Topeka, May, 1871, to April, 1873.	1864–1873	9
Orphans' Friend, Leavenworth (monthly).	1878–1892	14
The Western Homestead, Leavenworth (monthly).	1878–1882	3
The Workingman's Friend, Leavenworth.	1881–1883	2
Leavenworth Weekly Chronicle.	1883,1884	1
The Visitor, Leavenworth.	1882–1884	2
The Catholic, Leavenworth.	1885–1889	5
The Kansas Prohibitionist, Leavenworth.	1883,1884	1
Kansas Commoner, Leavenworth.	1884,1885	1
Truth, Leavenworth (monthly).	1886,1887	1
The Daily Sun, Leavenworth.	1887–1890	6
Leavenworth Post (daily).	1888–1892	10
Journal of the U. S. Cavalry Association, Leavenworth (quarterly).	1888–1892	5
The Leavenworth Advocate.	1888–1891	3
Taps, Leavenworth (monthly).	1889–1891	1
The Sentinel, Fort Leavenworth (Episcopal Church). (See Salina.)		
The Tonganoxie Mirror.	1882–1892	10
The Tonganoxie News, (changed from Linwood Leader,).	1885–1887	2
The Tonganoxie Sentinel.	1889–1892	4
The Linwood Leader.	1883–1884	1

BOUND NEWSPAPER FILES AND PERIODICALS, KANSAS—Continued.

NEWSPAPERS.	Years.	No. vols.
LINCOLN COUNTY.		
Lincoln County News, Lincoln Center	1873	1
Saline Valley Register, Lincoln Center	1876–1879	4
Lincoln Register, Lincoln Center	1879,1880	1
Saline Valley Register, Lincoln Center	1881–1883	2
Lincoln Banner, Lincoln Center	1884–1886	2
Lincoln Republican, Lincoln Center	1886–1892	7
The Argus and Beacon, Lincoln Center	1880	1
The Beacon of Lincoln County, Lincoln Center	1881–1884	3
The Lincoln Beacon, Lincoln Center	1884–1892	9
Lincoln County Democrat, Lincoln	1886–1890	4
Lincoln County Farmer, Lincoln	1890–1892	1
The Sylvan Grove Sentinel	1887–1892	5
Barnard Times	1888–1892	3
LINN COUNTY.		
La Cygne Weekly Journal	1876–1892	17
La Cygne Leader	1887,1888	1
Border Sentinel, Mound City	1866–1874	8
Linn County Clarion, Mound City	1876–1892	17
Mound City Progress	1884–1892	9
The Torch of Liberty, Mound City	1888–1892	5
The Pleasanton Observer	1876–1892	17
The Pleasanton Herald	1882–1892	11
The Prescott Eagle	1883–1888	5
The Prescott Republican	1888,1889	1
Prescott Enterprise	1889	1
The Blue Mound Sun	1883–1892	9
The Parker Pilot	1889–1891	3
The Pilot and Graphic, Parker	1891,1892	1
Goodrich Graphic	1890,1891	2
LOGAN COUNTY.		
The Oakley Opinion	1885–1889	4
The Oakley Republican	1887,1888	1
Oakley Saturday Press	1888	1
Logan County Times, Oakley and Russell Springs	1887,1888	1
Oakley News Letter	1889	1
Oakley Graphic	1889–1892	3
The Courier, Ennis and Monument	1886–1888	2
The Monument Obelisk	1888,1889	2
The Monument Observer	1890	1
The Scout, Gopher and Winona, (bound with Winona Messenger,)	1886–1888	3
The Winona Clipper	1887–1892	5
Winona Messenger	1887–1889	2
McAllaster Weekly Record	1887,1888	1
Augustine Herald	1887–1891	3
The Leader, Russell Springs	1887–1889	2
The Record, Russell Springs	1887	1
The Logan County Republican, Russell Springs	1888–1892	5
Page City Messenger	1889,1890	1
LYON COUNTY.		
Emporia News	1865–1889	24
Emporia Daily News	1878–1889	22
Kansas Educational Journal, Emporia, (see Leavenworth county.)		
Emporia Ledger	1876–1880	5
The Hatchet (monthly), Emporia	1877,1878	1
The Educationalist (monthly), Emporia	1879,1880	2
Emporia Sun	1878,1879	2
The Kansas Greenbacker, and the National Era, Emporia	1878,1879	2
The Emporia Journal	1880,1881	2
The Kansas Sentinel, Emporia	1880–1892	3
Daily Bulletin, Emporia	1881	1
Emporia Daily Republican	1881–1892	23
The Emporia Republican	1886–1892	6
Emporia Democrat	1882–1889	8
The Primitive Friend, Emporia	1883–1885	2
Emporia Daily Globe, (1888 lacking,)	1886–1889	3
The Fanatic, Emporia	1887,1888	1
The Weekly News-Democrat, Emporia	1889,1890	1
Emporia News-Democrat (daily)	1889,1890	1
The Semi-Weekly Miniature, Emporia	1887	1
The Normal Quarterly, Emporia	1889–1892	3
Kansas Workman, Emporia, (see Butler county.)		
College Life, Emporia	1890–1892	3
The Emporia Standard	1890–1892	2

BOUND NEWSPAPER FILES AND PERIODICALS, KANSAS—CONTINUED.

NEWSPAPERS.	Years.	No. vols.
LYON COUNTY — *Concluded.*		
The Baptist Visitor (monthly), Emporia	1891,1892	2
The Columbia, Emporia	1890–1892	1
The Emporia Zeitung (monthly)	1888–1891	2
The Emporia Daily Gazette	1890–1892	5
The Hartford Enterprise	1879,1880	1
The Hartford Weekly Call	1879–1891	11
Hartford News	1890–1892	3
Americus Weekly Herald	1881,1882	1
The Americus Ledger	1885–1889	4
The Americus Greeting	1890–1892	1
The Neosho Vivifier, Neosho Rapids	1885,1886	1
The Neosho Valley Press, Neosho Rapids	1886,1887	1
The Neosho Rapids Pilot	1889–1891	2
The Admire City Free Press	1887,1888	1
Admire Independent	1891,1892	1
The Allen Tidings	1887–1892	4
MCPHERSON COUNTY.		
The McPherson Independent	1876–1879	4
The McPherson Freeman	1878–1891	14
Freeman-Vim, McPherson	1891,1892	1
McPherson Daily Freeman	1887,1888	2
The McPherson Republican	1879–1892	13
McPherson Daily Republican	1887–1892	12
The Comet, McPherson	1881,1882	1
Industrial Liberator, McPherson	1882	1
The McPherson Independent	1882–1884	4
The McPherson Press	1884,1885	1
The McPherson County Champion, McPherson	1885–1887	2
The Democrat, McPherson	1886–1892	6
Kansas State Register, McPherson	1887	1
The McPherson Anzeiger	1887–1890	4
Our Opinion, McPherson	1888–1890	2
School, Fireside, and Farm, McPherson	1888	1
The Educator and Companion	1889–1892	4
The Industrial Union, McPherson	1890–1891	1
Kansas Vim, McPherson	1888–1891	2
People's Advocate, McPherson and Galva	1891,1892	1
Lindsborg Localist	1879–1883	3
Smoky Valley News, Lindsborg	1881–1888	7
Kansas Posten, Lindsborg	1882,1883	1
Framat, Lindsborg	1889	1
The Lindsborg News	1889–1892	4
The Canton Monitor	1880	1
Canton Carrier	1885–1888	3
The Republican, Canton	1889,1890	2
The Canton News	1891,1892	1
The Windom Record	1884–1886	2
The Windom Enterprise	1886–1888	2
The Roundridge Leader	1887–1892	6
Marquette Monitor	1887,1888	2
Marquette Tribune	1889–1892	4
Galva Times	1888–1892	3
The Inman Independent	1891,1892	1
Inman Review	1892	1
MARION COUNTY.		
Marion County Record, Marion Center	1875–1892	17
The School Galaxy, Marion Center	1877	1
Central Kansas Telegraph, Marion Center	1880	1
Marion Banner, Marion Center	1880,1881	2
Marion Graphic, Marion Center	1882,1883	1
Marion County Democrat and Independent, Marion Center	1883,1884	1
The Marion Register, Marion	1885–1888	2
The Marion Tribune	1886,1887	1
The Cottonwood Valley Times, Marion, (lacking Sept., 1889, to Nov., 1890,)	1887–1892	5
Marion Daily Times	1888	2
The School Glenner, Marion	1889,1890	1
The Rural Kansan, Marion	1889,1890	2
The Scimeter, Marion	1890	1
The Marion County Anzeiger, Marion and Hillsboro	1887–1892	5
The Central Advocate, Marion	1891	1
The Peabody Gazette	1876–1892	17
The Peabody Daily Gazette	1887	1
Peabody Reporter	1880	1
The Peabody Post	1882	1
Marion Graphic, Peabody	1883–1890	7

BOUND NEWSPAPER FILES AND PERIODICALS, KANSAS — CONTINUED.

NEWSPAPERS.	Years.	No. vols.
MARION COUNTY — *Concluded.*		
Florence Herald, (1886 lacking,)	1876–1892	15
Florence Tribune	1884–1886	2
Florence Weekly News	1886,1887	1
The Florence Weekly Bulletin	1887–1892	6
Hillsboro Phonograph	1881	1
The Intelligencer, Hillsboro	1881,1882	1
Freundschafts-Kreis, Hillsboro	1885,1886	2
Hillsboro Herald	1886–1888	3
Der Kansas Courier, Hillsboro	1891,1892	1
Canada Arcade	1887	1
Lincolnville Star	1887,1888	1
The Weekly Courier, Lost Springs	1888,1889	1
Burns Monitor	1889,1890	1
MARSHALL COUNTY.		
The Marysville Enterprise, (volumes 1 and 3,)	1866,1868	2
The Lantern, Marysville	1876	1
The Marshall County News, Marysville	1876–1892	17
Kansas Staats-Zeitung, Marysville	1879–1881	2
Marysville Signal	1881–1883	2
Marysville Post (German)	1881–1892	11
Marshall County Democrat, Marysville	1883–1892	10
The Bugle Call, Marysville	1885,1886	1
The True Republican, Marysville	1886–1890	4
The Daily Free Press, Marysville	1889,1890	3
Evening Democrat, Marysville	1890,1892	2
The People's Advocate, Marysville	1890–1892	2
The Waterville Telegraph, (1874 and 1875 lacking,)	1870–1892	21
Blue Rapids Times	1876–1892	17
The Blue Rapids Lyre	1886,1887	1
Blue Rapids Weekly Motor	1890–1892	2
Blue Valley Gazette, Irving	1876–1878	3
The Irving Citizen	1880	1
The Irving Leader	1886–1892	6
Frankfort Record	1876–1879	4
The National Headlight, Frankfort	1879–1881	2
The Frankfort Bee	1881–1892	12
The Frankfort Sentinel	1886–1892	5
The Beattie Boomerang	1883,1884	1
The North Star, Beattie	1884,1885	1
The Star, Beattie	1885–1891	6
Williamson's Beattie Eagle	1891,1892	1
The Visitor, Axtell	1883,1884	1
Axtell Anchor	1843–1892	9
The Summerfield Sun	1889–1892	4
The Oketo Sun and Herald	1889–1892	3
The Vermillion Record	1891,1892	1
MEADE COUNTY.		
The Pearlette Call	1879,1880	1
Fowler City Graphic	1885–1890	4
The Fowler City Advocate	1886	1
Meade County Globe, Meade Center	1885–1892	7
Meade Center Press	1885,1886	1
The Press-Democrat, Meade Center	1885–1890	4
Meade Center Telegram	1886	1
The Meade Republican, Meade Center	1887–1892	5
Meade County Democrat, Meade	1890–1891	1
Meade County Nationalist, Meade	1891,1892	2
The Hornet, Spring Lake, and Artois, Artesian City	1885–1889	4
The Guardian, West Plains	1886,1887	1
The West Plains News and Democrat	1887,1888	1
The West Plains Mascott	1888,1889	1
Meade County Times, Merilla	1886–1888	2
MIAMI COUNTY.		
The Western Spirit, Paola	1874–1892	19
The Miami Republican, Paola	1876–1892	17
Republican-Citizen, Paola	1878–1880	2
Miami Talisman, Paola	1881,1882	1
Paola Times, Miami Farmer, Times-Signal	1882–1892	11
The Miami School Journal, Paola	1889,1890	1
The Border Chief, Louisburg	1879–1881	2
Watchman, Louisburg	1881	1
The Louisburg Herald	1887–1892	5
Osawatomie Times	1880,1881	1
Osawatomie Gaslight	1887,1888	1

BOUND NEWSPAPER FILES AND PERIODICALS, KANSAS—Continued.

NEWSPAPERS.	Years.	No. vols.
MIAMI COUNTY—Concluded.		
Graphic, Osawatomie	1888–1892	5
Osawatomie Advertiser	1888–1890	1
Farmers' Signal, Osawatomie	1890,1891	1
Osawatomie Globe	1891,1892	1
Fontana News	1885–1889	4
MITCHELL COUNTY.		
Beloit Gazette, (dups. from April, 1872, to April, 1873; 1873, 1874 and 1875 lacking,)	1872–1892	17
Beloit Weekly Record	1877–1879	3
The Beloit Courier	1879–1892	14
Beloit Weekly Democrat	1878–1880	2
Western Democrat, Beloit, (1882 and 1883 lacking,)	1880–1890	7
The Western Nationalist, Beloit	1882,1883	2
Beloit Dental Herald	1888,1889	1
The Western Call, Beloit	1890–1892	2
The Harmonic (monthly), Beloit	1891,1892	1
The Echo, Cawker City	1876–1878	2
The Cawker City Free Press	1876–1883	5
Cawker City Journal	1880–1890	9
The Public Record, Cawker City	1883–1892	10
Cawker City Times	1888–1892	5
Glen Elder Key	1880	1
Glen Elder Herald	1885–1890	4
The Kansas Herald, Glen Elder	1890	1
The People's Sentinel, Glen Elder	1891,1892	2
Simpson Siftings	1884–1886	2
Scottsville Independent	1886–1889	4
Tri-County News, Scottsville	1889–1892	4
MONTGOMERY COUNTY.		
Independence Courier	1874,1875	2
Independence Kansan	1876–1884	9
The Star, Independence	1882–1884	3
The Star and Kansan, Independence	1885–1892	8
The South Kansas Tribune, Independence	1876–1892	17
The Workingman's Courier, Independence	1877–1879	3
The Living Age, Independence	1881	1
The Evening Reporter, and the Morning Reporter, Independence, (lacking from 1883 to February 17, 1886,)	1882–1892	15
The Independence News (daily and weekly)	1886	1
Montgomery Argus, Independence	1886	1
Coffeyville Journal	1876–1892	17
The Gate City Enterprise, Coffeyville	1884,1885	1
Gate City Gazette, Coffeyville	1886,1887	1
The Sun, Coffeyville	1886–1888	2
The Eagle, Coffeyville	1888–1890	1
The Index, Coffeyville	1889,1890	1
The News, Coffeyville	1890–1892	2
Afro-American Advocate, Coffeyville	1891,1892	1
Cherryvale Leader	1877	1
Cherryvale Globe	1879–1882	3
Cherryvale News	1881,1882	1
Cherry Valley Torch, Cherryvale	1882–1885	3
Cherryvale Globe-News	1882–1884	3
The Globe and Torch, Cherryvale	1885–1888	3
Daily Globe and Torch, Cherryvale	1885–1887	4
Cherryvale Bulletin	1884–1888	5
The Weekly Clarion, Cherryvale	1885	1
The Cherryvale Republican	1886–1892	6
The Cherryvale Champion	1887–1892	5
Southern Kansas Farmer, Cherryvale	1890,1891	1
The Kansas Commonwealth, Cherryvale	1891	1
The Morning Telegram, Cherryvale	1892	1
The Elk City Globe	1882–1887	5
The Elk City Star	1884–1886	1
The Elk City Democrat	1885,1886	1
The Elk City Eagle	1886–1890	4
Elk City Times	1887	1
The Elk City Enterprise	1889–1892	3
The Caney Chronicle	1883–1892	7
The Caney Times	1889–1892	4
The Havana Vidette	1885,1886	1
Havana Weekly Herald	1887,1888	1
The Havana Recorder	1889	1
The Havana News	1890	1
The Havana Press	1891,1892	1

BOUND NEWSPAPER FILES AND PERIODICALS, KANSAS—CONTINUED.

NEWSPAPERS.	Years.	No. vols.
MONTGOMERY COUNTY—*Concluded.*		
Liberty Light..	1886	1
The Liberty Review..	1886–1892	6
MORRIS COUNTY.		
Morris County Republican, Council Grove...	1876,1877	1
Council Grove Democrat..	1876,1877	2
Republican and Democrat, Council Grove..	1877–1879	2
Council Grove Republican...	1879–1892	14
Morris County Times, Council Grove	1880,1881	2
The Kansas Cosmos, Council Grove, (January to July, 1885, lacking; October 15, 1886, Cosmos consolidated with Council Grove Republican,).................................	1881–1886	6
The Council Grove Guard, and Herald Guard...	1884–1892	8
The Anti-Monopolist, Council Grove...	1888	1
Council Grove Courier..	1891,1892	1
Morris County Enterprise, Parkersville...	1878–1884	7
The Parkersville Times...	1887,1888	1
The Morris County News, White City...	1886–1888	2
The White City News	1888,1889	1
White City Register	1889–1892	4
The Dwight Wasp...	1887–1891	5
The Dunlap Courier	1889–1891	2
Wilsey Bulletin..	1890	1
MORTON COUNTY.		
Frisco Pioneer..	1886,1887	1
Morton County Democrat, Frisco..	1886–1888	1
The Richfield Leader...	1886,1887	1
The Leader-Democrat, Richfield...	1888,1889	1
The Richfield Republican..	1887–1890	2
The Monitor-Republican, Richfield...	1890,1891	3
The Great Southwest, Richfield..	1887,1888	1
The Morton County Star, Richfield...	1891,1892	2
The Taloga Star	1887–1890	3
Cundiff Journal..	1888,1889	1
The Morton County Monitor, Morton..	1888–1890	1
The Westola Wave...	1888,1889	1
NEMAHA COUNTY.		
Seneca Weekly Courier...	1875–1884	10
Seneca Courier-Democrat..	1885–1892	8
The Seneca Tribune...	1875–1892	14
Our Mission, Seneca...	1885,1886	1
The Seneca News..	1890–1892	2
Nemaha County Republican, Sabetha...	1876–1892	17
The Sabetha Advance..	1876,1877	2
Sabetha Weekly Herald...	1884–1892	9
The Oneida Journal...	1879–1882	3
The Oneida Chieftain, Democrat, and Dispatch...	1883,1884	1
The Oneida Monitor..	1885,1886	1
The Oneida World..	1892	1
The Wetmore Spectator, (lacking from August, 1884, to August, 1885,)...............	1882–1892	9
The Centralia Enterprise..	1883,1884	1
The Centralia Journal...	1885–1892	8
The Goff's News...	1887–1890	3
The Goff's Advance...	1892	1
The Bern Press...	1889–1892	4
NEOSHO COUNTY.		
Neosho County Journal, Osage Mission...	1876–1892	17
The Temperance Banner, Osage Mission..	1878–1880	2
Neosho Valley Enterprise, Osage Mission...	1880–1882	2
Neosho County Democrat, Osage Mission...	1883–1888	5
Neosho County Record, Erie...	1876–1886	11
Neosho County Republican, Erie...	1884–1886	3
The People's Vindicator, Erie..	1888,1889	1
Republican-Record, Erie..	1886–1892	6
The Erie Sentinel...	1889–1892	3
Chanute Times...	1876–1891	15
The Chanute Democrat...	1879,1882	3
The Chanute Chronicle...	1882,1883	2
Chanute Blade..	1884–1892	9
The Chanute Vidette...	1887–1890	3
Chanute Vidette-Times..	1891,1892	2
Railroad Employés' Companion, Chanute..	1889,1890	1
Chanute Daily Tribune...	1892	1
Head Light, Thayer...	1876–1892	16

BOUND NEWSPAPER FILES AND PERIODICALS, KANSAS — CONTINUED.

NEWSPAPERS.	Years.	No. vols.
NEOSHO COUNTY—*Concluded.*		
The Thayer Herald	1885, 1886	1
Thayer Independent News	1891, 1892	1
Star of Hope, Urbana	1878	1
The Stark Freeman	1890, 1891	1
NESS COUNTY.		
The Pioneer, Clarinda and Sidney	1879–1882	3
The Advance, Sidney	1882, 1883	1
Ness City Times	1880–1891	10
The Truth, Ness City	1883, 1884	1
The News, Ness City	1884–1892	8
The Ness City Graphic	1886	1
Walnut Valley Sentinel, Ness City	1886–1892	6
The Globe, Schoharie	1883, 1884	1
The Harold Record	1887–1889	3
Harold Boomer	1887	1
Nonchalanta Herald	1887, 1888	1
The Bazine Register	1887, 1888	1
Bazine Leader	1889	1
NORTON COUNTY.		
Norton County Advance, Norton	1878–1882	5
Norton County People, Norton	1880–1883	2
The Norton Courier	1883–1892	10
Norton Champion	1884–1892	8
The Norton Democrat	1886–1888	2
Weekly New Era, Norton	1889–1891	2
The Farmers' Advance, Norton	1890	1
The Lenora Leader	1882–1888	6
The Kansas Northwest, Lenora	1884, 1885	1
The Kansas Monitor, Lenora	1885, 1886	1
The Common People, Lenora	1886, 1887	1
The Lenora Record	1887–1890	3
The Norton County Badger, and } The Edmond Times, Edmond, }	1886–1890	5
The Almena Star	1885–1889	3
Almena Plaindealer	1888–1892	5
The Almena Advance	1889, 1890	1
The Oronoque Magic	1886	1
The Calvert Gazette	1889, 1890	1
OSAGE COUNTY.		
Osage County Chronicle, Burlingame, (1872 lacking,)	1868–1892	23
Osage County Democrat, Burlingame	1881–1887	4
Burlingame Herald	1881–1884	2
Burlingame Independent, (changed from Carbondale Calendar, Jan. 28 to April 1, 1886; Carbondale Independent, April 8 to May 13, 1886; then moved to Burlingame,)	1886–1888	2
Burlingame News (amateur)	1886–1889	1
The Burlingame Democrat	1888–1890	1
The Burlingame Echo, National Echo (monthly)	1888–1892	3
Osage City Free Press	1876–1892	17
The Kansas Times, Osage City, (moved from Lyndon,)	1879–1884	3
The Osage City Republican	1882, 1883	1
Osage County Democrat, Osage City	1886, 1887	1
The Kansas People, Osage City	1887–1890	4
Kansas People (daily), Osage City	1887, 1888	3
Lyndon Times	1876–1879	3
The Lyndon Journal	1882–1892	10
The Lyndon Leader	1882, 1883	2
Kansas Plebeian, Lyndon and Scranton	1882	1
Osage County Graphic, Lyndon	1888–1892	4
The People's Herald, Quenemo and Lyndon	1890–1892	2
Osage County Times, Scranton and Burlingame	1888–1891	4
The Scranton Gazette	1890–1892	3
The Carbondale Journal	1879	1
Carbondale Independent	1882–1884	2
Astonisher and Paralyzer, Carbondale	1885–1887	2
The Carbondalian, Carbondale	1887–1892	6
The Carbondale Record	1888	1
Kansas Workman, Scranton and Quenemo	1883–1888	5
Osage County Republican and Sentinel, Quenemo	1886–1892	6
Quenemo Republican	1892	1
The Quenemo Leader	1889, 1890	2
Melvern Record	1884–1890	6
The Melvern Review	1891, 1892	2
Overbrook Herald	1889–1892	4

BOUND NEWSPAPER FILES AND PERIODICALS, KANSAS—CONTINUED.

NEWSPAPERS.	Years.	No. vols.
OSBORNE COUNTY.		
Osborne County Farmer, Osborne	1876–1892	17
The Truth Teller, Osborne	1880	1
Daily News, Osborne	1881	1
Osborne County News, Osborne	1883–1892	10
Western Odd Fellow (monthly), Osborne	1886–1888	1
Osborne County Journal, Osborne	1886–1889	3
Bull's City Post	1890	1
Osborne County Key, Bull's City	1881,1882	1
The Western Empire, Bull's City	1883–1885	2
The Western Empire, Alton	1885–1892	8
Downs Times	1880–1892	13
Downs Chief	1886–1891	5
Downs Globe	1888–1890	2
Portis Patriot	1881–1890	9
The Whisperer, Portis	1890	1
OTTAWA COUNTY.		
The Solomon Valley Mirror, Minneapolis	1874–1886	12
The Sentinel, Minneapolis	1876–1883	8
Minneapolis Messenger, (successor to Sentinel,)	1883–1892	8
The Daily Messenger, Minneapolis	1887	1
Minneapolis Independent	1876–1881	6
Ottawa County Index, Minneapolis	1880–1833	4
The Progressive Current, Minneapolis	1883,1884	1
Solomon Valley Democrat, Minneapolis	1884–1891	7
The Daily Institute, Minneapolis, Nos. 1 to 20	1885	1
Kansas Workman (monthly), Minneapolis	1885–1892	8
Minneapolis School Journal	1885,1886	1
The Sprig of Myrtle (monthly), Minneapolis, (moved from Columbus, Cherokee county,)	1886–1892	6
Ottawa County Commercial, Minneapolis	1886,1887	1
Minneapolis Commercial	1887–1892	5
Kansas Union, Ottawa County Index, Minneapolis	1890–1892	2
The Review, Minneapolis	1891,1892	1
The Delphos Herald	1879,1880	2
Delphos Carrier	1881–1888	7
The Delphos Republican	1888–1892	4
Bennington Star	1883–1888	4
The Bennington Journal	1885	1
Herald and Star, Bennington	1889–1891	2
Ottawa County Democrat, Bennington	1891,1892	1
The Tescott Herald	1887–1891	3
PAWNEE COUNTY.		
Larned Press	1876–1878	3
The Pawnee County Herald, Larned	1877,1878	2
The Larned Enterprise-Chronoscope	1878–1888	11
Larned Chronoscope	1889–1892	4
Larned Daily Chronoscope	1887,1888	3
The Larned Optic	1878–1884	6
The Larned Weekly Eagle-Optic	1885–1892	8
The Labor News, Larned	1888,1889	1
Pawnee County Republican, Larned	1886,1887	1
Tiller and Toiler, Larned	1892	1
Garfield Letter	1885,1886	1
The Garfield News	1887,1888	1
The Burdett Bugle	1886–1888	2
PHILLIPS COUNTY.		
The Kirwin Chief	1876–1891	15
Kirwin Progress and Kirwin Democrat	1877,1878	2
The Independent, Kirwin	1880–1888	8
The Independent, Kirwin (second)	1889–1892	3
Kirwin Republican	1883,1884	1
Kirwin Graphic	1889	1
The Kirwin Globe	1891,1892	1
Phillips County Herald, Phillipsburg	1878–1892	15
The Phillipsburg Times	1884,1885	1
The Phillipsburg Dispatch	1886–1892	6
Phillipsburg Democrat	1887–1891	4
Logan Enterprise	1879–1883	5
Phillips County Freeman, Logan	1883–1890	7
The Logan Republican	1886–1892	7
The Long Island Argus	1845	1
Long Island Leader	1886–1892	
Phillips County Democrat, Long Island	1886	

BOUND NEWSPAPER FILES AND PERIODICALS, KANSAS — Continued.

NEWSPAPERS.	Years.	No. vols.
PHILLIPS COUNTY—*Concluded.*		
Phillips County Inter-Ocean, Long Island	1887–1891	4
Marvin Monitor	1886,1887	1
Woodruff Gazette and Republican	1886,1887	1
POTTAWATOMIE COUNTY.		
Pottawatomie Gazette, Louisville, (vols. 1, 2, 3, 4, and duplicate vol. 1,)	1847–1870	4
Kansas Reporter, Louisville	1870–1887	17
Pottawatomie County Herald, Louisville	1879	1
The Louisville Republican (and The Semi-Weekly Republican)	1882–1886	5
The Louisville Indicator	1887–1889	3
Pottawatomie County Times, Louisville	1889–1892	3
Weekly Kansas Valley, Wamego	1869–1871	2
The Wamego Blade	1876	1
The Wamego Tribune	1877–1882	6
Kansas Agriculturist, Wamego	1879–1892	14
Wamego Democrat	1885,1886	1
The Daily Wamegan, Wamego	1887–1889	5
The Kansas Teacher, Wamego	1889,1890	1
St. Mary's Times	1876,1877	2
St. Mary's Democrat	1878	1
Pottawatomie Chief, St. Mary's	1878,1879	2
St. Mary's Express	1880–1888	7
St. Mary's Star	1884–1892	9
St. Mary's Gazette	1888–1891	3
The Dial, St. Mary's	1890–1892	3
Inkslingers' Advertiser, Westmoreland	1878	1
The Weekly Period, Westmoreland	1882–1885	3
The Westmoreland Recorder	1885–1892	8
The Westmoreland Iudicator	1889–1891	1
The Alliance News, Westmoreland	1890–1892	2
The Onaga Journal	1878–1885	8
The Onaga Democrat	1885–1889	3
The Onaga Herald	1890–1892	3
Independent and Morning News, Havensville	1880–1882	2
The Havensville Register	1889,1890	1
The Havensville Torchlight	1891,1892	1
The Olsburg News-Letter	1887–1892	6
The Belvue Dodger	1889	1
Butler City News	1889,1890	1
PRATT COUNTY.		
The Stafford Citizen	1877,1878	1
Pratt County Press, Iuka	1878–1887	9
Pratt County Times, Iuka	1881–1892	11
The Iuka Traveler	1886–1888	1
The Saratoga Sun	1885–1887	3
Pratt County Democrat, Saratoga	1885,1886	1
The Cullison Banner	1886–1888	2
Cullison Tomahawk	1888–1890	1
Pratt County Register, Pratt	1886–1890	4
The Pratt County Republican, Pratt	1888–1892	5
Pratt County Union, Pratt	1890–1892	3
The Preston Herald	1887,1888	1
The Preston Plain Dealer	1889–1892	3
Springvale Advocate	1888	1
RAWLINS COUNTY.		
Atwood Pioneer	1879–1882	3
Republican Citizen, Atwood	1880–1892	12
Rawlins County Democrat, Atwood and Blakeman	1885–1892	7
The Atwood Journal	1888	1
The Ludell Settler	1884–1887	3
Ludell Gazette	1887–1892	4
The Celia Enterprise	1885–1888	3
The Blakeman Register	1887–1892	5
The Herndon Courant	1888–1890	3
McDonald Times	1888–1892	4
RENO COUNTY.		
Hutchinson News	1876–1892	17
Hutchinson Daily News	1886–1892	11
Hutchinson Herald	1876–1885	9
The Interior, Hutchinson	1877–1885	8
The Interior-Herald, Hutchinson	1885–1892	8
Hutchinson Daily Interior-Herald	1887	1

BOUND NEWSPAPER FILES AND PERIODICALS, KANSAS — CONTINUED.

NEWSPAPERS.	Years.	No. vols.
RENO COUNTY — *Concluded.*		
The Sunday Democrat, The Dollar Democrat, The Democrat, and The Hutchinson Democrat	1883–1890	8
The Hutchinson Call (daily)	1888	1
Hutchinson Republican	1889,1890	2
The Hutchinson Times-Republican	1889–1892	3
The Clipper, Hutchinson	1889–1892	4
Kansas Herald, Hutchinson (German)	1888–1890	2
Alliance Gazette, Hutchinson	1890–1892	2
The South Hutchinson Leader	1886,1887	1
The Saturday Review, South Hutchinson	1887–1890	2
The Journal, South Hutchinson	1888,1889	1
The Argosy, Nickerson	1878–1892	14
The Nickerson Register and The Nickerson Industry	1884–1891	6
The Nickerson Daily Register	1887	1
The Arlington Enterprise	1885–1892	7
Sylvia Telephone	1886–1889	2
The Sylvia Herald	1889,1890	2
The Sylvia Banner	1889–1892	3
The Haven Independent	1886–1892	5
The Turon Rustler	1888–1889	2
Turon Headlight	1889–1892	4
Partridge Cricket and Press	1886,1887	1
Lerado Ledger	1886–1888	1
The Weekly Press, Olcott	1889	1
The Torch Light, Plevna	1888,1889	1
REPUBLIC COUNTY.		
The Belleville Republic	1876	1
The Belleville Telescope	1876–1892	17
The Weekly Record, Belleville	1883–1885	2
The Belleville Democrat	1886–1890	4
Republic County Press, Belleville	1889,1890	1
Republic County Freeman, Belleville	1890–1892	2
The Belleville Democrat	1890–1892	1
Scandia Republic	1877	1
The Republic County Journal, Scandia	1878–1880	4
Republican-Journal, Scandia	1881	1
Scandia Journal	1882–1892	11
Republic County Independent, Scandia	1883,1884	1
Republic County Chief, Scandia	1885,1886	1
The Scandia Independent	1887–1889	2
White Rock Independent	1879	1
Republic City News	1883–1892	9
Conservative Cuban, Cuba	1884–1886	2
Republic County Pilot, Cuba	1885–1888	4
The Cuba Union, and The Union Pilot, Cuba	1888–1890	2
The Cuba Daylight	1890–1892	3
The Alliance Sun, Cuba	1891	1
Cesky Lev, Cuba (Bohemian)	1891,1892	1
The Wayne Register	1885–1887	3
The Warwick Leader	1886,1887	1
Cortland Register	1889–1892	4
RICE COUNTY.		
Rice County Gazette, Sterling	1876–1880	5
Sterling Gazette	1881–1891	10
Weekly Bulletin, and The Sterling Bulletin	1877–1891	13
The Bulletin and Gazette, Sterling	1891,1892	2
Sterling Weekly Champion	1888–1892	4
The Daily Bulletin, Sterling	1887,1888	2
Sterling Republican (weekly)	1886,1887	1
Sterling Republican (daily)	1887	1
The Arkansas Valley Times, Sterling	1888	1
The Saturday Republican, Sterling	1888	1
The Lyons Republican	1879–1892	13
The Daily Republican, Lyons	1892	1
The Lyons Daily Republican	1887,1888	3
Central Kansas Democrat, Lyons, (1882, 1883, 1888, 1889 lacking,)	1879–1892	10
Central Kansas Democrat (daily), Lyons	1886,1887	2
The Lyons Prohibitionist	1885–1890	4
The Soldiers' Tribune, Lyons	1887,1888	1
The Lyons Tribune	1888–1892	4
Rice County Eagle, Lyons	1890	1
The Lyons Democrat	1889,1890	1
The Rural West, Little River	1881,1882	2
The Little River Monitor	1886–1892	6
The Comet, Little River	1891	1

BOUND NEWSPAPER FILES AND PERIODICALS, KANSAS — CONTINUED.

NEWSPAPERS.	Years.	No. vols.
RICE COUNTY—*Concluded.*		
The Chase Dispatch	1884,1885	1
The Weekly Record, Chase	1886–1892	6
Geneseo Herald	1887–1892	6
The Raymond Independent	1887,1888	1
The Cain City Razzooper	1887,1888	1
Partridge Press	1887	1
Independent, Frederick	1888,1889	1
Rice County News, Frederick	1890–1892	2
The Alden Herald	1888	1
RILEY COUNTY.		
Manhattan Express	1859–1862	3
The Kansas Radical, Manhattan, (duplicate of 1867 and 1868,)	1866–1868	3
The Manhattan Independent, (1865 lacking,)	1864–1868	3
The Manhattan Standard, (triplicate of 1869 and duplicate of 1870,)	1868–1870	3
Manhattan Homestead (occasional)	1869–1892	9
The Nationalist, Manhattan, (eleven duplicates,)	1870–1892	22
The Literary Review, Manhattan	1872	1
Manhattan Beacon, (two duplicates,)	1872–1875	3
The Industrialist, Manhattan, (twelve duplicates,)	1875–1892	18
Manhattan Enterprise	1876–1882	6
The Kansas Telephone (monthly), Manhattan	1881–1892	12
The Manhattan Republic	1882–1892	11
Manhattan Daily Republic	1887–1891	8
The Independent, Manhattan	1883	1
The Mercury, Manhattan	1884–1892	8
The Golden Cresset (monthly), Manhattan	1884,1885	1
The Journal of Mycology (monthly), Manhattan, (moved to Washington, D. C.,)	1885–1888	3
The Saturday Signal, Manhattan	1888,1889	1
The Signal, Manhattan	1890	1
The Midget, Manhattan	1890	1
Randolph Echo	1882–1887	5
The Randolph Enterprise	1888–1892	4
The Independent, Riley Center	1879–1882	2
The Riley Times	1887–1889	2
The Riley Regent	1889–1892	3
Leonardville Monitor	1884–1892	9
Bala City Advance	1890,1891	1
ROOKS COUNTY.		
The Stockton News, and the Western News, (except 1881, see Plainville News,)	1876–1892	15
Rooks County Record, Stockton	1879–1892	13
Stockton Democrat	1885–1889	4
Stockton Eagle	1887,1888	1
Stockton Academician (quarterly)	1888–1892	3
The Teacher (monthly), Stockton	1891,1892	1
Alliance Signal, Stockton	1891,1892	2
The Plainville News, (moved from Stockton for one year,)	1881	1
The Plainville Press	1885,1886	1
Plainville Echo	1884–1886	2
Plainville Times	1886–1892	7
Webster Eagle	1885–1887	2
Webster Enterprise	1888	1
Woodston Saw and Register	1886–1889	3
Cresson Dispatch	1887,1888	1
RUSH COUNTY.		
Rush County Progress, Rush Center, and La Crosse Eagle	1877,1878	2
La Crosse Chieftain	1882–1892	11
La Crosse Clarion	1889–1892	3
La Crosse Democrat	1887–1891	3
The Western Economist, La Crosse	1891,1892	2
The Blade, Walnut City	1878–1882	5
The Herald, Walnut City	1883–1886	4
Walnut City Gazette, Rush Center	1880–1883	3
The Democrat, Walnut City	1886–1888	2
Walnut City News (daily)	1887,1888	2
Rush Center Gazette	1888–1890	3
Rush County News, Rush Center	1888–1891	3
The McCracken Enterprise	1887–1892	6
RUSSELL COUNTY.		
Russell County Record, Russell	1876–1892	17
Russell County Advance, Russell	1878	1
Russell Independent	1879–1881	2

BOUND NEWSPAPER FILES AND PERIODICALS, KANSAS—CONTINUED.

NEWSPAPERS.	Years.	No. vols.
RUSSELL COUNTY — *Concluded.*		
The Russell Hawkeye	1882,1883	1
Russell Live-Stock Journal, and Russell Journal	1885-1892	8
Russell Review, and Democratic Review, Russell	1886-1888	1
Russell County School Signal (monthly), Russell	1889-1892	4
Bunker Hill Advertiser	1880,1881	2
Bunker Hill Banner	1882,1883	1
Bunker Hill Banner (second)	1884,1885	1
The Bunker Hill News	1887,1888	1
Bunker Hill Gazette	1888,1889	1
The Dorrance Nugget	1886-1890	2
Luray Headlight	1887-1890	3
The Lucas Advance	1888-1892	5
Waldo Enterprise	1888-1890	2
ST. JOHN COUNTY. (See Logan.)		
The Oakley Opinion	1885,1886	1
SALINE COUNTY.		
The Salina Herald	1876-1892	17
Salina Daily Herald	1887,1888	3
Saline County Journal, Salina	1876-1892	17
Saline County Daily Journal, Salina	1887,1888	2
Farmers' Advocate, Salina	1876-1879	4
The Weekly Democrat, Salina	1878,1879	1
Svenska Heroiden, Salina	1878-1881	3
The Salina Independent	1882-1885	3
The Salina Republican	1886-1892	7
Salina Daily Republican	1888-1892	8
The Rising Sun, Salina	1885-1889	4
The Salina Sun	1889-1892	3
Wesleyan Advocate, Salina	1883,1889	2
The Normal Register (quarterly and monthly), Salina	1885-1892	3
Vade Mecum (monthly), Salina	1890,1891	1
Woman's Mission Star, Salina	1889,1890	1
Western Odd Fellow (monthly), Salina	1888-1891	2
The Evening News, Salina	1889-1891	5
Salina Gazette	1889	1
The Weekly Tidings, Salina	1887-1892	6
The Sentinel, and Kansas Churchman (monthly), Salina	1888-1891	2
The Salina Union	1890-1892	2
The Salina Weekly News	1891	1
The Agora (quarterly), Salina	1891,1892	2
Brookville Independent	1880	1
Brookville Transcript	1881-1890	9
Brookville Times	1887,1888	1
The Earth, Brookville	1891,1892	2
Chico Advertiser	1886,1887	1
The Gypsum Banner	1886,1887	1
Gypsum Valley Echo	1886-1890	4
Gypsum Advocate	1891,1892	2
Assaria Argus	1887-1889	2
SCOTT COUNTY.		
Western Times, Scott City	1885,1886	1
Scott County News, Scott City	1886-1892	7
Scott County Herald, Scott City	1886-1888	3
The Scott Sentinel, Scott City	1886-1888	2
The Sentinel-Herald, Scott City	1889,1890	2
Scott County Lever, Scott City	1891,1892	2
Grigsby City Scorcher	1887	1
The Pence Phonograph	1887-1889	2
SEDGWICK COUNTY.		
Wichita Vidette, (August 25, 1870, to March 11, 1871,)	1870,1871	1
Wichita City Eagle, (1873-1876 lacking,)	1872-1892	18
Wichita Daily Eagle	1884-1892	17
Wichita Weekly Beacon	1874-1892	19
The Wichita Daily Beacon, (the Evening News-Beacon, 1889-'90, 3 volumes,)	1884-1892	17
Wichita Herald	1877-1879	3
Stern des Westens, Wichita	1879	1
National Monitor, Wichita	1879,1880	1
Daily Republican, Wichita	1880,1881	2
Wichita Republican	1880,1881	1
Wichita Daily Times	1881-1884	7
Sedgwick Jayhawker and Palladium, Wichita	1882,1883	2
The New Republic, Wichita	1883-1890	8

BOUND NEWSPAPER FILES AND PERIODICALS, KANSAS—CONTINUED.

NEWSPAPERS.	Years.	No. vols.
SEDGWICK COUNTY—*Concluded.*		
Wichita Daily Evening Resident	1886	2
The Arrow, Wichita	1886–1892	7
Kansas Staats-Anzeiger, Wichita	1886–1892	7
Wichita Herold	1885–1892	7
The Wichita Citizen, Labor Union, Labor Union Press, and Independent	1886–1888	2
The Wichita District Advocate	1886–1888	1
Sunday Growler, Wichita	1880–1888	2
Wichita Daily Journal	1887–1890	7
Wichita Daily Call	1887	1
Wichita Daily Globe	1887	1
Western Evangelist, Wichita	1887,1888	1
The Leader (prohibition), Wichita, (see Topeka,)	1888	1
The Wichita Commercial	1887–1889	1
The Mirror, Wichita	1888–1892	4
The Journal, Wichita	1888–1890	3
The Democrat, Wichita	1890	1
Wichita Opinion	1889–1892	2
Western Methodist, Wichita	1889–1892	3
The Leader (monthly), Wichita	1890–1892	2
Wichita Newspaper Union, and Record	1890–1892	2
Kansas Commoner, Wichita	1891,1892	2
The Kansas Star, Wichita	1890–1892	2
The Wichita Price Current	1891,1892	1
Cheney Journal	1884–1886	5
The Cheney Weekly Blade	1888–1890	3
The Cheney Herald	1891,1892	1
Valley Center News	1885–1890	5
The Mount Hope Mentor	1885–1892	7
Clearwater Leader	1886–1888	3
The Clearwater Sun	1888–1890	2
The Colwich Courier	1887–1892	6
Garden Plain Herald	1887,1888	1
The Weekly Report, Goddard	1889,1890	1
SEQUOYAH COUNTY. (See Finney county.)		
The Garden City Paper	1879	1
The Irrigator, Garden City	1882	1
SEWARD COUNTY.		
The Prairie Owl, Fargo Springs	1885–1888	2
Seward County Democrat, Fargo Springs	1886–1888	3
The Fargo Springs News	1886–1888	2
Springfield Transcript	1886–1889	3
Springfield Soap-Box	1887,1888	1
Springfield Republican	1889–1892	4
Seward County Courant, Springfield	1887,1888	1
Seward Independent	1887,1888	1
The Arkalon News	1888–1892	5
The Liberal Leader	1888–1890	3
Southwest Chronicle, Liberal	1888–1890	1
The Liberal Lyre	1890–1892	2
SHAWNEE COUNTY.		
Daily Kansas Freeman, Topeka, (October 24 to November 7,)	1855	1
The Kansas Tribune, Topeka	1855–1858	2
Topeka Tribune, (two sets,)	1858–1861	4
The Topeka Tribune (second)	1866,1867	1
Topeka Daily Tribune, (January 12 to March 1,)	1864	1
The Congregational Record, Topeka, (see Douglas county.)		
Weekly Kansas State Record, Topeka, (1863–1867 lacking, 7 duplicates,)	1859–1875	'16
Daily Kansas State Record, Topeka, (January to June, 1870, lacking, 10 duplicates,)	1868–1871	8
Fair Daily Record, Topeka, (duplicate volume,)	1871	1
The Kansas Farmer, monthly, (Topeka, vol. 1, 1863 and 1864, 3 numbers lacking; Lawrence, January, 1865, to July, 1867; Leavenworth, September, 1867, to December, 1873; Topeka, weekly, since 1873, 8 duplicates,)	1863–1892	20
Kansas Educational Journal, Topeka, (see Leavenworth county.)		
Topeka Leader, (1866 and 1867, duplicates,)	1865–1869	6
Commonwealth, daily, Topeka, (46 duplicates; January 1, 1870, to February 14, 1871, lacking,)	1860–1888	37
The Weekly Commonwealth, Topeka, (13 duplicates,)	1874–1888	13
Tanner and Cobbler, Topeka	1872	1
Kansas Magazine (monthly), Topeka	1872,1873	4
Topeka Daily Blade, (1874 not published, 1 duplicate,)	1873–1879	10
Topeka Weekly Blade	1876–1879	4
Kansas State Journal (daily), Topeka	1879–1892	27
Kansas Weekly State Journal, Topeka, (lacking 1887–1891,)	1879–1892	8

BOUND NEWSPAPER FILES AND PERIODICALS, KANSAS—Continued.

NEWSPAPERS.	Years.	No. vols.
SHAWNEE COUNTY — *Continued.*		
Kansas Democrat, Topeka	1874–1882	8
American Young Folks (monthly), Topeka	1876–1882	7
Times (daily), Topeka	1876	1
The Kansas Churchman (monthly), Topeka, (1883–1885, Lawrence,)	1876–1887	8
Commercial Advertiser, Topeka	1877	1
Educational Calendar (monthly), Topeka	1877,1878	1
Colored Citizen, Topeka	1878,1879	2
Der Courier, Topeka, (see Atchison.)		
The Daily Capital, Topeka	1879–1892	28
Weekly Capital and Farmers' Journal, Topeka	1883–1892	9
Kansas Staats-Anzeiger, Topeka	1879–1881	2
The Kansas Methodist and Kansas Methodist-Chautauqua, Topeka, (mo. 1879, 1880, and weekly 1881–1886,)	1879–1888	10
The Topeka Tribune	1880,1881	3
The Topeka Post (daily)	1880	1
The Whim-Wham, Topeka	1880,1881	2
The Educationist, Topeka	1880–1884	4
Western School Journal (monthly), Topeka	1885–1892	8
The Kansas Telegraph, Topeka	1881–1892	12
Good Tidings, Topeka	1881–1886	5
Daily Democrat and Daily State Press, Topeka	1881,1882	1
The Colored Patriot, Topeka	1882	1
The Evening Herald, Topeka	1882	1
The Faithful Witness (semi-monthly), Topeka	1882–1886	4
The National Workman, Topeka	1882	1
Saturday Evening Lance, Topeka	1883–1892	9
The Kansas Newspaper Union, Topeka	1883–1892	9
The Topeka Tribune	1883–1885	2
Anti-Monopolist, Topeka	1883,1884	1
The Daily Critic, Topeka	1884	1
New Paths in the Far West (German monthly), Topeka	1884,1885	1
Light (Masonic monthly), Topeka	1884–1889	5
The Kansas Knight and Soldier (semi-monthly), Topeka	1884–1889	4
The Spirit of Kansas, Topeka	1884–1892	6
Western Baptist	1884–1889	5
City and Farm Record and Real Estate Journal (monthly), Topeka	1884–1889	5
The Kansas Law Journal, Topeka	1885–1887	4
The Citizen (daily), Topeka	1885,1886	1
The Washburn Argo (monthly), Topeka	1885–1891	6
The Washburn Reporter, Topeka	1887–1892	5
The Argo-Reporter (monthly, weekly), Topeka	1892	1
The Kansas Democrat (daily), Topeka	1886–1892	14
Our Messenger (monthly), Topeka	1886–1892	7
Welcome, Music and Home Journal (monthly), Topeka	1883–1888	3
Kansas Home (monthly), Topeka	1886–1888	1
The Lantern, Topeka	1887,1888	1
The Printer Girl, Topeka	1888,1889	1
The Christian Citizen, Topeka	1888,1889	1
The Association Reflector, Topeka	1888–1890	1
The Kansas Financier, Topeka	1888–1891	2
The Jeffersonian, Topeka	1889,1890	2
Villa Range, Topeka	1890	1
Sunday Ledger, Topeka	1888–1891	3
The United Presbyterian (monthly), Topeka	1888–1891	2
The Topeka Republican	1889–1892	3
The Western Veteran, Topeka	1889–1892	4
The Advocate, Meriden, Topeka	1889–1892	3
The Alliance Tribune, Topeka	1889–1892	2
Kansas Medical Journal, Topeka	1889–1892	4
The Western Poultry Breeder, Topeka	1889–1892	3
The Detective World (monthly), Topeka	1890,1891	1
Kansas Church Tidings (monthly), Topeka	1890,1891	1
The Grand Army Journal, Topeka	1890–1892	1
Lucifer—the Light-Bearer (bi-weekly), Topeka	1890–1892	2
Kansas Trade Journal (monthly and bi-monthly), Topeka	1890–1892	1
The Budget, and Budget and News, Topeka	1890–1892	2
The Farmer's Wife (monthly), Topeka	1891,1892	1
The Times-Observer (colored), Topeka	1891,1892	1
Daily Topics, Topeka	1891,1892	2
The Western Odd Fellow (monthly), Topeka	1891,1892	1
Merchants' Weekly Journal, Topeka	1891,1892	1
The Topeka Call (colored)	1891,1892	1
The Daily Sentinel, Topeka	1892	1
Topeka Times, North Topeka, (March, 1873, to February, 1874, lacking,)	1871–1874	3
North Topeka Times	1876–1885	10
North Topeka Daily Argus, and Times	1880,1881	3
The Evening Republic, North Topeka	1882	1
North Topeka Mail	1882–1892	10

—6

NEWSPAPERS.	Years.	No. vols.
SHAWNEE COUNTY — *Concluded.*		
North Topeka Daily Courier	1887,1888	1
The North Topeka News	1888–1892	4
News (daily), North Topeka	1888	1
Kansas Valley Times, Rossville	1879–1882	4
The Rossville News	1883,1884	1
Carpenter's Kansas Lyre, Rossville	1884–1888	4
The Rossville Times	1888–1892	4
Silver Lake News	1882	1
The Future (monthly), Richland	1885–1887	2
Potwin Tribune, Potwin Place	1889,1890	1
Oakland News	1890–1892	2
Shawnee county dailies, short lived, vol. 1: Topeka Daily Times, North Topeka, Nov. 6, 1878; The Tattler, Topeka, Feb. 13 to 22, 1879; The Daily Pantagraph, Topeka, Jan. 5 to 21, 1881; The North Topeka Daily Courier, July 1 to Oct. 17, 1888; The Topeka Daily Mail, North Topeka, Mar. 1 and 2, 1888; The Daily Leader, Topeka, Oct. 6 to Nov. 3, 1888; The Daily Sunflower, North Topeka, Oct. 19 to Nov. 5, 1888; Topeka Daily Globe, July 15 to Aug. 2, 1889; The Daily Epworthian, Topeka, June 21 to 30, 1892; Daily Truth, Topeka, Oct. 28 to Nov. 7, 1892	....	1
Shawnee county weeklies and monthlies, short lived, vol. 1: Star of Empire (monthly), Topeka, July, 1870; Kansas Advertiser and Agriculturist (monthly), Topeka, May to June, 1876; Bazaar News (monthly), Topeka, April, 1877; The Free Discussion (monthly), Topeka and Eskridge, Aug. 20, 1878; Sept., 1879; Jan., 1880, to Aug., 1881; Jan., 1886, to Feb., 1887; The Liberal Advocate, Topeka, Oct. 14 to 28, 1879; The Living Age, Topeka, Oct. 8 to Nov. 5, 1880; Religious Evolutionist (monthly), Topeka, Mar., 1881; The Western Reform Advocate, Topeka, Aug. 28, 1882; Railway Telegraph College, Topeka, Oct. 15, 1882; Saturday Night, Topeka, Nov. 11 to Dec. 2, 1882; Chips, Topeka, Apr. 28, 1883; The Mayflower, Topeka, Mar. 16, 1883; Fire and Hammer (monthly), North Topeka, Nov., 1883, to Aug., 1885; Church & Co.'s Monthly, Topeka, Apr. and May, 1884; The Watchword (monthly), Topeka, July, 1885; The Budget, Topeka, Nov. 15, 1884, to Jan. 5, 1888; The Boycotter, Topeka, Dec. 25, 1885, to Feb. 19, 1886; Our Herald, North Topeka, Jan. 9, 1885; Topeka Business College Journal (bi-monthly), Sept., 1885, to Nov. 15, 1889; The Kansas Democrat, Topeka, Feb. 4 to 13, 1886; The Kansas Home, Topeka, Feb. 15, 1886, to Dec. 13, 1890; The Topeka Trade Gazette (monthly), Aug. and Sept., 1886, and The Kansas Journal of Commerce (monthly), Topeka, Oct. 1887, to May, 1889; The Little Messenger, Topeka, Nov. 2, 1886; The Season Signal (monthly), Topeka, Dec. 20, 1886; Apr. 15, 1887; Sept., 1888; Sept., 1889; The Bee (monthly), Topeka, Aug., 1887, to Apr., 1888; Topeka Argus (weekly and monthly), May 18, 1888; May and June, 1889; Topeka Bulletin, North Topeka, Nov. 29 to Dec. 27, 1888; H. N. Washburn's Christmas Courier, Topeka, 1888	....	1
Shawnee county weeklies and monthlies, short lived, vol. 2: The Silver Lake Echo, Jan. 26 and Feb. 9 1889; The Topeka Commercial Bulletin (monthly), May, 1889; The Monthly Messenger, Topeka, Dec., 1889; Kansas Siftings (monthly), Topeka, June, 1889, to Apr. 22, 1890; The Potwin Tribune, Potwin Place, Sept. 28, 1889, to Sept. 26, 1890; Our State, Topeka, Oct. 12, 1889, to Feb. 15, 1890; Monday Morning Herald, Topeka, Oct. 28 to Dec. 23, 1889; Topeka Signal (monthly), Nov. and Dec., 1889; Ham and Eggs, or the Hog and the Hen (monthly), Topeka, July, 1890, to Feb., 1891; The Detective World (monthly), Topeka, Aug., 1890, to June, 1891; The Oakland Item, Dec. 21, 1889, to Mar. 29, 1890; Kansas Church Tidings (monthly), Topeka, Feb. 21, 1890, to July 18, 1891; The Bee, Topeka, Mar. 30 to Aug. 31, 1890; The Illustrated Companion, Topeka, Aug. 21, 1890; The Oratorious (occasional), Topeka, Jan. to Sept., 1891: The Independent, Topeka, Feb. 27 and Mar. 13, 1891; The Boanerges Reporter, Topeka, Mar. 21 to May 2, 1891; American Buyer and Seller (monthly), Topeka, Nov and Dec., 1891; The Sumner Times (bi-monthly), Topeka, Nov. 24 to Dec. 22, 1891; New Age, Topeka, (1st,) vol. 1, No. 1, Feb. 13, 1892; (2d,) vol. 1, No. 1, Feb. 27, 1892	....	1
SHERIDAN COUNTY.		
Sheridan County Tribune, Kenneth	1881,1882	1
Weekly Sentinel, Kenneth and Hoxie	1884–1892	8
Democrat, Kenneth and Hoxie	1885–1891	6
The Hoxie Palladium	1891,1892	1
The Sheridan County Democrat, Hoxie	1892	1
Sheridan Times	1887,1888	1
Selden Times	1889,1890	2
SHERMAN COUNTY.		
The New Tecumseh, Gandy, Leonard, and Itasca	1885,1886	1
Sherman County Republican and Republic, Itasca, Sherman Center, and Goodland	1886–1892	5
Sherman Center News, Sherman Center and Goodland	1886,1887	1
The Goodland News	1887–1892	5
Voltaire Adviser	1885,1886	1
Sherman County News, Voltaire	1886–1888	2
Sherman County Dark Horse, Eustis and Goodland	1886–1892	6

BOUND NEWSPAPER FILES AND PERIODICALS, KANSAS—CONTINUED.

NEWSPAPERS.	Years.	No. vols.
SHERMAN COUNTY—*Concluded.*		
Sherman County Democrat, Eustis	1887–1889	2
State Line Register, Lamborn	1888–1890	2
Sherman County Farmer, Goodland	1890–1892	1
SMITH COUNTY.		
Smith County Pioneer, Smith Centre	1876–1890	15
The Daily Pioneer, Smith Centre	1887, 1888	2
The Kansas Free Press, Smith Centre	1879–1881	2
Smith County Record, Smith Centre	1882, 1883	2
Smith County Weekly Bulletin, Smith Centre	1884–1890	7
The Pioneer-Bulletin, Smith Centre	1890–1892	2
The Bazoo, Smith Centre	1885–1889	4
Stewart's Bazoo, Smith Centre	1889–1892	4
Northwest Expositor (monthly), Downs, Cawker City, Smith Centre	1890–1892	2
Smith County Journal, Smith Centre	1890–1892	2
Light of Liberty (monthly), Smith Centre, Lebanon	1891, 1892	1
Gaylord Herald	1879–1892	13
The Toiler and Independent, Harlan	1879, 1880	1
The Harlan Weekly Chief	1884, 1885	2
The Harlan Advocate	1885–1887	1
The Harlan Enterprise	1887, 1888	1
The Cedarville Telephone	1883	1
The Cedarville Review	1884, 1885	1
Cedarville Globe	1886–1890	4
The Dispatch, Reamsville	1884–1886	1
The People's Friend, Reamsville and Athol	1887, 1888	1
The Cora Union	1886, 1887	3
The Lebanon Criterion	1887–1892	3
Lebanon Journal	1889–1892	3
The Union Labor Trumpet, Kensington	1885–1890	2
The Kensington Mirror	1888–1892	4
The Athol News	1888, 1889	1
STAFFORD COUNTY.		
Stafford County Herald, Stafford, (1887 and 1888 lacking,)	1879–1892	9
Stafford County Republican, Stafford	1886–1890	5
Stafford County Democrat, Stafford	1885–1888	3
The Weekly Telegram, Stafford	1886–1888	2
The Alliance Herald, Stafford	1890	1
Plain Truth, Stafford	1889	1
The Alliance Herald, Stafford	1890–1892	1
The St. John Advance	1880–1892	12
The Sun, St. John	1885–1888	3
County Capital, St. John	1887–1892	6
Stafford County Rustler, St. John	1889, 1890	1
St. John Weekly News	1888–1892	4
The Stafford County Bee, Milwaukee	1882, 1883	1
The Macksville Times	1886–1888	3
Macksville Telephone	1889, 1890	1
The Macksville Independent	1891, 1892	1
The Cassoday Herald	1886, 1887	1
The Cassoday Mirage	1887–1889	1
Seward Independent	1889, 1890	1
STANTON COUNTY.		
Veteran Sentinel, and Johnson City and Syracuse Sentinel	1886	1
The Johnson City World	1886–1888	2
Stanton County Eclipse, Johnson City	1887, 1888	4
Johnson City Journal	1888–1892	5
Stanton Telegram, Gognac and Johnson City	1888, 1889	2
Stanton County Republican, Johnson City	1889, 1890	1
Johnson City Sun	1891, 1892	1
The Mitchellville Courier	1887, 1888	1
The Border Rover, Borders	1887–1889	1
STEVENS COUNTY.		
Hugo Herald, Hugoton	1886–1889	4
Hugoton Hermes	1887–1890	2
Woodsdale Democrat	1887–1889	1
Woodsdale Sentinel	1889–1892	3
Stevens County Tribune, Woodsdale	1890–1892	2
Dermot Enterprise	1887, 1888	1
The Voorhees Vindicator	1887–1890	3
Zella Gazette and Moscow Review	1887, 1888	1

BOUND NEWSPAPER FILES AND PERIODICALS, KANSAS—Continued.

NEWSPAPERS.	Years.	No. vols.
SUMNER COUNTY.		
Sumner County Press, Wellington	1873–1892	19
Wellington Daily Press	1886, 1887	3
Sumner County Democrat, Wellington	1877–1879	3
The Wellington Semi-Weekly Vidette	1879	1
The Wellingtonian, Wellington	1881–1885	5
The Wellington Democrat	1882–1884	2
Sumner County Standard, Wellington	1884–1892	8
Daily Standard, Wellington	1887–1889	5
The Daily Postal Card, Wellington	1886, 1887	2
The Republican, Wellington	1886	1
The Wellington Monitor	1886–1892	6
The Monitor-Press, Wellington	1892	1
Kansas Weather Observer, Wellington	1886	1
Wellington Morning Quid Nunc (daily)	1887, 1888	3
Wellington Quid Nunc	1887, 1888	1
Wellington Daily Telegram	1887	1
The Christian Reminder, Wellington	1888–1891	2
The Daily Mail, Wellington	1889–1892	5
Wellington Gazette (daily)	1889, 1890	2
The Methodist News, Wellington	1890–1892	1
The Public School Journal, The Weekly Journal, Wellington	1891, 1892	1
Oxford Independent	1876–1879	4
Oxford Reflex and Weekly	1880, 1881	1
The Mocking Bird, Oxford	1888–1892	5
The Oxford Register	1884–1888	4
Caldwell Post	1879–1883	5
Caldwell Journal	1883–1892	10
Caldwell Commercial	1880–1883	3
Caldwell Daily Journal	1887	1
Oklahoma War Chief, Wichita, January 12 to March 9, 1883; Geuda Springs, March 23 to July 19, 1883; Oklahoma Territory, April 26 and May 3, 1884; Arkansas City, May 10, 1884; Geuda Springs, August 30, 1884; South Haven, October 23 to December 4, 1884; Arkansas City, February 3 to June 11, 1885; Caldwell, June 18, 1885, to August 12, 1885	1883–1886	3
Caldwell Standard	1884	1
The Free Press, Caldwell	1885, 1886	1
Times, Caldwell	1886, 1887	1
The Caldwell News (daily and weekly)	1887–1892	5
The Industrial Age, Caldwell	1887–1889	1
Geuda Springs Herald	1882–1892	10
Belle Plaine News	1879–1892	13
The Kansas Odd Fellow, Belle Plaine	1882, 1883	1
The Resident, Belle Plaine	1885, 1886	2
Mulvane Herald	1880–1882	2
Mulvane Record	1885–1892	8
The Mulvane Graphic	1891, 1892	1
Argonia Clipper	1884–1892	9
People's Voice, Argonia	1890–1892	2
Conway Springs Star	1885–1892	7
The Weekly News, South Haven	1885, 1886	1
The South Haven New Era	1886–1892	7
The South Haven Rustler	1889, 1890	1
The Patrick Henry, South Haven	1890, 1891	1
The Milan Press	1892	1
THOMAS COUNTY.		
Thomas County Cat, Colby	1885–1891	6
The Democrat, Colby	1886–1888	2
The Free Press, Colby	1889–1892	3
The Colby Tribune	1888–1892	5
The Hastings and Brewster Gazette	1888	1
The Brewster Gazette	1889, 1890	2
TREGO COUNTY.		
The Wa Keeney Weekly World	1879–1892	14
Kansas Leader, Wa Keeney	1879, 1880	1
Trego County Tribune, Wa Keeney	1885–1889	5
Trego County Gazette, Wa Keeney	1887, 1888	1
Trego County Republican, Wa Keeney	1889	1
Globe, Cyrus	1882, 1883	1
WABAUNSEE COUNTY.		
The Wabaunsee County Herald, Alma	1869–1871	2
The Alma Weekly Union	1871, 1872	1
Wabaunsee County News, Alma	1876–1892	17
The Blade, Alma	1877, 1878	1

BOUND NEWSPAPER FILES AND PERIODICALS, KANSAS—Continued.

NEWSPAPERS.	Years.	No. vols.
WABAUNSEE COUNTY — *Concluded.*		
Wabaunsee County Herald, Alma	1879–1881	2
The Alma Enterprise	1884–1892	8
The Alma Signal	1889–1892	3
The Laud-Mark, Eskridge, (not published from December, 1874, to June 30, 1883,)	1873–1883	2
The Home Weekly, Eskridge	1881–1888	7
The Eskridge Star	1883–1892	9
Wabaunsee County Democrat, Eskridge	1886	1
Free Discussion, monthly, Eskridge, (see Shawnee county, Topeka.)		
The Alta Vista Register	1887–1889	1
The Alta Vista Bugle	1889,1890	1
The Alta Vista Record	1890–1892	3
The Paxico Courier	1888,1889	1
WALLACE COUNTY.		
Wallace County Register, Wallace	1886–1890	4
Wallace County News	1886,1887	1
Wallace Weekly Herald	1888,1889	1
Wallace County Gazette, Wallace	1890–1892	3
The Western Times, Sharon Springs	1886–1892	6
Sharon Springs Leader	1887–1890	4
The Weskansan, Weskan	1888–1892	4
WASHINGTON COUNTY.		
Western Observer, and Washington Republican, (broken files,)	1869,1870	1
Washington Republican and Watchman	1870,1871	2
Washington Republican	1876–1892	17
Washington County Register, Washington	1881–1892	11
The Washington County Daily Register, Washington	1884,1885	2
Weekly Post, Washington	1883–1892	9
Washington Daily Post	1887	1
Washington Daily Times	1887,1888	1
Western Independent, Hanover	1876,1877	2
Washington County Sun, and Hanover Democrat	1878	1
The Hanover Democrat	1878–1892	15
Grit, Hanover	1884–1885	1
The Clifton Localist	1878	1
Clifton Journal and Review	1878–1880	3
Clifton Review	1881–1892	11
The Local News, and The Semi-Weekly News, Clifton	1885–1890	5
The Greenleaf Journal	1881–1883	3
The Greenleaf Independent	1882,1883	1
The Independent-Journal, Greenleaf	1883–1887	4
Greenleaf Journal	1887–1892	5
Greenleaf Herald	1883–1889	6
The Haddam Weekly Clipper	1883–1892	9
The New Era, Haddam	1886,1887	1
Haddam Politician	1889	1
Palmer Weekly Globe	1884	1
Palmer Pioneer	1888–1890	3
The Barnes Enterprise	1885–1892	7
The Record, Hollenberg	1889	1
The Linn Gazette	1889,1890	1
Linn Local Record	1890–1892	2
WICHITA COUNTY.		
Wichita Standard, Bonasa and Leoti City	1885–1892	7
Leoti Lance	1886,1887	1
Wichita County Democrat, Leoti City	1886,1887	1
The Leoti Transcript, Leoti City	1887–1890	2
The Western Farmer, Leoti	1889,1890	2
The Western Kansan, Leoti	1891,1892	2
Wichita County Herald, Coronado	1886,1887	1
The Coronado Star	1886–1888	1
Wichita County Farmer, Coronado, Farmer City, and Leoti	1888	1
The Selkirk Graphic	1889–1891	1
WILSON COUNTY.		
Wilson County Citizen, Fredonia	1870–1892	23
Fredonia Tribune	1878,1879	1
Fredonia Democrat	1882–1890	9
The Times, Fredonia	1883–1885	1
Fredonia Chronicle	1885–1888	3
Amicus Life-Line, (monthly,) Fredonia	1891,1892	1
The Alliance Herald, Fredonia	1891,1892	2
Neodesha Free Press	1876–1882	7
Neodesha Gazette	1881,1882	1

BOUND NEWSPAPER FILES AND PERIODICALS, KANSAS — Concluded.

NEWSPAPERS.	Years.	No. vols.
Wilson County—*Concluded.*		
Neodesha Register.........	1883–1892	9
Neodesha Independent...........	1887,1888	1
Wilson County Sun, Neodesha.........	1891,1892	2
Altoona Advocate.........	1886,1887	1
Altoona Journal.........	1887–1893	6
The Benedict Echo.........	1886–1890	3
Buffalo Clipper.........	1887	1
Buffalo Express.........	1888	1
The Buffalo Advocate.........	1889–1892	4
The Coyville Press.........	1887,1888	1
Woodson County.		
Woodson County Post, Neosho Falls.........	1873–1883	10
Neosho Falls Post	1883–1892	10
Woodson County Republican and Independent, Neosho Falls.........	1886,1887	1
Weekly News, Yates Center, and The Yates Center News	1877–1892	16
Yates Center Argus.........	1882,1883	2
Woodson Democrat, Yates Center.........	1884–1892	8
The Sun and Independent-Sun, Yates Center.........	1886–1888	2
Yates Center Tribune.........	1889	1
The Farmers' Advocate, Yates Center.........	1891,1892	2
The Toronto Topic	1883–1888	5
Register, Toronto.........	1886,1887	1
The Toronto Republican.........	1888–1892	4
Wyandotte County.		
Quindaro Chindowan.........	1857,1858	1
Wyandotte Gazette, (1869 and 1873 lacking,).........	1866–1888	19
Wyandotte Herald, (1873 lacking,).........	1872–1892	20
The Pioneer, Kansas City.........	1878–1880	3
The Kansas Pilot, Kansas City.........	1879–1881	2
The Stock Farm and Home Weekly, Kansas City.........	1880	1
The Spy, Kansas City.........	1881,1882	1
The Kawsmouth Pilot, Wyandotte.........	1881	1
Equitable Aid Advocate (monthly), Wyandotte.........	1881–1883	3
Wyandotte Republican (daily and weekly).........	1881,1882	2
The Wyandotte Chief.........	1883–1885	2
Kansas Pioneer, Wyandotte.........	1883–1889	5
The Globe and The Sun and Globe, Kansas City	1884–1886	2
Light, Kansas City	1884–1886	1
The Kansas City Daily Gazette	1887–1892	12
The Kansas City Gazette	1889–1892	4
The Kansas Weekly Cyclone, Kansas City.........	1887,1888	1
The Naturalist, Kansas City.........	1889,1890	1
The Chronicle, Kansas City.........	1890–1892	2
Kansas Herald (German), Kansas City.........	1890	1
The Kansas Catholic, Leavenworth and Kansas City.........	1890–1892	3
The Weekly Press, Kansas City.........	1890–1892	3
The Kansas City Sun.........	1891,1892	2
The American Citizen, Kansas City.........	1891,1892	2
Cromwell's Kansas Mirror, Kansas City.........	1891,1892	2
Der Waechter, Kansas City.........	1892	1
The Wasp, Rosedale	1884,1885	1
Rosedale Record	1888	1
Rosedale Era.........	1889,1890	1
Argentine Republic.........	1887–1892	5
The Argentine Advocate.........	1888	1
The Labor Review, Argentine.........	1891,1892	1
Argentine Eagle.........	1892	1
Cromwell's Kansas Mirror, Armourdale, (see Kansas City,).........	1887–1890	3

BOUND NEWSPAPERS, ETC., OF OTHER STATES AND COUNTRIES.

NEWSPAPERS.	Years.	No. vols.
Alabama.		
The Nationalist, Mobile.........	1865–1868	0
Alaska.		
The Alaska Free Press, Juneau.........	1889–1891	2
The Alaskan, Sitka.........	1889–1892	3

BOUND NEWSPAPERS, ETC., OF OTHER STATES AND COUNTRIES—Continued.

NEWSPAPERS.	Years.	No. vols.
ARIZONA.		
Arizona Weekly Journal-Miner, Prescott	1887–1892	5
ARKANSAS.		
The Jacksonian, Heber	1890–1892	2
The Rainbow, Eureka Springs	1891,1892	1
CALIFORNIA.		
California Teacher, San Francisco	1865	1
Overland Monthly, San Francisco (f. s.)	1868–1875	15
Overland Monthly, San Francisco (s. s.)	1883–1892	20
San Francisco Weekly Post	1879–1888	11
The Alaska Appeal, San Francisco	1879,1880	1
The Pacific Rural Press, San Francisco	1882–1890	8
California Patron and Agriculturist, San Francisco	1886–1888	3
The California Prohibitionist, San Francisco	1889,1890	1
American Sentinel, Oakland	1886–1889	4
Signs of the Times, Oakland	1886–1892	7
Pacific Health Journal (monthly), Oakland	1886–1892	6
The West American Scientist (monthly), San Diego	1887–1892	4
The Orange Belt (monthly), Alessandro, (Riverside P. O.,)	1891,1892	2
California miscellaneous newspapers		1
COLORADO.		
Silver World, Lake City	1877–1888	11
Hinsdale Phonograph, Lake City	1888,1889	1
Weekly Rocky Mountain News, Denver	1878–1892	15
The Rocky Mountain Presbyterian, Denver and Cincinnati	1879,1880	1
Denver Daily Tribune	1884	2
The Denver Republican (daily)	1887–1892	10
The Queen Bee (monthly), Denver	1887–1890	2
Colorado School Journal, Denver	1887–1889	1
The Commonwealth (monthly), Denver	1889–1891	3
The Great Divide (monthly), Denver	1889–1892	7
The Denver Press	1889–1892	4
The Gunnison Review (weekly)	1880,1881	2
The Gunnison Daily and Tri-Weekly Review-Press	1882–1891	13
Gunnison Tribune	1891,1892	2
Mountain Mail (semi-weekly), Salida	1880–1892	12
Grand Junction News	1884	1
Grand Valley Star, Grand Junction	1890–1892	3
White Pine Cone	1884–1892	8
The Otero County Eagle, La Junta	1889,1890	1
The Otero County Republican, La Junta	1890,1891	1
Law and Gospel (monthly), Springfield	1886–1890	2
The Fruita Star	1889,1890	1
The West Side Citizen, Villa Park, Colfax	1890–1892	2
The Edgewood Sun, Colorado Springs	1891,1892	1
The Idaho Springs News	1891,1892	1
CONNECTICUT.		
The Connecticut Courant, Hartford	1796–1799	3
Quarterly Journal of Inebriety, Hartford	1876–1892	16
Travelers Record (monthly), Hartford	1886–1892	7
Hartford Seminary Record (bi-monthly)	1890–1892	2
Middlesex Gazette, Middletown, (1804, 1805, and 1817,)	1804–1817	3
Silliman's Journal of Science and Arts, New Haven, vols. 1 and 37 to 48 (bi-monthly)	1818–1869	13
Connecticut Common School Journal, New Britain	1864,1865	2
The Connecticut Valley Advertiser, Moodus	1892	1
DAKOTA. (See North and South Dakota.)		
Dakota Teacher, Huron	1885,1886	1
Bismarck Weekly Tribune	1887–1890	3
Pierre Daily Capital	1890	2
DISTRICT OF COLUMBIA.		
Kendall's Expositor, Washington	1841	1
The National Era, Washington	1847–1859	13
The Council Fire, Washington	1879–1882	3
The Alpha, Washington	1881–1888	8
The Washington World	1882–1884	2
National Tribune, Washington, (1885 and 1887 lacking,)	1883–1892	6
United States Government publications, monthly catalogue, Washington	1885–1892	8
The Official Gazette of the United States Patent Office, Washington	1885–1892	39
Public Opinion, Washington and New York	1887–1892	11
The American Anthropologist (quarterly), Washington	1888–1892	5

· BOUND NEWSPAPERS, ETC., OF OTHER STATES AND COUNTRIES — Continued.

NEWSPAPERS.	Years.	No. vols.
District of Columbia — *Concluded.*		
The Washington Book Chronicle (occasional).............	1889–1892	1
The Woman's Tribune, Washington, and Beatrice, Neb.............	1890–1892	2
The National Bulletin (monthly), Washington................	1890–1892	1
National Farm and Fireside, Washington..................	1891,1892	2
U. S. Official Postal Guide, Washington...................1880,	1886–1892	8
Florida.		
The Florida Dispatch, Farmer, and Fruit Grower, Jacksonville.............	1885–1892	7
The Advertiser, Apopka................	1890	1
The Monthly Bulletin, Tallahassee.................	1889–1891	2
Georgia.		
Southern Industrial Record (monthly), Atlanta................	1885–1892	7
Atlanta Constitution....	1887,1888	1
Spelman Messenger (monthly), Atlanta.....	1888–1892	4
Illinois.		
Illinois Teacher (monthly), Chicago	1864,1865	2
Religio-Philosophical Journal, Chicago, (1878 to 1890, lacking,)...........	1868–1892	11
National Sunday School Teacher (monthly), Chicago............	1869–1881	13
Land Owner, Chicago..................	1870–1873	4
Chicago Advance, (files for 1872, 1873, 1874, 1875, 1877, 1879, 1884, and one duplicate,)	1872–1884	7
The Inter-Ocean, Chicago.................	1874–1881	8
Semi-Weekly Inter-Ocean, Chicago...........	1879–1892	14
Faith's Record (monthly), Chicago.............	1874–1881	6
Commercial Advertiser, Chicago	1877–1879	2
American Antiquarian (quarterly), Chicago............	1878–1892	14
Weekly Drovers' Journal, Chicago............	1879–1892	13
Industrial World and Commercial Advertiser, Chicago...........	1880–1882	3
Industrial World and Iron Worker, Chicago...........	1882–1892	10
The Standard, Chicago.............	1880–1892	12
Farmers' Review, Chicago................	1880,1881	2
Chicago Journal of Commerce............	1881	1
The Dial (monthly), Chicago...............	1881–1892	12
The Western Trail (quarterly), Chicago..........	1882–1891	7
The Hebrew Student (monthly), Chicago............	1882	1
Brown and Holland's Short-Hand News (monthly), Chicago............	1882–1884	4
The Watchman (semi-monthly), Chicago, (see Young Men's Era,)........	1882–1890	7
The Weekly Magazine, Chicago............	1882–1885	3
The New Era, Chicago..........	1888–1892	3
The Old Testament Student (monthly), Chicago............	1883–1886	3
The Weekly News, Chicago..............	1884–1886	2
Svenska Amerikanaren, Chicago............	1885–1892	8
The Unitarian (monthly), Chicago...........	1886, 1887	1
The Union Signal, Chicago.............	1886–1892	7
The Penman's Gazette (monthly), Chicago and New York........	1886	1
Pravada (monthly and weekly), Chicago.............	1886–1892	6
The Western Trail (monthly), Chicago...........	1884–1890	2
Gaskell's Magazine (monthly), Chicago............	1887,1888	1
The Open Court, Chicago..........	1887–1892	6
The Comrade (bi-monthly), Chicago....	1887,1888	2
Soldier and Citizen (monthly), Chicago............	1889,1890	1
The National Educator (monthly), Chicago................	1887,1888	2
The Kindergarten, Chicago...........	1888–1892	4
The Chicago Express............	1888–1892	5
Newspaper Union (monthly), Chicago	1888–1892	4
Unity, Chicago..............	1889,1890	1
National Journalist (monthly), Chicago............	1889–1892	4
The Inland Printer (monthly), Chicago.............	1889–1892	4
Humane Journal (monthly), Chicago.............	1889–1892	3
The Monist (quarterly), Chicago............	1890–1892	2
Young Men's Era, Chicago................	1890–1892	3
National Reveille, Chicago.................	1890–1892	3
The Lever, Chicago................	1890–1892	3
National Stenographer (monthly), Chicago............	1891,1892	2
Columbia, Chicago..............	1891,1892	1
The Young Crusader (monthly), Chicago.............	1891,1892	2
The Orange Judd Farmer, Chicago............	1891,1892	1
The Graphic, Chicago................	1891,1892	3
National W. C. T. U. Bulletin, Evanston............	1889–1891	1
The Odd Fellows' Herald (semi-monthly), Bloomington........	1883–1892	9
The Western Plowman (monthly), Moline............	1885–1892	8
The Grange News, River Forest................	1885,1886	1
The Gospel Messenger, Mt. Morris................	1889–1892	3

BOUND NEWSPAPERS, ETC., OF OTHER STATES AND COUNTRIES—CONTINUED.

NEWSPAPERS.	Years.	No. vols.
INDIAN TERRITORY.		
The Cherokee Advocate, Tahlequah	1881–1892	11
The Cheyenne Transporter, Darlington	1883–1886	4
Indian Chieftain, Vinita	1884–1892	9
Minco Minstrel	1890–1892	2
The Territorial Topic, Purcell	1890–1892	2
Purcell Register	1891,1892	2
INDIANA.		
Indiana State Journal, Indianapolis	1878–1892	15
The Millstone and The Corn Miller (monthly), Indianapolis	1884–1892	8
Western Sportsman, Indianapolis	1891	1
Western Horseman, Indianapolis	1891,1892	1
American Tribune, Indianapolis	1891,1892	1
American Nonconformist, Indianapolis	1891,1892	1
Our Herald, La Fayette	1882,1883	2
Mennonitische Rundschau, Elkhart	1886–1892	7
Indiana Student (monthly), Bloomington	1886–1888	2
IOWA.		
Davenport Gazette	1878	1
The Weekly Hawk-Eye, Burlington	1881–1885	4
The Burlington Hawk-Eye (daily)	1882–1885	5
The Iowa Historical Record (quarterly), Iowa City	1885–1892	8
The Christna (semi-monthly), Tabor	1889–1891	2
The Brethren Evangelist, Waterloo	1891,1892	1
KENTUCKY.		
Weekly Courier-Journal, Louisville	1878–1880	2
Southern Bivouac (monthly), Louisville	1886,1887	1
LOUISIANA.		
South-Western Christian Advocate, New Orleans	1879–1892	13
The Times-Democrat (daily), New Orleans	1883–1885	5
The Sugar Bowl and Farm Journal, New Orleans	1891,1892	1
MAINE.		
Oxford Observer, Paris	1824–1826	2
Oxford Democrat, Paris	1871–1876	6
Maine Advertiser, Norway	1872–1875	2
The Kennebec Journal, Augusta	1889–1892	3
First Maine Bugle (quarterly), Rockland	1891,1892	1
MARYLAND.		
Johns Hopkins University Circular, Baltimore, (1882 and 1884 lacking,)	1879–1892	8
Johns Hopkins University Studies in Historical and Political Science (monthly), Baltimore	1882–1892	10
Jottings (monthly), Baltimore	1887,1888	2
The American Journal of Psychology, Baltimore (quarterly), (moved to Worcester, Mass.,)	1888	1
MASSACHUSETTS.		
The Boston Chronicle, December 21, 1767, to December 19, 1768	1767,1768	1
Federal Orrery, Boston, October 20, 1794, to April 18, 1796, and scattering duplicates from October 20, 1794, to October 12, 1795	1794–1796	2
Massachusetts Mercury, Boston, May 11, 1798, to August 9, 1799	1798,1799	2
The Independent Chronicle and the Universal Advertizer, Boston, from January 1, 1798, to December 17, 1801	1798–1801	4
The Independent Chronicle, Boston, December 21, 1801, to December 30, 1804	1801–1804	3
Boston Patriot, from April 7, 1809, to September 12, 1810; from March 2 to December 25, 1811; from March 14, 1812, to September 8, 1813; and scattering duplicates from March 3, 1809, to March 10; 1813	1809–1813	7
Independent Chronicle and Boston Patriot (semi-weekly), January 11, 1832, to August 10, 1837	1832–1837	4
Columbian Centinel and Massachusetts Federalist, Boston, from June 29, 1799, to August 31, 1805; from January 3, 1807, to October 3, 1810; from January 2, 1811, to July 1, 1812; and scattering duplicates from February 28, 1801, to December 29, 1802	1799–1812	13
Boston Gazette, from January 9 to October 29, 1804; from August 19, 1815, to August 19, 1816; from December 27, 1817, to December 25, 1819; from April 23, 1827, to November 28, 1828	1804–1828	6
Boston Commercial Gazette (daily), from December 29, 1817, to December 25, 1819	1817–1819	2
Boston Spectator, from January 4, 1814, to February 5, 1815	1814,1815	1
North American Review, Boston, (Nos. 3–5, 10, 11, 13, 14, 15, 19, 20, 21 and 130 lacking,)	1815–1890	118
The Missionary Herald, Boston, vols. 17–80	1821–1884	63

BOUND NEWSPAPERS, ETC., OF OTHER STATES AND COUNTRIES — Continued.

NEWSPAPERS.	Years.	No. vols.
MASSACHUSETTS — *Continued.*		
New England Galaxy, Boston, from October 31, 1823, to December 26, 1828; and scattering duplicates from October 15, 1824, to April 6, 1827......................................	1823–1828	7
Christian Examiner, Boston, vols. 1–19, 1824–1836, and 16 vols. between 1840 and 1867,	1824–1868	35
Quarterly Register and Journal of the American Education Society, Boston, (1830 published at Andover,)............	1830–1842	13
Boston Recorder, from January 2, 1832, to December 25, 1835...................................	1832–1835	4
The Liberator, Boston, (lacking 1834–1837 and 1839,)...................................	1833–1865	28
Abolitionist, Boston..............	1833	1
Evening Journal, Boston, from Jan. 3, 1837, to Dec. 30, 1843; from Jan. 4 to Dec. 30, 1844; and from Feb. 4 to Dec. 30, 1845...............	1837–1845	9
The Commonwealth (daily), Boston, from Jan. 1 to July 3, 1851; and from Jan. 1 to Sept. 21, 1854...............	1851–1854	3
The Commonwealth, Boston, from Sept. 1, 1866, to Aug. 28, 1869......................	1866–1869	3
Youth's Companion, Boston, from Oct. 21, 1852, to April 17, 1856, and 1886–1890.........	1852–1892	11
Evening Telegram (daily), Boston, from Sept. 27, 1854, to March 31, 1855..............	1854,1855	1
Quarterly Journal of the American Unitarian Association, Boston............	1854–1859	5
Monthly Journal of the American Unitarian Association, Boston............	1860–1869	9
Anglo-Saxon, Boston, from Jan. 5 to Dec. 16, 1856............	1856	1
The Atlantic Monthly, Boston, vols. 1–50............	1857–1882	50
The Atlas and Daily Bee, Boston, from June 15 to Dec. 31, 1858............	1858	1
Boston Investigator, (1864, 1873, 1876 lacking,)............	1859–1892	14
Massachusetts Teacher (monthly), Boston............	1864,1865	2
Zion's Herald, Boston, (1868, 1869, 1870, 1878, 1880, 1883, 1884, 1890,)............	1868–1890	8
Bulletin of the Boston Public Library (quarterly and occasional)............	1868–1892	10
Banner of Light, Boston............	1869–1872	4
Boston Journal of Chemistry............	1873–1877	4
The New England Historical and Genealogical Register (quarterly), Boston.........	1876–1892	15
The Woman's Journal, Boston............	1879–1892	14
Civil Service Record, Boston............	1881,1882	2
United States Official Postal Guide (monthly), Boston.........	1881–1886	6
Our Dumb Animals (monthly), Boston............	1882–1885	2
The Citizen (monthly), Boston............	1883–1885	6
Journal of Education, Boston............	1883	1
The Popular Science News, Boston............	1885–1890	5
The Unitarian Review, and The Unitarian, (monthly,) Boston...................	1885–1892	8
The Evening Traveler (daily), Boston, from January to June, 1886............	1886	1
Political Science Quarterly, (see New York.)		
Library Notes (monthly), Boston............	1886–1889	3
The Writer (monthly), Boston............	1887–1892	6
The Estes & Lauriat Book Bulletin (monthly), Boston............	1887,1888	1
American Teacher (monthly), Boston............	1887–1890	3
Spelling (quarterly)............	1887,1888	1
Evening Gazette, Boston............	1888–1892	5
The New Jerusalem Magazine (monthly), Boston............	1888–1892	5
Journal of American Folk-Lore (quarterly, monthly), Boston............	1888–1892	5
Technology Quarterly, Boston............	1888–1890	4
The Golden Rule, Boston............	1890–1892	3
The Unitarian (monthly), Boston............	1890–1892	2
Daily Advertiser, Boston............	1891,1892	2
Living Issues (monthly), Boston............	1891,1892	1
The Dawn (monthly), Boston............	1891,1892	1
The New Nation, Boston............	1891,1892	2
The Weekly Bulletin, Boston............	1891,1892	1
The Woman's Column, Boston............	1891,1892	1
United States Investor, Boston, New York, Philadelphia............	1891,1892	1
The National Ægis, Worcester, Dec. 2, 1801, to Dec. 25, 1811; from Jan. 20, 1813, to May 4, 1814; from Jan. 5, 1815, to Dec. 25, 1816; from Dec. 15, 1824, to June 8, 1825, and years 1825, 1830, 1833–1840............	1801–1840	19
Worcester Evening Gazette, from January to December, 1866; from January, 1867, to July 18, 1881; and from January, 1882, to December, 1885............	1868–1885	38
Ægis and Gazette, Worcester, (part of 1877 lacking,)............	1875–1880	5
Massachusetts Spy or Worcester Gazette............	1805,1806	2
The Massachusetts Spy (weekly), Worcester............	1822	1
Worcester Daily Spy, from January to December, 1859; from January, 1868, to December, 1884; and from July, 1885, to July, 1886............	1859–1886	38
Daily Transcript, Worcester, from February, 1853, to December, 1855............	1853–1855	6
Worcester Daily Press, from June, 1873, to December, 1876............	1873–1876	7
The American Journal of Psychology (quarterly), Baltimore and Worcester.........	1887–1892	4
Light, Worcester............	1890–1892	2
Essex Register, Salem, from Jan. 1 to Dec. 17, 1817............	1817	1
Historical Collections of the Essex Institute, Salem............	1859–1889	26
Bulletin of the Essex Institute, Salem, (1873 and 1874 lacking,)............	1869–1892	22
The Salem Press and Historical and Genealogical Register............	1890–1892	2
Harvard University Bulletin (occasional), Cambridge............	1880–1892	7
Harvard Register (April to July)............	1881	1
Science, Cambridge, (see New York,)............	1883–1885	6
Gazette and Courier, Greenfield............	1885–1891	6

BOUND NEWSPAPERS, ETC., OF OTHER STATES AND COUNTRIES—CONTINUED.

NEWSPAPERS.	Years.	No. vols.
MASSACHUSETTS — *Concluded.*		
Martha's Vineyard Herald, Cottage City................................	1887,1888	1
Dedham Historical Register (quarterly)..................................	1890	1
Hyde Park Historical Record (quarterly)................................	1891,1892	1
Massachusetts miscellaneous newspapers................................		1
MICHIGAN.		
The Fireside Teacher (monthly), Battle Creek.........................	1886–1889	3
The Advent Review and Sabbath Herald, Battle Creek	1886–1892	6
The Unitarian (monthly), Ann Arbor...................................	1887–1890	3
The Plaindealer, Detroit..	1889–1892	4
Pernin's Monthly Stenographer, Detroit...............................	1891,1892	1
MINNESOTA.		
Pioneer-Press, St. Paul and Minneapolis.............................	1878,1879	1
The Illustrated Monthly Northwest Magazine, St. Paul............	1890–1892	3
The St. Paul Dispatch (daily)...	1891,1892	3
The Gospel Message (monthly), St. Paul.............................	1892	1
The Free Baptist, Minneapolis..	1891,1892	2
The American Geologist (monthly), Minneapolis....................	1892	1
Medical Argus (monthly), Minneapolis................................	1892	1
MISSOURI.		
The Western Journal (and Civilian, monthly), St. Louis...........	1848–1854	11
Organ and Reveille, St. Louis...	1851	1
American Journal of Education (monthly), St. Louis, (1889 lacking,)....	1873–1892	17
The Great Southwest (monthly), St. Louis, vols. 1, 2, 3, 6, and 7....	1874–1880	5
Fonetic Teacher (monthly), St. Louis, vol. 2.........................	1881	1
The Communist and Altruist (bi-monthly), St. Louis...............	1881–1892	6
American Journalist (monthly), St. Louis.............................	1883–1885	1
The St. Louis Evangelist...	1887,1888	1
The St. Louis Globe-Democrat (daily).................................	1887–1892	10
The Central Christian Advocate, St. Louis...........................	1888–1892	5
The Christian Evangelist, St. Louis....................................	1889–1892	4
Colman's Rural World, St. Louis..	1881–1891	9
National Reformer (monthly), St. Louis...............................	1890–1892	2
Broom-Corn Reporter (monthly), St. Louis and Chicago..........	1891,1892	1
St. Joseph Free Democrat...	1860	1
St. Joseph Herald, daily, (1878 and to July 1, 1879, lacking)......	1876–1892	26
St. Joseph Herald...	1877–1892	16
St. Joseph Gazette...	1877–1892	15
Kansas City Times, daily, (1875 lacking,)............................	1878–1892	34
Kansas City Evening Times..	1890,1891	2
The Kansas City Review of Science and Industry (monthly)......	1877–1885	9
Weekly Journal of Commerce, Kansas City...........................	1877–1879	3
Kansas City Daily Journal...	1879–1892	28
Mirror of Progress, Kansas City..	1879–1881	3
Kansas City Price Current	1880,1881	1
Santa Fé Trail (monthly), Kansas City, vol. 1, Nos. 1 to 8........	1880,1881	1
Camp's Emigrant Guide to Kansas, Kansas City	1880–1884	4
American Home Magazine, Kansas City...............................	1881,1882	3
Kansas City Live-Stock Indicator.......................................	1882–1892	11
The Mid-Continent, Kansas City and St. Louis	1882–1892	11
Svenska Herolden, Kansas City	1882–1884	3
Western Newspaper Union, Kansas City..............................	1883–1892	10
The Centropolis, Kansas City...	1883–1888	4
The Kansas City Medical Index (monthly)............................	1884–1887	6
Lanphear's Kansas City Medical Index (monthly)...................	1888–1892	5
Kansas City Live-Stock Record and Price Current..................	1884–1888	4
The Kansas City Record...	1885–1892	6
Missouri and Kansas Farmer (monthly), Kansas City..............	1886–1892	6
Kansas City Star...	1890–1892	3
The Kansas City Star (daily)..	1886–1892	13
The Faithful Witness (monthly), Kansas City........................	1886,1887	1
The Herald, Kansas City..	1886–1889	3
The Kansas Magazine (monthly), Kansas City.......................	1886–1888	2
The Church Builder, Kansas City......................................	1888,1889	1
The Evening News, Kansas City..	1888–1890	5
The Kansas City Daily Traveler...	1888,1889	3
Hoisington Bank Reporter (semi-monthly), Kansas City...........	1889–1892	3
Christian Era, Kansas City..	1889,1890	1
Kansas City Globe...	1889–1891	5
The Naturalist (monthly), Kansas City...............................	1889,1890	1
Border's Odd Fellow (monthly), Kansas City........................	1890–1892	2
Weekly Progress, Kansas City..	1890,1891	1
Real Estate Journal (occasional), Kansas City......................	1890–1892	2

BOUND NEWSPAPERS, ETC., OF OTHER STATES AND COUNTRIES—Continued.

NEWSPAPERS.	Years.	No. vols.
Missouri — Concluded.		
Insurance Magazine (monthly), Kansas City	1891, 1892	1
Christian Endeavor Monitor (monthly), Kansas City	1891, 1892	1
The National Dairyman (monthly), Kansas City	1892	1
The Daily Mail, Kansas City	1892	1
The Amoret Chief	1890, 1891	1
The Border Chief, Amsterdam	1891, 1892	1
Worland Watchman	1892	1
Missouri miscellaneous newspapers		1
Nebraska.		
The Western Newspaper Union, Omaha	1886–1892	5
The Woman's Tribune (monthly and weekly), Beatrice	1883–1890	7
Western Resources (monthly), Lincoln	1887–1892	6
Nebraska State Journal (daily), Lincoln	1887–1892	8
Nebraska State Journal (weekly and semi-weekly), Lincoln	1887–1892	5
Nebraska Congregational News (monthly), Lincoln	1887–1892	4
Daily Christian Advocate (N. E. Conference), Omaha	1892	1
New Jersey.		
The Journal of American Orthoëpy (monthly), Ringos	1884–1892	8
Orchard and Garden (monthly), Little Silver	1887–1892	6
New Mexico.		
Santa Fé New Mexican	1881–1883	4
Daily New Mexican, Santa Fé	1887–1892	10
New Mexican Mining News, Santa Fé	1881–1883	2
The Santa Fé Weekly Leader	1885, 1886	2
Albuquerque Weekly Journal	1881–1886	6
The Daily Citizen, Albuquerque	1887–1892	11
Mining World, Las Vegas	1880–1882	2
Las Vegas Weekly Optic	1883–1884	1
Las Vegas Daily Optic	1888–1892	8
San Marcial Reporter	1889–1892	4
New York.		
New York American, New York city	1827, 1828	2
Anti-Slavery Record, New York	1836	1
The Emancipator, New York, (from Feb. 3, 1837, to Feb. 14, 1839,)	1837–1839	2
The New Yorker, New York	1837–1840	3
The Diamond, New York	1840–1842	3
Workingman's Advocate, New York	1844, 1845	1
New York Evangelist	1845–1847	2
Scientific American, New York, (lacking from 1861 to 1884,)	1849–1892	22
New York Daily Tribune, (May to Aug., 1878, scattering; Aug., 1878, to July, 1879, lacking,)	1849–1892	90
New York Weekly Tribune, (lacking 1871–1878,)	1869–1884	8
New York Semi-Weekly Tribune, (lacking 1876, 1883, 1884,)	1871–1887	14
Propagandist, New York	1850, 1851	1
The Home Missionary (monthly), New York	1850–1892	42
Harper's Monthly Magazine, New York	1851–1854	8
Harper's Weekly, New York	1857–1888	32
New York Illustrated News	1853	2
The Industry of all Nations, New York	1853	1
Putnam's Monthly, New York	1853–1857	14
Daily Times, New York, (incomplete,)	1854–1856	4
The Phonographic Intelligencer, New York	1857	1
Historical Magazine (monthly), Boston, New York city, and Morrisania, (1864–1866 lacking,)	1857–1873	18
The Printer, New York	1858–1863	4
American Agriculturist (monthly), New York, (lacking 1862–1866, 1870–1890,)	1860–1892	6
New York Independent, New York, (1874 duplicate,)	1859–1887	33
American Phrenological Journal (monthly), New York city	1864	1
U. S. Service Magazine (monthly), New York	1864–1866	5
The Galaxy (monthly), New York	1866–1877	24
The Nation, New York, (July to December, 1879, lacking,)	1866–1890	57
American Educational Monthly, New York	1867–1869	3
The Revolution, New York	1868–1870	5
The Spectator, New York and Chicago	1870–1880	11
Scribner's Monthly and The Century Magazine, New York	1870–1888	36
Popular Science Monthly, New York	1872–1891	35
Christian Union, New York	1874–1887	14
The Iron Age, New York	1876	1
The Library Journal (monthly), New York	1876–1892	17
The Magazine of American History (monthly), New York	1877–1892	28

BOUND NEWSPAPERS, ETC., OF OTHER STATES AND COUNTRIES — Continued.

NEWSPAPERS.	Years.	No. vols.
New York — *Continued.*		
Brown's Phonographic Monthly, New York	1878–1883	6
The National Citizen and Ballot-Box, (from May, 1878, to Oct., 1881,) New York. (See Ballot-Box, Ohio.)	1878–1881	4
The Daily Register, New York	1879–1888	20
The Sheltering Arms (monthly), New York	1879–1892	13
The Publishers' Weekly, New York	1879–1892	23
The American Missionary (monthly), New York	1880–1892	13
Appleton's Literary Bulletin (bi-monthly), New York	1881–1889	6
Bulletin of the American Museum of Natural History (occasional), New York	1882–1890	2
John Swinton's Paper, New York	1883–1887	4
The Coöperative Index to Periodicals (monthly), New York	1883–1889	4
Science, New York	1883–1890	14
Phonetic Educator, New York and Cincinnati	1884,1885	1
The Literary News, New York	1884–1892	10
The Student's Journal (phonographic monthly), New York	1884–1892	9
Insurance, New York, (lacking 1886–1891,)	1884–1892	3
The Phonographic World (monthly), New York	1885–1892	8
New York Weekly Witness	1885–1892	7
The Irish World, New York	1885–1892	7
The Christian Advocate, New York, (from April, 1885, to Dec. 30, 1886,)	1885,1886	3
The American Book-Maker (monthly), New York	1885,1886	2
The New Princeton Review (semi-monthly), New York	1886–1888	6
Sabbath Reading, New York	1886–1892	6
The Delineator (monthly), New York	1886	1
Electrical Review (monthly), New York	1886–1892	7
Scribner's Magazine (monthly), New York, (1889 lacking,)	1887–1891	8
Political Science Quarterly, New York	1886–1892	7
Agricultural Science (monthly), New York	1887–1889	3
The Swiss Cross (monthly), New York	1887–1889	5
The Voice, New York	1887–1892	6
The Decorator and Furnisher (monthly), New York	1887–1892	7
The Public Service Review (monthly), New York	1887,1888	1
Home Knowledge (monthly), New York	1887,1888	2
New York Pioneer	1887–1891	3
The Curio, New York	1887,1888	1
Judge, New York	1888	1
Garden and Forest, New York	1888,1889	1
Demorest's Monthly, New York	1888	1
Tariff League Bulletin, New York	1888	1
The Standard, New York	1888–1892	7
The Saturday Globe, New York	1888–1891	4
Magazine of Christian Literature (monthly), New York	1889–1892	6
The School of Mines Quarterly, New York	1888–1892	4
Public Opinion, New York. (See District of Columbia.)		
The Critic, New York	1887–1889	1
College for the Training of Teachers (leaflet), New York	1887–1891	3
The Silver Cross (monthly), New York	1889–1892	3
Twentieth Century, New York	1889–1892	6
The Business Woman's Journal (bi-monthly), New York	1889–1892	4
Magazine of Western History (monthly), New York, (see Cleveland, Ohio,)	1889–1891	5
Literary Digest, New York	1890–1892	3
American Economist, New York	1880–1892	3
The American Sentinel, New York	1890–1892	3
The Temperance Teacher (monthly), New York	1890,1891	1
Microcosm (monthly), New York	1889–1891	2
Scientific American Supplement (monthly), New York	1890–1892	6
Building and Loan News (monthly), New York and London	1890–1892	2
The American Bookseller, New York	1891,1892	2
The Farmers' Pioneer, New York	1891,1892	2
Goldthwaite's Geographical Magazine (monthly), New York	1891,1892	4
Free Russia (monthly), New York	1891,1892	1
Educational Review (monthly), New York	1891,1892	4
War Cry, New York	1891,1892	1
Our Animal Friends (monthly), New York	1891,1892	1
The National Magazine, New York	1891,1892	2
The Journalist, New York	1891,1892	1
The School Bulletin (monthly), New York	1891,1892	1
Scientific American, architects' and builders' edition, (monthly,) New York	1891,1892	3
Review of Reviews (monthly), New York	1891,1892	4
The Forum (monthly), New York	1891,1892	2
The Standard Extra, New York	1891,1892	1
The Engineering Magazine (monthly), New York	1891,1892	2
The Charities Review (monthly), New York	1891,1892	1
Appleton & Co.'s Monthly Bulletin, New York	1891,1892	1
Kawkab America (Persian and English), New York	1891,1892	1
The International Bookseller, New York	1892	1
Evangelical Magazine, Utica, (vols. 2 and 3,)	1828,1892	2

BOUND NEWSPAPERS, ETC., OF OTHER STATES AND COUNTRIES—CONTINUED.

NEWSPAPERS.	Years.	No. vols.
NEW YORK—*Concluded.*		
Evangelical Magazine and Gospel Advocate, Utica, (vols. 4, 5, and 9, 1833, 1834, and 1838,)	1833–1838	3
The Jeffersonian, Albany	1838,1839	2
The Northern Light, Albany	1841–1843	1
The Cultivator and Country Gentleman, Albany	1879,1880	2
The Union, Brooklyn	1879–1882	3
Fruit Recorder and Cottage Gardener, Palmyra	1874–1876	3
The Bee Keepers' Exchange (monthly), Canajoharie	1879–1882	4
The Husbandman, Elmira and Binghamton	1886–1892	7
Library Bulletin of Cornell University (occasional), Ithaca	1882–1892	3
New York miscellaneous newspapers		1
NORTH DAKOTA.		
Dakota Teacher, Huron	1885,1886	1
Bismarck Weekly Tribune	1887–1892	5
Bismarck Daily Tribune	1890–1892	4
OHIO.		
The Ohio Cultivator, Columbus	1845,1846	2
The Crisis, (from January 31, 1861, to January 28 1863,) Columbus	1861–1863	2
Ohio Educational Monthly, Columbus	1865	1
National Teacher (monthly), Columbus	1872	1
Ohio Archæological and Historical Quarterly, Columbus	1887–1889	1
Weekly Phonetic Advocate, Cincinnati	1850–1853	4
Phonetic Advocate Supplement, Cincinnati	1850–1852	2
The Masonic Review, Cincinnati	1858–1862	17
Type of the Times, Cincinnati	1854,1855	2
American Phonetic Journal, Cincinnati	1858	1
National Normal (monthly), Cincinnati	1869	1
Cincinnati Weekly Times	1878–1892	15
The Phonetic Educator, Cincinnati	1878–1883	5
The Christian Press (monthly), Cincinnati	1880–1892	12
Journal of Cincinnati Society of Natural History (quarterly)	1881–1892	13
The American Journal of Forestry, Cincinnati	1882,1883	1
The Christian Standard, Cincinnati	1883–1892	10
The American Grange Bulletin, Cincinnati	1886–1892	7
Phonographic Magazine (monthly), Cincinnati	1887	1
Christian Educator (quarterly), Cincinnati	1889–1892	3
Cincinnati Nonpareil (monthly)	1891,1892	1
Coöperative News (semi-monthly), Cincinnati	1892	1
The Ballot-Box, (from June, 1876, to May, 1878,) Toledo, (see National Citizen, New York,)	1876–1878	2
Nachrichten aus der Heidenwelt, Zanesville	1877–1880	4
Bibliotheca Sacra (quarterly), Oberlin	1877–1889	13
Magazine of Western History (monthly), Cleveland	1884–1889	9
Farm and Fireside (semi-monthly), Springfield	1884–1891	6
Womankind, Springfield	1891,1892	1
Herald of Gospel Liberty, Dayton	1889–1892	4
Le Pasteur (quarterly), Dayton	1889–1892	4
American Farm News (monthly), Akron	1891,1892	1
OKLAHOMA TERRITORY.		
The Oklahoma Capital, Guthrie	1889–1892	4
The Oklahoma Daily Capital, Guthrie	1889	1
Oklahoma Optic, Guthrie	1889	1
Evening Democrat, Guthrie	1890	2
The West and the South, Guthrie	1891,1892	1
The Oklahoma School Journal (monthly), Guthrie	1891,1892	1
Oklahoma Standard, Stillwater	1889,1890	1
The New World, Kingfisher	1889–1891	1
Kingfisher News	1891,1892	1
Free Press, Kingfisher	1891,1892	1
The Frisco Herald	1890,1891	1
Hennessey Clipper	1890–1892	3
The Courier, Hennessey and Kingfisher	1890	1
The Evening Gazette, Oklahoma	1889–1892	7
Oklahoma Daily Journal	1890,1891	3
Oklahoma City Daily Times	1890,1891	3
Oklahoma Daily Times-Journal, Oklahoma City	1891,1892	3
The Norman Transcript	1890–1892	2
Edmund Sun	1890–1892	2
The Oklahoma Congregational News (monthly), Downs	1891,1892	1
Langston City Herald	1891,1892	1
Yukon Courier	1891,1892	1
Canadian County Courier, El Reno	1892	1
The Mulhall Monitor	1890,1891	1

BOUND NEWSPAPERS, ETC., OF OTHER STATES AND COUNTRIES—Continued.

NEWSPAPERS.	Years.	No. vols.
OKLAHOMA— *Concluded.*		
Oklahoma short lived, vol. 1: The Oklahoma Chief, Rock Falls, Aug. 7, 1884; Guthrie Getup, April 29 to Aug. 29, 1889; Guthrie Republican, Sept. 5 to Nov. 7, 1889; Oklahoma Daily State Herald, Guthrie, Oct. 14 to Nov. 30, 1889; Oklahoma Farmer, Guthrie, Oct. 18, 1889, to Jan. 3, 1890; Guthrie Weekly News, Nov. 25, 1889; Guthrie Daily News, April 9 to May 9, 1890; Oklahoma Hawk, Payne, March 15 to Aug. 26, 1890—4 Nos.; The Hardesty Times, May 31 to Aug. 16, 1890—5 Nos.; Oklahoma Weekly Farmer, Stillwater, Aug. 30, 1890; El Reno Herald, Oct. 9, 1890, to Jan. 16, 1891		1
OREGON.		
Fire and Hammer, the Way, the Truth, and the Light (monthly), Portland	1890–1892	1
PENNSYLVANIA.		
The American Naturalist, Philadelphia	1867–1880	14
Lossing's American Historical Record, Philadelphia	1872–1874	3
Potter's American Magazine, Philadelphia	1876	1
The Press (daily), Philadelphia	1878–1880	6
Progress, Philadelphia	1878–1885	7
Public Ledger (daily), Philadelphia	1879–1892	28
Faith and Works (monthly), Philadelphia	1879–1891	11
Sunday School Times, (files for 1879, 1880, 1884, 1886, 1891, 1892,) Philadelphia	1879–1892	7
Naturalist's Leisure Hour (monthly), Philadelphia	1880–1892	11
Dye's Government Counterfeit Detector, Philadelphia	1886–1889	3
The Building Association and Home Journal (monthly), Philadelphia	1887–1889	3
The Book Mart (monthly), Philadelphia	1887–1890	3
Paper and Press (monthly), Philadelphia	1888–1892	5
Weekly Press, Philadelphia	1889	1
Book News (monthly), Philadelphia	1889–1892	3
Food, Home, and Garden, Philadelphia	1889–1892	3
The Sugar Beet (monthly), Philadelphia	1890–1892	3
Annals of the American Academy of Political and Social Science (quarterly), Philadelphia	1890–1892	2
Farm and Fireside (bi-weekly), Philadelphia	1891,1892	2
University Extension (monthly), Philadelphia	1891,1892	1
The Microscopical Bulletin and Science News (monthly), Philadelphia	1891,1892	1
Stowell's Petroleum Reporter (monthly), Philadelphia	1891,1892	1
Lithographic Journal (monthly), Philadelphia	1892	2
Eadle Keatah Toh — the Morning Star and the Red Man (monthly), Carlisle	1881–1892	11
Historical Register (vols. 1 and 2), Harrisburg	1883,1884	2
The Farmers' Friend, Mechanicsburg	1886–1892	7
American Manufacturer and Iron World, Pittsburg	1887–1892	7
Poultry Keeper (monthly), Parkersburg and Philadelphia	1888–1892	4
Zion's Watch Tower, Allegheny	1892	1
Pennsylvania miscellaneous newspapers		1
RHODE ISLAND.		
Magazine of New England History (quarterly), Newport	1891,1892	1
SOUTH DAKOTA.		
Pierre Daily Capital	1890–1892	...
TENNESSEE.		
Bulletin State Board of Health (monthly), Nashville	1885–1892	8
TEXAS.		
Live-Stock Journal, Fort Worth	1882–1892	11
Texas Wool Grower, Fort Worth	1882,1883	2
El Paso Times (daily)	1883	1
Texas Review (monthly), Austin	1886	1
The Canadian Free Press	1887–1889	2
The Canadian Crescent	1888,1889	1
Southern Mercury, Dallas	1888–1892	4
Velasco Daily Times	1891,1892	2
Velasco Weekly Times	1891,1892	1
Houston Daily Post	1892	1
Houston Weekly Post	1892	1
UTAH.		
The Irrigation Age (semi-monthly)	1891,1892	..
VERMONT.		
The Woman's Magazine (monthly), Brattleboro	1885–1890	5
The National Bulletin (monthly), Brattleboro	1886,1887	1

BOUND NEWSPAPERS, ETC., OF OTHER STATES AND COUNTRIES— Concluded.

NEWSPAPERS.	Years.	No. vols.
Virginia.		
The Richmond Standard...	1880,1881	1
Southern Workman and Hampton School Record...	1886–1892	8
Washington.		
Whatcom Reveille..	1884–1886	2
West Virginia.		
The Mountain Echo, Keyser...	1889,1890	1
Wisconsin.		
Wisconsin State Journal, Madison...	1878–1889	11
Western Farmer and Wisconsin Grange Bulletin, Madison...............................	1886	1
Wisconsin Journal of Education (monthly), Madison..	1863–1865	2
Wyoming.		
Laramie Boomerang (daily)..	1889–1892	5
The Wyoming Commonwealth, Cheyenne..	1890,1891	1
Australia.		
Agricultural Gazette of New South Wales, Sydney...	1890,1891	2
Alliance Record, Melbourne...	1891	1
England.		
London Illustrated News...	1842–1879	62
Diplomatic Review, (vols. 1–25,) London...	1855–1877	25
The Labour Standard, London..	1832–1884	3
Forestry, a magazine for the country (monthly), Edinburgh and London.........	1834,1885	3
The Fonetic Journal, Bath..	1879	1
France.		
Bulletin de la Société Protectrice des Animaux (monthly), Paris.....................	1878–1882	5
Bulletin de la Société de Geographie, Paris..	1878–1892	15
Société de Geographie compte rendu des Séances de la Commission Centrale (semi-monthly), Paris.......	1882–1892	11
Chronique de la Société des Gens des Lettres (monthly), Paris.......................	1879–1892	14
Bulletin Mensuel de la Société des Gens des Lettres, Paris.............................	1878–1880	1
Bulletin des Séances de la Société Nationale d'Agriculture de France (monthly), Paris........	1879–1892	14
Bulletin de la Société de Geographie Commerciale de Paris (quarterly)..........	1888–1892	4
Bulletin Ministère de l'Agriculture, Paris..	1889	1
Revue Savoisienne, Journal Publié par la Société Florimontane d'Annecy (quarterly)........	1878–1880	2
Bulletin de la Société de Geographie Commerciale de Nantes (quarterly)........	1889,1890	2
Bulletin de la Société de Geographie de Rochefort (quarterly)........................	1889,1890	1
Recueil des Publications de la Société Havraise d'Etudes Diverses, Havre......	1890,1891	2
Société de Geographie Commerciale du Havre (monthly).................................	1891,1892	2
Bulletin de la Société.de Geographie de Toulouse (quarterly).........................	1891	1
Mexico.		
La Revista Agricola (bi-monthly), City of Mexico..	1891,1892	2
El Hijo del Ahuizote, City of Mexico..	1891,1892	1

KANSAS NEWSPAPERS.

The following is a list of the newspapers and periodicals published in Kansas, corrected to January 1, 1893. The regular issues of these, with very few exceptions, are now being received by the Kansas State Historical Society. They are the free gift of the publishers to the State. They are bound in annual or semi-annual volumes, and are preserved in the library of the Society in the State Capitol for the free use of the people. They number 792 in all. Of these 33 are dailies, 1 semi-weekly, 678 weeklies, 66 monthlies, 3 are semi-monthlies, 2 are bi-monthly, 7 are quarterlies, and 2 are occa-

sional. They come from all of the 106 counties of Kansas, and record the history of the people of all the communities and neighborhoods.

ALLEN COUNTY.

Humboldt Union, Republican; W. T. McElroy, publisher and proprietor, Humboldt.

Humboldt Herald, Democratic; S. A. D. Cox, editor and publisher, Humboldt.

Iola Register, Republican; Chas. F. Scott, editor and publisher, Iola.

The Farmers' Friend, People's Party; S. D. Bartlett, editor, S. D. Bartlett and —— Webber, publishers, Iola.

The Allen County Herald, Democratic; P. J. Talbot, editor and manager, Iola.

The Moran Herald, Republican; Geo. D. Ingersoll, editor and proprietor, Moran.

ANDERSON COUNTY.

The Republican-Plaindealer, Republican; Howard M. Brooke, editor and publisher, Garnett.

Garnett Journal, Democratic; J. T. Highley, editor and publisher, Garnett.

Garnett Eagle, Republican; W. A. Trigg, editor and publisher, Garnett.

Kansas Agitator, People's Party; W. O. Champe, editor and publisher, Garnett.

The Greeley News, independent; W. H. McClure, manager, Greeley Printing Company, publishers, Greeley.

The Greeley Graphic, Republican; Carl Brann, editor and publisher, Greeley.

The Light (monthly), Prohibition; Prohibition Club, publishers, L. N. Judd, chairman, Greeley.

The Free Press, Republican; S. L. Tathwell, editor, Colony Printing and Publishing Company, publishers, Colony.

The Westphalia Times, Democratic; Ancil F. Hatten, editor and publisher, Westphalia.

The Kincaid Dispatch, independent; J. E. Scruggs, jr., editor, and Scruggs Bros., publishers, Kincaid.

ATCHISON COUNTY.

The Atchison Champion (daily and weekly), Republican; A. J. Felt, editor and publisher, Atchison.

Atchison Patriot (daily and weekly), Democratic; S. F. Stambaugh, editor, The Patriot Publishing Company, publishers, Atchison.

The Atchison Daily Globe, independent; Edgar W. Howe, editor and publisher, Atchison.

The College Review (monthly), educational; A. G. Coonrood and C. T. Smith, editors and publishers, Atchison.

The Kansas Churchman (monthly), religious; Rev. F. K. Brooke, editor and publisher, Atchison.

The Midland (monthly), college; edited by Faculty and students of Midland College, Atchison.

The New Kansas Magazine (monthly), literary; W. H. Wynn, editor, Kansas Magazine Company, publishers, Atchison.

The Atchison Blade, Republican; Nat. T. Langston, editor, Blade Publishing Company, publishers, Atchison.

The Student, educational; students of St. Benedict's College, Atchison.

The Baptist (monthly), religious; Wilbur H. Park, local editor, City Mission Publishing Company, Pittsburg, Pa., publishers, Atchison.

Muscotah Record, neutral; Fred. W. Badger, editor and publisher, Muscotah.

The Graphic, People's Party; W. O. Adkins, editor and publisher, Effingham.

—7

The Weekly Journal, educational; George Mesigh, editor and proprietor, Effingham.

The Huron Herald, Republican; Frank I. White editor and publisher, Huron.

BARBER COUNTY.

Medicine Lodge Cresset, Republican; L. M. Axline, editor and publisher, Medicine Lodge.

The Barber County Index, People's Party; Leon E. Beals, editor and manager, Medicine Lodge.

Hazelton Express, independent; W. F. Hatfield, editor and publisher, Hazelton.

The Kiowa Journal, Republican; J. E. Hall, proprietor, R. S. Kelly, editor, Kiowa.

The Kiowa Review, People's Party; C. C. Hudson, editor, Hudson & Watrus, proprietors, Kiowa.

BARTON COUNTY.

The Great Bend Register, Republican; Morgan Caraway, editor and publisher, Great Bend.

Great Bend Tribune, Republican; C. P. Townsley, editor and publisher, Great Bend.

Barton County Democrat, Democratic; Will E. Stoke, editor, publisher, and proprietor, Great Bend.

Evening News (daily), neutral; C. P. Townsley, editor and publisher, Great Bend.

Barton Beacon, People's Party; D. T. Armstrong, editor and publisher, Great Bend.

Kansas Educator (monthly), educational; D. T. Armstrong, editor and proprietor, Great Bend.

Pawnee Rock Leader, Republican; M. E. Heynes, editor and publisher, Pawnee Rock.

The Ellinwood Advocate, Democratic; W. D. Wilkinson, editor and publisher, Ellinwood.

The Hoisington Dispatch, Republican; Ira H. Clark, editor, publisher, and proprietor, Hoisington.

The Hoisington Blade, Republican; Joe H. Borders, editor and publisher, Hoisington.

Barton County Banner, Republican; O. E. O'Bleness, editor and proprietor, Claflin.

BOURBON COUNTY.

Fort Scott Monitor (daily and weekly), Republican; W. R. Biddle, editor, D. F. Peffley, associate editor, H. C. Loucks, manager, The Monitor Company, publishers, Fort Scott.

Fort Scott Tribune, (daily and weekly), Democratic; J. B. Chapman, editor, Geo. W. Martin and J. B. Chapman, proprietors, Fort Scott.

The Fort Scott Journal, independent; Ralph Richards, editor, Fort Scott.

Fort Scott Dispatch, Republican; H. S. Brimhall, editor, Brimhall & Webster, publishers, Fort Scott.

The Lantern, People's Party; J. Herrick and M. A. Waterman, editors, The Lantern Publishing Company, publishers, Fort Scott.

The Normal Journal, educational; D. E. Sanders, editor, Fort Scott.

The Bronson Pilot, neutral; H. E. Conflans, editor and proprietor, Bronson.

Fulton Independent, independent; A. W. Felter, editor and proprietor, Fulton.

Fulton Rustler (monthly), independent; S. B. De Lano, editor, Fulton.

Hiattville Weekly Optic, independent; Harry E. Bird and Ralph Richards, editors, Ralph Richards, proprietor, Hiattville.

BROWN COUNTY.

The Brown County World, Republican; Ewing Herbert, editor and publisher, Hiawatha.

The Kansas Democrat, Democratic; G. W. & W. P. Harrington, editors and proprietors, Hiawatha.

The Hiawatha Weekly Journal, People's Party; J. Frank Moore, editor, Journal Publishing Company, publishers, Hiawatha.

The Delta of Sigma Nu (bi-monthly), college fraternity; Grant W. Harrington, editor and publisher, Hiawatha.

The Horton Headlight, Republican; H. E. Whitaker, editor and proprietor, Horton.

Horton Commercial, Democratic; Clyde McManigal, editor, publisher, and proprietor, Horton.

Fairview Enterprise Democratic; S. O. Groesbeck, editor and proprietor, Fairview.

The Everest Enterprise, independent; Chas. R. Johnson, editor, N. F. Hess, proprietor, Everest.

The Morrill News, independent; C. E. Stains, editor and publisher, Morrill.

BUTLER COUNTY.

Walnut Valley Times (daily and weekly), Republican; Alvah Shelden, editor and proprietor, El Dorado.

El Dorado Republican, Republican; T. B. Murdock, editor and publisher, El Dorado.

The Industrial Advocate, People's Party; J. F. Todd, and J. C. Riley, jr., editors and proprietors, El Dorado.

Augusta Journal, Republican; Will H. Cady, editor and publisher, Augusta.

The Augusta Gazette, Democratic; Timothy Sexton and O. J. Bradfield, editors and publishers, Augusta.

The Leon Indicator, Republican; C. R. Noe, editor and publisher, Leon.

Douglass Tribune, Republican; J. M. Satterthwaite and W. P. Tucker, editors, and publishers, Douglass.

The Herald, People's Party; E. Davis, editor and proprietor, Towanda.

The White Water Tribune, Republican; H. W. Bailey, editor and publisher, White Water.

The Latham Times, independent; J. & R.W. Romig, editors and publishers, Latham.

CHASE COUNTY.

Chase County Leader, Republican ; Wm. A. Morgan, editor and publisher, Cottonwood Falls.

Chase County Courant, Democratic ; W. E. Timmons, editor and publisher, Cottonwood Falls.

The Reveille, People's Party; E. W. Ellis, editor and proprietor, Cottonwood Falls.

Strong City Derrick, neutral; C. W. White, editor; Dave Rettiger, publisher, Strong City.

CHAUTAUQUA COUNTY.

The Sedan Times-Journal, Republican; Adrian Reynolds, editor, publisher, and proprietor, Sedan.

The Sedan Lance, People's Party; A. S. Koonce, editor; D. E. Shartel, proprietor, Sedan.

The Cedar Vale Star, independent; Frank G. Kenesson, editor, publisher, and proprietor, Cedar Vale.

The Cedar Vale Commercial, Republican; W. M. Jones, editor, publisher, and proprietor, Cedar Vale.

CHEROKEE COUNTY.

Columbus Star-Courier, Democratic; N. T. Allison and W. P. Eddy, editors and proprietors, Columbus.

The Columbus Advocate, Republican; L. M. Dillman, editor, Asa Lea, proprietor and business manager, Columbus.

Modern Light, People's Party; M. A. Housholder and Anna Widman, editors and proprietors, Columbus.

Cherokee County Teacher (monthly), educational; Anna Widman, editor, Galena.

Short Creek Republican, Republican; L. C. Weldy, editor and publisher, Galena.

The Galena Times, Democratic; Chas. T. Dana, editor; Galena.Publishing Company, publishers, Galena.

Baxter Springs News, neutral; M. H. Gardner and Chas. L. Smith, editors and publishers, Baxter Springs.

Weir City Tribune, independent; H. Hayden, editor and proprietor, Weir.

The Weir Journal, Republican; T. G. Rolison, editor and proprietor, Weir.

The Globe-Miner, independent; Phil. L. Keener, editor and publisher, Scammon.

CHEYENNE COUNTY.

Bird City News, Republican; Emory T. Fraker, editor and publisher, Bird City.

Cheyenne County Rustler, Republican; C. E. Dennison, editor and publisher, St. Francis.

People's Defender, People's Party, W. A. Pyne, editor and publisher, St. Francis.

CLARK COUNTY.

Clark County Clipper, People's Party; W. L. Cowden, editor and publisher, Ashland.

The Ashland Weekly Journal, Republican; M. G. Stevenson, editor, Journal Company, publishers, Ashland.

Englewood Chief, Republican; J. M. Grasham, editor and publisher, Englewood.

CLAY COUNTY.

The Clay County Dispatch, People's Party; W. D. Vincent, editor, John B. Park, publisher, W. A. Davidson, business manager, Clay Center.

The Times, Republican; D. A. Valentine, editor, publisher, and proprietor, Clay Center.

The Western Record, religious; D. P. Zeigler, editor and publisher, Clay Center.

Uncle Sam's Live-Stock Journal (monthly); J. H. Morgan, editor and publisher, Clay Center.

The Clifton News, Republican; L. A. Palmer, editor, publisher, and proprietor, Clifton.

The Times, People's Party; C. D. Tolin, editor and publisher, Clifton.

Wakefield Advertiser, neutral; J. J. L. Jones, editor and publisher, Wakefield.

CLOUD COUNTY.

The Concordia Empire, Republican; T. A. Sawhill, editor and proprietor, Concordia.

The Concordia Blade, People's Party; J. M. Hagaman, editor and publisher, Concordia.

Concordia Daylight, Republican; E. Marshall, editor and proprietor; J. E. Marshall, publisher and manager.

The Alliant, People's Party; Ferd. Prince, editor and publisher, Concordia.

The Clyde Herald, Republican; J. B. & M. L. Rupe, editors, publishers, and proprietors, Clyde.

The Clyde Argus, independent; Chas. A. Morley and Fred. O. Ayers, editors and publishers, Clyde.

The Farmers' Voice, People's Party; J. J. Henley, editor, The Farmers' Voice Company, publishers, Clyde.

Jamestown New Era, independent; M. D. Sutherlin, editor and publisher, Jamestown.

The Glasco Sun, independent; L. E. Frankforther, editor, Frankforther Bros., proprietors, Glasco.

Miltonvale Press, |Republican; H. E. Stewart and B. F. Miller, editors and proprietors, Miltonvale.

The Miltonvale Echo, People's Party; W. R. Hall, editor and proprietor, Miltonvale.

COFFEY COUNTY.

Burlington Republican, Republican; C. O. Smith, editor, publisher, and proprietor, Burlington.

Burlington Independent, Democratic; John E. Watrous, editor, publisher, and proprietor, Burlington.

Burlington Nonpareil, Republican; A. D. Brown, editor, publisher, and proprietor, Burlington.

The Courier, People's Party; M. M. Bowmen and N. S. Mounts, editors and publishers, Burlington.

Le Roy Reporter, independent; Frank Fockele, editor, publisher, and proprietor, Le Roy.

Waverly Gazette, independent; A. A. Smith, editor and proprietor, Waverly.

The Lebo Enterprise, Republican; W. P. Evans, editor and proprietor, Lebo.

COMANCHE COUNTY.

The Western Star, People's Party; W. M. Cash, editor, publisher, and proprietor, Coldwater.

Coldwater Enterprise, Republican; J. E. Hutchinson, editor and proprietor, Coldwater.

COWLEY COUNTY.

The Winfield Courier (daily and weekly); Republican; Ed. P. Greer, editor, Courier Publishing Company, publishers, Winfield.

The Winfield Tribune, Democratic; E. B. Buck, editor, Buck & Harter, publishers, Winfield.

Winfield Newspaper Union; auxiliary publishers, Winfield.

The Industrial Free Press, People's Party; P. W. Craig, editor and publisher, Winfield.

Western Reveille (monthly), G. A. R.; A. H. Limerick, editor and publisher, Winfield.

Farmers' Advocate; W. A. Halloran, editor and publisher, Winfield.

Kansas Agriculturist, agricultural; W. A. Halloran, editor and publisher, Winfield.

Winfield Weekly Review, Winfield Newspaper Union, publishers, Winfield.

Republican Traveler (daily and weekly), Republican; T. W. Eckert and R. C. Howard, editors, Eckert, Howard & Co., publishers, Arkansas City.

Arkansas Valley Democrat, Democratic; Timothy McIntire, editor, L. M. McIntire, publisher, Arkansas City.

Canal City Dispatch (daily and weekly), People's Party; G. W. & B. A. Wagner, editors, publishers, and proprietors, Arkansas City.

The Pittsburg Headlight, Republican; Wm. Moore & Son, editors, publishers, and proprietors, Pittsburg.

Pittsburg Kansan, People's Party; J. C. Buchanan, editor and publisher, Pittsburg.

The Miners' Echo, People's Party; T. B. McGregor, editor and proprietor, Pittsburg.

Pittsburger Volkszeitung, German; Benno Muhlen, editor and publisher, Pittsburg.

The Pittsburg Advance, Prohibition; George B. Brewer, editor and publisher, Pittsburg.

Crawford County Democrat, Democratic; J. M. Mahr, editor and publisher, McCune.

Arcadia News, Republican; L. R. Jewell, editor and proprietor, Arcadia.

Walnut Journal, Republican; Lewis Martin, editor and publisher, Walnut.

DECATUR COUNTY.

Oberlin Herald, People's Party; W. D. Street, editor and publisher, Oberlin.

The Eye, Republican; C. Borin, editor and publisher, Oberlin.

Oberlin Opinion, Republican; F. W. Casterline, editor, publisher, and proprietor, Oberlin.

Alliance Times, People's Party; John Shields, editor and proprietor, Oberlin.

The Rathbone Family Historian (monthly), genealogical; F. P. Rathbone, editor and publisher, Oberlin.

The Norcatur Register, Republican; J. F. Hoskins, editor and publisher, Norcatur.

Jennings Echo, Republican; Geo. W. Shook, editor, and Geo. W. Shook & Co., publishers, Jennings.

Dresden Star; E. E. Van Epps, editor, J. J. Reichert, local editor, Dresden.

DICKINSON COUNTY.

Abilene Weekly Chronicle, Republican; George Burroughs, editor and publisher, Abilene.

Abilene Reflector (daily and weekly), Republican; Charles M. Harger, editor, Reflector Publishing Company, publishers, J. J. Cooke, president, O. L. Moore, vice-president, Richard Waring, secretary-treasurer, and Richard Waring, business manager, Abilene.

The Dickinson County News, Democratic; L. B. Strother and F. K. Strother, editors and publishers, Abilene.

The Abilene Monitor, People's Party; A. S. Phillips, editor, Phillips & Gaffney, publishers, Abilene.

The Evangelical Visitor, religious; Henry Davidson, editor, Brethren Publishing Company, publishers, Abilene.

Solomon Sentinel, Republican; E. B. Burnett, editor and publisher, Solomon City.

The Hope Dispatch, Republican; M. C. Hemenway, editor and publisher, Hope.

The Hope Star, People's Party; J. B. Milford, editor and publisher, Hope.

Chapman Howitzer, Republican; Fred. A. Freeland, editor and publisher, Chapman.

The Chapman Journal, Republican; M. H. Curts, editor and publisher, Chapman.

The Manchester Sun, Republican; Addison S. Green, editor and publisher, Manchester.

The Kansas Miller and Manufacturer (monthly); devoted to the industrial development of Kansas, Enterprise.

The Integral Coöperator; Derrill Hope, editor, The Credit Foncier Company, publisher, Enterprise.

The Enterprise Journal, Republican; C. M. Case, editor, Enterprise Publishing Company, publishers, Enterprise.

Central Expositor (monthly), religious; M. R. Myer, editor, Enterprise Publishing Company, publishers, Enterprise.

The Herington Times, Republican; A. M. Crary, editor and proprietor, Herington.

Herington Journal (monthly), Republican; C. N. Hull, editor and publisher, Herington.

DONIPHAN COUNTY.

The Weekly Kansas Chief, Republican; Sol. Miller, editor, publisher, and proprietor, Troy.

The Troy Times, Democratic; H. B. Bishop, editor and publisher, Troy.

The Severance Weekly News, independent; P. L. Gray and W. J. Curtis, editors and proprietors, Severance.

Highland University Nuncio (bi-weekly), educational; F. M. Erickson, editor-in-chief, Leon C. Hills, business manager, Highland.

The Vidette, Republican; H. S. & Irvin Hogue, editors and publishers, Highland.

White Cloud Globe, Republican; John J. Faulkner, editor and manager, White Cloud.

DOUGLAS COUNTY.

Lawrence Journal (daily and weekly), Republican; O. E. Learnard, editor and proprietor, Lawrence.

Daily and Weekly Record, independent; Henry M. Greene, editor, E. Martindale, manager, Record Publishing Company, proprietors, Lawrence.

Lawrence World (daily and weekly), Republican; J. L. Brady, editor, World Publishing Company, proprietors, Lawrence.

Lawrence Germania (German), independent; Edward Grün, editor and publisher, Lawrence.

The University Review (monthly), college; Albert Fullerton, editor-in-chief, The Kansas University Publishing Company, publishers, Lawrence.

The Lawrence Gazette, Democratic; Frank L. Webster, editor, Gazette Publishing Company, publishers, Lawrence.

The Baker Beacon, college; S. B. Haskin, editor, Baker Beacon Company, publishers, Baldwin.

The School Times (monthly); E. W. Myler, editor, published by the teachers and pupils of the Baldwin public schools, Baldwin.

The Eudora News, independent, Geo. C. Brune, editor and publisher, Eudora.

The Lecompton Sun, independent Democrat; W. R. Smith, editor and proprietor, Lecompton.

The College Oracle (quarterly), college; C. M. Brooke, editor, published by Lane University, Lecompton.

EDWARDS COUNTY.

The Kinsley Graphic, People's Party; W. H. French, editor and proprietor, Kinsley.

The Kinsley Mercury, Republican; F. D. Smith, editor and proprietor, Kinsley.

ELK COUNTY.

The Howard Courant, Republican; Asa & Tom E. Thompson, editors and publishers, Howard.

Elk County Citizen, People's Party; C. L. McKesson, editor and manager; Elk County Publishing Company, publishers, Howard.

The Grenola Chief, neutral; T. W. Heylton, editor and proprietor, Grenola.

The Longton Gleaner, Republican; Ed. T. Chapman, editor and publisher, Longton.

The Moline Republican, Republican; Geo. C. Armstrong, editor and publisher, Moline.

ELLIS COUNTY.

Hays City Sentinel, Republican; W. P. Montgomery, manager, Hays City.

Free Press, People's Party; Harry Freese, editor and proprietor, Hays City.

The Republican, Republican; Geo. P. Griffith, editor and publisher, Hays City.

The Ellis Review-Headlight, Republican; Frank J. Brettle, editor, Ellis.

ELLSWORTH COUNTY.

Ellsworth Reporter, Republican; George Huycke, editor, publisher, and proprietor, Ellsworth.

Ellsworth Messenger, Democratic; G. A. Collett and F. S. Foster, editors and proprietors, Ellsworth.

The Wilson Echo, Republican; S. A. Coover, editor and publisher, Wilson.

The Kanopolis Kansan, People's Party, T. K. Griffith, editor and publisher, Kanopolis.

FINNEY COUNTY.

Garden City Sentinel, Republican; E. P. & E. L. Stephenson, editors and publishers, Garden City.

Garden City Herald, Republican; S. G. Norris and Homer Norris, editors and publishers, Garden City.

The Garden City Imprint, Republican; D. A. Mims, editor; D. A. Mims and E. N. Keep, publishers, Garden City.

Garden City Tribune, People's Party; H. H. Artz, editor, and Eugene Stotts, publisher, Garden City.

FORD COUNTY.

The Dodge City Times, People's Party; I. E. Voorhees, editor and proprietor, Dodge City.

The Globe-Republican, Republican; W. C. Shinn, editor, Globe Publishing Company, publishers, Dodge City.

The Dodge City Democrat, Democratic; W. F. Petillon, editor and publisher, Dodge City.

Bucklin Times-Ensign, independent; Grant Pettyjohn, editor and publisher, Bucklin.

FRANKLIN COUNTY.

The Ottawa Journal and Triumph, People's Party; E. H. Snow, editor, publisher, and proprietor, Ottawa.

The Ottawa Republican (daily and weekly), Republican; Clark Wilkinson, editor and proprietor, Ottawa.

The Ottawa Herald, Democratic; John B. Kessler, editor and publisher, Ottawa.

The Ottawa Lever, Prohibition; W. M. Preshaw, editor and proprietor, Ottawa.

Ottawa Tribune (daily and weekly), Republican; T. W. Fields, editor and publisher, Ottawa.

Ottawa Campus (monthly), college; W. H. Eaton, editor-in-chief, Ottawa University Oratorical Association, publishers, Ottawa.

Ottawa Chautauqua-Assembly Herald (monthly), educational; Rev. D. C. Milner, Mrs. Noble L. Prentis, Mrs. M. H. Gardner, and others, editors, Ottawa Chautauqua Assembly, publishers, Ottawa.

The Ottawa Baptist (monthly), religious; Chas. C. Corwin and John R. Newton, editors and publishers, Ottawa.

Ottawa Courier, Republican; John A. Frow, editor and proprietor, Ottawa.

The Educational Aid (monthly), educational; D. J. McManis and J. R. Newton, editors and publishers, Ottawa.

The Pomona Enterprise, independent; T. L. Newcomb, editor, The Enterprise Publishing Company, publishers, Pomona.

The Enterprise, neutral; A. D. Zimmerman, editor and proprietor, Williamsburg.

The Lane Leader, Republican; Carl Brann, editor and publisher, Lane.

Wellsville Globe, neutral; T. S. & W. F. Rice, editors and publishers, Wellsville.

GARFIELD COUNTY.

Ravanna Chieftain, independent; J. L. Wolf, editor and manager, Chieftain Publishing Company, publishers, Ravanna.

Garfield County Call, Republican; W. T. Williams, editor and publisher, Eminence.

GEARY COUNTY.

The Junction City Union, Republican; W. C. Moore, editor, John Montgomery, E. M. Gilbert, and W. C. Moore, publishers, Junction City.

The Junction City Tribune, People's Party; Chas. S. Davis, editor and proprietor, Junction City.

The Junction City Republican, Republican; Geo. A. Clark, editor, publisher, and proprietor, Junction City.

The Junction City Sentinel, Democratic; A. W. Chabin and Henry Litz, editors and publishers, Junction City.

The Kansas Wheelman's Library (monthly), road improvement; Kansas Division L. A. W., publishers, Junction City.

GOVE COUNTY.

Grainfield Cap Sheaf, Republican; J. B. Beal, editor and publisher, Grainfield.

Gove County Gazette, Republican; O. B. Jones and J. F. Jones, editors and publishers, Gove City.

Gove County Echo, Republican; J. L. Cook & Sons (Walter A. and Charles L.), editors and publishers, Gove City.

Quinter Republican, Republican; A. K. Trimmer, editor and proprietor, Quinter.

GRAHAM COUNTY.

Hill City Reveille, People's Party; H. D. Clayton, editor and proprietor, Hill City.

Hill City Republican, Republican; W. H. Hill, editor, W. R. & W. H. Hill, publishers, Hill City.

The People's Advocate, People's Party; L. C. Chase, editor and publisher, Hill City.

GRANT COUNTY.

Ulysses Tribune, People's Party; J. H. Lucas, editor, C. E. Watson & Co., publishers, Ulysses.

Grant County Republican, Republican; H. E. Evans, editor and publisher, Ulysses.

GRAY COUNTY.

Cimarron New West, Republican; N. B. Klaine, editor, New West Printing Company, publishers, Cimarron.

The Jacksonian, Democratic; Ellis S. Garten, editor, publisher, and proprietor, Cimarron.

Ingalls Union, Republican; R. H. Turner, editor, Union Publishing Company, publishers, Ingalls.

GREELEY COUNTY.

The Greeley County Republican, Republican; A. C. Hutchinson, editor and publisher, Tribune.

The Western Homestead (monthly), agricultural; Eugene Tilleux, editor and publisher, Tribune.

The Horace Headlight, People's Party; Thos. H. Orr, editor, Horace Printing Company, publishers, Horace.

GREENWOOD COUNTY.

The Eureka Herald, Republican; Z. Harlan, editor and proprietor, Eureka.

Democratic Messenger, Democratic, T. W. Morgan, editor and publisher, Eureka.

The Alliance Union, People's Party; W. L. Holcomb, Granville Giffith and Franklin Hall, editors and proprietors, Eureka.

The Severyite, Republican; C. G. Piece, editor and proprietor, Severy.

The Madison Star, Republican; W. D. Smith, editor, The Star Publishing Company, publishers, Madison.

Kansas Advocate, Republican; Lowry G. Gilmore, editor and publisher, Fall River.

HAMILTON COUNTY.

The Syracuse Journal, Republican; H. N. Lester, editor, H. N. Lester & Son, publishers and proprietors, Syracuse.

Hamilton County Bulletin, Republican; John W. Bishop, editor and proprietor, Syracuse.

The Democratic Principle, Democratic; F. M. Dunlavy, editor and publisher, Syracuse.

HARPER COUNTY.

The Anthony Republican, Republican; F. C. Raney, editor, F. C. Raney and S. A. Markwell, proprietors, Anthony.

Anthony Journal, Republican; J. R. & S. C. Hammond, editors and publishers, Anthony.

The Weekly Bulletin, People's Party; W. L. Hutchinson, managing editor, The Alliance Publishing Company, publishers, Anthony.

The Harper Sentinel, independent; Jonas Cook, editor and proprietor, Harper.

Harper Graphic, Republican; M. A. Hull, editor and publisher, Harper.

The Advocate, People's Party; L. A. Hoffman, editor, L. A. Hoffman & Son, proprietors and publishers, Harper.

Young Men's Voice (monthly), religious; Executive Committee of the Y. M. C. A. of Harper county, publishers, Harper.

Bluff City Independent, neutral; J. W. Randall, editor and proprietor, Bluff City.

Attica Tribune, neutral; Geo. W. Kelley, editor, Geo. W. Kelley & Son, publishers, Attica.

HARVEY COUNTY.

The Newton Republican (daily and weekly), Republican; W. S. Allen, editor, The Newton Publishing Company, publishers, Newton.

Newton Kansan (daily and weekly), Republican; C. H. Kurtz, editor, publisher, and proprietor, Newton.

The Newton Weekly Journal, Democratic; J. B. Fugate, editor and publisher, Newton.

The School Journal, Catholic educational magazine; Father Casey, editor, Catholic Educational Society, publishers, Newton.

Church Herald (monthly), religious; G. Lowther, editor, Chas. Lowther, publisher, Newton.

Der Hausfreund (monthly), religious; Rev. F. D. Rademacher, editor, City Mission Publishing Company, Pittsburg, Pa., publishers, Newton.

The Halstead Independent, Republican; E. J. Bookwalter, editor and publisher, Halstead.

Our Church Mirror (monthly), religious; J. W. Funk, editor, Claude O. Funk, publisher, Halstead.

The Burrton Weekly Graphic, Republican; J. W. Osburn, editor and publisher, Burrton.

The Free Lance, People's Party; L. I. Purcell, editor and proprietor, Burrton.

The Sedgwick Pantagraph, independent; Mack P. Cretcher, editor, Mack P. Cretcher and —— Bruce, proprietors, Sedgwick.

The Walton Reporter, Republican; W. D. Franklin, editor and publisher, Walton.

Harvey County Voice, Prohibition; B. M. House, editor, Newton.

Burrton Anzeiger, independent; J. C. Dick, editor and publisher, Burrton.

The Normal Advocate (monthly), educational; E. J. Hoenshel, editor and proprietor, Holton.

The Fraternal Aid (monthly), secret society; Chas. V. Hamm, editor and publisher, Holton.

The University Informer (bi-weekly), college; W. A. McKeever, editor and business manager, Holton.

Young People's Worker, church; Jno. F. Mick, editor, Holton.

The Whiting Weekly News, Republican; Jas. S. Martin and Fred. W. Badger, editors and publishers, Whiting.

The Clipper, Republican; Ben. L. and Minnie M. Mickel, editors and publishers, Soldier.

Kansas Bazaar, independent; S. W. McComas, editor and publisher, Circleville.

JEFFERSON COUNTY.

The Oskaloosa Independent, Republican; F. H. Roberts, editor and publisher, Oskaloosa.

The Oskaloosa Times, Democratic; A. G. Patrick, editor and publisher, Oskaloosa.

The Valley Falls New Era, Republican; E. P. Karr, editor and proprietor, Valley Falls.

The Farmers' Vindicator, People's Party; N. H. Harman, editor and proprietor, Valley Falls.

The Winchester Herald, Republican; Morton Alexander, editor and publisher, Winchester.

The Nortonville News, Republican; L. F. Randolph and R. M. Cook, editors and proprietors, Nortonville.

The McLouth Times, Republican; A. B. Mills, editor and publisher, McLouth.

Meriden Weekly Tribune, neutral; F. A. Hollingsworth and Mrs. F. A. Hollingsworth, editors and publishers, Meriden.

The Perry News, Prohibition; H. W. Spangler, editor, Kansas News Company, North Topeka, publishers, Perry.

JEWELL COUNTY.

Jewell County Monitor, Republican; R. F. Vaughan, editor and publisher, Mankato.

Jewell County Review, Republican; S. M. Weed, editor and publisher, Mankato.

The Western Advocate, People's Party; William E. Bush and Matie E. Convis, editors and proprietors, Mankato.

Jewell County Republican, Republican; W. C. Palmer and J. G. Bowman, editors and publishers, Jewell City.

Jewell County News, People's Party; Rarick & Forrest, editors and managers, News Publishing Company, publishers, Jewell City.

Burr Oak Herald, Republican; I. S. Drummond, editor and publisher, Burr Oak.

The Exponent, People's Party; P. H. & C. C. Kemp, editors, publishers, and proprietors, Randall.

The Esbon Leader, neutral; J. W. Mahaffey, editor and publisher, Esbon.

JOHNSON COUNTY.

The Olathe Mirror, Republican; H. A. Perkins, editor and publisher, Olathe.

The Kansas Patron, Grange; Geo. Black, editor, H. C. Livermore, manager, Johnson County Coöperative Association, publishers, Olathe.

The Kansas Star, industrial; published by the students of the Deaf and Dumb Institution, Olathe.

The Olathe Leader, People's Party; J. W. Sowers, editor and proprietor, Olathe.

Olathe Herald, Democratic; T. P. Fulton, editor and publisher, Olathe.

Spring Hill New Era, neutral; D. H. Bingham, editor and publisher, Spring Hill.

Gardner Graphic, neutral; W. F. Rice and T. S. Rice, editors and proprietors, Gardner.

KEARNY COUNTY.

Kearny County Advocate, Republican; C. O. Chapman, editor, L. P. Kimball, publisher, Lakin.

The Lakin Index, Republican; F. R. French, editor and proprietor, Lakin.

KINGMAN COUNTY.

Kingman County Democrat, Democratic; W. A. Eaton, editor and publisher, Kingman.

The Leader-Courier, Republican; Morton Albaugh, editor and proprietor, Kingman.

The Kingman Weekly Journal, People's Party; W. L. Brown, editor, H. H. Isley, publisher, Kingman.

Norwich News, Republican; J. O. Graham, editor and publisher, Norwich.

The Cunningham Herald, Republican; T. G. Elbury, editor and proprietor, Cunningham.

KIOWA COUNTY.

The Kiowa County Signal, Republican; Will. E. Bolton, editor and proprietor, Greensburg.

Kiowa County Times, People's Party; C. F. Mingenback, editor, Greensburg Publishing Company, publishers, Greensburg.

Republican Banner, independent; M. M. Lee and J. D. Beck, editors and publishers, Greensburg.

LABETTE COUNTY.

The Parsons Sun (daily and weekly), Republican; H. H. Lusk, editor, publisher, and proprietor, Parsons.

The Parsons Eclipse (daily and weekly), Democratic; C. A., H. A. & F. F. Lamb, editors and proprietors, Parsons.

Parsons Palladium, Democratic; Frank W. Frye, editor and publisher, Parsons.

Mills's Weekly World, People's Party; H. C. Sourbeer, editor and publisher, Parsons.

The Eye Opener, People's Party; E. M. Woods, editor, Parsons.

The Parsons Weekly Blade, Republican; S. O. Clayton, editor, Parsons Weekly Blade Publishing Company, publishers, Parsons.

The Chetopa Advance, Republican; J. M. Cavaness, editor and publisher, Chetopa.

The Chetopa Democrat, Democratic; J. J. Rambo, editor, publisher, and proprietor, Chetopa.

The Oswego Independent, Republican; M. A. & W. F. McGill, editors and publishers, Oswego.

Labette County Democrat, Democratic; J. M. Landis, editor and publisher, Oswego.

Labette County Times-Statesman, People's Party; R. B. Claiborne, editor and publisher, Oswego.

The American Crank; Harry Mills, editor, W. W. Whetstone, publisher, Oswego.

Golden Rod (monthly), scientific; W. S. Newlon, Oswego.

The Mound Valley Herald, Republican; W. F. Thrall, editor and publisher, Mound Valley.

The Edna Independent, People's Party; A. C. Veach, editor and publisher, Edna.

The Wilsonton Journal, neutral; Mrs. Augustus Wilson, editor and proprietor, Wilsonton.

LANE COUNTY.

The Dighton Herald, Republican; F. H. Lobdell, editor and publisher, Dighton.

LEAVENWORTH COUNTY.

The Leavenworth Times (daily and weekly), Republican; D. R. Anthony, editor, publisher, and proprietor, Leavenworth.

The Evening Standard, Democratic; Mrs. F. T. Lynch, editor, Standard Publishing Company, publishers, Leavenworth.

The Leavenworth Post (daily), Democratic; Max. Gronefeld, editor, German Printing and Publishing Company, publishers, Leavenworth.

The Home Record, (monthly), charitable; Mrs. C. H. Cushing, editor, Board of Managers of the Home for the Friendless, publishers, Leavenworth.

The Orphan's Friend (monthly), charitable; Mrs. Thos. Carney, editor, publisher, and business manager, Leavenworth.

The Art League Chronicle, (monthly), art; Mrs. Nevil Whitesides, editor, Art League Society, publishers, Leavenworth.

Leavenworth Labor News, Union-Labor; Mrs. E. M. Blackman, editor, Labor News Company, publishers, Leavenworth.

Leavenworth Journal of Commerce (semi-monthly), independent; Charles F. C. Smith, editor and publisher, Leavenworth.

Welcome News, independent; J. S. Harris and S. C. Chatham, editors and publishers, Leavenworth.

Journal of the United States Cavalry Association (quarterly), military; Wesley Merritt, editor, United States Cavalry Association, publishers, Fort Leavenworth.

The Tonganoxie Mirror, Republican; Wm. Heynen, editor, publisher, and proprietor, Tonganoxie.

Weekly Sentinel, People's Party; W. A. Brice, editor and proprietor, Tonganoxie.

The Prison Trusty; Penitentiary inmates, editors, Trusty Publishing Company, publishers, Lansing.

LINCOLN COUNTY.

The Lincoln Republican, Republican; Tell W. Walton, editor and proprietor, Lincoln.

The Lincoln Beacon, People's Party; W. S. & Anna C. Wait, editors and publishers, Lincoln.

The Sylvan Grove Sentinel, independent; W. H. Pilcher, editor and publisher, Sylvan Grove.

LINN COUNTY.

La Cygne Weekly Journal, Republican; J. P. Kenea and Ed. C. Lane, editors, publishers, and proprietors, La Cygne.

The Pleasanton Observer, Republican; J. Frank Smith, editor, J. P. Kenea, Ed. C. Lane, and J. Frank Smith, publishers, Pleasanton.

The Pleasanton Herald, People's Party; J. E. Latimer, editor and publisher, Pleasanton.

Linn County Clarion, Republican; C. J. Trigg, editor and publisher, Mound City.

Mound City Progress, Republican; N. Campbell and Frank Waymire, editors and publishers, Mound City.

The Torch of Liberty, People's Party; Geo. H. Townsley, editor and publisher, Mound City.

The Blue Mound Sun, Republican; J. N. Barnes, editor, J. N. & S. E. Barnes, proprietors, Blue Mound.

Pilot and Graphic, Republican; C. M. Brown, editor and proprietor, Parker.

LOGAN COUNTY.

Logan County Republican, Republican; J. F. Coulter, editor and proprietor, Russell Springs.

The Winona Clipper, Republican; Park R. Mitten, editor and proprietor, Winona.

The Oakley Graphic, Republican; C. V. Kinney, editor and publisher, Oakley.

LYON COUNTY.

Emporia Republican (daily and weekly), Republican; C. V. Eskridge, editor, publisher, and proprietor, Emporia.

The Emporia Gazette (daily and weekly), Republican; W. Y. Morgan, editor and publisher, Emporia.

The Tidings, People's Party; Major A. Paul, editor and proprietor, Emporia.

College Life, college; David S. Hibbard, editor; College of Emporia, publisher, Emporia.

The State Normal Quarterly, literary; Pres. A. R. Taylor, editor; Faculty State Normal School, publishers, Emporia.

The Baptist Visitor (monthly), religious; Rev. L. H. Holt, editor and publisher, Emporia.

The Hartford News, independent; C. C. Rogan, editor and publisher, Hartford.

Admire Independent, independent; B. E. Ogleby, editor and proprietor, Admire.

M'PHERSON COUNTY.

The McPherson Republican (daily and weekly), Republican; S. G. Mead, editor, publisher, and proprietor, McPherson.

The Freeman-Vim, Republican; J. M. Snyder, editor; Snyder Publishing Company, publishers, McPherson.

The Democrat, Democratic; Warren Knaus, editor and proprietor, McPherson.

The Educator and Companion, educational; J. M. Snyder, editor, S. Z. Sharp, educational editor, McPherson.

The Lindsborg News, Republican; Geo. E. Eberhardt, editor and publisher, A. Ringwald, proprietor, Lindsborg.

The Marquette Tribune, Republican; E. C. Crary, editor and publisher, Marquette.

The Moundridge Leader, independent; J. J. Sellers, editor and publisher, G. H. Wichman, proprietor, Moundridge.

The Inman Review, neutral; L. C. Heim, editor and publisher, Inman.

The Windom Enterprise, neutral; A. W. Newell, editor, publisher, and proprietor, Windom.

Canton Republican, Republican; H. F. Nolte, editor and publisher, Canton.

People's Advocate, People's Party; J. H. Baker, editor, Baker & Mason, proprietors, Galva.

MARION COUNTY.

Marion Record, Republican; E. W. Hoch, editor and publisher, Marion.

The Marion Times, People's Party; C. E. Foote and H. Kuhn, editors, Times Publishing Company, publishers, Marion.

The Advance, People's Party; Samuel Johnson, editor and proprietor, Marion.

The Peabody Gazette, Republican; W. H. Morgan, editor and proprietor, Peabody.

The Peabody Graphic, Republican; R. P. March, editor, publisher, and proprietor, Peabody.

Florence Weekly Bulletin, Republican; J. E. House, editor and publisher, Florence.

Hillsboro Anzeiger, Republican; J. F. Harms, editor and publisher, Hillsboro.

Der Kansas Courier, Democratic; Geo. P. Roth, editor and publisher, Hillsboro.

MARSHALL COUNTY.

The Marshall County News, Republican; Geo. T. Smith, editor, publisher, and proprietor, Marysville.

Marysville Post, Democratic; Ernst Denner, editor and publisher, Marysville.

Marshall County Democrat, Democratic; W. T. Ecks, editor and publisher, Marysville.

The People's Advocate, People's Party; Jas. P. Easterly, editor, Marshall County Printing Company, publishers, Marysville.

The Waterville Telegraph, Republican; Henry C. Willson, editor and publisher, Waterville.

The Blue Rapids Times, Republican; E. M. Brice, editor and publisher, Blue Rapids.

Blue Rapids Weekly Motor, People's Party; D. O. Munger, editor and proprietor, Blue Rapids.

The Frankfort Bee, Republican; M. B. Baldwin and G. W. Shedden, editors and publishers, Frankfort.

The Axtell Anchor, Republican; S. L. Wilson, editor and publisher, Axtell.

Williamson's Beattie Eagle, Republican; C. E. Williamson, editor and publisher, Beattie.

The Irving Leader, Republican; Hugh Thompson, editor and publisher, Irving.

The Summerfield Sun, Republican; W. H. Paine and F. W. Train, editors and publishers, Summerfield.

The Oketo Herald, Republican; R. B. & C. J. Moore, editors and proprietors, Oketo.

The Vermillion Record, Republican; F. W. Arnold, editor and proprietor, Vermillion.

MEADE COUNTY.

Meade County Globe, Republican; Frank Fuhr, editor and publisher, Meade.

Meade County Nationalist, People's Party; C. G. Allen, editor and publisher, Meade.

The Meade Republican, Republican; T. J. Palmer, editor and proprietor, Meade.

MIAMI COUNTY.

The Miami Republican, Republican; W. D. Greason, editor, publisher, and proprietor, Paola.

The Western Spirit, Democratic; B. J. Sheridan, editor and proprietor, Paola.

The Paola Times, People's Party, A. C. McCarthy and L. C. McCarthy-Hodges, editors and publishers, Paola.

The Louisburg Herald, Republican; R. H. Cadwallader, editor, publisher, and proprietor, Louisburg.

Osawatomie Graphic, Republican; J. P. & J. H. Bell, editors, Graphic Publishing Company, publishers, Osawatomie.

Osawatomie Globe, neutral; Kelley Mount, editor, publisher, and proprietor, Osawatomie.

Fontana News, Republican; B. Symonds, editor and publisher, Fontana.

MITCHELL COUNTY.

The Beloit Gazette, Republican; S. H. Dodge, editor and publisher, Beloit.

Beloit Weekly Courier, Republican; R. I. Palmer, manager and publisher, W. H. Caldwell, proprietor, Beloit.

The Western Call, People's Party; I. W. & J. S. Parks, editors and publishers, Beloit.

The Harmonic (monthly), educational; Irving Stanley, editor and publisher, Beloit.

Public Record, Republican; L. L. Alrich, editor, publisher, and proprietor, Cawker City.

The Times, Republican; J. W. McBride, editor and publisher, Cawker City.

Tri-County News, Republican; C. H. Sawyer, editor and publisher, Scottsville.

The People's Sentinel, People's Party; W. R. Baker and J. F. Ewing, editors and publishers, Glen Elder.

MONTGOMERY COUNTY.

The Star and Kansan, Democratic; Chas. T. Errett, editor, publisher, and proprietor, Independence.

South Kansas Tribune, Republican; W. T. & C. Yoe, editors, publishers, and proprietors, Independence.

The Morning Reporter, neutral; Walter S. Sickels, editor and publisher, Independence.

United Labor, People's Party; A. J. Miller, editor, E. W. Cox, publisher, Independence.

The Journal, Republican; D. Stewart Elliott, editor, Elliott Printing Company, publishers, Coffeyville.

News-Broadax, independent; Will. S. Irvin, editor and publisher, Coffeyville.

Afro-American Advocate, Republican; O. S. Fox and W. A. Price, editors, Afro-American Publishing Company, publishers, Coffeyville.

Coffeyville Daily Telegram, Republican; Joe Goodykoontz, editor and publisher, Coffeyville.

Cherry Vale Republican, Republican; D. R. Neville, editor and publisher, Cherry Vale.

Cherry Vale Champion, Republican; A. S. Duley, editor and publisher, Cherry Vale.

People's Party Plaindealer, People's Party; M. C. Handley, editor and publisher, Cherry Vale.

The Caney Chronicle, Republican; Dr. Jay Jasper Stone, editor and publisher, Caney.

—8

The Caney Times, People's Party; C. J. Reynolds, editor, Reynolds Publishing Company, proprietors, Caney.

The Elk City Enterprise, neutral; W. E. Wortman, editor and publisher, Elk City.

The Havana Press, Republican; R. B. Knock, editor and publisher, Havana.

MORRIS COUNTY.

The Council Grove Republican, Republican; W. F. Waller, editor, Republican Printing Company, publishers, Council Grove.

Council Grove Guard, Democratic; Dill & Bell, editors and publishers, Council Grove.

Council Grove Courier, People's Party; G. W. Coffin, jr., editor and publisher, Council Grove.

White City Register, Republican; J. D. & H. F. Parsons, editors and publishers, White City.

Morris County Republican, Republican; C. D. Hornbeck, editor and proprietor, Wilsey.

MORTON COUNTY.

The Morton County Star, Prohibition; H. W. Worthington, editor and publisher, Richfield.

The Monitor-Republican, Republican; Glenn S. Van Gundy, editor, Frank B. Van Gundy, business manager; Frank W. Trask, publisher, Richfield.

NEMAHA COUNTY.

Seneca Courier-Democrat, Democratic; A. P. Herold and C. H. Herold, editors and publishers, J. M. Cober, business manager, Seneca.

The Seneca Tribune, Republican; W. H. & G. J. Jordan, editors and publishers, Seneca.

The Seneca News, People's Party; James M. Jones, editor and proprietor, Seneca.

Nemaha County Republican, Republican; James B. Goode, editor and publisher, Sabetha.

The Sabetha Herald, Republican; Flora P. Hogbin, editor, A. C. Hogbin, publisher, Sabetha.

Nemaha County Spectator, Republican; J. T. Bristow, editor and proprietor, Wetmore.

Centralia Journal, neutral; A. J. Birchfield, editor, Journal Publishing Company, publishers, Centralia.

The Bern Press, Democratic; John Ford, editor and manager, W. J. McLaughlin, proprietor, Bern.

The Oneida World, Republican; W. W. Cohoon, editor and publisher, Oneida.

The Goffs Advance, Republican; Fred. Haughawout, editor and publisher, Goffs.

NEOSHO COUNTY.

The Osage Mission Journal, Republican; E. B. Park, editor, E. B. Park and E. L. Conklin, publishers, Osage Mission.

Chanute Vidette-Times, Republican; G. M. Dewey, editor and publisher, Chanute.

Chanute Blade, Democratic; J. A. Cross, editor and publisher, Chanute.

Chanute Daily Tribune, Republican; H. P. Hutton, editor, G. M. Dewey, publisher, Chanute.

Republican-Record, Republican; Chas. E. Harbaugh, editor and proprietor, Erie.

The Erie Sentinel, People's Party; C. E. Allison, editor and publisher, Erie.

Thayer Independent-News, neutral; M. A. Mitchell, editor, A. L. Palmer, proprietor, Thayer.

NESS COUNTY.

Ness County News, Republican; J. K. Barnd, editor and proprietor, Ness City.

Walnut Valley Sentinel, Democratic; Mrs. J. W. Brown, editor, manager, and proprietor, Ness City.

The Lance, Republican; R. Hathaway, editor and publisher, Ness City.

NORTON COUNTY.

The Norton Courier, Republican; F. M. Duvall, editor and publisher, Norton.

The Champion, Republican; J. W. Conway, editor, publisher, and proprietor, Norton.

The Almena Plaindealer, People's Party; J. B. Dyatt, editor and publisher, Almena.

The Liberator, People's Party; D. W. Hull, editor and publisher, Norton.

The Republican, Republican; Drummond & Wallace, publishers, Norton.

OSAGE COUNTY.

The Osage County Chronicle, Republican; Max Buek and E. G. Pipp, editors, Chronicle Publishing Company, publishers, Burlingame.

The National Echo (monthly), S. of V., D. of V., and Ladies' Aid Society; Wm. H. Mundy, editor, and publisher, Burlingame.

The Burlingame Herald, Republican; J. N. McDonald, editor and publisher, Burlingame.

The Osage City Free Press, Republican; D. J. Roberts, editor, D. J. Roberts and R. J. Hill, proprietors, Osage City.

The Public Opinion, Democratic; —— Blain and —— Rockford, editors and publishers, Osage City.

The Lyndon Journal, Republican; W. A. Madaris, editor and publisher, Lyndon.

Osage County Graphic, Republican; R. A. Miller, editor, Graphic Publishing Co., publishers, Lyndon.

The People's Herald, People's Party; Geo. Rogers, editor, People's Publishing Association, publishers, Lyndon.

The Carbondalian, Republican; R. F. Playford, editor, and proprietor, Everett Veatch, publisher, Carbondale.

The Overbrook Herald, Republican; S. A. Stauffer, editor, M. R. Stauffer, publisher, Overbrook.

The Osage County Sentinel, People's Party; Logan & Logan, editors and publishers, Quenemo.

Quenemo Republican, Republican; T. A., C. E. & J. J. Ellis, editors, Republican Publishing Company, publishers, Quenemo.

Scranton Gazette, Republican; Ralph M. Parker and O. K. Stakebake, editors and publishers, Scranton.

The Melvern Review, neutral; Isaac & J. E. Farley, editors, A. R. Ball, publisher, Melvern.

OSBORNE COUNTY.

Osborne County Farmer, Republican; W. S. Tilton and C. W. Landis, editors and proprietors, Osborne.

Osborne County News, People's Party; S. E. Ruede, editor and publisher, Osborne.

The Downs Times, Republican; H. M. Fletcher, editor and publisher, Downs.

Western Empire, Republican; Harmon D. Wilson, editor, H. M. Fletcher & Co., publishers, Alton.

OTTAWA COUNTY.

Minneapolis Messenger, Republican; A. P. Riddle, editor, publisher, and proprietor, Minneapolis.

Kansas Workman (monthly), A. O. U. W.; A. P. Riddle, editor and proprietor, Minneapolis.

The Review, People's Party; Tom Brewer, editor, Review Publishing Company, proprietors, Minneapolis.

The Sprig of Myrtle (monthly), K. of P.; A. P. Riddle, editor and proprietor, Minneapolis.

Ottawa County Index, People's Party; J. C. Cline, editor and publisher, Minneapolis.

Ye Pedagogue (monthly), educational; O. B. Fleming, editor, Review Publishing Company, publishers, Minneapolis.

The Souvenir (monthly), Epworth League; C. E. Waters, editor, Minneapolis.

Ottawa County Democrat, Democratic; D. B. Loudon, editor and proprietor, Bennington.

The Delphos Republican, Republican; J. M. Waterman and W. W. Waterman, editors and proprietors, Delphos.

PAWNEE COUNTY.

The Larned Weekly Eagle-Optic, Democratic; T. E. Leftwich, managing editor, Optic Steam Printing Company, publishers, Larned.

Larned Weekly Chronoscope, Republican; F. J. Davis, editor, Larned Printing Company, publishers, Larned.

Tiller and Toiler, People's Party; W. P. McMahon, editor and publisher, Larned.

PHILLIPS COUNTY.

The Independent, People's Party; H. W. & S. C. Landes, editors and proprietors, Kirwin.

The Kirwin Globe, Republican; A. Barron, editor and proprietor, Kirwin.

Phillipsburg Herald, People's Party; E. E. Brainard and G. W. Danforth, editors and proprietors, Phillipsburg.

The Phillipsburg Dispatch, Republican; John M. McNay, editor and publisher, Phillipsburg.

Long Island Leader, Republican; C. E. Booher, editor and publisher, Long Island.

The Logan Republican, Republican; F. F. Mende, editor, Logan Publishing Company, publishers, Logan.

POTTAWATOMIE COUNTY.

The Kansas Agriculturist, Republican; Ernest A. Weller, editor and proprietor, Wamego.

Pottawatomie County Times, independent, Sylvester Fowler, editor and publisher, Wamego.

St. Mary's Star, Democratic; P. L. Jackson and Clint. Graham, editors and publishers, St. Mary's.

The Dial (monthly), college; Francis E. Kehoe, editor-in-chief; published by the students of St. Mary's College, St. Mary's.

The Westmoreland Recorder, Republican; W. F. Hill, editor and publisher, Westmoreland.

The Alliance News, People's Party; J. C. Stanley, editor and publisher, Westmoreland.

The Olsburg News-Letter, Republican; Lewis Havermale, editor, publisher, and proprietor, Olsburg.

The Onaga Herald, Republican; F. S. Haughawout, editor and proprietor, Onaga.

The Havensville Torchlight, Republican; E. D. Anderson, editor and publisher, Havensville.

PRATT COUNTY.

The Pratt County Republican, Republican; L. C. Miller, editor, F. A. Lanstrum and L. C. Miller, publishers, Pratt.

Pratt County Times, Republican; James Kelly, editor, James Kelly and J. W. Naron, publishers, Pratt.

The Pratt County Union, People's Party; Joel Reece, editor and publisher, Pratt.

The Preston Plaindealer, independent; J. G. Oliver, editor and publisher, Preston.

RAWLINS COUNTY.

The Republican Citizen, Republican; James D. Greason, editor and publisher, Atwood.

The Times, People's Party; J. W. Morphy, editor, John F. Price, publisher and proprietor, Atwood.

Rawlins County Democrat, Democratic; M. W. Mikesell, editor and publisher, Atwood.

The Ludell Gazette, Republican; W. M. Dimmick, editor and manager, Gazette Publishing Company, publishers, Ludell.

The Blakeman Register, Republican; J. C. Work, editor and publisher, Blakeman.

RENO COUNTY.

Hutchinson News (daily and weekly), Republican; A. L. Sponsler, editor, The News Publishing Company, publishers, Hutchinson.

Weekly Interior Herald, Republican; Fletcher Meridith, editor and proprietor, Hutchinson.

The Clipper, society; W. A. Loe, editor and proprietor, Hutchinson.

The Hutchinson Times, Democratic; J. B. Crouch, editor and proprietor, Hutchinson.

Alliance Gazette, People's Party; Warren Foster, editor, Warren & Horace S. Foster, publishers, Hutchinson.

The Nickerson Argosy, Republican; W. F. Hendry and J. E. Humphrey, editors and publishers, Nickerson.

Arlington Enterprise, Republican; H. J. Haskard, editor and publisher, J. E. Eaton, proprietor, Arlington.

Haven Independent, People's Party; C. A. Hamlin, editor and publisher, Haven.

Turon Headlight, People's Party; S. Bacon, editor and publisher, Turon.

The Sylvia Banner, People's Party; Jeff. Bower, editor and proprietor, Sylvia.

REPUBLIC COUNTY.

The Belleville Telescope, Republican; J. C. Humphrey, editor, publisher, and proprietor, Belleville.

Republic County Freeman, People's Party; H. N. Boyd, editor and publisher, Belleville.

The Belleville Democrat, Democratic; John McLaury, editor and publisher, Belleville.

Scandia Journal, Republican; Geo. F. Page, editor and publisher, Scandia.

Republic City News, Republican; Gomer T. Davies, editor, publisher, and proprietor, Republic City.

The Cuba Daylight, Republican; Will. M. Shrouf, editor and publisher, Cuba.

The Courtland Register, People's Party; Geo. H. Litsinger, editor and publisher, Courtland.

RICE COUNTY.

The Bulletin and Gazette, Republican; J. E. Junkin, editor, J. E. Junkin and S. H. Steele, publishers, Sterling.

Sterling Weekly Champion, People's Party; T. L. Powers, editor and proprietor, Sterling.

The Lyons Republican (semi-weekly), Republican; Clark Conkling, editor, Frank E. Hoyt, associate, Clark Conkling, publisher, Lyons.

Central Kansas Democrat, Democratic; Fred. N. Cooper, editor, Minnie Wood Cooper, publisher, Lyons.

Rice County Eagle, People's Party; D. P. Hodgdon, editor and publisher, Lyons.

The Lyons Tribune, Republican; Elbert W. Hoyt, editor and proprietor, Lyons.

The Chase Record, Republican; Chas. O. Smith, editor, publisher, and proprietor, Chase.

The Little River Monitor, Republican; W. G. Greenbank, editor, publisher, and proprietor, Little River.

Geneseo Herald, Republican; J. E. Guier, editor, Geo. C. Sheets, proprietor, Geneseo.

Rice County News, Democratic; H. T. Murray, editor and publisher, Frederick.

The Frederick Republican, Republican; James A. Underwood, editor and publisher, Frederick.

Cooper Courier (monthly), college; A. C. Rees, editor-in-chief, Chrestomatheon Literary Society of Cooper Memorial College, publisher, Sterling.

RILEY COUNTY.

Manhattan Nationalist, Republican; R. D. Parker, editor and proprietor, Manhattan.

Manhattan Homestead (monthly) real estate; L. R. Elliott, editor and publisher, Manhattan.

The Industrialist, educational and agricultural; edited by the Faculty and students of the State Agricultural College, State Agricultural College, Printing Department, publishers, Manhattan.

The Manhattan Republic, People's Party; A. A. Stewart, editor and publisher, Manhattan.

The Kansas Telephone, (monthly), religious; R. D. Parker, editor and publisher, Manhattan.

Manhattan Mercury, Democratic; J. J. Davis, editor and publisher, Manhattan.

Randolph Enterprise, People's Party; Isaac Moon, editor and publisher, Randolph.

Leonardville Monitor, Republican; P. S. Loofbourrow, editor and publisher, Leonardville.

The Riley Regent, Republican; Chas. A. Southwick, editor and publisher, Riley.

Milford Times, independent; W. R. Bard, editor, and D. P. Zeigler, publisher, Milford.

ROOKS COUNTY.

The Western News, Republican; E. Owen, editor, E. & O. T. Owen, publishers and proprietors, Stockton.

Rooks County Record, Republican; W. L. Chambers, editor, publisher, and proprietor, Stockton.

The Alliance Signal, People's Party; F. M. Case, editor and publisher, Stockton.

Stockton Academician (monthly), educational; F. E. Sherman, editor, published by Stockton Academy, Stockton.

The Teacher (monthly), educational; H. J. Lambert, editor and publisher, Stockton.

The Christian Call (monthly) religious; B. Hill, editor and publisher, Stockton.

The Plainville Times, independent; I. O. Middaugh, editor, publisher, and proprietor, Plainville.

RUSH COUNTY.

La Crosse Clarion, Republican; A. Clay Whiteman, editor and proprietor, La Crosse.

La Crosse Chieftain, Republican; La Crosse Publishing Company, publishers, J. B. Morris, manager, La Crosse.

Western Economist, People's Party; Reform Publishing Company, publishers, T. F. Mulroy, manager, La Crosse.

Pythian Sisters News (monthly), secret society; Will. M. Goodwin, Laura A. Goodwin, publishers, La Crosse.

The McCracken Enterprise, Republican; F. R. Newton, editor and publisher, McCracken.

RUSSELL COUNTY.

The Russell Record, Republican; Arthur C. Jones, editor and publisher, Russell.

Russell Journal, Republican; S. H. Haffa, editor and proprietor, Russell.

Russell County School Signal (monthly), educational; J. R. Bickerdyke, editor and publisher, Russell.

The Lucas Advance, Republican; F. T. Naylor, editor, F. T. & N. Naylor, proprietors, Lucas.

SALINE COUNTY.

Saline County Journal, Republican; C. B. Kirtland, editor, C. B. Kirtland Publishing Company, publishers, Salina.

The Salina Herald, Democratic; J. H. Padgett, editor and publisher, Salina.

The Republican (daily and weekly), Republican; J. L. Bristow, editor and proprietor, Salina.

The Normal Register (monthly), educational; L. O. Thoroman, managing editor, C. B. Kirtland Publishing Company, publishers, Salina.

The Salina Sun, Republican; W. H. Johnson, editor, publisher, and proprietor, Salina.

The Weekly Tidings, religious; Rev. A. N. See, editor-in-chief, A. N. See & Co., publishers, Salina.

The Salina Union, People's Party; J. S. Cobb and Frank Honeywell, editors and proprietors, Salina.

The Advance (monthly), college; J. C. Postlethwaite, editor, J. L. Bristow, publisher, Salina.

Gypsum Advocate, Republican; J. Wayne Amos, editor and publisher, Gypsum City.

The Earth, Republican; Mord. S. Amos, editor and publisher, Brookville.

SCOTT COUNTY.

Scott County News-Lever, People's Party; J. C. Starr, editor and publisher, Scott City.

The Republican; B. F. Rochester, editor, Scott City.

SEDGWICK COUNTY.

The Wichita Eagle (daily and weekly), Republican; M. M. Murdock, editor, R. P. Murdock, business manager, M. M. Murdock & Bro., publishers and proprietors, Wichita.

The Wichita Beacon (daily and weekly), Democratic; Frank B. Smith and John S. Richardson, editors and publishers, Wichita.

Der Wichita Herold, (German); John Hoenscheidt, editor and publisher, Wichita.

Kansas Staats Anzeiger, (German); John Hoenscheidt, editor and publisher, Wichita.

The Leader (monthly), reform; G. W. Collings, editor; Forest City Printing Company, publishers, Wichita.

The Telegrapher (monthly), telegraphy; L. B. Jones, editor and publisher, Wichita.

Christian Helper (monthly), religious; Geo. H. Sims, editor and publisher, Wichita.

The Colwich Courier, independent; J. A. Mahuran, editor and proprietor, Colwich.

The Cheney Herald, Republican; J. A. Maxey, editor and publisher, Cheney.

Clearwater Echo, Republican; J. W. Parker, editor, I. E. Parker, publisher, Clearwater.

The Arkalon News, Republican; A. K. Stoufer, editor and proprietor, Arkalon.

Springfield Republican, Republican; R. C. Calvert, editor and publisher, Springfield.

The Liberal Lyre, Republican; M. Carleton Brosius, editor and publisher, T. J. McDermott, proprietor, Liberal.

The Topeka Capital (daily and weekly), Republican; J. K. Hudson, editor-in-chief; The Topeka Capital Company, publishers, Topeka.

The Topeka State Journal (daily and weekly), Republican; Frank P. MacLennan, editor and publisher, Topeka.

The Kansas Democrat, (daily and weekly), Democratic; C. K. Holliday, jr., editor, H. O. Garvey, manager, Kansas Democrat Publishing Company, publishers, Topeka.

The Daily Sentinel, Republican; W. P. Tomlinson, editor and proprietor, Topeka.

The Kansas Farmer, agricultural; H. A. Heath, president and manager, E. B. Cowgill, vice-president, D. C. Nellis, Secretary, Kansas Farmer Company, publishers, Topeka.

Western School Journal (monthly), educational; John MacDonald, editor and publisher, Topeka.

The Topeka Mail, Republican; Frank A. Root, editor and proprietor, Topeka.

Kansas Telegraph (German), Democratic; H. von Langen, editor, Leo von Langen, publisher, Topeka.

Kansas Newspaper Union, newspaper list; F. P. Baker, editor and publisher, Topeka.

The Lance, society and literary; Eugene L. Smith and Cora B. Zook, editors and publisher, Topeka.

The Argo-Reporter, college; F. S. Ditto, editor-in-chief; Argo-Reporter Company, publishers, Topeka.

Western Veteran, G. A. R.; O. H. Coulter, editor, Western Veteran Publishing Company, publishers, Topeka.

The Kansas Methodist (bi-weekly), religious; James Lawrence, editor and publisher, Topeka.

Our Messenger (monthly), W. C. T. U.; Olive P. Bray, editor and publisher, Topeka.

The Budget and News, neutral; J. F. Daniels, editor and publisher, Topeka.

The Sunday Ledger, literary; Geo. W. Reed, editor and publisher, Topeka.

The Spirit of Kansas, Prohibition; G. F. Kimball, editor and publisher, Topeka.

The Farmer's Wife (monthly), People's Party; Mrs. Emma D. Pack, editor, I. W. Pack, publisher, Topeka.

The Kansas Medical Journal (monthly); J. E. Minney, editor-in-chief; W. E. McVey, publisher, Topeka.

The Western Poultry Breeder (monthly), Thos. Owen, editor; Thos. Owen and A. M. Owen, publishers, Topeka.

The Advocate and Topeka Tribune, People's Party; S. McLallin, editor, Advocate Publishing Company, publishers, Topeka.

The Topeka News, Prohibition; G. F. Kimball, editor and publisher, Topeka.

Topeka Republican, society; M. R. Chesney and F. S. Fluke, editors and proprietors, Topeka.

The Western Odd Fellow (monthly), I. O. O. F.; A. L. Voorhis, editor and proprietor, Topeka.

Lucifer—the Light Bearer, free thought; Moses Harman, editor and proprietor, Lillie D. White, assistant editor and publisher, Topeka.

The Merchant's Journal, trade; F. P. Baker, editor and publisher, Topeka.

The Topeka Call, Republican; W. M. Pope, editor-in-chief, J. Hume Childers, associate editor, Topeka.

The Kansas Christian Advocate, religious; Geo. E. Dougherty, editor, W. T. Randolph, publisher, Topeka.

The Waif (monthly), charitable; Walter L. Russ, editor and publisher, Topeka.

The Agora (quarterly) historical and literary; T. E. Dewey, editor, Geo. W. Crane & Co., publishers, Topeka.

The Illustrated Weekly, literary; E. L. Shelton, editor and publisher, Topeka.

Kansas Arts and Industries (occasional), architecture; Jerome Winchell, editor and publisher, Topeka.

Kansas Farmers' Alliance and Industrial Union (monthly), People's Party; officers of Kansas State F. A. and I. U., editors and publishers, W. H. Biddle, president, W. S. Hanna, business manager, Topeka.

Topeka Populist, People's Party; A. J. R. Smith and Geo. A. Urie, editors and publishers, Topeka.

The Kansas State Ledger, Republican; F. L. Jeltz, editor and proprietor, Topeka.

The Santa Fé Reporter, People's Party; H. S. Montgomery, editor; The Santa Fé Reporter Publishing Company, publishers, Topeka.

Journal of Commerce (monthly), advertising; T. Brower Peacock, editor and publisher, Topeka.

Kansas State Sunday School Journal (quarterly); Jas. S. Drake, secretary and editor, Topeka.

The Congregationalist (monthly), religious; Rev. W. L. Byers, editor; published by the North Topeka Congregational Church, North Topeka.

The Rossville Times, neutral; Geo. A. Weller, editor and publisher, Rossville.

The Weekly Critic, Democratic; Byron C. Mitchner, editor; E. W. Gumert, proprietor, Rossville.

SHERIDAN COUNTY.

Hoxie Sentinel, Republican; W. S. Quisenberry, editor and proprietor, Hoxie.

The Hoxie Palladium, People's Party; L. S. Sprague, proprietor, Hoxie.

The Sheridan County Democrat, Democratic; J. Vedder, editor and publisher, Hoxie.

SHERMAN COUNTY.

Sherman County Dark Horse, Republican; J. H. Tait, editor and proprietor, Goodland.

The Goodland Republic and Sherman County Farmer, People's Party; J. H. Stewart, editor and publisher, Goodland.

The Goodland News, Democratic; E. F. Tennant, editor and publisher, Goodland.

SMITH COUNTY.

The Pioneer-Bulletin, Republican; W. H. Nelson and John Q. Royce, editors and publishers, Smith Centre.

Stewart's Bazoo, Democratic; Jack Stewart, editor and publisher, Smith Centre.

Smith County Journal, People's Party; Scott Rice, editor and publisher, Smith Centre.

Gaylord Herald, Republican; Lew. C. Headley, editor and publisher, Gaylord.

The Lebanon Criterion, Republican; Webb McNall, editor and proprietor, Lebanon.

Lebanon Journal, People's Party; W. L. Wright, editor and publisher, Lebanon.

Light of Liberty, People's party; M. L. & K. Lockwood, editors and publishers, Lebanon.

The Kensington Mirror, Republican; O. L. Reed, editor and publisher, Kensington.

STAFFORD COUNTY.

Stafford Republican, Republican; Geo. W. Akers, editor, Geo. W. & Art. B. Akers, publishers, Stafford.

The People's Paper, People's Party; E. G. Nettleton, editor and publisher, Stafford.

St. John Weekly News, Republican; W. A. Potter, editor and proprietor, St. John.

The Advance, Republican; W. K. P. Dow, editor and publisher, St. John.

County Capital, People's Party; J. B. Hilmes, editor, Mary J. Hilmes, publisher, St. John.

The Musical Mishap (occasional), music; P. D. Lamoreux, editor and publisher, St. John.

STANTON COUNTY.

Johnson City Journal, Republican; John A. Webster, editor and proprietor, Johnson City.

The Stanton County Sun, Democratic-Populist; A. B. Wallis, editor and proprietor, Johnson City.

STEVENS COUNTY.

Tribune-Sentinel, People's Party; A. A. Dunmire, editor and publisher, Woodsdale.

Hugoton Hermes, Republican; C. M. Davis, editor and publisher, Hugoton.

SUMNER COUNTY.

The Monitor-Press, Republican; J. G. Campbell and Chas. Hood, editors and proprietors, Wellington.

Sumner County Standard, Democratic; Luke Herring, editor and publisher, Wellington.

Wellington Daily Mail, independent; Fred. Bohanna, editor and publisher, Wellington.

People's Voice, People's Party; O. M. Howard, managing editor, Lyman Naugle, proprietor, Wellington.

The Weekly Journal, juvenile; Eddie Tinkham, editor; Eddie & Andrew Tinkham, publishers, Wellington.

Weekly Juvenile, juvenile; Henry K. Cowen, editor and proprietor, Wellington.

The Caldwell Journal, People's Party; Frank Walling, editor; H. R. Walling & Son, publishers, Caldwell.

The Daily Breeze; Journal Company, publishers, Caldwell.

The Caldwell News, Republican; R. T. & P. C. Simons, editors; Robert T. Simons, publisher, Caldwell.

The Belle Plaine News, independent; G. M. Turley, editor and publisher, Belle Plaine.

Geuda Springs Herald, Republican; W. C. Barnes, editor and proprietor, Geuda Springs.

Mulvane Record, independent; G. L. Reed, editor and publisher, Mulvane.

The Mulvane Graphic, independent; E. P. & E. L. Stephenson, editors and publishers, Mulvane.

The Argonia Clipper, independent; S. W. Duncan, editor and publisher, Argonia.

Conway Springs Star, independent; E. L. Cline, editor and publisher, Conway Springs.

The South Haven New Era, independent; C. A. Branscombe, editor, publisher, and proprietor, South Haven.

The South Haven Rustler, People's Party; W. J. McKinley, editor and publisher, South Haven.

The Mocking Bird, independent; J. M. Morgan, editor and publisher, Oxford.

The Milan Press, independent; M. O. Cissel, editor and publisher, Milan.

THOMAS COUNTY.

The Colby Tribune, Republican; P. A. Troutfetter, editor and proprietor, Colby.

The Free Press, People's Party; C. E. Dedrick, editor and proprietor, Colby.

The Colby News, neutral; E. E. Van Epps, editor and publisher, Colby.

TREGO COUNTY.

Western Kansas World, Republican; S. A. Cowick and A. D. Crooks, editors and publishers, Wa Keeney.

The Sun, People's Party; A. J. Kellogg, editor, G. E. Kellogg and D. P. Ziegler, publishers, Wa Keeney.

WABAUNSEE COUNTY.

The Alma News, People's Party; I. D. Gardiner, editor and publisher, Alma.

Alma Enterprise, Republican; Frank I. Sage and O. W. Little, editors and proprietors, Alma.

The Alma Signal, Democratic; Matt. Thomson, editor, publisher, and proprietor, Alma.

The Eskridge Star, Republican; W. H. Melrose, editor, publisher, and proprietor, Eskridge.

The Alta Vista Record, Republican; S. M. & J. C. Padgett, editors and publishers, Alta Vista.

WALLACE COUNTY.

The Western Times, Republican; Kate B. Doering, editor and proprietor, Western Times Publishing Company, publishers, Sharon Springs.

Leoti Standard, Republican; C. S. Triplett, editor and publisher, Leoti.

The Western Kansan, People's Party; J. B. Milford, editor and publisher, Leoti,.

Wilson County Citizen, Republican; John S. Gilmore, editor and publisher, Fredonia.

The Alliance Herald, People's Party; J. M. Kennedy, editor, published by Alliance Publishing Company, Fredonia.

Neodesha Register, labor; J. Kansas Morgan, editor and publisher, Neodesha.

Wilson County Sun, Democratic; Grant Shaw, editor and publisher, Neodesha.

The Buffalo Advocate, independent; C. E. & P. B. Cowdery, editors and publishers, Buffalo.

Altoona Journal, independent; M. A. Rhea, editor and proprietor, Altoona.

The Neosho Falls Post, Republican; J. N. Stout, editor and publisher, Neosho Falls.

The News, Republican; C. C. Clevenger, editor, Richard Trueblood and Frederick Stephenson, publishers, Yates Center.

Woodson Democrat, Democratic; R. R. Wells, editor and publisher, Yates Center.

The Farmers' Advocate, People's Party; A. E. & N. S. Macoubrie, editors and publishers, Yates Center.

The Toronto Republican, Republican; N. B. & C. A. Buck, editors and publishers, Toronto.

The Kansas City Gazette (daily and weekly), Republican; Geo. W. Martin, editor, W. L. Witmer, business manager, Gazette Publishing and Printing Company, publishers, Kansas City.

The Wyandotte Herald, Democratic; V. J. Lane & Co., editors and publishers, Kansas City.

The Kansas City Catholic, religious; John O'Flanagan, editor and publisher, Kansas City.

Cromwell's Kansas Mirror, Republican; Mark Cromwell, editor and proprietor, Kansas City.

The American Citizen, independent; C. H. J. Taylor, editor and publisher, Kansas City.

The Weekly Press, Republican; J. B. Hipple, editor and publisher, Kansas City.

The Kansas City Sun, People's Party; E. F. Heisler, editor, Sun Printing Company, publishers, Kansas City.

Der Waechter, independent; C. D. Heinrich, editor and publisher, Kansas City.

The Kansas City Age; M. H. Donoho, editor, The Age Printing Company, publishers, Kansas City.

Kansas City Call, Kansas City.

The Argentine Republic, neutral; Jos. T. Landrey, editor and publisher, Argentine.

The Labor Review, United Labor; David Hunt, editor, Review Publishing Company, publishers, Argentine.

The Argentine Eagle, Republican; J. M. Asher and Henry B. Funk, editors and publishers, Argentine.

The Baptist Banner (monthly), religious; Rev. W. B. Lile, editor, Eagle Publishing Company, publishers, Argentine.

NEWSPAPERS AND PERIODICALS NOW RECEIVED FROM OTHER STATES AND COUNTRIES.

ALASKA.

The Alaskan, neutral; C. H. Schaap, editor and publisher, Sitka.

ARKANSAS.

The Jacksonian, Democratic; Geo. W. Reed, editor and proprietor, Heber.

The Rainbow (monthly), Democratic; Jno. C. Betten, editor and publisher, Eureka Springs.

ARIZONA.

Arizona Weekly Journal-Miner, Republican; J. C. Martin, editor and proprietor, Prescott.

CALIFORNIA.

Overland Monthly, literary; The Overland Monthly Publishing Company, publishers, San Francisco.

Signs of the Times, religious; M. C. Wilcox, editor, Oakland.

Pacific Health Journal and Temperance Advocate (monthly); W. H. Maxson and M. C. Wilcox, editors, Pacific Press Company, publishers, Oakland.

The West American Scientist (occasional); C. R. Orcutt, editor and publisher, Los Angeles, Orcutt, and San Diego.

Public Library Bulletin (monthly); published under the supervision of the Board of Directors of the Library, Los Angeles.

The Orange Belt (monthly); L. M. Holt, managing editor, The Orange Belt Publishing Company, publishers, Rialto.

COLORADO.

Rocky Mountain Weekly News, People's Party; Thos. M. Patterson and John Arkins, editors and proprietors, Denver.

The Denver Republican (daily), Republican; Republican Publishing Company, publishers, Denver.

The Denver Press, Republican; V. P. Wilson, editor, V. P. Wilson & Son, publishers, Denver.

The Great Divide (monthly), literary; Stanley Wood, editor, The Great Divide Publishing Company, publishers, Denver.

Books (monthly), literary; J. C. Dana, editor, R. L. Harper, business manager, Denver.

The Gunnison Tribune, Republican; Chas. E. Adams and Henry Corum, editors and publishers, Gunnison.

The Salida Mail (semi-weekly), Republican; Howard Russell, editor, J. F. Erdlen and Howard Russell, proprietors, Salida.

White Pine Cone, People's Party; Geo. S. Irwin, editor and publisher, White Pine.

The West Side Citizen, Republican; Lewis L. Gray, editor and publisher, Colfax.

Grand Valley Star, People's Party; Grand Junction.

The Idaho Springs News, independent; M. J. Brown, editor and publisher, Idaho Springs.

The Edgewood Sun (juvenile), Republican; D. R. & F. J. Wood, editors and publishers, Colorado Springs.

CONNECTICUT.

The Quarterly Journal of Inebriety (quarterly), temperance; T. D. Crothers, M. D., editor, published by The American Association for the Cure of Inebriates, Hartford.

The Travelers Record (monthly), insurance; Travelers Insurance Company, publishers, Hartford.

The Hartford Seminary Record (bi-monthly), theological; edited and published by the Faculty of the Hartford Theological Seminary, Hartford.

The Connecticut Valley Advertiser, neutral; Jos. E. Selden, editor and publisher, Moodus.

FLORIDA.

The Florida Dispatch, Farmer, and Fruit Grower, agriculture and horticulture; Stephen Powers, editor, Da Costa & Powers, publishers, Jacksonville.

DISTRICT OF COLUMBIA.

The Official Gazette of the U. S. Patent Office (weekly); published by authority of Congress, Washington.

U. S. Official Postal Guide (monthly); Brodix Publishing Company, publishers, Washington.

Public Opinion; Public Opinion Company, publishers, Washington and New York.

The Washington Book Chronicle and Bulletin of Government Publications (quarterly); W. H. Lowdermilk & Co., publishers, Washington.

The National Tribune, G. A. R.; George E. Lemon, editor, Washington.

U. S. Government Publications (monthly catalogue); J. H. Hickcox, editor, W. H. Lowdermilk & Co., publishers, Washington.

The American Anthropologist (quarterly; Henry W. Henshaw, editor, Anthropological Society of Washington, publishers, Washington.

The National Geographic Magazine (bi-monthly); National Geographic Society, publishers, Washington.

Monthly Weather Review; Mark W. Harrington, chief of Weather Bureau, published by authority of the Secretary of Agriculture, Washington.

The Woman's Tribune, equal suffrage; Clara Bewick Colby, editor and publisher, Washington, D. C., and Beatrice, Neb.

National Watchman, People's Party; N. A. Dunning, managing editor, Congressional Committee, People's Party, publishers, Washington.

Summary Statement of the Imports and Exports of the United States (monthly); published by the Treasury Department, Bureau of Statistics, S. G. Brock, chief of bureau, Washington.

Statement of Foreign Commerce and Immigration (monthly); published by the Treasury Department, Bureau of Statistics, S. G. Brock, chief of bureau, Washington.

Exports of Mineral Oils and Cotton (monthly); published by the Treasury Department, Bureau of Statistics, S. G. Brock, chief of bureau, Washington.

Exports of Breadstuffs (monthly); published by the Treasury Department, Bureau of Statistics, S. G. Brock, chief of bureau, Washington.

Exports of the Principal Articles of Domestic Provisions (monthly); published by the Treasury Department, Bureau of Statistics, S. G. Brock, chief of bureau, Washington.

National Farm and Fireside, independent; Alex. J. Wedderburn, editor and publisher, Washington.

GEORGIA.

Railroad Record and Engineering Journal (monthly), manufacturing; R. F. Hartford and F. C. Hand, editors, Record Publishing Company, publishers, Atlanta.

Spelman Messenger (monthly), college; L. H. Upton and M. J. Packard, editors, E. O. Werden, publisher, Atlanta.

ILLINOIS.

The Semi-Weekly Inter-Ocean, Republican; Inter-Ocean Publishing Company, publishers, Chicago.

The Standard, religious; Justin A. Smith, editor, Edward Goodman, E. R. and J. S. Dickerson, proprietors, Chicago.

The Weekly Drovers' Journal, trade; Harvey L. Goodall, proprietor, Chicago.

Svenska Amerikanaren, Swedish; Jakob Bouggren, editor, Swedish-American Printing Company, publishers, Chicago.

The Lever, Prohibition; Monitor Publishing Company, publishers, Chicago.

Columbia (Welsh); W. J. Jones, treasurer, Chicago.

Industrial World and Iron Worker, manufacturing; David H. Mason, editor, Industrial World Company, publishers, Chicago.

Pravda, mission work; E. A. Adams, editor and publisher, Chicago.

The Orange Judd Farmer, agricultural; Orange Judd, editor, Orange Judd Farmer Company, publishers, Chicago.

The Religio-Philosophical Journal; Mary E. Bundy, editor and publisher, Chicago.

The Union Signal, W. C. T. U.; Frances E. Willard, Lady Henry Somerset, and Mary Allen West, editors, Woman's Temperance Publishing Association, publishers, Chicago.

The Open Court; Dr. Paul Carus, editor, The Open Court Publishing Company, publishers, Chicago.

Young Men's Era, Y. M. C. A.; Young Men's Era Publishing Company, publishers, Chicago.

The National Reveille (bi-weekly), Sons of Veterans; James I. Lyons, editor and proprietor, Chicago.

The Express, People's Party; Express Printing Company, publishers, Chicago.

The Graphic (illustrated); The Graphic Company, publishers, Chicago.

The Advance, religious; H. S. Harrison, editor, Advance Publishing Company, publishers, Chicago.

The Inland Printer (monthly), typographical; The Inland Printer Company, publishers, Chicago.

The National Journalist (monthly), journalism; B. B. Herbert, editor, National Journalist Publishing Company, publishers, Chicago.

The Humane Journal (monthly); Albert W. Landon, editor and publisher, Chicago,

The Newspaper Union (monthly); J. F. Cramer, president, C. E. Strong, manager, Chicago.

The Dial (semi-monthly), literary; Francis F. Browne, editor, A. C. McClurg & Co., publishers, Chicago.

The National Stenographer (monthly); Isaac S. Dement, editor and publisher, Chicago.

The Kindergarten (monthly); Cora L. Stockham and Andrea Hofer, editors, Kindergarten Publishing Company, publishers, Chicago.

The Young Crusader (monthly), W. C. T. U.; Alice M. Guernsey, editor, Woman's Temperance Publishing Association, publishers, Chicago.

Oak and Ivy Leaf (monthly), Y. W. C. T. U.; Jennie A. Stewart, editor, Woman's Temperance Publishing Association, publishers, Chicago.

Responsive Readings (monthly), W. C. T. U.; Woman's Temperance Publishing Association, publishers, Chicago.

Bible Readings (monthly), religious; Woman's Temperance Publishing Association, publishers, Chicago.

The Specimen (monthly), printing; F. J. Hurlbut, editor, Marder, Luse & Co., publishers, Chicago.

The Advance Guard (monthly), religious; Woman's Temperance Publishing Association, publishers, Chicago.

The American Antiquarian and Oriental Journal (bi-monthly); Stephen D. Peet, editor and publisher, Chicago.

The Western Trail (quarterly); published in the interest of the Chicago, Rock Island & Pacific Railway, Chicago.

The Monist (quarterly), philosophy, religion, science, and sociology; Dr. Pau Carus, editor, Open Court Publishing Company, publishers, Chicago.

The Publishers' Auxiliary (monthly), printing; A. N. Kellogg Newspaper Company, publishers, Chicago.

Quarterly Calendar of the University of Chicago (quarterly); The University Press of Chicago, publishers, Chicago.

The Western Plowman and South and West (semi-monthly), agricultural; J. W. Warr, editor, L. B. Kuhn, manager, Moline.

The Odd Fellows Herald, I. O. O. F.; C. F. Mansfield, editor and proprietor, Mansfield.

The Gospel Messenger, religious; H. B. Brumbaugh, editor and publisher, Mt. Morris, Ill., and Huntington, Pa.

INDIANA.

The Indiana State Journal, Republican; Indianapolis Journal Newspaper Company, publishers, Indianapolis.

Milling (monthly), manufacturing; D. H. Ranck Publishing Company, publishers, Indianapolis.

The Western Horseman; Dr. S. W. McMahan and R. J. Stukey, editors and proprietors, Indianapolis.

The American Nonconformist, People's Party; Vincent Bros., editors, publishers, and proprietors, Indianapolis.

The American Tribune, G. A. R.; W. R. Holloway, editor, American Tribune Company, publishers, Indianapolis.

Mennonitische Rundschau; Mennonite Publishing Company, publishers, Elkhart.

INDIAN TERRITORY.

The Cherokee Advocate, official organ of Cherokee Nation, Republican; H. M. Adair, editor, Wm. Eubanks, translator, W. T. Leoser, foreman and business manager, Talequah.

The Indian Chieftain; D. M. Marrs, editor, Chieftain Publishing Company, publishers, Vinita.

Minco Minstrel, Democratic; Lewis N. Hornbeck, editor, Minstrel Publishing Company, publishers, Minco, Chickasaw Nation.

The Purcell Register; Case & Walker, editors and publishers, Purcell, Chickasaw Nation.

IOWA.

- The Iowa Historical Record (quarterly); published by the State Historical Society, Iowa City.

The Brethren Evangelist (religious); W. R. Holsinger, editor, Brethren Publishing Company, publishers, Waterloo.

LOUISIANA.

Southwestern Christian Advocate, religious; E. W. S. Hammond, editor, Methodist Book Concern, publishers, New Orleans.

The Sugar Bowl and Farm Journal, devoted to the sugar industry and general agriculture; J. Y. Gilmore, editor and proprietor, New Orleans.

MAINE.

The Kennebec Journal, Republican; Clarence B. Burleigh and Chas. F. Flint, editors and publishers, Augusta.

First Maine Bugle (quarterly); Edward P. Tobie, editor, First Maine Cavalry Association, publishers, Rockland.

MARYLAND.

Johns Hopkins University Circulars (monthly); published with the approbation of the Board of Trustees, and printed by John Murphy & Co., Baltimore.

Johns Hopkins University Studies in Historical and Political Science (monthly); Herbert B. Adams, editor, The Johns Hopkins Press, publishers, Baltimore.

Tax Reform (monthly), single tax; Tax Reform Publishing Company, W. J. Atkinson, secretary, Chestertown.

MASSACHUSETTS.

Boston Daily Advertiser; Advertiser Newspaper Company, publishers, Boston.

Saturday Evening Gazette; B. E. Wolf, editor, Wm. Baker, business manager, Boston.

The Woman's Journal, equal suffrage; Lucy Stone, H. B. Blackwell, and Alice Stone Blackwell, editors, Boston.

The Woman's Column, equal suffrage; Alice Stone Blackwell, editor, Boston.

The Boston Investigator; Lemuel K. Washburn, editor, Ernest Mendum, proprietor, Boston.

The New Nation; Edward Bellamy, editor, Boston.

The Golden Rule, Young People's Society Christian Endeavor; Francis E. Clark, editor, Golden Rule Publishing Company, publishers, Boston.

The Weekly Bulletin of Newspaper and Periodical Literature; J. Morris Fuller, editor and publisher, Boston.

—9

United States Investor, finance; The Investor Publishing Company, publishers, Boston.

The Youth's Companion; Perry Mason & Co., publishers, Boston.

The New Jerusalem Magazine (monthly), religious; Massachusetts New Church Union, publishers, Boston.

The Unitarian (monthly), religious; J. T. Sunderland, editor, Geo. H. Ellis, publisher, Boston.

The Green Bag (monthly), for lawyers; Horace W. Fuller, editor, Boston Book Company, publishers, Boston.

The Dawn, Christian socialism; W. D. P. Bliss, editor and proprietor, Boston.

Living Issues (monthly); W. D. P. Bliss, editor and proprietor, Boston.

Journal of American Folk-Lore (quarterly); Wm. Wells Newell, editor, published for the American Folk-Lore Society, by Houghton, Mifflin & Co., Boston.

Bulletin of the Boston Public Library (quarterly); published by the trustees, Boston.

The Well Spring (Sunday school); Congregational Sunday-school and Publishing Society, Boston.

The Writer, (monthly); W. H. Hills, editor and publisher, Boston.

Dedham Historical Register (quarterly); Julius H. Tuttle, editor, Dedham Historical Society, publishers, Dedham.

The Hyde Park Historical Record (quarterly); Edmund Davis, editor, Hyde Park Historical Society, publishers, Hyde Park.

The American Journal of Psychology (quarterly); G. S. Hall, editor, J. H. Orpha, publisher, Worcester.

The Pedagogical Seminary (three times a year); G. S. Hall, editor, J. H. Orpha, publisher, Worcester.

The Worcester Despatch; Despatch Publishing Company, Worcester.

Harvard University Bulletin (occasional); Justin Winsor, editor, Cambridge.

Bulletin of the Essex Institute (occasional); Henry M. Brooks, secretary, Salem.

MICHIGAN.

The Plaindealer, Republican; The Plaindealer Company, publishers, Detroit.

Pernin's Monthly Stenographer; H. M. Pernin, editor and publisher, Detroit.

The Quarterly Register of Current History (quarterly); Alfred S. Johnson, editor, Evening News Association, publishers, Detroit.

The Advent Review and Sabbath Herald, religious; Uriah Smith, editor, Seventh Day Adventist Publishing Association, publishers, Battle Creek.

MINNESOTA.

The Northwest Magazine (monthly); E. V. Smalley, editor and publisher, St. Paul.

The Gospel Message (monthly); religious; T. C. Horton, editor, Gospel Union Publishing Company, publishers, St. Paul.

The Free Baptist, religious; J. T. Ward, editor, Western Free Baptist Publishing Society, publishers, Minneapolis.

The American Geologist (monthly); The Geological Publishing Company, publishers, Minneapolis.

Medical Argus (monthly); F. F. Casseday, editor and proprietor, Minneapolis.

MISSOURI.

The Kansas City Daily Times, Democratic; Kansas City Times Newspaper Company, publishers, Kansas City.

Kansas City Daily Journal, Republican; The Journal Company, publishers, Kansas City.

The Kansas City Star (daily and weekly), independent; Kansas City.

The Kansas City Mail (daily), Democratic; The Mail Printing Company, publishers, Kansas City.

Kansas City Live-Stock Indicator; Indicator Publishing Company, publishers, P. D. Etue, secretary and manager, Kansas City.

The Kansas City Record, list of newspapers; A. N. Kellogg Newspaper Company, publishers, Kansas City.

Western Newspaper Union, list of newspapers; Western Newspaper Union, publisher, Kansas City.

Lanphear's Kansas City Medical Index (monthly); Emory Lanphear, editor and publisher, Kansas City.

Missouri and Kansas Farmer (monthly), agricultural; Cliff M. Brooke, editor and publisher, Kansas City.

The Insurance Magazine (monthly); D. W. Wilder, editor and publisher, Kansas City.

The National Dairyman (monthly); Spencer & Barrick, editors and publishers, Kansas City.

Christian Endeavor Monitor (monthly), Y. P. S. C. E.; Bess M. Page, editor, local Union of Christian Endeavor, publishers, Kansas City.

U. S. Department of Agriculture Weather Map, Precipitation Chart (daily); published by authority of Secretary of Agriculture, Mark W. Harrington, chief, Kansas City.

St. Louis Globe-Democrat (daily), Republican; Globe Printing Company, publishers, St. Louis.

Central Christian Advocate, religious; Jesse Bowman Young, editor, Cranston & Curts, publishers, St. Louis.

The Christian Evangelist, religious; J. H. Garrison and B. W. Johnson, editors, Christian Publishing Company, publishers, St. Louis.

The Mid-Continent, religious; Meade C. Williams, editor, Presbyterian Newspaper Company, publishers, St. Louis and Kansas City.

American Journal of Education and National Educator (monthly); J. B. Merwin, managing editor, St. Louis.

The Altruist (monthly), devoted to common property and community homes; Alcander Longley, editor and publisher, St. Louis.

Missouri, Kansas, Nebraska and Illinois Broom-Corn Reporter (monthly); Solomon Schulein, editor and publisher, St. Louis and Chicago.

The National Reformer (monthly), People's Party; W. S. Morgan, editor, St. Louis.

The St. Joseph Herald (daily and weekly), Republican; Herald Publishing Company, publishers, St. Joseph.

St. Joseph Weekly Gazette, Democratic; C. F. Cochran, editor and manager, Gazette Publishing Company, publishers, St. Joseph.

The Border Chief, Democratic; J. J. Trickett, editor and publisher, Amsterdam.

The Triple Link (semi-monthly), I. O. O. F.; J. B. Jewell, editor and publisher, Carrollton.

Minden Itemizer, independent; Geo. W. Hammond and Ralph Richards, editors, Minden Mines.

Foster News, independent Democratic; W. D. Sylvester, editor, Sylvester Bros., publishers, Foster.

NEBRASKA.

Nebraska State Journal (daily and semi-weekly), Republican; State Journal Company, publishers, Lincoln.

Western Resources, stock; H. S. Reed, editor and general manager, Lincoln.

New York Tribune (daily), Republican; New York.

New York Weekly Witness, religious; John Dougall & Co., editors and publishers, New York.

The Irish World, Republican; Patrick Ford, editor and proprietor, New York.

The Voice, Prohibition; Funk & Wagnalls Company, publishers, New York.

Kawkab America (the Star of America), an Oriental weekly; Dr. A. J. and N. J. Arbeely, editors and publishers, New York.

Scientific American, manufacturing; O. D. Munn and A. E. Beach, editors and proprietors, New York.

Scientific American Supplement, manufacturing; O. D. Munn and A. E. Beach, editors and proprietors, New York.

Scientific American, Architects' and Builders' edition (monthly); O. D. Munn and A. E. Beach, editors and proprietors, New York.

War Cry, official organ of the Salvation Army in America; Wm. H. Cox, editor, Ballington Booth, proprietor, New York.

Electrical Review, illustrated; Chas. W. Price, editor, New York.

Twentieth Century; Joseph Fitzgerald, editor; Humboldt Publishing Company, publishers, New York.

The Literary Digest; Funk & Wagnalls Company, publishers, New York.

Sabbath Reading, religious; John Dougall & Co., publishers, New York.

The American Sentinel, religious; Alonzo T. Jones, editor, New York.

The Publishers' Weekly, a book trade journal; R. R. Bowker, manager, New York.

The Journalist; Allen Forman, editor and proprietor, New York.

American Economist; American Protective Tariff League, publishers, New York.

Insurance; S. H. Davis, editor, S. H. Davis and Chas. D. Lakey, publishers, New York.

The International Bookseller; Hugh Craig, editor, N. R. Monachesi, publisher, New York.

Beadle's Dime Library; Beadle & Adams, publishers, New York.

Beadle's Half-Dime Library; Beadle & Adams, publishers, New York.

Magazine of American History (monthly); Mrs. Martha J. Lamb, editor, New York.

The National Magazine (monthly), historical; The National History Company, publishers, New York.

The Review of Reviews (monthly), American edition; Albert Shaw, editor, The Review of Reviews, publishers, New York.

Goldthwaite's Geographical Magazine (monthly); Wm. M. Goldthwaite, editor and publisher, New York.

The Engineering Magazine (monthly); The Engineering Magazine Company, publishers, New York.

The Forum (monthly); The Forum Publishing Company, publishers, New York.

The Library Journal (monthly), official organ of the American Library Association; C. A. Cutter and R. R. Bowker, editors, New York.

The Literary News (monthly); A. H. Leypoldt, editor, New York.

Newspaperdom (monthly); Chas. S. Patterson, editor and proprietor, New York.

D. Appleton & Co.'s Monthly Bulletin; D. Appleton & Co., editors and publishers, New York.

The American Bookseller (monthly); The American Bookseller, publishers, New York.

The Phonographic World (monthly), phonograpy; E. N. Miner, editor, E. N. Miner and F. R. Madeira, publishers, New York.

The Students' Journal (monthly), phonography; Andrew J. Graham, editor and publisher, New York.

The American Woman's Journal (monthly); Mary F. Seymour, editor and publisher, New York.

The National Temperance Advocate (monthly); National Temperance Society and Publication House, publishers, New York.

The Magazine of Christian Literature (monthly); The Christian Literature Company, publishers, New York.

The American Missionary (monthly); American Missionary Association, publishers, New York.

The Home Missionary (monthly); American Home Missionary Society, publishers, New York.

The Silver Cross (monthly); published by the Central Council of the International Order of the King's Daughters and Sons, New York.

Our Animal Friends (monthly), humane; published by the American Society for the Prevention of Cruelty to Animals, New York.

The Sheltering Arms (monthly), an official advertiser for charitable societies and institutions; The Sheltering Arms, publishers, New York.

The Charities Review (monthly); Charity Organization Society of the city of New York, publishers, New York.

Educational Review (monthly), educational; Nicholas Murray Butler, editor, Henry Holt & Co., publishers, New York.

Good Roads (monthly); Isaac B. Potter, managing editor, League Roads Improvement Bureau, New York.

The Decorator and Furnisher (monthly), arts; The Art-Trades Publishing and Printing Company, publishers, New York.

Building and Loan News (monthly), devoted to the interests of the building associations; Building and Loan News Company, publishers, New York.

Free Russia (monthly); published monthly by the Society of Friends of Russian Freedom, New York.

The American Agriculturist (monthly); Orange Judd Company, publishers, New York.

Notes on New Books (quarterly); G. P. Putnam's Sons, publishers, New York.

The Journal of the Cincinnati Society of Natural History (quarterly); David L. James, editor, Cincinnati.

The Christian Educator (quarterly), religious; J. C. Hartzell and Geo. W. Gray, editors, Cincinnati.

Herald of Gospel Liberty, religious; J. P. Watson, editor, Geo. E. Merrell, publishing agent, Dayton.

Le Pasteur (quarterly); published by the Pasteur-Chamberland Filter Company, Dayton.

American Farm News (monthly), agricultural; Akron Printing and Publishing Company, publishers, Akron.

Womankind (monthly); Josephine Hill, managing editor, Hosterman Publishing Company, publishers, Springfield.

Cincinnati Nonpareil (monthly); Milo J. Harris, editor, Nonpareil Publishing Company, publishers, Camden.

OKLAHOMA.

The Evening Gazette, Democratic; Evening Gazette Company, publishers, Oklahoma.

Oklahoma Daily Times-Journal, Republican; J. J. Burke and E. E. Brown, editors and publishers, Oklahoma.

Oklahoma State Capital, Republican; Frank H. Greer, editor, State Capital Printing Company, publishers, Guthrie.

Canadian County Courier, Democratic; G. W. McClintick, editor and publisher, El Reno.

The Kingfisher Free Press, Republican; Jas. L. Admire, editor and proprietor, Kingfisher.

The Edmond Oklahoma Sun, Republican; J. E. Quein, editor and publisher, Edmond.

The Norman Transcript, Republican; Ed. P. Ingle, editor and proprietor, Norman.

Hennessey Clipper, Republican; J. B. Campbell, editor and publisher, Hennessey.

The Langston City Herald, Republican; W. L. Eagleson, editor, Herald Publishing Company, publishers, Langston.

OREGON.

The Way, The Truth, The Life (monthly), religious; W. T. Ellis, editor and publisher, Portland.

PENNSYLVANIA.

Public Ledger (daily), Republican; Geo. W. Childs, editor and publisher, Philadelphia.

The Sunday School Times, religious; John D. Wattles, editor and publisher, Philadelphia.

Farm and Fireside (bi-monthly), agriculture; Mast, Crowell & Kirkpatrick, publishers, Philadelphia.

Paper and Press (monthly), devoted to printing, etc.; Wm. M. Patton, publisher and proprietor, Philadelphia.

Lithographers' Journal (monthly); Wm. M. Patton, publisher and proprietor, Philadelphia.

University Extension (monthly), educational; The American Society for the Extension of University Teaching, publishers, Philadelphia.

Sunday School Missionary (monthly), religious; The American Sunday School Union, publishers, Philadelphia.

Book News (monthly); John Wanamaker, publisher, Philadelphia.

Food, Home, and Garden (monthly); Henry S. Clubb, editor, Vegetarian Society of America, publishers, Philadelphia.

The Naturalist's Leisure Hour and Monthly Bulletin (monthly); A. E. Foote, editor and publisher, Philadelphia.

The Sugar Beet (bi-monthly); Lewis S. Ware, editor, Henry Carey Baird & Co., publishers, Philadelphia.

The Microscopical Bulletin and Science News (bi-monthly); Edward Pennock, editor, Jas. W. Queen & Co., publishers, Philadelphia.

Annals of the American Academy of Political and Social Science (bi-monthly); Edmund J. James, editor, American Academy of Political and Social Science, publishers, Philadelphia.

American Manufacturer and Iron World; Joseph D. Weeks, editor, National Iron and Steel Publishing Company, publishers, Pittsburg.

Farmers' Friend and Grange Advocate, Grange; R. H. Thomas, editor, Mechanicsburg.

Zion's Watch Tower (bi-monthly), religious; C. T. Russell, editor, Tower Publishing Company, publishers, Allegheny.

The Poultry Keeper (monthly); P. H. Jacobs, editor, Poultry Keeper Company, publishers, Parkesburg.

The Red Man (monthly), published in the interest of Indian education; printed by Indian boys at Indian Industrial School, Carlisle.

The People's Magazine (monthly), story; Franklin News Company, publishers, Philadelphia.

The Christian Statesman, religious; Rev. Wilbur F. Crafts and Rev. J. T. McCrory, editors, published by the Reform Bureau, Philadelphia.

RHODE ISLAND.

Magazine of New England History (quarterly); R. H. Tilley, editor and publisher, Newport.

SOUTH CAROLINA.

The Centenary (monthly); A. W. Moore, editor, C. H. Prince, publisher, Florence.

TENNESSEE.

State Board of Health Bulletin (monthly); J. Berrien Lindsley, secretary, Nashville.

TEXAS.

The Houston Daily Post, Democratic; Houston Printing Company, publishers, Houston.

Texas Live-Stock and Farm Journal; Geo. B. Loving, editor and manager, Stock Journal Publishing Company, publishers, Fort Worth.

The Southern Mercury, People's Party; Milton Park, editor and manager, Dallas.

Texas School Journal (monthly), education; J. E. Rodgers, editor and publisher, Dallas.

The Velasco Times, Democratic; The Times Publishing Company, publishers, Velasco.

The Alvin Sun; J. D. Battle, editor and publisher, Alvin.

UTAH.

The Irrigation Age (bi-monthly); Smythe, Britton & Poore Company, publishers, Denver, Salt Lake, and San Francisco.

VIRGINIA.

Southern Workman and Hampton School Record (monthly); S. C. Armstrong, Helen W. Ludlow, Alice M. Bacon, Cora M. Folsom, and Eli Whitney Blake, jr., editors, Hampton.

WEST VIRGINIA.

Southern Historical Magazine (monthly); Virgil A. Lewis, publisher, Charleston.

WYOMING.

The Daily Boomerang, People's Party; Boomerang Publishing Company, publishers, Laramie.

FRANCE.

Société de Géographie Comptes Rendus des Seances de la Commission Centrale (semi-monthly); Paris.

Chronique de la Société des Gens de Lettres (monthly); Paris.

Bulletin de la Société de Géographie (quarterly); Paris.

Bulletin de la Société de Géographie Commerciale (quarterly); Paris.

Bulletin des Seances de la Société Nationale d'Agriculture du France (monthly); Paris.

Bulletin de la Société de Géographie de Lyon (monthly); Lyon.

Bulletin de la Société de Géographie de l'Est (quarterly); Nancy.

Bulletin de la Société de Géographie Commerciale (bi-monthly); Havre.

Bulletin de la Société de Géographie de Rochefort (quarterly); Paris et Rochefort.

Bulletin de la Société de Géographie de Toulouse (bi-monthly); Toulouse.

Union Geographique du Nord de la France (quarterly); Donai.

MEXICO.

La Revista Agricola (semi-monthly), agriculture; A. A. Portillo & Co., editors, published under the auspices of the Secretaria de Fomento, City of Mexico.

El Hyo del Ahuizote (illustrated political weekly); Daniel Cabrera, director and proprietor, City of Mexico.

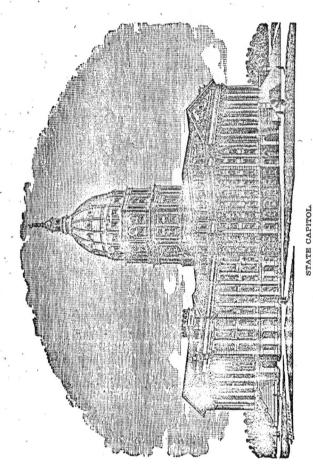

STATE CAPITOL.

NINTH BIENNIAL REPORT

OF THE

BOARD OF DIRECTORS

OF THE

KANSAS STATE HISTORICAL SOCIETY,

FOR THE PERIOD

COMMENCING NOVEMBER 16, 1892, AND ENDING NOVEMBER 20, 1894.

ALSO

PROCEEDINGS OF THE MEETINGS, 1895.

———

TOPEKA.
PRESS OF THE HAMILTON PRINTING COMPANY:
EDWIN H. SNOW, State Printer.
1895.

OFFICERS FOR THE YEARS 1893-'95.

PERCIVAL G. LOWE............Leavenworth..........*President, 1893.*
VINCENT J. LANE..............Kansas City..........*President, 1894.*
SOLON O. THACHER...........Lawrence.............*President, 1895.*
LEVI DUMBAULD..............Hartford.............*Vice President, 1893.*
VINCENT J. LANE...............Kansas City..........*Vice President 1983.*
W. L. BROWN................Kingman..............*Vice President, 1894.*
JAS. B. ABBOTT.................De Soto..............*Vice President, 1894–'95.*
HARRISON KELLEY...........Burlington............*Vice President, 1895.*
FRANKLIN G. ADAMS..........Topeka..............*Secretary, 1893–'95.*
T. DWIGHT THACHER..........Topeka..............*Treasurer, 1893.*
JOHN GUTHRIE................Topeka..............*Treasurer, 1894–'95.*

EXECUTIVE COMMITTEE:

E. N. MORRILL. C. K. HOLLIDAY. F. P. BAKER. WILLIAM SIMS. S. McLALLIN.

LEGISLATIVE COMMITTEE:

C. K. HOLLIDAY. F. P. BAKER. E. J. DALLAS. E. F. WARE. A. R. GREENE.
W. L. BROWN. W. J. COSTIGAN. E. B. COWGILL. A. J. FELT.
T. A. McNEAL. ARTHUR CAPPER. J. S. EMERY.

NOMINATING COMMITTEE:

S. A. KINGMAN. P. McVICAR. A. B. WHITING. F. P. MacLENNAN. F. WELLHOUSE.

COMMITTEE ON MEMORIALS:

V. J. LANE. D. R. ANTHONY. JOHN GUTHRIE.

COMMITTEE ON PROGRAM AND ADDRESSES:

E. F. WARE. D. W. WILDER. G. W. MARTIN. A. R. GREENE. CHAS. F. SCOTT.

BOARD OF DIRECTORS.

TABLE OF CONTENTS.

REPORT.

THE ninth biennial report of the Board of Directors of the Kansas State Historical Society is herewith presented. It shows the work of the Society during the two years from November 15, 1892, to November 20, 1894. Its publication has been delayed owing to deficiency in funds in the state printing department.

This Society has been engaged in its work for 19 years. For this period it has been intrusted by the people of the state with the duty of collecting the scattered materials of the eventful history of Kansas and, taking these materials as a basis of making up in the state capitol a general library of reference for the use of the people. The Society was formed by the Kansas State Editorial Association in 1875. That association, then embracing in one body a large representation of the intelligent and thoughtful people of the whole state, at the annual meeting held at Manhattan in April of that year appointed a committee to organize a State Historical Society. The committee organized this Society. Work was begun by the beginning of the centennial year (1876). That year the collections into the library numbered 408 bound and unbound volumes, including volumes of newspaper files. From this small beginning the library has grown to the number of 79,900 volumes, besides an almost innumerable collection of manuscripts, pictures, and historical relics and memorials of every description.

During the period covered by the report there have been added to the library 1,460 volumes of books; 5,346 unbound volumes and pamphlets; 2,776 volumes of newspapers and periodicals; 481 single newspapers containing matter of special historical interest; 326 maps, atlases, and charts; 2,891 manuscripts; 312 pictures and other works of art; 17 pieces of scrip, currency, and coin; 2 war relics; and 387 miscellaneous contributions.

Thus, to the library proper, of books, pamphlets, newspapers, and periodicals, during the two years have been added 9,582 volumes. Of these, 9,073 have been procured by gift and exchange, and 509 by purchase.

The total of the library at the present time is as follows: 15,874 bound volumes of books, 48,617 unbound volumes and pamphlets, 15,409 bound newspaper files and volumes of periodicals; in all, 79,900 volumes.

YEARLY GROWTH OF THE LIBRARY.

The following statement shows the yearly growth of the library during the 19 years from 1876 to 1894, inclusive.

YEAR.	Volumes books.	Volumes newspapers and magazines.	Pamphlets.	Total yearly accessions.	Yearly total of the library.
1876	280	54	74	408	408
1877	115	150	501	766	1,174
1878	1,237	710	1,184	3,131	4,305
1879	290	275	491	1,056	5,361
1880	448	448	1,146	2,042	7,403
1881	414	375	1,127	1,916	9,319
1882	1,669	513	2,721	4,903	14,222
1883	307	403	1,088	1,798	16,020
1884	782	807	2,763	4,802	20,322
1885	1,088	678	2,033	3,799	24,121
1886	1,772	1,573	7,975	11,320	35,441
1887	753	1,007	1,543	3,303	38,744
1888	866	988	7,707	9,561	48,305
1889	1,269	1,053	2,248	4,570	52,875
1890	991	1,100	2,960	5,051	57,926
1891	719	1,280	4,591	6,590	64,516
1892	1,464	1,219	3,119	5,802	70,318
1893	709	1,197	1,968	3,874	74,192
1894	751	1,579	3,378	5,708	79,900
Totals	15,874	15,409	48,617	79,900	

Of the accessions of books and pamphlets during the two years, 385 volumes have been purchased and 6,421 have come by gift and exchange. Of newspapers and magazines, 189 volumes have been purchased and 2,587 have been donated to the Society. The lists and tables in the report show the sources from which all the accessions of the different classes have come.

KANSAS NEWSPAPERS.

To the bound volumes of newspapers and magazines published in Kansas, 1,635 volumes have been added during the two years. These have all been donated to the Society by the publishers. The library now contains on its shelves 10,689 bound volumes of Kansas newspapers and magazines. This is a larger collection of local historical materials of this class than is contained in any other library in the world. Of newspapers and magazines published in other states, the library contains 4,720 volumes.

SOURCES—LEGAL REQUIREMENTS.

The accessions to the library come by gift, by exchange, and by purchase. Those by gift and exchange come largely from societies and institutions, and from state, government, municipal and other public authorities. The purchases come from booksellers. These three means of building up the library are contemplated in the law which recognized our Historical Society as an institution of the state and provided for its maintenance and the care of its

collections—the act of the legislature of 1879. In the language of the act, it is the duty of the Society to procure, "by gift and exchange, scientific and historical reports of the legislatures of other states, of railroads, reports of geological and other scientific surveys, and of such other books, maps, charts, and materials as will facilitate the investigation of historical, scientific, social, educational and literary subjects," and "to purchase books to supply deficiencies in the various departments of its collections."

The Society had been engaged in its work three years before its duties were specifically defined by law. The law was evolved from the experience of those three years. With little money expended, by 1879 a library of 4,300 volumes had been made up by the Society in the statehouse. It had grown almost wholly from gifts and exchanges. Now the state by law provided for the care of the library, and for its future growth. To enable the Society to augment its collections through exchanges, the legislature provided that, with one exception, there should be given it 60 bound copies of all of the publications of the state and of its institutions. It made the Society "the trustee of the state," imposed upon it definite duties in the discharge of its trust, and, with the Society's consent, took its library and collections into its keeping as the property of the state.

The legislature made it the duty of the Society to continue as hitherto in its work of making up a library of reference in history, science, education, politics, and in the various departments of human knowledge, by soliciting gifts and making exchanges, and by purchasing such books as might be necessary to supply the deficiencies in the various departments. Purchases had become quite necessary. A foundation had been made for a large library of general reference in all departments. Experience had shown that the growth by gift and exchange was resulting in making a library very incomplete in its various departments. As a consequence, in the use of the library, there would be found but incomplete sets of books upon any subject of investigation. The law, for this reason, provided that purchases should be made to supply the deficiencies in such sets, so that a well-rounded and well-filled library of reference should be made up for the use of students, investigators, and writers upon all subjects of common inquiry.

PURCHASES INSUFFICIENT.

Up to the present time, the appropriations for purchases have been wholly inadequate to supply deficiencies. They have been usually but $500 annually. This is a trifling and insignificant amount compared with the accessions by gift, and compared with what is being expended by other states for such purchases. Wisconsin, Minnesota, Illinois, and Iowa, for example, give for the purchase of books for their historical libraries from $3,000 to $5,000 annually.

Take one class of gifts alone—that of newspapers and magazines. The newspaper publishers of Kansas are giving to the library, annually, about 860 volumes. These, at the rates paid by subscribers, would give to the pub-

lishers an aggregate of at least $1,000 per year. This sum is thus being do-
nated annually to the state by one class of our citizens to aid in building up
the historical library of Kansas. The generosity of these givers stands in
striking contrast with the meagerness of the state appropriations for accessions to the library. This library is for the use of all the people of the state.
No other part of the library is being so much consulted as are the newspaper
files. In them, search is made by citizens of all parts of the state for legal
notices, for dates and details of occurrence of events, for facts concerning the
organization and movement of political and social bodies, and, in fact, concerning all the numberless subjects which enter into the busy life of our people, and which find so full a record in our local newspapers.

Our library contains the files of the newspapers of every county in the
state. Considering the small proportion in numbers which the class of newspaper publishers bears to the number of citizens of the state at large, the
generosity of the one class by no means finds proper recognition. These newspaper people were the founders of the State Historical Society. To them the
state owes the existence of a library already unequaled, in the value of its
local historical material, by that of any state of the union. It is certainly
demanded that the state should respond to the liberality of the newspaper
publishers, by adequate appropriations for making this library complete in
all its departments.

NEWSPAPERS AS MATERIALS OF HISTORY.

It cannot be said that these newspaper files are not worth in this library
the price of their subscription rates. They contain the history of Kansas.
No part of Kansas history can be written without consulting these files.
Hon. Nelson Case, of Oswego, the author of the recently published history
of Labette county, one of the most complete histories yet written of any
Kansas county, says:

"I think that anyone who has considered the matter, and especially anyone who has had any experience in writing local history, will agree with me
in saying there is no help so complete and accurate as the home newspaper
in giving the happenings in any community."

Says Hon. John Maloy, the very capable historian of Morris county:

"Speaking of the importance of the newspaper files in your Society's
rooms, I do not think the history of any county in our state could be written without consulting them. . . . I could not now do anything in the
way of sketching the history, biography or incidents of Morris county
without having recourse to the files of your library. I regard the State
Historical Society as one of the indispensable institutions of our state: one,
however, too little appreciated and too begrudgingly aided and fostered by
legislation."

In a recent article in the *Forum* magazine, President Eliot, of Harvard
University, says of the American newspapers of the present time, that,

"Taken together with magazines and the controversial pamphlets, they

shed more light on the social, industrial and political life of the people of the United States than was ever shed before on the doings and ways of any people. Many people," he says, "are in the habit of complaining bitterly of the intrusion of the newspaper reporter into every nook and corner of the state, and even into the privacy of the home; but in this extreme publicity is to be found the means of social, industrial and governmental reform and progress."

The newspaper which thus enlightens the public becomes an enduring record of history when preserved in a library. It carries down to the succeeding generations the story of the social, industrial and political life of the people, as the world moves forward in change and progress. For Kansas, all the newspapers published in the state are thus being preserved. A newspaper association established the Society, and newspaper publishers are making the most valuable additions to its library.

Our Society stands foremost among the historical societies in this country in the work of saving newspapers as materials of local history. Various causes have prompted the Society to diligence and thoroughness in this work; chiefly, that the Society was established by newspaper men; that the newspaper men of the state have always comprised the principal membership of the Society; and that they have always taken a pride and interest in the work which the Society is doing for the state. Historical societies and librarians have always valued this library feature. But it would seem that never, until in the instance of our Society, has an institution been so constituted as that sufficient attention and labor have been given to this department to make its work thorough and complete.

Twenty-two years ago, Hon. A. R. Spofford, the distinguished librarian of Congress, the foremost of all library makers, said, in the Centennial History of Libraries in the United States, 1876:

"The modern newspapers and other periodical publications afford the truest, the fullest, and, on the whole, the most impartial image of the age we live in that can be derived from any single source. Taken together, they afford the richest materials for the historian, or the student of politics, of society, of literature, and of civilization in its various aspects. What precious memorials of the day even the advertisements and brief paragraphs of the newspapers of a century ago afford us. . . .

"While the files of the journals of any period furnish unquestionably the best instruments for the history of that epoch, it is lamentable to reflect that so little care has ever been taken to preserve a fair representation of those of any age. The destiny of nearly all newspapers is swift destruction, and even those which are preserved commonly survive in a provokingly fragmentary state. These poor journals of to-day, which everybody is ready to stigmatize as trash, not worth the room to store or the money to bind, are the very materials which the man of the future will search for with eagerness, and for some of which he will be ready to pay their weight in gold. These representatives of the commercial, industrial, inventive, social, literary, political, moral and religious life of the times should be preserved and handed down to posterity with sedulous care. No historian, or other writer on any subject, who would write conscientiously or with full information, can afford to

neglect this fruitful mine of the journals, where his richest materials are frequently to be found."

Said our own lamented governor, John A. Martin, referring to the files of his own newspaper, afterwards mainly destroyed by fire:

"Piled up in the corner of the *Champion* office is the most complete history of Atchison that will ever be written. It is comprised in 35 bound volumes of the *Champion*, weekly and daily, from the first issue made by the present proprietor, February 20, 1858, up to the present time. In these papers — many of them beginning to take on the yellow hue of age — every essential fact connected with the growth and development and daily life of the city of Atchison is recorded — marriages and deaths; the establishment of business and manufacturing enterprises, and their changes; transfers of property; the erection of all important buildings; the results of elections; the opening of streets; the building of railroads; fires and floods; the municipal policies suggested, discussed, and adopted; and the daily life, thoughts, hopes, triumphs and disappointments of an aspiring and energetic community are all embodied in these files."

SOME CLASSES OF BOOKS.

It must not be thought that our Society, in its high appreciation of its newspaper work, is neglecting other departments. Within its means, it is making up a very full library of reference in every department. Into this library is being brought everything published in Kansas upon all subjects. In its general library, it is becoming very full in works relating to the discovery, exploration and settlement of the Western country, and of this class contains no less than 835 volumes; in works relating to Indian history, 442 volumes; in general history, United States history, and the history of the several states, we possess 2,875 volumes; in biography, 1,026 volumes; in science, 4,088 volumes; in education, 1,956 volumes; in political science and political economy, 3,910 volumes; relating to trade and commerce, 1,120 volumes; to agriculture, 1,154 volumes; in religion, 1,206 volumes; relating to charitable subjects, 1,417 volumes.

The history of this country during the last 40 years has hinged upon the history of Kansas. The industry and efficiency of the Kansas State Historical Society, in collecting the materials of Kansas history and of the history of the country in all respects, has attracted the attention of appreciative people everywhere. Hence, around our nucleus of local history has grown up, mainly by gift and exchange, the publications of almost every society and institution throughout this country and of many in the old world. The lists of donations contained in our ninth biennial report show that accessions, chiefly of books and pamphlets, come from more than a thousand different sources.

WAR BOOKS.

In respect to special features of library collections, there are two classes of books in which the library should be made very complete: First, all books written about Kansas history, and books of Kansas authorship of all kinds;

and second, books written upon the history of the war of the rebellion. As to the first class, the library is being made complete by the generous gifts of Kansas authors and publishers. In respect to the latter class, it is far from being made complete. It may be said that the period of the early history of Kansas, during which our people struggled through unsurpassed difficulties into a state existence, was but a prelude to the war of the rebellion. The war for the preservation of the union and of its free institutions raged for six years in Kansas; was fought almost single-handed here by our pioneer settlers before it was taken up by the nation and fought out to its glorious end.

Every well-written book pertaining to the war should be brought into the state historical library. A nucleus for such a library of war history has been gathered in, numbering 511 volumes. There are yet hundreds of volumes pertaining to the details of the war, written in large part by the actors in it, which should be brought into the library in order that it shall be made a complete library of reference as to the history of the great epoch in which Kansas history formed so considerable a feature. A very moderate estimate would call for a present expenditure of a sum of not less than $1,000 for the purchase of books of this class.

SPECIAL GIFTS.

Of the 2,891 manuscript papers and books of special interest given the Society during the two years, may be mentioned those given by Mr. Orville C. Brown, of Adams, N. Y. Mr. Brown was, more than any other person, the founder of Osawatomie. He was a prominent citizen of Kansas during the entire territorial period, and active in public affairs in many useful ways. He met with serious losses from pro-slavery depredations and outrages. His manuscripts given the Society relate, in large part, to matters of early Kansas history.

Hon. J. C. Burnett gives some interesting papers relating to political affairs at important crises in Kansas history.

Prof. I. T. Goodnow before his death, which occurred less than a year ago, added to his former gifts many manuscripts of much interest relating to public affairs in the later '50s, especially relating to the founding of the State Agricultural College — an institution to the establishment of which he, perhaps, contributed more of wise effort than any other person.

Gen. John A. Halderman has again given bountifully from his stores of papers saved through a long period of public life, extending from the earliest Kansas days to the present time. Among these papers are many letters written by Gov. Andrew H. Reeder and other prominent public men of Kansas territorial times, and by many others in different parts of this country and of the world.

The manuscript papers of the late Hon. James Hanway, which have for a number of years been in the possession of the Society as a conditional deposit, have, through the generosity of his son, Mr. John S. Hanway, of Lane,

been brought permanently into the collections of the Society. These papers are of great interest as reflecting the life work of an earnest student, industrious writer, and faithful public servant, for many years an active citizen of Kansas and a zealous promoter of her best institutions.

Col. R. J. Hinton has contributed important additions to his former gifts, including many papers relating to early Kansas free-state immigration, to measures of resistance against pro-slavery aggression, to John Brown history, and to the war of the rebellion.

Rev. J. D. Knox has given valuable manuscript papers and books relating to the history of the freedmen's exodus from the Southern states to Kansas, and to the work of the Kansas Freedmen's Relief Association in caring for the exiles in 1879–'81.

Miss Eva Ryan, of Hiawatha, has given some autograph poems of the late Mrs. Ellen P. Allerton.

J. B. Whitaker, of Topeka, has given a large number of official papers, which illustrate the methods of the pro-slavery party in harassing and persecuting free-state settlers.

The Kansas Baptist convention, at its late session at Winfield, upon the suggestion of Rev. J. B. Thomas, of Topeka, voted to place the important papers of the convention, not needed for immediate use, in the custody of our Society. These have been brought into our collections, numbering 261 pamphlets, containing the minutes and proceedings of Kansas Baptist associations and conventions; 2,202 manuscript papers, and 37 manuscript books. Mr. Thomas contributed from his own collection 72 pamphlets. This denomination publishes more largely than any other the proceedings of its local organizations.

This is the third instance in which ecclesiastical bodies of Kansas have chosen to place in our state archives the materials of the early history of their organization and work. The two former deposits were made by conferences of the Methodist Episcopal church — the parent organization, the Kansas Conference, and the South Kansas conference. Church organizations have always been powerful promoters of the immigration of the better class of settlers into the new states. The circumstances attending the settlement of our own state invited the incoming of people imbued with religious principles and enthusiasm. The organizations of these bodies were effected at the time our earliest political organizations were being formed. The ministers of the churches were among the active men in political movements. The nature of their calling brought them into the closest relations with the people in their homes, in their social intercourse, in their educational movements, and in all the higher relations of our best elements of civilization. The history of Kansas churches is, in large part, the history of the better Kansas. Our Society has reason to feel a great degree of gratification at the confidence reposed in it as the custodian of the records of these bodies. Taken together with the very large body of original records of the work of

the early missionaries of Kansas, of Meeker, McCoy, Pratt, Johnson, Simmerwell, and others, which have been brought into our library, and of which frequent mention has been made in these reports, it may be doubted if any library in the Mississippi valley now contains so great a fund of materials of missionary and religious history as are crowded into our limited fireproof receptacle. The scantiness of the room for the placing of these precious memorials calls loudly for more ample provision for their keeping.

Rev. Lewis Bodwell, of Clifton Springs, N. Y., has given the Society a very interesting set of views of the oldest Congregational church buildings erected in Kansas, together with portraits of the pastors and their wives. Rev. L. P. Broad, included in a large gift of materials showing his recent work as missionary of the Congregational churches in Kansas, has also given pictures of two Congregational churches, one of them that of a sod church in Osborne county.

An interesting relic of war history is a map made by Col. William Tweeddale, of Topeka, showing the mode of construction of the New Madrid canal, a device which led to the capture of Island No. 10, in the Mississippi river, April 7, 1862. The canal was planned by the donor of this map and it was constructed under his supervision.

In this connection may be mentioned a set of church charts brought into the library through the World's Columbian Exposition. These charts contain data and statistics pertaining to the founding and history of 178 churches and Sunday schools of all denominations in the various counties of Kansas, in many instances with portraits of pastors and views of church edifices. These form a unique and interesting collection of materials of Kansas church history. In the gathering of this history an ingenious blank chart devised by Mrs. J. C. Trotter, of Wichita, has been used. Mrs. A. M. Clark, secretary of the World's Fair board of managers, is deserving of great credit for the interest taken by her in bringing these charts into our library.

Orville C. Brown, of Adams, N. Y., has given a large number of interesting views and portraits. Supt. W. M. Davidson, of Topeka, has given a large number of views of schoolhouses in different portions of the state. Warren Foster, of Hutchinson, has placed in our collection a very interesting memorial descriptive of Abraham Lincoln's home in Kentucky and relating to his marriage. Col. R. J. Hinton has given an interesting collection of John Brown portraiture. A very fine portrait of the late Hon. John C. Vaughan has been given the Society by Hon. Joseph Medill, of Chicago.

A life-sized portrait of Governor Lewelling has been added to our collection of portraits of Kansas governors, the gift of friends of the governor among the state officers and others.

A fine oil-painted portrait of the late Henry J. Adams, the gift of members of his family, has also come into the collections. Mr. Adams was among the most prominent of the early settlers of Kansas, was elected governor under the Leavenworth constitution in 1858, and held many positions of honor and trust. The portrait is the work of the artist George M. Stone.

In compliance with the request of the Society, Maj. James S. Phillips, of the U. S. navy, has added to our picture gallery a fine oil-painted portrait of his father, the late Col. Wm. A. Phillips.

Messrs. Pennell & Zellner, photographers, Junction City, have contributed some excellent views taken at Fort Riley and vicinity, and H. S. Stevenson, photographer, Leavenworth, has given like views of the vicinity of Leavenworth and the fort.

Dr. L. F. Wentworth, of Osawatomie, has added to our picture collection a very fine set of views taken at Osawatomie, including those of the buildings of the state insane asylum, representing various stages of the history of the growth of that institution, a view of the John Brown monument, also of the house of Rev. S. L. Adair, built by him in 1855, in which he still resides, and in which John Brown made his home during his tarrying in Osawatomie, from 1855 to 1859.

Valuable newspaper files have been given by Hon. Joel K. Goodin, of Ottawa, John S. Hanway, of Lane, A. S. Huling, of Topeka, V. J. Lane, of Kansas City, Z. F. Riley and F. A. Root, of Topeka, Gov. A. J. Smith, of the soldiers' home, Leavenworth, Mrs. Jenny M. Ward, of Ottawa, and others.

An interesting relic of the barbarism from which our country escaped during the period of the history of Kansas, is a slave shackle taken by Joseph McFarland, now of Wichita, from the ankle of a negro slave in Missouri, a short time before the war of the rebellion, and brought by donor to Kansas and deposited by him in the collections of our Society. Geo. J. Remsburg, of Atchison, has added to his former gifts of mound-builders' relics. R. J. Traver, of Leoti, has given some very interesting relics from an Indian burial receptacle in Wichita county.

Capt. P. H. Coney has added interesting relics of the Lapland exhibit at the World's Fair. Many interesting relics of the investment of the state-house by the state militia in February, 1893, have been given by various persons of the different parties who took part in the interesting events of that brief period; among these is the sledge hammer used by Speaker George L. Douglass in opening the door of the house of representatives, and which has been deposited by him in our collections.

Among the objects of interest displayed at the World's Columbian Exposition, at Chicago, several have been deposited in the collections of our Historical Society. Among them may be mentioned that deposited by Mrs. Elizabeth Magie, of Girard, for the Grand Chapter of the Order of the Eastern Star in Kansas, being a large banner, in an elaborately carved oak frame, and showing on its face representations of the local chapters throughout the state; an elegant banner deposited by the Woman's Columbian Club of Jewell county, at the hands of Mrs. A. M. Clark; a fine carved and upholstered chair, exhibited by the Woman's Columbian Club of Nemaha county, and deposited by Mrs. Mary E. Todd, secretary; design executed on oak, in carved work and oils, for the Woman's Relief Corps, department of

Kansas, Mrs. Edith M. Wood, president, together with the six national flags used in its decoration.

Among the donors of books and pamphlets worthy of special mention, the following may be named: Kansas Baptist state convention, Rev. L. P. Broad, O. C. Brown, Mrs. A. M. Clark, F. D. Coburn, Chas. S. Davis, Henry T. Drowne, Dr. Samuel A. Green, R. J. Hinton, Indian Rights Association, C. M. Light, George T. Pierce, Z. F. Riley, Frank A. Root, Royal Academy (Stockholm, Sweden), Rev. C. S. Sheffield, Mrs. K. W. Shepperd.

OBITUARY.

During the last two years death has made sad inroads upon the prominent membership of the Society.

Col. William A. Phillips died November 30, 1893, at Fort Gibson, while on a business trip to the Indian Territory. He had always been a prominent figure in Kansas history and had been President of this Society. Memorial proceedings were had at the annual meeting in 1894.

Hon. Timothy Dwight Thacher died January 17, 1894. He had been a citizen of Kansas, with only a brief absence, since 1857, and had all the time taken a leading part in public affairs. He had been President of the Society, and always one of the most useful counselors in the conduct of its work.

Joseph C. Hebbard died January 22, 1894. He was an early citizen of Kansas, and an early member of this Society and of its Board of Directors. As a journalist, he had learned to value, more perhaps than any other, the collections of the Society, as furnishing data upon which to base exact statements in journalistic work in all matters pertaining to Kansas. His loss to the Society cannot be estimated.

Prof. Isaac T. Goodnow died March 20, 1894. He was one of the earliest settlers in Kansas, and was one of the numerous class who came to the new territory with the high purpose of aiding to establish good institutions in the new state to be founded. He came well equipped in learning and maturity of good character to perform a useful part in carrying out such aims. During his life here he occupied many positions of honor and usefulness. He was one of the most active members of the State Historical Society, and one of the most bountiful contributors to its collections.

Ex-Gov. James M. Harvey died April 15, 1894. He was a Kansas soldier in the war for the preservation of the union, a legislator, for two terms governor of the state, and a United States senator from Kansas. For a number of years he was a member of the Board of Directors of this Society, and always manifested an interest in its work.

Ex-Gov. Charles Robinson died August 17, 1894. His name, from the very beginning of the settlement up to the day of his death, was conspicuously linked with the history of Kansas. He ranked foremost among the founders of the state, and for more than a generation was one of the most

prominent of its leading citizens. One of the earliest Presidents of this Society, he was always among the most useful of its members. At our last annual meeting he was present with the Board of Directors, of which he had always been a member, and took an active and interested part in the pro-ceedings.

Memorial proceedings respecting these late distinguished members of our Society have been initiated by our Board of Directors.

PHONOGRAPH.

The Board has ventured upon an experiment with the Edison phonograph as a means of making and preserving historical records. The experiment has been carried to the extent of procuring the records of the voices of Ex-Governors Crawford, Osborn, Glick, and Lewelling, and of Chief Justice Horton. Unfortunately, Governor Robinson was not reached in time to procure a record of his voice; but, upon request, Mrs. Robinson consented to read into the phonograph a portion of Governor Robinson's inaugural address; and thus her voice was put on record in lieu of that of her recently deceased husband's. Brief extracts from the inaugural or other official addresses have been recorded upon phonographic cylinders, to be preserved for use at any time, and for all time, as unique historical records of the voices of the representative officers of the state in the earlier period of her history. It is for the Society and the legislature to determine whether the experiment has so far demonstrated the utility of this mode of preserving history as to warrant its continuance, within such prudent limits as may be established.

ROOMS.

The subject of rooms for the accommodation of the library and collections of the Historical Society is still one of the most important that can engage the Society's attention. The legislature at its last session, 1893, granted three additional rooms, in the south wing of the statehouse, and made an appropriation for furniture and shelving for the same. These added rooms, though far short of supplying our present needs, have greatly facilitated the placing of the library and the general work of the Society.

The grant was made under a concurrent resolution in the following words:

Resolved, That the rooms now occupied by the supreme court commissioners, in the basement of the south wing of the capitol building, be assigned for the additional and temporary use of the State Historical Society, and that it shall be the duty of the state executive council to cause suitable shelving and furniture to be immediately supplied to said rooms for such use.

The Society began its work nearly 19 years ago, without need of room, except desk room for the Secretary and room for a bookcase. These simple needs were found in the state offices, generously and encouragingly given. From time to time since, as needs demanded and as far as the unfinished condition of the statehouse would admit, rooms have been provided, so that now

the Society occupies more room than any other department in the statehouse. It would occupy twice as much as now if its library and collections were suitably placed. The rooms now occupied are in different parts of the basement portion of the capitol building, widely separated, and situated in every way inconvenient for use and access to the public.

In view of the contemplated provision for the completion of the capitol building, it is urgently demanded that plans should now be adopted for permanent and ample rooms for the Society. During the last session of the legislature this subject of permanent rooms was brought before that body, and the state architect was consulted by a legislative committee; but as no action was taken for the completion of the building, nothing was done toward providing permanent quarters for the Society.

In estimating for room space for our library and collections, we have taken the rooms of the Wisconsin state historical library as in considerable measure an index of our needs. That society occupies three floors of a wing of the state capitol building at Madison, built mainly for the use of the society, and completed in 1884. Each floor containing these rooms is 106 feet in length by 62 feet in breadth. The floor space of the three floors is nearly 20,000 square feet. The area of the floor space occupied by our Society at present is about 3,000 feet. Thus, the Wisconsin society occupies nearly seven times as much room as our Society. The library of the Wisconsin society contains 160,000 volumes. Our library contains 79,000 volumes; our library being nearly one-half as large as the Wisconsin library, but possessing but about one-seventh as much room. The Wisconsin society occupies three and a half times the room of one of the floors of a wing of our state capitol building.

These statements show that our library should have provided, for its present and future needs, room space at least equal to that of two entire floors of a wing in our statehouse. These statements are based upon actual measurements. They are made in accordance with library experience and library rules derived from experience. At our present rate of increase, all the space of two floors of one of the wings of our capitol building will be required to answer the needs of our Society within the next five years. A conference with the state architect on this subject has led to the opinion, that in view of existing plans for the completion and occupancy of the capitol building, and in view of assignment of room already made and contemplated, provision for the Historical Society can best be made in the east wing, the two main floors being given for that object. The rooms on those floors, as now understood, will be mainly or wholly vacated by the departments now occupying them by their removal into other portions of the building.*

---

* These recommendations as to room for the permanent home for the Society in the capitol building, as made by our Board of Directors at the November meeting, 1894, received the approval of the legislature of 1895, through the passage of a concurrent resolution directing that the two floors of the east wing of the capitol below the senate chamber be fitted up for the Kansas State Historical Society, when they shall be vacated by the present occupants.

Our Society has calls for present legislative action to supply its urgent needs, as follows: Provision for permanent rooms in the completed capitol building, additional temporary room, increased funds for the purchase of books, additional appropriation for clerk hire, and provision for present printing needs. Our clerical workers—always industrious, skillful, and faithful—have never been adequately paid. Some of them should have increased salaries. And there is an imperative demand for an additional clerk.

Provision should be made at the very outset of the session of the legislature for the printing of this report and for the printing of the catalogue of the Kansas portion of our library, now ready for the printer. Our Society, as before mentioned, in respect to the printing of this report, has fallen under the misfortune resulting from the scant printing appropriation made by the legislature of 1893.

MEETINGS, 1893–'94.

BOARD OF DIRECTORS' MEETING—JANUARY 17, 1893.

The meeting of the Board of Directors, preparatory to the seventeenth annual meeting of the Society, was held in the Society's rooms, January 17, 1893, at 3 P. M.

The following members were present: Hon. Jas. S. Emery, Hon. A. R. Greene, Hon. F. P. Baker, Hon. S. C. Wheeler, Col. D. R. Anthony, Hon. William Sims, Hon. T. D. Thacher, M. Weightman, Hon. Geo. W. Martin, Hon. S. A. Kingman, Hon. V. J. Lane, Hon. P. G. Lowe, Mrs. S. N. Wood, Col. C. K. Holliday, George D. Hale, Dr. P. McVicar, Hon. W. H. McBride, Hon. John Guthrie, and Secretary F. G. Adams.

A. R. Greene, Vice President, presided, in the absence of Gov. Thos. A. Osborn, the President.

The Secretary stated the business of the meeting to be the consideration of reports of committees.

Judge Emery, for the committee previously appointed on the World's Columbian Exposition, made a verbal report, stating that the committee recommend that an exhibit be made from the collections of the Society, consisting of the portraits of prominent Kansans, of pictures illustrating the history of the state, a full collection of books by Kansas authors, as complete a collection as possible of newspapers published in one or two of the older and newer counties, and of mound-builder, Indian and other relics peculiar to Kansas history. Judge Emery mentioned that various private collections had been offered the Society by Kansas citizens for display in connection with the Historical Society's exhibit.

On motion of Mr. Baker, the committee was continued, with full power to act in all matters pertaining to the Society's exhibit, including the presentation of a bill asking the legislature for an appropriation to defray the

actual expenses of such exhibit, with the understanding that no salary should be paid from such appropriation.

The Secretary then read the report of the Committee on Nominations.

The committee appointed to make arrangements for a Whittier celebration reported that, owing to lack of time, they had done nothing in the matter, and, at their request, the committee was discharged.

A resolution was adopted requesting the incoming officers and Executive Committee to appoint a Committee on Legislation.

The Secretary presented the subject of needed additional room for the Society. On motion of Colonel Anthony, a resolution was adopted requesting the Legislative Committee to act with the President and Secretary to frame a bill for presentation to the legislature making provision for room sufficient for the present and future needs of the Society.

On motion of Judge Kingman, the President appointed the following committee of three to draft resolutions on the services and death of Col. Samuel N. Wood, viz.: Col. D. R. Anthony, Hon. J. C. Hebbard, and Hon. George W. Martin.

ANNUAL MEETING OF THE SOCIETY—JANUARY 17, 1893.

The seventeenth annual meeting of the Society was held in the Senate chamber, the evening of January 17, 1893; Vice Pres. Albert R. Greene in the chair.

The Secretary read an abstract of the eighth biennial report of the Society.

Hon. W. H. T. Wakefield, of Lawrence, read a paper on "Squatter Courts in Kansas."

Colonel Holliday then gave a brief history of the origin and of the events of the "Wakarusa War."

A paper written by Mrs. Lois H. Walker (formerly Mrs. George W. Brown) was then read, relating to the bringing into Lawrence, by herself and Mrs. S. N. Wood, of ammunition from the house of Mrs. J. B. Abbott, for the use of the free-state men during the Wakarusa war, and Mrs. Wood made a brief verbal statement of her memories of the event.

The portrait of Col. S. N. Wood was then presented to the Society by his widow, Mrs. Margaret L. Wood, in the following words:

MR. PRESIDENT: One whom the people of Kansas will never forget; one who was a true friend of Kansas, and consequently a true friend of the State Historical Society, and an earnest worker for the objects for which it was instituted; one who was a friend to his fellow-men, and whose heart held a wealth of tenderness and compassion for all who suffer from wrong, oppression, and poverty; one to whom the hand of want never reached out in vain. He may have had faults; I have forgotten what they were. They called him a fighter, and a foe to be dreaded; but whether friend or foe, in the face of want and suffering, his heart was as tender as the heart of a child. That you may keep his features in mind; that you may not in this life forget him, and may know him when you meet him on the blest immortal shore of a better land, I present you this portrait of Samuel N. Wood.

Secretary Adams accepted the portrait in behalf of the Society.

Colonel Anthony read the following resolutions, which were unanimously adopted by the Society:

WHEREAS, By the hand of a cowardly assassin, the Hon. Samuel N. Wood has been taken from us; and

WHEREAS, Colonel Wood was an earnest and most useful member of this Society; a man who himself helped to make Kansas history; a leader and a tower of strength in the early struggles against slavery; a strong, earnest, aggressive laborer in the cause of right, as he saw the right; a bitter, unrelenting foe to every wrong that presented itself to him as wrong: therefore,

Resolved, That it is with deep sorrow that we have heard of the untimely and tragic death of Colonel Wood; and

Resolved, That it is our opinion that there is a radical defect in laws that are impotent to punish his assassin; and

Resolved, That we extend to his bereaved widow, who stood by him for so many years, and was in truth his helpmate in every good work, our heartfelt sympathy, and hereby express the sincere hope that she may continue long to supplement his faithful work, to which she herself so largely contributed; and

Resolved, That these resolutions be spread upon the minutes of this Society, and a copy of them be furnished to Mrs. Margaret L. Wood, the widow.

The Kansas poems of John G. Whittier were then read by Hon. T. D. Thacher. Mr. Thacher prefaced the reading by appropriate remarks relating to the character of Whittier and his great sympathy with the people of Kansas in their efforts to plant the institutions of freedom upon the soil of the new territory. The poems read were the following: "The Kansas Emigrant's Song," "Le Marais du Cygne," "The Burial of Barber," and verses relating to John Brown.

The President offered the following resolution, which was adopted, relating to the subject of private exhibits offered the Society for use at the Chicago exhibition:

Resolved, That the World's Fair committee be authorized and instructed to accept from private donors contributions to the Kansas historical collections in the Kansas building at the World's Fair exhibition, such objects of historical interest as the owners may present for that purpose, the committee to use its discretion as to accepting or rejecting such offers.

The following members of the Board of Directors were then elected, for the term of three years, ending January 21, 1896: Jas. B. Abbott, Lucien Baker, W. L. Brown, J. B. Chapman, E. B. Cowgill, Chas. S. Davis, Mrs. Anna L. Diggs, Levi Dumbauld, A. G. Forney, Warren Foster, H. N. Gaines, J. M. Hagaman, J. C. Hebbard, E. W. Hoch, J. K. Hudson, McCown Hunt, Mrs. Laura M. Johns, L. D. Lewelling, J. T. Little, Dr. S. McLallin, Dr. Peter McVicar, P. B. Maxson, Sol. Miller, M. M. Murdock, N. L. Prentis, J. B. Remington, William Rogers, Chas. F. Scott, Robert H. Semple, A. A. Stewart, S. O. Thacher, W. H. T. Wakefield, A. B. Whiting, and C. A. Woodworth; the latter to fill vacancy caused by the removal of Rev. J. W. D. Anderson from the state.

On the adjournment of the annual meeting, a meeting of the Board of Directors was held, and the following officers of the Society were elected: President, P. G. Lowe; Vice Presidents, Levi Dumbauld and V. J. Lane; Treasurer, T. D. Thacher; Secretary, F. G. Adams.

Mrs. S. N. Wood then introduced Mr. C. H. Dickson as the "boy" who assisted Mrs. Brown and herself in securing the ammunition for the Wakarusa war. Mr. Dickson gave an interesting account of his recollections of the affair.

President Lowe appointed the following committees:

Executive Committee.—C. K. Holliday, L. D. Lewelling, F. P. Baker, William Sims, and S. McLallin.

Legislative Committee.—J. C. Hebbard, John Guthrie, Jas. B. Abbott, Jas. F. Legate, and A. B. Whiting.

Nominating Committee.—F. P. Baker, Albert R. Greene, E. B. Cowgill, B. F. Simpson, and T. D. Thacher.

The persons whose names were presented at the meeting of the Board of Directors in the afternoon for nomination as members of the Society were unanimously elected, as follows:

Honorary Members.—Rev. Jas. H. Defouri, Santa Fé, N. M.; Hon. Chas. Francis Adams, jr., Boston, Mass.; Rev. Dr. J. A. Lippincott, Philadelphia, Pa.; Gen. Eugene A. Carr, Washington, D. C.

Corresponding Members.—Orville C. Brown, Adams, N. Y.; Sylvester H. Clarke, Clyde, N. Y.; Rev. J. W. D. Anderson, Hot Springs, S. D.; Hon. Samuel F. Tappan, Washington, D. C.; Hon. William Hutchinson, Washington, D. C.; Alfred S. Roe, Esq., Worcester, Mass.; Samuel Bernstein, Cincinnati, Ohio; Mrs. W. T. Keith (Eliza Meeker), Oakland, Cal.; Franklin P. Rice, Esq., Worcester, Mass.

Active Member.—Arthur Clark, Esq., Wichita.

The eighteenth annual meeting of the Board convened in the east rooms of the Society, Tuesday, January 16, 1894, at 2 P. M.; President Lowe in the chair.

The following members of the Board were present: Col. Percival G. Lowe, Col. Cyrus K. Holliday, Judge Samuel A. Kingman, Gov. Chas. Robinson, Hon. W. L. Brown, Hon. John Speer, Prof. E. B. Cowgill, Dr. Stephen McLallin, Hon. John Guthrie, Warren Foster, Esq., Hon. Floyd P. Baker, Dr. Peter McVicar, Hon. McCown Hunt, Col. D. R. Anthony, Hon. J. C. Hebbard, and Secretary F. G. Adams.

The Secretary read the report of the World's Fair committee, as follows, which was adopted:

The committee appointed by the Board of Directors to take charge of the Society's exhibit at the World's Columbian Exposition have to report, that

—2

on the application of the committee, the Kansas board of managers, which was appointed under the act of the legislature making an appropriation for the general Kansas exhibit, granted to the Society the sum of $500 for use in making a historical exhibit in the Kansas building. From the library and collections of the Society a selection was made of Kansas books and pictures, and these were shipped to Chicago and placed in the rooms assigned for the Society's use. It is believed that the historical exhibit so made contributed no inconsiderable share to the interest which attached to the Kansas exhibits. Herewith is given a detailed statement (see daybook No. 2, p. 82) of the expenditures in placing, caring for, and returning the exhibit to the rooms of the Society, from which it will be seen that less than the entire sum of $500 was expended, the balance remaining in the hands of the board of managers, being the sum of $51.02.

Respectfully submitted.   C. K. HOLLIDAY.
F. G. ADAMS.
J. S. EMERY.

Mr. Brown moved that, as Mr. Thacher, Major Simpson, and Mr. Greene, members of the Nominating Committee, were not present, their places be supplied by three members to be appointed by the chair. The motion was adopted, and Messrs. Robinson, Anthony and McVicar were appointed.

On motion of Colonel Holliday, the report of the Committee on Nominations was approved, for submission to the annual meeting.

The Secretary then read the annual report for the year ending November, 1893, for the consideration and action of the Board, and for submission to the annual meeting. On motion of Judge Kingman, the report was approved.

Nominations of corresponding and honorary members were then made, for the action of the evening meeting of the Board of Directors, including the following resolution, offered by Governor Robinson:

Resolved, That the chancellors and presidents of all chartered Kansas universities and colleges should, by virtue of their office, be considered as corresponding members of the Historical Society, and that certificates to that effect should be issued to such officers by the Secretary.

Judge Kingman then offered the following resolution, which was adopted:

Resolved, That the members of the State Historical Society have learned with profound regret of the sudden and dangerous illness of our late esteemed President, T. Dwight Thacher, and extend to him our best wishes for his speedy relief, and to his family the warmest sympathy in their anxiety and trouble.

The Secretary was directed to forward the resolution immediately to Mrs. Thacher.

ANNUAL MEETING OF THE SOCIETY—JANUARY 16, 1894.

The eighteenth annual meeting of the Society convened in the hall of the house of representatives at 7:30 o'clock P. M., Tuesday, the 16th of January, 1894, and was called to order by President Lowe.

The Secretary read the annual report of the Board of Directors, including the following:

FINANCIAL STATEMENT.

Nov. 15, 1892.—Balance of appropriation to June 30, 1893...............		$3,467 89
Balance in hands of Treasurer, Society fees.............		103 00
Total balance...		$3,570 89
July 1, 1893.—Appropriation to June 30, 1894......................		5,680 00
Receipts from membership fees........................		30 00
Total..		$9,280 89

Expenditures.

Salaries and clerk hire.....................	$4,536 00	
Purchase of books......................	429 70	
Postage, freight, and contingent............	617 28	
Miscellaneous expenses, Treasurer's account..	47 98	5,630 96
Total balance...................................		$3,649 93

On motion, the report was adopted.

The Society then elected the following members of the Board of Directors, for the three years ending January 19, 1897: D. R. Anthony, F. P. Baker, John C. Caldwell, Arthur Capper, W. H. Carruth, F. D. Coburn, J. W. Davis, I. T. Goodnow, C. R. Green, A. R. Greene, Ewing Herbert, D. P. Hodgdon, J. E. Junkin, Samuel A. Kingman, James F. Legate, E. C. Little, Timothy McIntyre, F. P. MacLennan, F. C. Montgomery, Russell S. Osborn, A. B. Paine, A. P. Riddle, Edward Russell, Charles Robinson, E. H. Snow, John Speer, Eugene F. Ware, M. Weightman, D. W. Wilder, B. P. Waggener, J. D. Walters, and Mrs. Margaret L. Wood.

On motion of Hon. John Guthrie, the names of T. E. Dewey, Esq., of Abilene, and Dr. William Bishop, of Salina, were added to the nominations for corresponding members.

Colonel Lowe, President of the Society, then read his annual address, relating to affairs in Kansas prior to the settlements.

The President announced that next in order were the memorial proceedings relative to the late Col. William A. Phillips, an eminent citizen of Kansas and a former President of the Society, lately deceased. Dr. William Bishop, of Salina, then delivered an able and exhaustive address, relating to the life, character and public services of Col. William Addison Phillips, who died at Fort Gibson, I. T., November 30, 1893. At the close of the address, on motion of John Guthrie, the thanks of the Society were extended to Doctor Bishop.

Clifford C. Baker, Esq., of Topeka, then read a fragment of a memorial address on Colonel Phillips, which had been prepared by Hon. T. Dwight Thacher. At the conclusion of Mr. Thacher's paper, Mr. Baker added some appropriate remarks on the subject.

Prof. E. B. Cowgill, of Topeka, read a brief paper relating to his early memories of Colonel Phillips's correspondence in the New York *Tribune.*

On motion of Hon. John Guthrie, the President appointed Hon. John Guthrie, Hon. John Speer and Col. D. R. Anthony to draft resolutions relating to the death of Col. William A. Phillips. The committee, after a brief conference, reported the following, which were adopted:

It having pleased Almighty God to remove from this life Hon. William

Addison Phillips, a distinguished member and who was one of the Presidents of this Society, and who for nearly 40 years was conspicuous in the history of the state and the nation by his achievements and services as a journalist, soldier, statesman, and author, a gentleman eminent alike for rich and varied learning, elegant scholarship, and refined taste, as well as for high attainment in all the gifts, graces and accomplishments of genuine manhood and unimpeachable character:

Resolved, That we cherish a profound veneration for the talents, virtues and services of our late associate, comrade, and friend; that we tender to the family of the deceased the expression of our sincere sympathy on the occasion of their irreparable loss, and that the foregoing preamble and resolutions be unanimously adopted and ordered to be entered upon the records of the State Historical Society; and

Resolved, That a copy of these resolutions be presented to the family of the deceased and published in the papers of the city.

Brief remarks relative to the life and work of Colonel Phillips were then made by Col. D. R. Anthony, Hon. John Speer, Rev. J. B. McAfee, and Hon. Jas. F. Legate.

On motion of Colonel Anthony, the Secretary was instructed to endeavor to procure a portrait of Colonel Phillips for the Historical Society.

BOARD OF DIRECTORS' MEETING—JANUARY 16, 1894.

On the adjournment of the annual meeting of the Society, a meeting of the Board of Directors was called by President Lowe.

The Board proceeded to the election of the officers of the Society nominated at the afternoon meeting of the Board, as follows: President, Vincent J. Lane, Kansas City; Vice Presidents, W. L. Brown, Kingman, and Jas. B. Abbott, De Soto.

President Lane then took the chair.

On motion, the honorary and corresponding members nominated at the afternoon and evening meetings were then elected, as follows:

Honorary.—Rev. William Copley Winslow, D. D., LL. D., Boston; Edwin F. Townsend, colonel twelfth infantry and commandant infantry and cavalry school, Leavenworth; Robert Treat Paine, Boston; Hon. Galusha A. Grow, of Pennsylvania.

Corresponding.—Samuel Bradlee Doggett, Boston, Mass.; Thomas Emmett Dewey, of Abilene; Dr. William Bishop, of Salina.

The resolution offered by Governor Robinson at the afternoon meeting of the Board, relating to corresponding membership of chancellors and presidents of Kansas universities and colleges, was then adopted.

BOARD OF DIRECTORS' MEETING—MARCH 30, 1894.

At a called meeting of the Board of Directors, March 30, 1894, the following members were present: President, Hon. V. J. Lane, Col. D. R. Anthony, Hon. John Guthrie, Dr. Peter McVicar, D. P. Hodgdon, F. D. Coburn, Chas. S. Davis, L. R. Elliott, and Secretary Adams.

Hon. John Guthrie was elected Treasurer of the Society to fill the vacancy caused by the death of Hon. T. Dwight Thacher, the former Treasurer.

Hon. W. A. Harris, of Linwood, was elected a member of the Board of Directors to fill the vacancy caused by the death of J. C. Hebbard; Hon. Harrison Kelley, of Burlington, was elected to fill the vacancy caused by the declination of Robert Hay; Hon. D. N. Heizer, of Great Bend, was elected to fill the vacancy caused by the death of T. Dwight Thacher; and Fletcher Meridith was elected to fill the vacancy caused by the death of Prof. I. T. Goodnow.

A resolution was adopted, expressive of the great loss of the Society by death, since the annual meeting, in January last, of Hon. T. Dwight Thacher, Prof. I. T. Goodnow, and J. C. Hebbard, all of whom had long been members of the Board, and prominent in the work of the Society.

On motion of Doctor McVicar, President Lane, Colonel Anthony and John Guthrie were appointed a committee to make preparations for suitable memorial proceedings in relation to these deceased members at the next annual meeting of the Society.

BOARD OF DIRECTORS' MEETING — NOVEMBER 20, 1894.

At a meeting of the Board of Directors of the Society, held November 20, 1894, to consider the ninth biennial report of the Board of Directors, preparatory to its publication, and for the transaction of other business, the following members were present: Vincent J. Lane, Kansas City; A. R. Greene, Lecompton; J. E. Junkin, Sterling; R. R. Hays, Osborne; C. R. Green, Lyndon; James S. Emery, Lawrence; Albert B. Paine, Fort Scott; Floyd P. Baker, John Guthrie, E. B. Cowgill, F. D. Coburn, Arthur Capper, Fred. Wellhouse, Albert H. Horton, Samuel A. Kingman, and F. G. Adams, Topeka.

The meeting was called to order by the President, Hon. V. J. Lane.

The report, as prepared by the Secretary, was read and approved.

Mr. Baker, from the Executive Committee, reported that the committee had examined the accounts of the Society for the year ending October 31, 1894, and found them to be correct.

Mr. Cowgill moved that the Secretary be authorized and empowered to have a synopsis of the report printed in pamphlet, the expense to be paid from the private fund of the Society. The motion was adopted.

Mr. Baker moved that the memorial committee be authorized and directed to prepare, or cause to have prepared, suitable biographical sketches of the deceased members of the Board of Directors, such sketches to be submitted to the committee for their approval before being accepted, and when accepted the committee shall file the matter with the Secretary for printing in the collections of the Society, and that memorial exercises at the annual meeting be dispensed with. The motion was adopted.

On motion of the Secretary, Mr. Cowgill, Mr. Baker, Mr. Greene and Mr. Coburn were appointed to assist the Secretary in preparing a program for the coming annual meeting, January 15, 1895.

MEETINGS, 1895.

[The delay in the printing of this report arising from the deficiency of funds in the state printing department permits of the publication of the following proceedings for 1895.]

BOARD OF DIRECTORS' MEETING—JANUARY 15, 1895.

The nineteenth annual meeting of the Board of Directors was held in the west rooms of the Society, January 15, 1895.

In the absence of Pres. V. J. Lane, Vice Pres. W. L. Brown presided. There were present: Jas. B. Abbott, W. L. Brown, A. R. Greene, F. P. Baker, D. R. Anthony, L. R. Elliott, William Sims, J. S. Emery, P. McVicar, Adrian Reynolds, John Speer, F. D. Coburn, Eugene Ware, N. L. Prentis, E. J. Dallas, C. R. Green, J. C. Caldwell, Jas. F. Legate, Arthur Capper, J. E. Junkin, Mrs. Margaret L. Wood, John K. Wright, John Guthrie, C. K. Holliday, Fred. Wellhouse, and F. G. Adams.

On motion, the President appointed F. P. Baker, D. R. Anthony and Fred. Wellhouse a Committee on Nominations.

At the suggestion of the Secretary, the by-laws of the Society were revised, amended, and adopted by sections, and the Secretary authorized to number them in the proper manner, as follows:

BY-LAWS.

I. There is hereby created an Executive Committee of the Board of Directors of the Society, to consist of five members, to be appointed subsequent to the annual meeting of the Society, and to hold their office until the next annual meeting.

II. The Executive Committee shall audit all accounts presented against the Society, and all warrants drawn on the Treasurer shall be upon sworn vouchers approved by a majority of the members of the Executive Committee.

III. The Executive Committee shall examine and audit the accounts and vouchers of the Treasurer annually before the time of the annual meeting, and at the annual meeting they shall make a written report to the Board of Directors.

IV. The Executive Committee shall determine the character of the published reports of the Society, and shall decide what papers from its transactions and collections the biennial report shall contain.

V. The Executive Committee shall take such action as the interests of the Society shall from time to time demand in relation to providing and furnishing suitable rooms for its collections, and shall consult with the Secretary, and with him decide upon the purchasing of books to augment the Society's library.

VI. There shall be a Committee on Program and Addresses, to consist of five members of the Board; and it shall be the duty of the committee to provide for the addresses and proceedings of annual and other meetings, and to take such action as may be deemed advisable in reference to the delivery from time to time of lectures and addresses on historical subjects at the state capital or elsewhere.

VII. There shall be a Committee on Legislation, to consist of three or more members of the Society; and it shall be the duty of the committee to confer with the members and committees of the legislature, and present for their consideration and action the matters of legislation which the Board of Directors shall recommend.

VIII. There shall be a Committee on Nominations, to consist of five members of the Board; and it shall be the duty of the committee, annually, at some time previous to the annual meeting of the Society, to make a selection of persons whom they deem proper to recommend for members of the Board of Directors, and shall present the same for the action of the Society at the annual meeting.

IX. All committees shall be appointed by the President.

The subject of permanent room for the Society in the completed capitol building was discussed at length, and, on motion of Colonel Holliday, the following resolution was adopted:

Resolved, That the State Historical Society adheres to the position formerly taken, that the legislature shall be asked to assign and have prepared for the use of the Society, through the state executive council, the first and second floors of the east wing of the capitol building, so soon as the same shall be vacated by the present occupants, on the completion of the main portion of the building.

The report of the Committee on Nominations was approved.

Honorary, corresponding and active members were then nominated, for election at the evening meeting of the Board.

Dr. William Bishop, of Salina, made some remarks regarding the library of the late Col. William A. Phillips, expressing the hope that it might be purchased by the state for the Historical Society. No action was taken by the Board of Directors.

The chair renewed the appointment of the present committee on memorials for the coming year.

ANNUAL MEETING OF THE SOCIETY—JANUARY 15, 1895.

The nineteenth annual meeting convened in the hall of the house of representatives, at 7:30 o'clock P. M., Tuesday, the 15th of January, 1895.

In the absence of the President, Hon. V. J. Lane, Vice Pres. W. L. Brown presided, and made a brief address.

The Secretary read an abstract of the report of the Board of Directors, including the following financial statement:

The finances of the Society for the year ending November 20, 1894, are as follows:

Nov. 21, 1893.—Balance of appropriation to June 30, 1894		$3,564 91
	Balance in hands of Treasurer, Society fees	85 02
	Total balance	$3,649 93
July 1, 1894.—Appropriation to June 30, 1895		5,680 00
	Receipts from membership fees	38 00
	Total	$9,367 93

Expenditures.

Salaries and clerk hire......................	$4,670 00
Purchase of books.......................	622 30
Postage, freight, and contingent...........	425 18
	$5,717 48
Total balance......................................	$3,650 45

The following members of the Board of Directors were then elected, for the term of three years, ending January 18, 1898: F. G. Adams, J. Ware Butterfield, Alex. Caldwell, J. R. Clark, E. J. Dallas, L. R. Elliott, J. S. Emery, Chas. S. Gleed, John Guthrie, H. C. F. Hackbusch, John G. Haskell, R. R. Hays, D. N. Heiser, C. K. Holliday, Scott Hopkins, A. H. Horton, V J. Lane, P. G. Lowe, John Maloy, George W. Martin, E. N. Morrill, John M. Price, Adrian Reynolds, B. F. Simpson, William Sims, W. H. Smith, W. R. Spicknall, Edmund Stanley, William B. Sutton, A. E. True, Fred. Wellhouse, Archie L. Williams, and John K. Wright.

For the term of two years, ending January 19, 1897: Mrs. Sara T. L. Robinson was elected in place of Gov. Charles Robinson, deceased.

For the term of one year, ending January 21, 1896: A. L. Sponsler was elected in place of Warren Foster, of Hutchinson, removed from the state.

The following program was then had: Address by Hon. A. R. Greene, "Chimney Corner Chat on the Battle of Wilson's Creek." Address by Prof. Oscar E. Olin, "Romance of Kansas History." Address by Hon. John Speer, "Incidents of the Pioneer Conflict. Music by the McNary quartette.

BOARD OF DIRECTORS' MEETING—JANUARY 15, 1895.

At the close of the annual meeting, the Board of Directors convened, and elected the following officers, nominated at the afternoon meeting: President, Solon O. Thacher; Vice Presidents, Maj. Jas. B. Abbott and Harrison Kelley; Treasurer, John Guthrie; Secretary, F. G. Adams.

The following members of the Society, nominated at the afternoon meeting, were elected:

Honorary Members.—Mrs. Mary Ann Bickerdyke [Mother Bickerdyke], Rusell, Kas.; Rev. George Lewis Platt, Episcopal minister, Tivoli, N. Y.; Hon. Alden Speare, Boston, Mass.; Senator Joseph R. Hawley, Hartford, Conn.

Corresponding Members.—Rev. William Piggott, D. D., Gainsborough, England; Rev. Harry Frank Tracey, D. D., vicar of Dartsmouth, South Devon, England.

Active Members.—J. H. Hunt, Topeka; Col. William Watson Houston, Garnett; Dr. H. D. Fisher, Westmoreland; Hon. Noah C. McFarland, Topeka; Prof. Oscar E. Olin, Manhattan.

LEGISLATIVE COMMITTEE'S MEETING—FEBRUARY 15, 1895.

At a meeting of the legislative committee, held in the catalogue room, at 2 o'clock P. M., February 5, 1895, there were present: Col. C. K. Holliday, F. P. Baker, E. J. Dallas, A. R. Greene, W. L. Brown, E. B. Cowgill, W. J. Costigan, and Arthur Capper.

The Secretary presented for the consideration of the committee a draft of a concurrent resolution, which, on motion, was approved, for presentation to the chairman of the committee on state affairs of the house of representatives.

The estimates for appropriations for each of the two ensuing fiscal years were also read and approved.

Other business of minor importance was transacted, when, on motion, the meeting adjourned.

DONORS OF BOOKS AND PAMPHLETS.

The following is a list of books and pamphlets given the Society by individuals and institutions, including those received in exchange, and Kansas state publications given the Society by the state for use in exchanges:

NAMES OF DONORS.	Bks.	Pam.
Abbott, A. J., Garden City..............................	....	1
Abbott, J. B., De Soto	....	1
Academie de Macon, societie des arts, sciences, belles-lettres, et d' agriculture, France...............................	1	....
Academie des sciences, arts et belles-lettres de Dijon, France...........	1	....
Academy of natural sciences of Philadelphia, Pa......................	....	3
Adams, F. G., Topeka.................................	2	30
Adams, Dr. Harriet E., Topeka..........................	....	4
Agnew, F. A., Newton.................................	....	6
Alabama agricultural experiment station, Auburn..................	....	16
Alabama agricultural experiment station, Canebrake	....	1
Alabama geological survey, university of Tuscaloosa, Ala.............	1	7
Aldrich, Nelson W., Washington, D. C...................	....	1
Alrich, L. L., Cawker City.............................	....	3
American Bell telephone company, Boston, Mass................	....	2
American bimetallic league, Washington, D. C.................	....	1
American Congregational association, Boston, Mass..............	....	4
American dialect society, Boston, Mass......................	....	3
American folk-lore society, Cambridge, Mass..................	1	1
American forestry association, Washington, D. C..............	....	4
American forestry congress, Washington, D. C................	....	3
American historical assoc'n, Smithsonian institution, Washington, D. C...	3	3
American home missionary society, New York city.............	2	....
American institute of civics. Washington, D. C..............	....	1
American Jewish hist. soc., Smithsonian institution, Washington, D. C....	1	....
American museum of natural history, central park, New York city.......	2	2
American philosophical society, Philadelphia. Pa.................	....	3
American public health association, Brattleboro, Vt................	12	....
Anthropological society, Washington, D. C....................	....	2
Arizona agricultural experiment station, Tucson.................	....	8
Arizona weather service, Tucson......	....	23
Arkansas agricultural experiment station, Fayetteville.............	....	8
Arkansas weather bureau, Little Rock......................	....	52
Artz, Henry H., Topeka..............................	12	....
Associated charities of Boston, Mass......................	....	4

DONORS OF BOOKS AND PAMPHLETS—Continued.

NAMES OF DONORS.	Bks	Pam.
A. T. & S. F. railroad, Joseph W. Reinhart, president, Boston, Mass.......	....	11
Ayer, James B., Boston, Mass................................	1	....
Badger, Joseph E., jr., Frankfort.............................	....	8
Baker, Adelbert C., Topeka..................................	....	14
Baker, Mrs. C. S., Topeka..................................	....	2
Baker, F. P., Topeka......................................	....	1
Baker, Henry B., Lansing.................................	1	2
Balcom, George L., Claremont, N. H.........................	....	1
Bangor public library, Maine..............................	....	2
Baptist state convention. Kansas...........................	....	221
Barnes, Rev. R. H., Olathe.................................	....	1
Barrington, F. H., McCracken..............................	1	....
Bayley, Samuel, Hartford..................................	2	....
Becker, Geo. F., San Francisco, Cal.........................	....	2
Beebe, John W., Kingman..................................	1	....
Beer, William, New Orleans, La............................	....	2
Bellas, Capt. Henry H., Germantown, Pa.....................	1	....
Bernstein, Samuel, Cincinnati, Ohio........................	....	5
Betton, Frank H., Pomeroy................................	....	43
Bevelle, Harvey J., Topeka................................	....	5
Biddison, V. H., Marysville................................	....	1
Biddle, W. H., Topeka....................................	5	29
Biological society of Washington, D. C......................	....	18
Bishop, G. S., Haven.....................................	....	3
Black, George, Olathe....................................	....	2
Bland, Richard P., Washington, D. C........................	....	5
Bogue, Mrs. M. L., Manchester, Conn........................	....	15
Bonham, Jeriah, Peoria. Ill...............................	....	1
Boston public library, Massachusetts.......................	....	2
Bostonian society, Boston, Mass...........................	....	1
Boughton, J. S., Lawrence................................	1	....
Bowen, Clarence W., New York city.........................	1	....
Bowles, John, New York city..............................	1	....
Bowman, Mrs. T. E., Topeka...............................	....	1
Boyce, Elijah, Topeka....................................	....	1
Brackett, G. C., Lawrence................................	10	10
Bradbury, L. T., secretary, Paola..........................	....	1
Bradley, Rev. C. D., Boston..............................	1	18
Brazil, museu nacional do Rio de Janeiro....................	1	...
Breidenthal, John W., Topeka.............................	120	....
Brisbane department of agriculture, Queensland.............	1	7
Bristow, J. L., Topeka....................................	....	10
British museum, London, Eng..............................	7	4
Broad, Rev. L. P., Topeka.................................	....	120
Broderick, Case, Holton...................................	8	4
Brooke, C. M., Lecompton.................................	....	2
Brooklyn library, Brooklyn, N. Y...........................	....	13
Brooks, Frank, Topeka....................................	2	48
Brooks, Wm. Gray, Boston, Mass...........................	....	1
Brown, A. B., Manhattan.................................	2	5
Brown, Bestor G., Topeka.................................	1	....
Brown, Channing J., Topeka..............................	....	16
Brown, Mrs. Ella W., Holton..............................	....	1
Brown, Dr. Geo. W., Rockford, Ill..........................	....	1
Brown, H., Fort Scott....................................	....	5
Brown, H. H., Topeka....................................	....	1
Brown, John S., Lawrence................................	....	2
Brown, Orville C., Adams, N. Y............................	....	50
Bruce, H. E., McPherson.................................	....	1
Brush, Dr. Edmund Cone, Zanesville, Ohio..................	....	1

NAMES OF DONORS.	Bks.	Pam.
Bryan, Geo. D,. Charleston, S.C.	1	....
Bryan, William J., Washington, D. C.	....	3
Bryant, Dr. R. F., Lincoln	....	1
Buffalo historical society, New York	....	2
Bullene, Moore & Emery. Kansas City, Mo	....	1
Burnz, Mrs. Eliza, New York city	....	1
Byington, Dwight. Leavenworth	1	3
Bynum, W. D., Washington, D. C.	....	1
California agricultural experiment station, Berkeley	....	4
California historical society, San Francisco,	....	1
California state mining bureau, San Francisco	2	5
California state university. Berkeley	4	4
California weather service, Los Angeles	....	64
California weather service, Sacramento	....	16
Callaham, Dr. A. M., Topeka	....	5
Cambridge school for girls, Massachusetts	....	1
Campbell, A. B., Topeka	....	4
Campbell, Mathew Monroe, North Topeka	....	4
Campbell, W. P., Kingfisher, O. T	....	7
Canada geological survey, Ottawa	3	1
Canadian institute, Toronto, Canada	3	2
Cannon, J G., Washington, D. C.	....	1
Cantrall, C. R., secretary, Fredonia	....	2
Case, Mrs. A. H., Topeka	....	1
Case, Geo. H., Lansing	....	60
Case, Nelson, Oswego	1	4
Cavaness, J. M., Chetopa	....	2
Chamberlayne, Chas. F., Boston, Mass.	....	1
Chandler, Edward H., Boston	....	5
Chappel, R. C., Manhattan	....	1
Charles, Thomas, company, Chicago, Ill.	....	1
Chase, Lyman C., Hill City	1	....
Chase, S. W., Lansing	6	....
Chicago historical society, Illinois	....	3
Chicago kindergarten college, Illinois	....	1
Chicago public library, Illinois	....	18
Chicago university, Illinois	....	6
Cilley, Gen. J..P., Rockland, Me.	....	4
Cincinnati chamber of commerce, Ohio	2	....
Cincinnati public library, Ohio	....	3
Civil service reform association, New York	....	1
Clark, A. Howard, Washington, D. C.	....	1
Clark, Mrs. A. M., Topeka	45	166
Clark, Dr. A. W., Lawrence	....	1
Clark, Sylvester H., Clyde, N. Y.	1	1
Clark university, Worcester, Mass.	....	2
Clarke, Robert & Co., Cincinnati, Ohio	1	....
Clemens, G. C., Topeka	....	3
Cleveland public library, Ohio	....	1
Clevenger, C. C., Yates Center	....	7
Clothier, Geo. L., Alma	....	3
Coburn, F. D., Topeka	96	343
Cochran, W. Bourke, Washington, D. C.	....	1
Coffman, S., Jewell	....	2
Colby university, Waterville, Me.	1	2
Cole, George E., Girard	....	2
Collings, G. W., Wichita	1	....
Cullins, Ira F., Sabetha	....	1
Colorado bureau of labor statistics, Denver	1	3
Colorado scientific society, Denver	....	15

DONORS OF BOOKS AND PAMPHLETS — CONTINUED.

NAMES OF DONORS.	Bks.	Pam.
Colorado weather service, Denver	....	15
Columbia college, New York city	....	3
Cone, W. W., Topeka	3	31
Cone, Sylvester W., Portland, Me	....	1
Coney, P. H., Topeka	..	2
Congregational home missionary society, New York city	1	1
Congregational new west education commission, Chicago	....	1
Connecticut agricultural experiment station, New Haven	1	5
Connecticut historical society, Hartford	1	3
Conway, James William, Norton	1	....
Cornell university, Ithaca, N. Y	2	5
Cornell university agricultural experiment station, Ithaca, N. Y	2	5
Corner, Rev. W. H., Atchison	....	1
Corning, Eva L., Topeka	....	2
Cowles, A. H., Hiawatha	....	3
Cox, W. R., secretary United States senate, Washington, D. C	5	....
Cragin, F. W., Colorado Springs, Colo	2	11
Crane, Geo. W., Topeka	1	21
Cummins, Scott, Canema	....	1
Curtis, Charles, Washington, D. C	..	1
Dana, F. L., Denver, Colo	1	....
Daniels, Percy, Topeka	....	1
Danvers historical society, Massachusetts	....	1
Darling, Chas. W., Utica, N. Y	1	22
Darlow, Miss Grace, Topeka	..	2
Davenport academy of natural sciences, Iowa	1	....
Davidson, W. M., Topeka	5	....
Davis, Chas., Junction City	20	213
Davis, John, Washington, D. C	1	4
Davis, Mrs. John, Junction City	1	....
Deats, H. E., Flemington. N. J	1	....
Defouri, Rev. James H., Santa Fé, N. M	..	5
De Geer, Mrs. M. E., Chicago	....	1
Delaware agricultural experiment station, Newark	....	7
Dement, Isaac S., Chicago, Ill	....	1
Dennis, H. J., Topeka	5	16
Detroit public library, Michigan	....	3
DeWitt, Jacob, Salina	....	1
Dickson, C. M., secretary, Olathe	....	1
Dill, E. J., secretary, Council Grove	....	1
Dingley, Nelson, Washington, D. C	....	1
District of Columbia, superintendent of charities, Washington, D. C	....	1
Ditto, Frank S., Greencastle. Ind	2	14
Dodd, Mead & Co., New York	....	2
Doggett, Samuel Bradlee, Boston, Mass	1	....
Doniphan, Col. John, St. Joseph, Mo	....	1
Dougherty, George E., Topeka	....	16
Downing, R. F. & Co., New York city	..	2
Drew theological seminary, New York city	1	....
Drew theological seminary, Madison, N. J	....	1
Drowne, Henry, New York city	....	24
Dury, Chas., Avondale, Cincinnati, Ohio	....	2
Dykes, Henry A., Topeka	20	....
Eastman, Dr. B. D., Topeka	8	18
Eastman, W. H., Topeka	....	2
Edwards, Rev. Jonathan. Walla Walla, Wash	....	1
Eldridge, J. L., Topeka	....	2
Ellenbecker, J. G., Marysville	....	1
Elliott, Chas. S., Topeka	51	1
Elliott, David Stewart, Coffeyville	....	1

DONORS OF BOOKS AND PAMPHLETS — CONTINUED.

NAMES OF DONORS.	Bks.	Pam.
Elliott, L. R., Manhattan	....	1
Essex institute, Salem, Mass.	....	11
Ewing, Gen. Thomas, New York city	....	8
Fairchild, George T., Manhattan	....	99
Felt, J. S., Minneapolis	....	2
Ferguson, D. M., Paola	....	1
Fernow, B. E., Washington, D. C.	....	2
Ficken, Mayor John F., Charleston, S. C.	2	....
Field, Stephen J., Washington, D. C.	1	....
Filley, C. E., secretary, Burlingame	....	8
First regiment, Massachusetts volunteer militia, Boston	....	1
Fletcher, Thomas P., Elk Falls	1	....
Florida agricultural experiment station, Lake City	....	4
Florida weather service, Jacksonville	....	14
Folman, W. H., New York city	....	10
Foster, Rev. R. B., Stillwater, O. T.	....	1
Fowler, Sylvester, Lyndon	....	8
Fulton, M. R., Winchester	....	2
Funk & Wagnalls company, New York city	....	3
Gaines, H. N., Topeka	61	44
Galveston cotton exchange, Texas	....	24
Garfield university, Wichita	....	2
Gatschet, Albert S., Vinita, I. T.	....	5
Genet, T. E., Halstead	1	....
Georgia agricultural experiment station, Experiment	....	3
Georgia department of agriculture, Atlanta	....	8
Georgia historical society, Savannah	....	1
Georgia weather service, Atlanta	....	37
Gilmore, John S., Fredonia	....	1
Glore, D. H., secretary, Lane	....	2
Goodnow, Rev. I. T., Manhattan	3	63
Graham, I. D., Manhattan	....	20
Grandgent, C. H., Cambridge, Mass	....	1
Gray, I. J., Beloit	....	2
Greeley, Rev. Clarence, Scituate, Mass	....	1
Green, Charles R., Lyndon	1	8
Green, Samuel A., Boston, Mass	24	113
Greene, A. R., Lecompton	1	2
Griffin, Albert, Manhattan	....	2
Griffin, Mrs. D. L., Kansas City, Mo	....	4
Guild, H. R., Jamaica Plain, Mass	....	1
Guild, Mrs. Mary Stiles (Paul), Lynn, Mass	1	....
Gun, Robert, London, Eng	....	2
Gunn, Benjamin J., Girard	2	2
Gunn, O. B., Kansas City, Mo	....	2
Hackedorn, M. R., Horton	....	1
Hadley, Z. M., North Branch	....	2
Halderman, John A., Washington, D. C.	....	8
Hale, Geo. D., Topeka	....	2
Hamlin, Rev. C. H., Woodmont, Conn	....	1
Hanway, John S. and Brougham, Lane, from the library of the late Hon. James Hanway	6	96
Harman, Colfax B., Valley Falls	....	1
Harrington, Grant W., Hiawatha	....	4
Harris, Fred. J., Hays City	....	1
Harris, W. A., Washington, D. C.	7	1
Harter, Thomas O., Topeka	....	1
Hartford theological seminary, Connecticut	....	2
Harvard university, Cambridge, Mass	3	7
Haskell printing company, Atchison	....	1

DONORS OF BOOKS AND PAMPHLETS — Continued.

NAMES OF DONORS.	Bks.	Pam.
Hatch, D. R., Golden. Colo..	1	...
Hatch agricultural experiment station, Amherst, Mass..............	....	2
Hay, Robert, Junction City...	....	18
Hayden, Rev. Horace Edwin. Wilkes Barre, Pa.......................	....	9
Hebbard, Joseph C., North Topeka...................................	....	4
Henderson, M. D., Topeka..	....	9
Henrie, Chas. A., Topeka...	....	1
Higgins, L. L., Topeka...	....	4
Hill, Don Gleason, Dedham, Mass....................................	1	...
Hill, Nathaniel P., Denver, Colo.....................................	1	...
Hills, R. C., Denver, Colo..	....	1
Hinckley, H. V., Topeka..	....	1
Hinton, Richard J., Washington, D. C................................	....	74
Hirons, C. C., Topeka..	13	...
Historical and philosophical society of Ohio, Cincinnati............	1	1
Hitchcock, Prof. Albert S., Manhattan...............................	....	7
Hoad, Gertrude M., Lecompton.......................................	2	...
Hoenshel, E. J., Holton..	....	5
Hoepli, Ulrich, Milan, Italy..	....	6
Hoffman, Rev. R. A., Wilson..	....	3
Hogeboom, Dr. G. W., Topeka..	1	...
Hoisington, P. M., secretary, Newton................................	....	1
Holcomb, Walter L., Topeka...	....	1
Holden, James D., Emporia...	....	2
Holland society of New York city.....................................	1	...
Holman, Rev. Calvin, North Topeka..................................	....	1
Holt, Rev. L. H., Emporia...	....	4
Home for aged couples, Boston, Mass................................	....	1
Hopkins, L. L., Topeka..	....	3
Hornbeck, E. A., National City, Cal..................................	....	1
Horne, Miss Katie A., Mankato......................................	....	4
Hoss, George W., Tarkio, Mo..	....	1
Housantonic (care New York Tribune, New York city)...............	....	1
Hovey, Chas. M., Topeka..	1	38
Howard, O. Wilbert, Hiawatha.......................................	....	1
Hudson, J. K., Topeka...	1	...
Hudson, Thos. J., Washington, D. C..................................	....	9
Huffman, Mattie J., Emporia...	....	2
Hughes, J. W. F., Topeka..	....	1
Humbert, Pierre, jr., Boston, Mass...................................	....	1
Humphrey, Geo. P., Rochester, N. Y..................................	....	1
Huron, G. A., Topeka..	....	5
Hutchinson, William E., Ulysses.....................................	....	1
Idaho agricultural experiment station, Moscow.......................	....	5
Idaho, university of, Moscow...	....	4
Idaho state library, Boise City.......................................	3	...
Idaho weather service, Idaho Falls...................................	....	9
Iliff, Rev. J. M., Mound City...	....	3
Illinois agricultural experiment station, Champaign..................	..	11
Illinois bureau of labor statistics, Springfield.......................	2	1
Illinois historical library, Springfield...............................	....	5
Indian rights association, Philadelphia, Pa...........................	....	31
Indiana agricultural experiment station, Lafayette...................	....	4
Indiana bureau of statistics, Indianapolis............................	1	...
Indiana department of geology and natural resources, Indianapolis....	4	...
Indiana historical society, Indianapolis..............................	....	3
Indiana state board of health, Indianapolis...........................	2	...
Indiana state grange, Adams...	....	1
Indiana weather service, Lafayette...................................	....	2
Inman, Major Henry, Topeka...	....	2

DONORS OF BOOKS AND PAMPHLETS — Continued.

NAMES OF DONORS.	Bks.	Pam.
Interstate-commerce commission, Washington, D. C.	1	....
Iowa A. F. and A. M. grand lodge, Cedar Rapids.	....	1
Iowa geological survey, Des Moines.	3	....
Iowa history department, Des Moines.	1	1
Iowa railroad commission, Des Moines.	9	2
Iowa state board of health, Des Moines.	....	8
Iowa state historical society, Iowa City.	....	3
Iowa state university, Iowa City.	....	4
Iowa weather bureau, Des Moines.	2	70
Ireland, M. G., Springfield, Mass.	....	4
Ives, H. M., Topeka.	....	1
Ives, John N., Topeka.	....	62
Jay, Walter M., Salina.	....	3
Jennings, T. B., Topeka.	1	....
Jersey City public library, New Jersey.	....	2
Johns Hopkins university, Baltimore, Md.	....	4
Johnson, Rev. William W., North Greenfield, Wis.	1	....
Judd, C. P., Hoxie.	....	1
Junkin, J. E., Sterling.	....	4
Kansas bureau and news company, Topeka.	....	6
Kansas City, Fort Scott & Memphis railroad, Kansas City.	....	1
Kansas mutual life association, Topeka.	....	2
Kansas state board of railroad commissioners, Topeka.	2	13
Kansas Telegraph, Topeka.	....	1
Kansas weather service, Topeka.	....	59
Kellam book and stationery company, Topeka.	1	5
Kelley, Rev. Cland, Leavenworth.	....	1
Kellogg, Vernon L., Lawrence.	1	60
Kelton, Dwight H., Quincy, Mich.	....	2
Kentucky agricultural experiment station, Lexington.	....	9
Kentucky weather service, Louisville.	....	27
Kern, H. H., Bonner Springs.	5	....
Kimber, Sidney A., Boston, Mass.	1	....
King, James L., Topeka.	50	1
King, S S., Kansas City, Kas.	....	1
Kingsley, D. W., secretary, Independence.	1	....
Knapp, Frederick Bradford, Duxbury, Mass.	....	1
Knox, Rev. John D., Topeka.	....	6
Kyle, W. S., Plymouth, Mass.	....	2
Ladd, Rev. Horatio O., New York.	....	1
Lancaster, Rev. E. G., Eureka.	....	2
Lancaster town library, Massachusetts.	....	3
Lansdon, W. C., Fort Scott.	....	1
Lapham, Dr. W. B., Augusta, Me.	1	....
Lasher, Mrs. E., Topeka.	....	2
Lawrence academy, Groton. Mass.	....	2
Lawrence, C. H., secretary, Hiawatha.	....	5
Lawrence, W. H. H., Painesville, Ohio.	....	1
Leader, Wichita.	....	1
Leicester public library, Massachusetts.	....	1
Leland Stanford, jr., university, Palo Alto, Cal.	1	2
Lenox library, New York city.	....	1
Lewelling, Gov. Lorenzo Dow, Topeka.	1	1
Lewis, Mrs. Evelyn S., Topeka.	1	....
Lewis academy, Wichita.	....	1
Library association of Portland, Ore.	....	2
Library bureau, Chicago.	1	....
Library company of Philadelphia, Pa.	....	3
Light, C. M., Pittsburg.	16	224
Lindsay, Dr. W. S., Topeka.	....	1

DONORS OF BOOKS AND PAMPHLETS--CONTINUED.

NAMES OF DONORS.	Bks.	Pam.
Linehan, John C., Concord, N. H	1	....
Lockard, F. M., Norton	1	....
Locke, Rev. Edwin, Argentine	....	2
Logan, Dr. C. A., Chicago, Ill	3	1
Longley, Elias, Los Angeles, Cal	....	3
Lord, Mrs. A. G., Topeka	....	4
Los Angeles public library, California	....	1
Louisiana agricultural experiment station, Baton Rouge	....	4
Louisiana agricultural experiment station, Calhoun	....	3
Louisiana bureau of agriculture, Baton Rouge	....	6
Louisiana historical society, New Orleans	....	1
Louisiana weather service, New Orleans	....	12
Lovell, Miss Sue, Topeka	....	1
Lytle, John J., Philadelphia, Pa.	....	1
McBride, W. H., Topeka	....	35
McCandless, A. W., Hutchinson	....	1
McClure, W. T., Holton	....	1
McCormick theological seminary, Chicago	....	1
McDiarmid, Mrs. Clara A., Little Rock, Ark	1	1
McDonald, William, Brunswick, Me	....	1
McFadden, S. S., Topeka	2	....
McFarland, J. M., Topeka	....	1
McGrew, S. B., secretary, Holton	..	3
McIntosh, Duncan, Highland	...	2
McKee, Rev. C. U., Enterprise	...	3
McKinley, Dr. L. D., Topeka	....	1
McLallin, Dr. S., Topeka	....	2
Magers, J. S., secretary, La Cygne	....	5
Maine agricultural experiment station, Orono	....	16
Maine genealogical society, Portland	....	2
Maine historical society, Portland	4	....
Maine society of sons of the American revolution, Portland	....	1
Manchester, Rev. Alfred, Salem, Mass	....	1
Marder, Luse & Co., Chicago	1	....
Martin, John, Washington, D. C	....	7
Marty, J. J., Clay Center	....	3
Maryland agricultural experiment station, College Park	....	12
Maryland weather service, Baltimore	....	38
Massachusetts agricultural college, Amherst	....	3
Massachusetts agricultural experiment station, Amherst	4	6
Massachusetts agricultural experiment station, State Station	....	5
Massachusetts historical society, Boston	1	3
Massachusetts horticultural society, Boston	1	3
Massachusetts institute of technology, Boston	3	3
Massachusetts medical society, Boston	....	38
Massachusetts state board of agriculture, Boston	3	20
Massachusetts state board of health, Boston	3	....
Massachusetts state board of lunacy and charity, Boston	2	....
Matthews, George W., Cawker City	....	2
Matthews-Northrup company, Buffalo, N. Y.	....	23
Mayo, Rev. Henry M., Jewell City	....	2
Mead, J. R., Wichita	....	1
Mercantile library association, San Francisco. Cal.	....	1
Michigan agricultural experiment station, Agricultural College	....	14
Michigan bureau of labor, Lansing	1	....
Michigan historical society, Lansing	2	....
Michigan secretary of state, Lansing	1	23
Michigan state board of health, Lansing	....	20
Miles, John D., Lawrence	....	2
Miller, A. S., Wichita	....	2

DONORS OF BOOKS AND PAMPHLETS — Continued.

NAMES OF DONORS.	Bks.	Pam.
Miller, E., Lawrence	1	....
Miller, E. L., secretary, Seneca	....	1
Miller, Sol., Troy	....	2
Mills, Harry E., Topeka	1	....
Mills, T. B., Las Vegas, N. M.	1	....
Milton Bradley company, Springfield, Mass.	1	3
Milwaukee public library, Wisconsin	....	1
Milwaukee public museum, Wisconsin	....	11
Mims, D. A., Garden City	....	3
Minnesota agricultural experiment station, St. Anthony Park	....	4
Minnesota historical society, St. Paul	12	2
Minnesota secretary of state, St. Paul	12	....
Minnesota state university, St. Anthony Park	....	1
Minnesota weather service, Minneapolis	....	25
Minor, Rev. S. J., Sabetha	....	10
Mississippi agricultural experiment station, Agricultural College	....	7
Missouri agricultural experiment station, Columbia	....	3
Missouri geological survey, Jefferson City	1	....
Missouri medical association, Kansas City	....	2
Missouri Pacific railway company, St. Louis, Mo.	....	501
Missouri state board of agriculture, Columbia	....	2
Missouri weather service, Columbia	....	64
Missouri & Kansas telephone company, Topeka	....	1
Mitchell, John H., Washington, D. C	....	3
Modern Medicine publishing company, Battle Creek, Mich.	....	1
Mohler, Martin, Topeka	143	1751
Montana historical society, Helena	....	1
Moore, H. Miles, Leavenworth	....	2
Moore, W. H., Brockport, N. Y.	....	1
Morgan. Albert T., Topeka	..	2
Morgridge, G. O., Los Cerrillos, N. M	2	....
Morrill, Charles, Chicago	....	1
Morrill, E. N., Hiawatha	1	....
Mott, John M., Chicago	....	5
Mottram, Mrs. Myra, Ottawa	1	....
Munk, Dr. J. A., Los Angeles, Cal.	....	1
Murphy, E. F., Goodland	....	1
National civil service reform league, New York city	....	37
National divorce reform league, Auburndale, Mass	....	2
National editorial association, Washington, D. C.	....	1
National grange, patrons of husbandry, Washington, D. C	....	2
National temperance society, New York	....	1
National military home for disabled soldiers, Hartford, Conn	....	•7
Naylor, J. M., Wichita	....	7
Nazareth academy, Concordia	....	. 1
Nebraska agricultural experiment station, Lincoln	2	6
Nebraska bureau of labor, Lincoln	1	....
Nebraska historical society, Lincoln	1	1
Nebraska weather service, Doane college, Crete	....	32
Nebraska weather service, Omaha	....	13
Nevada agricultural experiment station, Reno	....	6
Nevada weather service, Carson City	....	12
New England historic genealogical society, Boston	....	4
New England hospital for women and children, Boston	....	2
New England weather service. Boston	....	46
New Hampshire agricultural experiment station, Durham	....	6
New Hampshire historical society, Concord	....	3
New Hampshire insurance commissioner, Concord	2	....
New Hampshire secretary of state, Concord	1	....
New Hampshire state board of agriculture, Concord	....	.1

—3

DONORS OF BOOKS AND PAMPHLETS—CONTINUED.

NAMES OF DONORS.	Bks.	Pam.
New Hampshire state library, Concord..	1	....
New Jersey agricultural experiment station, New Brunswick..............	....	13
New Jersey free public library, Jersey City..............................	1	....
New Jersey state historical society, Trenton............................	22	32
New Jersey statistics of labor and industries, Trenton..................	5	....
New Jersey weather bureau, New Brunswick...............................	2	34
New London county historical society, Connecticut......................	....	1
New Mexico agricultural experiment station, Las Cruces.................	....	1
New Mexico college of agriculture and mechanical arts, Las Cruces......	....	15
New Mexico weather service, Santa Fé...................................	....	20
New South Wales government board for international exchanges, Sidney..	1	....
New West educational commission, Chicago..............................	....	1
New York academy of sciences, New York city..........................	....	1
New York agricultural experiment station, Geneva......................	1	27
New York agricultural experiment station, Ithaca......................	....	1
New York bureau of statistics of labor, Albany........................	8	....
New York society for the suppression of vice, New York city..	....	20
New York state commission in lunacy, Albany..........................	4	....
New York state library, Albany.......................................	7	6
New York state meteorological bureau, Albany.........................	1	1
New York state university, Albany....................................	....	2
New York weather service, Ithaca.....................................	1	78
Newell, Mrs. F. D., Manhattan..	....	3
Newlin, W. H., Springfield, Ill......................................	....	1
Nissley, J. E., Abilene...	....	1
Noble, Frederick Perry, Chicago......................................	....	1
North Carolina agricultural experiment station, Raleigh..............	....	8
North Carolina weather service, Raleigh..............................	....	57
North Dakota agricultural college, Fargo.............................	....	1
North Dakota agricultural experiment station, Fargo..................	....	15
North Dakota weather service. Bismarck..............................	....	42
Northwestern university, Evanston, Ill...............................	2	....
Oak Lawn cemetery society, La Cygne....	....	1
Oates, W. C., Washington, D. C......................................	....	10
Oberlin college, Ohio..	....	50
O'Brien, Dr. M., Topeka..	1	....
Ohio adjutant general, Columbus.....................................	2	....
Ohio agricultural experiment station, Wooster.......................	....	7
Ohio archæological and historical society, Columbus.................	....	2
Ohio inspector of workshops, factories, and public buildings, Columbus..	1	....
Ohio meteorological bureau, Columbus................................	....	1
Ohio weather and crop report, Norwalk...............................	....	33
Oklahoma weather service, Oklahoma City............................	....	43
Old Colony historical society, Taunton, Mass........................	....	2
Omaha public library, Nebraska.....................................	....	8
Oneida historical society, Utica, N. Y..............................	....	5
Ontario agricultural college, Guelph................................	8	4
Ontario agricultural college experimental station, Guelph..........	2	64
Ontario bureau of industry, Toronto................................	....	2
Ontario department of agriculture, Toronto.........................	3	15
Oregon agricultural college, Corvallis..............................	....	2
Oregon agricultural experiment station, Corvallis..................	....	11
Oregon weather bureau, Portland....................................	1	5
Osborn, R. S., Topeka	241	155
Pabor, William E., Pabor Lake, Fla.................................	....	1
Paine, A. B., Fort Scott...	1	....
Parker, L. G., Oberlin..	....	4
Paris, department of statistics, France............................	12	....
Parvin, T. S., Cedar Rapids, Iowa..................................	....	2
Pattee, Rev. J. T., Meriden, Conn..................................	....	1

DONORS OF BOOKS AND PAMPHLETS—CONTINUED.

NAMES OF DONORS.	Bks.	Pam
Patterson, Geo. A., secretary, Oskaloosa	....	4
Pattison, Gov. Robert E., Harrisburg, Pa	7	....
Paxton, William M., Platte City, Mo	1	1
Payne, Gen. Walter S., Fostoria, Ohio	....	1
Peabody educational fund, Richmond, Va	....	1
Peabody institute, Baltimore, Md	....	2
Peabody museum of American archæology and ethnology, Cambridge, Mass	....	1
Peacock, T. Brower, Kansas City, Mo	....	1
Peck, Geo. Gottsberger, New York	1	....
Peet, Rev. Steven D., Avon. Ill	....	1
Peffer, W. A., Washington, D. C	1	....
Pelton, Dr. D. R., Topeka	1	....
Pence, Lafe, Washington, D. C	....	8
Pennsylvania agricultural experiment station, State College, Centre county,	2	5
Pennsylvania prison society, Philadelphia	....	1
Pennsylvania society of the American revolution, Harrisburg	....	1
Pennsylvania society to protect children from cruelty, Philadelphia	....	1
Pennsylvania state college, State College	1	....
Pennsylvania state penitentiary, inspectors for eastern dist., Philadelphia,	1	1
Pennsylvania state university, Philadelphia	....	8
Pennsylvania weather service, Philadelphia	....	30
People's party central committee, Topeka	....	8
Perkins, Bishop W., Washington, D. C	8	8
Philadelphia academy of natural sciences, Pennsylvania	....	1
Phillips, Milton E., Winfield	....	1
Phillips, W. P., New York city	1	....
Phonographic institute, Cincinnati, Ohio	....	6
Pierce, George T., Goodrich and Centreville	21	4
Pinkston, Mrs. Sallie A. (Lyon), Cottonwood Falls	....	1
Pipp, E. G., secretary, Burlingame	....	1
Plumb, Mrs. P. B., Emporia	1	1
Polk, R. L. & Co., Detroit, Mich	1	....
Pond, Chester E., Topeka	....	2
Pond, Jas. B., New York	....	2
Poole, W. F., Chicago, Ill	1	....
Pope, Albert A., Boston, Mass	....	2
Popenoe, E. A., Manhattan	....	1
Pounds, L. H., Topeka	....	1
Prather, Van B., Topeka	....	62
Pratt institute, Brooklyn, N. Y.	....	8
Presbyterian historical society, Philadelphia, Pa	....	8
Prescott, B. E., Concord, N. H.	1	....
Press, Daily, Topeka	....	1
Price, G. T., Osawatomie	8	1
Prosser, Prof. C. S., Schenectady, N. Y.	1	....
Providence athenæum, Providence, R. I.	....	50
Providence free kindergarten association, Providence, R. I.	....	2
Public Ledger Company, Philadelphia, Pa	....	1
Purdue agricultural experiment station, Lafayette, Ind	....	4
Queen, Rev. C. N., Fort Scott	....	12
Queensland department of agriculture, Brisbane, Australia	1	....
Ramabai association, Boston	....	2
Randolph, A. M. F., Topeka	1	....
Rathbone, F. P., Oberlin	....	1
Ratterman, H. A., Cincinnati, Ohio	....	1
Reed, Enos, Dodge City	....	60
Reed, N. A., jr., Chicago	1	....
Reed, Thomas B., Washington, D. C	....	1
Reid, Whitelaw, New York city	....	1

NAMES OF DONORS.	Bks.	Pam.
Remsburg, Geo. J., Atchison	....	7
Remsen, Daniel S., New York	....	2
Republican state central committee, Topeka	1	....
Reynolds library, Rochester, N. Y	....	4
Rhode Island agricultural experiment station. Kingston	1	7
Rhode Island bureau of industrial statistics, Providence	2	....
Rhode Island historical society, Providence	....	3
Rice, Harvey, Topeka	....	1
Richardson, Miss E. L., Cheshire, Mass	1	....
Riddle, Mrs. Ada F., Minneapolis	....	4
Ridgway, Chas. H., secretary, Ottawa	....	3
Riley, Z. F., Topeka	39	4
Ritchie, J. H., Independence	....	1
Roberts, J. W., Oskaloosa	1	....
Roby, Dr. Henry W., Topeka	....	1
Roe, Alfred S., Worcester, Mass	1	....
Romance publishing company, N. Y	....	1
Root, Frank A., North Topeka	....	60
Root, Geo. A., Topeka	....	95
Root, Mrs. George A., Topeka	....	3
Ropes, E., Astor, Fla.	....	2
Rosengarten, J. G., Philadelphia	....	1
Rowell, Geo. P. & Co., New York city	1	....
Rowley, A. A., North Topeka	....	4
Royal academy of belles-lettres, history, and antiquity, Stockholm, Sweden.	30	....
Royal academy of Canada, Ottawa	3	....
Royal society of Canada, Montreal	1	....
Ryan, Miss Eva, Hiawatha	....	2
St. Benedict's college, Atchison	....	1
St. Louis mercantile library association, Missouri	....	1
Salem public library, Massachusetts	....	2
San Francisco mercantile library, California	....	1
San Francisco produce exchange, California	....	2
San Francisco public library, California	....	1
Sanger, Mrs. Jane, Fort Scott	....	5
Scientific society of Washington, D. C.	....	1
Scott, William T., Holton	....	2
Scudder, T. W., Topeka	1	....
Seeds, Mrs. Alice M., Abilene	....	5
Senter, James M., Topeka	....	1
Sentinel, Harper	....	1
Seward, Theodore F., New York city	....	1
Sharp, S. Z., McPherson	....	2
Shawnee building and loan association, Topeka	....	2
Sheffield, Rev. C. S., Topeka	....	41
Shelden, E. J., Paola	....	2
Sheldon, Rev. C. M., Topeka	1	7
Sheldon, E. S., Chicago, Ill	....	1
Shepard, R. B., Salt Lake City, Utah	....	2
Shepperd, Mrs. K. W., Christchurch, New Zealand	....	26
Sherman, Rev. F. E., Stockton	....	3
Sherman, Porter, Kansas City, Kas.	....	4
Shull, D. S., Scranton	....	1
Sickles, Daniel E., Washington, D. C.	....	1
Simpson, B. F., Topeka	....	2
Simpson, Jerry, Washington, D. C.	....	2
Skelton, W. H. Salina	....	1
Slosson, A. L, Sabetha	....	2
Smith, B. F., Lawrence	....	1
Smith, Ed. R., Mound City	....	3

DONORS OF BOOKS AND PAMPHLETS,—Continued.

NAMES OF DONORS.	Bks.	Pam.
Smith, M. E., secretary, Osborne..	....	2
Smith, W. H., Marysville..	....	2
Smithsonian institution, Washington, D. C.............................	17	22
Smythe, B. B., Topeka...	70	10
Snider, S. H., Topeka...	12	....
Snow, Edwin H., Topeka...	3	70
Snow, Florence L., Neosho Falls.......................................	....	1
Snow, Chancellor Francis H., Lawrence.................................	5	210
Société archeologique du department de Constantine, Algeria, Africa.....	1	1
Société de géographie de Lyon, France.................................	....	1
Société havraise d'études, diverses, Le Havre, France..................	....	1
Société historique, litteraire, artistique et scientifique du cher, France...	2	....
Société nationale d' agriculture, Paris................................	1	....
Société nationale des antiquaires de France, Paris....................	5	....
Société neuchateloise de géographie, Neuchatel, France	1	....
Société des sciences naturelles de la charente inferieure, La Rochelle, France...	1	....
Society of American florists, Boston, Mass............................	....	1
Society of colonial wars, Boston, Mass................................	....	1
Society of the army of the Cumberland, Cincinnati, O..................	2	....
Sons of the American revolution, District of Columbia.................	....	1
Sons of the American revolution, Indiana society, Indianapolis..........	....	1
Sons of the American revolution, Iowa society, Marshalltown...........	....	2
Sons of the American revolution, Maine society, Portland..............	....	1
Sons of the American revolution, national society, Washington, D. C.....	....	2
Sons of the American revolution, New York society, New York city......	1	....
South Dakota agricultural experiment station, Brookings...............	1	8
South Dakota weather service, Huron..................................	....	18
Southern California bureau of information, Los Angeles................	....	1
Spelman seminary, Atlanta, Ga.......................................	....	1
Spofford, A. R., Washington, D. C....................................	....	1
Sponsler, A. L., Hutchinson..	....	2
Stannard, Rev. L. E., Ottawa...	....	1
Stark, J. M., Topeka...	1	....
Sterling, Wilson, Lawrence...	1	....
Stewart, John T., Scammon...	....	61
Stitler, William, Topeka..	....	16
Stocking, Mrs. Patty Miller, Washington, D. C........................	....	2
Stoner, Rev. J. A., Seneca..	1	....
Stover, S. G., Topeka..	....	120
Stryker, William, Great Bend...	1	5
Swensson, Rev. C. A., Lindsborg......................................	....	1
Swett, John, San Francisco, Cal......................................	....	1
Tappan, Samuel F., Washington, D. C.................................	....	3
Taylor, A. R., Emporia...	1	132
Telephone exchange, Topeka..	....	1
Tennessee weather service, Nashville.................................	....	11
Texas agricultural experiment station, College Station, Brazos county	....	8
Texas geological survey, Austin.......................................	2	7
Texas weather service, Galveston.....................................	....	115
Thomas Charles company, Chicago	....	1
Thomas, Rev. J. B., Topeka...	....	88
Thomas, J. F., Maple City..	....	2
Thomas, N. S., Topeka..	....	28
Thompson, Alton H., Topeka..	....	2
Thoroman, L. O. Salina...	....	4
Throckmorton, George, secretary, Burlington	....	1
Thurston, Mrs. S. A., Topeka...	....	5
Thwaites, Reuben G., Madison, Wis...................................	....	1
Tilton, Warner A., Oxford...	....	3

DONORS OF BOOKS AND PAMPHLETS—Continued.

NAMES OF DONORS.	Bks.	Pam.
Todd, J. F., Topeka...	121	....
Toner, J. M., M. D., Washington, D. C.........................	....	1
Tower Bible and tract society, Allegheny, Pa..................	....	4
Townsend, H. C., St. Louis	....	4
Tracy, Col. Robert. St. Joseph, Mo...........................	....	2
Troutman, James A., Topeka..................................	....	3
Troxel, C. R.. Lawrence.....................................	....	10
Tweeddale, William, Topeka..................................	....	1
Unknown..	1	3
U. S. army, adjutant general, Washington, D. C...............	2	....
U. S. board of Indian commissioners, Washington, D. C........	1	....
U. S. board of publication, Washington, D. C.................	1	....
U. S. bureau of American republics, Washington, D. C.........	10	19
U. S. bureau of education, Washington, D. C..................	11	6
U. S. bureau of ethnology, Washington, D. C..................	6	6
U. S. bureau of labor, Washington, D. C......................	1	1
U. S. census office, Washington, D. C........................	1	165
U. S. chief of engineers, U. S. A., Washington, D. C..........	6	....
U. S. chief of ordnance, U. S. A., Washington, D. C..........	2	....
U. S. commissioner of education, Washington, D. C............	11	4
U. S. commissioner of labor statistics, Washington, D. C......	9	....
U. S. commissioner of patents, Washington, D. C.............	1	....
U. S. director of the mint, Washington, D. C.................	4	....
U. S. fish commissioner, Washington, D. C....................	5	..
U. S. geological survey, Washington, D. C....................	19	28
U. S. life-saving service, Washington, D. C..................	2	....
U. S. lighthouse board, Washington, D. C....................	1	..
U. S. military academy. West Point, N. Y....................	....	2
U. S. national museum, Washington, D. C....................	2	....
U. S. naval academy, Annapolis, Md..........................	....	1
U. S. naval observatory, Washington, D. C....................	....	1
U. S. navy department, nautical almanac office. Washington, D. C........	2	1
U. S. navy department, bureau of navigation, Washington, D. C........	....	2
U. S. navy department, hydrographic office, Washington, D. C..........	2	6
U. S. secretary of agriculture, Washington, D. C.............	3	29
U. S. secretary of agriculture, bureau of animal industry.....	1	2
U. S. secretary of agriculture, division of botany...........	1	21
U. S. secretary of agriculture, division of chemistry........	4	13
U. S. secretary of agriculture, division of entomology.......	....	11
U. S. secretary of agriculture, division of ethnology........	....	1
U. S. secretary of agriculture, division of forestry.........	1	23
U. S. secretary of agriculture, division of ornithology......	3	9
U. S. secretary of agriculture, division of pathology........	1	4
U. S. secretary of agriculture, division of pomology.........	....	1
U. S. secretary of agriculture, division of statistics.......	....	28
U. S. secretary of agriculture, office of experiment stations..	1	27
U. S. secretary of agriculture. weather bureau..............	2	11
U. S. secretary of interior, Washington, D. C...............	256	60
U. S. secretary of state, Washington, D. C..................	33	18
U. S. secretary of state, bureau of rolls and library, Washington, D. C.....	2	2
U. S. secretary of the treasury, Washington, D. C...........	2	1
U. S. secretary of the treasury, bureau of statistics, Washington, D. C.....	3	23
U. S. secretary of war. Washington, D. C...................	32	1
U. S. secretary of war, library department, Washington, D. C	5	2
University extension. extension division....................	....	1
Utah agricultural experiment station, Logan	2	8
Utah weather bureau, Salt Lake..............................	....	33
Van Cleave, Miss Minnie, Topeka............................	....	8
Van Dorn, F., Mount Morris, N. Y...........................	4	....
Van Vliet, James B., secretary, Frankfort....................	....	6

NAMES OF DONORS.	Bks.	Pam.
Vermont agricultural experiment station, Burlington	....	4
Vermont state university, Burlington	....	1
Vincent, Henry, Chicago, Ill	1	....
Vincent publishing company, Indianapolis, Ind	....	1
Virginia agricultural experiment station, Blacksburg	....	15
Virginia department of agriculture, Lynchburg	....	1
Virginia weather bureau, Lynchburg	....	21
Votel, Henry J., St. Mary's	....	1
Vrooman, Rev. Walter, Boston, Mass	....	5
Wade, Spencer P., Topeka	....	3
Wait, Mrs. Anna C., Lincoln	....	4
Walker, Joseph B., Concord, N. H	1	....
Walker, S. T., Olathe	....	7
Walkinshaw, J. C., Leavenworth	1	15
Wall, Dr. G. A., Topeka	1	....
Wall, H. Briggs, Hutchinson	....	1
Wallace, C. P.. Melbourne, Australia	....	1
Walsh, J. DeWitt, Carthage, Mo	4	....
Wampler, J. W., Brazilton	....	60
Ward, Mrs. Jennie M., Ottawa	....	20
Ward, Dr. M. B., Topeka	....	1
Ware, Eugene F., Topeka	1	2
Warner, A. G., Washington, D. C.	....	1
Warren, Fisk, Boston, Mass	1	....
Washburn, Avery, Topeka	1	....
Washington and Jefferson college, Washington, Pa	1	....
Washington university, St. Louis, Mo	1	5
Washington weather service, Seattle	....	40
Waterhouse, Prof. S., St. Louis, Mo	....	7
Waterman, Myron A., Topeka	....	1
Waugh, Rev. Lorenzo, Alkiah, Cal	....	6
Webb, Leland J., Topeka	....	3
Webb, W. C., Topeka	5	51
Webb, W. Seward, New York city	2	....
Wedel, Rev. Cornelius H., Newton	....	1
Welch, R. B., Topeka	....	3
Wesleyan university, Middletown, Conn	1	....
West Virginia agricultural experiment station, Morgantown	....	4
West Virginia weather service, Parkersburg	....	31
Westchester county historical society, White Plains, N. Y	....	1
Western news bureau. Topeka	....	1
Whitaker, C. L., secretary, Iola	....	2
Whitaker. O. B., Lincoln	....	1
White, H. F., Topeka	....	10
White, M. L., Garnett	....	2
White, W. F., Topeka	....	2
Wickens, Mrs. Margaret Ray, Sabetha	1	....
Wiegant, J. H. E., Leavenworth	....	14
Wilcox, Miss Mary R., Washington, D. C.	1	....
Wilcox, P. P., Los Angeles, Cal	....	3
Wilder, Mrs. C. F., Manhattan	....	27
Wilder, Edward, Topeka	1	....
Wiles, Dr. C. K., Winfield	....	6
Willard, Miss Frances E., Chicago, Ill	....	26
Williams, A. C., Elk Falls	....	8
Williams, D. M., Huntley, Ill	....	1
Wilson, Albert K.. Topeka	1	....
Wilson, J. W., Atchison	....	1
Winans, Geo. W.. Edmond, O. T.	....	1
Wingart, H. J., Topeka	....	6

DONORS OF BOOKS AND PAMPHLETS — Concluded.

NAMES OF DONORS.	Bks.	Pam.
Winslow, William C., Boston, Mass...................................	....	1
Wisconsin academy of sciences, arts, and letters, Madison..............	5	....
Wisconsin agricultural experiment station, Eau Claire................	....	1
Wisconsin agricultural experiment station, Madison....................	....	6
Wisconsin bureau of labor statistics, Madison........................	1	....
Wisconsin state board of health, Madison.............................	1	....
Wisconsin state historical society, Madison..........................	1	9
Wisconsin state university, Madison..................................	....	1
Wisconsin weather bureau, Milwaukee.................................	....	21
Wolcott, Henrietta L., Dedham, Mass.................................	....	122
Wolf, Rev. Innocent, Atchison.......................................	....	1
Wood, Mrs. Margaret L., Topeka.....................................	1	....
Woodruff, Clinton Rogers, Philadelphia, Pa...........................	....	7
Woolworth, Charlotte E., New Haven, Conn...........................	1	....
Worcester public library, Massachusetts..............................	....	2
Worcester society of antiquity, Massachusetts........................	....	4
World, New York city..	1	....
World's Columbian exposition, British section, Chicago, Ill...........	1	....
World's congress auxiliary, Chicago, Ill..............................	....	1
Worral, Harvey, Topeka..	....	1
Wyoming commemorative association, Wilkes Barre, Pa...............	....	2
Yale university, New Haven, Conn....................................	2	....
Y. M. C. A. of Emporia college, Emporia.............................	....	1
Yonkers historical and library association, Yonkers, N. Y............	....	1
Youth's Companion, Boston...	....	1

DONORS OF MANUSCRIPTS.

Armstrong, John, Topeka: Manuscript reminiscences, containing an account of the Topeka cannon brought from Milwaukee to Kansas in 1856; also of the loss of the 24-pound howitzer taken from Topeka to Westport, Mo., in the Price raid, and captured by the rebels October 22, 1864.

Bailey, Mrs. E. A., Lawrence: Letter written by Abram Cutler from Ouray, Colo., January 30, 1879, to Hon. L. D. Bailey, relating to the massacre of Oliver F. Short, United States surveyor, by Indians in southwest Kansas, and to other subjects.

Bishop, G. S., Haven: List of sub-alliances in Kansas; three manuscript books; six manuscript papers, one containing biographical sketch of donor.

Bradlee, Rev. C. D., Boston, Mass.: Commission of George Gay, of Boston, justice of the peace for Suffolk county, Massachusetts, with autograph of Gov. Levi Lincoln, of Massachusetts, dated January 2, 1833; application of Benjamin G. Gay for a passport, addressed to the United States secretary of state, dated March 26, 1868.

Broad, Rev. L. P, Topeka: 31 manuscript copies of select hymns.

Brown, John, jr., Put-in-Bay, Ohio: Letters of Maj. H. N. Rust, of South Pasadena, Cal., and of the following sons and daughters of Capt. John Brown, namely: Jason Brown, South Pasadena; Sarah Brown, Saratoga, Cal.; Ruth B. Thompson, South Pasadena, and Annie B. Adams, Petrolia, Humboldt county, California, all relating to the John Brown exhibit made by Major Rust at the World's Columbian Exposition, 1893.

Brown, O. C., Adams, N. Y.: Manuscript containing brief sketches and incidents of donor's life; 53 pages; three manuscripts: one entitled Hill's Landing, 1855, one John Brown's birthplace, one a continuation of writer's reminiscences; let-

ter of W. W. Updegraff to donor, dated Chicago, April 23, 1861; 99 manuscript papers, relating chiefly to Kansas and the civil war; copy of the communication of donor to the Kansas Board of World's Fair Managers, in response to the invitation extended to him to be present and participate in the ceremonies incident to Kansas week at the exposition, September 11–17, 1893; poem in memory of William A. Phillips; a poem by donor, entitled "John Brown's Grave"; stanza on Kansas, suggested by viewing the picture of the Kansas state building in the Columbian album; collection of papers on political, literary and moral subjects by Noah Webster; poem by donor, written May 30, 1893, in memory of Spencer K. Brown; letter of Mrs. Grace Lewis, dated May 9, 1893, concerning a shingle taken by her from the house which was the birthplace of John Brown, in Torrington, Conn; letter of donor, dated Lawrence, Kansas Territory, September 1, 1856, giving an account of the sacking of Osawatomie.

Burnett, J. C., Topeka: Copy of a paper dated Lawrence, K. T., October 21, 1857, containing the resolution adopted by the free-state convention held at Lecompton October 19, 1857, signed by William Hutchinson, secretary, protesting against the assembling of the Lecompton constitutional convention and providing for the appointment of a committee to bring to "summary punishment" all found implicated in the recent election frauds; copy of a paper dated Topeka, Kas., April 15, 1861, containing an agreement of members of the state legislature to vote for a resolution to go into a joint convention for the purpose of electing two United States senators, signed by Josiah Miller, H. S. Sleeper, S. D. Houston, T. A. Osborn, J. A. Phillips, John Lockhart, J. C. Burnett, W. Spriggs, P. P. Elder, H. W. Farnsworth, H. N. Seaver, John A. Martin, and Edward Lynde.

Butterfield, J. Ware, Topeka: Copy of a letter of Henry Flood, of Marblehead, Mass., containing some account of the services of battery M, second artillery, U. S. A., at the dispersal of the free-state legislature, at Topeka, July 4, 1856, in which battery Mr. Flood was a sergeant.

Clark, Mrs. A. M., Jewell: The Kansas visitors' register used at the World's Fair, Chicago, 1893.

Clarke, Sylvester H., Clyde, N. Y.: Ode written for and sung at the first Fourth of July celebration in Council City (Burlingame), Kas., 1855.

Cone, Edward P., New York city: *Facsimile* of original letter written by John Winthrop, jr., governor of Connecticut, under date of March 2, 1657, to Peter Stuyvesant, governor of New Netherlands, at the request of Daniel Cone.

Cone, W. W., Topeka: Manuscript relating to the first members of the Kansas territorial legislature, also containing autobiographical sketch of Hon. John Martin.

Corgan, John N., McPherson: Two letters and one postal, written to donor by Blakeley Durant, of Grand Forks, N. D., relating to incidents in the war of the rebellion.

Corning, Miss Eva L., Topeka: Autobiographical sketch of donor.

Davidson, Prof. W. M., Topeka: Four visitors' registers, used in the rooms of the Kansas educational exhibit, World's Columbian Exposition, Chicago, 1893.

Davis, Chas. S., Junction City: Petition of 750 resident voters of Geary county, Kansas, praying the legislature of 1893 to restore to the county the name of Davis, in honor of the late Judge David Davis, of Illinois, in compliance with which petition the legislature provided for the submission of the proposition to the people of the county at the election November 7, 1893; petition for joint discussion between John A. Anderson and John Davis.

Ditto, Frank S., Topeka: Manuscript history of the organization of the First Presbyterian Church, Topeka.

Elting, R. O., Kansada: Autograph letter of Aaron Burr, written to donor's great-grandfather, Richard Oliver, of Ulster county, New York, dated November 10,

1803; table of coin weights adopted by the New York chamber of commerce May 4, 1784. Conditional deposit.

Faulkner, Chas. E., Atchison: Biographical sketch of donor; portion of the history and genealogical record of the Coryell. family in America; portion of the genealogical record of the Beach family in America.

Finley, Richard R., Kansas City, Kas.: Autobiography of donor, containing a certificate showing his right to freedom under the laws of Alabama, signed by numerous citizens of Benton county, Alabama, and certified under seal by the probate judge of the county, under date of September 15, 1852; pass signed by Zimri Henderson and John N. Wills, dated September 18, 1852; recommendation signed by John N. Wills, dated September 18, 1852; paper without date or place signed by the trustees of a municipal corporation, granting donor permission to remain within the limits of same; also a poem written by donor entitled "Watchman Calls," dated May 8, 1855.

Gardner, Mrs. Helen Ward, Greenleaf: Copy of report of Henry J. Adams to the territorial legislature of 1858, as president of the board of commissioners to investigate election frauds under the acts of 14, 22, January, 1858.

Goodner, Rev. W. M., Larned: Copy of the prayer of donor at the opening of the people's party state convention in Topeka, June —, 1894.

Goodnow, Rev. Isaac T., Manhattan: Three manuscript letters addressed to donor, dated Worcester, Mass., January 27, 1890, February 7, and March 15, 1891, relating to Gov. Chas. Robinson's book entitled "The Kansas Conflict;" 45 manuscripts, consisting of letters and papers of dates from 1860 to 1866, chiefly relating to the founding of the agricultural college, the drought of 1860, and to political, educational, temperance and religious affairs in Kansas during the period in which they were written, as follows: Letters by T. H. Baker, Topeka, 2; John S. Brown, Lawrence; J. W. Davidson, Fort Riley, 2; B. C. Dennis, Golden City, Colorado territory; Rev. L. B. Dennis, Lawrence, 5; Rev. I. T. Goodnow, Manhattan, 6; E. O. Haven, Boston, 3; Rev. I. N. Lee, Topeka, 2; Rev. James H. Lee, Hillsdale, Mich.; H. D. McCarty, Leavenworth; Robert McBratney, Junction City; Rev. D. P. Mitchell, Johnstown, Pa., 2; Prof. B. F. Mudge, Topeka, 2; Marcus J. Parrott, Washington; Simeon Perry, Stone Bridge, R. I.; S. C. Pomeroy, Washington, 2; Rev. N. O. Preston, Topeka; Rev. Charles Reynolds, Fort Riley, 2; B. Sears, Providence, R. I.; William Smyth, Brunswick, Me.; J. C. Trask, Lawrence; Rev. Thos. H. Vail, Atchison; J. S. Whitman, M. D., Agricultural College, Pa.; three Kansas relief papers, famine of 1860, including call for a meeting in New York, December 12, 1860, with autograph signatures of W. C. Bryant, Chas. W. Elliott, Peter Cooper, Chas. A. Dana, H. J. Raymond, Horace Greeley, Edgar Ketchum, William M. Evarts, Horace B. Claflin, Cyrus W. Field, J. Watson Webb, and others; proceedings of Blue Mont College trustees, appointing Rev. J. Dennison, president of the college, March 5, 1863; proceedings of students and faculty State Agricultural College, relating to the death of Prof. N. O. Preston.

Greene, A. R., Lecompton: Sketch of the Lecompton free-state prison of 1856 and 1857, with a description of the building.

Halderman, General John A., Washington, D. C., 208 letters and papers, chiefly from his Kansas correspondents, as follows: I. L. Abell, Oakland, California; F. G. Adams, Topeka; H. J. Adams and William Stanley, 3 certificates of shares in the Wyoming, Jefferson county, Kansas, town association, 1858; John A. Anderson, Washington, D. C., 5; D. R. Anthony, Leavenworth, 2; George T. Anthony, Leavenworth, 2; J. P. Bauserman, Leavenworth; R. A. Barker, Atchison; Chas. A. Birnie, New York city; R. H. Bishop, Salina; W. P. Borland, Leavenworth; David J. Brewer, J. McCahon, H. Miles Moore, H. M. Herman, E. Stil-

lings, F. P. Fitzwilliams, T. A. Hurd, G. H. English, J. L. Pendery, Robt. C. Foster, L. B. Wheat, J. C. Hemingray, H. T. Green, Leavenworth, petition; George W. Brown, Lawrence; O. H. Browne, near Lecompton, K. T., Ridgeway, 2; A. Caldwell, Leavenworth, 2; Thomas Carney, Topeka; Edward Carroll, Leavenworth; George R. Cathcart, New York city; Chas. Chadwick, Topeka, 2; Col. B. P. Chenoweth, Canton, China; E. Colombet, Bangkok, Siam; C. Coppens, St. Mary's; Miss Mary L. Cort, Denver, Colo.; George A. Crawford, New York city; Gov. Samuel J. Crawford, Topeka; W. H. H. Curtis, Severance; A. C. Davis, Wyandotte, K. T., 2; Willard Davis, Oswego; William Dean, Bangkok, Siam; William H. De Graff, Jerseyville; H. B. Denman, Leavenworth, 3; George W. Deitzler, Fort Scott; copy of petition signed by Geo. W. Deitzler and 18 others, urging the appointment of General Halderman for colonel of new regiment; Winnie Dick, Topeka; Frank H. Drenning, Elwood, 4; M. J. Durham, Washington, D. C.; S. Ensminger, Highland; Thomas Ewing, Kansas City, Mo.; Thomas P. Fenlon, Leavenworth, 2; W. H. M. Fishback, Olathe; Stephen Fiske, New York; Henry Foote, Indianapolis, Ind.; J. H. Gillpatrick, Junction City; John A. Halderman, Washington, 14; J. W. Hart, Abilene; William Higgins, Topeka; Albert H. Horton, Atchison; Jay A. Hubbell, Washington, D. C.; J. M. Huber, Mount Florence; Fred. R. Hunt, Leavenworth; T. A. Hurd, Leavenworth; C. C. Hutchinson, New York city; H. W. Ide, Leavenworth; John J. Ingalls, Washington, D. C.; A. J. Isacks, Leavenworth; Henry Jansen, Leavenworth; Thomas L Johnson, Topeka; A. C. Jones, Nagasaki, Japan; I. M. Kalloch, San Francisco; H. C. Keller, Leavenworth; J. Ketner, Camp Lincoln; Thos. W. Knox, New York city, 6; John B. Kurth, Atchison; Carson Lake, New York; C. A. Logan, Leavenworth; H. A. Louis, Topeka; James McCahon, Leavenworth; T. McCarthy, Topeka; N. McCracken, St. Louis; J. B. McCullah, St. Louis; A. McDonald, New York; Rev. N.A. McDonald, Mount Union; John McKee, Leavenworth; F.J. Marshall, Longmont, Colo.; George W. Martin, Topeka; John Martin, Topeka; Andrew J. Mead, Manhattan, 3; E. Miller, Lawrence; Sam. F. Miller, Washington; Sol. Miller, Troy; C. R. Morehead, jr., Leavenworth; Thos. Moonlight, Fort Leavenworth; E. N. Morrill, Washington, D. C.; John S. Mosby, Hong Kong, China; Rev. Ephraim Nute, Boston, 7; Oriental Bank Corporation, Singapore; Thomas A. Osborn, Topeka; William N. Page, Leavenworth; P. S. Parks, Martinsville, Ind.; Marcus J. Parrott, Leavenworth; A. G. Patrick, Oskaloosa; Findley Patterson, Junction City; P. B. Plumb, Emporia; Gen. P. S. Post, Wyandotte; J. B. Pond, New York city; B. M. Prentiss, Chillicothe, Mo., 2; A. H. Reeder, Easton, Pa., 9, also 12 papers relating to business with Governor Reeder; Frank Reeder, Easton, Pa.; C. V. Riley, St. Louis, 2; J. W. Ripley, Washington, D. C.; Chas. Robinson, Lawrence; W. H. Russell, Leavenworth; Thomas Ryan, Washington, D. C.; Byron Sherry, Leavenworth; D. B. Sickles, New York; His Royal Highness, Prince Krom Mun Devawongsa, Bangkok, Siam; His Royal Highness, Prince Sonapandit, king's secretary, Bangkok, Siam, 2; B. F. Simpson, Paola; Henry L. Slayton, Chicago; John P. Slough, Chicago; W. H. Smallwood, Topeka; Dr. G. S. Smith, Bangkok, Siam; William Stanley, Leavenworth city, K. T.; B. F. Stevens, London; N. L. Stout, Leavenworth, 2; A. G. Studer, Singapore; F. Swoyer, Leavenworth; Thomas B. Sykes, Lecompton, K. T.; Frank M. Tracy, St. Joseph, Mo.; Thomas H. Vail, Topeka; General Van Vliet, Shrewsbury; Frank Vincent, jr., San Salvador, 3; B. P. Waggener, Atchison; J. W. Whitfield, Kickapoo, 2; D. W. Wilder, Kansas City, Mo.; Andrew S. Wilson, Washington; J. C. Wilson, Topeka; R. P. C. Wilson, ———; Jacob Winter, Salt Creek Valley; General W. W. Wright, Philadelphia, Pa.; John Russell Young, minister to China; miscellaneous papers: The original manuscript, in the hand-

writing of General Halderman, of the appeal issued to the people of Leavenworth county in favor of the election of democratic members of the Lecompton constitutional convention who would favor the submission of the whole constitution to a vote of the people who at the time of the election should be actual, *bona fide* settlers of Kansas; fifty-one autograph signatures to the petition, namely: John A. Halderman, B. L. Burris, J. C. Hemingray, H. B. Callahan, J. B. Davis, John F. Richards, John Kerr, C. H. Vincent, R. W. Budd, Hartford T. Clark, William A. Swift, Wm. S. Yohe, S. F. Johnson, R. Jones, W. D. Kelly, Joel Hiatt, Geo. P. Johnson, Samuel Phillips, D. L. Henry, C. C. Redman, Wm. F. Dodd, T. F. Campbell, Wm. A. Shannon, V. B. Young, G. W. Clayton, Dr. M. S. Thomas, J. M. Taylor, A. Payne, Bennett Burnam, P. B. Stanberry, John M. Ferrell, John T. Dunn, J. G. Hamburg, Michael Kelly, G. F. Shannon, John G. Spivey, Perry Keith. Lafayette Mills, M. J. Fogarty, J. M. Reed, G. W. Vincent, N. Vincent, John M. Fáckler, G. E. Vinson, H. B. Denman, J. M. Alexander, Powell Clayton, Dr. Tiffin Sinks, Edward L. Berthoud, Wm. P. Shockley, W. L. Blair, C. B. Trowbridge, P. P. Ellmore; provost marshal's pass, Leavenworth, October 16, 1864; card of J. A. Halderman, attorney and counselor, Leavenworth; card, with portrait, of Geo. Francis Train, candidate for President, 1872; invitation card, opening excursion, Kansas Pacific railway, St. Louis to Denver, August 30, 1870, John D. Perry, president; invitation card, twenty-first anniversary battle Wilson's creek, Leavenworth, August 10, 1882.

Hanway, John S., Lane: Manuscript volume containing the roster of the officers of the third Indian home guards regiment, in service in the war of the rebellion, from June, 1863, to May, 1865.

Hanway, John S. and Brougham, Lane: The manuscript collections of the late Hon. James Hanway, of Lane—family and business correspondence, 489 pages; papers written for publication in newspapers, 180; manuscript volume containing original treatises and miscellaneous notes on the subjects of natural philosophy, metaphysics, anatomy, and other subjects; volume containing original poetry and prose; volume containing literary extracts and scientific studies; volume of original essays on men and things; record book of Pottawatomie township, Franklin county, from July 17, 1857, to ———, 1868; docket of James Hanway, justice of the peace, Pottawatomie township, from January 30, 1859, to February 25, 1869; docket of James Hanway, mayor of New Castine, Darke county, Ohio, from March 14, 1851, to March 2, 1852; records of the Congregational church of Mount Gilead, Anderson county, Kansas territory, from April 2, 1859, to April 28, 1860.

Hawkes, F. W., Chicago: A manuscript paper containing incidents of experiences in Kansas in territorial and war times, while connected with William Terry and others in the business of the Ohio Stage Company; mention of W. C. Quantrill.

Hiatt, Henry, Twin Mound: Account of the observations and experiences of donor in Kansas in 1856, including an account of one week's imprisonment at Lecompton, in August and September of that year.

Hinton, Richard J., Washington, D. C.: Manuscript papers relating to John Brown, namely: letter of Capt. Wm. F. Creitz, of East Portland, Ore., dated June 16, 1889, referring to the "Battle of the Spurs"; copy of a letter of Rev. A. N. Milligan to John Brown; letter of E. A. J. Lindsley to James Redpath; letter of A. R. Chapman to John Brown; letter of James F. Neff, of Topeka, to Redpath and donor jointly; letter of Mrs. Mary Avery to Aaron D. Stevens; *facsimiles* of autograph poems by Wm. D. Howells, Edna Dean Proctor, and Edmond C. Steadman; also, of the commission of George B. Gill as secretary of the treasury under John Brown's provisional government; poem entitled "Bury Me in a Free Land,"

written by Frances Ellen Watkins, and copied by Aaron D. Stevens January 15, 1860, while in prison in Charlestown jail, Virginia, awaiting his execution for complicity in the John Brown raid; reminiscences of the "Insurrectionist," a paper of 22 note-sheet pages, written by James Redpath, relating to affairs in Kansas in 1856, to incidents on the overland emigrant route to Kansas from Chicago, by way of Iowa and Nebraska, and to Aaron Dwight Stevens; also copy, in the handwriting of Hon. John Jay, of New York, of a letter written by John Brown to Mr. Jay, from Charlestown, Va., jail, dated November 26, 1859; a manuscript volume, being a portion of a journal kept by donor during a part of the year 1856, giving a partial account of his journey with the second company of free-state emigrants of that year from Massachusetts, which marched overland through Iowa and Nebraska into Kansas, bringing arms and supplies for the beleaguered free-state people of the territory, giving, also, some account of the principal events which occurred in Kansas during that year; notes in the handwriting of Richard Realf, being memoranda of lectures which he delivered; report of the speech of David R. Atchison at the pro-slavery camp near Lawrence, May 21, 1856, previous to the sacking of the town, the report said to have been written by or under the direction of Dr. Joseph P. Root, afterwards lieutenant governor of Kansas; sketch made by Col. George H. Hoyt, showing the interior of the Charlestown, Va., jail, the room in which Aaron D. Stevens was confined, the adjacent rooms, and the stations of the prison guards, the sketch having been made for the information of the members of an organization formed for the rescue of Stevens and his fellow-prisoners, of which organization Thomas W. Higginson, Frank B. Sanborn, Doctor Thayer, James Redpath, John W. Le Barnes and others were members; fragment of a letter written by Frank B. Sanborn to Colonel Hinton; paper relating to California politics; historical sketch of the Harper's Ferry rescue party organized in February, 1860, for the purpose of attempting the release of Aaron Dwight Stevens and Albert Hazlett, the last executed of the prisoners of the John Brown Harper's Ferry expedition; original draft (in the handwriting of Colonel Hinton, who prepared it) of the proclamation issued early in 1861, by Col. C. R. Jennison, of the seventh Kansas cavalry, to the people of Jackson, La Fayette, Cass, Johnson and Pettis counties, Missouri.

Huling, Alden S., Topeka: Sketch relating to the ancestry of donor's branch of the Huling family.

Jones, David, Garnett: Manuscript biographical sketches of Edward Jones and Sarah Jones, father and mother of donor, settlers in Lawrence in 1854, the manuscript being in pamphlet form, in seven typewritten pages; also the ground plans of both floors of the free-state hotel, built in Lawrence in 1854 and 1855, as drawn by Edward Jones, who planned and directed the erection of same; also the discharge granted to Edward Jones December 15, 1855, attesting his services in the Wakarusa liberty guards, Kansas volunteers, from November 27 to December 13, 1855, "in defending the city of Lawrence from demolition by foreign invaders," signed by H. F. Sanders, captain, Lyman Allen, colonel, James H. Lane, brigadier general, and Chas. Robinson, major general; also portion of a letter written by William Salters, of Burlington, Ohio, to Edward Jones, in July, 1856, referring to Kansas troubles.

Knox, Rev. John D., Topeka: Financial record of the Kansas Freedmen's Relief Association, showing cash expended for use of freedmen in Kansas coming from Southern states, from May 16 to June 25, 1879, three pages; also list of cash contributions received from September 12, 1879, to March, 1881, 62 pages — a large account book; a ledger of 245 pages, of accounts of the association,

1879–'81; minutes of the board of directors of the association from September 12, 1879, to April 15, 1881; miscellaneous papers: 83 bills and receipts; 5 insurance; 10 orders; 2 books in account with Treasurer J. D. Knox, April 11, 1881; 6 check books, stubs; 15 statements of J. D. Knox, treasurer, accompanied by 924 checks, July, 1879, to April, 1881; 14 other papers.

Lincoln, Louise Davenport, Ozone Park, Long Island: Statement concerning Cephas W. Parr, government scout, connected with the army on the plains in 1868; also biographical sketch of Mrs. Anna Brewster Morgan, who was captured by Indians in Ottawa or Lincoln county, Kansas, October 16, 1868.

Lovell, Miss Sue, Topeka: Statement of donor regarding Abraham Lincoln's cane.

McAfee, Rev. J. B., Topeka: Letter from donor, inclosing copy of letter written to Gov. A. H. Reeder by donor, May 7, 1856, relative to threat of Charles Dunn to take the governor's life.

McCoy, Miss Alice, Topeka: Historical sketch of the Central Congregational Church, Topeka, written by A. G. Carruth, and read by him at the anniversary meeting of the church, January, 1894.

Pinkston, Mrs. Sallie A. (Lyon), Cedar Point: Biographical sketch of donor.

Potter, Samuel J., Topeka: Diploma issued to Otis Potter by the Douglas County Agricultural Society at its first annual fair, October 6 and 7, 1859.

Price, A. C., Junction City: Letter of A. D. Moon, of Beloit, relating to a small cannon in the possession of the G. A. R. post at Beloit, which is said to have been taken to the Solomon valley for the defense of the settlers, about the year 1869.

Riley, Z. F., Topeka: Paper giving the family lineage of donor.

Root, George A., Topeka: A poem entitled "Government Claims"; a poem written for the *Mail*, signed "Kilmer Relics"; report of the directors of the Kansas state penitentiary for 1864; manuscript order for state printing, addressed by Henry Hopkins, warden of the state penitentiary, April 8, 1872, to S. S. Prouty, state printer; other papers relating chiefly to state printing.

Ryan, Miss Eva, Hiawatha: Autograph poems by Mrs. Ellen P. Allerton, entitled "Why do You Ask?" "The Haunted Palace," "Harvest," "Indiana," "To Mr. and Mrs. Elbridge Chase, upon their Twenty-fifth Anniversary."

Sherry, Mrs. Helen, Kansas City, Mo.: Letters giving some account of the French colony in Leavenworth during the early territorial period — 1854–1860.

Smith, Rev. Benjamin L., president of associated charities, Topeka: Statement of relief statistics of Topeka, winter of 1893–'94.

Speer, John, Garden City: Paper relating to the biography of James H. Lane.

Stallard, Miss C. E., Topeka: A manuscript volume of 48 pages, containing copies of the poems written by the ladies of Grace cathedral, showing how each earned $1 to add to the funds of the Grace Church Benevolent Society, read at their meeting, December 14, 1893. (An account of the proceedings of the meeting is contained in the Topeka *State Journal*, December 16, 1893.)

Stumbaugh, Col. F. S., Topeka: Reminiscences of donor relative to John Brown's residence at Chambersburg, Pa.. in 1859.

Tilton, Warner A., Oxford: Manuscript copy of charter of order of Equal Rights of America, Oxford assembly No. 1, state of Kansas, with names of charter members and officers; also, statement written by donor, giving a history of the organization.

Tomson, Mrs. T. K., Dover: Manuscript book, containing the diary of J. C. Miller, member of a New England Emigrant Aid party, written while coming to Topeka and after reaching Topeka, from March 3 to July 4, 1855.

Walker, Mrs. Lois H., Topeka: Reminiscences written by donor (formerly Mrs. Geo.

W. Brown, of Lawrence), giving an account of the adventures of herself and Mrs. S. N. Wood, in passing through the enemy's lines at Lawrence during the Wakarusa war, December, 1856, procuring ammunition and conveying the same to Lawrence for the use of the free-state forces.

Webb, Leland J., Topeka: Petition, pleadings, orders and testimony in the Morton county county-seat case, 1887, in three typewritten books.

Whitaker, J. B., Topeka: Fifty sheriff's warrants, issued in the year 1857, by the United States district court for the second district, Kansas territory, under the seal of the court, signed by L. McArthur, clerk, for the arrest of the following persons, charged with robbery and other political offenses: Isaac D. Sims, Doctor Ritchie, A. J. Smith, William Jesse, John Cleary, Isaac Southwick, William A. Spiror, Hanks Switchell, Martin Stowell, William Updegraph, Edward Updegraph, H. Wentworth, Andrew Watters, James Garvey, William Webb, Garland Webb, Chas. Whipple, Andrew White, Alford Curtis, Chas. W. Moffat, Erastus Moffat, Dr. S. Lewis, Dr. R. Jordan, James H. Lane, John H. Kagi, A. A. Jameson, Eli Huddleston, William Sackett, H. Alderman, Cyrus G. Howard, Daniel H. Horne, —— Gordon, Guilford Dudley, Samuel Dolman, Calvin Cutler, William Crites [Creitz], L. G. Cleveland, W. W. Bouton, Luther W. Allen, Asaph Allen, Adam White.

Wilder,, D. W., Hiawatha: A letter written to donor by Capt. H. C. Palmer, of the 11th Kansas regiment, war of the rebellion, relating to circumstances connected with the death of Rev. Thomas Johnson, near Westport, Mo., in 1864; two letters of Frank B. Sanborn, and one of R. J. Hinton, relative to Colonel Hinton's book entitled "John Brown and His Men."

Wood, Mrs. S. N., Strong City: Letter written to donor by George W. Brown, dated Rockford, Ill., December 3, 1892, referring to the imprisonment of Governor Robinson and himself, with others, at Lecompton, in 1856, and to circumstances relating to the founding of the city of Emporia.

DONORS OF MAPS, ATLASES, AND CHARTS.

Adams, F. G., Topeka: Map of a part of township 10 south, of range 8 east, Kansas, showing the site of the Kansas Indian village, as described by Prof. Thomas Say, of Major Long's exploring expedition, in 1819, and showing the situation of Indian lodges; mapped by donor in 1880. See Kas. Hist. Col., vols. 1 and 2, p. 287.

American Bell Telephone Company, Boston, Mass.: Map of lines and connections.

American Telephone and Telegraph Company, New York: Map of lines and connections, March 1, 1893.

Bishop, G. S., Haven: Map showing the location of the farms in Haven township, Reno county, and Eagle and Greeley townships, in Sedgwick county, with names of owners, 1873.

Bradlee, Rev. C. D., Boston: Maps of the city of Boston in 1885 and 1892; map of the town of Brookline, Mass., 1892.

Brown, Orville C., Adams, N. Y.: Lithograph map of Osawatomie, Kas., as surveyed by A. D. Searl in February, 1855.

Brown, W. S., Kansas City, Mo.: Two maps.

Coburn, F. D., Topeka: Atlas of the United States geological survey, to accompany the geology of the Comstock lode, and that to accompany the tertiary history of the Grand Cañon district; railroad map of Illinois, 1893.

Clark, Mrs. A. M., Jewell : Map of California; illustrated charts, vols. 1 to 7, showing the founding, history, portraiture, etc., of 178 churches in Kansas, by denominations : Vol. 1, Protestant Episcopal, 5 charts; vol. 2, Catholic, 7; vol. 3, Presbyterian, 37; vol. 4, Congregational, 21; vol. 5, Baptist, 23; vol. 6, Methodist, 53; vol. 7, minor churches, 32.

Ditto, Frank S., Greencastle, Ind.: Four geological maps of Ohio, 1870.

Geological survey of Alabama University, Tuscaloosa: Map of Cahaba coal field, 1890.

Hanway, John S. and Brougham, Lane: Portfolio containing 27 original geological drawings by James Hanway.

Haskell, J. G., Lawrence: Plans of main new east room of the library of the State Historical Society, as made by the state architect, 1893.

Heisler, E. F., Kansas City, Kas.: Outline map of Kansas City, Kas., and vicinity.

Indiana department of geology and natural history, Indianapolis: Natural-gas map of Indiana.

Indiana geological survey, Indianapolis: Geological map of Indiana, 1893.

Iowa railroad commission, Des Moines: Map of Iowa, prepared and printed for the railroad commissioners, 1878, 1881, 1887, 1892.

Kinney, F. G., Oakley: Map of the state of New York, published in 1804.

Light, C. M., Pittsburg: Twenty miscellaneous maps from the Kansas World's Fair educational exhibit.

Martin, Hon. John, Washington, D. C.: Map of the United States and territories, with adjacent parts of Canada and New Mexico and of West India islands, issued by the United States department of agriculture, Hon. Lewis A. Groff, commissioner.

Mott, John M., Chicago: Six charts relating to phonetic script alphabet, conforming to that recognized by the American Philological Association.

Ottawa Geological Survey, Canada: Five maps to accompany annual report, vol. 5, 1890-'91.

Pennsylvania weather service, Franklin Institute, Philadelphia, Pa.: 25 maps.

Prescott, B. F., Concord, N. H.: Railroad map of New Hampshire, 1892.

Riley, Z. F., Topeka: Township and sectional map of Oklahoma, 1890.

Root, Geo. A., Topeka: Duplicate railroad maps, showing extension in 1889 of lines in Kansas; sectional map of Phillips county; one atlas; three maps.

Townsend, H. C., general passenger agent, St. Louis: Map of the Missouri Pacific railway, 1893.

Tweeddale, William, Topeka: Map made by donor, showing the mode of construction of the New Madrid canal which led to the capture of Island No. 10, in the Mississippi river, April 7, 1862, and which was planned and constructed by donor.

U. S. geological survey, Washington, D. C.: Atlas to accompany monograph of the geology of the Eureka district, Nevada.

U. S. post-office department, topographer's office, Washington, D. C.: Post-route map of Kansas and Nebraska and adjacent territory, 1893.

U. S. secretary of war, board of publication, Washington, D. C.: Atlas to accompany the official records of the union and confederate armies, Nos. 9 to 30.

Wilcox, P. P., Los Angeles, Cal.: Map of Palmdale colony, Los Angeles county, Cal.

DONORS OF PICTURES.

Abbott. A. J., Garden City: Cabinet photo portrait of donor, judge twenty-seventh district.

Adams, Miss Margaret L., Topeka: Photo group of the graduating class of the Topeka kindergarten training school, June, 1893.

Adams, Mrs. Mary A., Waterville, Mrs. Helen W. Gardner, Greenleaf, Mrs. Elizabeth P. Johnson, Horton, Mrs. Louisa M. Campbell, F. G. Adams, and H. J. Adams, Topeka: Oil-painted portrait of Maj. Henry J. Adams, by George M. Stone.

Admire. W. W., Chicago: Photo copies of memorial proceedings of the state officers in the senate chamber, October 2, 1889, relative to the death of ex-Gov. John A. Martin.

Allerton, Mrs. Ellen P., Padonia: Cabinet photo portrait of donor.

Anderson, Martin, Topeka: Cabinet photo portrait of donor.

Barrington, F. H., McCracken: Cabinet photo portrait of donor.

Beebe, John W., Kingman: Cabinet photo portrait of donor.

Bickerdyke, J. R., Russell: Neatly framed crayon portrait of Mrs. Mary A. Bickerdyke—"Mother Bickerdyke"—army nurse, war of the rebellion.

Blanck, S., Topeka: Cabinet photo portraits of ex-state treasurers Samuel Lappin, H. R. Dutton, J. E. Hayes, and William Sims; and of ex-attorneys general Chas. Chadwick, A. L. Williams, B. F. Simpson, A. Danford, A. M. F. Randolph, W. A. Johnston, and J. N. Ives.

Bodwell. Rev. Lewis, Clifton Springs, N. Y.: Cabinet photo group, showing First Congregational Church building in Topeka, with portraits of the first two pastors and their wives—Rev. Lewis Bodwell, 1856 to 1860, Dr. Peter McVicar, 1861 to 1866; cabinet photo groups, showing Plymouth Church, Congregational, Lawrence, with portraits of first two pastors and their wives—Rev. S. Y. Lum, October 15, 1854, to spring of 1857, and Dr. Richard Cordley, from 1857 to 1875; First Congregational Church in Manhattan, with portraits of the first two pastors and their wives—Rev. C. E. Blood, April 22, 1855, to January, 1862, and Rev. Geo. A. Beckwith, January, 1862; First Congregational Church at Grasshopper Falls, with portraits of the first three pastors and their wives—Rev. O. L. Woodruff, July, 1857, to 1859, Rev. H. P. Robinson, 1860 to 1862, and Rev. A. M. Hooker, 1862.

Bradlee, Rey. C. D., Boston, Mass.: Engraving showing the residences of Rev. Phillips Brooks, at North Andover and Trinity; heliotype portrait of the late Prof. Geo. C. Shattuck, M. D.; photo picture, showing the reading desk of Christ's Church. Longwood, Brookline, Mass., with portrait of donor, the pastor.

Broad, Rev. L. P., Topeka: Photo view of the Congregational tabernacle, Pittsburg, Kas., 1892; also, photo view of the sod church, Mount Ayr, Osborne county, Kansas, 1891.

Brown, Kenneth, Kansas City, Kas.: Steel-engraved portrait of the late Hiram M. Northrup, of Kansas City, Kas.

Brown, Orville C., Adams, N. Y.: Eleven photos and views of members of donor's family, namely: Family group, consisting of Frederick Orville Brown and wife, Leila Isabella Brown, Morgan Bryan (son-in-law), Mrs. Cornelia Gould Bryan, Miss Grace Bryan, Lewis Morgan Bryan, jr.; a cabinet photo of Mrs. H. Dwight and husband, cousins of donor; Mrs. Mary Gould Crane, sister, and Mr. Charles H. Crane, brother-in-law, of donor; Mrs. Abigail Wood, sister of donor; Mrs. Julia Kinsley, sister-in-law of donor, Buffalo, N. Y.; house of Mrs. O. C. Brown, Adams, N. Y.; birthplace of John Brown, Torrington, Conn.; small card photo

—4

of Mrs. Kate Horton, sister of donor, Chicago, Ill.; unfinished painting of cavalier and horse.

Caldwell, Alexander, Leavenworth: Two cabinet-sized photo portraits of donor.

Campbell, John P., Abilene: Large gilt-framed crayon portrait of donor.

Case, Nelson, Oswego: Photo-print of donor.

Chase, Mrs. Geo. S., Topeka: Cabinet photo portrait of Hon. William R. Griffith, first Kansas superintendent public instruction.

Chase, Lyman C., Hill City: Cabinet photo portrait of donor.

Clark, Mrs. A. M., Jewell: Photo of the huge walnut log cut in Leavenworth county and exhibited at the World's Columbian Exposition, Chicago, 1893; three lithograph views of state buildings, World's Fair.

Clevenger, C. C., Yates Center: Photo group of sergeants-at-arms of the republican house of representatives and assistants, session of 1893, namely: C. C. Clevenger, G. Stein, Geo. Higgins, A. C. Jordan, H. W. Young, C. J. Points, C. P. Kern, and W. P. Wilcox.

Coburn, F. D., Kansas City: Cabinet photo portrait of donor; 200 steel engraved portraits of the late Hon. Alfred Gray.

Corning, Miss Eva L., Topeka: Cabinet photo portrait of donor.

Crane, Geo. W., Topeka: Steel engraved portraits of Hon. Joel Moody, Dr. F. L. Crane, and of donor.

Cummins, Scott, Canema: Small photo portait of donor.

Davidson, Prof. W. M., Topeka: Photographic album containing pictures prepared for and shown in the Kansas exhibit at the Paris Exposition, in 1878, also exhibited at the World's Columbian Exposition, Chicago, containing views of Chetopa high school, Fort Scott high school, Parsons high school, west side; Parsons grammar school, east side; Lincoln, Quincy and Harrison schools, Topeka; Bethany College, Topeka; Ottawa high school; graded school, Columbus; Morris school, High school, Third Avenue public school, colored public school, interior of a school room in Morris school, interior of the high-school assembly room, interior of a school room in the Third Avenue school, Leavenworth; State Normal School, Emporia; public school, Beattie.

Davis, John, Junction City: Cabinet photo-portrait of donor.

Davis, Mrs. Willard, Kansas City, Mo.: Photo portrait of Hon. Willard Davis.

Defouri, Rev. James H., Santa Fé, N. M.: Cabinet photo portrait of donor.

De Geer, Mrs. M. E., Scott City and Topeka: Crayon portrait of donor, neatly framed.

Downing, George, Topeka: Cabinet photo of the sledge hammer used by Speaker Geo. L. Douglass in opening the door of the house of representatives February 15, 1893.

Drowne, Henry T., New York city: Engraved portrait of Washington, after a painting by Edward Savage, in 1790; engraved portrait of Capt. William Drowne, born April 17, 1755, died August 9, 1786, Providence, R. I.

Dundar, W., Washington, D. C.: Copperplate portraits of Hon. J. D. Miller, Lincoln, Kas., and Hon. Geo. Woodruff. Litchfield, Conn.

Elson, A. W. & Co., Boston: Photogravure portrait of George Washington.

Erving, William, New York: Artotype portrait of E. B. Whitman.

Farnsworth, H. W., Topeka: Cabinet photo portrait of donor, born October 13, 1816.

Farrow, W. F., Topeka: 15 photograph views of the Kansas legislative war, February, 1893.

Foster, Warren, Hutchinson: Photo portrait of donor; engraving showing the old Lincoln cabin near Springfield, Washington county, Kentucky, and *facsimile* of the marriage certificate of Thomas Lincoln and Nancy Hanks, the parents of

Abraham Lincoln, together with a printed folder containing official papers relating to the marraige.

Fulton, M. R., Winchester: Photo group, containing portraits of Speaker Douglass and officers of the house of representatives, 1893; cabinet photo portrait of donor.

Glass, C. G., Coffeyville: Nine photographs, illustrating the Dalton tragedy at Coffeyville, October 5, 1892, viz.: Two views showing Condon & Co.'s bank; view of the Dalton camp grounds; portraits of Marshal C. T. Connelly, Robert Dalton, Grat Dalton, Emmet Dalton, Dick Broadwell, and Bill Powers.

Goodin, Joel K., Ottawa: Photo portraits of donor and of his brother, the late Hon. John R. Goodin.

Goodnow, Isaac T., Manhattan: Engraved portrait of donor, as published in Barnard's *American Journal of Education*, at the time donor was superintendent of public instruction for Kansas.

Greer, Mrs. S. W., Winfield: Cabinet photo portrait of Hon. Samuel W. Greer, Kansas territorial superintendent of public instruction, 1858-'61.

Grinstead, V. H., Dighton: Cabinet photo portrait of donor, judge thirty-third district.

Gunn, Benjamin J., Girard: Cabinet photo portrait of donor "at 26."

Guthrie, W. W., Atchison: Life-size crayon portrait of donor, attorney general for Kansas, 1863.

Herbert, Ewing, Hiawatha: Cabinet photo portrait of John Brown, by Chase, Hiawatha.

Hinton, R. J., New York city: Proof prints of portraits which appear in his book entitled "John Brown and His Men," namely: Two of John Brown, one each of Owen, Oliver and Watson Brown, A. D. Thompson, Lewis S. Leary, John E. Cook, O. P. Anderson, Aaron Dwight Stevens, William H. Leeman, Stewart Taylor, John H. Kagi, Chas. P. Tidd, F. J. Merriam, Albert Hazlett, Barclay Coppic, William Thompson, Dangerfield Newby, Edwin Coppic, J. G. Anderson, and William A. Copeland; views of St. Joseph and Hannibal, Mo., in 1857 and 1858.

Hitchcock, E. C., North Topeka: Eight engraved views of Kansas state reform school, Topeka.

Holmes, Jas. H., Lane: Photo portrait of donor.

Humphrey, Jas., Junction City: Cabinet photo portrait of donor, judge of eighth district.

Humphrey, Mrs. M. A., Junction City: Cabinet photo portrait of donor.

Hutchinson, William Easton, Ulysses: Cabinet photo portrait of donor, judge of thirty-second district.

Hyatt, Thaddeus, Boston, Mass.: Engraved portrait of donor.

Ingalls, John J., Atchison: Large photo portrait of donor.

Inman, Maj. Henry, Topeka: Specimen of the figures composing the engravings of mural paintings, Yucatan explorations.

Jackson, Alfred M., Howard: Cabinet photo portrait of donor, judge thirteenth district.

Jenkins, E. J., Concordia: Cabinet photo portrait of donor.

Journalist, Chicago, Ill.: Board of officers of the international league of press clubs.

Kellerman, Prof. W. A., Columbus, Ohio: Cabinet photo portrait of donor.

Kowen, Geo. W., Topeka: Portrait of Mrs. Mary E. Lease, painted by John Koehler, a patient at the Topeka insane asylum.

Lawhead, R. B., Guthrie, O. T.: Cabinet photo portrait of Gen. Joseph H. Lawhead, late superintendent of public instruction of Kansas.

Leamer, William, Lecompton: Pencil sketch of the surveyor general's office at Lecompton, Kas., 1857.

Lease, Mrs. Mary E., Wichita: Large crayon portrait of donor, by S. Blanck.

Lemmon, Allen B., Santa Rosa, Cal.: Cabinet photo of donor, formerly state superintendent of public instruction of Kansas.

Leonard, J. H., Topeka: Cabinet photos of Kansas state senators, representatives, state officers, etc.

McAfee, J. B., Topeka: Large crayon portrait of donor.

Mason, Mrs. Alice B., Chetopa: Cabinet photo portrait of her father, the late Col. John W. Horner.

May, Celeste, Nelson, Neb.: Cabinet photo portrait of donor.

Medill, Jos., Chicago, Ill.: Half life-size crayon portrait of the late Col. John C. Vaughan; donated at the solicitation of Samuel Bernstein, Cincinnati, Ohio.

Mills, Harry E., Topeka: Cabinet photo portrait of donor.

Minier, Fred. S., Highland: Photo of monument erected in Highland cemetery to the memory of Prof. Hugh D. McCarty, who died in Highland September 12, 1887.

Morgan, Miss Nina Lillian, Topeka: Cabinet photo portrait of donor.

Nonpareil, Camden, Ohio: The White House, a lithograph.

Osborn, Russell S., Stockton: Cabinet photo portrait of donor; large water-color lithograph of the World's Fair building, state of Washington.

Osmond, S. M., D. D., Philadelphia, Pa.: Cabinet photo portrait of donor.

Parrott, Miss Laulette L., Dayton, Ohio: Large engraved portrait of her father, the late Hon. Marcus J. Parrott, second delegate from Kansas to Congress, 1857–'61.

Patton, Mrs. Ellen, Atchison: Cabinet photo portrait of donor.

Peacock, T. B., Topeka: Cabinet photo portrait of donor.

Peffer, W. A., Washington, D. C.: Cabinet photo portrait of donor.

Pennell & Zellner, Junction City: Views in Fort Riley and vicinity, showing the Ogden monument; the old Pawnee territorial building; Comanche, long the only surviving horse of the Custer massacre; the administration, mess hall, and hospital buildings; interior of riding hall; view of target practice; hospital litter drill; mounted parade; Fort Riley avenue; interior of hospital lecture room.

Phillips, Maj. James S., New York city: Oil-painted portrait of donor's father, the late Col. W. A. Phillips.

Pile, Dan. M., Sedan: Photograph of the battle flag of the 84th Illinois volunteers.

Pinkston, Mrs. Sallie A. (Lyon), Cottonwood Falls: Photo portrait of donor, 1887.

Plumb, Mrs. P. B., Emporia: Framed photo picture of the old *Kansas News* building, at Emporia, in which the *Emporia News* was published, the first bank in Emporia, afterwards the Emporia National Bank was established, Senator Plumb, president, and in which was held the first railroad meeting in Emporia; the *Emporia News* was published continuously from 1857 to 1889.

Prentis, Noble L., Kansas City, Mo.: Cabinet photo portrait of donor.

Remsburg, Geo. J., Atchison: portrait of donor, surrounded by relics and accouterments of his art as an antiquarian student and explorer.

Rice, Martin, Lone Jack, Mo.: Lithograph portrait of donor.

Rider, B. L., Pine Hill, N. Y.: Cabinet photo portrait of H. R. Dutton, state treasurer, 1861–'63, appointed by Governor Robinson in place of Wm. Tholen, who declined the office and went into the army.

Riley, Z. F., Topeka: Photo group of the Riley family, framed.

Root, Geo A., Topeka: Two portraits and one view.

Semple, R. H., Ottawa: Photo group of officers of the people's party, house of representatives, 1893, namely, Speaker J. M. Dunsmore, Speaker *pro tem.* R. H. Semple, Chief Clerk Ben. Rich, Sergeant-at-Arms Leroy Dick.

Shaw, Rev. James, Atchison: Cabinet photo portrait of donor.

Sleeper, Miss Katherine, Kansas City, Mo.: Cabinet photo portrait of her father, the late Gen. Hiram S. Sleeper.

Smith, Gov. A. J., Soldiers' Home, Leavenworth county: Photo views of the buildings of the western branch national soldiers' home, near Leavenworth.

Snider, Solomon H., Topeka: Photo portrait of donor, state insurance commissioner.

Speer, John, Garden City: Photo views of the two sides of an Indian silver peace medal, found by Mr. Lewallan in the spring of 1893, six miles east of Garden City, near the Arkansas river, south side, nearly opposite "Point of Rocks."

Statehouse employés, Topeka: Life-size sepia portrait of Gov. L. D. Lewelling.

Steele, Mrs. L. A. B., Lawrence: Enlarged photo portrait of donor.

Stevenson, H. S., Leavenworth: Photographic views of soldiers' home and vicinity, viz.: Fort Leavenworth from Sheridan's drive; Grant monument, Fort Leavenworth; monument at Fort Leavenworth in honor of Colonel Hatch, U. S. army; the building of the western branch of the national soldiers' home, near Leavenworth.

Stewart, Milton, Wichita: Cabinet photo portrait of donor.

Taylor, A. R., Emporia: Photo view of State Normal School, Emporia.

Thacher, Solon O., Lawrence: Cabinet photo portrait of donor.

Thompson, J. F., Seneca: Cabinet photo portrait of donor, judge twenty-second district.

Thompson, R. F., Minneapolis: Cabinet photo portrait of donor, judge thirtieth district.

Thompson, Ruth B., Pasadena, Cal.: Cabinet photo portrait of donor, daughter of John Brown.

Todd, J. F., Topeka: Photo portrait of donor, chief of Kansas bureau of labor.

Trickett, J. T, Olathe: Photographic view showing a cabin said to have been John Brown's, as it stood in 1858, at the base of Spy mound in the eastern part of Linn county, Kansas, John Brown standing by the same; also, view of the dwelling house which now stands on the same land.

Vance, W. O., New Albany, Ind.: John Brown memorial, large lithograph group, containing many John Brown portraits.

Vandivert, S. W., Kinsley: Photo portrait of donor, judge-sixteenth district.

Vincent, Cuthbert, Indianapolis, Ind.: Cabinet photo portrait of donor.

Vincent, Leo, Indianapolis, Ind.: Cabinet photo portrait of donor.

Walker, S. T., Olathe: Portraits of Philip A. Emory and donor, superintendents, and T. F. Rhodes, president of board of trustees, of the Kansas institution for the deaf and dumb, at Olathe; two cuts showing the buildings of the institution, and 10 interior views showing students in various employments.

Wall, Henrietta Briggs, Hutchinson: Copy of her photo group entitled "American Woman and Her Political Peers."

Weightman, Matthew, Topeka: Photo views of the machinery, buildings and kilns of the Capital City Vitrified Brick and Paving Company, three miles west of Topeka.

Wentworth, Dr. L. F., Osawatomie: Photo views in and near Osawatomie, namely: View of the original frame building of the Osawatomie insane asylum; view of the present main building; view of the new detached cottage, with room for 300 patients, women (not yet occupied); view of the Knapp building, opened in 1892, now containing 300 patients; view of the John Brown monument, erected in 1877, upon one side of which the following inscription is shown in the picture: "This inscription is also in commemoration of the heroism of Capt. John Brown, who

commanded at the battle of Osawatomie, August 30, 1856, who died and con-
quered American slavery on the scaffold at Charlestown, Va., December 2, 1859 ";
view of the residence of Rev. S. L. Adair, built by him in 1855, and which was the
Osawatomie home of John Brown; interior view of the room which John Brown
occupied, with portrait of his brother-in-law, Rev. S. L. Adair, as seated in the
room, 1894.

Wilder, Mrs. C. F., Manhattan: Photo portrait of donor.

Wilder, D. W., Hiawatha: Photo portrait of donor.

Wilson, Mrs. Augustus, Wilsonton: Photo portrait of donor.

Winans, Geo. W., Junction City: Cabinet photo portrait of donor.

Woman's Hesperian Club, Cawker City: Picture exhibited by the club in the Kansas building at the World's Fair, Chicago, 1893, representing the public library
building at Cawker City.

Wood, Mrs. Margaret L., Strong City: Enlarged photo portrait of Col. Samuel N.
Wood, neatly framed; cabinet photo portrait of donor.

Woodward, Brinton W., Lawrence: Photo portrait of donor.

Worden, Mrs. L. J., Lawrence: Card photo portrait of Hon. S. M. Thorp, state superintendent of public instruction, 1862.

Wright, John K., Junction City: Monograph of members of the house of representatives of Kansas, 1868.

Yoe, W. T., Independence: Monogram of the legislature and state officers of 1869,
showing temporary capitol building, 1863, and east wing of permanent capitol.

Youth's Companion, Boston: The picture "Sweet Charity," presented to subscribers
of the Youth's Companion, 1894.

DONORS OF SCRIP, COINS, AND MEDALS.

Adams, Paul, Topeka: United States silver quarter dollar, dated 1853.

Bowman, Clarence W., secretary of committee, New York: Two copies of the Washington centennial medal, 1889.

Bradlee, Rev. Caleb D., Boston, Mass.: Bill of exchange, dated San Francisco, March
3, 1860; bank note of the denomination of $10, issued by the Wiscasset Bank,
Wiscasset, Mass., dated July 4, 1817; note of the bank of Roxbury, Mass., for
$1.25, dated March 26, 1838; certificate of 100 shares in the "Grand Prize" Min-
ing Company, Nevada, given to G. B. Bayley, and dated San Francisco, May 11,
1880.

Brown, Orville C., Adams, N. Y.: Certificate of share in the Osawatomie Town Company, chartered January, 1858, and signed by N. I. Roscoe, secretary, and O. C.
Brown, president, dated Osawatomie, May 28, 1858; claim certificate of Kansas
Territory, No. 273, for $1,000, in favor of donor, dated Lecompton, June 14, 1859,
and signed by H. J. Strickler, auditor.

Clark, Arthur, Leavenworth: Aluminum people's party campaign medal; on one side
the presidential ticket nominated at Omaha, July 4, 1892; on the reverse, portrait
of L. D. Lewelling, candidate for governor of Kansas, 1892.

Dudley, Coleman, Topeka: Certificate of two shares ($10 each) in Council City,
K. T., American Settlement Company, dated September 11, 1855, signed by
George Walter, general superintendent.

Foster, Charles A., Quincy, Mass.: Three-dollar note of the Merchants' Bank of Fort
Leavenworth, Kas., dated August 21, 1854.

Green, Lewis N., Burlington: Spanish silver quarter dollar, dated 1793.

Hubbell, W. J., Topeka: A Roman coin, date not known, and a pfennige copper, of date 1874.

Smith, Miss Gertrude A., Lincoln, Neb.: Two silver quarter dollars, of dates 1854 and 1877.

Stanley, T. A., Osawatomie: Confederate currency and state-bank notes, as follows: $20 confederate states note; North Carolina state-bank notes, one 25 cents, one 50 cents, three $1, one $2, one $3.

DONORS OF WAR RELICS.

Rogers, W. A., Topeka: Cannon ball, supposed to have been shot by the British across the Maumee river during the seige of Fort Meigs, in 1813. The ball was picked up by Joseph Rogers, grandfather of donor, at Fort Meigs, in 1818. (Conditional deposit.)

Shockley, Maj. William B., Soldiers' Home, Leavenworth county: An iron ball, 1¾ inches in diameter, a relic of the battle of New Orleans, January 8, 1815. The ball was found by donor in 1879 in an alluvial deposit, at a depth of 4½ feet, while digging a ditch in front of where General Jackson's line of breastworks of cotton bales was thrown up in preparation for the battle.

Smith, Geo. W., Lecompton: A cannon ball found by donor in a well on the site of the territorial capitol building at Lecompton. The ball is supposed to have belonged to the battery which was posted near the prison to guard against the escape of the Hickory Point and Topeka free-state prisoners confined there in 1856.

DONORS OF MISCELLANEOUS CONTRIBUTIONS AND RELICS.

Achenbach, H. R., Topeka: Card containing school work, Wichita school exhibit, World's Columbian Exposition, 1893.

Adams, F. G., Topeka: Pass to statehouse, given to donor by Gov. L. D. Lewelling, countersigned by Adj. Gen. H. H. Artz, dated February 16, 1893, used by donor in passing through the lines of the state militia, February 16 and 17, 1893, during the legislative war.

Alrich, Mrs. E. B., Cawker City: Badge worn at the ninth annual convention, W. R. C., at Pittsburg, February 21-23, 1893; badge worn by donor at the thirteenth annual encampment, G. A. R., Newton, February 20-22, 1894; badge worn by donor at the tenth annual encampment, W. R. C., held at Newton, February 20-22, 1894.

Atkins, C. S., secretary, Pleasanton: Newspaper slip containing the resolutions adopted by the Sixth Kansas Veteran Association at the tenth annual meeting, Olathe, September 21, 1894, relative to the death of Maj. John Arrell Johnson, which occurred June 30, 1894, and expressive of the gratification of the members of the association that Major Johnson had deposited with the State Historical Society the relics and memorials of the services of himself and of his regiment during the war for the preservation of the union.

Ballard, D. E , Ballard's Falls: Polished fragment of a 170-pound volcanic rock from a sand bar on the Little Blue, at Ballard's Falls, Kas., supposed by Prof. W. O. Crosby, of Boston, to have been brought with drift materials from the Lake Superior region.

Bayley, Samuel, Hartford: Fragments of pottery found on Walnut creek, Atchison

county; a small white quartz arrow head from South Carolina, also one from Ohio; a number of water-worn pebbles and a small quantity of sand from Lake Ontario; a seed vessel from a plant not identified; two flint scrapers and one fragment of Indian whetstone.

Bert, H. L., Quincy, Ill.: Fragment of petrified wood from the big stump, said to be 52 feet in circumference, at Florissant, Colo.

Biddle, W. H., Topeka: Specimen of the sap of the bark of a California redwood tree, 400 feet in height and 29 feet in diameter, felled in Tulare county, California. The bark as taken from the tree was said to have been 23 inches in thickness. Presented to donor by J. L. Buck.

Bishop, G. S., Haven: Address to voters; a list of sub-alliances in Kansas.

Bradley, Mrs. John, Topeka: Small block of wood from the famous charter-oak tree, Hartford, Conn.

Breese, C. M., Manhattan: Table for determination of minerals, for use of students in agricultural college.

Brown, H. H., Topeka: Two people's party badges, state convention, June 12, 1894.

Brown, Orville C., Adams, N. Y.: Shingle from the house in Torrington, Conn., where John Brown, the partisan leader in Kansas, was born, in the year 1800, procured by the granddaughter of donor, Mrs. Grace Bryan Lewis, in the spring of 1893; charm cut from a peach stone by Spencer Kellogg Brown, son of donor, while in Castle Thunder prison, Richmond, Va., under the false charge of being a union spy, and under which charge he was condemned, and was executed September 23, 1863; also a quartzite pebble taken by Spencer from the prison.

Burr, H. C., Griffin, Ga.; Shannon, John P., Elberton, Ga.; Wolihan, A. M. and W. A., Macon, Ga.: A grand chapter badge worn at the triennial convocation of the grand general chapter of R. A. M., held at Topeka, August, 1894.

Burt, Frank J., Wabaunsee: Scrap book made by Col. Chas. B. Lines, chiefly made up of cuttings of newspapers containing letters and communications written by Mr. Lines from about the year 1832 to 1879; in considerable part relating to the organization and settlement of the Connecticut colony in Wabaunsee in 1856.

Cantrall, C. R., secretary, Fredonia: Eight posters of the Wilson county agricultural fair, 1893, and six posters and dodgers of the fair of 1894.

Clark, Mrs. A. M., Jewell: Section of a cornstalk used as a gavel at the dedicatory ceremonies of the Kansas building, World's Columbian Exposition, Chicago, October 22, 1892.

Clark, Arthur, Leavenworth: Card of admission to Kansas house of representatives, issued to donor by Speaker Dunsmore, January 14, 1893.

Coney, Patrick H., Topeka: Twenty-three miscellaneous papers, tickets, passes, etc., illustrating the management of the Lapland exhibit at the World's Fair, 1893; pair Lapland winter shoes, made of reindeer skin; a Laplander's belt, of reindeer leather, artistically ornamented; pair of reindeer antlers; pair of Lapland snow-shoes, of birchwood.

Connell, Mrs. Fannie L., Lecompton: A wooden dating stamp, used at the Lecompton post office in territorial times, upon which are engraved the words. "Lecompton, K. T.;" also, the stamp used during the same period, upon which is engraved the word "Paid."

Crane, Geo. W., Topeka: Samples of badges worn by the extra assistant sergeants-at-arms of the Douglass house of representatives and of the deputy sheriffs of Shawnee county during the time of the investment of the state capitol by the Kansas state militia, under the proclamation of Governor Lewelling, issued February 16, 1893.

Doolittle, W. A., Alma: Aluminum badge worn by donor, worshipful master of Alma

lodge, as delegate to the annual meeting of the grand lodge, A. F. & A. M., at Topeka, February 21–23, 1894.

Douglass, Geo. L., Wichita: Sledge hammer used by Speaker Douglass in opening
the door of the house of representatives, February 15, 1893. (Conditional deposit.)

Drowne, Henry T., New York city: Copy of a card of invitation, upon which is
printed and written the following: "Peace, liberty, and independence; admit
bearer to the entertainment (No. 158); I. Murray; carry glass and spoon; April
25, 1783." Copy of a pass, as follows: "Permit Mr. Drowne and son to pass the
guards from headquarters; I. Ward, secretary; June 22, 1775."

Elting, R. O., Kansada: Scales and weights for weighing coins, used by N. Y. Chamber of Commerce, 1791. (Conditional deposit.)

Fair, Geo. H., Topeka: Club carried by donor while acting as deputy sheriff of
Shawnee county, in the seige in house of representatives, February 15–18, 1893.

Fairchild, George T., Manhattan: Invitation to the Kansas State Agricultural College commencement exercises, June, 1893.

File, Rev. W. F., Topeka: Badges worn by donor, (pastor Madison Street Baptist
Church, Topeka,) while serving as assistant sergeant-at-arms and deputy sheriff
during the legislative war in Kansas, February 16–18, 1893.

Filley, C. E., secretary, Burlingame: Poster of the Osage County Agricultural Society.

Filson, T. A., Atchison: Gavel that called the united house of representatives of
Kansas to order, February 28, 1893. (Conditional deposit.)

Frey, John, Menoken: Iron hatchet, or tomahawk, found by donor about 1877
partly imbedded in the earth in underbrush on his farm in Menoken township,
Shawnee county, section 6, township 11, range 15, about one mile north of the
Indian graveyard, in the vicinity of Pleasant Ridge Presbyterian Church.

Funk & Wagnalls Company, New York city: Plates of the John Brown Bibliography.

Green, Dr. Samuel A., Boston, Mass.: Proclamation of Gov. F. T. Greenhalge, of
Massachusetts, declaring April 19, Bunker Hill day, a legal holiday.

Greene, A. R., Lecompton: Brick from the chimney of the Lecompton free-state
prison of 1856 and 1857; badge worn by donor at the twelfth annual encampment, G. A. R., Pittsburg, February 21–23, 1893.

Halderman, John A., Washington, D. C.: Two cards.

Hall, Chas. E., Russell, and Buckles, J. A., Ulysses: A block of wood, a pounding-
block, of black walnut, used on the speaker's desk in the house of representatives,
in session of 1893, by the republican and populist speakers in calling their re-
spective houses to order.

Hanway, John S. and Brougham, Lane: Eight scrapbooks containing copies of
original articles written by James Hanway, and printed in Ohio and Kansas newspapers; scrapbook containing miscellaneous clippings, not original.

Histed, Thad. C., Weir City: The original first "pigeon bill" model for twine harvest
binders ever made. Invented by Frank McClure, of Junction City, Kas. Mod-
eled by donor at Junction City, in 1877; now in use throughout the civilized
world.

Hoad, Gertrude M., Lecompton: Sheet music, "Bird of the Wildwood," and "March
of the Sixty Thousand."

Hoepli, Ulrico, Milan, Italy: Plan of ancient Rome.

Holz, Frank. Topeka: A piece of palmetto from Marion county, Florida.

Howlett, Col. John H., Atchison: An Allen revolving pistol, of the pepper-box style.

Hubbell, W. J., Topeka: A Garfield and Arthur republican ticket, Kansas.

Illinois historical library, Springfield: Arbor-day proclamation of Governor Alt-geld, April 14, 1893.

Kiene, L. L., Topeka: A large Indian stone ax, 2x4x9 inches in size, found on farm of donor, section 4, township 12, range 14, Dover township, Shawnee county, Kansas, at or near the residence of the Pottawatomie chief Ma-zhe, in the Indian village of Wau-wau-suc, near Mission creek, Shawnee county. (Conditional deposit).

Johnson, Miss Vina, Topeka: Piece of sheet music, guitar solo, entitled "Echoes from the Casino."

Junkin, J. E., Sterling: Badge of the Kansas Editorial Association; invitation card and program, 1894, of the Kansas Editorial Association.

Kingsley, D. W., secretary, Independence: Posters, circulars, etc., of the Montgomery County Fair Association.

Lawrence, C. H., secretary, Hiawatha: Three posters of the Brown County Exposition Association.

Lewelling, Gov. L. D., Topeka: Pen with which donor signed the resolution submitting to vote the equal-suffrage amendment to the constitution of Kansas at the general election, 1894.

Lykins, Mrs. Cornelia V., Kansas City, Mo.: A pair of brass candlesticks, formerly used in the first state senate of Kansas after the admission of the state into the union, and obtained at the time by the husband of donor, Hon. W. H. R. Lykins.

McFarland, Joseph, Wichita: An iron slave shackle, placed by James Hicklin, of Lexington, Mo., upon the leg of his slave man, and to which was chained a log chain and ball of the weight of 20 or 25 pounds. The shackle was taken from the negro by donor, in the night, some time before the war of the rebellion, and the negro set free. Mr. McFarland preserved the shackle as a personal memento of his recollections of the barbarism of human slavery.

Magie, Mrs. Elizabeth, Girard: Banner of the Order of the Eastern Star in Kansas, with large, elaborately carved black-walnut frame, contributed by the grand chapter to the Kansas exhibit in the Kansas building at the World's Columbian Exposition, and returned to Topeka for deposit, conditionally, in the rooms of the State Historical Society.

Orey, William, Wichita: General Shields's cane. A heavy, peculiarly grown stick, formed into a cane, which belonged to and was used by Gen. James Shields, and given by him to donor at St. Joseph, Mo.

Ozias, J. W., McPherson: Sample of wheat straw cut in 1828, in a field harvested with sickles, there being 50 men employed in the field, cutting half an acre a day each. The field was on the farm of Michael Moyer, in the southeast corner of Dauphin county, Pennsylvania.

Pearson, Robert H., Black Jack: Sandstone concretion from strata near the site of the battle of Black Jack, fought June 2, 1856, at which battle Capt. John Brown with his free-state forces captured Henry Clay Pate and his pro-slavery party.

People's party central committee, Topeka, 1894: Three posters of meetings to be addressed by Gov. L. D. Lewelling; two posters of meetings to be addressed by R. S. Osborn, secretary of state.

Remsburg, George J., Atchison: Two Indian spear heads and seven arrow heads found by donor in Atchison county, Kansas; three flint arrow heads, 21 imperfect and fragmentary spear heads and scrapers, 33 flint chips and 27 fragments of pottery, from aboriginal village sites and workshops in Atchison county; burnt stone from a mound on Owl creek, in same county; a chip cut by a beaver from a tree at the mouth of Salt creek, in Leavenworth county; 14 fragments of bones,

one of pottery, and one of burnt clay, from the farm of E. P. Rose, Sugar Lake, Buchanan county, Missouri; also newspaper clipping describing the same.

Richardson,.W. F., Topeka: A small, rudely shaped iron hoe, of aboriginal use, found on the farm of Mrs. Kate Osenbaugh, in Mission township, Shawnee county, April 15, 1894.

Ridgway, Charles H., secretary, Ottawa: Two posters of the Franklin County Agricultural Society.

Root, Frank A., North Topeka: Thirty miscellaneous circulars, cards, etc.; 10 circulars and cards relating to printing; 12 job specimens, Topeka *Mail.*

Root, Frank A. & Son, Topeka: "Game of Kansas History," 84 cards.

Root, Geo. A., Topeka: Cards, circulars, programs, tickets, and prospectuses, 42 in all; a piece of bread furnished the members of the republican house of representatives during the siege, February 16–18, 1893.

Seward, Geo. M., Topeka: Republican political badge, brass sunflower and motto, "Stand up for Kansas, 1892."

Smith, Chas. W., Lawrence: Memorial tablet of Hon. Samuel Walker.

Speer, John, Garden City: Cut nails made by Robert Speer, father of donor, in 1815, before steam was applied to their manufacture; specimen of ornamental pine from Watkins's harbor, near the Gulf of Mexico, at Calcasieu Parish, La.

Stagg, W. J., Topeka: Trunk and remaining branches of a young tree, relic of the Williamstown, Jefferson county, Kansas, cyclone of June 21, 1893.

Thompson, Robert, Topeka: Fragment of glass from the Presbyterian church at Wellington, which was destroyed by a cyclone in 1892.

Throckmorton, George, secretary, Burlington: Three posters of the Coffey County Agricultural Association, 1893.

Todd, Mrs. Mary E., secretary, Seneca: Chair exhibited by the woman's Columbian club of Nemaha county, at the World's Columbian Exposition, Chicago, 1893. (Conditional deposit.)

Traver, R. J., Leoti: Relics and remains from an Indian grave or burial receptacle in the bluffs of Beaver creek, six miles north of Leoti, Wichita county, Kansas, as follows: 1 large skull entire; 1 skull nearly entire; 1 small frontal bone; 2 scapulæ; 2 femurs; 2 humeri; 1 ilium; 2 tibiæ; 1 sacrum; 16 small bones and fragments; 2 copper bracelets; 1 arrow head, of iron; 2 shell ornaments; 21 porcelain beads, and a large number of glass beads.

Van Vliet, James B., secretary, Frankfort: Posters, streamers, tickets, etc., Frankfort Fair Association, 1888,.1892, 1893.

Waugh, Rev. Lorenzo, San Francisco, Cal.: Acrostic, "Save the Children from the Evil Habits of our Day."

Welch, R. B., Topeka: One of the passes used on the night of Thursday, February 16, 1893, by which 250 fresh men were admitted through the lines of the militia to relieve the guards, fatigued from long duty in the hall of the house of representatives; also, sample of badge worn by the 670 assistant sergeants-at-arms, under command of donor, in the hall of the house of representatives, from Tuesday, February 14, to Friday, February 17, 1893.

White, H. F., Topeka: Funeral dirge of Topeka, Orient and Siloam lodges, Topeka lodges, A. F. & A. M.

White, M. L., Garnett: Three posters, 1893, and two streamers and one hanger, 1894, of the Anderson County Fair Association.

Williams, J. Fletcher, St. Paul, Minn.: Testimonial of the Minnesota Historical Society to donor.

Woman's Columbian club of Jewell county, by Mrs. A. M. Clark, secretary of the Kansas board of managers, Topeka: The elegant banner displayed at the Co-

lumbian exposition, inscribed as follows: "Jewell, the banner corn county of Kansas; her daughters commemorate her glory."

Woman's relief corps, department of Kansas, Mrs. Edith M. Wood, president, Pittsburg: The woman's relief corps design which was displayed in the Kansas building, World's Columbian Exposition, Chicago, together with six national flags for the decoration of the same; also, broadside containing explanation of the design.

Wooster, L. C., superintendent World's Fair educational exhibit: Circulars, blanks, etc., used in the collection and preparation of the educational exhibit at Columbian Exposition, 1893.

Worrall, Harvey, Topeka: Board found near Williamstown, Jefferson county, Kansas, shortly after the tornado of June 21, 1893, some distance from the house of Mrs. Zachariah Evans, which was destroyed. Mrs. Evans was killed in the destruction of the house.

DONORS OF SINGLE NEWSPAPERS.

Bishop, G. S., Haven: 15 miscellaneous newspapers, of dates from 1873 to 1888.

Bogue, Mrs. M. L., Manchester, Conn.: One newspaper, devoted to the promotion of social purity and the protection of the young.

Bradlee, Rev. C. D., Boston, Mass.: Copy of the Boston Journal, March 11, 1893, descriptive of the fire in Boston, March 10, 1893; copies of St. Andrew's Cross, November and December, 1892; Boston Herald, June 13, 1893, containing proceedings of dedication of the new home for aged couples, at Roxbury, Mass.

Brewer, Justice D. J., Washington, D. C.: Copy of The Independent, New York, July 13, 1893, containing an account of the Fourth of July celebration at Roseland Park, Woodstock, Conn.

Brown, Orville C., Adams, N. Y.: Copy of the Utica (N. Y.) Herald, March 11, 1862, containing an account of the fight between the Monitor and Merrimac, and also the special message from President Lincoln, relating to the emancipation of slaves in the District of Columbia, and the gradual emancipation in the United States; copy of Commercial Advertiser, N. Y., October 3, 1893, anniversary number, ninety-sixth year.

Campbell, M. T., North Topeka: Topeka Times, April 2, 1874, to March 10, 1876.

Carruth, C. W., Oakland, Cal.: San Francisco Chronicle, April 23, 1893, California World's Fair issue, containing 64 pages, exhibiting the history, resources and condition of California.

Case, Nelson, Oswego: Newspapers containing reports of the Oswego, Kas., M. E. Sunday school, tenth anniversary, 1879, and two copies of the silver jubilee, May, 1894.

Clarke, Sylvester H., Clyde, N. Y.: Brick Pomeroy's Democrat, September 20, 1885.

Clemens, G. C., Topeka: The Tramp, Topeka, vol. 1, No. 1, July, 1878.

Colegrove, Prof. F. W., Ottawa University, Ottawa: Chicago Standard, November 24, 1892, containing biographical sketch of donor.

Colorado Sunday Sun, publishers of, Denver: Copy of the Colorado Sunday Sun, June 11, 1893.

Cummins, Scott, Canema: A copy of the Boston Liberator, December 21, 1860; copy of Douglass's Monthly, April, 1863.

Elliott, L. R., Manhattan: Daily Christian Advocate, Omaha, May 18, 19, and 25, 1892, containing proceedings of the general conference of the M. E. church; copy of the Normal Register, Salina, January, 1892; The Western Settler, February 15, 1893; two copies of Riley County Educator, Manhattan, February and March,

1893; Prohibition Lance, Manhattan, vol. 1, Nos. 1, 2, 3, 1894; copies of the Golden Cresset, March, 1884, March, 1885; The First Methodist, Topeka, September 17-23, 1893; Riley County Educator, August and September, 1893.

Fox, W. H. H., Auburn: Daily Kansas Freeman, Topeka, K. T., vol. 1, No. 2, October 24, 1855.

Garrison, Francis J., Boston, Mass.: A copy of The Liberator, Boston, March, 6, 1846.

Halderman, John, Washington, D. C.: Copy of the Neues Politisches Volksblatt, February 7, 1888; copy of the Siam Free Press, September 1, 1893.

Hanway, John S. and Brougham, Lane: Fifty miscellaneous newspapers, Illinois, Ohio, Massachusetts, etc.; 136, Kansas.

Heisler, E. F., Kansas City, Kas.: Five copies Kansas City Sun, January 9, 1893, illustrated edition.

Hinton, R. J., Washington, D. C.: Newspaper clippings, as follows: Letter from Martin White, published in a Bates county (Mo.) newspaper, January 24, 1860; chapter from Wetherell's "Old John Brown," published in Davenport, Iowa, Gazette, 1877; "John Brown's Scaffold," Washington Post, November 13, 1892; "John Brown's Life at Richmond," Washington Star, 1892; "John Brown's Revolution," correspondence of James Redpath, Governor Robinson, William A. Phillips, R. J. Hinton, and others, New York Herald, April 10, 1860; "Life of John Brown," R. J. Hinton's reply to Rev. D. N. Utter, Chicago News, January 5, 1884; "John Brown's Men," R. J. Hinton, J. H. Kagi, Aaron D. Stevens, and others, St. Louis Globe-Democrat, January 20, 1890; communication from Governor Robinson relative to J. H. Lane, John Brown, and others, Kansas State Record, March 25, 1860; "Harper's Ferry," Evening Post; "The Fort Scott Difficulties and Governor Robinson," R. J. Hinton, Freeman's Champion, 1858; "The Truth of History — the Doy Rescue," R. J. Hinton, Washington Standard, March 25, 1868; "General Denver in Kansas," R. J. Hinton, New York Tribune, August 10, 1892; three copies of John Brown song; "Albert Pike as Confederate States Indian Commissioner in 1861," R. J. Hinton, in Milwaukee Sentinel, July 12, 1865.

Hubbell, Mrs. M. G., Topeka: Scattering numbers of the Paola Republican, 1871, 1874, 1876 — 74 numbers in all; Paola Democrat, September 28, 1871; Paola Spirit, eight issues, 1873, 1874, 1876 ; two copies of the Globe and one of the Globe Democrat, St. Louis, 1873, and 1876; four copies of the Lawrence Standard, 1879, and 1880; 12 copies of the Lawrence Republican Daily Journal, 1874, 1875, 1876, 1878; 307 copies of the Daily Journal, 1879, 1880, 1881.

Ingle, E. P., Norman, Oklahoma: The Norman (O. T.) Transcript, April 22, 1893, fourth anniversary souvenir edition.

Julien, Isaac H., San Marcos, Tex.: The People's Era, San Marcos, Tex., January 19, 1893, containing an editorial article relating to Major Israel B. Donaldson, United States marshal for Kansas Territory in 1856.

Keagy, Franklin, Chambersburg, Pa.: A copy of Public Opinion, Chambersburg, dated February 13, 1891, containing an article entitled "John Brown and his Men."

Kinney, F. G., Oakley: *Facsimile* of the first newspaper issued by Benj. Franklin (February 11, 1723), reprinted (September, 1856) on a press once used by Franklin.

Lasher, Mrs. E., Topeka: The G. A, R. edition of the Indianapolis Journal, September 2-8, 1893.

Marston, C. W., Argentine: The Argentine Republic, January 26, 1893, containing an article relating to the Kansas Historical Society.

Meridith, Fletcher, Hutchinson: Two copies of the Weekly Interior Herald, Hutch-

inson, October 28, 1893, containing an editorial entitled "Reno County Newspapers."

Moore, Ely, Lawrence: Copy of the Fort Smith New Era, Fort Smith, Ark., December 26, 1863.

Northrup, H. M., Kansas City, Kas.: Copy of Kansas City Journal, November 5, 1892. containing a communication by donor on the bullion question, addressed to Senator Bishop W. Perkins.

Oberlin College, Ohio: One newspaper.

Republic Publishing Company, Colorado Springs: Republic and Telegraph, Colorado Springs, December 31, 1892, containing prize essays and poems relating to Colorado Springs.

Root, Frank A., North Topeka: Thirty-four copies of the New York Herald, of dates from April 15 to July 19, 1865, and September 5, 1862; four miscellaneous newspapers.

Root, Geo. A., Topeka: Elmira (N. Y.) Telegram, May 28, 1893, containing memorial and other G. A. R. matter; 17 miscellaneous newspapers.

Sherry, Mrs. Helen, Kansas City, Mo.: Copy of L'Estafette du Kansas, a French newspaper, published in Leavenworth, December 11, 1858.

University Extension, Chicago, Ill.: The University Extension World, vols. 1–3, 1894.

Ward, Mrs. Jennie M., Ottawa: Supplement to Western School Journal, containing a historical sketch of the Ladies' Mount Vernon Association.

Whittemore, G. G., Cambria, Wyo.: Newcastle (Wyo.) News-Journal, August 3, 1894, containing proceedings of Wyoming republican state convention.

Wilcox, P. P., Los Angeles, Cal.: Land and Water, Los Angeles, June 14, 1894, and the Express, Los Angeles, June 29, 1894.

DONORS OF NEWSPAPER FILES AND MAGAZINES.

Baker, F. P., Topeka: File of the True Commonwealth, Washington, D. C., April 1, 1890, to March 1, 1891.

Benham, P. D., Chicago, Ill.: The Banner of Gold, Chicago, 1892–'93, bound file.

Bundy, Mrs. J. C., Chicago: Partial files of the Religio-Philosophical Journal, Chicago, from 1878–'91; most of the volumes nearly complete.

Clemens, G. C., Topeka: Whim-Wham, Topeka, vol. 1, from October 9, 1880, to May 7, 1881, and vol. 2, from May 14, 1881, to October 27, 1881.

Cragin, F. W., Colorado Springs, Colo.: File of the American Geologist, Minneapolis, Minn., vol. 7, 1891; American Naturalist, nine numbers of vol. 19, 1885.

Dickinson, Rev. Chas. A., Boston, Mass.: File of the Berkeley Beacon, Boston, vol. 5, 1893.

Goodin, Joel K., Ottawa: Bound file of the Journal, Minneola, Kas., from March 19, to September 3, 1864, and the Young America, Baldwin City, November. 1864, to May, 1865.

Hanway, John S. and Brougham, Lane, from the library of the late Hon. James Hanway: Bound files of the Kansas Farmer, vols. 2 and 3, January, 1865, to July, 1867; Kansas Spirit, vols. 1 and 2, from February, 1872, to September, 1873: Farmer's Review, Chicago, vols. 5 and 6, from December 23, 1880, to June 23, 1881; American Agriculturist, New York, vol. 26, 1867, and vol. 28, 1869; Mirror of Progress, Kansas City, Mo., vols. 1–3, from September 6, 1879, to October 22, 1881.

Hubbell, Mrs. M. G., Topeka: File of the Paola Republican, 1873.

Huling, A. S., Topeka: File of the Labor Inquirer, Chicago, February, 1887, to Au-

gust, 1888; the first two volumes of Henry George's Standard, 1887; and the Leader, New York, from September 28 to November 11, 1887.

Husbandman, Binghampton, N. Y.: Bound files of the Husbandman, Elmira, N. Y., from August 25, 1875, to August 10, 1888.

Iowa state board of health, Des Moines: Monthly bulletin, from vol. 1, No. 6, November, 1887, to vol. 6, No. 6, 1892.

Lane, V. J., Kansas City, Kas.: File of the Wyandotte Herald for 1873.

Riley, Z F., Topeka: File of Godey's Lady's Book for 1864.

Root, Frank A., Topeka: Files of the following Colorado newspapers: Crested Butte Republican, October 5, 1881, to July 19, 1882; Tin Cup Record, May 28, 1881, to July 22, 1882; Free Press, Gunnison, September 7, 1881, to July 29, 1882, 2 vols.; Garfield Banner and Tin Cup Banner, September 10, 1881, to July 29, 1882; Gunnison Democrat, August 4, 1880, to May 11, 1881; News and Democrat, Gunnison, April 24, 1880, to June 11, 1881; Pitkin Independent, July 30, 1880, to July 29, '1882; Elk Mountain Bonanza, Gothic, July 10, 1880, to March 26, 1881; Gothic Miner, April 2 to November 5, 1881; Silver Record, Gothic, June 24 to July 22, 1882; Elk Mountain Pilot, Irwin and Crested Butte, June 24, 1880, to December 11, 1884; Pitkin Mountain News, October 21, 1881, to July 28, 1882; Gunnison News-Democrat, July 17, 1881, to August 1, 1882, 2 vols.; miscellaneous Gunnison county newspapers, May, 1881, to October, 1886; miscellaneous Colorado newspapers, 1880 to 1886, 9 vols.; Gunnison Daily Review, October 11, 1881, to July 28, 1882; Gunnison Daily Review-Press, August 1, 1882, to June 30, 1886, 8 vols.; Gunnison Sun, 1 vol.; Gunnison Review, May 15, 1880, to July 29, 1882; Gunnison Review, May 15, 1880, to May 7, 1881, 3 files; files of the following Kansas newspapers: Holton Express, 15 vols.; Topeka Mail, October 22, 1885, to December 31, 1886, January 7, 1887, to December 30, 1892, January 6, 1888, to December 27, 1889, January 3, 1890, to December 30, 1892, January 2, 1891, to December 30, 1892 —14 vols.; file of the New York Weekly post.

Root, Geo. A., Topeka: New York Weekly Tribune, August 10, 1892, to September 20, 1893; The Week, December 21, 1888, to June 28, 1889, Toronto, Can.

Scales, James W., North Topeka: Bound file of the Carbondale Record, April 7 to November 17, 1888.

Shepperd, Mrs. K. W., Christchurch, New Zealand: The Prohibitionist, Christchurch, New Zealand, June 6, 1891, to May 21, 1892.

Smith, Andrew J., Leavenworth: Bound file of the Reveille, Soldiers' Home, Leavenworth, February 1, 1893, to January 15, 1894.

Snow, Francis H., Lawrence: Seminary Notes, vols. 1 and 2, May, 1891, to May, 1893.

Ward, Mrs. Jennie M., Ottawa: File of the Mount Vernon Record, Philadelphia, July, 1858, to June, 1861.

BOUND NEWSPAPERS AND PERIODICALS.

The following is a statement of bound newspaper files and bound volumes of periodicals in the library of the Society December 31, 1894, numbering 15,409 volumes; of which 10,689 are of Kansas, and 4,720 are of other states and countries. Of these, 2,776 have been added during the two years covered by this report, and of which added volumes 1,635 are of Kansas. Volumes not otherwise described are of weekly newspapers. Added to some of the county lists below are volumes which contain short-lived newspapers, such as suspended publication after a few issues, and which have been bound together in one book as indicated.

BOUND NEWSPAPERS AND PERIODICALS.

NEWSPAPERS.	Years.	No. vols
ALLEN COUNTY (88).		
Iola Register..	1873–1894	22
Allen County Independent, Iola..............................	1879,1880	1
Allen County Courant, Iola..................................	1884–1889	5
Allen County Democrat, Iola.................................	1886–1888	1
Democrat-Courant, Iola.....................................	1888	1
The Farmers' Friend, Iola..................................	1890–1892	3
Allen County Herald, Iola...................................	1890–1893	3
Friend-Herald, Iola...	1893,1894	2
The Rural Kansan, Humboldt.................................	1873,1874	1
Humboldt Union (* October 9 to December 11, 1869).........	1876–1894	19
Inter-State, Humboldt......................................	1878–1886	9
Independent Press, Humboldt...............................	1882	1
The Humboldt Herald.......................................	1887–1894	7
Moran Herald...	*1885–1894	9
Elsmore Eagle..	1890–1892	2
Savonburg Progress..	1891,1892	1
Allen county, short-lived, vol. 1:		
Neosho Valley Register, Iola, January 5 to December 8, 1869; The Rural Kansan, Humboldt, November, 1873, May and September, 1874; Daily Evening Courant, Iola, December 5–22, 1883...............	....	1
ANDERSON COUNTY (107).		
Garnett Weekly Journal....................................	1876–1894	19
Garnett Plaindealer (April to December, 1883, Anderson County Republican), (*October 13, 1869).........................	1876–1884	8
Anderson County Republican, Garnett.......................	1883,1884	1
Republican-Plaindealer, Garnett............................	1884–1894	11
Anderson County Democrat, Garnett........................	1885,1886	1
Garnett Eagle..	1886–1894	8
Kansas Agitator, Garnett...................................	1890–1894	4
The Kansas Sunflower (monthly), Garnett...................	1893,1894	1
The Greeley Tribune..	1880,1881	1
The Greeley News..	1881–1894	13
Greeley Graphic..	1892–1894	3
The Light, Greeley..	1892–1894	2
The Pastor's Visit (monthly), Greeley......................	1894	1
The Colony Free Press......................................	1882–1894	12
Westphalia Times...	1885–1894	9
Westphalia Independent and Democrat......................	1884,1885	1
Kincaid Kronicle (April, 1888, to September, 1889, lacking)..	1886–1892	6
The Kincaid Dispatch.......................................	1888–1894	6
Anderson county, short-lived, vol. 1:		
The Baptist Times, Garnett, January to April, 1892; Greeley Tribune, March 4 to June 17, 1892; The Harris News, June 29 to December 21, 1894.........	....	1
ATCHISON COUNTY (224).		
Squatter Sovereign, Atchison..............................	1856,1857	1
Freedom's Champion, Atchison (February 3, 1861, to February 14, 1862, lacking)..	1857–1863	4
Atchison Daily Free Press...................................	1865–1868	7
Atchison Weekly Free Press.................................	1865–1868	3
Champion and Press (weekly), Atchison......................	1868–1873	4
Atchison Daily Champion....................................	1876–1894	37
Atchison Weekly Champion (lacking from December, 1877, to June, 1885).... ...	1873–1892	12
Kansas Zeitung, Atchison...................................	1857,1858	1
Atchison Union (broken files)..............................	1859–1861	3
American Journal of Education. (See Missouri—St. Louis.)		
Atchison Patriot (daily), (from July, 1876, to July, 1879, lacking)....	1876–1894	32
Atchison Patriot (weekly)..................................	1874–1894	21
Atchison Courier...	1876–1879	3
Atchison Globe (daily)......................................	1878–1894	31
Atchisonian, Atchison......................................	1877	1
Atchison Banner..	1878,1879	1
The New West, Atchison....................................	1878–1880	2
The Sunday Morning Call, Atchison.........................	1880–1883	4
Kansas Telegraph (daily), Atchison........................	1880,1881	1
Kansas Staats-Anzeiger, Atchison..........................	1881–1885	4
Atchison Journal (daily)....................................	1881,1882	2
Western Mercury, Atchison.................................	1883–1886	2
The Western Recorder, Atchison †..........................	1884	1
The Trades-Union, Atchison................................	1885,1886	1
The Atchison Times (daily and weekly).....................	1887–1891	3
Midland College Monthly, Atchison........................	1891,1892	1
The Midland (monthly), Atchison...........................	1892–1894	3
Atchison Baptist (monthly).................................	1890–1893	3
The College Review (monthly), Lawrence and Atchison......	1891–1894	4
The Kansas Churchman (monthly), Atchison. (See Lawrence.)		

* In portfolio. † Not found.

BOUND NEWSPAPERS AND PERIODICALS -- Continued.

NEWSPAPERS.	Years.	No. vols
ATCHISON COUNTY — *Concluded.*		
Abbey Student (monthly), Atchison	1891–1894	3
The New Kansas Magazine (monthly), Atchison	1892, 1893	1
Atchison Blade	1892–1894	1
Missouri Valley Farmer, Atchison	1893, 1894	2
The Graphic, Atchison	1893, 1894	1
The Prairie Press, Lancaster	1888–1890	2
Muscotah Record (missing from August, 1886, to January, 1887)	1885–1894	8
The Effingham Enterprise	1886	1
The Effingham Times	1887–1891	4
The Graphic, Effingham	1891–1893	2
Huron Graphic	1890, 1891	2
The Huron Herald	1892–1894	3
Atchison county, short-lived, vol. 1:		
Daily Sumner Gazette, October 1, 1857; Real Estate Record, Atchison, July, 1869; Kansas Illustrated Monthly Souvenir, Atchison, February and June, 1873; Atchison Daily Globe, September 30 and October 12, 1873; Gardner's Real Estate Bulletin, Atchison, December, 1873; Short Line Advocate, Atchison, April 21, 1879; Der Courier, Atchison and Topeka, May 20, 1879; Muscotah News, June 16, 1880; Public Ledger, Atchison, August 19 and October 30, 1880; Western Farm and Home, Atchison, January to April, and October, 1881; Bible Investigator, Atchison. July to December, 1881; Atchison's Monthly, September, 1881; Sentinel of the Northwest, Atchison, January, 1883; Sunday Morning Facts, Atchison, September 2, 1883, to February 3, 1884; Humorist, Atchison, February 2, 1884; Huron Headlight, March 13, 1884; Atchison Sunday Morning Sermon, June 1 to July 27, 1884; The Huron Messenger, July 2, 1884; Atchison Advance, November 15, 1884, to January 3, 1885; Messachorean, Atchison, February to June, 1888; Atchison Daily Bee, March 25 to April 4, 1889; The Tradesman, Atchison, November 16, 1891; Effingham Weekly Journal, September 3, 1892, to February 23, 1893; People's Press, Atchison, August 5 to September 15, 1893		1
Atchison county, short-lived, vol. 2:		
Huron Times, April 4-25, 1891		1
BARBER COUNTY (74).		
Barber County Mail, Medicine Lodge	1878, 1879	1
Medicine Lodge Cresset	1879–1894	16
Barber County Index, Medicine Lodge	1881–1894	13
Medicine Lodge Chief	1886–1888	2
Barber County Herald, Medicine Lodge	1890, 1891	1
Hazelton Express	1884–1893	10
The Herald, New Kiowa	1884–1891	6
The Kiowa Journal	1886–1894	8
The Alliance Review, Kiowa	1891–1894	4
Sharon News	1884–1886	2
The Union, Sun City	1884–1888	4
The Ætna Clarion	1885–1887	2
Kansas Prairie Dog, Lake City	1885–1889	3
The Lake City Bee	1888, 1889	1
Barber county, short-lived, vol. 1:		
Independent Star, Medicine Lodge, February 21 to March 13, 1888; Barber County Democrat, Medicine Lodge, March 23 to July 6, 1888; Hazelton Bee, March 24 to September 8, 1894		1
BARTON COUNTY (109).		
Great Bend Register	1876–1894	18
Inland Tribune, Great Bend	1876–1894	18
Arkansas Valley Democrat, Great Bend	1877–1882	5
Kansas Volks Freund, Great Bend	1878, 1879	1
Barton County Democrat, Great Bend	1886–1894	8
Daily Graphic, Great Bend	1887, 1888	2
Evening News (daily), Great Bend	1890–1894	10
Barton County Beacon, Great Bend	1890–1894	4
Normal Weekly, Great Bend	1891, 1892	1
Pythian Sisters' News (monthly), La Crosse, Great Bend, and Erie	1892, 1893	1
The Rebekahian (monthly), Great Bend	1894	1
The Ellinwood Express	1878–1888	10
The Ellinwood Advocate	1888–1894	6
Pawnee Rock Leader	1886–1893	8
The Alliance Globe, Pawnee Rock	1891, 1892	1
The Echo, Hoisington	1887–1889	1
Hoisington Dispatch	1889–1894	6
The Hoisington Blade	1892, 1893	2
Claflin Gazette	1888	1
Barton County Banner, Claflin	1890–1894	4
Claflin Leader	1894	1

—5

BOUND NEWSPAPERS AND PERIODICALS—CONTINUED.

NEWSPAPERS.	Years.	No. vols
BARTON COUNTY—*Concluded.*		
Barton county, short-lived, vol. 1:		
The New West, Great Bend, September, 1888; Barton County Times, July 26 to September 27, 1883; The Crank, Pawnee Rock, March 7 to 28, 1888; Hoisington Mascot, August 17 to September 21, 1888; Morning Mascot, Hoisington, October 18, 1888; Fun, Pawnee Rock, February 2 to March 30, 1891; Normal Herald, February to May, 1892; Kansas Educator, Great Bend, September, 1892, to June, 1893; Evening Star, Great Bend, May 6 to June 27, 1893	....	1
BOURBON COUNTY (167)..		
Fort Scott Daily Monitor (December 8, 1891, to November 1, 1892, lacking)...	1880–1894	28
Fort Scott Weekly Monitor (1870 to June, 1876, November, 1891, to October, 1892, lacking)	1867–1894	20
Fort Scott Pioneer	1876–1878	2
Camp's Emigrants' Guide, Fort Scott	1877	1
New Century, Fort Scott	1877, 1878	1
Fort Scott Herald (Herald and Record, 1882 to 1884, 2 vols.)	1878–1885	8
Republican-Record, Fort Scott	1879–1882	4
Evening Herald (daily), Fort Scott	1882–1885	7
The Western Educational Review (monthly), Fort Scott	1881, 1882	1
Medical Index (monthly), Fort Scott	1881–1884	4
The Banner, Fort Scott	1882–1884	2
Fort Scott Daily Tribune	1884–1894	22
Fort Scott Weekly Tribune	1884–1894	10
Kansas Staats-Zeitung, Fort Scott	1886, 1887	2
The Fort Scott Union	1887, 1888	1
The Fort Scott Evening Globe (daily)	1888, 1889	1
The Sunday Call, Fort Scott	1889	1
Fort Scott Daily News	1889, 1890	2
The Spectator, Fort Scott	1890–1892	3
Fort Scott Industrial Union	1890, 1891	1
The Normal Journal (bi-monthly and monthly, scattering issues), Fort Scott	1883–1894	3
The Lantern, Fort Scott	1891, 1892	1
Fort Scott Dispatch	1892–1894	2
Western Medical Journal, Fort Scott	1893, 1894	1
Bronson Pilot	1884–1894	11
The Fulton Independent	1884–1894	10
The Fulton Rustler (monthly)	1890–1893	4
The Telephone, Uniontown	1885–1887	2
The Garland Gleaner	1886, 1887	2
The Telephone, Mapleton	1887–1889	2
Mapleton Dispatch (at Fort Scott in 1892–1894)	1889–1894	4
The Lantern, Mapleton	1890, 1891	1
Bourbon county, short-lived, vol. 1:		
Daily Fort Scott Post, October 16, December 14, 29, 30, 1869, January 4, 1870; Southern Kansas Immigrant, Fort Scott, May, October, and December, 1869; Fort Scott Land Record, September, November, 1870; Broom Corn Reporter, Fort Scott, September 15, 1886, to September 1, 1887; Fort Scott Weekly News, November 28, 1889, to March 27, 1890; Fort Scott Herold, April 3 to May 29, 1890; Southern Argus, Fort Scott, October 15, 1891, to February 4, 1892; Christian Sower, Fort Scott, October, 1892, to January, 1893,	....	1
BROWN COUNTY (100).		
Hiawatha Dispatch	1876–1882	6
The Hiawatha World and Brown County World	1882–1894	13
Brown County World (daily)	1891, 1892	1
Kansas Herald, Hiawatha	1876–1883	8
The Kansas Sun, Hiawatha	1879, 1880	1
Weekly Messenger, Hiawatha	1882–1884	2
The Kansas Democrat, Hiawatha	1883–1894	11
Free Press, Hiawatha	1887, 1888	1
The Hiawatha Journal	1889–1894	5
The Delta of Sigma Nu (bimonthly), Hiawatha, *see* Douglas county	1891–1894	2
The Sunflower Magazine (monthly), Hiawatha	1893, 1894	1
Kansas Newspaperdom and Kansas Newspaper World, Hiawatha	1894	1
Everest Reflector	1884–1886	2
The Everest Enterprise	1888–1894	6
Horton Headlight	1886–1894	8
Horton Daily Headlight (September, 1888, to October, 1889, lacking)	1887–1889	2
Horton Gazette	1887–1889	2
Horton Commercial	1887–1894	7
The Horton Railway Register	1888, 1894	1
Horton Daily Railway Register	1889	1
Horton Telegram	1889, 1890	1
Hamlin News Gleaner	1889, 1890	1
Fairview Enterprise	1888–1894	7

BOUND NEWSPAPERS AND PERIODICALS—Continued.

NEWSPAPERS.	Years.	No. vols
BROWN COUNTY— *Concluded.*		
Fairview Courier..	1893,1894	1
Morrill News..	1890-1894	5
The Robinson Reporter...	1891,1892	1
Brown county, short-lived, vol. 1:		
The North Kansan, Hiawatha, September 7 to November 30, 1878; The Morrill Journal, July 5 to October 18, 1882; Brown County Herald, Morrill, July 9 to August 20, 1886; Brown County Star, Horton, January 1 to April 23, 1889..	....	1
Brown county, short-lived, vol. 2:		
Brown County Sentinel, Hiawatha, September 9 to December 30, 1869; Interstate Advocate, Morrill, June 1, 1886, to April, 1888; Daily Brown County World, Hiawatha, October 4-7, 1887; Brown County Star, Horton, February 26, 1889; Horton Headlight. M. E. conference edition, March 5-10, 1890; The Academy Review, Hiawatha, December, 1892, to March, 1893...............	....	1
BUTLER COUNTY (165).		
Augusta Republican (1875–1880 lacking).............................	1873-1883	3
Southern Kansas Gazette, Augusta	1876-1887	11
Augusta Advance..	1883,1884	1
Augusta Electric Light..	1884-1886	2
Augusta Weekly Journal..	1887-1894	7
The Augusta News..	1889,1890	1
The Industrial Advocate, Augusta.................................	1890,1891	1
Augusta Gazette, No. 2..	1892-1894	2
The Sunflower, Augusta..	1894	1
Walnut Valley Times, El Dorado.................................	1874-1894	21
Daily Walnut Valley Times, El Dorado...............................	1887-1894	15
El Dorado Press...	1877-1883	7
El Dorado Daily Republican...	1885-1888	5
El Dorado Republican..	1883-1894	11
Butler County Democrat, El Dorado (lacking from Oct., 1888 to Nov., 1889).....	1881-1891	9
Butler County Jeffersonian, El Dorado (see Democrat).......................	1888,1889	1
The El Dorado Eagle..	1882,1883	1
Kansas Workman, Emporia and El Dorado...............................	1888-1890	1
The Daily Eli, El Dorado.........	1890,1891	2
Educational Advance (monthly), El Dorado.............................	1893,1894	2
Butler County Citizen, El Dorado......................................	1893,1894	1
The New Enterprise, Douglass..	1879,1880	2
Douglass Index..	1880-1883	3
The Douglass Tribune.....	1884-1894	11
Leon Indicator (missing from February to September, 1887)...................	1880-1894	13
The Leon Quill..	1886,1887	1
The Benton Reporter..	1884,1885	1
The Benton Call...	1893	1
The Towanda Herald (May to November, 1886, lacking).................	1885-1893	8
The Brainerd Sun..	1885,1886	1
The Brainerd Ensign..	1887-1889	2
Latham Journal..	1885,1886	1
Latham Signal...	1886-1890	3
The Latham Times...	1890-1893	3
The Beaumont Business...	1886,1887	1
Potwin Messenger..	1888,1889	2
White Water Tribune..	1889-1893	4
The Weekly Herald, White Water..	1893,1894	1
Butler county, short-lived, vol. 1:		
Augusta News, August 7 to November 13, 1886; El Dorado Daily Democrat, February 15 to 22, 1888; Daily Industrial Advocate, May 2 to June 13, 1892..	....	4
Butler county, short-lived, vol. 2:		
The Augusta Crescent, August 17, 1870: Church Record, February and March, 1881; the Elbing Hatchet, July 29, 1893, to January 13, 1894...................	....	4
CHASE COUNTY (61).		
Kansas Press, Cottonwood Falls (see Council Grove Press).....................	1859	1
Chase County Banner, Cottonwood Falls............................	1867-1869	1
Chase County Courant, Cottonwood Falls..............................	1874-1894	20
Chase County Leader, Cottonwood Falls...............................	1875-1894	20
The Reveille, Cottonwood Falls.......	1890-1894	4
The School News, Cottonwood Falls..........	1887,1888	1
Strong City Independent (September, 1884, to August, 1885, lacking)......	1881-1887	5
Chase County Republican, Strong City................................	1887-1892	4
Strong City Derrick.................	1892-1894	3
Matfield Mirror...	1893,1894	1
Chase county, short-lived, vol. 1:		
The Scalping Knife, Cottonwood Falls, September 15, 1874; The True Reformer, November 1, 1876; Valley Echo, Cottonwood, October 20, 1880, to January 27, 1881; Chase County Leader, daily, Cottonwood Falls, September 29 to October 2, 1886; Strong City Advance, September 7, 1893, to May 10, 1894..	....	1

NEWSPAPERS.	Years.	No. vols
CHAUTAUQUA COUNTY (63).		
Chautauqua Journal, Sedan...	1876–1884	9
The Chautauqua County Times, Sedan.................................	1878–1881	2
Sedan Times...	1881–1884	4
Sedan Times-Journal...	1885–1893	9
The Border Slogan, Sedan...	1883,1884	1
The Graphic, Sedan..	1884–1890	6
Chautauqua County Democrat, Sedan..................................	1884	1
Sedan Republican..	1890–1892	2
Chautauqua News, Peru (not published November, 1879, to October, 1880)........	1876–1880	3
The Peru Times..	1886,1887	1
The Weekly Call, Peru...	1888,1889	2
The Peru Eagle...	1890,1891	1
The Freemen's Lance, Peru...	1891	1
The Chautauqua Springs Spy...	1882,1883	1
Chautauqua Springs Mail...	1887	1
The Chautauqua Springs Express.......................................	1888,1889	1
The Cedar Vale Star...	1884–1893	10
Cedar Vale Commercial..	1889–1894	5
Elgin Clipper..	1891	1
The Horoscope, Niotaze..	1893,1894	1
Chautauqua county, short-lived, vol. 1: Cedar Vale Blade, August 24 to December 21, 1877; Cedar Vale Times, May 24 to December 6, 1878; Home Enterprise, Sedan (monthly), February to June, 1880; Our Paper, Sedan (monthly), October, 1885; Sedan Daily Republican, October 31, 1891........	....	1
CHEROKEE COUNTY (135).		
Republican-Courier, Columbus...	1876–1878	3
The Columbus Courier..	1878–1886	8
The Columbus Star-Courier (April 21 to December 15, 1887, lacking).............	1886–1892	7
The Columbus Democrat..	1876	1
The Columbus Vidette..	1877,1878	1
Border Star, Columbus (first)..	1876–1880	2
Border Star, Columbus (second)..	1882–1886	5
Kansas Bee-Keeper, Columbus..	1881–1885	5
The Times, Columbus...	1881–1886	5
Lea's Columbus Advocate...	1882–1884	2
The Columbus Advocate..	1885–1894	10
The Daily Advocate, Columbus...	1886,1887	2
The Daily News and the Weekly News, Columbus.......................	1882,1883	1
The Expository, Girard and Columbus..................................	1883,1884	1
The Sprig of Myrtle (monthly), Columbus, see Ottawa county...........	1883–1885	1
The Kansas Prohibitionist, Columbus...................................	1884–1886	1
Modern Light, Columbus...	1891–1894	4
Baxter Springs Republican, No. 1......................................	1876,1877	1
The Times, Baxter Springs...	1878–1880	2
Baxter Springs News...	1882–1894	13
Baxter Springs Delta...	1887	1
Cherokee County Republican, Baxter Springs..........................	1893,1894	1
Galena Miner..	1877–1881	4
Galena Miner (second)...	1888,1889	1
Short Creek Weekly Banner, Galena...................................	1878	1
The Galena Messenger..	1879	1
Short Creek Republican, Galena..	1883–1893	10
Galena Republican...	1893,1894	2
The Galena Times..	1890–1894	4
Empire City Echo..	1877–1879	2
Western Friend (monthly), Quakervale and Vareck.....................	1880–1890	10
Labor's Tribune, Weir...	1884–1887	2
Weir City Tribune...	1887–1894	8
Weir City Eagle..	1887,1888	1
The Weir Journal..	1889–1894	4
The Globe-Miner, Scammon..	1892–1894	2
Farlington Plaindealer...	1885,1886	1
Cherokee county, short-lived, vol. 1: The Workingman's Journal, Columbus and Girard, January 7, 1870; The Cherokee Sentinel, Baxter Springs, September 1, 1871, to June 22, 1872; Baxter Springs Examiner, September 14 to October 26, 1871; Columbus Journal, March 5, 1874, to March 17, 1875; Columbus Avalanche, October 28, 1875 (?); The Western Luminary, Columbus, January and February, 1877; The Rural Educationist, Columbus, March, 1877; Our School Journal, Columbus, December, 1877, to February and March, 1878; The Banner, Galena, and Short Creek Weekly Banner, Galena, October 12, to December 27, 1878; The Ionian Casket, Quaker Valley, December, 1878, to June, 1879; The Ionian Casket, Jr., Quaker Valley, October, 1879; The Christian Polemic, Galena, February to April, 1879; The Gospel Mirror, Columbus, September 18, 1880, to May 24, 1881; Our School Journal (second), Galena, 1881; The		

BOUND NEWSPAPERS AND PERIODICALS — CONTINUED.

NEWSPAPERS.	Years.	No. vols
CHEROKEE COUNTY—*Concluded.*		
Daily Courier, Columbus, November 28 to December 6, 1882; Daily News, Baxter Springs, October 7 to 11, 1884; Reunion Daily News, Baxter Springs, August 25 to 30, 1891, and August 30 to September 4, 1892; The Radical Democrat, Scammonville, October 31 to November 28, 1885; Baptist Banner, Columbus, April 8 to May 30, 1887; Cherokee County Teacher, Galena, November 16, 1891, to July 15, 1892; The Sunflower State, Baxter Springs, March 25, October 14 to December 9, 1893....................	....	1
Cherokee county, short-lived, vol. 2:		
Scammon Register, April 10 to November 20, 1891; Real Estate Guide, Galena, June 1, 1891; Southern Argus, Baxter Springs, June 18 to October 8, 1891; Scammon Miner, January 29 to June 25, 1892.........................	....	1
Cherokee county, short-lived, vol. 3:		
Banner, and the Short Creek Weekly Banner, Galena, October 12 to December 27, 1888; Labor Journal, Scammonville and Rosedale, March 21 to June 6, 1885	....	1
CHEYENNE COUNTY (29).		
Cheyenne County Rustler, Wano, St. Francis (January 8 to November 12, 1891, Rustler-Review)......................	1885–1894	9
Plaindealer, Wano and St. Francis...................	1887–1889	2
Bird City News......	1886–1894	8
Cheyenne County Democrat, Bird City......	1886–1889	3
Cynosure and The Gleaner, Guy and Jaqua......	1887,1888	1
Weekly Review, St. Francis......	1889,1890	1
Cheyenne County Herald, St. Francis and Bird City............	1889,1890	1
People's Defender, St. Francis......	1892–1894	3
The Frontiersman and The Herald of Independence, Bird City..............	1886,1887	1
CLARK COUNTY (36).		
Clark County Clipper, Ashland	1884–1894	10
Republican Herald, Ashland.......	1885–1887	2
Ashland Journal.......	1886–1894	8
Ashland Herald.......	1887,1888	1
Clark County Citizen, Ashland.............	1889,1890	1
Clark County Chief, Englewood	1885–1887	3
The Englewood Chief (suspended June 19, 1889, to August 19, 1891)............	1888–1892	2
Englewood Enterprise.......	1887–1889	1
Appleton Kansas Era.......	1886,1887	2
The Lexington Leader.......	1886–1888	2
The Minneola Era.......	1887,1888	1
Clark Republican, Minneola.......	1888,1889	1
Cash City Cashier.......	1886–1888	1
Clark county, short-lived, vol. 1:		
County Beacon, Lexington, June 4 to July 16, 1886; The Leader, Ashland, February 15 to April 5, 1889...........	....	1
CLAY COUNTY (86).		
Clay County Dispatch, Clay Center	1876–1894	19
The Localist, Clay Center.......	1879–1881	3
The Democrat, Clay Center.......	1879,1880	2
The Kansas Baptist, Clay Center.......	1881–1884	3
The Cresset, Clay Center	1882,1883	1
The Times, Clay Center	1882–1894	13
The Times (daily), Clay Center.......	1886–1888	5
The Monitor, Clay Center	1883,1884	1
Clay Center Firebrand.......	1883,1884	1
Weekly Argus, Clay Center.......	1885,1886	1
Clay Center Eagle.......	1885,1886	1
The Clay Center Democrat, Republican Valley Democrat, Clay Center (July, 1888, to July, 1889)...................	1886–1890	4
The Little Hatchet, Clay Center (second)...........	1886	1
The Holiness War News (monthly), Clay Center (see Marshall county, short-lived, vol. 1).		
The Weekly Sun, Clay Center.......	1890–1892	1
The Clay Center Critic.......	1890,1891	1
The Pentecost Trumpet, Clay Center.......	1891,1892	1
Western Record, Clay Center	1892,1893	1
Morganville News and Sunflower.......	1885–1887	3
The Clay County Sentinel, Morganville.......	1887–1891	4
Uncle Sam's Live-Stock Journal, Morganville and Clay Center	1891–1894	3
The Advance, Morganville.......	1891	1
The Idana Journal.......	1886,1887	1
Wakefield Advertiser.......	1886–1894	8
The Herald, Industry.......	1886,1887	1
Oak Hill Herald	1888,1889	1
Oak Hill Echo	1889	1

BOUND NEWSPAPERS AND PERIODICALS — CONTINUED.

NEWSPAPERS.	Years.	No. vols
CLAY COUNTY — *Concluded.*		
The Times, Clifton	1892,1893	2
Clay County Star, Green	1894	1
Clay county, short-lived, vol. 1:		
Clay County Independent, Clay Center, October 12, 1871; Little Hatchet, Clay Center (first), September 28, 1878, to June 80, 1883; Republican Valley Banner, Clay Center (monthly),) ay, 1880, to) ay, 1881; Daily Dispatch, Clay Center, September 16-18, 1885: The Outlook, Clay Center (monthly), November, 1886, to August, 1887; The Observer, Clay Center (monthly), July to September, 1887		1
CLOUD COUNTY (154).		
Republican Valley Empire, Clyde and Concordia	1870-1872	3
Concordia Empire	1876-1883	8
The Republican-Empire, Concordia	1883-1887	3
Concordia Empire	1887-1894	8
The Concordia Republican	1882,1883	2
The Concordia Expositor	1877-1881	5
The Cloud County Blade, Concordia	1879-1882	3
Kansas Blade, Concordia	1882-1894	13
Concordia Daily Blade (February, 1885, to) arch, 1887, suspended)	1884-1888	4
Cloud County Critic, Concordia (Kansas Critic, 1888)	1882-1888	6
The Concordia Times	1884-1891	8
Concordia Democrat and Daylight	1886	1
The Concordia Weekly Daylight	1886-1894	8
The Alliant, Concordia	1890-1894	4
The Clyde Herald (February to December, 1881, lacking)	1878-1894	16
Clyde Democrat	1880-1882	2
Cline's Press, Clyde	1884	1
The Clyde) ail	1884-1887	3
The Clyde Argus	1888-1894	7
The Farmers' Voice, Clyde	1891-1894	4
Glasco Tribune	1881,1882	1
The Glasco Sun	1883-1894	12
Cloud County Kansan, Jamestown (The New Era, 1890-1893)	1881-1894	13
The Quill, Jamestown	1888-1890	2
The) iltonvale News	1882-1891	9
) iltonvale Chieftain	1887,1888	1
) iltonvale Press	1892,1893	1
) iltonvale Tribune	1894	1
Ames Advance	1885,1886	1
The Ames Bureau	1887	1
Aurora News	1892,1893	1
Cloud county, short-lived, vol. 1:		
Glasco Banner, February 25 to July 10, 1880;) iltonvale Star, April 14 to August 26, 1886; Reformer, Concordia, September 15 to November 2, 1886; Weekly Courier, Ames, March 23 to June 29, 1888;) iltonvale Review, July 25 to November 14, 1889; Advance,) iltonvale, January 13 to April 6, 1892; Reporter,) iltonvale. February 25 to) arch 17, 1892;) iltonvale Echo, July -26, 1892, to January 6, 1893		1
Cloud county, short-lived, vol. 2:		
Clyde Star,) arch 14 to April 25, 1884; Daily Reporter, Concordia, August 8 to September 3, 1887; Western Rustler (monthly), Clyde, January and February, 1889;) iltonvale Leader, August 31, 1893, to January 4, 1894; District School (monthly), Aurora, December, 1893, to) arch, 1894		1
COFFEY COUNTY (104).		
Neosho Valley Register, Burlington	1859,1860	1
Kansas Patriot, Burlington	1864-1868	5
Burlington Patriot (*October 15, 1869, January 1, 1870)	1876-1886	10
Burlington Republican (Republican-Patriot, April, 1886, to December, 1887)	1882-1894	13
Burlington Daily Republican	1887	1
The Burlington Independent	1876-1894	18
The Burlington Nonpareil	1886-1893	7
The Farm Record, Burlington	1890-1892	1
The Courier, Burlington	1891-1894	4
Le Roy Reporter	1879-1894	15
The Le Roy Eagle	1887,1888	1
The Lebo Light	1884-1888	5
The Lebo Courier	1889-1891	2
The Lebo Enterprise	1891-1894	4
The Waverly News ( ) arch, 1884, to) arch, 1885, lacking)	1883-1889	5
The Gazette, Waverly	1889-1894	6
The Gridley Gazette	1887,1888	2
The Standard, Gridley	1889,1890	1
Gridley Herald	1894	1

* Portfolio.

BOUND NEWSPAPERS AND PERIODICALS — CONTINUED.

NEWSPAPERS.	Years.	No. vols
COFFEY COUNTY—*Concluded.*		
Coffey county, short-lived, vol. 1:		
Little Caisson, Burlington, February 15 to May 15, 1877; Burlington Daily Star, January 13 to February 3, 1878; Gridley Register, September 23 to October 23, 1886; Burlington Daily Nonpareil, April 4 to May 7, 1887............	....	1
Coffey county, short-lived, vol. 2:		
The Free West (bimonthly), Burlington, August, 1869, to November, 1870; Voice of the People, Burlington, September 9 to November 18, 1874; The Waverly Sun, August 2 to 30, 1894, January 11, 1895......................	....	1
COMANCHE COUNTY (46).		
The Western Kansan, Nescutunga..	1885,1886	1
Nescutunga Enterprise...	1886–1888	3
Coldwater Review..	1884–1891	6
The Western Star, Coldwater (February to July, 1885, lacking)...................	1884–1894	10
Republican, Coldwater	1885,1886	1
Coldwater Echo	1886–1891	6
Coldwater Enterprise..	1889–1894	6
The People's Advocate, Coldwater.....	1890,1891	1
Echo-Advocate, Coldwater..	1891,1892	1
Comanche County Citizen, Avilla...............................	1885–1887	2
The Avilla Democrat..	1886, 1887	1
Protection Echo..	1885,1886	1
The Protection Press.......................................	1886, 1887	1
Western Kansan, Protection...	1886,1887	1
Kansas Weekly Ledger, Protection......................................	1887	1
The Leader, Protection...	1888	1
Evansville Herald...	1885–1887	1
Comanche City News...	1886–1888	1
Comanche county, short-lived, vol. 1:		
Comanche Chieftain, Nescutunga, October 17, 1884, to January 9, 1885; Comanche Chief, Reeder, January 23 to March 27, 1886; Republican, Coldwater, January 6 to January 27, 1887; Western Advocate, Protection, May 8 to July 26, 1886; Coldwater Real Estate Journal (monthly), June and July, 1887; Comanche County Sun, Coldwater (semimonthly), September 10, 29, 1888; Coldwater Voice, January 3 to February 7, 1891; Protection Press (second), July 26 to October 22, 1891............................		1
COWLEY COUNTY (334).		
Winfield Courier (January to July, 1875, lacking)............................	1873–1894	20
Winfield Daily Courier	1885–1894	19
Winfield Plow and Anvil and Cowley County Democrat..........................	1876	1
Cowley County Telegram, Winfield (January to July 1882, lacking)..............	1876–1890	15
Winfield Daily Telegram (November, 1881, to March, 1887, lacking).............	1879–1888	9
Winfield Semi-Weekly	1879,1880	1
Cowley County Monitor, Winfield...	1880,1881	1
Cowley County Courant, Winfield...	1881,1882	1
Winfield Daily Courant.......	1881,1882	1
The Winfield Tribune (Saturday Evening Tribune, 1886–1889)..................	1884–1892	8
The Daily Visitor, Winfield..	1886–1889	6
The Winfield Visitor.......	1887–1899	1
The American Nonconformist, Winfield.......................................	1886–1891	5
Daily Tribune-Visitor, Winfield...	1889	2
The Winfield Daily Tribune (March to October, 1890, lacking).................	1890,1891	2
Industrial Free Press, Winfield..............................;	1890–1894	5
Winfield Newspaper Union...	1890–1894	4
The Monthly Herald (Baptist), Winfield.....................................	1890–1892	2
The Christna (semimonthly), Winfield, *see* Tabor, Iowa.		
Western Reveille (monthly), Winfield..	1891–1894	3
Kansas Agriculturist, Winfield...............................	1892–1894	2
Farmers' Advocate, Winfield..	1892–1894	2
Public Platform (monthly), Winfield....	1892–1894	2
Arkansas City Traveler and Republican-Traveler.....	1876–1894	19
Arkansas Valley Democrat, Arkansas City	1879–1894	15
Oklahoma War Chief, Arkansas City, *see* Sumner county.		
The Arkansas City Republican..	1884–1887	3
The Arkansas City Republican (daily)..	1886,1887	2
Republican-Traveler (daily), Arkansas City..................................	1887	1
Arkansas City Traveler (daily)...	1888–1894	14
Canal City Daily Dispatch, Evening Dispatch, Arkansas City...................	1887–1894	13
Canal City Dispatch (weekly), Arkansas City.................................	1887–1894	8
The Fair Play, Arkansas City.............	1888–1892	4
Daily Border Bulletin, Arkansas City.......................................	1892	1
Gate City Journal, Arkansas City...	1893,1894	1
The New Enterprise, Burden (for 1880, see Butler county)....................	1880,1881	2
Burden Enterprise (Burden Siftings, June and July, 1891)...................	1882–1891	9
Burden Eagle..	1885–1889	5
The Spirit of the West, Burden...	1891–1893	2

BOUND NEWSPAPERS AND PERIODICALS — Continued.

NEWSPAPERS.	Years.	No. vols
COWLEY COUNTY—*Concluded.*		
Burden Eagle (second)...	1892–1894	2
Cambridge Commercial...	1881	1
The Cambridge News (March, 1886, to March, 1888, lacking)........................	1882–1890	5
The Eye (Post, June to July, 1888) Dexter (November, 28, 1885, to September 10, 1887, lacking)..	1884–1888	3
Dexter Free Press..	1888–1890	2
The Udall Sentinel...	1885,1886	1
The Udall Record (March to December, 1888, lacking; not published from January 10 to June 19, 1891)..................................	1886–1893	7
Cowley county, short-lived, vol. 1:		
Winfield Daily News, February 19 to May 4, 1885; Atlanta Advertiser, September 25 to December 4, 1885; Bugle Call, Arkansas City and Howard; July 25 to September 22, 1888; Atlanta Cricket, October 4, 1888, to January 31, 1889; Atlanta Herald, March 28 to May 30, 1890; Daily Fair Play, Arkansas City, March 30 to April 7, 1891; People's Leader, Arkansas City, May 30 to October 31, 1891..................................		1
Cowley county, short-lived, vol. 2:		
Cowley County Teacher, Winfield, Oct. 8. 1879, to May, 1880; Southwestern Kansas Conference Daily, Winfield, March 10 to 15, 1887; The Spy Glass, Arkansas City, October, 1891; Dexter Delta, November 10, 1892, to September 7, 1893; Educational Index, Winfield, January to July, 1893; Sunday Morning Times, Arkansas City, February 26 to March 19, 1893; The Morning Star, Arkansas City, May 2, 1893; Cherokee Strip Guide, Arkansas City, May 20 to September 1, 1893; Poultry Voice (monthly): Burden, November, 1893, to July, 1894; Daily News, Arkansas City, February 1 to March 5, 1894.........		1
CRAWFORD COUNTY (168).		
Girard Press..	1874–1894	21
Crawford County News, Girard.......................................	1876–1880	4
Girard Herald (Western Herald, 1890–'94; July, 1882, to March, 1883, lacking)......	1880–1894	15
The Kansas Workman (monthly), Girard................................	1882–1885	4
The Daily World, Girard..	1894	2
The World (weekly), Girard...	1894	1
Cherokee Index..	1876,1877	2
The Young Cherokee, Cherokee.......................................	1876,1877	1
Cherokee Banner..	1877,1878	1
The Temperance Rural, Cherokee and Baxter Springs...................	1878,1879	1
Sentinel on the Border, Cherokee....................................	1879–1882	4
The Cherokee Sentinel...	1883–1894	11
The Cherokee Cyclone...	1884–1888	4
Cherokee Times-Miner...	1893	1
The Smelter, Pittsburg...	1881–1891	11
The Headlight, Pittsburg...	1886–1894	9
The Daily Headlight, Pittsburg......................................	1887,1888	2
Pittsburg Democrat (first)..	1887	1
Pittsburg Democrat (second)..	1888,1889	1
The Pittsburg Kansan..	1889–1894	5
The Weekly World, Pittsburg..	1890–1893	3
Pittsburg Daily World (not published from June, 1891, to August, 1892)...........	1891–1893	4
Pittsburg Herold..	1890,1891	1
Pittsburg Daily Star...	1891	1
Sunday Morning Mail, Pittsburg.....................................	1892	1
Penny Post, Pittsburg (daily).......................................	1892	1
The Miners' Echo, Pittsburg (weekly, daily, tri-weekly)...................	1892,1893	1
Pittsburg Messenger...	1893,1894	2
The McCune Standard...	1881,1882	1
The McCune Times..	1882–1891	9
The Brick, McCune and Pittsburg....................................	1886,1887	1
Crawford County Democrat, McCune.................................	1889–1893	4
McCune Leader...	1893	1
Walnut Journal (first), (not published from January to October, 1892)...........	1882–1894	11
Walnut Journal (second)...	1894	1
Educational Advocate, Walnut.......................................	1894	1
Walnut Comet..	1892	1
Walnut Eagle...	1894	1
The Arcadia Reporter..	1882–1888	6
The Christian Worker, Arcadia......................................	1888	1
Arcadia Democrat...	1888–1890	2
The Arcadian, Arcadia...	1888	1
Arcadia News...	1890–1894	4
The Hepler Leader (not published from January, 1884, to January, 1890)........	1881–1890	2
The Hepler Banner..	1887–1889	2
The Farlington Plaindealer..	1883,1884	1
Farlington Gem...	1886,1887	
Crawford county, short-lived, vol. 1:		
Walnut Herald, September 2 to December 23, 1882; Mulberry Grove Gazette June 19 to November 27, 1886; Arcadia Real-Estate Record, June, 1888;		

*BOUND NEWSPAPERS AND PERIODICALS — CONTINUED.

NEWSPAPERS.	Years.	No. vols
CRAWFORD COUNTY — *Concluded.*		
The Disciples at Work. Cherokee, July 11, 1887; Outlook, Girard, August, 1886; Daily Arcadian. Arcadia, November 7, 8, 9, 1888; Pittsburg Daily Smelter, June 28 to August 3, 1890; Pittsburg Daily Times, August 15 to September 5, 1891; Pittsburg Star, November 21, 1891, to March 12, 1892....	....	1
Crawford county, short-lived, vol. 2:		
People's Vindicator, Girard, August 18, 1870; Normal Record, Girard, July 8 to August 4, 1881; Educational Advocate, Burden, February, 1884; Conference Daily Press. South Kansas, Girard, March 10 to 14, 1891; Pittsburger Volks-Zeitung, November 11, 1892, to January 6, 1893; Pittsburg Advance, November 18, 1892. to January 20, 1893; McCune Republican, November 9, 1894, to January 25, 1895.........	....	1
DAVIS COUNTY, *see* Geary (47).		
Junction City Union (May to December, 1879, lacking)......................	1865–1889	24
The Junction City Daily Union.........................	1887	1
Junction City Tribune.........	1873–1889	15
Davis County Republican, Junction City........................	1882–1889	6
Davis county, short-lived, vol. 1:		
Junction Sentinel. Junction City, May 14, 1859; Real Estate Register, Junction City, September 1, December, 1870, March, 1871; Youth's Casket, Junction City, January to December, 1878; Parish Iris, Junction City, December, 1884, to June, 1885; Junction City Methodist, June, 1886, to June, 1887; Daily Junction City Tribune. September 21–26, 1886; Conference Daily Tribune, Junction City, March 17–22, 1887; Democrat, Junction City, October 28 to December 31, 1887; Insurance Messenger, Junction City, June, 1888, to June, 1889.........	....	1
DECATUR COUNTY (62).		
The Oberlin Herald (April to July, 1881, lacking).................	1879–1894	15
The Eye, Oberlin.........................	1883–1894	11
The Oberlin World and Democrat.........	1885,1886	1
Oberlin Opinion.........................	1886–1894	8
Alliance Times. Oberlin.........	1890–1894	4
The Rathbone Family Historian (monthly), Oberlin.........	1892–1894	3
The Norcatur Register.........	1886–1894	9
The Allison Breeze and Times.........	1887,1888	1
Jennings Echo.........	1888–1894	6
Jennings Times and Alliance Times.........	1888–1890	2
The Star, Dresden.........	1890–1893	3
Decatur county, short-lived, vol. 1:		
Oberlin Farmer (monthly), March, 1888, to August, 1889; Daily Oberlin Eye, October 12, 1886.........	....	1
DICKINSON COUNTY (177).		
Dickinson County Chronicle, Abilene (Chronicle-Journal, 1887)..................	1875–1894	19
Kansas Gazette, Enterprise (moved to Abilene).........	1876–1878	2
Abilene Gazette (not published from April, 1889, to June, 1894)..................	1878–1894	11
Abilene Daily Gazette.........	1866–1888	7
The Weekly Democrat, Abilene.........	1880–1882	2
The Abilene Reflector.........	1883–1894	11
The Abilene Daily Reflector.........	1887–1894	14
The Dickinson County News, Abilene.........	1888–1894	6
The Alliance Monitor, Abilene.........	1890–1892	1
Abilene. Monitor.........	1892,1893	2
Abilene Herald.........	1892,1893	2
Monitor-Herald, Abilene.........	1893,1894	1
The Dispatch, Abilene..	1893,1894	1
Evangelical Visitor (semimonthly), Abilene.........	1893,1894	2
The Solomon Sentinel, Solomon City.........	1879–1894	15
Enterprise Register.........	1883,1884	1
Kansas Miller and Manufacturer, Enterprise.........	1888–1893	5
Enterprise Independent.........	1888–1890	3
The Anti-Monopolist, Enterprise.........	1883–1888	4
*The Enterprise Journal.........	1890–1894	4
Expositor (monthly), Downs. Cawker City, Smith Centre, and Enterprise.........	1890–1894	5
The Integral Coöperator, Enterprise.........	1891–1894	3
The Chapman Star.........	1884–1886	2
The Chapman Courier.........	1887–1891	4
The Chapman Howitzer.........	1891,1892	2
Chapman Standard.........	1892–1894	2
The Herington Tribune.........	1884–1890	6
Herington Headlight.........	1888,1889	1
Herington Vindicator.........	1890	1
The Herington Times.........	1889–1894	5
The Herington Signal (first).........	1891,1892	1
Herington Journal (monthly).........	1892–1894	2
The Herington Signal (second).........	1893,1894	2

BOUND NEWSPAPERS AND PERIODICALS—Continued.

NEWSPAPERS.	Years.	No. vols
DICKINSON COUNTY—*Concluded.*		
The Hope Herald.........	1885–1892	7
The Hope Dispatch........	1886–1893	8
Hope Crescent........	1893,1894	1
Carlton Advocate........	1886–1888	2
The Banner Register, Banner City........	1887,1888	2
The Manchester Sun........	1887–1893	6
Dickinson county, short-lived, vol. 1: The Little Sand-Pounder, Abilene, August 14 to October 30, 1886; Herington Herald, November, 1886; Abilene Republican, November 12 to December 17, 1886; Union Labor Banner, Abilene, October 5 to December 14, 1888; Woodbine Tidings, May 25 to August 3, 1889; The Hope Star, August 18, 1892, to January 13, 1893.........	....	1
Dickinson county, short-lived, vol. 2: Western News, Detroit, February 11, 1870; Daily Herald, Hope, October 8, 1886; Enterprise Daily Journal, June 7 to 10, 1892; Chapman Journal, October 27 to December 8, 1892; Christian Endeavorer, Chapman, January 1, 1894.........	....	1
DONIPHAN COUNTY (91).		
White Cloud Chief and Weekly Kansas Chief, Troy........	1857–1894	37
White Cloud Review........	1880–1887	7
White Cloud Review (second)........	1888,1889	1
White Cloud Globe........	1892–1894	3
Troy Reporter........	1866,1867	1
Doniphan County Republican, Troy (August, 1872, to September, 1873, lacking)..	1871–1875	3
Troy Weekly Bulletin........	1877–1879	2
The Troy Times........	1886–1894	8
Elwood Advertiser........	1857,1858	1
Kansas Free Press, Elwood........	1858,1859	1
Elwood Free Press........	1859–1861	2
Wathena Reporter (April, 1868, to September, 1873, lacking)........	1867–1877	5
Wathena Advance........	1878	⎱ 1
Wathena Mirror........	1878	⎰
Wathena Gazette........	1889,1890	1
Highland Sentinel........	1878,1879	1
The Central State, Highland........	1880–1882	2
Highland University Nuncio (biweekly)........	1880–1894	4
The Vidette, Highland........	1892–1894	3
Enterprise, Severance (and Centralia, Nemaha county)........	1883	1
Severance News........	1889–1894	6
Doniphan county, short-lived, vol. 1: Kansas Constitutionalist, Doniphan, January 7, 1857; Geary City Era, August 1 to 15, 1857; Kansas Crusader of Freedom, Doniphan City, January 30 and March 6, 1858; The Weekly Highlander, Highland, January 1, 1859; The Palermo Leader, November 19, 1859; Doniphan County Patriot, Troy, April 11, 1863; Doniphan County Republican, Troy, October 23 and November 6, 1869, January 1, 1870, and August 16, 1873; The Western Emigrant, Brenner, June 8, 1878; Bible Investigator, Doniphan, January to September, 1882; Doniphan Weekly News, March 17 to August 25, 1882; The Times, Severance, August 30 to September 20, 1883; The Alumni Annual, Highland University, 1883, 1884; The Severance Advertiser, August 3, 1883, to May 2, 1884; Bendena Echo, July 13 to August 24, 1889; White Cloud News, June 15, 1891, to March 15, 1892........	....	1
DOUGLAS COUNTY (324).		
Herald of Freedom, Lawrence........	1854–1859	4
Kansas Free-State, Lawrence........	1855,1856	1
Lawrence Republican (1858–'62, scattering)........	1857–1862	2
The Congregational Record (monthly), Lawrence, January, 1859, to December, 1864; Topeka, June, 1865, to May, 1867........	1859–1867	8
Kansas State Journal, Lawrence (scattering)........	1861–1867	1
The Western Home Journal, Lawrence........	1869–1885	15
Lawrence Weekly Journal (January to July, 1886, lacking; 1890, called Journal-Tribune)........	1886–1894	8
Republican Daily Journal, Lawrence Daily Journal, and Lawrence Journal-Tribune (January, 1878, to June, 1879, lacking)........	1877–1894	32
Kansas Daily Tribune, Lawrence (lacking, February, 1871, to September, 1873; 1875; July, 1877, to December, 1879; called Evening News, Morning News, Morning News-Tribune, Morning Tribune, November, 1883, to July, 1884; Herald-Tribune, July, 1884, to May, 1886)........	1863–1890	39
Kansas Tribune, Lawrence (January to September, 1873; January, 1875, to April, 1877; January, 1880, to January, 1882, lacking)........	1867–1888	16
Semi-Weekly Tribune, and Weekly Herald-Tribune........	1884,1885	2
Spirit of Kansas, Lawrence (1874, 1875, 1883, 1884, scattering)........	⎰ 1872,1873 ⎱ 1876–1884	⎰ 9 ⎱
Kansas Collegiate, Lawrence........	1875–1879	5

BOUND NEWSPAPERS AND PERIODICALS — Continued.

NEWSPAPERS.	Years.	No. vols
DOUGLAS COUNTY — *Continued.*		
Colored Radical, Lawrence (see Leavenworth county, short-lived, vol. 1).		
The University Courier (monthly), Lawrence	1878,1879	1
University Courier (semi-monthly and weekly), Lawrence	1882–1894	12
Lawrence Standard	1877–1880	4
The Kansas Monthly, Lawrence	1878–1881	4
The Kansas Review (monthly), Lawrence	1879–1884	5
The University Review (monthly), Lawrence	1884–1894	10
The Daily Reporter, Lawrence	1879	1
Kansas Temperance Palladium, Lawrence	1879,1880	1
Die Germania, Lawrence (June, 1881, to February, 1883, lacking)	1880–1894	12
The Kansas Liberal (monthly), Lawrence, July to September, 1882 (see Valley Falls).		
Kansas Progress, Lawrence	1882,1883	1
The Lawrence Gazette	1882–1894	12
Lawrence Daily Gazette (first)	1884,1885	1
Western Recorder, Lawrence	1883,1884	2
Kansas Churchman (monthly), Lawrence (first) (see Shawnee county).		
Kansas Daily Herald, Lawrence	1883,1884	2
The Head Center and Daily Morning Sun, Lawrence	1883	1
Once a Week, Lawrence	1883–1884	2
The Kansas Zephyr, Lawrence	1884–1887	3
College Review, Lawrence	1885–1888	2
Sigma Nu Delta (bimonthly), Lawrence	1886–1889	2
Lawrence Daily Democrat	1888	1
Evening Telegram, Lawrence	1888	1
University Times, Lawrence	1888,1889	1
University Kansan, Lawrence	1889,1890	1
Progressive Educator, Lawrence	1889	1
The Daily Record, Lawrence	1889–1893	8
The Weekly Record, Lawrence	1890–1893	4
The Select Friend (monthly), Lawrence	1890–1894	4
The Jeffersonian, Lawrence	1890–1894	4
Kansas Churchman (monthly), Salina, Atchison, and Lawrence (second)	1891–1894	3
Smith's Small Fruit Farmer (quarterly), Lawrence	1891–1893	3
Seminary Notes (monthly), Lawrence	1891–1893	2
Lawrence Weekly Press	1891	1
University Quarterly, Lawrence	1892–1894	2
The World (daily), Lawrence	1892–1894	6
Lawrence Weekly World	1892–1894	3
The Student's Journal, Lawrence	1892–1894	2
Lawrence Daily Gazette (second)	1893,1894	3
North Lawrence Leader	1884,1885	1
Freeman's Champion, Prairie City	1857,1858	1
The Young America, Baldwin	1864,1865	1
Baldwin Criterion	1883–1885	1
The Baldwin Visitor	1884,1885	1
The Baldwin Ledger	1885–1894	10
The Baldwin Index, Baker University (some lacking numbers)	1881–1894	14
The Baker Beacon, Baldwin	1889–1894	5
Kansas New Era, Lecompton	1866,1867	1
Lecompton Monitor	1885,1886	1
College Echoes, Lecompton	1888–1891	2
The Lecompton Ledger	1889,1890	1
The Lecompton Sun	1891–1894	4
The College Oracle (quarterly), Lecompton	1892–1894	2
The Eudora News	1887–1894	7
Douglas county, short-lived, vol. 1: Kansas Pacific Homestead, Lawrence, 1876, February, 1877, and April, 1878; Daily Mirror, Lawrence, September 13 to 16, 1881; The Kansas Mirror, Lawrence, October 20, 1881, to January 19, 1882; The Kansas Witness, Lawrence, April, 1882; The Daily Hand Bill, Lawrence, April 23, 1883; The Southern Kansan, Lawrence, September, 1883, February, 1884, and January 15, 1886; Lawrence Daily Gazette, September 2 to October 30, 1885; The True Citizen, Lawrence, August 13, 1886, to February 19, 1887; The Baldwin Advance, January to May, 1887; University Breeze, Baldwin, April 24 to May 29, 1888; The Historic Times, Lawrence, July 11 to November 14, 1891		*
Douglas county, short-lived, vol. 2: The Lecompton Union, November 20, 1856, and February 21, 1857; Semi-Weekly Union, Lecompton, February 7, 1857; The Kansas Messenger, Baldwin City, January 1, 1859; The Kansas State Journal, Lawrence, May 29, 1862; The Kansas State Journal (second), Lawrence, October 8 and November 12, 1863; The Kansas Underwriter and Real Estate Journal, Lawrence, June, August, and October, 1869, and June, 1870; Democratic Standard, Lawrence, September 29, November 17, December 8 and 15, 1870; Kansas Pacific Homestead, Lawrence, 1875; The Standard of Reform, Lawrence, July 8 and August 26, 1875; The State Sentinel, Lawrence, September 16, October 7, and November 18, 1875; Observer of Nature, Lawrence, Decem-		

BOUND NEWSPAPERS AND PERIODICALS — CONTINUED.

NEWSPAPERS.	Years.	No. vols
DOUGLAS COUNTY — *Concluded.*		
ber 13, 1875; The Kansas Monthly, Lawrence, December, 1878; Our Schools, Lawrence, January, February, and May, 1879; Kansas Benevolent Society Record, Lawrence, January, April, and July, 1880; Bismarck Fair Daily, Lawrence. September 20, 1882; The Reunion Banner, Lawrence, September 21, 1882; The Commercial Educator, Lawrence, July, 1885; The Evening Tribune, Lawrence, March 6 to 13, 1889; College Life, Lawrence, March to May, 1890; School Times, Baldwin, February 12, 1892, to April 5, 1893......	....	1
EDWARDS COUNTY (39).		
Edwards County Leader, Kinsley.....................................	1877–1880	3
Valley Republican (bound with Kinsley Graphic, 1878).............	1877, 1878	1
Kinsley Republican..	1878–1881	4
The Kinsley Graphic (except 1882, 1888, 1889)....................	1878–1894	13
Kinsley Republican-Graphic..	1882	1
Edwards County Banner, Kinsley....................................	1887	1
Weekly Banner-Graphic, Kinsley...................................	1887–1890	2
Kansas Staats-Zeitung, Kinsley....................................	1878, 1879	1
The Kinsley Mercury...	1883–1892	8
Kinsley Daily Mercury...	1887, 1888	2
The Wendell Champion..	1885–1886	1
Wellsford Register, and Democrat and Watchman, Dowell and Wellsford, *see* Kiowa county.		
Edwards county, short-lived, vol. 1:		
Kinsley Reporter, January 11, 1877; Belpre Beacon, June 15 to September 28, 1888; Kinsley Chronicle (monthly), April to November, 1890............	....	1
ELK COUNTY (91).		
The Courant, Howard (except 1878).................................	1875–1880	5
Elk County Ledger, Howard...	1876, 1877	1
The Courant-Ledger, Howard..	1878	1
The Howard Courant..	1880–1894	14
Industrial Journal, Howard..	1878–1880	2
The Howard Journal..	1880–1883	3
Kansas Rural, Howard (second, *see* short-lived, vol. 1)..........	1881	1
Grip, Howard..	1883, 1884	1
The Howard Democrat...	1884–1891	6
Kansas Traveler, Howard...	1886, 1887	1
Howard Daily Traveler...	1887	1
The Broad Axe, Howard...	1888	1
Elk County Citizen, Howard..	1891–1894	3
Bugle Call, Howard, *see* Cowley county.		
Our Church Mirror, Howard, *see* Harvey county — Halstead.		
Elk County Ledger, Elk Falls......................................	1876	1
Elk Falls Signal..	1880–1882	2
The Pioneer, Longton..	1880, 1881	1
The Times, Longton..	1881–1892	11
Longton Leader..	1887	1
Longton Signal..	1890–1892	2
Longton Gleaner...	1892–1894	2
Moline News...	1880	1
Moline Mercury (September 29, 1882, to March 27, 1885, lacking)...	1882–1889	5
The Moline Free Press...	1883–1885	2
The Moline Republican...	1889–1894	5
The Grenola Argus...	1880–1882	2
Grenola Chief (February 14 to July 13, 1889, lacking; Weekly Crisis, October 11, 1890, to June 5, 1891).........	1883–1894	11
The Hornet, Grenola and Howard,)..................................	1884, 1885	1
The Cave Springs Globe *..	1882	1
The Cana Valley Herald, Grenola...................................	1882, 1883	1
Elk county, short-lived, vol. 1:		
Elk City Courant, June 17, 1874; Howard City Beacon, July 24 to December 11, 1875; Kansas Rural, Howard City (monthly, first), July to September, 1877; Weekly Examiner, Elk Falls, February 1 to June 21, 1878; Howard Clipper, August 20 to November 26, 1880; Elk County Herald, Howard, August 20 to October 14, 1881; Kansas Telephone, Elk Falls, September 3 to 24, 1887; Kansas Weekly Ledger, Elk Falls, July 20 to November 2, 1888; South Kansas Farmer, Moline, March 4 to April 1, 1890..................	....	•
Elk county short-lived, vol. 2:		
Our Church Mirror, November, 1890, to September, 1891.............	....	•
ELLIS COUNTY (66).		
Ellis County Star, Hays City (lacking from December, 1877, to April, 1879).......	1876–1882	5
Hays City Sentinel (Star-Sentinel, from May, 1882, to May, 1887; lack May, 1884, to May, 1885; May, 1886, to May, 1887)......................	1876–1894	16

* Not found.

BOUND NEWSPAPERS AND PERIODICALS — Continued.

NEWSPAPERS.	Years.	No. vols
ELLIS COUNTY — *Concluded.*		
German-American Advocate, Hays City (lack November, 1884, to June, 1885)......	1882–1886	3
The Advocate, November 22–29; The Advocate. and Ellis County Democrat, December 6–27, 1884: Ellis County Democrat and Advocate, January to December, 1885; Ellis County Democrat, January to May, 1886. Hays City.................	1884–1886	1
Ellis County Free Press and Democrat, Hays City...........................	1886–1888	3
Hays City Times............................	1886,1887	1
Democratic Times, Hays City...........................	1888–1891	3
The Republican, Hays City...........................	1888–1894	7
Hays City Free Press...........................	1888–1894	6
Ellis Weekly Headlight...........................	1890–1890	11
The Ellis Review-Headlight...........................	1890–1894	4
Ellis Review...........................	1886–1890	4
Walker Journal...........................	1887,1888	1
Ellis county, short-lived, vol. 1:		
Hays City Railway Advance, June 23, 1868; Standard, Ellis, September 22, October 27, 1877; Union, Hays City, January 25 to February 22, 1887; Alliance Pilot, September 18 to November 6, 1890; Hornet, Hays City, December 7, 1892, to February 8, 1893...............	....	1
ELLSWORTH COUNTY (71).		
Ellsworth Reporter...........................	1875–1894	20
Ellsworth Republican...........................	1880	1
The Ellsworth News...........................	1883,1884	2
The Ellsworth Democrat...........................	1885–1891	7
The Weekly Herald, Ellsworth...........................	1888–1890	1
The Ellsworth Republican (second)...........................	1890,1891	1
Ellsworth Messenger...........................	1891–1894	3
Wilson Index...........................	1878,1879	1
The Wilson Echo...........................	1880–1894	15
The Wilson Wonder...........................	1886,1887	2
The Wilson Hawkeye...........................	1887,1888	1
Wilson Eagle...........................	1888,1889	1
Cain City News (first)...........................	1882,1883	1
Cain City News (second)...........................	1884–1886	2
The Kanopolis Journal...........................	1886–1890	4
Kanopolis Kansan...........................	1890–1893	3
The Hollyrood Enterprise...........................	1887–1890	3
The Sentinel, Hollyrood...........................	1891,1892	1
Ellsworth county, short-lived, vol. 1:		
Ellsworth Land Journal, monthly, July, 1878; Ellsworth Times, May 3, 1879, to April 22, 1880: Rural West. Ellsworth, November 16, 1882, to February 28, 1883; Ellsworth Daily Evening Democrat, March 23 to April 23, 1887; The Weekly Review, November to December, 1894...............	....	1
FINNEY COUNTY, *see* Sequoyah county (64).		
The Garden City Paper...........................	1879	1
Garden City Herald (1884–'87 lacking)...........................	1882–1887	5
Garden City Herald (daily, lacking from October, 1888, to April, 1889)...........	1883–1894	6
Garden City Sentinel. July, 1887, to August, 1888, Sentinel and Cultivator)........	1886–1890	7
Garden City Sentinel (daily...........................	1884–1894	10
Cultivator and Herdsman, and Kansas Cultivator, Garden City (September, 1884, to May, 1886, lacking)...........................	1886–1888	6
The Western Times, Garden City and Scott City...........................	1884–1887	1
Finney County Democrat, Garden City...........................	1885	1
The Garden City Imprint...........................	1887–1891	4
The Lookout, Garden City...........................	1889–1894	6
Garden City Tribune...........................	1891,1892	1
Lakin Herald, *see* Kearny county...........................	1892–1894	2
The Pioneer Democrat, Lakin, *see* Kearny county...........................	1883,1884	1
Pierceville Courier...........................	1886,1887	1
Terry Enterprise...........................	1886,1887	1
The Terry Eye...........................	1886,1887	1
Ingalls Echo, *see* Gray county...........................	1887–1889	3
Ivanhoe Times, *see* Haskell county...........................	1886,1887	1
Montezuma Chief, *see* Gray county...........................	1886,1887	1
Santa Fé Trail, *see* Haskell county...........................	1886,1887	1
Ravanna Chieftain, *see* Garfield county...........................	1893,1894	2
The Hatfield News...........................	1887–1889	1
Finney county, short-lived, vol. 1:		
The Optic, Garden City, November 13, 1880; Bundle of Sticks, Garden City, (monthly), February 15, 1885, to February, 1886; Loco Motive, December 16, 1886, to March 17, 1887; Garden City Taxpayer, March 7 to April 25, 1891...	....	1
FOOTE COUNTY, *see* Gray county (3).		
The New West and The Optic, Cimarron...........................	1879–1881	2
The Signet, Cimarron...........................	1880,1881	1

BOUND NEWSPAPERS AND PERIODICALS — Continued.

NEWSPAPERS.	Years.	No. vols
FORD COUNTY (81).		
Dodge City Times (December 25, 1891, to September 16, 1892, lacking)...........	1877–1893	16
Times-Ensign, Dodge City and Bellefont....................................	1892	1
Ford County Globe, Dodge City................................	1878–1884	7
The Globe Live-Stock Journal, Dodge City.....................	1884–1887	4
Dodge City Democrat (May to December, 1889, lacking)......................	1884–1894	10
Kansas Cowboy, Dodge City..	1884,1885	1
The Sun, Dodge City.......................................	1886,1887	1
Ford County Republican Dodge City..............................	1887–1889	3
The Globe-Republican, Dodge City..............................	1889–1894	5
Speareville Enterprise, and Speareville News..................	1878–1880	2
Speareville Blade (August, 1890, to February, 1892, lacking)...............	1885–1892	6
Ford County Democrat, Speareville and Fonda..................	1886–1888	2
New West, Cimarron, see Gray county............................	1885–1887	2
Cimarron Herald, and Kansas Sod House, Cimarron, see Gray county...........	1885,1886	1
The Ryansville Boomer, and The Boomer, Ford City............	1885–1888	2
Ford Gazette..	1886–1890	4
Wilburn Argus.....................................	1886,1887	2
The Bucklin Herald..................................	1887,1888	1
The Bucklin Journal..................................	1888–1890	2
Bucklin Times-Ensign................................	1892,1893	1
Standard, Newkirk, Colcord, and Bucklin..................	1887,1888	1
The Weekly Telegram, Bloom..........................	1888,1889	2
Western Kansas Ensign, Bellefont.....................	1889–1891	3

Ford county, short-lived, vol. 1:

Prairie Homes, Speareville, May 15 and June 14, 1879; Speareville Echo, March 24 to April 28, 1881; Ford County Record, Speareville, September 29, 1885, to February 16, 1886; The Fonda Herald, August 25, 1886; Our Methodist, Dodge City, May, 1888, to May, 1889; Ford County Democrat, Dodge City, July 17 to August 28, 1888; Bucklin Weekly Bulletin, July 7 to September 8, 1892 .... | | 4

Ford county, short-lived, vol. 2:

Dodge City Messenger, February 26 to June 25, 1874; College Advocate (monthly), Dodge City, June 20, 1889, to March, 1890; Dodge City Echo, January 19 to April 29, 1893................................ | | 1

FRANKLIN COUNTY (175).		
Western Home Journal, Ottawa................................	1865–1868	3
Ottawa Journal (October, 1871, to March, 1872; March to September, 1873, lacking),	1870–1874	4
The Triumph, Ottawa..	1875–1877	2
Ottawa Journal and Triumph........	1877–1894	18
Ottawa Republican (1875 lacking)............................	1874–1894	20
Ottawa Daily Republican....................................	1879–1894	31
Kansas Home News, Ottawa..................................	1879,1880	1
Ottawa Gazette..	1879	1
Ottawa Leader (February, 1881, to August, 1882, not published)...............	1880–1883	2
Ottawa Campus (quarterly and monthly)......................	1884–1894	10
Jefferies' Western Monthly, Ottawa........................	1884,1885	1
Queen City Herald, Ottawa........	1886,1887	2
Daily Local News, Ottawa	1886–1888	5
Fireside, Factory, and Farm, Ottawa......................	1886–1888	2
The Kansas Lever, Ottawa................................	1887–1894	8
The Bee (daily and weekly), Ottawa../..................	1887,1888	1
Railroad Employés' Companion, Ottawa, Topeka, Chanute, and Wellington.....	1888–1890	2
Ottawa Tribune..	1889–1893	3
Ottawa Daily Tribune (scattering).........................	1890–1892	3
The Ottawa Herald	1889–1894	6
Ottawa Chautauqua Assembly Herald........................	1891–1894	3
The Ottawa Baptist (monthly)............................	1891–1893	2
Williamsburg Review.....................................	1879	1
Weekly Gazette, Williamsburg............................	1880–1883	2
The Eagle, Williamsburg................................	1885–1889	4
The Enterprise, Williamsburg...........................	1889–1893	4
Williamsburg Star.....................................	1894	1
Lane Advance......................................	1881,1882	1
The Commercial Bulletin, Lane...........................	1886–1888	3
The Lane Star..	1889,1890	1
The Lane Leader......................................	1890–1893	3
The Wellsville News (October, 1882, to March, 1884, called Transcript)...........	1882–1886	3
The Wellsville Transcript..............................	1882–1884	1
The Wellsville Exchange...............................	1887–1889	2
Wellsville Globe.....................................	1890–1894	4
The Pomona Enterprise (April, 1886, to September, 1887, not published)..........	1884–1894	9
Republican, Pomona....................................	1889,1890	1
Richmond Recorder....................................	1885–1888	3
Princeton Progress...................................	1885–1888	3

BOUND NEWSPAPERS AND PERIODICALS — CONTINUED.

NEWSPAPERS.	Years.	No. vols
FRANKLIN COUNTY — *Concluded.*		
Franklin county, short-lived, vol. 1:		
State Press, Ottawa, October 26, 1878, to March 15, 1879; Ottawa Free Trader (monthly), September, 1883, to October, 1884; Lane Leader (first), September 26, 1885, to January 9, 1886; Homewood Herald, December 18. 1885, to January 1, 1886; Runsomville Register, December 24, 1885; Agricola American, December 24, 1885, to January 1, 1886; Sunday Bee, Ottawa, January 8, to February 5, 1888; Shield of Reciprocity (monthly), Wellsville, March to June, 1891; Mission Banner, Ottawa, May 29, 1891...........	....	1
Franklin county, short-lived, vol. 2:		
Ottawa Bulletin, 1869, to August. 1870: Kansas Common School Record, Ottawa, November, 1890: Ottawa Daily Republican, South Kansas M. E. Conference, March 8 to 14, 1892; Educational Aid, Ottawa (monthly), October, 1892, to January, 1893; Richmond Reporter, July 6 to September 28, 1893; Times and Times-Leader, Ottawa, August 25 to November 3, 1893; Franklin County Star, Williamsburg, December 1, 1893, to March 29, 1894; Ottawa Commercial Bulletin, February 3, 1894...............................	....	1
GARFIELD COUNTY (22). (Incorporated into Finney county in 1893.)		
Kansas Sod-House, Ravanna....................	1886,1887	1
Ravanna Chieftain (*see* Hodgeman county)......................................	1887-1893	8
Ravanna Record...	1887-1889	2
The Ravanna Enquirer...	1887,1888	1
The Kalvesta Herald (*see* Hodgeman county).................................	1887,1888	1
The Essex Sunbeam...	1887	1
The Garfield County Call, Eminence	1887-1893	6
Garfield County Journal, Loyal...............................	1887-1889	2
GEARY COUNTY, *see* Davis (30).		
Junction City Union..........	1889-1894	6
Junction City Tribune.......................	1889-1894	6
Junction City Republican..........................	1889-1894	6
The Junction City Sentinel, The Democratic Sentinel and Sentinel Critic.........	1889-1894	6
The Mid-Continental Review (monthly), Junction City..................	1890,1891	3
The Kansas Wheelmen's Library (monthly), Junction City.....................	1891,1892	2
Geary county, short-lived, vol. 1:		
Milford Times. November 3 to 25, 1892..............................	....	1
GOVE COUNTY (43).		
Buffalo Park Express..........................	1880	1
Buffalo Park Pioneer...	1885-1887	3
Grainfield Republican..........................	1880	1
Cap-Sheaf, Grainfield..........................	1885-1894	9
The Golden Belt, Grinnell (April, 1888 to March, 1889, lacking)................	1885-1890	4
Gazette, Gove City..........................	1886-1894	9
Gove County Graphic, Gove City..........................	1887,1888	1
Gove County Republican, Gove City..........................	1888-1890	1
Gove County Echo, Gove City..........................	1891-1894	4
The Settler's Guide, Quinter..........................	1886-1889	2
Quinter Republican..........................	1889-1894	6
The Smoky Globe, Jerome..........................	1887,1888	1
Gove county, short-lived, vol. 1:		
Golden Belt Advance, Grainfield, June 21 to September 10, 1881..............	....	1
GRAHAM COUNTY (53).		
The Hill City Reveille (1893 *).......................	1884-1894	9
Hill City Democrat..........................	1887-1890	3
Hill City Sun..........................	1888,1889	1
Hill City Star..........................	1888,1889	1
Hill City Republican..........................	1890-1894	4
The People's Advocate, Hill City (March to October, 1891, lacking)...........	1891-1894	3
Graham County Lever, Gettysburg..........................	1879,1880	1
The Times, Gettysburg and Penokee..........................	1889,1890	1
The Millbrook Times..........................	1879-1889	10
Graham County Times, Millbrook	1889-1891	2
Millbrook Herald..........................	1882,1883	1
Millbrook Herald (second)..........................	1885-1888	3
The Graham County Democrat, Millbrook..........................	1885-1888	3
Roscoe Tribune..........................	1880,1881	1
Western Cyclone, Nicodemus..........................	1886-1888	2
The Fremont Star..........................	1886-1888	2
The Fremont Press..........................	1888,1889	1
Fremont Eagle..........................	1889,1890	1
The Bogue Signal..........................	1888-1890	2

* Not found.

BOUND NEWSPAPERS AND PERIODICALS—Continued.

NEWSPAPERS.	Years.	No. vols
Graham County—*Concluded.*		
Graham county, short-lived, vol. 1:		
The Western Star, Hill City, December 25, 1879, to June 10, 1880; Hill City Lively Times, June 16 to July 28, 1881; Graham Republican, Millbrook, August 6, 1881, to January 7, 1882; Nicodemus Enterprise, April 17 to December 28, 1887............		1
Grant County (25).		
Grant County Register, Ulysses............	1885–1890	5
Ulysses Tribune, Tribune-Commercial, and Grant County Register (Enfield, 1887)..	1887–1892	6
Ulysses Plainsman............	1889,1890	1
Grant County Republican, Ulysses............	1892–1894	3
The Post, Surprise (see Hamilton county).		
Shockeyville Eagle.	1887	1
Shockeyville Plainsman	1889	1
Golden Gazette............	1887–1889	3
Zionville Sentinel............	1887,1888	1
The Commercial, Cincinnati and Appomattox (see Ulysses Tribune)............	1887,1888	2
The Standard, Cincinnati and Appomattox............	1887,1888	1
Grant county, short-lived, vol. 1:		
Lawson Leader, October 28, 1887, to January 20, 1888; Conductor Punch, November 25, 1887, to February 3, 1888; Shockeyville Independent, December 7, 1887 to January 18, 1888; Daily Register, Ulysses, August 1 to 15, 1888....		1
Gray County (33).		
New West, Cimarron (first)............	1881,1882	1
Cimarron New West (second), (May, 1888, to February, 1891, called New West Echo)............	1887–1894	8
Gray County Echo, Cimarron............	1887,1888	1
Cimarron Herald and Kansas Sod House............	1885,1886	1
The Jacksonian, Cimarron............	1886–1894	9
Ingalls Union............	1887–1894	7
Gray County Republican, Ingalls............	1888	1
The Weekly Messenger, Ingalls............	1889,1890	1
The Montezuma Chief (see Finney county)............	1887–1889	2
Ensign Razzoop............	1887,1888	1
Gray county, short-lived, vol. 1:		
Gray County Republican, Montezuma............	1889	1
Greeley County (24).		
Greeley County Gazette, Greeley Centre and Horace............	1886–1888	2
Greeley County News, Greeley Centre and Horace............	1886–1888	1
Horace Messenger............	1888	1
Horace Champion	1888,1889	1
Horace Headlight............	1892,1893	2
Greeley County Tribune, Tribune and Reid............	1886,1887	1
Greeley County Enterprise, Tribune............	1887–1889	2
Greeley County Republican, Tribune............	1888–1894	6
Greeley County Journal, Tribune and Horace............	1890–1892	2
Western Homestead, Tribune............	1892–1894	3
Greeley County Republican, Reid	1887,1888	1
Colokan Graphic	1887,1888	1
Greeley county, short-lived, vol. 1:		
Hector Echo, April 1 to July 29, 1886; Greeley County New Era, Horace, October 11 to November 22, 1889............		1
Greenwood County (120).		
Eureka Censorial............	1876–1879	3
Eureka Herald (*October 30, 1868, October 15 and December 24, 1869)............	1876–1894	19
The Graphic, Eureka............	1879–1892	3
The Eureka Sun............	1879,1880	1
Greenwood County Republican, Eureka............	1880–1892	12
Greenwood County Democrat, Eureka†............	1882–1884	2
Democratic Messenger, Eureka............	1884–1894	11
The Academy Student, Eureka............	1889,1890	1
Kansas Alliance Union, Eureka............	1890–1894	5
Madison Times (first)............	1877,1878	1
The Madison News............	1879–1892	12
The Zenith, and The Madison Times (second)............	1886	1
Madison Times (third)............	1887,1888	1
Madison Star............	1892–1894	2
Fall River News............	1881–1891	10
Fall River Echo............	1883–1886	3
Fall River Courant	1886–1888	2

* Portfolio.   † Not found.

BOUND NEWSPAPERS AND PERIODICALS—Continued.

NEWSPAPERS.	Years.	No. vols
GREENWOOD COUNTY—Concluded.		
Saturday Morning Sun, Fall River....................................	1888,1889	1
The Pioneer, Gould and Severy.....................	1881–1883	2
Southern Kansas Journal, Severy............................	1883–1887	3
Severy Liberal..	1884–1886	2
Severy Record...	1887–1891	5
The Kansas Clipper, Severy...................................	1887–1889	1
Severyite, Severy..	1889–1892	6
The Severy Telegram (*,1891)..................................	1891,1892	2
The Sunflower, Reece...	1885,1886	1
Greenwood Review, Virgil......................................	1887–1892	4
The Hamilton Broadaxe..	1889,1890	1
Kansas Advocate, Fall River,..................................	1892–1894	2
Greenwood county, short-lived, vol. 1:		
Severy Leader, Severy and Gould City, February 27 to April 2, 1880; The Gould City News, April 9 to May 14, 1880; Real Estate Register, Eureka, August, 1883; Severy Enterprise, January 18 to February 15, 1884; Homeseekers' Guide, Fall River, May, 1887; Daily Republican, Eureka, August 10, 1888; Fall River Chief, June 6 to November 14, 1891; Republican Club, Eureka, August 18 to October 20, 1892............................	....	1
HAMILTON COUNTY (45).		
The Syracuse Journal...	1885–1894	9
Sentinel, Veteran, Johnson City and Syracuse....................	1886–1889	3
Syracuse Democrat..	1887	1
Democratic Principle, Syracuse..................................	1887–1894	7
Shockeyville Eagle..	1885–1887	1
The Hartland Times...	1886,1887	1
Hartland Herald (see Kearny county)............................	1886,1887	1
Border Ruffian, Coolidge.......................................	1886,1887	1
Coolidge Citizen...	1886–1890	4
Coolidge Times...	1887–1890	2
Hamilton County Bulletin, Coolidge and Syracuse................	1890–1893	3
Coolidge Inter State..	1893	1
Surprise Post (see Grant county)...............................	1886,1887	1
The Kendall Ken and The Signal................................	1886,1887	1
The Kendall Boomer..	1886–1889	4
Kendall Gazette...	1887	1
The Kendall Free Press...	1889,1890	1
Johnson City World...	1886,1887	1
Enfield Tribune (Enfield and Ulysses; see Grant county)....	1887	1
Hamilton county, short-lived, vol 1:		
Hamilton County Republican, Kendall, May 6 to September 29, 1886; West Kansas News, Syracuse, March 23 to June 29, 1887; Daily Citizen, Coolidge, October 23 to November 24, 1888................................	....	1
HARPER COUNTY (119).		
Anthony Journal (first)...	1878–1884	5
The Anthony Republican..	1879–1894	15
Anthony Daily Republican......................................	1886–1889	6
Harper County Enterprise, Anthony.............................	1885–1891	7
The Harper County Democrat, Anthony..........................	1886,1887	1
Anthony Free Press (daily)......................................	1887,1888	2
Anthony Free Press (weekly)....................................	1887,1888	1
Anthony Journal (second).......................................	1888–1894	5
Anthony Daily Journal..	1888	1
The Weekly Bulletin, Anthony..................................	1891–1894	3
Harper County Times, Harper...................................	1878–1885	7
The Sentinel, Harper...	1882–1894	12
The Daily Sentinel, Harper (Feb. 19 to May 21, 1887, lacking).....	1885–1888	5
Harper Graphic (suspended August, 1888, to September, 1890).....	1883–1892	7
Harper Daily Graphic...	1886	1
The College Journal, Harper....................................	1888–1890	2
The Prophet, Harper..	1888	1
The Alliance Bulletin, Harper..................................	1890,1891	1
The Advocate, Harper...	1891–1894	3
Bluff City Tribune..	1886–1888	2
Bluff City Herald...	1888–1890	2
Bluff City Independent...	1891–1894	3
The Danville Argus and Courant (November, 1882, to March, 1883, lacking)......	1882–1884	1
The Danville Express...	1885,1886	1
The Attica Advocate..	1885–1891	7
Attica Daily Advocate..	1887	1
Attica Bulletin...	1886–1888	2
Attica Tribune..	1891–1894	3
Freeport Leader..	1885–1891	5

*Not found.

—6

BOUND NEWSPAPERS AND PERIODICALS—CONTINUED.

NEWSPAPERS.	Years.	No. vols
HARPER COUNTY—Concluded.		
The Freeport Tribune.........	1886	1
Midlothian Sun...............	1885,1886	1
The Crisfield Courier.........	1885–1890	4
Crisfield News *.............	1889,1890	1
Harper county, short-lived, vol. 1:		
Anthony Weekly Herald, January 14 to May 8, 1886; Attica Record, March 24 to April 29, 1886; Harper Morning News, October 22 to November 3, 1886; Harper Weekly News, October 29, 1886; Harper Daily Republican, January 3 to February 26, 1889; Young Men's Voice, Harper, July, 1892, to July, 1893,	....	1
HARVEY COUNTY (160).		
Zur Heimath (semimonthly), Halstead, Summerfield, Ill., and St. Louis.........	1875–1881	7
Nachrichten aus der Heidenwelt (monthly), Halstead..........................	1877–1881	5
The Halstead Independent......................................	1881–1894	14
The Halstead Clipper.....................................	1884–1886	2
Halstead Herald..	1887,1888	2
The Halstead Tribune.........	1890–1892	2
Our Church Mirror, Halstead....................	1892–1894	2
Harvey County News, Newton................	1876–1879	4
The Newton Republican (changed from Harvey County News)................	1879–1894	15
Newton Daily Republican................	1886–1894	18
Newton Kansan................	1876–1894	19
Newton Daily Kansan (suspended September, 1888, to November, 1891)..........	1887–1894	6
The Golden Gate, Newton............................	1879–1882	3
Das Neue Vaterland, Newton........................	1879	1
The Newton Democrat...	1883–1887	4
Newton Anzeiger.............................	1887–1892	4
The Kansas Commoner, Newton..................	1887–1890	3
The Kansas Chronicle, Newton.................	1888	1
Newton Weekly Journal......................	1888–1894	5
The School Journal (monthly), Newton....................	1891–1893	2
Harvey County News (second), Newton.................	1893–1895	2
The Burrton Telephone........................	1878–1881	2
The Burrton Monitor........................	1881–1886	6
The Burrton Graphic........................	1886–1894	8
The Free Lance, Burrton........................	1890–1893	3
The Jayhawker and Palladium, Sedgwick................	1882–1884	2
The Pantagraph, Sedgwick................	1884–1894	11
Walton Independent........................	1886–1888	2
The Walton Reporter........................	1890–1893	3
Harvey county, short-lived, vol. 1:		
Halstead Record, March 9, 1877; The Newton Bee, June 7 to August 2, 1879; Arkansas Valley Democrat, March 30 to June 29, 1883; Burrton Real Estate Guide, April, 1885; Der Hausfreund, Newton, December, 1889, January and March, 1890, and October, 1892; The Halstead Daily Herald, March 15 to April 14, 1887; The Ladies' Magazine, Newton, August, 1891, to June, 1892; Church Herald, Newton, June, 1892, March, 1894; Harvey County Voice, Newton, October 15, 1892, to January 7, 1893; Der Burrton Anzeiger, October 31, 1892; Perfect Peace (monthly), Newton, January, 1894:..............	....	1
HASKELL COUNTY (16).		
Ivanhoe Times (see Finney county)	1887–1892	
Santa Fé Trail (see Finney county).		
Santa Fé Champion........................	1887,1888	1
Haskell County Review, Santa Fé.................	1887,1888	1
The Santa Fé Leader	1888	1
Santa Fé Monitor.................	1888–1894	6
Haskell county, short-lived, vol. 1:		
Haskell County Republican, Santa Fé, February 8 to May 30, 1888.............	....	1
HODGEMAN COUNTY (40).		
Agitator, Hodgeman Center	1879	1
Hodgeman County Herald, Hodgeman Center and Kalvesta (see Garfield county),	1886,1887	2
Republican, Fordham........................	1879	1
The Buckner Independent, Jetmore	1879–1881	2
The Jetmore Reveille........................	1882–1892	10
Hodgeman County Scimitar, Jetmore........................	1886–1889	4
Jetmore Siftings (October 27, 1887, to August 9, 1888, lacking)..............	1886–1894	7
Jetmore Journal	1887–1889	1
The Jetmore Sunflower........................	1889–1894	5
The Ravanna Chieftain (see Garfield county)................	1886,1887	1
The Cowland Chieftain	1885	1
The Orwell Times........................	1886	1
Western Herald, Jetmore........................	1892–1894	3

* Not found.

BOUND NEWSPAPERS AND PERIODICALS—Continued.

NEWSPAPERS.	Years.	No. vols
HODGEMAN COUNTY— *Concluded.*		
Hodgeman county, short-lived, vol. 1:		
Pawnee Valley Democrat, December 31, 1886, to March 25, 1887; Hanston Gazette, July 22 to October 21, 1887; Jetmore Republican, October 16 to 30, 1889,	....	1
JACKSON COUNTY (87).		
Jackson County News and Holton News	1872,1873	2
Holton Express..	1872–1875	3
Holton Recorder (1875–'77, Recorder and Express)....................	1875–1894	20
The Holton Argus	1877	1
The Holton Signal......................................	1878–1894	17
Normal Advocate, Holton (scattering, July, 1887, to December, 1890, lacking)....	1882–1894	8
Jackson County Federal, Holton............................	1886,1887	1
Independent Tribune, Holton	1890–1894	4
The Fraternal Aid (monthly), Holton.......................	1891–1894	3
University Informer, Holton..............................	1892,1893	1
Netawaka Chief..	1872–1874	2
The Bee (daily and weekly), Netawaka, Holton...............	1879,1880	1
Netawaka Star...	1893,1894	3
The Whiting Weekly News (January to June, 1891, lacking)	1883–1892	10
The Hoyt Times	1887	1
Soldier City Tribune	1888–1890	2
The Soldier City Clipper	1891–1894	4
The Denison Star..	1889,1890	1
Rural Advocate, Circleville...............................	1890	1
The Kansas Bazaar, Circleville	1891–1893	2
Jackson county, short-lived, vol. 1:		
Daily Holton Express, September 30 and October 1, 1873; Whiting Telephone, May 24. to July 5, 1878; Holton Daily Recorder, March 19 to 23, 1886; Hoyt Messenger, April, 1887; Denison News, June 8 to 29, 1888; Netawaka Reporter, September 1 to October 27, 1888; Home Doings, Soldier, September 11, 18, 1890..........	....	1
JEFFERSON COUNTY (139).		
The Kansas Educational Journal, Grasshopper Falls, *see* Leavenworth county.		
Valley Falls New Era....................................	1873–1894	21
The Valley Falls Liberal and the Kansas Liberal (weekly and monthly), Valley Falls and Lawrence..................................	1880–1883	3
Lucifer, the Light-Bearer, Valley Falls....................	1883–1890	7
Valley Falls Register....................................	1881–1891	11
Fair Play, Valley Falls..................................	1888–1890	2
Valley Falls Republican..................................	1889,1890	1
Farmers' Vindicator, Valley Falls.........................	1890–1894	4
The Oskaloosa Independent (lacking from January to September, 1876)........	1870–1894	24
Sickle and Sheaf. Oskaloosa..............................	1873–1879	6
Oskaloosa Weekly Sickle.................................	1879–1886	8
The Oskaloosa Times.....................................	1891–1894	4
The Winchester Argus....................................	1877–1888	9
The Winchester Herald...................................	1888–1892	5
Winchester Star...	1893,1894	2
The Kaw Valley Chief, Perry..............................	1879–1882	3
The Perry Monitor and Kaw Valley Chief (second), Perry..............	1883,1884	1
The Perry News...	1891,1892	2
The Nortonville News....................................	1885–1894	8
Meriden Report	1885–1889	4
Meriden Weekly Tribune..................................	1890–1894	4
The Meriden Ledger......................................	1894	1
The Osawkie Times......................................	1885,1886	1
The McLouth Times......................................	1887–1894	7
Jefferson county, short-lived, vol. 1:		
Grasshopper, June 12, 1858; Kansas Weekly New Era, Medina, May 29 to September 4, 1867; Kansas Weekly Statesman, Oskaloosa, December 17–31, 1869; Valley Falls Baptist, June, 1884; Social Reformer, Valley Falls (monthly), August, 1884, to January, 1885; Valley Falls Daily Register, September 1, 1885; The Perry Sun, October 18 to November 22, 1893..................	....	1
JEWELL COUNTY (97).		
Jewell County Diamond, Jewell City (* July 4, 1874)...............	1876,1877	2
Jewell County Republican, Jewell City....................	1879 1894	15
Jewell County Democrat, Jewell City......................	1885–1887	2
The Jewell County News, Jewell City......................	1891–1894	3
Jewell County Monitor, Jewell Center (* June 5, 1874)............	1876,1877	2
Jewell County Monitor and Diamond, Jewell Center..........	1878,1879	2
Jewell County Monitor, Jewell Center and Mankato..........	1880–1894	15
Jewell County Review, Jewell Center and Mankato (March, 1883, to December, 1885, called Mankato Review)............................	1879–1894	15

* Portfolio.

BOUND NEWSPAPERS AND PERIODICALS—CONTINUED.

NEWSPAPERS.	Years.	No. vols
JEWELL COUNTY— *Concluded.*		
Mankato Daily Review	1887	1
The Kansas Jewellite, Mankato	1882–1884	1
The Jacksonian, Mankato	1888–1890	3
The Labor Clarion, Mankato	1888,1889	1
White Rock Independent	1879	1
Jewell County Journal, Omio	1879,1880	1
Western Advocate, Omio	1882	1
The Omio Mail	1884	1
The Western Advocate, Burr Oak and Mankato	1890–1894	4
Burr Oak Reveille	1880–1884	4
Burr Oak Herald	1883–1894	12
The Thinker, Burr Oak, *see* McPherson county, short-lived, vol. 1.		
Burr Oak Rustler	1886	1
The Independent, Jewell County Independent, and Burr Oak Republican	1886,1887	1
Salem Chronicle	1882	1
Salem Argus (not published from January to June, 1889; called Kansas Labor Clarion, Mankato, from July 12, 1888, to January 17, 1889)	·1883–1890	6
The People's Friend, Salem	1885–1887	2
Randall Register	1885–1888	3
The Beacon, Randall	1889,1890	1
The Exponent, Randall	1891,1892	2
Esbon Leader	1892,1893	1
Jewell county, short-lived, vol. 1: Antimonopolist, Rubens, February 9, 1882; Randall Tribune, October 8 to December 31, 1887; Jewell County Republican (daily), Northwest Kansas Conference M. E. Church, Jewell City, March 27 to April 1, 1889; Formoso Times, October 4 to November 8, 1889; Institutionist, Dentonia (monthly), April to June, 1890; Webber Times, March 30 to May 11, 1894; Webber Herald, May 18 to June 1, 1894	....	4
JOHNSON COUNTY (87).		
Olathe Mirror (* October 25, 1862, October 29, 1864, September 3, 1868, October 24, 1869)	1866–1868	2
Mirror and News-Letter, Olathe	1876–1882	6
The Olathe Mirror (1883 to 1886, Mirror-Gazette,)	1882–1893	11
Olathe Republican Mirror	1893,1894	2
Western Progress, Olathe	1876–1880	4
Kansas Star, Olathe	1876–1894	10
Olathe Leader	1879–1881	2
Olathe Gazette	1879–1882	3
Kansas Patron, Olathe (March 10 to August 18, 1881, Patron and Farmer)	1881–1894	14
Johnson County Democrat, Olathe	1882–1891	10
The Olathe Republican	1884,1885	2
The Olathe Leader (second)	1891–1894	3
Alliance Echo, Olathe, and Olathe Tribune	1893,1894	1
Progressive Thought, Olathe (quarterly, monthly, and bimonthly)	1893,1894	1
Olathe Weekly Herald	1893,1894	1
Our Little Friend, Olathe	1893,1894	1
Kansas Register, Spring Hill	1878	1
Weekly Review, Spring Hill	1881,1882	1
Spring Hill New Era, Olathe, (January, 1885, to August, 1888, lacking)	1883–1894	7
The Young Kansan, Gardner	1889,1890	1
The Kansan, Gardner	1890,1891	1
Gardner Graphic	1891–1893	2
Johnson county, short-lived, and fragmentary papers, vol. 1: Kansas Central, Olathe, March 11, 1868; Olathe Evening Meteor, April 1 to 26, 1879; Educational Advocate, Olathe, March, 1880, to February, 1881; De Soto Signal, January, 1887; Kansas Plaindealer, Olathe, January 4 to May 3, 1887; Olathe Baptist Builder (monthly), May to September, 1887	....	1
KEARNY COUNTY (28).		
Lakin Herald	1882	1
The Kearny County Advocate, Lakin	1885–1894	9
Pioneer Democrat, Lakin	1887–1890	4
The Lakin Index	1890–1894	5
Hartland Times	1887	1
Hartland Herald, *see* Hamilton county	1887–1891	4
Kearny County Coyote, Chantilly, Omaha, and Hartland	1887–1890	3
Kearny county, short-lived, vol. 1: Lakin Eagle, May 20 to October 10, 1879; Standard, Hartland, December 24, 1888, to March 2, 1889	....	4
KINGMAN COUNTY (76).		
The Kingman Mercury	1878–1880	2
The Kingman County Citizen, Kingman	1879–1884	4

*Portfolio.

BOUND NEWSPAPERS AND PERIODICALS — CONTINUED.

NEWSPAPERS.	Years.	No. vols
KINGMAN COUNTY — *Concluded.*		
The Kingman County Republican, Kingman (Citizen-Republican, 1884)..........	1882–1884	3
The Kingman Blade...	1880	1
Southern Kansas Democrat, Kingman, and The Kingman County Democrat......	1883–1894	11
The Kingman Courier...	1884–1889	6
Kingman Daily Courier..	1887–1889	4
Kingman Leader..	1884–1889	5
Kingman Leader-Courier...	1889–1894	5
Kingman News...	1886–1888	1
Kingman Daily News (November, 1887 to February, 1888, lacking)...............	1886–1888	2
Voice of the People, Kingman.......................................	1888,1889	2
The Kingman Weekly Journal...	1890–1894	5
The Cleveland Star...	1881,1882	1
Norwich News..	1885–1892	9
Ninnescah and Cunningham Herald...................................	1886,1887	1
Cunningham Herald (not published January to May, 1891)...................	1887–1892	5
Cunningham Chronicle..	1893,1894	1
The Spivey Dispatch..	1887,1888	2
Spivey Index..	1889–1891	3
New Murdock Herald...	1887	1
The Penalosa News...	1887,1888	1
Kingman county, short-lived, vol. 1:		
The Nashville News. April 12 to July 12, 1888; Kingman Mercury, May 8 to June 13, 1890...	....	1
KIOWA COUNTY (34).		
Wellsford Republican...	1886,1887	1
Kiowa County Democrat, Wellsford...................................	1887,1888	2
Wellsford Register (second)...	1889,1890	1
Comanche Chief and The Kiowa Chief, Reeder...........................	1886	1
The Kiowa County Signal, Greensburg.................................	1886–1894	9
Greensburg Rustler..	1886–1888	3
Greensburg Republican (first).......................................	1887,1888	1
The Kiowa County Times, Greensburg.................................	1888–1894	6
The Republican, Greensburg (second).................................	1890,1891	1
Republican Banner, Greensburg......................................	1891–1895	4
Mullinville Mallet...	1886–1888	2
The Weekly Telegram, Mullinville....................................	1886,1887	1
The Haviland Tribune...	1887–1889	2
Kiowa county, short-lived, vol. 1:		
Wellsford Register (first), June 13, to November 21, 1885; Democrat and Watchman, Dowell and Wellsford, November 28, 1885, to August 14, 1886; Wellsford Reformer, December 29, 1888, to August 9, 1889...............	....	1
LABETTE COUNTY (221).		
Parsons Sun (November, 1876, to May, 1877, lacking)........................	1876–1894	18
Parsons Sun (daily)..	1884–1894	22
Parsons Eclipse..	1876–1894	19
Parsons Daily Eclipse...	1881–1894	27
Daily Outlook, Parsons..	1877,1878	1
Daily Infant Wonder, Parsons.......................................	1878–1880	3
Daily Republican, Parsons..	1880,1881	2
The Daily Evening Star, Parsons.....................................	1881	1
Parsons Palladium...	1883–1894	12
The Weekly Clarion, Parsons..	1888–1891	2
The Parsons Daily Journal...	1889,1890	1
The Daily Eli, Parsons..	1891	2
Kansas Workman and State Alliance, Parsons...........................	1891	1
Our Home Visitor (monthly), Parsons.................................	1891,1892	2
Mills's Weekly World, Parsons; Parsons World.........................	1891–1893	2
Parsons Independent...	1894	1
Southern Kansas Advance and Chetopa Advance........................	1876–1894	17
Chetopa Herald..	1876–1878	2
Chetopa Statesman..	1885–1880	4
The Chetopa Democrat..	1876–1894	7
Oswego Independent...	1876–1894	19
Labette County Democrat, Oswego....................................	1880–1894	15
The Oswego Republican...	1881–1886	5
The Oswego Daily Republican..	1881–1883	3
The Oswego Bee..	1887–1889	2
The Oswego Daily Bee..	1887,1888	4
Labette County Statesman and Times-Statesman, Oswego................	1889–1894	5
The Oswego Courant..	1889,1890	2
The Golden Rod (bimonthly), Oswego.................................	1891–1894	2
Union Blade, Oswego...	1894	1
Mound Valley Herald...	1885–1894	9
Mound Valley News..	1886,1887	1
The Altamont Sentinel	1886–1890	4

NEWSPAPERS.	Years.	No. vols
LABETTE COUNTY — *Concluded.*		
Mills's Weekly World, Altamont	1888–1891	3
Edna Enterprise	1887	1
The Edna Star	1887,1888	1
The Edna Independent	1890–1893	3
The Wilsonton Journal (monthly)	1888–1894	4
Labette county, short-lived, and fragmentary papers, vol. 1:		
The Oswego Register, July 30, 1869, December 6 and 12, 1873, July 10, 1874; Parsons Surprise, June 13, 1874, to January 20, 1875; The Settlers' Guide, Chetopa, April to October, 1877; Parsons Broadax, December 28, 1877, January 11, 1878; Coffin's Business Directory, Parsons, February, 1878; Kansas Christian Advocate, Oswego, December 14, 1881, to May 19, 1882; Mound Valley Times, December 16, 1881, to April 28, 1882; Oswego Daily Independent, December 15, 1882, to January 6, 1883; Chetopa Times, August 2, 1884; The Arbitrator, Parsons, September 10 to October 29, 1886; United Labor, Mound Valley, August 6, 1887; Labette County Times, Oswego, June 18 to July 9, 1892; The Eye Opener, Parsons, July 9 to 23, and December 26, 1892; The American Crank, Oswego, November 19, 1892, to March 11, 1893; The Railway Employé, Parsons, May 1, 1893	....	1
LANE COUNTY (24).		
Lane County Gazette, California	1880–1882	2
The Progress, Dighton Junction, and Western Progress, Dighton	1880	1
Lane County Herald, Dighton, and Dighton Herald	1885–1894	10
Dighton Journal	1886–1892	6
Dighton Republican	1887–1889	2
Lane County Farmer, Dighton	1890–1892	2
Lane county, short-lived, vol. 1:		
Western Advance (monthly), Dighton, March to June, 1890	....	1
LEAVENWORTH COUNTY (286).		
Kansas Herald, Leavenworth	1854–1859	5
Kansas Territorial Register, Leavenworth	1855	1
Leavenworth Conservative, daily (January to June, 1867, lacking)	1861–1868	14
Times and Conservative (daily), Leavenworth	1868–1870	4
Leavenworth Times, daily (July to October, 1878, lacking: *scattering issues, 1859 to 1864)	1870–1894	48
Leavenworth Times, weekly (March 14, 1857, and May 28, 1859, two issues)	1876–1881	5
Leavenworth Daily Commercial	1873–1876	4
The Kansas Educational Journal (monthly): Leavenworth, January, 1864 to August, 1865; Grasshopper Falls, September,1865, to January, 1866; Topeka, June, 1866, to August, 1867; Emporia. September, 1867, to April, 1871; Emporia and Topeka, May, 1871, to April, 1873; Leavenworth, May, 1873, to March, 1874	1864–1874	10
Kansas Freie Presse (weekly), Leavenworth, (June 2 and December 31, 1869; November 16, 1870,)	1876–1886	11
Kansas Freie Presse (daily), Leavenworth, (April, 1876, to December, 1879; May to June, 1881, lacking,)	1876–1886	14
Leavenworth Appeal (see short-lived, vol. 3, Sunday Herald)	1877,1879	3
Leavenworth Appeal (daily)	1876–1878	3
Leavenworth Appeal and Tribune	1879,1880	1
Home Record (monthly), Leavenworth	1876–1894	19
Public Press (weekly), Leavenworth	1877–1883	6
Public Press (daily), Leavenworth	1879–1882	8
Orphans' Friend (monthly), Leavenworth	1878–1894	16
The Western Homestead (monthly) Leavenworth	1878–1882	4
Democratic Standard (weekly), Leavenworth	1880–1882	2
Kansas Farmer (monthly), Leavenworth (see Shawnee county).		
Leavenworth Evening Standard	1881–1894	27
The Workingman's Friend, Leavenworth	1881,1882	2
The Visitor, Olathe and Leavenworth (monthly and weekly); The Catholic Visitor, The Catholic, and The Kansas Catholic, Leavenworth (see Wyandotte county)	1882–1890	7
Leavenworth Weekly Chronicle	1883,1884	1
The Kansas Prohibitionist, Leavenworth	1883,1884	1
Kansas Commoner, Leavenworth	1884,1885	1
Leavenworth Post (daily)	1887–1894	14
The Daily Sun, Leavenworth	1888–1890	6
Journal of the U. S. Cavalry Association (quarterly), Fort Leavenworth	1888–1894	7
The Leavenworth Advocate	1888–1891	3
Taps (monthly), Leavenworth	1889–1891	2
Art League Chronicle (monthly), Leavenworth	1891–1894	4
Leavenworth Labor News	1892–1894	3
Leavenworth Journal of Commerce (semimonthly)	1892–1894	2
The Leavenworth Herald	1894	1
The Sentinel, Fort Leavenworth (Episcopal Church). (See Salina.)		
The Reveille (semimonthly), Fort Leavenworth	1893,1894	2
The Tonganoxie Mirror	1882–1894	12
The Tonganoxie News (changed from Linwood Leader)	1885–1887	2

* In portfolio.

BOUND NEWSPAPERS AND PERIODICALS—CONTINUED.

NEWSPAPERS.	Years.	No. vols
LEAVENWORTH COUNTY—*Concluded.*		
Weekly Sentinel, Tonganoxie (November, 1893, to June, 1894, not published).....	1890–1894	5
The Linwood Leader..	1883,1884	1
The Prison Trusty, Lansing...	1892–1894	2
Leavenworth county, short-lived, and fragmentary papers, vol. 1: Kansas Pioneer, Kickapoo City, October 10, 1855: Leavenworth Journal, February 19, 1857; Kansas Free State, Delaware, July 25 to August 22, and October 31, 1857; Kansas Daily State Register, Leavenworth, November 5, 1859; Daily Leavenworth Herald, September 22, 1860; Leavenworth Daily Enquirer, December 19, 1862; Kansas Insurance ——, Leavenworth, 1867; Leavenworth Weekly Bulletin, January 29, 1868, and March 24, 1869; Daily Evening Call, Leavenworth, October 20, 1869, to February 26, 1872; Kansas Acorn, Leavenworth (monthly), December, 1869; Western Gardener, Leavenworth (monthly), October, 1870, to January, 1871; Western World, Leavenworth (monthly), August, 1873, to March 15, 1877; The Freeman, Leavenworth, November, 1873, to March, 1874; The Kansas Evangel, May 21 to December 24, 1874: State Sentinel, Leavenworth, March, 18, 1875; Colored Radical, Leavenworth and Lawrence, August 24 to November 16, 1876; The Central Record, May to August, 1878; Household Companion, November, 1879; National Tribune, Leavenworth, November 14, 1880, to January 23, 1881; Der Kansas Pioneer, Leavenworth (monthly), August 15, 1881, to September, 20, 1883; Tonganoxie Chronicle, December 23, 1881, to January 13, 1882; Tonganoxie Weekly Star, December 29, 1881, to March 18, 1882....	....	1
Leavenworth county, short-lived, vol. 2: Tonganoxie Chronicle, March 10, 1882; G. A. R., Leavenworth, August 10, 1882, to July 15, 1884; Sunday Free Lance, Leavenworth, February 3–24, 1884; Truth, Leavenworth (monthly), September, 1886, to July 30, 1887; Leavenworth Progress, June 9 to August 12, 1887; The Christian Recruiter, Tonganoxie (monthly), March to October, 1889; National Anti-Prohibition Journal, Leavenworth, October 4 to December 13, 1889; The Evening Republican, Leavenworth, June 17 to July 3, 1891; The Independent, Leavenworth (first), November 5–19, 1892; Welcome News, Leavenworth, November 26 to December 17, 1892...	....	1
Leavenworth county, short-lived, vol. 3: Leavenworth Sunday Herald, *see* Leavenworth Appeal, November 2 to December 14, 1879; The Independent, Leavenworth (second), February 11 to May 19, 1894..	....	1
LINCOLN COUNTY (51).		
Lincoln County News, Lincoln Center...	1873	1
Saline Valley Register, Lincoln Center (Lincoln County Register, September, 1879, to November, 1881)..	1876–1884	8
The Lincoln County Beacon, and Lincoln Beacon, Lincoln Center...............	1880–1894	15
Lincoln Banner, Lincoln Center..	1884–1886	2
Lincoln Republican, Lincoln Center..	1886–1894	9
Lincoln County Democrat, Lincoln...	1886–1890	5
Lincoln County Farmer, Lincoln..	1890–1892	1
Lincoln County Sentinel, Lincoln..	1894	1
The Sylvan Grove Sentinel (suspended, October, 1890, to March, 1892)...........	1887–1893	5
Barnard Times...	1888–1892	3
Beverly Star..	1893,1894	1
LINN COUNTY (122).		
La Cygne Weekly Journal (Journal-Clarion, Sept. 2, 1893 to Jan. 27, 1894)........	1876–1894	19
Border Sentinel, Mound City...	1866–1874	8
Linn County Clarion, Mound City..	1876–1893	17
Mound City Progress (lacking from January to June, 1886).....................	1884–1894	10
Torch of Liberty, Mound City (monthly, first).........................'.......	1886,1887	1
The Torch of Liberty, Mound City (second).....................................	1888–1894	7
The Pleasanton Observer...	1876–1894	18
The Pleasanton Herald...	1882–1894	13
The Prescott Eagle..	1883–1888	5
The Prescott Republican...	1888,1889	1
Prescott Enterprise...	1889	1
Prescott Sunflower..	1893	1
The Blue Mound Sun...	1883–1894	11
Farm Record, Blue Mound...	1890	1
The Parker Pilot..	1889–1891	3
The Pilot and Graphic, Parker...	1891–1894	3
Goodrich Graphic..	1880–1891	2
Linn county, short-lived, vol. 1: Free Press, Pleasanton, October, 1869; Linn County Weekly Press, Pleasanton, November 13, 1869, to January 8, 1870; Real Estate Banner, Pleasanton, January 1, 1870; Blue Mound Independent, February 9, March 2, 9, 1883; La Cygne Leader, January 13, 1887, to November 8, 1888; Goodrich Sentinel, September 19 to November 14, 1889; Visitor (monthly), La Cygne, September, 1890, to August, 1891...	....	4

BOUND NEWSPAPERS AND PERIODICALS—CONTINUED.

NEWSPAPERS.	Years.	No. vols
LOGAN COUNTY (40). (Changed from St. John, March, 1887.)		
The Oakley Opinion	1887–1889	3
The Oakley Republican	1887,1888	1
Oakley Saturday Press	1888	1
Oakley News Letter	1888,1889	1
Logan County Times, Oakley and Russell Springs	1886–1888	1
Oakley Graphic	1889–1894	5
The Courier, Ennis and Monument	1887,1888	1
The Monument Obelisk	1888,1889	1
The Monument Observer	1890	1
The Scout, Gopher and Winona, and Winona Messenger	1886–1889	2
The Winona Clipper	1887–1894	7
McAllaster Weekly Record	1887,1888	1
Augustine Herald	1887–1891	3
Logan County Leader, Russell Springs	1887–1889	2
The Record, Russell Springs	1887	1
The Logan County Republican, Russell Springs	1888–1894	7
Page City Messenger	1889,1890	1
Logan county, short-lived, vol. 1:		
Western Kansas Advocate, Ennis City, Monument post office (monthly), July, 1886, to January, 1887; Logansport Light, July 27 to September 3, 1887; Daily Leader, Russell Springs, December 12 to 14, 1887; Winona Daily Clipper, December 23, 1887		1
LYON COUNTY (183).		
Emporia News (lacking from January to October, 1873—*August 1, November 21, 1857, September 29, 1860)	1865–1889	24
The Weekly News-Democrat, Emporia	1889,1890	1
Emporia News-Democrat (daily)	1889,1890	1
Emporia Daily News	1878–1889	21
Kansas Educational Journal, Emporia, *see* Leavenworth county.		
Emporia Ledger	1876–1882	6
The Hatchet (monthly), Emporia	1877,1878	1
The Educationalist (monthly), Emporia	1879,1880	2
Emporia Sun	1878,1879	1
The Kansas Greenbacker, Emporia	1878,1879	1
*The National Era, Emporia	1879	1
The Emporia Journal	1880,1881	1
The Kansas Sentinel, Emporia	1880–1882	2
Daily Bulletin, Emporia	1881	1
Emporia Daily Republican	1882–1894	25
The Emporia Republican	1886–1894	8
Emporia Democrat	1882–1889	8
The Primitive Friend, Emporia	1883–1885	2
Emporia Weekly Globe	1886,1887	1
Emporia Daily Globe (1888 lacking; called Democrat from July to September, 1889)	1886–1889	3
The Fanatic, Emporia	1887,1888	1
The Semiweekly Miniature, Emporia	1887	1
The Emporia Zeitung (monthly; Anzeiger, May, 1888)	1888–1892	4
The Normal Quarterly, Emporia	1889–1894	5
Kansas Workman, Emporia, *see* Butler county.		
College Life, Emporia (Semiweekly Miniature, March to June, 1887)	1890–1894	5
The Emporia Standard, and Gazette	1890–1894	4
The Baptist Visitor (monthly), Emporia	1890–1894	4
The Columbia, Emporia	1890,1891	1
The Emporia Daily Gazette	1890–1894	9
The Tidings, Emporia	1892–1894	2
The Daily Tidings, Emporia (first few issues, Daily Populist)	1894	2
Lyon County Democrat, Emporia	1893,1894	2
The Hartford Enterprise	1879,1880	1
The Hartford Weekly Call	1879–1891	11
Hartford News	1890–1894	5
Americus Weekly Herald	1880–1882	1
The Americus Ledger	1885–1889	4
The Americus Greeting (suspended from April, 1892, to July, 1893)	1890–1894	3
The Neosho Vivifier, Neosho Rapids	1885,1886	1
The Neosho Valley Press, Neosho Rapids	1886,1887	1
The Leader, Neosho Rapids, *see* Topeka.		
The Neosho Rapids Pilot	1889–1891	2
The Admire City Free Press	1887,1888	1
Admire Independent	1891–1893	1
The Allen Tidings	1887–1892	5
Lyon county, short-lived, vol. 1		
Real-Estate Register, Emporia, March, 1869, to December, 1877; H. E. Norton & Co.'s Real-Estate Bulletin, Emporia, October, 1869; Emporia Tribune, December 29, 1869, to November 30, 1870; Land Buyer, Emporia, April, July,		

*Portfolio.

BOUND NEWSPAPERS AND PERIODICALS — Continued.

NEWSPAPERS.	Years.	No. vols
Lyon County — *Concluded.*		
1878; Daily Union Spy and Fair Bulletin, Emporia, September 7, 1880; Kansas State Sunday-School Journal, Topeka, Emporia (quarterly), January 1, 1883, to October, 1885; Christian Visitant, Emporia, October to December, 1886; Industrial Review, Emporia, October 2 to November 27, 1886; Herald, Emporia, January 16 to April 10, 1890; Advance, Admire, April 8 to 29, 1893; Real-Estate News, Emporia, February to March, 1894................	....	1
McPherson County (145).		
The McPherson Independent (lacking from September, 1876, to March, 1877)......	1876–1879	3
The McPherson Freeman..	1878–1801	13
Freeman-Vim, McPherson..	1801–1894	3
McPherson Daily Freeman...	1887,1888	2
The McPherson Republican..	1879–1894	15
McPherson Daily Republican...	1887–1894	16
The Comet, McPherson..	1881,1882	1
Industrial Liberator, McPherson...	1882	1
The McPherson Independent...	1882–1884	2
The McPherson Press..	1884,1885	1
The McPherson County Champion, McPherson................................	1885–1887	2
The Democrat, McPherson...	1886–1894	8
Kansas State Register, McPherson...	1887	1
The McPherson Anzeiger...	1887–1890	3
Our Opinion, McPherson...	1888–1890	2
School, Fireside, and Farm, and the Educator and Companion, McPherson (monthly, weekly)..	1888–1894	7
The Industrial Union, McPherson..	1890,1891	1
Kansas Vim, McPherson..	1889–1891	2
Alliance Index, January to April, 1891; People's Advocate, May to November, 1891, and People's Party Advocate, McPherson, November, 1891, to February 26, 1892; McPherson County Advocate, Galva, Canton, March to July 15, 1892; People's Advocate, Galva, April to August, 1893 (July, 1892, to April, 1893, lacking)..	1891,1892	2
McPherson County Times, McPherson..	1893	1
McPherson Opinion..	1893,1894	1
Lindsborg Localist..	1879–1883	4
Smoky Valley News, and Lindsborg News.....................................	1881–1894	13
Kansas Posten, Lindsborg...	1882,1883	1
Framat, Lindsborg..	1887–1889	2
The Canton Monitor...	1880,1881	1
Canton Carrier...	1885–1888	3
The Republican, Canton (first)..	1889,1890	2
Canton Republican (second)...	1892–1894	2
The Canton News..	1891,1892	1
The Windom Record...	1884–1886	2
The Windom Enterprise, (first)..	1886–1888	2
The Windom Enterprise (second)...	1892–1894	2
The Moundridge Leader...	1887–1894	7
Marquette Monitor..	1887–1889	2
Marquette Tribune..	1889–1894	6
Galva Times..	1888–1892	3
The Inman Independent...	1891,1892	1
Inman Review..	1892–1894	3
McPherson county, short-lived, vol. 1; Kansas State Tidning, Lindsborg, December 24, 1879, to February 18, 1880; McPherson County School Journal (monthly), McPherson, July to December, 1880; Canton Mirror, February 12 to March 26, 1881; McPherson Leader, March 24 to July 14, 1881; Dispatch, McPherson, May 26 to June 9, 1883; Pedagogue (monthly), Lindsborg, February, 1885, to April, 1886; Praktiken (No. 1), January 15, 1886; Indicator, McPherson, August, 1885; Lindsborg Daily News, May 31, to June 2, 1887; Israel at Work (monthly), McPherson, July and August, 1889; Galva Enterprise, February 5 to 26, 1892; Kansas Courier, McPherson, October 13 to November 10, 1893..............	....	1
Marion County (121).		
Marion County Record, Marion Center.......................................	1875–1894	19
Central Kansas Telegraph, Marion Center....................................	1880	1
Marion Banner, Marion Center..	1880–1882	2
Marion Graphic, Marion Center...	1882–1884	1
Marion County Democrat and Independent, Marion...........................	1883,1884	1
The Marion Register, Marion..	1886–1888	2
The Marion Tribune...	1886,1887	1
The Cottonwood Valley Times (Marion Times), Marion (lacking September, 1889, to November, 1890)..	1887–1894	7
Marion Daily Times...	1888	1
The School Gleaner, Marion...	1889,1890	1
The Rural Kansan (monthly), Marion..	1889,1890	2
The Scimeter, Marion...	1890	1
The Marion County Anzeiger, Marion.......................................	1887,1888	1

BOUND NEWSPAPERS AND PERIODICALS—CONTINUED.

NEWSPAPERS.	Years.	No. vols
MARION COUNTY—*Concluded.*		
Marion Weekly Globe.....	1890,1891	1
The Central Advocate, Marion.....	1891	1
The Peabody Gazette.....	1876–1894	19
The Peabody Daily Gazette.....	1887	1
Peabody Reporter.....	1880	1
The Peabody Post.....	1882	1
Peabody Graphic (Marion County Graphic, January to March, 1884).....	1884–1894	11
Florence Herald (June, 1885, to February, 1887, lacking).....	1876–1891	14
Florence Tribune.....	1884–1886	2
Florence Weekly News.....	1886,1887	1
The Florence Weekly Bulletin.....	1887–1894	8
Hillsboro Phonograph.....	1881	1
The Intelligencer, Hillsboro.....	1881,1882	1
Freundschafts-Kreis, Hillsboro.....	1885,1886	2
Hillsboro Herald.....	1886–1889	3
Hillsboro Anzeiger.....	1888–1894	6
Freie Presse, Hillsboro.....	1890	1
Der Kansas Courier, Hillsboro.....	1891–1893	2
Canada Arcade.....	1887	1
The Weekly Courier, Lost Springs.....	1888,1889	1
Burns Monitor.....	1889,1890	1
Burns Citizen.....	1893,1894	1
Marion county, short-lived, vol. 1: Des Farmers' Anzeiger, Hillsboro, Nos. 1, 2, 1883; School Galaxy, Marion Center, September 6, 1877, to January 3, 1878; Marion Daily Register, September 6, 1886; Lincolnville Star, July 16 to November 19, 1887; Lost Springs Journal, September 17 to November 26, 1887; Lower Light, (monthly), Marion, November, 1887 to October, 1889; Enquirer, Marion, March 15, 1890; Burns' Mirror, September 5, 1890, to January 16, 1891; Marion County Democrat, Marion, April 7 to May 26, 1892; Advance, Marion, October 1 to 18, 1892.....	.....	1
MARSHALL COUNTY (178).		
The Marysville Enterprise (vols. 3 and 4).....	1866–1868	2
The Lantern, Marysville.....	1876	1
The Marshall County News, Marysville.....	1876–1894	19
Kansas Staats-Zeitung, Marysville.....	1879–1881	2
Marysville Signal.....	1881–1883	3
Maysville Post (German).....	1881–1894	13
Marshall County Democrat, Marysville.....	1882–1894	12
The Bugle Call, Marysville.....	1885,1886	1
The True Republican, Marysville.....	1886–1890	4
The Daily Free Press, Marysville.....	1889,1890	3
Evening Democrat, Marysville.....	1890–1892	2
The People's Advocate, Marysville.....	1890–1894	4
The Waterville Telegraph (June, 1873, to January, 1876, lacking).....	1870–1894	22
Blue Rapids Times.....	1876–1894	19
The Blue Rapids Lyre.....	1886,1887	1
Blue Rapids Weekly Motor.....	1890–1894	4
Blue Valley Gazette, Irving.....	1876–1878	3
The Irving Citizen.....	1880	1
The Irving Leader.....	1886–1894	8
Frankfort Record.....	1876–1879	3
The Greenback Headlight, and National Headlight, Frankfort.....	1879–1881	2
The Frankfort Bee.....	1881–1894	13
The Frankfort Sentinel.....	1886–1892	6
Weekly Review, Frankfort.....	1893,1894	1
The Beattie Boomerang and Boomer.....	1883,1884	1
The North Star and The Star, Beattie.....	1884–1891	7
Williamson's Beattie Eagle.....	1891–1894	3
The Visitor, Axtell.....	1883,1884	1
Axtell Anchor.....	1883–1894	11
The Summerfield Sun.....	1889–1894	6
The Oketo Sun and Herald.....	1889–1894	5
The Vermillion Record.....	1891–1894	3
Marshall county, short-lived, vol. 1: Our New Home, Frankfort, December 2, 1869; Irving Recorder, December 10 to 31, 1869; Kansas Pilot, Blue Rapids (monthly), January and March, 1879; Daily Marshall County News, Marysville, October 2, 3, 1879, September 21 to 24, 1880; Marshall County Record, Marysville, October 8 to December 17, 1880; Marshall County Democrat, Marysville, October 21 to November 3, 1880; Kind Words, Vermillion (monthly), July to September, 1881; Marysville Pickings (monthly), January and February, 1883; Daily Institute, Marysville, July 7 to 31, 1884; Bugle Call, Marysville, December 10, 1885, to August 5, 1886; Western Breeder, Beattie (monthly), September, 1887, to May, 1891.....	.....	
Marshall county, short-lived, vol. 2: Holiness War News (monthly), Irving and Clay Center, November, 1890, to October 1, 1891.....	.....	

BOUND NEWSPAPERS AND PERIODICALS—CONTINUED..

NEWSPAPERS.	Years.	No. vols
MEADE COUNTY (39).		
The Pearlette Call (biweekly and weekly)	1879,1880	1
Fowler City Graphic	1885–1890	5
Meade County Globe, Meade Center	1885–1894	9
Meade Center Press, Meade County Press-Democrat, and Meade County Democrat,	1885–1891	5
Meade Center Telegram	1886	1
The Meade Republican, Meade Center	1887–1893	6
Meade County Nationalist, Meade	1891,1892	2
The Hornet, Spring Lake and Artesian City	1885–1889	3
The Guardian, West Plains	1886,1887	1
The West Plains News and Democrat	1887,1888	1
The West Plains Mascotte	1888,1889	1
Meade County Times, Mertilla	1886–1888	3
Meade county, short-lived. vol. 1:		
Fowler City Advocate, April 30 to July 9, 1886		1
MIAMI COUNTY (89).		
The Western Spirit, Paola (1874 to 1876, scattering)	1874–1894	20
Miami Republican, Paola (we have February 2, 1867; December 11, 1869; March 6, 1875; scattering, Nos. 71, 72, 74; 73 nearly complete; 1875 to April, 1876, lacking),	1876–1894	21
Republican-Citizen, Paola	1878–1880	2
Miami Talisman, Paola	1881,1882	1
Paola Times, Miami Farmer (Times-Signal, July 9, 1891, to January 21, 1892)	1882–1894	13
The Miami School Journal (monthly), Paola	1889–1891	2
The Border Chief and Border Watchman, Louisburg	1879–1881	2
The Louisburg Herald (*August 30, 1877)	1887–1894	7
Osawatomie Times	1880,1881	1
The Osawatomie Sentinel	1885	1
Osawatomie Gaslight	1887,1888	1
Graphic, Osawatomie	1888–1894	7
Osawatomie Advertiser	1888–1890	1
Farmers' Signal, Osawatomie	1890,1891	1
Osawatomie Globe	1891–1894	3
Fontana News	1885–1890	5
Miami county, short-lived. vol. 1:		
Border Tier Real Estate Bulletin (monthly), Paola, April and May, 1869; Paola Democrat, September 28, 1871; Journal of Didactics (monthly), Paola, January 15 to June, 1880		1
MITCHELL COUNTY (114).		
Beloit Gazette (April, 1873, to June, 1876, lacking)	1872–1894	19
Beloit Weekly Record	1877–1879	2
Beloit Weekly Democrat and Western Democrat, Beloit (1882 and 1883, Nationalist)	1878–1890	10
The Beloit Courier	1879–1894	16
The Western Nationalist. Beloit	1882,1883	2
The Western Call, Beloit	1890–1894	4
Kansas Woodman (monthly), Beloit	1893,1894	2
Cawker City Tribune	1873,1874	1
The Echo, Cawker City	1876–1878	2
The Cawker City Free Press	1878–1883	5
Cawker City Journal	1880–1890	10
The Public Record, Cawker City	1883–1894	12
Cawker City Times	1888–1894	7
Expositor, Cawker City (see Dickinson county).		
Glen Elder Key	1880,1881	1
Glen Elder Herald, The Kansas Herald, Glen Elder (May, 1885, to June, 1886, lacking)	1885–1890	4
The People's Sentinel, Glen Elder	1891–1894	4
Glen Elder Republican	1893,1894	1
Simpson Siftings	1884–1886	2
Scottsville Independent	1886–1889	3
Tri-County News, Scottsville	1889–1894	6
Mitchell county, short-lived, vol. 1.:		
Mitchell County Mirror, Beloit, May 17 to June 28, 1871; Cawker City Tribune, December 2 and 9, 1873; Cawker City Sentinel, April 3, 1874; Campfire (monthly), Cawker City, August, 1882, to September, 1883; Mitchell County Farmer, Beloit, July, 1884; Dental Herald, Beloit, January, 1888, to January, 1889; Beloit Trade Journal, May 8 to August 7, 1890; Harmonic, Beloit, September, 1892, to June, 1893		1
MONTGOMERY COUNTY (194).		
Coffeyville Courier	1874,1875	1
Coffeyville Journal	1875–1894	19
Coffeyville Daily Journal	1894	1
The Gate City Enterprise, Coffeyville	1884,1885	1
Gate City Gazette, Coffeyville	1886,1887	1

* Portfolio.

BOUND NEWSPAPERS AND PERIODICALS — CONTINUED.

NEWSPAPERS.	Years.	No. vols
MONTGOMERY COUNTY — *Concluded.*		
The Sun, Coffeyville...	1886–1889	3
The Eagle, Coffeyville..	1888–1890	1
The News, Coffeyville, and News-Broad-Ax........................	1890–1893	3
Afro-American Advocate, Coffeyville................................	1891–1893	2
Coffeyville Daily Telegram..	1893	1
The Kansas Blackman, Topeka and Coffeyville......................	1894	1
Independence Courier, The Weekly Courier (December, 1876, to April, 1877, lacking)...	1875–1877	2
The Workingman's Courier, Independence............................	1877–1879	2
Independence Kansan...	1876–1884	9
The Star, Independence (Coffeyville Star, April to October, 1881)...........	1881–1884	4
The Star and Kansan, Independence.................................	1885–1894	10
The South Kansas Tribune, Independence...........................	1876–1894	19
The Living Age, Independence.......................................	1881	1
The Evening Reporter, and the Morning Reporter, Independence (lacking from June, 1882, to February 17, 1884; from May, 1884, to February, 1886).........	1882–1894	19
The Independence News (daily and weekly).............................	1886	1
Montgomery Argus, Independence.....................................	1886,1887	1
United Labor, Independence..	1892–1894	3
Kansas Populist, Independence and Cherry Vale.....................	1893,1894	1
Cherry Vale Leader..	1877	1
Cherry Vale Globe (May, 1881, to January, 1882, lacking).............	1879–1882	2
Cherry Vale News..	1881,1882	1
Cherry Valley Torch, Cherry Vale....................................	1882–1885	3
Cherry Vale Globe-News..	1882–1885	3
The Globe and Torch, Cherry Vale...................................	1885–1888	3
Daily Globe and Torch, Cherry Vale (June, 1887, to December 9, 1888, lacking)..	1885–1889	5
Cherry Vale Bulletin..	1884–1888	1
The Cherry Vale Republican (January to July, 1893, lacking).........	1886–1894	8
The Cherry Vale Champion..	1887–1894	7
Southern Kansas Farmer, Cherry Vale................................	1890,1891	1
The Kansas Commonwealth, Cherry Vale...............................	1891	1
The Morning Telegram, Cherry Vale..................................	1892	1
Cherry Vale Republic..	1893	1
Republican-Plaindealer, Cherry Vale................................	1893	1
Daily Kansas Populist and Morning News, Cherry Vale...............	1894	2
Elk City Times..	1880	1
The Elk City Globe..	1882–1887	5
The Elk City Star...	1884,1885	1
The Elk City Democrat...	1885,1886	1
The Elk City Eagle..	1886–1890	4
The Elk City Enterprise...	1889–1894	3
The Caney Chronicle...	1885–1894	9
The Caney Times...	1889–1894	6
The Havana Vidette..	1885–1887	1
Havana Weekly Herald..	1887–1889	2
The Havana Recorder...	1889	1
The Havana Press and Torch..	1891–1893	2
Liberty Light...	1886	1
The Liberty Review..	1887–1892	6
Montgomery county, short-lived, vol. 1:		
Independence Pioneer, November 13, 1869, to January 1, 1870; Independence Itemizer, July 19 to August 5, 1879; Parish Churchman, Independence, November, 1880; Cherry Vale Home, Nos. 1, 2, 3, 1883 (?); Cherry Vale Advocate (quarterly), July and October, 1883, April and August, 1884, April and June, 1885, March, 1886; Caney Valley Home, May, 1884: Stewart's Southern Kansas Guide, Independence, April to October, 1884, March, 1885, January, 1886; Oklahoma Boomer, Coffeyville, January 21 to April 1, 1885; Weekly Clarion, Cherry Vale, October 1 to December 31, 1885; Buyers' Guide, April 3 to May 15, 1886; Montgomery Monitor, Independence, December 26, 1885, to January 30, 1886; Independence Weekly News, May 14 to July 23, 1886; Southern Kansas Journal and Land Buyers' Guide, March, 1887; Caney Sunbeam, September 30 to November 11, 1887...............	....	▲
Montgomery county, short-lived, vol. 2:		
The Daily Cent, Cherry Vale, November 22 to December 15, 1888; The Index, Coffeyville, October 1, 1889, to , 1891; Havana News, October 12 to August 2, 1890; Havana Globe, November 7, 1890, to January 2, 1891; The Broad-Ax, Coffeyville, December 31, 1891, to April 29, 1892; People's Party Plaindealer, Cherry Vale, September 14, 1892, to January 13, 1893; Ranch and Range, Coffeyville, January 5 to April 14, 1893; Gate City Independent, Coffeyville, August 18, 23, 1893...........	....	▲
Montgomery county, short-lived, vol. 3:		
The Evening Courier, Independence, March 7-19 to November 17, 1879........	....	1
MORRIS COUNTY (72).		
The Kansas Press, Council Grove (incomplete; Cottonwood Falls, May to August, 1859)..	1859–1865	3
The Council Grove Democrat (first).................................	1866	1

BOUND NEWSPAPERS AND PERIODICALS — CONTINUED.

NEWSPAPERS.	Years.	No. vols
MORRIS COUNTY — *Concluded.*		
Morris County Republican, Council Grove	1876,1877	2
Council Grove Democrat (second)	1876,1877	1
Republican and Democrat, Council Grove	1877–1879	2
Council Grove Republican	1879–1894	16
Morris County Times, Council Grove	1880,1881	2
The Kansas Cosmos, Council Grove (January to July, 1885, lacking)	1881–1886	4
The Council Grove Guard (Herald-Guard, January 2, 1891, to May 6, 1892)	1884–1894	10
The Anti-Monopolist, Council Grove	1888	1
Council Grove Courier	1891–1894	3
Morris County Enterprise, Parkersville	1873–1884	7
The Parkersville Times	1887,1888	1
White City Whig, Morris County News, and White City News	1885–1890	4
White City Register	1889–1894	5
The Dwight Wasp	1887–1891	4
The Dunlap Courier	1889–1891	2
Wilsey Bulletin	1889–1891	2
The Morris County Republican, The Morris County Independent, The Wilsey Independent (May, 1893, to March, 1894, lacking)	1892–1894	1
Morris county, short-lived, vol. 1:		
Council Grove Advertiser, December 25, 1869, to August 30, 1870; Dunlap Chief, March 3 to June 2, 1882; Temperance Banner, Council Grove, August 19 to November 4, 1882; Council Grove Vidette, May 19, 1883; Daily Republican, Council Grove, April 17–19, 1884; Field and Range, Kansas City, Mo., and Dwight, Kas. (monthly), July to October, 1887; Sweet Chariot, Dunlap, September 1 to December 31, 1887; Dunlap Reporter, scattering, July 20, 1883, March 21, 1884, to May 10, 1888; Daily Morning News, Council Grove, September 15–18, 1891, September 27–30, 1892; Dwight Independent, October 23 to December 11, 1891; Greeting, Dunlap, May 6 to June 17, 1892; Morris County Republican, Wilsey, October 6 to December 22, 1892		1
MORTON COUNTY (24).		
Frisco Pioneer	1886,1887	1
Morton County Democrat, Frisco	1886–1888	1
The Great Southwest, Richfield	1886,1887	1
The Richfield Leader	1886,1887	1
The Leader-Democrat, Richfield	1888,1889	1
The Richfield Republican	1887–1890	3
The Monitor-Republican, Richfield	1890–1894	5
Richfield News	1889,1890	1
The Morton County Star, Richfield	1891–1893	3
The Taloga Star	1887–1890	3
Cundiff Journal	1888,1889	1
The Morton County Monitor, Morton and Richfield	1888–1890	1
The Westola Wave	1888,1889	1
Morton county, short-lived, vol. 1:		
Westola Sunbeam, September 22 to December 1, 1887; Morton Herald, January 10 to 24, 1889		1
NEMAHA COUNTY (110).		
Seneca Weekly Courier (*October 21, 1869, May 16, 1873)	1875–1884	9
Seneca Courier-Democrat	1884–1894	10
The Seneca Tribune	1879–1894	15
Our Mission, Seneca	1884–1886	2
The Seneca News	1891–1894	4
Nemaha County Republican, Sabetha	1876–1893	17
The Sabetha Advance (May to August, 1874)	1876,1877	2
Sabetha Weekly Herald	1884–1893	9
Sabetha Republican-Herald	1893,1894	2
The Oneida Journal	1879–1882	3
The Oneida Chieftain, Democrat, and Dispatch	1883,1884	1
The Oneida Monitor	1895,1886	1
The Oneida World	1892	1
The Wetmore Spectator (lacking from August, 1884, to September, 1886)	1882–1894	10
The Centralia Enterprise	1883,1884	2
The Centralia Journal	1884–1894	10
Centralia Times	1893,1894	2
The Goff's News	1887–1890	3
The Goff's Advance	1892–1894	3
The Bern Press	1889–1894	6
Nemaha county, short-lived, vol. 1:		
Independent Press, Seneca, June 11, 1870; L'Etoile du Kansas, Neuchatel, January, 1873; Corning Chief, April 12 to July 12, 1884; Wetmore Register, July 31 to August 28, 1886; Oneida Owl, August 21, 28, 1886; Corning Independent, April 18 to July 10, 1890; Goff's Reporter, January 15 to 29, 1891		1

* Portfolio.

BOUND NEWSPAPERS AND PERIODICALS — Continued.

NEWSPAPERS.	Years.	No. vols
Neosho County (112).		
Neosho County Journal, Osage Mission..........	1876–1894	19
The Temperance Banner, Osage Mission (monthly, semimonthly)..............	1878–1880	2
Neosho Valley Enterprise, Osage Mission..................................	1880–1882	2
Neosho County Democrat, Osage Mission................	1883–1887	5
Neosho County Record, Erie, and Erie Record (June, 1884, to April, 1885, lacking),	1876–1886	9
Republican-Record, Erie...........................	1886–1894	8
Neosho County Republican, Erie.......................	1882–1886	4
The People's Vindicator, Erie	1888,1889	2
The Erie Sentinel.....................................	1889–1894	5
Pythian Sisters' News, Erie, *see* Barton county.		
Chanute Times....................................	1876–1891	15
The Chanute Democrat............................	1879–1882	3
The Chanute Chronicle..........................	1882,1883	2
Chanute Blade...................................	1883–1894	11
The Chanute Vidette	1887–1891	3
Chanute Vidette-Times.............................	1891–1894	4
Railroad Employés' Companion, Chanute, *see* Franklin county.		
Chanute Daily Tribune............................	1892–1894	5
Head Light, Thayer.................................	1876–1893	15
The Thayer Herald................................	1885,1886	1
Thayer Independent News...........................	1891–1894	3
The Stark Freeman.................................	1890,1891	1
Neosho county, short-lived, vol. 1:		
Star of Hope, Urbana, January to April, 1878; Chanute Recorder (monthly), October, 1882, to March, 1883; Galesburg Journal, April 22 to July 15, 1885; Stark Herald, June 14, 1888; Chanute Daily Times, June 14 to September 13, 1890; Hornet, Thayer, September 23 to November 4, 1892............	....	1
Neosho county, short-lived, vol. 2:		
Osage Mission Transcript, October 17 to November 7, 1873; January 9, February 27, March 20, 1874; Neosho County Chronicle, Chanute, June 22 to October 5, 1894..........	....	1
Ness County (44).		
The Pioneer, Clarinda and Sidney....................	1879,1880	1
The Advance, Sidney.............................	1882,1883	1
Western Central Kansas Cowboy, Sidney..............	1883,1884	1
Ness City Times.................................	1880–1891	11
The Truth, Ness City..............................	1883,1884	1
The News, Ness City..............................	1884–1894	10
The Sixteenth Amendment, Ness City...............	1885	1
The Ness City Graphic............................	1886	1
Walnut Valley Sentinel, Ness City, and Ness City Sentinel..........	1886–1893	7
Ness County Echo, Ness City....................	1893,1894	2
The Globe, Schoharie.............................	1883,1884	1
The Herold Record...............................	1887–1889	2
Herold Boomer....................................	1887	1
Nonchalanta Herald.............................	1887–1889	1
The Bazine Register.............................	1887,1888	1
Bazine Leader....................................	1889	1
Ness county, short-lived, vol. 1:		
Bazine Banner, June 29 to August 10, 1888; Lance, Ness City, October 19 to December 21, 1892..........	....	1
Norton County (70).		
Norton County Advance, Norton....................	1878–1882	4
Norton County People, Norton.....................	1880–1883	2
The Norton Courier..............................	1883–1894	12
Norton Champion................................	1884–1894	11
The Norton Democrat (April to June, 1886, Norton Reporter).............	1886–1888	2
Weekly New Era, Norton..........................	1888–1891	3
The Norton Republican	1892–1894	2
The Liberator, Norton.............................	1893,1894	2
The Lenora Leader................................	1882–1888	6
The Kansas Northwest, Lenora....................	1884,1885	1
The Kansas Monitor, Lenora......................	1885,1886	1
The Common People, Lenora......................	1886,1887	1
The Lenora Record...............................	1887–1890	3
The Norton County Badger, and ⟩		
The Edmond Times, Edmond, ⟩	1886–1890	5
The Almena Star (May to November, 1887, lacking)...........	1885–1889	3
Almena Plaindealer..............................	1888–1894	7
The Almena Advance (Farmers' Advance, Norton, June 12 to August 28, 1890)....	1889,1890	1
Almena Enterprise...............................	1894	1
The Oronoque Magic..............................	1886	1
The Calvert Gazette..............................	1889,1890	1
Norton county, short-lived, vol. 1:		
Norton County Bee, Norton, May 7, 1877; Densmore News, June 21 to September 27, 1888; Normal Instituter, Norton, August 13, 1888, to August 30, 1889;		

BOUND NEWSPAPERS AND PERIODICALS — CONTINUED.

NEWSPAPERS.	Years.	No. vols
NORTON COUNTY — *Concluded.*		
Densmore Dispatch, May 16 to July 26, 1889; Norton County Educator, Norton (monthly), January and March, 1890; Norton District Advocate, Norton (semimonthly), May 21, 1889; Lenora Sun, March 6 to June 26, 1890; Lenora Times, February 1 to June 3, 1893...........	....	4
OSAGE COUNTY (163).		
Osage County Chronicle, Burlingame (January, 1872, to September, 1873, lacking),	1868–1894	25
Osage County Democrat, Burlingame and Osage City...........................	1881–1887	5
Burlingame Herald..	1881–1884	2
Burlingame Independent...	1886–1888	2
The Burlingame Democrat...	1888–1890	1
The Burlingame Echo, National Echo (monthly).......................	1888–1893	4
Burlingame Herald, and Blade.......................................	1892,1893	1
The Plebeian, and The Chronicle (monthly magazine), Burlingame.........	1894	2
Osage City Free Press..	1876–1894	19
The Osage City Republican..	1882,1883	1
The Kansas People, Osage City......................................	1887–1891	4
Kansas People (daily), Osage City..................................	1887–1890	7
Public Opinion, Osage City...	1892–1894	2
Lyndon Times and Kansas Times (Osage City, August to November, 1879; not published November, 1879, to March, 1880)...........................	1876–1881	5
The Lyndon Journal..	1882–1894	13
The Lyndon Leader...	1882,1883	2
Kansas Plebeian, Lyndon and Scranton..............................	1882	1
Osage County Graphic, Lyndon......................................	1888–1894	6
Kansas Workman, Scranton and Quenemo.............................	1883–1888	5
Osage County Times, Scranton, Burlington, and Osage City...........	1888–1891	4
The Scranton Gazette...	1890–1894	5
The Carbondale Journal..	1879	1
Carbondale Independent..	1882,1883	2
Astonisher and Paralyzer, Carbondale..............................	1885–1887	2
The Carbondalian, Carbondale......................................	1887–1894	8
The Carbondale Record...	1888	1
Osage County Republican, Quenemo.................................	1886–1892	6
Quenemo Republican...	1892–1894	3
The Quenemo Leader...	1889,1890	1
The People's Herald, Quenemo and Lyndon...........................	1890–1894	4
Melvern Record..	1884–1890	7
The Melvern Review..	1891–1894	4
Overbrook Herald..	1889–1894	6
Osage county, short-lived, vol. 1:		
Osage County Real Estate Journal, Burlingame, September, 1869; The Shaft, Osage City, March 23 to April 13, 1872, November 1, 1873, to April 18, 1874, scattering; Burlingame News, June, 1886, to August, 1889; Rosemont Reflector, October 23 to December 16, 1887; Beech Brook Breeze, Burlingame, September, 1888, to March, 1889; Weekly Offering, Quenemo, January 17 to March 14, 1893..	....	4
Osage county, short-lived, vol. 2:		
Carbondale Calender, January 28 to April 1, 1886; Carbondale Independent (second), April 8 to 29, 1886....................................	....	1
OSBORNE COUNTY (85).		
Osborne County Farmer, Osborne (October to December, 1876)..........	1876–1894	19
The Truth Teller, Osborne..	1879–1881	1
Daily News, Osborne...	1881	1
Osborne County News, Osborne.....................................	1883–1894	12
Western Odd Fellow (monthly), Osborne (see Saline and Shawnee counties).....	1886–1888	1
Osborne County Journal, Osborne...................................	1886–1889	3
Bull's City Post..	1880	1
Osborne County Key, Bull's City....................................	1881,1882	1
The Western Empire, Bull's City, Alton, Osborne....................	1883–1894	12
Downs Times..	1880–1894	15
Downs Chief..	1885–1891	6
Downs Globe..	1888–1890	2
Expositor, Downs (see Dickinson county).		
Downs World..	1893,1894	1
Portis Patriot (Whisperer, April to July, 1890)....................	1881–1890	9
Osborne county, short-lived, vol. 1:		
The Friend, Osborne (monthly), May, 1880, to February, 1889; Daily News, Osborne, June 10 to August 13, 1881; Hulaniski's Saturday Evening Lamp, Downs, October 20, 1883, to November 10, 1883; Downs Headlight, June 30 to August 11, 1887; Osborne Evening News, October 19 to 31, 1888; Rustler, Portis, June, 1889; Farmers' Aid, Covert, May 22 to October 2, 1890.............	....	1
OTTAWA COUNTY (97).		
The Solomon Valley Mirror (monthly), Minneapolis....................	1874–1886	5
The Sentinel, Minneapolis..	1876–1883	7
The Minneapolis Messenger (successor to Sentinel)..................	1883–1894	11

BOUND NEWSPAPERS AND PERIODICALS—Continued.

NEWSPAPERS.	Years.	No. vols
OTTAWA COUNTY—*Concluded.*		
The Daily Messenger, Minneapolis	1887	1
Minneapolis Independent (October 25, 1870, in Ottawa, short lived, vol. 1)	1876–1880	4
Ottawa County Index. Minneapolis	1880–1883	4
The Progressive Current, Minneapolis	1883,1884	1
Solomon Valley Democrat, Minneapolis	1884–1891	7
Kansas Workman (monthly), Minneapolis	1885–1894	9
The Sprig of Myrtle (monthly), Minneapolis (moved from Columbus, Cherokee county)	1886–1894	8
Ottawa County Commercial, Minneapolis, and Minneapolis Commercial	1886–1892	6
Kansas Union and Ottawa County Index, Minneapolis	1890–1894	4
The Review, Minneapolis	1891–1894	3
Ottawa County Democrat, Minneapolis and Bennington	1891–1894	1
The Delphos Herald	1879,1880	2
Delphos Carrier	1881–1888	7
The Delphos Republican	1888–1894	6
Bennington Star (lacking from February, 1884, to July, 1886)	1883–1889	3
The Bennington Journal	1885	1
Herald and Star, Bennington	1889–1891	2
The Tescott Herald	1887–1891	4
Ottawa county, short-lived, vol. 1: Normal Institute Record, Minneapolis, July 15 to August 9, 1878: Ottawa County Loan and Insurance Record, Minneapolis, February, 1884; Minneapolis Republican, February 20 to March 6, 1885; Daily Institute, Minneapolis, July 7 to August 1, 1885: Minneapolis School Journal, December, 1885, to May, 1886; Bennington Mercury, July 27 to August 17, 1888; Schoolroom Journal, Minneapolis (monthly), September, 1888, to May, 1889; Ye Pedagogue, Minneapolis (monthly). December, 1801, to April, 1893; The Souvenir, Minneapolis, June 30, 1892, to May 31, 1893		1
PAWNEE COUNTY (50).		
Larned Press	1876–1878	2
The Pawnee County Herald, Larned	1877,1878	2
The Larned Enterprise-Chronoscope *	1878–1888	2
Larned Chronoscope	1880–1894	15
Larned Daily Chronoscope	1887,1888	3
The Larned Optic	1878–1884	6
The Larned Weekly Eagle-Optic	1885–1894	10
Pawnee County Republican, Larned	1886,1887	1
The Labor News, Larned	1888,1889	1
Tiller and Toiler, Larned	1892–1894	3
Garfield Letter	1885,1886	1
The Garfield News	1887,1888	1
The Burdett Bugle	1886–1888	2
Pawnee county, short-lived, vol. 1: Larned Democrat, October 26, 1888, to January 5, 1889; Larned Morning Tiller and Toiler, April 26 to May 19, 1803		1
PHILLIPS COUNTY (104).		
The Kirwin Chief	1876–1891	15
Kirwin Progress and Kirwin Democrat	1877,1878	2
The Independent, Kirwin	1880–1888	8
Kirwin Republican	1883–1885	2
The Independent, Kirwin (second)	1889–1894	5
The Kirwin-Globe	1891–1804	3
Phillips County Herald, Phillipsburg	1878–1894	17
The Phillipsburg Times	1884,1885	1
The Phillipsburg Dispatch	1886–1894	8
Phillipsburg Democrat	1887–1891	4
Logan Enterprise	1879–1884	4
Phillips County Freeman, Logan	1884–1890	7
The Logan Republican	1886–1894	8
The Long Island Argus	1885	1
Long Island Leader	1886–1894	8
Phillips County Democrat, Long Island	1886	1
Phillips County Inter-Ocean. Long Island	1887–1891	4
Marvin Monitor	1886–1888	
Woodruff Gazette and Republican	1886,1887	1
Agra Graphic and Kirwin Graphic	1889	1
Agra Politician	1890	1
Agra News	1803,1894	1
Phillips county, short-lived, vol. 1: Lively Times, Phillipsburg, June 27, July 4, 1874; Solomon Valley Democrat, Kirwin, August 14 to December 26, 1878; Rag Baby, Kirwin, October 7 to November 6, 1879; Iconoclast, Kirwin. November 13 to December 4, 1879; The Daily Herald, Phillipsburg, September 28, 29, 1882; Kirwin Daily Chief,		

*Not found.

BOUND NEWSPAPERS AND PERIODICALS—Continued.

NEWSPAPERS.	Years.	No. vols
PHILLIPS COUNTY—Concluded.		
July 17 to 20, 1883 (M. E. conference), March 25 to 30, 1886; Daily Northwest, Kirwin, August 7 to 14, 1883: Kansas Northwest, Kirwin, August 31, September 7, 1883; Marvin Democrat, September 29, October 5, 1883: Daily Democrat, Phillipsburg, September 27, 1887; Phillips County School Journal (monthly), Phillipsburg, May, 1889, to January, 1890; Woodruff News, May 9 to June 6, 1890; Alliance Watchman, Phillipsburg, July 11 to August 15, 1890........	....	1
POTTAWATOMIE COUNTY (149).		
Pottawatomie Gazette, Louisville (vols. 1, 2, 3, 4)................	1867–1870	4
Kansas Reporter, Louisville........	1870–1881	11
Pottawatomie County Herald, Louisville........	1879	1
The Louisville Republican (and The Semi-Weekly Republican)........	1882–1886	5
The Louisville Indicator........	1887–1889	2
Pottawatomie County Times, Louisville and Wamego........	1889–1893	4
Weekly Kansas Valley, Wamego........	1869–1871	2
The Wamego Blade........	1876, 1877	1
The Wamego Tribune........	1877–1881	4
Kansas Agriculturist, Wamego........	1879–1894	16
Kansas Reporter, Wamego (suspended, July, 1887, to August, 1888)........	1881–1889	7
Wamego Democrat........	1885,1886	1
The Daily Wamegan, Wamego........	1887–1889	5
Weekly Wamegan, Wamego........	1891	1
The Kansas Teacher, Wamego........	1889,1890	1
The Wamego Times........	1893,1894	1
St. Mary's Times........	1876–1878	2
St. Mary's Democrat........	1878,1879	1
Pottawatomie Chief, St. Mary's........	1878,1879	2
St. Mary's Express........	1880–1888	8
St. Mary's Star........	1884–1894	11
St. Mary's Gazette........	1888–1891	3
The Dial (monthly), St. Mary's........	1890–1894	5
St. Mary's Democrat (second)........	1893,1894	1
The Onaga Journal........	1878–1885	7
The Onaga Democrat (lacking December, 1887, to October, 1888)........	1885–1890	4
The Onaga Herald........	1890–1894	4
The Weekly Period, Westmoreland........	1882–1885	3
The Westmoreland Recorder........	1885–1894	10
The Westmoreland Indicator........	1889–1891	2
The Alliance News, Westmoreland........	1890–1894	4
The Independent, Havensville........	1880,1881	1
The Havensville Register........	1889,1890	1
The Havensville Torchlight........	1891–1894	3
The Olsburg News-Letter........	1887–1894	8
The Belvue Dodger........	1889	1
Butler City News........	1889,1890	1
Pottawatomie county, short-lived, vol. 1:		
Ink Slinger's Advertiser, Westmoreland, January 1 to May 11, 1878; Garrison Times, July 27 to September 7, 1880: Pottawatomie County Democrat, Wamego, November 13 to 20, 1880: Daily Agriculturist, Wamego, September 28 to 30, 1881; Daily Kansas Reporter, Wamego, September 5 to 9, 1882; Westmoreland Signal, August 3 to October 12. 1888: Kansas Teacher, Wamego (monthly), October, 1889, to July, 1890: School Mirror, Olsburg, February to May, 1890; Wamego Daily Times, June 7 to July 2, 1892................	....	1
Pottawatomie county, short-lived, vol. 2:		
The Morning News, Havensville, February 18 to September 2, 1882........	....	1
PRATT COUNTY (56).		
The Stafford Citizen (see Stafford county)........	1877,1878	1
Pratt County Press, Iuka........	1878–1887	9
Pratt County Times, Iuka and Pratt (January to April, 1886, lacking)........	1881–1894	13
The Iuka Traveler........	1886–1888	1
The Saratoga Sun........	1885–1887	3
Pratt County Democrat, Saratoga........	1885,1886	1
The Cullison Banner........	1886–1888	2
Cullison Tomahawk........	1888–1890	1
Pratt County Register, Pratt........	1886–1890	4
The Pratt County Republican, Pratt........	1888–1894	7
Pratt County Union, Pratt........	1890–1894	5
The Preston Herald........	1887,1888	1
The Preston Plain Dealer........	1889–1894	6
Springvale Advocate........	1888	1
Pratt county, short-lived, vol. 1:		
Saratoga Plaindealer, January 25 and February 10, 1888; Plaindealer, Pratt, July 14 to November 9, 1888........	....	1

BOUND NEWSPAPERS AND PERIODICALS — CONTINUED.

NEWSPAPERS.	Years.	No. vols
RAWLINS COUNTY (52).		
Atwood Pioneer......	1879,1880	1
Republican Citizen, Atwood (1880 to 1882, scattering; January to April, 1883, December, 1883, to February, 1884, lacking)......	1880–1894	12
Rawlins County Democrat, Atwood and Blakeman......	1885–1894	9
The Atwood Journal......	1888,1889	2
The Times, Atwood......	1891–1894	2
The Ludell Settler......	1884–1887	3
Ludell Gazette	1887–1894	6
The Celia Enterprise......	1885–1888	3
The Blakeman Register......	1887–1894	6
The Herndon Courant......	1888–1890	3
McDonald Times......	1888–1891	3
Rawlins county, short-lived, vol. 1:		
Review, Atwood, March 11 to April 15, 1881; Review, Ludell, April 29 to May 19, 1881; Ludell Review, June 8 to July 6, 1881......	......	1
RENO COUNTY (163).		
The Examiner, Hutchinson......	1876	1
Hutchinson News......	1876–1894	19
Hutchinson Daily News......	1886–1894	17
Hutchinson Herald......	1877–1885	8
The Interior, Hutchinson......	1877–1885	8
The Interior-Herald, Hutchinson......	1885–1894	10
Hutchinson Daily Herald......	1887	1
The Sunday Democrat, The Dollar Democrat, The Democrat, and The Hutchinson Democrat......	1883–1890	8
The Hutchinson Call (daily)......	1888	1
Kansas Herold, Hutchinson (German)......	1888–1890	2
Hutchinson Republican......	1889,1890	1
The Hutchinson Times (July 4, 1890, to December 4, 1891, Times-Republican)....	1889–1894	5
The Clipper, Hutchinson......	1889–1894	6
Alliance Gazette, Hutchinson......	1890–1894	4
The School Visitor (monthly), Hutchinson......	1893,1894	2
Hutchinson Headlight......	1893,1894	1
Hutchinson Patriot (daily)......	1893	1
Our Union and The Salt Workers' Journal, Hutchinson......	1893,1894	1
The South Hutchinson Leader......	1886,1887	1
The Saturday Review, South Hutchinson......	1887–1890	3
The Journal, South Hutchinson......	1888,1889	1
The Argosy, Nickerson......	1878–1894	16
The Nickerson Register and The Nickerson Industry......	1884–1891	6
The Nickerson Daily Register......	1887	1
The Arlington Enterprise......	1886–1894	9
Sylvia Telephone......	1886–1889	3
The Sylvia Herald......	1889	1
The Sylvia Banner......	1889–1894	5
The Haven Independent (June, 1888, to January, 1889, March to December, 1889, lacking)......	1886–1893	6
Haven Dispatch......	1888,1889	1
The Haven Item......	1894	1
The Turon Rustler......	1886–1889	2
Turon Headlight......	1889–1893	4
Partridge Cricket, and Press......	1886,1887	1
Lerado Ledger......	1886–1888	1
Abbyville Tribune......	1886,1887	1
The Weekly Press, Olcott......	1889	1
The Torch Light, Plevna......	1888,1889	1
Pretty Prairie Press......	1894	1
Reno county, short-lived, vol. 1:		
Reno Independent, Hutchinson, February 23, 1876; New Rural, Hutchinson, July 1, October 1, 1885; Kansas Veteran, Hutchinson, November 4, 1885, to February 17, 1886; Law and Gospel (monthly), Hutchinson, October, November, 1886; New Times, South Hutchinson, February 10, April 28, 1887; Weekly World, Hutchinson, December 19, 1889, to March 20, 1890; Real Estate Reporter, Hutchinson, June, 1891......	......	1
REPUBLIC COUNTY (95).		
The Belleville Republic......	1876	1
The Belleville Telescope (*October 14, 1870), July, 1876, to April, 1877, lacking..	1876–1894	14
The Weekly Record, Belleville......	1883–1885	2
The Belleville Democrat (lacking, December 12, 1890, to October 2, 1891), Democrat-Press, November 7 to December 5, 1890......	1886–1894	8
Republic County Press, Belleville......	1889,1890	1
Republic County Freeman, Belleville......	1890–1894	4
Scandia Republic......	1876,1877	1
The Republic County Journal, Scandia......	1878–1881	2

*Portfolio.

BOUND NEWSPAPERS AND PERIODICALS—CONTINUED.

NEWSPAPERS.	Years.	No. vols
REPUBLIC COUNTY—Concluded.		
Scandia Journal	1882-1894	13
Republic County Chief, Scandia	1885,1886	1
The Scandia Independent	1886-1889	3
White Rock Independent	1879	1
Republic City News	1883-1894	11
Conservative Cuban, Cuba	1884-1886	1
Republic County Pilot, Cuba	1885-1888	4
The Cuba Union, and The Union Pilot, Cuba	1888-1890	2
The Cuba Daylight (not published from March, 1889, to May, 1890)	1888-1894	5
The Alliance Sun, Cuba	1891	1
Cesky Lev, Cuba (Bohemian)	1891,1892	1
The Wayne Register (January to June, 1887, lacking)	1885-1887	2
The Warwick Leader, and Advanced Leader, Warwick	1886,1887	1
Cortland Register	1889-1894	6
Evangelistic War Cry, Kackley (see Saline county).		
The Western Record, Kackley	1893	1
The Leader, Kackley	1893,1894	1
The Narka News	1893,1894	1
Republic county, short-lived, vol. 1:		
Kansas Enterprise, Belleville, October 20, 1882; Republic County Independent, Scandia, September 13 to December 13, 1883; Wayne Register, January 6 to June 23, 1887; Narka Bazoo, April 5 to June 15, 1888; Farmers' Alliance, Cuba, August 7 to October 3, 1890; Calcium Light, Belleville, December 20, 1890, to March 12, 1891; Kansaské Noviny, Belleville, February 1 to May 17, 1892		1
RICE COUNTY (134).		
Rice County Gazette, Sterling, and Sterling Gazette	1876-1891	16
Weekly Bulletin, and The Sterling Bulletin	1877-1891	14
The Bulletin and Gazette, Sterling	1891-1894	3
Sterling Weekly Champion	1888-1894	6
The Daily Bulletin, Sterling	1887,1888	2
Sterling Republican (weekly)	1886,1887	1
Sterling Republican (daily)	1887	1
The Arkansas Valley Times, Sterling	1888	1
The Saturday Republican, Sterling	1888	1
Cooper Courier (monthly), Sterling	1892-1894	3
The Lyons Republican	1879-1894	15
The Daily Republican, Lyons	1882	1
The Lyons Daily Republican	1887,1888	3
Central Kansas Democrat, Lyons (May 12, 1881, to February 21, 1884, lacking; suspended November, 1887, to March, 1890)	1879-1894	11
Central Kansas Democrat (daily), Lyons	1887	1
The Lyons Prohibitionist	1885-1890	5
The Soldiers' Tribune, Lyons, and Lyons Tribune	1887-1893	6
The Lyons Democrat	1889,1890	1
Rice County Eagle, Lyons	1890-1894	5
The Rural West, Little River	1881,1882	2
The Little River Monitor	1886-1894	8
The Comet, Little River	1891	1
The Chase Dispatch	1884,1885	1
The Weekly Record, Chase	1886-1894	6
Geneseo Herald	1887-1894	8
The Raymond Independent	1887,1888	1
The Cain City Razzooper	1887,1888	1
Independent, Frederick	1888,1889	1
Rice County News, Frederick	1890-1894	4
Frederick Republican	1892,1893	1
Rice county, short-lived, vol. 1:		
Little River News, November 3, 1880, to January 26, 1881; Recorder, Sterling, March, 1881, to February, 1882; New Home, Sterling, December, 1880, to September 13, 1882; Valley Echo, Sterling, November 1, 1884; Raymond Advance, November 20, 1885, to April 29, 1886; Alden Herald, May 19 to September 29, 1888; Sterling News, February 23 to June 29, 1889; Cain City News, August 1 to December 6, 1889; Sterling Weekly World, July 21 to September 8, 1892		1
Rice county, short-lived, vol. 2:		
Church Worker, Chase (monthly), August, 1893, to March, 1894; Frederick Bulletin, September 28, 1893, to February 3, 1894		1
RILEY COUNTY (161).		
Manhattan Express	1859-1862	3
The Manhattan Independent (February, 1865, to September, 1866, lacking)	1864-1868	3
The Kansas Radical, Manhattan	1866-1868	2
The Manhattan Standard	1868-1870	2
Manhattan Homestead (occasional)	1869-1894	10
The Nationalist, Manhattan	1870-1892	24
The Literary Review, Manhattan	1872	1

BOUND NEWSPAPERS AND PERIODICALS—Continued.

NEWSPAPERS.	Years.	No. vols
RILEY COUNTY — *Concluded.*		
Manhattan Beacon	1872–1875	3
The Industrialist, Manhattan (July to December, 1886, and January to December, 1888, lacking)	1875–1894	19
Manhattan Enterprise	1876–1882	6
The Kansas Telephone (monthly), Manhattan	1880–1894	14
The Independent, Manhattan	1881–1883	1
The Manhattan Republic	1882–1894	12
Manhattan Daily Republic	1887–1891	8
The Mercury, Manhattan	1884–1894	10
The Journal of Mycology (monthly), Manhattan (moved to Washington, D. C.)	1885–1888	4
The Saturday Signal. Manhattan	1888–1891	3
Manhattan District Methodist (monthly)	1890	1
Riley County Educator (monthly), Manhattan	1893,1894	2
The Independent, Riley Center	1879–1881	2
The Riley Times	1887–1889	2
The Riley Regent	1889–1894	5
Randolph Echo (April to December, 1885, at Leonardville)	1882–1885	4
The Randolph Enterprise	1888–1894	6
Leonardville Monitor	1884–1894	11
Leonardville Echo	1885	1
Bala City Advance	1890,1891	1
Riley county, short-lived, vol. 1: Land Register, Manhattan, January, 1870; News, Manhattan, January 15 to May 1, 1876: Manhattan Enterprise, May 24, 1876, to March, 1880, scattering; Hygiene Miscellany and Medical News, Manhattan, June, 1877, to January, 1878; News Gleaner, Mayday, December, 1879, to November 26, 1880; Daily Nationalist, Manhattan, September 29, 1880: Manhattan National News, February 16 to July 30, 1881; Independent, Manhattan, April 6, 13, 1882; Golden Cresset, Manhattan, February, 1882, to April, 1885; Manhattan Signal, April, 1886: Manhattan Methodist (monthly), October to December, 1886; Argus, Manhattan, October, 1887, to third quarter, 1888; Manhattan District News (monthly), August to October, 1889; Kansas Presbyter, Manhattan, September, 1889, to September, 1890; Randolph Leader, October 10, 1889, to January 2, 1890; Midget, Manhattan, June 28 to October 4, 1890; Kansas Real Estate Journal, Riley, January 15, 1892; Tri-Weekly Nationalist, Manhattan, November 2–7, 1893: Manhattan Courier, vol. 3, No. 3		1
ROOKS COUNTY (67).		
The Stockton News and The Western News (May, 1881, to April, 1882, Plainville News)	1876–1894	17
Rooks County Record, Stockton	1879–1894	15
Stockton Democrat	1885,1886	1
Rooks County Democrat, Stockton (1886 and 1887 scattering)	1886–1889	3
Stockton Academician (quarterly and monthly)	1888–1894	6
Alliance Signal, Stockton	1891–1894	4
The Plainville News, *see* Stockton News.		
Plainville Echo	1884–1886	2
The Plainville Press	1885	1
Plainville Times	1886–1894	9
Webster Eagle and Stockton Eagle	1885–1888	3
Webster Enterprise	1888	1
Woodston Saw and Register	1886–1889	3
Rooks county, short-lived, vol. 1: Cresson Dispatch, December 8, 1887, to March 1, 1888; Stockton Clipper, August 20 to December 17, 1890: The Observer, Stockton, September 2 to November 4, 1890; Christian Call, Stockton, May 1 to December, 1892; Rooks County Teacher, Stockton, October 15, 1892, to June, 1893		4
RUSH COUNTY (50).		
La Crosse Clarion	1889–1894	3
La Crosse Democrat	1887–1891	2
La Crosse Chieftain (January, 1891, to July, 1892, lacking)	1882–1894	1
The Western Economist. La Crosse	1891–1894	4
Pythian Sisters' News, La Crosse, *see* Barton county.		
The Blade, Walnut City	1878–1880	2
The Herald, Walnut City	1883–1886	3
Walnut City Gazette	1886,1887	1
The Democrat, Walnut City	1886–1888	2
Walnut City News (daily)	1887,1888	2
Walnut City Gazette, Rush Centre Gazette	1887–1890	3
Rush County News, Rush Centre	1888–1891	3
The Walnut Valley Standard, Rush Centre	1893,1894	2
The McCracken Enterprise	1887–1894	8
Rush county, short-lived, vol. 1: Walnut Valley Standard (first), Rush Centre, December 24, 1874; Walnut Valley Standard (second), Rush Centre, December 13, 1876; Rush County Progress, Rush Centre and La Crosse, June 22 to November 2, 1877; Progress, La Crosse, November 9, 1877, to March 23, 1878; La Crosse Eagle, May 13 to		1

BOUND NEWSPAPERS AND PERIODICALS—CONTINUED.

NEWSPAPERS.	Years.	No. vols
RUSH COUNTY—*Concluded.*		
December 26, 1878; La Crosse Chieftain, January 18 to March 22, 1881; Rush County Democrat, Walnut City, Rush Centre, August 20 to September 24, 1886		1
RUSSELL COUNTY (88).		
Russell County Record, Russell	1876–1894	18
Russell County Advance, Russell	1878	1
Russell Independent	1879–1881	3
The Russell Hawkeye	1882,1883	1
Russell Live-Stock Journal, and Russell Journal	1884–1894	10
Russell Review, and Democratic Review, Russell	1886–1888	2
Russell County School Signal (monthly), Russell	1889–1892	3
Bunker Hill Advertiser	1880,1881	2
Bunker Hill Banner	1882	1
Bunker Hill Banner (second)	1884,1885	1
The Bunker Hill News	1887,1888	1
Bunker Hill Gazette	1888,1889	1
The Dorrance Nugget	1886–1889	2
Luray Headlight	1887–1890	3
Luray Star	1893	1
The Lucas Advance	1888–1894	6
Waldo Enterprise (July, 1889, to April, 1890, suspended)	1888–1890	1
Russell county, short-lived, vol. 1:		
Weekly Gazette, Russell, March 14 to June 13, 1889		1
ST. JOHN COUNTY, *see* Logan (2).		
The Oakley Opinion	1885–1887	1
Ennis City Courier	1886,1887	1
St. John County Times, *see* Logan County Times.		
The Scout, Gopher and Winona, *see* Logan county.		
Western Kansas Advocate (monthly), Ennis City, *see* Logan county.		
SALINE COUNTY (126).		
The Salina Herald	1876–1894	19
Salina Daily Herald	1887,1888	3
Saline County Journal, Salina	1876–1893	17
Saline County Daily Journal, Salina	1887,1888	2
Farmers' Advocate, Salina (Salina News, December 19, 26, 1879)	1876–1879	4
The Weekly Democrat, Salina	1878,1879	1
Svenska Herolden, Salina	1878–1881	3
The Salina Independent	1882–1885	3
The Salina Republican, and Republican-Journal	1885–1894	9
Salina Daily Republican	1888–1894	12
The Rising Sun, Salina, and The Salina Sun	1885–1894	9
The Normal Register (quarterly and monthly), Salina	1885–1892	3
Vade Mecum (monthly), Salina	1887–1891	4
Western Odd Fellow (monthly), Salina	1888–1891	3
The Sentinel, and Kansas Churchman (monthly), Fort Leavenworth, Salina, *see* Lawrence.	1889–1891	2
Wesleyan Advocate, Salina	1888,1889	3
Kansas Wesleyan Lance, Salina		
Woman's Mission Star, Salina	1889,1890	1
The Evening News, Salina	1889–1891	5
Salina Gazette (daily)	1889	1
The Weekly Tidings, Salina	1890–1893	4
The Salina Union	1890–1894	4
The Salina Weekly News	1891	1
The Agora (quarterly), Salina (continued in Shawnee county)	1891,1892	1
The Open Church (monthly), Salina	1893,1894	1
The Irrigation Farmer (monthly), Salina	1894	1
Brookville Independent	1880	1
Brookville Transcript	1881–1890	9
Brookville Times	1887,1888	1
The Earth, Brookville	1890–1894	4
Chico Advertiser	1886,1887	1
The Gypsum Banner	1886,1887	1
Gypsum Valley Echo	1886–1890	4
Gypsum Advocate	1890–1894	4
Assaria Argus	1887–1890	3
Saline county, short-lived, vol. 1:		
Kansas Central Advocate, Salina, December, 1873, and February, 1874; Kansas Central Land Journal, Salina, April, 1874, March and August, 1877, and February, 1878; N. E. Conference Daily, Salina, March 12 to 18, 1878; Morning News, Salina, July 4 to 31, 1878; Salina News, December 19, 1879, to October 2, 1880; Western Reformer (monthly), Salina, March to December, 1880; Salina Record, August 11 to 25, 1888; Baptist Times, Salina, July 26, 1892, to March 24, 1893; Salina Daily Journal, September 13 to 18, 1892		4
Saline county, short-lived, vol. 2:		
Evangelistic War Cry, Kackley and Salina, October 3, 1893, to May 3, 1894		4

BOUND NEWSPAPERS AND PERIODICALS — CONTINUED.

NEWSPAPERS.	Years.	No. vols
SCOTT COUNTY (23).		
Western Times, Scott City (see Finney and Wallace counties).		
Scott County News, Scott City	1886–1892	7
Scott County Herald, Scott City	1886–1888	3
The Scott Sentinel, Scott City	1886–1888	2
The Sentinel-Herald, Scott City	1889–1891	2
Scott County Lever, Scott City	1891,1892	2
Scott City Republican	1893,1894	2
Scott County News-Lever, Scott City	1893,1894	2
The Pence Phonograph..	1887–1889	2
Scott county, short-lived, vol. 1:		
Grigsby City Scorcher, November 26, 1886, to April 29, 1887.................	....	1
SEDGWICK COUNTY (234).		
Wichita Vidette (August 25, 1870, to March 11, 1871)	1870,1871	1
Wichita City Eagle (April, 1873, to April, 1874, lacking).................	1872–1894	22
Wichita Daily Eagle	1884–1894	21
Wichita Weekly Beacon...	1874–1894	20
The Wichita Daily Beacon (The Evening News-Beacon, 1889 and 1890, 3 vols.)..	1884–1894	20
Wichita Herald	1877–1879	2
Stern des Westens, Wichita..	1879	1
National Monitor, Wichita..	1879,1880	1
Daily Republican, Wichita...	1880,1881	2
Wichita Republican..	1880,1881	1
Wichita Daily Times...	1881–1884	6
The Wichita Daily Leader	1881,1882	1
The Leader (weekly), Wichita (see Topeka).		
Weekly Leader, Wichita	1882,1883	1
The New Republic, Wichita...	1883–1890	8
Wichita Times (lacking, October, 1883, to September, 1884)................	1883,1884	1
Oklahoma War Chief, Wichita (see Sumner county).		
Kansas Staats-Anzeiger, Wichita...	1886–1894	9
Wichita Herold..	1885–1894	10
Wichita Daily Evening Resident	1886	1
The Arrow, Wichita..	1885–1893	8
The Wichita Citizen, Labor-Union, Union Labor Press, and Independent.......	1886–1888	2
Sunday Growler, Wichita...	1886–1888	2
Weekly Nation, Wichita..	1886,1887	1
Wichita Daily Journal...	1887–1890	8
Wichita Daily Call..	1887	1
Wichita Daily Globe	1887	1
Wichita Globe	1887	1
The Kansas Globe, Wichita...	1887,1888	1
Western Evangelist, Wichita...	1887,1888	1
The Wichita Commercial	1887–1889	1
The Leader (prohibition), Wichita (see Topeka)	1888	1
The Wichita Independent...	1888,1889	1
The Mirror, Wichita...	1888–1894	6
The Journal, Wichita..	1888–1890	3
Wichita Opinion (September, 1890 to December, 1891, lacking)..............	1889–1893	3
Western Methodist, Wichita..	1889–1894	5
The Democrat, Wichita...	1890	1
The Leader (monthly), Wichita...	1890–1894	4
Wichita Newspaper Union and Record..	1890–1894	4
The Kansas Star, Wichita..	1890–1894	4
Kansas Commoner, Wichita..	1891–1894	4
The Wichita Price Current...	1891–1894	4
Jiber Jab (monthly), Wichita..	1894	1
Cheney Journal	1884–1886	3
The Cheney Weekly Blade...	1888–1890	3
The Cheney Herald (Wichita, March 3 to April 7, 1894).....................	1891–1894	3
The Cheney Sentinel...	1894	1
Valley Center News	1885–1890	5
The Mount Hope Mentor (suspended, July to December, 1892).................	1885–1894	8
Clear Water Leader..	1886,1887	1
The Clear Water Sun	1888–1890	2
Clear Water Echo..	1892,1893	1
The Colwich Courier	1887–1892	6
Sedgwick County Reporter, Colwich...	1893	1
Garden Plain Herald	1887,1888	1
Derby Dispatch..	1889,1890	1
The Weekly Report, Goddard..	1889,1890	1
Sedgwick county dailies, short-lived, vol. 1:		
Wichita Evening News, November 26, 1885, to February 24, 1886; Wichita Daily Democrat, September 21 to October 3, 1887; Daily Commoner, Wichita, July 23 to 30, 1892...	....	1
Sedgwick county weeklies and monthlies, short-lived, vol. 1:		
Wichita Tribune, April 22 to July 15, 1881; Arkansas Valley Sunshine, Wichita,		

BOUND NEWSPAPERS AND PERIODICALS—CONTINUED.

NEWSPAPERS.	Years.	No. vols
SEDGWICK COUNTY— *Concluded.* September 17 to November 5, 1881: Sunday Morning Enquirer, Wichita, January 4 to March 15, 1885; Saturday Evening Call, Wichita, December 19, 1885, to April 24, 1886; Wichita District Advocate (monthly), July, 1886, to June, 1887; Y. M. C. A. Echoes (monthly), Wichita, July 15, 1886, to February 15, 1887; Colwich Rambler, February 10 to March 10, 1887; University Review (monthly), Wichita, March, 1887, to March, 1888; Wichita Globe, April 8, 1887; Wichita Breeze, November 5, 1887, to January 21, 1888; Wichita Diocesan News (monthly), January 20 to November, 1888; Wichita Weekly Express, October 13 to December 8, 1888		1
Sedgwick county weeklies and monthlies, short-lived, vol. 2: Clear Water Times, November 26, 1886, to January 21, 1887; Clear Water Independent, October 1 to December 31, 1887; Wichita Commercial Bulletin, September 29, 1888, to March 2, 1889; National Detective Review, Wichita, April to October, 1889; Burton Baptist (monthly), North Wichita, May, 1889, to January, 1890; Southwestern Business Journal (monthly), Wichita, March to August, 1889; Business Informer, Wichita, November 1, 1889; Wichita World, February 16 to March 30, 1889; Wichita Price Current, August 10, 1889, to January 11, 1890; Southwestern Specimen, Wichita, February 8 to April 19, 1890; Wichita Poultry Home (monthly), November, 1890, to May 15, 1891; Kansas Sunflower, Wichita, September 26 to November 7, 1890; Kansas Cultivator and Stockman, Wichita, December 10 to 24, 1890; Derby Mimeogram, October 1, 1891, to May 5, 1892; Grand Army Forum, Wichita, October 1, 1891, to February 25, 1892; Valley Center Journal, February 26 to May 27, 1892; Wichita Key (monthly), April, 1892; Telegrapher (monthly), Wichita, May to September, 1892; Christian Helper, Wichita, August 1, 1892, to July 1, 1893		1
SEQUOYAH COUNTY. (See Finney county.)		
The Garden City Paper	1879	
The Irrigator, Garden City	1892	
The Optic, Garden City, November 13, 1880, *see* Finney county, short-lived, vol. 1.		
SEWARD COUNTY (34).		
The Prairie Owl, Fargo Springs	1885–1888	2
Seward County Democrat, Fargo Springs	1886–1888	3
The Fargo Springs News	1886–1888	2
Springfield Transcript	1886–1889	3
Springfield Soap-Box	1887,1888	1
Seward County Courant, Springfield	1887,1888	1
Springfield Republican	1889–1893	5
Western Vidette, Springfield	1890	1
The Arkalon News	1888–1892	5
The Liberal Leader	1888–1890	2
Southwest Chronicle, Liberal	1888–1890	2
The Liberal Lyre	1890–1893	3
Liberal News	1892–1894	2
Seward county, short-lived, vol. 1: Chronicle, Jr., Liberal (Christmas)	1888	1
SHAWNEE COUNTY (586).		
Daily Kansas Freeman, Topeka (October 24 to November 7)	1855	1
The Kansas Tribune, Lawrence and Topeka (incomplete)	1855–1858	3
Topeka Tribune	1858–1861	3
The Topeka Tribune (second)	1866,1867	1
Topeka Daily Tribune (January 12 to March 1)	1864	1
The Congregational Record, Topeka, *see* Douglas county.		
Weekly Kansas State Record, Topeka (1863 to 1867 lacking)	1859–1875	9
Daily Kansas State Record, Topeka	1868–1871	7
The Kansas Farmer (monthly, Topeka, vol. 1, 1863 and 1864, 3 numbers lacking; Lawrence, January, 1865, to July, 1867; Leavenworth, September, 1867, to December, 1873; Topeka, weekly, since 1873; January to June, 1875, and August, 1875, to April, 1876, lacking)	1863–1894	30
Kansas Educational Journal, Topeka, *see* Leavenworth county.		
Topeka Leader (suspended from April, 1869, to September, 1876)	1865–1876	4
Mills & Smith's Real Estate Advertiser (monthly), Topeka	1867–1871	4
Commonwealth (daily), Topeka (January 1, 1870, to February 14, 1871, lacking)	1869–1888	37
The Weekly Commonwealth, Topeka (1869, 1870, and 1872, scattering numbers)	1874–1888	13
Kansas Magazine (monthly), Topeka	1872,1873	4
Topeka Daily Blade (1874 not published)	1873–1879	10
Topeka Weekly Blade	1876–1879	4
Kansas State Journal (daily), Topeka	1879–1894	30
Kansas Weekly State Journal, Topeka (lacking October, 1885, to November, 1891)	1879–1894	9
Kansas Democrat, Topeka	1874–1882	8
American Young Folks (monthly), Topeka	1875–1882	7
The Kansas Churchman (monthly), Topeka (June, 1883, to March, 1885, Lawrence; not published from March to November, 1885)	1876–1887	10
Commercial Advertiser, Topeka	1877	1
Educational Calendar (monthly), Topeka	1877,1878	1

BOUND NEWSPAPERS AND PERIODICALS—Continued.

NEWSPAPERS.	Years.	No. vols
SHAWNEE COUNTY—*Continued.*		
Colored Citizen, Topeka......	1878–1880	2
Der Courier, Topeka, *see* Atchison.		
The Daily Capital, Topeka (Capital-Commonwealth, November, 1888, to April, 1889)	1879–1894	31
Weekly Capital and Farmers' Journal, Topeka ,semiweekly, 1894; 1883 to 1885, incomplete)	1883–1894	11
Kansas Staats-Anzeiger, Topeka....	1879–1881	2
The Kansas Methodist and Kansas ~~eth dist~~-Chautauqua, Topeka (monthly, 1879, 1880, and weekly, 1881-1888).......	1879–1888	10
The Santa Fé Trail (occasional), Topeka,........	{ 1880–1883 1892	} 2
The Topeka Tribune (colored).............	1880, 1881	1
The Topeka Post (daily)...........	1880	1
The Whim-Wham, Topeka............	1880, 1881	1
The Educationist, Topeka...........	1880–1884	4
Western School Journal (monthly), Topeka....	1885–1894	10
The Kansas Telegraph, Topeka....	1881–1894	14
Good Tidings, Topeka and North Topeka....	1881–1886	4
Daily Democrat and Daily State Press, Topeka....	1881, 1882	1
The Faithful Witness (monthly and semimonthly), Topeka (December, 1885, to July, 1886, lacking).....	1882–1887	4
The National Workman, Topeka....	1882	1
Saturday Evening Lance, Topeka....	1883–1894	11
The Kansas Newspaper Union, Topeka....	1883–1894	11
The Topeka Tribune, Western Recorder, and Tribune-Recorder (colored)........	1883–1885	2
Anti-Monopolist, Topeka....	1883, 1884	1
The Daily Critic, Topeka....	1884	1
Bulletin Washburn Laboratory of Natural History (occasional), Topeka....	1884–1890	2
New Paths in the Far West (German monthly), Topeka....	1884, 1885	1
Light (Masonic monthly), Topeka....	1884–1889	5
The Kansas Knight and Soldier (semimonthly), Topeka....	1884–1889	4
The Spirit of Kansas (incomplete), Topeka....	1884–1892	5
Western Baptist (suspended July, 1889, to January, 1890), Topeka....	1884–1890	5
Western Real Estate Journal and City and Farm Record (monthly and weekly), Topeka (September, 1888, to January, 1889, and August, 1889, to December, 1890, lacking)....	1884–1891	6
Topeka Volks Freund (daily)....	1885, 1886	1
The Kansas Law Journal, Topeka....	1885–1887	2
The Citizen (daily), Topeka....	1885, 1886	2
The Washburn Argo (monthly). Topeka....	1885–1891	6
The Washburn Reporter, Topeka....	1887–1892	4
The Argo-Reporter (biweekly, weekly), Topeka....	1892, 1893	2
The Kansas Democrat (daily), Topeka....	1886–1894	17
The Weekly Kansas Democrat. Topeka....	1892, 1893	1
Welcome, Music and Home Journal (monthly), Topeka........	1885–1889	4
Our Messenger (monthly), Topeka....	1886–1894	9
The Labor Chieftain, Topeka....	1886, 1887	1
The Lantern, Topeka....	1887	1
American Citizen, Topeka....	1888	1
Topeka Post....	1888	1
Railroad Employés Companion, Topeka, *see* Franklin county.		
The Leader, Wichita, Topeka, and Neosho Rapids....	1888, 1889	2
The Printer Girl, Topeka....	1888, 1889	1
The Christian Citizen, and Midland Christian Advocate, Topeka....	1888–1890	1
The Association Reflector, Topeka....	1888–1890	2
The Kansas Financier (monthly), Topeka....	1888–1891	4
Sunday Ledger, Topeka (September to November, 1890; January, February, September, 1891, to October, 1892, lacking)....	1888–1894	6
The United Presbyterian (monthly), Topeka....	1888–1891	3
The Topeka News (daily)....	1888	1
The Jeffersonian, Topeka	1889, 1890	2
Villa Range, and Ladies' Home Journal (monthly), Topeka....	1889, 1890	1
The Topeka Republican....	1889–1894	5
The Western Veteran, Topeka....	1889–1893	5
The Advocate. Meriden, Topeka....	1889–1894	4
The Alliance Tribune, Topeka......	1889–1892	3
Kansas Medical Journal (monthly and weekly), Topeka........	1889–1894	6
The Western Poultry Breeder (monthly), Topeka....	1889–1894	6
Kansas Trade Journal (monthly and bimonthly), Topeka....	1889–1892	3
The Grand Army Journal, Topeka....	1890–1892	2
Lucifer, the Light-Bearer, Topeka, *see* Valley Falls....	1890–1894	4
The Budget, and Budget and News, Topeka (incomplete)....	1890–1894	3
Baptist Visitor (monthly), Topeka....	1891–1894	4
Kansas Methodist Times, and Kansas Methodist (biweekly), Topeka and Manhattan....	1891, 1892	2
The Farmer's Wife (monthly), Topeka....	1891–1894	3
The Times-Observer (colored). Topeka....	1891, 1892	1
Daily Topics, Topeka....	1891, 1892	2

BOUND NEWSPAPERS AND PERIODICALS—CONTINUED.

NEWSPAPERS.	Years.	No. vols.
SHAWNEE COUNTY—*Continued.*		
The Western Odd Fellow (monthly), Topeka...............................	1891–1894	4
Merchants' Weekly Journal, Topeka......................................	1891–1894	4
The Topeka Call (colored), incomplete...................................	1891–1894	2
The Daily Sentinel, Topeka...	1892,1893	1
Topeka Populist...	1892,1893	2
The Agora (quarterly), Salina and Topeka...............................	1892–1894	2
The Waif, and The Western Youth (monthly), Topeka.....................	1892,1893	2
The Epworthian, and The Kansas Christian Advocate, Topeka.............	1892–1894	3
Kansas State Ledger (colored), Topeka.................................	1892–1894	2
Kansas State Sunday School Journal (quarterly and monthly), Topeka.....	1892–1894	2
The Congregationalist, and The Pilgrim (monthly), Topeka..............	1892–1894	2
The Western Jewel and Home Journal (monthly), Topeka.................	1893,1894	1
The Washburn Mid-Continent (weekly and monthly), Topeka..............	1893,1894	1
Foundation Principles (semimonthly), Topeka	1893,1894	1
Railroad Register, Topeka...	1893–1895	2
The Topeka Daily Press..	1893,1894	4
The Topeka State Press..	1893,1894	2
The Kansas Worker (semimonthly), Topeka..............................	1893,1894	1
The People, and The New Era, Topeka..................................	1893–1895	2
Ottawa Journal (Topeka edition).......................................	1894	1
The Kansas Breeze, Topeka..	1894	1
Smith's Fruit Farmer (monthly), Topeka...............................	1894	1
The Christian Endeavorer (monthly , Topeka...........................	1894	1
Topeka Times, North Topeka (March, 1873, to February, 1874, lacking)..	1871–1876	4
North Topeka Times...	1876–1883	9
North Topeka Daily Argus, and Times..................................	1880,1881	3
North Topeka Mail..	1882–1894	12
The North Topeka News...	1888–1892	3
The North Topeka Evening News.......................................	1888	1
Kansas Valley Times, Rossville..	1879–1882	4
The Rossville News..	1883,1884	1
Carpenter's Kansas Lyre, Rossville.....................................	1884–1885	3
The Rossville Times...	1888–1894	6
The Weekly Critic, Rossville...	1892,1893	1
Silver Lake News and Topeka Sentinel.................................	1882	1
The Future (monthly), Richland.......................................	1885–1887	2
Richland Argosy..	1893–1894	2
Oakland News..	1890–1892	2
Shawnee county dailies, short-lived, vol. 1:		
Topeka Daily Times, North Topeka, November 6, 1878; The Tattler, Topeka, February 13 to 22, 1879; The Daily Pantagraph, Topeka, January 5 to 21, 1881; The North Topeka Daily Courier, July 1 to October 17, 1888; The Topeka Daily Mail, North Topeka, March 1 and 2, 1888; The Daily Leader, Topeka, October 6 to November 3, 1888; The Daily Sunflower, North Topeka, October 19 to November 5, 1888; Topeka Daily Globe, July 15 to August 2, 1889; The Daily Epworthian, Topeka, June 21 to 30, 1892; Daily Truth, Topeka, October 28 to November 7, 1892......................		1
Shawnee county dailies, short-lived, vol. 2:		
Kansas Daily Tribune, Topeka, March 7, 8, 11, 15, 1856; Kansas State Fair Advance, Topeka, September, 1873; Topeka Daily Bulletin, February 2 to 7, 1874; Topeka Daily Times, May 4, 1875, to January 27, 1876, scattering; Topeka Daily Argus, May 8 to 10, 1876; Daily Programme of the Shawnee County Fair, Topeka, September 28 and 29, 1876; Daily Whim-Wham, Topeka, September 17 to October 27, 1881; Conference Daily (M. E. Church), Topeka, March 14 to 21, 1888; Daily Populist, Topeka, January 10 to 31, 1893; Evening Call, Topeka, May 17 to July 8, 1893; Daily Ledger, Topeka, June 13 to 20, 1893..		1
Shawnee county dailies, short-lived, vol. 3:		
Daily Fair Record, Topeka, September 11–15, 1871; Evening Herald, Topeka, July 10 to December 5, 1882; Evening Republic, North Topeka, August 7 to September 20, 1882; North Topeka Daily Courier, scattering issues from December 16, 1887, to April 18, 1888..		1
Shawnee county weeklies and monthlies, short-lived, vol. 1:		
Kansas Advertiser and Agriculturist (monthly), Topeka, May to June, 1876; Bazaar News (monthly , Topeka, April, 1877; The Free Discussion (monthly), Topeka and Eskridge, August 20, 1878, September, 1879, January, 1880, to August, 1881, January, 1886, to February, 1887; The Liberal Advocate, Topeka, October 14–28, 1879; The Living Age, Topeka, October 8 to November 5, 1880; Religious Evolutionist (monthly), Topeka, March, 1881; The Western Reform Advocate, Topeka, August 28, 1882; Railway Telegraph College, Topeka, October 15, 1882; Saturday Night, Topeka, November 11 to December 2, 1882; Chips, Topeka, April 28, 1883; The Mayflower, Topeka, March 16, 1883; Fire and Hammer (monthly), North Topeka, November, 1883, to August, 1885; Church & Co.'s Monthly, Topeka, April and May, 1884; The Watchword (monthly), Topeka, July, 1885; The Budget, Topeka, November 15, 1884, to January 5, 1888; The Boycotter, Topeka, December 25, 1885, to February 19, 1886; Our Herald, North Topeka, January 9, 1885; Topeka Business College Journal (bimonthly), September, 1885,		

NEWSPAPERS.	Years.	No. vols
SHAWNEE COUNTY — *Concluded.*		
to November 15, 1889; The Kansas Democrat, Topeka, February 4-13, 1886; The Kansas Home (monthly), Topeka, February 15, 1886, to December 13, 1890; The Topeka Trade Gazette (monthly), August and September, 1886, and The Kansas Journal of Commerce (monthly), Topeka, October, 1887, to November, 1892; The Little Messenger, Topeka, November 2, 1886; The Season Signal (monthly), Topeka, December 20, 1886, April 15, 1967, September, 1888, September, 1889; The Bee (monthly), Topeka, August, 1887, to April, 1888; Topeka Argus (weekly and monthly), May 18, 1888, and May and June, 1889; Topeka Bulletin. North Topeka. November 29 to December 27, 1888; H. J. Washburn's Christmas Courier, Topeka, 1888	....	1
Shawnee county, weeklies and monthlies, short-lived, vol. 2:		
The Silver Lake Echo. January 26 and February 9, 1889; The Topeka Commercial Bulletin (monthly), May, 1889; The Monthly Messenger, Topeka, December, 1889; Kansas Siftings (monthly), Topeka, June, 1889, to April 22, 1890; The Potwin Tribune, Potwin Place, September 28, 1889, to September 26, 1890; Our State, Topeka, October 12, 1889, to February 15, 1890; Monday Morning Herald, Topeka, October 28, to December 23, 1889; Topeka Signal (monthly), November and December, 1889; Ham and Eggs, or the Hog and the Hen (monthly), Topeka, July, 1890, to February, 1891; The Detective World (monthly), Topeka, August, 1890, to June, 1891; The Oakland Item, December 21, 1889, to March 29, 1890; Kansas Church Tidings (monthly), Topeka, February 21, 1890, to July 18, 1891; The Bee, Topeka, March 30 to August 31, 1890; The Illustrated Companion, Topeka, August 21, 1890; The Oratorius (occasional), Topeka, January to September, 1891; The Independent, Topeka, February 27 and March 13, 1891; The Boanerges Reporter, Topeka, March 21 to May 2, 1891; American Buyer and Seller, (monthly), Topeka, November and December, 1891; The Sumner Times (bimonthly), Topeka, November 24 to December 22, 1891; New Age, Topeka (first), vol. 1, No. 1, February 13, 1892; (second), vol. 1, No. 1, February 27, 1892	....	1
Shawnee county weeklies and monthlies, short-lived, vol. 3:		
Kansas Freeman, Topeka, November 14, 1855, January 9, 1856; Truth Teller, Topeka, February 17 to March 4, 1862; Topeka Real Estate Bulletin, February 15, 1866, March 1, 1867; Star of Empire. Topeka, January, 1869, to December, 1870; Kansas Monthly Souvenir, Topeka, September, November, 1872; Kansas Quarterly Review of Real Estate, Topeka, January, 1873; Kansas Evangel (monthly), Topeka. October, December. 1873, February, March, 1874; Kansas School Journal, Topeka, August 15, September 15, 1874; Kansas State Grange Bulletin (quarterly), Topeka, May 10, 1875; New Era, Topeka, 1876 (?); Bazaar News, Topeka, May, 1876; American Journal of Education, Topeka, May to October, 1876; Kansas Agriculturist, July, August, 1876; Kansas Capital, Topeka, December 24, 31. 1876; Holiday Visitor, Topeka, December 25, 1876: San Juan Guide, Topeka, 1877; The Tramp, Topeka, July 28, 1878; Sunday Morning Salute, Topeka, July 28, 1878: Tri-Weekly Topeka Tribune, October 26, 1878; Topeka Sun, March 3, 1879; Topeka Commercial, March 5, 1879; Liberal Advocate, Topeka, November 4, 1879, to February 17, 1880; Town and Country, Topeka, 1879; Kansas Temperance Palladium, January 22, 1880; Reunion Banner, Topeka, October 30, 1881, September 16, 1882; Western Reform Advocate, Topeka, August 28, 1882; Real Estate News, September 18, 1882; Weekly Topeka Purchasers' Guide, November 14, 1885; Topeka Trade Gazette, July, 1887; Kansas Chautauqua Assembly, July 19, 1887; Health Messenger, Topeka, 1888; Kansas News (monthly), Topeka, September 15, October 25, 1888; Topeka Commercial Bulletin, Topeka, May, 1889; Topeka Wasp, June, 1889; Monthly Balance, Topeka, August to October, 1891; Kansas Arts and Industries, Topeka, October, 1891, to March, 1892; Western Cumberland Presbyterian (monthly), Topeka, June to September, 1892; Santu Fé Reporter, September 24, 1892, to February 25, 1893; Christian Church Helper (monthly), Topeka, April, June, 1893; Topeka Signal (monthly), June, September, 1893; Busy Bee Magazine, Topeka, February, March, 1893; Topeka Sensation, 1893; High School Budget (monthly), Topeka, October 27, 1893, to March, 1894..	....	
Shawnee county weeklies and monthlies, short-lived, vol. 4:		
Tanner and Cobbler, Topeka, August 13, to November 2, 1872; Weekly Kansas Herald, Topeka, January 30, February 6, 1880; Herald of Kansas, Topeka, February 13 to June 11. 1880; Colored Patriot, Topeka, April 20 to June 22, 1882; Benevolent Banner. North Topeka, May 21 to October 22, 1887; American Citizen, Topeka, January 11 to July 11, 1889; First Methodist, Topeka, September to November, 1893; Shawnee County District School (monthly), Topeka, September, 1893. to April, 1894; Baptist Headlight (semimonthly), Topeka, September 15, 1893, to August 8, 1894; Topeka Hurykain, December 23, 1893, to March 10, 1894; Topeka Signal (monthly), March, 1894; Kansas Blackman, Topeka, April 20 to June 29, 1894.....................	....	1
SHERIDAN COUNTY (27).		
Sheridan County Tribune, Kenneth.....................	1881,1882	1
Weekly Sentinel, Kenneth and Hoxie......	1884–1894	10
Democrat, Kenneth and Hoxie.....................	1885–1891	6
The Hoxie Palladium.....................	1891–1894	3

BOUND NEWSPAPERS AND PERIODICALS — CONTINUED.

NEWSPAPERS.	Years.	No. vols
SHERIDAN COUNTY — *Concluded.*		
The Sheridan County Democrat, Hoxie...	1892–1894	3
Sheridan Times..	1887,1888	1
Selden Times..	1888–1890	2
Sheridan county, short-lived, vol. 1:		
Sheridan County Times, Kenneth, June 25 to July 2, 1885; Sheridan Times, May 12 to June 23, 1887; Times. Hoxie, June 22, 1892; Selden Courant, March 11, 18, May 13, June 10, 1893	....	1
SHERMAN COUNTY (35).		
The New Tecumseh. Gandy, Leonard, and Itasca.................................	1885–1887	1
Sherman County Republican and Republic, Itasca, Sherman Center, and Goodland,	1886–1894	8
Sherman Center News..	1886,1887	1
Voltaire Adviser..	1885,1886	1
Sherman County News, Voltaire..	1886–1888	2
Sherman County Dark Horse, Eustis and Goodland..............................	1886–1894	8
Sherman County Democrat, Eustis and Goodland.................................	1887–1889	3
The Goodland News	1887–1894	7
Sherman County Farmer, Goodland..	1891,1892	1
State Line Register, Lamborn..	1888–1891	2
Sherman county, short-lived, vol. 1:		
Goodland Daily Republican, September 24 to October 24, 1889	....	1
SMITH COUNTY (101).		
Smith County Pioneer, Smith Centre (Pioneer-Bulletin from July 24, 1890, to March 2, 1892; 1876, 1877, incomplete)	1876–1894	19
The Daily Pioneer, Smith Centre...	1887,1888	2
The Independent, Smith Centre and Harlan..	1879,1880	1
The Kansas Free Press, Smith Centre..	1879–1881	2
Smith County Record, Smith Centre..	1892–1884	3
Smith County Weekly Bulletin, Smith Centre......................................	1884–1890	6
The Bazoo, and Stewart's Bazoo, Smith Centre...................................	1885–1894	9
Northwest Expositor (monthly), Smith Centre, *see* Dickinson county.		
Smith County Journal, Smith Centre..	1890–1894	4
Light of Liberty (monthly and weekly), Smith Centre, Lebanon..............	1891–1894	3
Gaylord Herald..	1879–1894	15
The Harlan Weekly Chief..	1883–1885	2
The Harlan Advocate..	1885–1887	2
The Harlan Enterprise..	1887,1888	1
The Cedarville Telephone	1883	1
The Cedarville Review	1884,1885	1
Cedarville Globe	1886–1890	4
The Dispatch, Reamsville..	1884,1885	1
The People's Friend, Reamsville and Athol...	1887,1888	1
The Cora Union	1886,1887	1
The Lebanon Criterion..	1887–1894	7
Lebanon Journal..	1889–1894	5
The Union Labor Trumpet, Kensington...	1888–1890	2
The Kensington Mirror..	1888–1894	7
The Athol News (Union Labor Trumpet, November 17, 1888)	1888,1889	1
Smith county, short-lived, vol. 1:		
The Toiler, Smith Centre, October 11 to November 7, 1879; True Voter, Smith Centre, October 6 to 27, 1880; Smith County Daily Bulletin, Smith Centre, September 13 to 18, 1887...	....	1
STAFFORD COUNTY, *see* Pratt county (68).		
Stafford County Herald, Stafford (first)..	1879–1885	6
Stafford County Democrat, Stafford..	1885–1888	3
Stafford County Republican, Stafford..	1886–1894	9
The Weekly Telegram, Stafford..	1887,1888	2
Stafford County Herald, Stafford (second)...	1889,1890	1
The Alliance Herald, Stafford	1890–1892	2
Plain Truth, Stafford	1889	1
People's Paper, Stafford..	1892–1894	2
The St. John Advance (August, 1884, to April, 1885, July, 1888, to May, 1889, missing)...	1880–1893	12
The Sun, St. John...	1885–1888	3
County Capital, St. John..	1887–1894	8
St. John Weekly News..	1888–1894	6
Stafford County Rustler, St. John...	1889,1890	1
The Stafford County Bee, Milwaukee...	1882,1883	1
The Macksville Times...	1886–1888	3
Macksville Telephone..	1889,1890	1
The Macksville Independent..	1891,1892	1
Macksville Sun...	1893	1
The Cassoday Herald...	1886,1887	1
The Cassoday Mirage..	1887–1889	1
Seward Independent..	1887–1890	2

BOUND NEWSPAPERS AND PERIODICALS—Continued.

NEWSPAPERS.	Years.	No. vols
STAFFORD COUNTY — *Concluded.*		
Stafford county, short-lived, vol. 1.		
Bedford Pilot, October 20 to November 3, 1881; School Journal, Stafford, December 24, 1888, to March 9, 1889; Musical Mishap, St. John, April, 1892....	....	1
STANTON COUNTY, *see* Hamilton county (18).		
The Johnson City World........................	1887,1888	1
Stanton County Eclipse, Johnson City..................................	1887,1888	1
Johnson City Journal........................	1888-1894	7
Stanton Telegram, Goguac and Johnson City.........	1888,1889	2
Stanton County Republican, Johnson City............	1889-1891	1
Stanton County Sun, Johnson City..................	1891-1894	2
The Mitchellville Courier..........................	1887,1888	1
The Border Rover, Borders..........................	1887-1889	1
Stanton county, short-lived, vol. 1:		
Stanton County Herald, West Haven, May 13 to June 3, 1887; Gazette, Eli, August 18 to October 7, 1887..........................	....	1
STEVENS COUNTY (22).		
Hugo Herald, Hugoton...........................	1886-1889	4
Hugoton Hermes..........................	1887-1890	2
Woodsdale Democrat..........................	1887-1889	2
Woodsdale Sentinel..........................	1889-1892	3
Stevens County Tribune, Woodsdale..................	1890-1892	2
Tribune-Sentinel, Woodsdale..........................	1892,1893	1
Stevens County Sentinel, Woodsdale.................	1893,1894	2
Dermot Enterprise..........................	1887,1888	1
The Voorhees Vindicator..........................	1887-1890	3
Moscow Review..........................	1888	1
Stevens county, short-lived, vol. 1:		
Woodsdale Times, October 15 to November 27, 1888; Stevens County Eagle, Woodsdale, March 28 to May, 1889	....	1
SUMNER COUNTY (229).		
Sumner County Press, Wellington	1873-1892	18
Wellington Daily Press	1886,1887	3
Sumner County Democrat, Wellington..................	1877-1881	4
The Wellington Semi-weekly Vidette..................	1879	1
The Wellingtonian, Wellington	1881-1885	5
The Daily Wellingtonian, Wellington..................	1885	1
The Wellington Democrat	1882-1884	2
The Kansas Weather Observer, Wellington............	1885,1886	1
Sumner County Standard, Wellington	1884-1894	10
Daily Standard, Wellington..........................	1887-1889	4
The Daily Postal Card, Wellington..................	1886,1887	2
The Republican, Wellington..........................	1886	1
The Wellington Monitor..........................	1886-1892	6
The Monitor-Press, Wellington..........................	1892-1894	3
Wellington Morning Quid Nunc (daily)............	1887,1888	3
Wellington Quid Nunc..........................	1887,1888	2
Wellington Daily Telegram..........................	1887	1
The Christian Reminder, Wellington (monthly)......	1888-1891	3
The Daily Mail, Wellington..........................	1889-1894	10
The Wellington Gazette (daily)..........................	1889,1890	2
Railroad Employés' Companion, Wellington (see Franklin county).		
The Methodist News, Wellington	1890-1892	1
People's Voice, Wellington	1890-1894	4
Weekly Journal, Wellington..........................	1892,1893	1
Primitive Christian, Wellington	1893,1894	1
Oxford Independent..........................	1876-1878	2
Oxford Weekly Reflex	1890	1
Oxford Register (Mocking Bird, April, 1888, to August, 1893).........	1884-1894	5
The Mocking Bird, Oxford..........................	1888-1893	6
Caldwell Post..........................	1879-1883	4
Caldwell Commercial..........................	1880-1883	3
Caldwell Journal (September, 1891, to May, 1892, lacking)..............	1883-1894	11
Caldwell Daily Journal..........................	1887	1
Oklahoma War Chief, Wichita, January 12 to March 9, 1883; Geuda Springs, March 23 to July 19, 1883; Oklahoma Territory, April 26 and May 3, 1884; Arkansas City, May 10, 1884; Geuda Springs, August 30, 1884; South Haven, October 23 to December 4, 1884; Arkansas City, February 3 to June 11, 1885; Caldwell, June 18, 1885, to August 12, 1886..........................	1883-1886	4
Caldwell Standard..........................	1884	1
The Free Press, Caldwell..........................	1885,1886	1
Times, Caldwell	1886,1887	1
The Daily News, Caldwell..........................	1887	1
The Caldwell News (weekly)..........................	1887-1894	8
The Industrial Age, Caldwell and Wellington........	1887-1889	1
Geuda Springs Herald (not published from August 13 to November 27, 1886).....	1882-1894	13

BOUND NEWSPAPERS AND PERIODICALS — Continued.

NEWSPAPERS.	Years.	No. vols
SUMNER COUNTY — *Concluded.*		
Geuda Springs News	1884,1885	1
Belle Plaine News	1879-1894	15
The Kansas Odd Fellow, Belle Plaine	1882,1883	1
The Resident, Belle Plaine	1885,1886	1
Belle Plaine Voice	1894	1
Mulvane Herald	1880-1882	2
Mulvane Record	1885-1894	10
The Mulvane Graphic	1891-1893	2
Mulvane Voice	1894	1
Argonia Clipper	1884-1894	11
People's Voice, Argonia	1890-1892	2
The People's Press, Argonia, and Milan	1891,1892	1
Argonia Voice	1894	1
Conway Springs Star	1885-1894	9
The Weekly News, South Haven	1885,1886	1
The South Haven New Era	1886-1894	9
The Patrick Henry, South Haven	1890-1891	1
South Haven Voice	1894	1
The Hunnewell Rustler, and South Haven Rustler	1889,1890	1
Hunnewell Voice	1894	1
The Milan Press	1892-1894	3
Mayfield Voice	1894	1
Corbin Voice	1894	1
Sumner county, short-lived, vol. 1:		
Caldwell Daily Standard, June 20 to July 2, 1884; Rambler, Wellington, April, May, 1886; Crank, Geuda Springs, September 4 to November 6, 1886; Stars and Stripes, Wellington, May, 1888, to July, 1890; Weekly Gazette, Wellington, January 3 to 31, 1890; Public School Journal (monthly), Wellington, October 25, 1890, to April, 1892; Weekly Juvenile, Wellington, August 5, 1892, to March 25, 1893: South Haven Rustler, September 24 to December 31, 1892; Bandman (monthly), Wellington, February to July, 1893	....	1
Sumner county, short-lived, vol. 2:		
Oxford Weekly, December 18, 1880, to March 11, 1881	....	1
THOMAS COUNTY (26).		
Thomas County Cat, Colby	1885-1891	6
The Democrat, Colby	1886-1889	3
The Colby Tribune	1888-1894	7
The Free Press, Colby	1889-1894	5
Colby News	1892,1893	1
The Hastings Gazette	1888	1
The Brewster Gazette	1888-1890	2
Thomas county, short-lived, vol. 1:		
Quickville Courier, January 6 to February 24, 1888	....	1
TREGO COUNTY (29).		
The Wa Keeney Weekly World and Western Kansas World	1879-1894	16
Kansas Leader, Wa Keeney	1879-1881	2
Trego County Tribune, Wa Keeney	1885-1890	4
Trego County Gazette, Wa Keeney	1887,1888	1
Trego County Republican, Wa Keeney	1887-1889	2
Omnicrat, Wa Keeney	1893,1894	2
Globe, Cyrus	1882,1883	1
Trego county, short-lived, vol. 1:		
Tregola Index, August 7 to October 23, 1886; Ogallah News, May 21, 1887; The Sun, Wa Keeney, November 4, 1892, to February 2, 1893	....	1
WABAUNSEE COUNTY (70).		
The Wabaunsee County Herald, Alma	1869-1871	2
The Alma Weekly Union	1871,1872	1
Weekly Alma Union	1872	1
Wabaunsee County News, Alma	1876-1894	18
The Blade, Alma	1877,1878	1
Wabaunsee County Herald (second), Alma	1879-1881	2
The Alma Enterprise	1884-1894	10
The Alma Signal	1889-1894	5
The Land-Mark, Eskridge (not published from December, 1874, to June 30, 1888)	1873-1883	2
The Home Weekly, Eskridge	1881-1888	7
The Eskridge Star	1883-1894	11
Free Discussion (monthly), Eskridge (see Shawnee county, Topeka).		
The Alta Vista Register	1887-1889	2
The Alta Vista Bugle	1889,1890	1
The Alta Vista Record	1890-1894	5
The Paxico Courier	1888,1889	1
Wabaunsee county, short-lived, vol. 1:		
Wabaunsee Patriot, September 7 to October 19, 1861; Wabaunsee County Sun, Eskridge, October 11 to November 29, 1888	....	1

BOUND NEWSPAPERS AND PERIODICALS—Continued.

NEWSPAPERS.	Years.	No. vols
Wallace County (32).		
Wallace County Register, Wallace....................................	1886–1890	4
Wallace County News...	1886, 1887	1
Wallace Weekly Herald...	1888, 1889	1
Wallace County Gazette, Wallace...	1890, 1891	1
The Western Times, Sharon Springs (May 13 to September 16, 1886, Scott City)..	1886–1894	9
Sharon Springs Leader..	1887–1891	5
Alliance Echo, Sharon Springs...	1890, 1891	1
People's Voice, Sharon Springs..	1892–1894	3
The Weskansan, Weskan...	1888–1894	6
Wallace county, short-lived, vol. 1:		
Rose of Sharon, Sharon Springs, April 28 to September 9, 1886; Western Kansas Rustler, Wallace, August 17 to September 30, 1886.....................	....	1
Washington County (144).		
Western Observer and Washington Kansas Daily Republican (broken files).......	1869, 1870	1
Kansas Magnet, Washington Republican, and Republican Valley Watchman, Washington...	1870, 1871	1
Washington Republican..	1876–1894	18
Washington Republic...	1894	1
Washington County Register, Washington...................................	1881–1894	13
The Washington County Daily Register, Washington........................	1884, 1885	2
Weekly Post, Washington..	1883–1894	9
Washington Daily Post...	1887	1
Washington Daily Times..	1887, 1888	1
Washington Palladium..	1893	1
Western Independent, Hanover..	1876, 1877	1
The Hanover Democrat (Washington County Sun, October, 1877, to April, 1878)..	1878–1894	17
Grit, Hanover..	1884, 1885	1
The Clifton Localist...	1878	1
Clifton Review	1879–1892	13
The Local News and The Semi-Weekly News, Clifton......................	1885–1894	9
The Greenleaf Journal and Independent-Journal, Greenleaf.................	1881–1894	14
The Greenleaf Independent...	1882, 1883	1
Greenleaf Herald..	1883–1889	6
The Haddam Weekly Clipper..	1883–1894	11
The New Era, Haddam...	1886, 1887	1
Haddam Investigator..	1888, 1889	1
Haddam Politician..	1889	1
Palmer Pioneer (first)...	1888–1890	3
The Palmer Index...	1894	1
The Barnes Enterprise...	1885–1894	9
Barnes Chief...	1894	1
The Record, Hollenberg...	1889	1
The Linn Gazette..	1889, 1890	1
Linn Local Record...	1890, 1891	1
Washington county, short-lived, vol. 1:		
Washington County Answer, Washington, February 1, 1882; Palmer Weekly Globe, February 23 to August 23, 1884; Morning and Day of Reform (monthly), Washington, July and August, 1884; Argus, Hollenberg, May 15, 1885; Washington Daily Post, September 21 to 25, 1886; Greenleaf Safeguard, September 22, 1887, to January 20, 1888; Haddam City Times, March 1 to 15, 1890..	....	1
Washington county, short-lived, vol. 2:		
Hanover Enterprise, May 24, 1873; Clifton Journal, May 18 to June 22, 1878; The Haddam Gazette, November 22, 1879; Palmer Pioneer (second), November 29, 1890, February 13 to March 6, 1891......................	....	..
Wichita County (25).		
Wichita Standard, Leoti City, and Leoti Standard.........................	1885–1894	9
Leoti Lance..	1886, 1887	1
Wichita County Democrat, Leoti City.......................................	1886, 1887	1
The Leoti Transcript, Leoti City...	1887–1890	3
The Western Kansan, Leoti..	1891–1894	5
The Western Farmer, Farmer City and Leoti...............................	1889, 1890	2
Wichita County Herald, Coronado..	1886, 1887	1
The Coronado Star...	1886, 1887	1
The Selkirk Graphic...	1889–1891	1
Wichita county, short-lived, vol. 1:		
Coronado Chronicle, January 12 to March 15, 1888; Wichita County Farmer, Coronado, February 9 to March 1, 1888.....................................	....	..
Wilson County (86).		
Wilson County Citizen, Fredonia...	1870–1894	24
Fredonia Tribune	1878, 1879	1
Fredonia Democrat...	1882–1890	9
The Times, Fredonia...	1883–1885	1
Fredonia Chronicle...	1885–1888	3
The Alliance Herald, Fredonia..	1891–1894	4

BOUND NEWSPAPERS AND PERIODICALS—Continued.

NEWSPAPERS.	Years.	No. vols.
Wilson County— *Concluded.*		
Neodesha Free Press.............................	1876–1883	7
Neodesha Gazette................................	1881,1882	1
Neodesha Register (March, 1893, to March, 1894, lacking)...........	1883–1894	10
Neodesha Independent...........................	1887–1889	2
Wilson County Sun, Neodesha....................	1891–1894	4
Altoona Advocate................................	1886,1887	1
Altoona Journal.................................	1887–1894	7
The Benedict Echo...............................	1886–1890	3
Buffalo Clipper.................................	1887	1
Buffalo Express................................	1888	1
The Buffalo Advocate............................	1889–1894	6
Wilson county, short-lived, vol. 1:		
South Kansas Prohibitionist, Neodesha, July 22 to October 5, 1882; Wilson County Teacher (monthly), Fredonia, December, 1885, to July, 1886; La Fontaine Spy, February 10 to May 26, 1887; Coyville Press, October 7, 1887, to January 6, 1888; Amicus Life-Line (monthly), Fredonia, October, 1891, to July, 1892...........	....	1
Woodson County (72).		
Woodson County Post, Neosho Falls...............	1873–1894	21
Woodson County Republican and Independent, Neosho Falls........	1886,1887	1
Weekly News, Yates Center, and The Yates Center News........	1877–1894	16
Yates Center Argus..............................	1882–1884	3
Woodson Democrat, Yates Center..................	1884–1894	10
The Sun and Independent-Sun, Yates Center.......	1886–1888	2
Yates Center Tribune............................	1889,1890	1
The Farmers' Advocate, Yates Center.............	1891–1894	4
The Toronto Topic...............................	1883–1888	6
Register, Toronto...............................	1886,1887	1
The Toronto Republican..........................	1888–1894	6
Woodson county, short-lived, vol. 1:		
The Young Jayhawker, Neosho Falls, April, May, July 30, 1877; Our School Review (monthly), Neosho Falls, May, 1878; People's Herald, Neosho Falls, August 14 to October 23, 1878; Weekly Record, Neosho Falls, August 12 to September 9, 1879; District Fair Daily News, Neosho Falls, September 23, 1880; Land Mark, Yates Center, April, 1883; The Woodson Republican, November 15, 1894, to January 10, 1895...........	... .	1
Wyandotte County (145).		
Quindaro Chindowan..............................	1857,1858	1
Wyandotte Gazette (October 3, 1872, to October 17, 1873, lacking)..........	1866–1887	19
Wyandotte Herald...............................	1872–1894	23
The Pioneer, Kansas City........................	1878–1880	2
The Kansas Pilot, Kansas City...................	1879–1881	2
The Stock Farm and Home Weekly, Kansas City.....	1880	1
The Spy, Kansas City............................	1881,1882	1
The Kawsmouth Pilot, and The Kawsmouth, Wyandotte............	1881	1
The Kawsmouth Pilot (daily), Wyandotte..........	1881	1
Equitable Aid Union Advocate (monthly and semimonthly), Wyandotte........	1881–1884	8
Wyandotte Republican (daily)....................	1881,1882	1
Wyandotte Republican (weekly)...................	1881,1882	1
The Wyandotte Chief.............................	1883–1885	2
Kansas Pionier (German), Wyandotte..............	1883–1889	6
Kansas Pionier (English edition), Wyandotte.....	1887,1888	1
The Kansas Globe, and The Kansas City Sun and Globe............	1884–1886	2
Light, Kansas City..............................	1884–1887	2
The Kansas City Daily Gazette...................	1887–1894	16
The Kansas City Gazette.........................	1887–1894	8
The Kansas Weekly Cyclone, Kansas City..........	1887,1888	1
The Chronicle, Kansas City......................	1890–1892	3
Kansas Herold (German), Kansas City.............	1890,1891	1
The Kansas Catholic, Leavenworth and Kansas City...........	1890–1894	4
The Weekly Press, Kansas City (1889 to 1890, scattering,).......	1889–1894	4
The American Citizen, Kansas City (June 6, 1890, to February 20, 1891)........	1880–1894	5
The Kansas City Sun.............................	1891–1894	4
Cromwell's Kansas Mirror, Kansas City...........	1891–1894	4
Der Waechter, Kansas City.......................	1892–1894	3
Kansas City Age.................................	1892,1893	1
American Eagle, Kansas City.....................	1892–1894	2
The Bethany Visitor (monthly), Kansas City......	1893,1894	2
Argentine Republic..............................	1887–1894	7
The Argentine Advocate..........................	1888	1
The Labor Review, Argentine.....................	1891,1892	1
Argentine Eagle................................	1892–1894	3
Rosedale Record, and Rosedale Era...............	1888–1890	2
Cromwell's Kansas Mirror, Armourdale, *see* Kansas City...........	1887–1890	3

BOUND NEWSPAPERS AND PERIODICALS—CONCLUDED.

NEWSPAPERS.	Years.	No. vols
WYANDOTTE COUNTY—*Concluded.*		
Wyandotte county, short-lived, vol. 1:		
Iron City Press, Rosedale, January 25 to February 8, 1883; Wasp, Rosedale, September 15, 1883, to November 7, 1885 (scattering); Kansas City Ledger, June 6 to June 27, 1885; Armourdale News, May 1 to October 2, 1885; Argentine Siftings, January 9 to May 29, 1886; Methodist Record (monthly), Kansas City, July, 1887, to March, 1888; Argentine Weekly Argus, August 25 to December 1, 1887; Armourdale Advocate, December, 15, 22, 29, 1888; Armourdale Daily Advocate, January 5 to March 4, 1889; Rosedale Bee, December 5, 1889, to September 18, 1890 (scattering); Rosedale Enquirer, January 25 to June 14, 1890; Kaw Valley News, Bonner Springs, February 28 to April 4, 1890; Bonner Springs Citizen, April 18 to July 11, 1890; The Owl, Kansas City, July 12 to September 18, 1890; The Age, Riverview, July 12 to September 13. 1890; Glad Tidings, Kansas City, May to July, 1891; Delphian, Kansas City, January to March, 1892.............	....	1
Wyandotte county, short-lived, vol. 2:		
Wyandotte City Register, July 25, 1857; Kansas Real Estate Herald, Wyandotte, May, 1869; Stockman and Farmer, Kansas City, October 30 to November 27, 1880; Monthly Clipper, Armourdale, September, 1886; Kansas City Daily Sun, May 28, 1892; Baptist Banner, Argentine, September 7 to 28, 1892; Kansas City Republican, March 15 to April 26, 1894.....................	....	1

BOUND NEWSPAPERS, ETC., OF OTHER STATES AND COUNTRIES.

NEWSPAPERS.	Years.	No. vols
ALABAMA (3).		
The Nationalist, Mobile.................................	1865–1868	3
ALASKA (7).		
The Alaska Free Press, Juneau...................	1889–1891	2
The Alaskan, Sitka.................................	1889–1894	5
ARIZONA (7).		
Arizona Weekly Journal-Miner, Prescott...........	1887–1894	7
ARKANSAS (6).		
The Jacksonian, Heber........................	1890–1894	4
National Reformer (monthly), Hardy............	1893,1894	1
Arkansas miscellaneous newspapers............	....	1
CALIFORNIA (92).		
California Teacher, San Francisco (incomplete).....	1864–1867	2
Overland Monthly, San Francisco (f. s.).........	1868–1875	15
Overland Monthly, San Francisco (s. s.).........	1883–1894	24
San Francisco Weekly Post...................	1878–1888	11
The Alaska Appeal, San Francisco............	1879,1880	1
The Pacific Rural Press, San Francisco.........	1892–1890	8
California Patron and Agriculturist. San Francisco..	1886,1887	2
The California Prohibitionist, San Francisco......	1890	1
Irrigation Age, San Francisco, *see* Colorado.		
American Sentinel, Oakland..................	1886–1889	4
Signs of the Times, Oakland.................	1886–1894	9
Pacific Health Journal (monthly). Oakland......	1886–1894	8
The West American Scientist (monthly), San Diego (April, 1892 to June, 1893, suspended)......................	1887–1894	4
The Orange Belt (monthly), Alessandro (Riverside P. O.), Rialto, and Los Angeles.	1891–1893	2
California miscellaneous newspapers...........	....	1
COLORADO (176).		
Weekly Rocky Mountain News, Denver (1875 to 1877, lacking).....	1874–1892	16
The Rocky Mountain Presbyterian and Presbyterian Home Missions (monthly), Denver, New York, and Cincinnati...............	1879–1886	3
The New West (quarterly) Omaha and Denver.............	1881–1883	2
Denver Daily Tribune.......................	1884	1
The Denver Republican (daily)...............	1887–1894	14
The Queen Bee, Denver....................	1888–1890	2
Colorado School Journal, Denver............	1887–1889	2
The Commonwealth (monthly), Denver........	1880–1891	4
The Great Divide (monthly), Denver..........	1889–1892	8
The Denver Press........................	1889–1894	6
Denver Public Library Bulletin, and Books (monthly).........	1890–1894	4

BOUND NEWSPAPERS, ETC., OF OTHER STATES AND COUNTRIES — CONTINUED.

NEWSPAPERS.	Years.	No. vols
COLORADO — *Concluded.*		
Irrigation Age (semimonthly), Denver, Salt Lake City, and San Francisco, *see*		
Illinois........	1891–1893	3
The Woman Voter, and The Western Woman, Denver.............................	1894	2
Silver World, Lake City..	1877–1888	10
Hinsdale Phonograph, Lake City..	1888,1889	1
The Gunnison Review, and Review-Press, *see* Saturday edition of daily....	1880–1891	11
The Gunnison Daily Review..	1881,1889	7
The Gunnison Daily and Tri-Weekly Review-Press...............................	1882–1889	15
The Gunnison News and Democrat..	1880,1881	1
Gunnison Democrat...	1880,1881	1
Gunnison Daily News-Democrat..	1881,1882	2
Free Press, Gunnison...	1881,1882	1
The Sun, Gunnison...	1883,1884	1
Gunnison county miscellaneous, vol. 1	1880–1886	1
Gunnison Tribune...	1891–1894	4
Salida Mail (weekly and semiweekly; 1886 lacking)..............................	1880–1894	13
Elk Mountain Pilot, Irwin and Crested Butte	1880–1884	2
Crested Butte Republican..	1881,1882	1
Pitkin Independent..	1880–1882	2
Pitkin Mining News..	1881,1882	1
The Tin Cup Record..	1881,1882	1
Garfield Banner, and Tin Cup Banner..	1881,1882	1
Elk Mountain Bonanza, Gothic Miner, and Silver Record, Gothic.............	1881,1882	1
White Pine Cone...	1883–1892	9
Grand Junction News..	1884,1885	1
Grand Valley Star, and Star-Times, Grand Junction..............................	1890–1894	4
The Horticulturist (quarterly), Grand Junction	1894	1
The Otero County Eagle, La Junta...	1889,1890	1
The Otero County Republican, La Junta..	1890,1891	1
Law and Gospel (monthly), Springfield, *see* Reno county, Kansas.		
The Fruita Star..	1889,1890	1
The West Side Citizen, Villa Park, Colfax.......................................	1890–1894	4
The Edgewood Sun, Colorado Springs..	1891–1893	2
The Idaho Springs News	1891–1894	3
The Fulford Signal...	1893	1
Du Bois Chronicle..	1894	1
Colorado miscellaneous newspapers, vols. 1–11.................................	....	11
CONNECTICUT (93).		
The Connecticut Courant, Hartford (scattering)................................	1776–1799	1
American Mercury, Hartford (scattering from October 17, 1796, to July 24, 1797)..	1796,1797	1
Quarterly Journal of Inebriety, Hartford.......................................	1876–1894	16
Travelers' Record (monthly), Hartford..	1886–1894	9
Hartford Seminary Record (bimonthly)...	1890–1894	4
Middlesex Gazette, Middletown (1804, 1805, and 1817).........................	1804–1817	2
American Journal of Science and Arts, Silliman (bimonthly and monthly), New Haven, 1 to 3 series...	{ 1818 { 1864–1894	}56
American Journal of Education (quarterly), Hartford, vols. 1, 2, 4, and 5........	1855–1858	4
Connecticut Common School Journal, New Britain...............................	1864,1865	2
The Connecticut Valley Advertiser, Moodus.....	1892–1894	3
DAKOTA, *see* North and South Dakota (1).		
Dakota Teacher, Huron...	1885,1886	1
DISTRICT OF COLUMBIA (169).		
Latter Day Luminary (monthly), Washington and Philadelphia (incomplete)....	1819–1824	2
African Repository and Colonial Journal (semimonthly), Washington (scattering),	1839–1841	1
Kendall's Expositor, Washington...	1841	1
The National Era, Washington...	1847–1859	13
Summary Statement of the Imports and Exports of the United States (monthly), Washington..	1879–1894	13
The Council Fire (monthly), Washington.	1879–1881	2
United States Official Postal Guide (monthly supplements), Washington..........	{ 1880 { 1886–1894	}10
The Alpha (monthly), Washington...	1881–1888	7
The Washington World...	1882–1884	2
Union Volunteer (monthly), Washington..	1882,1883	1
The Official Gazette of the United States Patent Office, Washington (July, 1883, to December, 1884, lacking)...	1883–1894	41
Statement of Foreign Commerce and Immigration (monthly), Washington (incomplete)..	1883–1893	8
National Tribune, Washington (1885 lacking)....................................	1883–1894	11
Washington Grit...	1884	1
Health and Home (monthly), Washington.......................................	1884–1887	2
United States Government Publications, Monthly Catalogue, Washington........	1885–1894	10
Public Opinion, Washington and New York.....................................	1887–1894	14
The American Anthropologist (quarterly), Washington..........................	1888–1894	7
National Geographical Magazine (occasional), Washington......................	1888–1894	6

—8

BOUND NEWSPAPERS, ETC., OF OTHER STATES AND COUNTRIES—Continued.

NEWSPAPERS.	Years.	No. vols
DISTRICT OF COLUMBIA — *Concluded.*		
The Washington Book Chronicle (quarterly)	1889–1894	1
The Woman's Tribune, Washington, and Beatrice, Neb	1890–1894	5
The National Bulletin (monthly), Washington	1890–1894	1
The True Commonwealth (monthly), Washington	1890, 1891	1
National Farm and Fireside, Washington	1891–1894	3
National Watchman, Washington	1892–1894	2
Good Government (monthly), Washington and New York	1893, 1894	1
Principal Articles of Domestic Export (monthly), Washington	1893, 1894	1
The American Farmer (monthly), Washington	1893, 1894	2
FLORIDA (15).		
The Florida Dispatch, Farmer, and Fruit Grower, Jacksonville	1884–1894	10
The Monthly Bulletin, Tallahassee	1889–1891	2
The Advertiser, Apopka	1890	1
Pabor Lake Pineapple (monthly)	1892–1894	2
GEORGIA (17).		
Southern Industrial Record (monthly), Atlanta	1884–1893	9
Atlanta Constitution	1887, 1888	1
Spelman Messenger (monthly), Atlanta	1888–1894	7
ILLINOIS (447).		
Times and Seasons (biweekly), Nauvoo	1841, 1842	1
Emery's Journal of Agriculture, and Prairie Farmer, Chicago	1858	1
Illinois Teacher (monthly), Chicago (scattering issues, 1867 to 1870)	1864, 1865	2
Rounds' Printers' Cabinet (quarterly), Chicago	1867–1877	4
Religio-Philosophical Journal, Chicago (1868 to 1888 incomplete)	1868–1894	28
Chicago Specimen (quarterly), Chicago (incomplete)	1868–1880	7
National Sunday School Teacher (monthly), Chicago	1868–1882	13
Land Owner (monthly), Chicago (incomplete)	1870–1877	5
Chicago Advance (incomplete)	1870–1894	33
National Live-Stock Journal, Chicago	1871, 1872 1875, 1876	3
The Inter-Ocean, Chicago (incomplete)	1874 1881, 1885	4
Semi-Weekly Inter-Ocean, Chicago	1879–1893	15
Foundling's Record and Faith's Record (monthly), Chicago (1875 to 1876, lacking)	1874–1881	5
Commercial Advertiser, Chicago	1877–1879	4
Industrial World and Commercial Advertiser, Chicago	1880–1882	5
Industrial World and Iron Worker, Chicago	1883–1894	25
American Antiquarian (quarterly), Chicago	1878–1894	16
Weekly Drovers' Journal, Chicago	1879–1894	15
Rockford Gazette	1879–1881	1
Farmers' Review, Chicago	1880, 1881	2
The Standard, Chicago	1880–1894	14
The Dial (monthly and semimonthly), Chicago	1880–1894	14
Chicago Journal of Commerce	1881	1
The Hebrew Student, and Old-Testament Student (monthly), Chicago	1882–1886	4
The Western Trail (quarterly), Chicago	1882–1894	10
Brown & Holland's Short-Hand News (monthly), Chicago	1882–1885	4
The Watchman (semimonthly), Chicago	1882–1889	7
Young Men's Era, Chicago	1890–1894	5
The Weekly Magazine, Chicago	1882–1885	3
The New Era, Chicago	1883–1885	2
The Weekly News, Chicago	1884–1886	2
The National Educator (monthly), Chicago, Peoria, and Springfield	1885–1888	2
Svenska Amerikanaren, Chicago	1885–1894	10
The Union Signal, Chicago	1886–1894	9
The Penman's Gazette (monthly), Chicago and New York	1886	1
Pravda (monthly and weekly), Chicago	1886–1894	8
The Comrade (bimonthly), Chicago	1886–1888	2
The Unitarian, Chicago (see Boston).		
The Labor Enquirer, Chicago	1887, 1888	2
Gaskell's Magazine (monthly), Chicago and New York	1887, 1888	1
The Open Court, Chicago	1887–1894	8
The Inland Printer (monthly), Chicago (October, 1888, to September, 1889, lacking)	1887–1894	8
Humane Journal (monthly), Chicago	1888–1894	6
The Kindergarten, Chicago	1888–1894	6
The Chicago Express	1888–1894	7
Newspaper Union (monthly), Chicago	1888–1894	6
Unity, Chicago	1888–1890	2
National Journalist, and National Printer Journalist (monthly), Chicago	1889–1894	6
Soldier and Citizen (monthly), Chicago	1889–1890	1
The Monist (quarterly), Chicago	1890–1894	4
Young Men's Era, Chicago	1890–1894	5
National Reveille, Chicago	1890–1894	5
The Lever, Chicago	1890–1894	5

BOUND NEWSPAPERS, ETC., OF OTHER STATES AND COUNTRIES—Continued.

NEWSPAPERS.	Years.	No. vols
ILLINOIS — *Concluded.*		
National Stenographer (monthly), Chicago	1891–1893	3
Columbia, Chicago	1891–1894	2
The Young Crusader (monthly), Chicago	1891–1894	4
The Orange Judd Farmer, Chicago	1891–1894	3
The Graphic, Chicago	1891–1894	6
The Athena (monthly), Chicago	1891,1892	1
Milling (monthly), Chicago	1892–1894	3
Publisher's Auxiliary (monthly), Chicago	1892–1894	2
Oak and Ivy Leaf (monthly), Chicago	1892–1894	2
Quarterly Calendar of the University of Chicago	1892–1894	3
Bible Reading (monthly), Chicago	1892–1894	3
Responsive Readings (monthly), Chicago	1892–1894	3
Banner of Gold, Chicago	1892,1893	4
The Specimen (monthly), Chicago	1892–1894	1
Chicago Daily Record	1893	1
The Western Settler (quarterly), Chicago	1893	1
Chicago Daily Tribune	1893,1894	4
The Progressive Thinker, Chicago	1893,1894	1
Child Garden (monthly), Chicago	1893,1894	2
Irrigation Age, (monthly) Chicago (*see* Colorado)	1893,1894	2
New Occasions (monthly), Chicago	1893,1894	2
Journal of Geology (semiquarterly), Chicago	1893,1894	2
University Extension World (monthly and quarterly), Chicago	1893,1894	3
The Odd Fellows' Herald (semimonthly), Bloomington	1883–1894	11
The Western Plowman (monthly), Moline	1882–1894	13
The Grange News, River Forest	1885,1886	1
The Gospel Messenger, Mount Morris	1889–1894	5
National W. C. T. U. Bulletin. Evanston	1889–1891	1
The Christian Life (quarterly), Morton Park	1891–1894	2
INDIAN TERRITORY (37).		
The Cherokee Advocate, Tahlequah	1881–1894	13
The Cheyenne Transporter, Darlington	1883–1886	4
Indian Chieftain, Vinita	1883–1894	11
Minco Minstrel	1890–1894	4
The Territorial Topic, Purcell	1890,1891	1
Purcell Register	1891–1894	4
Alfred Monitor, *see* Oklahoma Territory.		
INDIANA (56).		
Indiana State Journal, Indianapolis	1878–1894	17
The Millstone and The Corn Miller (monthly), Indianapolis (see Milling, Ill.)	1884–1892	8
Western Sportsman. Indianapolis	1891	1
Western Horseman, Indianapolis	1891–1894	4
American Tribune, Indianapolis	1891–1894	3
American Nonconformist, Indianapolis	1891–1894	3
Our Herald, La Fayette	1882–1885	3
Mennonitische Rundschau. Elkhart	1885–1894	9
Sunday-School Lesson Helps (quarterly). Elkhart	1894	1
Young People's Paper (biweekly), Elkhart	1894	1
The Hoosier Naturalist (monthly), Valparaiso	1885–1887	2
Indiana Student (monthly), Bloomington	1886–1888	2
The Archæologist (monthly), Waterloo	1893,1894	2
IOWA (35).		
North Western Review, Keokuk	1857,1858	1
Davenport Gazette	1877,1878	1
Phonetic Magazine, Oskaloosa, *see* Piqua, Ohio.		
The Weekly Hawk-Eye, Burlington	1881–1885	4
The Burlington Hawk-Eye (daily)	1882–1885	5
The Iowa Historical Record (quarterly), Iowa City	1885–1894	10
Monthly Bulletin of Iowa State Board of Health, Des Moines	1887–1894	7
Farmers' Tribune, Des Moines	1893,1894	1
Annals of Iowa (quarterly), Des Moines	1893,1894	1
The Christian (semimonthly), Tabor, and Winfield, Kas	1889–1891	2
The Brethren Evangelist, Waterloo	1891–1893	2
Marne Free Press	1893	1
KENTUCKY (3).		
Weekly Courier-Journal, Louisville	1878,1879	2
Southern Bivouac (monthly), Louisville	1886,1887	1
LOUISIANA (29).		
New Orleans Weekly Picayune	1841–1846	6
South-Western Christian Advocate, New Orleans	1879–1894	15
The Times-Democrat (daily), New Orleans	1883–1885	5
The Sugar Bowl and Farm Journal, New Orleans	1891–1893	2
New Orleans miscellaneous newspapers		1

BOUND NEWSPAPERS, ETC., OF OTHER STATES AND COUNTRIES—Continued.

NEWSPAPERS.	Years.	No. vols
MAINE (22).		
Oxford Observer, Paris........................	1824–1826	2
Oxford Democrat (incomplete), Paris....................	1856–1876	7
Oxford Observer, Norway..........................	1829–1832	3
Maine Advertiser, Norway.........................	1872–1875	2
The Kennebec Journal, Augusta......................	1889–1893	5
First Maine Bugle (occasional), Rockland........	1874–1893	3
MARYLAND (30).		
The Weekly Register, Baltimore......................	1811,1812	2
Spirit of the Nineteenth Century (monthly), Baltimore............	1842	1
Rural Register (semimonthly), Baltimore.................	1859–1861	2
Johns Hopkins University Circular, Baltimore (1882 and 1884 lacking)..........	1879–1894	12
Johns Hopkins University Studies in Historical and Political Science (monthly), Baltimore	1882–1894	12
Jottings (monthly), Baltimore........................	1887,1888	3
The American Journal of Psychology, Baltimore, *see* Worcester, Mass.		
MASSACHUSETTS (811)		
The Boston Chronicle, December 21, 1767, to December 19, 1768..............	1767,1768	1
Federal Orrery, Boston, October 20, 1794, to April 18, 1796............	1794–1796	2
Massachusetts Mercury, Boston, May 11, 1798, to August 9, 1799..........	1798,1799	1
The Independent Chronicle and The Universal Advertizer, Boston, from January 1, 1798, to December 17. 1801	1798–1801	4
Columbian Centinel and Massachusetts Federalist, Boston. from June 29, 1799, to August 31, 1805: from January 3, 1807, to October 3, 1810; from January 2, 1811, to July 1, 1812 (incomplete)...........	1799–1812	5
The Independent Chronicle, Boston, December 21, 1801, to December 30, 1804....	1801–1804	3
New England Quarterly Magazine, Boston...............	1802	1
The Massachusetts Missionary Magazine (monthly), Boston (incomplete)........	{ 1804–1808 } { 1814,1815 }	} 3
Boston Gazette, from January 9 to October 29, 1804: from August 19, 1815, to August 19, 1816; from December 27, 1817, to December 25, 1819; from April 23, 1827, to November 28, 1828...........	1804–1828	6
The Panoplist, or Christian Armory (monthly), Boston...........	1805,1806	1
Panoplist and Christian Magazine (monthly), Boston............	1808,1809	1
Boston Patriot, from April 7, 1809, to September 12, 1810; from March 2 to December 25, 1811; from March 14, 1812, to September 8, 1813...........	1809–1813	5
Omnium Gatherum (monthly), Boston.................	1810	1
Boston Spectator, from January 4, 1814, to February 5, 1815..........	1814,1815	1
North American Review (quarterly and bimonthly), Boston (Nos. 3–6, 10, 11, 13, 14, 15, 19, 20, and 130, lacking, *see* New York city)....	1815–1877	117
American Baptist Magazine and Missionary Intelligencer (monthly), Boston....	1817,1818	1
Boston Commercial Gazette (semiweekly)...........	1819	2
The Missionary Herald (monthly), Boston (Nos. 17–80)............	1821–1824	64
New England Galaxy, Boston, from October 31, 1823, to December 26, 1828.......	1823–1828	5
Christian Examiner, Boston, vols. 1–19, 1824–1836, and 16 vols. between 1854 and 1867	1824–1868	35
Quarterly Register and Journal of the American Education Society, Andover, Boston.....................	1829–1843	14
Independent Chronicle and Boston Patriot (semiweekly), January 11, 1832, to August 10, 1837.................	1832–1837	6
Boston Recorder, from January 2, 1833, to December 25, 1835..............	1833–1835	3
The Liberator, Boston (lacking 1834–1837 and 1839).................	1833–1865	28
Abolitionist, Boston	1833	1
Baptist Missionary Magazine (monthly), Boston..........	1836	1
Evening Journal, Boston, from January 3, 1837, to December 30. 1843: from January 4 to December 30, 1844; and from February 4 to December 30, 1845 (incomplete)	1837–1845	4
Common School Journal (semimonthly), Boston............	1839	1
The Commonwealth (daily), Boston, from January 1 to July 8, 1851; and from January 1, 1853, to September 21, 1854...........	1851–1854	4
The Commonwealth, Boston, from September 1, 1866, to August 28, 1869...........	1866–1869	3
Youth's Companion, Boston, from October 21, 1852, to December, 1857, and 1886 to 1894	1852–1894	14
Evening Telegraph (daily), Boston...................	1854,1855	1
Quarterly Journal of the American Unitarian Association, Boston............	1854–1859	6
Anglo-Saxon, European and Colonial Gazette, Boston............	1855,1856	1
The Atlantic Monthly, Boston, vols. 1–50..............	1857–1882	50
The Atlas and Daily Bee, Boston.............	1858	1
Boston Investigator (April, 1863, to April, 1864; April, 1875, to April, 1877; April, 1883, to April, 1885, lacking).............	1859–1894	21
The Well Spring, Boston (incomplete)..................	1859–1894	3
Monthly Journal of the American Unitarian Association, Boston	1860–1869	9
Massachusetts Teacher (monthly), Boston...............	1864,1865	2
Zion's Herald, Boston, 1868, 1869, 1870, 1878, 1880, 1883, 1884, 1890........	1868–1890	8
Bulletin of the Boston Public Library (quarterly and occasional)............	1868–1894	13
Banner of Light, Boston.................	1869–1872	4
Christian Register, Boston.....	1869–1886	4

BOUND NEWSPAPERS, ETC., OF OTHER STATES AND COUNTRIES—Continued.

NEWSPAPERS.	Years.	No. vols.
MASSACHUSETTS—Continued.		
Life and Light for Heathen Women (monthly), Boston and Chicago (incomplete),	1872-1882	3
Boston Journal of Chemistry (monthly)	1873-1877	4
The Missionary Herald (monthly), Boston	1876	1
Knights of Honor Reporter (monthly), Boston	1878-1888	2
The New England Historical and Genealogical Register (quarterly), Boston	1878-1894	17
The Woman's Journal, Boston	1879-1894	16
Civil Service Record, Boston	1881,1882	2
United States Official Postal Guide, Boston, see District of Columbia.		
Our Dumb Animals (monthly), Boston (incomplete)	1882-1886	2
Journal of Education, Boston	1883	1
Boston Herald	1883-1885	3
Pilgrim Quarterly, Boston and Chicago	1883	1
Pilgrim Quarterly, International, Boston and Chicago (incomplete)	1885-1891	4
Pilgrim Quarterly, Sr., Boston and Chicago (incomplete)	1885-1891	3
Bay State Monthly, Boston	1884-1885	3
New England Magazine (monthly), Boston	1886-1891	7
The Williams Athenæum (biweekly)	1884,1885	1
The Williams Fortnight	1885,1886	1
The Popular Science News, Boston	1885-1890	5
The Unitarian Review (monthly), Boston	1885-1891	13
The Evening Traveler (daily), Boston, from January to June, 1886	1886	1
The Citizen (monthly), Boston	1886,1887	4
Political Science Quarterly, see New York.		
Library Notes (monthly), Boston (lacking, No. 10 of vol. 3)	1886-1889	3
The Unitarian (monthly), Chicago, Ann Arbor, and Boston	1886-1894	9
The Writer (monthly), Boston (suspended April, 1892, to May, 1893)	1887-1894	7
American Teacher (monthly), Boston	1887-1890	3
Spelling (quarterly and occasional)	1887-1893	2
Technology Quarterly, Boston	1887-1894	7
Saturday Evening Gazette, Boston	1888-1893	6
The New Jerusalem Magazine (monthly), Boston	1888-1893	6
Journal of American Folk-Lore (quarterly and bimonthly), Boston	1888-1894	7
The Golden Rule, Boston	1890-1894	5
Daily Advertiser, Boston	1891-1894	6
Living Issues (monthly), Boston (incomplete)	1891-1894	1
The Dawn (monthly), Boston	1891-1893	1
The New Nation, Boston	1891-1893	3
The Weekly Bulletin, and Weekly Review, Boston	1891-1893	3
The Woman's Column, Boston	1891-1894	3
United States Investor, Boston, New York, Philadelphia	1891-1894	4
Bicycling World Bulletin, Boston	1891,1892	1
The Green Bag (monthly), Boston	1892,1893	1
Dorchester Beacon, Boston	1892-1894	2
Berkeley Beacon (monthly), Boston	1893,1894	1
Donahoe's Magazine (monthly), Boston	1894	2
The New-Church Review (quarterly), Boston	1894	1
Lend a Hand (monthly), Boston	1894	1
The National Ægis, Worcester (December 2, 1801, to December 25, 1811: from January 20, 1813, to May 4, 1814; from January 5, 1815, to December 25, 1816; from December 15, 1824, to June 8, 1825, and years 1825, 1830, 1838-1840 incomplete),	1801-1840	15
Massachusetts Spy or Worcester Gazette	1805,1806	2
The Massachusetts Spy (weekly), Worcester	1822	1
Worcester Daily Spy, from January to December, 1859; from January, 1868, to December, 1884; and from July, 1885, to July, 1866 (July to December, 1880, lacking)	1859-1886	36
Worcester Evening Gazette, from January to December, 1866; from January, 1867, to July 18, 1881; and from January, 1882, to December, 1885 (July to December, 1884, missing)	1868-1894	38
Ægis and Gazette, Worcester (May to December, 1877, lacking)	1875-1880	5
Massachusetts Yeoman, and Worcester Saturday Journal and Advertiser (1826 lacking)	1823-1830	6
Daily Transcript, Worcester	1853-1855	6
Worcester Daily Press	1873-1878	9
The American Journal of Psychology (quarterly), Baltimore and Worcester	1890-1892	6
Light, Worcester	1890-1892	6
Essex Register, Salem, from January 1 to December 17, 1817	1817	1
Historical Collections of the Essex Institute, Salem	1859-1884	31
American Naturalist (monthly), Salem, Boston, and Philadelphia	1867-1880	14
Bulletin of the Essex Institute, Salem	1869-1894	26
Putnam's Monthly Historical Magazine, Salem	1893,1894	1
Bibliotheca Sacra and Theological Review (quarterly), Andover	1844-1883	40
Harvard University Bulletin (occasional), Cambridge (1876 to 1879, incomplete)	1876-1894	7
Harvard Register, Cambridge (April to July)	1881	1
Science, Cambridge, see New York.		
The Prospect Union Review (semimonthly), Cambridgeport	1894	1
The True Educator, South Lancaster	1885-1888	2
Gazette and Courier, Greenfield	1885-1891	6
Winchester Record (occasional)	1886	1

BOUND NEWSPAPERS, ETC., OF OTHER STATES AND COUNTRIES—Continued.

NEWSPAPERS.	Years.	No. vols
MASSACHUSETTS—*Concluded.*		
Martha's Vineyard Herald, Cottage City...	1887,1888	1
The Sounding Board (monthly), Quincy...	1889,1890	1
Dedham Historical Register (quarterly)...	1890–1894	5
Hyde Park Historical Record (quarterly)...	1891,1892	2
The Kindergarten News (monthly), Buffalo, N. Y., and Springfield...............	1893,1894	2
Massachusetts miscellaneous newspapers..	....	1
MICHIGAN (20).		
The Fireside Teacher (monthly), Battle Creek.....................................	1886–1888	3
The Advent Review and Sabbath Herald, Battle Creek..........	1886–1894	8
Religious Liberty Library (monthly), Battle. Creek...............................	1892–1894	2
The Unitarian (monthly), Ann Arbor, *see* Boston.		
The Plaindealer, Detroit...v......................	1889–1893	4
Pernin's Monthly Stenographer, Detroit...	1891–1894	3
MINNESOTA (37).		
Pioneer-Press, St. Paul and Minneapolis............................'...............	1878,1879	1
Northwestern Railroader, St. Paul and Minneapolis............................	1888	2
The Northwest Illustrated Monthly Magazine, St. Paul........................	1890–1894	5
The St. Paul Dispatch (daily)...	1891–1894	7
The Gospel Message (monthly), St. Paul..	1892,1893	1
The American Geologist (monthly), Minneapolis (July to September, 1890, lacking)...	1888–1894	14
The Free Baptist, Minneapolis...	1891–1894	4
Medical Argus (monthly), Minneapolis...	1892–1894	3
MISSOURI (427).		
The Western Journal, and Civilian (monthly), St. Louis (vol. 6, old style, and vols. 6–8, new style)..	1848–1854	10
Daily Organ and Reveille, St. Louis...	1851	1
American Journal of Education (monthly), St. Louis.............................	1875–1894	20
Weekly Globe-Democrat, St. Louis..	1877–1880	3
The Phonetic Educator, St. Louis, *see* Cincinnati.		
Fonetic Teacher (monthly), St. Louis..	1879–1883	2
The Communist and Altruist (bimonthly), Cincinnati and St. Louis...........	1879–1894	15
American Journalist (monthly). St. Louis..	1883–1885	1
Colman's Rural World, St. Louis (1885 incomplete)...............................	1883–1891	7
The Central Christian Advocate. St. Louis...	1886–1894	8
The St. Louis Evangelist, and Christian Evangelist...............................	1887–1894	8
The St. Louis Globe-Democrat (daily)..	1887–1894	14
National Reformer (monthly), St. Louis...	1890–1892	2
Broom-Corn Reporter (monthly), St. Louis and Chicago.........................	1891–1893	1
Triple Link (semimonthly), St. Louis, Carrollton, and Springfield............	1892–1894	3
Daily Inquirer, Jefferson City..	1850,1851	1
St. Joseph Free Democrat...	1860	1
St. Joseph Herald (daily), (December. 1877, to September, 1878, lacking)........	1876–1894	37
St. Joseph Herald..	1877–1894	18
St. Joseph Gazette...	1877–1894	17
Kansas-City Times (daily), (March, 1875, to January, 1876, lacking)...........	1873–1894	40
Kansas-City Evening Times..	1890,1891	2
The Kansas City Review of Science and Industry (monthly).....................	1877–1885	9
Weekly Journal of Commerce, Kansas City...	1877–1879	2
Kansas City Daily Journal (November 14 to December 3, 1874).................	{ 1874 / 1879–1894	} 28
Mirror of Progress, Kansas City..	1879–1881	2
The Weekly Pioneer, Kansas City..	1880	1
Kansas City Price Current..	1880,1881	1
Santa Fé Trail (monthly), Kansas City, vol. 1, Nos. 1 to 8.......................	1880,1881	1
Camp's Emigrant Guide to Kansas, Kansas City....................................	1880–1884	4
The Western Advocate, or Camp's Emigrants' Guide (monthly), Kansas City...	1885–1888	3
American Home Magazine, Kansas City...	1881–1884	5
Kansas City Live-Stock Indicator...	1882–1894	13
The Mid-Continent, Kansas City and St. Louis.....................................	1882–1894	13
Svenska Harolden and Vestern, Kansas City...	1882–1885	3
Western Newspaper Union, Kansas City..	1883–1894	12
The Centropolis, Kansas City...	1883–1887	4
The Kansas City Medical Index Lanphear (monthly)...............................	1884–1894	11
Kansas City Live-Stock Record and Price Current, and Farmer..................	1884–1889	4
Missouri and Kansas Farmer (monthly), Kansas City (1889 lacking)...........	1884–1894	9
The Kansas City Record...	1885–1894	9
The Penny Press (daily), Kansas City..	1890	1
The Kansas City Star (daily)...	1886–1894	17
Kansas City Star (weekly)..	1890–1894	5
The Faithful Witness (monthly), Kansas City..	1886–1888	2
The Herald, Kansas City..	1886–1889	3
The Kansas Magazine (monthly), Kansas City.......................................	1886–1888	2
The Great West (monthly), Kansas City...	1888–1889	1
The Church Builder, Kansas City...	1888,1889	1

BOUND NEWSPAPERS, ETC., OF OTHER STATES AND COUNTRIES—CONTINUED.

NEWSPAPERS.	Years.	No. vols
MISSOURI—*Concluded.*		
The Evening News, Kansas City	1888–1890	5
The Kansas City Daily Traveler	1888,1889	3
Hoisington Bank Reporter (semimonthly), Kansas City	1889–1892	6
Christian Era, Kansas City	1889,1890	1
Kansas City Globe	1889–1891	5
The Naturalist (monthly), Kansas City	1889,1890	1
Borders' Odd Fellow (monthly), Kansas City	1890–1892	2
Weekly Progress, Kansas City	1890,1891	1
Real Estate Journal (occasional), Kansas City	1890–1893	3
The Kansas City Scientist (monthly)	1891	1
Insurance Magazine (monthly), Kansas City	1891–1894	7
Christian Endeavor Monitor (monthly), Kansas City	1891–1894	3
The National Dairyman (monthly), Kansas City	1892–1894	3
The Daily Mail, Kansas City (suspended from March to July, 1893)	1892–1894	5
Western Veteran, Kansas City	1893,1894	1
The Border Chief, Amsterdam	1891–1893	1
Minden Itemizer	1892,1893	1
Missouri miscellaneous newspapers		2
NEBRASKA (55).		
Nebraska Palladium, Belleview	1854,1855	1
The Little Blue, Jenkins Mills (bound with the Observer and Republican, Washington, Kas.)	1869,1870	1
The New West, Omaha (*see* Colorado)		
The Western Newspaper Union, Omaha	1886–1894	8
Daily Christian Advocate (M. E. Conference), Omaha	1892	1
The Gospel Message (monthly), Omaha	1893,1894	1
Omaha Mercury	1893,1894	2
The Woman's Tribune (monthly and weekly), Beatrice, *see* Washington, D. C.	1883–1889	6
Western Resources (monthly and weekly), Lincoln	1887–1894	8
Nebraska State Journal (daily), Lincoln	1887–1894	14
Nebraska State Journal (weekly and semiweekly), Lincoln	1887–1894	7
Nebraska Congregational News (monthly), Lincoln	1887–1894	7
NEW JERSEY (19).		
The Journal of American Orthoëpy (monthly), Ringos	1884–1894	10
Orchard and Garden (monthly), Little Silver	1887–1892	6
Library Record (monthly), Jersey City	1892–1894	2
The Jerseyman (quarterly), Flemington	1893	1
NEW MEXICO (66).		
Santa Fé Daily New Mexican (lacking from June, 1883, to December, 1887)	1881–1894	18
New Mexican Mining News, Santa Fé	1881,1882	2
Santa Fé New Mexican Review	1883	1
The Santa Fé Weekly Leader	1885,1886	2
El Boletin Popular, Santa Fé	1892–1894	2
Mining World, Las Vegas	1880–1882	2
Las Vegas Weekly Optic	1883,1884	1
Las Vegas Daily Optic	1888–1894	12
Albuquerque Weekly Journal, and Journal and Opinion	1881–1886	6
The Daily Citizen, Albuquerque	1887–1894	15
San Marcial Reporter	1889–1893	4
New Mexican miscellaneous newspapers		1
NEW YORK (1192).		
Academician (monthly and semimonthly), New York city	1818,1819	1
New York American, New York city (1829 lacking)	1827–1835	8
Anti-Slavery Record, New York city	1836,1837	2
The Emancipator, New York city (from February 23, 1837, to February 14, 1839)	1837–1839	2
The New-Yorker, New York city	1837–1841	8
The Diamond, New York city	1840–1842	2
Baptist Memorial and Monthly Chronicle, New York city	1842–1851	10
Workingman's Advocate, New York city	1844,1845	1
New York Evangelist	1845–1847	2
The American Review, a whig journal, and American Whig Review (monthly), New York city	1845–1852	16
The United States Magazine and Democratic Review (monthly), New York, n. s.	1846	1
American Protestant (monthly), New York city	1848	1
New York Daily Tribune (1848, 1849 incomplete: August, 1878, to August, 1879, lacking)	1848–1894	90
New York Weekly Tribune (lacking 1871–1878, 1885–1891; 1855–1858, 1861–1869 incomplete)	1870–1894	9
New York Semi-Weekly Tribune (lacking 1881, 1883, 1884; 1855, 1856, 1867, 1868, scattering issues)	1871–1888	18
Scientific American, New York city (lacking from 1861 to 1876, 1878, 1880 to 1884; scattering, 1867 to 1876)	1849–1894	37
Working Farmer (monthly), New York city	1849,1850	1

BOUND NEWSPAPERS, ETC., OF OTHER STATES AND COUNTRIES—Continued.

NEWSPAPERS.	Years.	No. vols
New York — *Continued.*		
Hunt's Merchants' Magazine (monthly), New York city	1849,1850 1852	5
The Anglo Saxon (monthly), New York city	1849,1850	1
Propagandist (semimonthly), New York city	1850,1851	
The Home Missionary (monthly), New York city	1850–1894	44
Harper's Monthly Magazine, New York city	1851–1854	8
Harper's Weekly, New York city	1857–1889	33
New York Illustrated News	1853	2
The Industry of all Nations, New York city	1853	1
Putnam's Monthly, New York city (first series)	1853–1857	10
Putnam's Monthly, New York city (second series; June, 1870, lacking)	1868–1870	6
Daily Times, New York city (incomplete)	1854–1856	4
Woodworth's Youth's Cabinet (monthly), New York city	1855,1856	1
The Phonographic Intelligencer, New York city	1857	1
Historical Magazine (monthly), Boston, New York city, and Morrisania (1864–1866 lacking)	1857–1873	19
Cosmopolitan Art Journal (monthly), New York city	1857,1858	2
The Printer (monthly), New York city	1858–1863	4
American Agriculturist (monthly), New York city (lacking 1862–1866, 1868, 1870–1875, 1877–1890; scattering issues, 1859 to 1876)	1860–1894	9
American Phrenological Journal (monthly), New York city	1864 1872–1874	7
United States Service Magazine (monthly) New York city	1864–1866	5
New York Herald (daily)	1865	1
New York Independent (1867 and 1869 lacking)	1866–1892	25
The Galaxy (monthly), New York city	1866–1877	24
The Nation, New York city (vols. 8, 10–12, 34, 35, 40, 41, 50–57 lacking)	1866–1893	38
New York Teacher and American Educational Monthly	1867–1869	3
The Commercial and Financial Chronicle, New York city	1867,1868	4
The Revolution, New York city	1868–1870	5
Typographic Messenger (monthly), New York city (incomplete)	1869–1875	1
The Spectator, New York city and Chicago	1870–1880	11
Scribner's Monthly, New York city	1870–1881	22
The Century Magazine (monthly), New York city	1881–1893	24
Scribner's Magazine (monthly), New York city (new series)	1887–1891	10
The Pig Tail (biweekly), New York city	1871,1872	1
Science of Health (monthly), New York city	1872–1873	6
Popular Science Monthly, New York city	1872–1891	40
Forest and Stream, New York city	1873–1875	1
Christian Union, New York city (earlier volumes incomplete)	1874–1893	28
Outlook, New York city	1893,1894	3
Pomeroy's Democrat, New York city	1874,1875	1
Frank Leslie's Boys' and Girls' Weekly, New York city	1875	1
The Iron Age, New York city	1875–1877	2
The Library Journal (monthly), New York city	1876–1894	19
The Magazine of American History (monthly), New York city	1877–1893	30
The Christian Advocate, New York city	1877,1878 1885,1886	2
North American Review (monthly), New York city (*see* Boston)	1878–1890	26
The Students' Journal (monthly), New York city (1883 lacking)	1878–1894	16
The Baptist Home Mission (monthly), New York city	1878–1893	15
The Speling Reformer (monthly), New York city	1878	1
Brown's Phonographic Monthly, New York city	1878–1883	6
The National Citizen and Ballot-Box (from May, 1878, to October, 1881), New York city (*see* Ballot-Box, Ohio)	1878–1881	3
The Daily Register, New York city	1879–1889	22
New York Law Journal (daily)	1890	1
The Sheltering Arms (monthly), New York city	1879–1894	16
The Publishers' Weekly, New York city	1879–1894	31
America, New York city	1879–1881	1
Our Union (monthly and semimonthly), New York city	1879–1882	3
American Missionary (monthly), New York city	1880–1894	15
The Phonetic Educator, New York city, *see* Cincinnati.		
Appleton's Bulletin (monthly, quarterly, and occasional), New York city (1890 lacking)	1881–1894	9
Bulletin of the American Museum of Natural History (occasional), New York city	1882–1893	5
John Swinton's Paper, New York city	1883–1887	4
The Coöperative Index to Periodicals (monthly), New York city	1883–1889	4
Science, Cambridge and New York	1883–1890	14
The Literary News, New York city	1884–1894	11
Insurance, New York city (lacking 1886–1891)	1884–1894	12
New York Weekly Witness	1884–1894	11
The Phonographic World (monthly), New York city	1885–1894	9
Dickerman's United States Treasury Counterfeit Detector (monthly), New York	1885	1
The Irish World, New York city	1885–1894	9
The American Book-Maker (monthly), New York city	1885,1886	2
The New Princeton Review (semimonthly), New York city	1886–1888	6
Sabbath Reading, New York city	1886–1894	8

BOUND NEWSPAPERS, ETC., OF OTHER STATES AND COUNTRIES—Continued.

NEWSPAPERS.	Years.	No. vols
NEW YORK—*Continued.*		
The Delineator (monthly), New York city (scattering numbers, 1883–1887)........	1886	1
Electrical Review, New York city......	1886–1894	16
The Menorah (monthly), New York city (incomplete)...........................	1886–1889	5
Gaskell's Magazine, New York city, *see* Chicago.		
Political Science Quarterly, New York city	1886–1894	9
The Voice. New York city...	1886–1894	8
The Swiss Cross (monthly), New York city.............	1887–1889	5
The Decorator and Furnisher (monthly), New York city....	1887–1894	15
The Public Service Review (monthly), New York city ....!	1887,1888	1
Home Knowledge (monthly), New York city ....·.......	1887,1888	2
New York Pioneer and The Farmer's Pioneer.........................	1887–1892	5
The Curio, New York city	1887,1888	1
The Standard, New York city (January to October, 1888, and September, 1889 to December, 1890, lacking).............................	1887–1892	7
The Standard Extra, New York city ....;......................	1891,1892	1
The Critic, New York city.......................................	1887–1889	1
New York Weekly Post..................................	1888	*1
The Book Buyer (monthly), New York city	1888–1890	2
Public Opinion, New York city, *see* District of Columbia.		
Judge, New York city.................................	1888,1889	2
Garden and Forest, New York city	1888,1889	1
Demorest's Monthly, New York city ....,.............	1888	1
Tariff League Bulletin, New York city	1888	1
The Saturday Globe, New York city	1888–1891	6
The School of Mines Quarterly, New York city	1888–1893	4
Magazine of Western History (monthly), New York city (*see* Cleveland, Ohio) ...	1888–1891	7
The National Magazine (monthly), New York city..........	1891–1894	6
Magazine of Christian Literature (monthly), New York city ....;.........	1889–1892	8
The Thinker (monthly), London and New York city	1893	2
Christian Literature and Review of the Churches (monthly), New York city	1894	1
Microcosm (monthly), New York city	1880–1891	2
American Economist, New York city...................	1889–1894	11
The Silver Cross (monthly). New York city.	1890–1894	6
Twentieth Century, New York city	1889–1894	10
The Business Woman's Journal (bimonthly), New York city...............,.....	1889–1894	8
Literary Digest. New York city..............................	1890–1894	9
The American Sentinel, New York city	1890–1894	5
The Temperance Teacher (monthly), New York city ......;.............	1890,1891	1
Scientific American Supplement,.New York city....................	1890–1894	8
Building and Loan News (monthly), New York city and London...............	1890–1894	4
The American Bookseller (semimonthly), New York city................	1891,1892	2
Goldthwaite's Geographical Magazine (monthly), New York city........	1891–1894	6
Free Russia (monthly). New York city	1891–1894	3
Educational Review (monthly). New York city...............................	1891–1893	4
War Cry, New York city...........................	1891–1894	3
The Journalist, New York city	1891–1894	6
Scientific American, architects' and builders' edition (monthly), New York city..	1891–1894	8
Review of Reviews (monthly), New York city....................	1891–1894	8
The Forum (monthly), New York city......................	1891–1894	6
. The Engineering Magazine (monthly). New York city................	1891–1894	6
The Charities Review (monthly). New York city......................	1891–1894	3
Kawkab America (Persian and English). New York city...................	1891–1894	3
Notes on New Books (quarterly), New York city.....	1891–1894	4
The Publisher (monthly). New York city	1891,1892	1
Our Animal Friends (monthly), New York city................	1892–1894	2
Humanity and Health (monthly), New York city...............	1892–1894	3
Good Roads (monthly), New York city and Boston................	1892–1894	6
Christian Unity (quarterly), New York city........................	1892,1893	1
Converted Catholic (monthly), New York city	1892–1894	3
Newspaperdom (monthly), New York city	1892–1894	3
The New City, [Topolobampo,] (biweekly), New York city...............	1892–1894	2
International Bookseller, New York city.....................	1892,1893	1
Book Reviews (monthly), New York city	1893,1894	1
Illustrated Africa, (monthly), New York city....................	1893,1894	2
The Irrigation Market (monthly), New York city....................	1893,1894	1
The Philanthropist (monthly), New York city	1894	1
Evangelical Magazine and Gospel Advocate, Utica (n. s., vols. 4 and 9)............	1833–1838	2
The Jeffersonian, Albany..........................	1838,1839	1
The Northern Light (monthly), Albany........................	1841–1843	2
The Gavel (monthly), Albany	1846,1847	1
The Cultivator and Country Gentleman, Albany....	1879,1880	1
Daily Morning Drum Beat, Brooklyn...............................	1864	1
The Union, Brooklyn...............................	1879–1882	3
Pratt Institute Monthly, Brooklyn.......................	1892–1894	2
Fruit Recorder and Cottage Gardener, Palmyra ......,.................	1874–1876	3
The Husbandman, Elmira and Binghampton (August, 1878, to August, 1879; August, 1881, to August, 1886, lacking...........................	1875–1893	13
The Bee Keepers' Exchange (monthly), Canajoharie	1879–1881	4

BOUND NEWSPAPERS, ETC., OF OTHER STATES AND COUNTRIES—CONTINUED.

NEWSPAPERS.	Years.	No. vols
NEW YORK—*Concluded.*		
Liberal Sentinel, Middletown....................	1881	1
Library Bulletin of Cornell University (occasional), Ithaca.....................	1882–1892	3
Agricultural Science (monthly), Geneva..	1887–1889	3
The School Bulletin (monthly), Syracuse...	1891–1894	3
The Chautauqua Collegian (quarterly), Buffalo......................	1892–1894	2
The Kindergarten News, Buffalo, *see* Massachusetts.		
New York miscellaneous newspapers	....	1
NORTH CAROLINA (1).		
The Laurensville Herald......................................	1881	1
NORTH DAKOTA (15).		
Bismarck Weekly Tribune....................................	1887–1894	7
Bismarck Daily Tribune.....................................	1890–1894	8
OHIO (170).		
Western Monthly Magazine, Cincinnati (*see* Columbus)...............	1835	1
The Western Academician and Journal of Education and Science, Cincinnati.....	1837,1838	1
American Pioneer (monthly), Cincinnati............................	1842,1843	2
Weekly Phonetic Advocate, Cincinnati	1850–1853	4
Supplement to the Weekly Phonetic Advocate, Cincinnati..................	1850–1852	2
The Masonic Review (monthly), Cincinnati..........................	1853–1862	18
Type of the Times, Cincinnati.....................................	1854,1855	2
American Phonetic Journal, Cincinnati.............................	1858	1
National Normal (monthly), Cincinnati............................	1868,1869	1
Cincinnati Weekly Times	1878–1894	17
The Phonetic Educator (quarterly and monthly), St. Louis, Cincinnati, and New York (vols. 1 to 5 incomplete).......................	1878–1885	2
The Christian Press (monthly), Cincinnati........................	1880–1894	14
Journal of Cincinnati Society of Natural History (quarterly)................	1881–1884	15
The American Journal of Forestry (monthly), Cincinnati............	1882,1883	1
The Christian Standard, Cincinnati...............................	1883–1894	12
Cincinnati Commercial Gazette; Times-Star........................	1884	1
The American Grange Bulletin, Cincinnati........................	1886–1894	9
Phonographic Magazine (monthly), Cincinnati......................	1887,1894	2
Christian Educator (quarterly), Cincinnati........................	1889–1894	5
Cincinnati Nonpareil (monthly), Camden..........................	1891–1893	2
Coöperative News (semimonthly), Cincinnati.......................	1892–1894	2
The Hesperian, or Western Monthly Magazine, Columbus and Cincinnati.....	1838,1839	3
The Ohio Cultivator (semimonthly), Columbus......................	1845,1846	2
The Crisis, Columbus (from January 31, 1861, to January 23, 1863)...............	1861–1863	2
Ohio Educational Monthly, Columbus.............................	1864,1865	2
National Teacher (monthly), Columbus............................	1872	1
Ohio Archæological and Historical Quarterly, Columbus..............	1887–1889	2
The Ballot-Box (from June, 1876, to April, 1878), Toledo (*see* National Citizen, New York).....................	1876–1878	2
Phonetic Magazine (monthly), Piqua, and Oskaloosa, Iowa	1878,1879	2
Bibliotheca Sacra (quarterly), Oberlin............................	1884–1889	6
Magazine of Western History (monthly), Cleveland.................	1884–1888	7
Farm and Fireside (semimonthly), Springfield and Philadelphia, Pa...............	1884–1894	10
Womankind (monthly), Springfield................................	1891–1894	3
American Farmer (monthly), Springfield...........................	1893,1894	2
Herald of Gospel Liberty, Dayton................................	1889–1894	6
Le Pasteur (quarterly), Dayton..................................	1889–1892	4
American Farm News (monthly), Akron...........................	1891,1892	1
The Brethren Evangelist, Ashland.................................	1893,1894	1
OKLAHOMA TERRITORY (75).		
The Oklahoma Capital, Guthrie..................................	1889–1894	6
The Oklahoma Daily Capital, Guthrie (September, 1889, to September, 1893, lacking)...................	1889–1894	4
Oklahoma Daily Optic, Guthrie..................................	1889	1
Evening Democrat, Guthrie......................................	1890	2
The West and South, Guthrie....................................	1891,1892	1
Oklahoma State Journal, Guthrie.................................	1891	1
Oklahoma Standard, Stillwater..................................	1889,1890	1
The New World, Kingfisher (October, 1889, to October. 1890, lacking).............	1889–1891	2
Free Press, Kingfisher..	1891–1894	2
The Evening Gazette, Oklahoma..................................	1889–1891	8
Oklahoma Daily Journal..	1890,1891	3
Oklahoma City Daily Times......................................	1890,1891	3
Oklahoma Daily Times-Journal, Oklahoma City	1891–1894	7
Press-Gazette (daily), Oklahoma City	1893,1894	2
Daily Oklahoman, Oklahoma City................................	1894	1
The Frisco Herald..	1890,1891	1
Hennessey Clipper...	1890–1894	5
The Courier, Hennessey and Kingfisher............................	1890	2
The Norman Transcript...	1890–1894	4

BOUND NEWSPAPERS, ETC., OF OTHER STATES AND COUNTRIES—Continued.

NEWSPAPERS.	Years.	No. vols
OKLAHOMA TERRITORY—*Concluded.*		
The Oklahoma School Herald (monthly), Norman............:	1892–1894	2
Edmond Sun..	1890–1894	4
Langston City Herald...	1891–1893	1
Yukon Courier..	1891,1892	1
Canadian County Courier, El Reno...	1892,1893	2
The El Reno Democrat..	1893,1894	1
The Mulhall Monitor (Alfred Monitor, I. T., April to May, 1890)..............	1890,1891	1
Cherokee Strip Guide, Ponca City and Cross..................................	1893,1894	1
The Ponca City Courier...	1893,1894	1
Newkirk Republican..	1893,1894	1
The Pond Creek Echo...	1893,1894	1
The Pond Creek Tribune..	1893,1894	1
Cherokee Sentinel, Pond Creek..	1894	⌐1
Oklahoma, short-lived, vol. 1:		
The Oklahoma Chief, Rock Falls, August 7, 1884; Guthrie Getup, April 29 to August 29, 1889; Guthrie Republican, September 5 to November 7, 1889; Oklahoma Daily State Herald, Guthrie, October 14 to November 30, 1889; Oklahoma Farmer, Guthrie, October 18, 1889, to January 3, 1890; Guthrie Weekly News, November 25, 1889; Guthrie Daily News, April 9 to May 9, 1890; Oklahoma Hawk, Payne, March 15 to August 26, 1890—4 Nos.; The Hardesty Times, May 31 to August 16, 1890—5 Nos.; Oklahoma Weekly Farmer, Stillwater, August 30, 1890; El Reno Herald, October 9, 1890, to January 16, 1891..............	....	1
Oklahoma, short-lived, vol. 2:		
Oklahoma School Journal (monthly), Guthrie, May, 1891, to January, 1892; Oklahoma Congregationalist (monthly), Downs, June to September, 1891; Kingfisher News, September 18 to November 19, 1891; Der Courier, El Reno, December 22, 1893, to May 25, 1894..............	....	1
OREGON (3).		
Fire and Hammer, the Way, the Truth, and the Light (monthly and quarterly), Portland..	1890–1894	3
PENNSYLVANIA (250).		
The Examiner and Journal of Political Economy (semimonthly), Philadelphia...	1833–1835	2
The Friend, Philadelphia (September 28, 1844, to September 19, 1846, lacking)....	1842–1847	3
Komstok's Fonelik Magazin (monthly), Philadelphia...........................	1846–1848	2
The Press (daily), Philadelphia (January to June, 1879, July to December, 1880, lacking).............	1857 1873–1880	5
Godey's Lady's Book and Magazine (monthly), Philadelphia.....................	1864	2
Printer's Circular (monthly, incomplete), Philadelphia.........................	1867–1875	3
The Proof Sheet (incomplete), Philadelphia..................................	1870–1878	3
The American Naturalist, Philadelphia, *see* Salem, Mass.		
Lossing's American Historical Record, Philadelphia...........................	1872–1874	3
Potter's American Monthly Illustrated Magazine, Philadelphia.................	1876,1877	2
Lippincott's Monthly Magazine, Philadelphia................................	1877	2
Sunday School Times, Scholars' Quarterly, Philadelphia.......................	1878–1880	2
Sunday School Times, Philadelphia (1881, 1882, 1887, 1888, lacking)...........	1878–1894	13
Progress, Philadelphia..	1878–1885	7
Public Ledger (daily), Philadelphia (April to July, 1880, lacking).............	1879–1884	31
Faith and Works (monthly), Philadelphia....................................	1879–1891	11
Naturalist's Leisure Hour (monthly), Philadelphia............................	1880–1894	14
Dye's Government Counterfeit Detector, Philadelphia (incomplete)............	1882–1892	5
The Microscopical Bulletin and Science News (bimonthly, incomplete), Philadelphia........	1886–1893	2
Book News (monthly), Philadelphia...	1887–1894	7
The Building Association and Home Journal (monthly), Philadelphia...........	1887–1889	3
The Book Mart (monthly), Philadelphia.....................................	1887–1890	3
American Catholic Researches (quarterly), Philadelphia.......................	1888–1894	7
Paper and Press (monthly), Philadelphia.....................................	1888–1894	14
Weekly Press, Philadelphia...	1889	1
Food, Home, and Garden, Philadelphia......................................	1889–1894	5
The Sugar Beet (quarterly and bimonthly), Philadelphia......................	1890–1894	5
Annals of the American Academy of Political and Social Science (bimonthly), Philadelphia....	1890–1894	4
Sunday School Missionary (monthly), Philadelphia...........................	1891–1894	3
Farm and Fireside, Philadelphia, *see* Springfield, Ohio.		
University Extension (monthly), Philadelphia................................	1891–1894	3
Lithographer's Journal (monthly), Philadelphia..............................	1892–1894	6
Pennsylvania Nationalist, Philadelphia......................................	1893,1894	1
The Conservator (monthly), Philadelphia....................................	1893,1894	1
The Stenographer (monthly), Philadelphia...................................	1893,1894	3
Pennsylvania School Journal (monthly), Lancaster............................	1863,1864	1
The Phonetic Friend (monthly), Montrose...................................	1879,1880	1
Eadle Keatah Toh—The Morning Star, and The Red Man (monthly), Carlisle.....	1880–1894	12
The Chautauquan (monthly), Meadville.....................................	1882,1883	1
Historical Register (monthly), Harrisburg...................................	1883,1884	2

BOUND NEWSPAPERS, ETC., OF OTHER STATES AND COUNTRIES—Continued.

NEWSPAPERS.	Years.	No. vols.
PENNSYLVANIA—*Concluded.*		
The Farmers' Friend, Mechanicsburg....................................	1886–1894	9
Zion's Watch Tower (monthly and biweekly), Pittsburg and Allegheny (1886–1891 lacking)......................	1881–1894	6
American Manufacturer and Iron World, Pittsburg..........................	1887–1894	13
Stowell's Petroleum Reporter (monthly, incomplete), Pittsburg..................	1890–1894	2
The Christian Statesman, Pittsburg and Allegheny............................	1892–1894	2
Poultry Keeper (monthly), Parkesburg and Philadelphia.......................	1887–1894	7
Pennsylvania, miscellaneous...		1
RHODE ISLAND (11).		
Journal of the Rhode Island Institute of Instruction (semimonthly), Providence..	1845,1846	1
Newport Historical Magazine, Rhode Island Historical Magazine, and Magazine of New England History (quarterly), Newport	1880–1893	10
SOUTH CAROLINA (1).		
The Centenary, Florence...	1891,1892	1
SOUTH DAKOTA (10).		
Pierre Daily Capital...	1890–1894	10
TENNESSEE (6).		
Bulletin of the State Board of Health (monthly), Nashville (July, 1886, to July, 1889, lacking)..	1885–1894	6
TEXAS (38).		
Live-Stock Journal, Fort Worth	1882–1894	12
Texas Wool Grower, Fort Worth...	1882–1884	2
El Paso Times (daily)...	1883	1
Texas Review (monthly), Austin *..	1886	1
The Canadian Free Press..	1887–1889	2
The Canadian Crescent..	1883,1889	1
Southern Mercury, Dallas...	1888–1894	6
Texas School Journal (monthly), Dallas...................................	1892–1894	2
Velasco Daily Times..	1891,1892	1
Velasco Weekly Times..	1891–1893	2
Houston Daily Post...	1892–1894	5
Houston Weekly Post.	1892	1
The La Porte Chronicle...	1893,1894	2
UTAH.		
The Irrigation Age, Salt Lake (see Denver).		
VERMONT (11).		
Vermont Historical Gazetteer (occasional), Burlington, Claremont [N. H.], Montpelier, and Brandon...	1867–1891	5
The Woman's Magazine (monthly), Brattleboro............................	1885–1890	5
The National Bulletin (monthly), Brattleboro............................	1886,1887	1
VIRGINIA (11).		
The Richmond Standard..	1881,1882	1
Southern Workman and Hampton School Record..........................	1885–1894	10
WASHINGTON (3).		
Whatcom Reveille...	1884–1886	2
The Beacon, Dungeness and Port Angeles................................	1892,1893	1
WEST VIRGINIA (3).		
The Mountain Echo, Keyser..	1889,1890	2
Southern Historical Magazine (monthly), Charleston.....................	1892	1
WISCONSIN (14).		
Wisconsin Journal of Education (monthly), Madison......................	1863–1865	2
Wisconsin State Journal, Madison......................................	1878–1889	11
Western Farmer and Wisconsin Grange Bulletin, Madison.................	1886	1
WYOMING (12).		
Laramie Boomerang (daily)...	1889–1894	11
The Wyoming Commonwealth, Cheyenne................................	1890,1891	1
AUSTRALIA (3).		
Agricultural Gazette of New South Wales, Sydney........................	1890,1891	2
Alliance Record, Melbourne..	1891	1
BRAZIL (3).		
Revista Agricola do Imperial Instituto Fluminense de Agricultura (quarterly), Rio de Janeiro...	1888–1893	4

* Not found.

BOUND NEWSPAPERS, ETC., OF OTHER STATES AND COUNTRIES—Concluded.

NEWSPAPERS.	Years.	No. vols.
CANADA (11).		
Canadian Illustrated Shorthand Writer (monthly), Toronto......................	1880,1881	1
Acadian Scientist (monthly), Wolfville, N. S......	1883	1
The Cosmopolitan Shorthand Writer and Shorthander (monthly), Toronto (1881 to 1883, scattering)..	1885-1887	2
Fonetic Herald (monthly), Port Hope, and The Herald, Toronto...................	1885-1889	5
The Week, Toronto...........	1888,1889	1
The Owl (monthly), Toronto................................ :........	1892-1894	2
ENGLAND (109).		
The Monthly Magazine or British Register, London (reprinted in Boston, scattering numbers, 1823 to 1840)..	1815,1816	2
British Quarterly Review, London (January, 1815, January, 1854)................	1815,1854	2
Diplomatic Review, London, vols. 1-25..	1858-1877	25
London Illustrated News..	1842-1879	69
The Phonographic Correspondent, London..........	1850	1
The Latter-Day Saints' Millennial Star (monthly), Liverpool....................	1851	1
The Fonografer (monthly), Bath..	1857,1858	1
The Fonetic Journal, London...	1879	1
The Labour Standard, London..	1881-1885	4
Forestry, a magazine for the country (monthly), Edinburgh and London.........	1883-1885	3
FRANCE (120).		
Bulletin de la Societe Protectrice des Animaux (monthly), Paris.................	1878-1883	5
Bulletin de la Societe de Geographie (monthly and quarterly), Paris............	1878-1894	20
Societe de Geographie compte rendu des Seances de la Commission Centrale (semimonthly), Paris...	1882-1894	13
Chronique de la Societe des Gens de Lettres (monthly), Paris (incomplete)......	1878-1893	15
Bulletin Mensuel de la Societe des Gens de Lettres, Paris	1878-1880	1
Bulletin des Seances de la Societe Nationale d'Agriculture de France (monthly), Paris (incomplete)..	1879-1894	15
Bulletin de la Societe de Geographie Commerciale de Paris (quarterly)..........	1888-1894	6
Bulletin Ministere de l'Agriculture, Paris	1889	1
Recueil des Publications de la Societe Havraise d'Etudes Diverses (quarterly; 1877, 1878, 1886, lacking)..	1876-1893	11
Societe de Geographie Commerciale de Havre (bimonthly)......................	1890-1894	5
Revue Savoisienne, Journal Publie par la Societe Florimontane d'Annecy (quarterly)..	1878-1880 1889 1890,1893	2 3
Bulletin de la Societe de Geographie Commerciale de Nantes (quarterly)........	1890,1893	3
Bulletin de la Societe de Geographie de Rochefort (quarterly)...................	1889,1890	1
Union Geographie du Nord de la France, Siege a Douai (quarterly)...............	1889-1893	5
Bulletin de la Societe de Geographie de Lyon (bimonthly; incomplete)...........	1890-1894	3
Bulletin de la Societe de Geographie de Toulouse (bimonthly; May to August lacking)..	1890-1894	5
Societie de Geographie de l' Est, Bulletin trimestriel, Nancy....................	1890-1894	5
Societie Languedocienne de Geographie, Bulletin (quarterly), Montpellier (incomplete)..	1890-1893	4
MEXICO (7).		
La Revista Agricola (bimonthly), City of Mexico...............................	1891-1894	4
El Hijo del Ahuizote, City of Mexico...	1891-1894	3
Miscellaneous foreign newspapers..		1

BOUND NEWSPAPERS, ETC.. OF OTHER STATES AND COUNTRIES—Concluded.

NEWSPAPERS.	Years.	No. vols.
CANADA (11).		
Canadian Illustrated Shorthand Writer (monthly), Toronto.	1880,1881	1
Acadian Scientist (monthly), Wolfville, N. S.	1883	1
The Cosmopolitan Shorthand Writer and Shorthander (monthly), Toronto (1881 to 1883, scattering).	1885–1887	2
Fonetic Herald (monthly), Port Hope, and The Herald, Toronto.	1885–1889	5
The Week, Toronto.	1888,1889	1
The Owl (monthly), Toronto.	1892–1894	2
ENGLAND (109).		
The Monthly Magazine or British Register, London (reprinted in Boston, scattering numbers, 1823 to 1840).	1815,1816	2
British Quarterly Review, London (January, 1815, January, 1854).	1815,1854	2
Diplomatic Review, London, vols. 1–25.	1838–1877	25
London Illustrated News.	1842–1879	69
The Phonographic Correspondent, London.	1850	1
The Latter-Day Saints' Millennial Star (monthly), Liverpool.	1851	1
The Fonografer (monthly), Bath.	1857,1858	1
The Fonetic Journal, London.	1879	1
The Labour Standard, London.	1881–1885	4
Forestry, a magazine for the country (monthly), Edinburgh and London.	1883–1885	3
FRANCE (120).		
Bulletin de la Societe Protectrice des Animaux (monthly), Paris.	1878–1883	5
Bulletin de la Societe de Geographie (monthly and quarterly), Paris.	1878–1894	20
Societe de Geographie compte rendu des Seances de la Commission Centrale (semimonthly), Paris.	1882–1894	13
Chronique de la Societe des Gens de Lettres (monthly), Paris (incomplete).	1878–1893	15
Bulletin Mensuel de la Societe des Gens de Lettres, Paris	1878–1880	1
Bulletin des Seances de la Societe Nationale d'Agriculture de France (monthly), Paris (incomplete).	1879–1894	15
Bulletin de la Societe de Geographie Commerciale de Paris (quarterly).	1888–1894	6
Bulletin Ministere de l'Agriculture, Paris	1889	1
Recueil des Publications de la Societe Havraise d'Etudes Diverses (quarterly; 1877, 1878, 1886, lacking).	1876–1893	11
Societe de Geographie Commerciale de Havre (bimonthly).	1890–1894	5
Revue Savoisienne, Journal Publie par la Societe Florimontane d'Annecy (quarterly).	1878–1880	2
Bulletin de la Societe de Geographie Commerciale de Nantes (quarterly).	1889 / 1890,1893	3
Bulletin de la Societe de Geographie de Rochefort (quarterly)	1890,1890	1
Union Geographie du Nord de la France. Siege a Douai (quarterly).	1889–1893	5
Bulletin de la Societe de Geographie de Lyon (bimonthly; incomplete).	1890–1894	3
Bulletin de la Societie de Geographie de Toulouse (bimonthly; May to August lacking).	1890–1894	5
Societie de Geographie de l' Est, Bulletin trimestriel, Nancy.	1890–1894	5
Societie Languedocienne de Geographie, Bulletin (quarterly), Montpellier (incomplete).	1890–1893	4
MEXICO (7).		
La Revista Agricola (bimonthly), City of Mexico.	1891–1894	4
El Hijo del Ahuizote, City of Mexico.	1891–1894	3
Miscellaneous foreign newspapers.		1

KANSAS NEWSPAPERS.

The following is a list of the newspapers and periodicals published in Kansas June 1, 1895. The regular issues of these, with very few exceptions, are now being received by the Kansas State Historical Society. They are the free gift of the publishers to the state. They are bound in annual or semiannual volumes, and are preserved in the library of the Society in the state capitol for the free use of the people. They number 788 in all. Of these 42 are dailies, 634 weeklies, 4 semiweeklies, 90 monthlies, 6 semimonthlies, 3 bimonthlies, 4 quarterlies, 2 occasional. They come from all of the 106 counties of Kansas, and record the history of the people of all the communities and neighborhoods.

ALLEN COUNTY.

The Humboldt Union, republican; W. T. McElroy, editor and proprietor, Humboldt.

The Humboldt Herald, democratic; S. A. D. Cox, editor and publisher, Humboldt.

The Iola Register, republican; Chas F. Scott, editor and publisher, Iola.

The Friend-Herald, populist; Chris. S. Ritter, editor, Iola.

The Western Sentinel, democratic; J. B. Goshorn, editor, Iola.

Southern Kansas Horticulturist (monthly); L. M. Pancoast, editor, E. S. Davis, publisher, Iola.

The Moran Herald, republican; J. E. Smith and Jay Matthews, editors and publishers, Moran.

The Trio-News, independent; E. A. Jordan, publisher, Savonburg.

ANDERSON COUNTY.

The Republican-Plaindealer, republican; Howard M. Brooke, editor and publisher, Garnett.

The Garnett Journal, democratic; Richardson & Milligan, proprietors, Garnett.

The Garnett Eagle, republican; W. A. Trigg, editor and proprietor, Garnett.

Kansas Agitator, populist; W. O. and Anna Champe, editors, J. M. Alexander and W. H. Ambrose, associate editors, Garnett.

Presbyterian Bulletin (monthly); Rev. E. L. Combs, editor, Garnett.

The Greeley News, independent; Ernest McClure and C. H. Lyon, editors and publishers, Greeley.

The Greeley Graphic, populist; Horace Grant, editor, Greeley.

The Light (monthly), prohibition; Prohibition Club, publishers, Thomas Mills, president, W. H. McClure, vice president and editor, Greeley.

The Pastor's Visit (monthly), religious; Rev. H. I. Dolson, editor, Greeley.

The Free Press, republican; C. H. Johnson, editor and publisher, Colony.

The Gleaner, independent; L. D. Russell, editor and manager, Colony.

The Westphalia Times, democratic; Ancil F. Hatten, editor, Westphalia.

The Kincaid Dispatch, republican; J. E. Scruggs, jr., editor, Scruggs Bros., publishers, Kincaid.

The Kincaid News, republican; R. R. Gillham, editor, Gillham Bros. (R. R. and E. L.), proprietors, Kincaid.

The Telephone, neutral; Telephone Publishing Company, Selma.

ATCHISON COUNTY.

The Atchison Champion (daily and weekly), republican; Andrew J. Felt, editor and proprietor, Atchison.

Atchison Patriot (daily and weekly), democratic; J. L. A. Anderson, editor and publisher, Atchison.

The Atchison Globe (daily and weekly), republican; Edgar W. Howe, editor and proprietor, Atchison.

Missouri Valley Farmer, republican; Ed. R. Felt, manager, Atchison.

The College Review (monthly), educational; A. G. Coonrod and C. T. Smith, editors, Atchison.

The Midland (monthly), college; faculty and students, publishers, E. B. Knerr, Sc. D., from faculty, Atchison.

Abbey Student (bimonthly), college; Wm. H. McCormick, editor in chief, Wm. L. Moore, editor, P. E. Boesen, business manager, Atchison.

Muscotah Record, independent; James S. Martin and Guy L. Stoddard, proprietors, Muscotah.

The New Leaf, republican; M. C. Klingman, editor, Mrs. Ina L. Klingman, associate editor, Effingham.

BARBER COUNTY.

Medicine Lodge Cresset, republican; L. M. Axline, editor and publisher, Medicine Lodge.

The Barber County Index, populist; C. C. Painter and Clayton Herr, editors and business managers, Medicine Lodge.

The Kiowa Journal, republican; H. E. Glenn, editor and proprietor, Kiowa.

The Kiowa Review, democratic; M. A. Hull, editor and manager, Kiowa.

BARTON COUNTY.

The Great Bend Register, republican; A. J. and Earl M. Hoisington, editors and proprietors, Joe H. Borders, assistant editor, Great Bend.

Great Bend Tribune, republican; C. P. Townsley, editor, Great Bend.

Evening News (daily), neutral; C. P. Townsley, editor, Great Bend.

Barton County Democrat, democratic; Will. E. Stoke, publisher and proprietor, Ella M. Stoke, city editor, Great Bend.

The Barton Beacon, populist; D. T. Armstrong, editor and publisher, Great Bend.

The Kansas Rebekah (monthly), society; Joe H. Borders, editor and publisher, Adelaide Schmidt Wayland and Minnie W. Brady, associate editors, Great Bend.

Ellinwood Advocate, democratic; W. D. Wilkinson, editor and proprietor, Ellinwood.

The Hoisington Dispatch, republican; Ira H. Clark, editor, Hoisington.

The Claflin Leader, republican; Joseph W. A. Cooke, editor, Claflin.

BOURBON COUNTY.

The Fort Scott Monitor (daily and weekly), republican; W. C. Lansdon, editor, Monitor Company, proprietors, Fort Scott.

Fort Scott Tribune (daily and weekly), democratic; Geo. W. Martin, editor and proprietor, George W. Marble, city editor, Fort Scott.)

The Lantern, populist; J. Herrick, editor and manager, Lantern Publishing Company, Fort Scott.

The Normal Journal (monthly), educational; D. E. Sanders and J. E. Monroe, editors, Fort Scott.

Western Medical Journal (monthly), medical; J. B. Carver, M.D., editor, H. V. Rice, manager, Western Medical Journal Company, publishers, Fort Scott.

The Bronson Pilot, neutral; H. E. Conflans, editor and proprietor, Bronson.

Fulton Independent, independent, A. W. Felter, editor and proprietor, Fulton.

Mapleton Dispatch, neutral; A. F. McCarty, editor and publisher, Mapleton.

BROWN COUNTY.

The Hiawatha Kansas World, republican; Ewing Herbert, editor and publisher, Hiawatha.

The Kansas Democrat, democratic; G. W. and W. P. Harrington, editors and proprietors, Hiawatha.

The Hiawatha Journal, populist; Ben. F. Hildebrand, editor and publisher, Hiawatha.

The Delta of Sigma Nu (bimonthly), college fraternity; Clarence E. Woods, editor, Richmond, Ky., Harrington Printing Company, Hiawatha.

The Sunflower Magazine (monthly), Sons of Veterans; Grant W. Harrington, editor, Hiawatha.

Kansas Newspaper World (monthly), neutral; Ewing Herbert, editor and proprietor, Hiawatha.

Horton Headlight, republican; Lucian H. Smyth, editor, Horton.

Horton Commercial, democratic; Clyde McManigal, editor and publisher, Horton.

Fairview Enterprise, independent; S. O. Groesbeck, editor and proprietor, Fairview.

The Courier, republican; The Fairview Publishing Company, publishers, Fairview.

Everest Enterprise, independent; Charles R. Johnson, editor and publisher, Everest.

The Morrill News, republican; Morrill.

The Morrill Vindicator, independent; T. K. Sawyer, editor, S. A. Haldeman and A. H. Eichelberger, publishers and proprietors, Morrill.

The Robinson Index, independent; C. R. Arries, editor, Robinson.

Powhattan Post, independent; H. J. Calnan, editor and publisher, Powhattan.

BUTLER COUNTY.

Walnut Valley Times (daily and weekly), republican; Alvah Shelden, editor, Geo. F. Fullinwider, local editor, El Dorado.

El Dorado Republican, republican; T. B. Murdock, editor and proprietor. S. S. Smith, business manager, El Dorado.

The Industrial Advocate, populist; J. D. Botkin, editor, W. H. Biddle, publisher, El Dorado.

The Visitor (monthly), religious; Rev. W. W. Curtis, Rev. John E. Earp, editors, El Dorado.

Augusta Journal, republican; Will. H. Cady, editor and proprietor, Mrs. W. H. Cady, local editor, Augusta.

The Augusta Gazette, democratic, Timothy Sexton, editor and proprietor, Augusta.

The Augusta Press, republican; John Bunyan Adams, editor, Augusta.

Douglass Tribune, republican; J. M. Satterthwaite, editor and proprietor, Douglass.

The Weekly Herald, republican; E. Davis, jr., editor and proprietor, White Water.

The Leon Indicator, republican; C. R. Noe, editor and proprietor, Leon.

CHASE COUNTY.

Chase County Leader, republican; W. A. Morgan, editor and proprietor, Cottonwood Falls.

Chase County Courant, democratic; W. E. Timmons, editor and proprietor, Cottonwood Falls.

The Reveille, populist; W. S. Romigh, editor and general manager, Reveille Publishing and Printing Company, Cottonwood Falls.

Strong City Derrick, democratic; J. B. Wilcox, editor and proprietor, Strong City.

The Pointer, A. B. Emerson, editor, J. Fred. Whiting, publisher, Cedar Point.

CHAUTAUQUA COUNTY.

The Weekly Times-Star, republican; Adrian Reynolds, editor, F. G. Kenesson, business manager, Sedan.

The Sedan Lance, populist; G. V. Johnson, editor, G. W. Ifland, business manager, Ifland & Johnson, publishers, Sedan.

Cedar Vale Commercial, republican; W. M. Jones, editor and proprietor, Cedar Vale.

The Chanticleer (monthly), poultry journal; Jasper Jay Stone, M. D., editor and publisher, Niotaze.

CHEROKEE COUNTY.

Columbus Star-Courier, democratic; J. Norman Cook and H. L. Gongwer, editors and publishers, N. T. Allison, associate editor, W. P. Eddy, J. M. Cook, and H. L. Gongwer, proprietors, Columbus.

The Columbus Advocate (daily and weekly), republican; J. M. McNay and Asa Lea, editors and publishers, Columbus.

Modern Light, populist; L. L. Hopkins, editor and manager, Modern Light Publishing Company, publishers, Columbus.

The Galena Republican, republican; L. C. Weldy, editor and proprietor, Galena.

The Galena Times, independent; E. E. Stevens, editor, The Galena Publishing Company, Galena.

The Galena Post, republican; W. G. Stevens, editor and proprietor, Galena.

Baxter Springs News, independent; M. H. Gardner and Charles L. Smith, editors and publishers, Baxter Springs.

Cherokee County Republican, republican; F. N. Newhouse, editor and proprietor, Baxter Springs.

Weir City Tribune, democratic; Horace Hayden, editor and publisher, Weir City.

The Weir Journal, republican; E. F. Caton, editor and publisher, Weir City.

Weir City Daily Sun, republican; J. W. Campbell, editor and proprietor, Weir City.

The Scammon Miner, democratic-populist; Phil. L. Keener, editor and publisher, Scammon.

CHEYENNE COUNTY.

The Kansas Eagle, populist; Geo. Lawless and D. L Loofbourrow, editors, W. K. Loofbourrow, manager, St. Francis.

Cheyenne County Rustler, republican: C. E. Dennison, editor and publisher, St. Francis.

CLARK COUNTY.

Clark County Clipper, populist; H. C. Mayse, editor and publisher, Ashland.

The Ashland Weekly Journal, republican; M. G. Stevenson, editor, Journal Company, publishers, Ashland.

—9

CLAY COUNTY.

The Clay Centre Dispatch, populist; Chas. A. Southwick, editor and publisher, Clay Centre.

The Times, republican; D. A. Valentine, editor and publisher, Clay Centre.

Uncle Sam's Live-Stock Journal, monthly; J. H. Morgan, editor and proprietor, Morganville.

Wakefield Advertiser, democratic; J. J. L. Jones, editor; F. F. Sheppard, business manager, Wakefield.

The Morganville Star, neutral; J. W. Mahaffey, editor and publisher, Morganville.

The Clifton News, republican; L. A. Palmer, editor and publisher, Clifton.

CLOUD COUNTY.

The Concordia Empire, republican; T. A. Sawhill, editor and publisher, Concordia.

Concordia Blade, populist; J. M. Hagaman, editor, Blade Publishing Company, publishers, Concordia.

The Concordia Daylight, republican; J. E. Marshall and Seward A. Jones, editors and publishers, Concordia.

The Kansan, populist; Frank Honeywell, editor and publisher, Concordia.

District School (monthly), educational; Clinton E. Rose, editor and publisher, Concordia.

The Clyde Herald, republican; J. B. and Mary L. Rupe, editors and publishers, Clyde.

The Clyde Argus, republican; Chas. A. Morley, editor and publisher, Clyde.

The Farmers' Voice, populist; J. J. Henley, editor and publisher, Clyde.

The Kansas Sunflower, local; F. O. Ayers, editor, Sunflower Publishing Company, publishers, Clyde.

The Kansas Optimist, independent; Mrs. Mary L. Burton, editor and publisher, Jamestown.

The Glasco Sun, independent; L. E. Frankforther, editor and publisher, Glasco.

COFFEY COUNTY.

The Burlington Republican, republican; C. O. Smith, editor and publisher, Burlington.

The Burlington Independent, democratic; John E. Watrous, editor and publisher, Burlington.

The Burlington Courier, populist; Otto O. Outcalt, editor and publisher, Burlington.

The Jeffersonian, independent; Dan. K. Swearingen, editor and publisher, Burlington.

Le Roy Reporter, democratic; Frank Fockele, editor and publisher, Le Roy.

Waverly Gazette, independent; C. L., Ada C. and P. B. Kendrick, editors and publishers, Waverly.

The Waverly Republican, republican; A. A. Smith, editor and publisher, Waverly.

The Lebo Enterprise, republican; W. P. Evans, editor and publisher, Lebo.

The Gridley Herald, neutral; C. T. Sherwood, editor and publisher, Gridley.

COMANCHE COUNTY.

The Western Star, populist; W. M. Cash, editor and publisher, Coldwater.

COWLEY COUNTY.

The Winfield Courier (daily and weekly), republican; Ed. P. Greer, editor, Courier Printing Company, publishers, Winfield.

The Industrial Free Press, populist; J. C. Bradshaw and J. E. Riley, editors and publishers, Winfield.

The Winfield Sentinel, independent; W. W. Vanpelt, editor, W. W. Vanpelt and G. Lowther, proprietors.

The Public Platform (monthly); John E. Riley & Co., editors and publishers, Winfield.

Christian Herald (monthly), religious; Rev. G. Lowther, editor, Winfield.

Southwestern Collegian (monthly), educational; Viola V. Price, editor, Chas. E. Lowe, business manager, Winfield.

The Kansas Fancier (monthly), poultry, etc.; Chas. J. Forsyth, editor, L. C. Ball and H. T. Cogdal, publishers, Winfield.

The Assembly Herald (monthly), Chautauqua; A. H. Limerick, editor and manager, Q. A. Glass, associate editor, Herald Publishing Company, Winfield.

Republican Traveler (daily and weekly), republican; T. W. Eckert, R. C. Howard & Co., editors and publishers, Arkansas City.

Arkansas Valley Democrat, democratic; T. McIntire, editor, T. McIntire and M. N. Sinnott, publishers, Arkansas City.

Canal City Dispatch, populist; Jesse C. Stanley, editor, publisher, and proprietor, Arkansas City.

The Gate City Journal, republican; E. Mattie Shawhan, editor and publisher, Arkansas City.

The Life Line (monthly), religious; M. La Blaney, editor and publisher, Arkansas City.

Burden Eagle, republican; J. G. Crawford, editor, Eagle Publishing Company, publishers, Burden.

Udall Reporter, neutral; J. A. Reed, editor and publisher, Udall.

CRAWFORD COUNTY.

The Girard Press (daily and weekly), republican; E. A. Wasser and D. C. Flint, editors and publishers, Girard.

The Western Herald, populist; H. B. Lucas, editor and publisher, Girard.

Girard World (daily and weekly), independent; Abe Steinberger, editor, World Company, publishers, Girard.

The Cherokee Sentinel, republican; J. F. and H. B. Price, editors and publishers, Cherokee.

Pittsburg Headlight (daily and weekly), republican; William Moore & Son, editors and publishers, Pittsburg.

Pittsburg Kansan, populist; J. C. Buchanan, editor and publisher, Pittsburg.

The Pittsburg Messenger, democratic; W. L. Yancey, editor and proprietor, Pittsburg.

Arcadia News, republican; Benjamin J. Gunn, editor and publisher, Arcadia.

Crawford County Democrat, democratic; J. M. Mahr, editor and publisher, McCune.

The Labor Review, reform; R. D. Oliver, editor and publisher, McCune.

The Walnut Eagle, republican; Lewis Martin, editor and publisher, Walnut.

DECATUR COUNTY.

Oberlin Herald, populist; E. M. Coldren, editor and publisher, Oberlin.

The Eye, republican; C. Borin, editor and publisher, Oberlin.

The Oberlin Opinion, republican; F. W. Casterline, editor and publisher, Oberlin.
The Oberlin Times, democratic; W. S. Langmade, editor and publisher, Oberlin.
The Norcatur Register, republican; H. H. Hoskins, editor and publisher, Norcatur.
Jennings Echo, republican; George W. Shook, editor and publisher, Jennings.

DICKINSON COUNTY.

The Abilene Weekly Chronicle, republican; George Burroughs, editor and publisher, Abilene.
Abilene Reflector (daily and weekly), republican; Chas. M. Harger, editor, Richard Waring, business manager, Reflector Publishing Company, publishers, Abilene.
The Abilene Dispatch, populist; A. S. Phillips, editor and publisher, Abilene.
The Dickinson County News, democratic; S. K. Strother and B. L. Strother, editors and publishers, Abilene.
The Abilene Monitor, populist; W. D. Struble, editor, Monitor Publishing Company, publishers, Abilene.
Evangelical Visitor (semimonthly), religious; H. Davidson, editor, Abilene.
The Gospel Message (monthly), religious; Geo. S. Fisher, president, Gospel Union Publishing Company, publishers, Abilene.
The School and Home (monthly), educational; D. F. Shirk, editor and publisher, Abilene.
Solomon Sentinel, republican; E. B. Burnett, editor and publisher, Solomon City.
The Hope Crescent, republican; Crescent Publishing Company, publishers, Hope.
The Western News, republican; Burton & Ross, editors and publishers, Hope.
Enterprise Journal, republican; T. A. Borman and R. O. Shadinger, editors and publishers, Enterprise.
Central Expositor (monthly), religious; J. A. Weller, editor, Enterprise.
The Integral Coöperator (occasional); C. F. Lindstrom, editor, Kansas-Sinaloa Investment Company, publishers, Enterprise.
The Christian Endeavorer (monthly), religious; Wilson C. Wheeler, editor and publisher, Chapman.
Chapman Standard, republican; J. C. and D. C. Russell, editors and publishers, Chapman.
Herington Times, republican; A. M. and B. C. Crary, editors and publishers, Herington.
The Herington Signal, republican; James B. Gallagher and Clarence Perry, editors and publishers, Herington.
The Dillon Republican (amateur), republican; Joseph W. Murray, editor and publisher, Dillon.

DONIPHAN COUNTY.

The Weekly Kansas Chief, republican; Sol. Miller, editor and proprietor, Troy.
The Troy Times, democratic; J. M. Halligan, editor and publisher, Troy.
The Severance News, independent; P. L. Gray, editor and proprietor; P. L. Gray and L. P. Johnson, publishers, Severance.
University Nuncio (monthly) educational; University Press, publishers, Highland.
Highland Vidette, republican; H. S. Hogue, editor and publisher, Highland.
White Cloud Globe, republican; Frank Newlin, editor and publisher, White Cloud.
The Leona Sun, independent; E. C. Mailler, editor and publisher, Leona.
The Denton Wheel, independent; C. E. Williamson, editor and publisher, Denton.

DOUGLAS COUNTY.

Lawrence Journal (daily and weekly), republican; O. E. Learnard, C. S. Finch, editors, Journal Company, publishers, Lawrence.

The Lawrence World (daily and weekly), republican; J. L. Brady, editor, W. O. Simons, associate editor, World Publishing Company, proprietors, Lawrence.

The Gazette (daily and weekly), democratic; Frank L. Webster, editor, Gazette Publishing Company, Lawrence.

Lawrence Germania (German), independent; Eduard Grün, editor and publisher, Lawrence.

The Jeffersonian, populist; E. Martindale, editor and proprietor, Lawrence.

The University Review (monthly), W. M. Lyon, editor in chief, C. T. Southwick, managing editor, C. H. Lease and H. T. Myers, business managers, Kansas State University Publishing Company, Lawrence.

The Student's Journal, college; E. T. Hackney, editor in chief, Stanton Olinger, business manager, Lawrence.

The University Courier, Rolla R. Mitchell, editor, John A. Edwards, managing editor, L. E. Thrasher and W. T. Perry, business managers, Courier Company, publishers, Lawrence.

The Kansas University Quarterly, scientific; W. H. Carruth, managing editor, university, publishers, Lawrence.

Kansas University Lawyer, faculty and students of law school; Galen Nichols, editor, Jno. Little, managing editor, Journal Company, printers and publishers, Lawrence.

The Kansas Churchman (monthly), religious; Rev. W. W. Ayres, editor and publisher, Lawrence.

The Select Friend (monthly), secret society; J. S. Boughton, editor and publisher, Lawrence.

The Western Economist (monthly), sociology; W. H. T. Wakefield, editor and publisher, Lawrence.

The Baker University Index (monthly), college; C. B. Dalton, editor, J. F. Roach, business manager, Index Publishing Company, Baldwin.

The Baker Beacon, college; J. L. Taylor, editor, W. F. Denious and E. T. Pendleton, business managers, Baker Beacon Company, publishers, Baldwin.

The Baldwin Ledger, republican; W. C. Markham, editor, Ledger Publishing Company, publishers, Baldwin.

The Eudora News, independent; Geo. C. Brune, editor and publisher, Eudora.

The Lecompton Sun, democratic; W. R. Smith, editor and publisher, Lecompton.

The College Oracle (monthly), college; Lane University faculty, publishers, Lecompton.

EDWARDS COUNTY.

The Kinsley Graphic, populist; J. M. Lewis, jr., editor and publisher, Kinsley.

Kinsley Mercury, republican; F. D. Smith, editor, A. E. Geer, manager, Kinsley.

ELK COUNTY.

The Howard Courant, republican; Asa and Tom. E. Thompson, editors and publishers, Howard.

Elk County Citizen, populist; F. C. Flory, editor, S. S. Logan, business manager, Howard.

Grenola Chief, neutral; Geo. C. Thompson, editor and publisher, Grenola.

The Longton Gleaner, republican; Ed. T. Chapman, editor and publisher, Longton.

The Moline Republican, republican; Geo. C. Armstrong, editor and publisher, Moline.

ELLIS COUNTY.

Hays City Sentinel, republican; W. P. Montgomery, editor and publisher, Hays City.

Free Press, populist; Harry Freese, editor and publisher, Hays City.

The Republican, republican; Geo. P. Griffith, editor and publisher, Hays City.

The Ellis Review-Headlight, republican; Frank J. Brettle, editor and publisher, Ellis.

ELLSWORTH COUNTY.

Ellsworth Reporter, republican; George Huycke, editor, publisher, and proprietor, Ellsworth.

Ellsworth Messenger, democratic; Frank S. Foster, editor and manager, Ellsworth.

The Wilson Echo, republican; S. A. Coover, editor, S. A. Coover and C. S. Hutchison, proprietors, Wilson.

Hollyrood Sun, independent; D. B. Downey, editor and publisher, Hollyrood.

FINNEY COUNTY.

The Garden City Sentinel, democratic; E. L. Stephenson, editor and publisher, Garden City.

Garden City Herald, republican; S. G. and Hamer Norris, editors and publishers, Garden City.

Garden City Imprint, republican; D. A. Mims, editor, D. A. Mims and E. N. Keep, publishers, Garden City.

The Irrigation Champion (monthly); A. W. Stubbs, editor and publisher, Garden City.

The Spectator, juvenile; Messrs. Seeds, Wolf & Shanklin, editors, Garden City.

Ravanna Chieftain, populist; F. C. Thomas, editor and manager, Eminence.

FORD COUNTY.

The Globe-Republican, republican; S. H. Connaway and C. P. Markley, editors and publishers, Dodge City.

The Dodge City Democrat, democratic; W. F. Petillon, editor and publisher, Dodge City.

The Ford County Leader, populist; J. E. Lucas, editor and publisher, Dodge City.

The College Advance (monthly), educational; Rev. E. H. Vaughan, editor and publisher, Dodge City.

FRANKLIN COUNTY.

Ottawa Journal and Triumph, populist; L. L. Porter, editor and lessee, C. J. Wilson, business manager, Ottawa.

The Ottawa Republican (daily and weekly), republican; W. H. Finch, editor and publisher, Ottawa.

The Ottawa Herald, democratic; John B. Kessler, editor and publisher, Ottawa.

Ottawa Campus (monthly) college; G. W. Beach, editor in chief, L. R. Foote, business manager, Ottawa.

Ottawa Chautauqua Assembly Herald (monthly), educational; Rev. D. C. Milner, Mrs. N. L. Prentis, and Dr. J. L. Hurlbut, editors, Ottawa.

The Ottawa Bulletin (triweekly), George D. and L. E. Rathbun, editors and publishers, Ottawa.

The High School Opinion (monthly), educational; Frank B. Parker, editor in chief, Samuel G. Tracy, business manager, Ottawa.

The Pomona Enterprise, independent; T. L., L. S. and A. R. Newcomb, editors and publishers, Pomona.

Williamsburg Star, neutral; Mrs. E. McCurdy, editor and publisher, Williamsburg.

The Lane Light, literary; Roy J. Bell, editor and publisher, Lane.

The Lane Graphic, neutral; Horace Grant, editor and publisher, Lane.

Wellsville Globe, neutral; E. P. Mills & Co., editors and publishers, Wellsville.

GEARY COUNTY.

The Junction City Union, republican; W. C. Moore, editor, John Montgomery, E. M. Gilbert, and W. C. Moore, publishers, Junction City.

Junction City Tribune, populist; Charles S. Davis, editor and proprietor, Junction City.

Junction City Republican, republican; Geo. A. Clark, editor and publisher, Junction City.

The Junction City Sentinel (daily and weekly), democratic; A. W. Chabin, editor and proprietor, Junction City.

GOVE COUNTY.

Gove County Leader, populist; Thomas Kirtley, editor and publisher, Gove City.

Gove County Gazette and Echo, republican; J. L. Cook & Sons, editors and publishers, Gove City.

Quinter Republican, republican; A. K. Trimmer, editor and proprietor, Quinter.

GRAHAM COUNTY.

People's Reveille, populist; —— Inlow and —— Emmons, publishers, Hill City.

Hill City Republican, republican; W. H. Hill, editor and proprietor, Hill City.

Hill City Democrat, democratic; F. P. and B. McGill, editors, publishers, and proprietors, Hill City.

GRANT COUNTY.

Grant County Republican, republican; H. E. Evans, editor and publisher, Ulysses.

GRAY COUNTY.

The New West, republican; John H. Whiteside, editor and publisher, Cimarron.

The Jacksonian, democratic; Ellis S. and C. B. Garten, editors and publishers, Cimarron.

Ingalls Union, republican; John Harper, editor and proprietor, Ingalls.

GREELEY COUNTY.

Greeley County Republican, republican; J. U. Brown and C. K. Gerard, editors and publishers, Tribune.

The Western Homestead (monthly), agricultural; Eugene Tilleux, editor and publisher, Tribune.

The Tribune Leader, populist; H. W. Milford, editor, N. Vannoy and H. W. Milford, publishers, Tribune.

GREENWOOD COUNTY.

The Eureka Herald, republican; Z. Harlan, editor and proprietor, Eureka.

The Democratic Messenger, democratic; Thomas W. Morgan, editor and publisher, Eureka.

The Eureka Times, populist; Charles E. Moore, editor and publisher, Eureka.

The Severyite, republican; C. G. Pierce, editor and publisher, Severy.

The Madison Star, republican; W. D. Smith and S. F. Wicker, editors and publishers, Star Publishing Company, Madison.

The Madison Index, populist; Will. Dungan, editor, Dungan & Yearout, publishers, Madison.

Kansas Advocate, neutral; Paul Wiley, editor and proprietor, Fall River.

The Leader, neutral; A. J. Howell, editor and proprietor, Virgil.

HAMILTON COUNTY.

The Syracuse Journal, democratic; Henry Block, editor and proprietor, Syracuse.

Syracuse Republican, republican, I. J. C. and C. S. Guy, editors and publishers, Syracuse.

The Coolidge Enterprise, neutral; R. H. Dunnington, editor; C. A. Crittenden, manager, Coolidge.

HARPER COUNTY.

The Anthony Republican, republican; F. C. Raney, editor and proprietor, Anthony.

Anthony Journal, republican; J. R. and S. C. Hammond, editors and publishers, Anthony.

The Weekly Bulletin, populist; T. H. W. McDowell and W. L. Hutchinson, editors and publishers, Anthony.

The Harper Sentinel, republican; C. I. Denny, editor and proprietor, Harper.

The Advocate, populist; A. B. Hoffman, editor and publisher, Harper.

Attica Tribune, neutral; Geo. W. and B. V. Kelley, editors and publishers, Attica.

HARVEY COUNTY.

The Newton Republican (daily and weekly), republican; John A. Reynolds, editor and publisher, Newton.

Newton Kansan, republican; Charles H. Kurtz, editor and publisher, Newton.

The Newton Semi-Weekly Journal, democratic; J. B. Fugate, editor and publisher, Newton.

The Halstead Independent, republican; E. J. Bookwalter, editor and publisher, Halstead.

The Sedgwick Pantagraph, independent; Mack. P. Cretcher, editor and publisher, Sedgwick.

The Burrton Graphic, independent; E. J. Bookwalter, editor and publisher, Burrton.

HASKELL COUNTY.

The Santa Fé Monitor, republican; John J. Miller, editor and publisher, Santa Fé. Santa Fé Trail.

HODGEMAN COUNTY.

Western Herald, republican; P. H. Hand, editor and publisher, Jetmore.

The Jetmore Republican, republican; C. E. Roughton, editor, and Q. M. Mack, business manager, Jetmore.

JACKSON COUNTY.

The Holton Recorder, republican; M. M. Beck, editor and proprietor, Holton.

The Holton Weekly Signal, democratic; Thomas A. Fairchild and Samuel Osterhold, editors and proprietors, Holton.

The Tribune, independent; J. Irwin Gabel, editor and publisher, Holton.

Normal Advocate (monthly), educational; E. J. Hoenshel, editor, Holton.

The University Informer (monthly), college, H. G. McKeever, editor and proprietor, Holton.

The Fraternal Aid (monthly), secret society; C. V. Hamm, editor and publisher, Holton.

The Soldier Clipper, republican; Ben. L. and Minnie M. Mickel, editors and publishers, Soldier.

The Wasp, independent; L. H. Pearson, editor and publisher, Netawaka.

The Sun, republican; E. E. Sanders, editor and proprietor, Whiting.

The Circleville Kicker, local; George T. Harrison, editor and publisher, Circleville.

JEFFERSON COUNTY.

The Oskaloosa Independent, republican; F. H. Roberts, editor and publisher, Oskaloosa.

The Oskaloosa Times, populist; Geo. Harman, editor and publisher, Oskaloosa.

Valley Falls New Era, republican; E. P. Karr, editor and publisher, Valley Falls.

The Farmers' Vindicator, populist; N. H. and Colfax Harman, editors and publishers, Valley Falls.

The Winchester Star, republican; W. C. Starr, editor and publisher, Winchester.

The Nortonville News, republican; L. F. Randolph and A. W. Robinson, editors and publishers, Nortonville.

The Royal Neighbor (monthly), secret society; Ira L. Maxson, editor and publisher, Nortonville.

The McLouth Times, republican; A. B. Mills, editor and publisher, McLouth.

The McLouth Tribune, independent; H. C. Stewart, editor, Frank Miller, publisher, McLouth.

The Meriden Tribune, populist; J. W. Cook, editor and publisher, Meriden.

The Meriden Ledger, republican; Chas. E. and Mrs. Laura Prather, editors and publishers, Meriden.

JEWELL COUNTY.

Jewell County Monitor, republican; R. F. Vaughan, editor and proprietor, A. C. Walch, local editor, Mankato.

The Jewell County Review, republican; Chas. A. Robertson, editor, J. F. Thompson, publisher, Mankato.

The Western Advocate, populist; William E. Bush, editor, Western Advocate Printing Company, publishers, Mankato.

Jewell County Republican, republican; W. C. Palmer, editor and proprietor, Jewell City.

Burr Oak Herald, republican; E. A. Ross, editor and publisher, Burr Oak.

Randall Independent, independent; W. A. Huff, editor and publisher, Randall.

JOHNSON COUNTY.

The Olathe Mirror, republican; W. A. Mitchell and John J. Lyons, editors and publishers, Olathe.

The Kansas Patron, grange; George Black, editor, H. C. Livermore, manager, Olathe.

Olathe Weekly Herald, democratic; J. F. Herman, editor and proprietor, Olathe.

The Olathe Tribune, populist; A. E. Macoubrie, general manager, Tribune Publishing Company, Olathe.

The Kansas Star, industrial; J. T. Trickett, editor, Kansas institution for the education of the deaf and dumb, publishers, Olathe.

Our Little Friend; Alfred H. Hubbell, editor, Kansas institution for the education of the deaf and dumb, publishers, Olathe.

Spring Hill New Era, republican; J. W. Sowers, editor and publisher, Spring Hill.

Kansas True Flag, independent; G. R. Hickok, editor and publisher, Gardner.

The Edgerton Gazette, republican; A. A. Smith, editor, Gazette Publishing Company, publishers, Edgerton.

KEARNY COUNTY.

Kearny County Advocate, republican; H. S. Gregory, editor and publisher, Lakin.

The Lakin Index, democratic; L. I. Purcell, editor and proprietor, Lakin.

The Lakin Union, republican; H. S. Gregory, editor and publisher, Lakin.

KINGMAN COUNTY.

The Leader-Courier, republican; Morton Albaugh, editor and publisher, Kingman.

The Kingman Weekly Journal, populist; W. L. Brown, editor, H. H. Isley, business manager, Kingman.

Norwich Courant, independent; N. I. Farris and U. S. Weaver, editors and publishers, Norwich.

KIOWA COUNTY.

The Kiowa County Signal, republican; Will. E. Bolton, editor and proprietor, Greensburg.

Kiowa County Times, populist; C. F. Mingenback, editor, T. C. Eberly, manager, Greensburg Publishing Company, Greensburg.

LABETTE COUNTY.

The Parsons Sun (daily and weekly), republican; H. H. Lusk, editor and publisher, Parsons.

The Parsons Eclipse (daily and weekly), independent; C. A., H. A. and F. F. Lamb, editors and proprietors, Parsons.

Parsons Palladium, democratic; Frank W. Frye, editor and publisher, Parsons.

The Parsons Independent, populist; A. G. Stacey, editor, Independent Publishing Company, Parsons.

The Parsons Weekly Blade (colored), republican; P. D. Skinner, editor in chief. Blade Publishing Company, Parsons.

The Chetopa Advance, republican; J. M. Cavaness, editor and publisher, Chetopa.

The Chetopa Democrat, democratic; J. J. Rambo, editor and publisher, Chetopa.

The Oswego Independent, republican; Mary A. and W. F. McGill, editors and proprietors, Oswego.

Labette County Democrat, democratic; Harry Mills, editor; Democrat Publishing Company, Oswego.

Labette County Times-Statesman, populist; R. B. Claiborne, editor and publisher, Oswego.

The Golden Rod (bimonthly), scientific; Dr. W. S. Newlon, editor and publisher. Oswego.

The Oswego News-Blade, populist; Sim. C. Steinberger, editor and publisher. Oswego.

The Mound Valley Herald, republican; W. F. Thrall, editor and publisher, Mound Valley.

The Wilsonton Journal (monthly), neutral; Mrs. Augustus Wilson, editor and proprietor, Wilsonton.

The White Banner (semimonthly), populist; J. L. Switzer, editor and proprietor, Wilsonton.

The Edna Sun, neutral; W. E. Staige, editor and proprietor, Edna.

The Altamont Gazette, neutral; H. Bristow, editor and publisher, Altamont.

LANE COUNTY.

The Dighton Herald, republican; F. H. Lobdell, editor and publisher, Dighton.

LEAVENWORTH COUNTY.

Leavenworth Times (daily and weekly), republican; D. R. Anthony, editor, publisher, and proprietor, Leavenworth.

The Leavenworth Standard (daily and weekly), democratic; T. A. Hurd, president, Mrs. Frank T. Lynch, secretary, Leavenworth.

Leavenworth Post (daily and weekly), democratic; Chas. F. C. Smith, editor and publisher, Leavenworth.

Art League Chronicle (monthly), art; Mrs. J. A. Lane, editor, Mrs. S. W. Jones, Mrs. G. W. Nelles, and Mrs. E. E. Murphy, business managers, Leavenworth.

The Home Record (monthly), charity; Mrs. C. H. Cushing, editor, Leavenworth.

The Orphans' Friend (monthly), charity; Mrs. John Van Fossen, editor and business manager, Mrs. Mary V. Baker, associate editor, Leavenworth.

The Leavenworth Labor News, populist; Mrs. Eva M. Blackman, editor and proprietor, Leavenworth.

The Labor Chronicle, organ trades and labor council; Wm. A. Doidge, Geo. W. Leek, and Chas. Sproul, committee on publication, Leavenworth.

Journal of the U. S. Cavalry Association (quarterly), military; Capt. W. H. Carter, editor, published by the association, Fort Leavenworth.

The Reveille (semimonthly), Keeley league; Edward A. Trader, editor, E. B. Wheeler, associate editor, Jerre Keller, business manager, National Military Home.

The Tonganoxie Mirror, republican; Wm. Heynen, editor and proprietor, Tonganoxie.

Weekly Sentinel, independent; W. A. Brice, editor and proprietor, Tonganoxie.

LINCOLN COUNTY.

The Lincoln Republican, republican; W. H. Pilcher and W. E. Menoher, editors and publishers, Lincoln.

The Lincoln Beacon, populist; W. S. and Anna C. Wait, editors and publishers, Lincoln.

The Lincoln County Sentinel, democratic; Geo. D. Abel, editor and publisher, Lincoln.

The Sylvan Alert, independent; E. D. Smith and H. V. Jeffers, editors and publishers, Sylvan Grove.

LINN COUNTY.

La Cygne Weekly Journal, republican; C. L. Shrake and J. W. Mitchell, editors and publishers, La Cygne.

Pleasanton Observer, republican; J. Frank Smith, editor and manager, Observer Publishing Company, Pleasanton.

The Pleasanton Herald, populist; J. E. Latimer, editor and publisher, Pleasanton.

Linn County Republic and Mound City Progress, republican; Nev. Campbell, editor and manager, Republic Publishing Company, Mound City.

The Torch of Liberty, populist; Laura L. Lowe, editor, L. L. and E. C. Lowe, publishers, Mound City.

The Blue Mound Sun, republican; J. N. Barnes, editor, J. N. and S. E. Barnes, proprietors, Blue Mound.

Parker Gazette.

LOGAN COUNTY.

The Logan County Banner, populist; U. P. Davis and A. C. Towne, editors, publishers, and proprietors, Russell Springs.

The Winona Clipper, republican; Park R. Mitten, editor and publisher, Winona.

The Oakley Graphic, republican; C. V. Kinney, editor and proprietor, Oakley.

LYON COUNTY.

The Emporia Republican (daily and weekly), republican; C. V. Eskridge, editor and proprietor, Emporia.

The Emporia Gazette (daily and weekly), republican; Will. A. White, editor and publisher, Emporia.

The Emporia Times, populist; P. F. Yearout and M. Q. Starr, editors and publishers, Emporia.

College Life, college; James A. Sankey, editor, Edward P. Shier and Harry H. Pratt, associate editors, Emporia.

State Normal Monthly, college; Pres. A. R. Taylor, editor, Emporia.

Students' Salute; Forrest Woodside, editor in chief, B. F. Carter and E. M. Carney, business managers, Students' Salute Publishing Company, Emporia.

The Independent League (monthly), nonpartisan reform; Reform Publishing Company, Jas. D. Holden, president, Ed. S. Waterbury, secretary, Emporia.

The Hartford News, neutral; C. C. Rogan, editor and publisher, Hartford.

The Americus Greeting, republican; D. C. Grinnell, editor and publisher, Americus.

The Reading Advance, neutral; S. H. Stratton, editor and publisher. Reading.

Neosho Rapids Times, neutral ; Times Publishing Company, Neosho Rapids.

The Allen Herald, neutral; L. C. Heim, editor and publisher, Allen.

McPHERSON COUNTY.

McPherson Republican (daily and weekly), republican; S. G. Mead, editor, publisher, and proprietor, McPherson.

The Freeman-Vim, republican; F. H. Potter and W. N. Snyder, editors and publishers, J. M. Snyder, associate editor, McPherson.

The Democrat, democratic; Warren Knaus, editor and proprietor, McPherson.

The Educator, educational; S. Z. Sharp and Daniel Vaniman, editors and proprietors, McPherson.

McPherson Opinion, populist; C. A. Hamlin, editor and proprietor, McPherson.

Game and Shooting (monthly), sporting; Ed. F. Haberlein, editor, Haberlein & Son, publishers, McPherson.

The Lindsborg News, republican; J. D. and Frank Nelson, editors and proprietors, Lindsborg.

Bethany Messenger (monthly), educational; Julius Lincoln, editor, C. A. Stone, business manager, Lindsborg.

The Marquette Tribune, republican; E. C. Crary, editor and publisher, Marquette.

The Journal, neutral; Orin Bartlett, editor and publisher, J. J. Toevs, proprietor, Moundridge.

The Inman Review, neutral; A. E. Duvall, editor and proprietor, Inman.

Canton Republican, republican; Bert Merrill, editor and publisher, Canton.

MARION COUNTY.

Marion Record, republican; E. W. Hoch, editor and proprietor, Marion.

The Marion Times, populist; H. Kuhn, editor and publisher, Marion.

Marion Baptist (monthly), religious; Rev. W. F. Allen, editor and publisher, Marion.

The Peabody Gazette, republican; Wm. H. Morgan, editor and proprietor, Peabody.

The Peabody Weekly Republican, republican; J. H. Ayers, editor, Ayers & McClure, proprietors and publishers, Peabody.

The Florence Bulletin, republican; Grant Shaw, editor and publisher, Florence.

The Burns Citizen, neutral; M. M. Phillips, editor, Phillips & Whiting (J. F.), proprietors, Burns.

The Hillsboro Anzeiger, republican; J. F. Harms, editor, Hillsboro.

Zions-Bote, religious; J. F. Harms, editor and publisher, Hillsboro.

MARSHALL COUNTY.

The Marshall County News, republican; George T. Smith, editor and proprietor, Marysville.

Marysville Post, democratic; Ernst Denner, editor and publisher, Marysville.

Marshall County Democrat, democratic; J. S. and L. S. Magill, editors and publishers, Marysville.

The People's Advocate, populist; C. A. Hammett, editor, Hammett Bros., proprietors, Marysville.

The Normal Herald (quarterly), educational; J. G. Ellenbecker and M. W. Street, editors, Marysville.

The Waterville Telegraph, republican; Henry C. Willson, editor and publisher, Waterville.

The Blue Rapids Times, republican; E. M. Brice and Livy B. Tibbetts, editors and publishers, Blue Rapids.

Blue Rapids Weekly Motor, populist; D. O. Munger, editor and proprietor, Blue Rapids.

The Frankfort Bee (semiweekly), republican; J. W. and —.—. Bliss, editors and publishers, Frankfort.

Weekly Review, neutral; G. W. Shedden, editor, Shedden & Shedden, proprietors, Frankfort.

The Axtell Anchor, republican; C. E. Stains, editor and publisher, Axtell.

The Beattie Eagle, republican; S. L. and R. D. Wilson, editors and publishers, Beattie.

The Irving Leader, republican; Hugh Thompson, editor and publisher, Irving.

The Summerfield Sun, republican; R. W. Hemphill, editor and publisher, Summerfield.

The Oketo Herald, republican; R. B. and C. J. Moore, editors and publishers, Oketo.

The Vermillion Record, republican; F. W. Arnold, editor and publisher, Vermillion.

MEADE COUNTY.

The Meade County Globe, neutral; Frank Fuhr, publisher, Meade.

MIAMI COUNTY.

The Miami Republican, republican; W. D. Greason, editor and proprietor, Paola.

The Western Spirit, democratic; B. J. Sheridan, editor and proprietor, Paola.

The Paola Times, populist; A. C. McCarthy, editor and publisher, Paola.

The Louisburg Herald, republican; R. H. Cadwallader, editor and publisher, Louisburg.

Osawatomie Graphic, republican; J. P. Bell, publisher and proprietor, Osawatomie.

The Osawatomie Globe, democratic; Frank Pyle, editor and proprietor, Osawatomie.

MITCHELL COUNTY.

The Beloit Gazette, republican; S. H. Dodge, editor and publisher, Beloit.

The Western Call, populist; I. W. and J. S. Parks, editors and publishers, Beloit.

Kansas Woodman (monthly), secret society; J. S. Parks and P. G. Chubbic, editors and publishers, Beloit.

Good Tidings (monthly), religious; Jean W. and Edith N. Honey, editors, Good Tidings Publishing Company, Beloit.

Public Record, republican; Levi L. Alrich, editor and publisher, Cawker City.

Tri-County News, republican; C. H. Sawyer, editor and publisher, Scottsville.

The People's Sentinel, populist; W. R. Baker, editor and publisher, Glen Elder.

MONTGOMERY COUNTY.

The Star and Kansan, populist; H. W. Young, editor and publisher, Independence.

South Kansas Tribune, republican; W. T. and C. Yoe, editors and publishers, Independence.

The Morning Reporter (daily), neutral; T. N. Sickels, editor and publisher, Independence.

The Coffeyville Journal (daily and weekly), republican; D. Stewart Elliott, editor, John B. Elliott, manager, Elliott Printing Company, Coffeyville.

The Twice-a-Week Independent, independent; C. W. Kent, publisher and proprietor, Coffeyville.

Cherry Vale Republican, republican; D. R. Neville, editor and publisher, Cherry Vale.

Cherry Vale Champion, republican; R. T. Webb and H. F. Thompson, editors and publishers, Cherry Vale.

Kansas Populist, populist; J. H. Ritchie, editor and publisher, Cherry Vale.

The Daily News; News Company, publishers, Cherry Vale.

Caney Chronicle, republican; C. O. Taylor and Harry Brighton, editors and publishers, Caney.

The Caney Times, populist; A. M. Parsons, editor and publisher, Caney.

The Elk City Enterprise, neutral; W. E. Wortman, editor and publisher, Elk City.

MORRIS COUNTY.

The Council Grove Republican, republican; William A. Miller and J. S. Carpenter, editors, Republican Printing Company, publishers, Council Grove.

Council Grove Guard, democratic; E. J. Dill and D. O. Bell, editors and proprietors, Council Grove.

Council Grove Courier, populist; J. C. Padgett and G. W. DeWald, editors and publishers, Council Grove.

White City Register, republican; J. D. and H. F. Parsons, editors and publishers, White City.

MORTON COUNTY.

The Monitor-Republic, republican; Ernest C. Wilson, editor and publisher, Richfield.

NEMAHA COUNTY.

Seneca Courier-Democrat, democratic; A. P. and C. H. Herold, editors and proprietors, Seneca.

The Seneca Tribune, republican; W. H. and G. F. Jordan, editors and proprietors, Seneca.

The Seneca News, populist; Jas. M. and Mrs. J. M. Jones, editors and proprietors, Seneca.

The Sabetha Republican-Herald, republican; J. A. Constant, editor and publisher, Sabetha.

Nemaha County Spectator, republican; J. T. Bristow, editor and publisher, Wetmore.

Centralia Journal, republican; Frank M. and A. B. Hartman, editors and publishers, Centralia.

The Centralia Times, independent; Times Publishing Company, A. B. Clippinger, president, P. K. Shoemaker, secretary, Centralia.

The Bern Press, democratic; W. J. McLaughlin, editor and proprietor, Bern.

The Goff's Advance, republican; Oscar C. Williamson, editor and publisher, Goff's.

The Corning Gazette, republican; Fred. Haughawout, editor and publisher, Corning.

NEOSHO COUNTY.

The Osage Mission Journal, republican; E. B. Park, editor and proprietor, Osage Mission.

Chanute Vidette-Times, republican; G. M. Dewey, editor and publisher, Chanute.

The Chanute Blade, democratic; J. A. Cross, editor and publisher, Chanute.

Chanute Daily Tribune, republican; G. M. Dewey, editor and publisher, Chanute.

Republican-Record, republican; Mrs. Charles E. Harbaugh, editor and proprietor, Erie.

The Erie Sentinel, populist; C. E. Allison, editor and publisher, Erie.

Thayer Independent News, neutral; A. L. Palmer, editor and proprietor, Thayer.

The Weekly Graphic, republican; E. L. Barnes, editor and proprietor, Thayer.

Galesburg Enterprise, independent; J. R. Schoonover, editor, Galesburg.

NESS COUNTY.

Ness County News, republican; J. K. Barnd, editor and proprietor, Ness City.

Ness County Echo, populist; M. Pembleton, editor and proprietor, Ness City.

The Ness County Republican, republican; Geo. E. and Geo. M. Nicholson, editors and proprietors, Ness City.

NORTON COUNTY.

The Norton Courier, republican; F. M. Duvall, editor and manager, Norton.

The Champion, republican; J. W. Conway, editor and publisher, Norton.

The Liberator, populist; D. W. Hull, editor and proprietor, Norton.

The Norton Republican, republican; A. L. and I. S. Drummond, editors and proprietors, Norton.

The Almena Plaindealer, republican; O. L. Reed, editor, Plaindealer Publishing Company, Almena.

OSAGE COUNTY.

The Osage County Chronicle, republican; E. G. Pipp, editor, Chronicle Publishing Company, Burlingame.

Chronicle Magazine (monthly), history and literature; Edwin G. Pipp, editor and publisher, Burlingame.

Debtor and Workingman, labor; F. M. Steves, editor, F. M. Steves & Co., publishers, Burlingame.

The Osage City Free Press, republican; James M. Mickey, editor, and R. J. Hill, business manager, Osage City.

The Public Opinion, democratic; J. M. Hedrick and Charles Stackhouse, editors and proprietors, Osage City.

The Lyndon Journal, republican; W. A. Madaris, editor and publisher, Lyndon.

Osage County Graphic, republican; R. A. Miller, editor, Graphic Publishing Company, Lyndon.

The People's Herald, populist; Sig. H. Gill, editor, S. H. Gill & Co., publishers, Lyndon.

The Carbondalian, republican; Everett Veatch, editor and publisher, Carbondale.

The Overbrook Herald, republican; S. A. and S. W. Stauffer, editors and publishers, Overbrook.

Quenemo Republican, republican; T. A., C. E. and J. J. Ellis, editors and proprietors, Republican Publishing Company, Quenemo.

Scranton Gazette, neutral; I. N. Grandon, editor and publisher, Scranton.

The Melvern Review, neutral; A. R. and W. P. Ball, editors and publishers, Melvern.

OSBORNE COUNTY.

Osborne County Farmer, republican; W. S. Tilton and C. W. Landis, editors and proprietors, Osborne.

Osborne County News, populist; C. W. Ames, editor, C. W. Ames and J. E. Eckman, publishers and proprietors, Osborne.

The Downs Times, republican; H. M. Fletcher and H. D. Wilson, editors and publishers, Downs.

American Schools (monthly), educational; Kansas Book Company, publishers, Downs.

Western Empire, republican; W. C. Brown and A. H. Goddard, editors and proprietors, Alton.

OTTAWA COUNTY.

Minneapolis Messenger, republican; A. P. Riddle, editor and proprietor, Minneapolis.

Kansas Workman (monthly), A. O. U. W.; A. P. Riddle, editor and proprietor, Minneapolis.

The Sprig of Myrtle (monthly), Knights of Pythias; A. P. Riddle, editor and proprietor, Minneapolis.

The Review, populist; Mrs. C. Ingersoll Tucker, editor, H. H. Tucker, business manager, Review Publishing Company, Minneapolis.

Ottawa County Index, populist; J. C. Cline, editor and proprietor, Minneapolis.

The Delphos Republican, republican; J. M. Waterman & Sons (W. W. and A. B.), editors and proprietors, Delphos.

PAWNEE COUNTY.

The Larned Eagle-Optic, democratic; T. E. Leftwich. managing editor, A. B. Leftwich, business manager, Optic Steam Printing Company, publishers. Larned.

Larned Weekly Chronoscrope, republican; F. J. Davis, editor and manager. Larned Printing Company, publishers, Larned.

Tiller and Toiler, populist; W. P. McMahon, editor and proprietor, Larned.

Western Kansas Voice (monthly), irrigation; Rob. N. Morehead, editor and publisher, Larned.

PHILLIPS COUNTY.

The Independent, populist; H. W. and S. C. Landes, editors and proprietors, Kirwin.

The Kirwin Globe, republican; A. Barron, editor and proprietor, Kirwin.

Phillipsburg Herald, populist; E. E. Brainerd and J. M. Tadlock, editors and proprietors, Phillipsburg.

The Phillipsburg Dispatch, republican; John Q. Royce, editor and publisher, Phillipsburg.

Long Island Leader, populist; E. M. Weed, editor and publisher, Long Island.

The Logan Republican, independent; E. J. Garner, editor and publisher, Logan.

Agra News, religious; J. H. Ebling, editor and publisher, Agra.

POTTAWATOMIE COUNTY.

The Kansas Agriculturist, republican; Frank A. Root, editor, Ernest A. Weller, business manager, Wamego.

The Wamego Times, republican; R. M. Chilcott, editor and publisher, Wamego.

The Presbyterian Herald (biweekly); Rev. N. D. Johnson, editor, Wamego.

St. Mary's Star, democratic; P. L. Jackson, editor and publisher, St. Mary's.

The Dial (monthly), college; Martin M. Monaghan and others, editors, Edmund F. Salland, business manager, St. Mary's.

St. Mary's Eagle, republican; M. M. Lee, editor and publisher; Lynn M. Christy, local editor, St. Mary's.

St. Mary's Journal, democratic; James Graham, editor, Graham Publishing Company, St. Mary's.

The Westmoreland Recorder, republican; W. F. Hill, editor and publisher, Westmoreland.

Westmoreland News, populist; C. A. and W. D. Wallace, editors and publishers, Westmoreland.

The Olsburg News-Letter, republican; G. W. Havermale, publisher and proprietor. A. L. Havermale, local editor and business manager, Olsburg.

The Onaga Herald, republican; C. C. Haughawout, editor, F. S. Haughawout, proprietor, Onaga.

The Havensville Torchlight, republican; E. D. Anderson, editor and publisher, Havensville.

PRATT COUNTY.

The Pratt County Republican, republican; J. K. Cochran, editor, F. A. Lanstrum, business manager, Republican Printing Company, publishers, Pratt.

Pratt County Union, populist; Joel Reece, editor, W. F. Brown, associate editor, Union Printing Company, publishers, Pratt.

The Preston Plain Dealer, independent; J. G. Oliver, editor and publisher, Preston.

RAWLINS COUNTY.

The Republican Citizen, republican; C. V. Woodard, editor and publisher, Atwood.

The Atwood Patriot, populist; W. K. Loofbourrow, editor and manager, Atwood Publishing Company, Atwood.

RENO COUNTY.

Hutchinson News (daily and weekly), republican; A. L. Sponsler, editor, News Publishing Company, Hutchinson.

Weekly Interior Herald, republican; Fletcher Meridith, editor and proprietor, Hutchinson.

—10

The Clipper, society; W. A. Loe and M. Stevens, publishers, Hutchinson.

The Hutchinson Democrat, democratic; O. S. Coffin, editor, M. R. Cain, business manager, McKinstry & Hutton, publishers and proprietors, Hutchinson.

Hutchinson Gazette, populist; Horace S. Foster and Lee A. Hutton, editors and publishers, Hutchinson.

School and Fireside (monthly), educational; F. J. Altswager, editor and publisher, Chas. P. Dawson, associate editor, Hutchinson.

The Normal Class (monthly), educational; A. P. George, editor, F. C. George, manager, Hutchinson.

The Nickerson Argosy, republican; W. F. Hendry and J. E. Humphrey, editors and publishers, Nickerson.

The Chronicle (monthly), religious; E. C. and O. E. Pollard, editors and publishers, Nickerson.

The Nickerson Record, republican; W. L. Brown and H. H. Brightman, editors and publishers, Nickerson.

The Haven Item, neutral; J. V. Mowder, editor and publisher, Haven.

The Sylvia Banner, independent; H. B. Watson, editor and publisher, Sylvia.

The Turon Weekly Press, republican; T. G. Elbury, editor and proprietor, A. A. Elbury, associate editor, Turon.

Arlington Enterprise, republican; M. L. Barrett, editor and publisher, Arlington.

REPUBLIC COUNTY.

The Belleville Telescope, republican; J. C. Humphrey, editor and proprietor, Belleville.

Republic County Freeman, populist; H. N. Boyd, editor and publisher, Belleville.

Scandia Journal, republican; Albert B. Kimball, editor and proprietor, Scandia.

Republic City News, republican; Gomer T. Davies, editor and proprietor, Republic City.

The County Teacher (monthly), educational; Chas. S. Earley, editor and proprietor, Republic City.

The Cuba Daylight, republican; Will. M. Shrouf, editor and proprietor, Cuba.

The Courtland Register, republican; H. A. Hoyt, editor and publisher, Courtland.

The Narka News, neutral; J. L. Addington and G. H. Stineback, editors and publishers, Narka.

Herald of Pentecost, religious; D. P. Zeigler, editor, B. S. Barton and H. W. Smith, corresponding editors, Kackley.

RICE COUNTY.

The Bulletin and Gazette, republican; J. E. Junkin, editor, J. E. Junkin and S. H. Steele, publishers, Sterling.

Cooper Courier (monthly), college; Talmon Bell, editor in chief, J. C. McCracken, business manager, Sterling.

The Lyons Republican, republican; Clark Conkling, editor and publisher, Frank E. Hoyt, manager, Lyons.

Central Kansas Democrat, democratic; Ed. W. Wood, editor, Minnie Wood Cooper and F. N. Cooper, publishers, Lyons.

Rice County Eagle, populist; D. P. Hodgdon, editor and publisher, Lyons.

Chase Record, independent; George W. Lowman, editor and publisher, Chase.

The Little River Monitor, independent; W. G. Greenbank, editor and publisher, Little Liver.

Geneseo Herald, republican; W. R. White, editor and publisher, Geneseo.

Rice County News, republican; W. R. White, editor and proprietor, Frederick.

RILEY COUNTY.

The Manhattan Nationalist, republican; H. J. Allen, editor and publisher, Manhattan.

Manhattan Homestead (monthly), real estate; L. R. Elliott, editor, F. B. Elliott, assistant editor, Manhattan.

The Industrialist, agricultural college; faculty and students, editors and publishers, Manhattan.

Manhattan Republic, populist; James P. Easterly, editor and publisher, Manhattan.

Manhattan Mercury, democratic; J. J. Davis, editor and publisher, Manhattan.

Riley County Educator (monthly), educational; C. G. Swingle, editor and publisher, Manhattan.

Randolph Enterprise, independent, Isaac Moon, editor and publisher, Randolph.

Leonardville Monitor, republican; Dr. J. W. Megan, editor and publisher, Leonardville.

The Riley Regent, populist; W. H. Remmele, local editor, Chas. A. Southwick, manager, Riley.

ROOKS COUNTY.

The Western News, republican; L. B. Powell and F. E. Young, editors, publishers, and proprietors, Stockton.

Rooks County Record, republican; W. L. Chambers, editor and publisher, Stockton.

Alliance Signal, populist; F. M. Case, editor and proprietor, Maggie Case, local editor, Stockton.

Stockton Academician (monthly), educational; F. E. Sherman, editor, Stockton.

Rooks County Journal, populist; W. E. Cox and G. E. Nichols, editors and publishers, Plainville.

RUSH COUNTY.

La Crosse Clarion, republican; A. Clay Whiteman, editor, J. B. Morris, manager, La Crosse.

La Crosse Chieftain, populist; John W. Torrey, editor and proprietor, La Crosse.

Walnut Valley Standard, independent; Fred. W. Miller, editor, F. C. Kirch, manager, Standard Publishing Company, Rush Centre.

Rush County Leader, republican; J. T. Nolan, editor, McCracken.

RUSSELL COUNTY.

The Russell Record, republican; James Jones, editor, Arthur C. Jones, publisher and proprietor, Russell.

The Journal, republican; S. H. Haffa, editor and publisher, Russell.

The Lucas Advance, republican; C. W. Deeble, editor, J. W. and H. Naylor, publishers and proprietors, Lucas.

SALINE COUNTY.

The Salina Herald, democratic; J. H. Padgett, managing editor, Salina.

Salina Republican-Journal (daily and weekly), republican; M. D. Sampson, editor and proprietor, Salina.

The Salina Sun, republican; W. H. Johnson, editor and proprietor, Salina.

The Salina Union, populist; H. N. Gaines, editor, Central Kansas Publishing Company, Salina.

The Wesleyan Advance (monthly), college; C. N. Poe, editor in chief, D. E. Blair, manager, Salina.

The Open Church (monthly), religious; W. B. Mucklow and T. V. Davies, editors and publishers, Salina.

The Irrigation Farmer (monthly), irrigation; J. L. Bristow, editor and publisher, Salina.

Forward, religious; Howard C. Rash, editor and business manager, Forward Publishing Company, Salina.

Salina Rustler.

The Gypsum Advocate, republican; E. G. Kinyon, editor and publisher, Gypsum.

The Earth, republican; W. H. Bush, editor and publisher, Brookville.

SCOTT COUNTY.

Scott County News-Lever, populist; J. C. Starr, editor, News-Lever Publishing Company, Scott City.

Scott City Republican, republican; W. O. Bourne, editor and publisher, Scott City.

SEDGWICK COUNTY.

Wichita Eagle (daily and weekly), republican; M. M. Murdock, editor. M. M. and R. P. Murdock, proprietors, Wichita.

The Wichita Beacon, (daily and weekly), democratic; H. J. Hagny, manager, Mrs. Frank B. Smith, owner, Wichita.

Der Wichita Herold (German); John Hönscheidt, editor and publisher, Wichita.

Kansas Staats Anzeiger (German); John Hönscheidt, editor and publisher, John M. Seitz, local editor, Wichita.

Kellogg's Wichita Record, auxiliary; A. N. Kellogg Newspaper Company, publishers, Wichita.

The Mirror, republican; John Carter, editor and publisher, Wichita.

The Kansas Commoner, populist; B. E. Kies, editor and manager, Wichita.

The Kansas Star, republican; J. L. Papes, editor and publisher, Wichita.

Western Methodist, religious; William M. Starr, editor and publisher, Rev. W. J. Martindale, assistant editor, Wichita.

The Wichita Price Current, trade; J. L. Papes, editor and publisher, Wichita.

The Leader (monthly) reform; G. W. Collings, editor, Leader Printing Company, publishers, Wichita.

The Wichita Times, republican; W. T. Burgess, editor, J. C. Richey, proprietor and manager, Wichita.

Western Newspaper Union, auxiliary; Wichita.

Our Church Mirror (monthly), missionary; Rev. Joseph W. Funk, editor and publisher, Wichita.

The Union Advocate, independent labor; W. T. Wisdom, publisher, Wichita.

The Kansas Freemason (monthly); Edgar B. Marchant, editor and publisher, Frank I. Bates, general agent, Wichita.

The Weekly Mount Hope Mentor, republican; H. D. Johnson, editor and publisher, Mount Hope.

The Cheney Sentinel, republican; J. A. Maxey, editor and lessee, Cheney.

The Maize Critic, independent; Orlie H. Reid, editor and publisher, Maize.

Maize Pointer.

Colwich Courier.

SEWARD COUNTY.

The Liberal News, republican; Abe K. Stoufer, editor and publisher, Liberal.

SHAWNEE COUNTY.

Topeka Capital (daily and semiweekly), republican; J. K. Hudson, editor in chief, H. T. Chase, associate editor, Dell Keizer, business manager, Topeka.

The Topeka State Journal (daily and weekly), republican; Frank P. MacLennan, editor and publisher, Topeka.

The Topeka State Press (daily and weekly), populist; J. B. Chapman, editor and publisher, Topeka.

The Daily Democrat, democratic; W. P. Tomlinson, editor and publisher, Topeka.

Kansas Farmer, agricultural; H. A. Heath, president and manager, E. B. Cowgill, vice president, D. C. Nellis, secretary, Kansas Farmer Publishing Company, Topeka.

The Topeka Mail, republican; Arthur Capper, editor and proprietor, Topeka.

Western School Journal (monthly), educational; John MacDonald, editor and publisher, Topeka.

Kansas Telegraph (German), democratic; H. Von Langen, editor, H. and Leo Von Langen, publishers, Topeka.

The Lance, society and literary; M. O. Frost, editor and publisher, Topeka.

Our Messenger (monthly), Kansas W. C. T. U.; Olive P. Bray, editor, Topeka.

The Sunday Ledger, literary; George W. Reed, publisher, Topeka.

The Shawnee Independent, independent; I. W. Pack, editor and publisher, Topeka.

The Kansas Medical Journal, scientific; W. E. McVey, editor, Medical Publishing Company, Topeka.

The Western Poultry Breeder (monthly), Thomas Owen, editor, Owen & Co., publishers, Topeka.

The Advocate, populist; S. McLallin, editor, Advocate Publishing Company, Topeka.

The Western Odd Fellow (semimonthly), secret society; H. C. Stevens, editor, F. S. Stevens, business manager, Topeka.

Lucifer, the Light-Bearer, free thought; Moses Harman, editor and publisher, Topeka.

The Merchants' Journal, trade; Charles P. Adams, manager, Merchants' Journal Publishing Company, Topeka.

The Weekly Call (colored), republican; William Pope, editor and publisher, Topeka.

Kansas Christian Advocate, religious; T. E. Stephens, editor, W. T. Randolph, publisher, Topeka.

The Agora (quarterly), historical and literary; T. E. Dewey, editor, George W. Crane & Co., publishers, Topeka.

The Helping Hand, and F. A. and I. U. (monthly); officers state F. A. and I. U., publishers, W. F. McHenry and M. R. Chesney, business managers, Topeka.

The State Ledger (colored), republican; F. L. Jeltz, editor, Topeka.

Kansas Sunday School Journal (monthly), religious; James F. Drake, editor, Kansas Sunday School Association, publishers, Topeka.

Topeka Pilgrim (monthly), religious; Rev. W. L. Byers, editor, Rev. L. Blakesley and Rev. C. M. Sheldon, associate editors, Topeka.

The Kansas Endeavorer (monthly), religious; L. L. Roby, editor and business manager, Topeka.

The Kansas Breeze, republican; T. A. McNeal, president, F. C. Montgomery, secretary, Kansas Breeze Company, publishers, Topeka.

Ottawa Journal and Triumph (Topeka edition), populist; E. H. Snow, editor and publisher, Topeka.

Illustrated Weekly (occasional); E. L. Shelton, publisher, Topeka.

The Washburn Mid-Continent (monthly), college; M. W. Axtell, editor in chief, M. P. Gould and W. R. Adams, business managers, Topeka.

The Baptist Visitor (monthly), religious; Gertrude Frazeur, editor, W. J. Reeks, business manager, Topeka.

The Kansas Worker (semimonthly), religious; Kansas Tract Society, Topeka.

The Western Jewell (monthly), I. O. O. F.; Ed. G. Moore & Son, editors and proprietors, Topeka.

The Kansas Bee Journal (monthly); Mrs. Edith Miller, editor, Miller & Dunham, publishers, Topeka.

American Horticulturist (monthly), horticultural; F. A. Waugh, editor, B. F. Smith, associate editor, Topeka.

The National Referendum, economics; National Referendum Publishing Company, Topeka.

The Columbian Herald (monthly), K. of C.; George W. Reed, editor and publisher, Topeka.

Shawnee Drum-Beat, reform; A. O. Grigsby, editor, J. F. Petrik, business manager, People's Publishing Association, publishers, Topeka.

Weekly Weather Crop Bulletin of the Kansas Weather Service; T. B. Jennings, director, Topeka.

Temple Klocken, Topeka.

Gospel Chariot, Topeka.

The Rossville Times, republican; N. J. Baker, editor and publisher, Rossville.

Richland Argosy, republican; W. A. Hunt, editor, C. W. and S. V. Searing, proprietors, Richland.

SHERIDAN COUNTY.

The Hoxie Sentinel, republican; Frank A. McIvor, editor, M. F. Shafer, publisher, Hoxie.

The Sheridan County Democrat, democratic; John Vedder, editor, publisher, and proprietor, Hoxie.

The Hoxie Palladium, populist; E. E. Hartley, editor and publisher, Hoxie.

SHERMAN COUNTY.

The Goodland News, democratic; E. F. Tennant, editor and publisher, Goodland.

The Goodland Republic, populist; F. H. Stewart, editor and publisher, Goodland.

SMITH COUNTY.

Smith County Pioneer, republican; W. H. Nelson, editor and publisher, Smith Centre.

Stewart's Bazoo, democratic; Art. Gentzler, editor, J. W. Stewart, proprietor, Smith Centre.

Smith County Journal, populist; E. S. Rice and Ben. T. Baker, editors and publishers, Smith Centre.

The Church Calendar, religious; Rev. D. Baines-Griffiths, editor and proprietor, Smith Centre.

The Gaylord Herald, republican; Lew. C. and Ed. Headley, editors and publishers, Gaylord.

The Lebanon Criterion, republican; Lew. C. Headley, editor and publisher. Lebanon.

Lebanon Journal, populist; W. L. and J. A. Wright, editors and publishers, Lebanon.

Light of Liberty, populist; M. L. and K. Lockwood, editors and publishers, Lebanon.

The Kensington Mirror, populist; Jas. Boyd, editor, Sanford & Boyd, publishers, Kensington.

STAFFORD COUNTY.

Stafford Republican, republican; Dr. Geo. W. Akers, editor, G. W. and Art. B. Akers, proprietors, Stafford.

The People's Paper, populist; E. G. Nettleton, editor and publisher, Stafford.

St. John Weekly News, republican; H. J. Cornwell, editor and proprietor, St. John.

County Capital, populist; John B. Hilmes, editor, Mary J. Hilmes, publisher, St. John.

STANTON COUNTY.

Johnson City Journal, republican; H. A. Lauman, editor, Ada L. Lauman, proprietor, Johnson City.

STEVENS COUNTY.

Hugoton Hermes, republican; C. M. Davis, editor and publisher, Hugoton.

SUMNER COUNTY.

The Monitor-Press, republican; J. G. Campbell and Chas. Hood, editors and publishers, Wellington.

Sumner County Standard, democratic; Wellington Printing Company, publishers, Wellington.

Wellington Daily Mail, independent; A. A. Richards, editor and publisher, Wellington.

The Sumner County Star, republican; A. A. Richards, editor and publisher, Wellington.

People's Voice, populist; Lyman Naugle, editor and publisher, Wellington.

The School Times (semimonthly), educational; Geo. Burk, editor, Irwin Burk, publisher, Wellington.

The Tri-Weekly Bee, juvenile; Harker Rhodes, editor, Ralph Burk, publisher, Wellington.

The Caldwell News, republican; Rob. T. Simons, editor and publisher, Caldwell.

Caldwell Weekly Advance, independent; John E. Wells, editor and publisher, Caldwell.

The Belle Plaine News, independent; J. Byron Cain, editor and publisher, Belle Plaine.

Geuda Springs Herald, independent; W. C. Barnes, editor and proprietor, Geuda Springs.

Mulvane Record, independent; G. L. Reed, editor and publisher, Mulvane.

The Argonia Clipper, independent; S. W. Duncan, editor and publisher, Argonia.

Conway Springs Star, independent; E. L. Cline, editor and publisher, Conway Springs.

The South Haven New Era, independent; C. A. Branscombe, editor and publisher, South Haven.

The Milan Press, independent; Mervin O. Cissel, editor and publisher, Milan.

Oxford Register, republican; C. B. MacDonald, editor and publisher, Oxford.

THOMAS COUNTY.

The Colby Tribune, republican; P. A. Troutfetter, editor and proprietor, Colby.

The Free Press, populist; C. E. Dedrick, editor and proprietor, Colby.

TREGO COUNTY.

Western Kansas World, republican; H. S. Givler and A. D. Crooks, editors and proprietors, Wa Keeney.

WABAUNSEE COUNTY.

Alma Enterprise, republican; Frank I. Sage and O. W. Little, editors and publishers, Alma.

The Alma Signal, democratic; Matt. Thomson, editor and publisher, Alma.

The Eskridge Star, republican; W. H. Melrose, editor and publisher, Eskridge.

The Alta Vista Record, republican; S. M. Padgett & Son, editors and publishers, Alta Vista.

WALLACE COUNTY.

The Western Times, republican; W. E. Ward, editor and publisher, Sharon Springs.

The People's Voice, populist; J. R. Gamble, editor and publisher, Sharon Springs.

. The Weskansan, republican; Ed. Carter, editor, P. A. Carter, proprietor and publisher, Weskan.

WASHINGTON COUNTY.

Washington Republic, populist; L. J. Sprengle, editor and proprietor, Washington.

The Washington Register, republican; E. N. Emmons, editor and publisher, Washington.

The Washington Post, republican; J. T. Hole, editor and proprietor, Otis B. Nesbit, city editor, Washington.

The Hanover Democrat, democratic; A. D. Campbell, editor and proprietor, Hanover.

Greenleaf Journal, republican; M. O. Reitzel, editor and proprietor, Greenleaf.

Greenleaf Sentinel, republican; Jas. C. Feeley, editor and proprietor. Greenleaf.

Haddam City Clipper, republican; R. O. Woody, editor and publisher, Haddam.

The Barnes Chief, republican; Irvin Hogue, editor and publisher, Barnes.

WICHITA COUNTY.

Leoti Standard, republican; G. W. Taylor, editor and publisher, Leoti.

The Western Kansan, populist; J. B. Milford, editor and publisher, Leoti.

WILSON COUNTY.

Wilson County Citizen, republican; John S. Gilmore, editor and proprietor. Fredonia.

The Alliance Herald, populist; J. M. Kennedy, editor and publisher, Fredonia.

Wilson County Sun, populist; C. E. Cowdery, editor, Cowdery Bros. & Brichler, proprietors, Neodesha. .

Neodesha Register, republican; J. Kansas Morgan, editor and manager, J. B. Morgan, proprietor, Neodesha.

The Student (monthly), college; Arthur Street, editor, Neodesha.

Buffalo Advocate, populist; P. B. Cowdery, editor, Cowdery & Brichler, proprietors, Buffalo.

Altoona Journal, independent; Geo. B. Sipe, editor and proprietor, Altoona.

WOODSON COUNTY.

The Neosho Falls Post, republican; J. N. Stout, editor and publisher, Neosho Falls.

The News, republican; Richard H. Trueblood and Fred. L. Stephenson, editors and proprietors, Yates Center.

The Farmers' Advocate, populist; A. E. and N. S. Macoubrie, editors and publishers, Yates Center.

Woodson Gazette, democratic; G. S. McCartney, editor and publisher, Yates Center.

The Toronto Republican, republican; A. B. Mann, editor, M. M. Buck & Son, proprietors, Toronto.

WYANDOTTE COUNTY.

The Kansas City Gazette (daily and weekly), republican; George W. Martin, editor, W. L. Witner, business manager, Gazette Publishing and Printing Company, Kansas City.

The Wyandotte Herald, democratic; V. J. Lane & Co., editors and proprietors, Kansas City.

The Kansas City Catholic, religious; John O'Flanagan, editor, Kansas Catholic Publishing Company, Kansas City.

Cromwell's Kansas Mirror, republican; Mark Cromwell, editor and publisher, Kansas City.

The American Citizen (colored), independent; George A. Dudley, managing editor, American Citizen Publishing Company, publishers, Kansas City.

The Weekly Press, independent; J. B. Hipple, editor and publisher, Kansas City.

The Kansas City Sun, populist; E. F. Heisler, editor and publisher, Kansas City.

The Bethany Visitor (monthly), charitable; Mrs. Helen D. Evans, editor, Kansas City.

The American Eagle, A. P. A.; J. W. Hile, editor and proprietor, Kansas City.

Kansas Tribune, republican; R. B. Armstrong, editor and publisher, Kansas City.

Kansas Staats-Zeitung (German); F. Gehring, editor, Jacob Frohwert, business manager, Staats-Zeitung Publishing Company, Kansas City.

The Search-Light (monthly); Allen V. Wilson, editor, H. Rowland Way, businsss manager, Search-Light Publishing Company, Kansas City.

Kansas City Topics.

The Argentine Republic, neutral; Joseph T. Landrey & Son, editors and publishers, Argentine.

The Argentine Eagle, populist; Thomas Wolfe and George A. Brooks, editors and publishers, Argentine.

The Kansas Citizen and Labor Record; Alex. Couch and Geo. A. Brooks, editors and publishers, Argentine and Kansas City.

NEWSPAPERS AND PERIODICALS NOW RECEIVED FROM OTHER STATES AND COUNTRIES.

ALASKA.

The Alaskan and Herald; E. O. Sylvester and E. Otis Smith, editors and publishers, Sitka.

ARKANSAS.

The Jacksonian, democratic; Geo. W. Reed, editor and proprietor. Heber.

National Reformer (monthly), populist; W. S. Morgan and Geo. A. Puckett, editors, C. V. Morgan, publisher, Hardy.

Arkansas Agricultural Experiment Station Bulletin; R. L. Bennett, director, Fayetteville.

ARIZONA.

Arizona Weekly Journal-Miner, republican; J. C. Martin, editor and proprietor, Prescott.

Bulletin of the Arizona Weather Service (monthly); W. R. Burrows, director, Tucson.

CALIFORNIA.

Overland Monthly, literary; Rounseville Wildman, editor, Overland Monthly Publishing Company, San Francisco.

Signs of the Times, religious; M. C. Wilcox, editor, Oakland.

Pacific Health Journal (monthly); W. H. Maxson, editor, Pacific Press Publishing Company, Oakland.

The Rural Californian (monthly); Henry W. Kruckeberg, editor, Los Angeles.

Monthly Meteorological Summary; Geo. E. Franklin, observer, United States department of agriculture, Los Angeles.

Monthly Bulletin of the California Weather Service; J. A. Barwick, director, State Agricultural Society, publishers, Sacramento.

Weekly Weather-Crop Bulletin of Southern California; Geo. E. Franklin, director, Los Angeles.

The West American Scientist (monthly); C. R. Orcutt, editor, San Diego.

COLORADO.

The Denver Republican (daily); Republican Publishing Company, Denver.

The Denver Press; W. S. Partridge, editor, E. H. Randell, manager, The Denver Press Publishing Company, Denver.

Books (monthly); J. C. Dana, editor, R. L. Harper, business manager and associate editor, The Carson-Harper Company, publishers, Denver.

The Woman Voter and the Western Woman; Woman Voter Publishing Company, Denver.

The Altrurian (monthly); T. O. Smith, editor, published by the directors of the Colorado Coöperative Colony, Denver.

Monthly Review of the Colorado Weather Service; F. H. Brandenburg, director, Denver.

Gunnison Tribune, republican; C. E. Adams, editor, Gunnison.

Salida Mail (semiweekly); Howard Russell, editor, Erdlen & Russell, proprietors, Salida.

The West Side Citizen; L. L. Gray, editor, Citizen Publishing Company, Colfax (Villa Park post office).

CONNECTICUT.

The Quarterly Journal of Inebriety, temperance; T. D. Crothers, M. D., editor, American Association for the Study and Cure of Inebriates, publishers, Hartford.

Travelers' Record (monthly), insurance; Travelers' Insurance Company, publishers, Hartford.

The Hartford Seminary Record (bimonthly), theological; edited and published by the faculty of Hartford Theological Seminary, Hartford.

The Connecticut Valley Advertiser; G. P. Lecrenier, editor, Fowler & Lecrenier, publishers, Moodus.

Biblia (monthly), American organ of Egypt and Palestine Exploration Funds; Dr. Charles H. S. Davis, Meriden.

DISTRICT OF COLUMBIA.

Public Opinion; Public Opinion Company, publishers, Washington and New York.

The National Tribune, G. A. R.; National Tribune Company, publishers, Washington.

The American Farmer (monthly); American Farmer Company, publishers, Washington.

National Farm and Fireside (biweekly); Alex. J. Wedderburn, editor, National Farm and Fireside, publishers, Washington.

National Watchman, people's party; N. A. Dunning, managing editor, National Watchman Company, publishers, Washington.

The Woman's Tribune, equal suffrage; Clara Bewick Colby, editor and publisher, Washington.

The American Anthropologist (quarterly), Frank Baker, editor in chief, Anthropological Society of Washington, publishers, Washington.

The National Geographical Magazine (occasional); National Geographical Society, publishers, Washington.

Good Government (monthly); National Civil Service Reform League, Carl Schurz, chairman committee on publication, Washington.

The Washington Book Chronicle (quarterly); W. H. Lowdermilk & Co., publishers, Washington.

Congressional Record (daily); United States Congress, Washington.

The Official Gazette of the United States Patent Office; published by authority of Congress, Washington.

Consular Reports (monthly); United States department of state, bureau of statistics, Washington.

Monthly Weather Review; Prof. Cleveland Abbe, editor, Mark W. Harrington, chief of weather bureau, United States department of agriculture, Washington.

Experiment Station Record (monthly); United States department of agriculture, A. C. True, editor, Washington.

Principal Articles of Domestic Exports (monthly); Worthington C. Ford, chief of bureau of statistics. treasury department, Washington.

Library Bulletin of United States Department of Agriculture (bimonthly); Washington.

Summary Statement of the Imports and Exports of the United States (monthly); Worthington C. Ford, chief of bureau of statistics, treasury department, Washington.

Imports, Exports and Immigration of the United States (monthly); W. C. Ford, chief of bureau of statistics, treasury department, Washington.

Insect Life (monthly); C. V. Riley and L. O. Howard, editors, United States department of agriculture, division of entomology, Washington.

Bulletin United States Department of Agriculture, Division of Entomology (occasional); C. V. Riley, entomologist, Washington.

Farmers' Bulletin (occasional); United States department of agriculture, Washington.

Bulletin of the United States Department of Agriculture, Division of Vegetable Pathology (occasional); B. T. Galloway, chief of division, Washington.

Bulletin of the United States Department of Agriculture, Division of Chemistry (occasional); H. W. Wiley, chemist, Washington.

Report of the Statistician (monthly); Henry A. Robinson, United States department of agriculture, division of statistics, Washington.

Miscellaneous Reports, United States Department of Agriculture, Division of Statistics (occasional); Henry A. Robinson, statistician, Washington.

FLORIDA.

Florida Farmer and Fruit Grower; S. Powers, publisher and proprietor, Jacksonville.

Florida Weather Service Report (monthly); United States department of agriculture, weather bureau, publishers, E. R. Demain, director, Jacksonville.

Pabor Lake Pineapple (monthly); W. E. Pabor, editor and publisher, Pabor Lake.

Bulletin Florida Agricultural Experiment Station (monthly); O. Clute, director, Lake City.

GEORGIA.

Spelman Messenger (monthly); L. H. Upton and M. J. Packard, editors, E. O. Werden, publisher, Atlanta.

Georgia Weather Service Report (monthly); United States department of agriculture, weather bureau, Geo. E. Hunt, director, Atlanta.

Georgia Experiment Station Bulletin (monthly); R. J. Redding, director, College of Agriculture and Mechanic Arts, publishers, Experiment.

ILLINOIS.

The Chicago Daily Tribune, republican; Chicago.

Chicago Daily Coin, Coin Publishing Company, Chicago.

Svenska Amerikanaren, Swedish; Jakob Bonggren, editor, Swedish American Printing Company, publishers, Chicago.

The Chicago Express, populist; L. D. Raynolds, publisher, Chicago.

The Chicago Searchlight, populist; Henry Vincent, editor and publisher, Chicago.

Industrial World and Iron Worker; F. W. Palmer, editor, Industrial World, publishers, Chicago.

The Weekly Drovers' Journal; Harvey L. Goodall, proprietor, Chicago.

The Orange Judd Farmer (central edition of American Agriculturist); Orange Judd Company, publishers, Chicago.

The Irrigation Age (monthly); Wm. E. Smythe, editor, Irrigation Age Company, publishers, Chicago.

The Inland Printer (monthly); A. H. McQuilkin, editor, Inland Printer Company, publishers, Chicago.

National Printer-Journalist (monthly); Benjamin B. Herbert, editor, National Printer-Journalist Company, publishers, Chicago.

The Publisher's Auxiliary (monthly); A. N. Kellogg Newspaper Company, publishers, Chicago.

The Newspaper Union (monthly); Chicago Newspaper Union, publishers, Chicago.

Dictation (monthly), phonography; Isaac S. Dement, editor and publisher, Chicago.

The Western Trail (quarterly); C. R. I. & P. railway, publishers, Chicago.

The Advance, religious; Advance Publishing Company, Chicago.

The Standard, religious; Justin A. Smith, D. D., editor, Goodman & Dickerson, publishers and proprietors, Chicago.

The Universalist, religious; J. S. Cantwell, editor, Universalist Publishing House, Chicago.

The Progressive Thinker; J. R. Francis, editor and publisher, Chicago.

The Religio-Philosophical Journal; B. F. Underwood, editor and publisher, Sara A. Underwood, associate editor, Chicago.

The Open Court, religion of science; Dr. Paul Carus, editor, E. C. Hegeler, publisher, Chicago.

Young Men's Era, Y. M. C. A.; J. E. Defebaugh, managing editor, Young Men's Era Publishing Company, Chicago.

Pravada, mission work; E. A. Adams, editor and publisher, Chicago.

Union Signal, W. C. T. U.; Frances E. Willard, editor in chief, W. T. P. Association. Chicago.

Bible Readings (monthly); W. T. P. Association, Chicago.

The Young Crusader (monthly); Ada M. Melville, editor, W. T. P. Association, Chicago.

Young Women (monthly); Jennie A. Stewart, editor, W. T. P. Association, Chicago.

The Advance Guard (monthly); W. T. P. Association, Chicago.

Responsive Readings for the W. C. T. U. (monthly); W. T. P. Association, Chicago.

The Lever, prohibition; James Lamont, editor, Monitor Publishing Company, Rockford and Chicago.

The Monist (quarterly), philosophy, religion, science, and sociology; Dr. Paul Carus, editor, E. C. Hegeler and Mary Carus, associates, Open Court Publishing Company. Chicago.

New Occasions (monthly), sociological; Chas. H. Kerr & Co., publishers, Chicago.

The Dial (semimonthly), literary criticism; Francis F. Browne, editor, The Dial Company, publishers, Chicago.

The Journal of Geology (semiquarterly); T. C. Chamberlin and others, editors. University of Chicago, publishers, Chicago.

The University Extension World (quarterly); Francis W. Shepardson, editor, University of Chicago, publishers. Chicago.

The Quarterly Calendar; University of Chicago, publishers, Chicago.

Child-Garden (monthly); Andrea and Amalie Hofer, editors, Kindergarten Literature Company, publishers, Chicago.

Kindergarten Magazine (monthly); Andrea and Amalie Hofer, editors, Kindergarten Literature Company, publishers, Chicago.

The Humane Journal (monthly); Albert W. Landon, publisher, Chicago.

National Reveille (semimonthly), Sons of Veterans; S. E. Thomason, editor and proprietor, Chicago.

The Public School Journal (monthly); Geo. P. Brown, editor, Public School Publishing Company, Bloomington.

The American Antiquarian (bimonthly), Rev. Stephen D. Peet, editor, Good Hope.

The Western Plowman (semimonthly); J. W. Warr, editor, Plowman Publishing Company, publishers, Moline.

The Odd Fellows' Herald (biweekly), I. O. O. F.; Jas. R. Miller and John H. Sikes, editors and proprietors, Springfield.

The Christian Life (quarterly), religious; J. B. Caldwell, editor, National Purity Association, publishers, Morton Park.

The Brethren's Missionary Visitor (quarterly); general missionary and tract committee, German Baptist Brethren Church, publishers, Mount Morris.

The Gospel Messenger; D. L. Miller and H. B. Brumbaugh, editors, Brethren's Publishing Company, Mount Morris.

Bulletin of the Agricultural Experiment Station (occasional); University of Illinois, publishers, Urbana.

INDIANA.

The Indiana State Journal, republican; Indianapolis Journal Publishing Company, Indianapolis.

The Western Horseman; S. W. McMahan, editor, Stukey & McMahan, editors and proprietors, Indianapolis.

The American Tribune, soldiers' paper; American Tribune Company, publishers, Indianapolis.

Mennonitische Rundschau, religious, Mennonite Publishing Company, Elkhart.

Young People's Paper (biweekly); M. S. Steiner, editor, J. S. Lehman, manager, Young People's Association, Elkhart.

Sunday-School Lesson Helps (quarterly); J. S. Coffman, editor, Mennonite Publishing Company, Elkhart.

Bulletins Purdue University Experiment Station (occasional); C. S. Plumb, director, Lafayette.

INDIAN TERRITORY.

The Cherokee Advocate, official organ Cherokee Nation; Geo. O. Butler, editor, Tahlequah.

The Indian Chieftain; D. M. Marrs, editor, Chieftain Publishing Company, Vinita.

The Purcell Register; W. H. Walker, editor, Case & Walker, publishers, Purcell.

Minco Minstrel; Lewis N. Hornbeck, editor and publisher, J. D. Rogers, manager, Minco.

IOWA.

Farmers' Tribune, populist; Thomas F. Byron, editor, Thos. Meredith, proprietor, Des Moines.

Annals of Iowa (quarterly); historical department of Iowa, publishers, Chas. Aldrich, curator and secretary, editor, Des Moines.

Iowa Health Bulletin (monthly); J. F. Kennedy, editor, state board of health, publishers, Des Moines.

Monthly Review of the Iowa Weather and Crop Service; J. R. Sage, director, Des Moines.

Midland Monthly, literary; Des Moines.

The Iowa Historical Record (quarterly); published by State Historical Society, M. W. Davis, secretary, Iowa City.

The Critic; J. E. Staudacher, manager, Matthew McCook, publisher, Dubuque.

KENTUCKY.

Bulletin of the Kentucky Agricultural Experiment Station (occasional); M. A. Scovell, director, Lexington.

LOUISIANA.

Southwestern Christian Advocate; E. W. S. Hammond, editor, Hunt & Eaton, publishers, New Orleans.

Louisiana Weather Journal and Agriculturist (monthly); Robert E. Kerkam, editor and publisher, New Orleans.

MAINE.

The Maine Bugle (monthly and quarterly), Maine Association, War of the Rebellion. J. P. Cilley, treasurer, Rockland.

MARYLAND.

Johns Hopkins University Studies in Historical and Political Science (monthly); Herbert B. Adams, editor, Baltimore.

Johns Hopkins University Circular (occasional); Baltimore.

Maryland State Weather Service Monthly Report; Prof. Wm. B. Clark, director, Baltimore.

MASSACHUSETTS.

Boston Daily Advertiser; Advertiser Newspaper Company, publishers, Boston.

The New England Historical and Genealogical Register (quarterly); John Ward Dean, editor, New England Historic Genealogical Society, publishers, Boston.

The Youth's Companion; Perry Mason & Co., publishers, Boston.

The Writer (monthly); William H. Hills, editor, Writer Publishing Company, Boston.

Good Roads (monthly); Sterling Elliott, managing editor, League of American Wheelmen, publishers, Boston.

American Journal of Numismatics (quarterly); Wm. T. R. Marvin and Lyman H. Low, editors, T. R. Marvin & Son, publishers, Boston.

The Journal of American Folk-lore (quarterly); William Wells Newell, editor, American Folk-lore Society, publishers, Boston and New York.

Technology Quarterly and Proceedings of the Society of Arts; Massachusetts Institute of Technology, publishers, H. W. Tyler, secretary, Boston.

Bulletin of the Public Library of the City of Boston (quarterly); published by the trustees, Boston.

Spelling (occasional); organ of Spelling Reform Association, Library Bureau, publishers, Boston.

The New England Kitchen Magazine (monthly); Mrs. Estelle M. H. Merrill and Miss Anna Barrows, editors, New England Kitchen Publishing Company, Boston.

Bulletin of the New England Weather Service (monthly); J. Warren Smith, director, Boston.

Massachusetts Crop Report (monthly bulletin); state board of agriculture, William R. Sessions, secretary, publisher, Boston.

The Woman's Journal, equal suffrage; H. B. and Alice Stone Blackwell, editors, Boston.

The Woman's Column, equal suffrage; Alice Stone Blackwell, editor, Boston and New York.

Lend a Hand (monthly), sociological reforms; Edward E. Hale and others, editors, J. Stilman Smith & Co., publishers, Boston.

The Boston Investigator, free speech; Ernest Mendum, editor and publisher, Boston.

The New-Church Review (quarterly), Swedenborgian; Theodore F. Wright, editor in chief, Massachusetts New-Church Union, publishers, Boston.

Donahoe's Magazine (monthly), religious; Donahoe's Magazine Company, publishers, Boston.

The Unitarian (monthly); George H. Ellis, publisher, Boston.

The Dawn (monthly), Christian socialism; W. D. P. Bliss, editor, The Dawn Company, publishers, Boston.

The Golden Rule, Y. P. S. C. E.; Golden Rule Company, publishers, Boston.

Berkeley Beacon (monthly), religious; Henry T. Richardson, editor, J. Edwin Everett, business manager, Boston.

United States Investor; Investor Publishing Company, Frank P. Bennett, treasurer, Boston, New York, and Philadelphia.

The Prospect Union Review (semimonthly); Alford W. Cooley, managing editor, published by Harvard students and wage-earners, Cambridgeport.

Bulletin of the Essex Institute (occasional); published by the Essex Institute. Salem.

Essex Institute Historical Collections (quarterly); Essex Institute, publishers, Salem.

Putnam's Monthly Historical Magazine and Magazine of New England History; Eben Putnam, editor and publisher, Salem.

The American Journal of Psychology (quarterly); G. Stanley Hall, editor, J. H. Orpha, publisher, Worcester.

Journal of Education; A. E. Winship, editor, New England Publishing Company, Boston.

American Teacher (monthly); A. E. Winship and W. E. Shelden, editors, New England Publishing Company, Boston.

The Pedagogical Seminary (three times a year); G. Stanley Hall, editor, J. H. Orpha, publisher, Worcester.

The Kindergarten News (monthly); Milton Bradley Company, publishers, Springfield.

Dedham Historical Register (quarterly); Julius H. Tuttle, editor, Dedham Historical Society, publishers, Dedham.

The Dorchester Beacon, republican; Dorchester Beacon Company, publishers. Dorchester.

Bulletin of Hatch Experiment Station of the Massachusetts Agricultural College (occasional); Henry H. Goodell, director, Massachusetts Agricultural College, publishers, Amherst.

MICHIGAN.

The Advent Review and Sabbath Herald; Uriah Smith, editor, Seventh-day Adventist Publishing Association, Battle Creek.

The Religious Liberty Library (monthly); International Religious Liberty Association, publishers, Battle Creek.

The Loyal American (monthly), initiative and referendum; D. A. Reynolds & Co., editors and publishers, Lansing.

Good Health (monthly); J. H. Kellogg, editor, Battle Creek.

Report of the Michigan Weather Service (monthly); C. F. Schneider, director, Lansing.

Michigan Crop Report (monthly); Washington Gardner, secretary of state, Lansing.

Bulletin of the Michigan State Agricultural College Experiment Station (occasional); Lewis G. Gorton, director, Agricultural College.

MINNESOTA.

St. Paul Dispatch (daily), republican; George Thompson, editor and publisher. St. Paul.

The Illustrated Monthly Northwest Magazine (historical); E. V. Smalley, editor and publisher, St. Paul.

The American Geologist (monthly); Chas. E. Beecher and others, editors, Geological Publishing Company, Minneapolis.

Medical Argus (monthly); Dr. F. F. Casseday, editor, Medical Argus Company, publishers, Minneapolis.

The Free Baptist (religious); J. T. Ward, editor, Western Free Baptist Publishing Society, Minneapolis.

Monthly Bulletin of the Minnesota Weather Service; Edward A. Beales, director, Minneapolis.

Bulletin of the University of Minnesota Agricultural Experiment Station (occasional); William M. Liggett, chairman, St. Anthony Park.

MISSOURI.

The Kansas City Times (daily), democratic; Kansas City Times Newspaper Company, publishers, Kansas City.

Kansas City Daily Journal, republican; The Journal Company, publishers, Kansas City.

The Kansas City Star (daily and weekly), independent; The Star Company, publishers, Kansas City.

· The Kansas City Mail (daily); M. W. and C. Hutchison, editors and managers, Kansas City Mail Newspaper Company, publishers, Kansas City.

Missouri and Kansas Farmer (monthly); Cliffe M. Brooke, editor and publisher, Kansas City.

Western Veteran (semimonthly), soldiers' paper; O. H. Coulter and W. F. Henry, editors and managers, Kansas City.

The Live Stock Indicator; Indicator Publishing Company, Kansas City.

The Kansas City Medical Index (monthly); Herman E. Pearse, editor and publisher, Kansas City.

The Insurance Magazine (monthly); D. W. Wilder, editor and publisher, Carter Wilder, manager, Kansas City.

Our Boys and Girls, juvenile; M. H. Tomlinson, business manager, Boys and Girls Publishing Company, Kansas City.

Kellogg's Kansas City Record, auxiliary; I. F. Guiwitz, resident manager, A. N. Kellogg Newspaper Company, publishers, Kansas City.

Western Newspaper Union, auxiliary; Western Newspaper Union, publishers, Kansas City.

The Western Stenographer (monthly); S. H. Snow, editor and publisher, Kansas City.

Weather Map, United States Department of Agriculture (daily); Mark W. Harrington, chief, Kansas City.

The Bee, local; T. W. Fields, publisher, Kansas City.

—11

St. Louis Globe-Democrat (daily), republican; The Globe Printing Company, publishers, St. Louis.

Central Christian Advocate, religious; Jesse Bowman Young, editor, Cranston & Curts, publishers, St. Louis.

The Christian Evangelist, religious; J. H. Garrison, editor, Christian Publishing Company, St. Louis.

The Mid-Continent, religious; Meade C. and David R. Williams, editors, Presbyterian Newspaper Company, publishers, St. Louis.

The Altruist (monthly); Alcander Longley, editor, The Altruist Community, publishers, St. Louis.

American Journal of Education (monthly); J. B. Merwin, editor, Perrin & Smith, publishers, St. Louis.

The St. Joseph Herald (daily and weekly), republican; Herald Publishing Company, St. Joseph.

The St. Joseph Weekly Gazette, democratic; C. F. Cochran, editor and manager, Gazette Company, publishers, St. Joseph.

The Triple Link (semimonthly), I. O. O. F.; J. B. Jewell, editor and publisher, Springfield.

Monthly Bulletin of the Missouri Weather Service; J. R. Rippey, director, A. E. Hackett, observer, Columbia.

Bulletin of the Missouri Agricultural College Experiment Station (occasional); Edward D. Porter, director, Columbia.

MONTANA.

Bulletin of the Montana Agricultural Experiment Station (occasional); S. M. Emery, director, Bozeman.

NEBRASKA.

The Nebraska State Journal (daily and semiweekly), republican; Nebraska State Journal Company, publishers, Lincoln.

Lincoln Newspaper Union, auxiliary; Lincoln Newspaper Union, publishers, Lincoln.

Nebraska Congregational News (monthly), religious; H. A. French, publisher, Lincoln.

Monthly Weather Review of the Nebraska Weather Service; G. D. Swezey, director, Lincoln.

Bulletin of the Agricultural Experiment Station of Nebraska (occasional); C. L. Ingersoll, director, University of Nebraska, publishers, Lincoln.

The Omaha Mercury, official paper Nebraska legal fraternity; H. N. McGrew, manager, J. C. Barnard, proprietor, Omaha.

NEVADA.

Monthly Review of the Nevada State Weather Service; Chas. W. Friend, director, Carson City.

NEW JERSEY.

Library Record (monthly); Free Public Library, publishers, Jersey City.

The Jurnal uv Orthoepi and Orthografi (monthly), phonetic; C. W. Larisun, editor and publisher, Ringos.

Bulletin of the New Jersey Agricultural College Experiment Station (occasional); Austin Scott, director, New Brunswick.

Bulletin of the New Jersey Weather Service (monthly); E. W. McGann, director, New Brunswick.

NEW MEXICO.

Santa Fé Daily New Mexican, republican; New Mexican Printing Company, publishers, Santa Fé.

El Boletin Popular (Spanish); José Segura, editor and publisher, Santa Fé.

Bulletin of the New Mexico Weather Service (monthly); H. B. Hersey, observer and chief, Santa Fé.

Las Vegas Daily Optic, republican; R. A. Kistler, editor and proprietor, Las Vegas.

The Albuquerque Daily Citizen, republican; Thos. Hughes, editor, W. T. McCreight, business manager and city editor, Albuquerque.

The New Mexican Single-Taxer; P. H. Smith, editor and publisher, Raton.

NEW YORK.

New York Daily Tribune, republican; Tribune Company, publishers, New York city.

The Irish World and American Industrial Liberator; Patrick Ford, editor and proprietor, New York city.

Twentieth Century, a weekly radical magazine; D. O'Loughlin, manager, Humboldt Publishing Company, New York city.

Pomeroy's Advance Thought (monthly), national reform; Mark M. Pomeroy, editor and publisher, New York city.

Kawkab America [The Star of America], an oriental weekly; Dr. A. J. and N. J. Arbeely, editors and publishers, New York city.

American Economist; The American Protective Tariff League, publishers, New York city.

The American Magazine of Civics (monthly); Andrew J. Palm, editor, H. R. Waite, associate editor, A. J. Palm & Co., publishers, New York city.

Political Science Quarterly; University Faculty of Political Science of Columbia College, editors, Ginn & Co., publishers, New York city.

The Basis, a journal of citizenship; Albion W. Tourgee, editor, Citizens' Publishing Company, Buffalo.

Insurance; S. H. Davis, editor, Davis & Lakey, publishers, New York city.

The Decorator and Furnisher (monthly); W. R. Bradshaw, editor, The Art Trades Publishing and Printing Company, New York city.

The Student's Journal (monthly), phonography; Andrew J. Graham & Co., editors and publishers, New York city.

Illustrated Phonographic World (monthly); E. N. Miner, editor and publisher, New York city.

The Journalist; Margherita Arlina Hamm, editor and proprietor, New York city.

Newspaperdom (monthly); Chas. S. Patteson, publisher, New York city.

The American Woman's Journal (monthly); Helen Kendrick Johnson and Cornelia K. Hood, editors, American Journal Publishing Company, New York city.

The Review of Reviews (monthly); Albert Shaw, editor, Review of Reviews Company, publishers, New York city.

The Forum (monthly); Walter H. Page, editor, Forum Publishing Company, New York city.

Publishers' Weekly, an American book trade journal; R. R. Bowker, manager, New York city.

The Literary Digest; Funk & Wagnalls Company, publishers, New York city.

Notes on New Books (quarterly); G. P. Putnam's Sons, publishers, New York city and London.

Book Reviews (monthly); Macmillan & Co., publishers, New York city.

D. Appleton & Co.'s Monthly Bulletin, literary review; D. Appleton & Co., publishers, New York city.

Literary News (monthly); A. H. Leypoldt, editor, New York city.

Scientific American, arts, sciences, mechanics, etc.; O. D. Munn and A. E. Beach, editors and proprietors, New York city.

Scientific American Supplement; Munn & Co., editors and proprietors, New York city.

Scientific American, building edition (monthly); Munn & Co., editors and proprietors, New York city.

Illustrated Electrical Review; Chas. W. Price, editor, Stephen L. Coles, associate editor, Electrical Review Company, publishers, New York.

The Engineering Magazine (monthly); John R. Dunlap, editor, Engineering Magazine Company, publishers, New York city.

The National Magazine (monthly), American history; New York History Company, publishers, New York city.

Spirit of '76 (monthly), American revolution; Wm. H. Brearley, editor, The Spirit of '76, publishers, New York city.

American History Leaflets (bimonthly); Albert B. Hart and Edward Channing, editors, A. Lovell & Co., publishers, New York city.

The Library Journal (monthly); official organ of the American Library Association, New York city.

Library Bulletin of Cornell University (occasional); Cornell University, publishers, Ithaca.

The American School Board Journal (monthly); Wm. Geo. Bruce, publisher and proprietor, New York city.

Teachers' World (monthly); Bemis Publishing Company, New York city.

The School Journal; E. L. Kellogg & Co., publishers, New York city and Chicago.

The Outlook, religious; The Outlook Company, publishers, New York city.

New York Weekly Witness, religious and political; John Dougall & Co., publishers, New York city.

War Cry, Salvation Army; Maj. Wm. H. Cox, editor, Ballington Booth, proprietor, New York city.

American Sentinel, religious liberty; Alonzo T. Jones and C. P. Bollman, editors, Pacific Press Publishing Company, New York city.

Christian Literature (monthly), religious; Christian Literature Company, publishers, New York city.

The Converted Catholic (monthly); James A. O'Connor, editor and publisher, New York city.

Illustrated Africa (monthly), missionary; Bishop William Taylor and Rev. Ross Taylor, editors, New York city.

The American Missionary (monthly); American Missionary Association, publishers, New York city.

The Home Missionary (monthly); Congregational Home Missionary Society, publishers, New York city.

Sabbath Reading; John Dougall & Co., publishers, New York city.

The Silver Cross (monthly), King's Daughters and Sons; Mary Lowe Dickinson. editor, Silver Cross Publishing Company, New York city.

The Voice, prohibition; Funk & Wagnalls Company, publishers, New York city.

The National Temperance Advocate, (monthly); J. N. Stearns, publishing agent, National Temperance Society, publishers, New York city.

The Sheltering Arms (monthly), official advertiser for charitable societies and institutions; Sheltering Arms, publishers, New York city.

The City Vigilant (monthly); C. H. Parkhurst, chairman committee of publication, City Vigilance League, publishers, New York city.

The Charities Review (monthly), sociology; Charity Organization Society of New York City, publishers, New York city.

The Philanthropist (monthly); Aaron M. and Mrs. Anna Rice Powell, editors, The Philanthropist Company, publishers, New York city.

Our Animal Friends (monthly); American Society for the Prevention of Cruelty to Animals, publishers, New York city.

Health and Beauty (monthly); Ella A. Jennings and W. A. Cooper, editors, Health and Beauty Publishing Company, New York city.

Beadle's Dime Library; Beadle & Adams, publishers, New York.

Beadle's Half-Dime Library; Beadle & Adams, publishers, New York.

The School Bulletin and New York State Educational Journal (monthly), C. W. Bardeen, editor and publisher, Syracuse.

Pratt Institute Monthly, art and science; Pratt Institute, publishers, Brooklyn.

The Cyclopedic Review of Current History (quarterly); Alfred S. Johnson, editor. Garreston, Cox & Co., publishers, Buffalo.

Monthly Report of the New York State Weather Bureau; E. A. Fuertes, director, Ithaca.

Bulletin of the Cornell University Agricultural Experiment Station (occasional); I. P. Roberts, director, Cornell University, publishers, Ithaca.

Bulletin of the New York Agricultural Experiment Station (monthly); Peter Collier, director, Geneva.

NORTH CAROLINA.

Bulletin of the North Carolina Agricultural Experiment Station (occasional); H. B. Battle, director, North Carolina College of Agriculture and Mechanic Arts, publishers, Raleigh.

Monthly Meteorological Report of the North Carolina State Weather Service; H. B. Battle, director, Raleigh.

NORTH DAKOTA.

Bismarck Tribune (daily and weekly); R. N. Stevens, editor and publisher, Bismarck.

Bulletin of the North Dakota Weather and Crop Service (monthly); B. H. Bronson, director, Bismarck.

OHIO.

Cincinnati Weekly Times, republican; The Times Company, publishers, Cincinnati.

The Journal of the Cincinnati Society of Natural History (quarterly); Davis L. James, editor, Cincinnati Society of Natural History, publishers, Cincinnati.

Christian Standard, religious; Standard Publishing Company, Cincinnati.

The Christian Educator (quarterly); J. C. Hartzell and J. W. Hamilton, editors, The Christian Educator, publishers, Cincinnati.

The Christian Press (monthly); Western Tract Society, publishers, Cincinnati.

Herald of Gospel Liberty, religious; J. J. Summerbell, editor, Christian Publishing Association, publishers, Cincinnati.

The Phonographic Magazine (semimonthly); Jerome B. Howard, editor, Phonographic Institute Company, publishers, Cincinnati.

The Coöperative News (semimonthly), official organ of the Ohio and Indiana

building association leagues; The Cöoperative News Company, publishers, Cincinnati.

American Grange Bulletin and Scientific Farmer; Frederick P. Wolcott and "Locksie Powell," editors, American Grange Bulletin and Scientific Farmer, publishers, Cincinnati.

Sound Money; Jacob S. Coxey, publisher and proprietor, Henry Vincent, editor, Massillon, Ohio.

Farm and Fireside (semimonthly); Mast, Crowell & Kirkpatrick, publishers, Springfield.

Womankind (monthly); conducted by Johnstone Murray, Hosterman Publishing Company, Springfield.

The Archæologist (monthly); Warren K. Morehead, editor, The Archæologist Company, publishers, Columbus.

Report of the Ohio Weather and Crop Service (monthly); W. W. Miller, director, Columbus.

Bulletin of the Ohio Agricultural Experiment Station (occasional); Charles E. Thorn, director, Wooster.

Brethren Evangelist, religious; A. D. Gnagey, editor, Brethren Book and Tract Committee, publishers, Ashland.

OKLAHOMA TERRITORY.

The Oklahoma Times Journal (daily); Brown Bros., editors and publishers, Oklahoma City.

The Daily Oklahoman; R. Q. Blakeney, editor and publisher, Oklahoma City.

Oklahoma Magazine (monthly); Frank McMaster, editor, The McMaster Printing Company, publishers, Oklahoma City.

Monthly Bulletin of the Oklahoma Weather Service; James I. Widmeyer, director. Oklahoma City.

The Oklahoma State Capital (daily and weekly); Frank H. Greer, editor, State Capital Printing Company, Guthrie.

The Kingfisher Free Press; Free Press Publishing Company, Kingfisher.

The El Reno Democrat; T. F. Hensley, editor and proprietor, El Reno.

The Hennessey Clipper; C. H. Miller, editor and proprietor, Hennessey.

The Edmond Sun-Democrat; Kirwin & Thomas, editors and proprietors, Edmond.

The Edmond News; B. L. Hanna, editor, News Publishing Company, Edmond.

The Pond Creek Tribune; R. N. McKay, editor and proprietor, Pond Creek.

Cherokee Sentinel; T. E. Myers, editor and proprietor, Pond Creek.

The Ponca City Courier; Bion S. Hutchins and Elbert W. Hoyt, editors, Elbert W. Hoyt, publisher, Ponca City.

Oklahoma School Herald (monthly); J. S. Griffin, editor, Ed. P. Ingle & Co., publishers. Norman.

The Norman Transcript; Ed. P. Ingle, editor and proprietor, Norman.

The Woodward News; W. E. Bolton, editor, News Publishing Company, publishers, Woodward.

The Live Stock Inspector (monthly); Will. E. Bolton, editor and publisher, Woodward.

Newkirk Republican; L. McKinlay, editor and publisher, Newkirk.

Oklahoma State Guide; A. C. Harding, publisher and proprietor, Newkirk.

OREGON.

Our Library (monthly); Library Association of Portland, publishers, Daniel F. W. Bursch, librarian, Portland.

The Way, the Truth, the Life (monthly); W. T. Ellis, editor and publisher, Portland.

Bulletin of the Oregon Agricultural Experiment Station (monthly); John M. Bloss, director, Corvallis.

PENNSYLVANIA.

Public Ledger (daily) republican; L. Clarke Davis, managing editor, George W. Childs Drexel, editor and publisher, Philadelphia.

The American Historical Register (monthly); gazette of the patriotic-hereditary societies of the United States; Chas. H. Browning, editor in chief, The Historical Register Publishing Company, Philadelphia.

Annals of the American Academy of Political and Social Science (bimonthly); Edmund J. James, editor, Roland P. Falkner, James H. Robinson, associate editors, American Academy of Social and Political Science, publishers, Philadelphia.

Woman's Progress (monthly), literature, politics, etc.; Jane Campbell, editor, Woman's Progress Company, publishers, Philadelphia.

University Extension (monthly); American Society for the Extension of University Teaching, publishers, Philadelphia.

The Conservator (monthly), an exponent of the world movement in ethics; Horace L. Traubel, editor, The Conservator, publisher, Philadelphia.

City and State, reform; Herbert Welsh, managing editor and publisher, W. J. Skillman, associate editor, Philadelphia.

The Stenographer (monthly); Francis H. Hemperley, editor, The Stenographer Printing and Publishing Company, Philadelphia.

The American Catholic Historical Researches (quarterly); Martin I. J. Griffin, editor and publisher, Philadelphia.

The Sunday School Times, religious; John D. Wattles & Co., editors and publishers, Philadelphia.

The Temple Magazine, religious; Walter J. Phillips, editor, George W. Bishop, publisher, Philadelphia.

Sunday School Missionary (monthly); American Sunday School Union, publishers, Philadelphia.

Paper and Press (monthly); Wm. M. Patton, publisher, Philadelphia.

Lithographers' Journal (monthly); W. M. Patton, publisher, Philadelphia.

Book News (monthly), book review; John Wanamaker, publisher, Philadelphia.

Food, Home, and Garden (monthly); Rev. Henry S. Clubb, editor, Vegetarian Society of America, publishers, Philadelphia.

The Sugar Beet (bimonthly); Lewis S. Ware, editor, Henry C. Baird & Co., publishers, Philadelphia.

Forest Leaves (bimonthly); Pennsylvania Forestry Association, publishers, Philadelphia.

The Nautilus (monthly); conchology; H. A. Pilsbry, editor, C. W. Johnson, associate editor, Pilsbry & Johnson, publishers, Philadelphia.

Proceedings of the Academy of Natural Sciences (three times a year); Edward J. Nolan, editor, Academy of Natural Sciences, publishers, Philadelphia.

The Naturalists' Leisure Hour and Monthly Bulletin; A. E. Foote, editor and publisher, Philadelphia.

United States Official Postal Guide (monthly); Geo. F. Lasher, printer, Philadelphia.

Monthly Weather Review of the Pennsylvania State Weather Service; T. F. Townsend, observer in charge, Philadelphia.

Golden Days, juvenile; James Elverson, publisher, Philadelphia.

Zion's Watch Tower and Herald of Christ's Presence (semimonthly), religious: Chas. T. Russell, editor, Mrs. C. T. Russell, associate editor, Tower Publishing Company, Allegheny.

Christian Statesman, religious; Rev. David McAllister, editor in chief, Philadelphia, Pittsburg, and Allegheny.

Old Theological Quarterly; Tower Bible and Tract Society, Allegheny.

American Manufacturer and Iron World; Joseph D. Weeks, editor, National Iron and Steel Publishing Company, Pittsburg.

The Pennsylvania School Journal (monthly); N. C. Schaeffer, editor, J. P. McCaskey, publisher, Lancaster.

Farmers' Friend and Grange Advocate; R. H. Thomas, editor, Farmers' Friend, publishers, Mechanicsburg.

The Red Man (monthly), devoted to Indian education and civilization; edited and published at Indian industrial school, Carlisle.

The Poultry Keeper (monthly); P. H. Jacobs, editor, Poultry Keeper Company, publishers, Parkesburg.

Bulletin of the Pennsylvania State College Agricultural Experiment Station (occasional); H. P. Armsby, director, State College.

RHODE ISLAND.

Publications of the Rhode Island Historical Society (quarterly); Amos Perry, editor, Rhode Island Historical Society, publishers, Providence.

Bulletin of the Agricultural Experiment Station of the Rhode Island College of Agriculture and Mechanic Arts (monthly); Chas. O. Flagg, director, Kingston.

SOUTH DAKOTA.

Pierre Daily Capital, Denton & Janes managers, Daily Capital Company, publishers, Pierre.

Monthly Meteorological Summary of the South Dakota Weather Service; Sam. W. Glenn, director, Huron.

TENNESSEE.

Tennessee Journal of Meteorology and Monthly Agricultural Review; J. B. Marberry, director Tennessee weather and crop service, editor and publisher, Nashville.

State Board of Health Bulletin (monthly); edited and published by the state board of health, Nashville.

TEXAS.

The Houston Daily Post, democratic; E. P. Hill, president, A. F. Sittig, secretary, Houston Printing Company, Houston.

Texas School Journal (monthly); T. G. Harris, editor and publisher, Houston.

Texas Stock and Farm Journal; Stock Journal Publishing Company, publishers, Fort Worth.

The Southern Mercury, populist; Milton Park, managing editor and general manager, The Southern Mercury, publishers, Dallas.

Monthly Bulletin of the Texas Weather Service; J. L. Cline and D. D. Bryan, directors, Galveston.

Weekly Weather Crop Bulletin of the Texas Weather Service; I. M. Cline, meteorologist, Galveston.

Bulletin of Texas Agricultural Experiment Station (occasional); J. H. Connell, director, College Station.

UTAH.

The Salt Lake Tribune (daily), gentile; C. C. Goodwin, editor, The Tribune Publishing Company, Salt Lake City.

The Inter-Mountain Advocate; Warren Foster, editor, N. B. Dresser, publisher, Salt Lake City.

Monthly Report of the Utah Weather Service; J. H. Smith, observer weather bureau, director, Salt Lake City.

The Logan Nation (semiweekly); A. N. Rosenbaum, editor and publisher, Logan.

Bulletin of the Utah Agricultural College Experiment Station (monthly); J. H. Paul, director, Logan

The Tooele Transcript; F. E. Gabriel, editor and proprietor, Tooele.

The Richfield Advocate; Meteer Bros., editors and publishers, Richfield.

The Manti Messenger; Joel Shomaker, editor, The Manti Printing and Publishing Company, Manti.

VERMONT.

Bulletin of the Vermont Agricultural Experiment Station (occasional); J. L. Hills, director, Burlington.

VIRGINIA.

Southern Workman and Hampton School Record (monthly); H. B. Frissell, Helen W. Ludlow, Alice M. Bacon, and Cora M. Folsom, editors, Hampton Normal and Agricultural Institute, publishers, Hampton.

Monthly Report of the Virginia Weather Service; Dr. E. A. Craighill, director, Lynchburg.

WASHINGTON.

Monthly Meteorological Report of the Washington State Weather Service; George N. Salisbury, director, Seattle.

Washington State Weather Reporter (monthly); Henry F. Alciatore, director, editor and publisher, Seattle.

WEST VIRGINIA.

Monthly Report of the West Virginia State Weather Service; H. W. Richardson, observer, Parkersburg.

Bulletin of the West Virginia Agricultural Experiment Station (occasional); John A. Myers, director, Morgantown.

WISCONSIN.

Mind and Body (monthly), physical education; Hans Ballin, managing editor, Freidenker Publishing Company. Milwaukee.

Wisconsin Weather and Crop Journal (monthly); S. C. Emery, director of Wisconsin service, editor, Milwaukee.

Hoard's Dairyman; W. D. Hoard, editor, W. D. Hoard Company, publishers, Fort Atkinson.

WYOMING.

The Daily Boomerang; Boomerang Company, publishers, Laramie.

FRANCE.

Société de Géographie Comtes Rendus des Seances de la Commission Centrale (semi-monthly), Paris.

Bulletin de la Société de Géographie (quarterly), Paris.

Bulletin de la Société de Géographie Commerciale de Paris (quarterly), Paris.

Bulletin des Seances de la Société Nationale d' Agriculture de France (monthly), Paris.

Lightning Source UK Ltd.
Milton Keynes UK
UKHW010921021118
331648UK00006B/88/P